Shooter's Bible®

No. 75
1984 Edition

Shooter's Bible

EDITOR:
Robert F. Scott

MANAGING EDITOR:
Frank R. North

LIBRARY RESEARCH:
Robert D. Scott

FIREARMS CONSULTANTS:
Frank Gologorsky • Frank Ercolino
Vincent A. Pestilli • Hermann Koelling
Robert A. Scanlon

FIREARMS RESEARCH:
Frank Russell • Gus Reinhardt

ARTISTS:
Kathryn Gracie • Fay Davey

PRODUCTION SUPERVISOR:
Diane Scheiblin

PRODUCTION ASSISTANTS:
Patricia Kirsch • Dave Hunt
Josephine Hussnatter

COVER PHOTOGRAPHER:
Ray Wells

TYPOGRAPHY AND COMPOSITION:
Daniel Stovall & Associates

DESIGN CONSULTANTS:
Saddle River Graphics

PUBLISHER:
Robert E. Weise

Stoeger Publishing Company

Published by Stoeger Publishing Company
55 Ruta Court
South Hackensack, New Jersey 07606

Library of Congress Catalog Card No.: 63-6200

International Standard Book No.: 0-88317-117-1

Manufactured in the United States of America

Distributed to the book trade and to the sporting goods trade by Stoeger Industries, 55 Ruta Court, South Hackensack, New Jersey 07606

In Canada, distributed to the book trade and to the sporting goods trade by Stoeger Trading Company, 165 Idema Road, Markham, Ontario, L3R 1A9.

Contents

*This 65 Anniversary Edition of
the SHOOTER'S BIBLE is
gratefully dedicated to
Howard Kicherer.*

*He served Stoeger from 1946, fresh out of the U.S. Coast Guard,
until his retirement as President in 1983. A loyal employee and
astute executive who guided Stoeger's destiny through good times
and bad, always a valued friend and sage counselor, Howard
Kicherer still continues to serve Stoeger as its "elder statesman."*

Foreword

*O*pponents of gun control scored a significant victory at the polls in California recently. This was no skirmish, but rather a major battle over Proposition 15, which would have become the toughest handgun control legislation on the books anywhere in the United States.

In samples of voter sentiment taken by pollsters six months before the election, victory seemed assured for proponents of gun control. Better than 60% of the voters favored Proposition 15. Yet on November 2nd, it took a drubbing at the polls.

First, let us look at what Proposition 15 was about. It would have registered every existing handgun in California. It would have imposed a mandatory jail term on anyone caught on the street with an unregistered handgun. And it would have limited the number of handguns in the state of California to the number which had been registered as of a year after the law went into effect. No one knows what this number would have been, but estimates placed it at about five million handguns.

Proposition 15 carefully skirted previous objections to similar legislation. It did not cover rifles or shotguns. It was not confiscatory. It was calculated to appeal to voters tired of seeing handguns associated with crime and violence. Had Proposition 15 passed in this, the nation's most populous state, a trend-setter in the traditionally free-wheeling West, other states could be expected to fall into line.

Proposition 15 was soundly trounced. It was almost as though the voters had heard the voice of wise old Ben Franklin saying, "Those who give up essential liberty to purchase a little temporary safety, deserve neither liberty nor safety."

What happened?

It is patently too easy to attribute the outcome to the relative amounts of money spent by each side, and this would be an insult to the intelligence of the voters of California. Great gobs of money could not assure victory to candidates in other parts of the country who outspent their rivals and still did not win. Other factors obviously played a role.

For one thing, Proposition 15 was intimidating by its sheer size. It ran to sixty printed pages in length. Moreover, as election time approached, it became apparent to California voters that Proposition 15 was aimed at the wrong target and ignored the real problem: crime. Most voters correctly recognized that Proposition 15 did nothing to address the festering sore of the crime problem.

There are more than twenty thousand gun-control laws already on the books nationwide. Yet there is little enforcement of existing gun-control laws and infrequent prosecution under them. California voters are to be complimented for perceiving that Proposition 15 would have injured the law-abiding citizen more than it would have punished the habitual criminal. Proposition 15 was a classic example of throwing the baby out with the bath water.

Voters soon realized that under Proposition 15 only law-abiding citizens would register their handguns. Criminals would, of course, continue to own and trade in unregistered handguns, taking their chances with the law if and when caught. That their chances of having anything more serious happen than confiscation of the weapon is borne out by the New York City experience. Playing on the fears of the city's crime-ridden residents and shopkeepers, New York's garrulous mayor trumpets that his city has the toughest gun law in the nation—like Proposition 15, it imposes a mandatory term (one year) for anyone found with an unregistered gun in his possession. Each year, some forty thousand unregistered guns are seized in New York City. What the mayor doesn't add is that their owners, all criminals by definition, are freed almost immediately by judges motivated not by compassion but by reality—the city's jail system is overcrowded to the point of explosion, and no relief is in sight. So much for "tough" gun-control laws.

Nevertheless, the proponents of similar legislation will be studying the lessons of Proposition 15 to make another assault on the civil liberties of law-abiding citizens. They will not make the same mistakes the second time around.

Be on the lookout for the following, among the expected tactics:

1. An attempt to portray lawful gun owners as the sole source of the weapons used in crimes. For this reason, responsible gun owners will want to continue to ensure the safety of the weapons they own. Each year, thousands of guns find their way into the hands of criminals as a result of thefts—thefts in transit; thefts from armories; thefts from firearms dealers, sporting goods stores or pawnshops; as well as thefts

from individual owners. Paradoxically, a gun is the only article of commerce that actually *increases* in value when it is stolen, making it more desirable as an object for theft. The thief who steals jewels, cameras, TV sets or a stereo system may get only ten cents on the dollar from a fence or other buyer of stolen merchandise, but a gun inevitably commands many times its actual value in the criminal underworld. Gun control will in no way reduce the traffic in such weapons.

2. An increased effort to enlist grass roots support for gun control will be mounted, perhaps linked to other issues. Control advocates envy the unanimity of the law-abiding gun owners and their presence at all levels of society, which makes for true grass roots strength.

3. A new Proposition 15—leaner, harder and more to the point—will certainly be offered to the voters again, backed this time by a bigger war chest.

Gun control is obviously not the answer. The real problem is—and always has been—crime. We need more and sterner and swifter and surer crime control—not more gun control. Moreover, not only do gun-contol laws fail to disarm criminals (New York's Sullivan Law is a classic example), they tend to make criminals of law-abiding citizens who, for philosophical reasons or on legal principles, see registration of handguns as a prelude to the registration of all guns and a first step toward eventual confiscation.

The misadventures of the Eighteenth (Prohibition) Amendment and its aftermath demonstrated that making the manufacture, transportation and sale of liquor a criminal act did not decrease the consumption of alcohol. If anything, more people drank, and they drank more liquor, liquor of doubtful quality, than ever before. Additionally, a criminally controlled underworld industry, bootlegging, was spawned as forty million gallons of illegal liquor were smuggled into the country annually. A veritable army of snooping government agents was powerless to stem the flow, at best intercepting only five percent of the bootleg liquor.

Gun control of the kind proposed by Proposition 15 will inevitably give rise to a similar criminal industry with the same consequences. Nor do we have reason to believe that the imposition and attempted enforcement of sterner gun-control laws will be any more successful than the government's current almost-futile effort to stem the rising tide of illicit drugs being smuggled into the United States by a vast criminal network and distributed openly by other criminals, a heinous trade that threatens to sap the very strength of this nation.

Wendell Phillips, in a not dissimilar context and quoting Thomas Jefferson, gave responsible gun owners their watchword: "Eternal vigilance is the price of liberty."

—ROBERT F. SCOTT

Articles

Getting Back to Basics: Matchlocks Then and Now

Robert Fisch

Would a reasonably prudent, rational, black powder enthusiast head for an afternoon's shooting pleasure on the range, knowing that in all probability he would return with holes burned in his clothing and maybe a few in his skin, black smears on his face, the latter perhaps covering a bruise on his cheek? He certainly would if he wanted to shoot a matchlock!

Although many people might think of matchlocks as primitive, one of the most important developments in firearms history was introduced during the matchlock era: the trigger. A man armed with a hand cannon had to start the ignition chain at the vent, get his hand back on the stock and aim the piece before the charge in the barrel was expelled. The development of the serpentine simplified this procedure.

At first the serpentine was a combination trigger and match holder. A piece of iron was formed into an "S" shape with a pivot slightly above center. A tube or clamp was formed on the upper end to hold the slowmatch and when the bottom half was pulled to the rear, the match was brought in contact with the vent. To facilitate ignition, a small receptacle was formed around the vent and filled with fine priming powder. No cover was provided for the pan and no springs were necessary to keep the arm of the "serpentine" vertical; the lower end was longer than the upper end and gravity did the job. We can presume holding the

musket vertically at "present arms" was not required when it was loaded and primed. Whether we interpret the serpentine as a primitive gunlock or simply an extended trigger, it certainly deserves a very high place on a list of significant developments in firearms history. It allowed the gunner the luxury of a good grasp on his piece, careful sighting and the discharge of the piece at the instant of his choosing.

Along with the introduction of the serpentine came a more advanced form of stock in comparison with hand cannons. The barrel was inset into the wood or at least clamped to it for most of its length, and the rear end of the stock was shortened so that it could be held in front of the man at eye level. The butt was too short and not properly shaped to be held against the shoulder, so the recoil could only be absorbed with both arms. If the shooter was wearing enough padding, the butt could be held against the breast, but was not as practical as "Cheeking" the stock.

It is believed that the first matchlocks with shoulder stocks originated in Spain in the middle of the 16th century. These 20-pound muskets were 8 to 10 gauge and fired up to 2-ounce charges of powder. Not only was a shoulder stock useful in firing these pieces, but a forked rest was also necessary to hold the barrel steady. The term "musket" denotes the larger of the shoulder arms and "caliver" the smaller. "Arquebus"

Illustration is from the Dutch *Wapenhandelinghe van Roers Musqyetten* by Jacob van Gheyn, printed in 1607. The musketeer is blowing the excess powder away from the pan before clamping the match into the serpentine.

is a term which was indiscriminately applied to either at times, but generally referred to calivers. A simple rule of thumb is—if the piece is so heavy to require a rest, it is a musket; if it can be comfortably held offhand, it is an arquebus or caliver. By the middle of the 17th century, muskets became lighter, averaging 14 to 16 pounds and these distinctions were no longer rigid.

After the introduction of the simple serpentine lock near the middle of the 15th century, several improvements were added which greatly facilitated its use. The flashpan was moved to the side of the barrel and a hinged cover was added to it. The common form of trigger used on crossbows, a long bar parallel to the stock, was connected to a simple lock mechanism. Internally the lock only consisted of a sear, link and spring, but the trigger pull was much shorter and the serpentine was drawn back out of the pan when the trigger was released. By the beginning of the 17th century, the standard "finger trigger" and trigger guard replaced the trigger bar and by the third quarter of the century, the pan was attached to the lockplate instead of to the barrel.

One departure from the simple form of matchlock mechanism which developed in the first half of the 16th century was the snapping lock. As the name suggests, the spring in this lock brings the serpentine to the pan instead of withdrawing it, as in the common matchlock. One might think such an improvement would completely supersede the earlier types, but such was not the case. Besides being more complicated and thus more expensive, they were more dangerous because the match is held closer to the pan encouraging accidental discharges. Worse yet, they could snap the match down into the pan and snuff it out or create a hangfire.

As unpopular as this lock was in Europe, it still was much used in another part of the world. This was the snapping type of matchlock which was brought to Japan in 1543 by Portuguese sailors. According to a Japanese account of the incident, a Chinese cargo ship landed at the island of Tanegashima. Three Portuguese adventurers aboard had two matchlocks among their possessions. The feudal master of Tanegashima, Lord Tokitaka, was so impressed with the possibilities of these guns, that he arranged to take shooting lessons from the Portuguese and within a month bought both pieces from them. He then ordered his chief swordsmith to copy them.

At this point, there is some confusion as to fact and legend, because it seems Yatsuita Kinbei, the swordsmith, was unable to duplicate the breechscrew. It is said that several months later a Portuguese ship stopped at Tanegashima and Kinbei gave his 17-year-

A hand cannoneer of the 15th-century taken from a woodcut in the "Rudimentum Noviciorum", Lübeck, 1475. The chain of ignition had to include a fuse in the vent to allow the cannoneer to get the hand holding the wire "touche" or slowmatch back on the "tiller" and aim the piece before it discharged.　　　　Illustration by Michael McAfee

old daughter to the captain of the ship in return for lessons from the ship's armorer. Kinbei made at least ten guns the first year and others began to copy them. Lord Tokitaka had all of his vassals equipped and trained by the middle 1540s, and large orders by other lords are a matter of record. By 1560, firearms were being used in battle, and it is recorded that a general wearing full armor died of a bullet wound that year. The use of firearms continued to expand until the last quarter of the 16th century. Then a regression began which not only limited the number of firearms that could be produced but also stifled any major improvements.

Those who have seen the television program or have read the book *Shogun* will be familiar with some of the customs and traditions of 16th–17th century Japan, especially the distinct classes among the

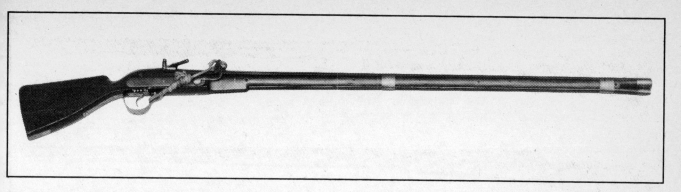

This German matchlock musket is .80 caliber and weighs almost 17 pounds. The form is generally of the first half of the 17th-century; it is provided with a steel band in the middle of the forend to reduce the wear on the stock from the forked rest.

West Point Museum Collections

people. The sword was said to be the soul of a samurai and years of training went into the use of swords and other "honorable" weapons. The method of fighting was different and even included strolling between the lines before a battle and boasting of one's past military exploits. It is said that at one battle which took place in 1548, the side with guns lost because of the guns. After the ritual of introductions, the side without guns attacked immediately and didn't give the other side time to ready their priming and matches. In subsequent battles, introductions had to be dispensed with, which obviously did not endear firearms in the eyes of those who had something to crow about. More and more noblemen were being removed from active campaigning by bullets fired from a distance by a peasant with only a few weeks' training. Beginning around 1587, repressive measures were taken.

The first step focused on removing the guns from the hands of civilians and was done quite craftily.

Lord Hideyoshi, the Regent of Japan, announced that he was going to build a gigantic statue of Buddha. Although mostly of wood, many tons of iron would be needed for the fixtures of it, and the $\frac{1}{8}$ of a square-mile-temple to house it. Farmers and monks were required to make their contributions of iron, and under the guise of religious devotion, disarmament began.

Firearms were still widely used for military purposes, but in 1607 edicts were proclaimed which would eventually give the edge back to those armed with cutlery. A Shogun, Lord Tokugawa Teyasu, ruled that Nagahama would be the central area in Japan for the gunmaking industry, and he began moving all of the gunsmiths there, except those of Sakai, where his power was not secure enough. He also required the gunsmiths to be licensed, appointing a commissioner of guns who would clear all orders for guns before the smiths could make them. Gradually the cutbacks

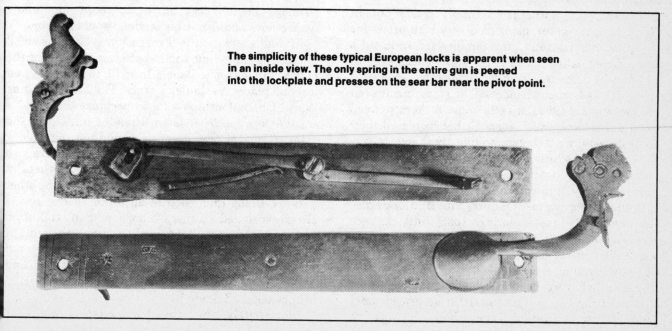

The simplicity of these typical European locks is apparent when seen in an inside view. The only spring in the entire gun is peened into the lockplate and presses on the sear bar near the pivot point.

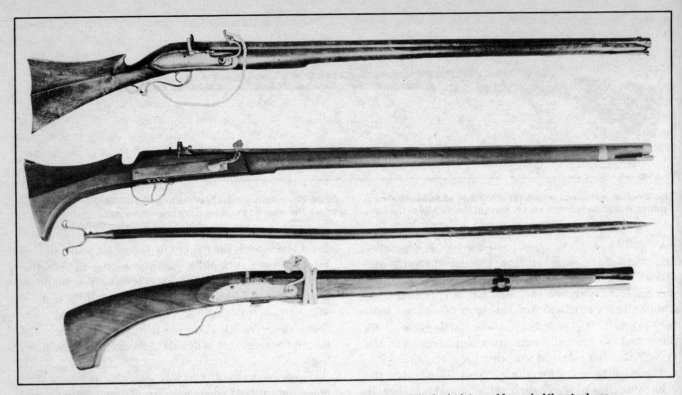

(Top) English military matchlock musket, c. 1670. The lock has an integral pan and the lockplate and forend of the stock are rounded, typical of a late matchlock. However, its 15-pound weight would still make the use of a forked rest desirable. (Middle) Austrian caliver and rest, late 16th-, early 17th-century. This .78 caliber caliver only weighs about 10 pounds and could be held comfortably without the rest. However, calivers were often equipped with rests simply to steady the aim of the shooter. The stock is beech, although chestnut, birch and fruitwood were also used. Walnut was seldom used on matchlocks, except those made in England. (Bottom) This reproduction 17th-century Spanish caliver was made in Spain about 25 years ago. It is a good example of the diversification in styling found on European matchlocks. The trigger is the type more popular in the 16th-century but has been combined with an integral pan lock of the late 17th-century.   **West Point Museum Collections**

began and by the 18th century production was limited to 35 large matchlocks in even years and 250 small matchlocks in odd years.

To keep the trade from totally dying out in Nagahama, the government paid very high prices for the guns and this kept a few families secure in their trade. Less qualified or talented gunsmiths stayed in business by doing repairs and making other articles of iron, such as farm implements. The government even offered guaranteed salaries to some makers to keep them in business, which even further increased their control over them. Understanding these events certainly explains why it is so difficult to find an average quality Japanese matchlock in fine condition today.

In the early 19th century, a very few progressive individuals began experimenting with flintlock arms. It is documented that as early as 1636, flintlocks were brought to Japan, but since the repressive measures were still in effect and no significant demand existed, business continued as usual at the few gunsmiths' forges still glowing. In 1855, when Commander John Rogers of the *U.S.S. Vincennes* led an armed party ashore on the island of Tanegashima, he was im-

pressed by the lack of knowledge among the people about firearms. The general term for firearm was "teppo," but the word for matchlock was "Tanegashima." Little did he or those inhabitants realize how significant his landing would become.

My indoctrination to Tanegashimas and the smell of burning rope came somewhat after the visit of the *U.S.S. Vincennes* to Japan. In 1976, to be exact, and in, of all places, Versailles, France. The Muzzleloading World Championships were in progress there and a small delegation from Japan attended to petition the International Committee to include a matchlock event in subsequent championships. They were also there to demonstrate matchlock shooting, perhaps in the hope of fostering interest in the event among other nations. Being interested in all forms of firearms, I already included a Tanegashima among my collection of muzzleloaders. Still, I never had serious thoughts of shooting anything quite so ancient. I had deciphered the Japanese characters on the barrel of my piece and knew that a gunsmith by the name of Matsunami Munashagi had made it.

Immediately after the demonstration was concluded, I approached a member of the Japanese delegation and offered to sell my Tanegashima to him. Not wanting to mix fountains of sparks and black powder and noticing the smoldering holes in his clothing, my instinct influenced my subconscious and wanted to remove temptation from my grasp. My description of the musket seemed to hold his attention until I mentioned the name Matsunami Munashagi at which time the conversation politely began to terminate with many explanations of the difficulty of owning firearms in Japan and especially of importing them. My thoughts were somewhat confused, but definitely included the opinion that among Japanese collectors, old Munashagi probably didn't even rate wall space.

One year later I was standing on the steps of the Schützen Haus in Zurich, a gold medal hanging from my neck and the Tanegashima Trophy in my hands, while several members of the Japanese Team offered their congratulations to me. My grin couldn't have been wider as two words came from my lips,

"Matsunami Munashagi," and I noticed the expression of one gentleman become rather grim. Undoubtedly that name has a special meaning for at least two people in the world.

Much had to be learned between September 1976 and September 1977. For example, the first thing anyone should do before firing an antique gun is examine it thoroughly. Upon removing the breechplug from Mr. Munashagi's creation, I found that he had not mastered the art of making screw threads. Since then I have unbreeched many others; all had plugs with 6 to 9 threads per inch and a thread angle of 100 to 120 degrees. They are made undersize and wrapped with thin sheet copper or brass to take up the slack, and most appear to be hand filed and scraped, both in the internal and external threads. Usually only bits and pieces of the sheet metal remain around the plug; even replacing it will not make a seal tight enough to completely eliminate gas leaks.

I proof-tested the musket with two balls and over 2½ times what I thought the normal load would be,

The author shooting a Tanegashima. The cloud of sparks generated at the moment of discharge looks like confetti, but many of them burn out before landing. The match has been blown out of the serpentine and the burning tip is just about to strike the shooting glasses. Eye protection is definitely recommended for this sport!

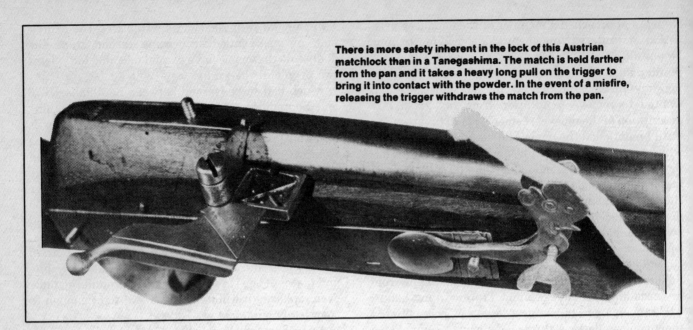

There is more safety inherent in the lock of this Austrian matchlock than in a Tanegashima. The match is held farther from the pan and it takes a heavy long pull on the trigger to bring it into contact with the powder. In the event of a misfire, releasing the trigger withdraws the match from the pan.

but eventually turned a new breechplug on my lathe because it was a nuisance to have fouling build up in the barrel channel with each shooting session. Others who are shooting these guns have done the same thing or else retapped the breech and then made a new plug or simply let the fouling build up in the threads to the point where it forms its own gas seal. The latter seems to have been the most popular Japanese method for 200 years.

Fortunately, the breechplug is usually the only screw you will encounter in a Japanese matchlock that has an external mainspring. The internal coil mainspring style will often have a second screw to hold the equivalent of the hammer and tumbler together, but everything else is held together by pins, dovetails, nails or friction alone. It's delightful to see the ingenuity used in assembling these guns.

As most of us do not include slowmatch among our stock of muzzleloading supplies, this is a primary consideration before heading for the range. Original slowmatch appears to be loosely woven plant fibers, cotton, flax and even bamboo in the case of Japanese match. A loose, almost fluffy core was surrounded by long firm strands around which thread was wound 2 or 3 turns to the inch. Usually, European match was nitrated and Japanese bamboo match was not. Today, it is far more expedient to make the slowmatch from cotton washline, ¼ - or $5/16$-inch diameter. Just be sure it does not have a synthetic core—otherwise it will not stay lit and will leave a gummy mess in your pan. It works best if the sizing has been removed so I prefer line which has been used about six months to a year. (Remember to buy a replacement before removing your wife's washline or your project will not be off to

a rousing start.) It must be nitrated, and the object is to get the nitrate to penetrate the entire rope without building up crystals on the outside.

I boil a two-pound coffee can of water and put six heaping tablespoons of potassium nitrate in it when it begins to boil. Then remove it from the stove and stuff as much washline in it as can be covered (20 to 25 ft.), let it soak for half a day. If crystals have formed on the outside, scrub them off—usually a dry brush will do it because they will "spark off" looking like miniature comets and occasionally ignite the priming at inopportune times. In the jargon of matchlock shooters, "zingers" are definitely to be avoided.

The remaining mechanics of shooting a Tanegashima are much the same as shooting other smoothbore weapons. A rifled European matchlock is extremely rare, but a rifled Tanegashima is unknown to me. A majority of shooters prefer to use a patched round ball, using the same rules of thumb as if it were rifled—including the powder charges. I embrace the opposite school of thought and use no patch, only a shotgun filler wad between the powder and ball. Most Tanegashimas are 40 to 50 caliber and a ¼ or $5/16$ inch wad such as the Alcan "Blue Streak" works very well. You might be tempted to try one of the larger caliber short-barrelled Tanegashimas, but you risk a swollen cheek and maybe even a visit to your dentist. Most likely you will have to make a wad cutter about .005 inches larger than bore size and cut oversize wads to fit.

If the wads are soaked in melted Crisco, the fouling will stay soft indefinitely without cleaning between shots. I pour about 30 wads in the Crisco at a time, sing one stanza from the overture of *The Mikado* very

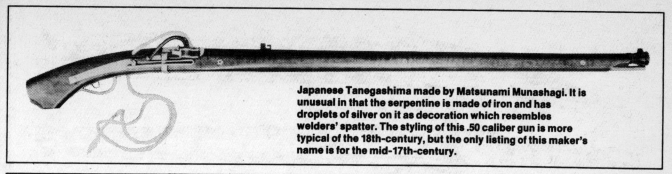

Japanese Tanegashima made by Matsunami Munashagi. It is unusual in that the serpentine is made of iron and has droplets of silver on it as decoration which resembles welders' spatter. The styling of this .50 caliber gun is more typical of the 18th-century, but the only listing of this maker's name is for the mid-17th-century.

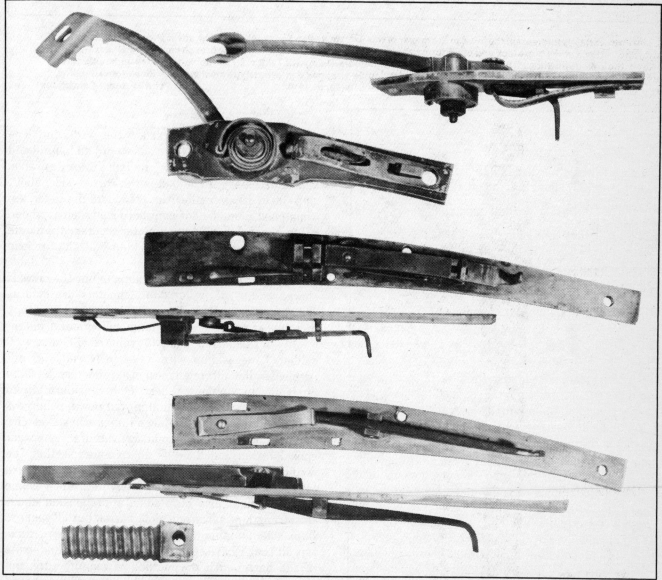

The inside views of these Tanegashima locks illustrate the three basic systems used by the Japanese. The lower lock has a sear that moves horizontally and simply hooks over the tail of the serpentine. The middle lock has a primary sear that moves parallel to the lockplate and is connected to a coiled flat spring which allows trigger pull adjustment. The secondary sear is "U" shaped and is pivoted at the bottom of the "U". The branches of the "U" protrude through the lockplate and hold the tail of the serpentine in the cocked position. The upper is the last type to be developed and is generally found on 19th-century guns. Although it has a simple laterally moving sear with the sear spring mounted over it, the power for the serpentine is supplied by a brass coiled flat spring. The breech plug is from an early 18th-century Tanegashima, but the coarse shallow threads are typical of all Japanese matchlocks.

West Point Museum Collections

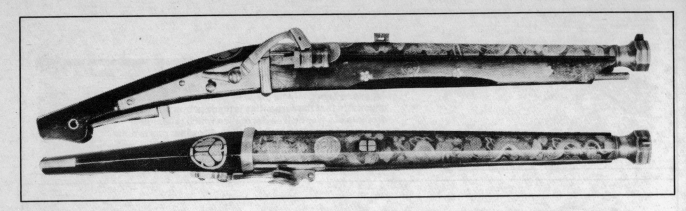

Quality was certainly foremost in the mind of the maker of this extremely fine Tanegashima. Gold, silver and brass were used in its decoration and the brass lock and other furniture were silver plated. On the stock at the breech can be seen the family crest of the Tokugawa Shogun, the barrel bears the crest of Uemura, Daimyo of Takatori. The rubbing from the underside of the barrel has been translated and indicates that the barrel is double-wrapped damascus-type steel made by Shichirobei Oshikaji, who used the pseudonym Shigehide. It was made at Sakae City about 1810.　　　　West Point Museum Collections

Kitae

Nijyu

Makibari

Oshikaji

Shichirobei

Shigehide

鍛二重巻張

噫鍛治七郎兵衛重燦㐵

quickly and immediately scoop the wads out. Too much lubricant makes the wads sloppy to handle and weakens them. A wad over the ball is not desirable, and unnecessary if the ball is the correct size, about .002–.003 inches smaller than the bore diameter. An unpatched round ball of semi-hard lead such as wheel-balance metal seems to give better accuracy than pure lead, but if you intend to patch your bullets, pure lead is a necessity.

A practical thing to remember is to put the powder charge under the bullet. Most shooters use 3FG in Japanese matchlocks and 2FG in European matchlocks because of the large calibers and poorer quality of the barrels. I use 45 grains of 3FG in my .50 caliber Tanegashima with a $5/16$ inch wad and un-patched bullet, although most other shooters use 50 to 60 grains in similar calibers. One consideration to keep in mind when determining your powder charge is that the gun is being used as a target arm so velocity and muzzle energy are secondary to accuracy. Another consideration which needs no reminder is that the recoil is being absorbed by your cheek and hands so a lower level of recoil is definitely desirable. Some shooters might also have some apprehension about the strength of a Tanegashima barrel, but all seem to be excellent quality. There are no proof marks as such, but all that I have seen are marked on the underside of the barrel with the method of manufacture and type of material. The usual process of making a barrel involved coiling a flat strip of metal around a mandril and forge-welding it in the same manner that twist barrels were made in Europe. However, the Japanese welded a second strip coiled in the opposite direction around the first; this adds quite a margin of strength to the barrel. Some of these early matchlock barrels

The ingredients: Alcan Blue Streak felt wads cut .005 over bore diameter and soaked in melted Crisco, bullets cast of wheel weights .003 under bore diameter and the sprues clipped, separate powder charges in fire-resistant containers and a non-metallic priming container with a minimum amount of powder in it.

were so sturdy that they were rifled and converted to breechloading bolt-action rifles in the late 19th century. It's understandable that any craftsman who could produce edged weapons of the quality of Japanese swords would not have any difficulty fashioning attractive and robust gun barrels.

With all of the components assembled, now the shooting can begin. It's a good idea and also a rule in international shooting to detach the match from the gun while loading. It should be placed in a fireproof container so spilled powder cannot reach it. A soda can with some holes punched in it for ventilation will do, but I prefer my little tin recipe box which has a clip riveted inside to suspend the match. The pan cover must be closed or the vent stopped with a pipe cleaner

or some other method as the vents are usually large enough to allow 3FG powder to escape when the ball is rammed. The loading and priming are accomplished in the same manner as a flintlock weapon, but after priming and closing the pan cover, one should "huff and puff" with enthusiasm around the pan to be sure that no loose powder is exposed. Then take the match and thread it through the match support hole in the stock, or secure it to the gun by wrapping it around the barrel, triggerguard or some other method. Some shooters nail the match to the bench or wall, but that method limits your movement.

Blow on the glowing tip to clear off the ash and insert it into the serpentine, taking care that the tip of the match will be brought into the center of the pan

First target after the winter layoff scores out to 88. In international matches no sighting shots are permitted but 13 rounds are fired and the highest 10 are scored. The 10 ring is 80 mm in diameter and each ring is 80 mm larger. The target adopted by the International Committee is the French Army 200M rifle target which accounts for the large black area. In using it at 50M, it is very easy to lose your sight picture in this big blob. In the four championships in which the Tanegashima match has been fired, the winning scores have been 87, 86, 95, 90. Twice the Gold Medal has been awarded to Wilhelm Weigner of West Germany and twice to the author.

serpentine and anchor point of the match to a minimum. On a Tanegashima, the match is anchored behind the serpentine so if the match is blown out of the serpentine upon discharging the piece, it is blown to the rear. If there is too much slack in the match, the burning tip kisses you in the face—a very unpleasant sensation.

Among other negative aspects, it is also advisable not to go shooting on a windy day. A stiff breeze increases the burning rate of the match to the point where sparks will be blown off it, and they have a nasty way of finding the powder as soon as you open the pan cover. Then you have to absorb the recoil with only one hand. I prefer to hold the musket at cheek level and aim it down range when uncovering the pan so any surprises will head in a safe area.

Conversely, on a still, muggy day, when the match is not burning very hot, ash will build up on the tip and the match will drop into the pan without igniting the powder. With luck, it might be a long hang fire but more often than not you can stare, make faces, curse at it and nothing will happen until you try to pull the match out of the pan. Actually it is best to count to about ten, get a good one-handed grip on the piece and then recock it by pressing on the tail of the serpentine behind the pivot point so your hand is not in line with the vent blast. Then count to at least ten again before brushing the powder and ash out of the pan and repriming. In such situations, the European type matchlock has the advantage, because releasing the trigger automatically withdraws the match from the pan.

when the serpentine falls. Do not extend the tip of the match beyond the edge of the serpentine more than necessary to align it, and keep the slack between the

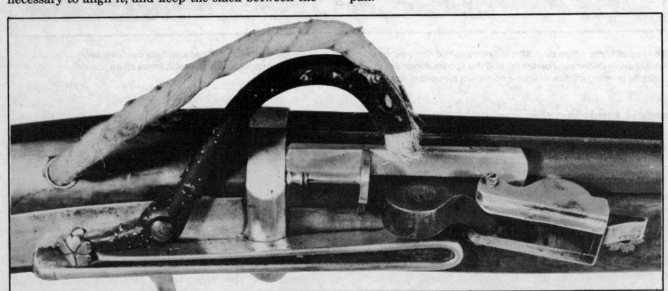

There is no automatic pan opener on a Tanegashima. Once the pan cover is swung forward you have fire three-quarters of an inch from your powder. The pan is welded to the barrel, whereas on European matchlocks it is dovetailed to the barrel or welded to the lockplate. The match is original 19th-century Japanese bamboo match. When hunting, a short piece of match was pinned to the serpentine through the holes in the socket and lighted from a main match carrier in a container when the quarry was sighted.

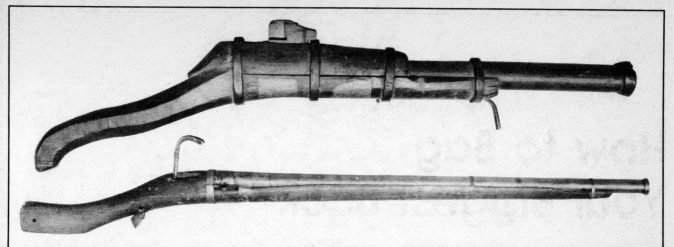

There are no time limitations on the manufacture and use of early styled crude weapons. Both of these arms were used against U.S. troops in this century. The 14th-century type hand cannon on top was captured from insurgents in the Philippines and the 15th-century-style matchlock shown below was captured at Peking during the Boxer Rebellion.

West Point Museum Collections

One final negative aspect of shooting matchlocks is the problem of finding one that has the potential to be a shooter. Most European matchlocks are of large caliber and seldom have shootable bores. They also seem to have been high on the menu priorities of wood worms and generally show their age. There is light at the end of the tunnel, though, because Navy Arms Company, of Ridgefield, New Jersey, is planning to reproduce European-style matchlocks. For the handyman, there is also the option of making one. A number of barrel makers today are offering smoothbore barrels for shotguns and trade muskets. The lock and furniture are rudimentary and the stock is also quite basic. Perhaps this would be the ideal project for someone who would like to build his first "scratch" gun.

A Japanese Tanegashima is a more demanding project and requires a wide selection of scrap brass. On most, only the barrel, integral pan and the breechplug are of ferrous metal. All else, including the springs, is brass or precious metal, and bamboo is sometimes used for the trigger and barrel pins. Until 1981 there was little reason to make a reproduction Tanegashima for shooting, since originals could be found at reasonable prices and international competition required that originals be used.

Since then, the rules have been altered to include a reproduction matchlock event, so there is now a small but worldwide market for these guns. Occasionally matchlocks can also be used in more local competition as many shooting matches which include smoothbore flintlock or percussion muskets will also allow matchlock shooters to participate. If the weather is favorable, the matchlock musketeer is at little or no disadvantage for the ignition can be very rapid and positive, the small bore of a Tanegashima is easier to control and it has no heavy lock action to jar the weapon at the moment of discharge.

Even if one has no interest in competing with matchlocks, shooting them can be instructive and fun. There is no better weapon for developing self discipline, mental management and a keen awareness of the need to follow safety procedures. Other shooters on the firing line will respect your turf. No one crowds a matchlock shooter and after a while, you will not even hear the shouts of "Pyromaniac!" from your friends.

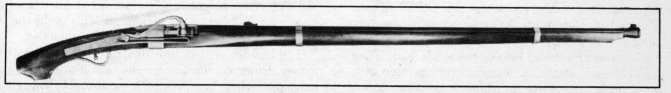

Although reproducing a Japanese Tanegashima might seem to be an overwhelming project to many people, Heinrich Schreiber of New Windsor, New York, made this Tanegashima in just over three weeks. The tapering flats on the Dixie Gun Works smooth bore .43 caliber barrel were milled but everything else was formed with hand tools. Those of us without a lifetime of experience in machining and blacksmithing could expect to spend a little more time on such a project. As far as is known by the author, this is the first reproduction Tanegashima made in the United States.

How to Bag Your Biggest Buck

Don Lewis

The hunter eased to a ridge overlooking a wide valley. For several minutes he glassed the opposite hillside. Suddenly, the unmistakable horizontal line of a deer's back became visible in a stand of small saplings. A long look through binoculars proved it was a legal buck.

Slipping into a sitting position, he rested the single-shot rifle against a tree and found the buck in the scope. The distance was over 200-yards, but he was prepared for a long shot, having scouted the area earlier. He had sighted the Ruger 7mm Magnum in two inches high at 100-yards. The 140-grain bullet would be on target across the valley. Seconds later, the buck moved into a clearing and the hunter froze the crosswire reticle on the ribcage and touched off the shot; it was a clean kill.

Undoubtedly, similar scenes are repeated thousands of times each year across the United States; whitetail deer hunting is the nation's number one big-game hunting sport. That is understandable, too. Early settlers depended heavily on the whitetail. They ate deer meat, stretched deerskin over log cabin windows, made clothes from deerhides and became proficient riflemen matching their shooting skills against the elusive whitetail. In a sense, deer made it possible for America to grow.

While the whitetail deer is part of America's history, it is actually an immigrant. Somewhere back in the distant past, whitetails crossed the Asian-American land bridge and survived the terrible droughts, glaciers and predators of the Pleistocene Period.

The proper name for this graceful animal is *Odecoileus virginiana,* and there are more than 25 subspecies in the United States and southern Canada. Basically, the whitetail's habitat lies east of the Mississippi. Mule deer rule the western states; the whitetail is rare in Nevada, Washington and California. In the east, New England, Pennsylvania, Wisconsin and Michigan are famous for their whitetail populations. Pennsylvania is not a large state, ranking 33rd in area, and has close to 12 million people, yet it maintains a herd of over 650,000 deer.

The whitetail is not really a big animal, but hunters tend to overestimate the size of it. An adult whitetail has a shoulder height of 30 to 40 inches, with most measuring well below the maximum. This is the distance from the ground to the top of the shoulder.

The bottom of the chest line runs from 18 to 24 inches. However, it's the weight that hunters can't judge properly. A hog-dressed 18-month-old Pennsylvania buck will seldom go over 110 pounds. In Maine, for instance, a buck of the same age could tip the scales up to 125 pounds.

The growth pattern of a deer is much like a tree; it

Photos by Helen Lewis

Mike Ondik, noted Pennsylvania deer biologist. Here Ondik checks a buck that has just shed its antlers. Note cavity above buck's eye.

grows rapidly through the spring, summer and early fall and then literally stops during the winter. A fawn will add about ⅓-pound per day and can double its weight during the first two weeks of its life.

One of the most intriguing aspects of a buck deer is its rack. There are probably more misconceptions on this subject than in all the rest of deer hunting. It's a common belief that a male deer is a spike buck the first year and adds points each year after that.

Pennsylvania's noted deer biologist Mike Ondik, who supervised the deer research program for the Pennsylvania State University for 20 years states research doesn't substantiate that belief. Ondik says that many deer biologists now believe the number of points is genetic and a characteristic of the species. From his own observations with hundreds of bucks he worked with, most mature 1½-year old bucks will have 8 points and will continue to have 8 points through their life span. A buck sheds it antlers after

the mating season.

This also holds true with other point spreads. If a buck had 5 points on its second year, it would always be a 5 point unless disease, parasites or an accident damaged the rack.

This doesn't mean the rack will always remain the same in physical dimensions. The length and thickness of the main beams and points are directly related to habitat. This is why a buck's age cannot be determined by the size of the rack. A very old buck can produce a massive rack if it lives in prime habitat. A very young buck can do the same thing. However, a buck living in an over-browsed area may never procude a large, heavy set of antlers.

During the thousands of hours Ondik spent studying deer, he learned there is a distinct correlation between rain and the time a doe chooses to drop her fawn. He found that during the fawning season, the birth rate would be low if the nights were bright and

1984 SHOOTER'S BIBLE 23

Bill Nichols, of De Young, Pennsylvania, spends more time watching than walking. Here he kneels to check the deer trail far ahead. He knows a buck could be watching its back trail. Rifle is a .257 Roberts in a Mauser action. Stock designed and built by Nichols. Scope is a 2½x7X Weaver.

Deer are polygamous, and a healthy buck will make with many does. The breeding season is called the "rut" and varies somewhat from North to South, but generally is from mid-October to early December. Bucks reach sexual maturity during their second year and become very aggressive during the rutting season. By this time, the rack is hard as bone and highly polished. The buck stakes out his territory by making "rubs" on small saplins. The rub is not part of the process of polishing the antler during the velvet stage; it's the "No Trespassing" sign for other bucks to heed. Once he stakes out his domain, he continues to make the rounds to each rub to see if another buck is challenging his right to that area.

During the mating season, when two bucks meet there is no backing down; conflict is inevitable. Each is ready for combat after weeks of sparring with saplings and small bushes that have hardened their neck muscles. At this point, the buck is swollen-necked and red-eyed. The contest seldom ends in death, but occasionally the horns will become "locked" and both deer will die from starvation.

The whitetail deer is a creature of the night. It seldom moves during the day unless disturbed. This means the hunter has to move the deer. Unfortunately, not many hunters know how to do this properly. It's safe to say the hunter is his own worst enemy. His prime mistake is not realizing the immense advantage a deer has over him.

Ondik put it this way. "A deer has the remarkable ability to pick out a disturbing smell from among many smells and respond to it alone. It can also distinguish one sound it knows means danger from a conglomerate of sounds."

Nichols was even more emphatic. "Most hunters don't know what they are looking for. The secret of success is always to be on the alert and constantly scan the land around them. A good deer hunter doesn't just look for a whole deer; he watches for a horizontal line that could be a deer's back, the curve of a hip or even the quick wag of an ear."

The prime requisite for any deer hunter is to learn the area to be hunted. The more the hunter knows about the terrain, the better the chances for success. Start with a topographical map and get a general view of the area. Know which way the streams and fire trails run. Once you are familiar with the overall picture, move into the area with a compass and learn the lay of the land firsthand. Find out where the deer run and where their trails cross. These indicate how the deer move when not disturbed. No hunter can be successful on his own unless he knows the land around him.

dry. Rain would trigger a chain reaction. Apparently, rain washes away much of the scent and makes it safer for the fawn.

Another old fable is that the hunter can tell the sex of a deer by its track. Veteran whitetail hunter and guide Bill Nichols, of De Young, Pennsylvania, claims this is not exactly the case. He found that the tracksize was not important, but experience has proved to him that the females have a tendency to walk in single file or in a straight line. The buck, being more cautious and wary, stays on the outside of the herd zig-zagging back and forth and turning often to watch his back track.

Ondik agrees that size doesn't mean a thing. He states, "I have measured hundreds of deer feet, and there are no distinguishing differences between the sexes. With experience, we could tell the very young from the adults, but the only sure thing the track tells the hunter is which way the deer is going."

Veteran deer hunter and guide Bill Nichols, of De Young, Pennsylvania, holds a nice Pennsylvania 6-point shot by his son Ken. On the wall are two nice bucks also taken by Nichols. On the left is a Pennsylvania 8-point; on the right a 4-point Wyoming Mule deer.

Note the horizontal line of a deer's back (second deer from left). Three deer are visible in this photo. In denser cover, the two deer on the left would be very hard to see.

During the hunt, move slowly and cautiously. When tracking, take plenty of time. The buck knows it is being followed and will spend minutes standing motionless watching its back trail. The hunter who moves too fast keeps the deer on the move and will never get within shooting range. It's wiser to spend more time watching than moving.

Snow is the page nature writes on during the winter. The hunter who has a comprehensive knowledge of his quarry carefully studies the "snow signs." Tracks that are frozen on the bottom are old, but a well-packed track with soft edges is fresh. Master deer hunter Bill Nichols takes advantage of everything written in the snow including "urine" signs. The doe urinates behind her rear legs while the bucks splashes his urine in front of his rear feet. Nichols admits this isn't an easy sign to read, but it does show that the experienced deer hunter must use a great deal of woodlore when matching his hunting skills against the wary whitetail.

Since most hunters are as much out of place in a deer woods as a deer would be in a department store, leaning against a large tree and being very still and acutely observant is the best success method. Choose an area that has several deer crossings within shooting range. Stay close to sections of woods that have several or more buck rubs. In early morning or late evening, the buck may make the rounds. In the South, hunters look for fresh "scrapes." Scrapes are made during the rutting season when the buck cleans away a small area right down to the fresh dirt and usually urinates on it to attract does. Normally, a buck returns to his scrape several times to check it and renew it with urine. In a sense, the scrape tells the hunter where the buck is going to be.

When it's raining, move quietly a few yards at a time and watch as far ahead as possible. A buck will pussyfoot ahead of the hunter in rainy conditions. A good practice is to stop by a tree for concealment and study the entire area in front and on both sides. It's amazing how easily a deer can circle around a hunter.

If a hunter knows the lay of the land, many times he can get out in front of a buck and wait until it passes. This will only work when conditions are right. A deer's sense of smell is incredible and can whiff the hunter's scent long before the deer is in view. The buck just circles the unsuspecting hunter. So always try to hunt with the wind coming from the deer.

As the season wears on, bucks become extremely cautious and will leave the main herd. The hunter should check out isolated spots such as crabapple thickets, grassy fields that contain a few trees and wooded gullies. It's unusual for a buck to desert his home range. Biologists claim a deer will live its entire life in an area less than 1½-miles square if habitat is good. It does know every square foot of its territory and will use every thicket, gulley or wooded area for a hiding place.

There's no better method for seeing deer than ridge hunting. Here the hunter moves along a ridge but stays twenty or thirty yards form the crest. Every fifty yards or so, the hunter moves quietly to the edge and studies the hollow below. The wind is seldom a factor since the hunter is much higher than the deer. This is a very slow method since most of the time is spent watching, but it does give the hunter a distinct advantage.

Deer hunting has many aspects. Organized drives, treestand watching or just the lone hunter following a track are a few of the methods used to hunt the whitetail deer. Weather conditions can spell success or failure—sit tight when the wood's floor is crackling dry and move cautiously when snow or rain deadens the hunter's footsteps. Deer hunting is a sport with many ingredients.

Of all the arguments in deer hunting, the controvery over choosing the proper cartridge leads the list. Actually, a variety of cartridges can be used. In the swamps of South Carolina, the shotgun with buckshot is a must when shots are under 25 yards. In the wide open West, long range Magnum cartridges are needed to cover the super-long shots. It's in the northeastern section of the United States where all the confusion begins. States such as Pennsylvania, New York and Maine have varying types of terrain and vegetation, and the deer hunter should use the cartridge he feels is best for his type of terrain. However, another hunter in the same area may decide a different cartridge is better.

If *Homo sapiens* were really a rational creature, the cartridge argument could be settled in relatively short order. Ballistically, it's as plain as day. The brush hunter whose shots are not more than 100 yards would stick with cartridges like the 30-30, 32 Winchester Special, 35 Remington or Winchester's two new creations, the 307 and the 356. What about sights for these close shots? That's really no problem. Simply stick with "peep" sights or use a 1½ × 4X variable power scope.

The hunter who favors open-terrain-type hunting won't be hard pressed for a good cartridge, either. The old .270 Winchester, 30-06 and 8mm along with several new creations like Remington's 7mm Express and 7mm-08 won't shortchange the hunter on shots up to 250 yards. For this type of shooting, open sights are pretty much out of the question, but the 2½ × 7X or

Ben Rogers Lee, of Coffeeville, Alabama, gets out of his self-climbing tree stand after bagging a nice ten-point Alabama buck. Rifle is a Browning semi-automatic 30-06 scoped with a Leupold 3 x 9X variable. Lee is a nationally recognized turkey hunter, noted for his ability to use a turkey call. He is also an avid deer hunter.

the 3 × 9X variable power scopes have this range of shooting written all over them.

Powerful super Magnum cartridges like the .300 Winchester Magnum, 300 H & H Magnum or the 8mm Remington Magnum have no place in the eastern deer woods. Deer are tough animals, but their skeletal makeup doesn't require heavy high-velocity bullets for penetration.

Other cartridges that classify as deer stoppers include the 6mm creations when 100-grain bullets are used, Weatherby's .270 Magnum and the Remington 7mm Magnum. Some chamberings that are no longer mass-produced but are top deer cartridges include the .257 Roberts, .284 Winchester and the .264 Winchester Magnum. From a true ballistic viewpoint, the .264 Winchester, .270 Weatherby and the 7mm Remington Magnum can't be clased with the larger Magnum shells. Hence, all are top-notch whitetail cartridges.

With such a wide selection to choose from, it doesn't seem possible there would be a clamor for something different. The trend today is for power, but that's not the total answer. Hunting history reveals the 30-30 Winchester cartridge has killed more deer than any other cartridge, and the 30-30 can't be considered powerful. What is the answer?

Some wise whitetail hunter claimed that any rifle is a good deer rifle in the hands of a good deer hunter, and there's a lot of truth in that. It's not the cartridge that makes the hunter. When all the dust and rhetoric have settled, ballistics take over.

In simple terms, the deer cartridge must produce sufficient killing power at long ranges, and its bullet has to meet certain constructional criteria. For many years, a bullet that produced 1300 foot pounds of energy at 100 yards was considered adequate in the power realm. That in itself is misleading; a lot of bullets large and small fall into that category. For instance, a 50-grain .224 bullet leaving the muzzle at 3,900 feet per second will produce more than 1,300 foot pounds of energy at 100-yards, but it's highly possible the tiny slug will disintegrate immediately

J. Wayne Fears, of Tuscaloosa, Alabama, examines a nice Alabama four point. Rifle is a Ruger M-77 .257 Roberts with a 3 x 9X Jason Empire scope.

Two new entries for the deer hunter. Left is Remington Model Seven 7mm-08 carrying a Burris 6X scope in Leupold mounts. Compact, lightweight (6¼-pounds) ideal for young, old or female hunter. Right is a Ruger Model M-77 RSI Mannlicher .308 topped with 2½ x 7 (V7W) Widefield and an Uncle Mike Cobra sling.

after impact. It isn't constructed to penetrate heavy bone and muscle and has little value in the deer woods.

There isn't an exact blueprint for determining a proper whitetail bullet, but it's fair to say it should weigh at least 100-grains, be designed to expand uniformly and retain the bulk of its weight after impact for penetration purposes.

Deer hunting can be long-or short-range shooting, although most deer are killed under 150 yards in the East. This is the paramount reason oldies such as the 30-30, 32 Winchester Special and 35 Remington still rank high in popularity. At 125 yards, these old cartridges are deadly.

The configuration of a deer rifle should meet the psychological requirements of the hunter. In all probability, he will match it to the terrain being hunted. In dense cover, a short carbine-type is just the ticket, and we're right back with the 94 Winchester, 336 Marlin lever outfits and the old 35 Remington pump. Lately, rifle manufacturers are offering compact, lightweight bolt-action outfits like the Ruger M-77 RSI Mannlicher and the Remington Model Seven. Neither rifle stretches beyond 39-inches in length or tips the scales above the 6¼-pound mark. Ideal deer outfits for older hunters and the distaff side of the family.

Remington's new slide action in their Model Four

and Six versions has a smoother working action and should fit the needs of the mobile hunter. Drop the detachable magazine out of the rifle, flip open the action and the pump rifle is empty.

There is no shortage of good rifles. The list runs from old standbys like the Savage 99 lever and the ex-military 30-40 Krag to new entries like the model 1500 Smith and Wesson and Thompson Arms' brand new single shot that accommodate five interchangeable barrels. Browning, Colt, Harrington & Richardson, and Weatherby are some of the American firms that offer top deer rifles. The discriminating hunter can have special outfits from DuBiel Arms Company, Sherman, Texas; Paul Jaeger, Jenkintown, Pennsylvania and Bighorn Rifles, Orem, Utah. Anything the hunter needs is available today.

The excitement shouldn't end when the whitetail is bagged. Deer meat is top quality red meat free from additives commonly found in domestic meats. Properly handled from the moment of the kill, deer meat has no peer; it is delicious.

Critics who claim it doesn't taste like beef are missing an important point—deer meat *shouldn't* taste like beef. It has a robust, invigorating flavor of its own. Pork, fowl and fish don't taste like beef, but this doesn't relegate them to the ranks of the unwanted. The truth is that a lot of deer meat is ruined

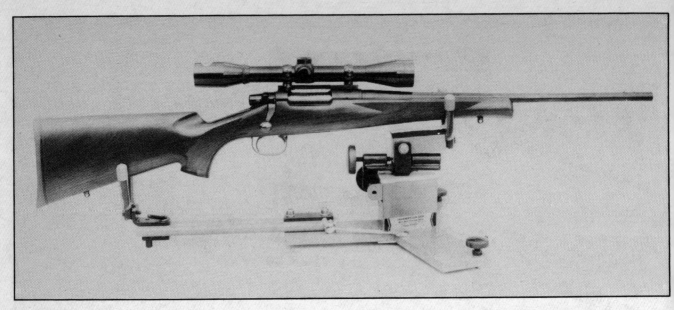

For the hunter who has a benchrest or heavy table to shoot from, the Cravener Micro-Benchrest allows precise metering both in elevation and windage. Rifle rest in two plastic covered V-Forks that eliminates much of the recoil. Rest is complete with leveling screws and rear V-fork adjusts for long or short stocks.

long before it gets to the chef.

Unlike domestic meat that is slaughtered under controlled conditions by professional butchers, a high percentage of deer are killed, field-dressed and cut up for freezing by people who have no knowledge of meat processing.

Deer hunters in Nichols' class make every attempt to shoot through the chest or rib cage. This vital-organ area is not only a fatal shot, but allows the animal to bleed-out internally. The only other shot that permits a deer to "bleed-out" is a neck shot. The latter type of shot immobilizes the deer without immediately stopping its heart.

Actually, deer meat can be spoiled before the hunter pulls the trigger. Organized "drives" produce deer, but if the deer are pushed hard, the steaks, tenderloin, chops and roasts are literally being charged with adrenalin. The same is true when a wounded deer is relentlessly pursued. The meat in most cases will have a strong, rank taste.

The hunter should make every effort not to arouse the animal. Stalk the quarry quietly and make one well-placed shot in the neck or chest cavity. With a clean kill, the hunter's next important task is field-dressing.

Approach a downed deer carefully from the back. Jab it several times with a long stick; a dying deer can seriously injure or kill a hunter with its flailing hoofs. A deer dies with its eyes open. If they are closed, it is probably only stunned and a finishing shot will be required.

As a precautionary move, it's wise to remove the tarsal (musk) glands on the inside of each hind leg. These glands produce a strong, sickening odor that will be transferred to the meat if it gets on the hands or knife. Start back under the hide a full inch from the glands and take plenty of time in cutting each gland free. Do not touch them or cut into the glands.

There are a number of methods for cleaning a deer. Make a slit from the breastbone to the aitchbone. Cut through the paper-thin diaphragm at the breastbone and reach up into the neck area as far as possible, and grasp the gullet and windpipe (the gullet is smooth and the windpipe feels like a gas-mask hose). With great care, reach up past the lungs with the knife and sever both tubes.

Some hunters break through the atichbone to free the rectum and urethra while others encircle the anus with a deep cut and pull the rectum into the body through the pelvic arch. The latter method is better since it doesn't expose a lot of good meat to dirt and drying. When all the minor attachments are cut free, roll the entire viscera on the ground.

If the bullet passed through the stomach or any part of the intestines, wash out the deer thoroughly as soon as possible. If water isn't available, use snow or even a rag to get the waste material out of the deer. In any case, wash the deer out before skinning it.

In the skinning process, hang the deer with the head down and peel the hide from the legs, body and neck and remove the head. It's next to impossible to skin a deer without getting hair on the meat, and it's difficult to see. An easy method for removing the hair is to use a common propane torch and a clean cloth.

Sweep the flame over a section of the body being careful not to overheat the meat. The heat crinkles the hair which can be wiped off. This is a time-consuming job. Inspect the deer for hidden or "buried" hairs. In the transparent fat, the hair is almost invisible. This writer works the torch over the meat during the packaging process.

Deer hunting has a humane side most anti-hunters never see. Those who see culling the herd as cruel and unnecessary do not understand the workings of nature. As man encroaches more and more on hunting lands, habitat vanishes. When deer are permitted to become overabundant and exceed the carrying capacity of their range, they literally eat the plants and preferred browse to death. Winter then becomes the grim reaper. In the North, deer huddle together in "yards" forsaking much of their range. Deer cannot navigate in deep snow, and in bitter conditions will not leave the yard area. Many starve within a mile of good food habitat. The fawns go first as malnutrition and pneumonia set in.

Herd management is the answer. Removing a predetermined number of deer each year keeps the herd size within the limits of the food supply and produces healthier deer. Those who attack deer management programs and cry "inhumane" for killing antlerless deer haven't seen the gaunt, puffed faces of helpless animals in the final stages of malnutrition. Buck shooting alone will never keep the number of deer at a level where all deer will get enough to eat.

Proof of the wisdom of deer management exists in Pennsylvania. For three decades, deer management has been a prime function of the Game Commission. Each season, a predetermined number of antlerless deer are removed from each county, and the practice has paid off. Executive Director Peter S. Duncan reported that of the 20 most successful buck seasons, 19 have occurred since 1963. During the 1982 seson, 72,113 bucks and 66,109 antlerless deer were harvested for a total of 138,222. Duncan says this is an impressive indication that the Commission's deer management program is working well.

Death is never a pleasant sight, weather it is a dying stockyard steer or a whitetail deer. We accept the killing of the steer as necessary for our survival but condemn the killing of antlerless deer as cruel and senseless. We fail to realize that flesh is a replaceable commodity. A forest strip-mined and bulldozed for the coal underneath is gone forever. Draining a swamp for an industrial complex destroys habitat and puts a severe strain on the entire ecosystem. Yet, unlike the forest and swamp that are beyond recall, we can alter the number of deer to be compatible with the food supply without suffering any long-term loss in population.

The majestic whitetail deer with its regal rack and waving white flag is for all hunters. No matter what walk of life the hunter comes from, deer hunting is not beyond his reach financially. It is not in some distant land—it's local, within a few miles even of the city dweller. Equipment is a matter of choice; a custom outfit for the affluent hunter or a simple single shot 30-30 for the farm lad. That's the beauty of this fascinating sport.

Author Don Lewis with ten-point mentioned in article. Rifle is a Ruger Number 1 chambered for the Remington 7mm Magnum cartridge. Scope is a 4 x 12X Redfield Variable power.

Photograph taken in 1841 of Simeon North at 76 years old — using the daguerreotype process invented in the 1830's.

Simeon North:
The First Fifty Years
of American Firearms

Frank R. North

B uyers of firearms are more than familiar with many names of illustrious arms manufacturers and inventors of years past. A list could include such names as Colt, Remington, Savage, Smith & Wesson, Winchester, Browning, Iver Johnson, and Mannlicher—and the list could go on and on. The name of one prolific arms maker though is sadly forgotten and won't be found on rifles or handguns displayed in gunshop cases or on racks in sporting goods stores.

Simeon North, a name unfamiliar to most, manufactured almost fifty thousand pistols, seven thousand rifles and close to thirty thousand breechloading rifles and carbines. Over a fifty-three year period, he made firearms for the U.S. Army, Navy and early state militias during the administrations of twelve presidents—from John Adams through Millard Fillmore. North's arms were carried by our armed forces in the Wars of Tripoli, War of 1812, Seminole Wars, the Black Hawk War and the Mexican War in 1848. Flintlock and percussion (converted) North pistols, rifles and carbines were even used during the Civil War.

A number of historical firsts mark the manufacturing career of Simeon North: he was awarded the *first* United States government contract for pistols (1799); he was the first arms maker to receive a U. S. government contract specifying the parts of each gun to be

interchangeable (1808); the *only* private manufacturer to produce Hall breechloading rifles and carbines under contract to the U. S. government—and in so doing was the first private contractor to manufacture arms interchangeable with those made at a national armory (1830). Simeon North also made the *first* percussion weapons adopted by *any* nation, as well as the first breechloading firearm to be so adopted (1834).

Military weapons have always found their way into private hands and with great luck a North firearm may still be resting in the recesses of your attic—squirreled away among Grandpa's dusty old treasures. Simeon North's Model 1799 pistols, the beginning of his long involvement in firearms manufacture, are today extremely rare. Less than one percent—or only fifteen to twenty of the original 2,000—are known to have survived. In fine condition, a Model 1799 flintlock pistol would be valued by collectors at around thirty thousand dollars. Even with today's inflation, that was not a bad investment if your great-great-grandfather had held on to one first purchased by the government for $6.00 in 1799.

Simeon North was born on July 13, 1765 in the village of Berlin, Connecticut. He was a sixth-generation descendant of John North, who sailed from England in 1635, the same year Hartford and Saybrook were settled on the Connecticut River. John North first landed in Boston, but later moved to Farmington, 8 miles southwest of Hartford, in 1653.

Simeon North grew up on his father's farm at the north end of Berlin and was only eleven when the colonies declared their independence from England. Young North watched with envy as his three older brothers marched off to serve in the Revolution and then with pride heard their tales of bloody skirmishes with the British.

One of his grandsons claimed that in 1781, when North was sixteen years old, he shouldered a gun and walked thirty miles to Saybrook to enlist. When he reached there, probably after Cornwallis' disastrous defeat and surrender at Yorktown in October, word of negotiations for peace had preceded him and he was not mustered into service.

As an industrious young man working on his father's farm, North's inclination towards things mechanical would naturally have led him to investigate forges and shops of craftsmen in and around his village in Connecticut—an area known for its clockmakers, nail-cutters and especially Berlin's numerous tinsmiths, who made various articles of tinware. It may have been at the forge and workbench of his older brother Levi that North first acquired the discipline and skills of blacksmithing and perhaps his introduction to gun repair.

His brother had been taken prisoner by the British during the Revolution while serving with the Connect-icut State Militia and, in prison, "was set at making tools and repairing weapons." After returning from the war, Levi probably looked discouragingly at life on the farm—the rocky soil of Connecticut made farming hard and unrewarding—and later encouraged the state's rapid industrial development. So, rather than become a farmer like his father, he decided to use the hard-earned experience gained in prison to become a blacksmith. He built a home in East Berlin and opened a shop there. Although records of assessment only show that he made scythes, he may also have continued to repair firearms.

Another likely source for North's introduction to firearms was at a relative's nearby gunsmith shop. Located just a scant mile north of his father's farm was an area known as the Beckley Quarter. North's great-aunt Martha lived there with her husband Daniel Beckley, whom she married in 1719. One of his cousins, Elias Beckley, operated a gunshop there, and after his death in 1816, his son Elias, Jr., ran the shop and "also a blacksmith's shop" where he made, "iron work, nails, latches, and hinges." Although they made long fowlers and muskets in the gunshop, their skill and New England ingenuity were probably more often put to repairing guns used by the villagers and farmers living nearby.

As is evident from many fine examples of firearms that have survived to this day, the craftsmanship and inventiveness exhibited by eighteenth-century gunsmiths was remarkable, especially in view of the crude tools and laborious hand methods they employed.

The Spruce Brook lazily wanders just east of Berlin, Connecticut. A sawmill built here in 1771 was used by Simeon North as a blacksmith's shop from 1795. In 1799, North began production of U.S. government pistols in a "factory" at this site. Remains of the stone foundation can be seen at right.

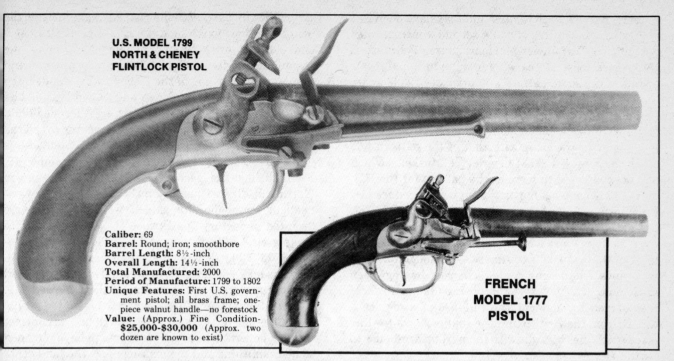

**U.S. MODEL 1799
NORTH & CHENEY
FLINTLOCK PISTOL**

Caliber: 69
Barrel: Round; iron; smoothbore
Barrel Length: 8½-inch
Overall Length: 14½-inch
Total Manufactured: 2000
Period of Manufacture: 1799 to 1802
Unique Features: First U.S. government pistol; all brass frame; one-piece walnut handle—no forestock
Value: (Approx.) Fine Condition-$25,000-$30,000 (Approx. two dozen are known to exist)

**FRENCH
MODEL 1777
PISTOL**

The North & Cheney Model 1799 pistols were patterned after the French Model 1777 pistols used during the American Revolution. The most obvious difference is the increase in barrel length one inch to 8½-inches. 2,000 .69 caliber smoothbore flintlock pistols were produced in the Berlin factory between 1799 and 1800.

How seriously North considered following in his father's footsteps we may never know. Certainly he had ample opportunity to learn blacksmithing as well as gunsmithing skills from his brother and his Beckley relatives. Records show he had acquired 66¼ acres of farmland in parts of Hartford and Middlesex counties before his twenty-first birthday.

In 1786, he married Lucy Savage and immediately began a family which would include seven children (the four oldest sons would later work in their father's factory).

In 1795, records show North purchased from his uncle Jacob Wilcox a one-ninth privilege to use the water at a sawmill on Spruce Brook, which flowed east of Berlin. He opened a blacksmith shop and, like his brother Levi, began making hickory-handled iron scythes—an indispensable farm implement in great demand and which he sold to farmers in Berlin and neighboring communities. He may have repaired guns for these same customers as well, as did many skilled blacksmiths.

Between June 1795 and May 1799, North made three separate purchases, obtaining the deed to a house, barn and five-acre lot, which included almost 13 acres of farmland located next to the mill site on the Spruce Brook. One of the deeds dated August 29, 1798, describes the house as, "now occupied by s[ai]d North."

The house was probably rented to one of his shop workers by that date, however, because in March of 1795, soon after acquiring the "sawmill privilege," he purchased and moved into another house on the other side of Spruce Brook. Interestingly, the first house was owned in 1801 by Elisha Cheney, the clockmaker and North's brother-in-law.(Cheney's son Olcott purchased the house in 1822, the deed reserving a mill right to Simeon North).

On April 2, 1794, at about the time North was considering purchase of the sawmill privilege for his blacksmith's shop, the U.S. Congress passed an act establishing the first government arsenals. The act authorized funds to begin manufacture of firearms for both the army and navy.

After production of U.S Model 1795 muskets was underway at the first national armory in Springfield, Massachusetts, it was decided to seek bids for manufacture by private contractors. By act of Congress, May 4, 1798, $800,000 was appropriated for firearms and ammunition. Eli Whitney, inventor of the cotton gin, was awarded the first contract for ten thousand muskets on January 14, 1798. On the same day that Nathan Starr signed a contract for swords, March 9, 1799, Simeon North, thirty-four years old, received the first U.S. government contract for pistols. He was to be paid $6.50 each for 500 horse pistols.

The Model 1799 pistols were patterned after the French Model 1777 pistols used during the Revolutionary War. Although a copy of the first government contract has not been located and may have been lost or destroyed by fire, North's second contract with Secretary of War James McHenry, dated February 6, 1800, does exist. It called for an additional 1,500 pistols of the same pattern at a price of $12.00 a pair.

Although basically patterned after the French Model 1777, certain differences from the pattern pistol were to be made. "The Bore or Calibre of the pistol is to be the same with that of the pattern [.69 cal. French Model 1763] Charleville Musket," which had been selected to serve as the pattern for the U.S. Model 1798 contract muskets then being produced by Eli Whitney, 26 miles south in New Haven. In 1777, the French, who had been supplying the new nation with money, ships and troops, shipped large quantities of these muskets to America. Although obsolete in France (numerous design changes having been made on service muskets then being used in France) they served to augment the supplies of arms "captured" from the British and the soldiers' own fowling pieces and rifles brought with them from farmhouse to battlefield.

North's pistol contract also specified the length of the barrel to be 8½ inches, one inch longer than the French pattern. Interestingly some of the pistols in collections today are known to measure up to ⅛ of an inch shorter than the contract length. An additional screw was to be added for holding the barrel to the frame, and "that that part of the Breech of the pistol which lies within the Brass may be formed round on the underpart instead of being square." On the underside of the frame, directly under the lock at the trigger guard stamped in a curve either "S. NORTH & E. CHENEY BERLIN" or "NORTH & CHENEY BERLIN." Information gleaned from serial numbers on known Model 1799 pistols suggests that the first 500 made were marked "S. NORTH AND E. CHENEY BERLIN " and the 1500 pistols made under the second contract were stamped without the initials.

Something of a mystery, though, has always existed regarding the role "E. CHENEY" played in North's early pistol manufacturing. Elisha Cheney was Simeon North's brother-in-law; he married North's sister Olive in 1793. The possibility exists that Eli Cheney's skills as a clockmaker led to more than just a financial relationship but rather to an actual working partnership for the manufacture of the first contract pistols. Perhaps North wanted to have someone at the workbench more skilled in the handcrafting of wood and brass, and turned to Cheney, an experienced clockmaker, to provide the deft craftsmanship North lacked as a village blacksmith.

There can be no doubt Cheney possessed the neces-

sary skills to have actually helped manufacture the pistols. And although he did *not* co-sign North's second contract on February 6, 1800, to produce the remaining Model 1799 pistols, he was present and witnessed the signing of the $9,000 surety bond, along with Simeon's brothers Noah and David North. The bond was given by Simeon North's father, Jedidiah, and Simeon's uncle, Jacob Wilcox (who was to sell the entire Spruce Brook mill/factory site to Simeon five years later). Later that same year, on December 19, 1800, during the second contract period, Simeon North and Elisha Cheney jointly advertised in a Connecticut newspaper for skilled workers. They were "wanted at factory" on Spruce Brook in Berlin, "to make guns." Why they would both advertise for factory help if North was the sole owner is not known. Records may yet be found in an archive or attic to end the speculation as to the nature of their relationship.

From September of 1802, when the last Model 1799 pistol was delivered, until 1808, North had no contract for U.S. government arms. He seems to have returned to blacksmithing and the making of scythes and other tools and hardware. On June 3, 1805, Jacob Wilcox sold him the mill site, "where s[ai]d North's blacksmith shop now stands, "for twenty-four dollars, where he built a "large factory" of two stories and a basement (used as a forging room). The Spruce Brook, which flows north past the factory, supplied the necessary water power.

On June 30, 1808, North signed a contract to manufacture a thousand pairs of pistols for the U.S. Navy. A second contract for an additional five hundred pairs of Model 1808 pistols was signed on December 4, 1810. The first contract of 1808, interestingly, was co-witnessed by Nathan Starr of Middletown, the same Starr who manufactured swords. Like North, Nathan Starr had received a government contract in 1799, and from the time of its completion until his next contract in 1808, had also, like North, returned to his regular business of making scythes (he also made felling axes and even fire engines).

The Model 1808 .64 caliber Navy pistols were priced at $11.75 a pair for the first thousand pairs and $12.00 a pair in the second contract calling for an additional five hundred pairs. Unlike the Model 1799 pistols, North's name is the only one to appear on the Model 1808 lockplates, which were stamped "S. NORTH" over "BERLIN" over "CON." Also, unlike the first contract pistols, which featured an all-brass frame, one-piece walnut handle and no forestock, the Model 1808 has a full-length pin-fastened walnut stock.

The Model 1808 was the first U.S Martial pistol to

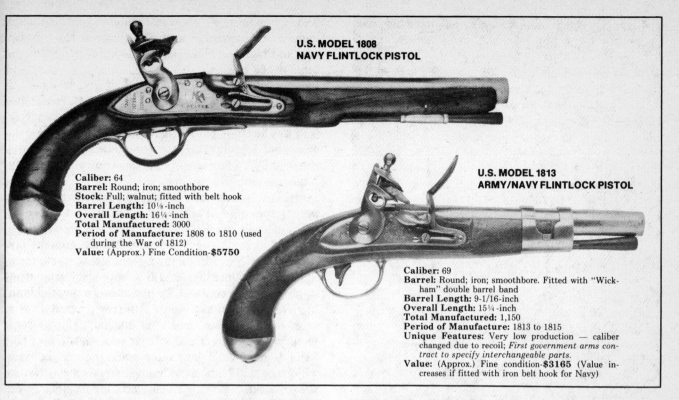

**U.S. MODEL 1808
NAVY FLINTLOCK PISTOL**

Caliber: 64
Barrel: Round; iron; smoothbore
Stock: Full; walnut; fitted with belt hook
Barrel Length: 10⅛-inch
Overall Length: 16¼-inch
Total Manufactured: 3000
Period of Manufacture: 1808 to 1810 (used during the War of 1812)
Value: (Approx.) Fine Condition-**$5750**

**U.S. MODEL 1813
ARMY/NAVY FLINTLOCK PISTOL**

Caliber: 69
Barrel: Round; iron; smoothbore. Fitted with "Wickham" double barrel band
Barrel Length: 9-1/16-inch
Overall Length: 15¼-inch
Total Manufactured: 1,150
Period of Manufacture: 1813 to 1815
Unique Features: Very low production — caliber changed due to recoil; *First government arms contract to specify interchangeable parts.*
Value: (Approx.) Fine condition-**$3165** (Value increases if fitted with iron belt hook for Navy)

feature an iron backstrap running from the tang to the unusual umbrella-shaped brass butt cap; and because this model was intended for use by the Navy, an iron belt hook was attached to the left side of the stock. Total production was 3,000 pistols.

The next contract was signed on November 18, 1811, for a thousand pairs of .69 caliber pistols; the same year North was commissioned a Lieutenant Colonel in the Connecticut State Militia. Except for differences in length and caliber (and the absence of a belt hook), these pistols were quite similar to the 1808; the Model 1811 was also made with the umbrella-shaped brass butt cap.

On February 24, 1811, North's wife, Lucy, died. With three young children still at home, it is not surprising that he remarried just a year later in 1812. His second wife, Lydia Huntington, was from Middletown. Located only six miles from Berlin on the Connecticut River, it was a much larger town and a principal inland port for trade with England and the West Indies. Probably because his oldest son Reuben had recently married and was starting a family of his own in the house near Spruce Brook, North moved to his late father-in-law's home in Middletown, which he purchased on March 11, 1812. North and his second wife had one child during their marriage, a daughter.

Before North had completed the thousand pairs of Model 1811 pistols then in production at the Spruce Brook factory, a change was ordered to be made to the

remainder of the contract. Marine T. Wickham, a U.S. Inspector of Arms for the Ordnance Department, suggested a different method for retaining the pistol barrels to the stocks. An iron double-strap band would replace the pin-fastening system originally specified. The Wickham "Improvement" was made on approximately five hundred of the original contract for two thousand and became known as the Model 1811 Transition pistols.

A few pistols were also produced during the later part of this contract period for sale to the civilian market. Because these pistols used a pin-fastened barrel, they may have been made before the change to Wickham barrel bands was ordered. They conform to the original pattern exactly, but were not approved so do not have government proofmarks or "U. States" stamped on the lock plate.

North received his next contract on April 16, 1813, almost immediately after completion of the Model 1811 pistols. Because of the ongoing war with England, production of arms was greatly increased. This contract, his largest to date, called for 20,000 pistols to be manufactured over a 5-year period. The Model 1813 pistols were similar in many respects to the Model 1811, but certain changes were specified. The distinctive brass butt cap was replaced with an oval-shaped cap of iron. The hickory ramrod with swelled front tip was retained, but with a threaded ferrule, added for use in cleaning and ball removal, and the

North purchased land in 1813 on the "West" River in the Staddle Hill section of Middletown, Connecticut. This picturesque waterfall was created by the dam North erected to provide power for his firearms factory.

barrel length was increased one-half inch to nine inches. Small changes were also made to the powder pan and hammer. The size of the bore remained the same at .69 caliber.

The most historically significant requirement of the Model 1813 contract, though, was that, "the component part of pistols, are to correspond so exactly that any limb or part of one Pistol, may be fitted to any other Pistol of the Twenty thousand." This was the *first* U.S. government firearms contract to specify interchangeability of parts.

Because production of 20,000 pistols would have been impossible in the Spruce Brook factory—production levels requiring additional space for machines and the hiring of new workers—North immediately began looking in Middletown for a site suitable for a new factory. On May 29, 1813, only six weeks after signing the new contract, he purchased a piece of land in an area known as Staddle Hill (the property was a short distance from the site of Nathan Starr's sword factory). It was described as "lying southerly along the eastside of river at low water mark (before the dam which the said North is to build shall be erected). Also the privilege of flowing on land on the east side of said West River [known today as the Arrawana River] so high as to accommodate the works which said North may erect." Whereas the Spruce Brook factory lacked sufficient water power for production of the new contract pistols, the river flowing around his new site offered water power in abundance. A year after, North acquired an additional, "thirteen acres of land lying westerly on land which was lately conveyed to him." While North's son, Reuben, remained in Berlin to superintend the old factory, North began construction of a three-story factory at the Middletown site. The basement and first floor were constructed of "dark gray sand-stone" and the two upper floors were of "fire-proof brick." The dam North built still stands.

Overall, the main building measured 84 feet long and 37 feet wide. Total cost to build the factory was said to have been $100,000. Although the main factory building has been torn down, remains of the stone foundation can still be seen by the side of the dam, and a low brick building across from the former factory site appears to stand on the foundation of one of the original factory storage buildings. (This river site and factory provided sufficient space and power for firearms manufacture well into the 1860s and was adapted successfully to woolen manufacturing, which continued on North's original site into the 1930s).

Actual construction of the new factory building may have begun during the summer of 1813, but it seems apparent that it was not fully operational for

This rare photograph, circa 1880, shows the Middletown factory Simeon North built in 1813. Described in 1816 as "a respectable establishment on a never failing stream. The principle workshop is of stone and brick, 86 by 36 feet, three stories high." Used during and after the Civil War by the Savage Revolving Arms Co., the site was purchased in 1882 by the Rockfall Woolen Co. which manufactured woolen horse blankets for the U.S. Army until the 1930's.

Recent photo shows "dark gray sand-stone" from the original factory foundation.

several months, if not longer.

Production of the Model 1813 pistols was started in Berlin so as not to delay deliveries while the Middletown factory was under construction. Records show that 140 pistols, some using locks made for the Model 1811 pistols and stamped "BERLIN," were delivered in an attempt to begin deliveries under the new contract. Although these pistols conformed to most of the contract specifications, they do not interchange with Model 1813 pistols manufactured later in the new Middletown factory. Because of the small number produced, these U.S. Transitional Model 1811-1813 pistols are quite rare and command a premium price.

Continued construction of the new factory and changes required to start production on the Model

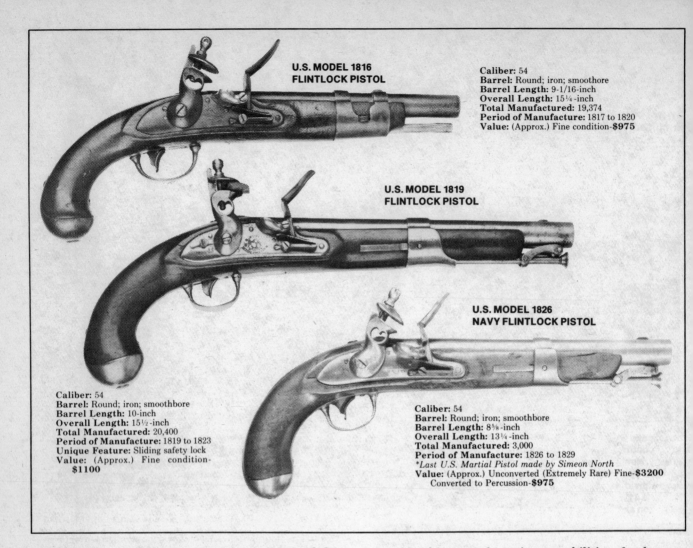

U.S. MODEL 1816 FLINTLOCK PISTOL

Caliber: 54
Barrel: Round; iron; smoothore
Barrel Length: 9-1/16-inch
Overall Length: 15¼-inch
Total Manufactured: 19,374
Period of Manufacture: 1817 to 1820
Value: (Approx.) Fine condition-**$975**

U.S. MODEL 1819 FLINTLOCK PISTOL

Caliber: 54
Barrel: Round; iron; smoothbore
Barrel Length: 10-inch
Overall Length: 15½-inch
Total Manufactured: 20,400
Period of Manufacture: 1819 to 1823
Unique Feature: Sliding safety lock
Value: (Approx.) Fine condition-**$1100**

U.S. MODEL 1826 NAVY FLINTLOCK PISTOL

Caliber: 54
Barrel: Round; iron; smoothbore
Barrel Length: 8⅝-inch
Overall Length: 13¼-inch
Total Manufactured: 3,000
Period of Manufacture: 1826 to 1829
Last U.S. Martial Pistol made by Simeon North
Value: (Approx.) Unconverted (Extremely Rare) Fine-**$3200**
Converted to Percussion-**$975**

1813 contract created numerous and unexpected delays in manufacture and delivery and shortages of cash. North attempted to explain his situation and obtain advances on his contract.

Fewer than 1200 of the 20,000 pistols had been delivered by June of 1815, more than two years after signing the contract. Production was just beginning to increase when the government decided to make changes in the pattern pistol. Because of a number of complaints regarding the severe recoil from the large .69 caliber of the Model 1813, the new bore specification became .54 inches. The barrel was changed from octagonal at the breech to round. Wickham's barrel-band was retained with a minor but distinct change to the base. Although the changes were intended as a revision to the contract of 1813, the new pistols became known as the Model 1816. In the spring of 1819, six years after production began in the Spruce Brook factory, North finally completed the twenty thousandth pistol—in Middletown.

The government was evidently convinced of Sim-

eon North's manufacturing capabilities, for he was awarded a second contract for twenty thousand pistols on July 21, 1819 at $8.00 each. Unlike the contract of 1813, North now had confidence in his ability to deliver all 20,000 within the five-year period specified.

These Model 1819 pistols were quite changed from any North had manufactured under previous contracts. With an increase in barrel length to ten inches, an overall length of 15½ inches and replacement of Wichham's two-ring barrel band with a single band, the pistols acquired a balanced, more graceful, curving shape. This pistol is preferred by many collectors over any of North's earlier contract pistols. Manufactured to conform to pattern pistols designed at Harper's Ferry, the Model 1819 pistol was the first and only U.S. martial pistol to feature a sliding safety lock, located on the lock plate just behind the hammer. A steel button-head swivel ramrod, similar to those used on contemporary British military pistols, replaced the hickory and iron ramrods of earlier contract models.

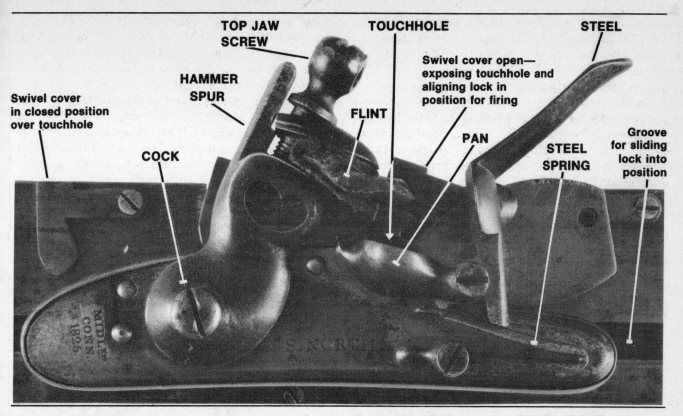

TOP JAW SCREW

HAMMER SPUR

Swivel cover in closed position over touchhole

COCK

TOUCHHOLE

Swivel cover open— exposing touchhole and aligning lock in position for firing

FLINT

PAN

STEEL

STEEL SPRING

Groove for sliding lock into position

Lock made in 1825 by Simeon North of Middletown, Connecticut — during production of his first rifle contract for U.S. Model 1817 "common" rifles. shown used on an Ellis-Jennings Sliding Lock 10-Shot Repeating Flintlock Rifle made by Reuben Ellis of Albany, New York under contract for 520 rifles for the militia of the state of New York. These unique U.S. military arms were covered by an 1821 patent given Isiah Jennings, New York. The barrel was designed to hold ten superposed loads. Touchholes have individual swivel covers which slide up to catch the lock and align and position it as it is moved back for each charge. Barrel length is 41½ inches, caliber .54. Considered extremely rare, and highly desirable, these rifles are valued between $6500 in good condition and $12,500 in fine condition. (This example formerly of Winchester Arms Collection.) **Courtesy Buffalo Bill Historical Center**

North's factory production went smoothly and deliveries were made ahead of schedule.

While work was proceeding on the Model 1819 pistols, North signed his first rifle contract, on December 10, 1823. Although he was first mentioned in 1810 by the U.S. Purveyor of Public Supplies as a possible supplier of muskets, it was felt at that time, "that he should confine his operations to pistols." The 1823 contract was for 6,000 Model 1817 "common" rifles to be delivered within five years, to be included with each a "ramrod, and Flint, including also, the proportion of bullet moulds, screw-drivers, Wipers, Ball screws, Spring vices, and flint caps." The addition of rifles to North's Middletown factory does not seem to have caused any kind of slowdown or delay in production. The contract was completed in 1827, one year earlier than specified. An additional twelve hundred rifles of the same model were contracted for on July 22, 1829, also at $14.50 each.

By this time, North's factory was using machinery for barrel-turning, machining stocks and milling of the various parts for locks. Technical advances at national armories and at private factories were quickly copied and adapted to speed up production; this in turn caused the manufacturing of interchangeable parts to spread throughout the entire industry. North's manufacturing techniques allowed for simultaneous production of pistols and rifles (Model 1819 pistols, Model 1817 rifles and Hall rifles) between 1823 and 1829. The financial problems he encountered on more than one occasion do not seem to have seriously affected his relationship with government departments and agencies or to have led to the loss of further contracts.

Few early armsmakers were prepared to manufacture all the parts of each gun. North was unique in that he never subcontracted production. Except for operations like polishing of barrels, which he gave at times to Nathan Starr's factory, a mile northeast of his, North tooled up to meet production needs whenever it became necessary.

On November 16, 1826, just as he was finishing production of his first rifle contract for six thousand Model 1817 rifles, North was awarded the first of three contracts for Model 1826 pistols; additional contracts for the same model were signed on December 12, 1827 and again on August 18, 1828, for a total of three thousand pistols. These would be the last U.S. martial pistols Simeon North would manufacture.

The Model 1826 was in many ways a smaller version of the Model 1819 and was a return to the look of North's earlier contract pistols. The contract specified an 8⅝-inch round barrel and overall length of 13¼ inches. The shorter barrel length and sharper curve to the grip of the Model 1826 resulted in a pistol more than two inches shorter than any other pistol North had manufactured.

Made for use by the U.S. Navy for $7.00 each, the .54 caliber smoothbore pistol continued use of the swivel-type ramrod with button-shaped head and was fitted with iron belt hooks on the left side of the stock. So many of the 3,000 Model 1826 Navy pistols were later converted from flintlock to percussion to prolong their usefulness that original unconverted pistols are scarce and are much sought after today by collectors.

Upon the last delivery of Model 1826 pistols, North's long history of manufacturing U.S martial pistols came to a close. With one exception, it seems he confined his final years of production to rifles and carbines. An extremely rare and unusual single-shot pistol made after North's final pistol contract is thought to be of his manufacture. From inspection marks on the pistol and correspondence between Simeon North and the U.S. Ordnance Department in 1833, it appears that the pistol was made to serve as a pattern for a new pistol contract North sought.

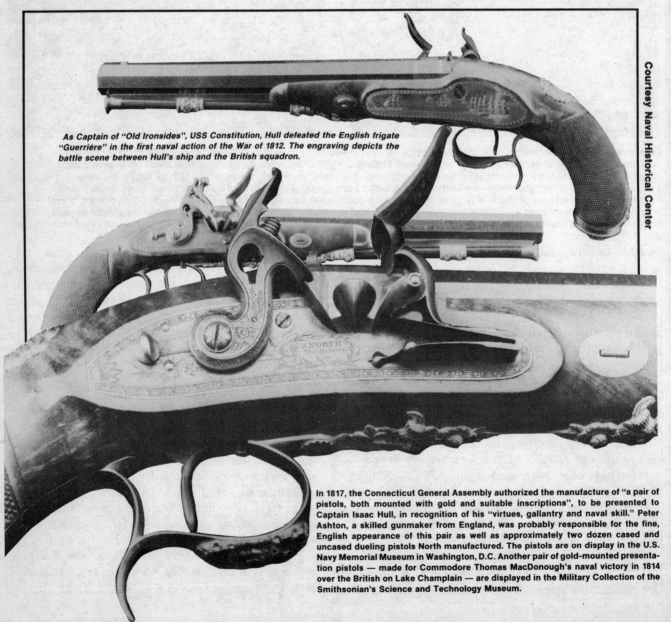

As Captain of "Old Ironsides", USS Constitution, Hull defeated the English frigate "Guerriére" in the first naval action of the War of 1812. The engraving depicts the battle scene between Hull's ship and the British squadron.

Courtesy Naval Historical Center

In 1817, the Connecticut General Assembly authorized the manufacture of "a pair of pistols, both mounted with gold and suitable inscriptions", to be presented to Captain Isaac Hull, in recognition of his "virtues, gallantry and naval skill." Peter Ashton, a skilled gunmaker from England, was probably responsible for the fine, English appearance of this pair as well as approximately two dozen cased and uncased dueling pistols North manufactured. The pistols are on display in the U.S. Navy Memorial Museum in Washington, D.C. Another pair of gold-mounted presentation pistols — made for Commodore Thomas MacDonough's naval victory in 1814 over the British on Lake Champlain — are displayed in the Military Collection of the Smithsonian's Science and Technology Museum.

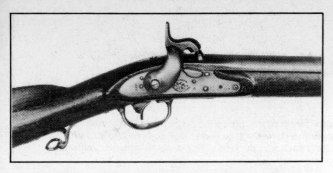

Under contracts of 1823 and 1829, North manufactured 7200 U.S. Model 1817 Flintlock "Common" rifles. Approx. Value: Fine condition-$2000; Converted to Percussion (As shown)-$725.

The gun incorporates parts from a Model 1826 flintlock pistol, but is a percussion breech-loader in .52 caliber; it resembles the breech-loading mechanism on the Model 1840 Hall carbines North manufactured from about 1839.

On December 15, 1828, toward the end of production of his second contract for Model 1817 "common" rifles, North signed a contract to "manufacture and deliver, for the military service of the United States, five thousand Hall flintlock rifles, with Bayonets and Ramrods complete; and it is further agreed, that the said rifles shall have that perfect uniformity of their respective component parts, and also, that the component parts may be exchanged in a similar manner, with the rifles made, or making, at the National Armory."

Because production of Hall's rifles at the national armories was not sufficient to meet the demands of both the regular army and state militia troops, the Secretary of War had authorized their manufacture at North's Middletown factory. The contract called for delivery at the rate of a thousand per year from July 1, 1829; the price per rifle was set at $17.50.

Maintaining interchangeability with Hall rifles made at the national armories was of the greatest importance to the Ordnance Department and of tremendous concern to John H. Hall.

Hall, inventor of the breech-loading system used on the rifles in production at the Harper's Ferry Arsenal *and* at Simeon North's private facility in Middletown, was extremely apprehensive and anxious that *North* rifles conform and interchange in every respect. His concern seems to have stemmed from anger that the U.S. government gave out *his* rifle for production to anyone other than himself. In a letter to Colonel George Bomford of the Ordnance Department on July 26, 1830, Hall wrote, "If irregularities of any kind should once be permitted in the construction of the arms it will prove utterly subversive of the utility of the plan now in operation, at this place [Harper's Ferry]."

After overcoming minor problems with irregular pattern rifles furnished him, North's Hall rifles met all specifications. In reply to one of Hall's letters of alarm, Colonel George Bomford wrote, "The only point in which Mr. North's work did not conform to the regulations, as stated by Mr. Dudley [a govern-

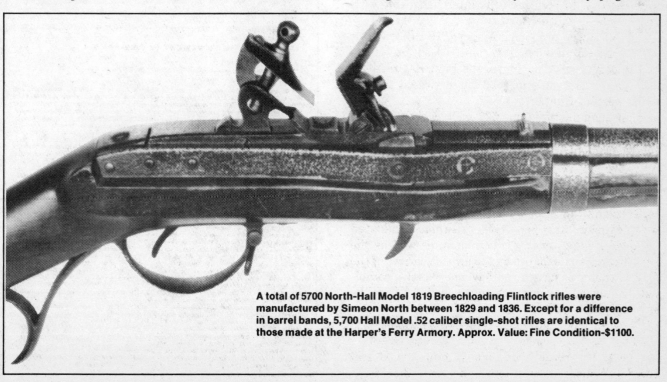

A total of 5700 North-Hall Model 1819 Breechloading Flintlock rifles were manufactured by Simeon North between 1829 and 1836. Except for a difference in barrel bands, 5,700 Hall Model .52 caliber single-shot rifles are identical to those made at the Harper's Ferry Armory. Approx. Value: Fine Condition-$1100.

North manufactured approximately 6000 Hall Model .52 caliber smoothbore, single-shot breechloading percussion carbines between 1840 and 1843. The Type II, "Fishtail" operating lever version shown is similar to the Model 1833 carbine. Approx. Value: Fine Condition-$1000.

ment inspector at North's Middletown factory], was the bayonet in some instances rested on the stud instead of the end of the stock. And that this defect did not interfere in the least with the free exchange of the bayonets nor render the arm less efficient."

As Hall probably feared would happen, North, always one to suggest new and better methods or devices, incorporated an innovation to Hall's original breech-loading design. Although patent No. 3686 was granted to North and Edward Savage on July 30, 1844, to protect the side-lever breach-loading mechanism, Hall rifles were manufactured in Middletown with this "Improvement in Firearms" as early as 1843.

During the production of North's first contract of December 15, 1828 for Hall's rifles, 5700 U.S. Model 1819 flintlock rifles were delivered; the last delivery was made on July 25, 1836. Of interest to those who compile lists of firsts will be the fact that these arms were the first to be made fully interchangeable with arms made at another factory.

In 1833, while producing Model 1819 rifles, North was asked to develop a carbine based on Hall's breechloading system, to arm the First Regiment of Dragoons (reactivated in 1833 for service on the nation's western frontier).

First manufactured in .577-inch caliber smooth bore in 1834, the caliber was changed to that of the .52 caliber pistol. The remainder of North-Hall carbines were made with this bore diameter until the last delivery in 1853.

The Model 1833 carbine again brings some historical significance to North's manufacturing, as this was the first military percussion firearm to be adopted for regular issue by any government, as well as the first firearm made for use by the armed services of the United States to have a rod bayonet. North's combination ramrod-bayonet design allowed for it to be stored in the stock.

Between 1833 and 1839, a total of 8171 Model 1833 carbines were delivered.

The Hall carbine North manufactured next featured two distinct variations. The first, the Model 1840, Elbow Lever Type, has been called the "Whitneyville Colt" among the various Hall model arms, because only 500 of this type were produced. As an improvement over the spur-type catch on the Model 1833 carbines, an L-shaped breech lever, first suggested to the Ordnance Department on March 23, 1839, was designed to overcome the disquieting problem of receivers being opened accidentally.

Although not entirely satisfied with the elbow lever mechanism, and still unsure of other changes still under consideration, the Ordnance Department gave the order for North to manufacture five hundred carbines. After the order had been given on January 23, 1840, however, they immediately requested elimination of the rod bayonets on these carbines, and a reduction of the barrel length from 23-3/16 inches to

UNITED STATES PATENT OFFICE.

EDWD. SAVAGE AND SIMEON NORTH, OF MIDDLETOWN, CONNECTICUT.

IMPROVEMENT IN FIRE-ARMS.

Specification forming part of Letters Patent No. **3,686**, dated July 30, 1844.

To all whom it may concern:

Be it known that we, EDWARD SAVAGE and SIMEON NORTH, of Middletown, in the county of Middlesex and State of Connecticut, have invented a new and useful Improvement in Fire-Arms; and we do hereby declare that the following is a full, clear, and exact description thereof, reference being had to the accompanying drawings, which form a part of our specification, in which—

Figure 1 is a representation of the breech-gun. Fig. 2 is a section. Fig. 3 shows the detached parts.

The nature of our invention consists in the apparatus by which the chamber is elevated and brought securely back into place again.

The barrel of the gun is made similar to others, with detached receiver-chambers, and from the breech end two straps or stays, *a*, of iron, project back on each side of the receiver *b*, and form a supporter or chamber to contain and sustain the receiver. At the end of this chamber next the barrel there is a recess on each side of the supporter, one of which is shown at *x*. Fig. 2, close to the butt of the barrel. In the left-hand side recess there is a permanent chock, *c*, attached to the supporter by a screw. This fits the recess behind, and in front, next the butt of the barrel, it is slanted off from the top to the bottom, down toward the barrel. Against this face there is a projection, *d*, on the receiver, that fits and slides, wedging the butt of the barrel against it with it. The receiver *b* is a square prism of metal, the end next the barrel being bored out about half the length to receive the charge, and in the other half the lock is contained it has a pin, *f*, passing through it horizontally,

which connects it with the supporter, **and** serves as a fulcrum on which it turns when raised to receive the charge. On the right side of this receiver, opposite the projection *d*, there is an elliptical-shaped one, *h*, and in the recess on the same side there is a tumbler-chock, *i*, that, when the receiver is down, just fits the projection *h* on the receiver. This chock turns on an axis at *k*, that runs through the supporter on that side, and is connected outside with a spring-lever, *l*, Fig. 1, which raises the receiver by being turned down and raising the tumbler-chock *i*, that acts on the projection *h*, as shown in Fig. 1. When brought back into place again, it catches on a wrist or catch, *m*, in the side of the supporter, to which the lever then lies parallel. A spring, *n*, is fastened on alongside of the barrel, that bears on the head of the lever and gives it steadiness of motion.

What we claim as our invention, and desire to secure by Letters Patent, is—

1. The combination of the tumbler-chock *i* with the receiver in the manner and for the purpose herein set forth.

2. In combination therewith, the permanent chock, constructed and arranged as herein set forth.

3. The lever and spring, in combination with the tumbler-chock and receiver, arranged substantially in the manner and for the purpose described.

Middletown, June 26, 1844.

EDW. SAVAGE.
SIMEON NORTH.

Witnesses:
KINGSBURY CADY,
JONATHAN BARNES.

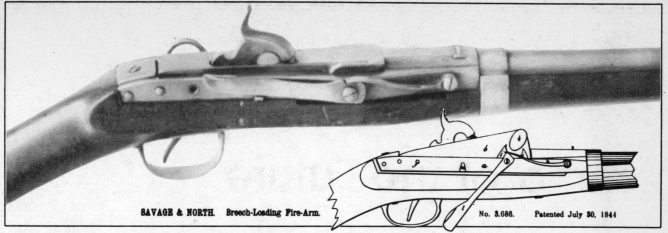

SAVAGE & NORTH. Breech-Loading Fire-Arm.   No. 3,686.   Patented July 30, 1844

This North-Hall .52 caliber breechloading percussion carbine incorporates North's patented side-lever design. A total of 11,000 were made in North's factory between 1843 and 1853. The breechlock mechanism operates by release of the lever on the right side which raises the lock for loading. The Hall carbine most commonly seen today, many were used by the U.S. Army during the Civil War. Approx. Value: Fine Condition-$800.

21 inches (thus shortening the carbines from 45 inches to 40 inches). The receiver would remain identical to the Model 1833. North made the changes before delivery on May 2, 1840.

Additional recommendations were made and after much deliberation, the second-type receiver opening-lever, the Fishtail, was adopted for the Model 1840 carbine. Six thousand carbines with the second-type modification and a slightly reworked ramrod retaining stud were delivered between August of 1840 and June 3, 1843. The price North received per carbine jumped from $18.00 to $18.50 after deliveries began; the latter price to cover the cost of installing a cavalry-type swivel bar and ring on the left side, which was ordered as still another change in April of 1841. During this period of War Department "decision-making"—at its most confusing for an arms supplier—an exasperated Simeon North found it necessary to inform the Chief of Ordnance, Colonel George Talcott, on *two* separate occasions, he would "suspend that part of business" until he received clarification of orders for the carbines he was *attempting* to manufacture.

During 1841 and 1842, North worked with Edward Savage to develop and refine a side-lever release mechanism they would later incorporate into the Model 1843 Hall carbines—this improvement eliminated the troublesome receiver catch altogether. As an addition to the original contract of May 22, 1839, North was told to deliver ten thousand carbines with the new side lever in 1843 and was paid $17.50 per carbine.

North was not to see final delivery on this contract.

Simeon North was seventy-nine years old when he and Edward Savage were granted U.S. Patent No. 3686 on July 30, 1844. Younger men, especially his grandson, Henry S. North, were following close behind with ideas and innovations of their own. Reuben, Simeon North's oldest son, to whom he had sold the Spruce Brook factory in 1826, was in failing health in 1843 and retired from the business in that year. North's grandson was obviously the one Simeon hoped would eventually take over and continue production at the Middletown factory.

On June 5, 1847, after working with Hall breech-loading mechanisms in his grandfather's factory, thirty-six-year-old Henry S. North received U.S. Patent No. 5141 for an improved breech-loading firearm. Just a year and a half later, January 20, 1848, Simeon North sold his land in Middletown "together with water privileges, dam, factory building and all the machinery and tools and implements of every kind and description" to his son James (Henry's father) and Edward Savage.

In reply to a letter of February 5, 1850, his *last* official correspondence, regarding a new order for three thousand carbines from the Ordnance Department, North wrote, "I have the same desire that I always had to do all in my power to improve and perfect the arms of our Country."

Simeon North listened with great pride—and perhaps just a touch of skepticism—as his grandson Henry excitedly described the new self-cocking double-action revolver he and Chauncey D. Skinner patented on June 1, 1852.

Simeon North, certain that development and manufacture of firearms would continue long after his own involvement had ended, died on August 25, 1852, at the age of 87. On February 26, 1853, six months after North's passing, final delivery was made on his last contract. Even in death, this remarkable arms pioneer fulfilled his commitments.

Ammo of the Future

Dick Eades

Infallible prediction of the future requires a very effective crystal ball or some other apparatus. A reasonable forecast, however, can be made simply. To determine what is likely in the future, one needs first to trace records of the past and then chart probable new developments. Barring some unforeseen but major breakthrough, ammo of the future will probably develop along already-established paths.

Since the development of the self-contained metallic cartridge and smokeless powder, few radical changes have been made in ammunition. Instead, there has been a steady progression of small improvements.

Probably one of the greatest improvements in ammunition for several decades has been better quality control. Shooters of the 1950s and 1960s thought they had the best ammo that could be made. Under conditions of the times, they were probably right, but the average cartridge from those days would be unacceptable by today's standards.

Without a doubt, current factory ammunition is fantastically accurate and consistent. This being the case, where do we go from here?

Some informed observers believe future developments in ammunition will bring about totally new types unknown to today's shooters. A few envision a complete departure from the conventional case/powder/primer/projectile ammo we now use. They feel ammo of the future will be in the form of energy projection; the "death ray" of science fiction, if you will!

Lasers are used for purposes their discoverers never dreamed and new methods of use are devised almost daily. At least one company is tinkering with techniques of "particle beam projection under military supervision." No, I can't explain how it works but have been told it could lead to a hand-held device capable of killing at ranges beyond those of a rifle. The "PBP" also could be aimed more easily than a projectile-firing weapon, since it would not be influenced by gravity. Without the need to consider gravitational forces, ballistic trajectories cease to exist and the path to the target would be as direct as a beam of light!

Obviously, such accomplishments are far in the future, if they come about at all. Of more interest to sport shooters is what may be in store in the reasonably near future. In the past, sporting ammunition has largely tracked military developments. New bullet metals, priming compounds and powders were often adopted by civilian shooters *before* the military got them, but initial research for most was funded by or on behalf of someone's army.

Sure, there have been some odd offshoots from ordinary ammo development but most have led short

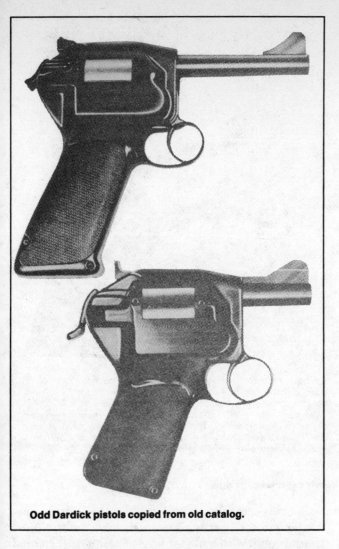

Odd Dardick pistols copied from old catalog.

and uneventful lives. Remember the Dardick? This gun/cartridge creation utilized a triangular bore and fired cartridges labeled "trounds." At the time, some reason for the odd shape was published, but I'm not able to locate anyone who remembers what it was. In preparing this article, I was unable to locate a single example of either the gun or cartridge for photographs.

Next, the Gyro-Jet was heralded as "the sporting arm of the future." More than anything, the G-J was simply a multi-shot rocket launcher. Both rifles and pistols were offered but neither enjoyed much success. The projectile was equipped with a series of angled vents on the base which were supposed to impart spin as the gasses generated by burning propellant were ejected rearward. My only experience with them led to the sad conclusion that the vents sometimes stopped up, causing a complete loss in stability of the projectile. Others complained that the projectile started off so slowly, accelerating as it moved down the bore and

after it left the muzzle, that excessive bore time caused a loss of accuracy. For whatever reasons, neither the Dardick nor the Gyro-Jet brought their developers lasting fame, glory or money.

One of the "hottest" items in military small arms development today is the caseless cartridge. Several companies have workable prototypes and one large contract has been accepted by a major military power. The idea of a caseless cartridge isn't new. One of the earliest efforts was recorded in the mid-1800s. The Volcanic pistol used a hollow-based bullet which held powder and detonator. Only semi-successful, the Volcanic set the stage for later experiments.

From a military point of view, caseless cartridges have several advantages over metal-cased cartridges. First, they weigh far less and a greater number can be carried by an individual soldier or be transported in bulk. Next, caseless cartridges represent a substantial saving in production expense. After all, the metallic case is the most expensive single component used in a cartridge and it is usually abandoned upon firing. Finally, a caseless cartridge can, in theory, be made to fire faster in automatic weapons. Without a fired case, the extraction and ejection cycles are eliminated and rate of fire is limited only by the capabilities of the feeding mechanism and the time a projectile remains in the weapon's bore.

Benelli Armi of Urbino, Italy, has developed and built a compact submachine gun firing caseless 9mm cartridges. The 139-grain projectiles are launched at a muzzle velocity of 1216 feet per second (fps) and the little gun spews them out at a cyclic rate of 1148 per minutes. Benelli employees refer to the new system as a submachine gun (SMG) with "autopropulsive projectiles." It has attracted the interest of several governments because of probable reduction of ammo cost and obvious weight savings in transportation.

The Benelli system uses a hollow-based bullet containing the propellant and a priming mixture which is distributed in a "girdle" surrounding the projectile near the center. It is ignited by a firing pin striking downward.

Another approach is being readied by Heckler & Koch and Dynamit Nobel of West Germany. Their system involves a bullet with propellant formed into a case-like structure at the rear. Samples of the cartridge (bullet?, round?) exhibited have the propellant formed with a square cross-section but the shape could be varied to suit different requirements. For most purposes, the square cross-section would be desirable due to its space-saving shape. In firing, both the priming device and propellant are almost completely consumed, eliminating the need for extraction

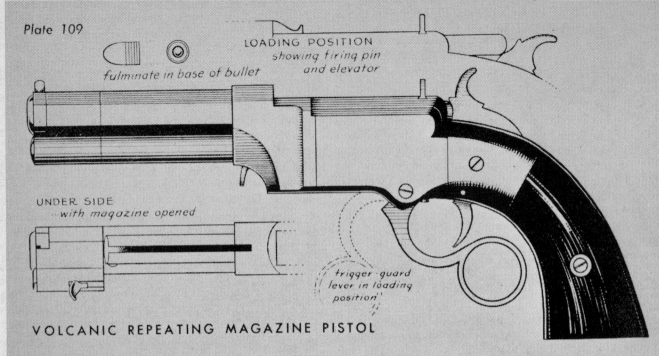

Plate 109

fulminate in base of bullet

LOADING POSITION
showing firing pin
and elevator

UNDER SIDE
--with magazine opened

trigger-guard
lever in loading
position

VOLCANIC REPEATING MAGAZINE PISTOL

Caliber .30. Nine inches in length . . . with 3-inch octagon barrel. Bronze frame, silver plated. Top of barrel marked, "NEW HAVEN CONN., PATENT FEB. 14, 1854." Five-shot magazine.

This interesting American arm was the forerunner of both the Henry and Winchester rifles. The same operating action used on this repeating pistol was later adopted for both rifles . . . that is the lever feeding the cartridges from a tube under the barrel into the chamber . . . and at the same time cocking the hammer with a bolt firing pin. This arm used no cartridge as such. A hollow base in the end of the bullet contained the powder and fulminate. Consequently, there was no extraction of cartridge case problem with this distinctive arm.

Drawing of the Volcanic pistol shows mechanism which was used with early caseless cartridge.

or ejection.

One criticism of caseless cartridges, especially those with external propellant, has been their lack of durability. The most recent commercial effort at a caseless cartridge was the Daisy V/L system, which was introduced in 1968 and discontinued in 1969. Announced as a great breakthrough in sporting arms, the V/L was not well accepted, in part, because of its fragile ammunition.

Daisy ammo was furnished in packs of 100; ten "sticks" of ten rounds each. Once removed from the plastic tube, or "stick," individual cartridges were delicate. The propellant was liable to break away from the projectile or to disintegrate if roughly handled.

The fragility of earlier caseless ammunition caused me to inquire about durability of the newer military product. In response, an employee of one of the military contractors drew a caseless cartridge from his pocket and handed it to me. It was burnished in spots and showed a few small nicks but was obviously serviceable. He then informed me that it had been in his pocket with coins and keys for almost two months. Okay, so the new stuff is tough!

Someday, maybe several years in the future, caseless ammo for sporting arms will be a reality. Next time around, with a higher level of technology behind it, the idea could be a commercial success. In that case, is it time for us to discard our reloading tools, dies and scales? Is the ammunition handloader a dying species? I think not. At least not within *our* lifetimes. For a long time to come, ammunition will remain reloadable with today's tools and equipment. Neither the equipment nor the handloader is yet obsolete.

Changes in conventional bullets may be most noticeable to the average handloader in the next few years. In addition to a variety of shapes, bullets will be seen with new coatings, inserts of various materials or possibly combinations of materials in the bullet itself.

We have already seen Teflon used as a bullet coating, and some startling new plastics may open the way for plastic-covered iron or mild steel as a bullet material. Several years ago, Winchester introduced a hollow-pointed pistol bullet with a small steel ball imbedded in the nose cavity. Intended for use at relatively low velocities, the steel ball helped feed the bullet into the chamber, then helped insure expansion

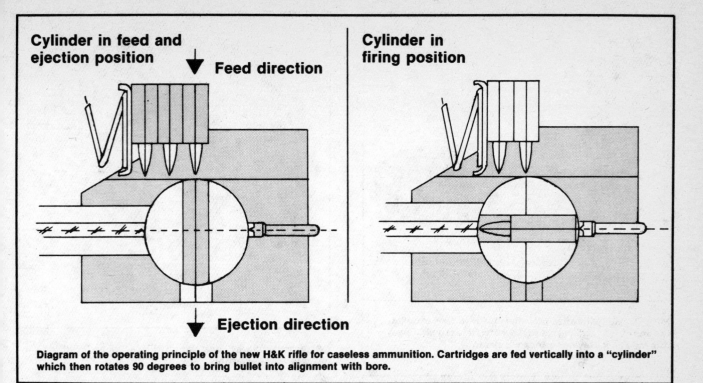

Cylinder in feed and ejection position

Feed direction

Cylinder in firing position

Ejection direction

Diagram of the operating principle of the new H&K rifle for caseless ammunition. Cartridges are fed vertically into a "cylinder" which then rotates 90 degrees to bring bullet into alignment with bore.

upon impact by being driven back into the bullet. Rifle bullets with lightweight metal or plastic wedges to create rapid expansion aren't unknown today and will probably be seen more frequently in the future. Such designs permit the use of thicker jackets and/or harder material, while maintaining reliable expansion characteristics. As prices of conventional jacket metals continue to rise, we will probably see additional efforts to employ less expensive metals in bullet jackets. Most of the required technology is already available. Don't be surprised to see new alloys of very soft iron.

No matter what may done with caseless ammunition, we will be using more or less traditional ammuni-

tion for sporting purposes for a long time to come. Aside from new bullet materials, major changes will probably be made in the cartridge case itself. Most changes will be aimed at cost reduction, either through use of less expensive materials or by achieving more efficient designs for ease of manufacturing.

The most common cartridge case material in use today is a simple brass alloy. Initially, brass was chosen because it was tougher than copper, easy to work, plentiful and inexpensive. It also offers a high degree of corrosion resistance compared to other available metals. Unfortunately, on today's market, brass is escalating in price to the point where other materials must be considered.

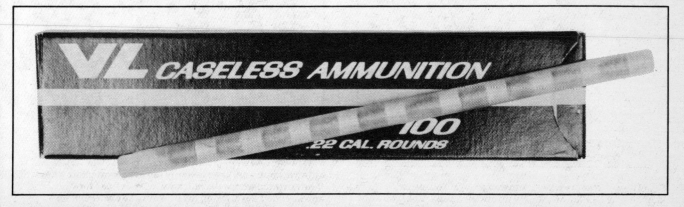

VL *CASELESS AMMUNITION*

100 .22 CAL. ROUNDS

Daisy VL caseless ammunition was packaged in sticks of 10 rounds each with 10 sticks to the box. After the plastic tube was opened, handling of the delicate rounds was troublesome.

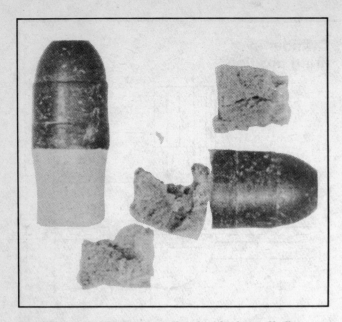

Daisy VL ammunition had propellant fused to base of bullet. Age and rough handling cause the material to crumble away from the bullet, leaving cartridge useless.

CCI Blazer ammo is headstamped with caliber and "NR" to indicate "non-reloadable."

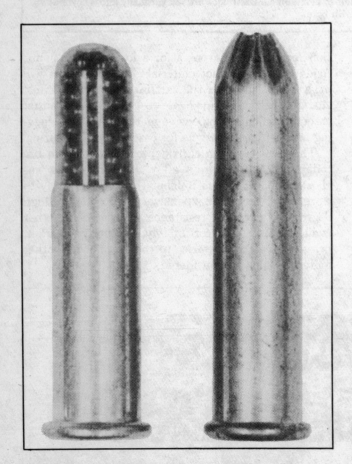

Small improvements are made in many ways. The terribly inefficient .22 rimfire shotshell with crimped case (right) has been overshadowed by CCI's .22 rimfire shotshell with shot capsule (left.)

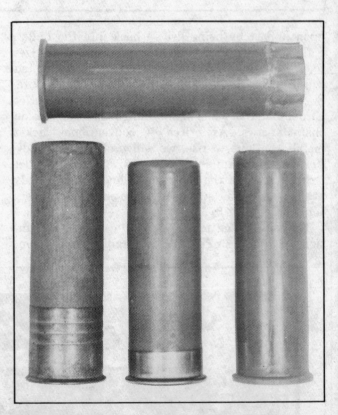

Brass heads on shotshells are becoming obsolete. At left, an old style paper hull used heavy brass head for reinforcement. Center, a modern plastic hull retains brass head for appearance's sake. Right, the new Eclipse shell eliminates brass head altogether. At top, a fired Eclipse shell shows conventional crimp.

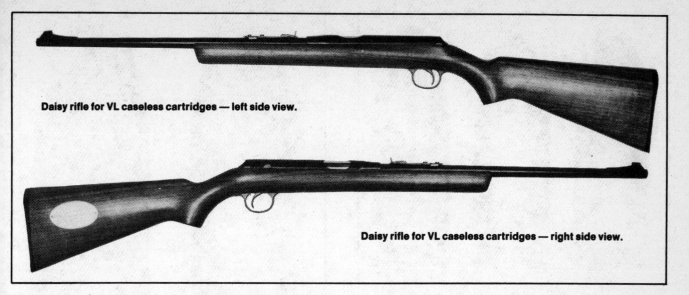

Daisy rifle for VL caseless cartridges — left side view.

Daisy rifle for VL caseless cartridges — right side view.

Handgun cartridges with cases of aluminum are now being marketed by CCI under the "Blazer" logo. These cases, while not reloadable, are quite serviceable for a single firing and offer a substantial price reduction by eliminating the use of costly brass. In order to discourage attempts at reloading, CCI has designed the case to use an odd-sized Berdan primer instead of the usual Boxer primer of most American ammunition.

At present, the aluminum alloy used by CCI in the Blazer line is not considered adequate for high-intensity rifle cartridges but don't disregard the possibility of further developments in this area. Experiments have also been conducted with exotic alloys of tin, zinc, low-copper-content metals and various coatings for steel.

As long ago as World War II, steel-cased ammunition was manufactured in large quantities. Some very serviceable 9mm Parabellum ammo was delivered by Germany early during the war. The United States produced large numbers of steel-cased .45 ACP ammunition and a lesser number of .30 carbine cartridges of similar material. After firing several thousand rounds of each, I have experienced no malfunctions traceable to the case metal.

The primary shortcoming of steel cases is their lack of resistance to rust and corrosion but this can easily be checked by use of modern coatings, plating or lubricants.

A second problem with steel cases has been their

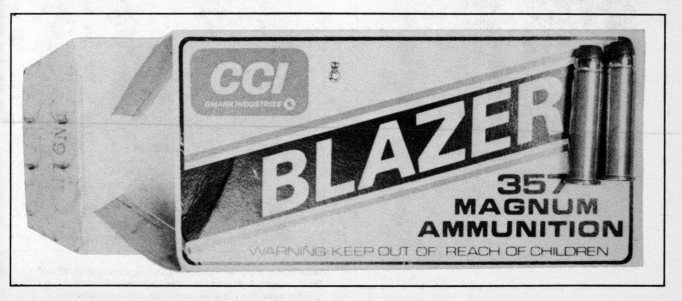

CCI's new Blazer ammo is packaged in a distinctive white-and-black package. The aluminum-cased ammunition is not reloadable but offers an attractive price compared to brass-cased cartridges.

Treated steel cases survive almost as well as brass. These three 9mm Parabellum cartridges bear a 1943 headstamp. The one on the left carries a standard full-jacketed bullet in steel case. In center, the case is brass and bullet has an ordinary gilding metal jacket. At right is a treated steel case with soft iron bullet. For identification, the iron bullet is colored black.

Brass-cased .45 ACP round (left) is headstamped 1943. The cartridge on right is also headstamped 1943 but has a steel case which has developed a bad case of rust and corrosion. Both have been stored under similar conditions for forty years.

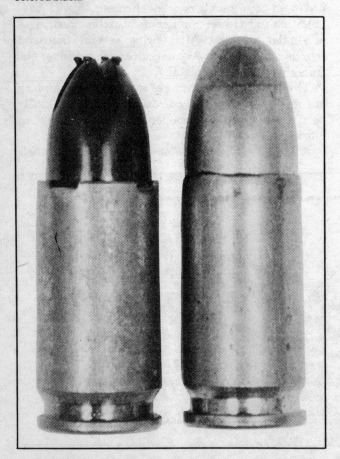

Brass-cased, plastic-bulleted 9mm practice round (left) is shown with FMJ military 9mm round.

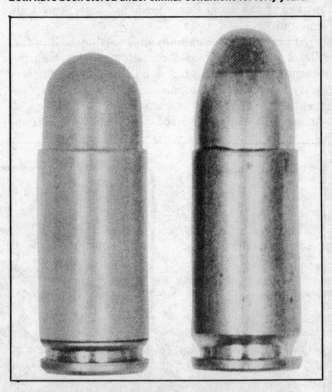

Plastics are now being used for training ammunition. At left, the plastic 9mm Parabellum is used for indoor shooting at short ranges. It is close enough in all dimensions to the standard 9mm (right) that it shoots very well. The plastic round will not operate the action of autoloading pistols.

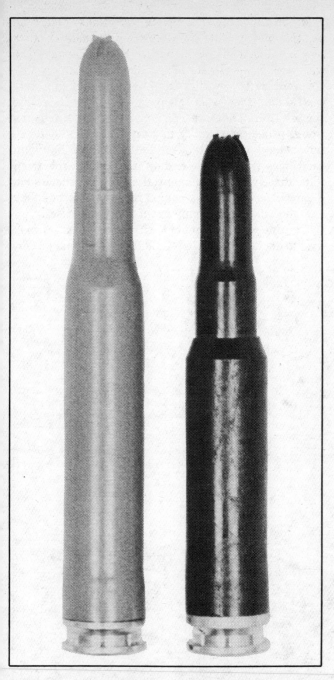

Plastic training rounds are available in several calibers. The light-colored cartridge on left is .30.06 and the darker one is for .308. Both use metal heads to facilitate extraction.

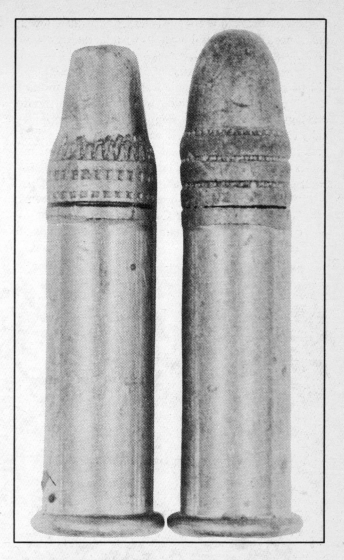

External change was slight but the Remington Yellow Jacket (left) drives its bullet at 1500 feet per second (fps) while the ordinary .22 RF loafs along at 1150/1250 fps. Advantages of the higher-velocity round are numerous.

failure to fully obturate upon firing. Highly ductile steels are now available that should not only produce an effective gas seal but should be reloadable by use of ordinary reloading tools and dies. Low-cost production processes for working steel into cases are possible.

Further use of plastics in shell-case manufacturing will continue to be developed. A few years ago, primitive plastic shotshell hulls were supported by heavy-duty brass shell heads. As plastics improved, the brass head served less and less as an essential part of the shell. Today, the brass head (sometimes plated steel) on a shotgun shell is largely for cosmetic purposes. Most manufacturers agree that the metal head is put there simply because shotgunners *expect* shells to have metal heads and rims.

At least one manufacturer has decided to publicly admit that the brass on shotshells is nothing more than eyewash. Eclipse Cartridge Corp., 26407 Golden Valley Rd., Saugus, Ca 91350 is vending a line of shotshells with hulls formed of a single piece of plastic. No metal head or rim, no reinforced primer pocket. What's more, the Eclipse line of shotshells is fully reloadable with no modification to existing loading tools. Durability seems to be no problem and loading effort is no greater than that for any other shotshell. Prices for Eclipse shells are 15%-20% lower than those for comparable shells with metal heads. So who needs brass on shotshells?

In discussing possible use of plastics for handgun or rifle cartridges with officials from two large manufacturing companies, I received two distinctly different opinions. The head of one company declared emphatically that no existing plastic could withstand the heat generated by even a modest handgun load. He considers experiments with plastics for rifle and pistol cartridges a complete waste of time and effort. In addition to the lack of heat resistance, he deems plastic to be far too weak for reliable functioning in any cartridge developing more than 15,000 pounds of operating pressure.

In response to the same questions regarding plastics, an official of another major manufacturer responsed that his company has been experimenting with plastic-cased pistol cartridges for several years. He went on to say that they have developed a successful case for use in revolvers up to and including the .45 Colt. They are not convinced that the cases would prove satisfactory in heavy magnum loadings but believe they could market a line of handgun cartridges in the low end of the power spectrum immediately. At the moment, they do not believe such a cartridge would be a commercial success but they can and will start production if the need arises.

Continued experiments with various plastics may lead to development of a type suitable for more power-

The author holds Benelli SMG designed for caseless cartridge. The little gun has a high cyclic rate of fire and produces slightly greater muzzle velocity/energy than conventional 9mm parabellum.

ful cartridges, including those for high-powered rifles. As an afterthought, the second manufacturer mentioned that plastic cases could be practical if rifles were designed with less need for the strength of a brass case. Considering the fact that caseless cartridges and the guns to use them are a reality, might not the design of a rifle for use with plastic cases be mere child's play?

Bullet on left is lubricated with almost invisible dry lubricant while other uses petroleum-based lube that must be applied while in semi-soft condition. Dry lube is more efficient as well as cleaner.

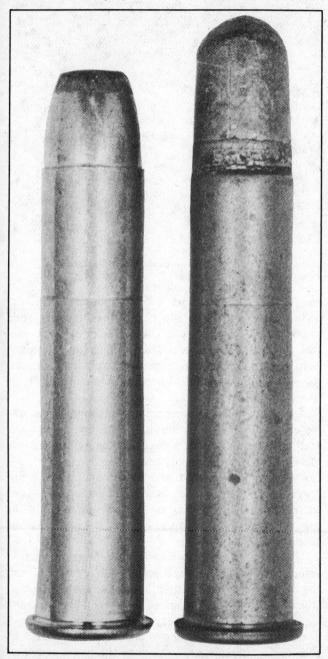

Propellant and bullet design have updated many older cartridges. Here, a modern .45-70 soft point (left) is shown with a black powder loading of the same cartridge. Even though the modern bullet is much lighter (300 grains vs. 500 grains), the newer cartridge is more potent.

Taurus bullets are covered with bonded-film dry lubricant that retards bore leading better than older, messy, petroleum lubes.

Headstamp on the Eclipse shell is moulded right into the plastic. The primer sits in a formed plastic pocket. Except for the primer and shot, these new shells contain no metal.

Development of new cartridges continues. Shown here, the .45 Winchester Magnum (left) compared to standard .45 ACP. The 9mm Winchester Magnum (third from left) offers ballistic superiority over the 9mm Parabellum (far right.)

Another cartridge component undergoing constant change is the propellant powder. In the age of firearms, smokeless powder is a relatively recent development but today's smokeless formulae are only distantly related to those of 75 years ago. Not only has the chemical content of the powders undergone drastic change, the choice of grain structure is amazing. Powder granules may be flakes, pebbles, rods or tubes, as well as almost perfectly shaped spheres. Burning rate is controlled by alteration of chemical content and by addition of various coatings, applied after the powder is formed. Chemists of the century past would not have been able to visualize the wizardry employed in manufacturing today's powders. If today's powder is smokeless, non-corrosive and non-abrasive, may not tomorrow's be flashless or even self-cleaning?

The final conventional ammunition component subject to improvement is the primer. Much has been done in the past few decades to improve both the mechanical functioning and chemical properties of primers. Those who have fired surplus ammunition from World War II may recall the heavy cleaning required to prevent corrosion. Non-corrosive priming was available then, but it was far less stable and resistant to aging than the chlorate primers preferred by the military. Thanks to the efforts of chemists, non-corrosive primers now exhibit the same long life once reserved for mercuric or chlorate materials. It's no longer necessary to clean after firing with soap and water or powerful solvents, then, check daily for several days to be sure rust from the primer residue hasn't set in. Some changes may be expected in moisture-proofing primers and rendering them less sensitive to cleaning solvents.

Along the same lines as primer improvements, we may find tomorrow's ammunition more weatherproof and solventproof than today's. Some of the newer plastic-based sealants will resist the ravages of solvents and indefinite immersion in water. There's no reason to doubt that they can be applied to an entire cartridge after completion of the manufacturing process. Weatherproof ammunition should be quite valuable to some hunters.

No matter what direction future ammunition developments may take, the changes will be gradual. For the immediate future, there's no need to sell your stock holdings in copper mines or to scrap your reloading equipment. Our factory ammunition, for a few years at least, will continue to be wrapped (mostly) in those shiny brass cases so dear to the heart of every handloader. One thing is certain, tomorrow's ammunition will be better than today's just as today's is better than yesterday's.

The Man Behind the Gun: Anthony Fiala

John C. Rhodes

Ask the average gun enthusiast if he's ever heard of the Fiala pistol and the chances are good he'll respond with, "I think so. Italian gun, wasn't it?"

The truth is the Fiala target pistol is as American as apple pie. It was one of a number of similar 22-caliber guns to appear in the period between the two world wars, guns that never quite made it in competition with the best-selling Colt Woodsman. The comparatively rare Fiala pistol has never been really appreciated by most collectors, partly because the story of Anthony Fiala, the man who gave his name to it, has never been told. This is the story of the search for the man behind the gun.

It all began with a letter that was received at the offices of the Stoeger Publishing Company several years ago, postmarked at Auckland, New Zealand. The writer had been offered a Fiala pistol and wanted to know something about the gun and the man who had made it.

The letter was routine enough. What made it so intriguing to Stoeger's editors was its place of origin. Anthony Fiala had been an Arctic explorer who later set himself up in the expedition-outfitting business. In the 1930s, Auckland was the jumping-off place for expeditions to Antarctica, most notably the expeditions of Admiral Richard E. Byrd to "Little America." Could this Fiala pistol have found its way to New Zealand as part of the kit of some member of such an expedition? The possibilities were there and they are exciting to contemplate.

The phrase "Renaissance Man" is an apt description of Anthony Fiala. Engineer, surveyor, cartographer, artist, soldier, explorer, lecturer, businessman, raconteur, devoted husband and father, Anthony Fiala was all of these. In many respects, he was ahead of his time in his enterprise and vision. Certainly his like will not come this way again.

Anthony Fiala was born in Hudson City (later it would become part of Jersey City), New Jersey on September 19, 1869. The name Fiala is not Italian—his father had come to America from Bohemia in what is now Czechoslovakia and had worked as a diamond setter in New York City, eventually settling in Brooklyn. Now the butt of jokes of radio and TV comics, in those days Brooklyn was a quiet little city, proud of its traditions and its churches, libraries and schools. Its newspaper, the *Brooklyn Eagle,* was world-renowned and on a par with any big-city daily, even maintaining its own corps of foreign correspondents. Walt Whitman had once been its editor.

Young Anthony Fiala began his career as a lithographic stone artist and soon graduated to the new processes of photoengraving and photogravure. When war with Spain threatened, he joined Troop C, a

Anthony Fiala in Arctic garb.

cavalry unit of the New York National Guard head-quartered in Brooklyn and under the command of Captain Bertram T. Clayton, a West Point graduate in the class of 1886.

In the spring of 1898, Troop C was mustered into federal service and left Brooklyn for the war zone. After a brief stay in Camp Black on Long Island and Camp Alger in Virginia, the khaki-clad citizen-soldiers reached Newport News, where they boarded a transport. Unfortunately, their ship ran aground at the entrance to the harbor of Ponce on the southern coast of Puerto Rico and the troops were transferred to a U.S. cruiser, which landed them on the beach. Equipped with Springfield carbines and Krag-Jorgensen carbines in saddle scabbards and .45 caliber revolvers in belt holsters, the troopers took part in skirmishes with the enemy at Coamo, Asomante and Aibonito. During this period young Fiala also served as a war correspondent and combat artist, sending back to the *Brooklyn Eagle* his letters and sketches of the war. These were later incorporated in his book, *Troop "C" in Service,* a lively account of his unit's war experiences, distinguished by a chapter contributed by Richard Harding Davis. Davis was perhaps the most celebrated war correspondent of the conflict that John Hay, U.S. ambassador to Great Britain, in a letter to Theodore Roosevelt had called "a splendid little war."

The Puerto Rican expedition, planned as one of the main campaigns of the war, had proceeded so smoothly that it turned out to be almost an anti-climax. An American force of 3300 men had faced and beaten 8233 Spanish regulars and 9107 volunteers. Thanks to the strategy of former Indian-fighting General Nelson A. Miles, the campaign lasted only a month, terminating when an armistice was signed.

Back in prosaic Brooklyn again, Anthony Fiala was commissioned a first lieutenant in the 14th Infantry, New York National Guard, and settled down to the routines of civilian life. But soon he was to pack up and be off once again, this time as the official photographer of the Baldwin-Ziegler Polar Expedition.

At the turn of the century, polar fever gripped the popular imagination of the United States. One who caught the bug was Evelyn Briggs Baldwin, who had had some experience in polar work with Robert E. Peary in Greenland. Although not a scientist, Baldwin had the knack of being able to obtain money from wealthy benefactors anxious to see the American flag raised at the top of the world. One man Baldwin succeeded in interesting in such a venture was William Ziegler, who had made a tremendous fortune through his ownership of the Royal Baking Powder Company.

Ziegler wanted an expedition bearing his name to attain the North Pole in the worst way—in fact, he wanted to buy it. He candidly told a reporter from the *London Daily Chronicle* in 1900, "I intend to plant the Stars and Stripes on the North Pole if it costs me a million dollars to do it."

Ziegler didn't spend a million, but he did lay out a quarter of a million dollars for the most lavishly equipped expedition ever sent to the Arctic. It included three ships, an electric heating plant, a telephone system, prefabricated buildings, message balloons, and 400 sled dogs and 15 Siberian ponies. The expedition roster totalled 42 men and even included Russian hostlers to care for the ponies.

The Baldwin-Ziegler Polar Expedition was a comedy of errors and mismanagement. Baldwin seems to have spent most of his time aboard the headquarters

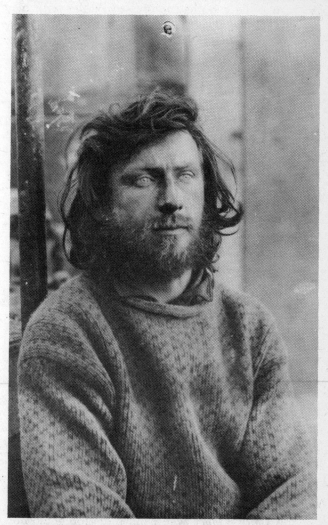

A rare photograph from an old negative: After several months of the Arctic winter, Anthony Fiala looked like this.

vessel, communicating with bases on shore by telephone. The following June, when he should have been readying for a dash for the pole from Franz Josef Land, northeast of Spitzbergen, Baldwin became nervous because the expected supply ship had not arrived. He set out for Norway, where he met Ziegler, waiting there for news of the attainment of the pole, and discovered that the supply ship had passed his ship en route. Stories of dissension began to surface, and Ziegler fired Baldwin on the spot.

Baldwin later tried unsuccessfully to organize other Arctic exploration ventures. Observers of the polar scene humorously remarked that Baldwin's greatest discovery seems to have been William Ziegler. Baldwin subsequently disappeared into obscurity as a minor government clerk.

In 1903, another Ziegler expedition was planned and fitted out, this time with a new commander, Anthony Fiala, who had impressed Ziegler with his zeal and resolve. Once again, the expedition's ship was the 400-ton steam yacht *America,* formerly the Dundee whaler *Esquimau.* Fiala chose William J. Peters, of Washington, D.C., as his chief scientist, and Russell W. Porter, of Springfield, Vermont, as Peters' assistant. Both men later had distinguished scientific careers. Captain Edwin Coffin of Edgartown, Massachusetts, was the ship's master.

Despite Anthony Fiala's resolve to avoid the problems of the previous expedition and to impose discipline, dissension broke out. To complicate matters, the expedition ship, frozen in the ice since November of 1903 off Franz Josef Land, was badly nipped by shifting ice and sank suddenly in January of 1904. Fortunately, supplies of food and fuel had been wisely removed on Fiala's orders and the expedition members were able to survive in reasonable comfort.

Two Fiala attempts on the Pole were turned back by bad weather and openings in the ice. Fiala was game for wintering over another winter, but democratically allowed his men to choose to retreat south for a prearranged rendezvous with the expedition supply ship. More men chose to head south than he had anticipated and Fiala later wrote, "The politicians in the retreating party used their influence and persuasiveness to enlarge their own party—until those to whom 'Northward!' had become a shibboleth became, like Gideon's band, fewer and fewer." The retreat turned out to be futile, for the rescue ship missed the meeting and the disgruntled men had to return to Fiala's base.

Apparently Fiala's even-handed discipline did not sit well with some of his men. In 1969, a Russian expedition visited Fiala's base camp and found an

Pastel portrait of a youthful Anthony Fiala clothed in expedition garb and holding an ice-axe.

electrically wired explosive device planted in the commander's quarters. The Russians also found a note signed by three defectors: "We, the opposition, are leaving the camp on Saturday, July 2, 1904, having 18 dogs, two ponies and an Indian Boat."

To make matters worse, benefactor Ziegler died suddenly in the spring of 1905. With financial support clouded, the Fiala expedition returned to Norway in the *Terra Nova,* a rescue ship chartered by William S. Champ, Ziegler's assistant. The scientific results of the Fiala-led Ziegler Polar Expedition were later published by the National Geographic Society and added considerably to knowledge of polar studies.

Fiala also wrote a lively account, *Fighting the Polar Ice,* in which he pointed out that, contrary to popular wisdom, money alone could not guarantee the success of a polar expedition. Arctic exploration also required luck, endurance and courage; all members of the expedition needed patience, "the highest qualities of Christian character." An Arctic explorer, he explained, "operates in a decidedly hostile and un-

On Theodore Roosevelt's River of Doubt expedition in Brazil, Anthony Fiala made this sketch of a dugout canoe running hazardous rapids.

cultivated territory, where there are no cornfields or henroosts along the line of march, but instead an active enemy in every wind that blows from the north, and opposition to his advance in every pressure ridge and water lane that crosses his path."

Fiala's next exploration venture was with ex-President Theodore Roosevelt's famous River of Doubt expedition (which Fiala also outfitted) in its penetration of the Brazilian jungle in 1913. As the leader of one of three sections of the expedition, Anthony Fiala surveyed, mapped and made motion pictures of the unknown region of central Brazil and explored the thousand-mile course of the Papagaio river and its lower reaches, the Juruena and Tapajos rivers. On one occasion, he narrowly escaped death when his dugout canoe capsized and sank. This was the expedition that broke Teddy Roosevelt's health; five years later the

former Rough Rider would be dead.

Fiala returned to the United States in 1914 and resumed the management of Rogers, Peet & Company's sporting goods department, which he had opened in 1909. Military life beckoned again in 1916, when Mexican bandit Pancho Villa raided across the border and hit Columbus, New Mexico, and the United States sent troops to the Mexican border. In this campaign, Anthony Fiala served as captain of the machine gun troop of the 1st New York Cavalry of the New York National Guard, serving at McAllen, Texas.

Upon the entrance of the United States into the first World War, Anthony Fiala was transferred to Spartanburg, South Carolina, as captain of D Company of the 102nd Ammunition Train. In July of 1918, he was promoted to the rank of Major and placed in charge of the Small Arms Proving Ground at the

Anthony Fiala's rough sketch of a canoe portage. Teddy Roosevelt appears in the upper right corner.

described as the Model 1920.

Early Fiala pistols had a fixed 7½-inch barrel, but Major Fiala, as he was called for the remainder of his life, added a choice of three barrels (3 inches and 20 inches, in addition to the "standard" barrel) plus an additional wooden buttstock. In this feature, Fiala's gun was not much different in concept or appearance from some of today's takedown survival guns. Advertisements called it "three guns in one." Customers could have the combination gun in a rough-and-ready canvas roll-up case or in a small leather or leatherette trunk-like case handsomely lined with purple plush. A silencer and a smooth-bore barrel were also offered. As his trademark, Fiala appropriately selected a polar bear.

The gun to which Anthony Fiala lent his name is interesting but was an anomaly from the start. In assessing the gun in his classic, *The Book of Pistols and Revolvers,* W.H.B. Smith wrote, "A combination of good balance, Patridge sights and four-grooved rifling as developed for the .22 Springfield rifle makes this an accurate target arm."

"In appearance this arm closely resembles the Colt Woodsman. With 7½-inch barrel it measures 11¼ inches overall and weighs about 31 ounces. It has a Woodsman-type magazine in the handle which holds ten cartridges," Smith wrote.

"However, it is *not* an automatic pistol," Smith pointed out. "It is a magazine pistol. When a loaded magazine is inserted in the handle a bolt lock on the receiver must be pushed in to release the breechblock

Springfield Armory. Known as the Borden Brook Range, this facility was located near Blandford, Massachusetts, about 20 miles west of Springfield. Major Fiala was apparently in demand as a public speaker; a photograph in the October 1918 issue of the Springfield Armory magazine *The Armorer,* shows him addressing a large and enthusiastic Liberty Bond rally in Springfield.

Undoubtedly this service at the Springfield Armory gave Major Fiala a first-hand familiarity with small arms that was to stand him in good stead in his next venture. He left the army in June 1919 and severed his connection with Rogers, Peet & Company, to establish the Fiala Arms & Equipment Company in New York City and New Haven, Connecticut. In the latter place, he became associated with James E. Schall in the manufacture of his Fiala Target Pistol, probably around 1920, because the first guns produced were

Because of his arctic explorations, Anthony Fiala appropriately chose a polar bear as his trademark.

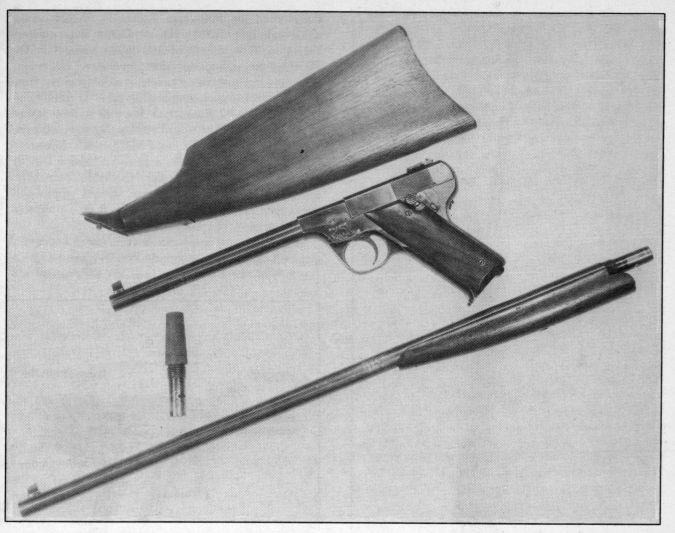

Typical Fiala set included three barrels (3-, 7½- and 20-inch) and a wood shoulder-stock and can be considered a forerunner of today's survival guns.

Photo courtesy Charles E. Petty

slide. The slide is then drawn to the rear to clear the top of the magazine and permit a cartridge to rise in line. As the arm does not have a recoil spring, the slide must be pushed forward to chamber the cartridge. Each time the pistol is fired the slide must be unlocked and drawn back to extract and recock, then thrust forward to chamber and lock the breech. A disconnector prevents the arm from being fired unless the breech is fully closed."

We shall probably never know what attracted Anthony Fiala to a gun that did not possess automatic capabilities. The Colt Woodsman, a true automatic, and a gun which the Fiala and other pistols of the period resembles, was first manufactured on March 29, 1915, thus antedating the others.

When a true automatic is fired, the slide is blown back to eject the empty cartridge case, cock the hammer and compress the recoil spring, and then moves forward to reload the firing chamber with another round from the magazine. After the Fiala has been fired, it is necessary to press in and release the slide lock at the breech, then to pull the slide back manually using the free hand to eject the empty case, to recock the hammer and to clear the top of the magazine so the slide may go home to pick up a loaded cartridge and insert it in the chamber. It has been suggested that Anthony Fiala's Arctic experience may have prejudiced him against genuine automatic weapons, which often malfunction under conditions of extreme cold. But his experience may have also blinded him to reality—the Colt Woodsman was selling like hotcakes; in 1920, Colt produced 5500, a figure that was to rise to 11,000 in 1921, before dropping back to 4500 in 1922 in response to economic conditions.

Let us now turn our attention to the inventor and

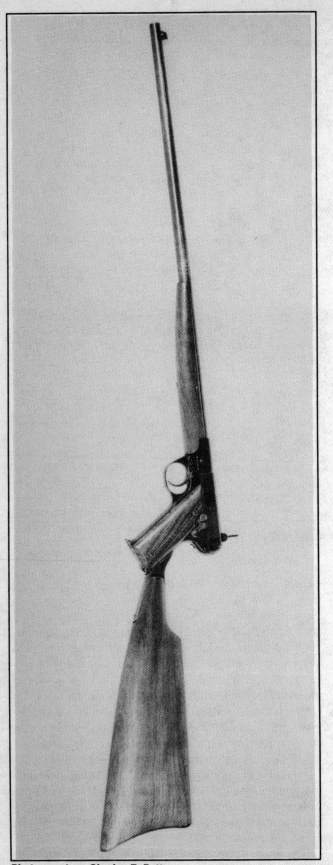

Photo courtesy Charles E. Petty

designer of the Fiala gun, Lucius N. Diehm, about whom relatively little is known. Diehm lived on Vera Street in West Hartford and listed himself in the Hartford city directories as an "inventor." His inventiveness extended over a period of a dozen years, from 1913 to 1925 (see accompanying table of patents issued to Lucius N. Diehm). Of the nine patents issued to Diehm between 1916 and 1925, seven were assigned in part to Berkley C. Stone, a Middletown, Connecticut, dealer in automobile accessories. Stone had an interest in a war-born company, the Middletown Firearms and Specialty Company, which apparently subsidized Diehm's work. Whether it ever produced any firearms is not known.

In addition to competition from more successful guns, another factor that undoubtedly played a role in the fate of the Fiala pistol was the widespread un-

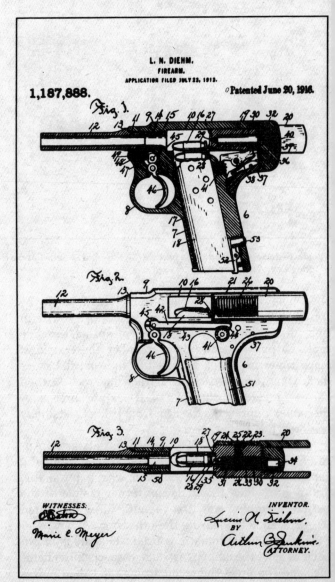

UNITED STATES PATENT OFFICE.

LUCIUS N. DIEHM, OF WEST HARTFORD, CONNECTICUT, ASSIGNOR OF ONE-HALF TO BERKLEY C. STONE, OF MIDDLETOWN, CONNECTICUT.

FIREARM.

Specification of Letters Patent.   Patented June 20, 1916.

1,187,888.   Application filed July 23, 1913.   Serial No. 780,711.

To all whom it may concern:
Be it known that I, Lucius N. Diehm, a citizen of the United States, and a resident of the county of Hart-

receiving chamber 15 for the reception of cartridges 16.
A magazine opening 17 is formed lengthwise through the handle 7, this opening extending from the lower end of the handle into the breech bolt opening 10, and to receive a magazine 18 of

The Patents of Lucius N. Diehm

Number	Application Date	Issue Date	Item
1,187,888	July 23, 1913	June 20, 1916	Firearm
	Assigned one-half to Berkley C. Stone, Middletown, Connecticut		
1,226,478	August 6, 1915	May 15, 1917	Automatic firearm
	Assigned two-thirds to Berkley C. Stone		
1,271,678	October 6, 1916	July 9, 1918	Firearm
1,285,954	July 21, 1917	November 26, 1918	Trigger mechanism
	Assigned as follows: 39/624 to Dayton A Baldwin, 307/624 to Berkley C. Stone, 115/624 to Fred I. Hodge, 40/624 to Franklin Turner, all of Middletown Connecticut		
1,405,765	September 4, 1920	February 7, 1922	Pistol
	Assigned one-half to Berkley C. Stone		
1,489,989	May 17, 1919	April 8, 1924	Firearm
	Assigned one-half to Berkley C. Stone		
1,511,509	February 26, 1921	October 14, 1924	Firearm
	Assigned one-half to Berkley C. Stone		
1,511,510	August 6, 1921	October 14, 1924	Firearm
	Assigned one-half to Berkley C. Stone		
1,557,435	February 24, 1925	October 13, 1925	Firearm

employment in 1921 and the accompanying postwar depression. Presaging similar situations in the future, on August 16, 1921, the Department of Labor released figures showing that 5,735,000 American workers were unemployed—a record number.

Whatever the reason, by 1922, like many other American businesses, the Fiala Arms & Equipment Company was in the hands of a receiver, David A. Lederer, of New Haven. Somewhat more than four thousand Fiala pistols had been made, according to Anthony Fiala, a figure that is at odds with the existence of Fiala pistols serially numbered around 5600. Some later pistols bore the names SCHALL & CO, BOTWINIK BROTHERS and COLUMBIA.

This was not unprecedented. The Fiala Arms & Equipment Company had no manufacturing facilities of its own. According to various sources, the frames were made by the Blakeslee Drop Forging Company of Hartford, Connecticut, and the guns were assembled by James E. Schall & Company in New Haven, Connecticut.

To demonstrate the difficulty of reconstructing even relatively recent history, Hartford city directories show no such Blakeslee company in Hartford. Yet New Haven directories show James E. Schall, with offices on Grant Street near Plymouth Street, to be the "local representative, Blakeslee Drop Forging Company." If that information is correct, in what city

Patented Oct. 13, 1925.   1,557,435

UNITED STATES PATENT OFFICE.

LUCIUS N. DIEHM, OF WEST HARTFORD, CONNECTICUT.

FIREARM.

Application filed February 24, 1925. Serial No. 11,275.

To all whom it may concern:

Be it known that I, LUCIUS N. DIEHM, a citizen of the United States, and a resident of West Hartford, in the county of Hartford and State of Connecticut, have invented new and Improved Firearms, of which the following is a specification.

My invention relates more especially to that class of firearms that are customarily held in the hand and that are otherwise unsupported while being fired, and which are commonly known as pistols, and an object of my invention, among others, is the production of a firearm of this class having novel features of construction with respect to the firing mechanism.

One form of a firearm embodying my invention and in the construction and use of which the objects herein set out, as well as others, may be attained is illustrated in the accompanying drawings, in which—

Figure 1 is a side view of the frame of a firearm embodying my invention.

Figure 2 is a view in section on a plane denoted by the dotted lines 2—2 of Figure 5.

Figure 3 is a bottom view of the breech bolt.

Figure 4 is a view in side elevation of the upper rear end of the frame with the thumb lever for actuating the breech-bolt stop broken off.

Figure 5 is a cross section on a plane denoted by the dotted line 5—5 of Figure 2.

In the accompanying drawings the numeral 6 denotes the stock or handle comprising a portion of the frame of my improved

said hole being closed as by a screw threaded plug 15. A hole 16 is formed through the rear end of the breech-bolt into the recess 13, said hole being somewhat smaller in diameter than that of the recess and providing a shoulder at the bottom of the recess to receive the thrust of a spring support 17 located in the recess and having a push lug 18 extending therefrom through the hole 16, and as shown in Figure 2 of the drawings.

A breech-bolt stop 19 is located in a recess 20 in the receiver or upper part of the frame, said stop being seated upon a spring 21, and said stop being held within the recess as by means of a pin 22. The upper end of the stop projects into a breech-bolt stop recess 23 located in the under surface of the breech-bolt at the back part thereof, a hammer recess 24 opening at the bottom of the breech-bolt stop recess, and as shown in Figure 3 of the drawings, the end of a firing pin 25 projecting into the recess 24 to be struck by the hammer 26 in a manner that will be readily understood.

A slot 27 extends through the bottom of the recess 23 into the breech-bolt actuating spring recess 13, and a spring retainer 28, in the form of a nose extending from the end of the breech-bolt stop 19, passes through said slot and into an opening 29 in the under surface of the spring support 17. A breech-bolt stop actuating lever 30 is pivotally mounted on the side of the receiver or upper part of the frame, this lever having a breech-bolt stop actuating pin 31 extending through a slot 32 in the side of

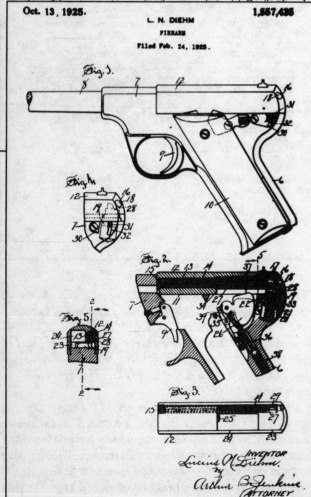

Oct. 13, 1925.   1,557,435

L. N. DIEHM

FIREARM

Filed Feb. 24, 1925.

INVENTOR
Lucius N. Diehm
by
Arthur B. Jenkins
ATTORNEY

(Left) The last pistol patent issued to Lucius Diehm — on Oct. 13, 1925 — covering an improvement to the firing mechanism. **(Above)** Stampings on Fiala pistols — "SCHALL & CO. NEW HAVEN, CONN. U.S.A." — after Fiala Arms Co. went into receivership in 1922.

or town was the Blakeslee company located?

The addition of other names can be easily explained. If large numbers of Fiala guns were in various stages of manufacture at the time the Fiala company got into financial difficulty, the roll-stamping of other names after assembly would have been commonplace, especially if Schall's company and Botwinik Brothers were creditors attempting to realize some part of the money owed to them.

Schall, of course, had been in the iron and steel business and later (1925) made universal joints for automobiles as the New England Auto Products Corporation. Botwinik Brothers (not Botwinick, as some sources have it) was a large and prosperous firm selling new and used machinery and factory supplies, with offices at 21 Sylvan Avenue in New Haven, Connecticut, and a branch in Bridgeport, Connecticut, at 28-42 Drouve Street.

Lucius N. Diehm was later to play a role in the Hartford Arms & Equipment Company, which was founded in 1925 and manufactured a .22 caliber pistol in small quantities. The Hartford came in two versions: a single-shot model very similar in appearance to the Fiala but without provision for a magazine and a semi-automatic model quite similar in appearance to the Colt Woodsman and almost identical with the High Standard Model B. This latter fact is not surprising, since the bankrupt Hartford Arms & Equipment Company was acquired by High Standard (at that time not in the gun business) in 1932.

For some gun companies, the period between the two world wars was certainly not propitious. Considering the relatively small number of Fiala guns manufactured and their current scarcity, it is no exaggeration to say that on the used-firearms market, pistols like the Fiala are distinctly undervalued.

And what of Anthony Fiala? New York City directories for 1922/1923 show that he maintained two

(Top) Fiala pistol with 3-inch barrel. (Middle) Fiala pistol with 7½-inch barrel. (Bottom) Schall & Company version of Fiala pistol with barrel shortened to 6¾-inches.

Photo courtesy Charles E. Petty

business addresses: Fiala Outfits, at 25 Warren Street, just north of the city's financial district, and the Fiala Arms & Equipment Company, with midtown offices in room 702 at 342 Madison Avenue. What makes the latter address so interesting is that 1924/1925 directories show this to have been the address of the Columbia Arms Corporation, which may explain why some post-bankruptcy Fiala-type pistols have turned up roll-stamped COLUMBIA.

Secondary sources show Anthony Fiala to have been the president of the Fiala Arms & Equipment Company, with Clarence W. Sprague as vice-president and Alf W. Duckett, secretary-treasurer. Room 702 also housed the offices of A. W. Duckett & Company, steamship agents and brokers, of which Duckett was president and Sprague was vice-president. Business,

Left and right sides of Fiala target pistol with 7½-inch barrel. Right side is stamped "FIALA ARMS and EQUIPMENT CO INC NEW HAVEN CONN PATENTS PENDING [the patents were those of inventor Lucius N. Diehm] Model 1920 MADE IN U.S.A."
Left side is stamped FIALA ARMS; polar bear logo.
Photo courtesy Charles E. Petty

like politics, sometimes makes strange bedfellows: Room 702 was also the home of the Chalet Chocolate Company. In 1925, the Duckett company moved to 110 East 42nd Street, to become the Sprague-Duckett Corporation, dealers in general merchandise. By then, the Fiala pistol was almost forgotten by everyone. Family sources say that Anthony Fiala had wanted to move cautiously in manufacturing the gun, but was overruled by his business partners, who opted for producing the gun in large quantities.

In the early 1930s, Fiala Outfits moved to 47 Warren Street, moving again in the mid-1930s to 10 Warren Street, where it would remain. Anthony Fiala continued to take an active interest in the business. In later years, in addition to occasional old-fashioned

exploring expeditions, his outfitting clients included oil companies, mining and timber exploration companies scouring the world for riches on and under the surface.

Anthony Fiala died on April 8, 1950, at his home at 148 Eighty-third Street in the Bay Ridge section of the borough of Brooklyn, which had been a part of New York City since 1898. His passing marked the end of the old breed of explorers—men who were able to plunge into the unknown without benefit of radios, airplanes or helicopters and come out months or years later, undaunted by adversity and with expedition members in good health and numbers virtually intact. Surely the world could use some of these qualities right now to see us through the trying days ahead.

The Bianchi Cup: Handgunning's "World Series"

Mickey Fowler

The Bianchi Cup International Tournament of Champions is handgunning's richest and most prestigious event. The Ray Chapman Academy Range, located in Columbia, Missouri, hosts this world series of pistol shooting during the last week of May each year. Shooters from around the world compete for cash and prizes totaling over $150,000. Generous support from the firearms industry has made this possible; manufacturers such as Colt, Heckler & Koch, Tasco, Caswell, Aimpoint, and many others have made possible an event rivaling a professional golf tournament or tennis match in cash to the overall winner.

The "Cup," as it is called, is by invitation only—one must be a top competitor with a proven record in competition to receive one of the coveted invitations. And the list of competitors reads like a "who's who" of tournament pistoleros. Spectators get a unique opportunity to see top guns from pistol and revolver shooting compete in this world series of handgunning. Famous names like Ross Seyfried, 1981 IPSC World Champion; two-time NRA National Champion Joe Pascarella; former Police PPC National Revolver Champion Royce Weddle; two-time Second Chance Combat Champion Bill Wilson; 1982 World Speed Shooting Champion Mike Plaxco; two-time US National IPSC Champion John Shaw and others battle it out for the coveted "Bianchi Cup."

John Bianchi, owner and founder of the Bianchi Gunleather Company, wanted to create a handgun match which would allow the revolver shooter to compete on an equal basis with the pistol shooter. Ray Chapman, 1975 IPSC World Champion, was asked to design a challenging course of fire to cover as many different practical shooting skills as possible. Of equal importance was spectator appeal, which would eventually lead to television coverage. Most practical shooting matches require quick reloading during strings of fire. This, in effect, give the auto pistol an insurmountable advantage when tight time limits are used.

To eliminate this problem, Chapman designed four different courses of fire consisting of 48 rounds each. Strings of fire are limited to a maximum of six rounds. By eliminating the need to reload during the firing sequences, equality of the revolver and autopistol is achieved. In the interest of practicality, it was decided that the lower limit of caliber be 9mm. The lower limit of power is 158 grain 38 Special round-nosed, lead, factory police-loadings, chronographed from a six-inch barrel.

No limitations are set on handgun types, sights, ammunition capacity, barrel length or configuration. However, the handgun must be suitable for holster use. All strings of fire begin from the holster. For safety reasons holsters must be worn near waist level and suspended from a pants belt or gunbelt and must not allow the pistol to be pointed at spectators or competitors while worn or in drawing the pistol. Two types of targets are used in the four-match agregate, which makes up the overall championship portion of the event. A buff-colored cardboard target 30 inches high by 18 inches wide, with a rounded top cut on a nine-inch radius is used in three of the four matches; this target looks just like a tombstone.

The center of the target contains scoring rings: A four inch "X" ring or tie breaker, an eight-inch ten ring and a twelve-inch eight ring. Shots outside the scoring rings but still on the target score five points. Other targets are eight-inch diameter steel plates mounted on pivots. To score a hit, the targets must be knocked down and each hit is worth ten points. A miss is zero. An eight-inch ten ring may seem large and hard to miss but under the tight time limits for each string of fire and the added pressure of thousands of dollars riding on the shot, the targets can look very small indeed.

After the four individual matches making up the overall championship and a overall champion is decided, the top twenty finishers go on to compete in a special event, the Colt Speed Match. Targets for this match are Colt speed plates. Three-eighths-inch steel is cut into 12- by 28-inch pieces. The tops are 12-inch circles, but about a third of the way down these taper to 8½ inches and continue down to at the narrowest point to 4½ inches. These are mounted on pivots and must be knocked down to score a hit.

Match one: The Aimpoint Practical Event

This match, consisting of 48 rounds and a possible 480 points, is shot on the Bianchi Cup paper target. Shooters stand facing two targets downrange, spaced three feet apart edge to edge, with the tops approximately six feet above ground level. The shooter starts with his pistol holstered and loaded, both hands held shoulder high, and must remain upright while firing. The starting signal is a police-type whistle after the commands, "Stand by" and "Ready." Ranges are 10, 15, 25 and 50 yards. At 10 yards on the signal to commence fire, one shot is fired at each target in three seconds. At the second signal to fire, the shooters fire two shots at each target in four seconds. At the third signal to fire, competitors must fire three shots at each target, weak hand only (right-handed shooters use their left hand) in eight seconds. The draw and switch to the weak hand may be made with the strong hand, but all shots must be fired with the weak hand unsupported. The shooter then moves to the 15-yard line.

Competitor shooting stage one of the Guns and Ammo Barricade Event.

The first sequence is one shot on each target in four seconds. On the second signal, two shots are fired on each target in five seconds. The third string of fire is three shots on each target in six seconds. Now things start getting more difficult. From 25 yards, the shooter fires one shot on each target in five seconds, two shots on each target in six seconds and three shots on each target in seven seconds.

The last twelve shots are fired from 50 yards; this separates the men from the boys. The first string of fire is one shot on each target in seven seconds. The next string is two shots on each target in ten seconds. The stage is completed by firing three shots on each target in fifteen seconds.

Most competitors find the 25 and 50 yard stages the most difficult. Any error in sight alignment and trigger squeeze can cost valuable points. The 10-yard weak hand only stage can also cause problems. A fumbled draw or slightest flinch can cause shots to go completely off target. It is in these three stages that match one is generally won or lost.

The current record score on this event is 476 points out of a possible 480. This was achieved using a six-inch-long slide Colt 45 automatic pistol equipped with

Bomar open sights.

Match two: The Guns and Ammo Barricade Event

This is a 48-round match with a possible 480 points. The Bianchi Cup cardboard target is used and the distances are 10, 15, 25 and 35 yards. At each firing distance, there is a six-foot high by two-foot wide barricade placed in a line, one directly behind another. Each barricade has a clearly defined two-foot wide by three-foot long firing area on the uprange side. The commence-firing signal is a whistle, and no portion of the competitor's body or equipment may touch outside the firing area until the shooter has finishing firing the designated rounds.

Two targets down range are placed three feet off the center line of the barricades to their inside edges. The starting position for each string is with the pistol holstered and the palms of both hands on the face of the barricade. From 10 yards, on the signal to commence firing, the shooter fires six rounds at either target from the matching side of the barricade. At the second signal to fire, six shots are fired at the remaining target from the matching side of the barricade. The time limit for each 10-yard string of fire is six seconds. The competitor moves to 15 yards and re-peats the procedure used at 10 yards with the time limit increased to seven seconds per string. The 10- and 15-yard strings are frequently cleaned for points and occasionally even for X's by the top shooters.

As the range increases so does the difficulty. The competitor moves to the 25-yard barricades and fires six shots from each side of the barricade. Time limit is eight seconds. The final two strings of fire are from the 35-yard barricade. Six shots from the right side and six shots from the left side in nine second strings complete this event. The 35-yard stage is by far the most difficult and is rarely completed without dropping a few points.

It is worth noting that due to the tight time limits shooters hold their pistols in the same hand on both sides of the barricades. The record score for this event is a perfect 480 points with 42 X's. A specially modified Colt 45 automatic pistol with a muzzle brake was used to fire the record score.

Match three: The Shooting Times Moving Target Event

I rate this as one of the most difficult of the four events. This match is 48 rounds with a possible 480 points and is shot on the Bianchi Cup cardboard target. The distances are 10, 15, 20 and 25 yards. The

Tom Campbell, one of the great handgun shots of all time firing his Aimpoint equipped experimental 45 ACP caliber Smith and Wesson automatic pistol in the Guns and Ammo Barricade Event.

Two-time NRA National Bullseye Pistol Champion Joe Pascarella firing on the Shooting Times moving target event. The target is moving at 10 feet per second and is about halfway through its run.

target moves from behind a barricade and travels 60 feet in six seconds and then disappears behind another barricade. There are clearly marked three-foot-square firing areas at each stage. The firing boxes are at the center of the 60-foot run of the target. The shooter must remain within the designated firing square for each firing sequence.

When the competitor is ready to fire, both hands are raised to shoulder height. The appearance of the target from behind the barricade is the signal to commence firing. From 10 yards, the shooter fires six shots at the target which moves from right to left. On the second string of fire, the target moves from left to right and six more shots are fired. The contestant then moves to the 15-yard shooting box. Three shots are fired at a target which moves from right to left. At the second signal to fire the target moves from left to right and three more shots are fired. This whole procedure is repeated once again. The 20- and 25-yard stages are fired using the same procedure as the fifteen yard stage. Each stage of the moving target match has its own unique degree of difficulty. The 10-yard stage with its six shots per string of fire requires a smooth quick draw and rapid target acquisition. No time can be wasted between shots or the target will disappear behind the barricade before all shots are fired. At 15 yards, shots are reduced to three per string giving the shooter more time to track the target and squeeze the

trigger; one problem at this distance is the difficulty of keeping the proper lead with no clear aiming point of reference on the target. Light on the moving target range can obscure the scoring rings from view making the shooting even more difficult. From 20 yards most shooters hold their front sight on the leading edge of the target. This clear reference point makes this stage a bit easier than the others.

Back at 25 yards, the shooter is again faced with the problem of no clear aiming point. I hold about three inches off the leading edge of the target. This makes holding accurate elevation extremely difficult. Most points lost in this stage come from either high or low shots. For handgunners who want to know how far to lead the target at the various ranges, here are calculations based on an average bullet velocity of 800 feet per second: At 10 yards, 4½ inches off target center, at 15 yards, 6¾ inches. Twenty yards is 9 inches or on the leading edge. Back at the 25-yard shooting box, about 12 inches of lead is used. When shooting the moving target, the competitor must use the fundamentals of marksmanship, sight-picture, trigger squeeze, with the added necessity of smoothly swinging with the target. If the shooter fails to follow through on his swing, shots fall behind and off the target. The record for this event is 478 points out of a possible 480. A PPC bull-barreled revolver in 38 Special caliber was used to set this record.

Mark Duncan shooting his modified PPC revolver in the Shooting Times Moving Target Event. Mark has been a consistantly high finisher in the overall championship.

Match four: The Heckler & Koch Falling Plate Event

Once again, 48 shots are fired, with a perfect score adding up to 480 points. Targets are Bianchi cup falling plates. The distances are 10, 15, 20 and 25 yards. There are two sets of six target plates with each plate placed one foot apart edge to edge. The shooter stands with hands held shoulder high with pistol holstered. The starting signal is a police type whistle preceded by the commands, "Stand by" and "Ready." Plates are knocked down in two six-shot strings from each firing distance.

At 10 yards, six seconds are allowed per six shot string, at 15 yards it is seven seconds, eight seconds from 20 yards and the shooters finish at 25 yards in nine second strings. If a shooter knocks over all 48 plates, the 25-yard stage is repeated until one plate is missing during a six-shot string. This breaks any ties and determines the winner.

As of now, only six shooters have fired perfect scores on this event. This match is the last event fired by the top pistol shooters and decides who is the overall champion. The "fatal plates," as they have been nicknamed, have taken their toll of some of the world's finest pistoleros.

When $30,000 rides on every shot, strange things can happen inside one's head. The eight-inch plates, which even at 25 yards in practice sessions looked large, now appear to be the size of white bottle caps at the 10-yard distance when the pressure is on. Front sights have been seen to be shaking, as if the competitor's pistol was mounted in a weight-reduction clinic's vibrating machine.

In order to complete this test of skill and nerves successfully, the shooter must rely totally on fundamentals. Focus must be kept on the front sight at all times and a controlled, precise trigger squeeze must be

Bill Wilson, two-time Second Chance Combat match overall winner, firing on the moving target with his Wilson custom 45 Colt automatic with scope.

Fred Romero, one of this country's best revolver shots, shooting the Heckler and Koch Falling Plate Match.

1981 IPSC World Champion Ross Seyfrid qualifying for the Colt Speed Event.

maintained. The natural tendency of most pistol shooters when firing under extreme pressure is to look at the target instead of the front sight. This causes missed plates.

Unlike the Bianchi Cup cardboard target matches, where you still get a score for hits out of the eight-inch 10 ring, a missed plate is worth no points. Of the six competitors who have shot perfect scores on this match in actual competition, three used 38 Special PPC modified revolvers and three used modified 45 ACP caliber Colt Government Model automatics.

The four-match agregate takes three days to complete. One match is fired on Wednesday, one on Thursday and two matches on Friday, the last being the Heckler & Koch falling plates. Results are tabulated on a computer and then the overall champion is announced.

On Saturday morning, the top twenty finishers compete in the fifth match, the Colt Speed Event. The first place winner in this event receives $5,000 and a beautiful sterling silver trophy. Two sets of Colt speed plates are placed ten yards down range in banks of five targets each. There are two three-foot square firing areas which are spaced six feet apart, edge to edge. Each bank of five targets is positioned in a fan to the left of the left-side competitor and to the right side of the right-side competitor.

Start position is each shooter standing upright, with the pistol holstered. Both hands are held shoulder high while waiting for an audible electronic signal preceded by the commands, "Stand by" and "Ready."

Phase one: Qualification

Each of the twenty qualifiers fires a maximum of six shots at the targets. This is done two times in the left-side position and two times in the right-side position. All targets must be knocked down to score. The total of the four times makes up the competitor's score. The six fastest shooters from phase one continue on to phase two.

Phase two: The speed event

This is done in what is known as "man vs. man" style. Two competitors square off against identical setups, one in the left-side firing area and one in the right side firing area. The man who knocks down his targets quicker wins that sequence. The procedure is repeated until one shooter wins three times, alternating between right and left sides each time. This constitutes one bout. Each competitor completes one bout against every other competitor; the first shooter who wins three bouts is the winner of this event.

Equipment:

Which action type—double-action revolver or automatic pistol—is the best choice for the overall cup

Chip McCormick and Bill Wilson square off against one another in the Colt "Man vs Man" Speed Event.

Author (Mickey Fowler) qualifying for the Colt Speed event, "Man vs Man" Championship.

championship? There is no clearcut choice as to which is superior. As of now, modified Colt Government Models in 45 ACP caliber have finished first every year since 1979. Sounds like that's the way to go, right? In the last three years of competition, the PPC type revolver has finished in second place and the top ten finishers have been equally divided between both types. In the individual matches, the revolver holds the record on the moving target and falling plate matches. The automatic holds top scores on the barricade and practical matches.

John Bianchi and Ray Chapman have certainly designed a well-balanced course of fire! Let's look at a few of the common modifications done on both action types to ready them for this type of competition. Most of the 45 autos have extended slides or muzzle brake systems. This cuts down recoil and extends the sight radius. Bo-mar sights are either low mounted in the slide or a full sight rib is installed. After accuracy tuning, groups shot from a machine rest with match ammo at a distance of 50 yards will stay within one and one-half inch. Trigger pulls are smoothed and lowered to under three pounds.

A competitive pistol modified by a well-known pistolsmith costs anywhere from one thousand to fifteen hundred dollars. The top-finishing revolvers have heavy match six-inch bull barrels on which full length sight ribs are attached. The double-action pulls are smoothed and lightened.

The cost of a competition PPC revolver is considerably less than an automatic. Prices come to anywhere between four hundred and nine hundred dollars. It's not uncommon to see 50-yard machine-rest groups under one inch when these guns are tuned by top gunsmiths. Optical sights are starting to show up on revolvers and automatics. Pistol scopes of two power and less, with dot reticules, and the aimpoint sight with a battery-powered red dot as the sight are making their presence known. Improved scores at the longer firing distances are possible because the shooter who uses a scope doesn't have to concentrate on sight picture; you just look at the spot you wish your bullet to strike, put the dot on it and squeeze the trigger. If these devices are allowed to be used in the future, we might just see a perfect score of 1920 points.

Will a perfect score be fired in the Bianchi Cup match this year? No one can say, but one thing you can be sure of: on Memorial Day weekend two hundred of the world's best pistol shots will be competing for handgunning's richest purse. Whoever wins can indeed be proud of his victory.

A Guide to
Hunting Optics

Clair Rees

European sportsmen typically shoot game long after it would even be legal for an American deer hunter to fire. But many Americans make the mistake of giving up and going back to camp just as the best hunting begins. Trophy animals tend to move just as the last light is fading, or in the darkness just preceding dawn. With the right binoculars and a good rifle scope, the wise nimrod will be equipped to take advantage of what the Germans call "prime hunting light."

It's a fact that good optics can add several minutes to each end of the hunting day. Since dawn and dusk are by far the most productive times to hunt deer and other early- and late-feeding animals, it's only good sense to take full advantage of these low-light opportunities.

The ability to hunt early and late is but one advantage good optics afford—and it's one many sportsmen don't even recognize. Most shooters opt for optical sights simply to magnify the target image and help them better see the game they're shooting at. Similarly, binoculars and spotting scopes are most often used in bright daylight.

Good optical gear is of prime importance to hunters, and some of this equipment is in almost universal use. Today, most riflemen and an increasing number of handgunners rely on magnifying glass sights to help

them get their game.

While the scope sight is by far the most popular type of optical equipment used by modern nimrods, other kinds of optics can be equally important. Binoculars are used to find distant game the unaided eye might miss, while spotting scopes allow an even closer look. Such aids are invaluable in mountainous or plains country and are absolute musts for the trophy hunter.

Optical rangefinders are available to help you judge range and determine the holdover needed to put your bullet on target. Some riflescopes come equipped with rangefinding reticles and trajectory compensating adjustment devices. These depend on bracketing the chest cavity of an animal with adjustable stadia hairs to determine range, while the hand-held rangefinders being marketed can be used to gauge the distance to any object by superimposing dual images.

Hardened shooting glasses are an important accessory that can protect your eyes from injury. I own several pairs, including one that is permanently scarred by bits of metal blown from a failed cartridge case. Those pitted lenses are a constant reminder of what *can* happen, even though such accidents are extremely rare. Shooting glasses can also shade your eyes from too much sun or sharpen images on hazy days.

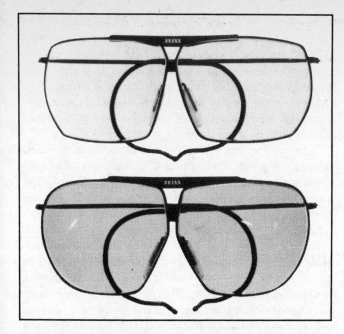

Shooting glasses come with lenses in different shades, are light, yet sturdy. Top: "Sportsman; Bottom: "Competition".

Other handy items include the optical collimators offered by Redfield, Bushnell and other manufacturers to help both professional and home gunsmiths bore-sight scopes after they've been mounted on a rifle. Bushnell also offers a pocket-sized bore sighter that hunters can use to recheck their rifle's zero without firing a shot. This little item costs only a few dollars and is invaluable for verifying crosshair alignment after your rifle has been bounced around by airline baggage handlers or bucked off a bad-tempered pack horse.

When buying most optical equipment, it's important to get the best you can afford. This is one time the old adage, "you get what you pay for" almost always applies. There are binoculars and rifle scopes available to fit almost any hunting budget, but the wise sportsman steers well clear of the bargain-priced models. Low-cost binoculars invariably cause eyestrain and—eventually—splitting headaches. Such glasses never provide the bright, sharp images you'll see through a top-quality set.

Budget-priced scopes lack the light-gathering qualities of more costly sights, and so aren't as effective early and late in the day. In addition they're more likely to "shoot loose" under heavy recoil, and fog up at inopportune moments. Economizing here can actually *cost* you money in the long run. When a bargain scope fails afield, the whole trip may be ruined. That $50 or $100 you saved at the sporting goods store won't compensate for the lost time, disappointment and other expenses (like gas, food and license costs)

you incurred to make the hunt.

As far as riflescopes are concerned, you'll usually be far better off mounting a quality scope on a budget-priced firearm than vice-versa. There are a number of relatively inexpensive rifles on the market that perform very well, even though they may not be as handsome as a much more costly model. Conversely, a low-priced scope may look every bit as nice as a top-of-the-line model; a glossy external finish is cheap and easily come by. The true quality is hidden under that brightly blued tube, and you have to examine the optics—or depend on the brand name—to determine how well a particular scope will perform. The same is true of binoculars. Beauty is only skin deep, and a handsome covering is no guarantee of honest quality and performance.

Fortunately, you don't have to be an optical engineer or a trained expert to determine the kind of optical performance you can expect from a piece of hunting glassware. Where binoculars are concerned, there are a couple of quick tests you can conduct while you're still in the store to double check on quality. The first is to hold the binocular at arms length, and look

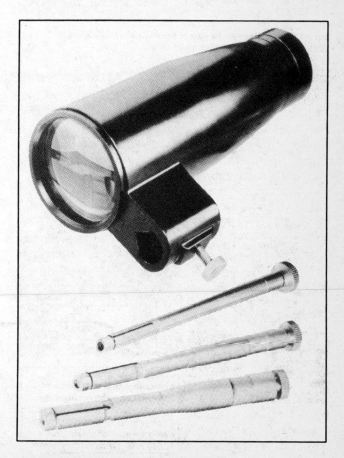

A collimator can be used by amateur and professional gunsmiths to bore-sight scopes.

Leupold now offers a new line of porro prism binoculars designed with the hunter in mind.

Two high-magnification binoculars that are light and compact enough for hunting: at right, Bausch & Lomb 9x35 mm Zephyr featuring porro prism design, and roof prism Zeiss 10x40 B/GA with rubber armor.

through the eyepiece against a source of light. The small circle you should see in each lens defines the exit pupils, and each image should be perfectly round, sharply defined and evenly illuminated. An oval, square, or flat-sided exit pupil image is evidence of undersized or poorly seated prisms, or of poor construction. Circles with indistinct borders or a pair of circles that overlap indicate poor optical design.

The twin barrels of a pair of binoculars must be properly aligned. If they're not, using them will cause eyestrain in a very few minutes. To check this out, first swing the two barrels together or apart until you see a single, perfectly round image through the lenses. Then hold the binoculars far enough away from your eyes so that you can see a pair of *separate* images. Hold the binoculars level and point them at a roofline or anything else that will provide an unbroken, horizontal line to look at. Finally, separate the barrels as far as the hinge will allow. If the horizontal viewing line shows identical continuity in the twin images, the barrels are properly aligned.

Failing either of these simple tests should disqualify a set of binoculars from further consideration, regardless of the price.

While there are other tests an expert can perform, your surest guide to quality lies in trusting to the top brands: Zeiss, Leitz, Swarovski, and Bausch & Lomb, to name just a few of the top-rated glasses. Good-quality optics are also available from Nikon, Pentax and other Japanese makers, and Leupold has just introduced a new line of hunting glasses that should offer good value. A really first-rate pair of full-sized binoculars will retail for anywhere from $400 to $1000 (and up), but when you consider that this represents a lifetime investment the cost really isn't excessive.

While quality is important, you must also consider the type and magnification of the binoculars you select. Most all-around hunting glasses fall in the 7 to 10X magnification range. Because a 9X or 10X glass is harder to hold steady, 7X or 8X models are usually preferred for general use. However, many serious hunters like slightly greater magnification. In addition to providing a larger image, the more powerful binoculars also deliver greater image brightness in poor light, all other things being equal.

When you shop for a pair of binoculars, you need to know what the identifying numbers signify. A 7 X 35 glass magnifies the viewing image 7 times, and has objective lenses (the ones up front) measuring 35mm in diameter.

You can determine the size of the exit pupil by dividing the objective lens diameter by the magnification. Thus, a pair of 7X35 binoculars have exit pupils

Rees uses rangefinder, tripod-mounted spotting scope when shooting ground squirrels at long range.

but wider overall design characteristic of these glasses.

Some binoculars are designed with long eye relief to accommodate eyeglass wearers, while other models offer only a limited field of view when used with such glasses. The Zeiss "B-type" binoculars and the Swarovski "S" models are examples of optics designed for use with eyeglasses.

Hunting binoculars are available with either center-focusing or individual-focusing systems. The first is more convenient and easier to use, while the second makes it easier to seal the optics against damaging moisture.

In addition to the full-sized binoculars most sportsmen use, you can also purchase miniature, shirt-pocket-sized models. I've owned a set of Bushnell 6X25 Custom Compacts for years, and seldom go afield without them. The advantage of compact binoculars lies in their handy portability—you always

measuring 5mm across, while a set of 7X50 glasses feature 7.1mm exit pupils. On a bright, sunlit day the pupil of a human eye contracts to a diameter of around 2mm; at night, it opens to around 7mm. This means that you can't really take advantage of the brightness offered by a large exit pupil in ordinary daytime viewing, and there's no need to tote a pair of bulky glasses with 50mm objective lenses. But for minimum light conditions, the larger binoculars are worthwhile.

For years, binoculars were rated for brightness by simply squaring the size of the exit pupil. Thus, a 6X30 glass was considered equally as bright as a set of 7X35 optics, since both had exit pupils measuring 5mm across, or relative brightness factors of 25.

A more accurate standard called the "twilight factor" is now used for comparison. This is determined by multiplying the magnification by the objective lens diameter, and taking the square root of the product. Using this scale, it's easy to see that magnification is an advantage in low-light situations.

Most binoculars offered for sale today are of either roof prism or porro prism design. With the former, the prisms are more or less in line, which makes for a slimmer, more streamlined binocular. Porro prism models feature offset prisms, resulting in the shorter,

This new 30X fixed power spotting scope is only 7.5 inches long and weighs 11.5 ounces, making it ideal for sheep, goat, antelope and varmint hunters, as well as competition shooters. It comes with a rugged and attractive two-compartment carrying case. Also available is an optional, lightweight tripod which can be used in the conventional manner, hand-held or clamped on an automobile window.

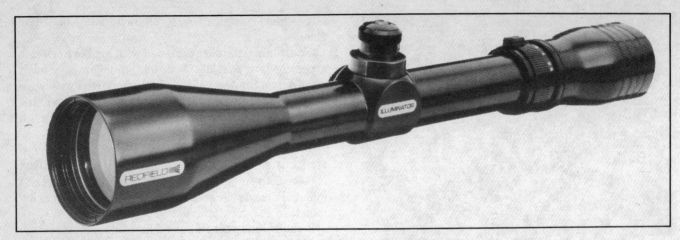

Redfield Illumnator 3-9X variable riflescope with rangefinding, trajectory compensating reticle.

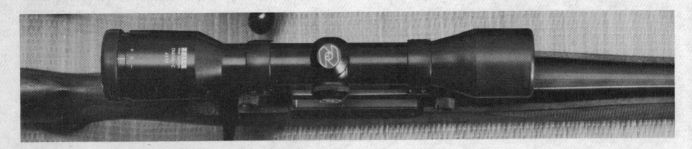

Zeiss 4X riflescope is fine for all-around hunting.

Outdoor writer Jon Sundra with 26-inch black Lechwe bagged with help of Zeiss 8X30 binoculars and Zeiss 4X riflescope.

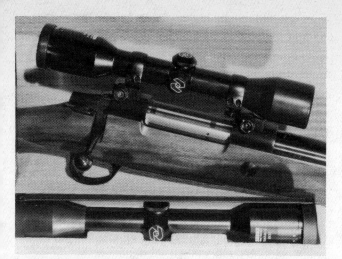

Zeiss riflescopes are expensive, but represent excellent value because of their proven high quality.

have them with you when you need them. However, serious glassing of distant game calls for full-sized binoculars.

Several different manufacturers now offer rubber-armored models. These are particularly popular with hunters because the rubber coating helps absorb shock, won't chip the finish from riflestocks, sheds water and makes the binoculars easier to grip.

Riflescopes are available in both fixed- and variable-magnification models, in a wide range of power ranges. For most deer-sized game, a good 4X glass will do the job, although some people prefer a little more (6X) or a little less (2½ or 3X) magnification. The greater a scope's magnification, the smaller the field of view—that's the tradeoff.

Many shooters today prefer a variable-power scope. Thus, the owner of a rifle wearing a 3-9X glass can use 3X or 4X magnification for medium-to-close-range hunting, and crank up a full 9X for long-distance shots. As a matter of fact, the 3-9X power range is by far the most popular, and nearly every scope manufacturer offers one or more such models. In my opinion, the 3-9X variable is at its best on a combination varmint-and deer-hunting rifle chambered for the

Zeiss 10X40 B/GA rubber-armored binoculars are paired with Sako-mounted Zeiss 4X riflescope as part of author's deer-hunting gear.

.243 Winchester, .25-06 Remington or other cartridge suitable for both kinds of hunting.

For dangerous game or when close shots may be offered, a 1½-4½X glass makes more sense. At the low end of the scale, the field of view is extremely wide for close, running shots. And at 4½X, the scope provides plenty of magnification for most practical purposes. The Austrian firm of Kahles now makes a 1.1-4.5X riflescope, and when this is at its lowest power setting you can shoot with both eyes open. The image isn't magnified enough to throw off your binocular vision, making this one of the fastest-sighting scopes on the market.

There are compact scopes for lightweight rifles, high-powered 8X, 10X and 12X scopes for varmint shooting, and long-eye-relief scopes for handgun use.

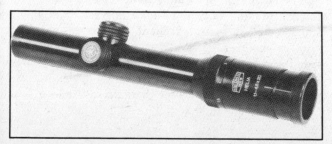

Kahles 1.1-4.5X variable makes a top choice for use on dangerous game. The low 1.1X setting allows you to use it with both eyes open.

With today's modern, flat-shooting rifles, a good scope sight is a must when hunting open country.

These pistol scopes range from 1¼ to 4X in power, and make long-range hunting accuracy feasible for handgunners shooting flat-trajectory rounds.

Again, you'd be well advised to buy a well-known brand when shopping for a riflescope: Leupold, Zeiss, Bausch & Lomb, Bushnell, Redfield, Weaver, Burris and the like. Some companies offer different grades to appeal to a broad range of buyers. For the best performance, select the best scope you can afford.

There are several fine spotting scopes on the market, ranging from relatively heavy, high-powered glasses best suited to target range or base camp use, to light, compact models ideal for the hunting sportsmen. Redfield has recently introduced an ultra-compact scope featuring a new cadadioptric lens system. This little 30X glass is only 7½ inches long and weighs just 11½ ounces. For hunting use, a 20X or 30X lens is just about ideal.

The right kind of hunting optics can go a long way toward making any hunt more successful. Today's sportsman has many excellent riflescopes, spotting scopes, shooting glasses and binoculars to choose from, and there's no reason for anyone to be poorly equipped with optical gear. The best optics are expensive, but represent a real bargain in the long run.

Still More Do's and Don'ts of Home Gunsmithing

John Traister

S cene: A gunsmith's shop.
Place: Anywhere in the United States or Canada.
Time: The present.

(The owner is frantically thumbing through a card-index file trying to locate a customer's gun.)

GUNSMITH: When did you say you brought the gun in?

CUSTOMER: The end of January or about the beginning of February.

(The search continues without success.)

CUSTOMER (impatiently): It had to be January because I bought a new car that same day and it's just six months old.

GUNSMITH: Oh, you mean January of *this* year. Hell, we haven't even gotten around to the guns that were brought in *last* year. That's how busy we are!

(Customer exits muttering, holding his retrieved, still rough-looking J.P. Sauer shotgun, a bottle of Belgian Blue and a book on firearms refinishing.)

So it goes. There are a lot of sick guns out there and not enough qualified repairmen to fix them . . . at least not in time to keep owners happy. For this and other reasons, more and more gun owners are setting up shop in basements, attics or garages and performing a lot of gunsmithing work themselves. Most of them usually start by cleaning their firearms; then

progress to perhaps refinishing a gunstock or touching-up some worn places on the metal with instant blue. The projects progress in complexity until, eventually, a gun ends up in a professional shop where the amateur's mistakes are corrected—usually at many times the cost of repairing the initial problem, because of the damage caused by attempting a project beyond the amateur's capabilities.

There is really nothing wrong with knowledgeable hobbyists trying some gun repair jobs at home. In fact, the practice should be encouraged . . . provided one knows one's capabilities and when and where to stop. Then, home gunsmithing can not only be fun, but can save you money and enable your firearms to have features not obtainable at discount houses.

Articles in the 1981, 1982 and 1983 SHOOTER'S BIBLES discussed basic requirements of the home gunsmith, such as selecting tools and safety precautions, and recommended reference books along with solutions to many problems encountered by the home gunsmith. Charts were presented in these articles that showed the reader at a glance what each job involved and whether it should be attempted or not by the hobbyist. (See "Do's and Don'ts of Home Gunsmithing," 1981 SHOOTER'S BIBLE, pp 52-62, "More Do's and Don'ts of Home Gunsmithing" 1982 SHOOTER'S BIBLE, pp 83-93, and "Still More Do's and Don'ts of

Each year more shooters are turning to home gunsmithing because there seems to be more sick guns than there are professionals to repair them.

Home Gunsmithing'' 1983 SHOOTER'S BIBLE, pp 55-67.) Still more do's and don'ts are included here, but before getting to them, let's review some recent experiences.

First of all, the most common problems that have come to my attention during the past year have been those caused by amateurs trying to disassemble their own firearms—for one reason or another. One local attorney apparently likes to remove and replace the screws in his Ruger Bearcat revolver because it has been in the shop a few times with loose and missing screws. "I was trying to tune her up a little bit, and somehow lost the screws" was his explanation.

Another gun enthusiast tried to remove the lug bolt from the bottom of his Remington Model 700. The screwdriver blade—which was too small—slipped and took a large gouge out of the bottom of the carefully inletted benchrest stock. A repair was made, but it cost the owner a lot—and could have been avoided if he had invested in a $10 screwdriver that fitted the screw perfectly.

The amateur can disassemble his firearms satisfactorily if he uses caution, obtains the correct tools, and has disassembly drawings and instructions close at hand. But most gun owners still rely on dime-store screwdrivers.

If you happen to be a serious hobbyist, one who does enough work or spends enough time in your shop to warrant the purchase of a metal-turning lathe, you will certainly want to investigate the Myford Super 7 lathe. Many machinists classify this model as strictly for the student or hobbyist, but for work under 7 inches in diameter or not longer than from about 18 to 30 inches, the Myford will do anything the "professional" lathes will do, and often do it better. I've been playing with one for the past couple of months, and for the price, I haven't seen anything to touch it. For information and prices, write to D & M Model Engineering, P.O. Box 400, Western Springs, Illinois 60558.

You should also send for a catalog from Blue Ridge Machine and Tool, Hurricane, West Virginia 25526. They sell quality home shop equipment at good prices, and their service is hard to surpass.

The following charts are designed to show hobbyists some of the projects that are most often considered practical for home gunsmithing. Better yet, they point out those projects which are most likely to get you into trouble, and should therefore not be attempted. As explained in previous editions, these are not totally guaranteed. You might have the tools and capabilities to do some of the don'ts. On the other hand, some of the do's may be don'ts for you. These are merely guides to help you get started.

If you should run into difficulty or are unclear about a certain procedure and want to know more, write to me at Traister Arms Co., Rt. 1, Box 300, Bentonville, VA 22610. A self-addressed, stamped envelope will be appreciated.

GENERAL GUN REPAIRS

Type of Project	Do	Don't	Comments	Tools Needed
Magazine repair				
1. Rewinding and replacing spring	X		Disassemble magazine. Use a wooden template and vise to wind spring.	Piano wire, bench vise, wooden or metal template.
2. Reshape feed lips		X	These must be just right for the gun to function properly. Replace magazine or take to pro.	
3. Straightening deformed floorplate	X		Rest on flat steel surface. Use flat-ended punch to restore shape.	Hammer, steel punch and flat steel surface.
4. Altering angle of follower		X	Must be angled exactly right for gun to feed properly. Correct angle difficult to obtain by amateur.	

The Myford Super 7 lathe is an excellent choice for the serious hobbyist.

GENERAL GUN REPAIRS

Type of Project	Do	Don't	Comments	Tools Needed
Repairing firing pin points				
1. By silver soldering		X	Amateur can leave the point either too soft or too brittle, causing the pin to break in short order.	
2. By drilling	X		Square broken pin, drill small hole in existing shaft. Insert new pin in drilled hole. Then drill smaller hole through side of existing shaft to cross-pin replacement pin.	
Making new striker for inexpensive arm.	X		Secure nail of proper size in drill motor. Turn nail head to proper diameter. Cut to required length. Harden with Kasenit hardening compound.	
Restoring shotguns with Damascus barrels				
1. For shooter		X	Damascus barrels are not considered safe with any load —even blackpowder shotshells.	
2. As wall-hanger	X		Restoring great-grandpap's old side-hammer shotgun is a good project for the hobbyists. A lot can be learned about the operation and other gunsmithing tasks.	Varies depending upon the extent of restoration.
3. Those with collector's value		X	Some English shotguns along with Parkers and others are more valuable left with original finish.	
Increasing length of shotgun chamber				
1. On expensive gun		X	Alteration may lower value.	
2. On inexpensive gun	X		Many older shotguns have chambers less than 2¾ inches. The amateur can lengthen these chambers with no power tools, to improve pattern and for safer operation.	Long forcing cone reamer, cutting oil, T-handle tap wrench. Order from Brownell's and follow instructions.
Increasing length of shotgun chamber to accept 3-inch magnum shells		X	Most guns are not designed, nor safe, to fire with magnum shells. Leave alone or else consult professional for advice.	

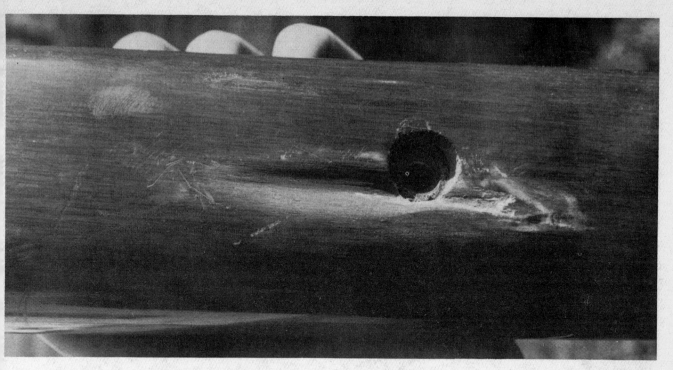

This disfiguring gouge was made by a screwdriver blade slipping out of the screw slot. Such damage can be avoided by using a screwdriver blade of the correct size.

GENERAL GUN REPAIRS

Type of Project	Do	Don't	Comments	Tools Needed
Parkerizing				
1. Rifle or shotgun		X	Requires stainless steel tank large enough to hold firearm. Too expensive for only one or two guns.	
2. Handgun	X		Relatively inexpensive kits are available enabling amateurs to do a good job at home. Have parts sand- or bead-blasted at local shop.	Parkerizing kit from The Dutchmen's, 4143 Taylor Blvd., Louisville, KY 40215.
Electroless Plating		X	Initial investment too expensive for only a couple of guns. Problems might develop requiring professional knowledge.	Equipment available from Brownells, Inc.
Polishing for Plating				
1. Inexpensive gun	X		Much of the work in plating handguns involves polishing the old finish. Some money can be saved by polishing all parts before taking to professional shop for plating.	Abrasive paper in grits from 80 to 400.

As a rule, barrel chambering is not suited for the home gunsmith. Equipment costs are high and the knowledge required is usually beyond that of the home mechanic.

GENERAL GUN REPAIRS

Type of Project	Do	Don't	Comments	Tools Needed
2. Expensive gun		X	Contours may be changed by amateur polishing as well as markings might be removed and would lower value.	
Fume Blueing				
1. Expensive gun		X	Collector's value might be ruined.	
2. Inexpensive gun	X		Disassemble, polish metal. Use equal portions (about 10 drops) of nitric acid and hydrocloric acid in plastic container to hold parts and acids. Extreme care must be exercised.	Plastic enclosure to seal parts and acids. Water tank and heat to boil parts. Steel wool to card parts between boilings.
Torch Coloring Metal		X	Although relatively easy to perform on polished metal, heat must be applied to critical parts and process is best left to professional.	

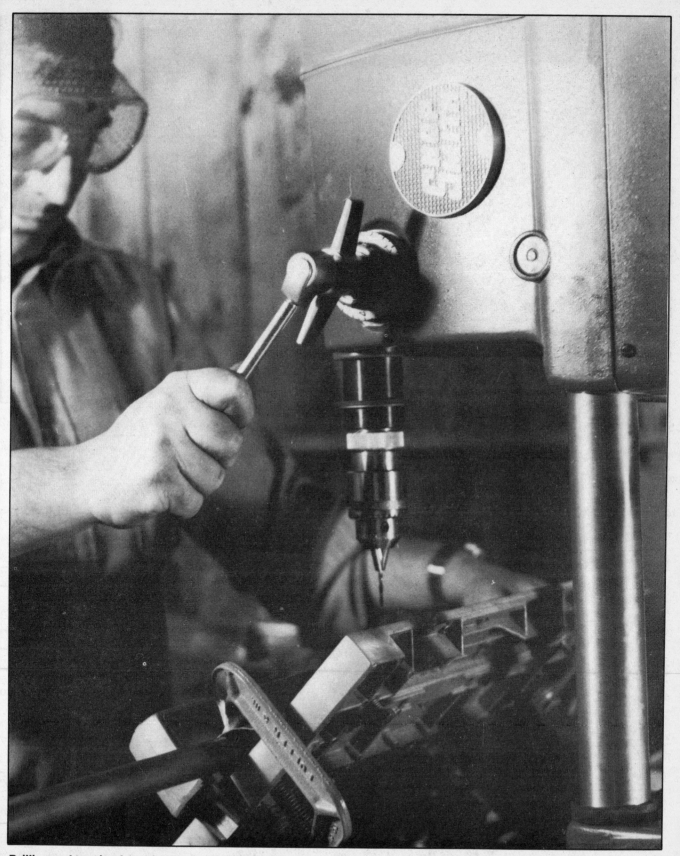

Drilling and tapping for a shotgun bead-sight is within the capabilities of the average craftsman.

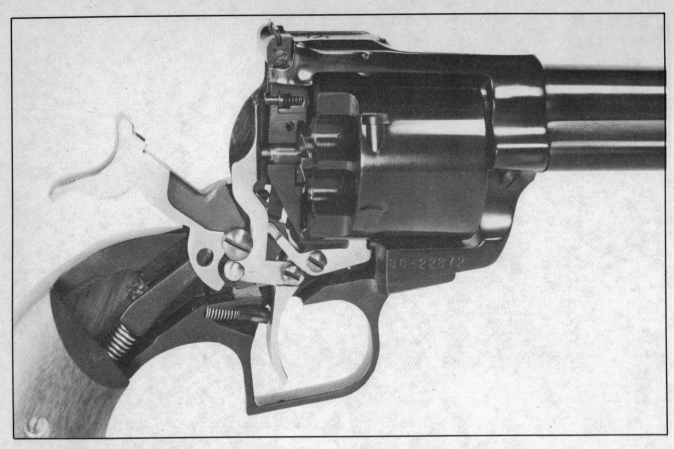

When disassembling firearms, always use all available reference materials and diagrams that will help.

GENERAL GUN REPAIRS

Type of Project	Do	Don't	Comments	Tools Needed
Rust removal				
1. Light rust (all surfaces)	X		Light rust can usually be easily removed by wiping with oil and cloth which will not affect bluing or other finishes.	Old towel and gun oil.
2. Heavy rust on working gun (not collector's items)	X		First try 4/0 steel wool, either dry or in combination with oil. Any commercial rust remover is okay, but gun's finish will also be removed. Will need to be refinished.	
3. Heavy rust on rare gun		X	Any type of rust removal by amateur is sure to lower value.	
Removing barrel bulges				
1. Valuable gun		X	There is a chance beginner will make the barrel worse. Leave job to professional restorer.	

A damaged gunstock can be repaired, but it takes skill and a keen eye to produce a job that is not easily detectable.

GENERAL GUN REPAIRS

Type of Project	Do	Don't	Comments	Tools Needed
2. Inexpensive hunting gun	X		Rest bulged portion of barrel on steel block; use ballpeen hammer to strike barrel as it is rotated. Use light taps only. Will take considerable time, so be patient.	
Correcting deformed screw heads 1. All guns but rarest	X		A good project for hobbyists. Method will vary with type of defect, but usually deepen screw slot first. Secure screw in drill chuck and spin. Use files and abrasive paper to polish.	Files, abrasive paper, electric drill.
Chamber throating		X	Much harm can be done by improper throating. Leave to pro.	

This B-Square Drill and Tap Guide does the trick.

GENERAL GUN REPAIRS

Type of Project	Do	Don't	Comments	Tools Needed
Making wood pistol grips	X		An excellent project for the home gunsmith. Use paper or cardboard to form pattern. Lay pattern on wood and cut out and shape. Finish.	Sharp knife, abrasive paper, hand drill, and finishing oil.
Repairing plastic rifle stocks	X		Such stocks are almost always on inexpensive guns. Use soldering iron to weld break inside and out. Finish with files and abrasive paper. For deep gouges, use plastic stick of same color to melt into the stock being repaired.	Soldering gun, files and abrasive paper.
Installing stock recoil reducer		X	These need careful fitting to operate correctly and should be done by a professional. Also the possibility of drilling through, or otherwise damaging stock during the installation.	

GENERAL GUN REPAIRS

Type of Project	Do	Don't	Comments	Tools Needed
Installing trap butt plate		X	The installation of this type of butt plate requires a considerable amount more fitting than a conventional butt plate and is best left to pro.	
Bedding for accuracy				
Inexpensive rifle	X		Use Brownell's Acra-Glas kit and follow directions.	
Expensive rifle		X	Stock modification may lower collector's value.	
Making wooden gun case	X		Good project for beginner, but use pine or other inexpensive wood on first attempt. When confident, more elaborate woods may be used.	Woodworking tools.
Splicing gouges in wood				
1. Expensive firearms		X	Takes skill and practice to make good splice which only top professional can do properly.	
2. Inexpensive firearms	X		Patience and a certain degree of skill will enable the hobbyist to perform a relatively good splice in gouged gunstocks.	Sharp knife, scrap wood, glue, chisels and abrasive paper. Also stock finishing kit for touching up repaired area.
Wood inlays		X	Requires a certain degree of skill and knowledge. Might be okay on cheap stock, but inlays look out of place on all but fancy gunstocks.	
Modifying stocks				
1. Expensive gun		X	Value can be lowered by amateur's work.	
2. Inexpensive gun	X		Certain custom work can be performed by hobbyist to enable a better stock fit such as shortening length of pull, streamlining military stock, etc.	Depending upon project. Mostly woodworking tools.

GENERAL GUN REPAIRS

Type of Project	Do	Don't	Comments	Tools Needed
Checkering pistol grips				
1. Modern handgun	X		A good project for the amateur to learn wood checkering.	Checkering tools, tooth-brush, and finishing oil such as Dem-Bart.
2. Obsolete handgun		X	Modification of factory grips may lower collector's value.	
Repairing plastic or hard rubber pistol grips	X		Grips that are broken rarily add anything to the handgun, so a repair is in order. Messing up would not hurt matters.	Epoxy and dye same color of original grip. Checkering tool to match existing pattern.
Cleaning hand files				
1. Rap file to remove chips		X	Damage to side teeth will occur.	
2. Using file brush	X			File card or brush.
Using measuring instruments.				
1. While work is moving in lathe, drill, or other power tools.	X		Expensive measuring instruments are delicate and must be handled accordingly.	
Polishing metal surfaces of tools.				
1. Polishing dry		X	Surface more apt to scratch.	
2. Polishing with oil	X		A surface polished with oil will keep clean much longer than one polished dry.	Oil, 4/0 steel wool, old towel.
Installing drill bits in electric hand drills				
1. While cord is plugged in, even though drill is not turning		X	Never!	
2. With cord unplugged	X		Tape chuck key to plug end of cord so that cord must be unplugged before chuck key may be used.	Electrical tape.

Great Weapons Museums: Museums of the State of Georgia

George M. Horn

The colony of Georgia was founded by James Oglethorpe acting for a group of English trustees and was named for King George II of England. Its coastal islands helped to maintain it as an English outpost in the centuries-old struggle between Spanish, French and English. From original settlements at Savannah, Brunswick and on the barrier islands, Georgia's colonists moved inland along the rivers to establish inland ports like Augusta and Columbus. At one time, Georgia extended from the Mississippi to the sea.

Georgia fitted well into the British mercantile system and was slow to join in the movement for independence. Gradually the radical element attracted enough Georgians to their cause to bring about the overthrow of the royal governor, James Wright. In 1776, three Georgians were among the signers of the Declaration of Independence, and Georgia later became the fourth of the original thirteen states.

No actual fighting took place in Georgia until 1778, when British forces attacked along the coast and from Florida. Savannah was captured on December 29, and American Gen. Robert Howe, who commanded the colony's forces, retreated into South Carolina. Sunbury and Augusta were taken in January 1779; by the end of that year every important Georgia town had fallen into the hands of the British. Only the sparsely settled northern region of Wilkes County was left unoccupied. The Revolutionary period in Georgia was not one of planned strategic warfare, but of incessant bloody guerilla strife. Confiscation, plunder, torture and outright murder for revenge were common occurrences.

When Georgia joined the Confederate States in 1861, a Georgian, Alexander H. Stephens, who had opposed secession, was chosen vice-president. His constitutional interpretation of the Civil War became the accepted Southern viewpoint. Although the question of the abolition of slavery and economic conflict between the North and South were factors, Stephens took the position that Georgia and the ten other states of the Confederacy were fighting for states' rights.

During the Civil War (still referred to as "The War Between the States" in the South), Georgia's lot was harsh. Much of the state, famous for its antebellum gentility, was devastated in Gen. William Tecumseh Sherman's famous 1864 march to the sea. Today, Georgia is a prosperous and bustling state, rich in history and memorabilia. For those interested in firearms or the art of warfare, every corner of this picturesque state provides fascinating museums, battlefields and historic shrines to visit.

Andersonville National Historic Site
Highway 49
Andersonville 31711
Telephone: (912) 924-0343
Founded: 1971
John N. Tucker, Superintendent
Hours: Daily, 8-5. Visitor Center closed Christmas Day.
Admission: Free.

On March 1, 1864, the Confederate Military Prison at Camp Sumter began to receive Union prisoners. Built to accommodate 10,000 men, during the 13 months it was in operation, 49,485 men were incarcerated here—as many as 33,006 at one time. As a result of unsanitary conditions caused by the overcrowding and poor diet, 12,462 prisoners died.

The parklike grounds of the Andersonville Historic Site.

The museum contains memorabilia of the Civil War, with emphasis on the daily life of the prisoners of war. The only weapons on display are an Austrian rifle musket bayonet and a LeMat revolver (Serial Number 1774) similar to the one carried by the stockade commander, Capt. Henry Wirz. Wirz was later hanged in Washington, D.C., after having been convicted of maliciously conspiring to torture and kill prisoners.

On the grounds, various northern states have erected monuments to honor their soldiers who were imprisoned at Andersonville. At the prison site are mounted 3-inch ordnance rifles and 12-pounder Napoleons (on reproduction carriages).

Le Mat revolver.

Navy Supply Corps Museum at Athens.

See also: Providence Spring, which bubbled from the ground after a heavy rain, was said to be the answer to the prisoners' prayers during the summer drought of 1864. The Sundial Monument commemorates the work of the Woman's Relief Corps in establishing the prison site as a memorial. Andersonville National Cemetery, a half mile north of the museum, contains the graves of Union soldiers who died in the prison camp and veterans of other wars.

Navy Supply Corps Museum
Navy Supply Corps School
Athens 30606
Telephone: (404) 354-7348
Founded: 1975
Richard P. Pawson, Capt., USN (Ret), Curator
Hours: Mon.-Fri., 9-5. Closed weekends and holidays.
Admission: Free.

Located in the former Carnegie Library built in 1910 to house the State Normal School's 4,000-volume library, the Navy Supply Corps Museum is dedicated to portraying the history of the Supply Corps and the United States Navy. Its collections include ship models, old guns and sabers, uniforms, and naval artifacts (including a piece of oak timber from the *USS Constitution*, better known as "Old Ironsides."

On the City Hall lawn in Athens is an unusual double-barreled cannon cast at the Athens Foundry in 1863 and believed to be the only double-barreled cannon in the world. Its inventors devised a scheme for chaining the balls together and mowing down great numbers of the enemy, but unfortunately failed to synchronize the firing of both barrels. One eyewitness to the trial shot stated that the chain broke; one ball demolished a Negro cabin; the other plowed up an acre of ground and killed a yearling calf in a distant field.

Atlanta Historical Society
3101 Andrews Drive
Atlanta 30355
Telephone: (404) 261-1837
Founded: 1926
Dr. Judson Ward, Director
Hours: Tues.-Sat., 10:30-4:30; Sun., 2-4:30. Closed first
  two weeks in January; holidays.
Admission: Free; donations accepted.

The museum gallery has an extensive collection of Civil War artifacts. The Society maintains the 1927-28 Swan House, which was inspired by the Palladian school of architecture and is located in the fashionable Buckhead residential district, as well as the restored 1840 Tullie Smith farmhouse, gardens, and slave cabin outbuildings.

Atlanta Museum

537-39 Peachtree Street, N.E.
Atlanta 30308
Telephone: (404) 872-8233
Founded: 1838
J.H. Elliott, Jr., Director
Hours: Mon.-Fri., 10-4. Closed Saturdays, Sundays, New
    Year's, July 4, Labor Day, Thanksgiving, Christmas.
Admission: Adults, $2.00; children, $1.00.

Housed in the 1900 Rose Mansion, last Victorian mansion
standing on Peachtree Street in the downtown area and
former home of the distiller of Four Roses whiskey, the
museum houses the original Eli Whitney cotton gin and the
Eli Whitney gun collection.

Cyclorama

800 Cherokee Avenue, S.E.
Atlanta 30315
Telephone: (404) 624-1071
Founded: 1898
David Palmer, Director
Hours: Daily, 9:30-4:40. Closed New Year's, Thanksgiving,
    Christmas.
Admission: Adults, $3.00; senior citizens, $2.50;
    children 6-12, $1.50.

Although no weapons or artifacts are displayed, the Cyclorama is well worth a visit. The Cyclorama of the battle of
Atlanta was painted in 1885-86 by a staff of German and
Polish artists, who executed similar gigantic canvases of the
battles of Gettysburg and Missionary Ridge, both of which
were accidentally destroyed. The painting is approximately
400 feet in circumference and 50 feet in height, and weighs
18,000 pounds. Its intense realism and attention to detail in
weapons, uniforms and topography must be seen to be
believed. The Cyclorama building also houses the "Texas,"
a famous railroad locomotive. With another engine, the

"General," on April 12, 1862, it took part in the famous
locomotive chase known as the Andrews Raid. (The "General" is now permanently enshrined in the Big Shanty
Museum, located six miles north of Marietta, Georgia via
Georgia Route 293 or U.S. Route 41 in Kennesaw, Georgia,
the spot where the Union raiders first stole her.)

Columbus Museum of Arts and Sciences

1251 Wynnton Road
Columbus 31906
Telephone: (404) 323-3617
Founded: 1952
William E. Scheele, Director
Hours: Mon.-Sat., 10-5; Sun., 2-5. Closed New Year's, July 4,
    Christmas.
Admission: Free.

The museum owns approximately 400 firearms displayed in
a gun gallery. Colt, Remington and Winchester guns are all
well represented in this exhibit, called the C. Dexter Jordan
Collection.

The James W. Woodruff Confederate Naval Museum

201 Fourth Street
Columbus 31902
Telephone: (404) 327-9798
Founded: 1964
Hours: Tues.-Sat., 10-5; Sun., 2-5. Closed Thanksgiving,
    Christmas.
Admission: Free; donations accepted.

Primary exhibits are the remains of two Confederate war-
ships, the ironclad ram *Jackson ("Muscogee")* and the
gunboat *Chattahoochee,* salvaged from the Chattahoochee
River near Columbus in the early 1960s. The museum also
displays relics salvaged from the gunboats, as well as other
exhibits relating to the history of the Confederate States
Navy. Also shown are several large naval guns associated
with the gunboats, including four Brooke guns.

Fort King George Historic Site near Darien.

Georgia Veterans Memorial Museum
Route U.S. 280
Cordele 31015
Telephone: (912) 273-2190
Founded: 1946
Gerald Evans, Superintendent
Hours: Tues.-Sun., 9-5; Closed New Year's, Thanksgiving, Christmas.
Admission: Free.

This 1307-acre park, nine miles west of Cordele, was founded to memorialize Georgia veterans of all wars. In addition to fishing, boating, waterskiing, swimming, picnicking, a museum displays weapons (small arms and field pieces), including a Stuart "Flaming Coffin" light tank (Model M3A1), a B-29 "Flying Fortress" and a Soviet Russian 85mm antitank gun captured in Vietnam.

Confederate Museum
Alexander Street
Crawfordville 30631
Telephone: (404) 456-2221
Founded: 1952
Evelyn Edwards, Superintendent
Hours: Tues.-Sat., 9-5; Sun., 2-5:30. Closed Thanksgiving, Christmas.
Admission: Adults, $1.00; children 12-17, $.50.

Housed in Liberty Hall, 1875 home of Alexander H. Stephens, the museum includes memorabilia and arms of the Civil War period. Displays include Minie balls picked up after the battle of Kennesaw Mountain, a Remington-Beals revolver and an unusual chair made at the Confederate Arsenal in Athens from gunstocks.

Fort King George Historic Site
Fort King George Drive
Darien 31305
Founded: 1961
Telephone: (912) 437-4770
Daniel Brown, Superintendent
Hours: Tues.-Sat., holiday Mondays, 9-5; Sun., 2-5:30. Closed Thanksgiving, Christmas.
Admission: Adults, $1.00; children, $.50.

Fort King George was built in 1721 by South Carolina Provincial Scouts near an abandoned Indian village and Spanish mission to block encroachment by the French and Spanish. This was the first English settlement in Georgia. The site of the fort, Indian village and Spanish mission have been preserved, and a museum interprets the successive periods of Indian, Spanish and British occupation, the settlement of nearby Darien by Scottish Highlanders, and the timber industry of Georgia.

National Infantry Museum
Building 396, Baltzell Avenue
Fort Benning 31905
Telephone: (404) 545-2958 or 544-4762
Founded: 1959
Dick D. Grube, Lt. Col. (Ret), Director
Hours: Tues.-Fri., 10-4:30; Sat.-Sun., 12:30-4:30. Closed New Year's, Thanksgiving, Christmas.
Admission: Free.

National Infantry Museum at Fort Benning.

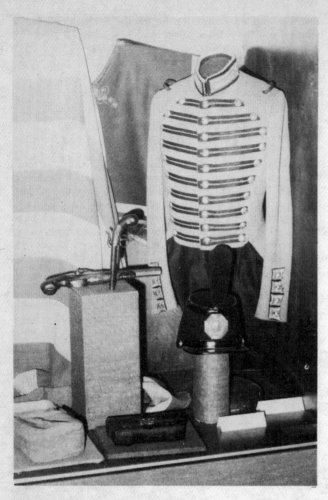

Uniforms and equipment of the 1880s.

Gatling gun exhibit, Fort Benning.

Exhibit of Japanese weapons and equipment, Fort Benning.

In the words of its director, this handsome museum is "more than just a collection of things painted green." The National Infantry Museum has a collection of some 2500 weapons, including an extensive group of 20th-century Japanese small arms, numbering about 450 items. One special collection traces the infantryman's basic weapon from the Committee of Safety pre-Revolutionary Brown Bess to the M-1 of Second World War fame. A study collection of M-16 rifles and 40mm rocket launchers demonstrates the testing of these weapons.

The museum has two Gatling guns, the classic long musket and the export, Spanish or Camel model. America's smallest atomic weapon, the Davy Crockett, is exhibited near a collection of caltrops, or "crow's feet" (iron points designed to impede cavalry), to show a dramatic contrast in weaponry.

The collection of uniforms, both U.S. and foreign, is rivalled in few museums today: An 18th-century blue and red Revolutionary War enlisted man's coat and vest, a Zouave

Warsaw Pact weapons at Fort Benning.

uniform worn by a New York regiment during the Civil War, the black-and-white striped coat of the Spanish-American War's 7th Colonial Volunteers, denim fatigues of the 1930s, pinks and greens of the 1940s, from paratroop jump suits worn in battle in Europe to the latest uniforms of the People's Republic of China.

There is something here for everyone, including a large military art collection, Oriental rugs, Victorian furniture, and a collection of military documents signed by each of the 40 American presidents. On the museum grounds is displayed a collection of field artillery weapons and armored vehicles.

U.S. Army Signal Museum
Fort Gordon 30905
Telephone: (404) 791-2818 or 3856
Founded: 1965
John Sherwin, Curator
Hours: Daily, 12-4. Closed New Year's, Labor Day,
   Christmas.
Admission: Free.

Fort Gordon is located nine miles south of Augusta, between U.S. Highways 1 and 78. The Signal Museum tells the story of the Army's Signal Corps from its beginnings in 1863 to the present. Among the items displayed are mementos of Brig. Gen. Albert J. Myer, the military surgeon who founded the Signal Corps. (Myer was also responsible for the establishment of the Weather Bureau.) Signal flags, telegraph, telephone and radio equipment are also dis-

played, together with examples of the most modern electronic devices. In all, there are about 300 displays.

Chickamauga and Chattanooga Military Park
U.S. Route 27
Fort Oglethorpe 30741
Telephone: (404) 866-9241
Founded: 1890
M. Ann Belkov, Superintendent
Hours: Daily, 8-4:45. Closed Christmas.
Admission: Free.

The Chickamauga and Chattanooga National Military Park is the oldest and largest such park, covering more than 8,000 acres in Georgia and Tennessee. The two-day battle fought here in 1863 was one of the bloodiest of the Civil War and was the high-water mark of the Confederacy in the west. Chickamauga Battlefield is one of 13 areas making up the National Military Park. Other areas include Point Park on Lookout Mountain, the Reservations on Missionary Ridge, Signal Point on Signal Mountain and Orchard Knob in Chattanooga, but these are all in Tennessee.

In the Visitor Center can be seen the impressive Claude E. and Zenado Fuller collection of American military firearms, containing examples of almost every type of long arm used by the military forces of the United States. This is the finest collection of American military shoulder arms anywhere in the world, and the 355 weapons displayed span a period of history beginning with the early colonists and terminating with the First World War. Among the highlights of this collection are a Sharps New Model 1863 Coffee Mill carbine and a Cochran 9-shot underhammer revolving turret rifle.

24th Infantry Division (Mech) and Fort Stewart Museum
Building 814, Wilson Avenue at Utility Street
Fort Stewart 31314
Telephone: (912) 767-4891
Founded: 1978
Dr. Ray J. Kinder, Curator
Hours: Mon.-Fri., 1-5; Sat., 2-5. Closed holidays.
Admission: Free.

Fort Stewart is outside Huntsville, Georgia, 40 miles southwest of Savannah. State routes 63, 67, 119, 129 and 144 pass through the reservation. Collections are organized around wars from the Revolution to the Vietnam War. Special collections include a Merrill's Marauders exhibit (one of two such in the U.S.), a rare Japanese battailion gun, unusual Japanese WW2 items (including a rare "belt of a thousand stitches" and ancestral tablets, an extensive collection of German WW2 small arms and side arms, decorations, insignia and awards, and a Vietnam War collection, which includes civilian as well as military items.

Of special interest will be a unique collection of Civil War cut-and-thrust weapons, weapons used by insurrectionists during the pacification of the Philippines, anti-tank small arms, sniper rifles, and Indian Wars arms and equipment. Because elements of the division served with distinction in battles on Biak, at Hollandia in New Guinea and at Breakneck Ridge on Leyte in the Philippines, the collection is unusually strong in materials relating to the Second World War in the Pacific.

Kennesaw Mountain National Battlefield Park
Junction of Stileboro Road and Old U.S. Highway 41
Marietta 30061
Telephone: (404) 427-4686
Founded: 1935
Marvin Madry, Superintendent
Hours: Daily, 8:30-5. Closed New Year's, Christmas.
Admission: Free.

Chicamauga and Chattanooga National Military Park features the Fuller collection of military shoulder arms.

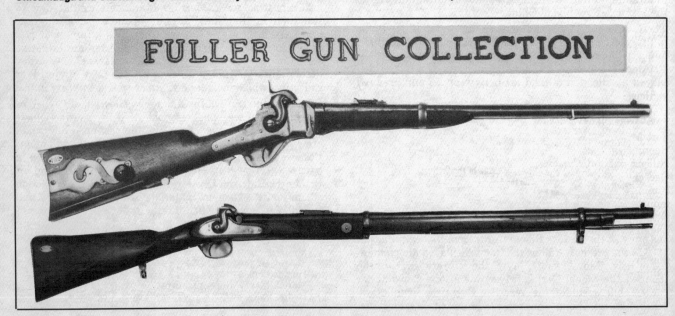

FULLER GUN COLLECTION

Temporarily stymied during his Atlanta Campaign flanking maneuvers, Maj. Gen. William T. Sherman attempted a frontal assault on June 27, 1864 to overwhelm Gen. Joseph E. Johnston's Confederates. Rough terrain, strong defensive fortifications, and determined Confederate resistance led to a bloody repulse for Sherman.

The collections in the Visitor Center are strong in uniforms, flags and weapons, including a Spencer carbine, 1860 Colt revolver, 1861 Springfield, 1840 cavalry saber, and the sword of Capt. Salathiel Neighbors, wounded at the "Dead Angle."

Sunbury Historic Site
Route 1
Midway 31320
Telephone: (912) 884-5888
Founded: 1951
Joseph Thompson, Superintendent
Hours: Tues.-Sat., holidays, 9-5; Sun., 2-5. Closed
    Thanksgiving, Christmas.
Admission: Free.

Ten miles from Midway, once called "The Cradle of the Revolution" by royal governor James Wright, is the site of Sunbury, which was established in 1758, soon after Mark Carr, friend of James Oglethorpe, had conveyed 300 acres of his original 500-acre grant to a group of trustees. They laid out a rectangular town with three public squares and 496 lots, and by 1769 Sunbury was a busy river port rivalling Savannah. Sunbury Academy, established in 1788, became the first in this part of Georgia.

The town began to decline with the shift of population westward and with the growing importance of Savannah. It is believed that one of the earliest Masonic lodge meetings in America was held here in 1734, with Oglethorpe as master. Here was located Fort Morris, built for defense in 1776. The Continental troops who garrisoned the fort offered spirited resistance to British attacks, but Sunbury was virtually destroyed.

Located in the Sunbury Historic Site are the 1814 earthworks, named Fort Defiance, which were built on the site of Fort Morris. The museum contains exhibits and artifacts from the fortifications and the town of Sunbury.

Fort McAllister Historic Site
Richmond Hill 31324
Telephone: (912) 727-2339
Founded: 1958
Roger S. Durham, Superintendent
Hours: Tues.-Sat., holiday Mondays, 9-5:30; Sun., 2-5:30.
    Closed Thanksgiving, Christmas.
Admission: Free.

Fort McAllister is located 25 miles south of Savannah, via Georgia 144 from I-95 or U.S. 17, 10 miles east of Richmond Hill off U.S. 17. Standing on the left bank of the Great Ogeechee River, this fort, built for the defense of Savannah, commands high ground between the city and the river's mouth. Its fall on December 13, 1864, marked the end of Gen. Sherman's March to the sea, rendering the defense of Savannah impossible.

Prior to this, Fort McAllister had demonstrated that such a massive earthwork could withstand the heaviest naval ordnance of its day. It protected the blockade runner *Nashville* from pursuit by Union gunboats and successfully resisted the attacks of Union *Monitor*-type ironclads. The

USS Montauk shelled the fort with the heaviest shells ever fired by a naval vessel against a shore position, but no casualties resulted. The Confederates made a gallant but unsuccessful attempt to defend the fort with only 230 men. Gen. Sherman called the overpowering of the garrison "the handsomest thing I have seen in this war." Today, the earthworks have been restored to resemble conditions during the Civil War. The museum contains mementos of the *Nashville* and the fort.

Fort Frederica National Monument
Route 4
St. Simon's Island 31522
Telephone: (912) 638-3639
Founded: 1959
Ellen Britton, Superintendent
Hours: Daily, 9-5. Closed Christmas.
Admission: Free.

Fort Frederica was one of the largest and costliest forts built by the British in North America. After selection of the site of the fort and town on a bluff overlooking the Frederica River, construction commenced in 1736. A regiment of 650 British soldiers arrived in 1738 to garrison it. The walls were strengthened with "tabby," a cement made of ground oyster shells, lime and sand. The adjacent town was enclosed by earth and timber walls up to 13 feet high, complete with towers and a moat.

Fort Frederica served as a base of operations for Oglethorpe's invasion of Florida. Other forts were built on St. Simons and other islands and attacks were made on Spanish outposts to the south. In July 1742, the Spanish launched an attack on Frederica, which was repulsed by Oglethorpe with an ambush, ending Spanish ambitions for Georgian territory. The fort and town flourished until peace came in 1748. With the withdrawal of British troops in the following year, the town began to decline and soon was no more.

The Visitor Center museum portrays the role Frederica played as an 18th-century garrison town. Among the military objects on display are a Scottish "targe" (shield) and Black Watch tartan, a British musket (long land pattern), and miscellaneous shot and shell fragments. Edged weapons are represented by Scottish and British infantry swords and bayonets.

Old Fort Jackson
1 Fort Jackson Road
Savannah 31404
Telephone: (912) 232-3945
Scott W. Smith, Director
Hours: Tues.-Sun., 9-5 (open every day in summer). Closed
    New Year's, Thanksgiving, Christmas.
Admission: Adults, $1.50; students, retired persons,
    military personnel, $1.00.

Fortified as early as the Revolutionary War because of its strategic position, in 1808 land was purchased here by the Federal government and the construction of Fort Jackson began. Old Fort Jackson (so called to distinguish it from Fort Jackson, located near Columbia, South Caroline) knew the tread of such greats as Robert E. Lee, Jefferson Davis and P.G.T. Beauregard. It was designed as a heavy artillery position to protect Savannah from attack by sea.

Guns were first mounted in 1812 and replaced as technological improvements were made in ordnance; the last guns

Aerial view of Fort Pulaski. Note the damage to the walls.

were removed in 1905 when the fort was abandoned. During the Civil War, six additional river batteries augmented the armament of the fort. In addition, four ironclads built in Savannah to break the Union blockade were eventually pressed into service as floating gun platforms. When Savannah fell in December of 1864, one vessel, the *Georgia,* was sunk intact in the river before Fort Jackson and remains there to this day awaiting salvage.

Fort Pulaski National Monument
  Tybee Island 31238
  Telephone: (912) 786-5787
  Founded: 1924
  Grady C. Webb, Superintendent
  Hours: June 30-Sept. 2, Daily, 8:30-6:45; Sept. 3-June 29,
    Daily, 8:30-5:30. Closed Christmas.
  Admission: $1.00 per car.

Fort Pulaski is 15 miles east of Savannah on U.S. 80. It occupies a strategic site on Cockspur Island at the mouth of the Savannah River. Here during an artillery siege in 1862, rifled cannon first breached the walls of a masonry fortification. Now restored to resemble its 19th-century appearance, the fort exhibits furnished casemates portraying life during its occupation by Confederate and Union troops. Rifled seacoast artillery as well as smoothbore cannon are exhibited. In the Visitor Center is a museum which in-terprets the significance of the fort, its strategic location and its role in the evolution of seacoast fortifications.

Tybee Museum
  Tybee Island 31328
  Telephone: (912) 786-4077 or 5693
  Founded: 1961
  Orville C. Rosen, Curator
  Hours: April 1-Sept. 30, Daily, 10-6; Oct. 1-March 31,
    Daily, 1-5.
  Admission: Over 12, $1.00; under 12, free.

The Tybee Museum is at the north end of the beach, opposite the Tybee lighthouse on U.S. 80. It is in the Garland Battery of Fort Screven, built for the Coast Artillery Corps in 1897 (26 similar locations had been recommended in 1886 by President Cleveland's Secretary of War, William C. Endicott.). Constructed with walls 20 feet thick and surrounded by as much as 30 feet of earth, the batteries were all but invisible from the sea, hidden behind enormous sand dunes. Equipped with 8-inch rifled guns, the batteries could fire thousand-pound shells a distance of up to eight miles. The museum houses a fine collection of antique guns, including a rare punt gun over ten feet long, used to hunt waterfowl from a punt, a shallow boat with flat bottom and square ends.

Scenes at Fort Pulaski.

Exterior view of the Tybee Museum showing the flags which have flown over Tybee Island in the past.

Tactics on Waterfowl

Ray Ovington

Waterfowling is the only form of hunting in which the game comes to the hunter. All other forms require the hunter to actually "hunt." Therefore, the tactics involved are quite different than most hunting experiences.

The upland gunner merely picks up his shotgun and heads for the woods or fields in search of grouse, woodcock, quail or pheasant. The deer hunter tramps the woods, as does the small game hunter.

But the duck and goose shooter sets up elaborate blinds; operates a small skiff, with or without motor, places decoys in specific locations and patterns on the water to attract ducks or geese. He also tries to attract inflying birds with a special kind of call and may be accompanied by a retriever dog that will bring back his downed trophy.

So, waterfowling is a much more involved "hunting" sport than any other form of game getting. The tactics are many and complicated at first, but in all the steps to be taken before the birds come by and the first shot is fired, there is a special kind of delight. The spin-offs are also many and involve artistic decoy making with some hunter-artists even painting or drawing their favortie species, making miniature models and owning and operating kennels for their specially trained retrievers.

Starting at the beginning, a general knowledge of the waterfowl species is required. The hunter must know the difference in species markings, because every season the regulations change and some species are protected in certain areas and at certain times. Knowing the game laws is rule one, and these can be obtained when your licence is purchased.

The duck species are divided into two basic catagories: the diving ducks and the puddle ducks. The habits of these two vary tremendously and, depending on which species inhabit or migrate through the territory where you live or hunt, knowledge of specific species is needed in order to understand their habits and habitat, their movements during migration through the area, the particular places in the marshlands or shorelines where they congregate to stop and feed or rest for the night while on their migration route.

In order to be able to take aim at any waterfowl, you must know how they fly. The divers take off from the water in a long into-the-wind path, while the puddle ducks bounce into the air immediately. When coming in, the divers usually take a long, straight path to their destination, while the puddlers may circle one or two times, whiffle in and set down near the decoys in an almost instantenous drop down from the sky.

Some ducks fly faster than others. A blue-winged teal for example is, or appears to be, a much faster

WOOD DUCKS
Alix sponsa

flier than a mallard, so the tactics now begin to involve the gunner with his shooting technique and choice of shotgun.

Any hunter who has gunned for upland game has some knowledge of instinctive shooting, knowing how much to lead a bird flying straight across or at an angle or coming straight in toward him. The gunner who has shot trap or skeet has had the training necesary to become a good waterfowler, though many good hunters have never shot either skeet or trap.

Knowing from what direction the birds will come to the blind is an all important item here and a definite rule can be applied. When coming in for a landing, birds always head into the wind just as airplanes do, so the relationship between the hunter in the blind, the layout of the shoreline and the placing of the decoys is the all important combined tactic which will give a positive shooting position. From then on, when the birds appear it is up to the shooter to determine their flight speed and the proper time to fire. Birds shot at too far out will either be missed or wounded. If shot at too close, they will be unduly mangled.

Since many upland gunners eventually try their

luck at waterfowling, they will already own a shot gun or two and have had extensive training in the field. All of that experience will be put to work in waterfowling and their talents will be strained to the extreme. Likewise their shotgun. There are definite recommendations as to the correct arm to use and if the hunter already owns such a shotgun and is familiar with it and comfortable with it, so much the better.

Today we are fortunate to have excellent domestic and foreign shotguns in both automatic and repeater slide actions. Some hunters also swear by the trusty old-style double, either side-by-side or over-and-under. While there are limitations and advantages among the three types, the doubles have the most restrictions. Unless the owner has a separate set of barrels, the usual modified and full choke has obvious limitations, because most shots at waterfowl are too far out for the modified choke pattern unless the ammo is #4 shot. The usual shot size is #6 used in 12 Ga, 12 Ga, Magnum, or 20 Ga. Magnum. Steel shot is preferred because the old lead pellets pollute the landscape.

As to the choice between the automatic and the slide action repeater, if you already own one or the other and are comfortable with it, stay with it in your waterfowling. If you are a beginning scatter gunner, arm yourself with a smooth-action automatic, since you can shoot faster at first than your companion banging away next to you with his slide action. The automatic also allows you to stay on your target and pull the trigger three times without having to lose aim while tugging on a slide-action mechanism.

Both the automatic and the slide action are one-barrel creations, so many hunters attach compensators that allow the adjustment from wide-open choke to full choke almost instantly. A gun so equipped can be used for all manner of hunting including the use of deer-hunting slugs. The one-gun man is then most fortunate. He can stick with one favored arm and learn to use it under any and all circumstances, including skeet and trap.

The gun must fit, and this takes a bit of doing if your body is at all unusual; arms too long or too short, long neck, short neck, big upper body or small upper body, etc. If you are starting out, try to select the proper arm and stock to fit you, just as you would select a pair of shoes carefully.

When it comes to actual shooting, most hunters find it difficult to judge distances, especially over water and under trying light conditions. Measure out 35 yards in an open place. Set up an old bed sheet (unless you have an old barn to shoot at). Fire and note the size of the pattern that will hopefully cover that duck out there at that distance. Try to memorize the distance by some familiar means. Football players, for example, know pretty well what ten yards are, so learn to focus in the same manner. Try to hold your fire to that approximate distance. When shooting at high-flying geese or ducks that are coming in right over your head, this can present a pesky problem. Only time and experience will help you to judge their distance by the size and species.

If you are fortunate enough to aim into a flock of ducks, you can merely gamble on the fact that at least one of the birds will come into your pattern, but this amounts to shoot-and-chance-it "luck." Sometimes that is all you can do. If the birds are coming in one ahead of the other or going away in a scatter formation, try to home in on the lead bird; if you miss it, you can take a smash at the followers.

Well before you are in the blind and the game is in the air, much preparation has to be made. It may seem a heavy trip to manage all the steps, remember that waterfowl hunting is a *complete* sport, involving more elements than any other form of hunting.

To begin with, the all-important hunting area must be located—preferably near where you live. The species of ducks that frequent that area during the fall migration and open season should be known, at least in theory. The map of the shoreline or hunting fields must be known and recognized and the blind placed in such a way as to face into the prevailing wind that usually blows at that time of the year. It is a very good idea to visit the area well before the season and get acquainted with it, marking range and distances either by placing sticks or floating markers to be used as guides later.

SHOVELLER DUCK
Spatula clypeata

We will come back to that scene after we get prepared for it with all our gear in order.

First, if needed, a duck boat. This can be a small rowboat, a specially designed duck-boat skiff or a usual outboard motor and boat combination used for fishing. Be prepared to row it into the shallows and even to use a paddle when necessary. The boat will have to be completely camouflaged with native grasses, tree branches or whatever natural cover you can obtain right nearby. If you embark well way from the area, there will be no need to cover the trailer or the car, but in the case where you park your boat and shoot from a shore blind, the boat should be kept as far away from the blind as possible, or heavily camouflaged if beached nearby. Because many shoot from boats, a shore blind is not necessary so their shooting platform will be self-contained.

Aboard that boat will be a long list of necessities. Comforts come first and depending on weather conditions, the proper underclothing and wind- and rain-protective outer garments must be included, even if not used at the same time. Waterfowling is a cold sport, even in Florida!

If hunting from the boat or even from a shoreline blind, you will need waders or at least hip boots in order to board and leave your boat, set out the decoys and possibly to act as your own retriever. Camouflage clothing is a must, and it is best to coat your shotgun so that it does not shine.

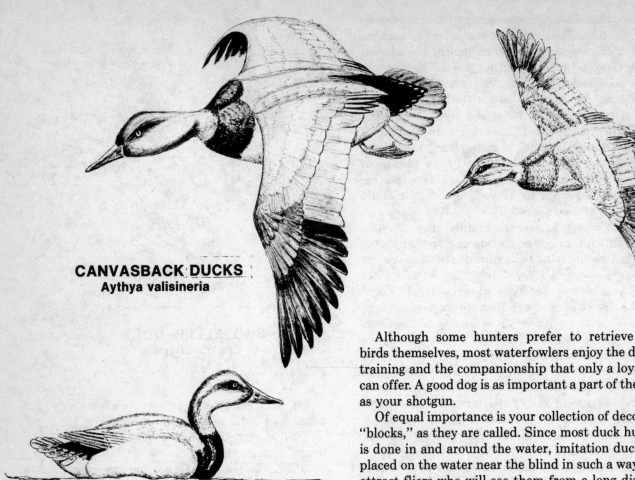

CANVASBACK DUCKS
Aythya valisineria

You'll need good refreshment and food aboard, for you may stay out longer than planned, or at the last minute an extra hunter may join you. Hot coffee (never any form of liquor) and plenty of it. Good protein-loaded sandwiches are also recommended for the larder.

Your best friend, your gun-dog retriever, must have his comforts, too, including some towels to dry him off after a ducking in the icy waters. Good warm meat soup and some dog biscuits are generally recommended while he's out there sharing the cold and wind and the fun of bagging your game.

Your good retriever will only be good if you have trained him carefully. Don't expect an upland dog to double in the blind the first time out. Rehearse him many times long before the season approaches. Get him used to the routine of in and out of the boat, resting, eating aboard, and retrieving. Don't take him for granted. Experienced duck and goose shooters train their dogs specifically for the duck blind or duck boat or both; when they are used to their surroundings and what is expected of them in performance, they will be your most anxious companion.

Although some hunters prefer to retrieve their birds themselves, most waterfowlers enjoy the days of training and the companionship that only a loyal dog can offer. A good dog is as important a part of the hunt as your shotgun.

Of equal importance is your collection of decoys, or "blocks," as they are called. Since most duck hunting is done in and around the water, imitation ducks are placed on the water near the blind in such a way as to attract fliers who will see them from a long distance away and mistake them for a happy flock that has settled down. If the decoys are placed correctly, the distance fliers will overfly the area and then circle into the wind and descend to join the party. If the birds are at all skittery, they may circle in, drop down to an almost committed landing and then, for some spooky reason, zoom back up into the air. The anxious shooter will often fall for this descent and shoot prematurely. Had he waited, the ducks might have recircled the area and then finally joined the blocks. Most of the time they will recognize the fraud and then take off, offering a second chance at them while on the wing. Only the very hungry ducker will shoot them while on the water.

Depending on the species and the conditions, a varied number of decoys are used. When hunting for canvasbacks and redheads, large flotillas of decoys are set out at the correct distance from the blind in order to fix the proper shooting range. For many other species, as few as six or eight decoys can be used. Quite often, smart hunters even place some of the decoys on the mud flats, grass tufts or shoreline to make the picture even more realistic and appealing.

Naturally, the decoys must act as naturally as

possible which involves the length of their line in relation to the depth of the water, allowing for tidal change. They should never be shiny. Duck and goose decoys can be bought in wood or plastic form and inflatable rubber ones are quite popular, thanks to their easy packing when deflated. Many artistically inclined hunters carve their own decoys and enjoy painting them as near to nature as possible. The art of decoy making is a tradition among waterfowlers and adds greatly to the off season, when thinking about duck and goose shooting is all that can be done.

An equally effective art is that of sound calling when the birds are almost within range. An experienced duck caller using one of the commercially made calls or utilizing his own vocal virtuosity can bring in scary and touchy birds, particularly those that tend to shy away from the decoys. That extra invitation made vocally often spells the difference between a shot and a hope. While there are countless species of birds, only a few basic calls are necessary to learn and recordings are available for study. Here again, an off-season art to be combined with the training of the dog, the making of the decoys, the sharpening up of the hunting and shooting accuracy and the constant improvement of the gear and equipment needed for the specific conditions under which you will be hunting.

It is quite impossible to detail specific situations in a short space, so the advice here is to study your bird species in the area in which you will be hunting, know your arm well and its range, have a well-trained dog with you, know your boat and motor and other equipment well and be prepared to operate all equipment in the dark and under sometimes very trying weather conditions.

Waterfowling is a unique combination of all these subjects. It is an involved sport with many aspects and

MALLARD DUCKS
Anas platyrhynchos

PINTAIL DUCK
Anas acuta

many conditions, some unexpected. But if you can learn to deal with them, you will be comfortable, safe and successful.

The most important tactic to follow is to become familiar with your area and prospects. Then it will be time to look up more-experienced waterfowlers in the area and earn their confidence in you so that they will readily begin to aid you in the selection of gear, the secrets of aim and lead and shooting prowess, the best decoys to use under known conditions, and the rest of their experience. If you can, get yourself invited to shoot with them.

One of the best sources of information and the way to get to know waterfowlers is to visit your local gun shop or sporting goods store. Chances are the shop

PINTAIL DUCK
Anas acuta

RING-NECKED DUCK
Aythya collaris

owner is a member of or even an officer of a local gun club. He wants you as his customer and will generally go the limit to get you into the sport and perhaps into the local club.

The most serious group of avid waterfowlers belongs to Ducks Unlimited, a conservation and shooting organization with members worldwide. They will indeed welcome you into the fold and hold out a generous invitation to join in their efforts to help wildfowl conservation efforts and also to enjoy the

shooting to be had in their area. They will happily guide you along the right path. Also, with their clubs all over the map, any time you wish to hunt in even a faraway place for an entirely new type of waterfowling experience, there will be someone in the area who will spread the welcome mat.

From Special Weapons to Tools of Terror

Jeff Arnold

I t was a scenario that could only have been penned by a madman, and yet it was played out on television screens for all the world to see. A head of state and Nobel Peace Prize winner was gunned down by Soviet-made AK47s wielded by a squad of his own soldiers who had leaped from a Soviet-built Zil truck that towed a North Korean antitank gun. As a backdrop to this weird scene, American M-60 tanks rumbled by, while a squadron of French-built Mirage jet fighters screamed overhead. It was the carefully planned and executed assassination of Egyptian President Anwar Sadat.

Nothing underscores the pervasiveness of the terrorist threat than this incident, coming as it did on the heels of assasination attempts on the lives of President Ronald Reagan and Pope John Paul. Can there be any doubt that the time has come to take note of this evil?

So long as there are terrorist fanatics who clothe themselves in the righteousness of self-determination, but who owe no allegiance to standards of fair play or the rules of war, no one is truly safe. (Comparisons are often made with the revolution that gained the American people their freedom, but that revolt was not characterized by the kind of bloody excesses that occur today with alarming regularity.) So long as Russian-made, shoulder-held, heat-seeking surface-to-air missiles can be openly bought in Middle Eastern countries, is there any place in the world where it will be safe for peaceable people to travel?

Terrorist weapons are long-lived. British writer Anthony Sampson described one chain of transfers in his book, *The Arms Bazaar*: "Ghana had a stock of Kalashnikovs bought from Nigeria, which had previously been bought by the Biafran army from Israel, which had captured them from the Egyptians and Syrians in the 1967 war. Ghana was now glad to sell them off profitably to the Lebanese Christians, and thus they returned to the Middle East."

By accident—the abandonment of millions of dollars' worth of military supplies by the United States in Vietnam—or by design—the running of guns to Third World countries by the Soviet Union and its surrogates (East Germany, Czechoslovakia and Bulgaria) or its stooges (Cuba)—the procurement of weapons by terrorists is not difficult.

We cannot show you their faces. Right now they mingle with you on the streets, in restaurants, in airport waiting rooms. They are students, businessmen, travelers, diplomats, so conventional-looking you won't even notice them. Their checked baggage often travels uninspected (as a rule, only carry-on luggage is examined by means of X-ray devices) or is subject to diplomatic immunity. But we can show you some of the tools of the terrorist's trade. Here, then, are the weapons of terror. They were intended for military purposes, but have fallen on evil ways.

In addition to their historic and technical interest because of widespread usage in the numerous undeclared brushfire wars that have sprung up since the end of World War II, these weapons commend themselves particularly to the attention of law enforcement officers, members of SWAT teams—in fact, to all responsible law-abiding citizens—in view of the potential for their increasing use by lawless elements at home.

A piece of popular modern folklore says that "you cannot ever be too rich or too thin," to which should be added, "or too knowledgeable." Knowledge is power.

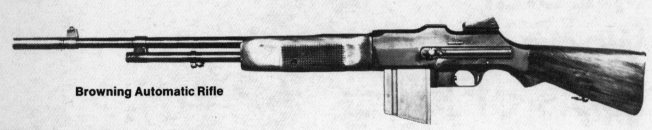

Browning Automatic Rifle

AUTOMATIC RIFLES

BELGIUM
FN FAL Automatic Rifle

Caliber: 7.62mm
System of operation: Gas
Type of fire: Selective
Overall length: 41.5 in.
Barrel length: 21.0 in.
Weight: 9.5 lbs.
Magazine: 20- or 30-round detachable box magazine
Sights: Front: Protected post, adjustable for elevation **Rear:** Unprotected aperture, adjustable for windage and elevation
Range: 600 meters
Rate of fire: 650-700 rpm (cyclic) 120 rpm (auto) 60 rpm (single shot)
Muzzle velocity: 2750 fps
Comments: This is probably the most successful of the designs produced by FN (Fabrique Nationale) and the FAL (Fusil Automatique Léger) has been sold to more than 70 countries, of which 8 have manufacturing licenses as well. It is produced in Great Britain as the L1A1 with the automatic feature removed and widely used by Dominion countries.

SOVIET UNION
RPK-74

Caliber: 7.62mm
System of operation: Gas
Type of fire: Selective
Overall length: 41.5 in.
Barrel length: 23.5 in.
Weight: 11 lbs.
Magazine: 40-round detachable box or 75-round detachable drum
Sights: Front: Protected post **Rear:** Tangent leaf
Range: 800 meters
Rate of fire: 600 rpm (cyclic) 50-150 rpm (practical)
Muzzle of velocity: 2410 fps
Comments: Basically developed from the AK-47 assault rifle, the RPK (Ruchnoy Pulemyot Kalashnikova) is replacing the older RPD as the squad automatic weapon of the Red Army. The finish on this gun is good and, like the AK, the bolt and bore are chrome-plated to reduce wear.

UNITED STATES
M-14E2

Caliber: 7.62mm
System of operation: Gas
Type of fire: Selective
Overall length: 44.3 in.
Barrel length: 22 in.
Weight: 12.75 lbs.
Magazine: 20-round detachable box magazine
Sights: Front: Protected blade **Rear:** Semi-protected adjustable aperture
Muzzle velocity: 2800 fps
Comments: The M-1 Garand rifle had served U.S. forces well in the Second World War and after. When the 7.62x51mm NATO round was selected in 1953, a new rifle design based on the Garand was adopted. The M-14 and M-14E2 had a relatively short service life and it is now relegated to National Guard units. Many are still in use around the world however, and it has been produced under license in Taiwan.

Browning Automatic Rifle

Caliber: .30 (.30-06)
System of operation: Gas
Type of fire: Selective fire or automatic only (Model 1918A2)
Overall length: M1918, M1918A1: 47 in. M1918A2: 47.8 in. M1922: 41 in.
Barrel length: 24 in. (18 in., Model 1922)
Weight: M1918: 16 lbs. M1918A1: 18.5 lbs. M1918A2: 19.4 lbs. M1922: 19.2 lbs.
Magazine: 20-round detachable box magazine
Sights: Front: Hooded or unprotected blade **Rear:** Protected adjustable aperture with battlesight notch
Range: 600 yds.
Rate of fire: 550 rpm (cyclic) 350 rpm (slow auto)
Muzzle velocity: 2805 fps
Comments: This workhorse of the U.S. Army was introduced in 1918 and can be regarded as a heavy automatic rifle or a light machine gun. Made until the Korean War, the BAR is still in use by the military forces of Costa Rica, Greece, Guatemala, Indonesia, Mexico, Norway and the Philippines. In the 1930s, it was built in Belgium under license by Fabrique Nationale and others were made in Poland and Sweden.

Vz58P

7.62mm Vzor 58 Assault Rifles

Vz58V

ASSAULT RIFLES

CZECHOSLOVAKIA
7.62mm Vzor 58 (Vz58P, Vz58V)
Assault Rifle

Caliber: 7.62mm
System of operation: Gas
Type of fire: Selective
Overall length: 33 in. (wooden stock) 25 in. (metal stock, folded) 33 in. (metal stock, fixed)
Barrel length: 15.8 in.
Weight: 8.75 lbs.
Magazine: 30-round detachable box magazine
Sights: Front: Protected post **Rear:** Tangent leaf, adjustable in 100-meter increments from 100 to 800 meters
Range: 300 meters
Rate of fire: 700-800 rpm
Muzzle velocity: 2300 fps
Comments: Introduced in 1958, this is the standard assault rifle of the Czechoslovakian army. Although it resembles the AK47 in outward appearance, the internal design is different. Accessories include a bayonet, flash-hider, bipod, sectional cleaning rod and magazine carrier. It can be equipped with the NSP-2 infrared sight for night use.

FRANCE
MAS Assault Rifle

Caliber: 5.56mm
System of operation: Delayed blowback
Type of fire: Selective (automatic or 3-shot bursts)
Overall length: 29.8 in.

Barrel length: 19.2 in.
Weight: 7.5 lbs. (without magazine)
Magazine: 25-round detachable box magazine
Sights: Front: Blade **Rear:** Aperture, 0-300 meters
Range: 300 meters
Rate of fire: 900-1000 rpm (cyclic) 3-shot bursts
Muzzle velocity: 3150 fps (960 mps)
Comments: A new design for the French army, utilizing a "bullpup" configuration and optional ejection to left or right. The overlarge plastic handle serves to protect the sights from damage; the butt is also of plastic.

GERMANY
MP-44 Assault Rifle

Caliber: 7.92mm
System of operation: Gas
Type of fire: Selective
Overall length: 37 in.
Barrel length: 16.5 in.
Weight: 11.5 lbs.
Magazine: 30-round detachable box magazine
Sights: Front: Hooded blade **Rear:** Tangent leaf, adjustable
Range: 400 meters (semi-auto) 200 meters (auto)
Muzzle velocity: 686 mps
Comments: This gun can be said to be the ancestor of modern assault rifles. Design of an automatic assault rifle was begun in 1938 in Germany and two companies, Haenel and Carl Walther, built prototypes. The MP-44 saw service during the last months of the war. Adolf Hitler is said to have conferred the name "Sturmgewehr" (assault rifle) on the gun, thus defining its role and touching off eventual Russian development of the AK Kalashnikov assault rifle.

MP-44 Assault Rifle

HK32 and HK32K Assault Rifles

Caliber: 7.62x39mm
System of operation: Delayed blowback
Type of fire: Selective
Overall length: 36.1 in. (HK32) 25.6 in. (HK32K, stock retracted) 33.9 in. (HK32K, stock extended)
Barrel length: 15.35 in. (HK32) 13.6 in. (HK32K)
Weight: 6.6 lbs.
Magazine: 30-round detachable box
Sights: Front: Hooded post **Rear:** Rotary diopter aperture, adjustable from 100 to 400 meters in 100-meter increments
Range: 400 meters
Rate of fire: 600-650 rpm (cyclic) 100 rpm (auto) 40 rpm (single shot)
Muzzle velocity: 920 mps
Comments: Heckler and Koch produced assault rifle variations of the NATO G3 rifle in caliber .223 (HK33 and HK33K) and 7.62x39mm Soviet M1943 cartridge (HK32 and HK32K)

SOVIET UNION
AK (Avtomat Kalashnikova) Assault Rifle

Caliber: 7.62x39mm
System of operation: Gas
Type of fire: Selective
Overall length: 34.25 in.
Barrel length: 16.34 in.
Weight: 10.58 lbs.
Magazine: 30-round detachable box magazine
Sights: Front: Protected post **Rear:** Tangent leaf
Range: 400 meters (semi-auto) 300 meters (auto)
Rate of fire: 600 rpm (cyclic) 100 rpm (auto) 40 rpm (semi-auto)
Muzzle velocity: 2330 fps
Comments: Designed shortly after the end of the Second World War by Mikhail Kalashnikov, the AK-47 began service with the Red Army in 1951. The AK-47 has to be acknowledged as one of the great gun designs. It has been manufactured outside of Russia in Bulgaria, Communist China, Czechoslovakia, East Germany, Finland, Hungary, North Korea, Poland, Rumania and Yugoslavia.

AK Assault Rifle

HK33 and HK33K Assault Rifles

Caliber: 5.56x45mm (.223)
System of operation: Delayed blowback
Type of fire: Selective
Overall length: 36.1 in. (HK33) 24.4 in. (HK33K, stock retracted) 32.7 in. (HK33K, stock extended)
Barrel length: 15.35 in. (HK33)
Weight: 6.6 lbs.
Magazine: 20-round detachable box magazine (HK33) 40-round detachable box magazine (HK33K)
Sights: Front: Hooded post **Rear:** Rotary diopter aperture, adjustable from 100 to 400 meters in 100-meter increments
Range: 400 meters
Rate of fire: 600-650 rpm (cyclic) 100 rpm (auto) 40 rpm (single shot)
Muzzle velocity: 920 mps
Comments: These are .223 caliber versions of the original G3 design (the "K" represents the word "Kurz," German for "short") and is a shorter version superseded by the HK33A2, HK33A3 and HK33KA1, but still encountered in large numbers.

SWITZERLAND
SIG540 and SIG542 Assault Rifles

Caliber: 5.56mm (SG540) 7.62mm (SG542)
System of operation: Gas
Type of fire: Selective
Overall length: (SG540) 37.5 in. (stock fixed) 28.7 in. (stock folded); (SG542) 38.9 in. (stock fixed) 30.1 in. (stock folded)
Barrel length: 19.31 in. (SG540) 19.5 in. (SG542)
Weight: 7.1 lbs. (SG540) 8.0 lbs. (SG542)
Magazine: 20-round box
Sights: Front: Protected post **Rear:** Rotating drum with apertures
Range: 400 meters
Muzzle velocity: 3215 fps (SG540) 2690 fps (SG542)
Comments: Made by the Schweizerische Industrie Gesellschaft, these rifles are simple in design and relatively easy to manufacture—stampings are used to reduce the cost of manufacture, heretofore a drawback with SIG products.

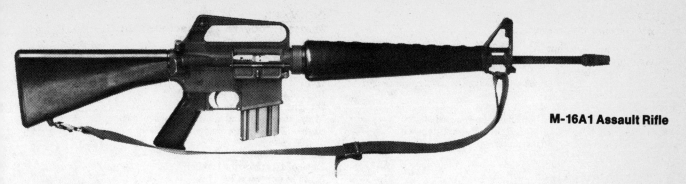

M-16A1 Assault Rifle

UNITED STATES
M-2 Carbine

Caliber: .30
System of operation: Gas
Type of fire: Selective
Overall length: 35.6 in. (fixed stock) 35.5 in. (folding stock
    extended) 25.4 in. (folding stock folded)
Barrel length: 18.0 in.
Weight: 5.5 lbs., 6.19 lbs. (with folding stock)
Magazine: 30-round detachable box magazine
Sights: Front: Protected blade **Rear:** Protected sliding aperture,
    adjustable from 100 to 300 yards
Range: 300 yds.
Rate of fire: 750 rpm (cyclic) 75 rpm (auto) 40 rpm (single shot)
Muzzle velocity: 1970 fps
Comments: The M-1 Carbine was designed before the Second
    World War to be used in place of the .45 pistol. Thanks to its
    greater magazine capacity, it increased the firepower of
    American troops. The M-2 was an automatic version of the semi-
    automatic M-1. The M-2 remains in service in Cambodia, Chile,
    Ethiopia, Honduras, Japan, Laos, Mexico, Norway, the
    Philippines, Taiwan and Tunisia.

M-16A1 Assault Rifle

Caliber: 5.56mm
System of opertion: Gas
Type of fire: Selective
Overall length: 39.0 in.
Barrel length: 20.0 in.
Weight: 6.3 lbs.
Magazine: 20- or 30-round detachable box magazine

Sights: Front: Protected post **Rear:** Protected L-type
Range: 400 yds.
Rate of fire: 750 rpm (cyclic)
Muzzle velocity: 3250 fps
Comments: The M-16A1 is the standard rifle of the U.S. Army.
    Widely exported and built under license in Singapore, South
    Korea and the Philippines, the M-16A1 is used by the armies of
    Jordan, Taiwan and Italy.

AR-18 Assault Rifle

Caliber: 5.56mm
System of operation: Gas
Type of fire: Selective
Overall length: 38.0 in. (stock extended) 28.75 in. (stock
    retracted)
Barrel length: 18.5 in.
Weight: 6.75 lbs.
Magazine: 20-round detachable box magazine
Sights: Front: Protected post **Rear:** Protected flip aperture with
    windage adjustment
Range: 300 yards
Rate of fire: 750-800 rpm (cyclic) 80 rpm (auto) 40 rpm (single
    shot)
Muzzle velocity: 3020 fps
Comments: Originally intended as a less-costly replacement for
    the M-16, the AR-18 was never accepted by the U.S. Army. It
    is produced in California, in Japan and in Great Britain.

M-2 Carbine

AUSTRIA
Mpi 69 Submachine Gun

Caliber: 9mm Parabellum
System of operation: Blowback
Type of fire: Selective
Overall length: 18.0 in. (stock retracted) 25.0 in. (stock extended)
Barrel length: 10.2 in.
Weight: 6 lbs.
Magazine: 25- or 32-round detachable box magazine
Sights: Front: Post with protecting ears **Rear:** L-type with apertures set for 100 and 200 meters.
Range: 400 meters
Rate of fire: 680 rpm (cycle)
Muzzle velocity: 1350 fps
Comments: Outwardly similar to the Israeli UZI in appearance, the Mpi 69 has many features, including an unusual trigger mechanism—a short squeeze gives single shots and a pronounced pull gives full automatic fire. Like the UZI, the Mpi 69 has a long barrel but a short overall length, thanks to a bolt that telescopes the barrel for about two-thirds of its length.

CZECHOSLOVAKIA
Vz-25 Submachine Gun

Caliber: 9mm Parabellum
System of operation: Blowback
Type of fire: Selective
Overall length: 34.4 in.
Barrel length: 12.8 in.
Weight: 8.7 lbs. (with 24-round magazine) 9.0 lbs. (with 40-round magazine)
Magazine: 24- and 40-round detachable box magazine
Sights: Front: Protected blade **Rear:** V-notch tangent graduated from 100 to 800 meters
Range: 150 meters (semi-auto) 100 meters (auto)
Rate of fire: 650 rpm (cyclic) 50 rpm (semi-auto) 80-100 rpm (auto)
Muzzle velocity: 1800 fps
Comments: The Vz-25 began service with the Czechoslovakian army after World War II. As the Vz-23 it had a fixed wooden stock. Many of these two models found their way to Cuba and the Middle East. The Vz-23 and Vz-25 were the first postwar submachine guns to demonstrate innovative design features.

M-61 (Vzor 61) "Skorpion" Submachine Gun

Caliber: 7.65mm
System of operation: Blowback
Type of fire: Selective
Overall length: 20.55 in. (with stock fixed) 10.62 in. (with stock folded)
Barrel length: 4.5 in.
Weight: 2.87 lbs.
Magazine: 10- or 20-round detachable box magazine
Sights: Front: Protected post **Rear:** Flip-over notch set for 75 and 150 meters.
Range: 100-200 meters
Rate of fire: 750 rpm (cyclic)
Muzzle velocity: 1040 fps
Comments: A machine pistol rather than a true submachine gun, the Skorpion fires a small-caliber bullet of doubtful combat effectiveness. It was apparently designed to give tank crews a holster weapon.

DENMARK
Madsen Model 50 Submachine Gun

Caliber: 9mm Parabellum
System of operation: Blowback
Type of fire: Automatic fire only
Overall length: 31.24 in. (stock extended) 21.0 in. (stock folded)
Barrel length: 7.87 in.
Weight: 7.6 lbs. (without magazine)
Magazine: 32-round detachable box magazine
Sights: Front: Unprotected blade **Rear:** Stamped aperture set for 100 meters.
Range: 100 meters
Rate of fire: 550 rpm (cyclic)
Muzzle velocity: 1200 fps.
Comments: One of the most unusual submachine gun designs ever produced and one of the last of the wooden-stocked models. One feature is the curious method of stripping by removing the magazine and barrel nuts after which the two receiver halves open sideways on two hinges at the rear. This gun was adopted by some of the smaller countries of South America and Asia and is made in Brazil as the Methralhadora de Mao .45 INA 953.

FINLAND
Suomi Model 31 Submachine Gun

Caliber: 9mm Parabellum
System of operation: Blowback
Type of fire: Selective
Overall length: 34 in.
Barrel length: 12.62 in.
Weight: 11.30 lbs. (with empty 50-round magazine)
Magazine: 70-round drum; 25- and 50-round box magazines.
Sights: Front: Blade **Rear:** Taugent graduated from 100 to 500 meters
Range: 200 meters
Rate of fire: 900 rpm (cyclic) 120 rpm (auto) 40 rpm (single shot)
Muzzle velocity: 1300 fps
Comments: Originally made in Finland by Oy Tikkakoski, the Model 31 was subsequently adopted by Norway, Sweden and Switzerland (as the MP 43/44). The designer was Aimo Lahtl, who designed the pistol of the same name.

FRANCE
MAT-49 Submachine Gun

Caliber: 9mm Parabellum
System of operator: Blowback
Type of fire: Automatic fire only
Overall length: 26.0 in. (stock extended) 18.3 in. (stock retracted)
Barrel length: 9.05 in.
Weight: 9.41 lbs.
Magazine: 32-round detachable box magazine
Sights: Front: Hooded blade **Rear:** L-type set for 100 and 200 meters
Range: 200 meters
Rate of fire: 600 rpm (cyclic)
Muzzle velocity: 1240 fps
Comments: The MAT-49 was adopted by the French army and was its standard submachine gun throughout the fighting in Indochina and Algeria. Many of these guns were captured by the North Vietnamese and were converted to fire the Tokarev 7.62mm pistol cartridge.

GERMANY
MP-5 (HK 54) Submachine Gun

Caliber: 9mm Parabellum
System of operation: Delayed blowback.
Type of fire: Selective
Overall length: 26 in. (fixed stock) 26 in. (retroctable stock, fixed) 19.3 in. (retractable stock, retracted)
Barrel length: 8.85 in.
Weight: 5.5 lbs.
Magazine: 30-round detachable box magazine
Sights: Front: Hooded post **Rear:** Flip-type
Range: 200-300 meters
Rate of fire: 650 rpm (cyclic) 100 rpm (auto) 50 rpm (cingle shot)
Muzzle velocity: 1310 fps
Comments: A shortened version of the H & K G3 rifle with which it shares many parts, the MP-5 is constructed largely of stampings with plastic components. It has yet to be adopted by any military force, but is used by the Bundespolizei and Bündesgrenzschütz (border guards) and is being evaluated by other agencies.

MPL and MPK Submachine Guns

Caliber: 9mm Parabellum
System of operation: Blowback
Type of fire: Automatic only
Overall length: (MPL) 29.42 in. (stock extended) 18.1 in. (stock folded) (MPK) 25.96 in. (stock extended) 14.75 in. (stock folded)
Barrel length: (MPL) 10.25 in. (MPK) 6.75 in.
Weight: (MPL) 6.62 lbs. (MPK) 6.27 lbs.
Magazine: 32-round detachable box magazine
Sights: Front: (MPL) Protected blade **Rear:** Flip-over notch set for 75 and 125 meters (MPK) **Front:** Protected blade **Rear:** Flip-over notch set for 75, 125 and 200 meters, 550 rpm (cyclic)
Range: 200 meters
Rate of fire: 550 rpm (cyclic)
Muzzle velocity: 1370 fps
Comments: The only difference between the two models lies in the length of the barrel. Making extensive use of stampings, these weapons were developed in 1963 but have only been adopted by the Mexican navy and some police forces.

MP-40 Submachine Gun

Caliber: 9mm Parabellum
System of operation: Blowback
Type of fire: Full automatic only
Overall length: 32.8 in. (stock extended) 24.8 in. (stock folded
Barrel length: 9.9 in.
Weight: 8.87 lbs. (MP-40)
magazine: 32-round detachable box magazine
Sights: Front: Hooded barleycorn **Rear:** Notched flip-over set for 100 and 200 meters
Range: 200 meters
Rate of fire: 500 rpm (cyclic)
Muzzle velocity: 1300 fps
Comments: The MP-40 was developed from the earlier MP-38 and was produced in great numbers during the Second World War. After the war it saw service with many nations; today it is used by few armies. In Norway it is named the Maskin 9mm M40. It is popular with guerrilla groups in Africa and Southeast Asia.

GREAT BRITAIN
STEN MK 11 Submachine Gun

Caliber: 9mm.
System of operation: Blowback
Type of fire: Selective
Overall length: 30 in.
Barrel length: 7.75 in.
Weight: 6.62 lbs.
Magazine: 32-round detachable box magazine
Sights: Front: Barleycorn **Rear:** Aperture set for 100 yards
Range: 200 yards
Rate of fire: 540 rpm
Muzzle velocity: 1280 fps
Comments: First introduced in 1940 and designed for easy manufacture, the STEN was produced in a variety of "marks," the most numerous of which was the Mark II. (It takes its name from the initial letters of the last names of its designers, Sheppard and Turpin, and the Royal Small Arms Factory at Enfield, England.) Great Britain had entered the Second World War without a submachine gun and the STEN was its emergency solution to the problem—a veritable workhorse of a gun.

Sterling MK 4 (LZA3) Submachine Gun

Caliber: 9 mm.
System of operation: Blowback
Type of fire: Selective
Overall length: 28 in. (stock extended) 19 in. (stock folded)
Barrel length: 7.8 in.
Weight: 6.0 lbs.
Magazine: 34-round detachable box magazine
Sights: Front: Blade with protecting ears. **Rear:** Flip-type aperture set for 100 and 200 meters
Range: 200 yards
Rate of fire: 550 rpm (cyclic)
Muzzle velocity: 1280 fps
Comments: The LZA3 is the military version of the Patchett machine carbine produced in the 1940s by the Sterling Armament Company of Dagenham, England. It has been in service with British and Canadian forces since 1954 and has been sold to more than 70 military forces around the world. The design is that of George W. Patchett.

ISRAEL
UZI Submachine Gun

Caliber: 9 mm. Parabellum
System of operation: Blowback
Type of fire: Selective
Overall length: 25.2 in. (wooden stock) 25.2 in. (metal stock, extended) 17.9 in. (metal stock folded)
Barrel length: 10.2 in.
Weight: 8.8 lbs. (with loaded 25-round magazine, wooden stock) 8.9 lbs. (with loaded 25-round magazine, metal stock)
Magazine: 25-, 32- and 40-round detachable box magazine
Sights: Front: Truncated cone with protecting ears **Rear:** L-type set for 100 and 200 yards
Range: 200 meters
Rate of fire: 550-600 rpm (cyclic) 128 rpm (auto) 64 rpm (single shot)

UZI Submachine Gun

Muzzle velocity: 1310 fps
Comments: The UZI was designed in 1949 by Major Uziel Gal of the Israeli Defense Forces and embodies a number of features adapted from Czech and other designs. One of its outstanding features is its short length because of the use of a bolt that telescopes forward over the barrel. Extensive use is made of stampings and heat-resistant plastics. West Germany, Iran, Venezuela and Thailand all use the UZI, as does the U.S. Secret Service in guarding the President.

ITALY
Beretta Model 12 Submachine Gun

Caliber: 9 mm Parabellum
System of operation: Blowback
Type of fire: Selective
Overall length: 25.39 in. (stock fixed) 18.43 in. (stock folded)
Barrel length: 7.9 in.
Weight: 6.6 lbs.
Magazine: 20-, 30- and 40-round detachable box magazine
Sights: Front: Protected blade **Rear:** Flip-over notch set for 100 and 200 meters.
Range: 200 meters
Rate of fire: 550 rpm (cyclic) 120 rpm (auto) 40 rpm (single shot)
Muzzle velocity: 1250 fps
Comments: Beretta developed a number of submachine guns in the 1950s to be successors to their earlier Model 4, still used by the Italian army. The Model 12 has been adopted by a number of countries and is also made in Indonesia.

SOVIET UNION
Shpagin Model 1941(PPSh) Submachine Gun

Caliber: 7.62 mm
System of operation: Blowback
Type of fire: Selective
Overall length: 33.15 in.
Barrel length: 10.63 in.
Weight: 11.99 lbs. (loaded drum magazine) 9.26 lbs. (loaded box magazine)
Magazine: 71-round detachable drum magazine or 35-round detachable box magazine
Sights: Front: Hooded post **Rear:** Tangent leaf or L-type (later models)
Range: 200 meters (short bursts) 100 meters (long bursts)
Rate of fire: 900 rpm (cyclic)
Muzzle velocity: 1640 fps
Comments: Developed during World War II and no longer used by the Red Army, the PPSh is employed in the Middle East and Asia. It has been built in Hungary, North Korea, North Vietnam and Communist China—all with minor modifications.

Shpagin Model 1941 Submachine Gun

**Sudayev M1943
Submachine Gun**

Sudayev M1943 (PPS) Submachine Gun

Caliber: 7.62 mm
System of operation: Blowback
Type of fire: Automatic fire only
Overall length: 32.72 in. (stock extended) 24.25 in. (stock folded)
Barrel length: 9.45 in.
Weight: 7.98 lbs.
Magazine: 35-round detachable box magazine
Sights: Front: Post with ears **Rear:** L-type
Range: 200 meters (short bursts) 100 meters (long bursts)
Rate of fire: 650 rpm (cyclic)
Muzzle velocity: 1600 fps
Comments: Developed from the earlier M1942, this gun is no
longer in first-line service in Russia or any Warsaw Pact
country. After the Second World War, Poland produced a model
of this gun with a wooden stock and known as the M43/52, which
is occasionally seen on TV news programs emanating from
Poland. It is also manufactured in Communist China.

SWEDEN
M45 Submachine Gun

Caliber: 9 mm Parabellum
System of operation: Blowback
Type of fire: Automatic fire only
Overall length: 31.8 in. (stock extended) 21.7 in. (stock folded)
Barrel length: 8 in.
Weight: 9.25 lbs. (loaded)
Magazine: 36-round detachable box magazine
Sights: Front: Protected post **Rear:** L-type

Range: 200 meters
Rate of fire: 550-600 rpm (cyclic)
Muzzle velocity: 1200 fps
Comments: Known as the "Carl Gustav," the M45 was first
produced in 1945 and is still being manufactured. This is the
standard Swedish submachine gun and is widely sold—Ireland
and Indonesia have been customers. The M45 was produced in
Egypt as the "Port Said." A silenced version was employed by
American Special Forces in Vietnam.

UNITED STATES
M-3 and M-3A1 Submachine Guns

Caliber: .45 ACP
System of operation: Blowback
Type of fire: Automatic
Overall length: 29.8 in. (stock extended) 22.8 in. (stock retracted)
Barrel length: 8 in.
Weight: 8.15 lbs.
Magazine: 30-round detachable box magazine
Sights: Front: Blade **Rear:** Fixed aperture
Range: 200 yards
Rate of fire: 450 rpm (cyclic) 120 rpm (auto)
Muzzle velocity: 920 fps
Comments: When the United States entered the Second World
War in 1941, submachine guns were in short supply (the
Thompson was difficult to mass-produce). The simple, all-metal
M-3 (dubbed "Grease Gun" by GIs) was the answer. The M-3
was superseded by the M-3A1, with the cocking handle replaced
by the unusual expedient of a finger hole in the bolt. It has been
widely made in other countries under license or merely copied.

M-3 Submachine Gun

Reising Model 50 Submachine Guns

Ingram M-10 Submachine Gun

Caliber: .45 ACP or 9mm Parabellum
System of operation: Blowback
Type of fire: Selective
Overall length: 22.0 in. (stock extended) 11.5 in. (stock retracted)
Barrel length: 5.84 in.
Weight: 7.1 lbs.
Magazine: 30-round (.45) and 32-round (9mm) detachable box magazine
Sights: Front: Protected post **Rear:** Unprotected aperture
Range: 100 yards
Rate of fire: 1145 rpm (cyclic) 90 rpm (auto) 40 rpm (single shot)
Muzzle velocity: 900 fps
Comments: Gordon B. Ingram has designed a number of extremely compact and lightweight guns, including the M-10, produced by the Military Armaments Corporation of Powder Springs, Georgia. The M-10 has been sold to Yugoslavia and Chile. Thanks to its light bolt, it has a high rate of fire. This, together with its compactness, have made it widely popular. A model 11 was also made, chambered for the 9mm short cartridge—the only submachine gun ever chambered for this round.

Reising Model 50 Submachine Gun

Caliber: .45 ACP
System of operation: Delayed blowback
Type of fire: Selective
Overall length: 35.75 in.
Barrel length: 11 in.
Weight: 6.75 lbs.
Magazine: 12- or 20-round detachable box magazine
Sights: Front: Blade **Rear:** Adjustable aperture
Range: 200 yards
Rate of fire: 550 rpm
Muzzle velocity: 2750 fps
Comments: This interesting gun was designed prior to the Second World War and mass-produced between 1941 and 1945, much of the production going to the U.S. Marine Corps. Although light and easy to shoot, the Model 50 was subject to jamming from dirt and the magazine design left something to be desired.

Thompson Model 1928A1 Submachine Gun

Caliber: .45 ACP
System of operation: Delayed blowback
Type of fire: Selective
Overall length: 33.75 in. (with buttstock) 25.0 in. (without buttstock)
Barrel length: 10.5 in.
Weight: 10.75 lbs.
Magazine: 20- or 30-round detachable box magazine
Sights: Front: Blade **Rear:** L-type with aperture or notched back sight
Range: 200 yards
Rate of fire: 700 rpm (cyclic) 120 rpm (auto) 40 rpm (single shot)
Comments: This was the first model of the Thompson submachine gun to be used in large numbers by the U.S. Army, Navy and Marine Corps. Unsuited for mass production, the Thompson was replaced after the war by more modern weapons. It can still be found in Egypt, Haiti and Yugoslavia and even in the hands of the IRA. During the war in Vietnam, numerous crude copies were produced in China for use by the North Vietnamese. The name "Tommy Gun" originated with the Thompson.

XM 177 E2 Submachine Gun

Caliber: 5.56
System of operation: Gas
Type of fire: Selective
Overall length: 39.0 in. (stock extended) 35.0 in. (stock retracted)
Barrel length: 11.5 in.
Weight: 7.12 lbs.
Magazine: 20- and 30-round detachable box magazine
Sights: Front: Protected post with elevation adjustment **Rear:** Protected L-type aperture with windage adjustment
Range: 200 yards
Rate of fire: 700-800 rpm (cyclic) 150-200 rpm (auto) 40-50 rpm (single shot)
Muzzle velocity: 2750 fps
Comments: Also known as the Colt Commando, this is a shortened version of the M-16 assault rifle intended to serve as a submachine gun. It was unsuccessful, largely because accuracy and handling characteristics were impaired because of the short barrel. Its future is uncertain.

Reference

Weapons and Military Museums of North America

ALABAMA
Dauphin Island. Ft. Gaines and Confederate Museum, 36528.
Daviston. Horseshoe Bend National Military Park, Rte. 1, Box 3, 36256.
Ft. McClellan. Military Police Corps Museum, Bldg. 3182, 36205.
  Women's Army Corps Museum, Bldg. 1077, 36025.
Ft. Rucker. U. S. Army Aviation Museum, Bldg. 6007, 36362.
Gulf Shores. Ft. Morgan Museum, Star Rte., Box 2780, 36542.
Huntsville. Alabama Space and Rocket Center, Tranquility Base, 35807.
Mobile. USS Alabama Battleship Commission, P.O.Box 65, 36601.
  Ft. Conde Museum, Royal Street, 36602.
Montgomery. Alabama Dept. of Archives and History, 624 Washington
  Ave., 36130.

ALASKA
Eagle. Eagle Historical Society Museum (Ft. Egbert), 99738.
Sitka. Sitka National Historical Park, P.O.Box 738, 99835.

ARIZONA
Bowie. Ft. Bowie National Historical Site, P.O.Box 158, 85605.
Camp Verde. Ft. Verde State Historic Park, P.O.Box 397, 86322.
Ft. Apache. Ft. Apache, White Mountain Culture Center, P.O.Box 507,
  85926.
Ft. Huachuca. Ft. Huachuca Historical Museum, P.O.Box 766, 85613.
Ganado. Hubbell Trading Post National Historic Site, Box
  150, 86505.
Phoenix. Arizona National Guard Historical Society Museum, 5636
  E. McDowell Rd., 85008.
Tombstone. Tombstone Courthouse State Historic Park, 219 Toughnut St.,
  85638.
Tucson. Arizona Historical Society, 949 E. 2nd St., 85719.
  Ft. Lowell Museum, 2900 N. Craycroft Rd., 85710.

ARKANSAS
Berryville. Saunders Memorial Museum, 113-15 Madison St., 72616.
Ft. Smith. Ft. Smith National Historic Site, P.O.Box 1406, 72902.
Gillett. Arkansas Post County Museum, Hwy.#1-The Great River Rd.,
  72055.
  Arkansas Post National Memorial, 72055.
Helena. Phillips County Museum, 623 Pecan St., 72342.
Jonesboro. Arkansas State Univ. Museum, Learning Resources Center,
  72401.
Little Rock. Arkansas History Commission, 1 Capitol Mall, 72202.
  Museum of Science and History, MacArthur Park, 72202.
Pea Ridge. Pea Ridge National Military Park, 72751.
Prairie Grove. Prairie Grove Battlefield State Park, P.O.Box 306, 72753.
Rogers. Daisy International Air Gun Museum, U. S. Hwy. 71, 72756.
Washington. Old Washington Historic State Park, 71862.

CALIFORNIA
Auburn. Placer County Museum, 1273 High St., Gold Country Fair Ground,
  95603.
Bakersfield. Cunningham Memorial Art Gallery, 1930 R St., 93301.
  Kern County Museum, 3801 Chester Ave., 93309.
Beverly Hills The Francis E. Fowler, Jr. Foundation Museum, 9215
  Wilshire Blvd., 90210.
Dorris. Herman's House of Guns, 204 S. Oregon St., 96023.
El Monte. El Monte Historical Museum, 3150 N. Tyler Ave., 91731.
Eureka. Fort Humboldt State Historic Park, 3431 Fort Ave.,
  95501.
Ft. Jones. Ft. Jones Museum, Main St., 96032.
Jenner. Fort Ross State Historic Park, 19005 Coast Hwy., 95450.
Lakeport. Lake County Museum, 255 N. Forbes St., 95453.
Lebec. Ft. Tejon State Historic Park, 93243.
Los Angeles. Amer. Society of Military History, Patriotic Hall, 1816 S.
  Figueroa St., 90015.
Monterey. Monterey State Historic Park, 210 Olivier, 93940.
  Presidio of Monterey Museum, Bldg. 113, 93940.
Port Hueneme. Civil Engineer Corps/Seabee Museum, Naval Construction
  Battalion Center, Code 2232, 93043.
San Diego. San Diego Historical Society, 2727 Presidio Dr., 92103.
San Francisco. Ft. Point and Army Museum Assn., Funston Ave. at Lincoln
  Blvd., 94129.
  Ft. Point National Historic Site, Presidio of San Francisco, 94129.
  Presidio Army Museum, Bldg. 2, Presidio of San Francisco, 94129.
  Wells Fargo Bank History Room, 420 Montgomery St., 94104.
Shasta. Shasta State Historic Park, P.O.Box 507, 96087.

Tiburon. Angel Island State Park, P.O.Box 318, 94920.
Wilmington. Drum Barracks Civil War Museum, 1055 Cary Ave., 90744.
Woodside. Woodside Store, 471 Kings Mountain Rd., 94062.

COLORADO
Colorado Springs. Pioneers' Museum, 215 S. Tejon, 80903.
Estes Park. Estes Park Area Historical Museum, Hwy. 36, 80517.
Ft. Carson. Ft. Carson Museum of the Army in the West, 849 Oconnel Blvd.,
  80913.
Ft. Garland. Old Fort Garland, P.O.Box 208, 81133.
Ft. Morgan. Ft. Morgan Heritage Foundation, P.O.Box 184, 80701.
Golden. Buffalo Bill Memorial Museum, Rte. 5, 80401.
Grand Junction. Museum of Western Colorado, 4th and Ute Sts., 81501.
Hugo. Lincoln County Museum, P.O.Box 626, 80821.
Julesburg. Ft. Sedgwick Depot Museum, 202 W. 1st St., 80737.
LaJunta. Bent's Old Fort National Historic Site, Box 581, 81050.
LaVeta. Ft. Francisco Museum, 81055.
Leadville. House with the Eye Museum, 127 W. Fourth St., 80461.
Meeker. The White River Museum, 565 Park St., 81641.
Sterling. Overland Trail Museum, Junction 1-76 and Hwy. 6 East, 80751.
USAF Academy. U.S.Air Force Academy Visitor Center, 80840.
Walsenburg. Ft. Francisco Museum, 119 E. Cedar St., 81089.

CONNECTICUT
Bristol. Memorial Military Museum, 61 Center St., 06010.
Groton. Submarine Force Library and Museum, Naval Submarine Base,
  06340
Gullford. Henry Whitfield Museum, Whitfield St., 06437.
Hartford. Museum of Connecticut History, Connecticut
  State Library, 231 Capitol Ave., 06115.
  Wadsworth Atheneum, 600 Main St., 06103.
Meriden. Meridan Historical Society, Inc., 424 W. Main St., 06450.
New London. U.S.Coast Guard Museum, 06320.
Norwich. The Slater Memorial Museum, 108 Crescent St., 06360.
Washington. Historical Museum of the Gunn Memorial Library,
  Wykeham Rd., 06793.
West Hartford. 76th Infantry Division Museum, 700 South Quaker Lane,
  06110.
West Redding. Colonial Museum, Putnam Memorial State Park,
  Connecticut Rte. 58, 06896.

DELAWARE
Delaware City. Ft. Delaware, Pea Patch Island in Delaware River, 19706.

DISTRICT OF COLUMBIA
Washington, D.C. Anderson House, Headquarters and Museum of the
  Society of the Cincinnati, 2118 Massachusetts Ave., N.W., 20008.
  Armed Forces Medical Museum, Bldg. 54 Armed Forces Inst.
  of Pathology, 6825 16th St., N.W., 20306.
  Bureau of Alcohol, Tobacco and Firearms Museum, 1200 Pennsylvania
  Ave., N.W., 20226.
  Daughters of the American Revolution Museum, 1776 D St., N.W., 20006.
  Ford's Theatre (Lincoln Museum), 511 10th St., N.W., 20004.
  National Air and Space Museum, 6th and Independence
  Aves., S.W., 20560.
  National Guard Heritage Gallery, 1 Massachusetts Ave.,
  N.W., 20001.
  National Museum of History and Technology, 14th St. and Constitution
  Ave., N.W., 20560.
  National Rifle Association Firearms Museum, 1600 Rhode Island
  Ave., N.W., 20036.
  Truxtun-Decatur Naval Museum, 1610 H St., N.W., 20006.
  U.S. Marine Corps Museum, Marine Corps Historical Center, Navy Yard,
  20374.
  U.S. Navy Memorial Museum, Bldg. 76, Washington Navy Yard, 20374.

FLORIDA
Boca Raton. Boca Raton Center for the Arts, Inc., 801 W. Palmetto Park
  Rd., 33432.
Eglin Air Force Base. U.S. Air Force Armament's Museum, 3201/AFAM,
  32542.
Fernandina Beach. Ft. Clinch State Park, 2601 Atlantic Avenue, 32034.
Ft. Pierce. St. Lucie County Historical Museum, 414 Seaway Dr., 33450.
Jacksonville. Ft. Caroline National Memorial, 12713 Ft. Caroline Rd.,
  32225.
Key West. East Martello Gallery and Museum, S. Roosevelt Blvd., 33040.

Fort Jefferson National Monument, c/o Supt.-Everglades National Park, P.O. Box 279, Homestead, Fla. 33030

Lighthouse Military Museum, 938 Whitehead at Truman, 33040.

Olustee. Olustee Battlefield State Historic Site, P.O.Box 2, U.S. 90, 2 miles east, 32072.

Orlando. Orange County Historical Commission, 812 E. Rollins St., 32803.

Pensacola. Naval Aviation Museum, U.S. Naval Air Station, 32508.

St. Augustine. Castillo de San Marcos National Momument, 1 Castillo Dr., 32084.

Ft. Matanzas National Monument, State Arsenal, 32084.

St. Petersburg. St. Petersburg Historical Museum, 335 2nd Ave., N.E., 33701.

GEORGIA

Andersonville. Andersonville National Historic Site, Hwy. 49, 31711.

Confederate Naval Museum, 201 4th St., 31902.

Athens. Navy Supply Corps Museum, 30606.

Atlanta. Atlanta Historical Society, 3101 Andrews Drive., N.W., 30355.

Atlanta Museum, 537-39 Peachtree St., N.E., 30308.

Cyclorama, Boulevard at Atlanta, 30303.

Columbus. Columbus Museum of Arts and Sciences, Inc., 1251 Wynnton Rd., 31906.

Cordele. Georgia Veterans Memorial Museum, 31015.

Crawfordville. Confederate Museum, Alexander H. Stephens State Park, 30631.

Darien. Ft. King George, P.O.Box 711, 31305.

Ft. Benning. National Infantry Museum, Bldg. 396, U.S. Army Infantry Center, 31905.

Ft. Gordon. U.S. Army Signal Museum, 30905.

Ft. Oglethorpe. Chickamauga-Chattanooga National Military Park, 30741.

Ft. Stewart. 24th Infantry Division and Ft. Stewart Museum, 31314.

Marietta. Kennesaw Mountain National Battlefield Park, Jct. Stilesboro Rd. and Old Hwy. 41, 30060.

Midway. Sunbury Historic Site, Rte. 1, 31320.

Richmond Hill. Ft. McAllister, P.O.Box 198, 31324

St. Simons Island. Ft. Frederica National Monument, Rte. 4, 31522.

Savannah. Old Ft. Jackson, Box 782, 31402.

Tybee Island. Ft. Pulaski National Monument, Box 98, 31328.

Tybee Museum, 31328.

HAWAII

Ft. DeRussy. U.S. Army Museum, Hawaii, Battery Randolph, Kalia Rd., 96815.

Pearl Harbor. Pacific Submarine Museum, Naval Submarine Base, 96860.

USS Arizona Memorial, 96860.

IDAHO

Rexburg. Upper Snake River Valley Historical Society, Rte. 2, 83440.

ILLINOIS

Aurora. Aurora Historical Museum, 304 Oak Ave., 60506.

G.A.R. Memorial & Veterans Museum, 23 E. Downer Pl., 60505.

Chicago. American Police Center & Museum, 1130 S. Wabash Ave., 60605.

Chicago Historical Society, Clark St. at North Ave., 60614.

Chicago Public Library Cultural Center, 78 E. Washington St., 60602.

George F. Harding Museum, 86 E. Randolph St., 60601.

Polish Museum of America, 984 N. Milwaukee Ave., 60622.

Clinton. The Homestead Museum, 219 E. Woodlawn St., 61727.

Edwardsville. Madison County Historical Museum, 715 N. Main St., 62025.

Ft. Sheridan. Ft. Sheridan Museum, Bldg. 33, 60037.

Kankakee. Kankakee County Historical Society Museum, 8th Ave. & Water St., 60901.

Marion. Williamson County Historical Society, 105 S. Van Buren, 62959.

Mendota. Time Was Village Museum, US 51-52, 4 Miles S., 61342.

Moline. Rock Island County Historical Society, 822 11 Ave., 61265.

Paxton. Ford County Historical Society, 145 W. Center St., 60957.

Prairie du Rocher. Ft. de Chartres Historic Site Museum, Ft. de Chartres Historic Site, 62277.

Rock Island. John M. Browning Memorial Museum, Rock Island Arsenal, 61299.

Sandwich. Stone Mill Museum, 315 East Railroad St., 60548.

Springfield. Memorial Hall of Flags, Centennial Bldg., 2nd and Edwards Sts., 62705.

Sterling. Sterling-Rock Falls Historical Society, 212 Third Ave., 61081.

Watseka. Iroquois County Historical Society Museum, Old Courthouse, 2nd & Cherry, 60970.

Wauconda. Andrew Cook Museum, North Main St., 60084.

Lake County Museum. Lakewood Forest Preserve, 60084.

Waukegan. Waukegan Historical Society, 1917 N. Sheridan Rd., 60085.

Wheaton. Cantigny, 1 S. 151 Winfield Rd., 60187.

Dupage County Historical Museum, 102 E. Wesley St., 60187.

INDIANA

Battle Ground. Battle Ground Historical Corp., Box 225, 47920.

Columbus. Bartholomew County Historical Society, 524 Third St., 47201.

Crawfordsville. General Lew Wallace Study (or Studio), East Pike St., 47933.

Evansville. Evansville Museum of Arts and Science, 411 S.E. Riverside Dr., 47713.

Ft. Wayne. Historic Fort Wayne, Inc., 46302.

Franklin. Johnson County Historical Museum, 150 W. Madison St., 46131.

Indianapolis. 38th Infantry Division Memorial Museum, 431 N. Meridian, 46204.

U.S. Finance Corps Museum, Army Finance and Accounting Ctr., 46249.

Kokomo. Howard County Historical Museum, 1200 W. Sycamore St., 46901.

La Porte. La Porte County Historical Museum, La Porte County Complex, Court House Square, 46350.

Lafayette. Tippecanoe County Historical Museum, 909 South St., 47901.

Mishawaka. Hannah Lindahl Children's Museum, 410 Lincoln Way East, 46544.

Peru. Puterbaugh Museum, 11 N. Huntington St., 46970.

Rensselaer. Jasper County Historical Society, 624 Clark St., 47978.

Richmond. Wayne County Historical Museum, 1150 North "A" St., 47374.

Salem. Washington County Historical Society, Inc., 307 E. Market St., 47167.

South Bend. The Northern Indiana Historical Society, 112 S. Lafayette Blvd., 46601.

Terre Haute. Historical Museum of the Wabash Valley, 1411 S. 6th St., 47802.

Versailles. Ripley County Historical Society Museum, P.O.Box 224, 47042.

Vincennes. George Rogers Clark National Historical Park, 401 S. Second St., 47591.

IOWA

Cedar Falls. Cedar Falls Historical Society Museum, 303 Clay St., 50613.

University of Northern Iowa Museum, 31st and Hudson Rd., 50614.

Decorah. Vesterheim, Norwegian-American Museum, 502 W. Water St., 52101.

Des Moines. Iowa State Historical Department Division of Historical Museum & Archives, E. 12th and Grand Ave., 50319.

Dubuque. Mathias Ham Museum, 2241 Lincoln Ave., 52001.

Ft. Atkinson. Fort Atkinson Museum, 52144.

Glenwood. Mills County Historical Society and Museum, Glenwood Lake Park, 51534.

Osage. Mitchell County Historical Museum, North 6th, 50461.

Sibley. McCallum Museum, City Park, 51249.

KANSAS

Abilene. Dickinson County Historical Society, 412 S. Campbell St., 67410.

Ashland. Pioneer Museum, 430 W. 4th, 67831.

Baldwin. Baker University, William A. Quayle Bible Collection, Spencer-Quayle Wing, Library, 8th St., 66006.

Old Castle Museum, 5th and Dearborn Sts., 66006.

Chanute. Martin and Osa Johnson Safari Museum, Inc., 16 S. Grant St., 66720.

Dodge City. Boot Hill Museum, Inc., 500 W. Wyatt Earp, 67801.

Ft. Leavenworth. Fort Leavenworth Museum, Reynolds & Gibbon Aves., 66027.

Ft. Riley. U.S. Cavalry Museum, United States Cavalry Museum, 66442.

Ft. Scott. Ft. Scott National Historic Site, Old Fort Blvd., 66701.

Fredonia. Wilson County Historical Society Museum, 416 N. 7th, 66736.

Garnett. Anderson County Historical Museum, Court House, 66032.

Kanopolis. Ft. Harker Museum, 67454.

Larned. Ft. Larned National Historic Site, Rte. 3, 67550.

Logan. Dane G. Hansen Memorial Museum, 67646.

Manhattan. Riley County Historical Museum, 2309 Claflin Rd., 66502.

Mankato. Jewell County Historical Museum, 66956.

Marysville. Original Pony Express Home Station, Inc., 809 North St., 66508.

North Newton. Kauffman Museum, E. 27th St., 67117.

Osawatomie. John Brown Memorial Museum, 10th and Main Sts., 66064.

Ottawa. Franklin County Historical Society, Inc., Box 145, 66067.

Phillipsburg. Old Ft. Bissell, 67661.

Republic. Pawnee Indian Village Museum, Rte. 1, 66964.

Salina. Smoky Hill Historical Museum, Oakdale Park, 67401.

Wichita. Wichita-Sedgwick County Historical Museum Assoc., 204 S. Main, 67202.

KENTUCKY

Bowling Green. Kentucky Museum, Western Kentucky University, 42101.
Columbus. Columbus-Belmont Civil War Museum, Columbus-Belmont State Park, 42032.
Ft. Campbell. Don F. Pratt Memorial Museum, Wickham Hall, 42223.
Ft. Knox. Patton Museum of Cavalry and Armor, Keyes Park, 40121.
Frankfort. Kentucky Historical Society, Broadway at the St. Clair Mall, 40602.
  Kentucky Military History Museum, East Main St., 40602.
Lexington. Waveland State Shrine, Higbee Mill Rd., 40503.
London. Mountain Life Museum, Levi Jackson Wilderness Road State Park, 40741.
Louisville. The Filson Club, 118 W. Breckinridge St., 40203.
  Museum of Natural History and Science, 727 W. Main St., 40202.
Middlesboro. Cumberland Gap National Historical Park, P.O.Box 840, 40965.
Perryville. Perryville Battlefield Museum, 40468.
Richmond. Ft. Boonesborough Museum, Ft. Boonesborough State Park, Route 5, 40475.
  Jonathan Truman Dorris Museum, Eastern Kentucky University, Perkins Bldg., 40475.

LOUISIANA

Chalmette. Chalmette National Historical Park, St. Bernard Hwy., 70043.
Ft. Polk. Ft. Polk Military Museum, Bldg. 917, 71459.
Mansfield. Mansfield State Commemorative Area, Hwy. 175, 3 miles SE of Mansfield, 71052.
Many. Ft. Jesup, Rt. 2, 71449.
New Orleans. Confederate Museum, 929 Camp St., 70130.
  Ft. Pike State Monument, Rte. 6, Box 194, 70119.
  Louisiana Military History and State Weapons Collection Museum, Jackson Barracks, 6437 St., Claude Ave., 70117.
  Louisana State Museum, 751 Chartres St., 70116.

MAINE

Augusta. Ft. Western Museum, Bowman St., 04330.
Bangor. Bangor Historical-Penobscot Heritage Museum, 159 Union St., 04401.
Brunswick. Pejepscot Historical Society, 11 Lincoln St., 04011.
Bucksport. Bucksport Historical Society, Inc., Main St., 04416.
Eastport. Border Historical Society, Inc., Washington St., 04631.
Newfield. Willowbrook at Newfield, Main St., 04056.
Portland. Maine Historical Society, 485 Congress St., 04101.
Prospect. Ft. Knox State Memorial, State Hwy. 174, 04981.
Rockland. Shore Village Museum, 104 Limerock St., 04841.
Waterville. Redington Museum, 64 Silver St., 04901.

MARYLAND

Aberdeen Proving Gound. U.S.Army Ordnance Museum, c/o U.S. Army Ordnance Center and School, 21040.
Annapolis. United States Naval Academy Museum, 21402.
Baltimore. Baltimore Seaport & the Baltimore Maritime Museum, Pier 4, Pratt St., 21202.
  Ft. McHenry National Monument and Historic Shrine, 21230.
  Star-Spangled Banner Flag House, 844 E. Pratt St., 21202.
  Walters Art Gallery, Charles and Centre Sts., 21201.
Big Pool. Ft. Frederick State Park, 21711.
Cumberland. George Washington's Headquarters, Dept. of Parks and Recreation, City Hall, 21502.
Ft. Meade. Ft. George G. Meade Army Museum, 4674 Griffin Ave., 20755.
Jefferson. Gathland Museum, 900 Arnoldstown Rd., 21755.
Oxon Hill. Ft. Washington Park, off Ft. Washington Rd., 20021.
Patuxent River. Naval Air Test and Evaluation Museum, 20670.
St. Michaels. Chesapeake Bay Maritime Museum, P.O. Box 636, 21663.
Scotland. Point Lookout State Park, Star Rt.
Sharpsburg. Antietam National Battlefield Site-Visitor Center, P.O.Box 158, 21782.

MASSACHUSETTS

Abington. Dyer Memorial Library, Centre Ave., 02351.
Berlin. Art and Historical Collections, 01503.
Beverly. Beverly Historical Society and Museum, 117 Cabot St., 01915.
Boston. Ancient and Honorable Artillery Company of Massachusetts, Faneuil Hall, 02109.
  USS Constitution Museum Foundation, Inc., Boston National Historical Park, 02129.
Canton. Canton Historical Society, 1400 Washington St., 02021.
Charleston. USS Constitution Museum, 02129.
Chelmsford. Chelmsford Historical Society, 40 Byam Rd., 01824.
Concord. Concord Antiquarian Society, 200 Lexington Rd., 01742.

Minute Man National Historic Park, P.O.Box 160, 01742.
Danvers. Danvers Historical Society, 13 Page St., 01923.
Deerfield. Memorial Hall Museum, Pocumtuck Valley Memorial Assn., Memorial St., 01342.
Duxbury. Duxbury Rural and Historical Society, Box 176, Snug Harbor Station, 02332.
Fall River. Fall River Historical Society, 451 Rock St., 02720.
  USS Massachusetts Memorial, Battleship Cove, 02721.
Fitchburg. Fitchburg Historical Society, 50 Grove St., 01420.
Groton. Groton Historical Society, Main St., 01450.
Longmeadow. Longmeadow Historical Society, 697 Longmeadow St., 01106.
Mattapoisett. Mattapoisett Museum and Carriage House, 5 Church St., 02739.
Middleborough. Middleborough Historical Association, Inc., Jackson St., 02346.
North Oxford. Clara Barton Birthplace, Clara Barton Rd., 01537.
Northborough. Northborough Historical Society, Inc., 52 Main St., 01532.
Oxford. Oxford Library Museum, 339 Main St., 01540.
Plymouth. Plimoth Plantation Inc., Warren Ave., 02360.
Salem. Salem Maritime National Historic Site, U.S. Customs House, Derby St., 01970.
Sandwich. Heritage Plantation of Sandwich, Grove St., 02563.
Scituate. Scituate Historical Society, 121 Maple St., 02066.
South Carver. Edaville Railroad Museum, Rochester Rd., 02366.
Springfield. Springfield Armory National Historic Site, 1 Armory Center, 01105.
Sturbridge. Old Sturbridge Village, 01566.
Taunton. Old Colony Historical Society, 66 Church Green, 02780.
Worcester. John Woodman Higgins Armory, Inc. 100 Barber Ave., 01606.
  Worcester Historical Museum, 39 Salisbury St., 01608.

MICHIGAN

Adrian. Lenawee County Historical Museum, 104 E. Church, 49221.
Copper Harbor. Ft. Wilkins State Park, 49918.
Dearborn. Dearborn Historical Museum, 915 Brady St., 48124.
Detroit. Ft. Wayne Military Museum, 6325 W. Jefferson Ave., 48209.
  Wayne State University Museum of Anthropology, Merrick and Anthony Wayne Dr., 48202.
Escanaba. Delta County Historical Society, Ludington Park, 49829.
Hastings. Charlton Park Village and Museum, 2545 S. Charlton Park Rd., 49058.
Leland. Leelanau Historical Museum, P.O.Box 246, 49654.
Ludington. Rose Hawley Museum, 305 E. Filer St., 49431.
Mackinac Island. Mackinac Island State Park Commission, Box 370, 49757.
Madison. Lac Qui Parle County Historical Society, West side of Fairgounds, 56256.
Manistee. Manistee County Historical Museum, 425 River St., 49660.
Marshall. Honolulu House Museum, P.O.Box 15, 49068.
Menominee. Menominee County Historical Museum, 904 11th Ave., 49858.
Niles. Ft. St. Joseph Museum, 508 E. Main St., 49120.
Plymouth. Plymouth Historical Museum, 155 S. Main St., 48170.
Port Sanilac. Sanilac Historical Museum, 228 S. Ridge St., 48469.
St. Ignace. Ft. de Buade Museum, Inc., 334 N. State St., 49781.

MINNESOTA

Bagley. Clearwater County Historical Society, 56621.
Brown Valley. Sam Brown Log House, 56219.
Carlton. Carlton County Historical Society, Dental Bldg., 55718.
Crookston. Polk County Historical Society, Hwy. 2, 56716.
Fairfax. Ft. Ridgely, R.R.1, 55332.
Grand Marais. Cook County Museum, 55604.
  Grand Portage National Monument, P.O. Box 666, 55604.
Henderson. Sibley County Historical Society, 56044.
Litchfield. G.A.R. Hall and Museum, Meeker County Historical Society, 318 N. Marshall, 55355.
Little Falls. Camp Ripley Museum, 56345.
Mantorville. Dodge County Old Settlers and Historical Society, 55955.
Morris. Stevens County Historical Museum, 6th & Nevada, 56265.
Preston. Fillmore County Historical Museum, 55965.
Red Wing. Goodhue County Historical Society, 1166 Oak St., 55066.
South St. Paul. Dakota County Historical Museum, 130 3rd Ave., N., 55075.
Stillwater. Washington County Historical Museum, 602 N. Main St., 55082.
Windom. Cottonwood County Historical Society, 812 Fourth Ave., 56101.

MISSISSIPPI

Biloxi. Beauvoir, the Jefferson Davis Shrine, Box 200 W. Beach Blvd., 39531.

Carrolton. Old Jail Museum, Carrolton Green & Magnolia Streets, 38917.

Columbus. The Columbus and Lowndes County Historical Society Museum, 316 7th St. No., 39701.

Holly Springs. Marshall County Historical Museum, P.O.Box 806, 38635.

Jackson. Mississippi Military Museum, 120 N. State St., 39201.

Lyman. JP Museum of Indian Artifacts, Hwy. 49, 39574.

Port Gibson. Grand Gulf Military State Park, Rte. 2, 39150.

Ship Island. Ft. Massachusetts.

Tupelo. Tupelo National Battlefield and Brices Cross Roads Battlefield Site, Natchez Trace Parkway, R.R.1, 38801.

Vicksburg. Old Court House Museum-Eva Whitaker Davis Memorial, 1008 Cherry St., 39180.
Vicksburg National Military Park, P.O.Box 349, 39180.

Washington. Historic Jefferson College, College St., 39190.

MISSOURI

Blue Springs. Lone Jack Civil War Battlefield Museum, 22807 Woods Chapel Rd., 64015.

Charleston. Mississippi County Historical Society, 403 N. Main, 63834.

Clayton. General Daniel Bissell Home, Jefferson Barracks Historical Park, 7900 Forsythe, 63105.

Hazelwood. Little Red School House, 450 Brookes Lane, 63042.

Kansas City. The Liberty Memorial Museum, 100 West 26th St., 64108.

Kennett. Dunklin County Museum, Inc., 122 College, 63857.

Kirksville. E.M. Violette Museum, Northeast Missouri State University, 63501.

Laclede. General John J. Pershing Boyhood Home State Historic Site, 64651.

Lexington. Battle of Lexington, State Historic Site, 64060.

Liberty. Clay County Historical Museum, 14 N. Main, 64068.

Lone Jack. Jackson County Civil War Museum and Battlefield, Jackson County Park Dept., 64070.

Mexico. Audrain County Historical Society, 501 S. Muldrow, 65265.

Point Lookout. The Ralph Foster Museum, School of the Ozarks, 65726.

Republic. Wilson's Creek National Battlefield, 521 No. Hwy. 60, 65738.

St. Charles. St. Joseph Museum, 11th and Charles, 64501.

St. Louis. Soldiers' Memorial, 1315 Chestnut St., 6310°.

Sedalia. Pettis County Historical Society, c/o Sedalia Public Library, Third & Kentucky, 65301.

Sibley. Ft. Osage, 4th and Osage Sts., 64088.

MONTANA

Billings. Yellowstone County Museum, Logan Field, 59103.

Crow Agency. Custer Battlefield National Monument, P.O. Box 39, 59022.

Ft. Benton. Ft. Benton Museum, 1801 Front St., 59442.

Missoula. Ft. Missoula Historical Museum, Bldg. 322, 59801.

Sidney. J.K.Ralston Museum & Art Center, 221 Fifth S.W., 59270.

Wisdom. Big Hole National Battlefield, P.O.Box 237, 59761.

NEBRASKA

Bellevue. Strategic Aerospace Museum, 2510 Clay St., 68005.

Burwell. Ft. Hartsuff State Historical Park, 68823.

Chadron. Museum of the Fur Trade, Rte. 2, 69337.

Crawford. Ft. Robinson Museum, Box 304, 69339.

Ft. Calhoun. Ft. Atkinson State Historical Park, Box 237, 68023.
Washington County Historical Museum, 14th and Monroe Sts., 68023.

Gering. North Platte Valley Historical Association, Inc., 11th and J Sts., near Hwy. 92 & 71, 69341.

Gothenburg. Pony Express Station, Ehmen Park, 69138.

Hastings. Hastings Museum, 1330 N. Burlington, 68901.

Kearny. Ft. Kearny State Historical Park, Rt. 4, 68847.

Lincoln. State Arsenal Museum, 17th and Court Sts., 68508.

North Platte. Buffalo Bill's Ranch, R.R. 1, 69101.
Sioux Lookout D.A.R. Log Cabin Museum, Memorial Park, 69101.

Omaha. General George Crook House, Ft. Omaha, 68111.
Union Pacific Historical Museum, 1416 Dodge St., 68179.

Osceola. Polk County Historical Museum, South end of Hawkey St., 68651.

Plattsmouth. Cass County Historical Society Museum, 644 Main St., 68048.

Red Cloud. Webster County Historical Museum, 721 W. 4th Ave., 68970.

Tecumseh. Johnson County Historical Society, Inc., Third and Lincoln Sts., 68450.

Weeping Water. Heritage House Museum, 68463.

Wilber. Wilber Czech Museum, Box 253, 68465.

York. Anna Palmer Museum, 211 E. 7th St., 68467.

NEVADA

Reno. Nevada Historical Society, 1650 N. Virginia St., 89504.

Silver Springs. Ft. Churchill Historical State Monument, 89429.

NEW HAMPSHIRE

Charlestown. Old Ft. Number 4 Associates, Rte. 11, 03603.

Dover. Annie E. Woodman Institute, 182-192 Central Ave., 03820.

Manchester. Manchester Historic Association, 129 Amherst St., 03103.

New London. New London Historical Society, Little Sunapee Rd., 03257.

Portsmouth. Portsmouth Historical Society, 43 Middle St., 03801.

NEW JERSEY

Camden. Camden County Historical Society, Park Blvd. & Euclid Ave., 08103.

Cape May Court House. Cape May County Historical Museum, Rte. 9-R.D. #1, 08210.

Ft. Monmouth. Communications-Electronics Museum, 07703

Freehold. Monmouth County Historical Association, 70 Court St., 07728.

Greenwich. Cumberland County Historical Society, YeGreate St., 08323.

Highlands. Sandy Hook Museum, P.O. Box 437, Gateway National Recreation Area, 07732.

Hopewell. Hopewell Museum, 28 E. Broad St., 08525.

Morristown. Morristown National Historical Park, Morris Ave. W. and Washington Pl., 07960.

Mount Holly. Historic Burlington County Prison Museum, 128 High St., 08060.

Neptune. Neptune Historical Museum, 25 Neptune Blvd., 07753.

Paterson. Passaic County Historical Society, Lambert Castle, Valley Rd., 07503.

Ridgewood. Paramus Historical and Preservation Society, Inc., 650 E. Glen Ave., 07450.

Ringwood. Ringwood Manor House Museum, Sloatsburg Rd., 07456.

Salem. Salem County Historical Society, 79-83 Market St., 08079.

Sussex. Space Farms Zoological Park and Museum, Beemerville Rd., 07461.

Titusville. Johnson Ferry Museum and Visitors Center, Washington Crossing State Park, 08560.

Trenton. Old Barracks Museum, S. Willow St., 08608.

Woodbury. Gloucester County Historical Society, 58 N. Broad St., 08096.

NEW MEXICO

Albuquerque. National Atomic Museum, Kirtland Air Force Base East, 87115.

Lincoln. Old Lincoln County Courthouse Museum, Lincoln State Monument, 88338.

Radium Springs. Fort Selden State Monument, Box 58, 58054.

Ramah. El Morro National Monument, 87321.

Taos. Governor Bent Museum, Bent St., 87571.

Watrous. Ft. Union National Monument, 87753.

NEW YORK

Albany. New York State Office of Parks and Recreation, Division for Historic Preservation, Executive Dept., Agency Bldg. No. 1, Nelson A. Rockefeller Empire State Plaza, 12238.

Auburn. Seward House, 33 South St., 13021.

Batavia. The Holland Land Office Museum, 131 W. Main St., 14020.

Bellport. Bellport-Brookhaven Historical Society-Museum, Bellport Lane, 11713.

Bronx. The Bronx County Historical Society, 3266 Bainbridge Ave., 10467.

Brooklyn. Harbor Defense Museum of New York City, Fort Hamilton, 11252.

Buffalo. Buffalo and Erie County Historical Society, 25 Nottingham Ct., 14216.

Caledonia. Big Springs Museum, Main St., 14423.

Canaan. Canaan Historical Society, Inc., Warner's Crossing Rd., 12029.

Castile. Castile Historical House, 17 E. Park Rd., 14427.

Cattaraugus. Cattaraugus Area Historical Center, 23 Main St., 14719.

Chazy. The Alice T. Miner Colonial Collection, Box 157, 12921.

Clayton. 1000 Islands Museum, 401 Riverside Dr., Old Town Hall, 13624.

Corning. The Rockwell-Corning Museum, Baron Steuben Pl., Market at Centerway, 14830.

Cortland. Cortland County Historical Society, Inc., 25 Homer Ave., 13045.

Crown Point. Crown Point State Historic Site, 12928.

East Durham. Durham Center Museum, Inc., 12423.

Elizabethtown. Adirondack Center Museum, Court St., 12932.

Elmira. Chemung County Historical Society, Inc., 304 Williams St., 14901.

Fablus. Pioneer's Museum, Highland Forest, 13063.

Fishers. Valentown Museum, Valentown Sq., 14453.

Fishkill. Van Wyck Homestead Museum, Rte. 9, 12524.

Ft. Edward. Ft. Edward Historical Association, P.O. Box 106, 12828.

Ft. Johnson. Montgomery County Historical Society, N.Y. Rte. 5, 12070.

Geneva. Geneva Historical Society and Museum, 543 S. Main St., 14456.

Gouverneur. Gouverneur Museum, Rte. 2, Leadmine Rd., 13642.

Hoosick Falls. Bennington Battlefield State Historic Site, State Rt. 67, 12090.

Hurleyville. Sullivan County Historical Society, Inc., P.O. Box 247, 12747.

Ilion. Remington Gun Museum, Catherine St., 13357.
Lake George. Ft. William Henry Museum, Canada St., 12845.
Little Falls. Herkimer House State Historic Site, Rte. 169, 13365.
Narrowsburg. Ft. Delaware, 12764.
Newburgh. Washington's Headquarters State Historic Site, 84 Liberty St., 12550.
New City. Historical Society of Rockland County, 20 Zukor Rd., 10956.
New York. Castle Clinton National Monument, 10005.
  Dyckman House and Museum, 204th St. & Broadway, 10021.
  Fraunces Tavern Museum, 54 Pearl St., 10004.
  General Grant National Memorial, Riverside Dr. and W. 122nd St's., 10031.
  Harbor Defense Museum, Ft. Hamilton, 11252.
  The Metropolitan Museum of Art, 5th Ave. at 82nd St., 10028.
  Museum of the City of New York, Fifth Ave. at 103rd St., 10029.
  New York City Police Academy Museum, 235 E. 20th St., 10003.
  The New-York Historical Society, 170 Central Park West, 10024.
Newburgh. Washington's Headquarters State Historic Site, 84 Liberty St., 12550.
Oriskany. Oriskany Battlefield State Historic Site, State Rte. 69, 13424.
Ossining. Ossining Historical Society Museum, 196 Croton Ave., 10562.
Owego. Tioga County Historical Society Museum, 110 Front St., 13827.
Oswego. Fort Ontario State Historic Site, East 7th St., 13126
Oyster Bay. Sagamore Hill National Historic Site, Cove Neck Road, 11771.
Riverhead. Suffolk County Historical Society, 300 W. Main St., 11901.
Rochester. Rochester Museum and Science Center, 657 East Ave., Box 1480, 14603.
Rome. Ft. Stanwix National Monument, 112 E. Park St., 13440.
Sackets Harbor. Pickering-Beach Historical Museum, 503 W. Main, 13685.
  Sackets Harbor Battlefield State Historic Site, 13685.
Sag Harbor. Suffolk County Whaling Museum of Sag Harbor, Long Island, Main St., 11963.
Schoharie. Old Stone Fort Museum & William W. Badgley Historical Museum, N. Main St., 12157.
Staten Island. Staten Island Historical Society, 441 Clarke Ave., 10306.
Stillwater. Saratoga National Historical Park, Box 113-C, 12170.
Stony Point. Stony Point Battlefield State Historic Site, U. S. 9W, 10980.
Tarrytown. The Historical Society of the Tarrytowns, Inc., 1 Grove St., 10591.
Ticonderoga. Ft. Mt. Hope, Burgoyne Rd., 12883.
  Ft. Ticonderoga, Box 390, 12883.
Tonawanda. Historical Society of the Tonawandas, Inc., 113 Main St., 14150.
Tuckahoe. Westchester County Historical Society, 43 Read Ave., 10707.
Vails Gate. Knox Headquarters State Historic Site, Box 207, 12584.
  New Windsor Cantonment State Historic Site, Temple Hill Rd., 12584.
Warsaw. Warsaw Historical Museum, 15 Perry Ave., 14569.
Warwick. Warwick Historical Society, P.O. Box 353, 10990.
Waterloo. Waterloo Library and Historical Society, 31 E. Williams St., 13165.
  Waterloo Memorial Day Museum, 35 E. Main St., 13165.
West Point. West Point Museum, United States Military Academy, 10996.
Westfield. History Center and Museum, Main and Portage St's., Center of Village Park, 14787.
Windsor. Old Stone House Museum, 10 Chestnut St., 13865.
Wyoming. Middlebury Historical Society Museum, 32 S. Academy St., 14591.
Youngstown. Old Ft. Niagara, Box 169, 14174.

NORTH CAROLINA
Burlington. Alamance Battleground State Historic Site, Rte. 1, 27215.
Currie. Moores Creek National Battlefield, P.O. Box 69, 28435.
Durham. Bennett Place State Historic Site, 4409 Bennett Memorial Rd., 27705.
Fort Bragg. 82nd Airborne Division War Memorial Museum, Ardennes St., 28307.
Greensboro. Guilford Courthouse National Military Park, New Garden Rd. & Old Battleground Rd., 27408.
Hickory. The Hickory Museum of Art, 3rd St. & First Ave., N.W., 28601.
Hillsborough. Orange County Historical Museum, King St., 27278.
King's Mountain. King's Mountain National Military Park, P.O. Box 31, 28086.
Kure Beach. Ft. Fisher State Historic Site, Box 68, 28449.
Manteo. Ft. Raleigh National Historic Site, Rt. 1, Box 675, 27954.
Murfreesboro. Murfreesboro, North Carolina Museum, P.O. Box 3, 27885.
Murphy. Cherokee County Historic Museum, Inc., Peachtree St., 28906.
Newton. Catawba County Historical Museum, 1716 S. College Dr., Hwy. 321, 28658.
Newton Grove. Bentonville Battleground State Historic Site, Box 27, 28366.
Raleigh. North Carolina Museum of History, 109 E. Jones St., 27611.
Shelby. Cleveland County Historical Museum, Courtsquare, 28150.
Southport. Brunswick Town State Historic Site, Box 356, 28461.

Wilmington. New Hanover County Museum, 814 Market St., 28401.
  USS North Carolina Battleship Memorial, Cape Fear River on Eagles Island, P.O. Box 417, 28402.

NORTH DAKOTA
Abercrombie. Ft. Abercrombie Historic Site, 58001.
Bismarck. Camp Hancock State Historic Site, First and Main St's., 58501.
  State Historical Society of North Dakota, North Dakota Heritage Center, 58505.
Ft. Ransom. Ransom County Historical Society, 58033.
Ft. Totten. Ft. Totten State Historic Site, 58335.
Jamestown. Ft. Seward Historical Society, Inc., 321 3rd Ave., 58401.
Kulm. White Stone Hill Battlefield State Museum, 58456.
Mandan. Ft. Abraham Lincoln State Historical Park, Rte. 2 Box 139, 58554.
  Great Plains Museum, Hwy. 1806, 58554.
Pembina. Ft. Pembina State Historical Museum, 58271.
Valley City. Barnes County Historical Museum, County Courthouse, 58072.
Williston. Ft. Buford State Historic Site, Buford Rt., 58801.
  Ft. Union Trading Post National Historic Site, Buford Rt., 58801.

OHIO
Bellefontaine. Logan County Historical Museum, W. Chillicothe Ave. at Seymour, 43311.
Bolivar. Ft. Laurens State Memorial, Rt. 1, 44612.
Burton. Geauga County Historical Society Century Village, 14653, E. Park St., 44021.
Cambridge. Guernsey County Museum, P.O. Box 741, 43725.
Carrollton. Carroll County Historical Society, P.O. Box 174, 44615.
Celina. Mercer County Historical Museum, The Riley Home, 130 E. Market, 45883.
Chillicothe. Mound City Group National Monument, 16062 State Rte. 104, 45601.
Franklin. Gen. Forrest Harding Memorial Museum, 302 Park Ave., 45005.
Fremont. The Rutherford B. Hayes Library and Museum, 1337 Hayes Ave., 43420.
Granville. Granville Historical Museum, Broadway, 43023.
Greenville. Garst Museum, 205 N. Broadway, 45331.
Marion. Stengel-True Museum, 504 S. State St., 43302.
Massillon. The Massillon Museum, 212 Lincoln Way, 44646.
Medina. Munson House, Medina County Historical Society, 231 E. Washington, 44256.
Niles. National McKinley Birthplace Memorial Association Museum, 40 N. Main St., 44446.
Norwalk. Firelands Historical Society Museum, 4 Case Ave., 44857.
Perrysburg. Ft. Meigs, P.O. Box 3, 43551.
Piqua. Piqua Historical Area, 9845 N. Hardin Rd., 45356.
Sheffield Lake. 103rd Ohio Volunteer Infantry Memorial Foundation, 5501 E. Lake Rd., 44054.
Tiffin. Seneca County Museum, 28 Clay St., 44883.
Urbana. Champaign County Historical Society Museum, 809 E. Lawn Ave., 43078.
Vermilion. Great Lakes Historical Society Museum, 480 Main St., 44089.
Wooster. Wayne County Historical Society, 546 E. Bowman St., 44691.
Wright-Patterson AFB. United States Air Force Museum, 45433.
Xenia. Greene County Historical Society, 74 W. Church St., 45385.
Zanesville. Dr. Increase Matthews House, 304 Woodlawn Ave., 43701.

OKLAHOMA
Bartlesville. Woolaroc Museum, State Hwy. 123, 74003.
Cheyenne. Black Kettle Museum, 73628.
Claremore. J. M. Davis Gun Museum, Fifth and Hwy. 66, 74017.
Cookson. Ft. Chickamauga, 74427.
Ft. Sill. U. S. Army Field Artillery and Ft. Sill Museum, 73503.
Okemah. Territory Town, Rte. 2, Box 297-A, 74859.
Oklahoma City. 45th Infantry Division Museum, 2145 N.E. 36th St., 73111.
  National Cowboy Hall of Fame and Western Heritage Center, 1700 N. E. 63rd St., 73111.
  Oklahoma Historical Society, Historical Bldg., 73105.
Sapulpa. Sapulpa Historical Museum, 100 E. Lee, 74066.
Tishomingo. Chickasaw Council House Museum, Rte. 1, Box 14, 73460.

OREGON
Astoria. Ft. Clatsop National Memorial, Rt. 3, Box 604, 97103.
Haines. Eastern Oregon Museum, Rte. 1, Box 109, 97833.
Hammond. Ft. Stevens Museum, Ft. Stevens State Park, 97121.
Kerby. Josephine County Kerbyville Museum, 24195 Redwood Hwy., Box 34, 97531.
Klamath Falls. Favell Museum of Western Art and Indian Artifacts, 125 W. Main St., 97601.

Lakeview. Schminck Memorial Museum, 128 "E" St., 97630.

Portland. Portland Children's Museum, 3037 S. W. 2nd Ave., 97201.

Roseburg. Douglas County Museum, Box 1550, County Fairgrounds, 97470.

The Dalles. Fort Dalles Museum, 16th St. & Garrison St., 97058.

PENNSYLVANIA

Athens. Tioga Point Museum, 724 S. Main St., 18810.

Boalsburg. Christopher Columbus Family Chapel, Boal Mansion and Museum, 16827.

Pennsylvania Military Museum, 28th Division Shrine, Box 148, 16827.

Carlisle Barracks. United States Army Military History Institute, 17013.

Easton. Northampton County Historical Society, 101 S. 4th St., 18042.

Gettysburg. Gettysburg National Military Park, 17325.

Harrisburg. Pennsylvania Historical and Museum Commission, 3rd & North Sts., 17120.

Haverford. Haverford Township Historical Society, Karakung Dr., Powder Mill Park, 19083.

Hellertown. Gilman Museum, at the Cave, 18055.

Jeannette. Bushy Run Battlefield, Bushy Run Rd., 15644.

Ligonier. Ft. Ligonier Memorial Foundation, Inc., S. Market St., 15658.

Meadville. Baldwin-Reynolds House Museum, 639 Terrace St., 16335.

Middleburg. The Snyder County Historical Society, Inc., Dr. Geo. F. Dunkleberger Memorial Library, 30 E. Market St., 17842.

Pennsburg. Schwenkfelder Museum, Seminary St., 18072.

Philadelphia. The Dandy First Museum, 103rd Engineer Battalion, 3205 Lancaster Avenue, 19104.

Independence National Historical Park, 313 Walnut St., 19106.

Philadelphia Maritime Museum, 321 Chestnut St., 19106.

War Library and Museum of the Military Order of the Loyal Legion of the United States, 1805 Pine St., 19103.

Pittsburgh. Ft. Pitt Blockhouse, Point State Park, 15222.

Ft. Pitt Museum, Point State Park, 15222.

Strasburg. Eagle Gun Museum, R. D. 1, 17579.

Sunbury. Ft. Augusta, 1150 N. Front St., 17801.

Valley Forge. The Valley Forge Historical Society, 19481.

Valley Forge National Historical Park, 19481.

Waterford. Ft. LeBoeuf Museum, 123 S. High St., 16441.

Wilkes-Barre. Wyoming Historical and Geological Society, 69 S. Franklin St., 18701.

Willow Grove. Antique Aircraft Display, Naval Air Station, 19090.

York. The Historical Society of York County, 250 E. Market St., 17403.

RHODE ISLAND

Bristol. Bristol Historical and Preservation Society, 48 Court St., 02809.

Newport. Naval War College Museum, Naval War College, Coasters Harbor Island, 02840.

Newport Artillery Company Museum, 23 Clarke St., 02840.

Providence. Rhode Island Historical Society, 52 Power St., 02906.

Rhode Island State Archives, Rm. 43, State House, Smith St., 02903.

Westerly. Westerly Public Library, Broad St., 02891.

SOUTH CAROLINA

Aiken. Aiken County Historical Museum, 226 Chesterfield, 29801.

Beaufort. Beaufort Museum, Craven St., 29902.

Blacksburg. Kings Mountain National Military Park, 29702.

Camden. Camden District Heritage Foundation, Historic Camden, P.O.Box 710, 29020.

Charleston. Citadel Archives-Museum, The Citadel, 29409.

Patriots Point Naval and Maritime Museum, 29464.

Powder Magazine, 79 Cumberland St., 29401.

Chesnee. Cowpens National Battlefield, 29323.

Columbia. South Carolina Confederate Relic Room and Museum, World War Memorial Bldg., 920 Sumter St., 29201.

South Carolina Criminal Justice Hall of Fame, 5400 Broad River Rd., 29210.

Florence. Florence Air and Missile Museum, U. S. Hwy. 301, North Airport Entrance, 29503.

Fort Jackson. Fort Jackson Museum, Bldg. 4442, 29207.

Greenwood. The Museum, Phoenix St., 29646.

Hampton. Hampton County Historical Society Museum, 1st West, 29924.

Mt. Pleasant. Patriot's Point Naval and Maritime Museum, P.O.Box 986, 29464.

Parris Island. Parris Island Museum, 29905.

Pendleton. Pendleton District Historical and Recreational Commission, 125 E. Queen St., 29670.

Spartanburg. Spartanburg County Regional Museum, 501 Otis Blvd. 29302.

Sullivan's Island. Ft. Sumter National Monument, Middle St., 29482.

Union. Union County Historical Museum, Drawer 220, 29379.

Winnsboro. Fairfield County Museum, South Congress St., 29180.

SOUTH DAKOTA

Chamberlain. Old West Museum, West Hwy. 16, 57325.

Deadwood. Adams Memorial Hall Museum, 54 Sherman, 57732.

Ft. Meade. Old Ft. Meade Museum, P.O. Box 134, 57741.

Lake City. Ft. Sisseton State Park Visitors Center, 57247.

Pierre. Robinson Museum, Memorial Bldg., 57501.

Rapid City. Horseless Carriage Museum, Box 2933, 57708.

Sturgis. Old Ft. Meade Museum and Historic Research Association, 1113 Poisley Terrace, 57785.

Watertown. Kampeska Heritage Museum, 27 First Ave. S.E., 57201.

TENNESSEE

Dover. Ft. Donelson National Military Park, Hwy. 79, 37058.

Franklin. Carter House, 1140 Columbia Ave., 37064.

Knoxville. Confederate Memorial Hall "Bleak House," 3148 Kingston Pike, 37919.

Murfreesboro. Stones River National Battlefield, Rte. 10, Box 401, Old Nashville Hwy., 37130.

Nashville. Association for the Preservation of Tennessee Antiquities, 110 Leake Ave., 37205.

Tennessee State Museum, War Memorial Bldg., 37219.

Shiloh. Shiloh National Military Park and Cemetery, 38376.

TEXAS

Austin. Texas National Guard Historical Center, Camp Mabry, 78756.

Texas State Library, 1201 Brazos St., 78711.

Cameron. Milan County Historical Museum, P.O. Box 966, 76520.

Canyon. Panhandle-Plains Historical Museum, 2401 Fourth Ave., 79015.

Cleburne. Layland Museum, 201 N. Caddo, 76031.

Del Rio. Whitehead Memorial Museum, 1308 S. Main St., 78840.

Denton. North Texas State University Historical Collection, West Mulberry and Ave. A, 76203.

Egypt. Northington-Heard Memorial Museum, Box 277, 77436.

El Paso. El Paso Museum of History, 12901 Gateway West, 79927.

Falfurrias. The Heritage Museum of Falfurrias, Inc., Box 86, 78355.

Ft. Bliss. Ft. Bliss Replica Museum, Pleasonton & Sheridan Rds. 79916.

Ft. Davis. Ft. Davis National Historic Site, Box 1456, 79734.

Ft. Hood. Second Armored Division Museum, 76546.

Ft. Worth. Ft. Worth Museum of Science and History, 1501 Montgomery St., 76107.

Museum of Aviation Group, 300 North Spur 341, 76108.

Pate Museum of Transportation, P.O. Box 711, 76101.

Fredericksburg. The Admiral Nimitz Center, 328 E. Main St., 78624.

Galveston. Galveston County Historical Museum, 2219 Market St., 77553.

Harlingen. Confederate Air Force, Rebel Field, 78550.

Hillsboro. Confederate Research Center and Gun Museum, P.O. Box 619, 76645.

Kingsville. John E. Conner Museum, Texas A&I University, 78363.

La Porte. Battleship Texas, 3527 Battleground Rd., 77571.

Livingston. Polk County Memorial Museum, 601 W. Church, P.O.Drawer 511, 77351.

Marshall. Harrison County Historical Museum, Old Courthouse, Peter Whetstone Square, 75670.

Nacogdoches. Stone Fort Museum, Stephen F. Austin University, 75962.

New Braunfels. Sophienburg Museum, 401 W. Coll St., 78130.

Newcastle. Ft. Belknap Museum and Archives, Box 68, 76372.

Ozona. Crockett County Museum, P.O.Drawer B, Courthouse Annex, 76943.

Panhandle. Carson County Square House Museum, 5th and Elsie Sts., 79068.

San Angelo. Ft. Concho National Historic Landmark, 213 East Ave. D, 76903.

San Antonio. The Alamo, Alamo Plaza, 78205.

Ft. Sam Houston Military Museum, Bldg. 123, 78234.

History and Traditions Museum, Military Training Center/LGH, Lackland Air Force Base, 78236.

Lone Star Brewing Company, Buckhorn Hall of Horns, Fins, Feathers and Boar's Nest, 600 Lone Star Blvd., 78297.

Memorial Bldg., 3805 Broadway, 78209.

San Jose Mission, 6539 San Jose Dr., 78214.

Sunset. Sunset Trading Post-Old West Museum, Rte. 1, 76270.

Teague. Burlington-Rock Island Railroad Museum, 218 Elm St., 75860.

Tyler. Goodman Museum, 624 N. Broadway, 75702.

Uvalde. Garner Memorial Museum, 333 N. Park St., 78801.

Van Horn. Culberson County Historical Museum, Main St., 79855.

Waco. Texas Ranger Hall of Fame and Museum, Ft. Fisher Park, 76703.

UTAH

Farmington. Pioneer Village, Box N, 84025.

Ft. Douglas. Ft. Douglas Museum, Bldg. 32, 84113.

Ft. Duchesne. Ute Tribal Museum, Hwy. 40, Bottle Hollow Resort, 84026.

Ogden. Ogden Union Station Museums, Rm. 212, Union Station, 25th & Wall Ave., 84401.

VERMONT
Brownington. The Old Stone House, 05860.
Hubbardton. Hubbardton Battlefield Museum, 05749.
Montpelier. Vermont Museum, Pavilion Bldg., 05602.
Northfield. Norwich University Museum, on Rte. 12 (Main St.) ¼ mile north of Jct. 12&12A, 05663.
Reading. Reading Historical Society, 05062.
Shelburne. Shelburne Museum, Inc., U.S. Rte. 7, 05482.
Windsor. Old Constitution House, North Main St., 05089.
Winooski. Vermont National Guard Museum, Bldg. 25, Camp Johnson, 05405.

VIRGINIA
Alexandria. Ft. Ward Museum and Park, 4301 W. Braddock Rd., 22304.
Appomattox. Appomattox Court House National Historical Park, P.O. Box 218, 24522.
Bridgewater. Reuel B. Pritchett Museum, Bridgewater College, East College St., 22812.
Charles City. Berkeley Plantation, Rte. 5, 23030.
Ft. Belvoir. U. S. Army Engineer Museum, Bldg. 1000, 16th St. and Belvoir Rd., 22060.
Ft. Eustis. U. S. Army Transportation Museum, 23604.
Ft. Lee. U. S. Army Quartermaster Corps Museum, A Ave. at 22nd St., 23801.
Ft. Monroe. Casemate Museum, Box 341, 23651.
Ft. Myer. 3rd U. S. Infantry (The Old Guard) Museum, 22211.
Fredericksburg. Fredericksburg National Military Park, 1301 Lafayette Blvd., 22401.
Front Royal. Warren Rifles Confederate Museum, 95 Chester St., 22630.
Glen Allen. Meadow Farm Museum, Mountain & Courtney Rds., 23060.
Lexington. George C. Marshall Library and Museum, Virginia Military Institute, 24450.
  Stonewall Jackson House, 8 E. Washington St., 24450.
  VMI Museum, Jackson Memorial Hall, Virginia Military Institute, Jackson Memorial Hall, 24450.
Manassas. Manassas National Battlefield Park, P.O. Box 1830, 22110.
New Market. New Market Battlefield Park, P.O. Box 1864, 22844.
Newport News. The Mariners, Museum Dr., 23606.
  The War Memorial Museum of Virginia, 9285 Warwick Blvd., Huntington Park, 23607.
Norfolk. General Douglas MacArthur Memorial, MacArthur Square, 23510.
  Naval Amphibious Museum, NAB Little Creek, 23521.
Petersburg. Centre Hill Mansion Museum, Franklin St., 23803.
  Petersburg National Battlefield, P.O. Box 549, 23803.
  Siege Museum, c/o Dept. of Tourism, 15 W. Bank St., 23803.
Portsmouth. Portsmouth Naval Museum, 2 High St., 23705.
Quantico. United States Marine Corps Aviation Museum, Brown Field, Marine Corps Base, 22134.
Richmond. Museum of the Confederacy, 1201 E. Clay St., 23219.
  Richmond National Battlefield Park, 3215 E. Broad St., 23223.
  Virginia Historical Society, 428 North Blvd., 23221.
Spotsylvania County. Spotsylvania Historical Associations, Inc., P.O. Box 64, 22553.
Williamsburg. Colonial Williamsburg, Goodwin Bldg., 23185.
Winchester. Winchester-Frederick County Historical Society, Inc., Box 58, 22601.
Yorktown. Colonial National Historical Park, P.O. Box 210, 23690.

WASHINGTON
Anacortes. Anacortes Museum, 1305 8th, 98221.
Bremerton. Naval Shipyard Museum, Washington State Ferry Terminal Bldg., 98310.
Brewster. Ft. Okanogan Interpretive Center, Bridgeport State Park, 98812.
Chinook. Fort Columbia State Park, P.O. Box 172, 98614.
Coulee Dam. Ft. Spokane Museum, Box 37, 99116.
Coupeville. Ft. Casey Coastal Defense Heritage Site, Ft. Casey State Park, 12805 Ft. Casey Rd., 98239.
Davenport. Ft. Spokane, Coulee Dam National Recreation Center, Star Rt., Box 30, 99122.
  Lincoln County Historical Museum, P.O. Box 585, 99122.
Ft. Lewis. Ft. Lewis Military Museum, Bldg. T4320, 98433.
Goldendale. Maryhill Museum of Fine Arts, 98620.
Grandview. Ray E. Powell Museum, 313 Division, 98930.
Ilwaco. Ft. Canby State Park, 98624.
Kelso. Cowlitz County Historical Museum, 5th & Allen St., 98626.
Keyport. Naval Museum of Undersea Warfare, Naval Undersea Warfare Engineering Station, 98435.

North Bend. Snoqualmie Valley Historical Museum, 222 North Bend Blvd., 98045.
Port Townsend. The Coast Artillery Museum at Ft. Worden, 98368.
  Jefferson County Historical Society, City Hall, 98368.
Prosser. Benton County Museum & Historical Society, Inc., P.O.Box 591, 99350.
Seattle. Museum of History and Industry, 2161 E. Hamlin St., 98112.
Spokane. Ft. Wright Historical Museum, W. 4000 Randolph Rd., 99204.
Tacoma. Ft. Nisqually Museum, Point Defiance Park, 98407.
Vancouver. Ft. Vancouver National Historic Site, 98661.
Walla Walla. Ft. Walla Walla Museum Complex, P.O.Box 1616, 99362.
White Swan. Ft. Simcoe Interpretive Center, Rte. 1, Box 39, 98952.
Yakima. Yakima Valley Museum and Historical Assocation, 2105 Tieton Dr., 98902.

WEST VIRGINIA
Ansted. Hawks Nest State Park, P.O.Box 417, 25812.
Charleston. West Virginia Dept. of Culture & History, Capitol Complex, 25305.
Harpers Ferry. Harpers Ferry National Historical Park, Shenandoah St., 25425.
Huntington. The Huntington Galleries, Inc., 2033 McCoy Rd., 25701.
Lewisburg. Ft. Savannah Inn, 204 N. Jefferson, 24901.
Weston. Jackson's Mill Museum, 26452.
Wheeling. Oglebay Institute-Mansion Museum, Oglebay Park, 26003.

WISCONSIN
Ashland. Ashland Museum, 500 W. 2nd St., 54806.
Beloit. Bartlett Memorial Historical Museum, 2149 St. Lawrence Ave., 53511.
Green Bay. Neville Public Museum, 129 S. Jefferson, 54301.
Hatfield. Vi Teeples' Thunderbird Museum, P.O. Merrillan, 54754.
Janesville. Rock County Historical Society, 10 S. High St., 53545.
  The Tallman Restorations, 440 N. Jackson St., 53545.
Kenosha. Kenosha County Historical Museum, 6300 3rd Ave., 53140.
King. Wisconsin Veterans Museum, Veterans Home, 54946.
Madison. Grand Army of the Republic Memorial Hall Museum, State Capitol, 419 N. 53702.
  State Historical Society of Wisconsin, 816 State St., 53706.
Milton. Milton House Museum, Hwy. 26 & 59, 53563.
Milwaukee. Milwaukee County Historical Society, 910 N. Third St., 53203.
  Milwaukee Public Museum, 800 W. Wells St., 53233.
New Glarus. Chalet of the Golden Fleece, 618 2nd St., 53574.
New Holstein. New Holstein Historical Society, 2025 Randolph Ave., 53061.
Oshkosh. Oshkosh Public Museum, 1331 Algoma Blvd., 54901.
Portage. Ft. Winnebago Surgeon's Quarters, R. R. 1, 53901.
Prairie du Chien. Villa Louis and Museum, Villa Rd. and Boilvin, 53821.
Racine. Racine County Historical Museum, Inc., 701 St. Main St., 53403.
River Falls. Area Research Center, Chalmer Davee Library, University of Wisconsin, 54022.
Stoughton. Stoughton Historical Society, 324 S. Page St., 53589.
Superior. Douglas County Historical Museum, 906 E. 2nd St., 54880.
Waupaca. Hutchinson House, P.O. Box 173, 54981.

WYOMING
Buffalo. Johnson County, Jim Gatchell Memorial Museum, 10 Fort St., 82834.
Casper. Ft. Caspar Museum and Historic Site, 14 Fort Caspar Rd., 82601.
Cheyenne. Warren Military Museum, Bldg. 210, Francis E. Warren Air Force Base, 82001.
  Wyoming State Museum, Barrett Bldg., 22nd & Central Ave., 82002.
Cody. Buffalo Bill Historical Center, Box 1020, 82414.
Douglas. Ft. Fetterman State Museum, 82366.
Ft. Laramie. Ft. Laramie National Historic Site, 82212.
Ft. Bridger. Ft. Bridger State Museum, 82933.
Gillette. Rockpile Museum, Hwy. 14-16 West Gillette, 82716.
Green River. Sweetwater County Museum, 50 W. Falming Gorge Way, 82395.
Guernsey. Guernsey State Museum, Guernsey State Park, 82214.
Jackson. Jackson Hole Historical Museum, 101 N. Glenwood, 83001.
Lander. Pioneer Museum, 630 Lincoln St., 82520.
Riverton. Riverton Museum, 700 E. Park, 82501.

PUERTO RICO
San Juan. Museum of Military and Naval History, Ft. San Jeronimo beside Caribe Hilton Hotel, 00905.

VIRGIN ISLANDS
Christiansted. Fort Christiansvaern, P.O.Box 160, 00820.

CANADA

ALBERTA

Calgary. Princess Patricia's Canadian Light Infantry Regimental Museum, Currie Barracks, T3E 1T8.
Drumheller. Homestead Antique Museum, P.O. Box 700, T0J 0Y0.
Ft. Macleod. Ft. Macleod Historical Association, Box 776, T0L 0Z0.
Wetaskiwin. Reynolds Museum, Hwy. 2A, Box 6780, T9A 2G4.

BRITISH COLUMBIA

Ft. Langley. Langley Centennial Museum & National Exhibition Centre, Mavis & King Sts., V0X 1J0.
Kamloops. Kamloops Museum, 207 Seymour, V2C 2E7.
New Westminister. The Regimental Museum/The Armory, 530 Queens Ave., V3L 1K3.
Powell River. Powell River Historical Museum Association, Museum Bldg., Box 42, V8A 425.
Prince Rupert. Museum of Northern British Columbia, Corner McBride St. and First Ave., V8J 3S1.
Vancouver. Pacific National Exhibition, British Columbia Pavilion, Exhibition Park, V5K 4A9.
  Regimental Museum, Seaforth Highlanders of Canada, 1650 Burrard St., V6J 3G4.
Vedder Crossing. Canadian Military Engineers Museum, Canadian Forces School of Military Engineering, Local 263, MP0 612, C.F.B. Chilliwack, V0X 2E0.
Victoria. Ft. Rodd Hill National Historic Park, 604 Ft. Rodd Hill Rd., V9C1B5.
  Maritime Museum of British Columbia, 28-30 Bastion Sq., V8W 1H9.

MANITOBA

Shilo. Royal Canadian Artillery Museum, Canadian Forces Base, R0K 2A0.
Winnipeg. Royal Winnipeg Rifles Museum, 969 St. Mathews Ave., R2C 1X8.

NEW BRUNSWICK

Aulac. Ft. Beausejour National Historic Park, E0A 3C0.
Oromocto. Canadian Forces Base Gagetown Museum, CFB Gagetown, E0G 1P0.
St. Andrews. Block House Historic Site and Centennial Park, 40 Town Hall, E0G 2X0.
St. John. Ft. Howe Blockhouse, P.O. Box 1971, E2L 4L1.
  The New Brunswick Museum, 277 Douglas Ave., E2K 1E5.

NEWFOUNDLAND

Placentia. Castle Hill National Historic Park, P.O. Box 10, Jerseyside, A0B 2G0.
St. John's. Cape Spear National Historic Park, P.O. Box 5879.

NOVA SCOTIA

Annapolis Royal. Ft. Anne National Historic Park, St. George St., B0S 1A0.
Halifax. Halifax Citadel National Historic Park, P.O. Box 1480, North Postal Station, B3K 5H7.
Halifax South. The Army Museum-Halifax Citadel, P.O. Box 3666, B3J 3K6.
Louisbourg. Fortress of Louisbourg National Historic Park, P.O. Box 160, B0A 1M0.

ONTARIO

Alliston. South Simcoe Pioneer Museum, Municipal Office, L0M 1A0.
Amherstburg. Ft. Malden National Historic Park, Laird Ave., Box 38, N9V 2Z2.
Borden. Base Borden Military Museum and Worthington Park, Canadian Forces Base, L0M 1C0.
Dundas. Dundas Historical Society Museum, 139 Park St., L9H 5G1.

Dunvegan. Glengarry Pioneer Museum, P.O. Box 5, K0C 1JC.
Gananoque. Gananoque Historical Museum, 10 King St., E, K7G 2T7.
Golden Lake. Algonquin Museum, Via Algonquin Park, K0J 1X0.
Guelph. Colonel John McCrae Birthplace Society, 102 Water St., N1H 6L3.
Kingston. Murney Tower Museum, P.O. Box 54, K7L 4V6.
  Old Ft. Henry, Box 213, K7L 4V8.
  Royal Military College of Canada Museum, K7L 2W3.
London. London Historical Museums, 325 Queens Ave., N6B 3L7.
  The Royal Canadian Regiment Museum, Wolseley Hall, Wolseley Barracks, N5Y 4T7.
Merrickville. Blockhouse Museum, R.R.4, P.O. Box 294, K0G 1N0.
Milton. Halton Museum, R.R.3, L9T 2X7.
Niagara-on-the-Lake. Ft. George National Historic Park, P.O. Box 787, L0S 1J0.
Ottawa. Canadian War Museum, 330 Sussex Dr., K1A 0M8.
  Regimental Museum, Governor General's Foot Guards, Drill Hall, Cartier Sq., K1P 5R3.
Penetanguishene. Historic Naval and Military Establishments, P.O. Box 160, Midland L4R 4K8.
Prescott. Ft. Wellington National Historic Park, 400 Dibble St., E., K0E 1T0.
St. Catharines. St. Catharines Historical Museum, 343 Merritt St., L2T 1K7.
Sutton. Eldon Hall, Sibbald Memorial Museum, Sibbald Point Park, R.R. 2 L0E 1R0.
Toronto. Black Creek Pioneer Village, 1000 Murray Ross Pkwy., M3N 1S4.
  Fort York Garrison Rd. at Fleet and Strachan Ave., M6K 3C3.
  Marine Museum of Upper Canada, Exhibition Place, M6K 3C3.
  Toronto Historical Board, Exhibition Park, M6K 3C3.
Windsor. Hiram Walker Historical Museum, 254 Pitt St. W., N9A 5L5.

PRINCE EDWARD ISLAND

Rocky Point. Ft. Amherst National Historic Park, C0A 1H0.

QUEBEC

Beebe. Stanstead County Historical Society, 110 Main St.
Chambly. Ft. Chambly National and Historic Parks, 2 Richelieu St., J3L 2B9.
Cookshire. Compton County Historical and Museum Society, J0B 1M0.
Coteau-du-Lac. Ft. Coteau-du-Lac.
Ile-aux-Noix. Ft. Lennox National Historic Park, St. Paul.
Knowlton. Brome County Historical Museum, P.O. Box 690, J0E 1V0.
Montreal. The Saint Helen's Island Museum, The Fort, H3C 2W9.
  Royal Canadian Ordnance Corps Museum, 6560 Hochelaga St., H3C 3H7.
Rigaud. Musee du College Bourget, 65 rue St. Pierre, J0P 1P0.

SASKATCHEWAN

Batoche. Batoche National Historic Site, S0M 0E0.
Battleford. Battleford National Historic Park, Box 70, S0M 0E0.
Regina. Royal Canadian Mounted Police Museum, Box 6500, S4P 3J7.
Riverhurst. F.T. Hill Museum, S0H 3P0.
Weyburn. Soo Line Historical Museum, 411 Industrial Lane, S.E.

Where to Hunt What in the World:
A Guide for All Who Hunt with Gun or Camera

NORTH AMERICA

Alaska
Deer, moose, caribou, mountain goat, mountain sheep, musk ox, bison, brown and grizzly bear, black bear, polar bear, wolf, wolverine, mink, marten, weasel, lynx, land otter, red, blue and white fox, muskrat, beaver, squirrel, coyote, grouse, ptarmigan, hare, rabbit, walrus, sea lion, porpoise, beluga, seal and waterfowl.

Canada
ALBERTA: Buffalo, moose, white-tailed deer, Rocky Mountain mule deer, elk, bighorn sheep, mountain goat, grizzly and black bear, mallard, pintail, blue-winged and green-winged teal, gadwall, baldpate and shoveller, Canadian goose, snow goose and white-front goose, sharp-tailed grouse, Hungarian partridge, blue grouse, Franklin grouse and ptarmigan.

BRITISH COLUMBIA: Moose, wapiti, caribou, wolf, mountain sheep, mountain goat, mule deer, white-tailed deer, grizzly and black bear, ptarmigan, prairie chicken, grouse, duck, goose, snipe, pheasant, partridge and quail.

MANITOBA: Moose, white-tailed deer, mule deer, bear, wolf, small game and wildfowl.

NEW BRUNSWICK: White-tailed deer, black bear, woodcock, partridge, ruffed grouse, duck and goose.

NEWFOUNDLAND: Moose, caribou, black bear, rabbit, snipe, wild goose and wild duck.

NORTHWEST TERRITORIES: Seal, moose, caribou, elk, grizzly and black bear, mountain sheep and mountain goat, upland game birds and waterfowl.

NOVA SCOTIA: Moose, white-tailed deer, black bear, wildcat, fox, raccoon, rabbit, woodcock, snipe, black duck, grouse, partridge, pheasant and Canadian wild goose.

ONTARIO: Deer, wolf, bear, moose, grouse, pheasant, woodcock, Hungarian partridge, quail, European hare, snowshoe and cottontail rabbits, blue goose, snow goose, Canada goose, pintail and black duck.

PRINCE EDWARD ISLAND: Hungarian partridge, ruffed grouse, ring-necked pheasant, wild duck and goose.

QUEBEC: Deer, black bear, wolf, wild duck, goose and partridge.

SASKATCHEWAN: Moose, black bear, mallard and pintail, Canadian and white-front goose, sharp-tailed grouse, Hungarian partridge, rough, spruce and sage grouse, willow ptarmigan, ring-necked pheasant, whitetail and mule deer.

YUKON TERRITORY: Mountain sheep, mountain goat, moose, barrenground and Osborn caribou, grizzly and black bear, grouse, ptarmigan, waterfowl.

THE CARIBBEAN AND THE BAHAMAS

Antigua
Deer (on the island of Barbuda).

Bahamas
Wild hog (on the islands of Abaco, Andros and Inagua).

Dominica
Wild hog, agouti and manique.

Martinique
Turtle dove, wood pigeon, small heron and a few species of North American duck.

Puerto Rico
Waterfowl, dove and pigeon.

Trinidad and Tobago
Agouti, armadillo, alligator, deer, lappe, opossum, mongoose, wild hog, squirrel, duck, crane, heron, the scarlet ibis and parrot.

U.S. Virgin Islands
ST. CROIX: Deer, dove and pigeon.

MEXICO AND CENTRAL AMERICA

British Honduras
Jaguar, puma, tapir, deer, antelope, ocelot, wild pig, monkey, iguana, alligator, crane and snakes.

Costa Rica
Deer, wild pig, saino, tapir, puma, jaguar, tepezquintle, rabbit, fox, ocelot, raccoon, wild goat, pizote, muskrat, ferret, otter, opossum, weasel, wild turkey, duck, quail, snipe, wild hen, band-tailed pigeon and the purple dove.

Guatemala
Jaguar, puma, javelina, deer, wild pig, wild turkey, monkey, alligator, quail, white-wing pigeon, dove, parrot and turtle.

Honduras
Jaguar, puma, wild pig, whitetail deer, monkey, wild turkey, alligator, quail, white-winged pigeon, parrot and waterfowl.

Mexico
Agouti, armadillo, bobcat, ring-tailed cat, chachalaca, coati, coyote, crane, curassow, brocket deer, whitetail deer, mule deer, dove, duck, gray fox, kit fox, goose grison, crested guan, iguana, jackrabbit, jaguar, jaguarundi, kinkajou, margay, ocelot, opossum, paca, collared peccary, white-lipped peccary, pigeon, upland plover, puma, quail, rabbit, raccoon, desert sheep, snipe, squirrel, tayra, tinamou, ocellated turkey, wild turkey, weasel and wolf.

Panama
Jaguar, black jaguar, ocelot, mangle cat, paca, agouti, deer, tapir, peccary, white-lipped peccary, wild turkey, alligator, iguana, pigeon, dove, grouse and duck.

SOUTH AMERICA

Bolivia
Jaguar, ocelot, puma, anteater, alligator, anaconda python, tapir, deer, wild boar, vicuña, guanaco, wolf, American tiger, bear and game birds.

Brazil
Tapir, otter, water buffalo, wild dog, wild pig, capivara, cotia, wildcat, arara, toucan, mutum, parrot, snowy owl, ocelot, alligator, wolf, painted jaguar, black jaguar, paca, sloth, fox, turtle, anteater, deer, stork, crane, flamingo, duck, pheasant, partridge and snake.

Colombia
Jaguar, puma, tapir, wild boar, deer, water hog, ape, alligator, anaconda, anteater, antelope, wild duck and wild turkey.

Guyana
Jaguar, puma, alligator, capybara, white-lipped peccary, monkey, parrot, lizard, several large bush fowl and snake.

Surinam
Deer, jaguar, tapir, alligator, wild boar, ocelot, black jaguar, puma, jungle hare, water buffalo, monkey, wild fox, otter, duck, parrot and tropical birds.

EUROPE

Austria
Roebuck, stag, chamois, red deer, moufflon, snipe, mountain and blackcock, pheasant, partridge, marmot, wild boar, fox, polecat, wild rabbit, weasel, sparrow hawk and heron.

Belgium
Stag, wild boar, ferret, badger, fox, partridge, pheasant, hare and rabbit.

Britain and Ireland
England and Wales: stag, hind, grouse and rabbit. Scotland: stag, hind, and grouse. Ireland: stag, hind, grouse, snipe, plover, duck, goose, pheasant and partridge.

Bulgaria
Stag, deer, fallow deer, wild boar, pheasant, hare, partridge and quail.

Czechoslovakia
Deer, fallow deer, moufflon, roe deer, wild boar, chamois, hare, wild rabbit, lynx, fox, bear, wood grouse, black grouse, the rare bustard, pheasant, partridge, snipe, lark.

Denmark
Hare, pheasant, fox.

Finland
Moose, lynx, hare, wolverine, wood grouse, heath grouse, ruffed grouse, white ptarmigan, wild duck.

France
Stag, deer, wild boar, wild hare, pheasant, quail, wild duck, moufflon, chamois, various partridge, plover, snipe, lark.

Germany
Red deer, fallow and sika deer, roe deer, wild boar, moufflon, chamois, marmot, hare, badger, otter, capercailzie, blackcock, hazel grouse, partridge, pheasant, wild pigeon, woodcock, snipe, wild goose, wild duck, buzzard and sea gull.

Hungary
Red deer, roe deer, fallow deer, wild pig, moufflon, hare, pheasant, wild bustard, wild duck and goose.

Iceland
Arctic ptarmigan, wild goose, wild duck, reindeer and sea birds.

Norway
Moose, reindeer, stag, polar bear, roe deer, fallow deer, capercailzie, black grouse, hazel grouse, ptarmigan, partridge, pheasant, snipe, woodcock, wild duck, wild goose, hare, fox and seal.

Poland
Red deer, fallow deer, roe deer, wild boar, lynx, wolf, fox, hare, rabbit, capercailzie, blackcock, hazelcock, pheasant, partridge, woodcock, ruff, snipe, wild duck and wild goose.

Portugal
Hare, turtledove, quail, snipe, wood pigeon, duck, woodcock, partridge, bustard and thrush.

Soviet Union
Stag, roebuck and wild boar.

Spain
Deer, buck, roebuck, wild goat, wild pig, bear, partridge, quail, turtledove, pheasant, grouse, wild rabbit, wild hare, dove, wild duck and goose.

Sweden
Moose, elk, stag, hare, woodcock, partridge, pheasant, duck.

Switzerland
Chamois, marmot, stag, buck, hare, wild duck, fox, badger, wild boar, pheasant, partridge, ibex, eagle, mountain cock and blackcock.

Yugoslavia
Stag, roebuck, chamois, bear, wild boar, hare, wood grouse, blackcock, pheasant, field and rock partridge, quail, snipe, hazel grouse, wild duck, wild goose, pigeon, turtledove.

ASIA

India
Tiger, panther, sambar, chital, blue bull, chinkara, black buck, wild pig, gaur, wild buffalo, wild bear, sloth bear, barking deer, four-horned deer, crocodile, pheasant, partridge, pigeon, quail, duck, goose and dozens of other bird species.

Indonesia
Barking deer, Java deer, wild pig, tiger, water buffalo, panther, elephant, dwarf deer, monkey, orangutan, crocodile, giant lizard, parrot, bird of paradise, cassowary, waterfowl and reptiles.

Iran
Red, fallow, spotted and roe deer, wild ass, gazelle, tiger, cheetah, wild sheep, wild goat, bear, leopard, wildcat, wolf, fox, jackal, hyena, wild boar, lynx, porcupine, pheasant, francolin, chukker partridge, all European waterfowl, sand grouse, wild pigeon, woodcock, snow partridge and quail.

Iraq
Wild boar, desert rabbit and duck.

Japan

Bear, brown bear, wild boar, deer, fox, racoon dog, badger, common and giant flying squirrel, marten, nutria, chipmunk, mink, hare, white-fronted and eastern bean goose, smew, three types of snipe, two types of sparrow, two types of crow, raven, woodcock, duck, pheasant, hazel grouse, quail, bamboo partridge, heron, coot and moor hen.

Jordan

Wild boar, ibex, gazelle, hare, lynx, porcupine, bustard, common partridge, sand partridge, rock dove, lark, sand grouse, coot, snipe, crane, quail, duck and goose.

Malaysia and Singapore

Tiger, leopard, wild boar and mouse deer.

Nepal

Tiger rhino, panther, black leopard, snow leopard, clouded leopard, sambar, swamp deer, musk deer, spotted deer, hog deer, barking deer, black buck, four-horned antelope, blue bull, blue sheep, Himalayan tahr, wild boar, sloth bear, elephant, bison, crocodile, peacock, swan, pheasant, marsh mugger, peafowl, duck and goose.

The Philippines

Carabao or water buffalo, wild boar, deer, crocodile, mouse deer, squirrel, anteater, porcupine, bearcat, pheasant, snipe, plover, sandpiper, curlew, godwit, jacana, lemur, dove, pigeon, partridge, quail, coot, rail, hornbill and wild duck.

Turkey

Bear, wild boar, red deer, ibex, wolf, dove, quail, chukar partridge, duck, goose and woodcock.

AFRICA

Algeria

Redleg partridge, hare, pin-tailed grouse, quail, turtle-dove, gazelle, snipe, pigeon, wild boar, starling, sheep and wild duck.

Angola

Elephant, buffalo, rhino, lion, leopard, sassaby, cape eland, wildebeest, impala, reedbuck, rean Antelope, red Lechwe, duiker steinbock, oribi, greater kudu, sable antelope, situtunga, warthog, cape buffalo, crocodile, partridge and guinea-fowl.

Botswana

Elephant, sable, black-maned lion, buffalo, greater kudu, situtunga, red lechwe, gemsbok, springbok and red hartebeest.

Cameroon

Giant eland, dwarf buffalo, roan, topis, waterbuck, giraffe, elephant, hippo, gorilla and birds.

Central African Republic

Elephant, bongo, situtunga, giant forest hog, red dwarf buffalo, red river hog, gorilla, bushbuck, duiker and small antelope.

Chad

White oryx, gazelle, Barbary sheep, cheetah, ostrich, bat-eared fox, antbear, wild dog and many varieties of birds in the desert. Giant eland, elephant, buffalo, lion, leopard, greater kudu, hippo, giraffe, roan, waterbuck, hartebeest, warthog, crocodile, python, goose and duck elsewhere.

Ethiopia

Nubian ibex, mountain nyala, Nile lichwe, oryx beisa, Soemmering's gazelle, gerenuk, roan antelope, greater and lesser kudu, elephant, buffalo, bushbuck, giant forest hog, waterbuck, hartebeest, tiang, hippopotamus, warthog, lion, leopard and game birds.

Gabon

Elephant, hippo, buffalo, situnga, waterbuck, gorilla, panther, bush pig, bongo and chimpanzee.

Gambia

Hartebeest, duiker, Gambian oribi, waterbuck, cob, reedbuck, antelope, bushbuck, river hog, giraffe, eland, elephant, hippo, Congo-Senegambian buffalo, waterfowl and plumed birds.

Kenya

Lion, cheetah, elephant, leopard, buffalo, gerenuk, eland, reedbuck, bushbuck, waterbuck, gazelle, oryx, hartebeest, zebra, blue and red duiker, impala, warthog, rhinoceros, hippopotamus, giraffe, ostrich, bongo, monkey and birds.

Libya

Partridge and gazelle.

Morocco

Wild boar, hare, partridge, turtledove, ring dove, thrush, wildfowl and fowl of passage.

Mozambique

The greater kudu, pitch-black sable, nyala, giraffe, rhino, lion, leopard, eland, zebra, duiker, crocodile, hippo and birds.

Rhodesia

Buffalo, bushbuck, duiker, eland, elephant, impala, kudu, leopard, lion, sable, antelope, warthog, waterbuck, wildebeest, zebra and game birds.

Senegal

Lion, panther, hippo, lamantin, chimpanzee, elephant, giraffe, derby eland, gazelle, buffalo, bubale, wild sheep, ostrich, stork, flamingo, aigrette, heron, pelican, jabiru, marabou, duck, alligator, warthog and hare.

Somali Republic

47 different species are found here, ranging from the rabbit to the elephant. Other animals include the bat-eared fox, lynx, crocodile, zebra, guenon, klipspringer, leopard, lion, kudu, porcupine and mongoose.

South Africa

Elephant, giraffe, rhino, eland, gemsbok, buffalo, hippo, lion, chettah, impala, kudu, zebra, blue wildebeest, reedbuck and birds.

South-West Africa

Giant oryx, greater kudu, cape hartebeest, mountain zebra, springbok, duiker, wildebeest, ostrich, eland, steinbok, and birds.

Sudan

Bushbuck, bush pig, many species of cob, dik-dik, four kinds of duiker, eland, gazelle, hartebeest, hippo, ibex, klipspringer, kudu, leopard, giraffe, cheetah, rhino and zebra.

Tanzania

Buffalo, elephant, lion, giraffe, rhino, hippo, zebra, dik-dik, rock rabbit, topi, pygmy antelope, birds and waterfowl.

Tunisia

Wild boar, hare, partridge, turtledove, ring dove, thrush, wildfowl and fowl of passage.

Uganda

Lion, cheetah, elephant, leopard, buffalo, gerenuk, eland, reedbuck, bushbuck, waterbuck, gazelle, oryx, hartebeest, zebra, blue and red duiker, impala, warthog, rhinoceros, hippopotamus, giraffe, ostrich, bongo, monkey, mountain gorilla and birds.

Zambia

Lion, sable, puku, oribi, elephant, warthog, cheetah, hartebeest, zebra, crocodile, leopard, roan, lechwe, duiker, hippo, eland, impala and buffalo.

AUSTRALIA, NEW ZEALAND AND HAWAII

Australia

Kangaroo, fox, dingo, camel, deer, goat, hare, buffalo wild pig, wallaby, donkey, crocodile, snipe, wedge-tail eagle, duck and goose.

New Zealand

Wapiti (elk), red deer, fallow deer, Virginia deer, Japanese deer, rusa deer, sambar deer, chamois, tahr, wild boar, Australian wallaby, and ferrel goat.

Hawaii

Axis deer, wild goat, wild pig, wild sheep, ring-necked pheasant, Japanese blue pheasant, California quail, Japanese quail, lace-necked dove, barred dove, chukar partridge and wild pigeon.

Federal, State and Provincial Agencies Concerned with Wildlife Protection and Exploitation

FEDERAL GOVERNMENT

Bureau of Sport Fisheries and Wildlife
Fish and Wildlife Service
Department of the Interior
18th and C Streets, N.W.
Washington, D.C. 20240

Environmental Protection Agency
401 M Street, S.W.
Washington, D.C. 20460

Forest Service
Department of Agriculture Building E
Rosslyn Plaza
Rosslyn, Virginia 22209

Migratory Bird Conservation Commission
Department of the Interior Building
Washington, D.C. 20240

National Zoological Park
Smithsonian Institution
Adams Mill Rd.
Washington, D.C. 20009

STATE GOVERNMENTS

ALABAMA
Game and Fish Division
Department of Conservation and
   Natural Resources
64 North Union Street
Montgomery, Alabama 36104

ALASKA
Department of Fish and Game
Subport Building
Juneau, Alaska 99801

ARIZONA
Game and Fish Department
2222 West Greenway Road
Phoenix, Arizona 85023

ARKANSAS
Game and Fish Commission
Game and Fish Commission Building
Little Rock, Arkansas 72201

CALIFORNIA
Department of Fish and Game
Resources Agency
1416 Ninth Street
Sacramento, California 95814

Wildlife Conservation Board
Resources Agency
1416 Ninth Street
Sacramento, California 95814

COLORADO
Division of Wildlife
Department of Natural Resources
6060 Broadway
Denver, Colorado 80216

CONNECTICUT
Fish and Wildlife Unit
Department of Environmental Protection
State Office Building
165 Capitol Avenue
Hartford, Connecticut 06115

DELAWARE
Division of Fish and Wildlife
Department of Natural Resources and
   Environmental Control
Tatnall Building
Legislative Avenue and D Street
Dover, Delaware 19901

DISTRICT OF COLUMBIA
Department of Environmental Services
1875 Connecticut Avenue, N.W.
Washington, D.C. 20009

FLORIDA
Game and Fresh Water Fish
   Commission
Farris Bryant Building
620 South Meridian Street
Tallahassee, Florida 32304

GEORGIA
Game and Fish Division
Department of Natural Resources
270 Washington Street, S.W.
Atlanta, Georgia 30334

HAWAII
Fish and Game Division
Department of Land and Natural
   Resources
1179 Punchbowl Street
Honolulu, Hawaii 96813

IDAHO
Fish and Game Department
600 South Walnut
P.O. Box 25
Boise, Idaho 83707

ILLINOIS
Wildlife Resources Division
Department of Conservation
605 State Office Building
400 South Spring Street
Springfield, Illinois 62706

INDIANA
Fish and Wildlife Division
Department of Natural Resources
State Office Building
Indianapolis, Indiana 46204

Land, Forests, and Wildlife
Resources Advisory Council
Department of Natural Resources
State Office Building
Indianapolis, Indiana 46204

IOWA
Fish and Wildlife Division
Conservation Commission
300 Fourth Street
Des Moines, Iowa 50319

KANSAS
Forestry, Fish and Game Commission
P.O. Box 1028
Pratt, Kansas 67124

KENTUCKY
Department of Fish and Wildlife
   Resources
State Office Building Annex
Frankfort, Kentucky 40601

LOUISIANA
Game Division
Wildlife and Fisheries Commission
Box 44095
Capitol Station
Baton Rouge, Louisiana 70804

MAINE
Department of Inland Fisheries
   and Game
284 State Street
Augusta, Maine 04330

MARYLAND
Wildlife Administration
Department of Natural Resources
Tawes State Office Building
580 Taylor Avenue
Annapolis, Maryland 21401

MASSACHUSETTS
Department of Natural Resources
Leverett Saltonstall Building
100 Cambridge Street
Boston, Massachusetts 02202

MICHIGAN
Wildlife Division
Department of Natural Resources
Mason Building
Lansing, Michigan 48926

MINNESOTA
Game and Fish Division
Department of Natural Resources
Centennial Office Building
St. Paul, Minnesota 55155

MISSISSIPPI
Game and Fish Commission
Game and Fish Building
402 High Street
P.O. Box 451
Jackson, Mississippi 39205

MISSOURI
Game Division
Department of Conservation
2901 North Ten Mile Drive
P.O. Box 180
Jefferson City, Missouri 65101

MONTANA
Game Management Division
Department of Fish and Game
Helena, Montana 59601

NEBRASKA
Game and Parks Commission
2200 North 33rd Street
P.O. Box 30370
Lincoln, Nebraska 68503

NEVADA
Department of Fish and Game
P.O. Box 10678
Reno, Nevada 89510

NEW HAMPSHIRE
Game Management and Research
Division
Department of Fish and Game
34 Bridge Street
Concord, New Hampshire 03301

NEW JERSEY
Wildlife Management Bureau
Fish, Game and Shellfisheries Division
Department of Environmental
Protection
Labor and Industry Building
P.O. Box 1809
Trenton, New Jersey 08625

NEW MEXICO
Game Management Division
Department of Game and Fish
State Capitol
Sante Fe, New Mexico 87503

NEW YORK
Division of Fish and Wildlife
Department of Environmental
Conservation
50 Wolf Road
Albany, New York 12233

NORTH CAROLINA
Wildlife Resources Commission
Albermarle Building
325 North Salisbury Street
P.O. Box 27687
Raleigh, North Carolina 27611

NORTH DAKOTA
Department of Game and Fish
2121 Lovett Avenue
Bismarck, North Dakota 58505

OHIO
Wildlife Division
Department of Natural Resources
1500 Dublin Road
Columbus, Ohio 43224

OKLAHOMA
Department of Wildlife Conservation
1801 North Lincoln Boulevard
P.O. Box 53465
Oklahoma City, Okalahoma 73105

OREGON
Wildlife Commission
1634 Southwest Alder Street
P.O. Box 3503
Portland, Oregon 97208

PENNSYLVANIA
Game Commission
P.O. Box 1567
Harrisburg, Pennsylvania 17120

RHODE ISLAND
Division of Fish and Wildlife
Department of Natural Resources
83 Park Street
Providence, Rhode Island 02903

SOUTH CAROLINA
Department of Wildlife Resources
1015 Main Street
P.O. Box 167
Columbia, South Carolina 29202

SOUTH DAKOTA
Department of Game, Fish and Parks
State Office Building No. 1
Pierre, South Dakota 57501

TENNESSEE
Game and Fish Commission
Ellington Agricultural Center
P.O. Box 40747
Nashville, Tennessee 37220

TEXAS
Fish and Wildlife Division
Parks and Wildlife Department
John H. Reagan State Office Building
Austin, Texas 78701

UTAH
Division of Wildlife Resources
Department of Natural Resources
1596 West North Temple
Salt Lake City, Utah 84116

VERMONT
Department of Fish and Game
Agency of Environmental Conservation
Montpelier, Vermont 05602

VIRGINIA
Commission of Game and Inland Fisheries
4010 West Broad Street
P.O. Box 11104
Richmond, Virginia 23230

WASHINGTON
Department of Game
600 North Capitol Way
Olympia, Washington 98501

WEST VIRGINIA
Division of Wildlife Resources
Department of Natural Resources
1800 Washington Street, East
Charleston, West Virginia 25305

WISCONSIN
Game Management Bureau
Forestry, Wildlife and Recreation Division
Department of Natural Resources
P.O. Box 450
Madison, Wisconsin 53701

WYOMING
Game and Fish Division
P.O. Box 1589
Cheyenne, Wyoming 82001

CANADA

ALBERTA
Alberta Fish and Wildlife Division
Natural Resources Building
9833 - 109th Street
Edmonton, Alberta T5K 2E1

BRITISH COLUMBIA
Environment and Land Use
Commission
Parliament Building
Victoria, British Columbia V8V 1X4

BRITISH COLUMBIA
Department of Land, Forest and
Water Resources
Parliament Building
Victoria, British Columbia V8V 1X4

MANITOBA
Department of Lands, Forests and
Wildlife Resources
9-989 Century Street
Winnipeg, Manitoba R3H 0W4

NEWFOUNDLAND
Canadian Wildlife Service
Sir Humphrey Gilbert Building
Duckworth St.
St. John's, Newfoundland A1C 1G4

Department of Tourism
Wildlife Division
Confederation Building, 5th Floor
St. John's, Newfoundland

NORTHWEST TERRITORIES
Game Management Branch
Government of the Northwest
Territories
Yellowknife, Northwest Territories

NOVA SCOTIA
Department of Environment
Box 2107
Halifax, Nova Scotia

Department of Land and Forests
Dennis Building
Granville Street
Halifax, Nova Scotia

ONTARIO
Wildlife Branch
Ministry of Natural Resources
Whitney Block
Toronto, Ontario M7A 1W3

PRINCE EDWARD ISLAND
Department of Fish and Wildlife
Environmental Control Commission
Box 2000
Charlottetown, Prince Edward Island
C1A 7N8

Department of Environment and
Tourism
Box 2000
Charlottetown, Prince Edward Island
C1A 7N8

QUEBEC
Department of Tourism, Fish and
Game
150 St. Cyrille East - 15th Floor
Quebec, Quebec G1R 4Y3

SASKATCHEWAN
Department of Natural Resources
Fisheries and Wildlife Branch
Administrative Building
Regina, Saskatchewan S4S 0B1

YUKON TERRITORY
Game Branch
Government of the Yukon Territory
Whitehorse, Yukon Territory

Organizations and Associations of Interest to the Hunter and Shooter

AMATEUR TRAPSHOOTING ASSOCIATION
P.O. Box 246, West National Road   Phone: (513) 898-4368
Vandalia, Ohio 45377
David D. Bopp, General Manager
Founded 1923
Members: 100,000

Persons interested in the sport of trapshooting. Sanctions and determines rules governing shoots held by local, state, and provincial trapshooting associations: maintains permanent records for each shooter participating in 16 yard, handicap and doubles classifications in registered class competitions in state and provincial meets. Sponsor of Grand American Trapshooting Tournament held annually at Vandalia, Ohio, where historical exhibit and Hall of Fame are maintained. Publications: (1) *Trap and Field Magazine,* monthly; (2) *Official Trapshooting Rules,* annual; (3) *Trap and Field Official ATA Averages,* annual.

AMERICAN COMMITTEE FOR INTERNATIONAL CONSERVATION
c/o Natural Resources Defense   Phone: (202) 737-5000
Council, Inc.
917 15th Street, NW
Washington, D.C. 20005
Thomas B. Stoel, Secretary-Treasurer
Founded 1930
Members: 20

A council of organizations concerned with international conservation of species and habitats. Serves as a national committee of the International Union for Conservation of Nature and Natural Resources (IUCN). Convention/Meeting: Annual.

AMERICAN COON HUNTERS ASSOCIATION
Ingraham, Illinois 62434   Phone: (618) 752-6691
Floyd E. Butler, Secretary
Founded 1948
Members: 500

Persons interested in coon hunting. To promote and encourage the great sport of coon hunting; to seek to encourage proper practices of conservation of our raccoons and their natural habitats; to encourage the propagation of raccoons; to encourage liberation of live raccoons so that their numbers will increase rather than decrease; to promote and maintain friendly relations between landowners and coon hunters, everywhere; to seek to restore decency and fairness in the sale of coonhounds, placing the ability to hunt, strike, trail and tree raccoons and stay treed, above all other qualities; to discourage the breeding of worthless ones; and so far as possible, place the coon-hunting fraternity upon the highest standard of sportsmanship so that it can pass on to posterity a sport unsurpassed in wholesome recreation, enjoyment, pleasure and delight. Convention/Meeting: World Championship for coon hounds held each year in October. Meeting held first day of World Championship.

AMERICAN DEFENSE PREPAREDNESS ASSOCIATION
1700 North Moore Street, Suite 900   Phone: (703) 522-1820
Arlington, Virginia 22209
Henry A. Miley Jr., President
Founded 1919
Members: 33,000
Staff: 25
Local groups: 48

Manufacturers, military personnel and engineers interested in industrial preparedness for the national defense of the United States. Divisions: Air Armament; Artillery; Chemical-Biological; Combat and Surface Mobility; Electronics; Fire Control; Management; Materials; Missiles and Astronautics; Packaging, Handling, and Transportability; Research; Small Arms Systems; Standards and Metrology; Technical Documentation; Underwater Ordnance; Cost and Value Management. Publications: (1) *Common Defense,* monthly newsletter; (2) *National Defense,* bimonthly magazine. Formerly: American Ordnance Association. Absorbed: (1965) Armed Forces Chemical Association; (1974) Armed Forces Management Association. Convention/Meeting: Annual—always June in Washington, D.C.

AMERICAN INSTITUTE OF BIOLOGICAL SCIENCES
1401 Wilson Boulevard   Phone: (703) 527-6776
Arlington, Virginia 22209
Arthur Gentile, Ph.D., Executive Director
Founded 1947
Members: 7,500

Federation of professional biological associations and individuals with an interest in the life sciences. To promote unity and effectiveness of effort among persons engaged in biological research, teaching or application of biological data; to further the relationships of biological sciences to other sciences, the arts, and industries. Conducts symposium series; arranges for prominent biologists to lecture at small liberal arts colleges and radiation biologists to visit certain medical schools; provides advisory committees and other services to the Atomic Energy Commission, Office of Naval Research, and National Aeronautics and Space Administration. Created in 1966 on Office of Biological Education which serves as a clearing-house for information and conducts programs relative to several facets of biological education. Maintains placement service. Committees: Education; Environmental Biology; Exobiology; Hydrobiology; Microbiology; Oceanic Biology; Physiology; Public Responsibilities. Publications: Scientific Manpower Commission. Publications: (1) *Bio-Science,* monthly; (2) *Directory of Bioscience Departments and Facilities in the U.S. and Canada.* Convention/Meeting: Annual.

AMERICAN PHEASANT AND WATERFOWL SOCIETY
Route 1   Phone: (715) 238-7291
Granton, Wisconsin 54436
Lloyd Ure, Secretary-Treasurer
Founded 1936
Members: 1,750

Hobbyists, aviculturists, zoos. To perpetuate all varieties of upland game, ornamental birds and waterfowl. Publications: (1) *Magazine,* bimonthly; (2) *Membership Roster,* irregular. Formerly: (1962) American Pheasant Society. Convention/Meeting: Annual.

AMERICAN SOCIETY OF ARMS COLLECTORS
c/o Robert F. Rubendunst
6550 Baywood Lane   Phone: (513) 931-5689
Cincinnati, Ohio 45224
Robert F. Rubendunst, Sec.-Treas.
Founded 1953
Members: 240

Advanced arms collectors, researchers, authors and museum directors interested in antique arms and weapons. Membership is by invitation only. Engaged in research on arms and arms makers; exchanges specimens in collections and acquires new specimens. Bestows grants toward publication of educational material in the field of arms collecting. Maintains 100 volume library on arms and armour; presents awards. Committees: Investment; Nominating. Publications: (1) *Bulletin,* semiannual; (2) *Membership Directory,* annual; also publishes monographs. Affiliated with: National Rifle Association of America. Convention/Meeting: Semiannual.

ASSOCIATION FOR CONSERVATION INFORMATION
c/o Arch Andrews   Phone: (316) 672-6473
Colorado Division of Wildlife
6060 Broadway
Denver, Colorado 80216
Arch Andrews, President
Members: 68

Professional society of officials of state and provincial conservation agencies. Sponsors annual awards program whereby winners in various categories of conservation education work are selected by a panel of judges. Publications: (1) *Balance Wheel,* bimonthly; (2) *Yearbook.* Convention/Meeting: Annual—always June or July.

ASSOCIATION OF AMERICAN ROD AND GUN CLUBS, EUROPE

First Perscom APO MSD
New York, New York 09081
Lee E. Miethke, Executive Officer
Founded 1952
Members: 65,000
Local groups: 70

Federation of rod and gun clubs connected with American military forces in Europe, North Africa and the Near East. To encourage hunting, fishing, archery and allied sports; to promote the principles of sportmanship and game conservation. Maintains library on conservation and European wildlife, with majority of books in German language. Publication: *Rod and Gun,* monthly. Convention/Meeting: Annual.

ASSOCIATION OF FIREARM AND TOOL MARK EXAMINERS

7857 Esterel   Phone: (714) 453-0847
LaJolla, California 92037
Eugene Bell, Sec.
Founded 1969
Members: 400

Firearm and tool mark examiners of law enforcement agencies and private laboratories; private consultants; others in related industries. Purposes are: to provide a ready means of communication between members concerning industry products, laboratory procedures and techniques; to advance the profession. Conducts annual seminar. Bestows awards. Publications: *Journal,* quarterly; also publishes Glossary. Convention/Meeting: Annual.

ASSOCIATION OF MIDWEST FISH AND GAME COMMISSIONERS

Forestry, Fish and Game Commission   Phone: (316) 672-6473
Box 1028
Pratt, Kansas 67124
Fred Warders, Treasurer
Founded 1934
Members: 17

Fish and game commissions and directors of 15 midwestern states and 3 Canadian provinces. Promotes conservation of wildlife and outdoor recreation. Sponsors Midwest Pheasant Council; Dove Committee. Committees: Federal-State Relations; Federal Aid; Legislation; Federal Farm Program; Wetlands. Publication: *Proceedings,* annual. Convention/Meeting: Annual.

BIG THICKET ASSOCIATION

Box 198   Phone: (713) 274-2971
Saratoga, Texas 77585
Gene Feigelson, President
Founded 1964
Members: 1,350

Conservationists and others interested in preserving the wilderness area of southeast Texas known as the "Big Thicket." The Thicket is one of the major resting places along the Gulf Coast for migratory birds; in addition, at least 300 species live there permanently, many of them endangered species. Members of the Association have succeeded in having parts of the area declared a national biological preserve. Other activities include assisting scientists with research projects, operating a tourguide service, helping to maintain a Big Thicket Museum at Saratoga, Texas, a Big Thicket collection at the Lamar University Library in Beaumont, Tex., and coordinating programs aimed at preserving the area with other conservation organizations. Publications: *Big Thicket Bulletin,* quarterly; also publishes informational pamphlets, a bibliography and other materials. Convention/Meeting: Annual—always first Saturday in June, Saratoga, Tex.

BIG THICKET COORDINATING COMMITTEE

225 Jague St.   Phone (817) 387-8948
Denton, Texas 76201
Peter Gunter, Chairman
Founded 1968
Members: 42

Representatives from various conservation groups united to support legislation to protect the Big Thicket National Preserve in southeastern Texas; to try to obtain funds for land purchase for the Preserve; to manage the Preserve; to help create a Big Thicket State Park and recreation area; to endeavor in all ways possible to protect and preserve the Big Thicket region. Convention/Meeting: Annual.

BOONE AND CROCKETT CLUB

205 Patrick Street   Phone (703) 548-7727
Alexandria, Virginia 22314
William H. Nesbitt, Administrative Director
Founded 1887
Members: limited to 100 by charter

A tax-exempt non-profit organization that works for the conservation of the wild animal life of North America and, so far as possible, encourages appropriate governmental and private actions to further that end. Sponsors graduate-level wildlife research and workshops to produce comprehensive summaries of big game species. Publication: *Records of North American Big Game,* at approximate six-year intervals. Meetings: Annual—always in December in New York City.

BOUNTY INFORMATION SERVICE

c/o Stephens College Post Office   Phone: (314) 474-6967
Columbia, Missouri 65201
H. Charles Laun, Director
Founded 1965
Members: 2,000

Individuals interested in the removal of wildlife bounties in the U.S. and Canada. Organizes bounty removal programs, publishes literature on the bounty system and methods for removal, compiles yearly summary of bounties in North America and executes individual studies of areas (i.e. cougar bounty in Texas). Maintains library. Publications: *Bounty News,* 1-3/year; has also published *Guide for the Removal of Bounties* and *A Decade of Bounties.* Convention/Meeting: Annual or Biennial.

BRIGADE OF THE AMERICAN REVOLUTION

The New Windsor Cantonment   Phone: (914) 561-1765
P.O. Box 207
Vails Gate, New York 12584
George Woodbridge, Commander
Founded 1962
Members: 1000
Staff: 9
Units: 80

The men and women of the Brigade are dedicated to the authentic re-creation of soldier life during the period of the American Revolution. The Brigade fosters and encourages the exhibition and display of crafts and skills of the 18th century in general and specifically those closely relating to the life of the armies of the time. Each member regiment assumes the identity and organization of an original unit known to have participated in the Revolutionary War. All clothing, arms and equipment are researched for historical accuracy and no substitutions or modern materials are permitted. Various performances of a pageant-like nature are staged, usually at some historic site, involving military drills and exercises and demonstrations of camp life and craft skills designed to educate and entertain. Publications: Quarterly journal, *The Brigade Dispatch;* Monthly newsletter. Convention/Meeting: Brigade events commence in March and generally take place every other weekend through November.

CITIZENS COMMITTEE FOR THE RIGHT TO KEEP AND BEAR ARMS

1601 114th Street SE, Suite 151   Phone: (206) 454-4911
Bellevue, Washington 98004
Alan M. Gottlieb, Chairman
Founded 1971
Members: 250,000
Staff: 24

A national independent non-profit mass membership organization concerned solely with preserving the right to keep and bear arms. The committee also maintains a public affairs office in the nation's capital (600 Pennsylvania Avenue, S.E., Suite 205). The Committee's National Advisory Council, made up of businessmen, educators, legislators, religious leaders, and includes 90 members of the U.S. Congress. Issues action bulletins, pro-gun rights brochures, bumper strips, decals, buttons and patches and legislative action materials. Supported by membership fees and voluntary contributions. Publication: *Point Blank,* monthly. Absorbed: Firearms Lobby of America. Formerly: (1975) National Citizens Committee for the Right to Keep and Bear Arms. Convention/Meeting: Annual.

COMMITTEE FOR HANDGUN CONTROL

109 N. Dearborn, 13th Fl.   Phone: (312) 641-5570
Chicago, Illinois 60602
Katherine Zartman, President
Founded 1973
Members: 200
National affiliates: 12

Individuals united to educate the public concerning the threat posed to American lives by the handgun, the accessible, concealable weapon; to encourage strong federal and local legislation restricting the manufacture, sale, distribution and importation of handguns. Conducts public forums, media presentations, legislative lobbying at local, state and federal levels. Bestows awards; maintains speakers bureau. Produces information kits. Publications: *Newsletter,* quarterly. Affiliated with: Handgun Control; National Coalition to Ban Handguns. Convention/Meeting: Annual symposium.

COMMITTEE FOR THE STUDY OF HANDGUN MISUSE

109 N. Dearborn St., 13th Fl.   Phone: (312) 641-5570
Chicago, Illinois 60602
Margaret Douaire, President
Founded 1973

Works to bring to the attention of citizens the effects of the use and abuse of handguns in American society. Conducts research; supplies information, speakers and statistics; sponsors conferences and seminars. Affiliated with: Committee for Handgun Control. Convention/Meeting: Annual.

COMPANY OF MILITARY HISTORIANS

North Main Street   Phone: (203) 399-9460
Westbrook, Connecticut 06498
Major William R. Reid, Administrator
Founded 1951
Members: 2,500
Staff: 4

Professional society of military historians, museologists, artists, writers, and private collectors interested in the history of American military units, organization, tactics, uniforms, arms, and equipment. Publications: (1) *Military Collector and Historian,* quarterly; (2) *Military Uniforms in America,* quarterly; (3) *Military Music in America* (records), irregular. Formerly: (1962) Company of Military Collectors and Historians. Convention/Meeting: Annual.

CONSERVATION EDUCATION ASSOCIATION

c/o Robert A. Darula   Phone: (414) 465-2480
School University Programs
University of Wisconsin, Green Bay
Green Bay, Wisconsin 54302
Robert A. Darula, Secretary-Treasurer
Founded 1947
Members: 950

Conservationists, educators and others interested in improving conservation education in public schools, teacher training institutions, and organization programs. Outstanding state, local and organizational conservation publications, especially those of normally limited distribution, are circulated bimonthly to members. Publications: (1) *Newsletter,* bimonthly; (2) *Proceedings,* annual. Formerly: (1953) National Committee on Policies in Conservation Education. Convention/Meeting: Annual—always August.

CONSERVATION FOUNDATION

1717 Massachusetts Avenue, NW   Phone: (202) 797-4300
Washington, D.C. 20036
William K. Reilly, President
Founded 1948
Staff: 50

Not a membership organization. Conducts research, education and information programs to develop knowledge, improve techniques, and stimulate public and private decision-making and action to improve the quality of the environment. Carries out environmental studies, demonstration planning programs, and offers a variety of conservation services at home and abroad. Publications: *Conservation Foundation Letter,* monthly; also publishes books, pamphlets, studies, guides, reports, and reprints.

CONSERVATION AND RESEARCH FOUNDATION

Box 1445   Phone: (203) 873-8514
Connecticut College
New London, Connecticut 06320
Richard H. Goodwin, President
Founded 1953

Not a membership organization. To encourage biological research and promote conservation of renewable natural resources. Makes research grants; offers Jeanette Siron Pelton Award for outstanding published contributions in experimental plant morphology. Publishes *Five Year Report* (last one in 1978). Convention/Meeting: Annual.

CONSERVATION SERVICES

Massachusetts Audubon Society
South Great Road
Lincoln, Massachusetts 01773
Wayne Hanley, Editor
Founded 1965
Members: 5
Staff: 5

Small Audubon and conservation groups, comprising 34,000 individual members. Purpose is to publish magazines, newsletters and environmental brochures for New England conservation organizations, and to develop television, radio and audiovisual materials that can be used in New England. Maintains extensive source files. Publications: (1) *Massachusetts Audubon Society Newsletter,* 10/year; (2) *Man and Nature Yearbook,* quarterly. Formerly: Conservation Services Center.

DEFENDERS OF WILDLIFE

1244 19th Street, NW   Phone: (202) 659-9510
Washington, D.C. 20036
John W. Grandy, IV, Executive Vice-President
Founded 1925
Members: 53,500

Persons interested in wildlife and conservation. To promote, through education and research, the protection and humane treatment of all mammals, birds, fish and other wildlife, and the elimination of painful methods of trapping, capturing and killing wildlife. Publication: *Defenders of Wildlife News,* bi-monthly. Formerly: Anti-Steel-Trap League; Defenders of Furbearers. Convention/Meeting: Semi-annual.

DESERT PROTECTIVE COUNCIL

P.O. Box 4294   Phone (714) 397-4264
Palm Springs, California 92263
Glenn Vargas, Executive Director
Founded 1954
Members: 700

Persons interested in safeguarding desert areas that are of unique scenic, scientific, historical, spiritual, and recreational value. Seeks to educate children and adults to a better understanding of the desert. Works to bring about establishment of wildlife sanctuaries for protection of indigenous plants and animals. The Desert Protective Council Education Foundation, a subdivision of the Council formed in 1960, handles educational activities and distributes reprints of desert and wildlife conservation articles. Publications: *El Paisano* (by Foundation), quarterly, and a yearly publication on a special topic. Convention/Meeting: Annual—October.

DUCKS UNLIMITED

P.O. Box 66300   Phone: (312) 299-3334
Chicago, Illinois 60666
Dale E. Whitesell, Executive Vice President
Founded 1937
Members: 390,000
Staff: 80
Regional Groups: 1,750
State groups: 50

Conservationists in the United States and Canada interested in migratory waterfowl conservation. To restore or build natural breeding habitats for migratory waterfowl primarily in the prairie provinces of Canada, which provides 80% of North America's wild geese and ducks. The American group raises funds for this construction and rehabilitation work, carried on by the field operating unit in Canada. Publications: (1) *Ducks Unlimited Magazine,* bi-monthly; (2) *Annual Report;* also publishes *The Ducks Unlimited Story.* Affiliated with: Ducks Unlimited (Canada). Absorbed: (1936) More Game Birds in America. Convention/Meeting: Annual.

FEDERATION OF WESTERN OUTDOOR CLUBS

208 Willard North   Phone: (415) 386-6544
San Francisco, California 94118
Winchell T. Hayward, President
Founded 1932
Members: 47

Outdoor clubs (41) in western United States with combined membership of 48,000, associate members 1300. Promotes conservation of forests, wildlife, and natural features. Publication: *Western Outdoor,* semi-annually. Convention/Meeting: Annual—always late August.

FIREARMS RESEARCH AND IDENTIFICATION ASSOCIATION

18638 Alderbury Dr.   Phone: (213) 964-7885
Rowland Heights, California 91748
John Armand Caudron, President
Founded 1978
Members: 12
State Groups: 1

Engineers, curators, safety professionals, insurance, finance and business consultants, medical technicians. Conducts research on the authenticity, history and development and accident analysis of firearms. Submits reports on defective weapons. Issues firearm certificates of authenticity and identification. Is currently developing certified test for firearm professionals. Maintains small library. Convention/Meeting: Annual—always May.

FRIENDS OF THE EARTH

124 Spear Street   Phone: (415) 495-4470
San Francisco, California 94105
David Brower, Founder & Board Chairman
Founded 1969
Members: 25,000
Regional groups: 50

International conservation organization which works to generate among people a new responsibility to the environment in which we live; to make the many important environmental issues that receive scant attention the subject of public debate; to select specific projects that offend the environment and hit these hard with every legal means possible. Lobbies before Congress and state governments; generates litigation and issue publications to further environmental goals. Departments: Legislative. Publications: (1) *Not Man Apart,* bimonthly; (2) *Soft Energy Notes,* bimonthly; also publishes numerous pamphlets and books. Convention/Meeting: Annual.

FRIENDS OF NATURE, INC.

Brooksville, Maine 04617
Martin R. Haase, Executive Secretary
Founded 1953

Conservationists "dedicated to maintaining the balance of nature for the mutual benefit of man and his plant and animal friends." Carries on educational work and maintains several nature sanctuaries. Holds annual meeting.

GAME CONSERVATION INTERNATIONAL

900 NE Loop, 410, Suite D-211   Phone: (512) 824-7509
San Antonio, Texas 78209
Bob Holleron, Executive Director
Founded 1967
Members: 1,000
Staff: 2

Individuals interested in wildlife conservation. Administers Hunters' Legal Defense Fund. Publication: *Hook 'n' Bullet,* quarterly. Convention/Meeting: Biennial Hunters and Fishermen's Conservation Conference.

HANDGUN CONTROL

810 18th St., NW, Suite 607   Phone: (202) 638-4723
Washington, DC 20006
Nelson T. Shields, Chairman
Founded 1974
Members: 60,000
Staff: 10

Public citizens' lobby working for legislative controls and governmental regulations on the manufacture, importation, sale, transfer and civilian possession of handguns. Compiles ongoing information on the handgun issue, including approaches, statistics, legislation introduced and research. Committees: National Advisory. Publications: (1) *Washington Report* (newsletter), quarterly; (2) *By This Time Tommorow. . .,* annual; also publishes *Victims Hotline* and special *Legislative Reports.* Formerly: (1979) National Council to Control Handguns.

INTERNATIONAL ASSOCIATION OF WILDLIFE AGENCIES

1412 16th Street, NW   Phone: (202) 232-1652
Washington, D.C. 20036
Jack H. Berryman, Executive Vice President
Founded 1902
Members: 384

State and provincial game, fish and conservation departments (68) and officials (316). To educate the public to the economic importance of conserving natural resources and managing wildlife properly as a source of recreation and a food supply; to seek better conservation legislation, administration and enforcement. Publications: (1) *Proceedings,* annual; (2) *Newsletter,* bimonthly. Formerly: (1917) National Association of Game Commissioners and Wardens. Convention/Meeting: Annual—always third week in September.

INTERNATIONAL BENCHREST SHOOTERS

c/o Evelyn Richards
411 North Wilbur Avenue
Sayre, Pennsylvania 18840
Robert A. White, President
Founded 1970
Members: 1,600
Staff: 1

Gunsmiths, research engineers, gun writers, other interested persons. "To develop the ultimate in gun accuracy." Sponsors tournaments with demonstrations of new inventions or idea developments in the field. Also sponsors seminars. Publication: *Precision Shooting Magazine,* monthly. Convention/Meeting: Annual.

INTERNATIONAL UNION FOR CONSERVATION OF NATURE AND NATURAL RESOURCES

CH-1196
Gland, Switzerland
Lee M. Talbot, Director General
Founded 1948
Members: 456

International federation of national governments (39) and national and international organizations (393) in 97 countries. For the preservation of the natural environment of man and the conservation of the world's natural resources. Serves as a forum for discussion of conservation problems and studies; sponsors international youth camps; intercedes with governments on conservation matters; maintains Van Tienhoven Library. Conducts research on measures to promote and protect national parks, nature reserves, wildlife and its habitat. Provides advisory field missions. Technical Commissions: Conservation Education; Ecology; Environmental Policy, Law and Administration; Landscape Planning; Law and Administration; National Parks and protected areas; Survival Service. Publications (must be ordered from Switzerland): (1) *IUCN Bulletin,* monthly; (2) *Proceedings* (of conferences); also publishes *Red Data Book* (endangered species), technical reports and a UN List of National Parks and Equivalent Reserves. Formerly: (1956) International Union for the Protection of Nature. General Assembly/Technical Meeting: Triennial.

INTERNATIONAL WILD WATERFOWL ASSOCIATION

Box 1075   Phone: (701) 252-1239
Jamestown, North Dakota 58401
Carl E. Strutz, Secretary
Founded 1958
Members: 500

Persons concerned with conservation and the preservation of wild waterfowl. Works toward protection, conservation and reproduction of any species considered in danger of eventual extinction; encourages the breeding of well known and rare species in captivity so that more people may learn about them by observation and enjoy them in the natural habitats created for this purpose. Has established Avicultural Hall of Fame. Publications: (1) *Newsletter,* irregular; (2) *Membership list,* annual; has published books on keeping cranes, wild geese, and wild ducks in captivity. Convention/Meeting: Annual.

IZAAK WALTON LEAGUE OF AMERICA

1800 North Kent Street, Suite 806   Phone: (703) 528-1818
Arlington, Virginia 22209
Jack Lorenz, Executive Director
Founded 1922
Members: 53,000
Staff: 18
State groups: 22
Local groups: 450

Promotes means and opportunities for educating the public to conserve, maintain, protect and restore the soil, forest, water and other natural resources of the U.S. and promotes the enjoyment and wholesome utilization of those resources. Committees: Energy Resources, Environmental Education, Fish and Wildlife, Public Lands, Urban Environment, Water and Wetlands, Water Quality, and Youth. Publication: *Outdoor America.* Absorbed: (1962) Friends of the Land. Convention/Meeting: Annual—always July.

J.N. "DING" DARLING FOUNDATION

209 South Village Drive   Phone: (515) 223-8850
West Des Moines, Iowa 50265
Mr. Sherry R. Fisher, Chairman
Founded 1962
Trustees: 38

"To initiate plans and to coordinate, guide and expedite programs, research and education which will bring about conservation and sound management of water, woods and soil; to restore and preserve historical sites; to create and assist in wildlife management plans; to improve and assure outdoor recreational opportunities for present and future generations." Established 1700-acre wildlife and waterfowl sanctuary on Sanibel Island, off the west coast of Florida. Awards scholarships at Iowa State University for wildlife management students. Named for the late J.N. "Ding" Darling, a professional cartoonist long active in conservation activities. Holds annual meeting.

LEAGUE TO SAVE LAKE TAHOE

Box 10110   Phone: (916) 541-5388
South Lake Tahoe, California 95731
James W. Bruner, Executive Director
Staff: 2

Membership comprised of individuals and organizations who give financial support to the League. Purpose is to "do all things and to perform all acts necessary to keep Lake Tahoe blue and to protect and preserve the natural beauty and grandeur of the Lake Tahoe area of California and Nevada; to promote and encourage the concept that all developments, improvements and man-made changes of any kind, which may be required to accommodate the proper and desirable growth of the area and provide the maximum recreational values, should place primary emphasis on preserving the natural beauty of the lake." Publication: *Newsletter,* quarterly. Convention/Meeting: Annual.

NATIONAL ASSOCIATION TO KEEP AND BEAR ARMS

P.O. Box 78336   Phone: (206) 226-0467
Seattle, Washington 98178
Gerry Unger, President
Founded 1967

Purposes are: "to support and defend the U.S. Constitutional principles at all government levels, primarily the Second Amendment; to strive for and ensure law and order for everyone, administered impartially and without regard to race, creed or color; to maintain and strengthen belief in Almighty God and in our national heritage." Presents awards. Maintains speakers bureau; supplies film strips and printed material to interested persons; compiles statistics. Maintains library of books and information primarily on the Second Amendment as well as files on persons and groups who hold an opposing point of view. Publications: *The Armed Citizen News,* monthly; also publishes special flyers.

NATIONAL AUDUBON SOCIETY

950 Third Avenue   Phone: (212) 823-3200
New York, New York 10022
Russell W. Peterson, President
Founded 1905
Members: 412,000
Local groups: 448
Affiliated groups: 131

Persons interested in conservation and restoration of natural resources, with emphasis on wildlife, wildlife habitats, soil, water, and forests. Sponsors four Audubon camps for teachers and youth leaders; nature lectures; and wildlife tours. Supports a force of 18 wardens to patrol wildlife refuge areas and sanctuaries; produces teaching materials for schools. Divisions: Educational Services; Lecture; Nature Centers; Research; Sanctuary; Service. Publications: (1) *Audubon Leader,* semimonthly; (2) *Audubon Magazine,* bimonthly; (3) *American Birds,* bimonthly; (4) *Nature Bulletins,* quarterly. Formerly: (1935) National Association of Audubon Societies for the Protection of Wild Birds and Animals, Inc. Convention/Meeting: Biennial.

NATIONAL BENCHREST SHOOTERS ASSOCIATION

5735 Sherwood Forest Drive   Phone: (216) 882-6877
Akron, Ohio 44319
Stella Buchtel, Secretary-Treasurer
Founded 1951

Rifle enthusiasts interested in precision shooting. Conducts registered shoots and certifies records. Sections: Bench Rest Rifle; Heavy Varmint; Light Varmint; Sporter Classes. Publication: *Rifle,* bimonthly. Holds annual directors' meeting.

NATIONAL BOARD FOR THE PROMOTION OF RIFLE PRACTICE

Room 1205   Phone: (202) 272-0810
Pulaski Building
20 Massachusetts Avenue, NW
Washington, D.C. 20314
Col. Jack R. Rollinger, Executive Officer
Founded 1903
Members: 25
Staff: 14
Local groups: 2,100

Civilian shooting clubs and marksmanship clubs in high schools and colleges. An agency of the U.S. Department of the Army, "to promote marksmanship training with rifled arms among able bodied citizens of the U.S. and to provide citizens outside the active services of the Armed Forces with means whereby they may become proficient with such arms." Provides arms and ammunition to member clubs; exhibits national marksmanship trophies; maintains records and distributes awards for national and international marksmanship competitions. Publication: *National Board Directory.* Convention/Meeting: Annual—always Washington, D.C.

NATIONAL COALITION TO BAN HANDGUNS

100 Maryland Ave., NW   Phone: (202) 544-7190
Washington, DC 20002
Michael K. Beard, Executive Director
Founded 1975
Members: 90,000
Staff: 4

Individuals, many of whom are members of the 30 national organizations (religious associations, citizen groups, educational organizations, professional societies, public interest groups) which support the Coalition. Purpose is to conduct a vigorous educational and legislative program on the need to ban handguns from importation, manufacture, sale, transfer, ownership, possession and use by the general American public. (Reasonable exceptions are the military, the police, security officers and pistol clubs where guns would be kept on the club's premises under secure conditions.) Encourages citizens to become more fully informed and to exercise their responsibilities regarding this issue; lobbies for legislation at the local, state and national levels; assists national, state and local groups; develops original educational materials including "The National Handgun Test" (film); relates to the media; undertakes field work assignments. Conducts research on effects of gun control laws around the country; does special analyses of statistics related to gun control; maintains speakers bureau. Publications: *Handgun Control News,* quarterly; also publishes *Resource List* and several informational and educational pamphlets and reports. Absorbed: National Gun Control Center.

NATIONAL MUZZLELOADING RIFLE ASSOCIATION

Friendship, Indiana 47021   Phone: (812) 667-5131
Maxine Moss, Office Manager-Editor
Founded 1933
Members: 25,000
Regional groups: 350

Persons interested in black powder shooting. To preserve the heritage left to us by our forefathers, and to promote safety in the use of arms. Maintains National Range located at Friendship, Ind. Sponsors Beef Shoot in Jan., Spring Shoot, National Shoot in the fall, and Turkey Shoot in Oct. Committees: Long Range Planning; Property; Fund Raising; Range Officers; Grounds; Commercial Row; Traffic; Safety; Camping; Memorial; Public Relations; Scoring; Award. Publication: *Muzzle Blasts,* monthly. Convention/Meeting: Semi-annual—always May and August.

NATIONAL PRAIRIE GROUSE TECHNICAL COUNCIL

College of Natural Resources   Phone: (715) 346-3665
University of Wisconsin
Stevens Point, Wisconsin 55481
Raymond K. Anderson, Chairman
Founded 1952
Members: 120
State groups: 17

Sponsors biennial meeting for technical personnel and administrators of state, provincial and federal agencies, and individuals from private groups involved in preservation, research, and management of the prairie chicken and sharp-tailed grouse. Conference makes possible exchange of information on current research and management of these species and reviews local and national legislation affecting the prairie grouse resource. Publications: (1) *P.G. News,* semiannual; (2) *Proceedings,* biennial. Formerly: (1956) National Committee on the Prairie Chicken; (1961) Prairie Chicken Technical Committee. Conference: Biennial.

NATIONAL RELOADING MANUFACTURERS ASSOCIATION

1221 S.W. Yamhill St.   Phone: (503) 227-3693
Portland, Oregon 97205
William J. Chevalier, Executive Secretary
Members: 29

Manufacturers and prime suppliers engaged in manufacturing and distribution of supplies used for handloading ammunition for revolvers, pistols, rifles, shotguns and similar small arms. Goals are: to promote interest in handloading of ammunition by all potential users; to encourage improvement of reloading tools, equipment and supplies; and to facilitate the means for better handloading. Promotes standardization of reloading equipment, supplies, tools and dies. Conducts consumer and trade promotion programs and publicity and provides educational materials. Publishes promotional and educational literature. Convention/Meeting: Annual.

NATIONAL RIFLE ASSOCIATION OF AMERICA

1600 Rhode Island Avenue, NW   Phone: (202) 828-6000
Washington, D.C. 20036
Harlan B. Carter, Executive Vice President
Founded 1871
Members: 1,800,000
Staff: 350
State groups: 54
Local groups; 11,000

Target shooters, hunters, gun collectors, gunsmiths, police officers, and others interested in firearms. Promotes rifle, pistol, and shotgun shooting, hunting, gun collecting, hunter and home firearms safety, conservation, etc. Encourages civilian marksmanship in interests of national defense. Maintains national records of shooting competitions; sponsors teams to compete in the Olympic Games and other world championships. Committees: Twenty-nine standing committees and four standing committees all with a charter of responsibilities to cover every phase of the shooting sport. Publications: (1) *The American Rifleman,* monthly; (2) *The American Hunter,* monthly; (3) *The American Marksman,* monthly. Other publications include a large variety of training, educational, and informational pamphlets, brochures, and pamphlets. Meeting: Annual.

NATIONAL SHOOTING SPORTS FOUNDATION

1075 Post Road   Phone: (203) 637-3618
Riverside, Connecticut 06878
Arnold H. Rohlfing, Executive Director
Founded 1961
Members: 135
Staff: 10

Chartered to promote in the American public a better understanding and more active participation in the recreational shooting sports. Organizes the annual observance of National Hunting and Fishing Day. Prints and distributes over 3 million copies of various shooting and hunting/conservation publications.

NATIONAL SKEET SHOOTING ASSOCIATION

P.O. Box 28188   Phone: (512) 688-3371
San Antonio, Texas 78228
Ann Myers, Executive Director
Founded 1935
Members: 18,000
Staff: 11
State groups: 54
Local groups: 650

Amateur skeet shooters. Registers competitive shoots and supervises them through formulation and enforcement of rules. Publication: *Skeet Shooting Review,* monthly. Convention/Meeting (World Championship Shoot): Annual—always last weekend in July/first week in August.

NATIONAL SPORTING GOODS ASSOCIATION

717 North Michigan Avenue   Phone: (312) 944-0205
Chicago, Illinois 60611
James L. Faltinek, Executive Director
Founded 1929
Members: 8,000
Staff: 50

Manufacturers, wholesalers, retailers, and importers of athletic equipment, sporting goods, and supplies. Provides data on cost-of-doing-business, store modernization, etc. Sponsors annual Gold Medal Award Program of the Sports Foundation for excellence in park and recreation management and in pollution control. Divisions: Athletic Goods Team Distributors; Awards Specialists; Outdoor Sports Stores; Ski Retailers International. Publications: (1) *Selling Sporting Goods,* monthly; (2) *Memo to Management,* monthly; (3) *NSGA Buying Guide,* annual; also publishes research and statistical studies. Convention/Meeting: Annual—always February, Chicago, Illinois.

NATIONAL TRAPPERS ASSOCIATION

15412 Tau Road   Phone: (616) 781-3472
Marshall, Michigan 49068
Don Hoyt Sr., President
Founded 1959
Members: 13,000
State groups: 55

Trappers of animals for the purpose of selling skins and furs; fur dealers, outdoorsmen. Researches animal control techniques; compiles statistics. Committees: Conservation. Publications: *Voice of the Trapper,* quarterly. Convention/Meeting: Annual.

NATIONAL WATERFOWL COUNCIL

c/o Arkansas Game and Fish   Phone: (501) 371-1145
  Commission
Game and Fish Building
Little Rock, Arkansas 72201
Steve Wilson, Chairman
Founded 1952
Members: 50

State and provincial fish and game departments. To coordinate waterfowl planning, research, and management. Convention/Meeting: Semiannual—March and August, held in conjunction with conventions of North American Wildlife Conference and Bureau of Sport Fish and Wildlife Service Waterfowl Regulations.

NATIONAL WILDLIFE FEDERATION

1412 16th Street, NW   Phone: (202) 797-6800
Washington, D.C. 20036
Thomas L. Kimball, Executive Vice President
Founded 1936
Members: 4,600,000
Staff: 400
Local groups: 6,500

Federation of 53 state conservation organizations and 1,748,000 associate members, plus individual conservationist-contributors. Represents in its structure 3.6 million supporters. To encourage the intelligent management of the life-sustaining resources of the earth, and to promote a greater appreciation of these resources, their community relationship and wise use. Gives organizational and financial help to local conservation projects; annually awards fellowships for graduate study of conservation; publishes conservation-education teaching materials. Compiles and distributes annual survey of compensation in the fields of fish and wildlife management. Maintains library of conservation publications. Sponsors National Wildlife Week; many public service television and radio announcements. Activities are financed by sales of Wildlife Conservation Stamps and nature-related materials. Publications: (1) *Conservation Report*, weekly; (2) *Conservation News*, semimonthly; (3) *Ranger Rick's Nature Magazine*, 10/year; (4) *National Wildlife Magazine*, bimonthly; (5) *International Wildlife Magazine*, bimonthly; (6) *Conservation Directory*, annual; also publishes numerous free and low-cost conservation materials. Convention/Meeting: Annual.

NATIONAL WILD TURKEY FEDERATION

Wild Turkey Building   Phone: (803) 637-3106
P.O. Box 467
Edgefield, South Carolina 29824
Tom Rodgers, Executive Vice President
Founded 1973
Members: 35,000
Staff: 10
Regional Groups: 75
State groups: 32
Local groups: 53

Wild turkey enthusiasts and biologists. Dedicated to the wise conservation and management of the American wild turkey as a valuable natural resource. Assists state game agencies, universities and other state or local organizations in conducting needed turkey research, management and restoration programs. Maintains financial assistance programs for agencies, organizations and individuals; offers placement service. Plans to establish a Wild Turkey Research Center and museum. Sponsors annual wild turkey stamp and print art contest. Bestows awards. Committees: Technical. Publications: (1) *Turkey Call* (magazine), bimonthly; (2) *Who's Who in Wild Turkey Management*, annual. Convention/Meeting: Annual directors meeting—always spring.

NATURAL RESOURCES COUNCIL OF AMERICA

Box 220
Tracys Landing, Maryland 20869
Michael Rawson, Executive Secretary
Founded 1946
Members: 46

Federation of national and regional conservation organizations and scientific societies interested in conservation of natural resources. Sponsors special natural resource studies and surveys. Committee: Scientific Advisory. Publications: (1) *Legislative News Service* (actions taken by Congress on natural resources), weekly; (2) *Executive News Service* (actions taken by Executive Branch on natural resources), weekly; also publishes books on selected natural resource topics. Convention/Meeting: Semiannual—always held with North American Wildlife and Natural Resources Conference.

NEW ENGLAND ADVISORY BOARD FOR FISH AND GAME PROBLEMS

115 Summit Avenue   Phone: (401) 821-9096
West Warwick, Rhode Island 02839
Theodore Boyer, Secretary
Founded 1951
Members: 64,200

Sportsmen. To promote and improve conservation, hunting, fishing and recreation in New England. All New England states affiliated. Convention/Meeting: Annual—always May.

NORTH AMERICAN WILDLIFE FOUNDATION

1000 Vermont Avenue, NW   Phone: (202) 347-1774
Washington, D.C. 20005
L.R. Jahn, Secretary
Founded 1911
Trustees: 50
Contributing members: 400
Trustees: 30

"To insure, through financial support, the continuity of practical and systematic investigation into management practices and techniques throughout North America, to the end that the latest, most effective local, national, and international programs for wildlife and other natural resources will be adopted in the public interest." Foundation is not an action organization and does not attempt the actual mechanics of wildlife restoration; works through cooperating agencies, organizations, institutions. Owns Delta Waterfowl Research Station in Manitoba, Canada. Maintains library of 450 volumes on natural science subjects and wildlife restoration and management. Formerly: (1935) American Game Protective Association; (1946) American Wildlife Institute; (1951) American Wildlife Foundation. Convention/Meeting: Annual.

NORTH-SOUTH SKIRMISH ASSOCIATION, INC.

Route 1, Box 226A   Phone: (703) 635-5715
Bentonville, Virginia 22610
John L. Rawls, Executive Secretary
Founded 1950
Members: 3,400
Regional groups: 12
Local groups: 178

"To pay tribute to the soldier on both sides in The War Between the States; to promote marksmanship with the small arms and artillery of the Civil War era, fired in the original manner." Sponsors semi-annual national skirmishes at Ft. Shenandoah, Virginia and some 40 regional skirmishes throughout the eastern United States, in which competitors, dressed as were Union and Confederate soldiers, compete. Skirmishes feature: individual matches with muskets, carbines, and revolvers; 6-man artillery matches; 5-man team carbine matches; and 8-man musket matches. Publication: *The Skirmish Line*, bimonthly. Affiliated with: National Rifle Association of America. Convention/Meeting: Semi-annual—always May and October.

OUTDOOR WRITERS ASSOCIATION OF AMERICA

4141 West Bradley Road   Phone: (414) 354-9690
Milwaukee, Wisconsin 53209
Edwin W. Hanson, Executive Director
Founded 1927
Members: 1,450
Staff: 3

Professional organization of newspaper, magazine, radio, television, and motion picture writers and photographers (both staff and free-lance) on outdoor recreation and conservation. Gives awards for outstanding writing and films in the field; conducts surveys for educational and industrial organizations; compiles market data for writer members, and offers liaison aid in writer assignments. Committees: Awards; Educational and Scholarship; Ethics; Youth Program. Publications: (1) *Outdoors Unlimited*, monthly; (2) *Outdoor Writers' Association of America Directory*; also publishes a writers instruction manual.

PACIFIC INTERNATIONAL TRAPSHOOTING ASSOCIATION

4408 Fourth Street, NW   Phone: (503) 364-1042
Puyallup, Washington 98371
Richard T. Stoner, Secretary-Manager
Founded 1928
Members: 6,000

Sponsors state, provincial, international and individual registered trapshoots. "Grand Pacific Trapshoot"/Meeting: Annual, Reno, Nevada—always July.

PHEASANT TRUST

Great Witchingham
Norwich, Norfolk, England
Philip Wayre, Honorary Director
Founded 1959
Members: 550
Staff: 3

Purposes are to breed rare and threatened species of game birds for release in suitable reserves in their native lands; to maintain the world's largest collection of rare pheasants for education and scientific research; to promote the conservation of rare game birds throughout the world. Has received several first breeding awards from Agricultural Society of Great Britain. Publication: Annual report. Formerly: Ornamental Pheasant Trust.

PRAIRIE CHICKEN FOUNDATION

4122 Mineral Point Road   Phone: (608) 233-5474
Madison, Wisconsin 53705
Paul J. Olson, President
Founded 1958

Persons dedicated to preservation of the prairie chicken in Wisconsin. Raises funds and acquires land to develop prairie chicken habitat in the state. Owns some 5000 acres; makes some purchases cooperatively with the Society Tympanuchus Cupido Pinnatus. Publication: *Prairie Chicken,* irregular.

RUFFED GROUSE SOCIETY
994 Broadhead Road, Suite 304   Phone: (412) 262-4044
Corapolis, Pennsylvania 15108
Samuel R. Pursglove Jr., Executive Director
Founded 1961
Members: 5,500
Staff: 5
State chapters: 12
Local groups: 16

Ruffed grouse hunters; game biologists; conservationists. Actively supports ruffed grouse and woodcock research and habitat improvement. Cooperates with state conservation departments, paper and pulp industries, and strip mining companies in habitat improvement and encourages conservation measures. Endows research into ecological aspects of the ruffed grouse and woodcock. Publications: *The Drummer,* bi-monthly. Convention/Meeting: Annual—always fall.

SAFARI CLUB INTERNATIONAL
5151 East Broadway, Suite 1680   Phone: (602) 747-0260
Tuscon, Arizona 85711
Holt Bodinson, Administrative Director
Founded 1970
Staff: 12
Regional groups: 59
Members: Regular, 2200; associate, 4700; affiliate, 500,000
Staff: 9
Regional groups: 39

To promote good fellowship among those who love the outdoors and the sport of hunting. To promote the conservation of the wildlife of the world through selective trophy hunting of aged and infirm animals, leaving prime animals to procreate. To educate youth in the safe and proper use of firearms and to interest them in the conservation and preservation of forests and animals, our natural heritage. Publication: *Safari* magazine. Convention/Meetings: Annual convention in Las Vegas; quarterly director's meetings; monthly chapter meetings.

SAINT HUBERT SOCIETY OF AMERICA
c/o Thomas C. Keister, Jr.   Phone: (212) 986-3180
Dean Witter Reynolds, Inc.
5 World Trade Center
New York, New York 10006
Thomas C. Keister Jr., President
Founded 1958
Members: 100

Individuals interested in wildlife, conservation, hunting, and the lore of the outdoors. "Dedicated to the promulgation of conservation, hunting, fishing, and the preservation of the great American heritage of the outdoors and those traditions of sportsmanship and fair play which have become associated with the American way of life." Sponsors outings for members including shoots, hunts, and fishing expeditions. Named in honor of the patron saint of hunters who was born in Belgium in the middle of the seventh century. Similar organizations have been in existence in Europe since the eighth century. Convention/Meeting: Annual—always third Thursday in April.

SECOND AMENDMENT FOUNDATION
1601 114th Ave., S.E., Suite 157   Phone: (206) 454-7012
Bellevue, Washington 98004
Alan M. Gottlieb, President
Founded 1974
Staff: 15

Individuals dedicated to promoting a better understanding of "our constitutional right to privately own and possess firearms." Activities include: producing a weekly pro-gun radio program distributed to 130 stations nationwide; distributing filmstrips analyzing the gun control debate; maintaining a legal aid hot-line servicing gun owners; and providing public service announcements through the media. Bestows annual Silver Bullet Award and James Madison Award. Maintains library and compiles statistics. Publications: (1) *Weekly Bullet;* (2) *Reporter,* bimonthly; also publishes monographs. Convention/Meeting: Irregular conferences.

SIERRA CLUB
530 Bush Street   Phone: (415) 981-8634
San Francisco, California 94108
Michael McCloskey, Executive Director
Members: 199,000
Staff: 130
Regional groups: 12
State groups: 53
Local groups: 276

All who feel the need to know more of nature, and know that this need is basic to man. "To protect and conserve the natural resources of the Sierra Nevada, the United States and the World; to undertake and publish scientific and educational studies concerning all aspects of man's environment and the natural ecosystems of the World; and to educate the people of the United States and the World to the need to preserve and restore the quality of that environment and the integrity of those ecosystems." Works on urgent campaigns to save threatened areas, wildlife, and resources; conducts annual environmental workshops for educators; schedules wilderness outings; presents awards; maintains library. Chapters and committees schedule talks, films, exhibits, and conferences. Committees: Economics; Energy; Environmental Education; Environmental Research; Forest Practices; International Environment; Mountaineering; National Land Use; National Water Resources; Native American Issues; Outings; Population; Wilderness; Wildlife and Endangered Species. Departments: Conservation; Outings. Publications: (1) *National News Report,* weekly; (2) *Sierra Club Bulletin,* monthly; (3) *Ascent,* Sierra Club mountaineering journal, annual; also publishes books and produces films, posters, and exhibits. Member of: United Nations (with non-government organization status). Convention/Meeting (Wilderness Conference): Biennial.

SOCIETY OF TYMPANUCHUS CUPIDO PINNATUS
433 East Michigan Street   Phone: (414) 271-6755
Milwaukee, Wisconsin 53202
Robert T. Foote, President
Founded 1960

Sportsmen dedicated to preserving the prairie chicken and to "doing so with humor, excellent taste, and efficiency—at the same time having a bit of fun along the way." (The prairie chicken or prairie hen, also called a pinneated grouse, is a game bird of the northern hemisphere, related to the pheasant and having mottled plumage. The Society calls itself by the scientific name for the prairie chicken.) Members' contributions are used to buy land for prairie chicken habitat, specifically to add acres to the Buena Vista Reservation in Portage County, Wisconsin. As of June, 1971, the Society had bought over 6300 acres of land, which is leased to the Wisconsin Conservation Department for clearing, restoration, and maintenance on chicken range. Only other organized activity is an annual cocktail party and business meeting held in December in Milwaukee where many of the members live. Publications: (1) *Boom,* quarterly; (2) *Membership Roll.* Convention/Meeting: Annual, always December, Milwaukee, Wisconsin.

SOUTHEASTERN ASSOCIATION OF FISH AND WILDLIFE AGENCIES
P.O. Box 40747   Phone: (615) 741-1431
Nashville, Tennessee 37204
Gary T. Myers, Secretary-Treasurer
Founded 1947
Members: 17

Directors of state game and fish commissions in 16 southern states and the Commonwealth of Puerto Rico. To protect the right of jurisdiction of southeastern states over their wildlife resources on public and private lands; study state and federal wildlife legislation and regulations as they affect the area; consult with and make recommendations to federal wildlife and public land agencies on federal management programs and programs involving federal aid to southeastern states; serve as a clearing house for exchange of ideas on wildlife management and research techniques. Sponsors statistical studies at North Carolina State University; Cooperative Fish Disease Study, Auburn University; and Cooperative Wildlife Disease Study, University of Georgia. Committees: Southeastern Dove Study; Waterfowl; Wildlife Disease Studies. Publications: (1) *Proceedings of Annual Conference;* (2) *Transactions,* annual. Formerly: (1977) Southeastern Association of Game and Fish Commissioners. Convention/Meeting: Annual.

SPORTING ARMS AND AMMUNITION MANUFACTURERS' INSTITUTE, INC.

P.O. Box 218   Phone: (203) 265-3232
Wallingford, Connecticut 06492
Harry L. Hampton Jr., Executive Director
Founded 1926
Members: 13
Staff: 4

Manufacturers of sporting firearms, ammunition and powder. Promotes shooting sports, safe handling of firearms, technical research, etc. Committees: Legislative and Legal Affairs; Promotional Guidance; International Trade; Traffic; Technical. Meeting: Semi-annual.

UNITED STATES REVOLVER ASSOCIATION

59 Alvin Street   Phone: (413) 734-5725
Springfield, Massachusetts 01104
Stanley A. Sprague, Executive Secretary
Founded 1900
Members: 1,350
Staff: 2

To foster and develop revolver and pistol shooting; to establish and preserve records; and to encourage and conduct pistol matches between members and clubs of this country as well as marksmen of other countries. Publication: *U.S. Handgunner*, bimonthly. Convention/Meeting: Annual—always Springfield, Mass.

WESTERN ASSOCIATION OF FISH AND WILDLIFE AGENCIES

P.O. Box 25   Phone: (208) 384-3771
Boise, Idaho 83707
Robert L. Salter, Secretary-Treasurer
Founded 1922
Members: 16

Officials of state and provincial game and fish agencies of western states and provinces. Promotes fish and game conservation in West. Publication: *Proceedings of WASGFC*, annual. Formerly: (1978) Western Association of State and Fish and Game Commissioners. Convention/Meeting: Annual—always July.

WILDERNESS SOCIETY

1901 Pennsylvania Avenue, NW   Phone: (202) 293-2732
Washington, D.C. 20006
William A. Turnage, Executive Director
Founded 1935
Members: 50,000
Staff: 35

Persons interested in preserving wilderness through educational programs, scientific studies, and cooperation with local and state citizen organizations in resisting the destruction of wildland resources and wildlife. Conducts leadership training programs for citizen conservationists. Sponsors book award program for young people. Sponsors "A Way to the Wilderness" trip program. Publication: *Living Wilderness*, quarterly; also publishes *Wilderness Reports*, notices, and conservation alerts on critical conservation issues. Convention/Meeting: Semi-annual.

WILDLIFE MANAGEMENT INSTITUTE

709 Wire Building   Phone: (202) 347-1774
Washington, D.C. 20005
Daniel A. Poole, President
Founded 1946
Staff: 18

To promote better management and wise utilization of all renewable natural resources in the public interest. Publications: (1) *Outdoor News Bulletin*, biweekly; (2) *Transactions of Annual North American Wildlife and Natural Resources Conference* (and cumulative index); also publishes various books and monographs. Holds annual conference.

WILDLIFE SOCIETY

7101 Wisconsin Avenue, NW, Suite 611   Phone: (301) 986-8700
Washington, D.C. 20014
Richard N. Denney, Executive Director
Founded 1937
Members: 7,500
Regional groups: 7

Professional society of wildlife biologists and others interested in resource conservation and wildlife management on a sound biological basis. Publications: (1) *Journal of Wildlife Management*, quarterly; (2) *Wildlife Society Bulletin*, quarterly; (3) *Wildlife Monographs*, irregular. Formerly: (1937) Society of Wildlife Specialists. Convention/Meeting: Annual—held with North American Wildlife and Natural Resources Conference.

WORLD WILDLIFE FUND

1601 Connecticut Avenue, NW   Phone: (202) 387-0800
Washington, D.C. 20009
Russell E. Train, President
Founded 1961
Staff: 33

Supported by contributions from individuals, funds, corporations, and foundations with a concern for conservation of wildlife and its habitat. Emphasizes preservation of endangered and vanishing species of wildlife, plants, and natural areas anywhere in the world. Makes grants for land acquisition, habitat protection and maintenance and scientific ecological research around the globe. Support is given existing conservation societies, agencies, and governments to carry out projects and services. Maintains small library. Committee: Scientific Advisory. Affiliated with: World Wildlife Fund International, and International Union for Conservation of Nature and Natural Resources, both headquartered at Morges, Switzerland. Holds quarterly board meetings. WWF includes 26 national affiliates.

(NOTE: Organizations and associations which are national in scope and who desire to be listed in this directory should send detailed information about themselves in the format shown here. Address: The Editor, SHOOTER'S BIBLE, 55 Ruta Court, South Hackensack, NJ 07606.)

The Shooter's Bookshelf

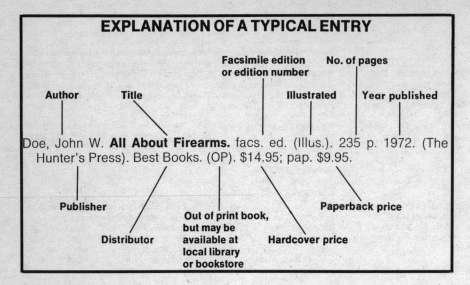

EXPLANATION OF A TYPICAL ENTRY

Facsimile edition or edition number

No. of pages

Author   Title

Illustrated   Year published

Doe, John W. **All About Firearms.** facs. ed. (Illus). 235 p. 1972. (The Hunter's Press). Best Books. (OP). $14.95; pap. $9.95.

Publisher

Paperback price

Distributor

Out of print book, but may be available at local library or bookstore

Hardcover price

AIR GUNS

Beeman, Robert. **Air Gun Digest.** 1977. pap. DBI Books. $7.95.

Churchill, Bob & Davies, Granville. **Modern Airweapon Shooting.** (Illus.). 1981. David & Charles. $18.95.

Walter, John. **The Airgun Book.** 1981. Stackpole. $21.95.

Wesley, L. **Air Guns and Air Pistols.** new and enl. ed. (Illus.). 1977. A.S. Barnes. (OP).

—**Air-Guns and Air-Pistols.** rev. by G. V. Carden. (Illus.) 1980. A. S. Barnes. (OP).

AMMUNITION

Barnes, Frank C. **Cartridges of the World.** 4th ed. pap. DBI Books. $9.95.

Central Intelligence Agency. **CIA Ammunition and Explosives Supply Catalog.** (Illus.) 1975. pap. Paladin Enterprises. $9.95.

—**CIA Explosives for Sabotage Manual.** (Illus.). 1975. pap. Paladin Enterprises. $7.95.

Goad, K.J. & Halsey, D. H. **Ammunition, Grenades & Mines.** 1982. Pergamon Press. $35.00; pap. $17.50.

Grennell, Dean A. **ABC's of Reloading.** 2nd ed. 1980. pap. DBI Books. $8.95.

Guns and Ammo Magazine Editors, ed. **Guns and Ammo Annual, 1981.** (Illus.). 1980. pap. Petersen Publishing. $6.95.

Hoyem, George A. **History and Development of Small Arms Ammunition, Vol. 1: Martial Long Arms, Flintlock through Rimfire.** (Illus.). 1981. Armory Pubns. $27.50.

—**History and Development of Small Arms Ammunition, Vol. II: Centerfire, Primitive and Martial Long Arms.** (Illus.). 1982. Armory Pubns. $34.50.

Labbett, Peter. **Military Small Arms Ammunition of the World, 1945-1980.** (Illus.). 1980. Presidio Press. $18.95.

Matunas, Edward. **American Ammunition and Ballistics.** (Illus.). 1979. Winchester Press. $15.95.

Parkerson, Codman **A Brief History of Bullet Moulds.** Pioneer Press. $1.75.

Sears & Roebuck Ammunition Catalog. (Illus.). pap. Sand Pond. $1.50.

Steindler, R. A. **Reloader's Guide.** 3rd ed. 1975. softbound. Stoeger. $7.95.

Suydam, Charles R. **U.S. Cartridges and Their Handguns: 1795-1975.** (Illus.). 1978. Beinfeld. $15.95; pap. $9.95.

Warner, Ken, ed. **Handloader's Digest.** 9th ed. 1981. pap DBI Books. $9.95.

—**Handloader's Digest Bullet and Powder Update.** 1980. $4.95 pap. DBI Books.

Williams, Mason. **The Law Enforcement Book of Weapons, Ammunition and Training Procedures; Handguns, Rifles and Shotguns** (Illus.). 1977. C. C. Thomas. $35.75.

Wootters, John. **The Complete Book of Practical Handloading.** (Illus.). 1977. softbound. Stoeger. $6.95.

—**The Complete Book of Practical Handloading.** (Illus.). 1976. Winchester Press. (OP).

ANTELOPES

Bere, Rennie. **Antelopes.** (Illus.). 1971. Arco. (OP).

Bronson, Wilfrid S. **Horns and Antlers.** (Illus.). 1942. Harcourt Brace Jovanovich. (OP).

Caton, John D. **The Antelope and Deer of America: A Scientific Treatise Upon the Natural History, Habits, Affinities and Capacity for Domestication of the Antilocapra and Cervidae of North America.** (Illus.). 1974. Repr. Arno Press. $22.00.

Chace, G. Earl. **Wonders of the Pronghorn.** (Illus.). (gr 3-7). 1977. Dodd, Mead & Co. $5.95.

ANTI-TANK GUNS

Chamberlain, Peter & Gander, Terry. **Anti-Tank Weapons.** (Illus.). 1975. Arco. (OP).

—**Self Propelled Anti-Tank and Anti-Aircraft Guns.** (Illus.). 1975 pap. Arco. $3.95.

Foss, Christopher. **Jane's Pocket Book of Towed Artillery.** 1979. pap. Macmillan. $7.95.

Hoffschmidt, E.J. **Know Your Antitank Rifles.** (Illus.). 1977. pap. Blacksmith Corp. $5.95.

Hoffschmidt, Edward J. & Tantum, William H. **German Tank and Antitank of World War Two.** 1968. Paladin Enterprises. $12.50.

ARCHERY

Adams, Chuck. **Bowhunter's Digest.** 2nd ed. pap. 1981 DBI Books. $9.95.

—**The Complete Book of Bowhunting.** (Illus.). 1978. Winchester Press. $14.95

American Alliance for Health, Physical Education & Recreation. **Archery: A Planning Guide for Group and Individual Instruction.** 1972. pap. AAHPER. (OP).

—**Archery Selected Articles, 1971.** pap. AAHPER. $.60.

Annarino, A. **Archery: Individualized Instructional Program.** 1973. pap. P-H. (OP).

Archery. 1976. pap. British Book Center. $2.50.

Archery-Fencing Guide 1978-80. 1978. pap. AAHPER. $2.50.

Ascham, Roger. **Toxophilus, The Schole of Shootinge,** 2 bks. 1969. Repr. of 1545 ed. Walter J. Johnson, Inc. $25.00.

—**Toxophilus, 1545.** Arber, Edward, ed. 1971. Repr. of 1895 ed. Scholarly Press. $29.00.

Barrett, Jean **Archery.** 3rd ed. 1980. Goodyear. (OP).

Barrett, Jean. **Archery.** 3rd ed. 1980. Scott, Foresman & Co. $6.95.

Barrett, Jean A. **Archery.** 2nd ed. 1973. pap. Goodyear. (OP).

Barrington, Daines. **Archery In England.** pap. British American Books. $3.95.

Bear, Fred. **Archer's Bible.** (Illus.). 1980. pap. Doubleday. $4.50.

—**Fred Bear's World of Archery.** (Illus.). 1979. Doubleday. $17.95.

Bilson, Frank. **Crossbows.** (Illus.). 1982. Hippocrene Books. $14.95.

Burke, Edmund. **Archery.** (Illus.). 1963. pap. Arc Books. (OP).

Burke, Edmund H. **Archery Handbook.** (Illus.). 1954. Arco. (OP).

—**Archery Handbook.** 1976. pap. Arco. (OP).

—**Field and Target Archery.** (Illus.). 1961. Arco. (OP).

—**History of Archery.** 1971. Repr. of 1957 ed. Greenwood Press. $15.75.

Butler, David F. **The New Archery.** rev. ed. (Illus.). 1973. A. S. Barnes. (OP).

Campbell, Donald W. **Archery.**. 1970. pap. Prentice-Hall. (OP).

Ford, Horace A. **Archery, Its Theory and Practice.** 1971. Repr. of 1856 ed. George Shumway Publisher. $10.00.

Foy, Tom. **Archery.** 1976. pap. Charles River Books. (OP).

—**A Guide to Archery.** (Illus.). 1981. Merrimack Book Service $14.95.

—**Beginner's Guide to Archery.** Transatlantic Arts, Inc. (OP).

Gillelan, G. Howard. **Archery at Home: How to Practice Daily and Stay Sharp for Target Shooting, Field Archery, and Bowhunting.** (Illus.). 1980. David McKay Co. (OP).

—**Complete Book of the Bow and Arrow.** rev. ed. 1981. Stackpole Books. $11.95.

Hargrove, E. **Anecdotes of Archery.** 1982. (Pub. by Falconiforme). State Mutual Book & Periodical Service. $30.00.

Heath, E. G. **Archery: A Military History.** 1981. State Mutual Book & Periodical Service. $39.00.

—**Archery: The Modern Approach.** rev. 2nd ed. (Illus.). 1978. pap. Faber & Faber. $6.50.

—**A History of Target Archery.** (Illus.). 1974. A.S. Barnes. (OP).

—**Better Archery.** 1976. International Pubns. Service. $8.50.

—**Better Archery.** 1976. Sportshelf. $16.95.

Helgeland, G. **Archery World's Complete Guide to Bowhunting.** (Illus.). 1975. pap. Prentice-Hall. $5.95.

Helgeland, Glenn. **Archery World's Complete Guide to Bowhunting.** 1977. Prentice-Hall. (OP).

Herrigel, Eugen. **Zen in the Art of Archery.** 1971. pap. Random House. $2.95.

Hochman, Louis. **Complete Archery Book.** (Illus.). 1957. Arco. $4.95.

Hodgkin, Adrian E. **The Archer's Craft.** 2nd ed. (Illus.). 1974. (Pub. by Faber & Faber). Merrimack Book Service $9.95.

Hougham, Paul. **Encyclopedia of Archery.** (Illus.). 1957. A. S. Barnes. (OP).

Johnson, Dewayne J. & Oliver, Robert A. **Archery.** 1980. pap. American Press. $2.95.

Klann, Margaret L. **Target Archery.** 1970. pap. Addison-Wesley. $7.95.

Latham, J. D., ed. **Saracen Archery.** (Illus.). Albert Saifer, Pub. $35.00.

Laubin, Reginald & Laubin, Gladys **American Indian Archery.** (Illus.). 1980. University of Oklahoma Press, $13.50.

Laycock, George & Bauer, Erwin. **Hunting with Bow and Arrow.** 1965. Arco. (OP).

Learn, C. R. **Bowhunter's Digest.** 1974. Follett. pap. (OP).

Lewis, Jack, ed. **Archer's Digest.** 2nd ed. (Illus.). 1977. pap. DBI Books. $7.95.

McKinney, Wayne C. **Archery.** 4th ed. 1980. pap. William C. Brown Co. Write for information.

Markham, Gervase. **The Art of Archerie.** facs. ed. 1968. Repr. of 1634 ed. George Shumway Publisher. $15.00.

Mosely, Walter M. **An Essay on Archery.** 1976. Charles River Books. $17.50.

Neade, William. **The Double Armed Man.** facs. ed. (Illus.). 1971. George Shumway Publisher. $10.00.

Niemeyer, Roy K. & Zabik, Roger. **Beginning Archery.** 3rd ed. 1978. pap. Wadsworth Publisher. $5.95.

Old Toxophilite. **The Archer's Guide.** 1982. (Pub. by Falconiforme). State Mutual Book & Periodical Service. $35.00.

Pszczola, Lorraine. **Archery.** 2nd ed. (Illus.). 1976. pap. Holt, Rinehart & Winston. $3.95.

Reichart, N. & Keasey, G. **Archery.** 3rd ed. (Illus.). 1961. Ronald Press. (OP).

Richardson, M. E. **Archery.** 1975. pap. David McKay Co. $4.95.

—**Teach Yourself Archery.** Sportshelf. (OP).

—**Teach Yourself Archery.** rev. ed. (Illus.). 1979. pap. David McKay Co. $4.95.

Roberts, Daniel. **Archery for All.** 1976. David & Charles. (OP).

Smith, Mike. **Archery.** 1978. Arco. (OP).

Stamp, Don. **Archery—an Expert's Guide.** pap. Wilshire Book Co. (OP).

—**Archery: An Expert's Guide.** pap. Borden. (OP).

—**Challenge of Archery.** (Illus.). 1971. International Publications Service. $16.50.

—**The Challenge of Archery.** 2nd ed. (Illus.). 1980. Transatlantic Arts, Inc. $16.95.

—**Field Archery.** (Illus.). 1980. Transatlantic Arts, Inc. $15.95.

Thompson, W.H. & Thompson, M. **How to Train in Archery.** 1982. (Pub. by Falconiforme). State Mutual Book & Periodical Service. $30.00.

Tinsley, Russell. **Bow Hunter's Guide.** (Illus.). 1975. softbound. Stoeger. $5.95.

Williams, John. **Archery for Beginners.** (Illus.). 1976. pap. Contemporary Books. (OP).

—**With Stick & String: Adventures with Bow and Arrow.** (Illus.). Avery Color Studios. $4.95.

Wood, Sir William. The Bowman's Glory or Archery Revived. 1976. Charles River Books. $7.50.

—**The Bowman's Glory or Archery Revived.** Repr. of 1969 ed. Ridgeway Books. $15.00.

ARMS AND ARMOR

Albion, Robert G. **Introduction to Military History.** (Illus.). 1971. Repr. of 1929 ed. AMS Press. $29.00.

American Machines & Foundry Co. **Accoustic Study Program.** (Illus.). 1972. pap. Paladin Press. (OP).

—**Silencers: Patterns & Principles, Vol. 2.** (Illus.). 1972. pap. Paladin Enterprises. $12.95.

Archer, Denis. **Infantry Weapons 1980-1981.** 1980. Franklin Watts. (OP).

Archer, Denis, ed. **Jane's Infantry Weapons 1977.** 1977. Franklin Watts, Inc. (OP).

—**Jane's Infantry Weapons 1978.** 1978. Franklin Watts, Inc. (OP).

Ashdown, Charles H. **Armour and Weapons in the Middle Ages.** (Illus.). Albert Saifer, Publisher. $18.00.

—**British and Continental Arms and Armour.** (Illus.). Peter Smith. $9.00.

—**British and Continental Arms and Armour.** (Illus.). 1970. pap. Dover. $4.00.

Bannerman's Catalogue of Military Goods. 1927 facsimile ed. 1981. DBI Books. $12.95.

Barker, A. J. **Russian Infantry Weapons of World War Two.** 1971. Arco. (OP).

Barnes, Duncan. **History of Winchester Firearms, 1866-1980.** rev. ed. (Illus.). 1980. Winchester Press. $21.95.

Bearse, Ray. **Sporting Arms of the World.** 1977. Harper & Row. $15.95.

Berenstein, Michael. **The Armor Book.** (Illus.). 1979. David McKay Co. (OP).

Birla Institute of Scientific Research, Economic Research Division & Agarwal, R. J. **Defense Production and Development.** 1978. Lawrence Verry, Co. $10.50.

Bivens, John. **Art of the Fire-Lock, Twentieth Century: Being a Discourse Upon the Present and Past Practices of Stocking and Mounting the Sporting Fire-Lock Rifle Gun.** 1982. Shumway. $40.00.

Blair, Claude. **European Armour: Circa 1066 to Circa 1700.** (Illus.). 1979. Beckman Publishers. $19.95.

Brassey's Infantry Weapons of the World. 2nd ed. 1978. Crane-Russak Co. (OP).

Brodie, Bernard & Brodie, Fawn M. **From Crossbow to H-Bomb.** rev. ed. (Illus.). 1973. pap. Indiana University Press. $6.95.

Central Intelligence Agency. **CIA Special Weapons Supply Catalog.** (Illus.). 1975. pap. Paladin Enterprises. $5.95.

Chappelear, Louis E. **Japanese Armor Makers.** 1978. Hawley, W. M. (OP).

Collier, Basil. **Arms and the Men: The Arms Trade and Governments.** (Illus.). 1980. (Pub. by Hamish Hamilton England). David & Charles. $37.00.

Cormack, A. J. **German Small Arms.** (Illus.). 1979. International Pubns. Service. $20.00.

Cowper, H. S. **The Art of Attack: Being a Study in the Development of Weapons and Appliances of Offense, from the Earliest Times to the Age of Gunpowder.** (Illus.). 1977. Repr. of 1906 ed. Rowman & Littlefield, Inc. $21.50.

Curtis, Howard M. **European Helmets, 800 B.C.-1700 A.D.** (Illus.). 1978. Beinfeld. (OP).

Curtis, Tony, ed. Lyle **Official Arms and Armour.** Review, 1981. (Illus.). 1980. Apollo. $24.95.

Daniel, Larry J. & Gunter, Riley W. **Confederate Cannon Foundries.** Pioneer Press, ed. Pioneer Press. $17.95.

De Gheyn, Jacob. **The Exercise of Arms.** (Illus.). 1976. Repr. of 1607 ed. Arma Press. (OP).

Diagram Group. **Weapons.** (Illus.). 1980. St. Martin's Press. $25.00.

Draeger, Donn F. **The Weapons and Fighting Arts of the Indonesian Archipelago.** (Illus.). 1972. C. E. Tuttle. (OP).

Dunnigan, James F. **How to Make War: A Comprehensive Guide to Modern Warfare.** (Illus.). 1981. Morrow, William & Co. $14.50.

Elgood, Robert, ed. **Islamic Arms and Armour.** (Illus.). 1979. Biblio Distribution Center. $175.00.

Fadala, Sam. **Black Powder Handgun.** 1981. pap. DBI Books. $9.95.

Featherstone, Donald. **Weapons and Equipment of the Victorian Soldier.** (Illus.). 1978. (Pub. by Blandford Press England). Sterling. $19.95.

Feist, Uwe. **Aero-Armor Series, Vol. 12.** 52 p. (gr. 7-12). 1980. pap. Aero Press. $4.95.

—**Armor Series, Vol. 13.** 1980. pap. Aero Press. $4.95.

Ffoulkes, Charles & Hopkinson, E. C. **Sword, Lance & Bayonet.** (Illus.). 1967. Arco. (OP).

Ffoulkes, Charles J. **Armourer and His Craft.** (Illus.). 1967. Repr. of 1912 ed. Arno Press. $18.50.

Finlay, Ian H. & Bann, Stephen. **Heroic Emblems.** (Illus.). 1978. pap. Z Press. $3.50.

Fitzsimons, Bernard, ed. **The Illustrated Encyclopedia of Twentieth Century Weapons and Warfare.** (Illus.). 1978. Purnell Reference Books. $466.00.

Foss. **Armour and Artillery 1979-1980.** 1980. Franklin Watts, Inc. (OP).

—**Combat Support Equipment 1980-1981.** 1980 Franklin Watts, Inc. $125.00.

Foss, Christopher. **Infantry Weapons of the World.** 1979. Scribner's. $12.50; Encore Ed. $4.50.

—**Infantry Weapons of the World.** 1981. (Pub. by Ian Allan). State Mutual Book & Periodical Service. $35.00.

Frost, H. Gordon. **Blades and Barrels: Six Centuries of Combination Weapons.** Walloon Press. $16.95; deluxe ed. $25.00; presentation ed. $50.00.

Funcken, Liliane & Funcken, Fred. **Arms and Uniforms: Lace Wars, Pt. 1.** 1978. Hippocrene Books. $17.95.

—**Arms and Uniforms: Lace Wars, Pt. 2.** 1978. Hippocrene Books. (OP).

—**Arms and Uniforms-Ancient Egypt to the Eighteenth Century.** Hippocrene Books. (OP).

—**Arms and Uniforms-Late Eighteenth Century to the Present Day.** Hippocrene Books. (OP).

—**Arms and Uniforms-The First World War, Pt. 1.** Hippocrne Books. (OP).

—**Arms and Uniforms-The First World War, Pt. 2.** Hippocrene Books. (OP).

—**Arms and Uniforms-The Napoleonic Wars, Pt. 1.** Hippocrene Books. (OP).

—**Arms and Uniforms-The Napoleonic Wars, Pt. 2.** Hippocrene Books. (OP).

—**Arms and Uniforms-the Second World War, Pt. 1.** Hippocrene Books. (OP).

—**Arms and Uniforms-the Second World War, Pt. 2.** Hippocrene Books. (OP).

—**Arms and Uniforms-The Second World War, Pt. 3.** Hippocrene Books. (OP).

—**Arms and Uniforms-The Second World War, Pt. 4.** Hippocrene Books. (OP).

—**British Infantry Uniforms from Marlborough to Wellington.** (Arms and Uniforms Ser.) (Illus.). 1977. pap. Hippocrene Books. (OP).

—**First World War, 2 pts.** (Illus.). 1974. International Pubns. Service. (OP).

—**The Lace Wars, Pt. 1.** (Illus.). 1977. International Pubns. Service. $17.50.

—**The Lace Wars, Pt. 2.** (Illus.). 1977. International Pubns Service. $17.50.

—**The Lace Wars, Pt. 1.** Beekman Publishers. (OP).

—**The Lace Wars, Pt. 2.** Beekman Publishers. (OP).

Gettens, Rutherford J., et al. **Two Early Chinese Bronze Weapons with Meteoritic Iron Blades.** (Illus.). 1971. pap. Freer Gallery of Art, Smithsonian Institution. $5.00.

Gordon, Don E. **Electronic Warfare: Element of Strategy & Multiplier of Combat Power.** (Illus.). 1981. Pergamon Press. $16.00.

Grancsay, Steven V. **Catalog of the John Woodman Higgins Armory Museum.** (Illus.). Mowbray Co. (OP).

Gruzanski, C. V. **Spike and Chain.** Wehman Brothers, Inc. $7.50.

Guthman, William, ed. **Guns and Other Arms.** (Illus.). 1980. pap. Mayflower Books. $7.95.

Halbritter, Kurt. **Halbritter's Arms Through the Ages: An Introduction to the Secret Weapons of History.** (Illus.). 1979. Viking Press. (OP).

—**Halbritter's Arms Through the Ages: An Introduction to the Secret Weapons of History.** Muir, Jamie, tr. (Illus.). 1980. pap. Penguin Books. (OP).

Hamilton, T. M. **Firearms on the Fronter: Guns at Fort Michilimackinac 1715-1781.** Armour, David A., ed. (Illus.). 1976. pap. Mackinac Island State Park Commission. $3.00.

Hart, Harold H., ed. **Weapons and Armor.** 1977. Hart. (OP).

Hawley, W. M. **Introduction to Japanese Swords.** 1973. pap. Hawley, W. M. $3.00.

Held, Robert, ed. **Arms and Armor Annual.** 1973. pap. DBI Books. (OP).

—**Arms and Armor Annual, Vol. 1.** 1973. pap. Arma Press. $9.95.

Hoff, Arne. **Feuerwaffen.** 2 Vols. (Illus.). 1976. Arma Press. Set (OP).

Hogg, I. V. **Military Pistols and Revolvers.** (Illus.). 1970. pap. Arco. $1.95.

Hogg, Ian V. **Military Small Arms of the Twentieth Century.** 1973. pap. Follett. (OP).

Hogg, Ian V. **The Encyclopedia of Infantry Weapons of World War 2.** (Illus.). 1981. Quality Books Illustrated. $9.98.

Holmes, Bill. **Home Workshop Guns for Defense & Resistance: The Handgun, Vol. 2.** 1979. pap. Paladin Enterprises. $10.00.

Hoyem, George A. **History & Development of Small Arms Ammunition: Black Powder Martial Long Arms, Volley Guns & Machine Guns, Vols. I & II.** 1982. Armory Pubns. $60.00.

—**History & Development of Small Arms Ammunition, Vol. 1: Martial Long Arms, Flintlock Through Rimfire.** 1981. Armory Pubns. $27.50.

—**History & Development of Small Arms Ammunition, Vol. 2: Ammunition: Centerfire, Primitive & Martial Long Arms.** 1982. Armory Pubns. $34.50.

Hughes, B. P. **Firepower: Weapon Effectiveness on the Battlefield, 1630-1815.** (Illus.). 1974. Scribner's. (OP).

Hulton, A. **Sword and the Centuries.** Wehman Brothers, Inc. (OP).

International Institute for Strategic Studies. **Military Balance 1980-1981.** 1980. Facts on File. $17.95.

Jane's Infantry Weapons: 1980. 1980. Franklin Watts, Inc. (OP).

Jane's Weapon Systems: 1980-81. 11th ed. 1980. Franklin Watts, Inc. (OP).

Johnson, Thomas M. **Collecting the Edged Weapons of the Third Reich.** 4 vols. Bradach, Wilfrid, tr. (Illus.). T. M. Johnson. Vol. 1: $18.50; pap. $10.00. Vol. 2: $18.50. Vol. 3: $20.00; Vol. 4: $25.00.

—**Wearing the Edged Weapons of the Third Reich.** Brodach, Wilfrid, tr. (Illus.). 1977. pap. T. M. Johnson $10.00.

Johnson, Thomas M. & Bradach, Wilfrid. **Third Reich Edged Weapons Accounterments.** (Illus.). 1978. pap. T. M. Johnson $10.00.

Joly, H. L. **Naunton Collection of Japanese Sword Fitting.** 1973. Repr. of 1912 ed. Hawley, W. M. $50.00.

Journal of the Arms and Armour Society. Vol. 1. (Illus.). 1970. George Shumway Publisher. $12.00.

Keller, May L. **The Anglo-Saxon Weapon Names, Treated Archaeologically and Etymologically.** 1967. Repr. of 1906 ed. International Pubns Service. $42.50.

Kelly, Francis M. & Schwabe, Randolph. **Short History of Costume and Armour, Chiefly in England 1066-1800.** 2 Vols. in 1. (Illus.). 1968. Repr. of 1931 ed. Arno Press. (OP).

—**A Short History of Costume and Armour 1066-1800.** 2 Vols. in 1. (Illus.). 1972. Arco. (OP).

Kemp, Anthony, **Weapons & Equipment of the Marlborough Wars.** (Illus.). 1981. Sterling. $24.95.

Kozen, S. **Manufacture of Armour and Helmets in Sixteenth Century Japan.** Albert Saifer, Publisher. $35.00.

Laking, Guy F. **A Record of European Armour and Arms Through Seven Centuries.** 5 vols. (Illus.). Repr. AMS Press. set $295.00.

Lewis, Jack. **Modern Gun Values.** 3rd ed. (Illus.). 1981. pap. DBI Books. $9.95.

Lindsay, Merrill. **The Lure of Antique Arms.** (Illus.). 1978. softbound. Stoeger. $5.95.

—**Miniature Arms.** (Illus.). 1976. Arma Press. (OP).

—**Twenty Great American Guns.** (Illus.). 1976. pap. Arma Press. $1.75.

Long, Franklin A. & Reppy, Judith, eds. **The Genesis of New Weapons: Decision Making for Military R&D.** 1980. Pergamon Press. $27.00.

McAulay, John D. **Carbines of the Civil War, 1861-1865.** 1981. Pioneer Press. $7.95.

Mango, Karin. **Armor: Yesterday and Today.** (Illus.). (gr. 4 up). 1980. Messner, Julian. $8.29.

Mason, Richard O. **Use of the Long Bow with the Pike.** 1970. limited ed. George Shumway Publisher. (OP).

Matunas, Edward. **Handbook of Metallic Cartridge Reloading.** (Illus.). 1981. Winchester Press. $15.95.

Mavrodin, Valentin, compiled by. **Fine Arms from Tula.** (Illus.). 1978. Harry N. Abrams, Inc. (OP).

Miller, Gene E. **The Art of Gun Collecting.** 1981. Carlton. $8.95.

Milton, Roger. **Heralds and History.** (Illus.). 1978. Hippocrene Books. (OP).

Mowbray, E. Andrew, ed. **Arms-Armor: From the Atelier of Ernst Schmidt, Munich.** (Illus.). 1967. Mowbray Co. $15.00.

Moyer, Frank A. **Special Forces Foreign Weapons Handbook.** (Illus.). 1970. Paladin Enterprises. (OP).

Neal, W. Keith & Back, D. H. **Great British Gunmakers 1740-1790: The History of John Twigg and the Packington Guns.** (Illus.).

1975. Biblio Distribution Center. $80.00.

Nickel, Helmut, et al. **The Art of Chivalry: European Arms & Armor from the Metropolitan Museum of Art.** 1982. pap. American Federation of Arts. $14.95.

Norman, A. V. & Pottinger, Don. **History of War and Weapons 449-1660: English Warfare from the Anglo-Saxons to Cromwell.** Orig. Title: **Warrior to Soldier: 449-1660.** 1967. T. Y. Crowell. (OP).

Oakeshott, Ewart. **European Weapons and Armour.** (Illus.). 1980. Beinfeld. $29.95.

Owen, J. I. ed. **Brassey's Infantry Weapons of the World.** (Illus.) 2nd ed. 1979. Pergamon Press. $61.00.

—**Brassey's NATO Infantry and Its Weapons.** 1976. Westview Press. (OP).

—**Brassey's Warsaw Pact Infantry and Its Weapons: Defence Publications.** 1976. Westview Press. (OP).

—**Infantry Weapons of the Armies of Africa, the Orient and Latin America.** 1980. pap. Pergamon Press. $24.00.

—**Infantry Weapons of the NATO Armies.** 2nd ed. 1980. pap. Pergamon Press. $24.00.

—**Infantry Weapons of the Warsaw Pact Armies.** 2nd ed. 1980. Pergamon Press. $24.00.

Peterson, Harold L. **The American Sword. 1775-1945.** (Illus.). 1977. Riling, Ray, Arms Books. $25.00.

Pierre, Andrew, J. **The Global Politics of Arms Sales.** 1981. Princeton University Press. $20.00; pap. $5.95.

Pretty, Ronald T., ed. **Jane's Weapon Systems.** 1976. Watts. Franklin, Inc. (OP).

—**Jane's Weapon Systems 1977-78.** (Illus.). 1977. Watts, Franklin, Inc. (OP).

Reid, William. **Arms Through the Ages.** (Illus.). Bonanza. (OP).

—**Arms Through the Ages.** (Illus.). 1976. Harper & Row. (OP).

Robinson, H. Russell. **The Armour of Imperial Rome.** (Illus.). 1974. Scribner's. (OP).

Robinson, H. Russell. **The Armour of Imperial Rome.** (Illus.). 1974. Scribner's. (OP).

Royal United Services Institute for Defense Studies, ed. **International Weapon Developments: A Survey of Current Developments in Weapon Systems,** 4th ed. (Illus.). 1980. pap. Pergamon Press. $14.25.

Rusi & Brassey's Defense Yearbook. 1978/79. 89th ed. 1979. Crane-Russak Co. $27.50.

Sampson, Anthony. **The Arms Bazaar: From Lebanon to Lockheed.** 1978. pap. Bantam Books. $2.95.

Schreeir, Konrad F., Jr. **Marbles Knives and Axes.** (Illus.). 1978. pap. Beinfeld. (OP).

Schroeder, Joseph J. Jr. ed. **Arms of the World: 1911.** (Illus.). 1976. pap. DBI Books. (OP).

Schuyler-Hartley-Graham Military Furnishers. **Illustrated Catalog Arms and Military Goods.** facs. ed. (Illus.). 1864. Flayderman, N. & Co. $9.50.

Seitz, Heribert. **Blankwaffen,** 2 vols. (Illus.). 1976. Arma Press. (OP).

Shepperd, G. A. **A History of War and Weapons, 1660-1918.** (Illus.). 1972. T. Y. Crowell. $8.95.

Snodgrass, A. M. **Arms and Armour of the Greeks.** (Illus.). 1967. Cornell University Press. $25.00.

Stephens, Frederick J. **Edged Weapons, a Collector's Guide.** (Illus.). 1977. Hippocrene Books. (OP).

Tantum, W. V. & Hoffschmidt, E. J. eds. **German Combat Weapons of World War II.** 1968. Sycamore Island Books. $12.95.

Tarassuk, Leonid & Blair, Claude, eds. **The Complete Encyclopedia of Arms & Weapons.** 1982. Simon & Schuster. $41.50.

Thomas, B., et al. **Armi e Armature Europee.** (Illus., Lt.). 1964. Arma Press. $64.50.

Thomas, Donald G. **U.S. Silencer Patents,** 2 vols. new ed. Brown, Robert K. & Lund, Peder C., eds. (Illus.). 1973. Paladin Enterprises. Incl. Vol 1. 1888-1935. Vol. 2 1936-1972. (OP).

—**Silencer Patents, Vol. III: European Patents, 1901-1978.** (Illus.). 1978. pap. Paladin Enterprises. $15.00.

Traister, John. **Learn Gunsmithing: The Troubleshooting Method.** (Illus.). 1980. Winchester Press. $15.95.

Truby, J. David. **Silencers, Snipers and Assassins.** Brown, Robert K. & Lund, Peder C., ed. (Illus.). 1972. Paladin Enterprises. $17.95.

—**Quiet Killers, Vol. 1.** (Illus.). 1972. pap. Paladin Enterprises. $8.00.

—**Quiet Killers II: Silencer Update** (Illus.). 1979. pap. Paladin Enterprises. $8.00.

U. S. Army Foreign Science & Technology Center, Washington, D. C. **Typical Foreign Unconventional Warfare Weapons.** 1976. Paladin Enterprises. Pap. (OP).

U. S. Army Munitions Command. **Silencers: 1896.** (Illus.). 1971. Paladin Enterprises. $13.95. pap. (OP).

U.S. Army Sniper Training Manual. (Illus.). 1975. Paladin Press. $14.95.

Vangen, Roland D. **Indian Weapons.** (Illus.). 1972. Filter Press. $4.50; pap. (OP).

Von Mellenthin, F. W. **Panzer Battles: A Study of the Employment of Armor in the Second World War.** Turner, L. C., ed. Betzler, H., tr. (Illus.). 1971. University of Oklahoma Press. $17.95.

Warry, John. **Warfare in the Classical World: An Illustrated Encyclopedia of Weapons, Warriors and Warfare in the Ancient Civilizations of Greece and Rome.** 1981. St. Martin. $19.95.

Werner, E. T. **Chinese Weapons.** Wehman Brothers, Inc. $3.50.

—**Chinese Weapons.** Alston, Pat, ed. (Illus.). 1972. pap. Ohara Pubns. $4.95.

West, Bill. **Junior Arms Library 1849-1970.** 5 vols. West, Bill. (OP).

—**U.S.A. Arms Manufacturers Catalogues, 1877-1900.** 3 vols. West, Bill. Set. $30.00.

Wilkinson. **Uniforms and Weapons of the Crimean War.** pap. David & Charles. $14.95.

Wilkinson-Latham, Robert. **Swords and Other Edged Weapons.** (Illus.). 1978. Arco. $8.95; pap. $5.95.

Williams, John. **Atlas of Weapons and War.** 1976. John Day. (OP).

Wintringham, Thomas H. **Story of Weapons and Tactics.** facs. ed. 1943. Arno Press. $16.00.

Woikinson, Frederick. **World War 1 Weapons and Uniforms.** (Illus.). Beekman Publishers. $14.95.

Yumoto, J.M. **Samurai Sword.** Wehman Brothers, Inc. $11.95.

ARTILLERY

Archer, Denis, ed. **Jane's Pocket Book of Naval Armament.** (Illus.). 1976. pap. Macmillan. $5.95.

Batchelor, John. **Artillery.** 1973. pap. Ballantine Books. (OP).

Batchelor, John H. & Hogg, Ian. **Artillery.** (Illus.). 1972. Scribner's. $9.95.

Behrend, Arthur. **As from Kemmel Hill: An Adjutant in France and Flanders, 1917 and 1918.** (Illus.). 1975. Repr. of 1963 ed. Greenwood Press. $15.00.

Bidwell, R. G., ed. **Brassey's Artillery of the World.** 2nd rev. ed. 1981. Pergamon Press. $49.50.

Bourne, William. **The Arte of Shooting in Great Ordnaunce.** 1969. Repr. of 1587 ed. W. J. Johnson. $13.00.

Chamberlain, Peter & Gander, Terry. **Heavy Artillery.** (Illus.). 1975. pap. Arco. (OP).

Foss, Christopher. **Artillery of the World.** 3rd rev. ed. (Illus.). 1981. Scribner's. $17.50.

—**Artillery of the World.** 1981 ed. (Pub. by Ian Allan). State Mutual Book & Periodical Service. $35.00.

—**Jane's Pocket Book of Towed Artillery.** 1979. pap. Macmillan. $7.95.

Gibbon, John, ed. **Artillerist's Manual.** Repr. of 1860 ed. Greenwood Press. $45.00.

Hogg, Ian. **Artillery in Color: 1920-1963.** (Illus.). 1980. Arco. $11.95; pap. $7.95.

—**Guns, 1939-45.** 1976. pap. Ballantine Books. (OP).

Hogg, Ian V. **British & American Artillery of World War Two.** (Illus.). 1979. Hippocrene Books. $24.95.

Hogg, Jan & Gander, Terry. **Artillery.** 1982. State Mutual Book & Periodical Service. $60.00.

Hogg, O. F. **Artillery: Its Origin, Heyday and Decline.** (Illus.). 1970. Shoe String Press. (OP).

Hughes, B. P. **Firepower: Weapon Effectiveness on the Battlefield, 1630-1815.** (Illus.). 1974. Scribner's. (OP).

Macchiavelli, Niccolo. **The Arte of Warre (Certain Wales of the Orderying of Souldiours).** Whitehorne, P., tr. 1969. Repr. of 1562 ed. W. J. Johnson. $42.00.

Marsden, E. W. **Greek & Roman Artillery: Technical Treatises.** 1971. Oxford University Press. (OP).

Norton, Robert. **The Gunner, Showing the Whole Practise of Artillerie.** 1973. Repr. of 1628 ed. W. J. Johnson. $40.00.

Patrick, John M. **Artillery & Warfare During the Thirteenth & Fourteenth Centuries.** 1961. pap. Utah State University Press. (OP).

Rogers, H. B. **A History of Artillery.** (Illus.). 1974. Citadel Press. $7.95.

Rogers, H. C. **A History of Artillery.** 1977. pap. Citadel Press. $4.95.

Simienowicz, Casimir. **The Great Art of Artillery.** 1976. Charles River Books. $20.00.

—**The Great Art of Artillery.** Chevlet, George, tr. from Fr. 1973. Repr. of 1729 ed. British Book Center. (OP).

Tousard, Louis De. **American Artillerists Companion.** 3 vols. 1809-1813. Repr. Set. Greenwood Press. $106.00.

BALLISTICS

Laible, Roy C. **Ballistic Materials & Penetration Mechanics.** 1980. Elsevier. $70.00.

Matunas, Edward. **American Ammunition and Ballistics.** (Illus.). 1979. Winchester Press. $13.95.

Wilber, Charles G. **Ballistic Science for the Law Enforcement Officer.** (Illus.). 1977. C. C. Thomas. $30.75.

—**Forensic Biology for the Law Enforcement Officer.** (Illus.). 1974. C. C. Thomas. $25.75.

Williams, M. **Practical Handgun Ballistics.** 1980. C. C. Thomas. $17.50.

BAYONETS

Carter, Anthony. **The History and Development of the Sword, Sabre and Knife Bayonet.** 1974. Scribner's. (OP).

Carter, J. Anthony. **Allied Bayonets of World War Two.** (Illus.). 1969. Arco. (OP).

Hardin, Albert N. **The American Bayonet: 1776-1964.** (Illus.). 1977. Hardin. $24.50.

Stephens, Frederick J. A. **A Collector's Pictorial Book of Bayonets.** (Illus.). 1976. pap. Hippocrene Books. (OP).

Walter, John. **The German Bayonet.** 1982. Stackpole. $19.95.

BIRD DOGS

Brown, William F. **National Field Trial Champions, 1956-1966.** (Illus.). 1966. A. S. Barnes. (OP).

—**Field Trials: History, Management and Judging Standards.** 2nd rev. ed. (Illus.). 1981. A. S. Barnes. $13.95.

Davis, Henry P. **Training Your Own Bird Dog.** rev. ed. (Illus.). 1970. Putnam. $8.95.

Evans, George Bird. **Troubles with Bird Dogs and What to Do About Them: Training Experiences with Actual Dogs Under the Gun.** (Illus.). 1975. Winchester Press. $15.95.

Falk, John R. **The Complete Guide to Bird Dog Training.** 1976. Winchester Press. $14.95.

—**The Practical Hunter's Dog Book.** (Illus.). 1975. softbound. Stoeger. $5.95.

—**The Practical Hunter's Dog Dook.** (Illus.). Winchester Press. $10.95.

Long, Paul. **All the Answers to All Your Questions About Training Pointing Dogs.** (Illus.). 1974. pap. Capital Bird Dog Enterprises. $5.95.

Mueller, Larry. **Bird Dog Guide.** rev. ed. (Illus.). 1976. softbound. Stoeger. $6.95.

Seminatore, Mike & Rosenburg, John M. **Your Bird Dog and You.** (Illus.). 1977. A. S. Barnes. (OP).

Webb, Sherman, **Practical Pointer Training.** (Illus.). 1974. Winchester Press. (OP).

BLACK POWDER GUNS

Buchele, William & Shumway, George. **Recreating The American Longrifle.** Orig. Title: **Recreating The Kentucky Rifle.** (Illus.). 1973. pap. George Shumway Publisher. $16.00.

Fadala, Sam. **The Black Powder Handgun.** 1981. pap. DBI Book. $9.95.

—**Blackpowder Hunting.** (Illus.). 1978. Stackpole. $10.95.

—**The Complete Black Powder Handbook.** 1979. pap. DBI Books. $9.95.

Lauber, George. **How to Build Your Own Flintlock Rifle or Pistol.** Seaton, Lionel, tr. from Ger. (Illus.). 1976. pap. Jolex. $6.95.

—**How to Build Your Own Percussion Rifle or Pistol.** Seaton, Lionel, tr. from Ger. (Illus.). 1976. pap. Jolex. $6.95.

—**How to Build Your Own Wheellock Rifle or Pistol.** Seaton, Lionel, tr. from Ger. (Illus.). 1976. Jolex. $6.95.

Lewis, Jack & Springer, Robert, eds. **Black Powder Gun Digest,** 2nd ed. (Illus.). 1977. pap. DBI Books. (OP).

National Muzzle Loading Rifle Association. **Muzzle Blasts: Early Years Plus Vol. I & II. 1939-41.** 1974. pap. George Shumway Publisher. (OP).

Nonte, George C., Jr. **Black Powder Guide.** 2nd ed. (Illus.). 1976. softbound. Stoeger. $7.95.

Nonte, George C., Jr. Author; Traister, John E., Ed. **Black Powder Guide,** 3rd Edition. (Illus.). 1982. Stoeger. $10.95.

—**Home Guide to Muzzle Loaders.** (Illus.). 1974. pap. Stackpole Books. (OP).

—**Home Guide to Muzzle Loaders.** 1982. pap. Stackpole Books. $14.95.

Steindler, R. A., ed. & illus. **Shooting the Muzzle Loaders.** (Illus.). 1975. Jolex. $11.95; pap. $6.95.

Walker, Ralph T. **Black Powder Gunsmithing.** 1978. pap. DBI Books. $8.95.

BOW AND ARROW

Adams, Chuck. **Bowhunter's Digest.** 2nd ed. pap. 1981. DBI Books. $9.95.

Barwick, Humphrey. **Concerning the Force and Effect of Manuall Weapons of Fire.** 1974. Repr. of 1594 ed. W. J. Johnson. $8.00.

Hamilton, T. M. **Native American Bows: Their Types and Relationships.** (Illus.). 1972. George Shumway Publisher. (OP).

—**Native American Bows.** 2nd ed. 1982. Missouri Archaeological Society. $10.00.

Hardy, Robert. **Longbow: A Social and Military History.** (illus.). 1977. Arco. (OP).

Mason, Richard O. **Use of the Long Bow with the Pike.** 1970. limited ed. George Shumway Publishers. (OP).

Maynard, Roger **Advanced Bowhunting.** (Illus.) 1982. softbound. Stoeger. $10.95.

Murdoch, John. **Study of the Eskimo Bows in the U.S. National Museum.** facs. ed. (Illus.). Repr. of 1884 ed. pap. Shorey. $1.95.

A New Invention of Shooting Fireshafts in Long-Bowes. 1974. Repr. of 1628 ed. W. J. Johnson. $3.50.

Pope, Saxton T. **Bows and Arrows.** 1974. University of California Press. $17.00.

Smythe, John. **Bow Versus Gun.** 1974. Repr. of 1590 ed. text ed. British Book Center. (OP).

Tinsley, Russell. **Bow Hunter's Guide.** (Illus.). 1975. softbound. Stoeger. (OP).

CARIBOU

Georgeson, C. C. **Reindeer & Caribou.** facs. ed. (Illus.). Repr. of 1904 ed. pap. Shorey. $2.95.

Murie, Olaus J. **Alaska Yukon Caribou.** facs. ed. (Illus.). 1935. pap. Shorey. (OP).

Rearden, Jim. **Wonders of Caribou.** (gr. 5 up). 1976. Dodd, Mead & Co. (OP).

CARTRIDGES

Barnes, Frank. **Cartridges of the World.** 4th ed. 1980. pap. DBI Books. $10.95.

Bartlett, W. A. & Gallatin, D. B. **B and G Cartridge Manual.** Pioneer Press. $2.00.

Datig, Fred A. **Cartridges for Collectors,** 3 vols. Borden. $8.95 ea.

Nonte, George. **The Home Guide to Cartridge Conversions.** rev. ed. Gun Room Press. rev. ed. $15.00.

Steindler, R. A. **Reloader's Guide.** 3rd ed. (Illus.). 1975. softbound. Stoeger. $7.95.

Suydam. **American Cartridge.** Borden. $8.50.

Suydam, Charles R. **U.S. Cartridges and their Handguns.** (Illus.). 1976. Beinfeld. $15.95; pap. $9.95.

—**U.S. Cartridges and their Handguns: 1795-1975.** (Illus.). 1978. DBI Books. (OP).

Thomas, Gough. **Shotguns and Cartridges for Game and Clays.** 3rd ed. (Illus.). 1976. Transatlantic Arts, Inc. $25.00.

Treadwell. **Cartridges, Regulation and Experiemental.** Pioneer Press. $2.00.

Whelen, Townsend. **Why Not Load Your Own?** (Illus.). A. A. Barnes. (OP).

COLLECTING

Chapel, Charles E. **The Gun Collector's Handbook of Values: 1980-81.** 13th rev. ed. (Illus.). 1979 Coward, McCann and Geoghegan. $16.95; pap. $8.95.

Liu, Allan J., ed. **The American Sporting Collector's Handbook.** (Illus.). 1977. softbound. Stoeger. $5.95.

COLT REVOLVERS

Bady, Donald B. **Colt Automatic Pistols,** rev. ed. 1973. Borden. $16.50.

Barnard, Henry **Armsmear: The Samuel Colt Biography.** (Illus.). 1978. Beinfeld. (OP).

Garton, George. **Colt's SAA: Post War Models.** Beinfeld. $17.95.

Keating, Bern. **The Flamboyant Mr. Colt and His Deadly Six-Shooter.** 1978. Doubleday. (OP).

Larson, E. Dixon. **Colt Tips.** Pioneer Press. (OP).

McClernan. John B. **Slade's Wells Fargo Colt.** (Illus.). 1977. Exposition Press. (OP).

Serven, James E. **Firearms from Eighteen Thirty-Six.** 1979. Stackpole Books. $29.95.

Shumaker, P. L. **Colt's Variations of the Old Model Pocket Pistol.** 1957. Borden. $8.95.

Smith, Loren W. **Home Gunsmithing: The Colt Single Action Revolvers.** (Illus.). 1971. Ray Riling Arms Books. (OP).

Swayze, Nathan L. **Fifty One Colt Navies.** (Illus.). 1967. Gun Hill. $15.00.

Virgines, George. **Saga of the Colt Six Shooter: And the Famous Men Who Used It.** 1969. Fell, Frederick, Publishers. (OP).

Wilson, R. L., **The Book of Colt Engraving.** 1978. Follett. (OP).

—**The Book of Colt Engraving.** 2nd ed. (Illus.). 1981. Beinfeld. $59.95.

CROSSBOWS

Bilsom, Frank. **Crossbows.** (Illus.). 1975. Hippocrene Books. (OP).

Payne-Gallwey, R. **Crossbow.** Newbury Books Inc. (OP).

Payne-Gallwey, Ralph. **Cross-Bow, Medieval and Modern.** Saifer, Albert, Pub. $55.00.

Wilbur, C. Martin. **History of the Crossbow.** (Illus.). Repr. of 1936 ed. pap. Shorey. $2.95.

DECOYS

Barber, Joel. **Wild Fowl Decoys.** (Illus.). pap. Dover. $6.00.

—**Wild Fowl Decoys.** (Illus.). Peter Smith. $12.50.

Becker, A. C., Jr. **Decoying Waterfowl.** (Illus.). 1973. A. S. Barnes. (OP).

Berkey, Barry R., et al. **Pioneer Decoy Carvers: A Biography of Lemuel and Stephen Ward.** (Illus.). 1977. Cornell Maritime, Press. $17.50.

Brown, Ercil. **Thrills of the Duck Hunt for the Officebound.** (Illus.). 1973. Dorrance. (OP).

Buckwalter, Harold R. **Susquehanna River Decoys.** (Illus.). 1978. Schiffer. $12.95.

Casson, Paul W. **Decoy-Collecting Primer.** (Illus.). pap. Eriksson, Paul S., Pubs. $5.95.

Connett, Eugene. **Duck Decoys.** 1980. Durrell. $12.50.

Coykendall, Ralf. **Duck Decoys and How to Rig Them.** (Illus.). 1965. Holt, Rinehart & Winston. (OP).

Decoys. (Illus.). 1974. Applied Arts. (OP).

Delph, John and Delph, Shirley. **Factory Decoys of Mason Stevens.** (Illus.). 1979. Schiffer. $35.00.

Earnest, Adele. **The Art of the Decoy.** (Illus.). 1965. Crown. $10.00.

—**The Art of the Decoy.** (Illus.). 1982. pap. Schiffer. $14.95.

Fleckenstein, Henry A. **Decoys of the Mid-Atlantic Region.** (Illus.). 1979. Schiffer. $19.95.

Frank, Charles W., Jr. **Louisiana Duck Decoys.** 1979. Pelican. $24.95.

Humphreys, John. **Hides, Calls and Decoys.** (Illus.). 1979. pap. International Pubns. Service. $7.50.

Johnsgard, Paul A. ed. **The Bird Decoy: An American Art Form.** (Illus.). 1976. University of Nebraska Press. $17.95.

Le Master, Richard. **Wildlife in Wood.** 1978. Model Technology, Inc. (OP).

—**Wildlife in Wood.** (Illus.). 1977. Contemporary Books. $35.00.

MacKay, William F., Jr. & Colio, Quinton. **American Bird Decoy.** (Illus.). 1979. Repr. of 1965 ed. Schiffer. $19.95.

MacKay, William, Jr. **American Bird.** (Illus.). 1979. Repr. of 1965 ed. Schiffer. $19.95.

McKinney, J. Evans. **Decoys of the Susquehanna Flats and Their Makers.** 1979. pap. Holly Press. $12.95.

Murphy, Charles F. **Working Plans for Working Decoys.** (Illus.). 1979. Winchester Press. $21.95.

Parmalee, Paul W. & Loomis, Forrest D. **Decoys and Decoy Carvers of Illinois.** 1969. pap. Northern Illinois University Press. $25.00.

Shourds, Harry V. & Hillman, Anthony. **Carving Duck Decoys.** 1981. pap. Dover. $4.25.

Spielman, Patrick. **Making Wood Decoys.** 1982. Sterling. $16.95; lib. bdg. $14.99; pap. $8.95.

Starr, George, R., Jr. **Decoys of the Atlantic Flyway.** 1974. Winchester Press. (OP).

—**How to Make Working Decoys.** (Illus.). 1978. Winchester Press. $21.95.

Webster, David S. & Kehoe, William. **Decoys at Shelburne Museum.** 1961. pap. Shelburne Museum, Inc. (OP).

Veasey, William & Hull, Cary S. **Waterfowl Carving: Blue Ribbon Techniques.** (Illus.). 1982. Schiffer. $35.00.

DEER HUNTING

Anderson, Luther A. **Hunting the Uplands with Rifle and Shotgun.** (Illus.). 1977. Winchester Press. $12.95.

Bauer, Erwin A. **The Digest Book of Deer Hunting.** (Illus.). 1979. pap. Follett. (OP).

—**Digest Book of Deer Hunting.** pap. DBI Books. $2.95.

Cartier, John O. **The Modern Deer Hunter.** (Illus.). 1977. T. Y. Crowell. (OP).

Conatser, Dean. **Bowhunting the Whitetail Deer.** Winchester Press. (OP).

Conway, Bryant W. **Successful Hints on Hunting White Tail Deer.** 2nd ed. 1967. pap. Claitors. $1.98.

Dalrymple, Bryon W. **Complete Book of Deer Hunting.** (Illus.). 1975. softbound, Stoeger. $6.95.

—**Complete Book of Deer Hunting.** 1973. Winchester Press. $12.95.

Dickey, Charley. **Charley Dickey's Deer Hunting.** (Illus.). 1977. pap. Oxmoor House. $3.95.

Donovan, Robert E. **Hunting Whitetail Deer.** (Illus.). 1978. Winchester Press. $15.95.

Elman, Robert, Ed. **All About Deer Hunting in America.** 1976. Winchester Press. $13.95.

Fischl, Josef & Rue, Leonard Lee, III. **After Your Deer is Down.** 1981. pap. Winchester Press. $9.95.

Hayes, Tom. **How to Hunt the White Tail Deer.** A. S. Barnes. rev. ed. pap. $6.95.

Hewett, H. P. **Fairest Hunting: Hunting and Watching Exmoor Deer.** 1974. British Book Center. (OP).

—**The Fairest Hunting.** (Illus.). J. A. Allen. (OP).

James, M. R. **Bowhunting: For Whitetail and Mule Deer.** 1976. Jolex. $6.95.

Kittredge, Doug & Wambold, H. R. **Bowhunting for Deer.** rev. ed. 1978. Stackpole Books. $12.95.

Koller, Lawrence, R. **Shots at Whitetails.** rev. ed. (Illus.). 1970. Knopf. (OP).

Laycock, George. **Deer Hunter's Bible.** rev. ed. (Illus.). 1971. pap. Doubleday. $3.95.

—**The Deer Hunter's Bible.** 2nd rev. ed. (Illus.). 1977. pap. Doubleday. $3.95.

McNair, Jack. **Shooting for the Skipper: Memories of a Veteran Deerstalker.** (Illus.). 1971. Reed, A. H. & A. W. Books. (OP).

Nelson, Norm. **Hunting the Whitetail Deer: How to Bring Home North America's Number-One Big Game Animal.** (Illus.). 1980. McKay, David, Co. (OP).

Outdoor Life Editors. **Outdoor Life's Deer Hunting Book.** (Illus.). 1975. Harper & Row. $10.95.

Sell, Francis E. **Art of Successful Deer Hunting.** 1980. pap. Willow Creek. $5.95.

Sisley, Nick. **Deer Hunting Across North America.** (Illus.). 1975. Freshet Press. $12.95.

Smith, Richard P. **Deer Hunting.** rev. ed. (Illus.). 1981. pap. Stackpole Books. $9.95.

Strung, Norman. **Deer Hunting.** (Illus.). 1973. Lippincott. (OP).

—**Deer Hunting.** (Illus.). 1982. pap. Mountain Press. $8.95.

Tillett, Paul. **Doe Day: The Antlerless Deer Controversy in New Jersey.** 1963. pap. Rutgers University Press. $5.95.

Tinsley, Russell. **Hunting the Whitetail Deer.** (Illus.). 1974. pap. Barnes & Noble. (OP).

—**Hunting the Whitetail Deer.** rev ed. (Illus.). 1977 Funk & Wagnalls. (OP).

—**Hunting the Whitetail Deer.** rev. ed. (Illus.). 1977 T. Y. Crowell. $9.95; pap. $4.50.

Wallack, L. R. **The Deer Rifle.** (Illus.). 1978. Winchester Press. $12.95.

Weiss, John. **The Whitetail Deer Hunter's Handbook.** (Illus.). 1979. pap. Winchester Press. $9.95.

Whitehead, Kenneth. **Hunting and Stalking Deer Throughout the Ages.** (Illus.). 1980. David & Charles. $45.00.

Wootters, John. **Hunting Trophy Deer.** 1977. Winchester Press. $15.95.

DUCK SHOOTING

Adams, Chuck. **The Digest Book of Duck and Goose Hunting.** (Illus.). pap. DBI Books. $2.95.

Barber, Joel. **Wild Fowl Decoys.** (Illus.). Peter Smith. $12.50.

—**Wild Fowl Decoys.** (Illus.). pap. Dover. $6.95.

Coykendall, Ralf. **Duck Decoys and How to Rig Them.** (Illus.). 1965. Holt, Rinehart & Winston. (OP).

Gresham, Grits. **The Complete Wildfowler.** (Illus.). 1975. softbound. Stoeger. $5.95.

Hinman, Bob. **The Duck Hunter's Handbook.** (Illus.). 1976. softbound. Stoeger. $8.95.

—**The Duck Hunter's Handbook.** 1974. Winchester Press. $12.95.

Jordan, James, M. & Alcorn, George T., eds. **The Wildfowler's Heritage.** (Illus.). 1981. JCP Corp. of Virginia. $46.50; deluxe $125.00.

DUCKS

Batty, J. **Domesticated Ducks and Geese.** 1981. (Pub. by Saiga). State Mutual Book & Periodical Service. $40.00.

Dethier, Vincent G. **Fairweather Duck.** 1970. Walker & Co. $4.95.

Ellis, Melvin R. **Peg Leg Pete.** 1973. Holt, Rinehart & Winston. (OP).

Holderread, Dave. **The Home Duck Flock.** rev. ed. (Illus.). 1980. pap. Garden Way Publishing. $7.95.

Hyde, Dayton. **Raising Wild Ducks in Capitivity.** 1974. Dutton. (OP).

Jaques, Florence P. **Geese Fly High.** (Illus.). 1964. Repr. of 1939 ed. University of Minnesota Press. $9.95.

Kortright, E. H. **Ducks, Geese and Swans of North America.** rev. by Frank C. Bellrose. (Illus.). 1981. Stackpole Books. $29.95.

McKane, John G. **Ducks of the Mississippi Flyway.** 1969. pap. North Star Press. $2.98.

Ogilvie, M. A. **Ducks of Britain and Europe.** 1975. R. Curtis Books. (OP).

—**Ducks of Britain and Europe.** (Illus.). 1975. Bueto. $18.00.

Ripley, Dillon. **Paddling of Ducks.** (Illus.). 1969. Smithsonian Institution Press. (OP).

Romashko, Sandra D. **Wild Ducks and Geese of North America.** (Illus.). 1978. pap. Windward Publishing. $2.95.

Saiga Editors. **Ducks and Geese.** 1981. State Mutual Book. $10.00.

Sowls, Lyle K. **Prairie Ducks: A Study of Their Behavior, Ecology and Management.** (Illus.). 1978. University of Nebraska Press. pap. $3.50.

Walters, John & Parker, Michael. **Keeping Ducks, Geese and Turkeys.** 1976. Merrimack Book Service. $8.95.

DUELING

Bacon, Francis. **The Charge of Sir F. Bacon Touching Duells.** Repr. of 1614 ed. Johnson, Walter J., Inc. $8.00.

Baldick, Robert. **The Duel: The History of Dueling.** (Illus.). 1966. Crown. $8.50.

Bennetton, Norman A. **Social Significance of the Duel in Seventeenth Century Drama.** Repr. of 1938 ed. Greenwood Press. (OP).

Coleman, J. Winston. **Famous Kentucky Duels.** (Illus.). 1969. Henry Clay. $3.95.

Douglas, William. **Duelling Days in the Army.** 1977. Scholarly Press. (OP).

Gamble, Thomas. **Savannah Duels & Duellists: 1733-1877.** (Illus.). 1974. Repr. of 1923 ed. $18.00.

Hutton, Alfred. **The Sword and the Centuries: or, Old Sword Days and Old Sword Ways.** (Illus.). 1973. Repr. of 1901 ed. C. E. Tuttle. $14.50.

McCarty, Clara S. **Duels in Virginia and Nearby Bladenburg.** 1976. Dietz Press. (OP).

Melville, Lewis & Hargreaves, Reginald. **Famous Duels and Assassinations.** (Illus.). 1974. Repr. of 1929 ed Gale Research Co. $27.00.

Risher, James F. **Interview with Honor.** 1975. Dorrance. (OP).

Sietz, Don C. **Famous American Duels.** facs. ed. 1929. Arno Press. $18.00.

Thimm, Carl A. **Complete Bibliography of Fencing and Dueling.** (Illus.). 1968. Repr. of 1846 ed. Arno Press. $23.00.

Trachtman, Paul. **The Gunfighters.** 1974. Silver Burdett Co. $12.96.

Williams, Jack K. **Dueling in the Old South: Vignettes of Social History.** Texas A & M University Press. $9.95.

FALCONRY

Allen, Mark. **Falconry in Arabia.** 1982. Greene. $40.00.

Ap Evans, Humphrey. **Falconry.** (Illus.). 1974. Arco. $15.00.

—**Falconry for You.** Branford. (OP).

Beebe, F. L. **Hawks, Falcons and Falconry.** (Illus.). 1976. Hancock House. $25.00.

Beebe, Frank L. & Webster, Harold M., eds. **North American Falconry and Hunting Hawks.** 4th ed. (Illus.). 1976. North American Falconry and Hunting Hawks. $30.00.

Berners, Juliana. **The Boke of Saint Albans Containing Treatises on Hawking, Hunting and Cote Armour.** 1976. Repr. of 1881 ed. Scholarly Press. $25.00.

—**The Book of Hawking, Hunting and Blasing of Arms.** 1969. Repr. of 1486 ed. W. J. Johnson. $42.00.

Bert, Edmund. **An Approved Treatise of Hawkes and Hawking Divided into Three Bookes.** 1968 Repr. of 1619 ed. W. J. Johnson. $16.00.

—**An Approved Treatise on Hawks and Hawking.** 1982. (Pub. by Falconiforme). State Mutual Book & Periodical Service. $50.00.

Blome, Richard. **Hawking or Falconry.** 1982. (Pub. by Falconiforme). State Mutual Book & Periodical Service. $50.00.

Brander, Michael. **Dictionary of Sporting Terms.** (Illus.). 1968. Humanities Press. (OP).

Burton, Richard F. **Falconry in the Valley of the Indus.** 1971. Falcon Head Press. $13.50.

Danielsson, Bror, ed. **Middle English Falconry Treatises, Pt. 1.** 1980. pap. Humanities Press. Write for info.

Fisher, Charles H. **Falconry Reminiscences.** 1972. Falcon Head Press. $15.00; deluxe ed. $25.00.

Fleming, Arnold. **Falconry and Falcons: Sport of Flight.** (Illus.). 1976. Repr. of 1934 ed. Charles River Books. (OP).

—**Falconry and Falcons: Sport of Flight.** (Illus.). Repr. text ed. Charles River Books. (OP).

Ford, Emma. **Falconry in News and Field.** (Illus.). 1982. Branford. $32.50.

Frederick Second of Hohenstaufen. **The Art of Falconry.** Wood, Casey A. & Fyfe, F. Marjorie, eds. (Illus.). 1943. Stanford University Press. $39.50.

Freeman, Gage E. & Salvin, Francis H. **Falconry: Its Claims, History and Practice.** 1972. Falcon Head Press. $12.50; deluxe ed. $25.00.

Glasier. **Falconry and Hawking.** David & Charles. $45.00.

Glasier, Philip. **Falconry and Hawking.** (Illus.). 1979. Branford. $15.50.

Gryndall, William. **Hawking, Hunting, Fouling and Fishing;** Newly Corrected by W. Gryndall Faulkener. 1972. Repr. of 1596 ed. Walter J. Johnson, Inc. $13.00.

Hands, Rachel, ed. **English Hawking and Hunting in the Boke of St. Albans.** facs. ed. (Illus.). 1975. Oxford University Press. (OP).

Harting, J.E. **Hints on the Management of Hawks and Practical Falconry.** 1982. (Pub. by Saiga). State Mutual Book & Periodical Service. $50.00.

Harting, James E. **Bibliotheca Accipitraria, a Catalogue of Books Ancient and Modern Relating to Falconry.** 1977. Repr. of 1963 ed. Oak Knoll Books. $45.00.

Humphries, Roy. **Hawking, Nineteen Twelve to Nineteen Sixty-One.** 1981. State Mutual Book & Periodical Service. $39.00.

Illingworth, Frank. **Falcons and Falconry.** 3rd rev. ed. 1964. British Book Center. (OP).

Jameson, Everett W., Jr. **The Hawking of Japan, the History and Development of Japanese Falconry.** (Illus.). Repr. of 1962 ed. Jameson & Peeters. $24.50.

Jameson, E. W. Jr. & Peeters, Hans J. **Introduction to Hawking.** 2nd ed. (Illus.). 1977. pap. E. W. Jameson, Jr. $8.95.

Lascelles, Gerald. **Art of Falconry.** (Illus.). 1971. Repr. of 1895 ed. Charles T. Branford, Co. $10.50.

Latham, Simon. **Lathams Falconry, 2 pts.** 1977. Repr. of 1615 ed. Walter J. Johnson, Inc. $32.50.

McElroy, Harry. **Desert Hawking.** (Illus.). 1977. H. C. McElroy. (OP).

Madden, D. H. **Chapter of Mediaeval History.** 1969. Repr. of 1924 ed. Kennikat. $15.00.

Mellor J. E. **Falconry Notes by Mellor.** 1972. Falcon Head Press. $8.50.

Michell, E. B. **Art and Practice of Hawking.** Bradford. (OP).

Phillott, D. C. & Harcourt, E. S., trs. from Persian Urdu. **Falconry—Two Treatises.** 1968. text ed. Falcon Head Press. $30.00.

Saiga Editors, ed. **Falconry.** 1981. State Mutual Book and Periodical Service. (OP).

Salvin, Francis H. & Broderick, William. **Falconry In the British Isles.** 1970. Repr. of 1855 ed. North American Falconry and Hunting Hawks. $22.50.

Samson, Jack. **Falconry Today.** (Illus.). 1975. Walck, Henry Z., Inc. (OP).

Schlegel, H. & Verster De Wulverhorst, J. A. **The World of Falconry.** 1980. Vendome Press. $60.00.

Schlegel, H. & Wulverhorst, A. H. **Traite De Fauconnerie: Treatise of Falconry.** Hanlon, Thomas, tr. (Illus.). 1973. Chasse Pubns. $32.50.

Stevens, Ronald. **Observations on Modern Falconry.** 1983. (Pub. by Falconiforme). State Mutual Book & Periodical Service. $55.00.

—**The Taming of Genghis.** 1982. (Pub. by Falconiforme). State Mutual Book & Periodical Service. $50.00.

Summers, Gerald. **The Lure of the Falcon.** 1973.

Simon & Schuster. $7.95.

Turberville, George. **The Books of Faulconrie or Hawking.** 1969. Repr. of 1575 ed. Walter J. Johnson, Inc. (OP).

Woodford, Michael H. **Manual of Falconry.** Branford, Charles T., Co. (OP).

FIREARMS

Ackley, Parker O. **Home Gun Care and Repair.** (Illus.). 1974. pap. Stackpole Books. $6.95.

Amber, John T. **Gun Digest Treasury.** 5th ed. 1977. pap. DBI Books. (OP).

Anderson, Robert S. **Metallic Cartridge Reloading.** (Illus.). 1982. pap. DBI Books. $10.95.

Askins, Charles. **Askins on Pistols and Revolvers.** Bryant, Ted & Askins, Bill, eds. 1980. National Rifle Association. $25.00; pap. $8.95.

Automatic and Concealable Firearms: Design Book, Vol. II. (Illus.). 1979. pap. Paladin Enterprises. $12.00.

Baer, L. R. **The Parker Gun: An Immortal American Classic.** (Illus.). 1978. Beinfeld. (OP).

Barker, A. J. **Principles of Small Arms.** (Illus.). 1977. pap. Paladin Enterprises. (OP).

Barnes, Leslie W. **Canada's Guns: An Illustrated History of Artillery.** (Illus.). 1979. pap. University of Chicago Press. $9.95.

Barwick, Humphrey. **Concerning the Force and Effect of Manuall Weapons of Fire.** 1974. Repr. of 1594 ed. W. J. Johnson. $8.00.

Bearse, Ray. **Sporting Arms of the World.** (Illus.). 1977. Harper & Row. $15.95.

Bianchi, John. **Blue Steel and Gunleather.** 1978. Follett. (OP).

Bird, Nicholas D. **Observer's Book of Firearms.** (Illus.). 1978. Scribner's. $3.95.

Bowman, Hank W. **Famous Guns from the Winchester Collection.** (Illus.). 1958. Arco. (OP).

Bristow, Allen P. **The Search for an Effective Police Handgun.** (Illus.). 1973. C. C. Thomas. $20.00.

Brophy, William S. **Krag Rifles.** (Illus.). Beinfeld. (OP).

Browne, Bellmore H. **Guns and Gunning.** (Illus.). Repr. of 1908 ed. pap. Shorey. $4.95.

Burch, Monte. **Gun Care and Repair.** 1978. Winchester Press. $15.95.

Cadiou, Yves & Richard, Alphonse. **Modern Firearms.** (Illus.). 1977. William Morrow & Co. $19.95.

Carlisle, G.L. & Stanbury, Percy. **Shotgun and Shooter.** rev. ed. 1981. (Pub. by Hutchinson). State Mutual Book & Periodical Service. $35.00.

Carmichel, Jim. **The Modern Rifle.** (Illus.). 1976. softbound. Stoeger. (OP).

Chant, Chris. **Armed Forces of the United Kingdom.** (Illus.). 1980. David & Charles. $14.95.

Chapel, Charles E. **Complete Guide to Gunsmithing: Gun Care and Repair.** rev. ed. (Illus.). 1962. A. S. Barnes. (OP).

Consumer Guide. **The Consumer Guide: Guns.** 1972. pap. Pocket Books. (OP).

Corbin,David R. **Discover Swaging.** 1979. Stackpole Books. (OP).

Courtney, Andrew. **Muzzle Loading Today.** (Illus). International Pubns. Service. $8.50.

Cromwell, Giles. **The Virginia Manufactory of Arms.** 1975. University Press of Virginia. $20.00.

Cullin, William H. **How to Conduct Foreign Military Sales: The 80-81 United States Guide.** 1980. Bureau of National Affairs. $95.00.

Daenhardt, Rainer, ed. **Espingarda Perfeyta; or The Perfect Gun: Rules for Its Use Together with Necessary Instructioons for Its Construction and Precepts for Good Aiming.** Daenhardt, Rainer & Neal, W. Keith, trs. from Port. (Illus., Eng. & Port.). 1975. Biblio Distribution Centre. $48.00.

Davis, John E. **Introduction to Tool Marks, Firearms and the Striagraph.** (Illus.). 1958. C. C. Thomas. $24.50.

Dewar, Michael. **Internal Security Weapons and Equipment of the World..** (Illus.). 1979. Scribner's. encore ed. $4.95.

Dunlap, Roy. The Gunowner's Book of Care, Repair & Maintenance. (Illus.). 1974. Harper & Row. $12.95.

Durham, Douglass. **Taking Aim.** 1977. Seventy-Six Press. $7.95.

Edsall, James. **The Story of Firearm Ignition.** Pioneer Press. $3.50.

—**Volcanic Firearms and Their Successors.** Pioneer Press. $2.50.

Educational Research Council of America. **Firearms Examiner.** Ferris, Theodore N. & Marchak, John P., eds. (Illus.). 1977. Changing Times Education Service. $2.25.

Ezell, Edward C. **Handguns of the World.** (Illus.). 1981. Stackpole Books. $39.95.

Ezell, Edward C. & Smith, W. H. **Small Arms of the World.** 11th ed. (Illus.). 1979. Repr. of 1943 ed. Stackpole Books. $29.95.

Fairbairn, W. E. & Sykes, E. A. **Shooting to Live.** 1974. Repr. of 1942 ed. Paladin Press. (OP).

Flayderman, Norm. **Flayderman's Guide to Antique Firearms and Their Values.** 1977. pap. DBI Books. (OP).

—**Flayderman's Guide to Antique American Firearms. 2nd ed.** (Illus.). 1980. pap. DBI Books. $15.95.

Foss, Christopher, **Infantry Weapons of the World.** rev. ed. (Illus.). 1979. Scribner's. (OP). encore ed. $4.95.

George, John N. **English Pistols and Revolvers.** Albert Saifer, Pub. $20.00.

Gottlieb, Alan M. **The Rights of Gun Owners.** 1981. softbound. Caroline House. $6.95.

Grennell, Dean A. **ABC's of Reloading.** 2nd ed. (Illus.). 1980. pap. DBI Books. $9.95.

Grennell, Dean A. & Lewis, Jack. **Law Enforcement Handgun Digest.** 2nd rev. ed. 1976. pap. Follett. (OP).

Grennell, Dean A. & Lewis, Jack. eds. **Pistol and Revolver Digest.** 2nd ed. 1979. pap. DBI Books. $8.95.

Guns and Ammo Magazine Editors, ed. **Guns and Ammo Annual.** 1982. (Illus.). 1981. pap. Petersen Publishing. $6.95.

Hacker, Rick. **The Muzzleloading Hunter.** 1981. Winchester Press. $16.95.

Hamilton, T. M. **Early Indian Trade Guns: 1625-1775.** (Contributions of the Museum of the Great Plains Ser.: No. 3). (Illus.). 1968. pap. Museum of the Great Plains Pubns. Dept. $4.00.

Hanauer, Elsie. **Guns of the Wild West.** (Illus.). A. S. Barnes. (OP).

Hatcher. **The Book of the Garand.** Gun Room Press. $15.00.

Hatcher, et al. **Firearms Investigation, Identification and Evidence.** 1977. Repr. Stackpole Books. $26.95.

Hatcher, Julian S. **Hatcher's Notebook.** rev. ed. (Illus.). 1962. Stackpole Books. $19.95.

Held, Robert. **Age of Firearms.** (Illus.). 2nd rev. ed. pap. DBI Books. (OP).

Helmer, William J. **The Gun That Made the Twenties Roar.** (Illus.). rev. and enl. ed. 1977. Gun Room Press. $16.95.

Hertzberg, Robert. **The Modern Handgun.** 1977. Arco. (OP).

Hoff, Arne. **Dutch Firearms.** Stryker, Walter A., ed. (Illus.). 1978. S. B. Bernet. $105.00.

Hoffschmidt, Edward J. **Know Your Gun, Incl. Know Your .45 Auto Pistols; Know Your Walther P. .38 Pistols; Know Your Walther P. P. and P. P. K. Pistols; Know Your M1 Garand Rifles; Know Your Mauser Broomhandle Pistol; Know Your Anti-Tank Rifle.** 1976. Borden pap. $5.95. ea.

Hogg, Brig., fwrd. by. **The Compleat Gunner.** (Illus.). 1976. Repr. Charles River Books. $10.50.

Hogg, Ian V. **The Complete Illustrated Encyclopedia of the World's Firearms.** (Illus.). 1978. A & W Pubs. $24.95.

—**Guns and How They Work.** (Illus.). 1979. Everest House. $16.95.

Hogg, Ian V. & Weeks, John. **Military Small Arms of the Twentieth Century.** 3rd ed. (Illus.). 1977. Hippocrene Books. (OP).

—**Military Small Arms of the Twentieth Century.** 4th ed. (Illus.). 1981. pap. DBI Books. (OP).

Home Workshop Silencers 1. 1980. pap. Paladin Enterprises. $12.00.

Howe, James V. **Amateur Guncraftsman.** (Illus.). 1967. pap. Funk & Wagnalls. (OP).

Howe, Walter J. **Professional Gunsmithing.** (Illus.). 1946. Stackpole Books. $24.95.

Huebner, Siegfried. **Silencers for Hand Firearms.** Schreier, Konrad & Lund, Peder C., eds. 1976. pap. Paladin Enterprises. $11.95.

Huntington, R. T. **Hall's Breechloaders: John H. Hall's Invention and Development of a Breechloading Rifle with Precision-Made Interchangeable Parts, and its Introduction into the United States Service.** (Illus.). 1972. pap. George Shumway Publisher. $20.00.

Ingram, M. V. **The Bellwitch.** Pioneer Press. (OP).

Jackson & Whitelaw. **European Hand Firearms.** 1978. Albert Saifer, Pub. $22.50.

James, Garry, ed. **Guns for Home Defense.** (Illus.). 1975. pap. Petersen Publishing. $3.95.

—**Guns of the Gunfighters.** (Illus.). 1975. pap. Peterson Publishing. (OP).

Journal of the Historical Firearms Society of South Africa. Vol. 1. (Illus.). 1964. Repr. of 1958 ed. Lawrence Verry Co. (OP).

Kennedy, Monty. **Checkering and Carving of Gunstocks.** rev. ed. (Illus.). 1952. Stackpole Books. $24.95.

Koller, Larry. **How to Shoot: A Complete Guide to the Use of Sporting Firearms—Rifles, Shotguns and Handguns—on the Range and in the Field.** rev. ed. Elman, Robert, ed. (Illus.). 1976. Doubleday. (OP).

Larson, E. Dixon. **Remington Tips.** Pioneer Press. $4.95.

Lauber, George. **How to Build Your Own Flintlock Rifle or Pistol.** Seaton. Lionel, tr. from Ger. (Illus.). 1976. pap. Jolex. $6.95.

—**How To Build Your Own Percussion Rifle or Pistol.** Seaton, Lionel, tr. from Ger. (Illus.). 1976. pap. Jolex. $6.95.

—**How To Build Your Own Wheellock Rifle or Pistol.** Seaton, Lionel, tr. from Ger. (Illus.). 1976. pap. Jolex. $6.95.

Lenk, Torsten. **Flintlock: Its Origin and Development.** Albert Saifer, Pub. $45.00.

The Lewis Gun. 1976. Paladin Enterprises. (OP).

Lewis, Jack. **Gun Digest Book of Modern Gun Values.** 3rd ed. pap. DBI Books. $9.95.

—**Law Enforcement Handgun Digest.** 3rd ed. 1980. pap. DBI Books. $9.95.

Lewis, Jack & Springer, Robert, eds. **Black Powder Gun Digest.** 2nd ed. (Illus.). 1977. pap. DBI Books. (OP).

Lindsay, Merrill. **Twenty Great American Guns.** (Illus.). 1976. Repr. pap. Arma Press. $1.75.

—**The Lure of Antique Arms.** (Illus.). 1978. softbound. Stoeger. $5.95.

Liu, Allan, J. **The American Sporting Collector's Handbook.** 1977. softbound. Stoeger. $5.95.

Miller, Martin. **Collector's Illustrated Guide to Firearms.** (Illus.). 1978. Mayflower Books. $24.95.

Muller, Heinrich. **Guns, Pistols and Revolvers.** 1981. St. Martin's Press. $29.95.

Murtz, Harold A. **Guns Illustrated, 1983.** 15th ed. (Illus.). 1982. pap. DBI Books. $10.95.

Murtz, Harold A., ed. **Gun Digest Book of Exploded Firearms Drawings.** 2nd ed. 1982. pap. DBI Books. $12.95.

Myatt, F. **An Illustrated Guide to Rifles and Automatic Weapons.** (Illus.). 1981. Arco. $8.95.

National Muzzle Loading Rifle Association. **Muzzle Blasts: Early Years Plus Vol. I and II 1939-41.** 1974. pap. George Shumway Publisher. $18.00.

Nonte, George C., Jr. Author; Traister, John E., Ed. **Black Powder Guide.** 3rd ed. (Illus.). 1982. Stoeger. $10.95.

—**Firearms Encyclopedia.** (Illus.). 1973. Harper & Row. (OP).

—**Handgun Competition.** (Illus.). 1978. Winchester Press. $14.95.

—**Handloading for Handgunners.** 1978. pap. DBI Books. $8.95.

—**Home Guide to Muzzle Loaders.** (Illus.). 1982. pap. Stackpole Books. $14.95.

—**Pistol Guide.** 1980. Stoeger. $8.95.

—**Revolver Guide.** 1980. Stoeger. $8.95.

Nonte, George C., Jr., & Jurras, Lee. **Handgun Hunting.** (Illus.). 1976. softbound. Stoeger. $5.95.

Nonte, George C., Jr. **Combat Handguns.** Jurras, Lee F., ed. (Illus.). 1980. Stackpole Books. $19.95.

Norton (R. W.) Art Gallery. **E. C. Prudhomme: Master Gun Engraver.** (Illus.). 1973. pap. Norton Art Gallery. $3.00.

Otteson, Stuart. **The Bolt Action: A Design Analysis.** (Illus.). Winchester Press. $12.95.

Owen, J. I., ed. **Brassey's Infantry Weapons of the World, 1975.** (Illus.). 1975. Westview Press. (OP).

—**Brassey's Infantry Weapons of the World.** 2nd ed. 1979. Pergamon Press. $61.00.

Page, Warren. **The Accurate Rifle.** 1975. softbound. Stoeger. $6.95.

Peterson & Elman. **The Great Guns.** 1977. Grosset & Dunlap. $10.95.

Peterson, Harold L. **Encyclopedia of Firearms.** (Illus.). 1964. E. P. Dutton. (OP).

Pollard, Hugh B. **The History of Firearms.** 1974. Burt Franklin, Pub. $29.50; pap. $8.95.

Price, Robert M. **Firearms Self-Defense: An Introductory Guide.** (Illus.). 1981. Paladin Enterprises. $19.95.

Rees, Clair F. **Beginner's Guide to Guns and Shooting.** (Illus.). 1978. DBI Books. $7.95.

Reese, Michael, II. **Nineteen Hundred Luger—U. S. Test Trials.** 2nd rev ed. Pioneer Press, ed. (Illus.). Pioneer Press. $4.95.

Rice, F. Phillip. **Outdoor Life Gun Data Book.** (Illus.). 1975. Harper & Row. (OP).

Richardson, H. L. & Wood, Wallis W. **Firearms and Freedom.** Seventy Six Press.

Riling, Ray. **Guns and Shooting: A Bibliography.** (Illus.). 1981. Ray Riling. $75.00.

Riviere, Bill. **The Gunner's Bible.** rev. ed. 1973. pap. Doubleday. $3.95.

Roberts, Willis J. & Bristow, Allen P. **Introduction to Modern Police Firearms.** Gourley, Douglas, ed. (Illus.). 1969. text ed. MacMillan. (OP).

Rosa, Joseph G. **Gunfighter: Man or Myth.** (Illus.). 1980. pap. University of Oklahoma Press. $8.95.

Russell, Carl P. **Firearms, Traps and Tools of the Mountain Men.** (Illus.). 1977. pap. University of New Mexico Press. $9.95.

—**Guns on the Early Frontiers: A History of Firearms from Colonial Times Through the Years of the Western Fur Trade.** 1980. University of Nebraska Press. $23.95; pap. $6.95.

Ryan, J. W. **Guns, Mortars and Rockets. Vol. 2.** (Illus.). 1982. Pergamon Press. $40.00; pap. $16.00.

Schroeder, Joseph J., Jr., ed. **Gun Collector's Digest.** 2nd ed. 1976. pap. DBI Books. (OP).

Schroeder, Joseph J., ed. **Gun Collector's Digest.** 3rd ed. 1981. pap. DBI Books. $9.95.

Schroeder, Joseph J. & Editors of Gun Digest, eds. **Gun Digest Book of Gun Accessories.** (Illus.). 1979. pap. DBI Books. $8.95.

Scott, Robert F., ed. **Shooter's Bible, 1983, No. 74.** 1982. (Illus.). softbound. Stoeger. $11.95.

Sell. **Handguns Americana.** 1973. Borden. $8.50.

Sherrill, Robert. **The Saturday Night Special.** 1975. pap. Penguin Books. (OP).

Shotgun Shooting. 4th ed. (Illus.). 1974. pap. Charles River Books. $2.50.

Smith, W. H. B. **Small Arms of the World.** (Illus.). 1975. pap. A & W Visual Library. (OP).

Smythe, John & Barwick, Humphrey. **Bow vs. Gun.** 1976. Repr. Charles River Books. $15.00.

Stack, Robert. **Shotgun Digest.** 1974. pap. DBI Books. (OP).

Stanford, J. K. **Complex Gun.** Sportshelf. $15.00.

Steindler, R. A. **Firearms Dictionary.** (Illus.). 1975. pap. Paladin Enterprises. $6.95.

—**Reloader's Guide.** (Illus.). 3rd ed. 1975. softbound. Stoeger. $7.95.

—**Rifle Guide.** (Illus.). 1978. softbound. Stoeger. $7.95.

Steindler, R. A., ed. & illus. **Shooting the Muzzle Loaders.** (Illus.). 1975. Jolex. $11.95; pap. $6.95.

Stockbridge, V. D. **Digest of U. S. Patents Relating to Breech-loading & Magazine Small Arms, 1836-1873.** (Illus.). 1963. N. Flayderman & Co. $12.50.

Suydam, Charles R. **U. S. Cartridges & Their Handguns: 1795-1975.** (Illus.). 1978. DBI Books. (OP).

—**U. S. Cartridges and Their Handguns.** (Illus.). 1976. Beinfeld. $15.95; pap. $9.95.

Sybertz, Gustav. **Technical Dictionary for Weaponry.** (ger.-Eng.). 1969. pap. French & European Pubns. Inc. $120.00.

Tappan, Mel. **Survival Guns.** 1978. Janus Press. (OP).

—**Survival Guns.** 1977. pap. Janus Press. $9.95.

Thielen, Thomas W. **The Complete Guide to Gun Shows.** 1980. pap. Loompanics Unlimited. $6.95.

Thomas, Donald G. **Silencer Patents, Vol. III: European Patents 1901-1978.** (Illus.). 1978. Paladin Enterprises. $15.00.

Traister, John E. **How To Buy and Sell Used Guns.** (Illus.) 1982. softbound. Stoeger. $10.95.

Truby, J. David. **The Lewis Gun.** (Illus.). 1977. Sycamore Island Books. (OP).

Truby, J. David & Minnery, John. **Improvised Modified Firearms.** 2 vols. Lund. Peder C. ed. (Illus.) 1975. Paladin Enterprises. $19.95 set.

Truby, J. David, et al. **Improved Modified Firearms.** 2 vols. 1975. Paladin Enterprises. $19.95 set.

U. S. Army. **Forty-MM Grenade Launcher: M79.** (Illus.). pap. Paladin Enterprises. $4.00.

U. S. Cartridge Company. **U. S. Cartridge Company Collection of Firearms.** (Illus.). Sycamore Island Books. $6.00.

Van Rensselaer, S. **American Firearms.** (Illus.). 1948. pap. Century House. $10.00.

Virgines, George E. **Famous Guns & Gunners.** (Illus.). 1980. Pine Mountain Press. $12.95; pap. $6.95.

Wahl, Paul. Author; Traister, John E., Ed. **Gun Trader's Guide.** (Illus.). 10th ed. pap. Stoeger. $10.95

Waite, M. D. & Ernst, Bernard. **The Trapdoor Springfield.** 1979. Beinfeld. (OP).

Warner, Ken. **The Practical Book of Guns.** (Illus.). 1978. Winchester Press. $15.95.

Warner, Ken, ed. **Gun Digest Nineteen Eighty Two.** 36th ed. (Illus.). 1981. pap. DBI Books. $9.95.

—**Handloader's Digest.** 8th ed. 1981. DBI Books. $9.95.

—**Handloader's Digest Bullet and Powder Update.** (Illus.). 1980. pap. DBI Books. $4.95.

West, Bill. **Know Your Winchesters: General Use, All Models and Types, 1849-1969.** (Illus.). B. West. $12.00.

—**Winchester, Cartridges, and History.** (Illus.). B. West. $29.00.

—**Winchester-Complete: All Wins & Forerunners, 1849-1970.** (Illus.). 1975. B. West. (OP).

—**Winchester Encyclopedia.** (Illus.). B. West. $15.00.

—**Winchester Lever-Action Handbook.** (Illus.). B. West. $25.00.

—**The Winchester Single Shot.** (Illus.). B. West. $15.00.

Weston, Paul B. **The New Handbook of Handgunning.** (Illus.). 1980. C. C. Thomas. $12.95.

Willett, Roderick. **Gun Safety.** (Illus.). 1967. International Pubns. Service. $5.25.

Williams, John J. **Survival Guns and Ammo: Raw Meat.** (Illus.). 1979. pap. Consumertronics. $19.00.

Williams, Mason. **The Law Enforcement Book of Weapons, Ammunition & Training Procedures: Handguns, Rifles and Shotguns.** (Illus.). 1977. C. C. Thomas. $35.75.

Winant, Lewis. **Firearms Curiosa.** (Illus.). 1961. Ray Riling, Arms Books. (OP).

Wirnsberger, Gerhard. **Standard Directory of Proof Marks.** Steindler, R. A. tr. from Ger. (Illus.). 1976. pap. Jolex. $5.95.

Wood, J. B. **The Gun Digest Book of Firearms Assembly-Disassembly: Centerfire Rifles, Pt. IV.** 1980. pap. DBI Books. $9.95.

—**Gun Digest Book of Firearms Assembly-Disassembly: Rimfire Rifles, Pt. I.** (Illus.). 1979. pap. DBI Books. $9.95.

—**Gun Digest Book of Firearms Assembly-**

Disassembly: Revolvers, Pt. II. (Illus.). 1979. pap. DBI Books. $9.95.

—**Gun Digest Book of Firearms Assembly-Disassembly: Rimfire Rifles, Pt. III.** (Illus.). 1980. pap. DBI Books. $9.95.

—**Gun Digest Book of Firearms Assembly-Disassembly: Shotguns, Pt. V.** (Illus.). 1980. pap. DBI Books. $9.95.

—**Gun Digest Book of Firearm Assembly-Disassembly: Law Enforcement Weapons, Pt. VI.** (Illus.). 1981. pap. DBI Books. $9.95.

—**Troubleshooting Your Handgun.** 1978. pap. DBI Books. $6.95.

Wootters, John. **The Complete Book of Practical Handloading.** (Illus.). 1977. softbound. Stoeger. $6.95.

—**Troubleshooting Your Rifle & Shotgun.** (Illus.). 1978. pap. DBI Books. $6.95.

—**The Complete Book of Practical Handloading.** (Illus.). 1976. Winchester Press. $13.95.

Wycoff, James. **Famous Guns That Won The West.** (Illus.). 1975. pap. Arco. (OP).

FIREARMS—CATALOGS

Bannerman Catalogue of Military Goods - 1927. replica ed. (Illus.). 1981. pap. DBI Books. $12.95.

Byron, D. **The Firearms Price Guide.** (Illus.). 1977. pap. Crown. $9.95.

Byron, David. **The Firearm's Price Guide.** rev. ed. (Illus.). 1980. pap. (Michelman Books.) Crown. $9.95.

Byron, David. **Official Price Guide to Antique and Modern Firearms.** (Illus.). 1982. pap. House of Collectibles. $9.95.

1862 Ordnance Manual. Pioneer Press. $1.50.

Guns, Value & Identification Guide. (Illus.). Wallace-Homestead Book Co. $2.95.

Hawkin, Peter. **Guide to Antique Guns & Pistols.** Newbury Books. $32.50.

Hoxie Bullet Catalog. Pioneer Press. $0.75.

Lewis, Jack. **Gun Digest Book of Modern Gun Values.** (Illus.). 3rd ed. 1981. pap. DBI Books. $9.95.

Murtz, Harold A., ed. **Guns Illustrated, 1982.** 14th ed. DBI Books. (OP).

Murtz, Harold A., ed. **Guns Illustrated 1981** 13th ed. 1980. pap. DBI Books. (OP).

Owen, J. I., ed. **Brassey's Infantry Weapons of the World, 1974-75: Infantry Weapons and Combat Aids in Current Use by the Regular and Reserve Forces of All Nations.** (Illus.). 1974. text ed. British Book Center. (OP).

Quertermous, Russel C. & Quertermous, Stephen C. **Modern Guns: Identifications & Values.** 1979. Crown. (OP).

Remington Gun Catalog 1877. Pioneer Press. $1.50.

Schroeder, Joseph J., ed. **Gun Collector's Digest.** 3rd ed. 1981. pap. DBI Books. $9.95.

Scott, Robert F., ed. **Shooter's Bible. No. 74. 1983.** (Illus.). 1982. softbound. Stoeger. $11.95.

Sears & Roebuck C1910 Ammunition Catalog. (Illus.). pap. Sand Pond. $2.00.

Sellers, Frank. **Sharps Firearms.** (Illus.). 1978. Follett. (OP).

Tarassuk, L. **Antique European and American Firearms at the Hermitage Museum.** Drapkin, R., tr. (Illus., Eng. & Rus.). 1973. Arco. (OP).

—**Antique European and American Firearms at the Hermitage Museum.** 1973. State Mutual Book and Periodical Service, Ltd. $15.00.

Tarassuk, Leonid, ed. **Antique European and American Firearms at the Hermitage Museum.** (Illus., Eng. & Rus.). 1976. Arma Press. ltd. ed. $40.00.

Tinkham, Sandra S., ed. **Catalog of Tools, Hardware, Firearms, and Vehicles.** 1979. Somerset House. pap. $30.00; incl. color microfiche. $260.00.

Traister, John E., ed. **How To Buy and Sell Used Guns.** (Illus.) 1982. softbound. Stoeger. $10.95.

United States Cartridge Co.-Lowell, Mass. 1891 Catalog. (Illus.). Sand Pond. $2.50.

U.S. Cartridge Company's Collection of Firearms. 1971. Paladin Enterprises. $6.00.

Wahl, Paul, Author; Traister, John E., ed. **Gun Trader's Guide.** (Illus.). 10th ed. 1982.

softbound. Stoeger. $10.95.

Warner, Ken, ed. **Gun Digest 1982** 36th ed. 1981. pap. DBI Books. $10.95.

—**Gun Digest Review of Custom Guns.** 1980. pap. DBI Books. $8.95.

West, Bill. **Remington Arms Catalogues, 1877-1899.** 1st ed. (Illus.). 1971. B. West. $8.00.

—**Stevens Arms Catalogues, 1877-1899.** 1st ed. (Illus.). 1971. B. West $8.00.

Wilson, Loring D. **The Handy Sportsman.** 1977. softbound. Stoeger. $5.95.

Winchester Shotshell Catalog 1897. (Illus.). pap. Sand Pond. $1.25.

FIREARMS—COLLECTORS AND COLLECTING

Akehurst, Richard. **Antique Weapons.** (Illus.). 1969. Arco. (OP).

Amber, John T. **Gun Digest Treasury.** 5th ed. 1977. pap. DBI Books. (OP).

—**Gun Digest 1978.** 32nd ed. pap. DBI Books. (OP).

Bowman, Hank W. **Antique Guns from the Stagecoach Collection.** (Illus.). 1964. lib. bdg. Arco. $3.50.

Byron, David. **Official Price Guide to Antique and Modern Firearms.** (Illus.). 1982. pap. House of Collectibles. $9.95.

Chapel, Charles E. **Gun Collector's Handbook of Values: 1980-1981.** 13th rev. ed. 1979. Coward, McCann & Geoghegan. $16.95; pap. $8.95.

Dicarpengna, N. **Firearms in the Princes Odescalchi Collection in Rome.** (Illus.). 1976. Repr. of 1969 ed. Arma Press. $20.00.

Dixie Gun Works Antique Arms Catalog. Pioneer Press. $1.50.

Early Firearms of Great Britain and Ireland from the Collection of Clay P. Bedford. (Illus.). 1971. Metropolitan Museum of Art. $17.50; pap. $4.95.

Flayderman, Norm. **Norm Flayderman's Book of Antique Gun Values.** 1977. pap. DBI Books. (OP).

—**Flayderman's Guide to Antique American Firearms and Their Values.** 2nd ed. (Illus.). 1980. pap. DBI Books. $15.95.

Gun Digest, 1983. 37th ed. (Illus.). 1982. pap. DBI Books. $12.95.

Guns, Value and Identification Guide. (Illus.). Wallace-Homestead Book Co. (OP).

Gusler, Wallace B. & Lavin, James D. **Decorated Firearms 1540-1870, from the Collection of Clay P. Bedford.** 1977. Universtiy Press of Virginia. $25.00.

Hake, Ted. **Six Gun Hero Collectibles.** 1976. Wallace-Homestead Book Co. (OP).

Hawkins, Peter. **Guide to Antique Guns and Pistols.** (Illus.). Newbury Books Inc. $32.50.

Hogg, Ian & Weeks, John. **Military Small Arms of the 20th Century.** 4th ed. (Illus.). 1981. DBI Books. $10.95.

Kennard. A. M. **French Pistols and Sporting Guns.** 1972. Transatlantic Arts Inc. $4.95.

Lewis, Jack. **Gun Digest Book of Modern Gun Values.** 3rd ed. (Illus.). pap. DBI Books. $9.95.

Lindsay, Merrill. **The Lure Of Antique Arms.** (Illus.). 1978. softbound. Stoeger. $5.95.

Liu, Allan J. **The American Sporting Collector's Handbook.** (Illus.). 1977. softbound. Stoeger. $5.95.

Madaus, H. Michael. **The Warner Collector's Guide to American Long Arms.** 1981. pap. Warner Books. $9.95.

Murtz, Harold A., ed. **Guns Illustrated 1983.** 15th ed. (Illus.). 1982. pap. DBI Books. $10.95.

Neal, Robert J. & Jinks, Roy G. **Smith and Wesson, 1857-1945.** rev. ed 1975. A. S. Barnes. (OP).

Nonte, George C., Jr., Author; Traister, John E., Ed. **Black Powder Guide,** 3rd Ed. (Illus.) 1982. $10.95.

Pocket Guide to Guns. (Illus.). 1980. pap. Collector Books. $2.50.

Quertermous, Russel & Quertermous, Steve. **Modern Guns, Identification and Values.** 3rd ed. 1980. pap. Collector Books. $11.95.

Quertermous, Russell & Quertermous, Steve. **Modern Guns, Identification and Values.**

(Illus.). pap. Wallace-Homestead Book Co. (OP).

Schroeder, Joseph J., Jr. ed. **Gun Collector's Digest.** 2nd ed. 1976. pap. DBI Books. (OP).

Schroeder, Joseph J. **Gun Collector's Digest.** 3rd ed. 1981. pap. DBI Books. $9.95.

Serven, James. **Rare and Valuable Antique Arms.** 1976. Pioneer Press. $4.95.

Shumaker, P. L. **Colt's Variations of the Old Model Pocket Pistol.** 1957. Borden. $8.95.

Steinwedel, Louis W. **Gun Collector's Fact Book.** 1975. pap. Arco. (OP).

Tarassuk, L. **Antique European and American Firearms at the Hermitage Museum.** Drapkin, R., tr. (Illus., Eng & Rus.). 1976. Arma Press. ltd. ed. $40.00.

Traister, John E. **How To Buy and Sell Used Guns** (Illus.) 1982. softbound. Stoeger. $10.95.

U. S. Cartridge Company's Collection of Firearms. 1971. Paladin Enterprises. $6.00.

Wahl, Paul. Author; Traister, John E., Ed. **Gun Trader's Guide.** 10th ed. (Illus.). softbound. Stoeger. $10.95.

Warner, Ken, ed. **Gun Digest Review of Custom Guns.** (Illus.). 1980. pap. DBI Books. $9.95.

Wilkinson, Frederick. **Antique Firearms.** (Illus.). 276 p. 1980. Sterling. $17.95.

Wilkinson-Latham, Robert. **Antique Guns in Color: 1250-1865.** (Illus.) 1978. Arco. $8.95; pap. $6.95.

Wilson, R. L. **The Book of Colt Engraving.** (Illus.). 1978. Beinfeld. (OP).

—**Colt—Christie's Rare and Historic Firearms Auction Catalogue.** (Illus.). 1981. Arma Press. $25.00.

FIREARMS—HISTORY

Ayalon, David. **Gunpowder and Firearms in the Mamluk Kingdom: A Challenge to Midaeval Society.** 2nd ed. 1978. Biblio Distribution Centre. $22.50.

Baer, L. R. **The Parker Gun: An Immortal American Classic.** (illus.). 1978. Beinfeld. (OP).

Barnes, Duncan. **The History of Winchester Firearms, 1866-1980.** (illus.). Winchester Press. $21.95.

Berger, Michael. **Firearms in American History.** (illus.). (gr. 5 up). 1979. Franklin Watts, Inc. $7.90.

Bianchi, John; Mason, James D., ed. **Blue Steel and Gunleather.** (Illus.). 1978. Beinfeld. $9.95

Blanch, H. J. A. **A Century of Guns: A Sketch of the Leading Types of Sporting and Military Small Arms.** (illus.). 1977. Repr. of 1909 ed. Charles River Books. $25.00.

Bowman, Hank W. **Famous Guns from the Smithsonian Collection.** (illus.). 1966. lib. bdg. Arco. (OP).

Bowman, Hank W. & Cary, Lucian. **Antique Guns.** 1953. pap. Arco. $2.50.

Brophy, William S. **Krag Rifles.** (Illus.). 1978. Beinfeld. (OP).

—**L.C. Smith Shotguns.** (Illus.). 1978. Beinfeld, (OP).

Brown, M. L. **Firearms in Colonial America: The Impact of History and Technology 1492-1792.** (Illus.). 1980. Smithsonian Institution Press. $45.00.

Buchele, W. & Shumway, G. **Recreating the American Long Rifle.** Orig. Title: **Recreating the Kentucky Rifle.** (Illus.). 1973. pap. George Shumway Publisher. $16.00.

Burrell, Brian. **Combat Weapons: Handguns and Shoulder Arms of World War 2.** (Illus.). 1974. Transatlantic Arts, Inc. $9.50.

Campbell, Hugh B. **The History of Firearms.** (Illus.). 1977. pap. B. Franklin. (OP).

Cooper, Jeff. **Fireworks: A Gunsite Anthology.** 1981. Janus Press. $19.95.

DuMont, John S. **Custer Battle Guns.** (Illus.). 1974. Old Army Press. (OP).

Editors of Outdoor Life, ed. **The Story of American Hunting and Firearms.** 1976. Dutton. (OP).

Fuller, Claude E. **Breech-Loader in the Service 1816-1917.** (Illus.). 1965. Flayderman, N. & Co. $14.50.

Fuller, Claude E. & Steward, Richard D. **Firearms of the Confederacy.** 1977. Repr. of 1944 ed. Quarterman. $25.00.

Gaier, Claude. **Four Centuries of Liege Gunmaking.** (Illus.). 1977. Arma Press. (OP).

Grancsay, Stephen V. & Lindsay, Merrill. **Master French Gunsmith's Designs from the XVII to the XIX Centuries.** (Illus.). 1976. Ltd. ed. (1000 copies) Arma Press. (OP).

Greener, William W. **The Gun and Its Development: With Notes on Shooting.** 1975. Repr. of 1881 ed. Gale Research Co. (OP).

Gusler, Wallace B. & Lavin, James D. **Decorated Firearms, 1540-1870 from the Collection of Clay P. Bedford.** 1977. (Colonial Williamsburg Foundation). University Press of Virginia. $25.00

Hackley, F.W. et al. **History of Modern U.S. Military Small Arms Ammunition: Vol. 2, 1940-1945.** Gun Room Press. $25.00.

Hamilton, T. M., ed. **Indian Trade Guns.** Pioneer Press. (OP).

—**Early Indian Trade Guns: 1625-1725.** 1968. pap. Museum of the Great Plains Pubns. $4.00.

Hartzler, Daniel D. **Arms Makers of Maryland.** (Illus.). 1976. George Shumway Publisher. $35.00.

Held, Robert. **Age of Firearms.** (Illus.). 2nd ed. rev. pap. DBI Books. (OP).

Helmer, William J. **The Gun That Made the Twenties Roar.** Gun Room Press. $16.95.

Hetrick, Calvin. **The Bedford County Rifle and Its Makers.** (Illus.). 1975. pap. George Shumway Publisher. (OP).

Hogg, Ian & Batchelor, John. **Naval Gun.** (Illus.). 1979. Sterling. (OP).

Holme, N. & Kirby, E. L. **Medal Rolls: Twenty-Third Foot Royal Welch Fusiliers, Napoleonic Period.** 1979. S. J. Durst. $39.00.

Hutslar, Donald A. **Gunsmiths of Ohio: 18th and 19th Centuries.** Vol. I. (Illus.). casebound. Geroge Shumway Publisher. $35.00.

Jackson, Melvin H. & De Beer, Charles. **Eighteenth Century Gunfounding.** (Illus.). 1974. Smithsonian Institution Press. $19.95.

Jinks, Roy G. **History of Smith and Wesson.** (Illus.). 1978. Beinfeld. (OP).

Kennet, Lee & Anderson, James L. **The Gun in America: The Origins of a National Dilemma.** (Illus., Orig.). 1975. Greenwood Press. $22.50; pap. $3.95.

Kindig, Joe Jr. **Thoughts on the Kentucky Rifle in its Golden Age.** 1982. casebound. George Shumway Publisher. $75.00.

Lindsay, Merrill. **The Kentucky Rifle.** (Illus.). 1976. Arma Press. $15.00.

—**The Lure of Antique Arms.** (Illus.). 1976. Arma Press. (OP).

—**The Lure of Antique Arms.** (Illus.). Stoeger. $5.95.

—**The New England Gun: The First 200 Years.** (Illus.). 1976. Arma Press. $20.00. pap. $12.50.

—**One Hundred Great Guns.** (Illus.). 1967. Walker & Co. (OP).

Neal, Keith W. & Back, D. H. **Great British Gunmakers 1740-1790: The History of John Twigg and the Packington Guns.** (Illus.). 1975. S. P. Bernet. $80.00

Nonte, George C., Jr. **Black Powder Guide.** (Illus.). pap. Stoeger. $7.95

North & North. **Simeon North: First Official Pistol Maker of the United States.** Repr. Gun Room Press. $9.95.

Oakeshott, Ewart. **European Weapons and Armour.** (Illus.). 1980. Beinfeld. $29.95

Peterson, Harold. **Historical Treasury of American Guns.** Benjamin Co. pap. $2.95.

Pollard, Hugh B. **History of Firearms.** (Illus.). 1974. B. Franklin. $29.50; pap. $8.95.

Reese. Michael II. **Nineteen-hundred Luger-U.S. Test Trials.** 2nd rev ed. (Illus.). pap. Pioneer Press. $4.95.

Ritchie, Carson I. **The Decorated Gun.** (Illus.). Date not set. A S. Barnes. (OP).

Rosebush, Waldo E. **American Firearms and the Changing Frontier.** 1962. pap. Eastern Washington State Historical Society. $3.00.

Rywell, Martin. **American Antique Pistols.** Pioneer Press. $2.00.

—**Confederate Guns.** Pioneer Press. $2.00.

Schreier, Konrad F., Jr. **Remington Rolling Block Firearms.** (Illus.). pap. Pioneer Press. $3.95.

Schroeder, Joseph J., Jr. **Arms of the World-1911.** 1972. pap. DBI Books. (OP).

Sellers, Frank M. **Sharps Firearms.** (Illus.). 1982. Sellers Pubns. $39.95.

Serven, James. **Two Hundred Years of American Firearms.** (Illus., Orig.). 1975. pap. Follett. (OP).

—**Colt Firearms from 1836.** 1974. Fountain Press. (OP).

—**Colt Firearms from 1836.** 1979. Stackpole Books. (OP).

—**Conquering the Frontiers.** 1974. Fountain Press. (OP).

Shelton, Lawrence P. **California Gunsmiths.** (Illus.). 302p. 1977. casebound. George Shumway Publisher. $29.65.

SIPRI. **Anti-Personnel Weapons.** 1978. Crane-Russak Co. $29.95.

Smythe, John & Barwick, Humphrey. **Bow Versus Gun: Certain Discourses, and a Breefe Discourse.** 1974. George Shumway Publisher. (OP).

—**Bow Versus Gun.** 1976. Repr. Charles River Books. $15.00.

Suydam, Charles R. **U. S. Cartridges and Their Handguns: 1795-1975.** (Illus.). 1978. Beinfeld. (OP).

Tarassuk, Leonid. **Antique European and American Firearms at the Hermitage Museum.** limited ed. (Illus., Eng. & Rus.) 1973. Arma Press. (OP).

—**Antique European and American Firearms at the Hermitage Museum.** 1973. State Mutual Book and Periodical Service, Ltd. (OP).

Tappan, Mel. **Tappan on Survival.** 1982. Caroline House Pubs. $7.95.

Tout, Thomas F. **Firearms in England in the Fourteenth Century.** (Illus.). 1969. pap. George Shumway Publisher. (OP).

West, Bill. **Browning Arms and History, 1842-Date.** (Illus.). 1972. B. West. $29.00.

—**Marlin and Ballard, Arms and History, 1861-1978.** (Illus.). 1978. B. West. $29.00.

—**Remington Arms and History, 1816-Date.** (Illus.). 1972. B. West. $29.00.

—**Savage Stevens, Arms and History, 1849-1971.** (Illus.). 1971. B. West. $29.00.

—**Winchester-Complete: All Wins and Forerunners, 1849-1970.** (Illus.). 1975. B. West. (OP).

Wilkinson, Frederick. **Antique Firearms.** 1978. Repr. Presidio Press. (OP).

—**Antique Firearms.** (Illus.). 1980. (Pub. by Guinness Superlatives England). Sterling. $17.95.

Wilkinson-Latham, Robert. **Antique Guns in Color: 1250-1865.** 1978. Arco. $8.95; pap. $6.95.

Williamson, Harry F. **Winchester: The Gun That Won The West.** (Illus.). A. S. Barnes. (OP).

Wilson, R. L. **The Colt Heritage: The Official History of Colt Firearms, 1836 to the Present.** 1979. Simon and Schuster. $39.95.

Wycoff, James. **Famous Guns that Won the West.** (Illus.). 1975. pap. Arco. (OP).

FIREARMS—IDENTIFICATION

Ahern, Jerry & Hart, Dave. **Peace Officer's Guide to Concealed Handguns.** 1978. pap. Follett. (OP).

Byron, David. **Gunmarks.** (Illus.). 1980. Crown. $10.00.

Grancsay, Stephen V. & Lindsay, Merrill.
—**Illustated British Firearms Patents, 1718-1853.** (Illus.). 1976. ltd. ed. Arma Press. $75.00.

Hill, Richard T. & Anthony, William E. **Confederate Longarms and Pistols: A Pictorial Study.** (Illus.). 1978. Confederate Arms. $29.95.

Madaus, H. Michael. **The Warner Collector's Guide to American Long Arms.** 1981. pap. Warner Books. $9.95.

Mathews, J. Howard. **Firearms Identification: Original Photographs and Other Illustrations of Hand Guns, Vol. 2.** 1973. Repr. of 1962 ed. C. G. Thomas. $56.75.

—**Firearms Identification: Original Photographs and Other Illustrations of Hand Guns, Data on Rifling Characteristics of Hand Guns & Rifles, Vol. 3.** Wilimovsky, Allan E., ed. (Illus.). 1973. C. C. Thomas. $88.00.

—**Firearms Identification: The Laboratory Examination of Small Arms, Rifling Characteristics in Hand Guns, and Notes on Automatic Pistols, Vol. 1.** 1973. Repr. of 1962 ed. C. C. Thomas. $56.75.

Quertermous, Russell & Quertermous, Steve. **Modern Guns, Identification and Values.** 3rd ed. (Illus.). 1980. pap. Collector Books. $11.95.

Quertermous, Russell & Quertermous, Steven. **Modern Guns.** 2nd ed. (Illus.). 1980. pap. Crown. (OP).

—**Modern Guns Identification and Values.** (Illus.). pap. Wallace-Homestead Book Co. (OP).

Suydam, Charles R. **U. S. Cartridges and Their Handguns.** (Illus.). 1976. Beinfeld. $15.95; pap. $9.95.

Wilber, Charles G. **Ballistic Science for the Law Enforcement Officer.** (Illus.). 1977. C. C. Thomas. $30.75.

The World's Submachine Guns. rev. ed. 1980. TBN Enterprises. $29.95.

FIREARMS—INDUSTRY AND TRADE

Bleile, C. Roger. **American Engravers.** (Illus.). 1980. Beinfeld. $29.95.

Farley, Phillip J., et al. **Arms Across the Sea.** 1978. Brookings Institution. $10.95; pap. $4.95.

Gervasi, Tom. **Arsenal of Democracy: American Weapons Available for Export.** (Illus.). 1978. Grove Press. (OP).

Grancsay, Stephen V. & Lindsay, Merrill. **Illustrated British Firearms Patents 1718-1853.** limited ed. (Illus.). Arma Press. $75.00.

Hanifhen, Frank C. & Engelbrecht, Helmuth C. **Merchants of Death: A Study of the International Armaments Industry.** Garland Pub. $38.00.

Hartzler, Daniel D. **Arms Makers of Maryland.** 1975. George Shumway Publisher. $35.00.

Kennett, Lee & Anderson, James L. **The Gun in America.** (Illus.). pap. Greenwood Press. $22.50; pap. $3.95.

Kirkland, Turner. **Southern Derringers of the Mississippi Valley.** Pioneer Press. $2.00.

Lindsay, Merrill. **One Hundred Great Guns.** (Illus.). 1967. Walker & Co. (OP).

Noel-Baker, Phillip. **The Private Manufacture of Armaments.** 1971. pap. Dover. $6.00.

Russell, Carl P. **Guns on the Early Frontiers: A History of Firearms from Colonial Times through the Years of the Western Fur Trade.** 1980. Universtiy of Nebraska Press. $23.95. pap. $6.95.

Smith, Merritt R. **Harper's Ferry Armory and the New Technology: The Challenge of Change.** (Illus.). 1977. Cornell University Press. $29.50. pap. $8.95.

Stockholm International Peace Research Institute (SIPRI). **The Arms Trade Registers.** 1975. MIT Press. $18.00.

—**Arms Trade with the 3rd World.** rev. ed. (Illus.). 1975. Holmes & Meier. $29.50.

West, Bill. **Browning Arms and History, 1842-1973.** (Illus.). 1972. B. West. $29.00.

FIREARMS—LAWS AND REGULATIONS

Cook, Phillip J. & Lambert, Richard D., eds. **Gun Control.** 1981. American Academy of Political and Social Science. $7.50; pap. $6.00.

Davidson, Bill R. **To Keep and Bear Arms.** 2nd ed. 1979. Paladin Enterprises. $14.95.

Dolan, Edward F. Jr. **Gun Control: A Decision for Americans.** (Illus.). 1978. Watts, Franklin, Inc. $7.90.

Gottlieb, Alan. **The Rights of Gun Owners.** 1981. pap. Green Hill. $6.95.

Gottlieb, Alan B. **The Gun Owner's Political Action Manual.** 1976. pap. Green Hill. $1.95.

Gottlieb, Alan M. **The Rights of Gun Owners.** 1981. Softbound. Caroline House. (OP).

Gun Control. 1976. pap. American Enterprise Institute for Public Policy Research. $3.75.

Gun Control Means People Control. 1974. Independent American. (OP).

Kates, Don B., Jr. **Restricting Handguns: The Liberal Skeptic Speaks Out.** 1979. North River Press. $9.95.

Kennet, Lee & Anderson, James L. **The Gun In America.** (Illus.). text ed. pap. Greenwood Press. $22.50; pap. $3.95.

Krema, Vaclav. **Identification and Registration of Firearms.** (Illus.). 1971. C. C. Thomas. $19.75.

Kukla, Robert J. **Gun Control: A Written Record of Efforts to Eliminate the Private Possession of Firearms in America.** Orig. Title: Other Side of Gun Control. 1973. pap. Stackpole Books. $4.95.

Lindell, James W. **Handgun Retention System.** 1982. pap. Calibre Press. $12.50.

Sandys-Winsch, Godfrey. **Gun Law.** 1979. pap. (Pub. by Shaw & Sons). State Mutual Book & Periodical Service. $30.00.

Scalon, Robert A. ed. **Law Enforcement Bible.** (Illus.). 1978. softbound. Stoeger. $7.95.

—**Law Enforcement Bible No. 2.** (Illus.). 1981. softbound. Stoeger. $11.95.

Sherrill, Robert. **The Saturday Night Special.** 1975. pap. Penguin Books. (OP).

Whisker, James B. **The Citizen Soldier and U.S. Military Policy.** 1979. North River Press. $7.50; pap. $4.50.

FOWLING

Bauer, Erwin A. **Duck Hunter's Bible.** pap. Doubleday. $3.95.

Becker, A. C. Jr. **Waterfowl in the Marshes.** (Illus.). 1969. A. S. Barnes. (OP).

Begbie, Eric. **Modern Wildfowling.** 1981. (Pub. by Saiga). State Mutual Book & Periodical Service. $40.00.

Bell, Bob. **Hunting the Long Tailed Bird.** (Illus.). 1975. Freshet Press. $14.95.

Bourjaily, Vance. **Unnatural Enemy.** (Illus.). 1963. Dial Press. (OP).

Carroll, Hanson, et al. **The Wildfowler's World.** 1973. Winchester Press. (OP).

Day, J. Wentworth. **The Modern Fowler.** 1973. Repr. of 1934 ed. British Book Center. (OP).

Dickey, Charley. **Quail Hunting.** (Illus.). 1975. softbound. Stoeger. $3.95.

Duffey, David. **Bird Hunting Tactics.** 1978. pap. Willow Creek. $5.95.

Gresham, Grits. **The Complete Wildfowler.** (Illus.). 1975. softbound. Stoeger. $5.95.

Gryndall, William. **Hawking, Hunting, Fouling and Fishing; Newly Corrected by W. Gryndall Faulkner.** 1972. Repr. of 1596 ed. W. J. Johnson. $13.00.

Hastings, Macdonald. **Shooting—Why We Miss: Questions and Answers on the Successful Use of the Shotgun.** 1977. David McKay Co. (OP).

Hinman, Bob. **The Duck Hunter's Handbook.** (Illus.). 1976. softbound. Stoeger. $8.95.

Knap, Jerome, ed. **All About Wildfowling in America.** 1976. Winchester Press. (OP).

Petzal, David E., ed. **The Expert's Book of Upland Bird and Water-Fowl Hunting.** 1975. Simon & Schuster. (OP).

Rice, F. Phillip & Dahl, John. **Game Bird Hunting.** rev. ed. (Illus.). 1977. pap. T. Y. Crowell. $4.50.

Russell, Dan M. **Dove Shooter's Handbook.** 1974. Winchester Press. (OP).

Vance, Joel M. **Upland Bird Hunting. (Illus.).** 1982. E.P. Dutton. $16.95.

Waterman, Charles F. **Hunting Upland Birds.** (Illus.). 1975. softbound. Stoeger. $5.95.

Williams, Lovett E., Jr. **The Book of the Wild Turkey.** 1981. Winchester Press. $19.95.

Woods, Shirley E. Jr. **Gunning for Upland Birds and Wildfowl.** 1976. Winchester Press. $10.00.

Youel, Milo A. **Cook the Wild Bird.** (Illus.). 1976. A. S. Barnes. (OP).

GAME AND GAME BIRDS

Anderson, Luther A. **Hunting the Uplands with Rifle and Shotgun.** (Illus.). 1977. Winchester Press. $12.95.

Becker, A. C., Jr. **Game and Bird Calling.** (Illus.). 1972. A. S. Barnes. (OP).

Bell, Bob. **The Digest Book of Upland Game Shooting.** 1979. pap. Follett. (OP).

—**Hunting the Long Tailed Bird.** (Illus.). 1975. Freshet Press. $14.95.

Billmeyer, Patricia. **The Encyclopedia of Wild Game and Fish Cleaning and Cooking.** Yeshaby Pubs. $3.95.

Blair, Gerry. **Predator Caller's Companion.** 1981. Winchester Press. $15.95.

Brakefield, Tom. **The Sportsman's Complete Book of Trophy and Meat Care.** (Illus.). 1975. Stackpole Books. (OP).

Bristol, Stewart J. **Practical Wild Turkey Hunting.** (Illus.). 1982. pap. Stone Wall Press. $9.95.

Bucher, Ruth & Gelb, Norman. **The Book of Hunting.** (Illus.). 1977. Paddington Press. $60.00.

Burk, Bruce. **Game Bird Carving.** (Illus.). 1972. Winchester Press. (OP).

Colby, C. B. **Big Game: Animals of Americas, Africa and Asia.** (Illus.). (gr. 4-7). 1967. Coward, McCann & Geoghegan. (OP).

Cone, Arthur L. Jr. **The Complete Guide to Hunting.** (Illus.). 1978. softbound. Stoeger. $5.95.

Dalrymple, Byron. **How to Call Wildlife.** (Illus.). 1975. T. Y. Crowell. $8.95.

—**North American Big Game Hunting.** (Illus.). 1978. softbound. Stoeger. $5.95.

Dasmann, Raymond F. **Wildlife Biology.** 2nd ed. 1981. John Wiley & Sons, Inc. $19.95.

Dickey, Charley. **Charley Dickey's Dove Hunting.** (Illus.). 1976. Oxmoor House. $2.95.

—**Quail Hunting.** (Illus.). 1974. softbound. Stoeger. $3.95.

Elliott, Charles. **Care of Game Meat and Trophies.** (Illus.). 1975. T. Y. Crowell. $7.50; pap. $4.50.

Gage, Rex. **Game Shooting with Rex Gage.** (Illus.). 1977. pap. International Pubns. Service. $5.00.

Gooch, Bob. **Coveys and Singles.** (Illus.). 1980. A. S. Barnes. $10.95.

—**Squirrels and Squirrel Hunting.** Cornell Maritime Press. $6.00.

Gresham, Grits. **The Complete Wildfowler.** (Illus.). 1975. softbound. Stoeger. $5.95.

Hagerbaumer, David. **Selected American Game Birds.** 1972. Caxton. $30.00.

Hinman, Bob. **The Duck Hunter's Handbook.** (Illus.). 1976. softbound. Stoeger. $8.95.

McCristal, Vic. **Top End Safari.** Sportshelf & Soccer Associates. (OP).

Oldham, J. **The West of England Flying Tumbler.** 1981. State Mutual Book & Periodical Service. Ltd. $25.00.

Ormond, Clyde. **Small Game Hunting.** (Illus.). 1974. pap. Barnes & Noble. (OP).

—**How to Track and Find Game.** (Illus.). 1975. (Funk & Wagnall Book). T. Y. Crowell. $8.95. pap. $4.50.

Pettinger, Martin. **Sporting Birds.** State Mutual Book & Periodical Service. $60.00.

Poultry and Game Birds. (Illus.). 1982. pap. Yankee Books.

Rue, Leonard L. **Sportsman's Guide to Game Animals.** 1968. Harper & Row. (OP).

Rue, Leonard L., III. **Game Birds of North America.** (Illus.). 1973. times Mirror Mag. (OP).

Scheid, D. **Raising Game Birds.** 1974. Scribner's. (OP).

Scott, P. **Coloured Key to the Wildfowl of the World.** rev. ed. (Illus.). 1972. Heinman. $15.00.

Scott, Peter. **A Coloured Key to the Wildfowl of the World.** rev. ed. (Illus.). 1972. International Pubns. Service. $11.50.

—**A Colored Key to the Wildfowl of the World.** rev. ed. 1980. (Pub. by Witherby). State Mutual Book & Periodical Service. $15.00

Sherwood, Morgan. **Big Game in Alaska.** 1981. Yale University Press. $27.50.

Smith, Guy N. **Gamekeeping and Shooting for Amateurs.** 1982. State Mutual Book & Periodical Service. $40.00.

—**Hill Shooting and Upland Gamekeeping.** 1981. State Mutual Book & Periodical Service. $40.00.

—**Rating and Rabbiting for Amateur Gamekeepers.** State Mutual Book & Periodical Service. $25.00.

Smith, Capt. James A. **Dress 'Em Out,** Vol. 1 (Illus.). 1982. softbound. Stoeger. $11.95.

Waterman, Charles F. **Hunting Upland Birds.** (Illus.). 1975. softbound. Stoeger. $5.95.

Woods, Shirley E., Jr. **Gunning for Upland Birds and Wildfowl.** (Illus.). 1976. Winchester Press. $10.00.

Youel, Milo A. **Cook the Wild Bird.** (Illus.). 1976. A. S. Barnes. (OP).

GAME AND GAME BIRDS— FRANCE

Villenave, G. M. **Chasse.** (Illus., Fr.). Larousse & Co. (OP).

GAME AND GAME BIRDS—MEXICO

Tinker, Ben. **Mexican Wilderness and Wildlife.** (Illus.). 1978. University of Texas Press. $9.95.

GAME AND GAME BIRDS—NEW ZEALAND

Poole, A. L. **Wild Animals in New Zealand.** (Illus.). 1969. C. E. Tuttle. $12.75.

GAME AND GAME BIRDS— NORTH AMERICA

Alaska Magazine Editors. **Alaska Hunting Guide.** (Illus.). 1976. pap. Alaska Northwest Publishing Co. $3.95. (OP).

Bromhall & Grundle. **British Columbia Game Fish.** pap. International School Book Service. (OP).

Dalrymple, Byron. **North American Big Game Hunting.** (Illus.). 1974. softbound. Stoeger. $5.95.

—**North American Game Animals.** (Illus.). 1978. Crown. $14.95.

Dickey, Charley. **Quail Hunting.** (Illus.). 1974. softbound. Stoeger. $3.95.

Elman, Robert. **The Hunter's Field Guide.** 1974. Knopf. (OP).

Elman, Robert and Peper, George. **Hunting America's Game Animals and Birds.** (Illus.). 1980. Winchester Press. $15.95.

Gresham, Grits. **The Complete Wildfowler.** (Illus.). 1975. softbound. Stoeger. $5.95.

Hinman, Bob. **The Duck Hunter's Handbook.** (Illus.). 1976. softbound. Stoeger. $6.95.

Holland, Dan. **Upland Game Hunter's Bible.** (Illus.). pap. Doubleday. $3.95.

Jacques, Florence P. **Geese Fly High.** (Illus.). 1964. Repr. of 1939 ed. University of Minnesota Press. $9.95.

Johnsgard, Paul A. **North American Game Birds of Upland and Shoreland.** (Illus.). pap. University of Nebraska Press. $7.95.

Knap, Jerome. **All About Wildfowling in America.** 1976. Winchester Press. $13.95.

Leopold A. Starker & Darling, F. Fraser. **Wildlife in Alaska.** 1973. Repr. of 1953 ed. Greenwood Press. $15.00.

Mullin, John M., ed. **Game Bird Propagation.** 1978. North American Game Breeders & Shooting Preserves Association, Inc. (OP).

Nesbitt, W. H. & Wright, Phillip L., eds. **Records of North American Big Game.** 8th ed. 1981. Boone & Crockett Club. $29.50.

Phillips, John C. **American Game Mammals and Birds: A Catalog of Books, Sports, Natural History and Conservation. 1582-1925.** 1978. Repr. of 1930 ed. Arno Press. $37.00.

Rice, F. Phillip & Dahl, John I. **Game Bird Hunting.** (Illus.). 1974. pap. Barnes & Noble. (OP).

Rue Leonard L. **Game Birds of North America.** 1973. Harper & Row. (OP).

Rue, Leonard L., III. **Complete Guide to Game Animals: A Field Book of North American Species.** rev. ed. 1981. Van Nostrand Reinhold. $15.95.

Sanderson, Glen C., ed. **Management of Migratory Shore & Upland Game Birds in North America.** 1980. pap. University of Nebraska Press. $10.95.

Tinsley, Russell, ed. **Small-Game Hunting.** 1977. softbound. Stoeger. $5.95.

—ed. **All About Small-Game Hunting in America.** 1976. Winchester Press. $14.95.

Walsh, Harry M. **The Outlaw Gunner.** 1971. Cornell Maritime Press. $12.50.

Walsh, Roy. **Gunning the Chesapeake.** 1960. Cornell Maritime $10.00.

Waterman, Charles F. **Hunting Upland Birds.** (Illus.). 1975. softbound. Stoeger. $5.95.

Zim, Herbert S. & Sprunt, Alexander, 4th. **Game Birds.** 1961. Western Publishing. $11.54.

GAME COOKERY

Angier, Bradford. **Home Cookbook of Wild Meat and Game.** (Illus.). 1982. pap. Stackpole Books. $9.95.

Backus, David. **European Recipes for American Fish and Game.** 1978. pap. Willow Creek. $4.50.

Billmeyer, Pat. **The Encyclopedia of Wild Game Cleaning and Cooking.** (Orig.). 1979. pap. ABC Publishing. (OP).

Billmeyer, Patricia. **The Encyclopedia of Wild Game and Fish Cleaning and Cooking.** pap. Yesnaby Pubs. $3.95.

Candy, Robert. **Getting the Most from Game and Fish.** Hard, Walter, ed. (Illus.). 1978. pap. Garden Way Publishing. $12.95.

Cone, Joan. **Easy Game Cooking: One Hundred and Twenty-Four Savory, Home-Tested Money-Saving Recipes and Menus for Game Birds and Animals.** 1974. EPM Publications, spiral bdg. (OP).

—**Easy Game Cooking.** (Illus.). 1974. pap. Maryland Historical Society. $4.95.

—**Fish and Game Cooking.** 1981. pap. EPM Publications. $7.95.

Fink, Edith & Day, Avenelle, **Hot Birds and Cold Bottles.** 320p. 1972. Delacorte. (OP).

Goolsby, Sam. **Great Southern Wild Game Cookbook.** 193p. 1980. Pelican. $13.95.

Gorton, Audrey A. **Venison Book: How to Dress, Cut up and Cook Your Deer.** 1957. pap. Greene. $4.95.

Green, Karen & Black, Betty. **How to Cook His Goose (and other wild game.)** 1973. pap. Winchester Press. $7.95.

Hanle, Zack. **Cooking Wild Game.** 1974. Liveright. (OP).

Hargreaves, Barbara. **Sporting Wife Game and Fish Cooking.** 1980. State Mutual Book & Periodical Service. $25.00.

Hull, Raymond & Sleight, Jack. **Home Book of Smoke-Cooking Meat, Fish and Game.** 1971. Stackpole Books. $10.95.

Jenkins, Susan. **Wildgame: Florida's Panhandle Cookbook.** (Florida's Panhandle Cookbook Ser.: No. 3). (Illus.). 48p (Orig.). 1977. pap. Owen & Jenkins. $2.25.

Johnson, L. W., ed. **Wild Game Cookbook: A Remington Sportsmen's Library Bk.** pap. Benjamin Co. $3.95.

Knight, Jacqueline E. **The Hunter's Game Cookbook.** (Illus.). 1978. Winchester Press. $12.95.

Lamagna, Joseph. **Wild Game Cookbook for Beginner and Expert.** J. Lamagna. $6.95.

Marsh, Judy and Dyer, Carole, eds. **The Maine Way—a Collection of Maine Fish and Game Recipes.** (Illus.). 1978. DeLorme Pub. $3.95.

Michigan United Conservation Clubs. **The Wildlife Chef.** new ed. 1977. pap. Mich United Conserv. $3.95.

Orcutt, Georgia and Taylor, Sandra, eds. **Poultry and Game Birds.** 1982. pap. Yankee Books. $8.95.

Rojas-Lombardi, Felipe. **Game Cookery.** (Illus.). 1973. Livingston. dura. $2.95.

—**Game Cookery.** (Illus.). 1973. plastic bdg. Harrowood Books. $2.95.

Rywell, Martin. **Wild Game Cook Book.** 1952. pap. Buck Hill. $4.95.

Sleight, Jack & Hull, Raymond. **The Home Book of Smoke Cooking, Meat, Fish and Game.** 1975. pap. B.J. Pub Group. $1.50

Smith, Capt. James A. **Dress 'Em Out, Vol 1** (Illus.). 1982. softbound. Stoeger. $11.95.

Sparano, Betty and Vin Sparano, Ed. **Celebrity Fish and Game Cookbook.** 1983. softbound. Stoeger. $11.95.

Steindler, Geraldine. **Game Cookbook.** Revised Edition. 1982. softbound. Stoeger. $10.95.

Weiss, John. **Care and Cooking of Fish and Game.** 1982. Winchester Press. $12.95.

Wongrey, Jan. **Southern Wildfowl and Wildgame Cookbook.** 1976. Sandlapper Store. $5.95.

Youel, Milo A. **Cook the Wild Bird.** (Illus.). 1976. A. S. Barnes. (OP).

GATLING GUNS

Johnson, F. Roy and Stephenson, Frank, Jr. **The Gatling Gun and Flying Machine of Richard and Henry Gatling.** (Illus.). 1979. Johnson NC. $9.50.

Wahl, Paul & Toppel, Donald R. **The Gatling Gun.** (Illus.). 1978. pap. Arco. $5.95.

GUNS

Carmichel, Jim. **The Modern Rifle.** (Illus.). 1976. softbound. Stoeger. (OP).

Daenhardt, Rainer. **Espingarda Perfeyta: or the Perfect Gun: Rules of Its Use Together with Necessary Instructions for Its Construction and Precepts for Good Aiming.** Daenhardt, Raier, tr. from Port. (Illus., Eng. & Port.). 1975. (Pub. by S. P. Bernet). Biblio Distribution Center. $48.00.

George, John N. **English Pistols and Revolvers.** Albert Saifer, Pub. $20.00.

Lindsay, Merrill. **The Lure of Antique Arms.** (Illus.). 1978. softbound. Stoeger. $5.95.

Liu, Allan J., ed. **The American Sporting Collector's Handbook.** (Illus.). 1977. softbound. Stoeger. $5.95.

Luger Manual. (Reprint of original English. languish edition.) 1967. softbound. Stoeger. $1.95.

Mauser Manual. (Facs. ed. of early English language Mauser Catalog and Manual.) 1974. softbound. Stoeger. $1.95.

Nonte, George C., Jr. **Black Powder Guide.** 2nd ed. (Illus.). 1976. softbound. Stoeger. $7.95.

—**Pistol Guide.** (Illus.). softbound. Stoeger. $8.95.

—**Revolver Guide.** (Illus.). softbound. Stoeger. $8.95.

Nonte, George C., Jr., Author; Traister, John E., Ed. **Black Powder Guide,** 3rd Edition. (Illus.). 1982. $10.95.

O'Connor, Jack. **The Hunting Rifle.** (Illus.). 1975. softbound. Stoeger. $7.95.

Page, Warren. **The Accurate Rifle.** (Illus.). 1975. softbound. Stoeger. $6.95.

Peterson, Harold. **Historical Treasury of American Guns.** Benjamin Co. pap. $2.95.

Scott, Robert F., Ed. **Shooter's Bible, No. 74, 1983.** (Illus.). 1982. softbound. Stoeger. $11.95.

Steindler, R. A. **Rifle Guide.** (Illus.). 1978. softbound. Stoeger. $7.95.

Traister, John E. **How To Buy and Sell Used Guns** (Illus.). 1982. softbound. Stoeger. $10.95.

Wahl, Paul. **Gun Trader's Guide.** 9th ed. (Illus.). softbound. Stoeger. $9.95.

Wahl, Paul, Author; Traister, John E., Ed. **Gun Trader's Guide,** 10th Edition. (Illus.). softbound. Stoeger. $10.95.

GUNSMITHING

Ackley, Parker O. **Home Gun Care and Repair.** (Illus.). 1974. pap. Stackpole Books. $6.95.

Angier, R. H. **Firearms Blueing and Browning.** 1936. Stackpole Books. $12.95.

Bailey, De Witt and Nic, Douglas A. **English Gunmakers: The Birmingham and Provincial Guntrade in the 18th and 19th Century.** (Illus.). 1978. Arco. $18.95.

Bish, Tommy. **Home Gunsmithing Digest.** 2nd ed. 1971. pap. Follett. (OP).

Bowers, William S. **Gunsmiths of Pen-Mar-Va, Seventeen Ninety to Eighteen Forty.** (Illus.). 1979. Irwinton. (OP).

Burch, Monte. **Gun Care and Repair.** (Illus.). Winchester Press. $15.95.

Carmichel, Jim. **Do-It-Yourself-Gunsmithing.** (Illus.). 1978. Harper & Row. $18.22.

Chapel, Charles E. **Complete Guide to Gunsmithing: Gun Care and Repair.** Rev. ed. (Illus.). 1962. A. S. Barnes. (OP).

Demeritt, Dwight B., Jr. **Maine Made Guns and Their Makers.** (Illus.). Maine State Museum Pubns. $22.00.

Dunlap, Roy F. **Gunsmithing.** 1963. Stackpole Books. $24.95.

Gaier, Claude. **Four Centuries of Liege Gunmaking.** (Illus.). 1977. Biblio. Distribution Center. (OP).

—**Four Centuries of Liege Gunmaking.** (Illus.). 1977. Arma Press. $80.00.

Gill, Harold B., Jr. **Gunsmith in Colonial Virginia.** (Illus.). 1974. University Press of Virginia. $4.95; pap. $4.50.

Gill, Harold, Jr. **The Gunsmith in Colonial Virginia.** 1974. pap. Colonial Williamsburg Foundation. (OP).

Grancsay, Stephen A. & Lindsay, Merrill. **Master French Gunsmith's Designs: From the Twelfth to Fourteenth Century.** limited ed. (Illus.). Arma Press. (OP).

Hartzler, Daniel D. **Arms Makers of Maryland.** (Illus.). 1977. George Shumway Publisher. $35.00.

Howe, James V. **Amateur Guncraftsman.** (Illus.). 1967. pap. Funk & Wagnalls. (OP).

Howe, Walter J. **Professional Gunsmithing.** (Illus.). 1946. Stackpole Books. $24.95.

Hutslar, Donald A. **Sunsmiths of Ohio: 18th and 19th Centuries.** Vol. 1. (Illus.). 1973. George Shumway Publisher. $35.00.

Lindsay, Merrill. **The New England Gun: The First 200 Years.** (Illus.). 1976. David McKay Co. (OP).

MacFarland, Harold E. **Gunsmithing Simplified.** (Illus.). A. S. Barnes. (OP).

—**Introduction to Modern Gunsmithing.** (Illus.). 1975. pap. Barnes & Noble. (OP).

Mitchell, Jack. **Gun Digest Book of Pistolsmithing.** 1980. pap. DBI Books. $9.95.

—**Rifle Gunsmithing.** 1982. pap. DBI Books. $9.95.

Newell, A. Donald. **Gunstock Finishing and Care.** (Illus.). 1949. Stackpole Books. $22.95.

Norton Art Gallery. **Artistry in Arms: The Art of Gunsmithing and Gun Engraving.** (Illus.). 1971. pap. Norton Art Gallery. $2.50.

Shelton, Lawrence P. **California Gunsmiths.** (Illus.). 1977. George Shumway Publisher. $29.65.

Smith, Loren W. **Home Gunsmithing: The Colt Single Action Revolvers.** (Illus.). 1971. Ray Riling, Arms Books. (OP).

Steindler, Robert A. **Home Gunsmithing Digest.** 2nd ed. (Illus.). 1978. pap. DBI Books. (OP).

Stelle & Harrison. **The Gunsmith's Manual: A Complete Handbook for the American Gunsmith.** (Illus.). Repr. of 1883 ed. Gun Room Press. $12.95.

Traister, John. **Clyde Baker's Modern Gunsmithing.** (Illus.). 1981. Stackpole Books. $24.95.

Traister, John E. **Basic Gunsmithing.** (Illus.). pap. TAB Books. $9.95.

—**First Book of Gunsmithing.** (Illus.). 1981. Stackpole Books. $16.95.

—**Gun Digest Book of Gunsmithing Tools and Their Uses.** 1980. pap. DBI Books. $8.95.

—**Learn Gunsmithing: The Troubleshooting Method.** (Illus.). Winchester Press. (OP).

Walker, Ralph. **Hobby Gunsmithing.** (Illus.). 1972. pap. DBI Books. (OP).

—**Black Powder Gunsmithing.** 1978. pap. DBI Books. $8.95.

Wood, J.B. **Gunsmithing: Tricks of the Trade.** (Illus.). 1982. pap. DBI Books. $9.95.

—**Troubleshooting Your Handgun.** 1978. pap. DBI Books. $6.95.

—**Troubleshooting Your Rifle and Shotgun.** 1978. pap. DBI Books. $6.95.

GUNSTOCKS

Arthur, Robert. **Shotgun Stock: Design Construction and Embellishment.** (Illus.). 1970. A. S. Barnes. (OP).

HAWKEN RIFLES

Baird, John D. **Fifteen Years in the Hawken Lode.** (Illus.). Gun Room Press. $15.00.

—**Hawken Rifles. The Mountain Man's Choice.** Gun Room Press. $15.00.

HUNTING

Acerrano, Anthony J. **The Practical Hunter's Handbook.** (Illus.). 1978. pap. Winchester Press. $9.95.

Amory, Cleveland. **Man Kind? Our Incredible War on Wildlife.** 1974. Harper & Row. $12.50.

Anderson, Luther A. **Hunting the Uplands with Rifle and Shotgun.** (Illus.). Winchester Press. $12.95.

—**Hunting the Woodlands for Small and Big Game.** (Illus.). 1980. A. S. Barnes. $12.00.

Ardrey, Robert. **The Hunting Hypothesis.** 1977. pap. Bantam Books. (OP).

Babcock, Havilah. **Jaybirds Go to Hell on Friday.** 1964. Holt, Rinehart & Winston. (OP).

Bashine, L. James. ed. **The Eastern Trail.** (Illus.). 1972. Freshet Press. $8.95.

Bauer, Erwin. **Hunter's Digest.** DBI Books. 1973. pap. (OP).

Bauer, Erwin A., ed. **Hunter's Digest.** 2nd ed. (Illus.). 1979. pap. DBI Books. $8.95.

Beckford, Peter. **Thoughts on Hunting.** (Illus.). Repr. British Book Center. (OP).

Berners, Juliana. **The Boke of St. Albans Containing Treatises on Hawking, Hunting and Cote Armour.** 1976. Repr. of 1881 ed. Scholarly Press. (OP).

—**The Book of Hawking, Hunting and Blasing of Arms.** 1969. Repr. of 1486 ed. W. J. Johnson. $42.00.

Bourjaily, Vance. **Country Matters: Collected Reports from the Fields and Streams of Iowa and Other Places.** 1973. Dial Press. $8.95.

—**Unnatural Enemy.** (Illus.). 1963. Dial Press. (OP).

Bowring, Dave. **How to Hunt.** (Illus.). 1978. Winchester Press. (OP).

Brakefield, Tom. **Big Game Hunter's Digest.** 1977. pap. DBI Books. $7.95.

—**Small Game Hunting.** (Illus.). 1978. Lippincott. $10.00.

Brister, Bob. **Shotgunning: The Art and The Science.** 1976. Winchester Press. $15.95.

Bucher, Ruth and Gelb, Norman. **The Book of Hunting.** (Illus.). 1977. Paddington Press. (OP).

Buckle, Esme, compiled by. **Dams of National Hunt Winners, 1963-64.** pap. (Dist. by Sporting Book Center). J. A. Allen. (OP).

—**Dams of National Hunt Winners, 1966-73.** (Illus.). pap. (Dist. by Sporting Book Center) J. A. Allen. $17.50.

Cadman, Arthur. **A Guide to Rough Shooting.** (Illus.). 1975. David & Charles. (OP).

Capossela, Jim. **How to Turn Your Fishing-Hunting Experiences Into Cash: Twenty-Five Ways to Earn Cash from Your Hobbies.** 1982. pap. Northeast Sportsmans. $3.50.

Carlisle, G.L. & Stanbury, Percy. **Shotgun and Shooter.** rev. ed. 1981. (Pub. by Hutchinson). State Mutual Book & Periodical Service. $35.00.

Cartier, John O. Ed. **Twenty Great Trophy Hunts.** 1980. David McKay Co. $17.95.

Clarke, H. Edwardes. **The Waterloo Cup: (1922-1977).** 1981. (Pub. by Saiga Pub.) State Mutual Book and Periodical Service. $60.00.

Clarke, I. A. **An Introduction to Beagling.** (Illus.). 1974. British Book Center. (OP).

Clayton, Michael. **A-Hunting We Will Go.** 1972. British Book Center. (OP).

Cone, Arthur L., Jr. **The Complete Guide to Hunting.** (Illus.). 1978. softbound. Stoeger. $5.95.

—**Complete Guide to Hunting.** 1970. Macmillan. (OP).

Coon, Carleton S. **The Hunting Peoples.** (Illus.). 1979. (Pub. by Chatto-Bodley-Jonathan). Merrimack Book Service. $10.95.

—**The Hunting Peoples.** 1972. Rowman. (OP).

Dalrymple, Byron W. **The Complete Book of Deer Hunting.** (Illus.). 1976. softbound. Stoeger. $6.95.

—**North American Big Game Hunting.** (Illus.). 1975. softbound. Stoeger. $5.95.

DeRuttie, Andrew. **Hunting on a Budget—for Food and Profit.** 1975. pap. Major Books. $1.25.

Dickey, Charley. **Quail Hunting.** (Illus.). 1974. softbound. Stoeger. $3.95.

—**Charley Dickey's Bobwhite Quail Hunting.** (Illus.). 1975. Oxmoor House. (OP).

—**Charley Dickey's Bobwhite Quail Hunting.** (Illus.). 1974. pap. (Family Guide Book Series.) Oxmoor House. $3.95.

Dodd, Ed. **Mark Trail's Hunting Tips.** (Illus.). 1969. pap. Essandess. (OP).

—**Mark Trail's Hunting Tips.** pap. Pocket Books. $1.00. Dougherty, Jim. **Varmint Hunter's Digest.** 1977. pap. Follett. (OP).

East, Ben. **The Ben East Hunting Book.** (Illus.). 1974. Harper & Row. (OP).

Eggert, Richard. **Fish and Hunt the Back Country.** 1978. Stackpole Books. $9.95.

Elliott, William. **Carolina Sports by Land and Water: Incidents of Devil-Fishing. Wild-Cat, Deer and Bear Hunting.** 1978. Repr. of 1859 ed. Attic Press. $10.00.

Elman, Robert. **The Hunter's Field Guide to the Game Birds and Animals of North America.** 1982. Knopf. $12.95.

—**One Thousand One Hunting Tips.** (Illus.). 1978. Winchester Press. $17.95.

Elman, Robert. ed. **The Complete Book of Hunting.** (Illus.). 1981. Abbeville Press. $59.95.

Fadala, Sam. **Blackpowder Hunting.** 1978. Stackpole Books. $10.95.

Ferber, Steve. ed. **All About Rifle Hunting and Shooting in America.** (Illus.). 1977. Winchester Press. $15.95.

Field & Stream. **Field and Stream Reader.** facs. ed. 1946. Arno. $19.50.

Fielder, Mildred. **Fielder's Herbal Helper for Hunters, Trappers and Fishermen.** 1982. Winchester Press. $12.95.

Fischl, Josef & Rue, Leonard Lee, III. **After Your Deer is Down.** 1981. pap. Winchester Press. $9.95.

Frankenstein, Alfred. **After the Hunt.** (Illus.). 1974. University of California Press. $52.50.

Gilsvik, Bob. **All-Season Hunting.** (Illus.). 1977. softbound. Stoeger. $5.95.

—**The Guide to Good Cheap Hunting.** (Illus.). 1979. Stein & Day. pap. $5.95.

—**All Season Hunting.** 1976. Winchester Press. $11.95.

Gooch, Bob. **Coveys and Singles.** (Illus.). 1980. A. S. Barnes. $10.95.

—**Land You Can Hunt.** (Illus.). 1980. A. S. Barnes. $12.00.

Gresham, Grits. **The Complete Wildfowler.** (Illus.). 1975. softbound. Stoeger. $5.95.

Grey, Hugh, ed. **Field & Stream Treasury.** 1971. Holt, Rinehart & Winston. (OP).

Grey, Zane. **Zane Grey, Outdoorsman: Zane Grey's Best Hunting and Fishing Tales.** Reiger, George, ed. (Illus.). 1972. Prentice-Hall. (OP).

Grinnell, George B. & Sheldon, Charles, eds. **Hunting and Conservation.** 1970. Repr. of 1925 ed. Arno. $25.00.

Gryndall, William. **Hawking, Hunting, Fouling and Fishing: Newly Corrected by W. Gryndall Faulkener.** 1972. Repr. of 1596 ed. W. J. Johnson. $13.00.

Hacker, Rick. **The Muzzleloading Hunter.** 1981. Winchester Press. $16.95.

Hagel, Bob. **Game Loads and Practical Ballistics for the American Hunter.** (Illus.). 1978. Knopf. $13.95.

Hammond, Samuel H. Wild. **Northern Scene in Sporting Adventures with Rifle and the Rod.** (Illus.). 1979. Repr. of 1857 ed. Harbor Hill Books. $12.50.

Hanenkrat, William F. **The Education of a Turkey Hunter.** 1974. Winchester Press. (OP).

Harbour, Dave. **Hunting the American Wild Turkey.** (Illus.). 1975. Stackpole Books. (OP).

Harker, Peter & Eunson, Keith. **Hunting with Harker.** (Illus. 1976. Reed, A. H. & A. W. Books. (OP).

Hastings, Macdonald. **Churchill's Gameshooting.** 1974. (Pub. by Michael Joseph.) Merrimack Book Service. $19.95.

Heacox, Cecil E. & Heacox, Dorothy. **The Gallant Grouse: All About the Hunting and Natural History of Old Ruff.** (Illus.). 1980. David McKay Co. $14.95.

Hill, Gene. **A Hunter's Fireside Book: Tales of Dogs. Ducks, Birds and Guns.** (Illus.). 1972. Winchester Press. $12.95.

—**Mostly Tailfeathers.** 1975. Winchester Press. $12.95.

Hinman, Bob. **The Duck Hunter's Handbook.** (Illus.). 1976. softbound. Stoeger. $8.95.

Holden, Philip. **Hunter by Profession.** 1974. International Publications Service. $9.90.

Hunter Safety Handbook. (Illus.). 1982. Outdoor Empire. Student ed. $2.50; Instr. ed. $3.50.

Hunting Magazine Eds. ed. **Hunting Annual 1982.** (Illus.). 1981. pap. Petersen Publishing. (OP).

James, Davis & Stephens, Wilson, eds. **In Praise of Hunting.** (Illus.). 1961. Devin-Adair Co. $10.00.

Janes, Edward C. **Boy and His Gun.** (Illus.). (gr. 7-9). 1951. A. S. Barnes. (OP).

—**Ringneck! Pheasants and Pheasant Hunting.** (Illus.). 1975. Crown. $8.95.

Johnson, et al. **Outdoor Tips.** pap. Benjamin Co. $2.95.

Klineburger, Bert & Hurst, Vernon W. **Big Game Hunting Around the World.** (Illus.). 1969. Exposition Press. $8.95.

Knap, Jerome. **The Digest Book of Hunting Tips.** 1979. pap. Follett. (OP).

—**Hunter's Handbook.** 1973. Scribner's. (OP).

—**Where to Fish and Hunt in North America: A complete Sportsman's Guide.** (Illus.). Pagurian. $8.95.

Knap, Jerome, J. **Complete Hunter's Almanac: A Guide to Everything the Hunter Needs to Know About Guns, Game, Tracking and Gear with a Special Section on Hunting Locations in North America.** (Illus.). 1978. Pagurian Press.

—**Digest Book of Hunting Tips.** pap. DBI Books. $2.95.

Larocco, Rich. **Shopping at Home for Hunting and Fishing Equipment.** 1982. $15.95; pap. $9.95. Facts on File.

Laycock, George. **Shotgunner's Bible.** (Illus.). 1969. pap. Doubleday. $3.95.

Lindner, Kurt. **The Second Hunting Book of Wolfgang Birkner.** (Illus.). 1976. ltd. ed. Arma Press. $175.00.

Lingertwood, Kenneth. **Huntsman of Our Time.** Sportshelf & Soccer Associates. $15.00.

Liu, Allan J. **The American Sporting Collector's Handbook.** (Illus.). pap. Stoeger. $5.95.

Lovell, Mary S. **A Hunting Pageant.** 1981. (Pub. by Saiga). State Mutual Book & Periodical Service. $50.00.

McCristal, Vic. **Top End Safari.** Sportshelf & Soccer Associates. (OP).

McNair, Paul C. **The Sportsman's Crafts Book.** 1978. Winchester Press. $12.95.

Madden, D. H. **Chapter of Mediaeval History.** 1969. Repr. of 1924 ed. Kennikat Press. $15.00.

Madden, Dodgson H. **Diary of Master William Silence: A Study of Shakespeare and Elizabethan Sport.** 1970. Repr. of 1897. ed. Haskell Booksellers. $51.95.

Marchington, John. **Game Shooting: Management and Economics.** (Illus.). 1976. Merrimack Book Service. (OP).

Merrill, William K. **Hunter's Bible.** (Illus.). 1968. Doubleday. $4.50.

Mosher, John A. **The Shooter's Workbench.** 1977. Winchester Press. $13.95.

Mueller, Larry. **Bird Dog. Guide.** (Illus.). 1976. softbound. Stoeger. $6.95.

Needwood. **The Hunting Quiz Book.** pap. British Book Center. (OP).

Nonte, George C., Jr. & Jurras, Lee E. **Handgun Hunting.** (Illus.). 1976. softbound. Stoeger. $7.95.

—**Handgun Hunting.** (Illus.). 1975. Winchester Press. $10.95.

O'Connor, Jack. **The Hunting Rifle.** (Illus.). 1975. softbound. Stoeger. $7.95.

—**Sheep and Sheep Hunting.** (Illus.). 1974. Winchester Press. $12.95.

—**Shotgun Book.** (Illus.). 1978. Knopf. $16.95; pap. $9.95.

Ormond, Clyde. **Complete Book of Hunting.** rev. ed. (Illus.). 1972. Harper & Row. (OP).
—**Small Game Hunting.** 1970. Dutton. $4.95. (OP).
—**Out-doorsman's Handbook.** 1975. pap. Berkeley Publishing. $1.95.
Page, Warren. **One Man's Wilderness.** 1973. Holt, Rinehart & Winston. (OP).
Petzal, David E. ed. **Experts' Book of the Shooting Sports.** Simon & Schuster. $9.95.
Pollard, Hugh B. **The Mystery of Scent.** 1972. British Book Center. (OP).
Pollard, Jack. **Straight Shooting.** Sportshelf & Soccer Associates. $17.50.
Pryce, Dick. **Hunting for Beginners.** (Illus.). 1978. softbound. Stoeger. $5.95.
Pulling, Pierre. **Game and the Gunner: Common-Sense Observations on the Practice of Game Conservation and Sport Hunting.** 1973. Winchester Press. (OP).
Randolph, J. W. **World of Wood, Field and Stream.** 1962. Holt, Rinehart & Winston. (OP).
Rees, Clair & Wixom, Hartt. **The Penny-Pinching Guide to Bigger Fish and Better Hunting.** (Illus.). 1980. Winchester Press. $9.95.
Robinson, Jerome B. **Hunt Close!** (Illus.). 1978. Winchester Press. (OP).
Rue, Leonard L. **Furbearing Animals of North America.** (Illus.). 1981. Crown. $19.95.
Scharff, Robert. **Hunter's Game, Gun and Dog Guide.** 1963. pap. Macmillan. $1.95.
Schwenk, Sigrid, et al. eds. **Multum et Multa: Beitraege zur Literatur, Geschichte und Kultur der Jagd.** (Illus.). 1971. De Gruyter. $75.00.
Scott, Robert F., Ed. **Shooter's Bible No. 74 1983.** (Illus.). 1982. softbound. Stoeger. $11.95.
Sell, Francis. **Art of Small Game Hunting.** 1973. pap. Stackpole Books. (OP).
Shaughnessy, Patrick and Swingle, Diane. **Hard Hunting.** (Illus.). Winchester Press. $12.95.
Smith, James A. **Dress 'Em out.** (Illus.). 1982. pap. Stoeger. $11.95.
Sparano, Vin T. **The Complete Outdoors Encyclopedia.** (Illus.). 1980. Harper & Row. $16.95.
Spiller, Burton. **Grouse Feathers.** (Sportsmen's Classics Ser.). (Illus.). 1972. Crown. (OP).
Spiller, Burton L. **More Grouse Feathers.** (Illus.). 1972. Crown. (OP).
Stehsel, Donald L. **Hunting the California Black Bear.** (Illus.). pap. Donald Stehsel. $7.00.
Strung, N. **Complete Hunter's Catalog.** (Illus.). 1978. pap. Lippincott.
Tapply, Horace G. **Sportsman's Notebook.** 1964. Holt, Rinehart & Winston. (OP).
Taylor, Zack. **Successful Waterfowling.** (Illus.). 1974. Crown. (OP).
Tinsley, Russell. **Bow Hunter's Guide.** (Illus.). 1975. softbound. Stoeger. (OP).
—**Small-Game Hunting.** (Illus.). 1977. softbound. Stoeger. $5.95.
Trueblood, Ted. **The Ted Trueblood Hunting Treasury.** (Illus.). 1978. David McKay Co. (OP).
Washburn, O. A. **General Red.** (Illus.). Jenkins. $5.50.
Waterman, Charles F. **Hunter's World.** (Illus.). 1970. Random House. (OP).
—**Hunting Upland Birds.** (Illus.). 1975. softbound. Stoeger. $5.95.
—**The Part I Remember.** (Illus.). 1974. Winchester Press. (OP).
Wehle, Robert G. **Wing and Shot.** (Illus.). 1964. Country Press. $12.00.
Whisker, James B. **The Right to Hunt.** 1980. Caroline House. (OP).
—**The Right to Hunt.** 1981. North River Press. $8.95.
Willett, Roderick. **Gun Safety.** (Illus.). 1967. International Publications Service. $5.25.
Wilson, James. **The Rod and the Gun.** (Illus.). 1973. Repr. of 1844 ed. British Book Center. (OP).
Wilson, Loring. **The Handy Sportsman.** (Illus.). 1977. softbound. Stoeger. $5.95.
Wilson, Loring D. **The Handy Sportsman.** 1976. Winchester Press. $12.95.
Woodcock, E. N. **Fifty Years a Hunter and Trapper.** pap. A. R. Harding. $3.00.

Woolner, Frank. **Timberdoodle: A Thorough Guide to Woodcock Hunting.** (Illus.). 1974. Crown. (OP).
Woolner, Lionel. **Hunting of the Hare.** 1972. British Book Center. (OP).
Young, Ralph W. **Grizzlies Don't Come Easy.** (Illus.). 1981. Winchester Press. $15.95.
Zumbo, Jim. **Hunting America's Mule Deer.** 1981. Winchester Press. $14.95.
Zutz, Don. **Handloading for Hunters.** 1977. pap. Winchester Press. $9.95.

HUNTING—DICTIONARIES

Brander, Michael. **Dictionary of Sporting Terms.** (Illus.). 1968. Humanities Press. (OP).
Burnand, Tony. **Dictionnaire chasse. (Dictionnaires de l'homme du vingtieme siecle.** (Fr.) 1970. Larousse & Co. $8.50.
—**Dictionnaire de la Chasse.** 250p (Fr.) 1970. pap. French & European Pubns. Inc. $7.50.
Frevert, W. **Woerterbuch der Jaegerei.** 4th ed. (Ger.) 1975. French & European Pubns. Inc. $12.00.
Kehrein, Franz. **Woerterbuch der Weldmannssprache.** (Ger.) 1969. French & European Pubns. Inc. $36.00.
Kirchoff, Anne. **Woerterbuch der Jagel. (Ger., Eng. & Fr. Dictionary of Hunting).** 1976. French & European Pubns. Inc. $27.50.
Sisley, Nick. **All About Varmint Hunting.** (Illus.). 1982. pap. Stone Wall Press. $8.95.
Sparano, Vin T. **The Sportsman's Dictionary of Fishing and Hunting Lingo.** (Illus.). 1980. David McKay Co. (OP).
Wisconsin Hunting Encyclopedia. 1976. pap. Wisconsin Sportsman. $2.95.

HUNTING—HISTORY

Allison, Colin. **The Trophy Hunters.** 1981. Stackpole Books. $24.95.
Butler, Alfred J. **Sport in Classic Times.** (Illus.). 1975. W. Kaufman. (OP).
Cheney, Roberta & Erskine, Clyde. **Music, Saddles and Flapjacks: Dudes at the Oto Ranch.** 1978. Mountain Press. $12.95.
Danielsson, Bror, ed. **William Twiti's the Art of Hunting, Vol. 1.** (Illus.). 1977. pap. Humanities Press. $31.50.
Goodall, Daphne M. **Huntsmen of a Golden Age.** 1980. (Pub. by Wifherby). State Mutual Book & Periodical Service. $12.00.
Greene, Robert. **The Third and Last Part of Conny-Catching.** 1923. Arden Library. $12.50.
Harding, Robert S. ed. **Omnivorous Primates: Gathering and Hunting in Human Evolution.** Teleki, Geza P. (Illus.). 1981. Columbia University Press. $45.00.
Petersen, Eugene T. **Hunters' Heritage: A History of Hunting in Michigan.** Lowe, Kenneth S., ed. (Illus.). 1979. Michigan United Conservation Clubs. $4.65.
Rick, John W. **Prehistoric Hunters of the High Andes.** (Studies in Archaeology Ser.) 1980. Academic Press. $27.50.
Spiess, Arthur E. **Reindeer and Caribou Hunters: An Archaeological Study.** (Studies in Archaeology Ser.). 1979. Academic Press. $30.00.

HUNTING—PRIMITIVE

Clarke, Grahame. **Stone Age Hunters.** 1967. McGraw-Hill. pap. $2.95.
Coon, Carleton. **The Hunting Peoples.** 1971. Little, Brown & Co. (OP).
—**The Hunting Peoples.** (Illus.). 1979. Merrimack Book Service. $10.95.
Frison, George C. **Prehistoric Hunter of the High Plains.** 1978. Academic Press. $29.50.
Gerstacker, Friedrich. **Wild Sports in the Far West.** Steeves, Edna L. & Steeves, Harrison R., eds. 1968. Duke University Press. $16.25.
Lee, Richard B. & De Vore, Irven. eds. **Man the Hunter.** 1968. pap. Aldine. $15.95.
Marks, Stuart A. **Large Mammals and a Brave People: Subsistence Hunters in Zambia.** (Illus.). 1976. University of Washington Press. $17.50.
Sergeant, R. B. **South Arabian Hunt.** 1976. text ed. Verry, Lawrence Co. $20.00.

Service, Elman R. **The Hunters.** 2nd ed. (Illus.). 1979. pap. Prentice-Hall. $8.95.

HUNTING—AFRICA

Capstick, Peter H. **Death in the Long Grass.** (Illus.). 1978. St. Martin's Press. $11.95.
Cloudsley-Thompson, J. L. **Animal Twilight, Man and Game in Eastern Africa.** (Illus.). 1967. Dufour Editions, Inc. $12.00.
Findlay, Frederick R. N. & Croonwright-Schreiner, S. C. **Big Game Shooting and Travel in Southeast Africa: Account of Shooting Trips In the Cheringoma and Gorongoza Divisions of Portuguese South-East Africa and in Zululand.** Repr. of 1903 ed. Arno. $40.25.
Gilmore, Parker. **Days and Nights by the Desert.** Repr. of 1888 ed. Arno. $20.50.
Haardt, Georges M. & Audouin-Dubreuil, Louis. **Black Journey: Across Central Africa with Citroen Expedition.** (Illus.). Repr. of 1927 ed. Negro University Press. Greenwood. $20.25.
Hemingway, Ernest. **Green Hills of Africa.** 1935. Scribner's. $17.50. pap. $5.95.
Herne, Brian. **Uganda Safaris.** 1980. Winchester Press. $12.95.
Holub, Emil. **Seven Years in South Africa.** 2 vols. 1881. Set. Scholarly Press. $45.00.
—**Seven Years in South Africa: Travels, Researches and Hunting Adventures Between the Diamond Field and the Zambesi, 1827-79.** 2 vols. 1971. Repr. of 1881 ed. Johnson Reprint Corp. $57.00.
MacQueen, Peter. **In Wildest Africa.** 1909. Scholarly Press. $29.00.
Mazet, Horace S. **Wild Ivory.** 1971. Galloway. (OP).
Mohr, Jack. **Hyenas In My Bedroom.** (Illus.). 1969. A. S. Barnes. (OP).
Nassau, Robert H. **In an Elephant Corral: And Other Tales of West African Experiences.** Repr. of 1912 ed. Negro University Press. $10.00.
Pohl, Victor. **Farewell the Little People.** (Illus.). 1968. pap. Oxford University Press. (OP).
Wynne-Jones, Aubrey. **Hunting: On Safari in East and Southern Africa.** (Illus.). 1982. International Scholarly Book Service. $29.95.

HUNTING—ALASKA

Alaska Hunting Guide 1978-79. rev. ed. (Illus.). pap. Alaska Northwest. (OP).
Alaska Magazine Editors. **Selected Alaska Hunting and Fishing Tales. Vol. 4.** 1976. pap. Alaska Northwest. $4.95.
Hubback, T. R. **Ten Thousand Miles to Alaska for Moose and Sheep.** facs. ed. repr of 1921 ed. Shorey. $1.95.
Joll, Gary. **To Alaska to Hunt.** (Illus.). 1978. pap. International Publications Service. $8.50.
Keim, Charles J. **Alaska Game Trails with a Master Guide.** pap. Alaska Northwest. $6.95.
Waugh, Hal & Keim, Charles J. **Fair Chase with Alaskan Guides.** (Illus.). 1972. pap. Alaska Northwest. $3.95.

HUNTING—ARTIC REGIONS

Nelson, Richard K. **Hunters of the Northern Ice.** 1972. University of Chicago Press. $25.00; pap. $5.95.
Stefansson, Vilhjalmur. **Hunters of the Great North.** Repr. of 1922 ed. AMS Press. $27.50.

HUNTING—AUSTRALIA

Byrne, Jack. **Duck Hunting in Australia and New Zealand.** (Illus.). 1974. Reed, A. H. & A. W., Books. (OP).
Stewart, Allan. **The Green Eyes are Buffaloes.** Sportshelf & Soccer Associates. $17.50.

HUNTING—BRITISH COLUMBIA

Shaughnessy, Patrick & Swingle, Diane. **Hard Hunting.** 1978. Winchester Press. $12.95.

HUNTING—FRANCE

Villenave, G. M. **Chasse.** (Illus., Fr.). Larousse & Co. (OP).

HUNTING—GREAT BRITAIN

Danielsson, Bror, ed. **William Twiti's the Art of Hunting.** Vol. 1. (Illus). 1977. pap. text ed. Humanities Press. $31.50.

Edward of Norwich. **Master of Game: Oldest English Book on Hunting.** Baillie-Grohman, William A. & Baillie-Grohman, F. eds. (Illus). Repr. of 1909 ed. AMS Press. $45.00.

Hands, Rachel, ed. **English Hawking & Hunting in the Boke of St. Albans.** facs ed. (Illus). 1975. Oxford University Press. (OP).

Hewitt, H. P. **Fairest Hunting: Hunting and Watching Exmoor Deer.** 1974. British Book Center. (OP).

Jeffries, Richard. **The Gamekeeper at Home and the Amateur Poacher.** 1978. pap. Oxford University Press. $5.95.

Thomas, William B. **Hunting England: A Survey of the Sport and of its Chief Grounds.** 1978. Repr. of 1936 ed. R. West. $30.00.

Watson, J. N. **British and Irish Hunts and Huntsmen: Vols. I & II.** (Illus). 1981. David & Charles. Set. $50.00 ea.; set $85.00.

HUNTING—GREECE

Butler, Alfred J. **Sport in Classic Times.** (Illus). 1975. W. Kaufmann. (OP).

Hull, Denison B. **Hounds and Hunting in Ancient Greece.** (Illus). 1964. University of Chicago Press. (OP).

HUNTING—INDIA

Jaipal. **Great Hunt.** 1980. Carlton Press. $9.50.

Taylor, John. **Wild Life in India's Tiger Kingdom.** 1980. Carlton Press. (OP).

HUNTING—NEW ZEALAND

Byrne, Jack, **Duck Hunting in Australia and New Zealand.** (Illus). 1974. Reed, A. H. & A. W., Books. (OP).

Forrester, Rex & Illingworth, Neil. **Hunting in New Zealand.** (Illus). 1967. Reed, A. H. & A. W., Books. (OP).

Joll, Gary. **Big Game Hunting in New Zealand.** (Illus). 1968. International Publications Service. $9.00.

Roberts, Gordon. **Game Animals in New Zealand.** (Illus). 1968. Reed, A. H. & A. W., Books. (OP).

HUNTING—NORTH AMERICA

Anderson, Luther A. **How to Hunt American Small Game.** (Illus). 1969. Funk & Wagnalls. (OP).

Cadbury, Warder, frwd. by. **Journal of a Hunting Excursion to Louis Lake, 1851.** (Illus). 1961. Adirondack Museum. $4.95.

Cartier, John O. **Hunting North American Waterfowl.** (Illus). 1982. Dutton. $17.95.

Dalrymple, Byron W. **North American Big Game Hunting.** (Illus). 1975. softbound. Stoeger. $5.95.

Elman, Robert. **The Hunter's Field Guide.** 1974. Knopf. (OP).

Elman, Robert & Peper, George, eds. **Hunting America's Game Animals and Birds.** (Illus). 1975. Winchester Press. (OP).

Holland, Dan. **Upland Game Hunter's Bible.** (Illus). pap. Doubleday. (OP).

Knap, Jerome. **Where to Fish and Hunt in North America: A Complete Sportsman's Guide.** (Illus). Pagurian Press. $8.95.

Leopold, Luna B., ed. **Round River: From the Journals of Aldo Leopold.** (Illus). 1972. pap. Oxford University Press. $3.95.

O'Connor, Jack. **The Art of Big Game Hunting in North America.** 2nd ed. 1977. Knopf. (OP).

Ormond, Clyde. **Small Game Hunting.** rev. ed. (Illus). 1977. Thomas Y. Crowell. $8.95.

Petzal, David E. **The Expert's Book of Big Game Hunting in North America.** 1976. Simon & Schuster. (OP).

Smith, **The One-Eyed Poacher.** 1980. Repr. Down East. $4.50.

HUNTING—U.S.

Abbott, Henry. **Birch Bark Books of Henry Abbott: Sporting Adventures and Nature Observations in the Adirondacks in the Early 1900s.** (Illus., Repr. of 1914 & 1932 eds.).

1980. Harbor Hill Books. $19.95.

Babcock, H. **My Health is Better in November.** (Illus). 1960. Holt, Rinehart & Winston. (OP).

Baily's Hunting Directory. 1978-79. (Illus). 1978. J. A. Allen. $36.00.

Cadbury, Warder, intro by. **Journal of a Hunting Excursion to Louis Lake. 1851.** (Illus). 1961. Syracuse University Press. $8.95.

Cone, Arthur L. **The Complete Guide to Hunting.** (Illus). 1978. softbound. Stoeger. $5.95.

Cory, Charles B. **Hunting and Fishing in Florida, Including a Key to the Water Birds.** 1970. Repr. of 1896 ed. Arno. $14.00.

Dalrymple, Bryon W. **The Complete Book of Deer Hunting.** (Illus). 1975. softbound. Stoeger. $6.95.

—**North American Big Game Hunting.** (Illus). 1975. softbound. Stoeger. $5.95.

Duffy, M. **Hunting and Fishing in Louisiana.** 1969. Pelican. (OP).

Elman, Robert, ed. **All About Deer Hunting in America.** 1976. Winchester Press. $13.95.

Gilsvik, Bob. **All-Season Hunting.** (Illus). 1976. softbound. Stoeger. $5.95.

—**The Guide to Good Cheap Hunting.** (Illus). 1979. pap. Stein & Day. $5.95.

Gohdes, Clarence, ed. **Hunting in the Old South: Original Narratives of the Hunters.** (Illus). 1967. Louisiana State University Press. (OP).

Kaplan, Meyer A. **Varmint Hunting.** 1977. pap. Monarch Press. $2.95.

Lang, Varley. **Follow the Water.** (Illus). 1961. John F. Blair. $6.95.

Lowenstein, Bill. **Hunting in Michigan: The Early 80's.** Arnold, David A., ed. 1981. pap. Michigan Natural Resources Michigan. $6.95.

McTeer, Ed. **Adventures in the Woods & Waters of the Low Country.** Beaufort Book Co. $5.95.

Mitchell, John G. **The Hunt.** 1980. Knopf. $11.95.

—**The Hunt.** 1981. pap. Penguin. $4.95.

Murray, William H. **Adventures in the Wilderness.** Verner, William K., ed. (Illus). 1970. Repr. Syracuse University Press. $10.50.

O'Connor, Jack. **The Hunting Rifle.** (Illus). 1975. softbound. Stoeger. $7.95.

Palliser, John. **Solitary Rambles and Adventures of a Hunter in the Prairies.** (Illus). 1969. Repr. of 1853 ed. C. E. Tuttle. $5.00.

Pryce, Dick. **Hunting for Beginners.** (Illus). 1978. softbound. Stoeger. $5.95.

Rearden, Jim, ed. **Alaska Magazine's Alaska Hunting Guide.** (Illus). 1979. pap. Alaska Northwest. $5.95.

Richardson, Larry. **A Guide to Hunting in Tennessee.** (Illus). pap. Thomas Press.

Roosevelt, Theodore. **Hunting Trips of a Ranchman.** 1970. Repr. of 1885 ed. Gregg Press. (OP).

—**Hunting Trips of a Ranchman.** Repr. of 1885 ed. Irvington. $17.50.

—**Outdoor Pastimes of an American Hunter.** 1970. Repr. of 1905 ed. Arno Press. $24.00.

—**Ranch Life and the Hunting-Trail.** 1970. Repr. of 1901 ed. Arno Press. $12.00.

—**Ranch Life and the Hunting-Trail.** 1966. Repr. of 1899 ed. University Microfilms International. (OP).

—**Ranch Life in the Far West.** (Illus). 1968. Northland Press. (OP).

—**Ranch Life in the Far West.** 1978. pap. Outbooks. $4.95.

—**Theodore Roosevelt's America.** Wiley, Farida, ed. (Illus). 1955. Devin-Adair Co. $10.00.

—**Wilderness Hunter.** 1970. Repr. of 1900 ed. Irvington. $16.00.

Sandoz, Mari. **The Buffalo-Hunters: The Story of the Hide Men.** 1978. pap. University of Nebraska Press. $6.50.

Tillett, Paul. **Doe Day: The Antlerless Deer Controversy in New Jersey.** 1963. Rutgers University Press. pap. $5.95.

Tome, Philip. **Pioneer Life or Thirty Years a Hunter: Being Scenes and Adventures in the Life of Phillip Tome.** (Illus). 1971. Repr. of 1854 ed. Arno Press. $15.00.

Wootters, John. **A Guide to Hunting in Texas.** 1979. pap. Pacesetter Press. $5.95.

HUNTING DOGS

Baily's Hunting Directory 1974-1975. 1975. British Book Center. $22.50.

Bernard, Art. **Dog Days.** 1969. Caxton. $5.95.

Brown, William F. **Field Trials: History, Management and Judging Standards.** 2nd rev. ed. (Illus). 1981. A. S. Barnes $13.95.

Drabble, Phil. **Of Pedigree Unknown: Sporting and Working Dogs.** (Illus). 1977. Transatlantic Arts, Inc. $8.75.

Duffey, David M. **Hunting Dog Know-How.** (Illus). 1972. Winchester Press. $11.95.

—**Hunting Hounds: How to Choose, Train and Handle America's Trail and Tree Hounds.** (Illus). 1972. Winchester Press. (OP).

—**Dave Duffey Trains Gun Dogs.** (Illus). 1974. Dreenan Press. (OP).

—**Expert Advice on Gun Dog Training.** 1977. Winchester Press. $13.95.

Erlandson, Keith. **Gundog Training.** 1978. Barrie & Jenkins. (OP).

Falk, John R. **The Complete Guide to Bird Dog Training.** 1976. Winchester Press. $14.95.

—**The Practical Hunter's Dog Book.** (Illus). 1975. softbound. Stoeger. $5.95.

—**The Practical Hunter's Dog Book.** (Illus). 1971. Winchester Press. $10.95.

Goodall, Charles. **How to Train Your Own Gun Dog.** (Illus). 1978. Howell Book House, Inc. $10.95.

Hartley, Oliver. **Hunting Dogs.** pap. A. R. Harding Pub. $3.00.

Henschel, Stan. **How to Raise and Train a Chesapeake Bay Retriever.** 1965. pap. TFH Pubns. $2.50.

—**How To Raise and Train a Coonhound.** pap. TFH Pubns. $2.50.

—**How to Raise and Train a Labrador Retriever.** (Illus). pap. TFH Pubns. $2.50.

Irving, Joe. **Training Spaniels.** (Illus). 1980. David & Charles. $16.95.

Knap, Jerome. **The Digest Book of Hunting Dogs.** (Illus). 1979. pap. DBI Books. (OP).

Lent, Patricia A. **Sport with Terriers.** (Illus). 1973. Arner Publications. $9.95.

Moxon, Peter. **Gundogs: Questions and Answers.** (Illus). 1980. pap. International Publications Service. $7.50.

Mueller, Larry. **Bird Dog Guide.** (Illus). 1976. softbound. Stoeger. $6.95.

Rice, F. Philip & Dahl, John. **Hunting Dogs.** 1967. Harper & Row. (OP).

—**Hunting Dogs.** rev. ed. (Illus). 1978. T. Y. Crowell. (OP).

Roebuck, Kenneth C. **Gun-Dog Training Spaniels and Retrievers.** 1982. Stackpole. $12.95.

Russell, Joanna. **All About Gazehounds.** (Illus). 1976. Merrimack Book Service. $9.95.

Salmon, H. M. **Gazehounds and Coursing.** (Illus). 1977. North Star Press. $18.50.

Smith, Guy N. **Sporting and Working Dogs.** 1981. (Pub. by Saiga). State Mutual Book and Periodical Service. $40.00.

Stetson, Joe. **Handbook of Gundogs.** 1965. pap. TFH Pubns. (OP).

—**Hunting with Flushing Dogs.** 1965. pap. TFH Pubns. (OP).

—**Hunting with Scenthounds.** 1965. pap. TFH Pubns. (OP).

Tarrant, Bill. **Best Way to Train Your Gun Dog: The Dalmar Smith Method.** 1977. David McKay Co. $10.95.

Wehle, Robert G. **Wing and Shot.** 1964. Country Press NY. $12.00.

Whitney, Leon F. & Underwood, Acil B. **Coon Hunter's Handbook.** Hart, Ernest, ed. (Illus). 1952. Holt, Rinehart & Winston. $5.95.

Wolters, Richard A. **Gun Dog. Revolutionary Rapid Training Method.** (Illus). 1961. Dutton. $12.50.

HUNTING DOGS—POINTERS

Hart, Ernest H. **How to Raise and Train a Pointer.** (Illus). 1966. TFH Pubns. (OP).

Pet Library Ltd. **Know Your Setters and Pointers.** (Illus). pap. Doubleday. (OP).

McCarty, Diane, ed. **German Shorthaired Pointers.** (Illus). 1980. TFH Pubns. (OP).

Maxwell, C. Bede. **The New German Shorthaired Pointer.** 4th ed. Howell Book House. $14.95.

Pata, Jan L. **Pointer Champions: 1889-1980.** (Illus). 1981. pap. Pata Pubns. $19.95.

Spirer, L. Z. & Spirer, H. F. **German Short-Haired Pointer.** 1970. TFH Pubns. $11.95.

Steinfeldt, Cecilia. **The Onderdonks: A Family of Texas Pointers.** 1975. Trinity University Press. (OP).

Stetson, Joe. **Hunting with Pointing Dogs.** 1965. pap. TFH Pubns. (OP).

HUNTING DOGS—RETRIEVERS

Coykendall, Ralph W., Jr. **You and Your Retriever.** (Illus). 1963. Doubleday. (OP).

Fowler, Ann & Walters, D. K., eds. **Charles Morgan on Retrievers.** (Illus). 1968. October House. $17.50.

Free, James L. **Training Your Retriever.** 5th rev. ed. (Illus). 1974. Coward, McCann & Geoghegan. $12.95.

Kersley, J. A. **Training the Retriever: A Manual.** (Illus). 1971. Howell Book House. $12.95.

Leclerc, Maurice J. **Retriever Trainer's Manual.** (Illus). 1962. Ronald Press. (OP).

Pet Library Ltd. **Know Your Retriever.** (Illus). pap. Doubleday. (OP).

Stetson, Joe. **Hunting with Retrievers.** pap. TFH Pubns. (OP).

Wolters, Richard A. **Water Dog.** (Illus). Dutton. $12.50.

HUNTING DOGS—SETTERS

Pet Library Ltd. **Know Your Setters and Pointers.** (Illus). pap. Doubleday. (OP).

HUNTING STORIES

Alaska Magazine Editors. **Selected Alaska Hunting and Fishing Tales.** Vol. 3. 1974. pap. Alaska Northwest. (OP).

Bear, Fred. **Fred Bear's Field Notes.** Doubleday. $17.95.

Brister, Bob. **Moss, Mallards and Mules: And Other Hunting and Fishing Stories.** 1973. Winchester Press. (OP).

Hill, Gene. **Hill Country: Stories About Hunting and Fishing and Dogs and Such.** (Illus). 1978. Dutton. $13.50.

Holden, Philip. **Backblocks.** (Illus). 1974. International Publications Service. (OP).

McManus, Patrick. **They Shoot Canoes, Don't They?** 1981. Holt, Rinehart & Winston. $10.95.

MacQuarrie, Gordon. **Stories of the Old Duck Hunters.** 1979. pap. Willow Creek Press. $5.95.

Neasham, V. Aubrey. **Wild Legacy: California Hunting and Fishing Tales.** (Illus). 1973. Howell-North. (OP).

HUNTING WITH BOW AND ARROW

Adams, Chuck. **Bowhunter's Digest.** 2nd ed. (Illus). 1981. pap. DBI Books. $9.95.

—**The Complete Book of Bowhunting.** (Illus). 1978. Winchester Press. $14.95.

Bear, Fred. **Archer's Bible.** (Illus). 1980. pap. Doubleday. $4.50.

Conaster, Dean. **Bowhunting the White-Tailed Deer.** (Illus). 1977. Winchester Pres. (OP).

Elliot, Cheri. **The Digest Book of Bowhunting.** (Illus). 1979. pap. DBI Books. $2.95.

—**Archer's Digest.** 3rd ed. (Illus). 1982. pap. DBI Books. $9.95.

Gillelan, G. Howard. **Complete Book of the Bow and Arrow.** rev. 3rd ed. (Illus). 1981. Stackpole Books. $11.95

Helgeland, Glenn. **Archery World's Complete Guide to Bowhunting.** 1975. pap. Prentice-Hall. $5.95.

James, M. R. **Bowhunting for Whitetail and Mule Deer.** (Illus). 1976. pap. Jolex. $6.95.

Kittredge, Doug & Wambold, H. R. **Bowhunting for Deer.** rev. ed. 1978. Stackpole Books. $12.95.

Laycock, George & Bauer, Erwin. **Hunting with Bow and Arrow.** 1965. ARco. (OP).

Learn, C. R. **Bow Hunter's Digest.** 1974. pap. DBI Books. (OP).

Maynard, Roger, **Advanced Bowhunting.** (Illus). 1982. softbound. Stoeger. $10.95.

Schuyler, Keith C. **Bow Hunting for Big Game.** (Illus). 1977. Stockpole Books. $7.95.

Smythe, John & Barwick, Humphrey. **Bow Vs. Gun.** 1976. Repr. Charles River Books. $15.00.

Tinsley, Russell. **Bow Hunter's Guide.** (Illus). 1975. softbound. Stoeger. $5.95.

KNIFE-THROWING

Collins, Blackie. **Knife Throwing: Sport..Survival.. Defense.** (Illus). 1978. pap. Knife World. $3.00.

Echanis, Michael D. **Knife Fighting, Knife Throwing for Combat.** (Illus). 1978. pap. Ohara Publications. (OP).

McEvoy, H. K. **Knife-Throwing.** Wehman Brothers, Inc. $3.95.

McEvoy, Harry K. **For Knife Lovers Only.** (Illus). 1979. pap. Knife World. $4.95.

—**Knife Throwing: A Practical Guide.** (Illus). 1973. pap. C. E. Tuttle. $3.95.

KNIVES

Barney, Richard W., and Loveless, Robert W. **How to Make Knives.** 1977. pap. Beinfeld Pub. (OP).

Blandford, Percy. **How to Make Your Own Knives.** (Illus). 1979. pap. TAB Books. (OP).

Boye, David. **Step-by-Step Knifemaking.** 1977. softbound. Stoeger. $7.95.

—**Step-by-Step Knifemaking.** 1977. Rodale Press. $14.95; pap. $10.95.

Cassidy, William. **Knife Digest.** Peterson, Harold L., et al. eds. (Illus). 1974. Knife Digest. (OP).

Cassidy, William L. **The Complete Book of Knife Fighting.** Lund, Peder C., ed. 1975. Paladin Enterprises. (OP).

—**Knife Digest: Second Annual Edition.** (Illus). 1976. pap. Paladin Enterprises. $12.95.

Ehrhardt, Larry. **Encyclopedia of Pocket Knives: Book Three: Winchester-Marbles-Knives and Hardware.** (Illus). 1974. Heart of America Press. $6.95.

Erhardt, Roy & Ferrell, J. **Encyclopedia of Pocket Knives: Book One and Book Two Price Guide.** rev. ed. (Illus). 1977. Heart of America Press. $6.95.

Hardin, Albert N., Jr. & Hedden, Robert W. **Light but Efficient: A Study of the M1880 Hunting and M1890 Intrenching Knives and Scabbards.** (Illus). 1973. Albert N. Hardin. $7.95.

Hughes, B. R. **American Hand-Made Knives of Today.** Pioneer Press. $9.95.

Ingber-Irvin, Beth. **Knifemakers Guild Directory.** (Illus). 1981. pap. Beinfeld. $12.95.

Knife World Publications. **The Best of Knife World, Vol. 1.** 1980. pap. Knife World. $3.95.

Latham, Sid. **Knifecraft.** Stackpole Books. $24.95.

—**Knives and Knifemakers.** (Illus). 1974. pap. Macmillan. $7.95.

—**Knives and Knifemakers.** 1973. Winchester Press. $17.95.

Levine, Bernard R. **Knifemakers of Old San Francisco.** (Illus). 1978. Badger Books. $12.95.

Lewis, Jack & Hughes, B. R. **Gun Digest Book of Folding Knives.** 1977. pap. DBI Books. $7.95.

McEvoy, Harry K. **For Knife Lovers Only.** (Illus). 1979. pap. Knife World. $4.95.

Mayes, Jim. **How to Make Your Own Knives.** (Illus). 1979. Everest House. $10.95; pap. $7.95.

Parker & Voyles. **Official 1982 Price Guide to Collector Knives.** 3rd ed. (Illus). pap. Stoeger. $9.95.

—**Official Guide to Pocket Knives.** 2nd rev. ed. 1979. pap. House of Collectibles. (OP).

Parker, James & Voyles, Bruce. **Official Price Guide to Collector Pocket Knives.** 4th ed. (Illus). pap. Wallace-Homestead. (OP).

—**Official Price Guide to Collector Knives.** 3rd ed. (Illus). 1980. pap. House of Collectibles. (OP).

Parker, James F. & Voyles, J. Bruce. **The Official 1981 Price Guide to Collector Knives.** 4th ed. 1982. pap. House of Collectibles. $9.95.

Parker-Voyles. **Official Price Guide to Collector Knives.** 5th ed. 1982. pap. House of

Collectibles. $9.95.

Peterson, Harold L. **American Knives.** 1975. pap. Scribner's. $6.95.

—**American Knives.** 1980. Gun Room Press. $15.00.

—**History of Knives.** (Illus). 1966. Scribner's (OP).

Pocket Knives. 1983. pap. Dell. $2.95.

Riaz, Yvan D. **The Book of Knives.** (Illus). 1982. Crown. $30.00.

Schreir, Konrad F., Jr. **Marble Knives and Axes.** (Illus). 1978. pap. Beinfeld Pub. $4.50.

Schroeder, William. **A Collector's Illustrated Price Guide to Pocket Knives.** 1977. pap. Collector Books. (OP).

Steele, David E. **Secrets of Modern Knife Fighting.** (Illus). 1975. Phoenix Associates. $15.95; pap. $9.95.

Stephens, Frederick J. **Fighting Knives.** (Illus). 1980. Arco. $14.95.

Strung, Norman. **The Encyclopedia of Knives.** (Illus). 1976. Lippincott. (OP).

Tappan, Mel, ed. **Guide to Handmade Knives and the Official Directory of the Knifemaker's Guild.** limited ed. Janus Press. $9.95.

—**A Guide to Handmade Knives and the Official Directory of the Knifemaker's Guild.** (Illus). 1977. Janus Press. (OP).

Wallace, George B. **Knife Handling for Self-Defense.** 1973. pap. Walmac Books. (OP).

Warner, Ken. **Practical Book of Knives.** (Illus). 1976. softbound. Stoeger. $7.95.

—**Practical Book of Knives.** 1976. Winchester Press. $12.95.

Warner, Ken. ed. **Knives '81.** 1980. pap. DBI Book. (OP).

—**Knives '82.** (Illus). 1981. pap. DBI Books. (OP).

—**Knives '83.** (Illus). 1982. pap. DBI Books. $8.95.

LEE-ENFIELD RIFLES

Chamberlain, Peter & Gander, Terry. **Machine Guns.** (Illus). 1975. Arco. (OP).

LUGER PISTOLS

Luger Manual. (Reprint of Original English-language edition.). 1967. softbound. Stoeger. $1.95.

Walter, John. **Luger.** 1977. Arms & Armour Press. (OP).

MAUSER PISTOLS

Belford & Dunlap. **Mauser Self-Loading Pistol.** Borden. $13.50.

Holland, Claude V. **The Military Four.** pap. Holland Bks. $4.95; pap. $2.98.

Mauser Manual. (Facs. ed. of early English language Mauser Catalog and Manual). 1974. softbound. Stoeger. $1.95.

Pender. **Mauser Pocket Pistols: 1910-1946.** Borden. (OP).

MOOSE

Berry, William D. **Deneki: An Alaskan Moose.** 1965. Macmillan. (OP).

Jenkins, Marie M. **Deer, Moose, Elk and Their Family.** (Illus). 1979. Holiday House. $8.95.

Mason, George F. **Moose Group.** (Illus). (gr. 6-9). 1968. pap. Hastings House Pubs. $2.95.

Peterson, Randolph L. **North American Moose.** 1955. University of Toronto Press. pap. $12.50.

Van Wormer, Joe. **The World of the Moose.** (Illus). 1972. Lippincott. (OP).

NATURAL HISTORY—OUTDOOR BOOKS

Barrus, Clara, ed. **The Heart of Burrough's Journals.** 1979. Repr. of 1928 ed. Arden Lib. $30.00.

Bedichek, Roy. **Adventures with a Texas Naturalist.** (Illus). 1961. pap. University of Texas Press. $8.95.

Beston, Henry. **The Outermost House.** 1976. pap. Penguin Books. $3.95.

Borland, Hal. **Beyond Your Doorstep.** (Illus). 1962. Knopf. (OP).

—**Hal Borland's Book of Days.** 1976. Knopf. $10.95.

Borland, Hal G. **This Hill, This Valley.** 1963. Lippincott. (OP).

Brown, Vinson. **How to Explore the Secret Worlds of Nature.** (Illus.). 1962. Little, Brown & Co. (OP).

—**Knowing the Outdoors in the Dark.** (Illus.). 1973. pap. Macmillan. (OP).

Burroughs, John. **Under the Apple—Trees.** 1916. Folcroft. (OP).

—**Wake-Robin.** 1896. Folcroft. (OP).

—**Winter Sunshine.** 1879. Folcroft. $15.00.

—**A Year in the Fields.** 1901. Folcroft. $15.00.

Cooper, Susan F. **Rural Hours.** (Illus.). 1968. Repr. of 1887 ed. Syracuse University Press. $8.95.

Davids, Richard C. **How to Talk to Birds and Other Uncommon Ways of Enjoying Nature the Year Round.** (Illus.). 1972. Knopf. (OP).

Errington, Paul L. **The Red Gods Call.** (Illus.). 1973. Iowa State University Press. $6.95.

Fuller, Raymond T. **Now That We Have to Walk: Exploring the Out-of-Doors.** facsimile ed. Repr. of 1943 ed. Arno Press. $17.00.

Gibbons, Euell. **Euell Gibbons' Beachcombers Handbook: Field Guide Edition.** 1967. pap. David McKay Co. (OP).

Halle, Louis J. **Spring in Washington.** Peter Smith. (OP).

—**Spring in Washington.** (Illus.). 1963. pap. Atheneum. $1.25.

Hanenkrat, Frank T. **Wildlife Watcher's Handbook.** (Illus.). 1979. Winchester Press. $9.95; pap. $7.95.

Harrison, Hal H. **Outdoor Adventures.** (Illus.). Vanguard. (OP).

Jefferies, Richard. **Old House at Coate.** 1948. Arno Press. $16.00.

Kieran, John F. **Nature Notes.** facs. ed. 1941. Arno Press. $14.50.

Leopold, Aldo. **Sand County Almanac: With Other Essays on Conservation from Round River.** (Illus.). 1966. Oxford University Press. $15.95.

—**Sand County Almanac Illustrated.** new ed. 1977. Tamarack Press. $25.00.

O'Kane, Walter C. **Beyond the Cabin Door.** 1957. William L. Bauhan, Inc. (OP).

Olson, Sigurd F. **Listening Point.** (Illus.). 1958. Knopf. $13.45.

—**Open Horizons.** (Illus.). 1969. Knopf. $10.95.

—**Singing Wilderness.** (Illus.). 1956. Knopf. (OP).

—**Sigurd F. Olson's Wilderness Days.** (Illus.). 1972. Knopf $17.95.

Ormond, Clyde. **Complete Book of Outdoor Lore.** (Illus.). 1965. Harper & Row. (OP).

—**The Complete Book of Outdoor Lore and Woodcraft.** (Illus.). 1982. Harper & Row. $21.95.

Pearson, Haydn S. **Sea Flavor.** facs. ed. 1948. Arno Press. $15.00.

Quinn, John R. **The Winter Woods.** (Illus.). 1976. Chatham Press. $8.95.

Rood, Ronald, et al. **Vermont Life Book of Nature.** Hard, Walter, Jr., et al. (Illus.). 1967. Stephen Greene Press. (OP).

Rowlands, John J. **Cache Lake County.** (Illus.). 1959. W. W. Norton & Co. $12.95.

Sharp, Dallas L. **Face of the Fields.** facs. ed. 1911. Arno Press. $15.00.

—**Sanctuary! Sanctuary!** facs. ed. 1926. Arno Press. $10.00.

Sharp, William. **Where the Forest Murmurs.** 1906. Arno Press. $19.50.

Shepard, Odell. **Harvest of a Quiet Eye: A Book of Digressions.** facs. ed. Repr. of 1927 ed. Arno Press. $19.50.

Teale, Edwin W. **American Seasons.** 4 Vols. (Illus.). 1966. Dodd, Mead & Co. Set. (OP).

—**Autumn Across America.** (Illus.). 1981. pap. Dodd, Mead & Co. $8.95.

—**Journey Into Summer.** (Illus.). 1981. pap. Dodd, Mead & Co. $8.95.

—**North With the Spring.** (Illus.). 1981. pap. Dodd, Mead & Co. $8.95.

—**Wandering Through Winter.** (Illus.). 1981. pap. Dodd, Mead & Co. $8.95.

Wiley, Farida, ed. **John Burroughs' America.** (Illus.). Devin-Adair Co. $10.50; pap. $5.25.

Wood, Robert S. **Mountain Cabin.** (Illus.). 1977. pap. Chronicle Books. (OP).

Working from Nature. (Color Crafts Ser.). 1975. Franklin Watts, Inc. (OP).

ORDNANCE

Bruce, Robert V. **Lincoln and the Tools of War.** (Illus.). 1974. Repr. of 1956 ed. Greenwood Press. $17.25.

Carman, W. Y. **History of Firearms from Earliest Times to 1914.** 1955. St. Martin's Press. (OP).

Chamberlain, Peter & Gander, Terry. **Infantry, Mountain and Airborne Guns.** 1975. Arco. (OP).

—**Light and Medium Artillery.** (Illus.). 1975. Arco. pap. (OP).

—**Mortars and Rockets.** 1975. Arco. (OP).

Cipolla, Carlo M. **Guns, Sails and Empires: Technological Innovation and the Early Phases of European Expansion 1400-1700.** Funk & Wagnalls. pap. (OP).

Colby, C. B. **Civil War Weapons: Small Arms and Artillery of the Blue and Grey.** (Illus.). 1962. Coward, McCann & Geoghegan. $5.29.

Derby, Harry L. **The Hand Cannons of Imperial Japan.** Reidy, John and Welge, Albert, eds. 1981. Derby Publishing Co. $37.50.

Ffoulkes, Charles. **The Gun Foundaries of England.** (Illus.). 1969. George Shumway Publisher. (OP).

Foss, Christopher. **Infantry Weapons of the World.** rev. ed. (Illus.). 1979. Scribner's encore ed. $4.95.

Hoffschmidt, Edward J. & Tantum, William H. **Second World War Combat Weapons: Japanese Combat Weapons, Vol. 2.** (Illus.). We Inc. (OP).

Lewis, Ernest A. **The Fremont Cannon: High Up and Far Back.** 1981. Arthur H. Clark. $32.50.

Marchant-Smith, D. J. & Haslem, P. R. **Small Arms and Cannons.** 1982. Pergamon Press. $26.00; pap. $13.00.

Norton, Robert. **The Gunner, Shewing the Whole Practise of Artillerie.** 1973. Repr. of 1628 ed. W. J. Johnson. $40.00.

Office of Strategic Service. **OSS Sabotage and Demolition Manual.** (Illus.). 1973. pap. Paladin Enterprises. $12.95.

Simon, Leslie E. **Secret Weapons of the Third Reich: German Research in World War II.** (Illus.). 1970. We Inc. (OP).

—**Secret Weapons of the Third Reich: German Research in World War II.** (Illus.). 1970. Paladin Enterprises. pap. $8.95.

Tomlinson, Howard. **Guns and Government: The Ordnance Office Under the Later Stuarts.** 1979. Humanities Press. $42.50.

ORIENTATION

Atkinson, George & Bengtsson, Hans. **Orienteering for Sport and Pleasure.** (Illus.). 1977. pap. Stephen Greene Press. $9.95.

Baker, R. Robin. **Human Navigation and the Sixth Sense.** 1982. pap. Simon and Schuster. $4.95.

Brown, Terry & Hunter, Rob. **The Concise Book of Orienteering.** 1979. pap. Vanguard. $2.95.

Disley, John. **Orienteering.** (Illus.). rev. 2nd ed. 1979. Stackpole Books. pap. $8.95.

Fraenkel, Gottfried & Dunn, Donald L. **The Orientation of Animals.** Peter Smith. $8.50.

Henley, B. M. **Orienteering.** (Illus.). 1976. Charles River Books. $6.95.

Kjellstrom, Bjorn. **Be Expert with Map and Compass: The Orienteering Handbook.** 1976. pap. Scribner's. $7.95.

Mooers, Robert L., Jr. **Finding your Way in the Outdoors.** 1972. Dutton. (OP).

—**Orienteering.** 1976. British Book Center. pap. $2.50.

Rand, Jim & Walker, Tony. **This is Orienteering.** (Illus.). 1977. Transatlantic Arts Inc. (OP).

Ratliff, Donald E. **Map, Compass and Campfire.** (Illus.). 1970. Binford & Mort Pubs. pap. $2.50.

Rutstrum, Calvin. **Wilderness Route Finder.** 1973. Macmillan. pap. $1.95.

Vassilevsky, B. **Where is the North?** 1977. pap. Imported Pubns. $3.95.

Watson, J. D. **Orienteering.** (Illus.). 1975. Charles River Books. pap. $2.50.

OUTDOOR COOKERY

Allen, Gale & Allen, Robert F. **The Complete Recreational Vehicle Cookbook: For Campers, Motor Homes, RV's and Vans.** Moulton, Jocelyn, ed. 1977. Celestial Arts. pap. $4.95.

Ames, Mark & Ames, Roberta. **Barbecues.** 1973. pap. Warner Books. (OP).

Anderson, Beverly M. & Hamilton, Donna M. **The New High Altitude Cookbook.** (Illus.). 1980. Random House. $14.95.

Anderson, Ken. **The Sterno Outdoor Living Book.** 1977. Dorison House. $5.95.

Angier, Bradford. **Food-from-the-Woods-Cooking.** (Illus.). 1973. Macmillan. pap. (OP).

—**Wilderness Cookery.** (Illus.). 1970. pap. Stackpole Books. (OP).

Antell, Steven. **Backpacker's Recipe Book.** (Illus.). 1980. pap. Pruett. $5.50.

Banks, James E. **Alfred Packer's Wilderness Cookbook.** (Illus.). 1969. Filter Press. $7.00. pap. $1.50.

Barker, Harriett. **The One-Burner Gourmet.** rev. ed. 1981. pap. Contemporary Books. $7.95.

—**The One Burner Gourmet.** 1975. pap. Contemporary Books. $6.95.

Bartmess, Marilyn A., ed. **Woodall's Campsite Cookbook.** 1971. pap. Simon & Schuster. (OP).

Bates, Joseph D., Jr. **Outdoor Cook's Bible.** (Illus.). 1964. Doubleday. $3.95.

Beard, James A. **Fireside Cookbook.** (Illus.). 1969. Simon & Schuster. $15.95.

Beardsley, Richard. **Trail and Camp Cooking with the Chinese Wok.** (Illus.). 1982. pap. Pruett. $2.95.

Berglund, Berndt & Bolsby, Clare. **Wilderness Cooking.** 1973. Scribner's (OP).

Better Homes & Gardens Editors. **The Better Homes & Garden All-Time Favorite Barbecue Recipes.** 1980. pap. Bantam. $2.25.

Betz, Eleanor P., et al. **Summertime Eating for a Healthy Heart: Cook Out—Camp Out—Eat Out The Low Cholesterol Way.** 1981. pap. $3.95.

Blanchard, Marjorie, P. **The Outdoor Cookbook.** (Illus.). 1977. Franklin Watts, Inc. $5.90.

Bock, Richard. **Camper Cookery.** 1977. pap. Lorenz Press. $5.95.

Bond, Jules. **The Outdoor Cookbook.** 1976. pap. Pocket Books. (OP).

Brent, Carol D., ed. **Barbecue: The Fine Art of Charcoal, Gas and Hibachi Outdoor Cooking.** (Illus.). 1971. Doubleday. (OP)

Bultmann, Phylis. **Two Burners and an Ice Chest: The Art of Relaxed Cooking in Boats, in Campers and Under the Stars.** (Illus.). 1977. Prentice-Hall. pap. $5.95.

Bunnelle, Hasse. **Food for Knapsackers: And Other Trail Travelers.** 1971. pap. Sierra Club Books. $4.95.

Bunnelle, Hasse & Sarvis, Shirley. **Cooking for Camp and Trail.** 1972. pap. Sierra Club. $4.95.

Burros, Marian & Levine, Lois. **The Summertime Cookbook.** 1980. pap. Macmillan. $4.50.

Carhart, Arthur H. **Outdoorsman's Cookbook.** rev. ed. 1962. pap. Macmillan. (OP).

Crocker, Betty. **Betty Crocker's New Outdoor Cookbook.** (Illus.). 1967. Western Publishing. (OP).

Cross, Margaret & Fiske, Jean. **Backpacker's Cookbook.** 1973. Ten Speed Press. $3.00.

Culinary Arts Institute Editorial Staff. **The Master Chef's Outdoor Grill Cookbook.** 1975. pap. Grosset & Dunlap. (OP).

Dawson, Charlotte. **Recreational Vehicle Cookbook.** (Illus., Orig.). 1970. Trail-R Club of America. $3.95.

—**Trailerists Cookbook.** Trail-R Club of America. $3.50.

Dodd, Ed. **Mark Trail's Cooking Tips.** 1971. pap. Essandess. (OP).

Douglas, Luther A. & Douglas, Conda E. **The Explorers Cookbook.** (Illus.). 1971. Caxton Printers. (OP).

Drew, Edwin P. **The Complete Light-Pack Camping and Trail-Food Cookbook.** 1977. pap. McGraw-Hill. $3.95.

Elmont, Nancy. **Good As All Outdoors: A Barbecue Cookbook.** (Illus.). 1981. Dorison House. (OP).

Fadala, Sam. **The Complete Guide to Game Care and Cookery.** 1981. pap. DBI Books. (OP).

Farm Journal's Food Editors. **Farm Journal's Picnic and Barbecue Cookbook.** Ward, Patricia, ed. (Illus.). 1982. Farm Journal. $13.95.

Farmer, Charles. **The Digest Book of Outdoor Cooking.** (Illus.). 1979. pap. DBI Books. (OP).

Farmer, Charles J. & Farmer, Kathy, eds. **Campground Cooking.** 1974. pap. DBI Books. (OP).

—**Digest Book of Outdoor Cooking.** pap. DBI Books. $2.95.

Fears, J. Wayne. **Backcountry Cooking.** (Illus.). 1980. East Woods Press. $11.95; pap. $7.95.

Ferguson, Larry & Lister, Priscilla, eds. **The Outdoor Epicure.** (Illus.). 1979. pap. Signpost Book Publishing. $2.95.

Fitzgerald, Don. **Easy to Bar-B-Q Cook Book: A Guide to Better Barbecuing.** pap. Pacifica House. (OP).

Fleming, June. **The Well-Fed Backpacker.** 1979. pap. Victoria House. $4.95.

—**The Well-Fed Backpacker.** (Illus.). 1981. pap. Random House. $3.95.

Groene, Janet. **Cooking on the Go.** rev. ed. (Illus.). 1980. W.W. Norton & Co. (OP).

Hemingway, Joan & Maricich, Connie. **The Picnic Gourmet.** (Illus.). 1977. Random House. (OP).

—**The Picnic Gourmet.** (Illus.). 1978. pap. Random House. $7.95.

Holm, Don. **Old-Fashioned Dutch Oven Cookbook.** 1969. pap. Caxton Printers. $5.95.

Holsman, Gale T. & Holsman, Beverly. **The Great Outdoors Cookbook.** 1980. pap. Bantam. (OP).

Hughes, Stella. **Chuck Wagon Cookin'.** 1974. pap. University of Arizona Press. $8.50.

Hunter, Rob. **Backpacking and Camping Cookbook.** 1981. State MutualBook and Periodical Service. $12.00.

—**Camping and Backpacking Cookbook.** (Illus.). 1978. pap. Hippocrene Books. $2.95.

Jones, Phil. **Cooking over Wood.** 1976. pap. Drake Pubs. (OP).

Kaatz, Van. **The Thrifty Gourmet's Chopped Meat Book.** (Illus.). 1976. pap. Major Books. $1.50.

Kamins, James. **The Cookout Conspiracy.** Young, Billie, ed. 1974. Ashley Books. (OP).

Kinmont, Vikki & Axcell, Claudia. **Simple Foods for the Pack.** (Illus.). 1976. pap. Sierra Club Books. $5.95.

Kirschbaum, Gabrielle. **Picnics for Lovers.** 1980. Van Nostrand Reinhold. $12.95.

Kitchin, Frances. **Cook-Out.** (Illus.). 1978. David & Charles. $6.95.

Knap, Alyson. **The Outdoorsman's Guide to Edible Wild Plants of North America: an Illustrated Manual.** (Illus.). 1975. Pagurian Press. $8.95.

Logan, Barbara. **Barbecue and Outdoor Cookery.** (Illus.). 1978. pap. Beekman Publishers. (OP).

Lund, Duane R. **Camp Cooking ... Made Easy and Kind of Fun.** Adventure Publications. 1978. $4.45.

MacDonald, Barbara and Culinary Arts Institute Staff. **Outdoor Cookbook.** (Illus.). 1975. pap. Delair Consolidated. $3.95.

McElfresh, Beth. **Chuck Wagon Cookbook.** pap. Swallow Press. (OP).

McHugh, Gretchen. **The Hungry Hiker's Book of Good Cooking.** (Illus.). 1982. Alfred A. Knopf. $17.50; pap. $7.95.

Macklin, Harvey. **Backpacker's Cookbook: A Complete Manual and Handbook for Cooking Freeze-Dried and Wild Foods on the Trail and in the Wilderness.** (Illus.). 1978. Pagurian Press.

Macmillan, Diane D. **The Portable Feast.** (Illus.). 1973. 101 Productions. pap. $4.95.

McMorris, Bill & McMorris, Jo. **The All Outdoors Cookbook.** (Illus.). 1974. David McKay Co. (OP).

McNair, James K. **The Complete Book of Picnics.** 1980. pap. Ortho Books. $4.95.

Mandeville, Terry M. **Backpacking Menus.** 1980. pap. Price Guide. (OP).

Marshall, Mel. **Cooking Over Coals.** 1975. softbound. Stoeger. $5.95.

—**Cooking Over Coals.** 1971. Winchester Press. $9.95.

—**The Family Cookout Cookbook.** 1973. pap. Ace Books. (OP).

Martin, George W. **The Complete Book of Outdoor Cooking.** (Illus.). 1975. A. S. Barnes. (OP).

Mendenhall, Ruth D. **Backpack Cookery.** (Illus.). 1974. pap. La Siesta. $1.95.

Messner, Yvonne. **Campfire Cooking.** (Illus., Orig.). 1973. pap. David C. McKay Publishing Co. (OP).

Miller, Dorcas S. **The Healthy Trail Food Book.** rev. ed. (Illus.). 1980. pap. East Woods Press. $3.95.

Mohney, Russ. **Trailside Cooking.** (Illus.). 1976. pap. Stackpole Books. $2.95.

Morris, Dan & Morris, Inez. **The Complete Fish Cookbook.** (Illus.). 1978. softbound. Stoeger. $5.95.

—**Complete Outdoor Cookbook.** 1979. Dutton. (OP).

Nagy, Jean. **Brown Bagging It: A Guide to Fresh Food Cooking in the Wilderness.** 1976 pap. Marty-Nagy Bookworks. $2.50.

The Outdoor Cookbook. (Illus.). 1976. Oxmoor House. (OP).

Popper, Kathryn. **Honorable Hibachi.** (Illus.). 1965. Simon & Schuster. (OP).

Powledge, Fred. **The Budget Backpacker's Food Book: How to Select and Prepare Your Provision from Supermarket Shelves with Over 50 Trail-Tested Recipes.** 1977. pap. David McKay Co. (OP).

Prater, Yvonne & Mendenhall, Ruth D. Gorp, **Glop and Glue Stew: Favorite Foods from 165 Outdoor Experts.** (Illus.). 1981. pap. Mountaineers. $6.95.

Raup, Lucy G. **Camper's Cookbook.** 1967. pap. C. E. Tuttle. $3.75.

Reimers, Emil. **Cooking for Camp and Caravan.** 1976. British Book Center. (OP).

Riviere, William A. **Family Campers Cookbook.** (Illus.). 1965. Holt, Rinehart & Winston. (OP).

Roden, Claudia. **Picnic.** 1981. State Mutual Book & Periodical Service. $40.00.

Schubert, Ruth L. **The Camper's Cookbook.** 1974. pap. Little, Brown & Co. $3.50.

Smith, Capt. James A. **Dress 'Em Out, Vol. 1** (Illus.). 1982. softbound. Stoeger. $11.95

Sparano, Betty and Vin Sparano, Ed. **Celebrity Fish and Game Cookbook.** 1983. softbound. Stoeger. $11.95.

Steindler, Geraldine. **Game Cookbook.** (Illus.). 1965. softbound. Stoeger. $7.95.

—**Game Cookbook,** Revised Edition. 1982. softbound. Stoeger. $10.95

Strom, Arlene. **Cooking on Wheels.** (Illus.). 1970. pap. Bond Wheelwright Co. $3.95.

Tarr, Yvonne Y. **The Complete Outdoor Cookbook.** (Illus.). 1973. Times Books. $8.95.

Taylor, Joan C. **Picnics.** (Illus.). 1979. Random House. $4.95.

Thomas, Dian. **Roughing It Easy: A Unique Ideabook on Camping and Cooking.** (Illus.). 1974. pap. Brigham Young University Press. $8.95. pap. $6.95.

Tonn, Maryjane H., ed. **Ideals Outdoor Cookbook.** 1975. pap. Ideals. (OP).

Wallace, Aubrey. **Natural Foods for the Trail.** 1977. Vogelsang Press. $3.95.

Western Publishing Editors, ed. **Betty Crocker's New Outdoor Cookbook No. 10.** 1976. pap. Bantam Books. (OP).

Wilder, James A. **Pine-Tree Jims's Jack-Knife Cookery: A Classic of Outdoor Lore.** 1982. pap. Siemens Communication Graphics. $7.95.

Wood, Jane. **Elegant Fare from the Weber Kettle.** (Illus.). 1977. Western Publishing. $6.95.

Woodall's Campside Cookbook. pap. Woodali. $3.95.

Woodruff, Leroy L. **Cooking the Dutch Oven Way.** (Illus.). 1980. pap. ICS Books. $6.95.

OUTDOOR LIFE

Acerrano, Anthony. **The Complete Woodsman's Guide.** (Illus.). 1981. Winchester Press. $16.95.

—**The Outdoorsman's Emergency Manual.** 1976. softbound. Stoeger. $7.95.

—**The Outdoorsman's Emergency Manual.** 1976. Winchester Press. $12.95.

Allison, Linda. **The Sierra Club Summer Book.** (Illus.). 1977. Sierra Book Club. (OP).

Andreson, Steve. **The Orienteering Book.** (Illus.). 1977. pap. World Pubns. (OP).

—**The Orienteering Book.** (Illus.). 1980. pap. Anderson World. $3.95.

Angier, Bradford. **Food-from-the-Woods-Cooking.** (Illus.). 1973. pap. Macmillan. (OP).

—**How to Live in the Woods on Pennies a Day.** (Illus.). 1971. pap. Stackpole Books. (OP).

—**How to Stay Alive in the Woods.** Orig. Title: **Living off the Country.** 1962. pap. Macmillan. $2.95.

—**One Acre and Security: How to Live off the Earth Without Ruining It.** 1973. pap. Random House. $4.95.

—**Skills for Taming the Wilds: A Handbook of Woodcraft Wisdom.** 1972. pap. Pocket Books. (OP).

—**Survival with Style.** (illus.). 1974. pap. Random House. $4.95.

—**Wilderness Gear You Can Make Yourself.** (Illus.). 1973. pap. Macmillan. (OP).

—**The Master Backwoodsman.** 1979. pap. Fawcett Book Group. $4.95.

—**The Master Backwoodsman.** 1978. Stackpole Books. $10.95.

Angier, Bradford & Angier, Vena. **Wilderness Wife.** (Illus.). 1976. Chilton Book Co. (OP).

Bauer, Erwin & Peggy. **Camper's Digest.** 3rd ed. pap. DBI Books. $7.95.

Bourjaily, Vance. **Country Matters: Collected Reports from the Fields and Streams of Iowa and other Places.** 1973. Dial Press. $8.95.

Boy Scouts of America. **Boy Scout Fieldbook.** new ed. (Illus.). 1978. pap. Workman Publishing. $4.95.

Bradford, William. **Survival Outdoors.** 1977. pap. Macmillan. (OP).

Bridge, Raymond. **High Peaks and Clear Roads: A Safe and Easy Guide to Outdoor Skills.** (Illus.). 1978. Prentice-Hall. (OP).

Brittain, William. **Survival Outdoors.** (Illus.). 1977. pap. Monarch Press. $2.95.

Brown, Terry & Hunter, Rob. **Map and Compass.** rev. ed. (illus.). Hippocrene Books. $2.95.

Brown, Vinson. **Knowing the Outdoors in the Dark.** (Illus.). 1973. pap. Macmillan. (OP).

—**Knowing the Outdoors in the Dark.** 1972. Stackpole Books. (OP).

—**Reading the Outdoors at Night.** (Illus.). 1982. pap. Stackpole Books. $9.95.

Carrighar, Sally. **Home to the Wilderness.** (Illus.). 1973. Houghton Mifflin. $7.95.

Cartier, John O. **The Modern Deer Hunter.** (Illus.). 1977. Crowell. (OP).

Colby, C. B. **Camper's and Backpacker's Bible.** (Illus.). 1977. softbound. Stoeger. $7.95.

Crawford, John S. **Wolves, Bears and Bighorns: Wilderness Observations and Experiences of a Professional Outdoorsman.** (Illus.). 1981. Alaska Northwest. $19.95; pap. $12.95.

Eastman, P. F. **Advanced First Aid for All Outdoors.** 1976. pap. Cornell Maritime Press. $6.00.

Elliott, Cheri. **Backpacker's Digest.** 3rd ed. 1981. pap. DBI Books. $8.95.

Explorers Limited, compiled by. **Explorers Ltd. Source Book.** (Illus.). 1977. Harper & Row. (OP).

Farmer, Charles J. **The Digest Book of Canoes, Kayaks and Rafts.** pap. DBI Books. $5.95.

Fear, Daniel E., ed. **Surviving the Unexpected: A Curriculum Guide for Wilderness Survival and Survival from Natural and Man Made Disasters.** (Illus.). 1974. Survival Education Association. $5.00.

Fleming, June, ed. **The Outdoor Idea Book.** (Illus.). 1978. pap. Victoria House. $6.50.

Fodor's Outdoors America. (Illus.). 1980. David McKay Co. $12.95; pap. $9.95.

Frederickson, Olive A. & East, Ben. **The Silence of the North.** 1973. pap. Warner Books. (OP).

Gearing, Catherine. **Field Guide to Wilderness Living.** 1973. pap. Southern Publishing Association. (OP).

Gode, Merlin. **Winter Outdoor Living.** 1978. pap. text ed. Brighton Publishing. $2.95.

Gregory, Mark. **The Good Earth Almanac.** 1973. pap. Grosset & Dunlap. (OP).

Grow, Laurence. **The Old House Book of Outdoor Living Places.** (Illus.). 1981. Warner Books. $15.00; pap. $8.95.

Hall, Bill. **A Year In the Forest.** (Illus.). 1975. McGraw-Hill. (OP).

Hamper, Stanley R. **Wilderness Survival.** 3rd ed. 1975. Repr. of 1963 ed. Peddlers Wagon. $1.79.

Hanley, Wayne. **A Life Outdoors: A Curmudgeon Looks at the Natural World.** (Illus.). 1980. Stephen Greene Press. pap. $5.95.

Heacox, Cecil E. **The Education of an Outdoorsman.** 1976. Winchester Press. $9.95.

Henderson, Luis M. **Campers' Guide to Woodcraft and Outdoor Life.** Orig. Title: **Outdoor Guide.** 1972. pap. Dover. $3.50.

Hickin, Norman. **Beachcombing for Beginners.** 1976. pap. Wilshire Book Co. $2.00.

Hollatz, Tom. **The White Earth Snowshoe Guidebook.** (Illus.). 1973. North Star Press. $5.00; pap. $3.50.

Humphreys, J. **Living Off The Land.** (Illus.). 1979. pap. International Pubns. Service. $8.50.

Hunter, Rodello. **Wyoming Wife.** 1969. Knopf. (OP).

Jeneid, Michael. **The Outdoors Adventure Book.** (Illus.). 1975. Henry Z. Walck. (OP).

Johnson, et al. **Outdoor Tips: A Remington Sportsman's Library Book.** pap. Benjamin Co. $2.95.

Jones, James C., ed. **The National Outdoor Living Directory, No. 2.** (Illus.). 1975. Live Free. (OP).

Kephart, Horace. **Camping and Woodcraft.** (Illus.). 1948. Macmillan. $10.95

Kodet, E. Russel & Angier, Bradford. **Being Your Own Wilderness Doctor.** (Illus.). 1975. Stackpole Books. $7.95.

Labostille, Anne. **Woodswoman.** (Illus.). 1978. pap. E. P. Dutton. (OP).

Lamoreaux, Bob & Lamoreaux, Marcia. **Outdoor Gear You Can Make Yourself.** (Illus.). 1976. pap. Stackpole Books. (OP).

Lueders, Edward. **The Clam Lake Papers: A Winter In The North Woods.** 1977. Harper & Row. $7.95.

McGuire, Thomas. **Ninety-Nine Days on the Yukon: An Account of What Was Seen and Heard In The Company Of Charles A. Wolf, Gentleman Canoeist.** 1977. pap. Alaska-Northwest. (OP).

McManus, Patrick. **A Fine and Pleasant Misery.** 1978. Holt, Rinehart & Winston. $7.95.

McPhee Gribble Publishers. **Out in the Wilds.** (Illus.). 1977. pap. Penguin Books. $2.25.

Merrill, W. K. **The Survival Handbook.** (Illus.). 1972. Winchester Press. $12.95.

Mitchell, Jim and Fear, Gene. **Fundamentals of Outdoor Enjoyment: Text or Teaching Guide for Coping with Outdoor Environments, All Seasons.** (Illus.). 1976. pap. Survival Education Association. $5.00.

Mohney, Russ. **Wintering: The Outdoor Book for Cold-Weather Ventures.** 1976. pap. Stackpole Books. $3.95.

Nichols, Maggie. **Wild, Wild Woman.** 1978. pap. Berkeley Publishing. $4.95.

Olsen, Larry D. **Outdoor Survival Skills.** rev. ed. 1973. Brigham Young University Press. $7.95.

—**Outdoor Survival Skills.** 1981. pap. Pocket Books. $2.95.

Olson, Sigurd F. **Olson's Wilderness Days.** (Illus.). 1972. Knopf. $17.95.

Ormond, Clyde. **Complete Book of Outdoor Lore.** (Illus.). 1965. Harper & Row. (OP).

—**The Complete Book of Outdoor Lore and Woodcraft.** 1982. Harper & Row. $21.12.

—**Outdoorsman's Handbook.** 1971. E. P. Dutton. (OP).

—**Outdoorsman's Handbook.** 1975. pap. Berkley Publishing. (OP).

Outdoor Living Skills Instructor's Manual. 1979. pap. American Camping Association. $5.00.

The Outdoors Survival Manual. (Illus.). 1978. pap. Sterling. (OP).

Owings, Loren C., ed. **Environmental Values, 1860-1972: A Guide to Information Sources.** 1976. Gale Research Co. $40.00.

Patmore, J. Allan. **Land and Leisure In England and Wales.** 1971. Fairleigh Dickinson. $27.50

Peppe, Rodney. **Outdoors.** 1981. Watts. $3.95.

Petzoldt, Paul. **The Wilderness Handbook.** (Illus.). 1977. pap. W. W. Norton & Co. $6.95.

Platten, David. **The Outdoor Survival Handbook.** David & Charles. $6.95.

Rae, William E. **A Treasury of Outdoor Life.** (Illus.). 1976. Harper & Row. $12.95.

Rand, William M. **Just Fishin' and Huntin'.** 1978. Vantage Press. (OP).

Rawick, George P. **From Sundown to Sunup.** 1972. pap. Greenwood Press. $15.00; pap. $4.45.

Roberts, Harry. **Keeping Warm and Dry.** (Illus.). 1982. pap. Stone Wall Press. $7.95.

Robinson, David. **The Complete Homesteading Book: Proven Methods for Self-Sufficient Living.** 1974. Garden Way Publishing. (OP).

Rood, Ronald. **It's Going to Sting Me: A Coward's Guide to the Great Outdoors.** 1977. pap. McGraw-Hill. $3.95.

Rutstrum, Calvin. **Backcountry.** 1981. ICS Books. $12.95.

—**New Way of the Wilderness.** (Illus.). 1966. pap. Macmillan. $2.95.

—**Once Upon a Wilderness.** (Illus.). 1973. Macmillan. $10.95.

Ruxton, George F. **Adventures in Mexico and the Rocky Mountains.** Rio Grande Press. (OP).

Scharff, Robert. **Projects for Outdoor Living.** 1981. Reston. $7.95.

Shepherd, Laurie. **A Dreamer's Log Cabin: A Woman's Walden.** (Illus.). 1981. Dembner Books. $8.95.

Thomas, Gordon. **Mostly in Fun: Rhymes and Reflections on Outdoor Experiences.** (Illus.). 1977. pap. Signpost Book Publishing. (OP).

Van Der Smissen, Betty, et al. **Leader's Guide to Nature-Oriented Activities.** 3rd ed. (Illus.). 1977. pap. Iowa State University Press. $7.95.

Vogt, Bill. **How to Build a Better Outdoors: The Action Manual for Fishermen, Hunters, Backpackers, Hikers, Canoeists, Riders, and All Other Outdoor Lovers.** (Illus.). 1978. David McKay Co. (OP).

Waterman, Charles F. **The Part I Remember.** (Illus.). 1974. Winchester Press. (OP).

Woolner, Frank. **My New England.** (Illus.). 1972. Stone Wall Press. (OP).

Wurman, Richard S. et al. **The Nature of Recreation: A Handbook in Honor of Frederick Law Olmstead.** 1972. pap. MIT Press. $5.95.

PISTOLS

Archer, Denis, ed. **Jane's Pocketbook of Pistols and Submachine Guns.** 1977. pap. Macmillan. $6.95.

Askins, Charles. **Askins on Pistols and Revolvers.** Bryant, Ted & Askins, Bill, eds. 1980. National Rifle Association. $25.00; pap. $8.95.

Best, Charles W. **Cast Iron Toy Pistols, 1870-1940: A Collector's Guide.** (Illus.). 1973. Best Antiques. (OP).

Bianchi, John. **Blue Steel and Gun Leather.** 1978. Beinfeld. (OP).

Blair, Claude. **Pistols of the World.** (Illus.). 1969. Viking Press. (OP).

Chamberlain, Peter & Gander, Terry. **Allied Pistols, Rifles and Grenades.** 1976. pap. Arco. $4.95.

—**Axis Pistols, Rifles and Grenades.** 1977. pap Arco. $4.95.

Datig, Fred A. **Luger Pistol.** rev. ed. Borden. $12.50.

Dixon, Norman. **Georgian Pistols: The Art and Craft of the Flintlock Pistol, 1715-1840.** 1972. George Shumway Publisher. $22.50.

Dunlap, H. J. **American, British and Continential Pepperbox Firearms.** (Illus.). 1967. Repr. of 1964 ed. Pacific Books. (OP).

Dyke, S. E. **Thoughts on the American Flintlock Pistol.** (Illus.). 1974. George Shumway Publisher. $6.50.

Grennell, Dean, ed. **Pistol and Revolver Digest.** 3rd ed. (Illus.). 1982. pap. DBI Books. $9.95.

Grennell, Dean A. **Pistol and Revolver Digest.** 1976. pap. DBI Books. (OP).

—Grennell, Dean A. & Lewis, Jack. **Pistol & Revolver Digest.** 2nd ed. (Illus.). 1979. pap. DBI Books. (OP).

Hertzberg, Robert. **Modern Handbuns.** (Illus.). 1977. Arco. (OP).

Hoffschmidt, E.J. **Know Your Forty-Five Caliber Auto Pistols.** (Illus.). 1973. pap. Blacksmith Corp. $5.95.

—**Know Your Walther PP and PPK Pistols.** (Illus.). 1975. pap. Blacksmith Corp. $5.95.

—**Know Your Walther P. 38 Pistols.** (Illus.). pap. 1974. Blacksmith Corp. $5.95.

Hogg, I. V. **Military Pistols and Revolvers.** (Illus.). 1970. Arco. $3.50; pap. $1.95.

Holland, Claude V. **The Military Four.** Hol-Land Books. $4.95; pap. $2.98.

Horlacher, R., ed. **The Famous Automatic Pistols of Europe.** Seaton, L. & Steindler, R. A., trs. from Ger. (Illus.). 1976. pap. Jolex. $6.95.

Kirkland, Turner. **Southern Derringers of the Mississippi Valley.** Pioneer Press. $2.00.

Klay, Frank. **The Samuel E. Dyke Collection of Kentucky Pistols.** 1980. Gun Room Press. $2.00.

Koch, R. W. **The FP-45 Liberator-Pistol 1942-45.** (Illus.). 1977. Research. $10.00.

Landskron, Jerry. **Remington Rolling Block Pistols.** (Illus.). 1981. Rolling Block Press. $34.95; deluxe ed. $39.95.

Leithe. **Japanese Hand Pistols.** Borden. $9.95.

Luger Manual. (Reprint of original English-language edition.) 1967. softbound. Stoeger. $1.95.

Mauser Manual. (Facs. ed. of early English language **Mauser Catalog and Manual.**) 1974. softbound. Stoeger. $1.95.

Millard J. T. **A Handbook on the Primary Identification of Revolvers and Semi-Automatic Pistols.** (Illus.). 1974. C. C. Thomas. $13.50; pap. $10.25.

Mitchell, Jack. **The Gun Digest Book of Pistolsmithing.** 1980. pap. DBI Books. $9.95.

Myatt, F. **An Illustrated Guide to Pistols and Revolvers.** 1981. Arco. $8.95.

Neal, Robert J. & Jinks, Roy G. **Smith & Wesson 1857-1945.** 1972. A. S. Barnes. (OP).

Nonte, George C. Jr. **Pistol Guide.** (Illus.). 1980. Stoeger. $8.95.

—**Pistol and Revolver Guide.** 3rd ed. (Illus.). 1975. softbound. Stoeger. (OP).

Nonte, George C., Jr. **Combat Handguns.** Jurras, Lee F. ed. (Illus.). 1980. Stackpole. $19.95.

—**Pistolsmithing.** (Illus.). 1974. Stackpole. $19.95.

Nonte, George C., Jr. & Jurras, Lee E. **Handgun Hunting.** (Illus.). 1976. softbound. Stoeger. $5.95.

—**Handgun Hunting.** (Illus.). 1975. Winchester Press. $10.95.

North & North. **Simeon North: First Official Pistol Maker of the United States.** Repr. Gun Room Press. $9.95.

Olson, John, compiled by. **The Famous Automatic Pistols of Europe.** (Illus.). 1975. Jolex. (OP).

Reese. Michael. **Collector's Guide to Luger Values.** 1972. pap. Pelican. $1.95.

Reese, Michael, II. **Luger Tips.** 1976. Pioneer Press. $6.95.

Sawyer, Charles W. **United States Single Shot Martial Pistols.** 1971. We Inc. $5.00.

Seaton, Lionel, tr. **Famous Auto Pistols and Revolvers, Vol. II.** (Illus.). 1971. Jolex. $6.95.

Van Der Mark, Kist & Van Der Sloot, Puype. **Dutch Muskets and Pistols.** (Illus.). 1974. George Shumway Publisher. $25.00.

Wallack, L. R. **American Pistol and Revolver Design and Performance.** 1978. Winchester Press. $16.95.

Whittington, Robert D. **German Pistols and Holsters, 1943-45: Military-Police-NSDAP.** (Illus.). Gun Room Press. $15.00.

Wilkerson, Frederick. **British and American Flintlocks.** 1972. Transatlantic Arts, Inc. $4.95.

Wilkinson, F. J. **Flintlock Pistols.** (Illus.). 1976. pap. Hippocrene Books. $2.95.

Williams, Mason. **The Sporting Use of the Handgun.** (Illus.). 1979. C. C. Thomas. $14.75.

Wood, J. B. **Gun Digest Book of Firearms Assembly-Disassembly. Pt. 1: Automatic Pistols.** (Illus.). 1979. pap. DBI Books. $9.95.

—**Troubleshooting Your Handgun.** (Illus.). 1978. pap DBI Books. $6.95.

RELOADING

Anderson, Robert S., ed. **Reloading for Shotgunners.** 1981. pap. DBI Books. $8.95.

Grennell, Dean A. **ABC's of Reloading.** 2nd ed. (Illus.). 1980. pap. DBI Books. $9.95.

Matunas, Edward. **Handbook of Metallic Cartridge Reloading.** (Illus.). 1981. Winchester Press. $15.95.

Scott, Robert F., ed. **Shooter's Bible 1983, No. 74.** 1982. softbound. Stoeger. $11.95.

Steindler, R. A. **Reloader's Guide.** 3rd ed. (Illus.). 1975. softbound. Stoeger. $7.95.

Warner, Ken, ed. **Handloader's Digest.** 9th ed. 1981. pap. DBI Books. $9.95.

—**Handloader's Digest Bullet and Powder Update.** 1980. pap. DBI Books. $4.95.

Wootters, John. **The Complete Book of Practical Handloading.** (Illus.). 1977. softbound. Stoeger. $6.95.

REVOLVERS

Askins, Charles. **Askins on Pistols and Revolvers.** Bryant, Ted & Askins, Bill, eds. 1980. National Rifle Association. $25.00; pap. $8.95.

Chamberlain, W. H. & Taylorson, A. W. **Adams' Revolvers.** 1978. Barrie & Jenkins. (OP).

Dougan, John C. **Know Your Ruger Single Action Revolvers: 1953-1963.** Amber, John T., ed. 1981. Blacksmith Corp. $35.00.

Grennell, Dean A. **Pistol and Revolver Digest.** (Illus.). 1976. pap. DBI Books. (OP).

—**Pistol and Revolver Digest.** 2nd ed. (Illus.). 1979 pap. DBI Books. (OP).

—**Pistol and Revolver Digest.** 3rd ed. (Illus.). 1982. pap. DBI Books. $9.95.

Hertzberg, Robert. **Modern Handgun.** (Illus.). 1977. Arco. (OP).

Hogg, I. V. **Military Pistols and Revolvers.** (Illus.). 1970. Arco. $3.50; pap. $1.95.

James, Garry, ed. **Guns of the Gunfighters.** (Illus.). 1975. pap. Petersen Publishing. (OP).

Jinks, Roy G. **History of Smith & Wesson.** (Illus.). 1978. Beinfeld. (OP).

Lewis, Jack. **Gun Digest Book of Single-Action Revolvers.** (Illus.). 1982. pap. DBI Books. $9.95.

Millard, J. T. **A Handbook on the Primary Identification of Revolvers and Semi-Automatic Pistols.** (Illus.). 1974. C. C. Thomas. $13.50; pap. $10.25.

Myatt, F. **An Illustrated Guide to Pistols and Revolvers.** 1981. Arco. $8.95.

Neal, Robert J. & Jinks, Roy G. **Smith and Wesson, 1857-1945.** 1975. A. S. Barnes. $25.00.

Nonte, George C. Jr. **Revolver Guide.** (Illus.). 1980. Stoeger. $8.95.

—**Pistol and Revolver Guide.** 3rd ed. (Illus.). 1975. softbound. Stoeger. (OP).

Nonte, George C., Jr. & Jurras, Lee E. **Handgun Hunting.** (Illus.). 1976. softbound. Stoeger. $5.95.

Report of Board on Tests of Revolvers and Automatic Pistols 1907. (Illus.). Sand Pond. $3.50.

Seaton, Lionel, tr. **Famous Auto Pistols and Revolvers, Vol. II.** (Illus.). 1979. Jolex. $6.95.

Wallack, L. R. **American Pistol and Revolver Design and Performance.** (Illus.). 1978. Winchester Press. (OP).

Williams, Mason. **The Sporting Use of the Handgun.** (Illus.). 1979. C. C. Thomas. $14.75.

Wood, J. B. **Gun Digest Book of Firearms Assembly/Disassembly. Pt. 1: Automatic Pistols.** (Illus.). 1979. pap. DBI Books. $9.95.

—**Gun Digest Book of Firearms Assembly/Disassembly. Pt. II: Revolvers.** (Illus.). 1979. pap. DBI Books. $9.95.

RIFLES

Archer, Denis, **Jane's Pocket Book of Rifles and Light Machine Guns.** 1977. pap. Macmillan. (OP).

Beard, Ross E., Jr. **Carbine: TheStory of David Marshall Williams.** 1977. Sandlapper Store. ltd. ed. signed. $25.00.

Behn, Jack. **45-75 Rifles.** Repr. of 1956 ed. Gun Room Press. (OP).

Bivins, John. **Art of the Fire-Lock Rifle.** 1983. George Shumway Publisher. $40.00.

—**British Rifles: A Catalogue of the Enfield Pattern Room.** 1981. State Mutual Book & Periodical Service.

Brophy, William S. **Krag Rifles.** (Illus.). 1978. Beinfeld. $24.95.

Buchele, William and Shumway, George. **Recreating the American Longrifle.** Orig. Title: **Recreating the Kentucky Rifle.** (Illus.). 1973. pap. George Shumway Publisher. $16.00.

Carmichel, Jim. **The Modern Rifle.** (Illus.). 1976. softbound. Stoeger. $5.95.

—**The Modern Rifle.** (Illus.). 1975. Winchester Press. $13.95.

Chamberlain, Peter & Gander, Terry. **Allied Pistols, Rifles and Grenades.** 1976. pap. Arco. $4.95.

—**Axis Pistols, Rifles and Grenades.** 1977. pap. Arco. $4.95.

—**Submachine Guns and Automatic Rifles: World War II Facts.** 1976. pap. Arco. (OP).

Chapman, John R. **Improved American Rifle.** (Illus.). 1978. Beinfeld. (OP).

Colby, C. B. **First Rifle: How to Shoot It Straight and Use It Safely.** (Illus.). 1954. Coward, McCann & Geoghegan. $5.99.

Davis, Henry. **A Forgotten Heritage: The Story of the Early American Rifle.** 1976. Repr. of 1941 ed. Gun Room Press. $9.95.

De Haas, Frank. **Bolt Action Rifles.** Amber, John T., ed. 1971. pap. DBI Books. (OP).

—**Bolt Action Rifles.** 1971. pap. DBI Books. (OP).

—**Single Shot Rifles and Actions.** (Illus.). 1979. pap. DBI Books. $9.95.

Dillin, John G. **The Kentucky Rifle.** 5th ed. (Illus.). 1967. George Shumway Publisher. (OP).

Editors of Gun Digest. **NRA Collector's Series: 1885-1888-1906-1923.** pap. DBI Books. (OP).

Edsall, James. **The Golden Age of Single Shot Rifles.** Pioneer Press. $2.75.

—**The Revolver Rifles.** Pioneer Press. $2.50.

Grant, James J. **More Single Shot Rifles.** (Illus.). Gun Room Press. $15.00.

—**Single-Shot Rifles.** Gun Room Press. $25.00.

—**Still More Single Shot Rifles.** 1979. Pioneer Press. $17.50.

Hanson. **The Plains Rifle.** Gun Room Press. $15.00.

Hatcher, Julian S. **The Book of the Garand.** Edwards, Douglas & Wick, Patricia, eds. (Illus.). 1977. Repr. of 1948 ed. Pine Mountain Press. $22.50.

Hoffschmidt, E.J. **Know Your M-1 Garand Rifles.** 1976. pap. Blacksmith Corp. $5.95.

Huddleston, Joe D. & Shumway, George. **Rifles in the American Revolution.** 1978. George Shumway Publisher. (OP).

Huddleston, Joe D. **Colonial Riflemen in the American Revolution.** (Illus.). 1978. George Shumway Publisher. $18.00.

Kindig, Joe. Jr. **Thoughts on the Kentucky Rifle in Its Golden Age.** (Illus.). 1971. George Shumway Publisher. (OP).

—**Thoughts on the Kentucky Rifle in Its Golden Age.** annotated 2nd ed. (Illus.). 1982. George Shumway Publisher. $75.00.

Klinger, Bernd., ed. **Rifle Shooting As a Sport.** 1981. A.S. Barnes. $15.00.

Lachuk, John. **The Gun Digest Book of the .22 Rimfire.** 1978. pap. DBI Books. $7.95.

Lindsay, Merrill. **The Kentucky Rifle.** 1976. Arma Press. (OP).

Mauser Manual (Facs. ed. of early English language Mauser Catalog and Manual.) 1974. softbound. Stoeger. $1.95.

McAulay, John D. **Carbines of the Civil War, 1861-1865.** 1981. Pioneer Press. $7.95.

Mallory, Franklin B. & Olson, Ludwig. **The Krag Rifle Story.** 1980. Springfield Research Service. $20.00.

Myatt, F. **An Illustrated Guide to Rifles and Automatic Weapons.** (Illus.). 1981. Arco. $8.95.

O'Connor, Jack, et al. **Complete Book of Shooting: Rifles, Shotguns and Handguns.** 1966. Harper & Row. (OP).

—**Complete Book of Rifles and Shotguns.** rev. ed. (Illus.). 1966. Harper & Row. (OP).

—**The Hunting Rifle.** (Illus.). 1975. pap. Stoeger. $7.95.

—**The Hunting Rifle.** (Illus.). 1970. Winchester Press. $14.95.

—**The Rifle Book.** 3rd ed. (Illus.). 1978. Knopf. $13.95; pap. $10.95.

Olson, John. **John Olson's Book of the Rifle.** (Illus.). 1974. pap. Jolex. $6.95.

Otteson, Stuart. **The Bolt Action: A Design Analysis.** 1976. Winchester Press. $12.95.

Page, Warren. **The Accurate Rifle.** (Illus.). 1975. softbound. Stoeger. $6.95.

—**The Accurate Rifle.** Winchester Press. $13.95.

Perkins, Jim. **American Boys Rifles.** (Illus.). 1980. pap. Collector Books. $9.95.

Petzal, David. **The .22 Rifle.** (Illus.). 1973. Winchester Press. $9.95.

Pullum, Bill and Hanenkrat, Frank T. **Position Rifle Shooting.** (Illus.). 1975. softbound. Stoeger. $5.95.

Roberts, Ned H. **The Muzzle-Loading Cap Lock Rifle.** (Illus.). 1978. Repr. George Shumway Publisher. $24.50.

Rywell, Martin. **American Antique Rifles.** Pioneer Press. $2.00.

—**U. S. Muskets, Rifles and Carbines.** Pioneer Press. $2.00.

Schedelman, Hans. **Vienna Kunsthistorisches Die Grossen Buchsenmacher.** (Illus.). 1976. Arma Press. (OP).

Shumway, George. **Pennsylvania Longrifles of Note.** (Illus.). 1977. pap. George Shumway Publisher. $7.50.

—**Rifles of Colonial America.** 2 vols. incl. Vol. 1; Vol. 2. (Illus.). 1980. casebound. George Shumway Publisher. ea. $49.50.

Steindler, R. A. **Rifle Guide.** (Illus.). 1978. softbound. Stoeger. $7.95.

Taylor. **African Rifles and Cartridges.** Gun Room Press. $16.95.

U.S. Rifle Caliber .30 Model 1903. Pioneer Press. $2.00.

U.S. Rifle Model 1866 Springfield. Pioneer Press. $0.75.

U.S. Rifle Model 1870 Remington. Pioneer Press. $0.75.

Wahl, Paul. **Carbine Handbook.** (Illus.). 1964. Arco. (OP).

Waite, M. O. & Ernst, Bernard D. **The Trapdoor Springfield.** (Illus.). 1980. Beinfeld. $29.95.

Wallack, L. R. **American Rifle Design and Performance.** 1977. Winchester Press. $16.95.

—**The Deer Rifle.** (Illus.). 1978. Winchester Press. $12.95.

Waterman, Charles. **The Treasury of Sporting Guns.** (Illus.). 1979. Random House. $24.95.

Womack, Lester. **The Commercial Mauser Ninety Eight Sporting Rifle.** Angevine, Jay B., Jr., ed. (Illus.). 1981. Womack Assoc. $20.00.

Wood, J. B. **Gun Digest Book of Firearms Assembly/Disassembly. Pt. III: Rimfire Rifles.** (Illus.). 1980. pap. DBI Books. $8.95.

—**Gun Digest Book of Firearms Assembly/Disassembly. Part IV: Centerfire Rifles.** (Illus.). 1979. pap. 8.95.

—**Troubleshooting Your Rifle and Shotgun.** (Illus.). 1978. pap. DBI Books $6.95.

SHARPS RIFLES

Manual of Arms for the Sharps Rifle. Pioneer Press. $1.50.

Rywell, Martin. **Sharps Rifle: The Gun That Shaped American Destiny.** Pioneer Press. $2.95.

Sellers, Frank. **Sharps Firearms.** (Illus.). 1978. Beinfeld. (OP).

SHIELDS

Chase, G. H. **The Shield Devices of the Greeks In Art and Literature.** (Illus.). 1978. Repr. of 1902 ed. Arno Press. (OP).

—**The Shield Devices of the Greeks in Art and Literature.** (Illus.). 1978. Repr. of 1902 ed. Ares. $15.00.

Davison, Betsy. **Shields of Ancient Rome.** (Illus.). 1969. pap. Westerfield. Malter-Westerfield. (OP).

Wright, Barton. **Pueblo Shields.** (Illus.). 1976. Northland Press. (OP).

SHOOTING

Anderson, Gary. **Marksmanship.** 1972. pap. Simon & Schuster. $2.95.

Arnold, Richard. **Clay Pigeon Shooting.** (Illus.). International Pubns Service. $12.50.

—**Clay Pigeon Shooting.** (Illus.). 1974. text. ed. Sportshelf & Soccer Associates. (OP).

—**Shooter's Handbook.** Sportshelf & Soccer Associates. (OP).

Bell, Bob. **The Digest Book of Upland Game Shooting.** 1979. pap. DBI Books. $2.95.

Brister, Bob. **Shotgunning: The Art and the Science.** (Illus.). 1976. Winchester Press. $15.95.

Carmichel, Jim. **The Modern Rifle.** (Illus.). 1976. softbound. Stoeger. $5.95.

Chapman, John R. **Improved American Rifle Instructions to Young Marksmen.** (Illus.). 1978. pap. DBI Books. (OP).

Cogwell & Harrison. **Shooting.** 1973. pap. McKay, David, Co. (OP).

Davidson, Bill R. **To Keep and Bear Arms.** 2nd ed. Sycamore Island Books. (OP).

—**To Keep and Bear Arms.** 2nd ed. 1979. Paladin Enterprises. $14.95.

Day, J. Wentworth. **The Modern Shooter.** 1976. Repr. of 1952 ed. Charles River Books. $15.00.

—**The Modern Shooter.** 1976. Repr. Dynamic Learn Corp. (OP).

Evans, G. P. **Small Game Shooting.** Sportshelf & Soccer Associates. $14.50.

Ferber, Steve, ed. **All About Rifle Hunting and Shooting in America.** 1977. Winchester Press. $15.95.

Fuller, W. H. **Small-Bore Target Shooting.** rev. ed. Palmer, A. J., ed. 1978. Barrie & Jenkins. (OP).

Gates, Elgin. **Gun Digest Book of Metallic Silhouette Shooting.** 1979. pap. DBI Books. $7.95.

Grennel, Dean A. **ABC's of Reloading.** 2nd ed. (Illus.). 1980. pap. DBI Books. $9.95.

Hastings, MacDonald. **Shooting—Why We Miss: Questions and Answers on the Successful Use of the Shotgun.** 1977. pap. McKay, David, Co. $3.95.

Hickey, Bob. **Mental Training.** (Illus.). 1979. pap. Totem Shooters. $19.50.

Janes, Edward C. **Boy and His Gun.** (Illus.). 1951. A. S. Barnes. (OP).

Johnson, A. B. **Shooting Wood Pigeon.** Sportshelf & Soccer Associates. $14.25.

Koller, Larry. **How to Shoot: A Complete Guide to the Use of Sporting Firearms—Rifles, Shotgun, and Handguns— on the Range and in the Field.** (Illus.). 1976. Doubleday. (OP).

Lind, Ernie. **Complete Book of Trick and Fancy Shooting.** (Illus.). 1972 pap. Citadel Press. $3.95.

—**Complete Book of Trick and Fancy Shooting.** (Illus.). 1972. Winchester Press. (OP).

McCawley, E. S. **Shotguns and Shooting.** 1965. pap. Van Nos Reinhold. $5.95.

McGivern, Ed. **Fast and Fancy Revolver Shooting.** New Century. $14.95.

Marchington, John. **Shooting: A Complete Guide for Beginners.** (Illus.). 1972. Merrimack Book Service. (OP).

—**Shooting: A Complete Guide for Beginners.** (Illus.). 1982. pap. Faber & Faber. $6.95.

Mason, James D. **Combat Handgun Shooting.** (Illus.). 1980. C. C. Thomas. $14.95.

Merkley, Jay P. **Marksmanship with Rifles: A Basic Guide.** (Illus.). pap. American Press. $2.95.

Missildine, Fred & Karas, Nick. **Score Better at Trap and Skeet.** (Illus.). 1977. softbound. Stoeger. $6.95.

Montague, Andrew A. **Successful Shotgun Shooting.** (Illus.). 1971. Winchester Press. (OP).

Mosher, John A. **The Shooter's Workbench.** (Illus.). 1977. Winchester Press. $13.95.

Nonte, Major George C., Jr. **Handgun Competition.** (Illus.). 1978. Winchester Press. $14.95.

O'Connor, Jack. **Complete Book of Shooting: Rifles, Shotguns, Handguns.** (Illus.). 1966. Harper & Row. (OP).

—**Hunting Rifle.** (Illus.). 1970. Winchester Press. $14.95.

—**Rifle Book.** 2nd rev. ed. (Illus.). 1978. Random House. (OP).

—**Shotgun Book.** (Illus.). 1978. Knopf. $16.95; pap. $9.95.

O'Connor, Jack, et al. **Complete Book of Shooting: Rifles, Shotguns, Handguns.** (Illus.). 1975. Times Mirror Mag. (OP).

Page, Warren. **The Accurate Rifle.** (Illus.). 1975. softbound. Stoeger. $6.95.

—**The Accurate Rifle.** Winchester Press. $11.95.

Parish, David & Anthony, John. **Target Rifle Shooting.** (Illus.). 1982. Sterling. $12.95.

Petzal, David E., ed. **Experts' Book of the Shooting Sports.** Simon & Schuster. $9.95.

Pryce, Dick. **Hunting for Beginners.** 1978. softbound. Stoeger. $5.95.

Pullum, Bill & Hanenkrat, Frank T. **Position Rifle Shooting.** (Illus.). 1975. softbound. Stoeger. $5.95.

Rees, Clair F. **Beginner's Guide to Guns & Shooting.** 1978. DBI Books. $7.95.

Reynolds, E. G. & Fulton, Robin. **Target Rifle Shooting.** 1978. Barrie & Jenkins. (OP).

Riling, Ray. **Guns and Shooting: A Bibliography.** (Illus.). 1981. Ray Riling. $75.00.

Riviere, Bill. **Gunner's Bible.** 1973. pap. Doubleday. $3.95.

Roberts, Willis J. & Bristow, Allen P. **Introduction to Modern Police Firearms.** Gourley, Douglas, ed. (Illus.). 1969. Glencoe. (OP).

Ruffer, J. E. **The Art of Good Shooting.** (Illus.). 1976. David & Charles. (OP).

—**Good Shooting.** (Illus.). 1980. David & Charles. $22.50.

Salisbury, R.W. **Shooting for Beginners.** 1981. (Pub. by Saiga). State MutualBook & Periodical Service.

—**Set Your Sights: A Guide to Handgun Basics.** (Illus.). 1982. Outdoor Empire. $1.95.

Scott, Robert F., ed. **Shooter's Bible No. 74, 1983.** (Illus.). 1982. softbound. Stoeger. $11.95.

Sherrod, Blackie. **Blackie Sherrod ... Scattershooting.** 1975. Strode. $6.95.

The Shooting Handbook. 1981. (Pub. by Parrish-Rogers). State Mutual Book and Periodical Service. $18.00.

Shotgun Shooting. 1976. pap. British Book Center. $2.50.

Smith, Guy N. **Shooting and Upland Gamekeeping.** 1981. (Pub. by Saiga). State Mutual Book and Periodical Service. $40.00.

Stanbury, Percy & Carlisle, G. L. **Shotgun Marksmanship.** rev. ed. (Illus.). 1978. Barrie & Jenkins. (OP).

Steindler, R. A. ed. **Shooting the Muzzleloaders.** (Illus.). 1975. Jolex. $11.95; pap. $6.95.

Weston, Paul B. **Combat Shooting for Police.** 2nd ed. (Illus.). 1978. C. C. Thomas. $12.75.

Wilkinson, Frederick, ed. **The Book of Shooting for Sport and Skill.** (Illus.). Crown. $19.95.

Willett, Roderick & Grattan, Gurney A. **Rough Shooting.** (Illus.). 1975. Merrimack Book Service. (OP).

Yochem, Barbara. **Barbara Yochem's Inner Shooting.** 1981. By By Productions. $6.95; pap. $3.95.

SHOTGUNS

Anderson, Robert S. L., ed. **Reloading for Shotgunners.** 1981. DBI Books. $8.95.

Arthur, Robert. **Shotgun Stock: Design, Construction and Embellishment.** (Illus.). 1970. A. S. Barnes. (OP).

Baer, L. R. **The Parker Gun: An Immortal American Classic.** (Illus.). 1978. Beinfeld. (OP).

Baer, Larry L. **The Parker Gun.** rev. ed. 1980. Beinfeld. $24.95.

Barker, A. J. **Shotguns and Shooting.** new ed.

Brown, Robert K. & Lund, Peder C., eds. (Illus.). 1973. Paladin Enterprises. $8.00.

Boy Scouts of America. **Rifle and Shotgun Shooting.** (Illus.). 1967. pap. Boy Scouts of America. $0.85.

Brister, Bob. **Shotgunning: The Art and the Science.** (Illus.). 1976. Winchester Press. $15.95.

Brophy, William S. **L. C. Smith Shotguns.** (Illus.). 1977. Beinfeld. $24.95.

Burch, Monte. **Shotgunner's Guide.** (Illus.). 1980. Winchester Press. $15.95.

Carlisle, G.L. & Stanbury, Percy. **Shotgun and Shooter.** rev. ed. 1981. (Pub. by Hutchinson). State Mutual Book Periodical Service. $35.00.

Crudgington, I. M. & Baker, D. J. **The British Shotgun: 1850-1870.** Vol. 1. (Illus.). 1978. Barrie & Jenkins. (OP).

Garwood, G. T. **Gough Thomas's Gun Book.** (Illus.). 1970. Winchester Press. (OP).

—**Gough Thomas's Second Gun Book.** (Illus.). 1972. Winchester Press. (OP).

Hastings, Macdonald. **Shooting—Why We Miss: Questions and Answers on the Successful Use of the Shotgun.** 1977. pap. McKay, David, Co. (OP).

—**The Shotgun: A Social History.** 1981. David & Charles. $29.95.

Hinman, Bob. **Golden Age of Shotgunning.** (Illus.). 1972. Winchester Press. (OP).

Jinks, Roy G. **History of Smith and Wesson.** (Illus.). 1978. Beinfeld. $29.95.

Knight, Richard A. **Mastering the Shotgun.** (Illus.). 1975. Dutton, E. P. (OP).

Laycock, George. **Shotgunner's Bible.** (Illus.). 1969. pap. Doubleday. $3.95.

Lewis, Jack & Mitchell, Jack. **Shotgun Digest.** 2nd ed. 1980. pap. DBI Books. $9.95.

McCawley, E. S. **Shotguns and Shooting.** 1976. pap. Van Nos Reinhold. $5.95.

McIntosh, Michael. **The Best Shotguns Ever Made in America.** 1980. McKay, David, Co. (OP).

—**The Best Shotguns Ever Made in America: Seven Vintage Doubles to Shoot and to Treasure.** 1981. Scribner's. $17.95.

Marshall-Ball, Robin. **The Sporting Shotgun.** 1982. (Pub. by Saiga). State Mutual Book & Periodical Service. $40.00.

O'Connor, Jack. **Shotgun Book.** (Illus.). 1965. Knopf. $16.95; pap. $9.95.

Olson, John. **John Olson's Book of the Shotgun.** (Illus.). 1975. Jolex. $6.95.

Robinson, Roger H. **The Police Shotgun Manual.** (Illus.). 1973. C. C. Thomas. $14.75.

Skillen, Charles R. **Combat Shotgun Training.** (Illus.). 1982. C.C. Thomas. $26.75.

Stanbury, Percy & Carlisle, G. L. **Shotgun Marksmanship.** (Illus.). Barrie & Jenkins. (OP).

—**Shotgun and the Shooter.** 1978. Barrie & Jenkins. (OP).

Thomas, Gough. **Shotgun Shooting Facts.** 1979. Winchester Press. (OP).

—**Shotguns and Cartridges for Game and Clays.** 3rd ed. (Illus.). 1976. Transatlantic Arts, Inc. $25.00.

Wallack, L. R. **American Shotgun Design and Performance.** 1977. Winchester Press. $16.95.

Waterman, Charles. **The Treasury of Sporting Guns.** (Illus.). 1979. Random House. $24.95.

Whillett, Roderick F. **The Good Shot.** 1980. A. S. Barnes. (OP).

Williams, Mason. **The Defensive Use of the Handgun: For the Novice.** rev. ed. (Illus.). C. C. Thomas. $12.75; pap. $7.75.

Wood, J. B. **Gun Digest Book of Firearms Assembly-Disassembly: Part V, Shotguns.** 1980. pap. DBI Books. $8.95.

—**Troubleshooting Your Rifle and Shotgun.** (Illus.). 1978. pap. DBI Books. $6.95.

—**World's Fighting Shotguns.** 1980. TBN Enterprises. $29.95.

Zutz, Don. **The Double Shotgun.** (Illus.). 1978. Winchester Press. $17.50.

SURVIVAL

Acerrano, Anthony J. **The Outdoorsman's Emergency Manual.** (Illus.). 1977. softbound. Stoeger. $5.95.

Allaby, Michael. **The Survival Handbook.** Tension, Marika H.; ed. (Illus.). 1977. State Mutual Book & Periodical Service. (OP).

Allen, Ray & Thackery, Gerald. **The Last Survival Manual: A Citizen's Guide to Nuclear Survival.** (Illus.). 1980. American Research Press. $24.95.

Angier, Bradford. **How to Stay Alive in the Woods.** Orig. Title: **Living Off the Country.** 1962. pap. Macmillan. $2.95.

—**Survival with Style.** (Illus.). 1972. Stackpole Books. (OP).

Belisle, David A. **The American Family Robinson: The Adventures of a Family Lost in the Great Desert of the West.** 1976. Repr. of 1854 ed. Scholarly Press. (OP).

Benson, Ragnar. **Live Off The Land In The City and Country.** (Illus.). 1981. Paladin Enterprises. $16.95.

Biggs, Don. **Survival Afloat.** (Illus.). 1976. David McKay, Co. (OP).

Boswell, John. **The Complete Survival Manual.** 1980. Times Books. (OP).

Boswell, John & Reiger, George, eds. **The U. S. Armed Forces Survival Manual.** rev. ed. 1981. Rawson Wade. $15.95; pap. $8.95.

Brown, Terry & Hunter, Rob. **The Concise Book of Survival and Rescue.** 1978. pap. Vanguard Press. (OP).

—**Survival and Rescue.** 1981. State Mutual Book & Periodical Service. $12.00.

Clayton, Bruce D. **Life After Doomsday: A Survivalist Guide to Nuclear War and Other Disasters. (Illus.). 1981. pap. Dial Press. $8.95.**

Colby, C. B. **Survival: Training In Our Armed Services.** (Illus.). 1965. Coward, McCann & Geoghegan. $5.29.

Dalrymple, Byron. **Survival in the Outdoors.** 1972. Dutton, E. P. $6.95.

Deen, Thalif & Browning, Earl S. **How to Survive a Nuclear Disaster.** (Illus.). 1981. New Century. $12.95.

Dennis, Lawrence. **Operational Thinking for Survival.** 1969. R. Myles. $5.95.

Dept. of the Air Force. **Survival: Air Force Manual 64-5.** (Illus.). 1976. pap. Paladin Enterprises. $8.00.

Fear, Daniel E., ed. **Surviving the Unexpected: A Curriculum Guide for Wilderness Survival and Survival from Natural and Man Made Disasters.** (Illus.). rev. ed. 1974. Survival Education Association. $5.00.

Fear, Eugene H. **Surviving the Unexpected Wilderness Emergency.** 6th ed. (Illus.). 1979. pap. Survival Education Association. $5.00.

Fear, Gene. **Where Am I: A Text and Workbook for Personal Navigation Anywhere.** 1974. pap. Survival Education Association. (OP).

Freeman, Daniel B. **Speaking of Survival.** (Illus.). pap. Oxford University Press. $5.95.

Gibbons, Euell. **Stalking the Good Life.** 1971. David McKay Co. (OP).

Graves, Richard. **Bushcraft: A Serious Guide to Survival and Camping.** (Illus.). 1972. pap. Schocken Books. (OP).

—**Bushcraft: A Serious Guide to Survival and Camping.** (Illus.). 1978. pap. Warner Books. $3.50.

Greenbank, Anthony. **A Handbook for Emergencies: Coming Out Alive.** (Illus.). 1976. Doubleday. $8.95; pap. $4.95.

Hal, Betty L. **Survival Education.** 1976. pap. Binford. $4.50.

Hersey, John R. **Here to Stay.** 1963. Knopf. (OP).

Jones, Tristan. **Ice!** 1978. Sheed, Andrews & McMeel. $8.95.

Koller, James, ed. **The Best of Live Free.** (Illus.). 1977. pap. Live Free. (OP).

LaValla, Rick. **Survival Teaching Aids.** 1974. pap. Survival Education Association. (OP).

Lee, E. C. & Lee, Kenneth. **Safety and Survival at Sea.** (Illus.). 1980. W. W. Norton & Co. $17.95.

Merrill, Bill. **The Survival Handbook.** 1974. pap. Arc Books. (OP).

Nelson, Dick & Nelson, Sharon. **Desert Survival.**

(Illus.). 1977. pap. Tecolote Press. $3.95.

Nesbitt, Paul, et al. **Survival Book.** (Illus.). 1969. pap. Funk & Wagnalls. (OP).

Olsen, Larry D. **Outdoor Survival Skills.** 4th rev. ed. 1973. Brigham Young University Press. $7.95.

—**Outdoor Survival Skills.** 1981. pap. Pocket Books. $2.95.

Platt, Charles. **Outdoor Survival.** (Illus.). 1976. Franklin Watts, Inc. (OP).

Read, Piers Paul. **Alive: The Story of the Andes Survivors.** (Illus.). 1974. pap. Harper & Row. $12.50.

Reader, Dennis J. **Coming Back Alive.** (Illus.). 1981. Random House. $8.95; PLB $9.99.

Shea, John G. **Perils of the Ocean and Wilderness: Or, Narratives of Shipwreck and Indian Captivity, Gleaned from Early Missionary Annals.** 1976. Repr. of 1857 ed. lib. bdg. Garland Publishing. $44.00.

Stoeffel, Skip. **Disaster-Survival Education Lesson Plans.** 1974. pap. Survival Education Association. (OP).

Stoffel, R. & Lavalla, Patrick. **Survival Sense for Pilot and Passengers.** (Illus.). 1980. pap. Survival Education Assn. $7.95.

Szczelkun, Stefan A. **Survival Scrapbook 1: Shelter.** (Illus.) pap. Shocken Books. $3.95.

Thygerson, Alton L. **Disaster Survival Handbook.** (Illus.). 1979. pap. Brigham Young University Press. $7.95.

Troebst, Cord-Christian. **Art of Survival.** Coburn, Oliver, (tr. from Ger.). (Illus.). 1975. pap. Doubleday. (OP).

Vignes, Jacques. **The Rage to Survive.** Voukitchevitch, Mihailo, tr. (Illus.). 1976. Morrow, William & Co. $6.95.

Western Electric. **Survival in the North.** Wehman Brothers, Inc. (OP).

SWORDS

Akehurst, Richard. **Antique Weapons.** (Illus.). 1969. Arco. (OP).

Campbell, Archibald. **Scottish Swords from the Battlefield at Culloden.** 1971. Mowbray, E. Andrew, ed. (Illus.). Mowbray Co. $5.00.

Castle, Egerton. **Schools and Masters of Fence from the Middle Ages to the Eighteenth Century.** (Illus.). 1969. casebound. George Shumway Publisher. (OP).

Dobree, Alfred. **Japanese Sword Blades.** 3rd ed. (Illus.) 1971. pap. George Shumway Publisher. (OP).

Draeger, Donn F. & Warner, Gordon. **Japanese Swordsmanship: Technique and Practice.** (Illus.). 1981. C. E. Tuttle. $29.95.

Ffoulkes, Charles & Hopkinson, E. C. **Sword, Lance and Bayonet.** (Illus.). 1967. Arco. (OP).

Gunsaulus, H. C. **Japanese Sword-Mounts.** (Illus.). 1923. pap. Kraus Reprint. $16.00.

Hamilton, John. **Collection of Japanese Sword Guards with Selected Pieces of Sword Furniture.** 1975. pap. Peabody Museum of Salem. $12.50.

Hawley, W. M. **Koto Swords Scrapbook.** 1976. W. M. Hawley. $7.50.

Hawley, Willis M. **Japanese Swordsmiths.** 2 vols. 1966-67. W. M. Hawley. Vol. 1 $15.00; Vol. 2. (OP).

Hutton, Alfred. **The Sword and the Centuries; or, Old Sword Days and Old Sword Ways.** (Illus.). 1973. Repr. of 1901 ed. C. E. Tuttle. $14.50.

Japanese Swordsmiths. rev. ed. 1980. W. M. Hawley. $75.00.

Johnson, Thomas M. **Collecting the Edged Weapons of the Third Reich.** Vol. 3 Bradach, Wilfred, tr. (Illus.). 1978. T. M. Johnson. $20.00.

—**Wearing the Edged Weapons of the Third Reich.** Bradach, Wilfrid, tr. 1977. pap. T. M. Johnson. $10.00.

Joly, Henri. **Shosankenshu: Japanese Sword Mounts.** Albert Saifer Pub. $35.00.

Joly, Henry. **Japanese Sword Fittings.** (Illus.). 1978. Albert Saifer, Pub. $75.00.

Kammer, Reinhard, ed. **Zen and Confucius in the Art of Swordsmanship.** Fitzgerald, Betty, tr. (Illus.). 1978. Routledge & Kegan. cased $16.00.

North, Anthony. **European Swords.** (Illus.). 1982. Stemmer House. $9.95.

Ogasawara, Nobuo. **Japanese Swords.** Kenny, Don, tr. from Jap. (Illus.). 1976. pap. $3.95. Japan Publications. (OP).

Peterson, Harold L. **The American Sword, 1775-1945.** (Illus.). 1977. Ray Riling Arms Books. $25.00.

Rankin, Robert H. **Small Arms of the Sea Services: A History of the Firearms and Edged Weapons of the U. S. Navy, Marine Corps and Coast Guard from the Revolution to the Present.** (Illus.). 1972. N. Flayderman & Co. $14.50.

Rawson, Philip S. **Indian Sword.** (Illus.). 1967. Arco. (OP).

Sasano, Mesayki. **Early Japanese Sword Guards: Sukashi Tsuba. (Pierced Work).** (Illus.). 1972. Japan Publications. (OP).

Schnorr, Emil. **Japanese Sword Guards.** (Illus.). 1976. pap. C. E. Tuttle. (OP).

Silver, George. **Paradoxes of Defence, Wherein Is Proved the True Grounds of Fight to Be in the Short Ancient Weapons.** 1968. Repr. of 1599 ed. Walter J. Johnson. $8.00.

Southwick, Leslie. **The Price Guide to Antique Edged Weapons.** (Illus.). 1981. Antique Collector's Club. $44.50.

Tsuba, Sukashi. **Early Japanese Sword Guards.** Wehman Brothers, Inc. (OP).

Wilkinson-Latham, Robert. **Swords and Other Edged Weapons.** 1978. Arco. $8.95. pap. $5.95.

Yumoto, John M. **Samuri Sword: A Handbook.** (Illus.). 1958. C. E. Tuttle. $11.00.

TAXIDERMY

Brakefield, Tom. **The Sportsman's Complete Book of Trophy & Meat Care.** (Illus.). 1975. Stackpole Books. (OP).

Cappel, Leo J. **A Guide to Model Making and Taxidermy.** (Illus.). 1973. C. E. Tuttle. pap. $5.25.

Farnham, Albert B. **Home Taxidermy for Pleasure and Profit.** (Illus.). pap. A. R. Harding Publishing. $3.00.

Grantz, Gerald J. **Home Book of Taxidermy and Tanning.** (Illus.). 1970. Stackpole Books. $10.95.

Harrison, James M. **Bird Taxidermy.** (Illus.). 1977. David & Charles. $12.50.

Haynes, Michael D. **Haynes on Air Brush Taxidermy.** (Illus.). 1979. Arco. $12.50.

Labrie, Jean. **The Amateur Taxidermist.** (Illus.). 1972. Hart. (OP).

McFall, Waddy F. **Taxidermy Step by Step.** (Illus.). 1975. Winchester Press. $12.95.

Maurice, Michael. **Complete Taxidermist's Guide to Books, Instructions and Supplies.** 1975. pap. Reel Trophy. $1.00.

Migdalski, Edward C. **Fish Mounts and Other Fish Trophies: The Complete Book of Taxidermy.** 2nd ed. 1981. Wiley. $15.95.

—**How to Make Fish Mounts and Other Fish Trophies.** 1960. Ronald Press. (OP).

Moyer, John W. **Practical Taxidermy: A Working Guide.** (Illus.). 1953. Ronald Press. (OP).

—**Practical Taxidermy.** 2nd ed. 1979. Wiley. $15.95.

Phillips, Archie & Philips, Bubba. **How to Mount Deer for Profit or Fun.** (Illus.). 1981. Stackpole. $21.95.

—**How to Mount Fish for Profit or Fun.** (Illus.). 1981. Stackpole. $21.95.

Pray, Leon L. **Taxidermy.** (Illus.). 1943. Macmillan. $9.95.

Roberts, Nadine H. **The Complete Handbook of Taxidermy.** (Illus.). 1979. pap. TAB Books. $9.95.

Saiga Editors, ed. **Taxidermy.** 1981. (Pub. by Saiga). State Mutual Book & Periodical Service. $10.00.

Smith, Capt. James A. **Dress 'Em Out, Vol. 1.** (Illus.). 1982. softbound. Stoeger. $11.95

Tinsley, Russell. **Taxidermy Guide.** 2nd ed. (Illus.). 1977. softbound. Stoeger. $7.95.

TRAP AND SKEET SHOOTING

Campbell, Robert, ed. **Skeet Shooting with D. Lee Braun.** pap. Benjamin Co. $4.95.

—**Trap and Skeet Shooting with D. Lee Braun.**
1981. W.H. Smith, Pubs. $16.95.
—**Trapshooting with D. Lee Braun and the Remington Pros.** pap. Benjamin Co. $5.95.
Chapel, C. E. **Field, Skeet and Trapshooting.** pap. Funk & Wagnalls. (OP).
—**Clay Pigeon Shooting.** 1981. (Pub. by Saiga). State Mutual Book & Periodical Service. $30.00.
Hartman, Barney. **Hartman on Skeet.** (Illus.). 1973. Stackpole Books. (OP).
Migdalski, Edward C. **Clay Target Games.** (Illus.). 1978. pap. Winchester Press. (OP).
Missildine, Fred with Nick Karas. **Score Better at Trap and Skeet.** (Illus.). 1977. softbound. Stoeger. $6.95.
—**Score Better at Trap.** (Illus.). 1978. Winchester Press. $7.95; pap. $5.95.
Rees, Clair F. **The Digest Book of Trap and Skeet Shooting.** 1979. pap. DBI Books. (OP).
Sports Illustrated Staff. **Sports Illustrated Book of Shotgun.** (Illus.). Lippincott. (OP).

TRAPPING

Argus Archives. **Traps and Trapping: Furs and Fashion.** 1977. pap. Argus Archives. (OP).
Bateman, J. E. **Trapping: A Practical Guide.** (Illus.). 1979. Stackpole Books. $14.95.
Bateman, James A. **Animal Traps and Trapping.** (Illus.). 1971. Stackpole Books. $12.95.
Chansler, Walter S. **Successful Trapping Methods: A Guide to Good Trapping.** 2nd ed. (Illus.). 1968. pap. Van Nos Reinhold. $5.95.
Clawson, George. **Trapping and Tracking.** (Illus.). 1977. Winchester Press. $13.95.
Dearborn, Ned. **Trapping on the Farm.** Repr. of 1910 ed. pap. Shorey. $3.95.
Errington, Paul L. **Muskrats and Marsh Management.** (Illus.). 1978. University of Nebraska Press. $13.50; pap. $3.25.
Fielder, Mildred. **Fielder's Herbal Helper for Hunters, Trappers and Fishermen.** 1982. Winchester Press. $12.95.
Finnerty, Edward W. **Trappers, Traps and Trapping.** (Illus.). 1976. A. S. Barnes. (OP).
Gilsvik, Bob. **The Complete Book of Trapping.** 1976. Chilton Book Co. $12.50.
—**The Modern Trapline: Methods and Materials.** 1980. Chilton Book Co. $12.50.
Glendinning, Richard. **When Mountain Man Trapped Beaver.** (Illus.). 1967. Garrard. (OP).
Harbottle, Jeanne & Credeur, Fern. **Woman in the Bush.** Pelican. $6.00.
Harding, A. R. **Deadfalls and Snares.** (Illus.). pap. A. R. Harding Publishing. $3.00.
—**Fox Trapping.** (Illus.). pap. A. R. Harding. Publishing. $3.00
—**Mink Trapping.** (Illus.). pap. A. R. Harding Publishing. $3.00.
—**Steel Traps.** (Illus.). pap. A. R. Harding Publishing. $4.00.

—**Trappers' Handbook.** 1975. pap. A. R. Harding Publishing. $1.50.
—**Trapping as a Profession.** 1975. pap. A. R. Harding Publishing. $1.50.
—**Wolf and Coyote Trapping.** (Illus.). pap. A. R. Harding Publishing. $3.00.
Karras, A. L. **North to Cree Lake.** (Illus.). 1971. Trident Press. (OP).
Kreps, E. **Science of Trapping.** (Illus.). pap. A. R. Harding Publishing. $3.00.
Lindsey, Neil M. **Tales of A Wilderness Trapper.** 1973. pap. A. R. Harding Publishing. $1.50.
Lynch. V. E. **Trails to Successful Trapping.** pap. A.R. Harding Publishing. $3.00.
McCracken, Harold & Van Cleve, Harry. **Trapping.** (Illus.). 1974. A. S. Barnes. $8.95.
Mascall, Leonard. **A Booke of Fishing with Hooke and Line.** 1973. Repr. of 1590 ed. Walter J. Johnson. $9.50.
Mason, Otis T. **Traps of the American Indians.** facs. ed. (Illus.). 1901. pap. Shorey. $2.95.
Russell, Andy. **Trails of a Wilderness Wanderer.** 1975. Knopf. $10.95.
Russell, Carl. **Firearms, Traps and Tools of the Mountain Men.** (Illus.). 1967. Knopf. (OP).
—**Firearms, Traps and Tools of the Mountain Men.** 1977. pap. University of New Mexico Press. $9.95.
Russell, Osborne, **Journal of a Trapper.** Haines, Aubrey L., ed. (Illus.). 1965. University of Nebraska Press. Holiday House. (OP).
Ruxton, George F. **Mountain Men.** Rounds, Glen, ed. & illus. (Illus.). (OP).
Sandoz, Mari. **The Beaver Men: Spearheads of Empire.** (Illus.). 1978. pap. University of Nebraska Press. $5.95.
Simms, Jeptha R. **Trappers of New York.** 1980. Repr. of 1871 ed. Harbor Hill Books. $15.00.
Smith, Guy N. **Ferreting and Trapping for Amateur Game Keepers.** 1981. (Pub. by Saiga). State Mutual Book & Periodical Service. $25.00.
Speck, F. G. et al. **Rappahannock Taking Devices: Traps, Hunting and Fishing.** (Illus.). 1946. University Museum of the University of Pennsylvania. $1.00.
The Trapper's Companion. (Illus.). pap. A. R. Harding Publishing. $2.00.
Walters, Keith. **The Book of the Free Trapper.** 1981. Pioneer Press. $7.95.
Woodcock, E. N. **Fifty Years a Hunter and Trapper.** pap. A. R. Harding Publishing. $3.00.

WHITE-TAILED DEER

Conatser, Dean. **Bowhunting the White-Tailed Deer.** (Illus.). 1977. Winchester Press. $12.95.
Conway, Bryant W. **Successful Hints on Hunting White Tail Deer.** 2nd ed. 1967. pap. Claitors. $1.98.

Hayes, Tom. **How to Hunt The Whitetail Deer.** new and rev. ed. A. S. Barnes. $8.95; pap. $6.95.
Koller, Lawrence R. **Shots at Whitetails.** rev. ed. (Illus.). 1970. Knopf. (OP).
La Bastille, Anne. **White-Tailed Deer.** Bourne, Russell & Lawrence, Bonnie S., eds. (Illus.). 1973. National Wildlife Federation. (OP).
Mattis, George. **Whitetail: Fundamentals and Fine Points for the Hunter.** rev. ed. 1980. Van Nostrand Reinhold Co. $15.95.
Rue, Leonard L. **World of the White-Tailed Deer.** 1962. Lippincott. $8.95.
—**World of the White-Tailed Deer.** 1962. Harper & Row. $10.95.
Stadtfeld, Curtis K. **The Whitetail Deer: A Year's Cycle.** (Illus.). 1975. Dial Press. (OP).
Tinsley, Russell. **Hunting the Whitetail Deer.** (Illus.). 1974. pap. Barnes & Noble. (OP).
—**Hunting the Whitetailed Deer.** 1977. T. Y. Crowell. (OP).

WINCHESTER RIFLES

Barnes, Duncan. **History of Winchester Firearms, 1866-1980.** rev. ed. (Illus.). 1980. Winchester Press. $21.95.
Butler, David F. **Winchester 1873 and 76: The First Repeating Centerfire Rifles.** (Illus.). 1970. Winchester Press. (OP).
Colby, C. B. **Firearms by Winchester: A Part of U. S. History.** (Illus.). 1957. Coward, McCann & Geoghegan. $5.99.
Madis, George. **The Winchester Book.** 3rd ed. (Illus.). 1979. Art & Reference House. $39.50.
—**The Winchester Handbook.** (Illus.). 1981. Art & Reference House. $19.50.
Watrous, George R. **History of Winchester Firearms 1866-1966.** 1975. Winchester Press. (OP).
West, Bill. **Know Your Winchester: General Use, All Models and Types, 1849-1969.** (Illus.). B. West. $12.00.
—**Winchester-Complete: All Wins and Forerunners, 1849-1976.** (Illus.). 1975. B. West. (OP).
—**Winchester Encyclopedia.** (Illus.). B. West. $15.00.
—**Winchester Lever-Action Handbook.** (Illus.). B. West. $25.00.
—**Winchester Single Shot.** (Illus.). B. West. $15.00.
—**Winchesters, Cartridges and History.** (Illus.). B. West. $29.00.
Williamson, Harry F. **Winchester: The Gun That Won The West.** (Illus.). 1978. pap. A. S. Barnes. $14.95.
Winchester Complete, Volume One: All Early Winchester Arms, 1849-1919. 1981. B. West. $29.00.
Winchester Complete, Volume Two: All Winchester Arms 1920-1982. 1981. B. West. $29.00.

The Shooter's Magazine Rack

Alaska (M)
Established 1935
Circulation: 182,000
Robert A. Henning, Editor and Publisher
Alaska Northwest Publishing Company
Box 4-EEE
Anchorage, Alaska 99509
(907) 274-0521

Alaska Geographia (Q)
Established 1972
Circulation: 15,000
Robert A. Henning, Editor
The Alaska Geographic Society
Box 4-EEE
Anchorage, Alaska 99509
(907) 279-1723

The American Blade (BM)
Established 1973
Circulation: 20,000
Bruce Vogles, Editor
The American Blade Corporation
112 Lee Parkway Drive
Chattanooga, Tennessee 37421
(615) 894-0339

American Field (W)
Established 1874
Circulation: 15,000
W.F. Brown, Editor
American Field Publishing Company
222 West Adams Street
Chicago, Illinois 60606
(312) 372-1383

American Firearms Industry (11 x yr.)
Established 1972
Circulation: 20,000
Tom McNulty, Editor
National Association of Federally
  Licensed Firearms Dealers
7001 North Clark Street
Chicago, Illinois 60626
(312) 338-7600

American Handgunner (BM)
Established 1976
Circulation: 100,000
Jerome Rakusan, Editor
Publishers' Development Corporation
591 Camino de la Reina, Suite 200
San Diego, California 92108
(714) 297-5350

The American Hunter (M)
Established 1973
Circulation: 312,000
Earl Shelsby, Managing Editor
National Rifle Association of America
1600 Rhode Island Avenue, NW
Washington, D.C. 20036
(202) 828-6000

The American Marksman (M)
Established 1945
Circulation: 17,000
Samuel B. Sutphin, II, Editor
National Rifle Association of America
1600 Rhode Island Avenue, NW
Washington, D.C. 20036
(202) 828-6000

The American Rifleman (M)
Established 1871
Circulation: 1,100,000
William F. Parkerson, III, Editor
National Rifle Association of America
1600 Rhode Island Avenue NW
Washington, D.C. 20036
(202) 828-6000

The American Shotgunner (M)
Established 1973
Circulation: 124,000
Bob Thruston, Editor
Celebrity Sports
P.O. Box 3351
Reno, Nevada 89505
(702) 356-7396

The American West (BM)
Established 1964
Circulation: 22,000
Thomas W. Pew Jr., Editor
American West Publishing Company
3033 N. Campbell Avenue
Tucson, Arizona 85717
(602) 881-5850

Archery World (BM)
Established 1952
Circulation: 95,000
Robert Brandan, Editor
Market Communications, Inc.
225 E. Michigan Ave.
Milwaukee, Wisconsin 53202
(414) 276-6600

The Arizona Shooter (M)
Established 1979
Circulation: 6,000
Norma Jankofsky, Editor and Publisher
5931 E. Sharon Drive
Scottsdale, Arizona 85254
(602) 996-2606

Army (M)
Established 1904
Circulation: 108,000
L. James Binder, Editor
Association of the U.S. Army
2425 Wilson Boulevard
Arlington, Virginia 22201
(703) 841-4300

Bow & Arrow (BM)
Established 1963
Circulation: 104,000
Cheri Elliott, Editor
Gallant Publishing Company, Inc.
34249 Camino Capistrano
Capistrano Beach, California 92624
(714) 493-2101

Bowhunter (BM)
Established 1971
Circulation: 105,000
M.R. James, Editor
9715 Saratoga Road
Fort Wayne, Indiana 46804
(219) 744-1373

Ducks Unlimited Magazine (BM)
Established 1937
Circulation: 327,000
Lee D. Salber, Editor
Ducks Unlimited, Inc.
P.O. Box 66300
Chicago, Illinois 60666
(312) 299-3334

Enforcement Journal (Q)
Established 1963
Circulation: 43,000
Frank J. Schira, Editor
National Police Officers Association of
  America
609 West Main Street
Louisville, Kentucky 40202
(502) 845-4141

Field & Stream (M)
Established 1895
Circulation: 2,019,000
Jack Samson, Editor
CBS Consumer Publishing
1515 Broadway
New York, N.Y. 10036
(212) 975-7435

Fins & Feathers (M)
Established 1972
Circulation: 110,000
Steve Grooms, Editor
318 West Franklin Avenue
Minneapolis, Minnesota 55404
(612) 874-8404

Fishing and Hunting News (W)
Established 1944
Circulation: 122,000
Vence Malernee, Editor
Outdoor Empire Publishing, Inc.
511 Eastlake Avenue E.
Seattle, Washington 98109
(206) 624-3845

Florida Sportsman (M)
Established 1969
Circulation: 81,000
Karl Wickstrom, Editor
Wickstrom Publishers, Inc.
2701 S. Bayshore Dr.
Miami, Florida 33133
(305) 858-3546

Fur-Fish Game (Harding's Magazine) (M)
Established 1905
Circulation: 190,000
A.R. Harding, Editor
A.R. Harding Publishing Co.
2878 East Main Street
Columbus, Ohio 43209
(614) 231-9585

Gray's Sporting Journal (7 x yr.)
Established 1975
Circulation: 46,000
Edward Williams, Editor
Gray's Sporting Journal Company
1330 Beacon Street
Hamilton, Massachusetts 01982
(617) 468-4486

Grit and Steel (M)
Established 1899
Circulation: 6,000
Mary M. Hodge, Editor
DeCamp Publishing Company
Drawer 280
Gaffney, South Carolina 29340
(803) 489-2324

Gun Dog (BM)
Established 1981
Circulation: n.s.
Dave Meisner, Editor and Publisher
Gun Dog Publications
P.O. Box 68
Adel, Iowa 50003
(515) 993-4006

The Gun Report (M)
Established 1955
Circulation: 8,500
Kenneth W. Liggett, Editor
World Wide Gun Report, Inc.
113-115 South College Avenue
Aledo, Illinois 61231
(309) 582-5311

Gun Week (W)
Established 1966
Circulation: 35,000
James C. Schneider, Editor
Hawkeye Publishing, Inc.
P.O. Box 411, Station C
Buffalo, New York 14209
(716) 885-6408

Gun World (M)
Established 1960
Circulation: 128,000
Jack Lewis, Editor
Gallant Publishing Company, Inc.
34249 Camino Capistrano
Capistrano Beach, California 92624
(714) 493-2101

Guns (M)
Established 1954
Circulation: 131,000
Jerome Rakusan, Editor
Publishers' Development Corporation
591 Camino de la Reina, Suite 200
San Diego, California 92108
(714) 297-5350

Guns and Ammo (M)
Established 1958
Circulation: 480,000
Howard French, Editor
Petersen Publishing Company
8490 Sunset Boulevard
Los Angeles, California 90069
(213) 657-5100

*Handloader: The Journal of Ammunition
   Reloading (BM)*
Established 1966
Circulation: 36,000
David R. Wolfe, Editor
Wolfe Publishing Company, Inc.
138 North Montezuma Street
Prescott, Arizona 86301
(602) 445-7810

Hobbies, The Magazine for Collectors (M)
Established 1931
Circulation: 46,000
Pearl Ann Reeder, Editor
Lightner Publishing Company
1006 South Michigan Avenue
Chicago, Illinois 60605
(312) 939-4767

Hunter Safety News (BM)
Established 1972
Circulation: 20,000
Leslie Hunter, Editor
Outdoor Empire Publishing, Inc.
511 Eastlake Avenue East
Seattle, Washington 98109
(206) 624-3845

Hunter's Horn (M)
Established 1921
Circulation: 10,000
George Slankard, Editor
The Hunter's Horn Publishing
   Company, Inc.
P.O. Box 426
Sand Springs, Oklahoma 74063
(918) 245-9571

Law and Order (M)
Established 1953
Circulation: 25,000
Scott Kingwell, Editor
Copp Organization, Inc.
5526 N. Elston Avenue
Chicago, Illinois 60630
(312) 792-1838

Man at Arms (BM)
Established 1978
Circulation: 13,000
E. Andrew Mowbray, Editor
   and Publisher
222 W. Exchange Street
Providence, Rhode Island 02903
(401) 861-1000

Michigan Out-of-Doors (M)
Established 1947
Circulation: 111,000
Kenneth Lowe, Editor
Michigan United Conservation Clubs, Inc.
P.O. Box 30235
Lansing, Michigan 48909
(517) 371-1041

Michigan Sportsman (BM)
Established 1976
Circulation: 27,000
Thomas Petrie, Editor
Michigan Sportsman, Inc.
P.O. Box 2483
Oshkosh, Wisconsin 54903
(414) 231-9338

Minnesota Sportsman (BM)
Established 1977
Circulation: 20,000
Thomas Petrie, Editor
Minnesota Sportsman, Inc.
P.O. Box 3003
Oshkosh, Wisconsin 54903
(414) 231-8160

Muzzle Blasts (M)
Established 1932
Circulation: 25,000
Maxine Moss, Editor
National Muzzle Loading Rifle Association
P.O. Box 67
Friendship, Indiana 47021
(812) 667-5131

The Muzzleloader (BM)
Established 1974
Circulation: 12,000
Oran Scurlock, Jr., Editor and Publisher
Route 5, Box 347-M
Texarkana, Texas 75503
(214) 832-4726

Mzuri Drumbeat (Q)
Established 1972
Circulation: 30,000
Bob Dill, Editor and Publisher
Dill & Associates
41 East Taylor
Reno, Nevada 89501
(702) 323-0779

National Defense (BM)
Established 1920
Circulation: 33,000
D. Ballow, Editor
American Defense Preparedness
   Association
Suite 900
1700 North Moore Street
Arlington, Virginia 22209
(703) 522-1820

Outdoor Life (M)
Established 1897
Circulation: 1,700,000
John Culler, Editor
Times Mirror Magazines, Inc.
380 Madison Avenue
New York, N.Y. 10017
(212) 687-3000

Outdoor Press (W)
Established 1966
Circulation: 6,000
Fred L. Peterson, Editor and Publisher
The Outdoor Press, Inc.
N. 2012 Ruby Street
Spokane, Washington 99207
(509) 328-9392

Outdoors Today (50 x yr.)
Established 1970
Circulation: 93,000
Ronald Olvera, Editor
Outdoors Today, Inc.
P.O. Box 6852
St. Louis, Missouri 63144
(314) 727-2722

Pennyslvania's Outdoor People (M)
Established 1959
Circulation: 70,000
Tom Price, Editor
Dardanell Publications, Inc.
610 Beatty Road
Monroeville, Pennsylvania 15146
(412) 373-7900

Petersen's Hunting (M)
Established 1973
Circulation: 242,000
Basil C. Bradbury, Editor
Petersen Publishing Company
8490 Sunset Boulevard
Los Angeles, California 90069
(213) 657-5100

Point Blank (M)
Established 1971
Circulation: 209,000
John M. Snyder, Editor
Citizens Committee for the Right
   to Keep and Bear Arms
Suite 151
1601 114th S.E.,
Bellevue, Washington 98004
(206) 454-4911

Police Magazine (BM)
Established 1974
Circulation: 27,000
David Anderson, Editor
801 Second Avenue
New York, N.Y. 10017
(212) 490-1913

The Police Marksman (Q)
Established 1975
Circulation: 19,000
James Collins, Editor
Police Marksman Association
217 South Court Street
Montgomery, Alabama 36104
(205) 262-5761

Police Times (M)
Established 1964
Circulation: 97,000
Donald Anderson, Editor
American Law Enforcement Officers'
   Association
1100 N.E. 125th Street
North Miami, Florida 33161
(305) 891-1700

Popular Mechanics (M)
Established 1902
Circulation: 1,696,000
John A. Linkletter, Editor
The Hearst Corporation
224 West 57th Street
New York, N.Y. 10019
(212) 262-4282

Popular Science (M)
Established 1872
Circulation: 1,914,000
Times Mirror Magazines, Inc.
380 Madison Avenue
New York, N.Y. 10017
(212) 687-3000

Precision Shooting (M)
Established 1956
Circulation: 2,500
A.H. Garcelon, Editor
Precision Shooting, Inc.
133 State Street
Augusta, Maine 04330
(207) 622-1711

Rifle: The Magazine for Shooters (BM)
Established 1969
Circulation: 25,000
David R. Wolfe, Editor
Wolfe Publishing Company, Inc.
138 North Montezuma Street
Prescott, Arizona 86301
(602) 445-7810

Saga (M)
Established 1950
Circulation: 209,000
David J. Elrich, Editor
Gambi Publishing Corporation
333 Johnson Avenue
Brooklyn, N.Y. 11206
(212) 456-8600

The Shooting Industry (M)
Established 1956
Circulation: 23,000
Jerome Rakusan, Editor
Publishers' Development Corporation
591 Camino de la Reina, Suite 200
San Diego, California 92108
(714) 297-5350

Shooting Times (M)
Established 1960
Circulation: 189,000
Alex Bartimo, Editor
PJS Publications, Inc.
P.O. Box 1790
Peoria, Illinois 61656
(309) 682-6626

Shootin' Trap (M)
Established 1979
Circulation: 15,000
Frank Kodl, Editor and Publisher
2500A Valley Road
Reno, Nevada 89512
(702) 329-4519

Shotgun News (SM)
Established 1946
Circulation: 160,000
Jim Weaver, Editor
Snell Publishing Company
P.O. Box 669
Hastings, Nebraska 68901
(402) 463-4589

Skeet Shooting Review (M)
Established 1946
Circulation: 18,500
Milo Mims, Editor
National Skeet Shooting Association
P.O. Box 28188
San Antonio, Texas 78228
(512) 688-3560

Soldier of Fortune (M)
Established 1975
Circulation: 160,000
Robert K. Brown, Editor and Publisher
Omega Group, Ltd.
P.O. Box 693
Boulder, Colorado 80302
(303) 449-3750

Southern Outdoors (8 x yr.)
Established 1953
Circulation: 157,000
Dave Ellison, Editor
Bass Anglers Sportsman Society
P.O. Box 17915
Montgomery, Alabama 36117
(205) 277-3940

Sporting Goods Business (M)
Established 1968
Circulation: 25,000
Robert Carr, Editor
Gralla Publications
1515 Broadway
New York, N.Y. 10036
(212) 869-1300

Sporting Goods Dealer (M)
Established 1899
Circulation: 16,000
C.C. Johnson Spink, Editor
Sporting Goods Publishing Co.
1212 North Lindbergh Boulevard
St. Louis, Missouri 63166
(314) 997-7111

Sports Afield (M)
Established 1887
Circulation: 572,000
Tom Paugh, Editor
The Hearst Corporation
250 W. 55th Street
New York, N.Y. 10019
(212) 262-8830

Sports and Recreation (BM)
Established 1946
Circulation: 35,000
Robert Bushnell, Editor
Nystrom Publishing Co.
9100 Cottonwood Lane
Maple Grove, Minnesota 55369
(612) 425-7900

Sports Merchandizer (M)
Established 1969
Circulation: 25,000
Eugene R. Marnell, Editor
1760 Peachtree Road, N.W.
Atlanta, Georgia 30357
(404) 874-4462

Sports Illustrated (W)
Established 1954
Circulation: 2,343,000
Gilbert Rogin, Editor
Time, Inc.
1271 Avenue of the Americas
New York, N.Y. 10020
(212) 586-1212

Texas Sportsman Magazine (BM)
Established 1971
Circulation: 25,000
R. Allan Charles, Editor and Publisher
Neptune Publications
P.O. Box 10411
San Antonio, Texas 78210
(512) 533-8991

Trap and Field (M)
Established 1890
Circulation: 24,000
John M. Bahret, Editor
Curtis Publishing Company
1100 Waterway Boulevard
Indianapolis, Indiana 46202
(317) 634-1100

Turkey Call (BM)
Established 1973
Circulation: 31,000
Gene Smith, Editor
The National Wild Turkey Federation
P.O. Box 467
Edgefield, South Carolina 29824
(803) 637-3106

West Virginia Hills and Streams (M)
Established 1971
Circulation: 1,400
Julia P. Young, Editor
West Virginia Hills and Streams, Inc.
Box 38
Durbin, West Virginia 26264
(304) 456-4789

Western Outdoor News (W)
Established 1953
Circulation: 77,000
Bill Rice, Editor
Western Outdoors Publications
3197 East Airport Loop Drive
Costa Mesa, California 92626
(714) 546-4370

Western Outdoors (M)
Established 1960
Circulation: 115,000
Burt Twilegar, Editor
Western Outdoors Publications
3197 East Airport Loop Drive
Costa Mesa, California 92626
(714) 546-4370

Wildlife Harvest (M)
Established 1973
Circulation: 1,600
John M. Mullin, Editor
North American Game Breeders &
   Shooting Preserves Association, Inc.
Goose Lake, Iowa 52750
(319) 577-2267

Wildlife Review (Q)
Established 1935
Circulation: 5,000
Kenneth J. Chiavetta, Editor
Aylesworth Hall, Room 263
Colorado State University
Fort Collins, Colorado 80523
(303) 491-7002

Wisconsin Sportsman (BM)
Established 1972
Circulation: 53,000
Thomas C. Petrie, Editor and Publisher
Wisconsin Sportsman, Inc.
P.O. Box 2266
Oshkosh, Wisconsin 54903
(414) 233-1327

Canadian Periodicals

B.C. Outdoors (M)
Established 1945
Circulation: 28,000
Donald Stainsby, Editor
S.I.P. Division of MacLean-Hunter, Ltd.
1132 Hamilton Street
Vancouver, British Columbia V6B 2S2
(604) 687-1581

Canada Gunsport (M)
Established 1975
Circulation: 20,000
G.N. Dentay, Editor
Canada Gun Sports
14th Avenue, RR2
Gormley, Ontario L0H 1G0
(416) 881-8446

**The Canadian Journal of
   Arms Collecting (Q)**
Established 1962
Circulation: 1300
S.J. Gooding, Editor
Museum Restoration Service
P.O. Box 390
Bloomfield, Ontario K0K 1G0
(613) 393-2980

Ontario Fisherman & Hunter (M)
Established 1967
Circulation: 32,000
Burton J. Myers, Editor
Ontario Fisherman and Hunter
5 Guardsman Road
Thornhill, Ontario L3T 2A1
(416) 881-1033

Sentier Chasse-Peche (M, French)
Established 1971
Circulation: 71,000
Les Publications Plein Air, Inc.
Jeannot Ruel, Editor
11440 Albert Houdon
Montreal-Nord, Quebec H1G 3J9
(514) 270-9241

Sporting Goods Canada (8 x yr.)
Established 1973
Circulation: 9,200
Dan Wilton, Editor and Publisher
Maclean-Hunter, Ltd.
481 University Avenue
Toronto, Ontario M5W 1A7
(416) 596-5955

Sporting Goods Trade (7 x yr.)
Established 1973
Circulation: 9,000
Gordon Bagley, Editor
Page Publications
380 Wellington Street West
Toronto, Ontario M5V 1E3
(416) 366-4608

Wildlife Crusader (M)
Established 1944
Circulation: 42,000
Paul F. Murphy, Editor
Stovel Advocate Press
1770 Notre Dame Avenue
Winnipeg, Manitoba R3E 3E6
(204) 633-3967

Explanation of Symbols: (M) Monthly; (BM) Bimonthly; (SM) Semimonthly; (W) Weekly; (Q) Quarterly

Firearms Curios and Relics

The Bureau of Alcohol, Tobacco and Firearms has determined that the following firearms are curios or relics as defined in 27 CFR 178.11 because they fall within one of the categories specified in the regulations.

Such determination merely classifies the firearms as curios or relics and thereby authorizes licensed collectors to acquire, hold or dispose of them as curios or relics subject to the provisions of 18 U.S.C. Chapter 44 and the regulations in 27 CFR Part 178. They are still "firearms" as defined in 18 U.S.C. 921(a) (3).

All original military bolt action and semiautomatic rifles manufactured between 1899 and 1946.

All properly marked and identified semiautomatic pistols and revolvers used by, or manufactured for, any military organization prior to 1946.

Armand Gevage .32ACP caliber semiautomatic pistols, as manufactured in Belgium prior to World War II.

Astra M 400 pistol, German Army Contract, caliber 9mm Bergmann-Bayard, Serial Number range 97351-98850.

Astra Model 400 semiautomatic pistol, second Germany Army Contract, caliber 9mm Bergmann-Bayard, in the serial number range 92851 through 97350.

Astra Model 1921 (400) semiautomatic pistols have slides marked Esperanzo Y Unceta.

Astra M 800 Condor Model, pistol, caliber 9mm Parabellum.

Baker Gun and Forging Company, all firearms manufactured from 1899 to 1919.

Bannerman Model 1937, Springfield rifle, caliber 30-06.

Bayard Model 1923 semiautomatic pistol, caliber 7.65mm or .380, Belgian manufacture.

Beretta Model 1915 pistols, caliber 6.35mm, 7.65 mm, and 9mm Glisenti.

Beretta Model 1915/1919 (1922) pistol (concealed hammer), caliber 7.65mm.

Beretta Model 1919 pistol (without grip safety), caliber 6.35mm.

Beretta Model 1923 pistol, caliber 9mm Glisenti.

Beretta Model 1932 pistol, having smooth wooden grips with "PB" medallion, caliber 9mm.

Beretta Model 1934 pistols, caliber 9mm post war variations bearing Italian Air Force eagle markings.

Beretta Model 1934 pistols, caliber 9mm, produced during 1945 or earlier and having serial numbers within the following ranges 500000 to 999999, F00001 to F120000, G0001 to G80000, 00001AA to 10000AA, or 00001BB to 10000BB. This classification does not include any post war variations dated subsequent to 1945 or bearing post war Italian proof marks.

Beretta Model 1934 pistol, light weight model marked "Tipo Alleggerita" or "A11" having transverse ribbed barrel, caliber 9mm.

Beretta Model 1935 pistol, Finnish Home Guard Contract, marked "SKY" on the slide, caliber 7.65mm.

Beretta Model 1935 pistols, caliber 7.65mm, produced during 1945 and earlier and having serial numbers below 620799.

Beretta M1951 pistol, Egyptian Contract, caliber 9mm Parabellum.

Beretta M1951 pistol, Israeli Contract, caliber 9mm Parabellum.

Bergmann-Bayard M1908 pistol, caliber 9mm Bergmann-Bayard.

Bernardelli Model 1956, experimental pistol, caliber 9mm Parabellum.

Bern Arsenal Experimental Gas Locked pistol, caliber 9mm Parabellum.

Bern Arsenal Experimental 16-shot pistol, caliber 9mm Parabellum.

FN Browning, Model 1902 (usually known as the Model 1903) semiautomatic pistol, caliber 9mm Browning long.

Browning Centennial Model High-Power Pistol, caliber 9mm Parabellum.

Browning Centennial Model 92 lever action rifle, caliber .44 Magnum.

Browning Superposed Centennial, consisting of a 20 gauge superposed shotgun, supplied with an extra set of .30-06 caliber superposed barrels.

Browning M1935 Hi-Power pistol, Canadian, Congolese, Indian and Nationalist Chinese Contracts, caliber 9mm Parabellum.

Browning "Baby" Model pistol, Russian Contract, caliber 6.35mm.

Browning Model 1922 pistol, caliber 7.65mm, bearing German NSDAP or RFV markings.

Browning Model 1922 pistol, caliber 7.65mm or 9mm Kurz, marked "C.P.I.M." denoting issue to the Belgian Political Police.

Browning Model 1922 pistol, caliber 7.65mm or 9mm Kurz, marked "S.P." and/or bearing the crest of the Kingdom Thailand.

Budischowsky, Model TP70, semiautomatic pistol, caliber .25 ACP, with custom serial number DB1.

Campo-Giro Model 1913 and 1913/16 pistol, caliber 9mm Largo.

Chinese Communist types 51 and 54 (Tokarev) pistols, caliber 7.62mm.

Chinese, Peoples Republic of China, copy of Japanese Type Sigiura Shiki semiautomatic pistol, caliber 7.65mm.

Chylewski semiautomatic pistol manufactured by S.I.G. Switzerland, caliber 6.35mm (.25 ACP)

Clement pistol, Belgian manufacture, caliber 5mm Clement.

Colt Ace Service Model semiautomatic pistol, caliber .22, manufactured by Colt from 1935 to 1945, serial number range from SM1 to SM13803 including those marked "UNITED STATES PROPERTY" on the right side of the frame.

Colt Ace semiautomatic pistol, caliber .22, manufactured by Colt from 1931 to 1947, serial number range from 1 to 10935 including those marked "UNITED STATES PROPERTY" on the right side of the frame.

Colt Aircrewman revolver produced between 1951 and 1959, caliber .38 Special, marked "Property of U.S. Air Force" on back strap, having Air Force issue numbers of 1 thru 1189 and in the serial number range 1902LW thru 90470LW.

Colt Army Model double action revolver, any caliber, manufactured between 1899 and 1907.

Colt Border Patrol Model Revolver, .38 Special Heavy Duty, Police Positive (D) style frame, serial number within the range 610000 through 620000.

Colt, Camp Perry Single Shot, Target Pistols, .22 long rifle or .38 Special caliber.

Colt Detective Special Model Revolver, Caliber .38, Serial Number 418162, owned by Colonel Charles A. Lindbergh.

Colt, First Model, Match Target Woodsman, caliber .22, semi-automatic pistol, manufactured from 1938 to 1944, serial numbers MT1 to MT15,000.

Colt Fourth Model Derringer, caliber .22 short rimfire, cased as a set of two pistols in a leather book titled "Colt Derringer, Limited Edition, by Colt," on the spine of the book and "A Limited Edition by Colt," on the cover.

Colt Government Model pistols in caliber .45 ACP, BB Series.

Colt, J frame, Officer's Model Match, .38 Special revolver manufactured from 1970 to 1972, identified by a J serial number prefix.

Colt, the Liege Number 1 Colt Single Action Army Revolver, Caliber .45, Serial Number Liege No. 1.

Colt Lightning Model double action revolver, any caliber manufactured between 1899 and 1909.

Colt, Match Target Woodsman Semiautomatic Pistol, Caliber .221r., Serial Number 128866S, owned by Ernest Hemingway.

Colt Model 1900 semiautomatic pistol, caliber .38, in orginal configuration.

Colt Model 1902 semiautomatic pistol, sporting model, caliber .38, in original configuration.

Colt Model 1902 semiautomatic pistol, military model, caliber .38, in original configuration.

Colt Model 1903 Pocket (exposed hammer), semiautomatic pistol caliber .38 ACP.

Colt Model 1903 Pocket (hammerless), semiautomatic pistol, caliber .32.

Colt Model 1908, caliber .25 ACP, hammerless semiautomatic pistol, having a grip safety, in serial number range 1 thru 409061.

Colt Model 1908 Pocket (hammerless) semiautomatic pistol caliber .380.

Colt Model 1911 Commercial semiautomatic pistols, caliber .45 ACP, serial numbers C1 thru C130,000.

Colt Model 1911-A1, commerical modek, in caliber .45 and bearing Egyptian inscription meaning police, on the upper forward right-hand side of the trigger guard and having serial numbers within the range of C186000 to C188000.

Colt Model 1911-A1, .45 caliber pistol, manufactured by Union Switch and Signal Company, prototype model, bearing serial number US & S Exp. 1 to US & S Exp. 100.

Colt Mk IV Series 70 semiautomatic pistols in all calibers, which were incorrectly marked at the factory with both Colt Government Model markings and Colt Commander markings.

Colt, New Frontier and Single Action Army Model revolvers originally ordered and shipped with factory engraving, accompanied by a confirming letter from the manufacturer confirming the authenticity of the engraving.

Colt New Service revolvers as manufactured between 1898 and 1944, all variations, all calibers.

Colt Official Police Revolver, Silver Inlaid and Engraved by Wilbur A. Glahn, Caliber .38, Serial Number 583469.

Colt Officers Model (1904-1930), .38 caliber revolver.

Colt Officers Model (1930-1949), .22 caliber revolver.

Colt Officers Model Match (1953-1969), .22 and .38 caliber revolvers.

Colt Officers Model Special (1949-1952), .22 and .38 caliber revolvers.

Colt Officers Model Target (1930-1949), .32 and .38 caliber revolvers.

Colt Sheriff's Model revolver, caliber .44 and .45.

Colt Single Action Army revolver, caliber .45, serial 85163A, Engraved and inlaid with a bust of President Abraham Lincoln.

Colt Python Revolver, .357 Magnum Caliber, Engraved and Inlaid with the Crest of the United Arab Emirates.

Colt Single Action Revolvers, Caliber .45, Engraved and Silver Inlaid for Presentation to Chuck Connors, Serial Numbers CC1 and CC2.

Colt, single action Army (Bisley, Standard, and target variations), all original, manufactured from 1899 to 1946, serial number range from 182000 to 357869.

Colt, Woodsman, caliber .22, semiautomatic target pistol, manufactured from 1915 to 1943, serial number 1 to 157,000.

Colt, Abercrombie and Fitch, "Trailblazer," .45 New Frontier.

Colt, Alabama Sesquicentennial, .22.

Colt, Alamo, .22 and .45.

Colt, Abilene, .22 (Kansas City-Cow Town).

Colt Age of Flight 75 Anniversary semiautomatic pistols, caliber .45.

Colt American Combat Companion, Enlisted Man's Model Caliber .45ACP pistol marked "1911 American Combat Companion 1981, 70 Years at America's Side."

Colt, Appomattox Court House Centennial, .22 and .45.

Colt, Arizona Ranger Model Commemorative, .22 revolver.

Colt, Arizona Territorial Centennial, .22 and .45.

Colt, Arkansas Territory Sesquicentennial, .22.

Colt, Battle of Gettysburg Centennial, .22.

Colt, Belleau Wood, .45 Pistol, (World War I Series).

Colt, John M. Browning Commemorative, .45 caliber, semiautomatic pistol, serial numbers JMB 0001 through JMB 3000 plus numbers GAS O JMB, PE CEW JMB, and 0003JMB, manufactured by Colt Industries.

Colt, Buffalo Bill Historical Center, Winchester Museum, Special Issue, Colt Single Action Revolver, Caliber .44-40, Serial Number 21BB.

Colt, California Bicentennial, .22.

Colt, California Gold Rush, .22 and .45.

Colt, Carolina Charter Tercentenary, .22 and .22/.45.

Colt, Chamizal Treaty, .22 and .45.

Colt, Chateau Thierry, .45 Pistol, (World War I Series).

Colt, Cherry's Sporting Goods 35th Anniversary, .22/.45.

Colt, Chisholm Trail, .22 (Kansas Series-Trails).

Colt, Civil War Centennial Single Shot, .22.

Colt, Coffeyville, .22 (Kansas Series-Cow Town).

Colt, Colorado Gold Rush, .22.

Colt, Colonel Samuel Colt, Sesquicentennial, .45.

Colt, Colt's 125th Anniversary, .45.

Colt, Columbus (Ohio) Sesquicentennial, .22.

Colt, H. Cook, "1 of 100," .22/.45.

Colt Custom Gun Shop's "Custom Edition Sheriff's Model" Single Action Revolver, Caliber .45 Colt, Serial Number 1 of 35.

Colt, Dakota Territory, .22.

Colt, Des Monies, Reconstruction of Old Fort, .22 and .45.

Colt, Dodge City, .22 (Kansas Series-Cow Town).

Colt, Wyatt Earp, Buntline Special, .45 (Lawman Series).

Colt, Wyatt Earp, .-2 and .45 (Lawman Series).

Colt, European Theater, .45 Pistol (World War II Series).

Colt, Florida Territory Sesquicentennial, .22.

Colt, General Nathan Bedford Forrest, .22.

Colt, Fort Findlay (Ohio) Sesquicentennial, .22.

Colt, Fort Hays, .22 (Kansas Series-Forts).

Colt, Fort Larned, .22 (Kansas Series-Forts).

Colt, Fort McPherson (Nebraska) Centennial Derringer, .22.

Colt, Fort Scott, .22 (Kansas Series-Forts).

Colt, Fort Stephenson (Ohio) Sesquicentennial, .22.

Colt, Forty-Niner Miner, .22.

Colt, Pat Garrett, .22 and .45 (Lawman Series).

Colt, Genesco (Illinois) 125th Anniversary, Derringer, .22.

Colt, Golden Spike Centennial, .22.

Colt, Wild Bill Hickok, .22 and .45 (Lawman Series).

Colt, General Hood, Tennessee Campaign Centennial, .22.

Colt, Idaho Territorial Centennial, .22.

Colt, Indiana Sesquicentennial, .22.

Colt, Kansas Centennial, .22.

Colt, Los Angeles Police Department (L.A.P.D.) Special Edition .45 caliber Government Model semiautomatic pistol

Colt, Maine Sesquicentennial, .22 and .45.

Colt, Bat Masterson, .22 and .45 (Lawman Series).

Colt, General George Meade, Pennsylvania Campaign, .22 and .45.

Colt, Meuse Argonne, .45 Pistol (World War I Series).

Colt, Montana Territory Centennial, .22 and .45.

Colt, Missouri Sesquicentennial, .22.

Colt, General John Hunt Morgan, Indiana Raid, .22.

Colt, Joaquin Murrieta, "1 of 100", .22/.45.

Colt, Nebraska Centennial, .22.

Colt, Ned Buntline Commenorative, caliber .45 revolver.

Colt, Nevada Centennial, .22 and .45.

Colt, Nevada Centennial "Battle Born," .22 and .45.

Colt, New Jersey Tercentenary, .22 and .45.

Colt, New Mexico Golden Anniversary, .22.

Colt, NRA Centennial, single action revolver, in calibers .357 Magnum and .45.

Colt, NRA Centennial, Gold Cup National Match pistol, in caliber .45.

Colt, Oklahoma Territory Diamond Jubilee, .22.

Colt, Oregon Trail, .22 (Kansas Series-Trails).

Colt, Pacific Theater, .45 Pistol (World War II Series).

Colt, Pawnee Trail, .22 (Kansas Series-Trails).

Colt, Peacemaker Commemorative, .22 and .45 revolver.

Colt, Pony Express, Russell, Majors and Waddell, Presentation Model .45.

Colt, Pony Express Centennial, .22.

Colt, Rock Island Arsenal Centennial Single Shot, .22.

Colt, St. Augustine Quadricentennial, .22.

Colt, St. Louis Bicentennial, .22 and .45.

Colt, Santa Fe Trail, .22 (Kansas Series-Trails).

Colt, Second (2nd) Marne, .45 Pistol (World War I Series).

Colt, Shawnee Trail, .22 (Kansas Series-Trails).

Colt, Texas Ranger, .45

Colt, "The Right to Keep and Bear Arms" commemorative, .22 caliber Peacemaker Buntline, single action revolver having a 7½-inch barrel with the inscription "The Right to Keep and Bear Arms" inscribed on the barrel and a serial number range of G0001RB thru G3000RB.

Colt, United States Bicentennial Commemorative, Python revolver caliber .357.

Colt, United States Bicentennial Commemorative, single action army revolver, caliber .45.

Colt, West Virginia Centennial, .22 and .45.

Colt, Wichita, .22 (Kansas Series-Cow Town).

Colt, Wyoming Diamond Jubilee, .22.

Colt, 1873 Peacemaker Centennial 1973, single action revolver, 44/.40 or .45.

Czechoslovakian CZ38, pistol caliber .380ACP

Czechoslovakian CZ50 pistol caliber 7.65mm.

Czechoslovakian CZ52 pistol, caliber 7.62mm.

Czechoslovakian Model 1952 and 1952/57, 7.62 x 45mm and 7.62 x 39mm caliber, semiautomatic rifles (Puska Vzor 52, 7.62 x 45mm, and Puska Vzor 52/57, 7.62 x 39mm)

Danish M1910/1921 Bayard, pistol, caliber 9mm BergmannBayard.

Davis Warner Infallible, semiautomatic pistol, caliber .32.

Dreyse Military Model 1910 pistol, caliber 9mm.

Egyptian Hakim (Ljungman) 7.92mm semiautomatic rifle as manufactured in Egypt.

Esser-Barratt, English manufacture, slide action rifle, caliber .303.

Fabrique Nationale Model SAFN49 semiautomatic rifles, any caliber.

French Model 1949, caliber 7.5mm, semiautomatic rifle (Fusil Mle. 1949 (MAS) 7.5mm).

German P38 pistols, caliber 9mm Parabellum manufactured prior to 1947.

Original German Model 1916 Grenatenwerfer spigot type mortars.

Hammond or Grant Hammond pistols, all models, variations or prototypes, made by Grant Hammond Corporation, New Haven, Connecticut.

Hammond/Hi-Standard semiautomatic pistols, in caliber .45.

Harrington and Richardson, Abilene Anniversary, .22 revolver.

Harrington and Richardson, Centennial Officer's Model Springfield rifle, .45-70 Govt.

Harrington and Richardson, Centennial Standard Model Springfield rifle, .45-70 Govt.

Harrington and Richardson, Self-loading semiautomatic pistol, caliber .32.

Hartford Arms and Equipment Company single shot target pistol, caliber .22LR.

Hartford Arms and Equipment Company repeating pistol, caliber .22LR.

Hartford Arms and Equipment Company Model 1928 pistol, caliber .22LR.

Hi-Standard experimental electric free pistol, caliber .22 long rifle.

Hi-Standard Model P38, semiautomatic pistol, caliber .38 special.

Hi-Standard experimental Model T-3 semiautomatic pistol, caliber 9mm Luger.

Hi-Standard experimental ISU rapid fire semiautomatic pistol, caliber .22 short.

Hi-Standard Model A pistol, caliber .22LR.

High Standard Model B pistol, caliber .22LR.

High Standard Model C pistol, caliber .22Short.

High Standard Model D pistol, caliber .22LR.

High Standard Model E pistol, caliber .22LR.

High Standard Model H-A pistol, caliber .22LR.

High Standard Model H-B pistol, first model, caliber .22LR.

High Standard Model H-B pistol, second model, caliber .22LR.

High Standard Model H-D pistol, caliber .22LR.

High Standard Model H-E pistol, caliber .22LR.

High Standard Model USA-HD pistol, caliber .22LR.

High Standard Model HD-Military pistol, caliber .22LR.

High Standard Model G-380 pistol, caliber .380.

High Standard Model G-B pistol, caliber .22LR.

High Standard Model G-D pistol, caliber .22LR.

High Standard Model G-E pistol, caliber .22LR.

High Standard Model G-O (First Model Olympic) pistol, caliber .22 Short.

High Standard Supermatic Trophy, Model 107, .22 pistol Olympic Commemorative Model.

Holland and Holland Royal Double Barrel Shotgun, .410 Gauge, Serial Number 36789.

Italian Brixia M1906, pistol, caliber 9mm Glisenti.

Italian Glisenti M1910, pistol, caliber 9mm Glisenti.

Ithaca double barrel shotguns actually manufactured in New York by the Ithaca Gun Company, Ithaca, New York. All gauges and all models, having barrels at least 18 inches in length and an overall length of at least 26 inches, manufactured before 1950.

Ithaca Gun Company single barrel trap guns, break open all gauges, all models actually manufactured at Ithaca, New York, before 1950.

Ithaca, St. Louis Bicentennial, Model 49, .22 Rifle.

Jieffeco pistol, Belgian manufacture, caliber 7.65mm.

Jieffeco, semiautomatic pistol, in caliber .25 ACP, marked "Davis Warner Arms Corp., N.Y."

Kimball pistols, all models, all calibers.

Kolibri pistols, calibers 2.7mm and 3mm Kolibri.

L. C. Smith Shotguns manufactured by Hunter Arms Company and Marlin Firearms Company from 1899 to 1971.

Lahti L-35 pistol, Finnish manufacture, caliber 9mm Parabellum.

Luger, pistol, all models and variations manufactured prior to 1946.

Luger, Mauser commercial manufacture, semiautomatic pistol, 70 Jahre, Parabellum-Pistole, Keiserreich Russland, commemorative, caliber 9mm.

Luger, Mauser commercial manufacture, semiautomatic pistol, 75 Jahre, Parabellum-Pistole, 1900-1975, commemorative, caliber 7.65mm.

Luger, Mauser commercial manufacture, semiautomatic pistol, 75 Jahre, Parabellum-Pistole, Konigreich Bulgarian, commemorative, caliber 7.65mm.

Luger, Mauser Parabellum, semiautomatic pistol, 7.65mm or 9mm Luger, 4 and 6 inch barrel, Swiss pattern with grip safety and the American Eagle stamped on the receiver. Made from 1970 to 1978.

MAB Model R pistol, caliber 9mm Parabellum.

Makarov pistol, Russian and East German, caliber 9mm Makarov.

Mannlicher pistol, M1900, M1901, M1903 and M1905, caliber 7.63mm Mannlicher.

Marlin 90th Anniversary, Model 39-A, .22 Rifle.

Marlin 90th Anniversary, Model 39-A, .22 Carbine.

Mauser, semiautomatic pistols manufactured prior to 1946, any caliber.

Mauser, Congolese Model 1950 rifles marked FP 1952 on the receiver, caliber .30/06.

Mauser Model 1935 rifle 7x57mm caliber with Chilean Police Markings.

Menz Liliput, German manufacture, caliber 4.25mm.

Menz PBIII, in caliber 7.65mm, manufactured by August Menz, Suhl, Germany.

Menz PBIIIA, in caliber 7.65mm, manufactured by August Menz, Suhl, Germany.

Menz PBIV, in caliber 7.65mm, manufactured by August Menz, Suhl, Germany.

Menz PBIVa, in caliber 7.65mm, manufactured by August Menz, suhl, Germany.

Menz Special, in caliber 7.65mm, manufactured by August Menz, Suhl, Germany.

Mexican Obregon, pistol, caliber .45 ACP.

Mugica Model 120, pistol, caliber 9mm Parabellum.

North Korean Type 1964, pistol, caliber 7.62mm Tokarev. Oerlikon 20mm Automatic Cannon, all variations manufactured in the United States prior to 1946.

PAF "Junior" semiautomatic pistol, caliber .25, manufactured by the Pretoria Arms Factory Ltd. of South Africa.

PAF pistol, marked "BRF," caliber .25, manufactured by the Pretoria Arms Factory Ltd. of South Africa.

Parker shotguns, all grades, all gauges, produced by Parker Brothers, Meridan, Connecticut, and Remington Arms, Ilion, New York, from 1899 through 1945.

Phoenix (U.S.A.), pistol, caliber .25 ACP.

Reising .22 caliber, semiautomatic pistol.

James Purdy Over and Under Shotgun, 12 Gauge, Serial Number 26819, Engraved and Gold Inlaid.

Remington Canadian Territorial Centennial, Model 742, Rifle.

Remington, Model 51, semiautomatic pistol, calibers .32 ACP or .380 ACP.

Remington 150th Anniversary Model 1100SA semiautomatic shotgun, caliber 12 gauge.

Remington 150th Anniversary Model 870SA slide action shotgun, caliber 12 gauge.

Remington 150th Anniversary Model 742ADL semiautomatic rifle caliber .30/06.

Remington 150th Anniversary Model 760ADL slide action rifle, caliber .30/06.

Remington 150th Anniversary Model 552A semiautomatic rifle, caliber .221r.

Remington 150th Anniversary Model 572A slide action rifle, caliber .221r.

Remington 150th Anniversary Model Nylon 66 semiautomatic rifle, caliber .221r.

Remington Montana Territorial Centenial, Model 600, Rifle.

Roth Steyr 1907, semiautomatic pistol, caliber 8mm.

Ruger Canadian Centennial, Matched No. 1 Rifle Sets, Special Deluxe.

Ruger Canadian Centennial, Matched No. 2 Rifle Sets.

Ruger Canadian Centennial, Matched No. 3 Rifle Sets.

Ruger Canadian Centennial, Model 10/22, carbine.

Ruger Falling Block Long Range Creedmore rifle, Caliber .45 (Sharps), Serial Number 130-06888, The Amber Silver - Jubilee.

Ruger, flattop, "Blackhawk" revolvers, calibers .44 Magnum and .357 Magnum, all barrel lengths, made from 1955 through 1962.

Ruger, flattop, single-six, .22 caliber revolvers with flat side loading gate, all barrel lengths, made from 1953 through 1956.

Sauer 38(h), pistol, caliber 7.65mm marked with Third Reich police acceptance stamps of Eagle C,F,K or L.

Savage Arms, semiautomatic pistols, caliber .45 ACP, all models.

Savage, Prototype pistols, caliber .25, .32 and .38 made between 1907 and 1927.

Savage, Model 1907 Pistols, caliber .32 and .380.

Savage, Model 1915 Pistol, caliber .32 and .380.

Savage, Model 1917 Pistol, caliber .32 and .380.

Smith and Wesson, U.S. Border Patrol 50th Anniversary Commemorative, Model 66, stainless steel, caliber .357 Magnum, revolvers.

Smith & Wesson, Model .22/32 Hand Ejector (Bekeart Model), caliber .22 LR, serial numbers 138220 to 534636 (no letter).

Smith & Wesson, K-22 Hand Ejector, caliber .22 LR, serial numbers 632132 to 696952 (no letter).

Smith & Wesson, K-32 Hand Ejector (K-32 Masterpiece), caliber .32 S&W Long, serial numbers 653388 to 682207 (no letter).

Smith & Wesson, .38 Hand Ejector Military and Police, caliber .38, serial numbers 1 to 241703 (no letter).

Smith & Wesson, .357 Magnum Hand Ejector, caliber .357 Magnum, serial numbers 45768 to 60000 (no letter).

Smith & Wesson, .44 Hand Ejector, all calibers, serial numbers 1 to 62488 (no letter).

Smith & Wesson, .455 Mark II Hand Ejector, caliber .455.

Smith & Wesson Mercox Dart Gun, caliber .22 rimfire, blank.

Smith & Wesson, .22/32 Kit Gun, caliber .22 LR, serial numbers 525670 to 534636 (no letter).

Smith & Wesson, .32 Double Action Top Break, caliber .32 S&W, serial numbers 209302 and higher.

Smith & Wesson, .32 Safety Hammerless Top Break (New Departure), caliber .32 S&W, serial numbers 91401 and higher.

Smith & Wesson, .38 Double Action Top Break, caliber .38 S&W, serial numbers 382023 and higher.

Smith & Wesson, .38 Double Action Top Break Perfected Model, caliber .38 S&W.

Smith & Wesson, .38 Safety Hammerless Top Break (New Departure), caliber .38 S&W, serial number 119901 and higher.

Smith & Wesson, pistol, caliber .35, all variations.

Smith & Wesson, 2nd Model, single shot pistol, calibers .22 rimfire, .32 S & W and .38 S & W.

Smith & Wesson, 3rd Model, single shot pistol, caliber .22 rimfire, .32 S & W and .38 S & W.

Smith & Wesson, 1st Model, Ladysmith revolver, caliber .22 rimfire long.

Smith & Wesson, 2nd Model, Ladysmith revolver, caliber .22 rimfire long.

Smith & Wesson, 3rd Model, Ladysmith revolver, caliber .22 rimfire long.

Smith & Wesson Model 39-1 (52-A), pistol, caliber 9mm Parabellum.

Smith & Wesson Model 39, steel frame pistol, caliber 9mm Parabellum.

Smith & Wesson, pistol, caliber .32 ACP.

Smith & Wesson Model Straight Line, single shot pistol, caliber .22 rimfire long rifle.

Smith & Wesson, Model 16 (K-32 Masterpiece), caliber .32 S&W Long, "K" serial number series.

Smith & Wesson, .38/44 Outdoorsman & Heavy Duty, caliber .38, serial numbers 36500 to 62023 (no letter).

Smith & Wesson, California Highway Patrol Commemorative Model 19 revolver, caliber .357.

Smith & Wesson, City of Los Angeles 200th Anniversary Commemorative Model 19 revolver, caliber .357.

Smith & Wesson 125th Anniversary Commemorative, Model 25, revolver, caliber .45. Marked "Smith & Wesson 125th Anniversary" and manufactured in 1977.

Smith & Wesson 150th Anniversary Texas Ranger Commemorative Model 19 revolver.

Standard Arms Co., rifle/shotgun combination, U.S., Model "Camp," slide action caliber .50.

Standard Arms Co., rifle Model G, slide action or gas operated, caliber unknown.

Standard Arms Co., rifle Model M, slide action caliber .25 .35, .30 Rem. and .35 Rem.

Steyr-Hahn M1912, pistol, caliber 9mm Steyr.

Steyr-Hahn M1912, pistol, caliber 9mm Parabellum marked with Third Reich police acceptance stamps of Eagle C,F,K or L.

Sosso pistols manufactured, by Guilio Sosso, Turin, Italy or Fabrica Nationale D'Armi, Brescea Italy, caliber 9mm.

Tauler Model military and police pistol.

Tokagypt 58, pistol, caliber 9mm Parabellum.

U.S. pistols, Model 1911-A1, caliber .45, manufactured by the Singer Manufacturing Company in 1942, serial number range from S800001 to S800500.

U.S. Model 1911-A1 semiautomatic pistol, caliber .45, manufactured by Remington Rand, bearing serial number prefix of ERRS.

U.S. Model 1911-A1 semiautomatic pistol, caliber .45, produced as original factory cutaways.

U.S. rifles, caliber .30, Model M-1, original military issue only, produced prior to 1956.

U.S. Rifle, caliber .30 MC-1952, equipped with telescopic sight mount MC, telescopic sight MC1, marked U.S.M.C. or kollmorgan.

Walther pistols, Manufactured at Zella -

Mehlis prior to 1946, all models any caliber.

Walther model PP & PPK semiautomatic pistols, in all calibers, manufactured in France and marked "manhurin". Webley Model 1909, pistol, caliber 9mm Browning Long.

Webley and Scott, Model 1910 and 1913 high velocity pistols, caliber .38 ACP.

Webley and Scott, M1913, Navy or Commercial, self-loading pistol, caliber .455.

Webley-Fosbury, semiautomatic revolvers, all calibers, all models.

Winchester 1980 Alberta Diamond Jubilee Commemorative carbines, Model 94, in caliber .38/55.

Winchester Alaskan Purchase Centennial, Model 1894, carbine.

Winchester Antlered Game Commemorative, Model 94, carbine, caliber .30-30.

Winchester Apache Commemorative carbine, commemorative edition of Model 1894 Winchester with serial number prefix of AC.

Winchester Bat Masterson commemorative, Model 94.

Winchester Bicentennial 76, Model 94 carbine.

Winchester Buffalo Bill, Model 1894, carbine.

Winchester Buffalo Bill, Model 1894, Rifle.

Winchester Calgary Stampede Commemorative, Model 94 carbine, caliber .32 Winchester Special.

Winchester Canadian 1967, Centennial Model 1894, carbine.

Winchester Canadian 1967, Centennial Model 1894, Rifle

Winchester Canadian Pacific Centennial, Model 94 carbine, caliber .32 Winchester Special.

Winchester Centennial, Model 1866, carbine.

Winchester Centennial, Model 1866, Rifle.

Winchester Comanche Commemorative carbine, commemorative edition of Model 1894 Winchester with serial number prefix of CC.

Winchester Cowboy Commemorative, Model 94, carbine.

Winchester "Ducks Unlimited" shotgun, Model 12, bearing serial numbers DU-001 through DU-800 (Commemorative).

Winchester Golden Spike, Model 1894, carbine.

Winchester, John Wayne Commerative, Model 94 carbine, caliber .32-40 W.C.F.

Winchester John Wayne Commemorative (Canadian Issue), Model 94 carbine, caliber .32-40.

Winchester Illinois Sesquicentennial, Model 1894, carbine.

Winchester Klondike Gold Rush Commemorative Model 94, carbine.

Winchester Legendary Lawman Commemorative, Model 94, carbine, caliber .30-30.

Winchester Legendary Frontiersman Model 94 rifle, caliber .38-55.

Winchester Limited Edition, Model 94 carbine, caliber .30-30, serial numbers 77L1 through 77L1500.

Winchester "Limited Edition I", Model 94.

Winchester "Limited Edition II" Model 94 rifle, caliber .30-30.

Winchester Little Big Horn Centennial, Model 94, carbine.

Winchester Lone Star Commemorative, Model 94, carbine.

Winchester Lone Star Commemorative, rifle, Model 94, .30-30.

Winchester "Matched Set of 1000," a cased pair consisting of a Winchester Model 94 rifle, caliber .30-30 and a Winchester Model 9422 rifle, caliber .22.

Winchester Model 21 Grand American Double Barrel Shotgun, Caliber 20 and 38 Gauge, Serial Number 32984, Engraved Custom Built by Winchester for Philip S. Rane.

Winchester Model 52, rifle, bearing serial numbers 1 to 6,500.

Winchester Model 53, all original, manufactured from 1924 to 1947 with 16 inch or longer barrel, and 26 inch or longer overall length.

Winchester Model 54, rifle, speed lock variation, caliber .270.

Winchester Model 63 selfloading rifles, caliber .22 rimfire.

Winchester models 64 and 65 lever-action rifles.

Winchester Model 70 Ultra Match Target Special Grade rifle, caliber .308.

Winchester rifles, Models 70, .308, .270 Winchester, and 30-06 caliber, 19 inch barrel and Mannlicher type stock, made from 1968 to 1971.

Winchester rifle, Model 70, caliber .308 rifle, 19 inch barrel and Mannlicher type stock, made from 1968 to 1971.

Winchester Model 71 all original, manufactured from 1936 to 1958, with 16 inch or longer barrel and 26 inch or longer overall length.

Winchester Model 1873, all original, manufactured from 1899 to 1925, with 16 inch or longer barrel and 26 inch or longer overall length.

Winchester Model 1885 (single shot rifle), all original, manufactured from 1899 to 1920, with 16 inch or longer barrel, and 26 inch or longer overall length.

Winchester Model 1886, all original, manufactured from 1899 to 1935, with 16 inch or longer barrel and 26 inch or longer overall length.

Winchester Model 1892, all original, manufactured from 1899 to 1947, with 16 inch or longer barrel and 26 inch or longer overall length.

Winchester Model 1894 rifles and carbines manufactured prior to January 2, 1964, and having a serial number of less than 2,700,000, provided their barrel length is at least 16 inches and their overall length at least 26 inches.

Winchester Model 1895, all original manufactured from 1899 to 1938, with 16 inch or longer barrel and 26 inch or longer overall length.

Winchester Model NRA Centennial, Model 94 carbine.

Winchester Mounted Police, Model 94, carbine.

Winchester Nebraska Centennial, Model 1894, carbine.

Winchester NRA Centennial rifle, Model 94, .30-30.

Winchester Northwest Territories Centennial rifle.

Winchester The Oliver F. Winchester commemorative, Model 94.

Winchester One of One Thousand European Rifle commemorative, Model 94.

Winchester Royal Canadian Mounted Police Centennial, Model 94 carbine.

Winchester Saskatchewan Diamond Jubilee Carbine commemorative, Model 94.

Winchester 150th Anniversary Texas Ranger Commemorative, Model 1894, carbine.

Winchester Theodore Roosevelt, Model 1894, carbine.

Winchester Theodore Roosevelt, Model 1894, Rifle.

Winchester United States Border Patrol Commemorative, Model 94 carbine, caliber .30-30.

Winchester Wells Fargo and Company Commemorative, Model 94 carbines.

Winchester Wyoming Diamond Jubilee, Model 94 carbine.

Winchester Yellow Boy Indian, Model 94 carbine.

National Firearms Act Weapons Removed from the Act as Collector's Items and Classified as Curios or Relics Under 18 U.S.C. Chapter 44

The Bureau has determined that by reason of the date of their manufacture, value, design and other characteristics, the following firearms are primarily collector's items and are not likely to be used as weapons and, therefore, are excluded from the provisions of the National Firearms Act.

Further, the Bureau has determined that such firearms are also curios or relics as defined in 27 CFR 178.11. Thus, licensed collectors may acquire, hold or dispose of them as curios or relics subject to the provisions of 18 U.S.C. Chapter 44 and 27 CFR Part 178. They are still "firearms" as defined in 18 U.S.C. 921(a)(3).

Pre-war Belgian manufactured Hi-Power pistols, in caliber 9mm having tangent sights graduated to 500 meters, slotted for shoulder stock, having serial numbers of less than 47,000 without letter prefixes or suffixes and accompanied by original Belgian manufactured detachable wooden flat board type shoulder stocks.

Beretta Model 1918/1930 semiautomatic carbine, caliber 9mm, having a barrel length of 12.5 inches and a magazine capacity of 25 rounds.

Beretta Model 1923 semiautomatic pistol, in caliber 9mm Kurz (.380), accompanied by original Italian detachable leather and metal holster/shoulder stock.

Bergmann-Bayard Pistol, Model 1908, 9mm Bergmann-Bayard with shoulder stock and 4 inch barrel.

Bergmann self-loading pistol, Mars Model 1903, with accompanying shoulder stock.

Blue Jacket Revolver with Shoulder Stock (Veterinarians's Pistol) Serial Number IRS-3600 Caliber .22 Rimfire. Marked Blue Jacket Patented 3-28-1871, 10-1-1876 and 1877, made by W Vurflein, Philadelphia.

Browning Pistol, Model 1903, 9mm Browning Long, with shoulder stock and 5 inch barrel.

Canadian Inglis No. I, Chinese Contract, Hi-Power pistols, caliber 9mm Parabellum, having a tangent rear sight adjustable from 50 to 500 meters, slotted for shoulder stock, and having the letters CH in the serial number and accompanied by original Canadian manufactured detachable wooden holster/shoulder stock.

Clement Pistol Carbine, Caliber 9mm.

Chinese manufactured copies of the Mauser Model 1896 semiautomatic pistol, produced prior to 1945, any caliber, accompanied by original Chinese manufactured detachable wooden holster/shoulder stocks.

Colt cutaway demonstrator lightning rifle, and all other original cutaway demonstrator lightning rifles produced by Colt.

Colt Pistol, Model 1905, .45 rimless, with leather holster/shoulder stock and 5 inch barrel.

Colt Officers Model, .38 Special caliber, double action revolver, with 6 inch barrel and a detachable, experimental skeleton shoulder stock and holster combination.

Colt Single Action Army revolver, serial number 354096, caliber .44/40 having a smooth bored barrel and a barrel length of 7½ inches.

Colt Single Action Army revolver, caliber .45, with original smoothbore barrel, serial number 325085.

Colt Model Woodsman, .22 Long Rifle caliber, semiautomatic pistol with an experimental 10 inch barrel and an experimental wooden detachable shoulder stock.

Colt Model Woodsman, .22 Long Rifle caliber, semiautomatic pistols, manufactured between 1915 and 1943, together with the original leather detachable holster stocks, manufactured by the N&S Corporation, Ventura, California.

Czechoslovakian Model CZ24 semiautomatic pistol, in caliber 9mm Kurz (.380) accompanied by original Czechoslovakian detachable wooden holster/shoulder stock.

Fiala Model 1920 repeating pistol, caliber .22LR in all barrel lengths with accompanying detachable shoulder stock; original copies of the Fiala repeating pistol, marked Schall, Columbia or Botwinick Brothers, caliber .22LR, with accompanying original detachable shoulder stock

Finnish Model L-35 Lahti Semiautomatic pistol, in caliber 9mm Parabellum, accompanied by original Finnish detachable wooden holster/shoulder stock.

Frommer Model 1912, semiautomatic pistol with Benke-Thiemann folding shoulder stock.

German (WWI) antitank rifle (PzAgew 1918), Model 1918, caliber 13.25mm.

German (Nazi) Belt Buckle Gun, .22 rimfire, marked "DRP Ausl Pat, Louis Marquis, W. Elberfeld."

German (Nazi) Belt Buckle Gun, 7.65mm, marked "D.R.P. Angem."

German anti-tank rifle, caliber 7.92mm, Gr 39, Granatbuchse, with 27mm grenade launcher cup.

German Kamphpistole Caliber 26.7mm.

German Leuchpistole, 26.7mm, Walter pattern, manufactured in or before 1945, with original 23mm rifle grenade launching adapter sleeve.

German Schiessbecher Grenade Launcher (G.Gr.Ger.), 27 mm, accompanied by a German Military Mauser 98 type rifle.

German VG1-5 (Volksgewehr) semiautomatic rifle, caliber 7.92mm Kurz, having a barrel length of 14.9 inches and an overall length of 34.8 inches.

Greener Cattle Killer (Original Model) No. B1201, .310 caliber.

Greener Cattle Killer (Pocket Pattern) No. B1203, .310 caliber.

Greener Safti Killer No. B1216, .22 caliber.

Greener Universal Safti Killer No. B1217,

.310 caliber.

Hamilton Model 7, Rifle

Hamilton Model 11, Rifle

Hamilton Model 15, Rifle

Hamilton Model 19, Rifle

Hamilton Model 23, Rifle

Hamilton Model 27 and 027, Rifle

Hamilton Model 31, Rifle

Hamilton Model 35, Rifle

Hamilton Model 39, Rifle

Hamilton Model 43, Rifle

Heal Rifle No. 10, caliber .22

Heal .22 rimfire caliber rifles, all models, manufactured prior to 1908, by the Heal Rifle Company or the Detroit Rifle Company.

High Standard Model C/S smoothbore .22 caliber shot semiautomatic pistols, bearing serial number 59279, 59473, 59478, 59460, or 59469.

High Standard Model S smoothbore .22 caliber shot semi-automatic pistols having slides marked: "HI-STANDARD MODEL "S" .22 L.R. SHOT ONLY," and bearing serial numbers 48142, 48143, 48144, 48145, 48146, 59474, 59496, 59458, or 59459.

"JGA" (J. G. Anchutz, Ulm, Germany), .22 Flobert single shot pistol.

Krupp Models 1902 and 1906 50mm Mountain Cannons as produced for the Siamese Government.

Luger, Artillery Model pistols having chamber dates of 1914 through 1918 plus the date 1920, having German Weimar Navy markings consisting of the letter M over an anchor and a German Navy property number accompanied by original Artillery Luger flat board stocks, bearing Geramn Weimar Navy markings of the letter M over an anchor with or without Navy property numbers.

Luger, the 1920 Commercial Artillery Model, pistols as manufactured by DWM or Erfurt, having undated chambers, commercial proofmarks, and bearing the inscription Germany or Made in Germany on the receiver and accompanied by original, German manufactured, artillery type, detachable wooden shoulder stocks.

Luger DWM Pistol, Model 1900, 1902, or 1906, in 7.65 Luger or 9mm Parabellum caliber, having the American Eagle chamber crest, and barrel lengths of either 4 inches or 4¾ inches with original detachable Ideal shoulder stocks and Ideal frame grips.

Original Models 1904, 1906, 1908, 1914 and 1920 DWM Luger Naval pistols in 9mm Parabellum or 7.65mm caliber, in both the Commerical and Naval military variations; in both altered and unaltered barrel lengths in the Model 1904 and in both altered and unaltered safety markings in the Model 1906; with original board-type detachable shoulder stocks bearing brass or iron discs, with or without markings, or, if without brass or iron discs, being of the Navy flat board-type. This exemption will apply only to the listed Naval Luger pistols if mated to the Naval Luger stock and will not apply if the Naval Luger pistol is mated to the

Artillery stock. The Naval stock has an overall dimension of 12¾ inches, a rear width of 4⅝ inches, a front width of 1½ inches, a rear thickness of $9/16$ inches, and a front thickness of $1^3/16$ inches.

Luger DWM Stoeger Model 1920 and 1923 semiautomatic pistols in 7.65mm or 9mm Parabellum caliber, in barrel lengths of 8, 10, 12, and 12½ inches, having either American Eagle chamber crests and/or Stoeger frame and/or upper receiver marks, having either standard, Navy or artillery rear sights, having extractors marked either "Loaded" or "Geladen" and having frame safety markings of either "Gesichert" or "Safe," together with original commercial flat board stocks of the artillery type, which bear no serial numbers or military proof marks; may include a "Germany" marking.

Luger DWM Pistol-Carbine, Model 1920, 7.65mm or 9mm Parabellum caliber, with accompanying original commercial type shoulder stock, with or without forearm piece, having barrel lengths of 11¾ inches to less than 16 inches.

Luger, German Model 1914 Artillery Model pistol, manufactured by DWM or Erfurt, having chambers dated 1914 through 1918, bearing Imperial German military proofmarks and accompanied by original, German manufactured, artillery type, detachable wooden shoulder stocks.

Luger Pistol-Carbine, Model 1902, 7.65mm Luger with original commercial type shoulder stock and forearm and 11¾ inch barrel.

Luger pistols, Persian (Iranian) Artillery Model, as manufactured by Mauser prior to 1945, accompanied by the original artillery type, detachable wooden shoulder stock, bearing a serial number in Farsi characters stamped into the wood on the left side.

Luger semiautomatic pistol, certain variations with Benke-Thiemann folding shoulder stock.

Luger, Swiss Model 1906, semiautomatic pistol, Serial Number E772, with original attachable shoulder stock known as "Stock System Benke-Thiemann".

MBA Gyrojet Rocket Guns, caliber 13mm, semiautomatic, version only, produced in 1968 or earlier, serial number ranges A0001 through A0032, A001 through A085, B010 through B411, and B5059 through B5692.

Manville, 18-shot-drum, 25mm, semi-automatic tear gas gun.

Marlin Baby carbines, having barrels measuring less than 15 inches in length, certain specific serial numbers, manufactured from 1883 to 1906. Information on individual serial numbers please write to the Firearms Technology Branch, Room B230, 1200 Pennsylvania Ave., NW, Washington, DC 20226.

Marlin, Model 93 carbine, caliber .32-40 WCF, with 15 inch barrel, serial number 426311.

Marlin, Model 94 carbine, caliber .38-40 WCF, with 15 inch barrel, serial number 384186.

Marlin Model 1894 carbine, serial number 325609, .32/20, with original 15 inch barrel.

Marlin Model 1894 carbine, serial number 397215, caliber .38-40, with 15 inch barrel.

Marlin Model 1894 carbine, caliber .44-40, with 15 inch barrel, serial numbers 324137, and 401374.

Marlin Model 1894 carbine, caliber .44 W.C.F., serial numbers 396987 and 423099, with 15-¼ inch barrel.

Mauser commercial Luger Artillery Model semiautomatic pistols caliber 9mm, Mauser banner marked, produced under contract for the Royal Thai Police accompanied by original, German manufactured, detachable wooden shoulder stocks.

Mauser Model 1896 semiautomatic pistol accompanied by original German manufactured detachable wooden holster/shoulder stocks, all semiautomatic German manufactured variations produced prior to 1940, any caliber.

Mauser pistol-carbine, Model 1896, 7.63mm, with shoulder stock and 11¾ inch to 16 inch barrel.

Mauser Model 1902, 6 and 10 - shot magazine capacity, semiautomatic pistols in caliber 7.63 x 25mm (.30 Mauser), having the distinctive hammer safety, barrel lengths of either 3.9 or 5.5 inches, and accompanied by an original detachable wooden holster/shoulder stock.

Mauser Pistol, Model 1912/14, 9mm Mauser short or .45 ACP, with original detachable wooden holster/shoulder stock and 5 inch barrel.

One Pocket Creedmores and other original pocket rifles with extension shoulder stocks, caliber .22, made by Samuel Watson Johnson (1838-1903).

E. Mayer single shot handgun, no serial number, caliber .38-55 smoothbore, barrel length 14-½ inches.

Military type Nambu pistol, Model 1904, caliber 8mm Nambu (Riku Shiki Nambu Kenju) with an accompanying original detachable telescoping wooden holster/shoulder stock.

OSS Glove Pistol, caliber .38 S & W or .38 special.

OSS "Liberator" pistol, .45 ACP or 9mm.

British PIAT (Projector, Infantry, Anti-tank).

Remington Flare (Very) Pistol, Mark III, 10 gauge.

Royal, semiautomatic pistol, Caliber 7.63 x 25mm (.30 Mauser) having an integral 10 or 20 round magazine, 5½ inch, 6¼ inch, or 7⅛ inch barrel, and accompanied by an original Spanish manufactured detachable holster/stock.

Sedgley, Mark V, 10 gauge, signal pistol (Remain Title I).

The Shatuck "Unique" palm gun in .22 and .32 caliber rimfire.

Smith and Wesson Model Military and Police revolver, caliber .38, serial number 112037, with original Ideal holster/shoulder stock.

Smith & Wesson Model 40 Light Rifle, caliber 9mm Parabellum.

Spanish Star Model A semiautomatic pistol in calibers 7.63 Mauser, 9mm Parabellum, 9mm Long, .38 ACP and .45 ACP, accompanied by original Spanish manufactured detachable wooden holster/shoulder stock.

Spanish manufactured copies of the Mauser Model 1896 semiautomatic pistol produced prior to 1946 in caliber 7.63mm or 9mm and having either integral or detachable magazines. Accompanied by original Spanish manufactured detachable wooden holster/shoulder stock.

Stevens Rifle, No. 20, with smooth bore barrel for .22 and .32 rimfire shot cartridges.

Stevens, Reliable Pocket Rifle, second issue, caliber .22 long rifle or .22 Stevens-Pope.

Stevens, New Model Pocket Rifle, first issue, caliber .22.

Stevens, New Model Pocket Rifle, second issue, caliber: .22 short, long or long rifle rimfire, .22 WRF, .32 long centerfire.

Stevens, New Model Pocket Rifle No. 40, caliber: .22 long rifle, .22 WRF, .22 Stevens-Pope, and .32 long centerfire.

Stevens, Hunter's Pet No. 34 Pocket Rifle, caliber .22 short rimfire to .44-40 WCF.

Stevens, Vernier Hunter's Pet No. 344/2 Pocket Rifle, caliber .22 short to 44-40 WCF.

Stevens, Vernier New Model Pocket Rifle No. 401/2, caliber .22 long rifle, .22 WRF, .22 Stevens-Pope, .32 long centerfire.

Stevens, 1898 New Model Pocket Shotgun, in calibers .38-40 and .44-40.

Stevens Number 39, New Model Pocket Shotgun, in calibers .38-40 and .44-40.

Steyr Hahn Model 1911/12 semiautomatic pistol, caliber 9mm Steyr or 9mm Parabellum having a 5 inch barrel and accompanied by an original European detachable holsterstock.

Swedish Model P-40 Lahti semiautomatic pistol, in caliber 9mm Parabellum, accompanied by original Swedish detachable wooden holster/shoulder stock.

The Taylor "Fur Getter" manufactured by the F.C. Taylor Fur Company, St. Louis, Missouri, .22 caliber rimfire.

U.S. Mark II, 10 gauge signal pistols.

Walther Pistol, Model 1937 "Armee Pistols," 9mm Parabellum, with original detachable shoulder stock and 4.9 inch barrel.

Webley & Scott Pistol, Mark I, No. 2, .455 caliber, with original detachable shoulder stock.

Winchester, Model 36 shotgun, 9mm rimfire.

Winchester, Model 1873, carbine, serial number 695081B, 32 W.C.F. caliber, with a barrel length of 14 inches.

Winchester, Model 1873, carbine, serial number 514709, 520569 caliber .38 W.C.F. with original 14-inch barrel.

Winchester Model 1873 carbine, serial number 719510B, caliber .44 W.C.F., with 14 inch barrel.

Winchester, Model 1873, carbine, serial number 127884, 247094B, 336514B, 380061, 486139, 92842A, 198040B, and 263826B caliber .44 W.C.F., original 15-inch barrel.

Winchester, Model 1873, carbine, serial number 382027 caliber .32 W.C.F. with original 15-inch barrel.

Winchester Model 1885 single shot rifle, serial number 104783, caliber .25/35, having a 15-inch number 3 round barrel, shotgun butt, plain pistol grip, and Winchester Express sight.

Winchester Model 92 carbine, caliber .44 W.C.F., serial number 954796, with 15 inch barrel.

Winchester Model 92 carbine, serial number 998845, caliber .38 WCF, with 14 inch barrel.

Winchester, Model 92 carbine, serial numbers 905158 and 998419, caliber .44-40, with original 15 inch barrel.

Winchester, Model 94 carbine caliber .30-30 WCF, with original 15 inch barrel, serial numbers 273691 and 758406.

Winchester Model 1892 Rifle, (Trapper version), caliber .25-20 W.C.F., with 14 inch barrel, serial number 940986.

Winchester Model 1892 Carbine, caliber .25-20 W.C.F., with 14 inch barrel, serial numbers 765952, 818777 and 859912.

Winchester, Model 1892 carbine, serial numbers 615287, 679709 and 826022, caliber .38 W.C.F., with 14 inch barrel.

Winchester, Model 1892 carbine, serial numbers 615287, 679709 and 826022, caliber .38 W.C.F., with 14 inch barrel.

Winchester Model 1892 carbine, serial number 850811, caliber .38 W.C.F., with 14 inch barrel.

Winchester, Model 1892 carbine, serial number 179252, 408307, 804878, 842788 and 843000, caliber .38 WCF, with 15 inch barrel.

Winchester, Model 1892 carbine, serial number 288562 and 848873, caliber .38-40, with original 14 inch barrel.

Winchester Model 1892 carbine, serial number 51976, 158145, 268828, 336549, 446526, 583403, 659700, 820170, 895062, 898938, 921643, 948932, 978462, 981212, 982483, 987239, 993799, 999398, caliber .44 WCF, with 14 inch barrel.

Winchester Model 1892 Carbine, caliber .44 W.C.F., with 15 inch barrel, serial numbers 381573, 95516, 977103, 998059, 998461, and 998679.

Winchester Model 1894 carbine, serial numbers 542097 and 589609, caliber .25-35 W.C.F., with 15 inch barrel.

Winchester Model 1894 carbine, serial numbers 505307, 793359, 805815 and 864415, caliber .30 W.C.F., with 14 inch barrel.

Winchester Model 1894 carbine, serial number 781211, caliber .32 Winchester Special, with 14 inch barrel.

Winchester, Model 1894 carbine, serial numbers 360587, 433426, 444269, 46404, 467286, 593839, 662192, 794467, 820101, 840123, 868769, 880845, 883055, 884272, 887409, 938370, 959421, 986621, 990851, 991114, 995675, 1004958, 1033973, 1033898, 1034037, 1017950, 1040905, 1046737, 1052851, 1066951, 1068292, and 1072755 caliber .30 WCF, with 15 inch barrel.

Winchester, Model 1894 carbine, caliber .30-30, serial numbers 701730 and 862245, with 15 inch barrel.

Winchester, Model 1894 carbine, serial number 1006715, caliber .32 Winchester Special, with 15 inch barrel.

Winchester, Model 1894 carbine, caliber .38-55 W.C.F., serial number 247646, with 15 inch barrel.

The following firearms were removed from the National Firearms Act as collector's items and classified as curios or relics under 18 U.S.C. Chapter 44. However, since they are antiques as defined in Chapter 44, they should not have been classified as curios or relics. Since they are no longer NFA weapons and are antiques under Chapter 44, they are not subject to GCA provisions:

Belgian Cane Gun, 41 caliber rimfire.

Bergmann Model 1897, caliber 7.65mm (7.8mm) pistol with accompanying shoulder stock.

Borchardt Model 1893, caliber 7.63mm pistol with accompanying shoulder stock.

Chicago palm pistol, caliber .32 rimfire extra short.

Frank Wesson Bicycle Rifle with accompanying shoulder stock.

Gaulois palm squeezer, 8mm short.

"Little All Right" palm pistol, .22 caliber rimfire patented by Edward Boardman and Andrew Peavey, January 18, 1876.

Mannlicher Pistol-Carbine, Model 1896, 7.63mm Mannlicher, with rifle type shoulder stock and forearm and 11¾ inch barrel.

Marveilleux squeezer pistol, 6mm and 8mm short.

Peavey, A.J., Knife Gun, .22 short rimfire.

Protector palm gun, .32 rimfire extra short, patented by Jacques Turbiaux, Patent No. 732644.

Quackenbrush Bicycle Rifle with telescopic wire stock, .22 caliber.

Remington Cane Gun, Model 1, .22 rimfire.

Remington Cane Gun, Model 2, .32 rimfire.

Stevens, Old Model Pocket Rifle, caliber .22 short or long rimfire.

Stevens, New Model Pocket Rifle, second issue, in caliber .25 Stevens or .32 long rimfire.

Stevens, Reliable Pocket Rifle, first issue, caliber .22 short, long or long rifle.

Stevens, New Model Pocket Rifle, first issue, in caliber .32 short or long rimfire.

Stevens, New Model Pocket Rifle No. 40, in caliber .25 Stevens or .32 long rimfire.

Stevens, Vernier, New Model Pocket Rifle, caliber .22 short, .22 long rifle, .22 WRF, .32 long rimfire.

Stevens, Vernier New Model Pocket Rifle No. 401/2, in caliber .25 Stevens or .32 long rimfire.

Tribuzio "Squeezer" invented by Catello Tribuzio of Turin, Italy, caliber 8mm short.

Winchester, Model 1873 carbine, serial number 380061, caliber .44 WCF, with 15 inch barrel.

Winchester, Model 1885, carbine, serial number 83304, caliber .44 W.C.F., with original 15 inch barrel.

Winchester, Model 1892 carbine, serial number 43844, caliber .38 WCF, with 15 inch barrel.

Winchester, Model 1892 carbine, serial number 158145, caliber .44 WCF, with 15 inch barrel.

Any pistol or revolver, manufactured in or before 1898, originally designed to accept a shoulder stock, and accompanied by an original shoulder stock.

Handguns

ASTRA PISTOLS & REVOLVERS

4-inch barrel

ASTRA 357 MAG.

Potent, powerful and smooth as silk: the Astra 357. Chambered for the hot 357 Magnum cartridge, this large-frame revolver also handles the popular 38 Special, making it equally suitable for the serious target shooter and for the sportsman.

All forged steel and highly polished to a rich blue, the Astra 357 has a heavyweight barrel with integral rib and ejector shroud. The rear sight is click-adjustable for windage and elevation. The hammer is of the wide-spur target type, and the trigger is grooved. The grips are of checkered hardwood. The cylinder is recessed, and the gun utilizes a spring-loaded, floating firing pin for additional safety.

The internal lockwork of the Astra 357 is as finely fitted and finished as the exterior, giving it a smoothness second to none. There's even a four-stage adjustment to control spring tension on the hammer.

The Astra 357 is available with 4-inch, 6-inch and 8½-inch barrel. The 4-inch and longer-barreled models have square butts and are supplied with comfortable, hand-filling oversized grips. Length overall with 6-inch barrel is 11¼ inches.

Barrel Length	Finish	Caliber	Weight	
4 in.	Blue	357 Mag.	38 oz.	$330.00
4 in.	Stainless	357 Mag.	38 oz.	390.00
8½ in.	Blue	357 Mag.	41 oz.	390.00

ASTRA CONSTABLE
22 L.R. & 380 ACP

The Astra Constable is a double-action, all steel small-frame auto, so you can safely carry it fully loaded with a round in the chamber and the safety off. A single pull of the trigger then cocks and fires the pistol without the necessity of cocking the hammer manually, as is necessary with most autos. The thumb safety completely blocks the hammer and actually locks the firing pin in place until released. The barrel is rigidly mounted in the frame for greater accuracy and the gun features quick, no-tool takedown, integral non-glare rib on the slide, push-button magazine release and a round, non-snagging hammer spur.

22 L.R. & 380 ACP Blue		$370.00/355.00
22 L.R. & 380 ACP Chrome		410.00/395.00
22 L.R. & 380 ACP Blue Eng.		520.00/500.00
22 L.R. & 380 ACP Chrome Eng.		530.00/510.00

*Checkered wood grips, $30.00 extra

Astra Model A-80

Double-action, semi-automatic pistol in 9mm Parabellum, .38 Super and .45 ACP.

Features include an advanced, smooth double-action mechanism, increased magazine capacity (15 rounds in 9mm and .38 Super, 9 rounds in .45 ACP), all-steel construction, compact size, loaded chamber indicator, combat-style trigger guard, optional right-side slide release $510.00

ASTRA MODEL 44 (not illus.)

Meet the Astra Model 44 Magnum. Designed around the popular lines of its forerunner, the Astra 357, this revolver features wide-spur target hammers and a four-position main spring adjustment device which allows for custom tuning of trigger pull. The Astra M44 has features all its own, too. For instance, oversized, beefed-up frame and target-style grips to provide balanced weight distribution and minimize the apparent recoil of the 44 Magnum round.

The revolver, finished in a deep astral blue, is available with a 6-inch barrel which features an integral sight rib and shrould for the ejector rod. Grooved triggers, ramp front sights and fully adjustable rear sights are standard on all 44 Magnum models.

Barrel Length	Finish	Caliber	
6 in.	Blue	44 Mag.	$450.00
6 in.	Blue	41 Mag.	450.00
6 in.	Blue	45 Colt	450.00

BERETTA PISTOLS

MODEL 70S PISTOL

This pistol is available in 22 Auto and 380 Auto and has a frame of steel alloy. Longer barrel guide; safety lever blocking the hammer; push button magazine release; sloping grip; sight and rear sight blade fixed on the breech block.

SPECIFICATIONS:

Total Length: 6.5 inches. **Barrel Length:** 3.5 inches. **Height:** 4.8 inches. **Weight (mag. empty):** 1 lb. 7 ozs. **Magazine Capacity, 380 Auto:** 7 rounds. **Magazine Capacity, 22 Auto:** 8 rounds.

Model 70S $274.00

MODEL 81/84 PISTOLS

These pistols are pocket size with a large magazine capacity. The lockwork is of double-action type. The first shot (with hammer down, chamber loaded) can be fired by a double-action pull on the trigger without cocking the hammer manually.

The pistols also feature a favorable grip angle for natural pointing, positive thumb safety (uniquely designed for both right- and left-handed operation), quick takedown (by means of special takedown button) and a conveniently located magazine release. The magazine capacity is 13 rounds in 380 caliber (Model 84) and 12 rounds in the 32 auto caliber (Model 81). Black plastic grips. Wood grips available at extra cost.

SPECIFICATIONS—Model M-81

Caliber: 32 Auto (7.65mm). **Weight:** 1 lb. 8 oz. **Barrel Length:** 3¾ inches. (Approx.) **Overall Length:** 6½ inches. (Approx.). **Sights:** Fixed — Front and Rear. **Magazine Capacity:** 12 Rounds. **Height, overall:** 4¼ inches. (Approx.).

SPECIFICATIONS—Model M-84

Caliber: 380 Auto (9mm Short). **Weight:** 1 lb. 7 oz. (Approx.). **Barrel Length:** 3¾ inches. (Aprox.) **Overall Length:** 6½ inches. (Approx.) **Sights:** Fixed — Front and Rear. **Magazine Capacity:** 13 Rounds. **Height, overall:** 4¼ inches. (Approx.).

Model 81 (with plastic grips) $408.00
Model 81 (with wood grips) 425.00
Model 84 (with plastic grips) 408.00
Model 84 (with wood grips) 425.00

MODEL 76 PISTOL

Designed for target shooting the M-76 features built-in, fixed, counterweight for correct balance and control of recoil; raised, matted rib on which both front and rear sights are solidly mounted; rear sight fully adjustable for windage and elevation; front sight supplied in three interchangeable widths. Trigger pull is factory adjusted to a weight between 3 lbs. 5 oz. and 3 lbs. 12 oz.

Grips are plastic, shaped and checkered to give a firm hold. Pistols are equipped with a positive thumb safety. All metal parts are finished in blue-black. Checkered wood grips available at extra cost.

SPECIFICATIONS:

Caliber: 22 L.R. **Magazine Capacity:** 10 Rounds. **Overall Length:** 8.8 inches. (223mm). **Barrel Length:** 6 inches. (150mm). **Sight Radius:** 6.9 inches. (176mm). **Weight (mag. empty):** 2 lbs. 1 oz. (930 grams). **Height:** 5.6 inches. (143mm). **Rifling:** 6 lands & grooves, R.H. pitch.

Model 76 (with plastic grips) $370.00
Model 76 (with wood grips) 415.00

MODEL 92S PISTOL

A heavy-duty handgun, chambered for the high-velocity 9mm Parabellum (Luger) cartridge. The pistol's unique "Hammer Drop" safety feature blocks the firing pin from the hammer, releases the hammer and breaks the connection between the trigger and sear. Double-action lockwork—pistol may be fired by a double-action trigger pull (with hammer down), as well as in the regular single-action mode. Magazine has extra-large capacity of 15 rounds, although of standard length (another cartridge may be carried in the chamber). Pistol is fully locked at time of firing. Extractor acts as loaded chamber indicator visually and by feel. Both front and rear sights are mounted on the slide. All metal parts are finished in blue-black. Grips are black plastic, checkered and grooved. Wood grips extra.

SPECIFICATIONS:

Caliber: 9mm Parabellum (Luger). **Magazine Capacity:** 15 Rounds. **Overall Length:** 8.54 inches. (217mm). **Barrel Length:** 4.92 inches. (125mm). **Sight Radius:** 6.1 inches. (155mm). **Weight (mag. empty):** 2 lbs. 1½ oz. (950 grams). **Height:** 5.39 inches. (137mm). **Width:** 1.45 inches. (37mm). **Rifling:** 6 lands & grooves, R.H. pitch.

Model 92S (with plastic grips) $515.00
Model 92S (with wood grips) 543.00
Model 92SB (with plastic grips) 600.00
Model 92SB (with wood grips) 620.00

BERNARDELLI PISTOLS

MODEL 80

Caliber: 22 L.R.—10 Shot; 380 ACP-7 Shot. **Barrel:** 3.54 inches. **O.A. Length:** 6.45 inches. **Weight:** 26.8 oz. **Stock:** Checkered plastic w/thumb rest (Wrap Around). **Sights:** Adjustable. **Features:** Hammer-blocking slide safety which locks firing pin to permit loading or clearing of chamber w/safety engaged. Loaded round indicator, adjustable rear sight. White outline rear sight and white dot front sight. Dual recoil buffer springs. Serrated trigger. Inertia type firing pin. Magazine follower interlock holds slide open after last round is fired.

Model 80 .... **$235.00**

MODEL 100

Caliber: 22 L.R. only—10 shot. **Barrel:** 5.9 inches. **O.A. Length:** 9.00 inches. **Weight:** 37.75 oz. **Features:** Target barrel weight included. Heavy sighting rib with interchangeable front sight. Rear sight adjustable for elevation and windage. Serrated trigger, inertia type firing pin. Comfortable checkered walnut grips with thumb rest. Accessories include cleaning equipment and assembly tools. Case included.

Model 100 .... **$425.00**

BROWNING AUTOMATIC PISTOLS

9mm HI-POWER

The Browning 9mm Parabellum, also known as the 9mm Browning Hi-Power has a 14-cartridge capacity and weighs two pounds. The push-button magazine release permits swift, convenient withdrawal of the magazine.

The 9mm is available with either a fixed blade front sight and a windage adjustable rear sight or a non-glare rear sight, screw adjustable for both windage and elevation. The front sight is a 1/8-inch wide blade mounted on a ramp. The rear surface of the blade is serrated to prevent glare.

In addition to the manual safety, the firing mechanism includes an external hammer so it is easy to ascertain whether the pistol is cocked.

Standard	**$519.95**
Standard with adjustable sights	**569.95**
Silver Chrome with adjustable sights	**594.95**
Extra magazine	**39.75**

SPECIFICATIONS:
Magazine Capacity: 10. **Overall length:** 10 7/8 inches. **Barrel length:** 6 3/4 inches. **Height:** 5 1/4 inches. **Weight:** 38 oz. **Sight radius:** 9 1/8 inches. **Ammunition:** 22 L.R. **Grips:** Impregnated hardwood. **Front sights:** 1/8 inch wide. **Rear sights:** Screw adjustable for vertical correction. Drift adjustable for windage.

BDA-380. A high-powered, double-action pistol with fixed sights in 380 caliber.

BDA-380 nickel	**$439.95**	BDA-380 std.	**$399.75**
Extra magazine	**27.00**	Extra magazine	**22.50**

AUTOMATIC PISTOL SPECIFICATIONS

	22 Challenger		9 mm Hi-Power		BDA 380
	Challenger III Sporter	III	Fixed Sights	Adjustable Sights	(Double Action)
Capacity of Magazine	10	10	13	13	12
Overall Length	10 7/8 in.	9 1/2 in.	7 3/4 in.	7 3/4 in.	6 3/4 in.
Barrel Length	6 3/4 in.	5 1/2 in.	4 21/32 in.	4 21/32 in.	3 13/16 in.
Height	5 1/4 in.	5 3/8 in.	5 in.	5 in.	4 3/4 in.
Weight (Empty)	39 oz.	35 oz.	32 oz.	32 1/5 oz.	23 oz.
Sight Radius	9 1/8 in.	8 in.	6 5/16 in.	6 3/8 in.	4 15/16 in.
Ammunition	22LR	22LR	9mm Luger	9mm Luger	380 Auto
Grips	Impregnated hardwood	Impregnated hardwood	Checkered walnut	Checkered walnut	Walnut
Front Sights	1/8 in. wide	1/8 in. wide	Fixed blade	1/8 in. wide blade on ramp	Fixed blade with white dot
Rear Sights	Screw adjustable for vertical correction. Drift adjustable for windage.	Screw adjustable for vertical correction. Drift adjustable for windage.	Drift adjustable for windage.	Screw adjustable horizontal and vertical.	White outlined square notch. Drift adjustable for windage.
Grades Available	Standard	Standard	Standard Nickel and Louis XVI	Standard Silver Chrome, Standard, Nickel and Louis XVI	Standard Nickel

BAUER PISTOLS

25 CALIBER AUTOMATIC
$136.40

SPECIFICATIONS:
Caliber: 25 automatic
Capacity: 6 shot
Barrel length(s): 2¼ inches
Weight: 10 oz.
Overall length: 4 inches
Safety: Positive manual
Grips: Pearl or genuine walnut
Finish: Neutral Satin Stainless

CHARTER ARMS REVOLVERS

POLICE BULLDOG
38 SPECIAL 6-SHOT REVOLVER

SPECIFICATIONS:
Caliber: 38 Special. **Type of action:** 6-shot single and double action. **Barrel length:** 2 and 4 inches. **Overall length:** 6¼ and 9 inches. **Height:** 5⅛ inches. **Weight:** 20½ ounces. **Grips:** Square butt, American walnut hand-checkered. **Sights:** Full-length ramp front; fully adjustable combat rear. **Finish:** High-luster Service Blue or Stainless Steel. **$245.00**

TARGET BULLDOG 357 MAG.
44 SPECIAL

SPECIFICATIONS:
Caliber: 357 Mag., 44 spl. **Type of action:** 5 shot, single and double action. **Barrel length:** 4 inches. **Overall length:** 9 inches. **Height:** 5⅛ inches. **Weight:** 20½ ounces. **Grips:** American walnut square butt. **Sights:** Full length ramp front sight; fully adjustable, milled channel, square notch rear sight. **Finish:** High-luster Service Blue.
357 Mag. **$215.50**
44 Special **225.00**

PATHFINDER
22 MAGNUM

SPECIFICATIONS:
Caliber: 22 Magnum. **Type of action:** 6 shot, single and double action. **Barrel length:** 3 or 6 inches. **Overall length:** 7¾ inches (3-inch bbl.), 10⅝ inches (6-inch bbl.). **Height:** 4¾-inches (3-inch bbl.), 5 inches (6-inch bbl.). **Weight:** 20 oz. (3-inch bbl.), 22½ oz. (6-inch bbl.). **Grips:** Hand-checkered square butt or checkered walnut panel. **Sights:** Patridge-type ramp front sight, fully adjustable notch rear sight. **Finish:** High luster Service Blue.

With 3-inch barrel **$200.00**
With 6-inch barrel **215.00**
With 3-inch barrel in Stainless Steel **250.00**

CHARTER ARMS REVOLVERS

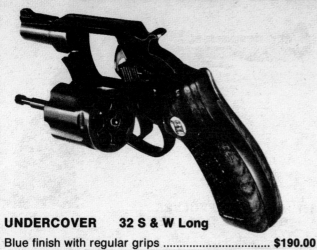

UNDERCOVER   32 S & W Long

Blue finish with regular grips **$190.00**

SPECIFICATIONS:
Caliber: 32 S & W Long. **Type of Action:** 6 Shot, single and double action. **Barrel Length:** 2 inches. **Overall Length:** 6¼ inches. **Height:** 4⅛ inches. **Weight:** 16 ounces. **Grips:** Checkered walnut panel. **Sights:** Wide Patridge type front; notch rear 9/64 inch. **Rifling:** One turn in 17 inches, right hand twist. **Finish:** High-luster Service Blue.

PATHFINDER   22 L.R.

Blue finish with regular grips
   3-inch barrel **$200.00**
Blue finish with square butt grips
   6-inch barrel **215.00**
Stainless Steel finish with regular grips
   3-inch barrel **250.00**

SPECIFICATIONS:
Caliber: 22 Long Rifle. **Type of Action:** 6 shot, single and double action. **Barrel Length:** 2, 3 or 6 inches. **Overall Length:** 6¼ inches. (2-inch bbl.). **Height:** 5 inches. **Weight:** 17 ounces. (2-inch bbl.). **Grips:** Checkered walnut panel or square butt. **Sights:** Fully adjustable rear; Patridge-type ramp front. **Rifling:** One turn in 16 inches, right hand twist. **Finish:** High-luster Service Blue or Stainless Steel.

UNDERCOVER 38 Special

2-inch barrel blue finish with
   checkered panel grips **$190.00**
2-inch barrel stainless steel finish
   with checkered panel grips **245.00**
3-inch barrel blue finish with
   checkered panel grips **190.00**

SPECIFICATIONS:
Caliber: 38 Special (Mid-Range & Standard). **Type of Action:** 5 shots, single and double action. **Barrel Length:** 2 or 3 inches. **Overall Length:** 6¼ inches (2-inch bbl.), 8 inches (3-inch bbl.). **Height:** 4¼ inches (2-inch bbl.), 4¾ inches (3-inch bbl.). **Weight:** 16 oz. (2-inch bbl.), 17½ oz. (3-inch bbl.). **Grips:** American walnut hand checkered. **Sights:** Patridge-type ramp front, square-notched rear. **Finish:** High-luster Service Blue or Stainless Steel.

BULLDOG 44 SPECIAL

Blue finish with Bulldog grips **$200.00**
Stainless Steel finish with Bulldog grips **260.00**

SPECIFICATIONS:
Caliber: .357 Mag. (2½ inch bbl.). 44 Special. **Type of Action:** 5 shot, single and double action. **Barrel Length:** 3 in. **Overall Length:** 7¼ or 7¾ inches. **Height:** 5 inches. **Weight:** 19 or 20 oz. **Grips:** Neoprene or American walnut hand-checkered bulldog grips. **Sights:** Patridge-type, 9/64-inch wide front; square-notched rear. **Finish:** High-luster Service Blue or Stainless Steel.

CHARTER ARMS REVOLVERS

22 LR SEMI-AUTO PISTOL EXPLORER II

Black or silvertone finish with regular grips
6-, 8- and 10-inch barrels $99.00

SPECIFICATIONS:
Caliber: 22 Long Rifle. **Type of Action:** 8-shot magazine. **Barrel Length:** 6-, 8- or 10-inch. **Overall Length:** 13½ inches. (6-inch bbl.), 15½ inches. (8-inch bbl.), 17½ inches. (10-inch bbl.) **Height:** 6½ inches. **Weight:** 28 ounces. **Grips:** Shur-hold, simulated walnut. **Sights:** Snag-free blade front; adjustable square-notched rear; elevation reference lines; definite click indicator. **Finish:** Black, heat cured, semi-gloss textured enamel or silvertone anti-corrosion.

357 MAGNUM REVOLVER BULLDOG "TRACKER"

Blue finish with Square Butt grips
2½-, 4- and 6-inch barrels $210.00

SPECIFICATIONS:
Caliber: 357 Magnum. **Type of Action:** 5 shot. **Barrel Length:** 2½-, 4- or 6-inches. **Overall Length:** 7½ inches. (2½-inch bbl.), 11 inches. (6-inch bbl.) **Height:** 5⅛ inches. **Weight:** 21 ounces (2½-inch.). **Grips:** Hand-checkered walnut, square butt design. **Sights:** Ramp front sight; adjustable square-notched rear; elevation reference lines; definite click indicator. **Finish:** Service Blue.

COLT REVOLVERS

PYTHON

357 MAGNUM & 38 SPECIAL

357 Magnum Barrels: 2½ inch, 4 inch, 6 inch and 8 inch
38 Special Barrel: 8 inch only
The Colt Python revolver, suitable for hunting, target shooting and police use, is chambered for the powerful 357 Magnum cartridge as well as the 38 Special. Python features include ventilated rib, fast cocking, wide-spur hammer, trigger and grips, adjustable rear and ramp-type front sights, ⅛ inch wide.

The sighting radius of the revolver with a 6-inch barrel is 7⅝ inches; overall length, 11¼ inches; weight, 43½ ounces. Both the 357 Magnum and the 38 Special come fitted with handsome fully checkered walnut stocks and a finish of either Colt royal blue or polished nickel.

6-INCH BARREL

Caliber	Barrel	Finish	Price
357 Mag.	2½ in.	Blue	**$540.50**
357 Mag.	3 in.	Blue	548.50
357 Mag.	4 in.	Blue	551.95
357 Mag.	4 in.	Nickel	585.95
357 Mag.	4 in.	St.S.	619.50
357 Mag.	6 in.	Blue	560.50
357 Mag.	6 in.	Nickel	587.95
357 Mag.	6 in.	St.S.	628.50
357 Mag.	8 in.	Blue	572.50
357 Mag.	8 in.	Nickel	600.50

COLT REVOLVERS

COLT DIAMONDBACK

22 L.R., 4-inch bbl.,
   blue $354.20
22 L.R., 6-inch bbl.,
   blue 362.50
38 Spec., 4-inch bbl.,
   blue 354.50
38 Spec., 6-inch bbl.,
   blue 362.50

The Colt Diamondback all-steel revolver was designed along the lines of the Python and includes the features of the bigger Python on a medium-size frame. These features include the ventilated rib, which dissipates barrel heat, reduces mirage effect and provides the preferred flat sighting plane . . . the wide spur target hammer which has a new cross-cut design which assures non-slip cocking . . . a grooved trigger and shrouded ejector rod, which protects the ejector rod and minimizes "barrel bounce."

The Diamondback is equipped with a fully adjustable rear sight for windage and elevation. The front sight is an integral ramp type.

SPECIFICATIONS:
Calibers: 22 L.R. and 38 Special
Barrel lengths: 4 inches and 6 inches
Sights: Adjustable rear sight, ramp-type front
Trigger: Smooth
Hammer: Wide-spur, checkered
Stocks: Checkered walnut target stock
Weights: 2½-inch bbl. 38 Spec. (24 ozs.):
4-inch bbl. 38 Spec. (27 oz.); 4-inch bbl. 22 L.R. (31¾ oz.)
Finish: Colt Blue. Polished nickel (38 only).

COLT DETECTIVE SPECIAL IN 38 SPECIAL WITH 2-INCH BARREL (All Steel)

Blue Finish 2" .... $352.95   3" $360.95
Nickel Finish 2" .... 388.50   3" 395.95

SPECIFICATIONS:
Caliber: 38 special
Barrel Length: 2- and 3-inches
Overall Length: 6⅞ inches (2-in. bbl.)
Weight: 21½ ounces
Sights: Fixed-type ramp-style, glare proofed
Trigger: Smooth
Stocks: Full checkered walnut, round butt
Finish: Colt Blue. Polished Nickel

COLT LAWMAN MK III and MK V 357 MAGNUM REVOLVER

SPECIFICATIONS:
Caliber: 357 Magnum
Barrel Lengths: 2 & 4 inches
Weight: 2-inch barrel 32 oz.; 4-inch barrel 35 oz.
Overall Length: 2-inch barrel 7¼ inches; 4-inch barrel
   9⅜ inches
Sights: Fixed blade front; fixed square notch rear
Hammer: Target
Stock: 2-inch barrel round-butt checkered walnut only;
   4-inch barrel square butt checkered walnut
Finish: Colt blue or polished nickel

Lawman MK III			
357	2 in.	Blue	$222.50
357	2 in.	Nickel	227.50
357	2 in.	Cltg.	213.95
357	4 in.	Blue	222.50
357	4 in.	Nickel	227.50
357	4 in.	Cltg.	213.95

Lawman MK V			
.357 Mag.	2 in.	Blue	$269.50
.357 Mag.	2 in.	Nickel	286.50
.357 Mag.	4 in.	Blue	269.50
.357 Mag.	4 in.	Nickel	286.50

COLT SINGLE-ACTION REVOLVERS

SINGLE ACTION ARMY

The Colt Single Action Army, also known as the original "Peacemaker," offers superb balance, rugged design and is equipped with fixed rear square notch and fixed front blades. In addition, all three models of this classic Colt feature authentic grips and three hammer positions: one for carrying, one for loading and one for firing.

Calibers: 357 Magnum, 44-Special, 44/40 and 45 Colt.
Barrel Length(s): 4¾ inches, 5½ inches, 7½ inches, 12 inches.
Weight: 45 caliber w/5½-inch barrel, 37 oz.; 357 caliber w/ 5½-inch barrel, 41½ oz.
Overall Length: 4¾-inch barrel, 10⅛ inches; 5½-inch barrel, 10⅞ inches; 7½-inch barrel, 12⅞ inches.
Sights: Fixed front blade; fixed rear square notch.
Stock: Black composite rubber or walnut.
Finish: Colt blue or polished nickel.

NEW FRONTIER SINGLE ACTION ARMY

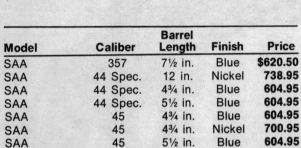

The Colt New Frontier Single Action Army Revolver is made in three calibers: 44-Special, 44/40 and 45 Colt. It features an adjustable rear sight with flat-top frame and ramp-front sight; also smooth trigger, knurled hammer spur and walnut stocks. Available in blue finish.

Calibers: 44-Special 44/40 and 45 Colt.
Barrel Lengths: 4¾ inches, 5½ inches and 7½ inches.
Overall Length: 12⅞ inches with 7½-inch bbl.
Weight: 39½ oz.
Sights: Ramp front; adjustable rear.
Sight Radius: With 7½-inch barrel—8⅝ inches.
Finish: Case-hardened frame; blued barrel, cylinder, trigger guard & backstrap.
Stock: Walnut.

Model	Caliber	Barrel Length	Finish	Price
SAA	357	7½ in.	Blue	**$620.50**
SAA	44 Spec.	12 in.	Nickel	**738.95**
SAA	44 Spec.	4¾ in.	Blue	**604.95**
SAA	44 Spec.	5½ in.	Blue	**604.95**
SAA	45	4¾ in.	Blue	**604.95**
SAA	45	4¾ in.	Nickel	**700.95**
SAA	45	5½ in.	Blue	**604.95**
SAA	45	7½ in.	Blue	**620.50**
SAA	44-40	4¾ in.	Blue	**604.95**
SAA	44-40	7½ in.	Blue	**620.50**

Model	Caliber	Barrel Length	Finish	Price
NF/SAA	44 Spec.	5½ in.	Blue	**$700.95**
NF/SAA	44 Spec.	7½ in.	Blue	**720.50**
NF/SAA	45	4¾ in.	Blue	**700.50**
NF/SAA	45	7½ in.	Blue	**719.50**
New Frontier	22 L.R.	4¾ in.	Blue	**276.95**
New Frontier	22 L.R.	6 in.	Blue	**278.95**
New Frontier	22 L.R.	7½ in.	Blue	**280.95**

COLT REVOLVERS & PISTOLS

TROOPER MK III and MK V
357 Mag., 22 Win. Mag. RF, 22 LR, Barrels: 4, 6 or 8 inch

Tremendous penetrating power in the Magnum caliber makes this handgun suitable for hunters of big game or for police officers. Its quick draw type, ramp-style front sight and adjustable rear sight makes this a target-sighted general purpose revolver. Features include: wide target trigger; wide serrated hammer; full checkered walnut stocks. Trooper MKIII, 357 Magnum, 22 Win. Mag. Rimfire, 22 Long Rifle. 4-; 6- or 8-inch barrel.

Specifications:
Caliber: 357 Magnum, 22 Win. Mag. RF, 22 LR. **Barrel Length:** 4 inches, 6 inches or 8 inches (357 Mag. only). With target stocks: ⅛ inch longer. **Weight (Oz.):** 39 oz. with 4-inch bbl. 42 oz. with 6-inch bbl. **Sights:** Fixed ramp-type front sight with ⅛-inch blade. Rear sight adjustable for windage and elevation. **Trigger:** Wide target trigger. **Hammer:** Wide checkered spur on target hammer. Target—case hardened finish. **Stocks:** Target stocks, checkered walnut. **Finish:** Colt blue and polished nickel finishes. **Cylinder Capacity:** 6 shot counterbored. **Overall Length:** 9½ inches with 4-inch barrel.

Trooper MK III

Caliber	Barrel	Finish	Price
357 Mag.	4 in.	Blue	$244.50
357 Mag.	4 in.	Nickel	250.95
357 Mag.	4 in.	Cltg.	235.95
357 Mag.	6 in.	Blue	246.50
357 Mag.	6 in.	Nickel	253.50
357 Mag.	6 in.	Cltg.	237.95
22 L.R.	4 in.	Cltg.	239.75
22 Mag.	4 in.	Cltg.	239.75
22 L.R.	6 in.	Blue	227.50
22 L.R.	6 in.	Cltg.	244.50
22 WMR	6 in.	Blue	227.50
22 Mag.	6 in.	Cltg.	244.50
357 Mag.	8 in.	Blue	252.95
357 Mag.	8 in.	Nickel	260.50
357 Mag.	8 in.	Cltg.	245.95

Trooper MK V

Caliber	Barrel	Finish	Price
357 Mag.	6 in.	Blue	$298.50
357 Mag.	6 in.	Nickel	316.50
357 Mag.	8 in.	Blue	299.50
357 Mag.	8 in.	Nickel	322.50

GOLD CUP NATIONAL MATCH
MK IV SERIES '70
45 ACP $560.95

SPECIFICATIONS:
Caliber: 45 ACP
Capacity: 7 rounds
Barrel length: 5 inches
Weight: 38½ oz.
Overall length: 8⅜ inches
Sights: Undercut front; Colt-Elliason adjustable rear
Hammer: Serrated target hammer
Stock: Checkered walnut
Finish: Colt blue

GOVERNMENT MODEL
MKIV/SERIES '70

These full-size automatic pistols, available exclusively with 5-inch barrels, may be had in 45 ACP, 9mm Luger, 38 Super and 22 LR. The Government Model's special features include fixed military sights, grip and thumb safeties, grooved trigger, sand-blasted walnut stocks and Accurizor barrel and bushing.

Caliber	Weight	Overall Length	Magazine Rounds	Finish	Price
45 ACP	38oz.	8⅜ in.	7	Blue	$419.95
				Nickel	448.50
				Satin Nickel	446.95
38 Super	39 oz.	8⅜ in.	9	Blue	434.50
9mm Luger	39 oz.	8⅜ in.	9	Blue	427.50
22 LR/"Ace"	42 oz.	8⅜ in.	10	Blue	454.95

Note: A 22 LR Conversion Unit containing 8 separate components converts 45 ACP and 38 Super Government Models to 22 LR **$246.50**

MK IV/ SERIES '70
GOVERNMENT MODEL

5-inch barrel only

COLT AUTOMATIC PISTOLS

LIGHTWEIGHT COMMANDER

This lightweight, shorter version of the Government Model offers increased ease of carrying with the firepower of the 45 ACP. The Lightweight Commander features alloy frame, fixed-style sights, grooved trigger, lanyard-style hammer and walnut stocks.

Weight	Overall Length	Magazine Rounds	Finish	Price
27 oz.	7⅞ in.	7	Blue	$415.50

LIGHTWEIGHT COMMANDER
4¼-inch barrel only

COMBAT COMMANDER

The semi-automatic Combat Commander, available in 45 ACP, 38 Super or 9 mm Luger, boasts an all-steel frame that supplies the pistol with an extra measure of heft and stability. This outstanding Colt also offers fixed square-notch rear and fixed blade front, lanyard-style hammer and thumb and grip safety.

Caliber	Weight	Overall Length	Magazine Rounds	Finish	Price
45 ACP	36 oz.	7⅞ in.	7	Blue	$419.95
				Satin Nickel	440.50
38 Super	36½ oz.	7⅞ in.	9	Blue	419.95
9mm Luger	36½ oz.	7⅞ in.	9	Blue	427.50

COMBAT COMMANDER
4¼-inch barrel only

EMF DAKOTA REVOLVERS

MODEL SA511E
1873 ARMY REVOLVER
$485.00

Custom engraved single-action revolver. Custom blue finish, one-piece walnut grips. Available with 5½- and 7½-inch barrels, in 357 Mag., 44/40, and 45 L.C.

MODEL SA511
$295.00

Genuine Dakota fast-draw single-action revolver with 4⅝-inch barrel. Exact shooting copy of the original Colt Single Action Revolver. Colt-type hammer with firing pin, beautiful blue finish, case-hardened frame, one-piece walnut grips and solid brass back strap and trigger guard. Available in 22 L.R., 32-20, 357 Mag., 30 MI, 38-40, 44/40, 45 L.C. Optional barrels available in 5½-, 7½- and 12-inch barrels.

DETONICS

DETONICS SUPER COMPACT D/A 9mm PARABELLUM

DETONICS SUPER COMPACT D/A 9mm PARABELLUM

Caliber: 9mm Parabellum, 7-shot magazine
Barrel: 3 inch
Weight: 22 oz. (empty)
Length: 5.7 inches overall, 4 inches high
Stock: Composition stock
Sights: Fixed sights
Features: Stainless Steel construction; ambidextrous firing pin safety; blowback action in double and single action; trigger guard hook for 2-hand shooting.
Price: Approx. **$425.00**

DETONICS SCOREMASTER

DETONICS SCOREMASTER

Caliber: .45 ACP, 7-shot clip; .451 Detonics Magnum, 7-shot clip.
Barrel: 5 inch heavy weight match barrel with recessed muzzle, 6 inch opt.
Weight: 41 oz. (empty)
Length: 8¾-inches overall, 5¼ inches high.
Stock: Pachmayr grips and M.S. housing
Sights: Low-Base Bomar Rear Sight
Features: Stainless Steel construction; self-centering barrel system; patented Detonics recoil system; combat tuned; ambidextrous safety; extended grip safety; National Match tolerances: extended magazine release.
Price: .45 ACP and .451 Detonics Magnum.................**$995.00**

DETONICS .45 PISTOL

DETONICS .45 PISTOL

Caliber: .45 ACP, 6-shot clip; 9mm Para., 7-shot clip; .38 Super, 7-shot clip; .451 Detonics Magnum, 6-shot clip.
Barrel: 3½-inch
Weight: 29 oz. (empty); MK VII is 26 oz.
Length: 6¾-inches overall, 4½-inches high
Stock: Checkered Walnut
Sights: Combat type, fixed; adj. sights available
Features: Has a self-adjusting cone barrel centering system, beveled magazine inlet, "full clip" indicator in base of magazine. Throated barrel and polished feed ramp. Mark MK V, MK VI, MK VII available in 9mm Para. and .38 Super; MC-1 available in 9mm Para..
Price:

MK V, matte stainless, fixed sights	$ 705.00
MK VI, polished stainless, adj. sights	754.00
MK VII, matte stainless, no sights	754.00
MC-1, non-glare combat stainless, fixed sights	632.00
MC-2, non-glare combat stainless, adj. sights	688.00
**9mm Para. and .38 Super; slightly higher	
MK VI and VII .451 Magnum	1280.00

FREEDOM ARMS

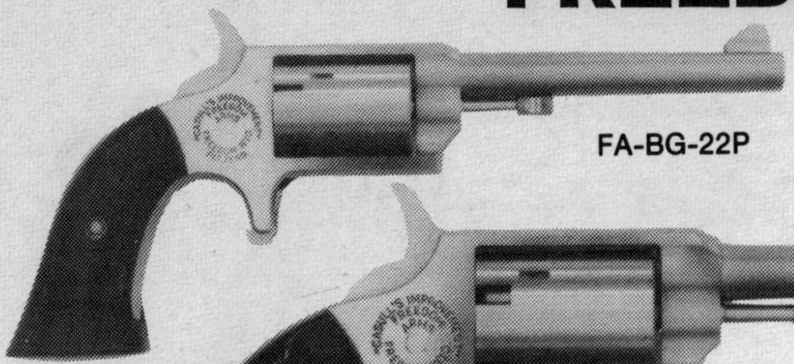

FA-BG-22P

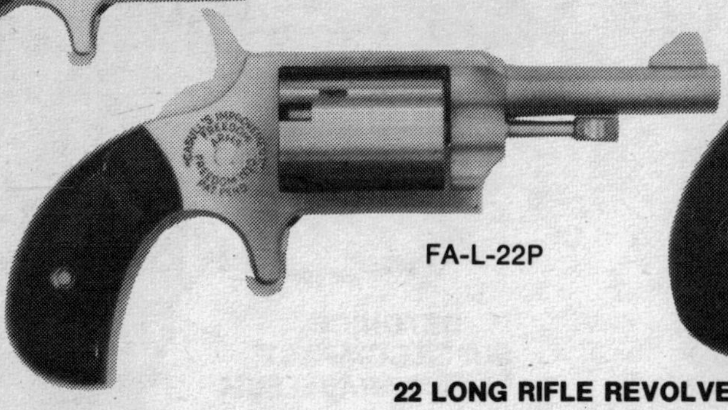

FA-L-22P

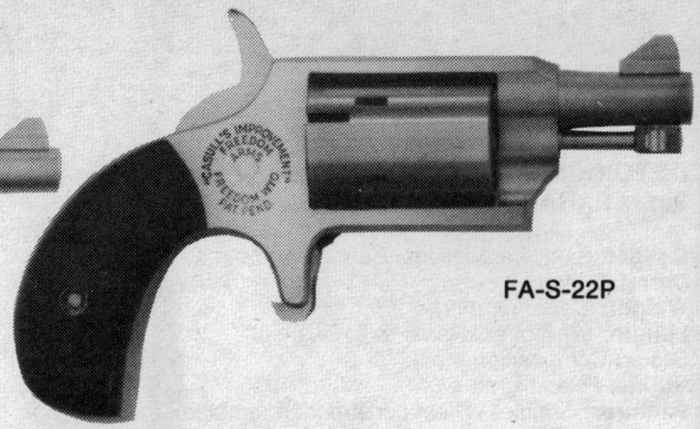

FA-S-22P

Model No.	22 LONG RIFLE REVOLVERS	Price
FA-S-22LR	Stainless Steel Mini-Revolver with 1-in. contoured barrel, partial high gloss finish. Caliber 22 Long Rifle.	$131.50
FA-L-22LR	Stainless Steel Mini-Revolver with ¾-in. contoured barrel, partial high gloss finish. Caliber 22 Long Rifle.	$136.50
FA-BG-22LR	Stainless Steel Mini-Revolver with 3-in. tapered barrel, partial high gloss finish, custom oversized grips. (Boot Gun) Caliber 22 Long Rifle.	$155.50

Above prices include soft zipper pouch.

	NEW 22 PERCUSSION REVOLVERS	
FA-S-22P	Stainless Steel Percussion Mini-Revolver with 1-in. contoured barrel, partial high gloss finish. Caliber 22.	$146.85
FA-L-22P	Stainless Steel Percussion Mini-Revolver with 1¾-in. contoured barrel, partial high gloss finish. Caliber 22.	$151.85
FA-BG-22P	Stainless Steel Percussion Mini-Revolver with 3-in. tapered barrel, partial high gloss finish, custom oversized grips. (Boot Gun) Caliber 22.	$167.90

All Percussion Revolver prices include the following: powder measure, bullet setting tool, twenty bullets and soft zipper pouch.

	22 WIN. MAGNUM REVOLVERS	
FA-S-22M	Stainless Steel Mini-Revolver with 1-in. contoured barrel, partial high gloss finish. Caliber 22 Win. Magnum Rimfire.	$152.50
FA-L-22M	Stainless Steel Mini-Revolver with 1¾-in. contoured barrel, partial high gloss finish. Caliber 22 Win. Magnum Rimfire.	$157.50
FA-BG-22M	Stainless Steel Mini-Revolver with 3-in. tapered barrel, partial high gloss finish and custom oversized grips. (Boot Gun) Caliber 22 Win. Magnum Rimfire.	$176.50
FA-LRCYL	22 Long Rifle cylinder fitted to Magnum Revolver (If Long Rifle cylinder is not ordered with new Magnum Revolver, gun must be returned to factory and a $10.00 fitting charge will be added.)	$22.15

Above prices include soft zipper pouch.

Model No.	.454 CASUL	Price
FA-4547	Standard Production .454 Casull, 7½'' barrel, stainless steel, brush finish, walnut grips.	$695.00
FA-45410	Standard Production .454 Casull, 10'' barrel, stainless steel, brush finish, walnut grips.	$695.00
FA-45412	Standard Production .454 Casull, 12'' barrel, stainless steel, brush finish, walnut grips.	$695.00

All standard production .454 Casull deliveries will commence in June 1983. Due to the tremendous amount of requests for this gun, a 50% deposit is required. Deliveries will be based upon receipt of deposit. Serial nos. will start at D07001.

H&R REVOLVERS

H&R Model 732
6-Shot Revolver

The H&R Model 732 features an easy-loading swing-out cylinder and comes with either 2½ or 4-inch barrel in blue finish.

2½ in.	**$116.50**
2½ in. (walnut grips)	**132.00**
4 in.	**116.50**

SPECIFICATIONS

Caliber: 32 S&W long
Capacity: 6 shots
Grips: Black Cycolac
Barrel Length: 2½ inches and 4 inches
Weight: 23½ oz., and 26 oz.

Action: Single and double
Swing-out cylinder
Sights: 4-inch barrels have windage adjustment on rear sight
Finish: H&R Crown-Lustre Blue

Also available in nickel as Model 733 at $10.00 over the above prices.

H&R Model 800 Series

These swing-out revolvers feature a 3-inch bull barrel. Weight: 27-29 oz.

Model 826 .... **$148.00**
Caliber: .22 Win. Mag.
Capacity: 6 rounds

Models 829/830 .... **$148.00-158.50**
Caliber: 22 LR
Capacity: 9 rounds
Models 832/833 .... **148.00-158.50**
Caliber: 32 S & W Long
Capacity: 6 rounds

H&R Model 999
9-Shot 22 Long Rifle

H&R's Model 999 is a break-open type 9-shot revolver featuring a wide hammer spur for fast and easy cocking. Made with unbreakable coil springs throughout.

With 6-inch fluted rib barrel **$196.00**
With 4-inch fluted rib barrel **196.00**
Engraved Model 999 with 6-inch fluted rib barrel **419.00**

Caliber: 22 short, long, and long rifle
Capacity: 9 shots
Grips: Checkered walnut
Barrel Length: 6 inch ventilated
Weight: 30 oz.

Action: Single and double
Top break-open
Sights: Adjustable front and rear
Finish: H&R Crown-Lustre Blue

H&R REVOLVERS

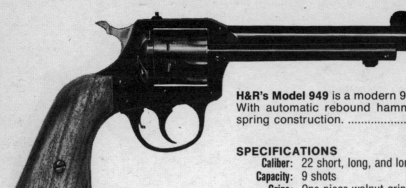

H&R Model 949

9-Shot 22 Long Rifle—Barrel: 5½ inches

H&R's Model 949 is a modern 9-shot, 22 caliber revolver with frontier features. With automatic rebound hammer, wide cocking spur and unbreakable coil spring construction. **$110.00**

SPECIFICATIONS

Caliber:	22 short, long, and long rifle
Capacity:	9 shots
Grips:	One-piece walnut grip
Barrel length:	5½ inches
Weight:	31 oz.

Action:	Single and double. Side loading and ejection
Sights:	Adjustable rear sight; Western type front blade sight
Finish:	H&R Crown-Lustre Blue; (or nickel)—Model 950 **$120.00**

H&R Model 929

9-Shot Revolver

9-Shot 22 Long Rifle—Barrel: 2½ inch, 4 inch & 6 inch

H&R's Model 929 revolver features a 9-shot swing-out cylinder. Made in 22 caliber, it is available with 2½-, 4- and 6-inch barrel lengths. The 4- and 6-inch barrels have windage adjustment on rear sight. Blue finish. 2½ inch, 4 inch and 6 inch **$116.50.** Walnut grips (2½ inches only) **$132.00.**

Model 930 has identical features, but it is finished in durable, protective nickel, and comes with 2½- or 4-inch barrels. Matte finish on top frame. 2½ inch and 4 inch **$127.00.** Walnut grips (2½ inches only) **$142.50**

SPECIFICATIONS

Caliber:	22 short, long, and long rifle
Capacity:	9 shots
Grips:	Black Cycolac
Barrel Length:	2½ inch, 4 inch, and 6 inch
Weight:	22 oz., 26 oz., and 28 oz.

Action:	Single and double Swing-out cylinder
Sights:	4- and 6-inch barrels have windage adjustment on rear sight.
Finish:	H&R Crown-Lustre Blue

H&R Model 649

Convertibles

SPECIFICATIONS
Caliber: 22 Long rifle; 22 Win. Magnum
Capacity: 6 shot
Barrel Length(s): 5½ inches, 7½ inches
Weight: 32 oz.
Sights: Western-type front blade sight; adjustable rear
Action: Single action and double action side loading and ejecting
Grips: One piece wrap around genuine walnut
Finish: H&R Crown Lustre Blue barrel, blue satin-finish frame
Price: $143.00
Model 650: Same as Model 649 except with nickel finish **$154.00**

H&R REVOLVERS

H&R Model STR 022

SPECIFICATIONS
Caliber: 22 blank. **Capacity:** 9 shots. **Grips:** Black Cycolac. **Barrel Length:** 2½ inches. **Weight:** 19 oz. **Action:** Single and double. Pull pin cylinder. **Finish:** Blue satin finished frame...**$79.00**
Available with nickel finish as Model STR 122 .... **84.50**
NOTE: *If a louder report is required, the 6-shot Model STR 032 is available at the same price, and with features identical to those of the Model STR 022. It is chambered for 32 caliber S&W center-fire, blank cartridges* **$79.00**
Available with nickel finish as Model STR 132 .... **84.50**

H&R Model 622

The H&R Model 622 is a 6-shot single and double action 22 caliber revolver which handles 22 long rifle and features a safety rim cylinder. Available in 2½- and 4-inch barrel lengths. Blue finish. **$94.50**

SPECIFICATIONS

Caliber:	22 long rifle		
Capacity:	6 shots	**Action:**	Single and double Pull pin cylinder
Grips:	Black Cycolac. Round Butt	**Sights:**	Blade front sight
Barrel length:	2½ inches and 4 inches	**Finish:**	Satin finished frame. H&R Crown-Lustre Blue barrel
Weight:	20 oz. and 26 oz.		

In 32 S&W Long as Model 632 2½ inches & 4 inches.
Blue Finish **$94.50**

In 22 WMR as Model 642 2½ inches & 4 inches.
Blue Finish **$158.50**

H&R Model 686

Double-action convertible with two cylinders and classic styling in 4½ inch, 5½ inch, 7½ inch, 10 inch and 12 inch barrels. Calibers: 22 & 22 LR and .22 WMRF.

4½ inch, 5½ inch, 7½ inch **$164.50**
10 inch, 12 inch **185.50**

HECKLER & KOCH PISTOLS

**P9S DOUBLE ACTION 45 ACP
& 9MM LUGER**

**VP7OZ DOUBLE-ACTION
AUTOMATIC PISTOL**

HK4 AUTOMATIC PISTOL

The HK4 provides the choice of 380, 32, 25 ACP or 22 LR. A dust-proof self-sealed auto with multiple safety features and double-action trigger.

SPECIFICATIONS:
Calibers: 380 - 22 LR -32 - 25
Length: 6-3/16 inches (157 mm)
Height: 4-21/64 inches (110 mm)
Width at Butt: 1-17/64 inches (32 mm)
Barrel Length: 3-11/32 inches (85 mm)
Sight Radius: 4-49/64 inches (121 mm)
Weight of Pistol: 16, 9 oz. (480 g)
Weight of Magazine: 1,4 oz. (40 g)
Magazine Capacity: 7 8 8 8

Model HK4 (380 cal.) $430.00
Model HK4 380 caliber with 22 caliber conversion kit 480.00
Model HK4 380 caliber with set of 3 conversion kits in
   22LR, 25, and 32 .... 590.00

MODEL P9S Cal. 45 ACP PISTOL

The P9S double action 45 ACP embodies the same features of the P9S 9mm—Polygonal rifling and the delayed roller-locked bolt system in the slide.

SPECIFICATIONS:
Caliber: 45 ACP
Magazine: 7 rounds (plus 1 in chamber)
Barrel Length: 4 inches
Length of Pistol: 7.6 inches
Height of Pistol: 5.4 inches
Sight radius: 5.8 inches
Weight without Magazine: approx. 30 oz.
Weight of Magazines Empty: 2.6 oz.

Model P9S Caliber 45 (w/Combat Sight) $550.00
Also available in 45 Target Model 630.00

HECKLER & KOCH PISTOLS
MODEL P9S AUTOMATIC PISTOL

The P9S is an automatic pistol with a stationary barrel and sliding delayed roller-locked system which reduces recoil. The polygonal twist barrel affords 5% to 6% increase in muzzle velocity.

SPECIFICATIONS:
Caliber: 9 mm parabellum (9 mm Luger)
Weight: 32 oz.
Barrel Length: 4 inches
Overall Length: 7⅝ inches
Magazine Capacity: 9 rounds
Sights: Fixed, square-blade quick-draw front; square-notch rear
Sights Radius: 5¾ inches
Rifling: Polygonal, right twist

Model P9S (w/Combat Sights) $550.00
Also available in Target pistol as Model P9S Target 630.00

VP7OZ DOUBLE-ACTION
AUTOMATIC PISTOL

The VP70 Automatic Pistol is recoil operated, with an inertia bolt and stationary barrel. The receiver is of solid plastic material. The parallel-type revolver trigger (double-action trigger only) and the direct firing pin ignition ensure constant **readiness to fire** and permit the weapon to be safely carried while **loaded and** uncocked until the trigger is pulled. The cartridges are fed from an 18-round magazine.

The sights on the VP70 are based on the light-and-shadow principle. Targets can be aimed at even under unfavorable lighting and vision conditions.

SPECIFICATIONS:
Magazine: 18 rounds
Caliber: 9 mm x 19 (Parabellum)
Sight, Front: Ramp type, channelled
Length of Pistol: 8.03 inches
Height of Pistol: 5.67 inches
Length of Barrel: 4.57 inches
Sight Radius: 6.89 inches
Pistol, without Magazine: 29 oz.
Weight of Magazine Empty: 3.5 oz.

Model VP7OZ (w/Combat Sights & Two 18-Round
Magazines) $399.00

HIGH STANDARD AUTO PISTOLS

VICTOR MILITARY MODEL TARGET PISTOL

High Standard's Victor is available with a restyled rib, and an interchangeable front sight. The rib, which reduces the overall weight of the 5½-inch Victor by three ounces is vented. The 5½-inch Victor, less barrel weight, is now ISU qualified. All models feature push button barrel takedown. The wide target trigger can be adjusted for travel and weight of pull. The rear sight is stationary (mounted on rib), and is micro adjustable for elevation and windage—adjustment screws are positive click spring loaded. The Victor comes fitted with checkered American walnut military grips with thumb rest. Front and backstrap are stippled for a positive grip. Equipped with positive double-action safety, and automatic slide lock, holding the action open after the last round has been fired. Additional features include 24-karat gold-plated trigger, safety and magazine release, with identifying roll marks gold-filled. Available with 5½-inch barrel, in blue finish **$415.00.**

FEATURES AND SPECIFICATIONS: Caliber: 22 L.R. **Capacity:** 10 rounds. **Barrel:** 4½- and 5½-inch, specially molded and contoured barrels. **Sights:** Adjustable micrometer rear sight mounted on rib. **Trigger:** Wide target trigger —2-2¼ lb. pull. **Grips:** Checkered walnut military. **Weight:** 47 oz. for 5½-inch model. **Overall Length:** 9¾ inches for 5½-inch model. **Finish:** Blue.

TROPHY GRADE—MILITARY MODEL AUTOMATICS

MILITARY TROPHY
10 Shot 22 L.R.
5½-inch Bull Barrel
$362.50

MILITARY TROPHY
10 Shot 22 L.R.
7¼-inch Fluted Barrel
$385.00

The High-Standard Trophy grade automatics come in military models only with a choice of a 5½-inch bull barrel, or a 7¼-inch fluted barrel. They differ only in length and style of barrel. The trigger pull is 2 to 2¼ lbs. and has a trigger travel adjustment, enabling the shooter to limit the amount of backward travel of trigger to a minute distance beyond the firing point. Also, there is a trigger-pull adjustment (a positive, click-stop adjusting screw) which adjusts the degree of tension on Trophy and Citation model triggers. A uniform trigger pull is achieved because the sear engages the hammer on the outside periphery, making the engaging surfaces further away from the hammer pivot point. The Trophy models are ground, polished,

buffed and blued and come with a gold, target-size trigger and gold identification. The back and front strap are stippled and the mechanical parts are machined and hand-honed. The rear sight is new in that the bracket is rigidly fixed to the frame—the slide moves through the yoke, making it completely vibration and shock free. The fixed ramp type front sight, dovetail slots in the barrel. The military grip is a faithful duplicate of the Military 45 and comes with thumbrest in checkered American walnut. Automatic slide lock holds action open after last shot is fired. When the safety is in position, the sear is blocked and the sear bar is disconnected, thereby completely disconnecting the firing mechanism. It cannot discharge.

SPECIFICATIONS FOR MILITARY TROPHY MODELS (5½-inch & 7¼-inch BARRELS)

Caliber: 22 Long Rifle
Capacity: 10 shot
Barrel: 5½-inch bull barrel; 7¼-inch fluted barrel
Sights: Stationary bracket type, deep notched rear; fixed ramp type dovetail front sight
Sight Radius: With 5½-inch barrel—8¾ inches; with 7¼-inch barrel —10 inches

Trigger: Wide target trigger, with trigger travel adjustment and trigger-pull adjustment (2-2¼ lbs.)
Safety: Double acting safety. Automatic side lock
Length Overall: With 5½-inch bbl.—9¾ inches; with 7¼-inch bbl.— 11½ inches
Weight: 44.5 ounces for both models
Finish: Ground, polished, buffed and blued

HIGH STANDARD AUTO PISTOLS

CITATION MILITARY MODEL AUTOMATICS

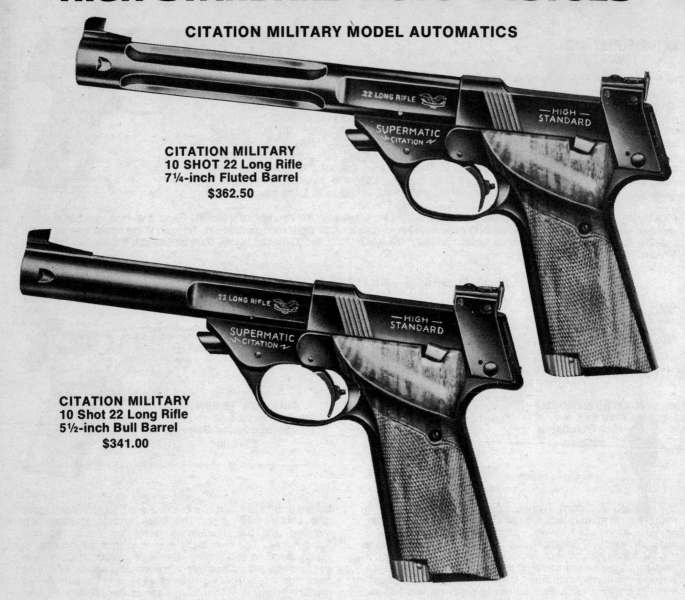

CITATION MILITARY
10 SHOT 22 Long Rifle
7¼-inch Fluted Barrel
$362.50

CITATION MILITARY
10 Shot 22 Long Rifle
5½-inch Bull Barrel
$341.00

The **Supermatic Citation** grade military models are available in two barrel lengths — 5½-inch bull barrel and 7¼-inch fluted barrel. The trigger pull and trigger travel adjustment are standard on all Citation models. The military models have a stationary-type rear sight with a dovetail, fixed ramp-type front sight. Back and front straps are stippled. The grips are checkered American walnut and come with thumbrest, in right- or left-hand design. All Citation models come with positive double-action safety and side lock features. Barrel interchangeability is also standard with all Citation models. Mechanical parts are machined and hand-honed.

SPECIFICATIONS

CALIBER: 22 Long Rifle
CAPACITY: 10 shot
BARREL: 5½-inch bull barrel; 7¼-inch fluted barrel
SIGHTS: Stationary bracket type, deep notched rear; fixed ramp type dovetail front sight
SIGHT RADIUS: With 5½-inch barrel—8¾ inches; with 7¼-inch barrel—10 inches
TRIGGER: Wide target trigger, with trigger travel adjustment and trigger-pull adjustment (2-2¼ lbs.)
SAFETY: Positive, double action. Side lock.
GRIPS: Military-type checkered American walnut with thumbrest
LENGTH OVERALL: With 5½-inch barrel—9¾ inches; with 7¼-inch barrel—11½ inches.
WEIGHT: 44.5 ounces for both models
FINISH: Ground, polished, blued

HIGH STANDARD REVOLVERS

HIGH SIERRA DELUXE
9-Shot 22 Long Rifle

The High Sierra Western-style revolver features a steel frame and comes with a 7-inch octagonal barrel with a custom blue finish, complemented by hand-rubbed walnut grips. Trigger guard and backstraps are gold-plated. Available with dual cylinders (22 L.R./22 Magnum). High Sierra deluxe comes equipped with an adjustable rear sight. High Sierra with adjustable rear sight and two cylinders (22LR/mag) **$290.00**

DOUBLE NINE
9-Shot 22 Long Rifle

The Double Nine with steel frame and 5½-inch barrel comes with interchangeable cylinders for standard 22 L.R. and 22 Magnum ammunition. Features include nine-shot capacity, double action and swing-out cylinders. Available with adjustable rear sight in blue finish. **$250.00.**

The Longhorn Deluxe: Same as Double Nine except with 9½-inch "Buntline" barrel. Available in trophy blue with dual cylinders with adjustable rear sights **$255.00.**

Western Revolvers (9-shot) Double Action

MODEL NO.	NAME	FEATURES	FINISH	CAL.	BBL. LGTH.
9324	Double Nine Deluxe	Adj. Rear Sight	Trophy Blue	2 Cyl 22 LR/mag	5½"
9328	Longhorn Deluxe	Adj. Rear Sight	Trophy Blue	2 Cyl 22 LR/mag	9½"
9375	High Sierra Deluxe	Adj. Rear Sight	Trophy Blue	2 Cyl 22 LR/mag	7" Oct

HIGH STANDARD PISTOLS

SPORT KING

Model: 9258 & 9259
Caliber: 22 L.R.
Barrel: 9258—4½ inches
   9259—6¾ inches
Weight: 4½ inches—39 oz.
   6¾ inches—42 oz.
Overall Length: 4½ inches—9¼ inches
   6¾ inches—11½ inches
Overall Height: 5 inches
Sights: Front—⅛ inch blade; Rear—⅛ inch square notch, adjustable for windage
Grips: Checkered walnut
Finish: Blue
Price: $290.00

MODEL 10-X
Custom-Made Target Pistol

Model: 9372
Caliber: 22 L.R.
Barrel: 5½-inch bull barrel
Sights: Adjustable rear sight mounted on the frame and free of the slide
Grips: Walnut
Finish: Non-reflective blue
Features: Military grip; target trigger with overtravel adjustment; trigger pull adjustment; stippled frontstrap and backstrap; automatic slide lock and two extra magazines
Price: $714.00

IVER JOHNSON PISTOLS

300 PONY

X300 PONY

All-steel, the X300 Pony is chambered for 380 ACP. The magazine holds six rounds. For maximum security, the pistol features an inertia firing pin, and the large thumb safety cams the hammer out of contact with the sear. The windage-adjustable rear sight is rounded on its outer dimensions so it won't snag on clothing. Grips are of solid walnut, and the backstop is extra long to protect a hand from being bitten by the hammer.
Length: 6 inches; **Height:** 4 inches

X300 PONY .380 AUTO PISTOL						
Model	Grips	Finish	Cal.	Barrel	Sights	Price
PO380B	Walnut	Blue	380	3 in.	Adjustable	$260.00
PO380M	Walnut	Military	380	3 in.	Adjustable	260.00
PO380N	Walnut	Nickel	380	3 in.	Adjustable	270.00
TP-25	Walnut	Blue	250	3 in.	Non-adjustable	140.00
TP-22	Walnut	Blue	22	3 in.	Non-adjustable	140.00

INTERARMS VIRGINIAN REVOLVERS

VIRGINIAN DRAGOON

Precision-machined from 4140 steel throughout. Rich, traditional color, case-treated frame, lock-fitted, spring-loaded floating firing pin. Durable, heavy-duty coiled mainspring. Standard model features classic frontier field sights. Fully adjustable rear sight and ramp-type Patridge front blade w/white dot optional for fast targeting in low-light-level conditions. Manufactured by Interarms Industries, Inc.

MODEL/FINISH	CALIBER/BARREL LENGTH	MODEL NO.	PRICE
VIRGINIAN DRAGOON SILHOUETTE MODEL	44 Magnum, 7½ in. Barrel	VAV15162	
Stainless Steel with Precision Metallic Silhouette Target Sight	44 Magnum, 8⅜ inch Barrel	VAV15172	**$425.00**
COMPLETE WITH EXTRA PACHMAYR RUBBER TARGET GRIPS AND TEST TARGET	44 Magnum, 10½ inch Barrel	VAV15182	
VIRGINIAN DRAGOON, ENGRAVED, BLUE	44 Magnum, 6 in. Barrel	VAV15136	
VIRGINIAN DRAGOON, ENGRAVED, BLUE	44 Magnum, 7 in. Barrel	VAV15166	**625.00**
VIRGINIAN DRAGOON, ENGRAVED, BLUE	45 Colt, 6 in. Barrel	VAV15036	
VIRGINIAN DRAGOON, ENGRAVED, BLUE	45 Colt, 7½ in. Barrel	VAV15066	
VIRGINIAN DRAGOON, ENGRAVED, STAINLESS STEEL	44 Magnum, 6 in. Barrel	VAV15137	
VIRGINIAN DRAGOON, ENGRAVED, STAINLESS STEEL	44 Magnum, 7½ in. Barrel	VAV15167	**625.00**
VIRGINIAN DRAGOON, ENGRAVED, STAINLESS STEEL	45 Colt, 6 in. Barrel	VAV15037	
VIRGINIAN DRAGOON, ENGRAVED, STAINLESS STEEL	45 Colt, 7½ in. Barrel	VAV15067	
VIRGINIAN DRAGOON "DEPUTY" MODEL	357 Magnum, 5 in. Barrel	VAV15700	
Blue and Color-Case Treated with Fixed Sight	45 Colt, 5 in. Barrel	VAV15000	**285.00**
	44 Magnum, 6 in. Barrel	VAV15100	
VIRGINIAN DRAGOON "DEPUTY" MODEL	357 Magnum, 5 in. Barrel	VAV15712	
Stainless Steel with Fixed Sight	45 Colt, 5 in. Barrel	VAV15012	**285.00**
	44 Magnum, 6 in. Barrel	VAV15112	
VIRGINIAN DRAGOON, STANDARD, BLUE	44 Magnum, 6 in. Barrel	VAV15130	
VIRGINIAN DRAGOON, STANDARD, BLUE	44 Magnum, 7½ in. Barrel	VAV15160	
VIRGINIAN DRAGOON, STANDARD, BLUE	44 Magnum, 8⅜ in. Barrel	VAV15170	
VIRGINIAN DRAGOON, STANDARD, BLUE	45 Colt, 5 in. Barrel	VAV15010	
VIRGINIAN DRAGOON, STANDARD, BLUE	45 Colt, 6 in. Barrel	VAV15030	**295.00**
VIRGINIAN DRAGOON, STANDARD, BLUE	45 Colt, 7½ in. Barrel	VAV15060	
VIRGINIAN DRAGOON, STANDARD, BLUE	357 Magnum, 6 in. Barrel	VAV15730	
VIRGINIAN DRAGOON, STANDARD, STAINLESS STEEL	44 Magnum, 6 in. Barrel	VAV15131	
VIRGINIAN DRAGOON, STANDARD, STAINLESS STEEL	44 Magnum, 7½ in. Barrel	VAV15161	
VIRGINIAN DRAGOON, STANDARD, STAINLESS STEEL	44 Magnum, 8⅜ in. Barrel	VAV15171	**295.00**
VIRGINIAN DRAGOON, STANDARD, STAINLESS STEEL	45 Colt, 6 in. Barrel	VAV15031	
VIRGINIAN DRAGOON, STANDARD, STAINLESS STEEL	45 Colt, 7½ in. Barrel	VAV15061	

LLAMA REVOLVERS

"Super Comanche"
44 Magnum $334.95
available in 6- and 8½-inch barrels

"Super Comanche"
357 Magnum $299.95
available in 4-, 6- and 8½-inch barrels

SUPER COMANCHE, LLAMA'S ALL-NEW 44 MAGNUM DOUBLE ACTION ... THE MOST RUGGED, ACCURATE REVOLVER BUILT

Three years of intensive product development and generations of prototypes evolved before final specifications were set for this all-new Super Comanche. If ever a handgun was conceived, designed and built to fit the exacting requirements of big-bore handgunners, this one is it.

Take the frame for example: it's massive. The most solid, most rugged of any other double-action revolver. Its weight and balance are such that the heavy recoil generated by the powerful 44 Magnum cartridge is easily and comfortably controlled, even when rapid firing in the double-action mode. In the single-action mode, the broad, serrated hammer-spur makes cocking easy and fast.

Instead of a single cylinder latch, the new Llama has two. In addition to the conventional center pin at the rear of the ratchet, there's a second latch up front which locks the crane to the frame at the underside of the barrel ring. Using this two-lock system, the cylinder and crane are locked in a more positive manner than can be achieved using the common detent/ball arrangement found on other revolvers.

Only coil springs are used throughout. Not only does this provide added strength in a critical area, but the added rigidity raises the gun's accuracy potential as well. Also aiding accuracy is the heavyweight barrel measuring .815-inch in diameter. A matte-finish rib reduces glare and helps get on target faster.

But building the strongest and most accurate revolver were only two of the three basic goals Llama engineers set for themselves; they also wanted to build the safest. To that end, the hammer is mounted on an eccentric cam, the position of which is controlled by the trigger. Only when the latter is fully depressed can the firing pin contact the primer. Accidental discharge is virtually impossible.

LLAMA REVOLVERS

NEW!
LLAMA "Super Comanche" 44 Magnum Revolver Specifications

CALIBER:	44 Magnum	44 Magnum
BARREL LENGTH:	6"	8½"
NUMBER OF SHOTS:	6 shots	
FRAME:	Forged high tensile strength steel	
ACTION:	Double action	
TRIGGER:	Smooth extra wide	
HAMMER:	Wide spur, deep positive serrations	
SIGHTS:	Rear-click adjustable for windage and elevation, leaf serrated to cut down on glare. Front-ramped blade.	
SIGHT RADIUS:	8"	10⅜"
GRIPS:	Oversized target, walnut. Checkered	
WEIGHT:	3 lbs., 2 ozs.	3 lbs., 8 ozs.
OVER-ALL LENGTH:	11¾"	14½"
FINISH:	High polished, deep blue	
SAFETY FEATURE:	The hammer is mounted on an eccentric cam, the position of which is controlled by the trigger. Only when the latter is fully depressed can the firing pin contact the primer.	

NEW!
LLAMA "Super Comanche" 357 Magnum Revolver

The 357 ammunition that is manufactured today is becoming more and more powerful. These hotter loads create additional recoil that causes undesirable battering of internal parts and excessive stretching of the frame. As a result, shooting accuracy as well as the average firing life of the traditional 357 has been decreased.

Llama engineers built this all new 357 on the big, brawny Super Comanche frame. This frame, forged for strength, absorbs the maximum amount of recoil, reduces muzzle jump, provides greater balance, control and accuracy, and a longer firing life.

For double added safety, Llama engineered an eccentric cam-hammer system that makes accidental discharge virtually impossible, and incorporated the "old reliable" triple lock crane cylinder support for additional locking strength.

And to satisfy those shooters who prefer a lighter, more compact gun, Llama engineers designed a second all-new 357, built on a medium weight frame, which also features the eccentric cam-hammer system, perfect balance and true accuracy.

Specifications

CALIBER:	357 Magnum		
BARREL LENGTH:	4"	6"	8½"
NUMBER OF SHOTS:	6 shots		
FRAME:	Forged high tensile strength steel		
ACTION:	Conventional double action		
TRIGGER:	Smooth extra wide		
HAMMER:	Wide spur, deep positive serrations		
SIGHTS:	Rear-click adjustable for windage and elevation, leaf serrated to cut down on glare. Front-ramped blade.		
SIGHT RADIUS:	6"	8"	10⅜"
GRIPS:	Oversized target, walnut. Checkered		
WEIGHT:	3 lbs.	3 lbs., 6 ozs.	3 lbs., 12 ozs.
OVER-ALL LENGTH:	9⅞"	11⅞"	14½"
FINISH:	High polished, deep blue		
SAFETY FEATURE:	The hammer is mounted on an eccentric cam, the position of which is controlled by the trigger. Only when the latter is fully depressed can the firing pin contact the primer.		

LLAMA REVOLVERS

NEW! *LLAMA* "Comanche"®

IN REVOLVERS TODAY, THERE'S A NEW NAME IN EXCELLENCE. IT'S THE LLAMA COMANCHE® SERIES. Designed for you and incorporating every feature worth having to make these Llamas the finest revolvers made today . . . at any price.

All the Comanche models—22 L.R. and the sledgehammer 357 Magnum caliber utilize massively forged solid-steel frames for tremendous strength and enduring reliability.

Up front, Llama added a precision-bored heavyweight barrel of target quality, complete with a solid shroud to protect the ejector rod, and a raised ventilated-rib that dissipates heat from the barrel to give you a clear, sharp sight image even when the action gets hot.

On the inside, everything is finely fitted and polished, for a double action that's slick and smooth, and a single-action trigger pull that's light, crisp and clean. Llama gave all Comanches a floating firing pin for greater safety and dependability.

Comanche
357 Mag.
Satin Chrome
4 in. and 6 in.

Comanche
357 Mag. in
Standard Blue
4- and 6-inch barrels

22 L.R. Standard Blue 6 in.	$199.95
357 Mag. Standard Blue 4 in., 6 in.	234.95
357 Mag. Satin Chrome 4 in., 6 in.	309.95

Specifications

	357 Magnum	.22 L.R.
CALIBERS:	357 Magnum	.22 L.R.
BARREL LENGTH:	4 and 6-inch	6-inch
NUMBER OF SHOTS:	6 shots	6 shots
FRAME:	Forged high hensile strength steel. Serrated front and back strap.	
ACTION:	Double-action. Floating firing pin.	
TRIGGER:	Wide grooved target trigger. Case-hardened.	
HAMMER:	Wide spur target hammer with serrated gripping surface. Case-hardened.	
SIGHTS:	Square notch rear sight with windage and elevation adjustments; serrated quick-draw front sight on ramp.	
SIGHT RADIUS:	With 4-inch barrel—5¾"; with 6-inch barrel—7¾".	
GRIPS:	Oversized target, walnut. Checkered.	
WEIGHT:	w/4" bbl.—2 lbs., 4 ozs. w/6" bbl.—2 lbs., 7 ozs.	2 lbs., 8 ozs.
OVER-ALL LENGTH:	With 4-inch barrel—9¼"; with 6-inch barrel—11".	
FINISH:	High-polished, deep blue. Deluxe models; satin chrome (.357 w/4" & 6" bbl.)	
SAFETY FEATURE:	The hammer is mounted on an eccentric cam, the position of which is controlled by the trigger. Only when the latter is fully depressed can the firing pin contact the primer.	

LLAMA AUTOMATIC PISTOLS

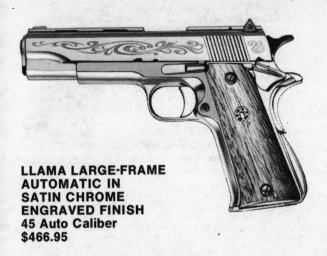

LLAMA LARGE-FRAME AUTOMATIC IN SATIN CHROME ENGRAVED FINISH
45 Auto Caliber
$466.95

9mm & 45 Std. Blue $249.95

Llama's time-proven design, enhanced by individual hand-fitting and hand-honing of all moving parts, has resulted in handguns that provide smooth operation, pinpoint accuracy and rugged reliability under the toughest conditions.

Deluxe features, all indicative of the extra care lavished on each gun, are found in all Llama handguns.

The small-frame Llama models, available in 22 L.R., 32 Auto. and 380 Auto., are impressively compact handguns. All frames are precision machined of high strength steel, yet weigh a featherlight 23 ounces. A full complement of safeties . . . side lever, half-cock and grip . . . is incorporated.

Every small-frame Llama is complete with ventilated rib, wide-spur serrated target-type hammer and adjustable rear sight.

The large-frame Llama models, available in potent 45 ACP and 9mm Parabellum, are completely crafted of high strength steel,

LLAMA LARGE-FRAME AUTOMATIC WITH DEEP BLUE FINISH
9mm & 45 Auto Caliber
$325.00

LLAMA SMALL-FRAME AUTOMATIC WITH DEEP BLUE FINISH
22 Caliber $200.95
32 & 380 Calibers 283.95

22 Std. Blue $166.95
380 Std. Blue   199.95
32 Std. Blue   216.95

LLAMA AUTOMATIC PISTOLS

machined and polished to perfection. Complete with ventilated rib for maximum heat dissipation, wide-spur checkered target-type hammer, adjustable rear sight and genuine walnut grips, make these truly magnificent firearms.

In addition to High Polished Deep Blue, these superb handguns are available in deluxe fancy finishes:

- High Polished Deep Blue Engraved (380 Auto., 45 ACP)
- Handsome Satin Chrome (22 L.R., 380 Auto., 45 ACP)
- Satin Chrome Engraved (380 Auto., 45 ACP)

Extra Magazine **$24.95**

**LLAMA LARGE-FRAME
AUTOMATIC PISTOL IN
BLUE ENGRAVED FINISH**
45 Auto Caliber
$433.95

**LLAMA LARGE-FRAME
AUTOMATIC PISTOL IN
SATIN CHROME FINISH**
45 Auto Caliber
$334.95

**LLAMA OMNI 9mm
DOUBLE-ACTION AUTOMATIC**
$434.95

LLAMA AUTOMATIC PISTOLS

LLAMA SMALL-FRAME AUTOMATIC PISTOL IN BLUE ENGRAVED FINISH
380 Caliber
$358.95

LLAMA SMALL-FRAME AUTOMATIC PISTOL IN SATIN CHROME FINISH
22 Caliber $249.95
380 Caliber   249.95

LLAMA SMALL-FRAME AUTOMATIC WITH SATIN CHROME ENGRAVED FINISH
380 Caliber
$366.95

LLAMA Automatic Pistol Specifications

TYPE:	Small Frame Auto Pistols			Large Frame Auto Pistols	
CALIBERS:	22 L.R.	32 Auto.	380 Auto.	9mm	45 Auto.
FRAME:	Precision machined from high strength steel. Serrated front strap, checkered (curved) backstrap.			Precision machined from high strength steel. Plain front strap, checkered (curved) backstrap.	
TRIGGER:	Serrated.			Serrated.	
HAMMER:	External. Wide spur, serrated.			External. Wide spur, serrated.	
OPERATION:	Straight blow-back.			Locked breech.	
LOADED CHAMBER INDICATOR:	No	Yes	Yes	Yes	Yes
SAFETIES:	Side lever thumb safety, half-cock safety			Side lever thumb safety, half-cock safety.	
GRIPS:	Modified thumbrest black plastic grips.			Genuine walnut on blue models. Genuine teakwood on satin chrome, satin chrome engraved and blue engraved models.	
SIGHTS:	Square notch rear, and Patridge-type front, screw adjustable rear sight for windage.			Square notch rear, and Patridge-type front, screw adjustable rear sight for windage.	
SIGHT RADIUS:	4¼"			6¼"	
MAGAZINE CAPACITY:	8-shot	7-shot	7-shot	9-shot	7-shot
WEIGHT:	23 ounces			2 lbs., 8 ozs.	
BARREL LENGTH:	3¹¹/₁₆"			5"	
OVER ALL LENGTH:	6½"			8½"	
HEIGHT:	4⅜"			5¼"	
FINISH:	Std. models; High-polished, deep blue. Deluxe models; satin chrome (22, 380, 45); satin chrome engraved (380, 45); blue engraved (380, 45)				

LLAMA AUTOMATIC PISTOLS

LLAMA Omni Double Action Automatic Pistol Specifications

TYPE:	Double Action Automatic Pistol	
CALIBER:	45 Auto	9mm
FRAME:	Precision machined from high tensile strength steel	
TRIGGER:	D A high strength steel	
HAMMER ACTION:	incorporates a bearing ball action hammer shoe	
OPERATION:	Split double action w/2 sear bars—one for double action and one for single action	
SAFETIES:	3 safeties—1 positive manual safety and 2 automatic safeties	
GRIPS:	Black ABS	
SIGHTS:	Front—ramped blade Rear—adjustable for windage and elevation	Front—ramped blade Rear—drift adjustable
SIGHT RADIUS:	6¹¹⁄₁₆″	6⅛″
MAGAZINE CAPACITY:	7 rounds	13 rounds
WEIGHT:	40 ounces	40 ounces
FIRING PIN:	Two-piece articulated firing pin	
BARREL LENGTH:	4¼″	4¼″
OVERALL LENGTH:	7¾″ (8″ with hammer cocked)	8″ (8¼″ with hammer cocked)
MAX. HEIGHT:	5⅜″	5½″
FINISH:	High polished deep blue	

OMNI 45

LLAMA OMNI

Omni 45 Std. Blue $533.95
Omni 9mm $434.95

Omni breaks the barrier in handgun design and function by incorporating every advanced feature offered by 20th century technology ... and more.

Llama's Omni is the one double action that dared go beyond conventional gun concepts and traditions to bring you, the American shooter, the highest standards of quality, safety, accuracy, reliability, dependability and durability. So durable, in fact, that we have enough confidence in our engineering and design accomplishments to guarantee the firing pin for life!

Extra magazine, 9mm (13 shot) **$31.95**
Extra magazine, 45 (7 shot) 26.95

Omni represents years of strenuous laboratory and field research and development, and independent testing by H.P. White Laboratories. Once you've had Omni in your hand and cycled its incredibly smooth action and trigger, you'll know the ultimate in gun technology.

LLAMA AUTOMATIC PISTOLS

OMNI FEATURE #1

DESIGN OBJECTIVE: To provide the most efficient, durable sear bar mechanism for greatest reliability.

BACKGROUND: In all other DA pistols you find just one sear bar (the linkage connecting the trigger and the sear). This one sear bar is a compromise as it must perform two distinct, stressful functions: cycle the firing mechanism in both the single and double action modes.

OMNI SOLUTION & BENEFITS: The new Omni's patented design mechanism avoids compromise by providing two sear bars. Each designed mechanism avoids compromise by providing two sear bars. Each is designed to excel at only one individual function:

   a. In the single-action mode, the left-side sear bar releases the already cocked hammer when the trigger is pulled.
   b. In the double-action mode, the right-side sear bar smoothly accomplishes the cocking of the hammer during the trigger pull.

Only Omni offers two separate and distinct sear bars to perform two separate functions. There is no compromise. This is the most durable trigger/sear linkage system for improved accuracy and greatest reliability in any DA pistol.

OMNI FEATURE #2

DESIGN OBJECTIVE: Create a firing mechanism that guarantees the smoothest action going.

BACKGROUND: In all other self-loading pistols, the hammer carrier mechanism assumes a slightly different position after each shot. This results in the following negative factors: inconsistent trigger pulls; excessive friction; different slide velocities; more wear and tear; and less reliability.

OMNI SOLUTION & BENEFITS: To correct all of these negative factors, Llama engineers placed 20 bearing balls in two columns, ten each, on either side of the newly created hammer carrier mechanism. This effectively eliminated all undesirable lateral motion of the hammer carrier mechanism greatly reducing unwanted friction, creating the optimal slide velocity. This guarantees the most effortless and smoothest action going.

Prove it to yourself. Manually cycle the slide and see how much less effort and energy is required over all other DA's. This same benefit holds true in the DA mode. There is also less wear and tear on the shooting mechansim, greater shooting life, incredible durability and reliability. No other DA but the Omni has this micro-bearing-ball system and no other one will, because it's patented.

OMNI FEATURE #3

DESIGN OBJECTIVE: To create a firing pin assembly so strong it could be guaranteed for life.

BACKGROUND: Common to all DA pistols is a one-piece tapered firing pin which is prone to breakage. The break normally occurs at the weakest point ... where the thin forward section of the firing pin joins the thicker rear section.

OMNI SOLUTION & BENEFITS: Through years of laboratory and field testing. Llama engineers solved the weakness problem of the one-piece firing pin. They developed a two-piece firing pin mechanism by "pre-breaking" the firing pin at its weakest point. To further assure the most reliable firing pin, a ball joint has been inserted between the two separate sections, thus, eliminating all vibration and stress transfer. Omni offers you the strongest known firing pin assembly available ... **guaranteed for life.**

LLAMA AUTOMATIC PISTOLS

OMNI FEATURE #4

DESIGN OBJECTIVE: To develop the strongest lock-up system for your greatest safety.

BACKGROUND: The conventional lock-up system found on all other DA pistols was not good enough for this revolutionary new Omni.

OMNI SOLUTION & BENEFITS: Llama engineers designed a superior barrel lock-up mechanism which yields greater strength and safety. This was accomplished by increasing the shear area (the area were the base of the locking lug joins the barrel) a full 50%. This innovative design maximizes the strength and rigidity of the two locking contact points. It is the strongest lock-up system, and virtually the safest, found on any pistol.

OMNI FEATURE #5

DESIGN OBJECTIVE: To redesign conventional rifling for higher, more uniform velocity and accuracy.

BACKGROUND: In all guns with conventional rifling, the trailing edges of the lands (the raised portions between the grooves of rifled bores) create excessive friction, unnecessary engraving of the bullet and increased barrel temperature.

OMNI SOLUTION & BENEFITS: Aiming to reduce the negative factors of conventional rifling, Llama engineers invented Buttress-Rifling. This innovative rifling was accomplished by streamlining the trailing edge of each land which minimizes friction between bullet and barrel contact surface; reduced friction; lowered barrel temperature and great accuracy.

The Omni, light years ahead in design and features, offers you shooting accuracy that cannot be found in any other double action.

Once you've held an Omni in your hand, you'll know why gun experts and enthusiasts have labeled the Omni the ultimate self-loading pistol of the century.

LUGER 22 AUTOMATIC PISTOLS

New Steel Frame

LUGER AUTOMATIC PISTOL
22 LR 4½-inch Barrel
$199.95

Chambered for the economical 22 LR, the newest Luger handles both standard and high velocity cartridges interchangeably. The Luger features a one-piece solidly forged and machined steel frame for total strength and accuracy, and all moving parts are engineered for steel-to-steel contact.

Luger Accessories:

Extra Luger Magazines $21.95
Luger Magazine Charger 4.95
Standard Luger Holster 21.95
Basket Weave Luger Holster 24.95
Carrying Case 21.95

LUGER 22 AUTOMATIC PISTOL

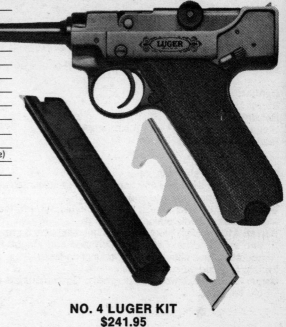

MODELS:	Standard Luger
CALIBER:	22 Long Rifle, standard or high-velocity
MAGAZINE:	Ten-shot capacity clip-type magazine
BARREL LENGTH:	4½"
SIGHTS:	Square bladed front sight with square notch, stationary rear sight
SIGHT RADIUS:	8"
FRAME:	High tensile strength steel
GRIPS:	Genuine American black walnut, fully checkered
APPROX. WEIGHT:	1 lb. 13½ ozs.
OVER ALL LENGTH:	8⅞"
SAFETY:	All models; Positive side lever safety, (Green Dot-Safe) (Red Dot-Fire)
FINISH:	Non-reflecting black

LIMITED EDITION
ONE-OF-ONE THOUSAND

A. F. STOEGER
AMERICAN EAGLE LUGER
$449.95

A Limited Edition of A. F. Stoeger's American Eagle Luger-first offered in 1923-serial numbered "1" through "1000"

• Limited production of original style A. F. Stoeger Lugar • Hand-polished with Deluxe blue finish • Receiver ring features gold roll-engraving of American Eagle motif; right side of frame gold roll-engraved with A. F. Stoeger markings • Gold safe marking back of frame by safety switch • Solid machined tapered pins and new style barrel; top of bolt contoured like A. F. Stoeger original • Handcrafted cherry hardwood fitted case with red lining and leather-like gold embossed A. F. Stoeger Luger logo on name plate.

Included in Case: Mark I magazine; Luger cleaning tool (as original)

Grips: Hand-selected from fine Herret stocks; Deluxe, individually hand-fitted

Serial Numbering: Front of frame as on A. F. Stoeger Lugers; numbers start with "1" and carry suffix "C" denoting Commemorative

Caliber: 22 Long Rifle, standard or high-velocity

NO. 4 LUGER KIT
$241.95

No. 4 Luger Kit contains Luger, complete with leather holster, easy loading magazine charger and extra magazine.

NO. 4 LUGER COMBO
$249.95

No. 4 Luger Combo (not illustrated) contains everything but the ammo. Includes Luger, leather holster, easy loading magazine charger, extra magazine and carrying case.

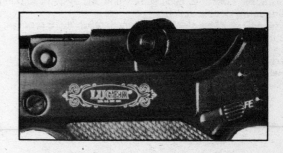

LIMITED EDITION ONE-OF-FIFTY

A. F. STOEGER
HAND-ENGRAVED
AMERICAN EAGLE LUGER
$915.95

Special features:
• Hand engraved by one of America's foremost firearms engravers
• Highly polished Deluxe Deep Blue finish
• Individually hand numbered "1" through "50"

ODI AUTOMATIC PISTOLS

VIKING COMBAT $579.00

Caliber: 9mm
Barrel Length: 4¼-inches
Hammer: Ring type
Weight: Balances at 2 lbs., 4 oz. (empty)
Magazine Capacity: 9 rounds

Magazine: 410 stainless steel
Construction: 17-4 and 400 Series stainless steels selected for maximum performance and reliability.
Operations: Locked breech semi-automatic system, featuring **Seecamp** double action.
Barrel: 410 stainless steel for maximum reliability. 6 grooves, 1 turn in 16 inches. Each barrel proofed and magno-flux inspected. Assembled weapon is function-fired.
Finish: Brushed satin, natural stainless.
Grips: Genuine teakwood for durability. Other materials available on request.

VIKING COMBAT

VIKING COMBAT $579.00

Caliber: .45 ACP
Barrel Length: 4¼-inches
Hammer: Ring type
Weight: Balances at 2 lbs., 4 oz. (empty)
Magazine Capacity: 7 rounds

Magazine: 410 stainless steel
Construction: 17-4 and 400 Series stainless steels selected for maximum performance and reliability.
Operations: Locked breech semi-automatic system, featuring **Seecamp** double action.
Barrel: 410 stainless steel for maximum reliability. 6 grooves, 1 turn in 16 inches. Each barrel proofed and magno-flux inspected. Assembled weapon is function-fired.
Finish: Brushed satin, natural stainless.
Grips: Genuine teakwood for durability. Other materials available on request.

VIKING

VIKING $579.00

Caliber: .45 ACP
Barrel Length: 5 inches
Hammer: Spur type
Weight: Balances at 2 lbs., 7 oz. (empty)
Magazine Capacity: 7 rounds

Caliber: 9mm
Barrel Length: 5 inches
Hammer: Spur type
Weight: Balances at 2 lbs., 7 oz. (empty)
Magazine Capacity: 9 rounds

Magazine: 410 stainless steel
Construction: 17-4 and 400 Series stainless steels selected for maximum performance and reliability.
Operations: Locked breech semi-automatic system, featuring **Seecamp** double action.
Barrel: 410 stainless steel for maximum reliability. 6 grooves, 1 turn in 16 inches. Each barrel proofed and magno-flux inspected. Assembled weapon is function-fired.
Finish: Brushed satin, natural stainless.
Grips: Genuine teakwood for durability. Other materials available on request.

ROSSI REVOLVERS

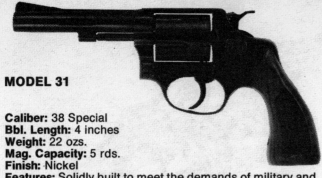

MODEL 31

Caliber: 38 Special
Bbl. Length: 4 inches
Weight: 22 ozs.
Mag. Capacity: 5 rds.
Finish: Nickel
Features: Solidly built to meet the demands of military and police service. Swing out 5-shot cylinder. Target trigger and wide-spur target hammer. Medium weight 4-inch barrel w/ramp front sight. Checkered wood grips. Crisp double-action and exceptional balance.
Model 31, blue **$150.00**
Model 31, nickel **155.00**

MODEL 51 SPORTSMAN

Caliber: 22 LR
Bbl. Length: 6 inches
Finish: Deep blue
Features: Checkered wood grips. Rear sight fully adjustable.
Model 51 Sportsman **$165.00**

MODELS 68, 69 & 70

Caliber: 22 short—mod. 70
  32 S&W—mod. 69
  38 Special—mod. 68
Bbl. Length: 3 inches
Weight: 22 ozs.
Mag. Capacity: 6 rds.—22 L.R. & 32 S&W; 5 rds.—38 Spec.
Features: Rugged, all-steel small frame. Smooth double-action pull and combat styling. Ramp front sight and low profile adjustable rear sight. Thumb-latch operated swingout cylinder. Checkered wood grips.

Model 68, blue	**$150.00**;	nickel	**$155.00**
Model 69, blue	145.00;	nickel	150.00
Model 70, blue	155.00;	nickel	160.00

RUGER REVOLVERS

POLICE SERVICE-SIX
357 Mag., 38 Special & 9mm

The Ruger Police Service-Six has all of the basic features built into the Ruger Security-Six revolvers. The grip of both the Police Service-Six and the Security-Six has been subtly redesigned to permit rapid, accurate double-action firing without any tendency for the revolver to shift during operation. The new Police Service-Six differs from the Security-Six in that it has fixed (non-adjustable) sights to eliminate any potential for accidental sight misalignment with resulting error in aim, and comes in 2¾-inch and 4-inch barrel lengths but not in 6-inch length. 357 Mag. w/2¾- & 4-inch barrel, blue only.

357 Mag., blue, 2¾-inch bbl., 4-inch bbl. &
  4-inch heavy bbl. **$217.50**
357 Mag., stainless steel, 4-inch bbl. &
  4-inch heavy bbl. **$239.50**
38 Special, blue, 4-inch bbl. 217.50
38 Special, stainless steel, 4-inch bbl. &
  4-inch heavy bbl. 239.50
9mm, blue, 4-inch bbl. 236.50

SECURITY-SIX 357 Mag.

SPECIFICATIONS: Six Shots. Calibers: 357 Magnum caliber (handles 38 Spec.), 38 Special. **Barrel:** 2¾-, 4- and 6-inch, five-groove-rifling 18¾-inch right twist. **Weight:** 33½ ounces (4-inch barrel). **Overall Length:** 9¼ inches (4-inch barrel). **Sights:** Ruger adjustable rear (elevation and windage adjustments). Front sight is ⅛ inch wide, serrated. **Grips:** Checkered walnut, semi-target style. **Finish:** Polished all over and blued. Stainless steel models have brushed satin finish.

357 Mag., blue, 2¾-inch bbl., 4-inch bbl.,
  4-inch heavy bbl. & 6-inch bbl. **$247.00**
357 Mag., stainless steel, 2¾-inch bbl., 4-inch bbl.,
  4-inch heavy bbl., & 6-inch bbl. 270.50
357 Mag., blue, big grip, 4-inch heavy bbl.&
  6-inch bbl. 266.00
357 Mag., stainless steel, big grip,
  4-inch heavy bbl. & 6-inch bbl. 290.00

RUGER REVOLVERS

SPEED-SIX
Double Action, Round Butt
(Checkered Walnut Grip Panels)

The **Speed-Six** is a round butt lightened version of the Security-Six, designed for the use by off-duty and plain-clothes officers where weight and concealability are essential. The Speed-Six is available on special order with a spurless hammer. The mechanism and construction are identical to the Security-Six. (Models 207 and 208 can be had with a spurless hammer.)

Blued
Model 208—38 Spec. Caliber-Fixed Sights
2¾-inch barrel $221.50

Model 207—357 Mag. Caliber-Fixed Sights
2¾-inch barrel $221.50
4-inch barrel 221.50

Model 209—9mm Caliber—Fixed Sights
2¾-inch barrel $240.50
4-inch barrel 240.50

Stainless Steel
Model 737—357 Mag. Caliber-Fixed Sights
2¾-inch barrel $246.00
4-inch barrel 246.00

Model 738—38 Spec. Caliber-Fixed Sights
2¾-inch barrel $246.00

SUPER SINGLE-SIX
(With two cylinders— 22 L.R. & 22 WMR)

Features: Ruger single-action mechanism. Transfer bar ignition. Interlocked gate, transfer-bar, cylinder latch functions. Gate-controlled loading. All stressed components hardened chrome-molybdenum steel. Music wire springs throughout. Improved patridge front sight. **Calibers:** 22 Short, Long, Long Rifle and 22 WMR. **Barrel:** 6 groove, 14-inch twist. **Cylinders:** 2-interchangeable. **Ignition mechanism:** transfer-bar. Independent-alloy steel firing pin mounted in frame.

Sights: Adjustable rear and ramp front blade sight. **Grips:** Genuine walnut.
Finish: Polished and blued or stainless steel.

NR4-4⅝-inch Barrel (with interchangeable 22 WMR cyl.) .$195.00	stainless steel	not available
NR5-5½-inch Barrel (with interchangeable 22WMR cyl.) ... 195.00	stainless steel	$265.00
NR6-6½-inch Barrel (with interchangeable 22WMR cyl.) 195.00	stainless steel	265.00
NR9-9½-inch Barrel (with interchangeable 22WMR cyl.) 195.00	stainless steel	not available

RUGER REVOLVERS

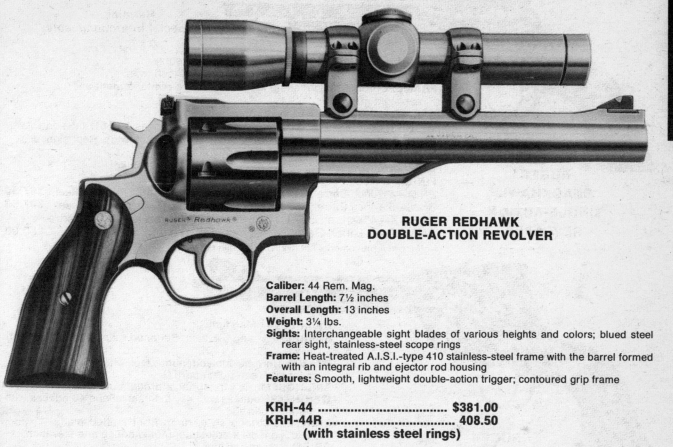

RUGER REDHAWK
DOUBLE-ACTION REVOLVER

Caliber: 44 Rem. Mag.
Barrel Length: 7½ inches
Overall Length: 13 inches
Weight: 3¼ lbs.
Sights: Interchangeable sight blades of various heights and colors; blued steel rear sight, stainless-steel scope rings
Frame: Heat-treated A.I.S.I.-type 410 stainless-steel frame with the barrel formed with an integral rib and ejector rod housing
Features: Smooth, lightweight double-aotion trigger; contoured grip frame

KRH-44 .... **$381.00**
KRH-44R 408.50
 (with stainless steel rings)

BLACKHAWK SINGLE-ACTION REVOLVER
(IN 30 CARBINE CALIBER) $237.50

Caliber: 30 Carbine
Barrel Length: 7½ inches, 6 groove rifling 20-inch twist
Overall Length: 13⅛ inches
Weight: 44 ounces
Springs: Unbreakable music wire springs used throughout; no leaf springs
Screws: For security, Nylok® screws are used at all five locations that might be affected by recoil
Sights: Patridge style, ramp front sight with ⅛ inch wide blade, matted to eliminate glare. Rear sight adjustable for windage and elevation
Ignition System: Independent alloy steel firing pin, mounted in frame, transfer bar
Frame: Same cylinder frame as 44 Mag. Super Blackhawk
Grips: Genuine walnut
Finish: Polished, blued and anodized

RUGER REVOLVERS

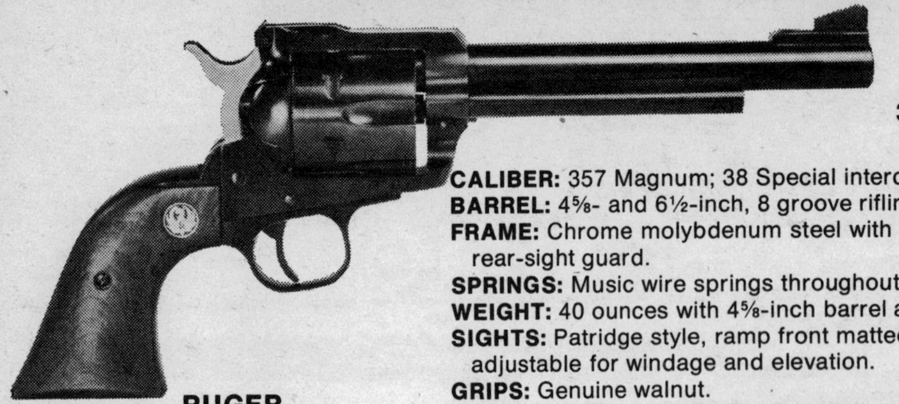

RUGER BLACKHAWK SINGLE-ACTION REVOLVER

Handles 38 Special Interchangeably

CALIBER: 357 Magnum; 38 Special interchangeably.
BARREL: 4⅝- and 6½-inch, 8 groove rifling, 16-inch twist.
FRAME: Chrome molybdenum steel with bridge reinforcement and rear-sight guard.
SPRINGS: Music wire springs throughout.
WEIGHT: 40 ounces with 4⅝-inch barrel and 42 ounces with 6½-inch barrel.
SIGHTS: Patridge style, ramp front matted blade ⅛ inch wide. Rear sight click adjustable for windage and elevation.
GRIPS: Genuine walnut.
FINISH: Polished and blued or stainless steel.
BN34—4⅝-inch Barrel, 357 Magnum caliber ..**$237.50** Stainless Steel **$307.50**
BN36—6½-inch Barrel, 357 Magnum caliber ... 237.50 Stainless Steel 307.50
BN34-X—4⅝-inch Barrel   fitted with 9mm Parabellum extra
BN36-X—6½-inch Barrel   cylinder. Walnut panels 260.00
Note: convertible model not available in stainless steel

RUGER BLACKHAWK SINGLE-ACTION REVOLVER

CALIBER: 41 Magnum.
BARREL: 4⅝- and 6½-inch. Buttoned rifling 1 turn in 20-inch twist.
FRAME: Chrome molybdenum steel with bridge reinforcement and rear-sight guard.
SPRINGS: Music wire springs throughout.
WEIGHT: 38 ounces with 4⅝-inch barrel and 40 ounces with 6½-inch barrel.
SIGHTS: Patridge style, ramp front matted blade ⅛ wide. Rear sight click adjustment for windage and elevation.
GRIPS: Genuine walnut.
OVERALL LENGTH: 12⅛ inches (6½-inch bbl.); 10¼ inches (4⅝-inch bbl.).
FINISH: Polished and blued.
BN-41—4⅝-inch Barrel **$237.50**
BN-42—6½-inch Barrel 237.50

RUGER SUPER BLACKHAWK SINGLE-ACTION REVOLVER

Handles 44 Special Interchangeably

CALIBER: 44 Magnum; 44 Special interchangeably.
BARREL: 7½ in., 10½ in.
FRAME: Chrome molybdenum steel with bridge reinforcement and rear sight guard.
SPRINGS: Music wire springs throughout.
WEIGHT: 48 ounces.
SIGHTS: Patridge style, ramp front matted blade ⅛ inch wide. Rear sight click and adjustable for windage and elevation.
GRIP FRAME: Chrome molybdenum steel enlarged and contoured to minimize recoil effect.
TRIGGER: Wide spur, low contour, sharply serrated for convenient cocking with minimum disturbance of grip.
OVERALL LENGTH: 13⅜ inches.
FINISH: Stainless Steel.

KS47N—7½-inch Barrel with steel grip frame **$325.00**
KS410N—10½-inch Barrel with steel grip frame 325.00
S47N—7½-inch Barrel, with steel grip frame **$250.00**
S410N—10½-inch Barrel, with steel grip frame 250.00

RUGER 22 AUTOMATIC PISTOLS

MARK II
STANDARD MODEL
AUTO PISTOL
$168.00

CALIBER: 22 Long Rifle only
BARREL: Length, 4¾- or 6-inch medium weight, 6 groove rifling, 14-inch twist.
SPRINGS: Music wire springs
WEIGHTS: 36 ozs. for 4¾-inch barrel; 38 ozs. for 6-inch barrel
OVERALL LENGTH: 8¾ inches or 10 inches depending on barrel length
SIGHTS: Front fixed; rear adjustable
MAGAZINE: Detachable, 9-shot capacity
TRIGGER: Grooved, curved finger surface, ⅜ inch wide. Two stage pull.
SAFETY: Locks sear and bolt. Cannot be put in safe position unless gun is cocked.
GRIPS: Hard rubber

MARK II
TARGET MODEL
PISTOL
$196.00

CALIBER: 22 Long Rifle only
BARREL: 5½-inch heavyweight bull barrel and 6⅞-inch barrel
OVERALL LENGTH: 9½ inches
SIGHTS: Patridge style, front blade, .125 inch wide, undercut Micro rear sight, click adjustments for windage and elevation
MAGAZINE: Detachable, 9-shot capacity
TRIGGER: Light crisp pull, no backlash
GRIPS: Hard rubber

SMITH & WESSON AUTO PISTOLS

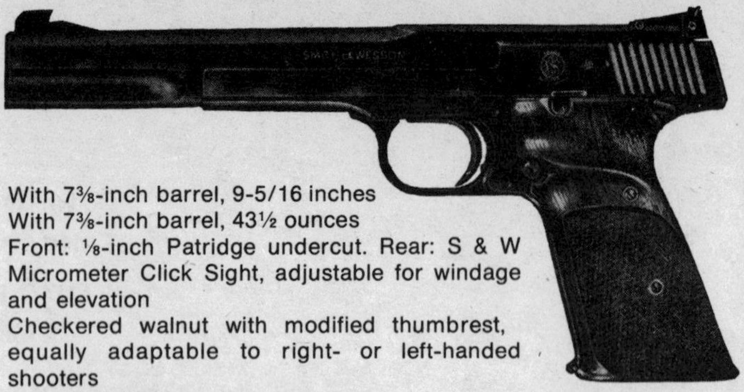

22 CAL. AUTOMATIC PISTOL
MODEL NO. 41

BLUE ONLY
(7⅜-inch BARREL)
$390.00

CALIBER:	22 Long Rifle
MAGAZINE CAPACITY:	10 rounds
BARREL:	5½ inches and 7⅜ inches
LENGTH OVERALL:	With 7⅜-inch barrel, 12 inches

SIGHT RADIUS:	With 7⅜-inch barrel, 9-5/16 inches
WEIGHT:	With 7⅜-inch barrel, 43½ ounces
SIGHTS:	Front: ⅛-inch Patridge undercut. Rear: S & W Micrometer Click Sight, adjustable for windage and elevation
STOCKS:	Checkered walnut with modified thumbrest, equally adaptable to right- or left-handed shooters
FINISH:	S & W Bright Blue
TRIGGER:	⅜-inch width, with S & W grooving and an adjustable trigger stop

NOTE: Model 41 is also available in 22 Short caliber for international shooting

38 MASTER MODEL NO. 52

CALIBER:	38 S & W Special for Mid Range Wood Cutter only
MAGAZINE CAPACITY:	5 rounds (2-five round magazines furnished)
BARREL:	5 inches
LENGTH OVERALL:	8⅝ inches
SIGHT RADIUS:	6-15/16 inches
WEIGHT:	41 oz. with empty magazine
SIGHTS:	Front: ⅛ inch Patridge on ramp base. Rear: New S & W Micrometer Click Sight with wide ⅞ inch sight slide
STOCKS:	Checkered walnut with S & W monograms
FINISH:	S & W Bright Blue with sandblast stippling around sighting area to break up light reflection
TRIGGER:	⅜-inch width with S & W grooving and an adjustable trigger stop

BRIGHT
BLUE ONLY
$573.50

9MM AUTOMATIC PISTOL
DOUBLE ACTION
MODEL 459/559

BLUE $424.50-451.00
NICKEL 457.00-483.50

Stainless Steel
Model 659
$431.50-458.00

CALIBER:	9mm Luger
MAGAZINE CAPACITY:	Two 14-round magazines, furnished
BARREL:	4 inches
OVERALL LENGTH:	7-7/16 inches

WEIGHT:	28 oz.
SIGHTS:	Front—square ⅛-in. serrated ramp; Rear—square notch rear sight blade fully Micrometer Click adjustable
STOCKS:	Checkered high-impact molded nylon grips
FINISH:	Blue or nickel

SMITH & WESSON AUTO PISTOLS

9MM AUTOMATIC PISTOL
DOUBLE ACTION
MODEL NO. 469

Price not set

CALIBER:	9mm Luger
MAGAZINE CAPACITY:	Two 12-round magazines furnished.
BARREL:	3½-inches
OVERALL LENGTH:	6⅞-inches
WEIGHT:	26 ounces
SIGHTS:	Front: yellow ramp Rear: dovetail mounted square-notch white inline
FINISH:	Sandblasted blue

9MM AUTOMATIC PISTOL
DOUBLE ACTION
MODEL 439/539

BLUE $370.50-397.00
NICKEL   402.00-428.50

CALIBER:	9mm Luger
MAGAZINE CAPACITY:	Two 8-round magazines, furnished
BARREL:	4 inches
OVERALL LENGTH:	7-7/16 inches
WEIGHT:	27 oz.
SIGHTS:	Front—square ⅛-in. serrated ramp; Rear—square notch rear sight blade fully Micrometer Click adjustable
STOCKS:	Checkered walnut grips with S & W monograms
FINISH:	Blue or nickel

**Stainless Steel
Model 639
$415.50-442.00**

SMITH & WESSON REVOLVERS

38 MILITARY & POLICE
(MODEL NO. 10)

CALIBER:	38 S & W Special
NUMBER OF SHOTS:	6
BARREL:	2,4,5 and 6 inches; also 4-inch heavy barrel
LENGTH OVERALL:	With 4-inch barrel, 9¼ inches
WEIGHT:	With 4-inch barrel, 30½ oz.
SIGHTS:	Front: Fixed, ⅛-inch serrated ramp. Rear: Square notch
STOCKS:	Checkered walnut Serivce with S & W monograms, round or square butt
FINISH:	S & W Blue or Nickel

**BLUE
$220.00
NICKEL
$238.00**

38 MILITARY & POLICE (AIRWEIGHT)
(MODEL NO. 12)

CALIBER:	38 S & W Special
NUMBER OF SHOTS:	6
BARREL:	2 or 4 inches
LENGTH OVERALL:	With 2-inch barrel and round butt, 6⅞ inches
WEIGHT:	With 2-inch barrel and round butt, 18 oz.
SIGHTS:	Front: Fixed, ⅛-inch serrated ramp. Rear: Square notch
STOCKS:	Checkered walnut Service with S & W monograms, round or square butt
FINISH:	S & W Blue or Nickel

**BLUE
$288.00
NICKEL
$326.50**

(Illus. with round butt)

357 MILITARY & POLICE (HEAVY BARREL)
(MODEL NO. 13)

CALIBER:	357 Magnum and 38 S&W Special
ROUNDS:	6-shot cylinder capacity
BARREL:	4 inches
LENGTH OVERALL:	9¼ inches
WEIGHT:	34 oz.
SIGHTS:	Front: ⅛-inch serrated ramp. Rear: Square notch
STOCKS:	Checkered walnut Service with S&W monograms, square butt
FINISH:	S&W Blue or Nickel

**BLUE
$224.00
NICKEL
$244.50**

9MM MILITARY & POLICE
(MODEL NO. 547)

CALIBER:	9mm
NUMBER OF SHOTS:	6
BARREL:	3 or 4 inches
OVERALL LENGTH:	8⅛ inches with 3-inch barrel; 9⅛ inches with 4-inch barrel
WEIGHT:	32 oz. with 3-inch barrel; 34 oz. with 4-inch barrel
SIGHTS:	Front is ⅛ inch serrated ramp; rear is ⅛ inch square notch
STOCKS:	Checkered walnut target round butt with speed-loader cutaway (3 inches); checkered square butt Magna Service (4 inches)
FINISH:	S&W Blue

BLUE ONLY $290.00

SMITH & WESSON REVOLVERS

38 COMBAT MASTERPIECE
WITH 4-INCH BARREL
(MODEL NO. 15)

CALIBER:	38 S & W Special
NUMBER OF SHOTS:	6
BARREL:	2 & 4 inches
LENGTH OVERALL:	9⅛ inches
WEIGHT LOADED:	With 4-inch barrel, 34 oz.
SIGHTS:	Front: ⅛-inch Baughman Quick Draw on plain ramp. Rear: S & W Micrometer Click Sight, adjustable for windage and elevation
STOCKS:	Checkered walnut Service with S & W monograms
FINISH:	S & W Blue or Nickel

BLUE $254.00
NICKEL $273.50
Blue with target hammer
and trigger, 4-inch barrel $282.50

K-22 MASTERPIECE
(MODEL NO. 17)

CALIBER:	22 Long Rifle
NUMBER OF SHOTS:	6
BARREL:	6, 8⅜ inches
LENGTH OVERALL:	With 6-inch barrel, 11⅛ inches
WEIGHT LOADED:	With 6-inch barrel, 38½ oz.; 8⅜-inch, 42½ oz.
SIGHTS:	Front: ⅛-inch plain Patridge. Rear: S & W Micrometer Click Sight, adjustable for windage and elevation
STOCKS:	Checkered walnut Service with S & W monograms.
FINISH:	S & W Blue.

BLUE ONLY
6 inches $321.00
8⅜ inches 335.00
with target hammer,
trigger and stocks
6-inch barrel $367.00
8⅜-inch barrel 381.00

22 COMBAT MASTERPIECE
WITH 4-INCH BARREL
(MODEL NO. 18)

CALIBER:	22 Long Rifle
NUMBER OF SHOTS:	6
BARREL:	4 inches
LENGTH OVERALL:	9⅛ inches
WEIGHT LOADED:	36½ oz.
SIGHTS:	Front: ⅛-inch Baughman Quick Draw on plain ramp. Rear: S & W Micrometer Click Sight, adjustable for windage and elevation
STOCKS:	Checkered walnut Service with S & W monograms
FINISH:	S & W Blue

BLUE ONLY
$310.50
With target hammer and trigger $339.00

"357" COMBAT MAGNUM
(MODEL NO. 19)

CALIBER:	357 Magnum (Actual bullet dia. 38 S & W Spec.)
NUMBER OF SHOTS:	6
BARREL:	2½, 4 and 6 inches
LENGTH OVERALL:	9½ inches with 4-inch barrel; 7½ inches with 2½-inch barrel; 11½ inches with 6-inch barrel
WEIGHT:	35 oz. (2½-inch model weighs 31 oz.)
SIGHTS:	Front: ⅛ inch Baughman Quick Draw on 2½- or 4-inch barrel, ⅛ inch Patridge on 6-inch barrel. Rear: S & W Micrometer Click Sight, adjustable for windage and elevation
STOCKS:	Checkered Goncalo Alves Target with S & W monograms.
FINISH:	S & W Bright Blue or Nickel

BRIGHT BLUE
OR NICKEL
$277.00-327.50

Price based on accessories such as round or square butt, adjustable sights, target trigger, target hammer, target stocks, white outline rear or red ramp front

1955 45 TARGET
(MODEL NO. 25)

CALIBER:	45 A C P
NUMBER OF SHOTS:	6
BARREL:	6½ inches
LENGTH OVERALL:	11⅞ inches
WEIGHT:	45 oz.
SIGHTS:	Front: ⅛-inch plain Patridge. Rear: S & W Micrometer Click Sight, adjustable for windage and elevation
STOCKS:	Checkered walnut target with S & W monograms
HAMMER:	Checked target type
TRIGGER:	Grooved target type
FINISH:	S & W Blue

BLUE ONLY
$391.00

Model No. 25-5

Available in heavy frame in 45 Colt caliber with 4-, 6- and 8⅜-inch barrels in blue or nickel finish **$409.00-423.50**

SMITH & WESSON REVOLVERS

357 MAGNUM
(MODEL NO. 27)

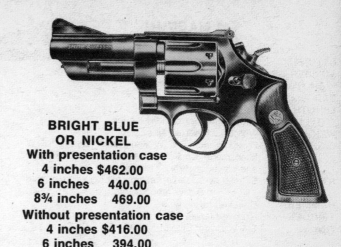

CALIBER: 357 Magnum (Actual bullet dia. 38 S & W Spec.)
NUMBER OF
  SHOTS: 6
BARREL: 3½, 5, 6 and 8⅜ inches
LENGTH
  OVERALL: With 6-inch barrel, 11¼ inches
WEIGHT: With 3½-inch barrel, 41 oz.; 5-inch, 42½ oz.; 6-inch, 44 oz.; 8⅜-inch, 47 oz.
SIGHTS: Front: Choice of any S & W target sight. Rear: S & W Micrometer Click Sight, adjustable for wind
STOCKS: Checkered walnut Service with S & W monograms
FRAME: Finely checked top strap and barrel rib
FINISH: S & W Bright Blue or Nickel

**BRIGHT BLUE
OR NICKEL
With presentation case
4 inches $462.00
6 inches 440.00
8¾ inches 469.00
Without presentation case
4 inches $416.00
6 inches 394.00
8¾ inches 423.00**

HIGHWAY PATROLMAN
(MODEL NO. 28)

CALIBER: 357 Magnum (Actual bullet dia. 38 S & W Spec.)
NUMBER OF
  SHOTS: 6
BARREL: 4 or 6 inches
LENGTH
  OVERALL: With 6-inch barrel, 11¼ inches
WEIGHT: With 4-inch barrel, 41¾ oz.; 6-inch, 44 oz.
SIGHTS: Front: ⅛ inch Baughman Quick Draw on plain ramp. Rear: S & W Micrometer Click Sight, adjustable for windage and elevation.
STOCKS: Checkered walnut Service with S & W monograms (walnut target stocks at additional cost)
FINISH: S & W Satin Blue with sandblast stippling or barrel rib and frame edging

**BLUE ONLY
$305.50
With target stocks (Illus.)
$327.00**

44 MAGNUM
(MODEL NO. 29)

CALIBER: 44 Magnum
NUMBER OF
  SHOTS: 6
BARREL: 4, 6, 8⅜ and 10⅝ inches (blue only)
LENGTH
  OVERALL: With 6½-inch barrel, 11⅞ inches
WEIGHT: With 4-inch barrel, 43 oz.; 6½-inch, 47 oz.; 8⅜-inch, 51½ oz.
SIGHTS: Front: ⅛ inch S & W Red Ramp. Rear: S & W Micrometer Click Sight adjustable for windage and elevation. White outline notch
STOCKS: Special oversize target type of checked Goncalo Alves; with S & W monograms
HAMMER: Checkered target type
TRIGGER: Grooved target type
FINISH: S & W Bright Blue or Nickel

**BRIGHT BLUE
OR NICKEL
With presentation case
4 and 6 inches $455.00
8⅜ and 10⅝ inches 469.50
Without presentation case
4 and 6 inches $409.00
8⅜ and 10⅝ inches 423.50**

SMITH & WESSON REVOLVERS

41 MAGNUM
(MODEL NO. 57)

CALIBER:	41 Magnum
NUMBER OF SHOTS:	6
BARREL:	4, 6 and 8⅜ inches
LENGTH OVERALL:	With 6-inch barrel, 11⅜ inches
WEIGHT:	With 6-inch barrel, 48 oz.
SIGHTS:	Front: ⅛-inch S & W Red Ramp, Rear: S & W Micrometer Click Sight adjustable for windage and elevation. White Outline notch
STOCKS:	Special oversize Target type of checked Goncalo Alves, with S & W monograms.
HAMMER:	Checked target type
TRIGGER:	Grooved target type
FINISH:	S & W Bright Blue or Nickel

**BRIGHT BLUE
OR NICKEL**
with presentation case
4 and 6 inches $455.00
8⅜ inches 469.50
without presentation case
4 and 6 inches $409.00
8⅜ inches 423.50

1953 22/32 KIT GUN
(MODEL NO. 34)

CALIBER:	22 Long Rifle
NUMBER OF SHOTS:	6
BARREL:	2, 4 inches
LENGTH OVERALL:	With 4-inch barrel and round butt, 8 inches.
WEIGHT:	With 4-inch barrel and round butt, 22¼ oz.
SIGHTS:	Front: 1/10-inch serrated ramp. Rear: S & W Micrometer Click Sight, adjustable for windage and elevation
STOCKS:	Checked walnut Service with S & W monograms, round or square butt
FINISH:	S & W Blue or Nickel

**BLUE
$263.00**

**NICKEL
$286.00**

STAINLESS STEEL MODELS

1977 22/32 KIT GUN
(MODEL NO. 63)

SPECIFICATIONS: Caliber: 22 Long Rifle. **Number of shots:** 6. **Barrel Length:** 4 inches. **Weight:** 24½ oz. (empty). **Sights:** ⅛-inch red ramp front sight. Rear sight is the black stainless steel S&W Micrometer Click square-notch, adjustable for windage and elevation. **Stocks:** Square butt. **Finish:** Satin.

**STAINLESS STEEL
$298.00**

38 CHIEFS SPECIAL STAINLESS
(MODEL NO. 60)

SPECIFICATIONS: Caliber: 38 S&W Special. **Number of shots:** 5. **Barrel:** 2 inches. **Length Overall:** 6½ inches. **Weight:** 19 oz. **Sights:** Front Fixed, 1/10-inch serrated ramp. **Rear:** Square notch. **Stocks:** Checked walnut Service with S&W monograms. **Finish:** Satin

**STAINLESS
STEEL
$289.50**

SMITH & WESSON REVOLVERS

38 MILITARY & POLICE STAINLESS
MODEL NO. 64

SPECIFICATIONS: Caliber: 38 S&W Special. **Number of Shots:** 6. **Barrel:** 4-inch heavy barrel, square butt. 2-inch regular barrel, round butt. **Length Overall:** With 4-inch barrel, 9¼ inches 2-inch barrel, 6⅞ inches. **Weight:** With 4-inch barrel, 34 ounces. **Sights:** Fixed, ⅛ inch serrated ramp front; square notch rear. **Stocks:** Checked walnut Service with S&W monograms. **Finish:** Satin. **Ammunition—** 38 S&W Special, 38 S&W Special Mid Range.

Stainless Steel
$243.50

357 Military & Police Stainless
Heavy Barrel
MODEL NO. 65

SPECIFICATIONS: Caliber: 357 Magnum and 38 S&W Special. **Rounds:** 6-shot cylinder capacity. **Barrel:** 4-inch heavy barrel. **Length Overall:** With 4-inch barrel, 9¼ inches. **Weight:** With 4-inch barrel, 34 oz. **Sights:** Fixed, ⅛-inch serrated ramp front; square notch rear. **Stocks:** Checked walnut Service with S&W monograms, square butt. **Finish:** Satin.

Stainless Steel
$254.00

357 COMBAT MAGNUM REVOLVER
MODEL NO. 66

SPECIFICATIONS: Caliber: 357 Magnum (Actual bullet dia. 38 S&W Spec.). **Number of shots:** 6. **Barrel:** 6 or 4 inch with square butt; 2½ inches with round butt. **Length Overall:** 9½ inches with 4-inch barrel; 7½ inches with 2½-inch barrel. **Weight:** 35 ounces with 4-inch barrel. **Sights:** Front: ⅛ inch Rear: S&W Red Ramp on ramp base, S&W Micrometer Click Sight, adjustable for windage and elevation. **Stocks:** Checked Goncalo Alves target with square butt with S&W monograms. **Finish:** Satin. **Trigger:** S&W grooving with an adjustable trigger stop. **Ammunition:** 357 S&W Magnum, 38 S&W Special Hi-Speed, 38 S&W Special, 38 S&W Special Mid Range.

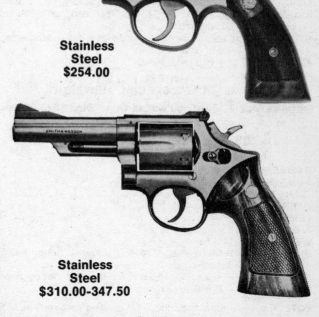

Stainless Steel
$310.00-347.50

K-38 COMBAT MASTERPIECE REVOLVER
MODEL NO. 67

SPECIFICATIONS: Caliber: 38 S&W Special. **Number of shots:** 6. **Barrel:** 4 inches **Length Overall:** 9⅛ inches with 4-inch barrel. **Weight Loaded:** 34 oz. with 4-inch barrel. **Sights:** Front: ⅛ inch Rear: S&W Red Ramp on ramp base, S&W Micrometer Click Sights, adjustable for windage and elevation. **Stocks:** Checked walnut Service with S&W Monograms square butt. **Finish:** Satin. **Trigger:** S&W grooving with an adjustable trigger stop. **Ammunition:** 38 S&W Special, 38 S&W Special Mid Range.

Stainless Steel
$301.00

SMITH & WESSON REVOLVERS

32 REGULATION POLICE
(MODEL NO. 31)

CALIBER:	32 S & W Long
NUMBER OF SHOTS:	6
BARREL:	2, 3 inches
LENGTH OVERALL:	With 4-inch barrel, 8½ inches
WEIGHT:	With 4-inch barrel, 18¾ oz.
SIGHTS:	Front: Fixed, 1/10-inch serrated ramp. Rear: Square notch
STOCKS:	Checked walnut Service with S & W Monograms
FINISH:	S & W Blue

BLUE ONLY
$263.00

38 CHIEFS SPECIAL
(MODEL 36)

CALIBER:	38 S & W Special
NUMBER OF SHOTS:	5
BARREL:	2 or 3 inches (3 inch—blue only)
LENGTH OVERALL:	With 2-inch barrel and round butt, 6½ inches
WEIGHT:	With 2-inch barrel and round butt, 19 oz.
SIGHTS:	Front: Fixed, 1/10-inch serrated ramp. Rear: Square notch
STOCKS:	Checked walnut Service with S & W monograms, round or square butt
FINISH:	S & W Blue or Nickel

BLUE
$235.00
NICKEL
$254.50

(MODEL NO. 37)
38 CHIEF'S SPECIAL AIRWEIGHT

Same as Model 36 except: weight 14 oz. **Blue $235.00; Nickel $265.50.**

38 BODYGUARD "AIRWEIGHT"
(MODEL No. 38)

CALIBER:	38 S & W Special
NUMBER OF SHOTS:	5
BARREL:	2 inches
LENGTH OVERALL:	6⅜ inches
WEIGHT:	14½ oz.
SIGHTS:	Front: Fixed, 1/10-inch serrated ramp. Rear: Square notch
STOCKS:	Checked walnut Service with S & W monograms
FINISH:	S & W Blue or Nickel

NOTE: The Bodyguard also supplied in all-steel construction, Model 49, weighing 20½ oz. Price: Blue, **$227.50;** Nickel, **$247.50.**

BLUE
$277.50
NICKEL
$313.50

K-22 MASTERPIECE M.R.F.
(MODEL NO. 48)

CALIBER:	22 Magnum Rim Fire
NUMBER OF SHOTS:	6
BARREL:	4, 6, 8⅜ inches
LENGTH OVERALL:	With 6-inch barrel, 11⅛ inches
WEIGHT:	With 6-inch barrel, 39 oz.
SIGHTS:	Front: ⅛-inch plain Patridge. Rear: S & W Micrometer Click Sight, adjustable for windage and elevation
STOCKS:	Checked walnut Service with S & W monograms
FINISH:	S & W Blue
	Auxiliary cylinder available in 22 LR.

BLUE ONLY
4 inches, 6 inches $330.00
8⅜ inches $345.50

SMITH & WESSON REVOLVERS
DISTINGUISHED COMBAT MAGNUM
MODELS 586 AND 686

CALIBER:	357 Magnum
NUMBER OF SHOTS:	6 **BARREL LENGTH:** 4 or 6 inches
OVERALL LENGTH:	9¾ inches with 4-inch barrel; 11½ inches with 6-inch barrel
WEIGHT:	42 oz. with 4-inch barrel; 46 oz. with 6-inch barrel
SIGHTS:	Front is S&W Red Ramp; rear is S&W Micrometer Click adjustable for windage and elevation; White outline notch. Option with 6-inch barrel only—plain Patridge front with black outline notch.
STOCKS:	Checkered Goncalo Alves with speedloader cutaway
FINISH:	S&W Blue or Nickel
MODEL 686,	Same as Model 586 except finish is stainless steel, $294.00-303.00

**BLUE, NICKEL OR SATIN
$294.50-330.00**

STAR AUTOMATIC PISTOLS

STAR PD
45 ACP BLUE

Chambered for the sledgehammer 45 ACP, the PD has the same capacity—7 rounds—as the U.S. Government Model, yet it weighs nearly a pound less, as well as being smaller in every dimension. Just a fraction over 7 inches long, it weighs only 25 ounces.
45 ACP Blue **400.00**

STAR BKM & BM
9mm LUGER BLUE
9mm LUGER CHROME

Overall Length: 7.17 inches. Barrel Length: 3.9 inches. Magazine Capacity: 8 rounds.
Model BM Blue 34.06 oz. **$330.00**
Model BM Chrome 34.06 oz. **360.00**
Model BKM Blue 25.59 oz. **330.00**

The Model BM offers all steel construction and the BKM offers a high strength, weight-saving duraluminum frame. An improved thumb safety locks both the slide and hammer with hammer cocked or uncocked; further, an automatic magazine safety locks the sear when the magazine is removed.

STERLING AUTOMATIC PISTOLS

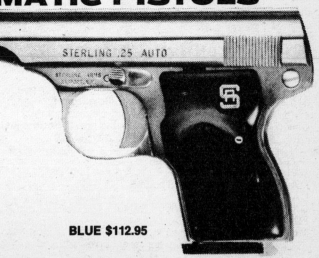

25 AUTO MODEL 300

Sterling Arms introduces the dependable MODEL 300, a personal sized automatic, constructed of ordnance steel, featuring indestructable Cycolac grips.

SIZE: 4½ inches x 3½ in.   **CONSTRUCTION:** All steel
WEIGHT: 13 oz.   **GRIPS:** Cycolac—Black
CAPACITY: 6 shots   **FINISH:** Blue or Stainless Steel
CALIBER: 25 ACP
Model 300S: Same as Model 300 except has stainless steel construction and finish. **$112.95**

BLUE $112.95

STERLING AUTOMATIC PISTOLS

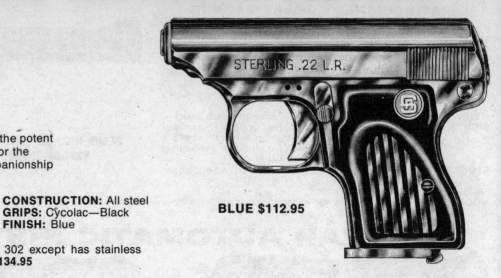

22 AUTO MODEL 302

Performance and standards of the potent little MODEL 302, chambered for the 22 LR cartridge, provides companionship above the ordinary.

SIZE: 4½ inches x 3½ inches
WEIGHT: 13 oz.
CAPACITY: 6 shots
CALIBER: 22 Long Rifle
CONSTRUCTION: All steel
GRIPS: Cycolac—Black
FINISH: Blue

Model 302S: Same as Model 302 except has stainless steel construction and finish. **$134.95**

BLUE $112.95

380 DOUBLE ACTION
AUTO MODEL 400 MK II

Your security is assured with the MODEL 400 featuring both double and single action, combined with the powerful 380 cartridge.

SIZE: 6½ in. x 4¾ in.
WEIGHT: 26 oz.
CAPACITY: 7 shots
CALIBER: 380
CONSTRUCTION: All ordnance steel
GRIPS: Walnut hand checkered
FINISH: Blue

Model 400S: Same as Model 400 except has stainless steel construction and finish. **$260.95**

BLUE $225.95

32 DOUBLE ACTION
MODEL 402S MK II

This slim and compact automatic pistol is ideal for police and security use. Features a low-profile, target-type rear sight fully adjustable for windage and elevation; safety is a rolling block design; slide lock remains open after the last shot; hammer is a low-profile serrated type.

SIZE: 6½ inches x 4¾ inches
WEIGHT: 26 oz.
MAGAZINE CAPACITY: 8 rounds
CALIBER: 32 ACP
GRIPS: Checkered American walnut
FINISH: Stainless Steel
Model 402 MK II: Same as Model 402S MK II except has deep blue finish with stainless steel barrel. **$225.95**

STAINLESS $260.95

STEYR PISTOLS

STEYR GB
Semi-Auto Pistol
$585.00

Caliber: 9mm Parabellum
Magazine Capacity: 18 rounds
Action: Double. Gas-operated, blowback delayed action
Barrel Length: 5.4 inches
Overall Length: 8.9 inches
Weight: 2.09 lbs. (empty)
Height: 5.7 inches
Sights: Fixed, open. Notch rear, post front
Trigger Pull: Approx. 4 lbs. (with hammer cocked);
approx. 14 lbs. (with hammer uncocked)
Muzzle Velocity: 1,184 fps

TAURUS PISTOLS

MODEL PT 99 THE PROTECTOR

Caliber: 9mm Parabellum
Action: Semi Automatic Double Action.
Hammer: Exposed
Barrel Length: 4.92 inches
Length: 8.54 inches
Height: 5.39 inches
Width: 1.45 inches
Weight: (with empty magazine) 34 oz.
Rifling: R.H., 6 grooves
Front Sight: Blade integral with slide
Rear Sight: Notched Bar Dovetailed to slide
Safeties: (a) Manual safety locking trigger mechanism and
slide in locked position
(b) Half cock position
(c) Inertia operated firing pin.
(d) Chamber loaded indicator.
Magazine: Staggered 15 shot capacity
Slide: Hold open upon firing last cartridge.
Finish: Blue
Grips: Thermo Plastic Pollanimide Resin in black color.

MODEL PT 99
$364.30 (Blue)
380.00 (Satin)

MODEL PT 92

SPECIFICATIONS:
Caliber: 9mm Parabellum
Action: Semi Automatic Double Action.
Hammer: Exposed.
Barrel Length: 4.92 inches
Length: 8.54 inches
Height: 5.39 inches
Width: 1.45 inches
Weight: (with empty magazine): 34 oz.
Rifling: R.H., 6 grooves
Front Sight: Blade Integral with slide
Rear Sight: Micrometer Click adjustable for elevation
and windage
Safeties: (a) Manual safety locking trigger mechanism and
slide in locked position
(b) Half cock position
(c) Inertia operated firing pin
(d) Chamber loaded indicator magazine: staggered, 15
shot capacity
Slide: Hold open upon firing last cartridge
Finish: Blue
Grips: Smooth Brazilian walnut. **Price: $391.50**

MODEL PT 92
$325.00

TAURUS REVOLVERS

MODEL 73

$187.40 (Blue)

199.50 (Satin)

SPECIFICATIONS:
Caliber: 32 Special
Capacity: 6 shot
Barrel length: 3-inch Heavy barrel
Weight: 20 oz.
Sights: Rear, square notch
Action: Double
Stock: Standard checkered
Finish: Blue or satin

MODEL 83

$187.40 (Blue)

199.50 (Satin)

SPECIFICATIONS:
Caliber: 38 Special
Action: Double
Number of Shots: 6
Barrel Length: 4 inches only
Weight: 34½ oz.
Sights: 2/8 inches on Ramp, Front. Rear Micrometer Click Adjustable for Windage and Elevation
Finish: Blue or satin
Stocks: Checkered walnut target

MODEL 86
Target Master
$230.00 (Blue)

SPECIFICATIONS:
Caliber: 38 Special
Capacity: 6 shot
Barrel length: 6 inches
Weight: 34 oz.
Sights: Patridge-type front; micrometer click adjustable rear for windage and elevation
Action: Double
Stock: Checkered walnut target
Finish: Bright royal blue

Model 96 Target Scout: Same as Model 86 Target Master except 22 L.R. caliber. Blue.

SPECIFICATIONS:
Caliber: 38 Special
Capacity: 6 shot
Barrel lengths: 3 inches, 4 inches
Weight: 33 oz.
Action: Double
Stock: Checkered walnut
Finish: Blue or satin

MODEL 80

$170.90 (Blue)

183.00 (Satin)

SPECIFICATIONS:
Caliber: 38 Special
Capacity: 6 shot
Barrel lengths: 3 inches, 4 inches
Weight: 34 oz.
Action: Double
Stock: Checkered walnut
Finish: Blue or satin

MODEL 82
Heavy Barrel
$170.90 (Blue)

183.00 (Satin)

TAURUS REVOLVERS

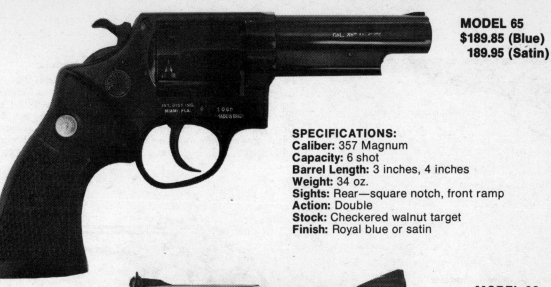

MODEL 65
$189.85 (Blue)
189.95 (Satin)

SPECIFICATIONS:
Caliber: 357 Magnum
Capacity: 6 shot
Barrel Length: 3 inches, 4 inches
Weight: 34 oz.
Sights: Rear—square notch, front ramp
Action: Double
Stock: Checkered walnut target
Finish: Royal blue or satin

MODEL 66
$226.00 (Blue)
226.00 (Satin)

SPECIFICATIONS:
Caliber: 357 Magnum
Capacity: 6 shot
Barrel Length : 3 inches, 4 inches, 6 inches
Weight: 35 oz.
Sights: Serrated ramp, front. Rear Micrometer Click adjustable for windage and elevation
Action: Double
Stock: Checkered walnut magna grips (3 inches); checkered walnut target grips (4 inches & 6 inches)
Finish: Royal blue or satin

MODEL 85 "Protector"
$190.00 (Blue)
207.00 (Satin)

SPECIFICATIONS:
Caliber: 38 Special
Capacity: 5 shot
Barrel Length: 3 inches
Weight: 21 oz.
Sights: Notch rear sight, fixed sight
Action: Double
Stock: Brazilian hardwood
Finish: Blue or satin

THOMPSON/CENTER

CONTENDER

Ventilated Rib/Internal Choke Models:

Featuring a raised ventilated (7/16 inch wide) rib, this Contender model is available in either 357 or 44 Magnum caliber. Its rear leaf sight folds down to provide an unobstructed sighting plane when the pistol is used with Hot Shot Cartridges. A patented detachable choke (1⅞ inches long) screws into muzzle internally. Overall barrel length 10 inches **$280.00**

Standard Models:

This Contender may be purchased with a standard barrel of your choice, in any of the standard calibers listed. Barrel is available in 10-inch length. 357 or 44 Magnum calibers are available either with or without patented choke. All standard barrels are supplied with iron sights; however, the rear sight may be removed for scope mounting. 357 and 44 Magnum calibers are available with the Thompson/Center patented detachable choke for use with the Hot Shot Cartridge. When the choke is removed, standard factory ammo may be fired from the same barrel without accuracy loss **$255.00**

6.5mm T.C.U., 7mm T.C.U., 22 Long Rifle, 22 Win. Mag., 22 Hornet, 221 Fireball, 222 Rem., 223 Rem., 256 Win. Mag., 30/30 Win., 357 Mag. with and without choke, 41 Mag., 44 Mag. with and without choke, 45 Colt with and without choke.

Bull Barrel Models:

This pistol with 10-inch barrel features fully adjustable Patridge-style iron sights.

Standard and Custom calibers available:
22 Long Rifle, 22 Hornet, 221 Fireball, 222 Rem., 223 Rem., 256 Win. Mag., 7mm T.C.U., 30/30 Win., 30 Herrett, 357 Herrett, 357 Mag., 41 Mag., 44 Mag., 45 Colt and 45 Win. Mag.
Less internal choke **$265.00**
Standard calibers available with internal choke: 357 Mag., 44 Mag., 45 Colt **$270.00**

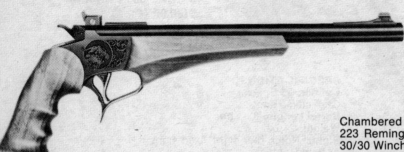

CONTENDER
SUPER "14" MODELS

Chambered in twelve calibers (22 L.R., 222 Remington and 223 Remington, 6.5mm T.C.U., 7mm T.C.U., 30 Herrett, 30/30 Winchester, 357 Herrett, 35 Remington, 41 Mag., 44 Mag. and 45 Win. Mag.), this gun is equipped with a 14-inch bull barrel, fully adjustable target rear sight and ramped front sight (Patridge Style). It offers a sight radius of 13½ inches, beavertail forend and grips designed by Steve Herrett. Overall length is 18¼ inches; weight is 3½ lbs. **$285.00**

WALTHER PISTOLS

DOUBLE ACTION AUTOMATIC PISTOLS

The Walther double action system combines the principles of the double action revolver with the advantages of the modern pistol . . . without the disadvantages inherent in either design. Published reports from independent testing laboratories have cited Walther superiority in rugged durability, positive performance and reliability. Special built-in safety design and a simple disassembly procedure combine to make these one of the safest and most easily maintained handguns.

Models PP and PPK/S differ only in the overall length of the barrel and slide. Both models offer the same features, including compact form, light weight, easy handling and absolute safety—both models can be carried with a loaded chamber and closed hammer, but ready to fire either single or double action. Both models in calibers 32 ACP and 380 ACP are provided with a live round indicator pin to signal a loaded chamber. An automatic internal safety blocks the hammer to prevent accidental striking of the firing pin, except with a deliberate pull of the trigger. Sights are provided with white markings for high visibility in poor light. Rich Walther blue/black finish is standard and each pistol is complete with extra magazine with finger rest extension. Available in calibers 22 L.R., 32 ACP and 380 ACP.

The Walther P-38 is a double action, locked breech, semi-automatic pistol with an external hammer. Its compact form, light weight and easy handling is combined with the superb performance of the 9mm Luger Parabellum cartridge.

The P-38 is equipped with both a manual and automatic safety, which allows it to be safely carried while the chamber is loaded.

Available in calibers 9mm Luger Parabellum, 30 Luger and 22 L.R. with either a rugged non-reflective black finish or in a polished blued finish.

Overall length: model PP (6.7 inches); PPK/S (6.1 inches); P-38 (8½ inches) P-38IV (8 inches). Height: models PP, PPK/S (4.28 inches); P-38 (5.39 inches) P-38IV (5.39); P-38K (5.39). Weight: model PP (23.5 oz.); PPK/S (23 oz.); P-38 (28 oz.) P-38IV (29 oz.).

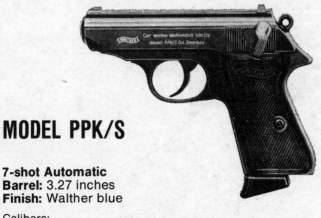

MODEL PPK/S

7-shot Automatic
Barrel: 3.27 inches
Finish: Walther blue

Calibers:
Model PPK/S American, 380ACP **$370.00**
Note: Engraved models—prices on request.

MODEL PP

7-shot Automatic
Barrel: 3.86 inches
Finish: Walther blue

Calibers:
    22 Long Rifle (8 Shot Magazine) **$520.00**
    32 Automatic **500.00**
    380 Automatic **500.00**
Note: Engraved models—prices on request.

MODEL P-38

8-shot Automatic
Barrel: 4-15/16 inches (9mm & 30 Luger)
         5-1/16 inches (22 L.R.)
Finish: matte

Calibers:
22 Long Rifle **$750.00**
30 Luger **680.00**
9mm Luger **680.00**
Note: Engraved models—prices on request

P-38IV AUTO-PISTOL

8-shot Automatic
Barrel: 4½ inches
Finish: Matte

Caliber:
9mm Luger **$650.00**
Same as the discontinued P-38K except for longer barrel, O.A. length and weight. Sights are non-adjustable

WALTHER PISTOLS

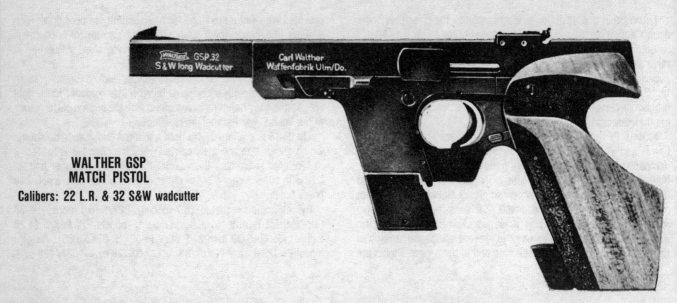

**WALTHER GSP
MATCH PISTOL**

Calibers: 22 L.R. & 32 S&W wadcutter

WALTHER OSP

22 Short only
$1095.00
with carrying case

Walther match pistols are built to conform to ISU and NRA match target pistol regulations. The model GSP, caliber 22 L.R. is available with either 2.2 lb. (1000 gm) or 3.0 lb. (1360 gm) trigger, and comes with 4½-inch barrel and special hand-fitting design walnut stock. Sights consist of fixed front, and adjustable rear sight. The GSP-C 32 S&W wadcutter center fire pistol is factory tested with a 3.0 lb. trigger. The 22 L.R. conversion unit for the model GSP-C consists of an interchangeable barrel, a slide assembly and two magazines. The 22 caliber model weighs 44.8 oz.; 32 S&W weighs 49.4 oz. Overall length is 11.8 inches. Magazine capacity is 5 shot.

Models:

GSP—22 Long Rifle w/carrying case	**$ 950.00**
GSP-C—32 S&W wadcutter w/carrying case	**1075.00**
22 caliber L.R. conversion unit for GSP-C	**645.00**
22 Short Cal. Conversion Unit for GSP-C	**695.00**

DAN WESSON REVOLVERS

.357 MAGNUM w/6-inch BARREL

357 MAG. REVOLVER

Introduced in 1935, the .357 Magnum is still the top selling handgun caliber. It makes an excellent hunting sidearm, and many law enforcement agencies have adopted it as a duty caliber. Take your pick of Dan Wesson .357's; then, add to it's versatility with an additional barrel assembly option to alter it to your other needs.

Specifications:
Six shot double and single action. **Ammunition:** .357 Magnum, .38 Special Hi-speed, .38 Special Mid-range. **Typical Dimension:** 4″ barrel revolver — 9¼″ x 5¾″. **Trigger:** Smooth, wide tang (⅜″) with overtravel adjustment. **Hammer:** Wide spur (⅜″) with short double action travel. **Sights:** Models 14 — 714 — ⅛″ fixed serrated front. Fixed rear integral with frame. Models 15 & 715 — ⅛″ serrated interchangeable front blade. Red insert standard. Yellow and white available. Rear — standard white outline, adjustable for windage and elevation. Graduated click. **NOTE:** 10″, 12″, 15″ barrel assemblies have special front sights and instructions. **Rifling:** Six lands & grooves, right-hand twist, one turn in 18.75 inches (2½″ thru 8″ lengths). Six lands and grooves, right-hand twist, one turn in 14 inches (10″, 12″, 15″ lengths). **NOTE:** All 2½″ guns shipped with undercover grips. 4″ guns are shipped with service grips and the balance have oversized target grips.

PRICE
$219.50-458.05

MODEL	CALIBER	TYPE	BARREL LENGTHS & WEIGHT IN OUNCES							FINISH
			2½″	4″	6″	8″	10″	12″	15″	
14-2	.357 Magnum	Service	30	34	38	NA	NA	NA	NA	Satin Blue
14-2B	.357 Magnum	Service	30	34	38	NA	NA	NA	NA	Brite Blue
15-2	.357 Magnum	Target	32	36	40	44	50	54	59	Brite Blue
15-2V	.357 Magnum	Target	32	35	39	43	49	54	59	Brite Blue
15-2VH	.357 Magnum	Target	32	37	42	47	55	61	70	Brite Blue
714	.357 Magnum	Service	30	34	40	NA	NA	NA	NA	Satin Stainless Steel
715	.357 Magnum	Target	32	36	40	45	50	54	59	Satin Stainless Steel
715-V	.357 Magnum	Target	32	35	40	43	49	54	59	Satin Stainless Steel
715-VH	.357 Magnum	Target	32	37	42	49	55	61	70	Satin Stainless Steel

22 REVOLVER

Built on the same frame as our .357 Magnum, have the heft and balance of a fine target revolver. Affordable fun for the beginner or the expert.

Specifications:
Six shot double and single action. **Ammunition:** Models 22 & 722 — .22 Long Rifle; Models 22M & 722M .22 Win Mag. **Typical Dimension:** 4″ Barrel Revolver — 9¼″ x 5¾″. **Trigger:** Smooth, wide tang (⅜″) with overtravel adjustment. **Hammer:** Wide spur (⅜″) with short double action travel. **Sights:** Front — ⅛″ serrated, interchangeable blade. Red insert standard. Yellow and white available. Rear — Standard white outline adjustable for windage and elevation. Graduated click. **Rifling:** Models 22 & 722 — Six lands and grooves, right-hand twist, one turn in 12 inches. Models 22M & 722M — Six lands and grooves, right-hand twist, one turn in 16 inches. **NOTE:** All 2½″ guns are shipped with undercover grips. 4″ guns are shipped with service grips and the balance have oversized target grips.

PRICE
$272.50-407.40

MODEL	CALIBER	TYPE	BARREL LENGTHS & WEIGHT IN OUNCES					FINISH
			2¼″	4″	6″	8″	10″	
22	.22 L.R.	Target	36	40	44	49	54	Brite Blue
22-V	.22 L.R.	Target	36	40	44	49	54	Brite Blue
22-VH	.22 L.R.	Target	36	41	47	54	61	Brite Blue
22-M	.22 Win Mag	Target	36	40	44	49	54	Brite Blue
22M-V	.22 Win Mag	Target	36	40	44	49	54	Brite Blue
22M-VH	.22 Win Mag	Target	36	41	47	54	61	Brite Blue
722	.22 L.R.	Target	36	40	44	49	54	Satin Stainless Steel
722-V	.22 L.R.	Target	36	40	44	49	54	Satin Stainless Steel
722-VH	.22 L.R.	Target	36	41	47	54	61	Satin Stainless Steel
722M	.22 Win Mag	Target	36	40	44	49	54	Satin Stainless Steel
722M-V	.22 Win Mag	Target	36	40	44	49	54	Satin Stainless Steel
722M-VH	.22 Win Mag	Target	36	41	47	54	61	Satin Stainless Steel

DAN WESSON REVOLVERS

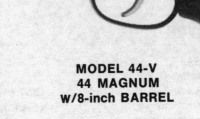

44 MAG. REVOLVERS

The Dan Wesson .44 Magnum is available with our patented "POWER CONTROL" to reduce muzzle flip. Both the .41 and the .44 have a one piece frame and patented gain bolt for maximum strength.

Specifications:
Six shot double and single action. **Ammunition:** Models 41 & 741 — .41 Magnum: Models 44 & 744 — .44 Magnum and .44 Special. **Typical Dimension:** 6″ barrel revolver — 12″ x 6″. **Trigger:** Smooth, wide tang (⅜″) with overtravel adjustment. **Hammer:** Wide checkered spur with short double-action travel. **Sights:** Front —⅛″ serrated interchangeable blade. Red insert standard. Yellow and white available. Rear — Standard white outline adjustable for windage and elevation. Click graduated. **Rifling:** Eight lands and grooves, right-hand twist, one turn in 18.75 inches. **NOTE:** 4″,6″, and 8″ .44 Magnum guns will be shipped with unported and POWER CONTROL barrels. 10″ .44 Magnum guns available only without POWER CONTROL. **NOTE:** Only jacketed bullets should be used with the .44 Mag. POWER CONTROL or excessive leading will result.

PRICE $373.40-473.60   * 10″ Nominal, 9.7″ Actual

MODEL 44-V
44 MAGNUM
W/8-inch BARREL

MODEL	CALIBER	TYPE	BARREL LENGTHS & WEIGHT IN OUNCES				FINISH
			4″	6″	8″	10″*	
41-V	.41 Magnum	Target	48	53	58	64	Brite Blue
41-VH	.41 Magnum	Target	49	56	64	69	Brite Blue
44-V	.44 Magnum	Target	48	53	58	64	Brite Blue
44-VH	.44 Magnum	Target	49	56	64	69	Brite Blue
741-V	.41 Magnum	Target	48	53	58	64	Satin Stainless Steel
741-VH	.41 Magnum	Target	49	56	64	69	Satin Stainless Steel
744-V	.44 Magnum	Target	48	53	58	64	Satin Stainless Steel
744-VH	.44 Magnum	Target	49	56	64	69	Satin Stainless Steel

38 REVOLVER

For decades a favorite of security and law enforcement agencies, the .38 special still maintains it's reputation as a fine caliber for sportsmen and target shooters. Dan Wesson gives you a choice of many barrel lengths in either the service or target configuration.

Specifications:
Six shot double and single action. **Ammunition:** .38 Special Hi-speed, .38 Special Mid-range. **Typical Dimension:** 4″ barrel revolver — 9¼″ x 5¾″. **Trigger:** Smooth, wide tang (⅜″) with overtravel adjustment. **Hammer:** Wide spur (⅜″) with short double action travel. **Sights:** Models 8 — 708 — ⅛″ fixed serrated front. Fixed rear integral with frame. Models 9 & 709 — ⅛″ serrated interchangeable front blade. Red insert standard. Yellow and white available. Rear — standard white outline, adjustable for windage and elevation. Graduated click. **Rifling:** Six lands & grooves, right-hand twist, one turn in 18.75 inches. **NOTE:** All 2½″ guns shipped with undercover grips. 4″ guns are shipped with service grips and the balance have over-sized target grips.

PISTOL PAC

PRICE $375.85 - 598.85

MODEL	CALIBER	TYPE	BARREL LENGTHS INCL.				Extra Grips	Addt'l. Sight Blades	Carry Case	Wrench & Gauge	Patch & Buckle
P-22	.22 L.R.	Target	2½	4	6	8	X	4	X	X	X
P-722	.22 L.R.	Target	2½	4	6	8	X	4	X	X	X
P-22M	.22 Win Mag	Target	2½	4	6	8	X	4	X	X	X
P-722M	.22 Win Mag	Target	2½	4	6	8	X	4	X	X	X
P-8-2	.38 Special	Service	2½	4	6	·	X	·	X	X	X
P-8-2B	.38 Special	Service	2½	4	6	·	X	·	X	X	X
P-9-2	.38 Special	Target	2½	4	6	8	X	4	X	X	X
P-708	.38 Special	Service	2½	4	6	·	X	·	X	X	X
P-709	.38 Special	Target	2½	4	6	8	X	4	X	X	X
P-14-2	.357 Magnum	Service	2½	4	6	·	X	·	X	X	X
P-14-2B	.357 Magnum	Service	2½	4	6	·	X	·	X	X	X
P-15-2	.357 Magnum	Target	2½	4	6	8	X	4	X	X	X
P-714	.357 Magnum	Service	2½	4	6	·	X	·	X	X	X
P-715	.357 Magnum	Target	2½	4	6	8	X	4	X	X	X
P-41	.41 Magnum	Target	·	·	6	8	X	2	X	X	X
P-741	.41 Magnum	Target	·	·	6	8	X	2	X	X	X
P-44*	.44 Magnum	Target	·	·	6	8	X	2	X	X	X
P-744*	.44 Magnum	Target	·	·	6	8	X	2	X	X	X

*Standard .44 pac includes a gun with 8″ unported barrel; an 8″ "POWER CONTROL" barrel; and two 6″ barrels—one unported and one "POWER CONTROL" with appropriate shroud.

PRICE
$219.50-375.20

MODEL	CALIBER	TYPE	BARREL LENGTHS & WEIGHT IN OUNCES				FINISH
			2½″	4″	6″	8″	
8-2	.38 Special	Service	30	34	38	N/A	Satin Blue
8-2B	.38 Special	Service	30	34	38	N/A	Brite Blue
9-2	.38 Special	Target	32	36	40	44	Brite Blue
9-2V	.39 Special	Target	32	35	39	43	Brite Blue
9-2VH	.38 Special	Target	32	37	42	47	Brite Blue
708	.38 Special	Service	30	34	38	N/A	Satin Stainless Steel
709	.38 Special	Target	32	36	40	44	Satin Stainless Steel
709-V	.38 Special	Target	32	35	39	43	Satin Stainless Steel
709-VH	.38 Special	Target	32	37	42	47	Satin Stainless Steel

Rifles

ANSCHUTZ RIFLES

MODEL 1422 D CLASSIC

Classic and Custom Grade Sporter Rifles

Specifications	Classic 1422D 1522D	Classic 1432D 1532D	Custom 1422D 1522D	Custom 1432D 1532D
Length—Overall	43 in.	42½ in.	43 in.	43 in.
Barrel	24 in.	23½ in.	24 in.	24 in.
Pull	14 in.	14 in.	14 in.	14 in.
Drop at—Comb	½ in.	½ in.	½ in.	½ in.
Monte Carlo			½ in.	½ in.
Heel	1¼ in.	1¼ in.	1¼ in.	1¼ in.
Average Weight	7¼ lbs.	7¾ lbs.	6½ lbs.	6½ lbs.
Rate of Twist Right Hand—one turn in 16.5 in. for .22LR; 1-16 in. for .22 Mag & .22 Hornet; 1-14 in. for .22 Rem.				
Take Down Bolt Action	•	•	•	•
Swivel Studs	•	•	•	•

Features	Classic 1422D 1522D	Classic 1432D 1532D	Custom 1422D 1522D	Custom 1432D 1532D
Grooved for Scope	•	•	•	•
Tapped for Scope	•	•	•	•
Sights—Front—Hooded Ramp	•		•	•
Rear—Folding Leaf	•		•	•
Trigger—Single Stage	•	•	•	•
Adjustable for Creep & Pull	•	•	•	•
Factory Set for Approx. 2.6 lbs. Pull	•	•	•	•
Clip Magazine	•	•	•	•
Safety—Wing	•	•	•	•
Stock—Monte Carlo			•	•
Roll Over Cheek Piece			•	•

MODEL 1416 D DELUXE

Deluxe Sporting Rifles

Features	Deluxe 1416D 1516D	Deluxe 1418D 1518D	Model 520/61 Auto
Grooved for Scope	•	•	•
Tapped for Scope			
Sights—Front—Hooded Ramp	•	•	•
Rear—Folding Leaf	•	•	•
Trigger—Single Stage	•	•	•
Adjustable for Creep & Pull	•	•	
Factory Set for Approx. 2.6 lbs. Pull	•	•	
Clip Magazine	•	•	•
Safety—Slide	•	•	
Rotary			•
Stock—Monte Carlo	•		•
Cheek Piece	•	•	
Roll Over Cheek Piece			

Specifications	Deluxe 1416D 1516D	Deluxe 1418D 1518D	Model 520/61 Auto
Length—Overall	41 in.	38 in.	43 in.
Barrel	22½ in.	19¾ in.	24 in.
Pull	14 in.	14 in.	14 in.
Drop at—Comb	¾ in.	¾ in.	1 in.
Monte Carlo	1 in.	1 in.	1½ in.
Heel	2 in.	2 in.	2½ in.
Average Weight	6 lbs.	5½ lbs.	6½ lbs.
Rate of Twist Right Hand—one turn in 16.5 in. for .22 LR; 1-16 in. for .22 Mag & .22 Hornet; 1-14 in. for .222 Rem. & .223 Rem.			
Take Down Bolt Action	•	•	
With Removable Firing Pin	•	•	
¾ in. Swivels		•	
Swivel Studs	•		•

ANSCHUTZ RIFLES

Match Rifles

MODEL MARK 2000

Specifications and Features

	Mark 2000	1403
Barrel	Precision rifled 22 long rifle only.	
Length	25¼-in. ¾-in. dia.	25¼-in. medium heavy 11/16-in. dia
Action	Single Shot. Large loading platform.	
Trigger	Factory set for crisp trigger pull. 3 lbs.	1.1 lbs. Single stage, adjustable for weight of pull, take-up, over-travel.
Safety	Slide safety locks trigger.	Slide safety locks sear and bolt.
Stock	Walnut finished hardwood.	Walnut finished hardwood Cheek-piece/Swivel Rail.
Sights	Front-Insert type globesight. Rear-(Micrometer click adjustments) available separately.	Takes Anschutz 6723 sights. Barrel drilled and tapped for blocks.
Overall Length	44 in.	44 in.
Weight (avg.)	7½-lbs	8.6 lbs. with sights

MODEL 64MS

MODEL 54.18MS

Metallic Silhouette Rifles

Specifications and Features

	64MS	54.18MS	54.18MSL
Grooved for scope		•	•
Tapped for scope mounts	•	•	•
Overall length	39.5 in.	39 in.	39 in.
Barrel length	21¼ in.	20 in.	20 in.
Length of pull	13½ in.	13¾ in.	13¾ in.
High cheek piece with Monte Carlo	•	•	•
Drop at Comb	1½ in.	1½ in.	1½ in.
Average weight	8 lbs.	8 lbs. 6 oz.	8 lbs. 6 oz.
Trigger:			
Two stage	Model 5091	Model 5018	Model 5018
Factory adjusted weight	5.3 oz.	3.9 oz.	3.9 oz.
Adjustable weight	4.9-7 oz.	2.1-8.6 oz.	2.1—8.6 oz.
Safety	Slide	Slide	Slide

ANSCHUTZ RIFLES

MODEL 1813

MODEL 1811

MODEL 1807

MODEL 1808ED

International Match Rifles

Specifications and Features

	1813	1811	1810	1807	1808ED-Super
Barrel Length	27¼ in.	27¼ in.	27¼ in.	26 in.	(19 in.)23½ in.
O/D	1 in.	1 in.	1 in.	⅞ in.	⅞ in.
Stock	Int'l.-Thumb Hole Adj. Palm Rest Adj. Palm Rest	Prone	Int'l.-Thumb Hole	Standard	Thumb Hole
Cheek Piece	Adj.	Adj.	Adj.	Removable	Adj.
Butt Plate	Adj. Hook 10 Way Hook	Adj. 4 Way	Adj. Hook 10 Way Hook	Adj. 4 Way	Adj. 4 Way
Recommended Sights	6720, 6723	6720,6723	6720,6723	6720,6723	Grooved Tapped Scope Mounts
Overall Length	45 in.-46 in.	45 in.-46 in.	45 in.-46 in.	43¾ in.-44½ in.	42 in.
Overall Length to Hook	49.6 in.-51.2 in.		49.6 in.-51.2 in.		
Weight without sights (approx.)	15.4 lbs.	11.9 lbs.	13.9 lbs.	10 lbs.	9¼ lbs.
True Left Hand Version	1813L	1811L	1810L	1807L	1808L
Recommended Sights for Above Models	6720L	6720L	6720L	6720L	Scope

ANSCHUTZ RIFLES

MODEL 1432 D CUSTOM

MODEL 520

TARGET RIFLES

1808ED Super - Running Target **$790.00	**1427B Biathlon w/6723 (Rear 6707) ...... $ 998.00**
**1808ED Super L - Running Target 868.00	**1427BL Biathlon w/6723 (Rear 6707) 1137.00

Without sights and sling swivel

1403 ...... 379.00	**1810 ...... 999.50
**1403L (Left Stock) 399.00	**1810L 1099.50
1807 ...... 706.00	1811 ...... 774.00
**1807L (Left Hand) 775.00	**1811L 850.00
**1809 ...... 930.00	1813 ...... 1124.00
**1809L 1022.00	**1813L 1235.00
2000 w/out sights 206.00	64MS 365.00
	54.18MS 682.00
**Available on special non-cancellable factory order.	54.18MSL 747.00

SPORTER RIFLES:

1416D	22 LR	370.00			
1516D	22 M	380.00	1518D	22 M	533.50
1422D	22 LR	634.50	1422D CL	22 LR	598.00
1522D	22 M	634.50	1522D CL	22 M	598.00
1432D	22 H	698.00	1432D CL	22 H	655.00
1532D	222 R	698.00	1532D CL	222 R	655.00
1418D	22 LR	521.50	520	22 LR	259.00
1433D	22 H	800.00			

BAUER RIFLE

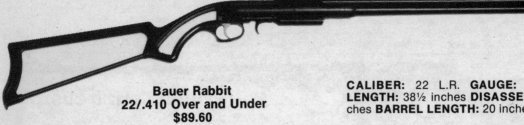

Bauer Rabbit
22/.410 Over and Under
$89.60

All metal construction, all American-made. The Rabbit features a special rust- and wear-resistant finish on stock, barrel and receiver. Quickly, the lightweight Rabbit can be taken down to a compact length of only 20 inches and easily snaps together to an assembled length of 38½ inches. Ideal for stowing in a backpack, private plane, fishing boat, recreation vehicle or in your favorite pick-up truck. The Rabbit also features selective single trigger for

CALIBER: 22 L.R. **GAUGE:** .410/3 inch **OVERALL LENGTH:** 38½ inches **DISASSEMBLED LENGTH:** 20 inches **BARREL LENGTH:** 20 inches **WEIGHT:** 4¾ lbs.

easy choice of either 22 cal. rifle or .410 shotgun. Ideal for the camper, trapper, coon hunter and plinker. With a .410 slug and rust-resistant finish it's dynamite as a shark gun.

All parts are precision machined and meticulously fitted to assure smooth, dependable and lasting performance. Bauer Firearms also prides itself on a fast and dependable warranty repair service.

BEEMAN RIFLES

BEEMAN/WEIHRAUCH HW 60 SMALLBORE RIFLE
FROM $495.00

22-caliber LR, single shot. Improved bolt action. Adjustable match trigger with push button safety. Precision rifled barrel. Stippled forearm and pistol grip. Precision aperture sights, hooded front sight ramp. Barrel length: 26.8 inches. Length: 45.7 inches. Weight: 10.8 lbs.

BEEMAN/FWB 2000
FROM $795.00

22-caliber long rifle. Micrometer match aperture sights. Foresight with interchangeable inserts. Meets ISU standard rifle specifications. Short lock time. Precision match trigger adjustable for weight, release point, finger length, lateral position, etc. Barrel length: 22 inches and 26¼ inches. Length: 39 inches and 43¾ inches. Weight 9⅛ lbs. and 9¾ lbs.

BEEMAN/FWB 2000
SUPER MATCH

$1285.00 mech. trigger   **$1505.00 Elect. trigger**

Developed from the highly successful design of the FWB 2000. Available with same outstanding mechanical trigger of the 2000 or the new electronic trigger. Anatomically correct thumbhole stock, accessory rails for moveable weights and adj. palm rest, adj. cheekpiece, adj. hooked buttplate, superb match sights.

BROWNING AUTOMATIC RIFLES

22 RIFLE SPECIFICATIONS

	22 Automatic	BL-22	BAR-22 Long Rifle	BRP-22 Magnum
Models	22 Long Rifle: Grade I, II, III. 22 Short: Grade I only.	Grades I, II.	Grades I, II.	Grades I, II.
Action	Self loading and ejecting. Shoots as rapidly as trigger is pulled. Double extractors. Bottom ejection.	Short throw lever. Travels an arc of only 33° carrying trigger with it, thereby preventing finger pinch.	Self loading and ejecting. Shoots as rapidly as trigger is pulled. Side ejection.	Short, positive pump stroke. Finger must be released and re-applied to trigger at end of stroke. Side ejection.
Barrel	22 Long Rifle: 19¼ in. 22 Short: 22 in. Crowned muzzle.	Both models: 20 in. Recessed muzzle.	20¼ in. Recessed muzzle.	20¼ in. Recessed muzzle.
Overall Length	22 Long Rifle: 37 in. 22 Short: 40 in.	Both models: 36¾ in.	38¼ in.	38¼ in.
Magazine	Tubular. Loading port in stock.	Tubular. Loading port under barrel.	Tubular. Latch closes from any position.	Tubular. Latch closes from any position.
Magazine Capacity	22 Long Rifle: 11 22 Short: 16	22 Long Rifle: 15 22 Long: 17 22 Short: 22	22 Long Rifle: 15	22 Magnum: 11
Stock	Select walnut. Finely checkered pistol grip and forearm.	Select walnut. Grade II: Grip and forearm finely checkered.	French walnut. Stock and forearm with cut checkering.	French walnut. Pistol grip and forearm with cut checkering.
Stock Dimensions	Length of pull 13¾ in. Drop at comb 1-3/16 in. Drop at heel 2⅝ in.	Length of pull 13½ in. Drop at comb 1⅝ in. Drop at heel 2¼ in.	Lenth of pull 13¾ in. Drop at comb 1½ in. Drop at heel 2¼ in.	Length of pull 13¾ in. Drop at comb 1½ in. Drop at heel 2¼ in.
Safety	Cross bolt safety system on forward section of trigger guard. Left hand optional at no extra cost when specifically ordered.	Disconnect system prevents firing during level cycle; exposed hammer with half-cock postion; inertia firing pin prevents firing due to accidental blow on hammer.	Cross bolt style safety on rear of trigger guard.	Cross bolt style safety on rear of trigger guard.
Sights	Front: Gold bead. Rear: Folding leaf with calibrated adjustments.	Front: Bead. Rear: Folding leaf with calibrated adjustments.	Front: Bead. Rear: Folding leaf with calibrated adjustments.	Front: Gold bead. Rear: Folding leaf with calibrated adjustments.
Sight Radius	Long Rifle: 16¼ in. Short 19 in.	15⅜ in.	16 in.	16 in.
Approximate Weight	22 Long Rifle: 4 lbs. 12 oz. 22 Short: 4 lbs. 15 oz.	5 lbs.	5 lbs. 13 oz.	6 lbs. 4 oz.
Recommended Scope and Mounts	4 x 22 Riflescope. Barrel drilled and tapped to accept Scope Mount Base.	4 x 22 Riflescope. Receiver grooved to accept Scope Mount Base.	4 x 22 Riflescope. Receiver grooved to accept Scope Mount Base.	4 x 22 Riflescope. Receiver grooved to accept Scope Mount Base.

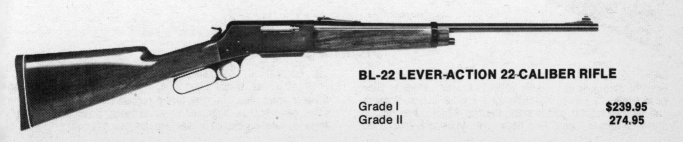

BL-22 LEVER-ACTION 22-CALIBER RIFLE

Grade I	**$239.95**
Grade II	**274.95**

BROWNING AUTOMATIC RIFLES

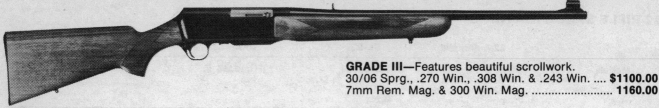

GRADE I—Quiet Browning quality.
30/06 Sprg., .270 Win., .308 Win. & .243 Win. **$499.95**
7mm Rem. Mag. & 300 Win. Mag. 549.95

GRADE III—Features beautiful scrollwork.
30/06 Sprg., .270 Win., .308 Win. & .243 Win. **$1100.00**
7mm Rem. Mag. & 300 Win. Mag. **1160.00**

Grade IV—The ultimate big-game rifle. The stock on this rifle is the very finest, highly figured French walnut.
30/06 Sprg., .270 Win., .308 Win. & .243 Win. **$2090.00**
7mm Rem. Mag. & 300 Win. Mag. **2150.00**

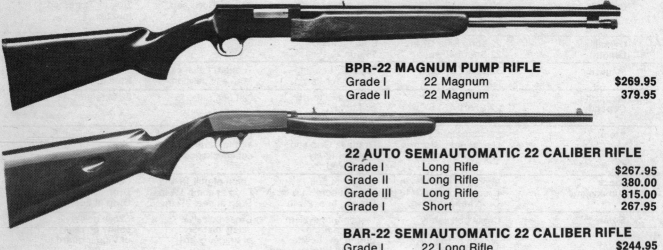

BPR-22 MAGNUM PUMP RIFLE

Grade I	22 Magnum	$269.95
Grade II	22 Magnum	379.95

22 AUTO SEMIAUTOMATIC 22 CALIBER RIFLE

Grade I	Long Rifle	$267.95
Grade II	Long Rifle	380.00
Grade III	Long Rifle	815.00
Grade I	Short	267.95

BAR-22 SEMIAUTOMATIC 22 CALIBER RIFLE

Grade I	22 Long Rifle	$244.95
Grade II	22 Long Rifle	349.95

Left hand safety optional at no extra charge if specified when placing order.

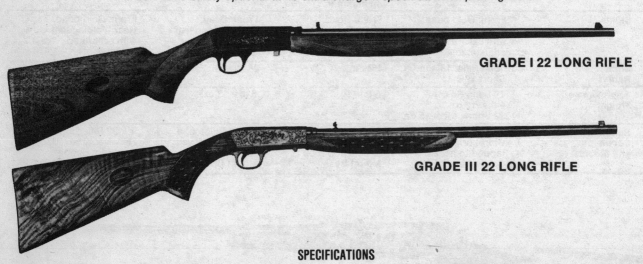

GRADE I 22 LONG RIFLE

GRADE III 22 LONG RIFLE

SPECIFICATIONS

Caliber: 22 Long Rifle in Grades I, II, III; 22 Short in Grade I only. **Action:** Semiautomatic, double extractors with bottom ejection. **Barrel length:** 22 LR, 19¼ inches; 22 Short, 22 inches. **Magazine:** Tubular with loading port in stock. **Capacity:** 22 LR, 11 rounds; 22 Short, 16 rounds. **Sights:** Gold bead front. Adjustable, folding leaf rear. **Length of pull:** 13¾ inches. **Overall length:** Long Rifle, 37 inches. Short, 40 inches. **Weight:** Long Rifle, 4 lbs. 12 oz.; Short, 4 lbs.15oz. **Grade II**—(not illus.) Chrome plated receiver in satin finish with small game scenes, engraved on all surfaces. Select walnut and forearm, hand-checkered in diamond design.

BROWNING RIFLES

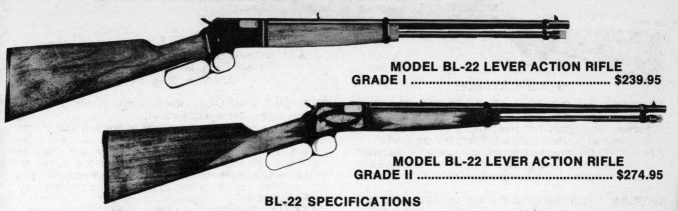

MODEL BL-22 LEVER ACTION RIFLE
GRADE I $239.95

MODEL BL-22 LEVER ACTION RIFLE
GRADE II $274.95

RIFLES

BL-22 SPECIFICATIONS

ACTION — Short throw lever action. Lever travels through an arc of only 33 degrees and carries the trigger with it, preventing finger pinch between lever and trigger on the upward swing. The lever cycle ejects the fired shell, cocks the hammer and feeds a fresh round into the chamber.

MAGAZINE — Rifle is designed to handle 22 caliber ammunition *in any combination* from tubular magazine. Magazine capacity is 15 Long Rifles, 17 Longs and 22 Shorts. The positive magazine latch opens and closes easily from any position.

SAFETY — A unique disconnect system prevents firing until the lever and breech are fully closed and pressure is released from and reapplied to the trigger. An inertia firing pin and an exposed hammer with a half-cock position are other safety features.

RECEIVER — Forged and milled steel. Grooved. All parts are machine-finished and hand-fitted.

TRIGGER — Clean and crisp without creep. Average pull 5 pounds. Trigger gold-plated on Grade II model.

STOCK AND FOREARM — Forearm and straight grip butt stock are shaped from select, polished walnut. Hand checkered on Grade II model. Stock dimensions:

Length of Pull .... 13½ in.
Drop at Comb .... 1⅝ in.
Drop at Heel .... 2¼ in.

SIGHTS — Precision, adjustable folding leaf rear sight. Raised bead front sight.

SCOPES — Grooved receiver will accept the Browning 22 riflescope (Model 1217) and two-piece ring mount (Model 9417) as well as most other groove or tip-off type mounts or receiver sights.

ENGRAVING — Grade II receiver and trigger guard are hand-engraved with tasteful scroll designs

BARREL — Recessed muzzle. Barrel length: 20 inches.

OVERALL LENGTH — 36¾ inches

WEIGHT — 5 pounds

BLR RIFLE
22-250 Rem., 243 Winchester, 308 Winchester &
358 Winchester
$394.95

BLR SPECIFICATIONS

CALIBERS: 22-250 Rem., 243 Win., 257 Roberts, 7mm-08 Rem., 308 Win. and 358 Win.

APPROXIMATE WEIGHT: 6 pounds, 15 ounces

OVERALL LENGTH: 39¾ inches

ACTION: Lever action with rotating head, multiple lug breech bolt with recessed bolt face. Side ejection.

BARREL: Individually machined from forged, heat treated chrome-moly steel. Length: 20 inches. Crowned muzzle. Rifling: 243 Win.—one turn in 10 inches. 308 and 358 Win.—one turn in 12 inches.

MAGAZINE: Detachable, 4-round capacity

TRIGGER: Wide, grooved finger piece. Short crisp pull of 4½ pounds. Travels with lever.

RECEIVER: Non-glare top. Drilled and tapped to accept most top scope mounts. Forged and milled steel. All parts are machine-finished and hand-fitted. Surface deeply polished.

SIGHTS: Low profile, square notch, screw adjustable rear sight. Gold bead on a hooded raised ramp front sight. Sight radius: 17¾ inches.

SAFETY: Exposed, 3-position hammer. Trigger disconnect system. Inertia firing pin.

STOCK AND FOREARM: Select walnut with tough oil finish and sure-grip checkering, contoured for use with either open sights or scope. Straight grip stock. Deluxe recoil pad installed.

Length of pull .... 13¾ inches
Drop at comb .... 1¾ inches
Drop at heel .... 2⅜ inches

ACCESSORIES: Extra magazines are available as well as sling swivel attachment for forearm bolt and butt-stock eyelet for sling mounting. **$21.75**

BROWNING RIFLES

BBR BOLT ACTION RIFLE
**Calibers—25-06 Rem., 270 Win., 30-06 Sprg.,
7mm Rem. Mag., 300 Win. Mag.,
338 Win. Mag. $469.95**

SPECIFICATIONS:

ACTION: Short throw bolt of 60 degrees. The large diameter bolt and fluted surface reduce wobble and friction. The rotary bolt head has 9 engaging locking lugs and a recessed bolt face. Plunger-type ejector.
MAGAZINE: Detachable. Depress the magazine latch and the hinged floorplate swings down. The magazine can be removed from the floorplate for reloading or safety reasons.
TRIGGER: Adjustable within the average range of 3 to 6 pounds. Also grooved to provide sure finger control.
STOCK AND FOREARM: Anti-warp inlays of structural aluminum ⅛ inch thick and 8 inches long in the barrel channel. Stock is select grade American walnut cut to the lines of a Monte Carlo sporter with a full pistol grip and high cheek piece. Stock dimensions:

Length of Pull .... 13⅜ in.
Drop at Comb .... 1⅝ in.
Drop at Heel .... 2⅛ in.

SCOPES: Closed. Clean tapered barrel. Receiver is drilled and tapped for a scope mount.
BARREL: Hammer forged rifling where a precision machined mandrel is inserted into the bore. The mandrel is a reproduction of the rifling in reverse. As hammer forces are applied to the exterior of the barrel, the barrel is actually molded around the mandrel to produce flawless rifling and to guarantee a straight bore. 24 inches long.
OVERALL LENGTH: 44½ inches   **WEIGHT:** 8 pounds

SHORT ACTION BBR
**Calibers—22-250 Rem., 243 Win., 257 Roberts,
7mm-08 Rem., 306 Win. $469.95**

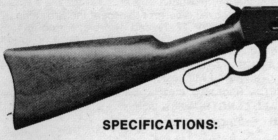

BROWNING 92
**Calibers—357 Mag., 44 Rem. Mag.,
Grade I $324.95**

SPECIFICATIONS:

ACTION: Lever operated with double verticle locks. Exposed 3 position hammer with half-cock position. Top ejection.
RECEIVER: Forged and milled from high strength steel.
BARRELS: Machined from forged, heat-treated billets of steel. Chambered and rifled for 357 Mag. and 44 Rem. Mag. caliber. Rifling twist 1 turn in 38 inches. Barrel length 20 inches.
SIGHTS: Classic cloverleaf rear with notched elevation ramp. Steel post front. Sight radius 16⅝ inches.

TRIGGER: Gold plated. Trigger pull approximately 5½ lbs.
MAGAZINE: Tubular. Loading port in right side of reciever. Magazine capacity 11 rounds.
STOCK AND FOREARM: Seasoned French walnut with high gloss finish. Straight grip stock and classic forearm style. Steel modified crescent butt plate.
Length of pull—12¾ in.
Drop at comb—2 in.
Drop at heel—2⅞ in.
OVERALL LENGTH: 37½ inches
APPROXIMATE WEIGHT: 5½ lbs.
HAND-ENGRAVED RECEIVER: Hand-engraved scrollwork on both receiver sides.

CHARTER AR-7 EXPLORER RIFLE

**MODEL 9220
EXPLORER RIFLE
(22 Long Rifle Caliber)**

**$98.00 (black finish)
101.00 (satin finish)**

The Explorer rifle is a semiautomatic 22 Long Rifle caliber with a 16-inch barrel and is fitted with a plastic stock which floats if accidentally dropped in water. For transport, the Explorer compacts into its own stock, measuring 16½ inches overall. The rear sight is a hooded peep with the aperture adjustable for elevation changes. Windage may be accomplished by moving the front sight back and forth.

CALIBER: 22 Long Rifle. **ACTION:** Semiautomatic. **LOAD:** Detachable box, magazine fed. **SIGHTS:** Square blade front, adjusting rear peep. **CAPACITY:** 8 rounds. **BARREL** High test alloy with rifled steel liner. **STOCK:** Full pistol grip, recessed to carry barrel and action. **WEIGHT:** 2¾ pounds. **OVERALL LENGTH:** 34½ inches. **LENGTH STOWED:** 16½ inches.

COLT HIGH POWER RIFLES

COLT SAUER SPORTING RIFLE
standard calibers $1172.95
magnum calibers $1212.50

Caliber: 25-06, 270, 30-06, 7mm Rem. Mag., 300 Win. Mag., 300 Weatherby Mag.
Capacity: 3 round with detachable magazines
Barrel length(s): 24 inches
Weight: Standard 8 lb.; mag. 8 lbs. 10 oz.
Overall length: 43¾ inches
Sights: Drilled and tapped for scope mounts

Action: Bolt action
Safety: Tang-type safety that mechanically locks the sear
Stock: American walnut, cast-off Monte Carlo design with cheekpiece; forend tip and pistol-grip cap are rosewood with white line spacers, hand-checkering and black recoil pad
Features: Unique barrel/receiver union, non-rotating bolt with 3 internal articulating locking lugs

COLT SAUER SHORT ACTION
$1172.95

Caliber: 22-250, 243 and 308 (7.62 mm NATO)
Barrel Length: 24 inches
Overall Length: 43¾ inches
Barrel Type: Krupp Special Steel, hammer forged
Stock: American walnut, Monte Carlo cheekpiece with rosewood forend tip and pistol grip cap
Weight (empty): 7 lbs. 8 oz.
Safety: Tang
Sights: Drilled and tapped for scope mounts

Magazine Capacity: 3 rounds in detachable magazine
Finish: Colt Blue with polyurethane
FEATURES: Now the Colt Sauer Rifle is available in 22-250, 243 and 308. Features the same revolutionary non-rotating bolt with three large locking lugs. American walnut stock with high-gloss finish, 18-line-per-inch checkering, rosewood forend tip and grip cap, black recoil pad. Cocking indicator, loaded chamber indicator, and Safety-on bolt opening capability.

COLT SAUER GRAND AFRICAN
$1304.95

Caliber: 458 Win. Mag. **Capacity:** 3 rounds with detachable magazines
Barrel length(s): 24 inch round tapered
Weight: 10 lbs. without sights
Overall length: 44½ inches
Sights: Hooded ramp style front; fully adjustable rear
Action: Bolt action
Safety: Tang type that mechanically locks the sear

Stock: Solid African bubinga wood, cast-off Monte Carlo design with cheek piece, contrasting rosewood, forend tip and pistol-grip cap with white line spacers, and checkering on the forend and pistol grip. **Features:** Unique barrel/receiver union, non-rotating bolt with 3 internal articulating locking lugs.

COLT SAUER GRAND ALASKAN
$1245.50

Caliber: 375 H&H. **Capacity:** 3 rounds with detachable magazine. **Barrel length:** 24 inches. **Weight:** 8 lbs. 10 oz. **Overall length:** 43¾ inches. **Sights:** Drilled and tapped for scope mounts. **Safety:** Tang. **Stock:** American walnut, Monte Carlo cheekpiece with rosewood forend tip and pistol grip cap and black recoil pad.

H&R CARBINES

MODEL 171 DELUXE
SPRINGFIELD CAVALRY CARBINE
$375.00

Caliber: 45-70 GOVT.
Stock: American walnut with saddle ring and bridle
Action: Trap door, single shot
Weight: 7 lbs.

Barrel Length: 22 inches
Overall Length: 41 inches
Sights: Blade front sight; original military-style rear
Metal Finish: Blue-black and color cased. Engraved action.

MODEL 174
LITTLE BIG HORN COMMEMORATIVE
SPRINGFIELD CARBINE
$375.00

Caliber: 45-70 GOVT.
Stock: American Walnut with metal grip adapter
Action: Trap door, single shot
Barrel Length: 22 inches

Sights: Tang mounted aperture sight adjustable for windage and elevation. Blade front sight.
Weight: 7 lbs. 8 oz.
Overall Length: 41 inches
Metal Finish: Barrel—Blue-Black
Action—Color case hardened

H&R CENTERFIRE RIFLES

BOLT-ACTION MODEL 340
$395.00

Caliber: 243 Win., 270 Win., 30-06, 308 Win., 7mm Mauser
Capacity: 5 round magazine.
Stock: One-piece genuine American walnut stock with rollover cheekpiece and pistol grip. Hand checkered, contrasting wood on forearm tip. Pistol grip cap. Rifle recoil pad.
Action: Mauser-type bolt action with hinged floor plate and adjustable trigger.

Barrel Length: 22-inches, tapered
Weight: 7¼ lbs.
Sights: Fully adjustable rear sight drilled and tapped for scope mounts and receiver sight. Gold bead front sight grooved for hood.
Overall Length: 43 inches
Safety: Sliding safety.

H&R RIMFIRE RIFLES
MODEL 865 $89.50

Caliber: 22 long rifle; standard and high velocity cartridge
Capacity: 5-round magazine
Weight: 5 lbs.
Barrel Length: 22-inches, tapered. **Overall Length:** 39 inches
Stock: Walnut-finished American hardwood. Hard rubber buttplate, white liner

Action: Self-cocking bolt action
Safety: Side thumb level
Sights: Blade front; open rear sight with elevator; grooved for tip-off scope mounts

H&R RIMFIRE RIFLES

MODEL 700 22 WMR $185.00

Caliber: 22 WMRF
Capacity: 5-round clip
Barrel Length: 22 inches
Weight: 6½ lbs.
Overall Length: 43¼ inches

Sights: Blade front; folding leaf rear; drilled and tapped for scope bases
Stock: Walnut stock
Finish: Blue-black barrel and receiver

Model 700 Deluxe, 22 caliber WMRF with 22-inch barrel, scope and mounts **$295.00**

MODEL 750 $79.00

Caliber: 22 long rifle; standard and high velocity cartridge
Capacity: Single shot   **Weight:** 5 lbs.
Barrel Length: 22-inch tapered. **Overall Length:** 39 inches

Stock: Walnut-finished American hardwood. Hard rubber buttplate, white liner
Action: Self-cocking bolt action
Safety: Side thumb lever
Sights: Blade front; open rear sight with elevator; grooved for tip-off scope mounts

MODEL 5200 MATCH $325.00

Caliber: 22 long rifle match
Action: Turn bolt, single shot   **Weight:** 11 lbs.
Barrel Length: 28 inches. **Overall Length:** 46 inches

Stock: American walnut, semi-gloss finish
Sights: None supplied with rifle. Receiver drilled and tapped for receiver sight. Barrel drilled and tapped for front sight. Scope bases supplied.
Metal Finish: Polished blue-black

H & R COMBO SHOTGUN/RIFLE

**MODEL 258 Handy Gun II
Combination Gun $149.50**

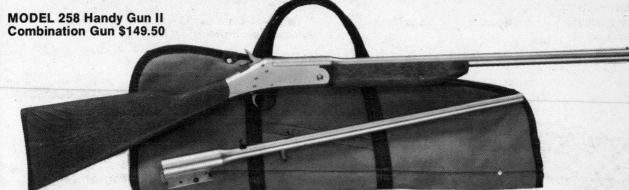

Average Weight: 6½ pounds. With case and accessory barrel 9¼.
Sights: Shotgun, bead front sight. Rifles, ramp mounted blade front sight and adjustable folding leaf rear sight. Drilled and tapped for scope mounts.
O/A Length: 37 inches
Stock Dimensions: Length 13¾ inches, drop at comb 1½ inches, drop at heel 2½ inches.

Gauge/Bbl./Length/Choke: 20/22 inches Mod.
Chamber Length: 20 Gauge 3 inches
Accessory 22in. Rifle Barrels: 22 Hornet, 30-30 Win., 357 Mag. (38 Spl.) 44 Mag.
Stock: Straight grip stock with semibeavertail forend in walnut-finished American hardwood.
Metal Finish: Barrels and all parts, inside and out, in H&R Hard-Guard electro-less matte nickel process.

RIFLES

H & R COMBO SHOTGUN/RIFLE

MODEL 058 COMBO GUN
20 gauge and 30-30 Win., 22 Hornet, 357 Mag. or 44 Mag.
$122.00

Gauge: 20-gauge modified-choke shotgun
Barrel length(s): 26 inches mod. Rifle 22 inches
Weight: 5¼ lbs., 6 lbs. with rifle barrel
Overall length: Shotgun barrel, 41½ inches; rifle barrel, 37½ inches

Sights: Front bead on shotgun barrel; blade front, folding leaf rear on rifle barrel
Action: Single shot
Stock: Walnut-finished hardwood with hard-rubber butt plate
Finish: Blue-black; color cased frame
Accessories: 30-30 Win. or 22 Hornet 22-inch barrels

H & R SINGLE-SHOT RIFLES

MODEL 157
30-30 Win., 22 Hornet
$122.00

Caliber: 30-30 Win., 22 Hornet
Barrel length: 22 inches
Weight: 6¼ lbs.
Overall length: 37 inches
Sights: Blade front; folding leaf rear; drilled and tapped for scope bases

Action: Single shot
Stock: Walnut-finished hardwood with hard-rubber butt plate
Finish: Blue-black barrel with color-cased frame
Accessories: Swivels front and rear

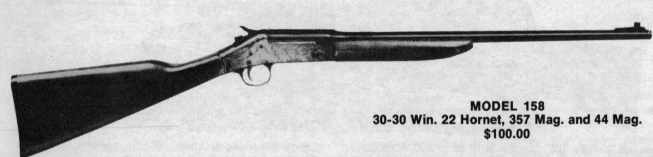

MODEL 158
30-30 Win. 22 Hornet, 357 Mag. and 44 Mag.
$100.00

Sights: Blade front with ramp; folding leaf rear; drilled and tapped for scope bases
Action: Single shot
Stock: Walnut finished hardwood with a hard-rubber butt plate
Finish: Blue-black barrel with color case-hardened frame

Caliber: 30-30 Win., 22 Hornet, 357 Mag., 44 Mag.
Barrel length: 22 inches
Weight: 6 lbs.
Overall length: 37 inches

HECKLER & KOCH RIFLES

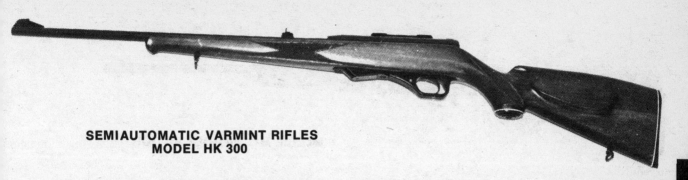

SEMIAUTOMATIC VARMINT RIFLES
MODEL HK 300

The Model HK 300 features a European walnut checkered stock. All metal parts are finished in a high-luster custom blue. The receiver is fitted with special bases for a HK 05 quick snap-on clamp mount with 1-inch rings that will fit all standard scopes. The positive locking action of the HK 05 provides for instant scope mounting with no change in zero, even after hundreds of repetitions. The rifle has a V-notch rear sight, adjustable for windage, and a front sight adjustable for elevation. Scope mounts are available as an additional accessory.

Caliber: 22 Winchester Magnum.
Weight: 5.7 lbs.

Barrel: Hammer forged, polygonal profile
Overall length: 39.4 inches
Magazine: Box type, 5 and 15 rounds capacity
Sights: V-notch rear, adjustable for windage; post front, adjustable for elevation
Trigger: Single stage, 3½ lb. pull
Action: Straight blow-back inertia bolt
Stock: Top-grade European walnut, Monte Carlo style with cheek rest, checkered pistol grip and forearm
Accessories: HK 05 clamp mount with 1-inch rings to fit most U.S. made telescopic sights **$113.00**
Model HK 300 .... **350.00**

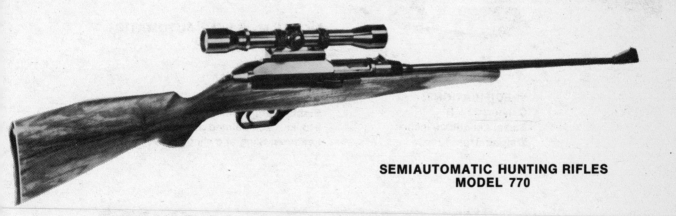

SEMIAUTOMATIC HUNTING RIFLES
MODEL 770

SPECIFICATIONS:
Caliber: 308 Win.
Weight: (308 cal.) 8 lbs.
Barrel: Hammer forged, standard or polygonal profile.
Overall Length: 44.5 inches
Magazine: 3 and 10 rounds
Sights: V-notch rear, adjustable for windage; post front, adjustable for elevation

Trigger: Single stage
Action: Delayed Roller locked
Stock: European walnut with Monte Carlo cheek rest

Model 770 .... **$560.00**
Model 940 same as **Model 770,**
except is 30-06 caliber **580.00**
Model 630 same as **Model 770**
except is .223 caliber.. **560.00**

KASSNAR RIFLES

MODEL M-1500 BOLT ACTION

SPECIFICATIONS:
Caliber: 22 mag., 22 MRF
Barrel: Tapered sporter-weight barrel
Weight: 6½ lbs.
Sights: Open sight sporter-type

Action: Bolt
Safety: Positive sliding thumb safety
Stock: Nato wood, with Monte Carlo comb. Receiver grooved for tip-off scope mount.

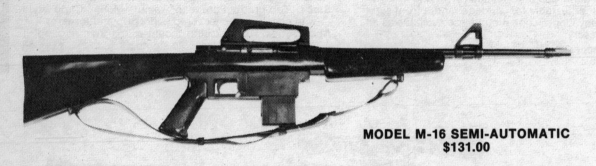

MODEL M-16 SEMI-AUTOMATIC
$131.00

SPECIFICATIONS:
Caliber: 22 L.R.
Barrel Length: 19 inches
Weight: 6 lbs. 12 oz.

Sights: Ramp front; adjustable peep rear sight
Stock: Black painted mahogany
Features: Sling and sling swivels included

MODEL M-1400 BOLT ACTION
$129.00

SPECIFICATIONS:
Caliber: 22 L.R.
Barrel: Tapered sporter weight barrel
Weight: 6 lbs.
Sights: Hooded ramp front sight; open rear sporter-type

Action: bolt
Safety: Positive sliding thumb safety
Stock: Hand-checkered nato wood, with Monte Carlo comb. Receiver grooved for tip-off scope mount.

KASSNAR RIFLES

MODEL M-20S SEMIAUTOMATIC
$99.95

SPECIFICATIONS:
Caliber: 22 L.R.
Capacity: 15-round clip
Barrel Length(s): 19½ inches

Weight: 5 lbs. 14 oz.
Sights: Open sights sporter-type
Safety: Positive sliding thumb safety
Stock: Nato wood, receiver grooved for tip-off scope mount. Hand-checkered.

KASSNAR/PARKER-HALE

PARKER-HALE SUPER

SPECIFICATIONS:
Caliber: 22/250, 243, 6mm, 25/06, 270, 30/06, 308, 7mm Mag., 300 Mag.
Capacity: 5 shot, Magnum,4 shot
Barrel Length(s): 24 inches
Overall Length: 45 inches
Sights: Hooded bead front sight; folding adjustable rear sight
Action: Bolt action. Receiver drilled and tapped for standard scope mounts
Safety: Slide thumb safety, locks trigger, bolt and sear
Stock: Two-tone walnut stock with a rollover Monte Carlo cheekpiece, skip-line checkering and rosewood at forend and grip cap
Standard calibers $369.95
Magnum calibers 374.95

PARKER-HALE VARMINT

SPECIFICATIONS:
Caliber: 22/250,243, 6mm, 25/06
Capacity: 5 shot
Barrel Length(s): 24 inches
Overall Length: 45 inches
Action: Glass-bedded, bolt action. Receiver drilled and tapped for standard scope mounts
Safety: Slide thumb safety, locks trigger, bolt and sear
Stock: Two-tone European walnut stock has high comb with rollover cheek piece, skip checkering, Wundhammer grip and ventilated recoil pad $374.95

KASSNAR/PARKER-HALE MIDLAND RIFLE

SPECIFICATIONS:
Caliber: 243, 270, 30/06, 308
Capacity: 4 shot

Barrel Length: 24 inches
Overall Length: 45 inches
Sights: Bead front sight, folding adjustable rear sight
Action: Long Mauser-type non-rotating claw extractor and one-piece forged construction with an extra safety lug
Safety: Tang safety catch which locks sear and trigger
Stock: Hand-checkered seasoned walnut
Price: (including 1-inch scope mounts, base blocks and fixing screws) $249.95

KIMBER RIFLES

KIMBER MODEL 82 CLASSIC

KIMBER MODEL 82

The Model 82 bolt-action, 22-caliber rifle is available in two styles, the Classic version with a satin sheen finish and plain buttstock or the Cascade model with Monte Carlo comb and cheekpiece. Both styles feature hand-checkered walnut stock, checkered steel buttplate, polished steel pistol grip and a one-piece trigger guard and floorplate. The trigger is adjustable for weight of pull, overtravel and depth of sear engagement. Accidental readjustment after setting is avoided because of two adjustment lock screws within the action housing.

The LR Sporter is available with a 4- or 10-shot magazine; the Magnum Sporter, available with a 4-shot magazine only. The barrel is 22 inches and has 6-groove, right-hand twist rifling with a pitch of one turn in 16 inches. Special Kimber one-inch scope mount rings, machined from steel to fit the dove-tailed receiver, are available in two heights. Also offered are open iron sights, hooded ramp front sight with bead and adjustable folding leaf rear sight.

Model 82 Classic, 22 LR Sporter, plain barrel, without sights **$495.00**
Model 82 Cascade, 22 LR Sporter, plain barrel, without sights **505.00**
Model 82 Classic, 22 Magnum Sporter, plain barrel, without sights **505.00**
Model 82 Cascade, 22 Magnum Sporter, plain barrel, without sights **515.00**

KLEINGUENTHER RIFLES

K-15 INSTA-FIRE IMPROVED $995.00

Available in Calibers:
243; 25-06; 270; 7X57; 30-06; 308 Win.; 308 Norma; 300 Win. Mag.; 7mm Reg. Mag.; 375 H and H Mag.; 270 Weatherby Mag.; 300 Weatherby Mag.; 257 Weatherby Mag.

SHORTEST IGNITION TIME: Striker travels 158 thousandths of one inch only . . . The extremely light striker is accelerated by a powerful striker spring . . . A patented two cocking cam design enables a very light and smooth cocking of the striker assembly . . . Two-piece firing pin.
CLIP FEATURE: Also will feed from top.
3 LOCKING LUGS: With large contact area as found on designs with multiple locking lugs involved . . . Providing perfect fit . . . a feature which cannot be duplicated by designs with multiple lugs . . . also Stellite locking insert.
60-DEGREE BOLT LIFT ONLY: For fast reloading
SAFETY: Located on right hand side . . . locking trigger and sear . . . Most convenient location . . . Also locks bolt . . . Combined with cocking indicator.
FINE ADJUSTABLE CRISP TRIGGER: 2 lbs. – 7 lbs. . . . Two major moving parts only.
STOCKS: American & European Walnut Monte Carlo stock with 1-inch recoil pad . . . Rosewood forend with white spacer . . . Rosewood pistol grip cap . . . 20-line hand-checkering . . . Quick detachable swivels . . . Bedded with three major contact points to metal . . . Barrel has one contact area, other than that it is free floating . . . High luster finish or full oil finish . . . Choice of wood color, blond thru dark. Available in right or left-hand stocks . . . AAA grade stocks available as an option.
SPECIFICATIONS: Barrel length—Standard-24 inches, Magnum-26 inches . . . Trigger pull weight—Micro-adjustable between 2-7 lbs. . . . Magazine capacity—Standard-5 cartridges, Magnum-3 cartridges . . . Trigger pull lengths—14⅜ inches. Overall length—Standard 44⅞ inches, Magnum 46⅞ inches . . . Overall weight 7 lbs. 8 to 10 oz.
RECEIVER DRILLED AND TAPPED FOR FOLLOWING SCOPE MOUNTS: Buehler two-piece and one-piece base mounts. Redfield one-piece base mount, Conetrol mount . . . Three different Kleinguenther two-piece base mounts and Quick Detachable.
OPTIONS: Iron sights . . . Set trigger . . . Engravings, wood carvings, wood inlays, etc.

MARLIN LEVER-ACTION CARBINES

MARLIN 444S $283.95

Caliber: 444 Marlin
Capacity: 4-shot tubular magazine
Action: Lever-action; solid top receiver; side ejection; gold-plated steel trigger; deeply blued metal surfaces; receiver top sand-blasted to prevent glare.

Stock: Two-piece genuine American black walnut with fluted comb; rubber rifle butt pad; full pistol grip; white butt plate and pistol grip spacers; tough Mar-Shield® finish; quick detachable sling swivels and leather carrying strap.
Weight: 7½ lbs.
Barrel: 22 inches with Micro-Groove® rifling (12 grooves)

Sights: Adjustable folding semi-buckhorn rear, hooded-ramp front sight with brass bead and Wide-Scan™ front sight hood; solid top receiver tapped for scope mount or receiver sight; offset hammer spur for scope use— works right or left.
Overall Length: 40½ inches

GOLDEN 39

MARLIN GOLDEN 39A

RIFLES

The Marlin lever action 22 is the oldest (since 1891) shoulder gun still being manufactured.

Solid Receiver Top. You can easily mount a scope on your Marlin 39 by screwing on the machined scope adapter base provided. The screw-on base is a neater, more versatile method of mounting a scope on a 22 sporting rifle. The solid top receiver and scope adapter base provide a maximum in eye relief adjustment. If you prefer iron sights, you'll find the 39 receiver clean, flat and sand-blasted to prevent glare. **Exclusive Brass Magazine Tube.**

Micro-Groove® Barrel. Marlin's famous rifling system of multi-grooving has consistently produced fine accuracy because the system grips the bullet more securely, minimizes distortion, and provides a better gas seal.
And the Model 39 maximizes accuracy with the heaviest barrels available on any lever-action 22.

MARLIN GOLDEN 39A $242.95 (less scope)

Caliber: 22 Short, Long and Long Rifle
Capacity: Tubular magazine holds 26 Short, 21 Long and 19 Long Rifle Cartridges
Action: Lever action; solid top receiver; side ejection; one-step takedown; deeply blued metal surfaces; receiver top sand-blasted to prevent glare.
Stock: Two-piece genuine American black walnut with fluted comb; full pistol grip and forend. Blued-steel forend cap; sling swivels; grip cap; white butt plate and pistol-grip spacers; tough Mar-Shield® finish.
Barrel: 24 inches with Micro-Groove® rifling (16 grooves)
Sights: Adjustable folding semi-buckhorn rear, ramp front sight with new Wide-Scan™ hood. Solid top receiver tapped for scope mount or receiver sight; scope adapter base; offset hammer spur for scope use—works right or left.
Overall Length: 40 inches
Weight: About 6½ lbs.

MARLIN GOLDEN 39M $242.95 (less scope)

Caliber: 22 Short, Long and Long Rifle.
Capacity: Tubular magazine holds 21 Short, 16 Long or 15 Long Rifle Cartridges.
Action: Lever action with square finger lever; solid top receiver; side ejection; one-step takedown; deeply blued-metal surfaces; receiver top sand-blasted to prevent glare.
Stock: Two-piece straight-grip genuine American black walnut with full forend. Blued steel forend cap; sling swivels; white butt plate spacer; tough Mar-Shield® finish.
Barrel: 20 inches with Micro-Groove® rifling (16 grooves)
Sights: Adjustable folding semi-buckhorn rear, ramp front sight and new Wide-Scan™ hood. Solid top receiver tapped for scope mount or receiver sight; scope adapter base; offset hammer spur for scope use—works right or left.
Overall Length: 36 inches
Weight: About 6 lbs.

MARLIN LEVER-ACTION CARBINES

MARLIN 1895S $349.95

Caliber: 45/70 Government
Capacity: 4-shot tubular magazine.
Action: Lever action; solid top receiver; side ejection; deeply blued metal surfaces; receiver top sandblasted to prevent glare.
Weight: About 7½ lbs.

Stock: Two-piece genuine American black walnut with fluted comb; rubber rifle butt pad; full pistol grip; white butt and pistol grip spacers; tough Mar-Shield® finish; quick-detachable sling swivels and leather carrying strap.
Barrel: 22 inches with Micro-Groove® rifling (12 grooves); honed chamber.

Sights: Adjustable semi-buckhorn folding rear, ramp front sight with brass bead and Wide-Scan™ hood. Solid top receiver tapped for scope mount or receiver sight; offset hammer spur for scope use; adaptable for right- or left-hand use.
Overall Length: 40½ inches

MARLIN 1894 $262.95

Caliber: 44 Rem. Magnum
Capacity: 10-shot tubular magazine
Action: Lever action with traditional squared finger lever; solid top receiver; side ejection; deeply blued metal surfaces; receiver top sandblasted to prevent glare.

Stock: Two-piece straight-grip genuine American black-walnut butt plate white spacer; blue-steel forend cap; tough Mar-Shield® finish.
Barrel: 20 inches with Micro-Groove® rifling (12 grooves). Honed chamber.

Sights: Adjustable semi-buckhorn folding rear, hooded-ramp front sights; solid top receiver tapped for scope mount or receiver sight; offset hammer spur for scope use—works right or left.
Overall Length: 37½ inches
Weight: About 6 lbs.

MARLIN 1894C 357 MAGNUM $262.95

Caliber: 357 Magnum
Capacity: 9-shot tubular magazine
Action: Lever action; side ejection; solid top receiver; deeply blued metal surfaces; receiver top sandblasted to prevent glare.

Stock: Straight-grip two-piece genuine American black walnut with white butt plate spacer.
Barrel: 18½ inches with modified Micro-Groove® rifling (12 grooves)

Sights: Adjustable semi-buckhorn folding rear, bead front. Solid top receiver tapped for scope mount or receiver sight; offset hammer spur for scope use —adjustable for right- or left-hand use.
Overall Length: 36 inches
Weight: 6 lbs.

MARLIN LEVER-ACTION CARBINES

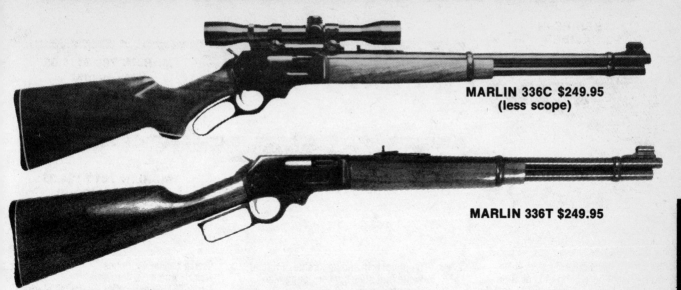

MARLIN 336C $249.95
(less scope)

MARLIN 336T $249.95

The 336C with full pistol grip and the 336T saddle gun both feature side-ejecting, solid top receivers, heat-treated machined steel forgings, American black-walnut stock with Mar-shield® finish, Micro-Groove® rifling, and folding semi-buckhorn rear sights.

Marlin 336C Specifications
Caliber: 30/30 Win. or 35 Rem.
Capacity: 6-shot tubular magazine
Action: Lever action; solid top receiver tapped for scope mount or receiver sight; offset metal surfaces; receiver top sandblasted to prevent glare.

Stock: Two-piece genuine American black walnut with fluted comb and full pistol grip. Grip cap; white butt plate and pistol-grip spacers; tough Mar-Shield® finish
Barrel: 20 inches with Micro-Groove® rifling (12 grooves)
Sights: Adjustable semi-buckhorn folding rear, ramp front sight with brass bead and Wide-Scan™ front sight hood. Solid top receiver; side ejection; gold-plated steel trigger; deeply blued hammer spur for scope use—works right or left.
Overall Length: 38½ inches
Weight: About 7 lbs.

Marlin 336T Specifications
Same action as 336C, available in 30/30 Win. only, with straight-grip stock, squared finger lever, and 18½-inch barrel. Approx. 6¾ lbs.

Overall Length: 37 inches

Forgings: Marlin uses six forged parts in the manufacture of all high rifles; receiver, lever, trigger plate, carrier, hammer and locking bolt.

MARLIN 375 $283.95

Caliber: 375 Winchester
Capacity: 5-shot tubular magazine
Action: Lever action; side ejection; solid top receiver; gold-plated steel trigger; deeply blued metal surfaces; receiver top sand-blasted to prevent glare.
Stock: Two-piece genuine American black walnut, with fluted comb, full pistol grip and rubber rifle butt pad. Pistol grip cap, white pistol grip and butt spacers. Tough Mar-Shield® finish, quick-detachable sling swivels and leather carrying strap.
Barrel: 20 inches with Micro-Groove® rifling (12 grooves).
Sights: Adjustable, folding semi-buckhorn rear, ramp front sight with brass bead and Wide-Scan™ hood. Solid top receiver tapped for scope mount or receiver sight; offset hammer spur for scope use; adaptable for right- or left-handers.
Overall Length: 38½ inches
Weight: About 6¾ lbs.

MARLIN BOLT-ACTION RIFLES

700 SERIES IN 22 CALIBER

MARLIN 780 $119.95
(less scope)

MARLIN 781 $124.95
(less scope)

Marlin 780 Specifications
Caliber: 22 Short, Long or Long Rifle
Capacity: Clip magazine holds 7 Short, Long or Long Rifle Cartridges.
Action: Bolt action; serrated, anti-glare receiver top; positive thumb safety; red cocking indicator.
Stock: Monte Carlo genuine American black walnut with full pistol grip; checkering on pistol grip and underside of forend; white butt plate spacer; tough Mar-Shield® finish.
Barrel: 22 inches with Micro-Groove® rifling (16 grooves)
Sights: Adjustable folding semi-buckhorn rear, ramp front, Wide-Scan™ front sight hood; receiver grooved for tip-off scope mount.

Overall Length: 41 inches
Weight: About 5½ lbs.
Marlin 781. Specifications same as Marlin 780, except with tubular magazine that holds 25 Short, 19 Long or 17 Long Rifle Cartridges. Weight: About 6 lbs.

700 SERIES IN 22 MAGNUM

MARLIN 783 MAGNUM
$138.95
(less scope)

Marlin 783 Magnum Specifications
Caliber: 22 Win. Magnum Rimfire (Not interchangeable with any other 22 cartridge)
Capacity: 12-shot tubular magazine with patented closure system
Action: Bolt action; serrated, anti-glare receiver top; positive thumb safety; red cocking indicator.
Stock: Monte Carlo genuine American black walnut with full pistol grip; checkering on pistol grip and underside of fore-end; white butt plate spacer; sling swivels and handsome leather carrying strap; tough Mar-Shield® finish.
Barrel: 22 inches with Micro-Groove® rifling (20 grooves)
Sights: Adjustable folding semi-buckhorn rear, ramp front with new Wide-Scan™ hood; receiver grooved for tip-off scope mount.
Overall Length: 41 inches
Weight: About 6 lbs.

MARLIN 782 MAGNUM
$133.95
(less scope)

Marlin 782 Magnum Specifications
Same as 783 Magnum, except with 7-shot clip magazine.

MARLIN RIFLES

MARLIN 990 $125.95

SPECIFICATIONS:
Caliber: 22 Long Rifle
Action: Semiautomatic
Capacity: 18-shot tubular magazine
Barrel: 22 inches with Micro-Groove® rifling (16 grooves)
Stock: Monte Carlo genuine American black walnut with fluted comb and full pistol grip; checkering on pistol grip and forend; tough Mar-Shield® finish.

Sights: Adjustable folding semi-buckhorn rear, ramp front sight with brass bead; Wide-Scan™ hood.
Overall Length: 40¾ inches
Weight: About 5½ lbs.
Features: Receiver grooved tip-off scope; bolt hold-open device; cross-bolt safety.

MARLIN 995 $117.95

SPECIFICATIONS:
Caliber: 22 Long Rifle
Action: Semiautomatic
Capacity: 7-shot clip magazine
Barrel: 18 inches with Micro-Groove® rifling (16 grooves)
Stock: Monte Carlo genuine American black walnut with full pistol grip; checkering on pistol grip and forend.

Sights: Adjustable folding semi-buckhorn rear; ramp front sight with brass bead; Wide-Scan™ front sight hood.
Overall Length: 36¾ inches
Weight: About 5½ lbs.
Features: Receiver grooved for tip-off scope mount; bolt hold-open device; cross-bolt safety.

MARLIN 15 $92.95

SPECIFICATIONS:
Caliber: 22 Short, Long or Long Rifle
Action: Bolt
Capacity: Single shot
Barrel Length: 22 inches (16 grooves)
Weight: 5½ lbs.
Overall Length: 41 inches
Sights: Adjustable open rear, ramp front sight

Features: Receiver grooved for tip-off scope mount; checkering on pistol grip; thumb safety; red cocking indicator.
Stock: One-piece walnut finished hardwood Monte Carlo stock with full pistol grip; checkering on pistol grip.

MARLIN MODEL 25
7-Shot Repeater $101.95

RIFLES

MARLIN RIFLES

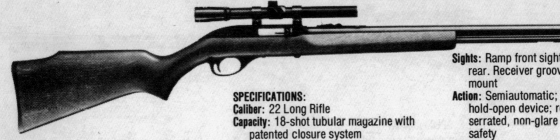

MARLIN 60 $97.95
(less scope)

SPECIFICATIONS:
Caliber: 22 Long Rifle
Capacity: 18-shot tubular magazine with patented closure system
Barrel Length: 22 inches
Weight: 5½ lbs.
Overall Length: 40½ inches

Sights: Ramp front sight; adjustable open rear. Receiver grooved for tip-off scope mount
Action: Semiautomatic; side ejection; bolt hold-open device; receiver top has serrated, non-glare finish; cross-bolt safety
Stock: One-piece walnut-finished hardwood Monte Carlo stock with full pistol grip
Shown here with Glenfield 200C, 4X scope

MODEL 30A $232.95
(less scope)

SPECIFICATIONS:
Caliber: 30/30 Win.
Capacity: 6-shot tubular magazine
Barrel Length: 20 inches
Weight: 7 lbs.
Overall Length: 38¼ inches

Sights: Ramp front sight; adjustable open rear. Solid top receiver tapped for scope mount or receiver sight; offset hammer spur for scope use—adaptable for right- or left-handed use
Action: Lever action; solid top receiver; side ejection; deeply blued metal surfaces; blued steel trigger; receiver top sandblasted to prevent glare
Stock: Two-piece walnut-finished hardwood stock with full pistol grip
Shown here with Glenfield 400 A, 4X scope

MARLIN 70 $97.95

SPECIFICATIONS:
Caliber: 22 Long Rifle
Capacity: Chrome-plated 7-shot clip magazine
Barrel Length: 18 inches
Weight: 4½ lbs.
Overall Length: 36½ inches
Sights: Adjustable open rear, ramp front sight. Receiver grooved for tip-off scope mount

Action: Semiautomatic; side ejection; bolt hold-open device; receiver top has serrated, non-glare finish; cross-bolt safety
Stock: One-piece walnut finished hardwood Monte Carlo stock with full pistol grip; sling swivels

MOSSBERG RIFLES

MODEL 144

Caliber: 22 Super Target Rifle
Capacity: 7-shot clip magazine; also loads as single shot
Barrel Length: 27 inches
Weight: About 8 lbs. with sights
Overall Length: 44½ inches
Sights: Lyman 17A hooded front sight with 7 interchangeable inserts. Receiver grooved for scope mounting; furnished with Mossberg S331 receiver peep sight

Action: Hammerless bolt action; grooved trigger with adjustable trigger pull
Stock: American walnut; beavertail forend, cheekpiece, adjustable hand stop pistol grip and special 1¼-inch target sling swivels

MOSSBERG RIFLES

22 CALIBER RIMFIRE

MODEL 377 PLINKSTER

Action—Semiautomatic. **Caliber**—22 Long Rifle. **Capacity**—15 Long Rifle Cartridges. Brass tubular magazine through buttstock; bright orange follower. **Barrel**—20-inch tapered with AC-KRO-GRUV rifling; ordnance steel. **Stock**—Straight-line, molded one-piece thumb hole of modified polystyrene foam, Monte Carlo comb and roll-over cheekpiece. Sling swivel studs and forend checkering. Serrated, non-slip butt plate. **Color**—Walnut finish with blued barrel and receiver. Black butt plate and trigger guard. **Sight**—4 power scope with cross hair reticle. **Safety**—Positive, thumb operated; bolt locks in open position. **Receiver**—Milled ordnance steel, complete with scope mount base. Shell deflector included. **Length**—40 inches. **Weight**—About 6.25 lbs. with scope.

MODEL 353

With exclusive two-position, extension forend of black Tenite for steady firing from the prone position, up to 7 shots in less than 2 seconds. **Action**—Shoots 22 cal. Long Rifle, regular or High Speed cartridges. Automatic self-loading action from 7-shot clip. Receiver grooved for scope mounting.

Stock—Genuine American walnut with Monte Carlo. Checkered at forend and pistol grip. Sling swivels and web strap on left of stock. Butt plate with white liner. **Barrel**—18 inches AC-KRO-GRUV® 8-groove rifled barrel. **Sights**—Open rear with "U" notch, adjustable for windage and elevation; ramp front with bead. **Weight**—About 5½ lbs. Length overall 38½ inches.

MODEL 341

Action—Hammerless bolt rifle action with Mossberg's "Magic 3-Way" 7-shot clip magazine which adjusts instantly to load, Short, Long or Long Rifle cartridges. Positive safety at side of receiver. Receiver grooved for scope mounting, tapped and drilled for peep sights. (Mossberg No. S330 receiver peep sight.) **Stock**—Genuine American walnut with Monte Carlo and cheekpiece. Custom checkering on pistol grip and forend. Sling swivels. Butt plate with white line spacer. **Barrel**—24 inches AC-KRO-GRUV® 8-groove rifled barrel. **Sights**—Open rear with "U" notch, adjustable for windage and elevation; ramp front with bead. **Weight**—About 6¼ lbs. Length overall 43½ inches.

MODEL 377 PLINKSTER   MODEL 353   MODEL 341

RIFLES

MANUFACTURER DOES NOT LIST SUGGESTED RETAIL PRICES

REMINGTON AUTOLOADING 22 RIFLES

NYLON 66 • MOHAWK BROWN
$129.95
WITH 4x SCOPE
$142.95

The Nylon 66 Autoloading rifle is chambered for 22 Long Rifle cartridges. Tubular magazine thru butt stock holds 15 long rifle cartridges. Remington's Nylon 66 receiver parts, stock and barrel are interlocked with steel and structural nylon. There's no need for lubrication because friction-free parts glide on greaseless bearings of nylon. Barrel made of Remington proof steel. Stock is made of DuPont "Zytel" nylon, a new gunstock material. Resembles wood, weighs less than wood, outwears, outlasts wood. Stock features fine-line non-slip checkering, white diamond inlays and white line spacers at grip cap, butt plate and forend tip and has a lifetime warranty. Receiver is grooved for "tip-off" scope mounts.

Nylon 66 Black Diamond	**$129.95**
Nylon 66 Black Diamond w/4x Scope	142.95
Sling Strap and Swivels Installed	13.25

The Nylon 66 is also made in an Apache Black deluxe model. The stock is jet black nylon and both the barrel and the receiver cover are chrome-plated. **$133.95**

	NYLON 66 MOHAWK BROWN	NYLON 66 APACHE BLACK
ACTION	Autoloading.	Autoloading.
CALIBER	22 Long Rifle RimFire.	22 Long Rifle RimFire.
CAPACITY	Tubular magazine thru butt stock. Holds 15 long rifle cartridges.	Tubular magazine thru butt stock. Holds 15 long rifle cartridges.
STOCK	DuPont "ZYTEL" nylon, checkered grip & forend with white diamond inlays, white line spacers on butt plate, grip cap & fore-end. Black forend tip.	DuPont "ZYTEL" nylon, checkered grip & forend with white diamond inlays, white line spacers on butt plate, grip & forend.
SIGHTS	Rear sight adjustable for windage and range, blade front, common sight line for iron sights and scope.	Rear sight adjustable for windage and range, blade front, common sight line for iron sights and scope.
SAFETY	Top-of-grip, Positive.	Top-of-grip, Positive.
RECEIVER	Grooved for "tip-off" scope mounts. Double extractors.	Grooved for "tip-off" scope mounts. Double extractors. Chrome-Plated Receiver and Barrel.
OVERALL LENGTH	38½ inches	38½ inches
WEIGHT	4 lbs.	4 lbs.

MODEL 541-S "CUSTOM" SPORTER • Clip Repeater

Remington Model 541-S "Custom" Sporter	**$373.95**
Extra 5-Shot Clip Magazine	5.75
Extra 10-Shot Clip Magazine	6.75
Sling Strap and Quick Release Swivels Installed ..	21.75

A customized 22 rimfire rifle. An excellent choice for rimfire metallic silhouette shooting. American walnut stock with fine-line-cut checkering in an attractive, raised diamond pattern, and protected by Du Pont's rugged RK-W finish. Receiver and bowed trigger guard handsomely scroll engraved. Matching rosewood-colored forend tip, pistol grip cap and checkered butt plate fitted with white line spacers.

Hand-polished exterior metal surfaces richly blued to a tasteful, medium high lustre. Receiver is drilled and tapped for regular scope mounts or receiver sights as well as grooved for "tip-off" type mounts. Barrel also drilled and tapped for open sights. Supplied with a 5-shot clip magazine. 5- and 10-shot extra magazines are available.

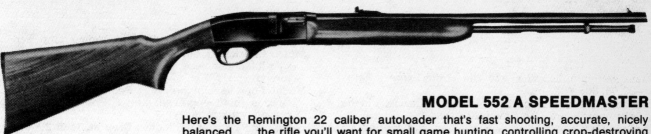

MODEL 552 A SPEEDMASTER

Here's the Remington 22 caliber autoloader that's fast shooting, accurate, nicely balanced . . . the rifle you'll want for small game hunting, controlling crop-destroying and marauding pests, or for just plain fun-shooting. The Model 552 has every feature the shooter wants, such as: twenty shots as fast as you can squeeze the trigger, rich walnut stock, cross bolt safety, receiver grooved for "tip-off" scope mounts **$174.95**

MODEL 552 BDL Deluxe

A deluxe model with all the tried and proven dependable mechanical features on the inside, plus special design and appearance extras on the outside. The 552 BDL includes new tasteful Remington custom impressed checkering on both stock and for new DuPont RK-W tough lifetime finish that brings out the lustrous beauty of the walnut while protecting it, and rugged big-game type fully adjustable rear sight with ramp front sight **$197.95**   Sling Strap and Swivels installed **$20.00**

ACTION:	Autoloading. Tubular Magazine.	**SAFETY:**	Positive cross bolt
CALIBER:	22 Short, Long and Long Rifle rimfire	**RECEIVER:**	Grooved for "tip-off" scope mounts
CAPACITY:	Holds 20 Short, 17 Long, 15 Long Rifle cartridges	**OVERALL LENGTH:**	40 inches
STOCK:	American Walnut. DuPont RK-W tough lustrous finish and fine-line custom checkering	**BARREL LENGTH:**	21 inches
SIGHTS:	552 A —Adjustable rear, bead front. 552 BDL—Fully adjustable rear, ramp front. Screw removable.	**AVERAGE WEIGHT:**	5¾ lbs.

REMINGTON AUTOLOADING RIFLES

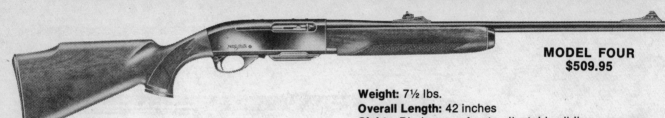

MODEL FOUR
$509.95

Calibers: 6mm, 243 Win., 270 Win., 7mm Express Rem., 30-06, 308 Win.
Capacity: 5-shot in all calibers (4 in the magazine, 1 in the chamber); extra 4-shot magazine available
Action: Gas operated; receiver drilled and tapped for scope mounts; positive safety switch
Barrel Length: 22 inches

Weight: 7½ lbs.
Overall Length: 42 inches
Sights: Blade ramp front; adjustable sliding ramp rear
Stock: Checkered American walnut; Monte Carlo stock with full cheekpiece; pistol grip; flared and checkered forend
Model Four special order: D Peerless and F Premier Grades (both engraved) and F Premier Grade (engraved with gold inlay)
Length of Pull: 13-5/16 inches **Drop at Heel:** 2½ inches **Drop at Comb:** 1-11/16 inches (with Monte Carlo: 1-13/16 inches)

MODEL 7400
$461.95

Calibers: 6mm Rem., 243 Win., 270 Win., 7mm Express Rem., 30-06 and 308 Win.
Capacity: 5 centerfire cartridges (4 in the magazine, 1 in the chamber); extra 4-shot magazine available
Action: Gas operated; receiver drilled and tapped for scope mounts

Barrel Length: 22 inches
Weight: 7½ lbs.
Overall Length: 42 inches
Sights: Standard blade ramp front, sliding ramp rear
Stock: Checkered American walnut stock and forend; curved pistol grip
Length of Pull: 13⅜ inches **Drop at Heel:** 2¼ inches **Drop at Comb** 1-13/16 inches

REMINGTON BOLT-ACTION RIFLES

MODELS 581 & 582 IN 22 L.R. CALIBER

The 581 series 22 Long Rifle rimfire bolt-action rifles feature the look, feel and balance of big-game centerfire rifles. They are available in styles—a clip repeater with single-shot adapter, and a tubular-magazine repeater. The bolt is an artillery type with rear lock-up and has six extra-heavy, rotary locking lugs at the back that engage grooves in the solid-steel receiver. A bolt cover at rear keeps dirt and bad weather outside. Two extractors are standard on this 581 series of 22 rifles. Hunting-type trigger is wide and the trigger guard is roomy enough to accommodate a gloved finger. The stock is Monte Carlo style with pistol grip suitable for use with or without a scope. Sights consist of a bead front sight and U-notch lock-screw adjustable rear. Precise bedding into the stock is achieved by a new round receiver. The receiver is also grooved for tip-off scope mounts. There are no slots or notches cut into the receiver and the bolt handle isn't used as lock-up lugs. The barrel is of ordnance steel, crowned at the muzzle, polished and blued. The non-slip thumb safety is located at the right rear of the receiver. With positive safety.

MODEL 581 BOYS' RIFLE $148.95

REMINGTON BOLT-ACTION RIFLES

MODEL 581 CLIP REPEATER WITH SINGLE SHOT ADAPTER
$141.95

Sling Strap and Swivels Installed	**$19.00**
Extra 5-shot clip	**5.75**
Extra 10-shot clip	**6.75**
Model 581 left-hand Clip Repeater with single shot adapter	**146.95**

MODEL 582 TUBULAR REPEATER
$173.95

MODEL 581 & MODEL 582

SPECIFICATIONS:
Stock & Forend: Walnut-finished hardwood with Monte Carlo, full size, black butt plate. Single-screw takedown.
Receiver: Round, ordnance steel, grooved for scope mounts.
Capacity: M/581 6-shot clip repeater with single-shot adapter. M/582 20 Short, 15 Long, 14 Long Rifle cartridges.
Sights: Front: bead, dovetail adjustable. Rear: U-notch type, lock-screw adjustable.
Safety: Positive, serrated thumb-type. Left-hand safety on left-hand model.
Weight: M/581 4¾ lbs.; M/582 5 lbs.
Overall Length: 42⅜ inches
String Strap and Swivels Installed **$14.50**

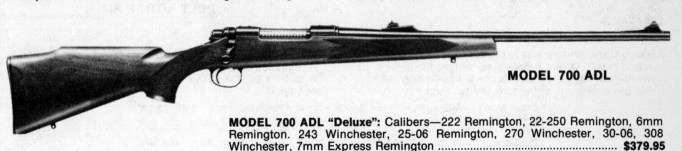

MODEL 700 ADL

MODEL 700 ADL "Deluxe": Calibers—222 Remington, 22-250 Remington, 6mm Remington. 243 Winchester, 25-06 Remington, 270 Winchester, 30-06, 308 Winchester, 7mm Express Remington **$379.95**
MODEL 700 ADL "Deluxe" MAGNUM: Caliber—7mm Rem. Mag. **396.95**

MODEL 700BDL

MODEL 700 BDL "Custom Deluxe": Calibers—222 Remington, 22-250 Remington, 6mm Remington, 243 Winchester, 25-06 Remington, 7mm-08 Remington, 270 Winchester, 30-06, 308 Winchester, 7mm Express Remington **$446.95**
17 Remington caliber **463.95**
Left-Hand Model in 270 Win. & 30-06 .... **463.95**
MODEL 700 BDL "Custom Deluxe" MAGNUM: Calibers—7mm Remington Mag., 8mm Rem. Mag., 300 Winchester Mag. **463.95**
Left-Hand Model in 7mm Rem. Magnum **480.95**
MODEL 700 SAFARI in 375 H&H Mag., 458 Win. Mag. **762.95**

REMINGTON BOLT-ACTION RIFLES

Caliber: 7mm Rem. Mag., 300 H&H Mag. $421.95

MODEL 700 CLASSIC
Calibers: 22-250 Rem., 6mm Rem., 243 Win., 270 Win., 30-06 & 30-06 Accelerator
$404.95

MODEL 700 C-CUSTOM
MODEL 700 D-PEERLESS
MODEL 700 F-PREMIER

SPECIFICATIONS:
Calibers: Same as Model 700 BDL except 17 Remington, 375 H&H Mag. and 458 Win. Mag.
Capacity: Same as Model 700 BDL.
Barrel: Choice of 22- or 24-inch length in Remington quality ordnance steel. With or without sights. Not available with stainless steel barrel.
Bolt: Jeweled with shrouded firing pin.
Receiver: Drilled and tapped for scope mounts. Fixed magazine with or without hinged floor plate.
Stock: Cut-checkered selected American walnut with quick detachable sling swivels installed. Recoil pad standard equipment on Magnum rifles. Installed at extra charge on others.

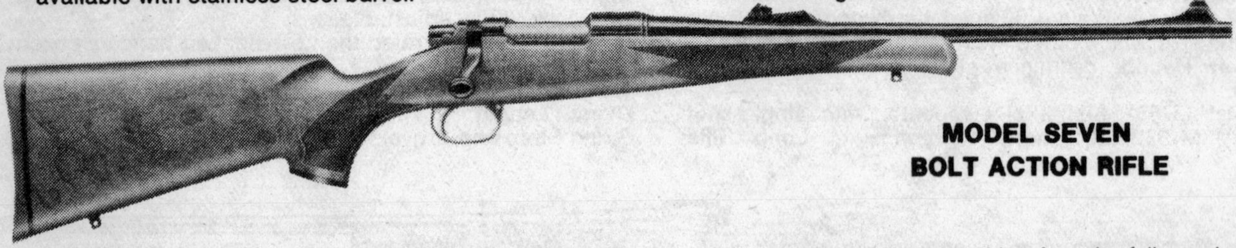

MODEL SEVEN
BOLT ACTION RIFLE

Every Model Seven is built to the accuracy standards of our famous Model 700, and is individually test fired to prove it. Its 18½" Remington special steel barrel is free-floating out to a single pressure point at the fore-end tip. And there is ordnance-quality steel in everything from its fully enclosed bolt and extractor system to its steel trigger guard and floor plate. Ramp front and fully adjustable rear sights, sling swivel studs are standard.

Standard Stock Dimensions: 13½ inch length of pull, 1 inch drop at heel, ⅝ inch drop at comb (measured from centerline of bore).

Calibers:	222 Rem.	243 Win.	7mm-08 Rem.	6mm Rem.	308 Win.
Clip Mag. Capacity	5	4	4	4	4
Barrel Length	18½ in.	18½ in.	18½ in.	18½ in.	18½ in.
Overall Length	37½ in.	37½ in.	37½ in.	37½ in.	37½ in.
Twist R-H (1 turn in)	14 in.	9⅛ in.	9¼ in.	9⅛ in.	10 in.
Average Weight (lbs.)	6¼	6¼	6¼	6¼	6¼

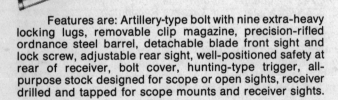

MODEL 788
CLIP REPEATER
Calibers: 223 Rem., 22-250 Remington, 243 Win., 308 Win., 7mm-08 Rem.
$288.95

Features are: Artillery-type bolt with nine extra-heavy locking lugs, removable clip magazine, precision-rifled ordnance steel barrel, detachable blade front sight and lock screw, adjustable rear sight, well-positioned safety at rear of receiver, bolt cover, hunting-type trigger, all-purpose stock designed for scope or open sights, receiver drilled and tapped for scope mounts and receiver sights.

Calibers	Clip Mag. Cap.	Barrel Length	Overall Length	Av. Wt. Lbs.
222 Remington	4	24"	43⅝"	7¼
223 Remington	4	24"	43⅝"	7½
22-250 Remington	3	24"	43⅝"	7½
243 Winchester	3	18½"	38½"	7¼
308 Winchester	3	18½"	38½"	7¼
7mm-08 Remington	3	18½"	38½"	7¼

REMINGTON BOLT-ACTION RIFLES

MODEL 700 BDL
HEAVY BARREL VARMINT SPECIAL $467.95

**Calibers: 222 Rem., 223 Rem., 22-250 Rem., 25-06 Rem.,
6mm Rem., 243 Win., 308 Win. and 7mm-08 Rem.**

The Model 700 BDL heavy barrel "Varmint Special" version comes equipped with a 24-inch heavy target-type barrel with target-rifle (Remington 40XB) scope bases. The "Varmint Special" is available in a wide range of popular high velocity, varmint calibers which include the 222 Rem., 223 Rem., 22-250 Rem., 25-06 Rem., 6mm Rem., 308 Win., 243 Win. calibers and 7mm-08 Rem. The "Varmint Special" was designed for maximum-range precision shooting—suitable for chucks, foxes and other varmints. Features include hinged floor plate; quick release, swivels and strap; crisp trigger pull; American walnut stock, Monte Carlo style with cheekpiece, positive cut skip-line checkering on grip and all three sides of forend, grip cap with white line spacer and butt plate; Du Pont developed RK-W wood finish. Stock dimensions are as follows: 13⅜-inch length of pull; 1⅜-inch drop at heel; ½-inch drop at comb (from open sight line). The safety is a thumb-lever type and is serrated. The bolt knob is oval shaped, serrated top and bottom. As in the Model 700 BDL, the cartridge head is completely encased by the bolt face and is supported by three rings of steel when the action is closed. The model is a very popular choice for metallic silhouette shooting.

Calibers	Clip Mag. Cap.	Barrel Length	Overall Length	Av. Wt. Lbs.
22-250 Remington	5	24"	43½"	9
222 Remington	6	24"	43½"	9
223 Remington	6	24"	43½"	9
25-06 Remington	5	24"	44½"	9
6mm Remington	5	24"	43½"	9
243 Winchester	5	24"	43½"	9
308 Winchester	5	24"	43½"	8¾
7mm-08 Remington	5	24"	43½"	8¾

REMINGTON PUMP-ACTION RIFLES

MODEL SIX $453.95

Overall Length: 42 inches
Sights: Blade ramp front sight; adjustable sliding ramp rear
Stock: Cut-checkered American walnut Monte Carlo stock with full cheekpiece; flared forend has full wraparound positive-cut checkering
Length of Pull: 13-5/16 inches **Drop at Heel:** 2½ inches **Drop at Comb:** 1-11/16 inches (with Monte Carlo: 1-13/16 inches)
Model Six special order: D Peerless and F Premier Grades (both engraved) and F Premier Grade (engraved with gold inlay)

Calibers: 6mm Rem., 243 Win., 270 Win., 30-06 and 30-06 "Accelerator," and 308 Win. and "Accelerator"
Capacity: 5-shot capacity in all six calibers (4 in the removable clip, 1 in the chamber)
Action: Pump action
Barrel Length: 22 inches
Weight: 7½ lbs.

MODEL 7600 $405.95

Barrel Length: 22 inches
Weight: 7½ lbs.
Overall Length: 42 inches
Sights: Standard blade ramp front sight; sliding ramp rear, both removable
Stock: Checkered American walnut
Length of Pull: 13⅜ inches. **Drop at Heel:** 2⅛ inches. **Drop at Comb:** 1-11/16 inches

Calibers: 6mm Rem., 243 Win., 270 Win., 30-06 and 30-06 "Accelerator," 308 Win. and 308 "Accelerator"
Capacity: 5-shot capacity in all six calibers (4 in the removable magazine, 1 in the chamber)
Action: Pump action

REMINGTON PUMP-ACTION RIFLES

MODEL 572 A FIELDMASTER • 22 Short, Long, Long Rifle

For the shooter who likes a pump-action 22-caliber rifle, the "Fieldmaster" Model 572 A is best . . . Exclusive cartridge-feeding design prevents jamming, permits easy single loading. By simply removing the inner magazine tube, parent or instructor can convert the Model 572 into a single-shot rifle for the beginning shooter; when shooter is experienced, magazine tube can be put back again to make the Model 572 a repeater.
.... **$181.95**

MODEL 572 BDL Deluxe • 22 Short, Long, Long Rifle

Features of this rifle with big-game feel and appearance are: DuPont beautiful but tough RK-W finish, centerfire-rifle-type rear sight fully adjustable for both vertical and horizontal sight alignment, big-game style ramp front sight, beautiful Remington impressed checkering on both stock and forend.

Model 572 BDL DELUXE **$204.95**
Sling Strap & Swivels Installed **17.75**

ACTION:	Pump repeater
CALIBER:	22 Short, Long and Long Rifle rimfire
CAPACITY:	Tubular magazine holds 20 Short, 17 Long, 15 Long Rifle cartridges
STOCK AND FOREND:	A—Walnut finished hardwood BDL—American Walnut with DuPont RK-W tough lustrous finish and fine line custom checkering
SIGHTS:	A—Adjustable rear, bead front BDL—Fully adjustable rear, ramp front Screw removable
SAFETY:	Positive cross bolt
RECEIVER:	Grooved for "tip-off" scope mounts
OVERALL LENGTH:	40 in.
BARREL LENGTH:	21 in.
AVERAGE WEIGHT:	5½ lbs

MODEL "XP-100" — Order Numbers & Specifications

"XP-100" (221 Rem. "Fire Ball")	**$338.95**
"XP-100" (7mm BR Remington)	**381.95**

Overall Length: 16¾ inches with 10½-inch barrel; 21¼ inches with 14¾-inch barrel. **Weight:** 3¾ lbs. with 10½-inch barrel; 4⅛ lbs. with 14¾-inch barrel.

The Model -' XP-100".

Here's the unique single-shot centerfire, bolt-action pistol that has become a legend for its strength, precision, balance and accuracy. Still chambered for the 221 Remington "Fire Ball" with a vent rib 10½-inch barrel, it's also available in 7mm BR Rem. with a 14¾-inch barrel. In this latter configuration you have what has been called the perfect factory-made metallic silhouette handgun for "unlimited" events.

Both "XP-100" handguns have one-piece DuPont "Zytel" nylon stocks with universal grips, two-position thumb safety switches, receivers drilled and tapped for scope mounts or receiver sights, and match-type grooved triggers.

REMINGTON TARGET RIFLES

MODEL 40-XB "RANGEMASTER"
CenterFire Rifle

Barrels are unblued stainless steel. Choice of either standard weight or heavy barrel. Comb-grooved for easy bolt removal. Mershon White Line non-slip rubber butt plate supplied.

MODEL 40XB-BR • Bench Rest CenterFire Rifle

Built with all the features of the extremely accurate Model 40-XB-CF but modified to give the competitive bench rest shooter a standardized rifle that provides the inherent accuracy advantages of a short, heavy, extremely stiff barrel. Wider, squared off forend gives a more stable rest on sandbags or other supports and meets weight limitations for the sporter and light-varmint classes of National Bench Rest Shooters Association competition.

	MODEL 40-XB CENTERFIRE	MODEL 40XB-BR CENTERFIRE
ACTION	Bolt—Single shot in either standard or heavy barrel versions. Repeater in heavy barrel only. Receiver bedded to stock. Barrel is free floating	Bolt, single shot only
CALIBERS	See listing below	222 Rem., 22 Bench Rest Rem., 7.62 NATO (308 Win.), 6mm Bench Rest Rem., 223 Rem., 6x47
SIGHTS	No sights supplied. Target scope blocks installed	Supplied with target scope blocks
SAFETY	Positive thumb operated	Positive thumb operated
RECEIVER	Drilled and tapped for scope block and receiver sights	Drilled and tapped for target scope blocks
BARREL	Drilled and tapped for scope block and front target iron sight. Muzzle diameter S2—approx. ¾", H2—approx. ⅞". Length: 27¼". Unblued stainless steel only	Unblued stainless steel only. 20" barrel for Light Varmint Class. 24" barrel for Heavy Varmint Class.
TRIGGER	Adjustable from 2 to 4 lbs. pull. Special 2 oz. trigger available at extra cost. Single shot models only	Adjustable from 1½ to 3½ lbs. Special 2 oz. trigger available at extra cost
STOCK	American Walnut. Adjustable front swivel block on rail. Rubber non-slip butt plate	Selected American Walnut. Length of pull—12"
OVERALL LENGTH	Approx. 47"	38" with 20" barrel. 42" with 24" barrel
AVERAGE WEIGHT	S2—9¼ lbs. H2—11¼ lbs.	Light Varmint Class (20" barrel) 9¼ lbs. Heavy Varmint Class (24" barrel) 12 lbs.

MODEL 40-XB CENTER FIRE	PRICE
40XB-CF-S2 Stainless steel, standard weight barrel	
	$847.95
40XB-CF-H2 Stainless steel, heavy barrel	

CALIBERS: Single-shot: 222 Rem., 22-250 Rem., 6mm Rem., 243 Win., 7.62mm NATO (308 Win.), 30-06, 30-338 (30-7mm Mag.), 300 Win. Mag., 25-06 Rem., 7mm Rem. Mag.

MODEL 40-XB CENTERFIRE	PRICE
Heavy barrel version only Extra for repeating models	$55.75
CALIBERS: Repeating 222 Rem., 22-250 Rem., 6mm Rem., 243 Win., 7.62mm NATO (308 Win.).	
Single shot version only Extra for two ounce trigger	93.95

MODEL 40XB-BR CENTER FIRE	
40XB-BR Heavy barrel without sights	893.95
Extra for two-ounce trigger	93.95

REMINGTON TARGET RIFLES

MODEL 40-XR
RimFire Position Rifle

Stock designed with deep forend for more comfortable shooting in all positions. Butt plate vertically adjustable. Exclusive loading platform provides straight line feeding with no shaved bullets. Crisp, wide, adjustable match trigger. Meets all International Shooting Union standard rifle specifications **$664.95**

MODEL 40-XC National Match Course Rifle

Chambered for the 7.62mm NATO cartridge solely, this match rifle was designed to meet the needs of competitive shooters firing the national match courses. Postion style stock, five-shot repeater with top-loading magazine, anti-bind bolt and receiver and in the bright stainless steel barrel. Meets all International Shooting Union Army Rifle specifications **$916.95**

	MODEL 540-XR, 540-XRJR RIMFIRE POSITION RIFLE	MODEL 40-XR RIMFIRE POSITION RIFLE
ACTION	Bolt action single shot	Bolt action single shot
CALIBER	22 Long Rifle rim fire	22 Long Rifle rim fire
CAPACITY	Single loading	Single loading
SIGHTS	Optional at extra cost. Williams Receiver No. FPTK and Redfield Globe front match sight	Optional at extra cost. Williams Receiver No. FPTK and Redfield Globe front match sight
SAFETY	Positive serrated thumb safety	Positive thumb safety
LENGTH OF PULL	540-XR—Adjustable from 12¾" to 16" 540-XRJR—Adjustable from 11" to 14¼".	13½"
RECEIVER	Drilled and tapped for receiver sight	Drilled and tapped for receiver sight or target scope blocks
BARREL	26" medium weight target barrel countersunk at muzzle. Drilled and tapped for target scope blocks. Fitted with front sight base.	24" heavy barrel
BOLT	Artillery style with lock-up at rear. 6 locking lugs, double extractors	Heavy, oversized locking lugs and double extractors
TRIGGER	Adjustable from 1 to 5 lbs.	Adjustable from 2 to 4 lbs.
STOCK	Position style with Monte Carlo, cheekpiece and thumb groove. 5-way adjustable butt plate and full length guide rail	Position style with front swivel block on fore-end guide rail
OVER-ALL LENGTH	540-XR—Adjustable from 42½" to 46¾" 540-XRJR—Adjustable from 41¾" to 45"	42½"
AVERAGE WEIGHT	8 lbs. 13 oz. without sights. Add 9 oz. for sights	10 lbs. 2 oz.

MODEL 540-XR
RimFire Position Rifle

An extremely accurate 22-caliber single-shot match rifle. Extra fast lock time contributes to this fine accuracy. Specially designed stock has deep forend and 5-way adjustable butt plate for added comfort and better scores in all positions.

Pistol grip designed to eliminate wrist-twisting and assures straight-back trigger pull. Adjustable match trigger. Match-style sling strap with adjustable front swivel block and set sight available as accessories at extra charge **$358.95**

MODEL 540-XR, 540-XRJR
Front Swivel Block and Sling Strap Assembly (Optional Accessory at Extra Charge). **$15.50**

MODEL 540-XRJR • Junior Rim Fire Position Rifle

A match rifle with all the features of the Model 540-XR but fitted with 1¾ inches shorter stock to fit the junior shooter **$358.95**

ROSSI RIFLES

ROSSI SLIDE-ACTION GALLERY MODEL
Standard or Carbine

The tubular magazine holds 20 short, 16 long and 13 long rifle 22 rimfire cartridges interchangeably. Available in blue finish.

Model	Finish	Weight	Barrel Length	Price
Standard	Blue	5¾ lbs.	23 in.	$160.00
Standard	Nickel	5¾ lbs.	23 in.	180.00
Carbine	Blue	5½ lbs.	16½ in.	160.00
Carbine	Nickel	5½ lbs.	16½ in.	180.00

ROSSI SADDLE-RING LEVER ACTION CARBINE
357 Mag. or 38 Special

Model	Finish	Weight	Barrel Length	Price
Carbine	Blue	5¾ lbs.	20 in.	$230.00
Carbine	Engraved	5¾ lbs.	20 in.	290.00

RUGER CARBINES

No. 3 CARBINE SINGLE-SHOT $284.00

Caliber: 45/70, 223, 44 Magnum, Single-shot
Barrel: 22 inches
Weight: 6 pounds
Overall Length: 38½ inches
Rear Sight: Folding leaf adjustable
Front Sight: Gold bead
Safety: Sliding tang
Stock and Forearm: Solid American Walnut

Scope not included

RUGER MINI-14
Mini-14/5 Blued $335.00
K-Mini-14/5 Stainless Steel $375.00
Mini-14/5R (with int. dovetails)
Ranch Rifle $362.50

MATERIALS—Heat-treated Chrome molybdenum and other alloy steels, as well as music wire oil springs, are used throughout the mechanism to ensure reliability under field operating conditions.

SAFETY—The safety blocks both the hammer and sear. The slide can be cycled when the safety is on. The safety is mounted in the front of the trigger guard so that it may be set to Fire position without removing finger from trigger guard.

FIRING PIN—The firing pin is retracted mechanically during the first part of the unlocking of the bolt. The rifle can only be fired when the bolt is safely locked.

STOCK—One-piece American hardwood reinforced with steel liner at stressed areas. Handguard and forearm separated by air space from barrel to promote cooling under rapid-fire conditions.

MINI-14
SPECIFICATIONS—CALIBER: 223 (5.56mm). **LENGTH:** 37¼ inches. **WEIGHT:** 6 lbs. 4 oz. **MAGAZINE:** 5 round, detachable box magazine. 10-shot and 20-shot magazines **BARREL LENGTH:** 18½ inches.

FIELD STRIPPING—The Carbine can be field stripped to its eight (8) basic subassemblies in a matter of seconds and without use of special tools.

RANCH RIFLE
SPECIFICATIONS:—CALIBER: 223 (5.56mm) **LENGTH:** 37¾ inches **WEIGHT:** 6 lbs. 8 oz. **MAGAZINE:** 10-shot and 20-shot magazines available. **BARREL LENGTH:** 18½ inches.

RUGER AUTOLOADING CARBINES
IN 22 LONG RIFLE AND 44 MAGNUM CALIBERS

10-Shot Rotary Magazine

STANDARD CARBINE
10/22 Carbine (22 L.R. cal.) $134.50

STANDARD CARBINE
44 Carbine (44 Mag. cal.) $332.00

DELUXE SPORTER
10/22 Deluxe Sporter (22 L.R. cal.) $163.00

Model 10/22 Carbine
22 LONG RIFLE CALIBER

Identical in size, balance and style to the Ruger 44 Magnum Carbine and nearly the same in weight, the 10/22 is a companion to its high-power counterpart. Construction of the 10/22 Carbine is rugged and follows the Ruger design practice of building a firearm from integrated sub-assemblies. For example, the trigger housing assembly contains the entire ignition system, which employs a high-speed, swinging hammer to insure the shortest possible lock time. The barrel is assembled to the receiver by a unique dual-screw dove-tail system that provides unusual rigidity and strength—and accounts, in part, for the exceptional accuracy of the 10/22.

Specifications: Caliber: 22 long rifle, high-speed or standard velocity loads. **Barrel:** 18½-inch length. Barrel is assembled to the receiver by unique dual-screw dove-tail mounting for added strength and rigidity. **Weight:** 5 pounds. **Overall Length:** 37 inches. **Sights:** 1/16-inch gold bead front sight. Single folding leaf rear sight, adjustable for elevation. Receiver drilled and tapped for scope blocks or tip-off mount adapter. **Magazine:** 10-shot capacity, exclusive Ruger rotary design. Fits flush into stock. **Trigger:** Curved finger surface, ⅜ inch wide. **Safety:** Sliding cross-button type. Safety locks both sear and hammer and cannot be put in safe position unless gun is cocked. **Stocks:** Solid American walnut, oil finished. Available in 2 styles. The Standard Carbine and The Sporter. **Finish:** Polished all over and blued or anodized.

Model 44 Carbine
44 MAGNUM CALIBER

The carbine is gas-operated, with the slide energized by a short-stroke piston driven by a very small quantity of gas tapped from the barrel during firing. The mechanism is exceptionally smooth in operation, strong, reliable and safe; the breech remains locked until it is opened automatically *after* the bullet has left the barrel. The receiver is machined from a solid block of hot-rolled chrome molybdenum steel. The tubular magazine is located in the forend, capacity is 4 shots, with an additional shot in the chamber. When the last shot has been fired, the breech remains open until it is released by operating the latch located just ahead of the trigger guard.

Specifications: Caliber: 44 Magnum only, using all factory loads. The use of jacketed bullets is recommended to insure optimum accuracy and maximum stopping power. **Barrel:** 18½ inches long, 12-groove rifling, 38-inch twist. Barrel is permanently assembled to the receiver by 20 pitch screw threads. **Weight:** 5 pounds, 12 ounces. **Overall Length:** 36¾ inches. **Sights:** 1/16-inch gold bead front sight. Single folding leaf rear sight, adjustable for elevation. Receiver drilled and tapped. **Magazine:** Fixed, tubular type located in forend. **Capacity:** 4 rounds plus 1 round in chamber. **Trigger:** Two-stage pull. Curved finger surface ⅜-inch wide. **Safety:** Sliding cross-button type. Safety locks both sear and hammer and cannot be put in safe position unless gun is cocked. **Stock:** Genuine American walnut.

RUGER M-77 BOLT-ACTION RIFLE

**MODEL No. M77R (TELESCOPE NOT INCLUDED)
COMPLETE WITH 1-inch STEEL RUGER RINGS (NO SIGHTS)**

**MODEL No. M77RS COMPLETE WITH 1-inch
STEEL RUGER RINGS AND OPEN SIGHTS**

Calibers: 22-250 Remington, 243 Winchester, 6mm Remington, 25-06 Remington, 220 Swift, 257 Roberts 250-3000, 7x57 mm, 270 Winchester, 30-06, 7mm Remington Magnum, 300 Winchester Mag., 338 Winchester Mag., and 458 Win. Magnum.

Action. The M-77 is available in two action lengths—the Short Stroke and the Magnum.

The Short Stroke action is designed to take advantage of the accuracy and ballistic efficiency of the modern short series of cartridges. (Magazine box length: 2.920 inches) The Magnum action—about ½ inch longer than the Short Stroke—assures smooth and faultless feeding of the versatile long series of cartridges. (Magazine box length: 3.340 inches)

The M-77 short stroke is available in calibers 22-250, 243, 6mm, 220 Swift, and 308. The M-77 Magnum is chambered for 270, 25-06, 7x57mm 30-06, 7mm Rem. Magnum, 300 Win. Mag., 338 Win. Mag. and 458 Win. Magnum. Also available in calibers 22-250, 220 Swift, 243 Win., 6mm Remington, 25-06, and 308 with a heavy 24-inch barrel, drilled and tapped for target-scope blocks, and supplied with 1-inch Ruger steel rings. 26-inch barrel in 220 Swift.

The M-77 Round top (Magnum Action only) is equipped with open sights. The receiver is shaped and tapped to accommodate standard commercial scope mount bases. The Round top is not milled for Ruger scope rings. Available only in 25/06, 270, 30-06, 7mm Rem. Mag., and 300 Win. Mag.

In the rare event of a cartridge case failure, the mechanism of the Model 77 has been provided with numerous vents to minimize the effect of escaping gas. A vent of the usual type is provided on the right side of the receiver. Gas which flows along the locking lug channel is largely diverted by the rugged bolt stop and vented through a special opening. In addition, the substantial flange on the bolt sleeve is designed to deflect gas away from the shooter. The one-piece bolt of the Model 77 avoids the brazed joints which are now commonly used as an economy measure. Two massive front locking lugs and a positive long extractor, combined with one-piece construction, result in extraordinary strength and reliability.

The external bolt stop, held in position by a strong hidden spring, is conveniently located on the left rear of the receiver. No tools are needed to open the bolt stop and remove the bolt.

The serrated steel-trigger is adjustable to a minimum pull of 3½ pounds. Trigger action is smooth, crisp and free from creep at all adjustments.

The safety, which is securely mounted in the heavy metal of the tang, is of the desired shotgun type; positive and readily accessible.

For added safety and convenience, the magazine floor plate is hinged to allow emptying of the magazine without having to work the cartridges through the action. The floor plate can be easily opened by pressing the release lever located at the inside front of the trigger guard.

Specifications:

ACTION: Short Stroke or Magnum lengths. **BOLT:** One-piece construction, with two massive locking lugs. **EXTRACTOR:** Long external type. **BOLT STOP:** Left side of receiver, coil spring action. **TRIGGER:** Serrated steel, adjustable for weight of pull. **SPRINGS:** Music wire coil springs throughout (except for special magazine follower spring). **MAGAZINE:** Staggered box type with stainless steel follower and quick release hinged floor plate. **CAPACITY:** Five rounds (plus one in chamber, three rounds in Magnum calibers. **BARREL:** 22 inches Chrome-molybdenum alloy steel. Except calibers 25/06, 300 Win. Mag., 338 Win. Mag., 458 Win. Magnum and 7mm Remington Magnum and all M77V which are 24 inches. **SAFETY:** Sliding shotgun-type mounted on receiver tang. **STOCK:** Genuine American Walnut, thoroughly seasoned, hand-checkered, and hand rubbed. Pistol grip cap with Ruger medallion. Swivel studs. Live rubber recoil pad. **STOCK DIMENSIONS:** Drop at heel: 2⅛ inches. Drop at comb: 1⅝ inches. **LENGTH OF PULL:** 13¾ inches. **STOCK BEDDING:** Ruger diagonal-front-mounting-screw system (Patented) insures consistent bedding of receiver barrel assembly in stock. **OVERALL LENGTH:** 42 inches. **WEIGHT:** Approximately 6½ pounds without scope. (M77V 9 lbs.) and 458 Mag. model, approx. 8¾ lbs.

MODELS AND PRICES

M77R — with scope rings only	**$393.00**
M77ST — (Round Top) with open sights	393.00
M77R — 338 Mag.	393.00
M77RS — with rings and sights	414.00
M77RS — 338 Win. Mag.	414.00
M77RS — 458 Win. Mag.	496.50
M77V — with 24-inch heavy barrel	393.00
M77B/A — Barreled actions	$319.00 to 433.50
D71 — Ruger 1-inch Steel Extra Rings (pr.)	25.50

RUGER NO. 1 SINGLE-SHOT RIFLES

These five illustrations show the variations which are currently offered in the Ruger No. 1 Single-Shot Rifle. Orders for variations or calibers other than those listed are not available from Ruger. The Ruger No. 1 rifles come fitted with selected American walnut stocks. Pistol grip and forearm are hand-checkered to a borderless design. Price for any listed model is **$405.00**. Barreled action is **$286.50**.

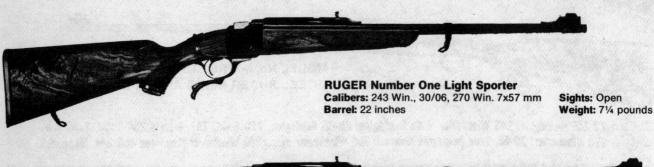

RUGER Number One Light Sporter
Calibers: 243 Win., 30/06, 270 Win. 7x57 mm
Barrel: 22 inches
Sights: Open
Weight: 7¼ pounds

RUGER Number One Medium Sporter
Calibers: 7mm Rem. Mag., 300 Win. Mag. 45/70, 338 Mag.
Barrel: 26 inches (22 inches in 45/70)
Sights: Open
Weight: 8 pounds (7¼ in 45/70)

RUGER Number One Standard Rifle
Calibers: 22/250, 243 Win., 6mm Rem. 25/06, 270 Win., 30/06, 7mm Rem. Mag., 300 Win. Mag. 220 Swift, 338 Mag., 280, 223, 257 Roberts
Barrel: 26 inches
Sights: Ruger steel tip-off scope rings, 1 inch
Weight: 8 pounds

RUGER Number One Special Varminter
Caliber: 22/250, 25/06, 220 Swift, 223, 243, 6mm, 280
Barrel: 24 inches
Sights: Ruger Steel blocks and Tip-off scope rings, 1 inch
Weight: 9 pounds

RUGER Number One Tropical Rifle
Calibers: 375 H&H Mag., 458 Win., Mag.
Barrel: 24 inches
Sights: Open
Weight: 8¼ pounds for 375, 9 pounds for 458

RUGER NO. 1 SINGLE-SHOT RIFLES

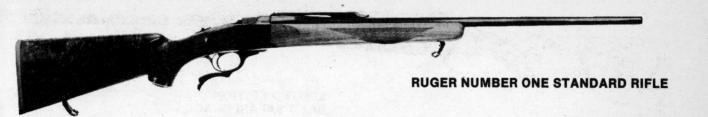

RUGER NUMBER ONE STANDARD RIFLE

General Description   The RUGER No. 1 SINGLE-SHOT action belongs in the under-lever, falling-block category and follows in many characteristics the Farquharson design. In all mechanical details, however, the RUGER No. 1 action is completely new and is in no sense a replica of any older action. The action has been engineered to use the most powerful of the modern magnum cartridges with safety and reliability.

Receiver Design.   The heart of the design is the massive receiver which forms a rigid connection between the barrel and butt stock. The butt stock is mortised into the receiver in such a way as to reinforce the grip section against splitting or cracking. A longitudinal bolt which passes through the butt stock binds the butt stock and receiver together into a solid, rigid structure. Projecting forward from the main part of the receiver and lying directly below the barrel is a heavy steel extension formed integrally with the receiver to facilitate forearm attachment. Because of this forearm hanger, it is possible to arrange the forearm to be completely clear of the barrel or to have any desired pressure on the barrel. The side walls of the receiver are .218-inch thick; these side walls are joined behind the breech block by a massive solid section. It is in this area that the RUGER No. 1 receiver represents the major improvement over the Farquharson type. In these older actions, there is only a thin web of steel effectively joining the side walls behind the breech block.

Firing Pin Hammer Design.   The advantages of the No. 1 hammer-firing pin design are:
1. The mainspring located in the forearm, is in an area where ample space is available for a large, lightly stressed spring.
2. Mounting of the hammer on the lever pivot simplifies the mechanism.
3. Hammer notch located on the periphery of the hammer greatly reduces the pressure on the sear.
4. The swinging transfer block, located in the upper interior of the breech block, functions to virtually lock the firing pin in its forward position against gas pressure during firing.
5. The ignition mechanism requires no openings in the rear of the breech block and, accordingly, no gas can issue in the direction of the shooter's face as it might in some older designs where some leakage can pass along the sides of the firing pin and exit at the rear surface of the breech block.
6. The hammer is retracted upon the first opening motion of the lever and can never actuate the firing pin unless the breech block is fully elevated into firing position.

Ejector Design.   The provisions for removal of fired cartridge cases from the chamber are particularly complete. The action readily handles any type of cartridge case i.e., rimmed, semi-rimmed, belted, rimless, etc. The extractor-ejector mechanism is designed to provide great leverage between the hand-lever and the point where the ejector actually engages the rim or groove of the cartridge case. It is so powerful, in fact, that if the case does not come out, the extractor will usually pull through the rim by use of a moderate force on the lever. With this mechanism, the shells will be thrown clear of the gun when the action is opened and the mechanism is in effect, a powerful spring-actuated automatic ejector. However, if the auto ejector feature is not desired, the ejector spring may be removed.

Trigger and Safety.   The trigger mechanism is adjustable for sear engagement, over travel, and weight of pull. The minimum pull at the present time is slightly under three pounds. The mechanism is free of take-up motion and trigger release is notably crisp. The crispness of this pull is attained by simply establishing leverages which greatly multiply, at the point of sear engagement, the movement of the trigger finger. The safety engages both the sear and the hammer directly to provide an absolute maximum of real security. The safety cannot be put on if the hammer is not cocked, but the action may be opened and closed whether the safety is on or off. The safety is of the sliding shotgun type.

Sights.   The mounting of telescopic sights has been carefully studied in connection with the RUGER No. 1 Single Shot. The rifle is sold complete with scope mounts of RUGER design, made particularly for this rifle. These mounts are split horizontally and fit 1-inch diameter scope tubes. They are the tip-off type, made entirely of steel. RUGER No. 1 rifles are equipped with ¼ rib scope mount only, unless open sights are also ordered. This ¼ rib functions primarily as a base for the RUGER scope mounts and may also be used for mounting open sights which are optional.

Two forearms are available: a semi beaver-tail modern type of forearm and a short slender design patterned after the typical designs of Alexander Henry.

When the short Henry type forearm is used, the front sling swivel is mounted on a barrel band and a sling in this event would be regarded as primarily a carrying sling. The front swivel is mounted in the forearm.

Both pistol grip and forearm are hjand-checkered in an ample area to a borderless design. The finish completely reveals the character and grain of the carefully selected American walnut from which the stocks and forearms are made.

SAKO RIFLES

LIMITED EDITION SAKO SAFARI GRADE

Features extended magazine for storing four back-up rounds plus one in the chamber; barrel band swivel; express-type rear sight rib for extra strength; a satin or matte bluing for extra durability.

**Available in 300 Win. Mag.,
338 Win. Mag., 375 H&H Mag.** **$1995.00**

SAKO CLASSIC GRADE

This incredibly accurate Sako C assic Grade is the rifle by which all others are judged. Sports blued, satin-finished barrel and is fashioned from select grade American walnut.

Available in the following:
AII 243 Win. .... $ 975.00
AIII 270 Win., 30-06 .... 1020.00
AIII 7 mm Rem. Mag. 1035.00

SAKO SUPER DELUXE

Sako offers the Super Deluxe to the most discriminating gun buyer. This one-of-a-kind beauty is available on special order.

**Special order. Available in AI,
AII, AIII Calibers** **$1995.00**

SAKO RIFLES

STANDARD RIFLE—AI

AI (short action) cal: 17 Rem. $758.95
222 Rem., 223 Rem. 725.00

STANDARD RIFLE—AII

AII (medium action) cal: 22-250 Rem.,
243 Win., 308 Win. $725.00

STANDARD RIFLE—AIII

AIII (long action) cal: 25-06
Rem., 270 Win., 30-06 ....$741.95
7mm Rem. Mag., 300 Win.
Mag., 338 Win. Mag. 758.95
375 H&H Mag. 775.00

THE SAKO TRIGGER IS A RIFLEMAN'S DELIGHT . . . SMOOTH, CRISP AND FULLY ADJUSTABLE.

If these were the only Sako features, it would still be the best rifle available. But the real quality that sets Sako apart from all others is its truly outstanding accuracy.

While many factors can affect a rifle's accuracy, 90% of any rifle's accuracy potential lies in its barrel. And the creation of superbly accurate barrels is where Sako is unique.

The care that Sako takes in the cold-hammering processing of each barrel is unparalleled in the industry. As an example, after each barrel blank is drilled, it is diamond-lapped and then optically checked for microscopic flaws. This extra care affords the Sako owner lasting accuracy and a finish that will stay "new" season after season.

You can't buy an unfired Sako. Every gun is test fired using special overloaded proof cartridges. This ensures the Sako owner total safety and uncompromising accuracy. Every barrel must group within Sako specif-

ications or it's scrapped. Not recycled. Not adjusted. Scrapped. Either a Sako barrel delivers Sako accuracy, or it never leaves the factory.

And hand-in-hand with Sako accuracy is Sako beauty. Genuine European walnut stocks, flawlessly finished and checkered by hand.

Sako rifles are available in the following:
- Standard, with AI, AII and AIII actions.
- Deluxe, with AI, AII and AIII actions.
- Varmint, with heavy-barrel and Varminter forend in AI and AII actions.
- Carbine—with full-length stock. AI action in 222 Rem. AII action in 243 and 308 Win. AIII action in 270 and 30-06.
- Super Deluxe, with AI, AII and AIII actions.
- Classic Grade, with AII (243), and AIII action in 270, 30-06, and 7mm Rem. Mag.
- Safari Grade, with AIII Mag. calibers: 300 Win. Mag., 338 Win. Mag. and 375 H&H Mag.

SAKO RIFLES

SAKO CARBINE

Caliber: 222 Rem., 243 Win., 270 Win., 308 Win., 30-06 .... **$825.00**

SAKO VARMINT (HEAVY BARREL)

AI (short action) cal: 222 Rem., 223 Rem. **$875.00**
AII (medium action) cal: 22-250 Rem., 243 Win., 308 Win. **875.00**

SAKO FINSPORT 2700

Caliber: 270, 30-06, 7mm Rem. Mag., 300 Win. Mag. **$866.95**

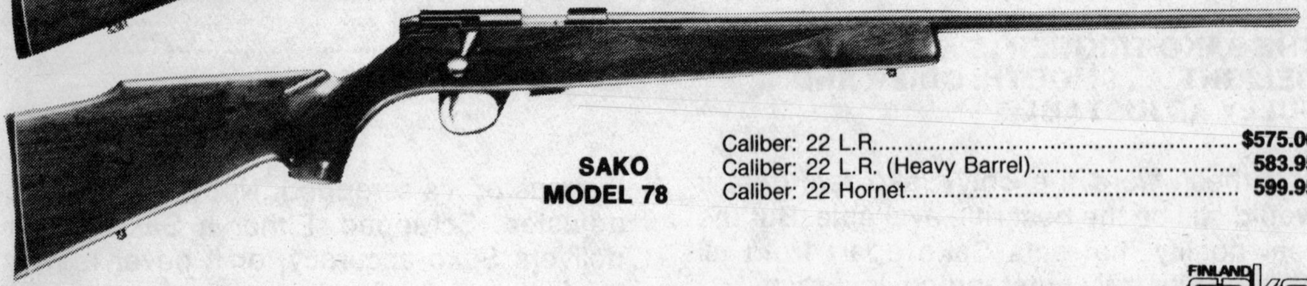

SAKO MODEL 78

Caliber: 22 L.R. **$575.00**
Caliber: 22 L.R. (Heavy Barrel) **583.95**
Caliber: 22 Hornet **599.95**

FINLAND sako

Specifications
COMPLETE RIFLES:

Calibers	Available Models	Action Type	Magazine Capacity	Barrel Length	Approx. Wt.: S, D, SD, CL,	Approx Wt. (Varmint)	Approx. Wt. (Carbine)	Approx. Wt. (Safari)	Twist R.H. 1 Turn-in	Length of Pull
.22LR	78	78	5	22½″	6¾ lbs.				16½″	13½″
.22LR HVY BBL	78	78	5	22½″	7¼ lbs.				16″	13½″
.22 Hornet	78	78	4	22½″	6¾ lbs.				14″	13½″
.17 Rem*	S/SD	AI·1	5	23½″	6½ lbs.				9″	13½″
.222**	S/D/V/SD/C	AI·1	5	23½″	6½ lbs.	8¼ lbs.	7 lbs.		14″	13½″
.223**	S/D/V/SD	AI·1	5	23½″	6½ lbs.	8¼ lbs.			13″	13½″
.22-250**	S/D/V/SD	AII·3	5	23½″	7¼ lbs.	8½ lbs.			14″	13½″
.243**	S/D/V/C/CL/SD	AII·1	5	23″ (20″C)	7¼ lbs.	8½ lbs.	7½ lbs.		10″	13½″
.308**	S/D/V/SD/C	AII·1	5	23″	7¼ lbs.	8½ lbs.	7 lbs.		12″	13½″
.25-06**	S/D/SD	AIII·1	5	24″	8 lbs.				10″	13½″
.270**	S/F/D/C/CL/SD	AIII·1	5	24″ (20″C)	8 lbs.		7½ lbs.		10″	13½″
.30-06**	S/F/D/C/CL/SD	AIII·1	5	24″(20″C)	8 lbs.		7½ lbs.		10″	13½″
7mm Rem. Mag.**	S/F/D/CL/SD	AIII·2	4	24″	8 lbs.				9½″	13½″
.300 Win Mag.**	S/F/D/SD/SF	AIII·3	4	24″	8 lbs.			8 lbs.	10″	13½″
.338 Win. Mag.**	S/D/SD/SF	AIII·3	4	24″	8 lbs.			8 lbs.	10″	13½″
.375 H&H Mag.**	S/D/SD/SF	AIII·4		24″	8 lbs.			8 lbs.	12″	13½″

*CODE: S = Standard F = Finsport D = Deluxe SD = Super Deluxe V = Varmint 78 = Model 78 C = Carbine CL = Classic Grade SF = Safari Grade

**Sako Super Deluxe Rifles are available for these calibers on special order only.

Stock: Standard — European walnut, high gloss finish, hand checkered, 20 lines to the inch. Deluxe — European walnut, high gloss finish, French-type hand checkered, 22 lines to the inch, rosewood grip cap and forend tip, semi-beavertail forend. Super Deluxe — Select European walnut, high gloss finish, deep oak leaf hand engraved design. Classic Grade — Select American walnut, oil finish, hand checkered, 20 lines to the inch. Safari Grade — European walnut, oil finish, hand checkered, 20 lines to the inch. Carbine — Full length stock, European walnut, oil finish, hand checkered, 20 lines to the inch. Varmint — European walnut, oil finish, hand checkered, 20 lines to the inch, bull beavertail forend.

Metal finish: Carbine, Varmint, Standard, Classic Grade, Safari Grade: Blued satin finish. Deluxe, Super Deluxe: super high polished deep blue finish.

SAKO RIFLES

SAKO HIGH-POWERED RIFLES ARE UNIQUE IN THAT THEY ARE MADE IN THREE DIFFERENT ACTIONS:
• AI (Short action) • AII (Medium action) • AIII (Long action)

Each action is customized to fit a specific set of individual hunting needs, each designed, engineered and scaled for a specific range of cartridges:

• AI (Short action) 17 Rem., 222 Rem., 223 Rem.

• AII (Medium action) 22-250 Rem., 243 Win., 308 Win.

• AIII (Long action) 25-06 Rem., 270 Win., 30-06, 7mm Rem. Mag., 300 Win. Mag., 338 Win. Mag., 375 H&H Mag.

Every Sako rifle, regardless of caliber, is built on an action with no unnecessary bulk or excess weight and with a bolt action as short as it is smooth.

Not only is the action scaled to the cartridge, the entire rifle is beautifully proportioned and perfectly scaled.

SAKO DELUXE RIFLES

AI (short action)
cal: 222 Rem., 223 Rem. **$995.00**

AII (medium action)
22-250 Rem., 243 Win., 308 Win. ... **$995.00**

AIII (long action)
cal: 25-06 Rem., 270 Win., 30-06 . **$ 995.00**
7mm Rem. Mag. .. **1120.00**
300 Win. Mag. **1120.00**
338 Win. Mag. **1120.00**
375 H&H Mag. **1020.00**

• The Sako AI, (Short action) chambered for 222 Rem., will weigh an easy-to-carry 6½ lbs.

• The Sako AII (Medium action), chambered for 243 Win., comes in at 7¼ lbs.

• The Sako AIII (Long action), chambered for the big 375 H&H Mag., will tip the scales at a recoil-absorbing 8 lbs.

As a result, every Sako delivers better handling, faster swing and less fatigue.

The scope mounting system on these Sakos is among the strongest in the world. Instead of using separate bases, a tapered dovetail is milled right into the receiver, to which the scope rings are mounted. A beautifully simple system that's been proven by over twenty years of use. Sako scope rings are available in: low (2½ to 3-power scopes); medium (4-power scopes) and high (6-power scopes). Available in 1 inch only.

SAKO RIFLES

AI (SHORT ACTION)
CALIBERS:
17 Rem.
222 Rem.
222 Rem. Mag.
223 Rem.
In white only $325.00

AII (MEDIUM ACTION)
CALIBERS:
22-250 Rem.
243 Win.
308 Win.
In white only $325.00

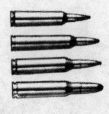

AIII (LONG ACTION)
CALIBERS:
25-06 Rem.
270 Win.
30-06
7mm Rem. Mag.
300 Win. Mag.
338 Win. Mag.
375 H&H Mag.
In white only $342.00

SAVAGE CENTERFIRE RIFLES

MODEL 99-C
Calibers: 308 & 243 Winchester,
7mm/08 Remington

The 99-C North American Classic features select walnut stock designed with a high Monte Carlo and deeply fluted comb. Stock and grooved forend skip-line checkered. Stock is fitted with whiteline recoil pad and pistol-grip cap. Detachable hooded ramp front sight, rear sight adjustable for elevation and windage. **$399.95**

MODEL 99-E
Calibers: 250, 300 Savage,
243 and 308 Winchester

The 99-E lever-action carbine comes with a 22-inch barrel. The fully enclosed box-type magazine with rotary carrier has a 5-shot capacity; plus one in chamber. With blued steel lever, grooved trigger and corrugated butt plate. Walnut finished Monte Carlo stock has grooved forend. Finger tip safety on right side of trigger locks trigger and lever. **$319.50**

SPECIFICATIONS—FEATURES

MODEL	Barrel Length	Barrel Steel	Steel Receiver	Tapped For Top Mount Scope	Sights Front	Sights Rear	Cocking Indicator	Magazine Type	Cartridge Counter	Capacity	Safety	Stock and Forend	Checkered	Flut. Comb.	Capped Grip	Butt Plate	Avg. Wgt. (Lbs.)
99-C	22"	Chrome Moly	Blued	X	Removable Hooded Ramp	Removable Adjustable	X	Clip		5	Top Tang	Select Walnut	X	X	X	Hard Rubber	7
99-E	22"	Chrome Moly	Blued	X	Removable Ramp	Removable Adjustable	X	Rotary		6	Slide Bottom Tang	Wal. Fin. Hardwood	X	X		Hard Rubber	7

MODELS 99 A, C and E Stock: Length 13½ inches; Drop at Comb 1⅜ inches (1½ inches for 99-A); Drop at Monte Carlo 1½ inches; Drop at Heel 2½ inches. Overall Length 41¾ inches.

RATE OF TWIST (R.H.) 1 turn in 9½ inches for 7mm/08; 1 turn in 10 inches for 243 and 250 Savage; 1 turn in 12 inches for 300 Savage, 375 and 308.

SAVAGE CENTERFIRE RIFLES

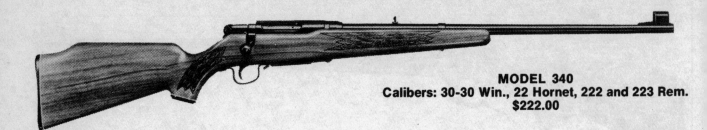

MODEL 340
Calibers: 30-30 Win., 22 Hornet, 222 and 223 Rem.
$222.00

The Savage 340 bolt-action centerfire rifle comes in calibers 30-30 Win., 22 Hornet, 222 and 223 Remington. The bolt locks up in front, assuring strength and accuracy. The barrel is precision-rifled and the muzzle is crowned.

The bolt handle is curved. Features include a Monte Carlo style stock of American walnut; checkering; pistol-grip cap. Other features include detachable clip magazine and metal open sights.

SPECIFICATIONS—FEATURES

MODEL	Barrel Length	Tapped for Scope Mount	Sights Front	Sights Rear	Thumb Safety	Clip Magazine	Capacity	Checkered Stock Select Walnut	Checkered Stock Fluted Comb.	White Line Butt Plate	White Line Grip Cap	Monte Carlo Stock	Roll-Over Cheek Piece	Butt Plate	Avg. Wgt. (Lbs.)
340	22 Hornet, 223, 222:24"	Side Mount	Hooded Removable Ramp	Folding Leaf	X	X	5	X	X			X		Hard Rubber	6¾
	30-30 22"	Side Mount	Hooded Removable Ramp	Folding Leaf	X	X	4	X	X			X		Hard Rubber	6½

MODEL 340 Stock: Length 13½"; drop 1¾" at comb, 1¾" at Monte Carlo, 2½" at heel.
RATE OF TWIST (R.H.) 1 turn in 12" for 30-30 and 14" for 222, 223, 22 Hornet.

MODEL 110 BOLT-ACTION CENTERFIRE RIFLES

MODEL 110-C (right hand)
MODEL 110-CL (left hand)

Features ejector clip magazine for convenient loading and unloading. To unload, press the recessed button and out pops the clip with the shells neatly held and tips protected. An extra loaded clip provides additional fire power. Exclusive twin gas ports in receiver, gas baffle lugs on bolt, and bolt end cap give most complete protection. Extra clip, **$10.50** (specify caiber).

Calibers for right and left hand; 30-06 Sprg., 270 Win. & 243 Mag. Caliber: 7mm Rem. Mag. Right hand only: 25-06, 22-250 Rem. 24-inch barrels only

Standard calibers: ....right hand **$366.50**
                left hand 375.50
Magnum caliber: ....right hand 371.50
                left hand 380.00

SAVAGE CENTERFIRE RIFLES

SPECIFICATIONS — FEATURES

MODEL	Free Floating Barrel		Steel Receiver	Gas Ports	Tapped For Top Mount Scope	Sights		Satin Slide Bolt	Recessed Bolt Face	Safety Gas Baffles	Cocking Indicator	Magazine	Capacity	Top Tang Safety	Checkered Stock	Cheek Piece	Butt Plate	Avg. Wgt. (Lbs.)
	Barrel Length	Barrel Steel				Front	Rear											
110-C,CL	22″*	Chrome Moly	Blued	2	X	Hooded Removable Ramp	Removable Adjustable	X	X	3	X	Clip	5	X	Select Walnut	X	Recoil Pad	7
110-C,CL (Mag)	24″	Chrome Moly	Blued	2	X	Removable Ramp	Removable Adjustable	X	X	3	X	Clip	4	X	Select Walnut	X	Recoil Pad	7¾

LEFT-HAND rifles built to same specifications, except with left-hand stock and action.
ALL MODELS Stock: Length 13½″; drop 1⅝″ at comb, 1½″ at Monte Carlo. 2¼″ at heel. Length over-all: 42½″-45″.

*RIGHT HAND 25-06, 22-250 Rem. 24″ barrel only.
RATE OF TWIST (R.H.) 1 turn in 9½″ for 7mm Rem. Mag.; 1 turn in 10″ for 25-06, 243, 30-06 and 270; 1 turn in 14″ for 22-250; 1 turn in 12″ for 308.

MODEL 110-S Silhouette Rifle
Caliber: 308 Win., 7mm/08 Rem.
$319.50

Features: A heavy 22-inch tapered barrel, ⅞-inch diameter at muzzle, allows for great accuracy. Receiver is drilled and tapped for scope mounting, satin blue finish on receiver to reduce light reflection. The barrel is free floating in special "Silhouette" stock of select walnut, has high fluted comb, hand filling, Wundhammer swell pistol grip for both right- and left-hand use. Stippled checkering on pistol grip and under forend. Stock is fitted with rifle recoil pad.

LENGTH	OVERALL	43 in.
	BARREL	22 in.
	STOCK	13½ in.
DROP AT	COMB	1⅜ in.
	MONTE CARLO	1¼ in.
	HEEL	2¼ in.
AVERAGE WEIGHT (LBS.)		(MAX. 8 lbs. 10 oz.)
CARTRIDGE CAPACITY		5

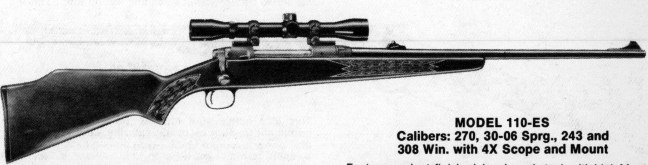

MODEL 110-ES
Calibers: 270, 30-06 Sprg., 243 and 308 Win. with 4X Scope and Mount

Features walnut-finished, hardwood stock with high Monte Carlo cheekpiece and 5-shot internal box magazine. Removable, adjustable rear sight and removable front ramp sight. **$296.00**
Model 110-E: Same as Model 110-ES but without 4X Scope and Mount. **$241.50**

SAVAGE/STEVENS 22 RIFLES

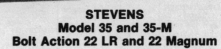

STEVENS
Model 35 and 35-M
Bolt Action 22 LR and 22 Magnum

Economical 22 Cal bolt action rifle chambered for 22 LR and 22 Magnum. **ACTION:** Streamlined bolt, cocks on opening. Thumb safety locks trigger. Double extractors for positive extraction and ejection. Recessed bolt face. **MAGAZINE:** 5-shot detachable clip, **STOCK:** Walnut finish hardwood, Monte Carlo, impressed checkering, corrugated butt plate. **SIGHTS:** Sporting front and rear sights with elevation adjustment. **BBL LENGTH:** 22 inches, **OA LENGTH:** 41 inches, **APPROX WEIGHT:** 5 lbs. **CALIBER:** 22 LR and 22 Magnum.

Model 35 . . . . $92.50
Model 35-M 96.50

STEVENS MODEL 987-T AUTOLOADER
22 Long Rifle with 1541 4X Scope and Mount
$106.50

The Model 987-T has top tang safety and 15-shot capacity tubular magazine. Autoloading is with 22 long rifle only. Trigger must be pulled and released for each shot. Monte Carlo stock is walnut-finished hardwood.
Model 987 22 Long Rifle: Same as Model 987-T except without 4X Scope and Mount. **$100.50**

STEVENS 72 CRACKSHOT
22 Long, Short and Long Rifle
$126.50

This unique falling block action is a pleasure to handle, shoot or simply admire. It has balance, smooth functioning and safety. This popular 22 rifle is truly in the great Stevens tradition. It features an octagonal barrel, case hardened frame, walnut stock and forend with oil finish.

STEVENS 89
22 Short, Long and Long Rifle
$85.00

This little single shot has the balance and feel of a traditional western carbine. Featuring western-style lever action with a rugged Martini-type breech block, automatic ejection. Hammer must be cocked by hand independent of the lever prior to firing. Ideal for that young beginner.

STEVENS MODEL 125
(not illus.)
$88.50

STEYR MANNLICHER RIFLES

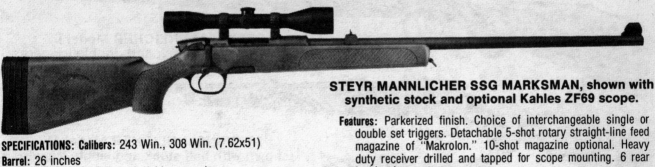

SPECIFICATIONS: Calibers: 243 Win., 308 Win. (7.62x51)

Barrel: 26 inches

Weight: 8.6 lbs. (9.9 lbs. with Kahles scope)

Overall Length: 44.5 inches

Stock: Choice of synthetic half stock of ABS "CYCOLAC" or walnut. Removable spacers in butt section adjusts length of pull from 12¾ inches to 14 inches.

Sights: Hooded blade front; folding rear leaf sight.

STEYR MANNLICHER SSG MARKSMAN, shown with synthetic stock and optional Kahles ZF69 scope.

Features: Parkerized finish. Choice of interchangeable single or double set triggers. Detachable 5-shot rotary straight-line feed magazine of "Makrolon." 10-shot magazine optional. Heavy duty receiver drilled and tapped for scope mounting. 6 rear locking lugs.

Cycloac half stock .... **$ 765.35**
Walnut half stock 887.30
Cycloac half stock, with mounted Kahles ZF69 scope 1482.00
Optional 10-shot magazine 66.00
Spare 5-shot magazine 25.00

STEYR MANNLICHER SSG MATCH

Same as the Model SSG MARKSMAN, except with 26-inch heavy barrel, match bolt, Walther target peep sights, and adjustable rail in forend to adjust sling travel. Weight: 11 lbs.

Cycolac half stock .... **$ 996.00**
Walnut half stock 1106.00
Spare 5-shot magazine 25.00

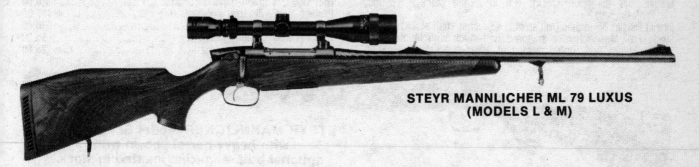

**STEYR MANNLICHER ML 79 LUXUS
(MODELS L & M)**

SPECIFICATIONS: Calibers:

Model L (standard calibers) 22-250 Rem., 6mm Rem., 243 Win., 308 Win.

Model L (optional metric calibers) 5.6x57

Model M (standard calibers) 25-06 Rem., 270 Win., 7x57, 7x64, 30-06

Model M (optional metric calibers) 6.5x55, 6.5x57, 7.5x55, 9.3x62

Barrel: 20 inches (full stock); 23.6 inches (half stock)

Weight: 6.8 lbs. (full stock); 6.9 lbs. (half stock)

Overall Length: 39 inches (full stock); 43 inches (half stock)

Stock: Hand-checkered walnut with Monte Carlo cheekpiece. Either full Mannlicher or half stock. European hand-rubbed oil finish or high gloss lacquer finish.

Sights: Ramp front—adjustable for elevation; open U-notch rear— adjustable for windage.

Features: Single combination trigger (becomes hair trigger when moved forward before firing). Detachable 3-shot steel straight-line feed magazine (6-shot optional). 6 rear locking lugs. Drilled and tapped for scope mounts.

Full stock .... **$ 1172.00**
Half stock 1097.00
Optional metric calibers add 55.00
Spare 3-shot magazine 41.50
Spare 6-shot magazine 77.35

STEYR MANNLICHER RIFLES

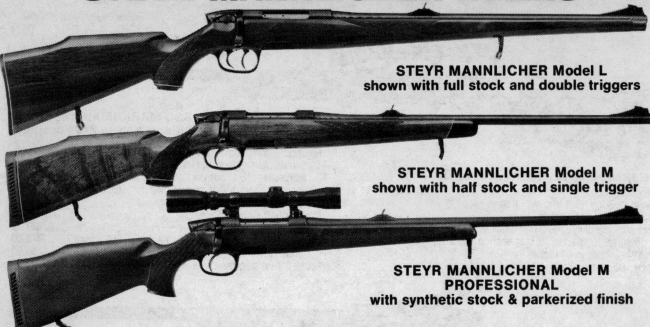

STEYR MANNLICHER Model L
shown with full stock and double triggers

STEYR MANNLICHER Model M
shown with half stock and single trigger

STEYR MANNLICHER Model M PROFESSIONAL
with synthetic stock & parkerized finish

SPECIFICATIONS:

Calibers:
Model SL (standard calibers only) 222 Rem., 222 Rem. Mag., 223 Rem.
Model L (standard calibers) 22-250 Rem., 6mm Rem., 243 Win., 308 Win.
Model L (optional metric caliber) 5.6x57
Model M (standard calibers) 25-06 Rem., 270 Win., 7x57, 7x64, 30.06 Spr.
Model M (optional metric calibers) 6.5x55, 6.5x57, 7.5x55, 8x57JS, 9.3x62

Barrel: 20 inches (full stock); 23.6 inches (half stock)
Weight: 6.8 lbs. (full stock); 6.9 lbs. (half stock); 7.5 lbs. (Professional)
Overall Length: 39 inches (full stock); 43 inches (half stock)
Stock: Full Mannlicher or standard half stock with Monte Carlo cheekpiece and rubber recoil pad. Hand-checkered walnut in skip-line pattern. The Model M with half stock is also available in a "Professional" version with a parkerized finish and synthetic stock made of ABS "CYCOLAC" (made with right-handed action only). Note: Model M is available with left-handed action in full stock and half stock.

Features: Choice of fine-crafted single or double set triggers. Detachable 5-shot rotary magazine of "Makrolon." 6 rear locking lugs. Drilled and tapped for scope mounting.

Full stock .... $ 958.00
Full stock, with left-handed action 1082.00
Half stock 893.00
Half stock, with left-handed action 1020.00
Professional, with iron sights 737.00
Professional, without sights 690.00
Optional metric calibers add 55.00
Spare magazine 25.00

STEYR MANNLICHER Model S/T Magnum
with heavy barrel shown with
optional butt magazine inletted in stock

SPECIFICATIONS:

Calibers:
Model S—257 Weatherby Mag., 264 Win. Mag., 300 Win. Mag., 338 Win. Mag., 7mm Rem. Mag., 300 H&H Mag., 375 H&H Mag.
Model S (Optional calibers)—6.5x68, 8x68S, 9.3x64
Model S/T (Heavy barrel)—375 H&H Mag., 458 Win. Mag.
Model S/T (Optional caliber)—9.3x64

Barrel: 26 inches Model S/T (with 26-inch heavy barrel)
Weight: 8.4 lbs. (Model S); 9.02 lbs. (Model S/T); add .66 lbs. for butt mag. opt.
Overall Length: 45 inches

Stock: Half stock with Monte Carlo cheekpiece and rubber recoil pad. Hand-checkered walnut in skip-line pattern. Available with optional spare magazine inletted in butt stock.

Features: Choice of fine-crafted single or double set triggers. Detachable 4-shot rotary magazine of "Makrolon." 6 rear locking lugs. Drilled and tapped for scope mounting.

Model S or S/T .... $ 62.00
Model S or S/T, with opt. butt magazine 1012.00
Optional calibers add 55.00
Spare magazine 25.00

STEYR MANNLICHER RIFLE

STEYR MANNLICHER VARMINT
Models SL & L $965.00

SPECIFICATIONS:
Calibers:
Model SL Varmint—222 Rem.
Model L Varmint—22-250 Rem., 243 Win., 308 Win.
Model L (Optional caliber)—5.6x57

Barrel: 26-inch heavy barrel
Weight: 7.92 lbs.
Overall Length: 44 inches/L (Varmint)
Sights: without sights.
Features: Choice of interchangeable single or double set triggers, 5-shot detachable "Makrolon" rotary magazine; 6 rear locking lugs; drilled and tapped for scope mounts.
Optional caliber **$55.00**
Spare magazine 25.00

THOMPSON/CENTER SINGLE-SHOT RIFLE

American Made—Lifetime Warranty

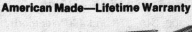

Barrels quickly interchange from one caliber to the next!

THOMPSON/CENTER SINGLE SHOT RIFLE
Calibers: 223 Rem., 22/250 Rem., 243 Win., 7mm Rem. Mag., or 30-06
$425.00
ACCESSORY BARREL $140.00

Chambered for five popular hunting cartridges, this superbly accurate sports rifle offers the simplicity and strength of a break open design coupled with the unique feature of interchangeable barrels. Triggers function double set or single stage. A positive lock cross bolt safety offers maximum security. Wood is hand selected American Black Walnut from the Thompson/Center mill. All barrels are equipped with iron sights which may be removed for scope mounting.

TIKKA RIFLES

MODEL 4601 Cal. 30-06	$650.00
4602 Cal. 308	615.00
4603 Cal. 270 Win.	650.00
4604 Cal. 243 Win.	615.00
4605 Cal. 7mm Mag.	650.00
4606 Cal. 300Win. Mag.	650.00
4607 Cal. 222 Rem.	615.00

The new Tikka Bolt Action Rifles, "Finland's finest", combine aesthetic beauty, perfect balance, and hard rugged construction for bolt action shooting. The barrels, made from Bofors ordnance steel, are rifled by the cold forging method, hand lapped for perfect shooting. The double lugged chrome moly bolt rides smoother and easier on double rails for perfect ejection, locking. The beautifully finished select grain walnut stock and palm swelled grip are enhanced by the reassuring hand cut checkering on both grip and forestock. Trigger adjustment can be done without action removal. Extra magazine clips are available. Sling swivels and front sight hood are packed with each gun.

TIKKA DELUXE TURKEY GUN
MODEL NO. 4651, 12 GAUGE, 8-in. MAG.
OVER .222 REM. $750.00

The ever popular Tikka Turkey Gun with mono block design has a switch type barrel selector and rebounding hammer. This combination over and under Turkey Gun as a 12 ga. shotgun barrel mounted over a .222 Remington rifle barrel equipped with muzzle break. A perfect gun for both long and close shots. Its beautifully finished hand

checkered walnut stock adds to its unique design. The Turkey Gun has a folding rear sight, and dove tailed front sight mounted on a ventilated rib. Sling swivels are packed with each gun.

WEATHERBY RIFLES

VARMINTMASTER $729.95
Calibers: 22-250 Rem. & 224 W.M.
(without sights)

Mark V VARMINTMASTER—Calibers: 22-250 Rem. and 224 Weatherby Magnum. **Action:** Mark V bolt action scaled down, six locking lugs, enclosed cartridge case head, three gas ports. **Sights:** shown with 3X to 9X Weatherby Variable Scope on Buehler Mount. **Stock:** Monte Carlo with cheekpiece and hand-checkering. Forend tip, pistol grip and rubber butt pad.

MARK V DELUXE RIFLE
Calibers: 240 W.M., 257 W.M., 270 W.M.
7mm W.M., 300 W.M., 340 W.M.,
378 W.M., 460 W.M. & 30-06

MARK V DELUXE RIFLE—Calibers: 257, 270, 7mm, 300, 340, 378 and 460 Weatherby Magnum and 30-06 calibers. **Action:** Weatherby Mark V with recessed bolt face, nine locking lugs, three gas escape ports. 54° bolt lift. **Sights:** shown with hooded ramp front sight and receiver peep sight. **Stock** Monte Carlo with cheekpiece and checkering, forend tip, pistol grip cap, fitted rubber recoil pad.
   Mark V Deluxe Rifle, less sights, in 240, 257, 270, 7mm, 300 W.M. and 30-06 calibers **$749.95.** In 340 W.M., less sights **$769.95;** 378 W.M. less sights **$924.95;** and in 460 W.M. caliber less sights **$1063.95.** Rifles with factory-mounted scopes at extra cost.

MARK V CUSTOM RIFLE

MARK V CUSTOM RIFLE—Specifications same as Deluxe rifle except with fancy grade walnut stock and full metal engraving. Mark V Custom rifle shown is equipped with 3X to 9X Weatherby Variable scope on Buehler mount. Customs require approximately 18 months to produce.

RIFLE SPECIFICATIONS

CALIBER	224	22/250	240	257	270	7mm	30-06	300	340	378	460
Model	Right hand 24" or 26" bbl. Left hand model not available.		Right or left hand 24" bbl. Right hand 26" bbl. Left hand 26" bbl. **available in 300 cal. only**						Right or left hand 26" bbl. only.	Right or left hand 26" bbl. only.	Right or left hand 26" bbl. only.
Weight w/o sights	6½ lbs.		7¼ lbs.						8½ lbs.		10½ lbs.
Overall length	43¼" or 45¼" dependent on barrel length		44½" or 46½" dependent on barrel length						46½"		
Capacity	5 shots: 4 in magazine; 1 in chamber	4 shots: 3 in mag.; 1 in chamber	6 shots: 5 in mag.; 1 in chamber	4 shots: 3 in magazine; 1 in chamber			5 shots: 4 in mag.; 1 in chamber	4 shots: 3 in magazine; 1 in chamber		3 shots: 2 in magazine; 1 in chamber	
Barrel	24" standard or 26" semi-target		24" standard or 26" #2 contour						26" #2 contour	26" #3 contour	26" #4* contour
Rifling	1-14" twist		1-10" twist	1-10" twist		1-10" twist		1-10" twist	1-10" twist	1-12" twist	1-16" twist
Sights	Scope or iron sights extra										
Stock	American walnut, individually hand-bedded to assure precision accuracy. High-lustre, durable stock finish. Quick detachable sling swivels. Basket weave checkering. Monte Carlo style with cheek piece, especially designed for both scope and iron sighted rifles. Length of pull 13½". Length of pull of 460-13⅞".										French walnut only.
Action	A scaled-down version of the popular Mark V action with 6 precision locking lugs in place of 9.		Featuring the Mark V action. The nine locking lugs have almost double the shear area of the lugs found on conventional bolt rifles. The cartridge case head is completely enclosed in the bolt and barrel. 460 action includes hand honing, bolt knob fully checkered, bolt and follower damascened, custom engraved floor plate.								
Safety	Forward moving release accessible and positive										

BARRELED ACTION SPECIFICATIONS

CALIBER	224	22/250	240	257	270	7mm	30-06	300	340	378	460
Model	Right hand 24" or 26" bbl. Left hand model not available.		Right or left hand 24" bbl. Right hand 26" bbl. Left hand 26" bbl. **available in 300 cal. only**						Right or left hand 26" bbl. only.	Right or left hand 26" bbl. only.	Right or left hand 26" bbl. only.

*Pendleton Dekicker is an integral part of the barrel. Prices for barreled action models 22-250 and 224 Varmintmaster calibers $400.00, 240 W.M., 257 W.M., 270 W.M., 7mm W.M., 300 W.M., and 30-06 calibers $415.00, 340 W.M. $425.00, 378 W.M. $495.00, 460 W.M. $550.00.

WEATHERBY RIFLES

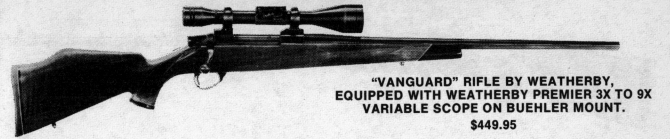

"VANGUARD" RIFLE BY WEATHERBY, EQUIPPED WITH WEATHERBY PREMIER 3X TO 9X VARIABLE SCOPE ON BUEHLER MOUNT.
$449.95

The Vanguard by Weatherby is now available in the following calibers: 243 Win., 25-06, 270 WCF 7mm Rem. Mag., 30-06, and 300 Win. Mag.

The "hammer-forging" method of barrel manufacture guarantees a glass-smooth bore with optimum dimensional stability from breech to muzzle. It is this "hammer-forging" technique which gives the Vanguard rifle its accuracy and long life.

The Vanguard action is based on one of the most highly acclaimed designs in the gun industry, yet sports many of the modern safety advancements. The bolt face is recessed and it in turn is recessed into the barrel forming 3 concentric bands of steel around the cartridge case head. In addition to this case support, the Vanguard also features a completely enclosed bolt sleeve to prevent escaping gases from flowing back through the bolt into the shooter's face. Other safety features include a gas ejection port, two massive bolt lugs, and side operated safety lever.

The action has a knurled bolt knob for a better grip, a hinged floor plate for easy removal of loaded cartridges from the magazine, and a drilled and tapped receiver for simplified scope installation. The action is forged out of high strength chrome moly steel, polished and blued to a rich deep hue. The trigger guard and floor plate are black chromed for maximum durability.

The Vanguard has a fully adjustable trigger mechanism providing a crisp and clean pull down to 3 pounds.

The Vanguard stock is made of select American walnut and bedded for accuracy, it sports a Weatherby butt pad, 45° rosewood forend tip and pistol grip cap, white line spacers, and the traditional Weatherby diamond inlay. The finish of the Vanguard stock is the same high luster type found on the Mark V . . . scratch resistant and impervious to water, perspiration or solvents. The Vanguard stock has a 13½-inch pull and just the right amount of cast-off and drop for the average shooter.

SPECIFICATIONS
Vanguard Rifles available in right-hand models only

Calibers	243 Win.	25-06 Rem.	270 WCF	7mm Rem. Mag.	30-06	300 Win. Mag.
Weight (approximate)	7 lb. 14 oz.	7 lb. 14 oz.	7 lb. 14 oz.	7 lb. 14 oz.	7 lb. 14 oz.	7 lb. 14 oz.
Overall Length	44 "	44½"	44½"	44½"	44½"	44½"
Magazine Capacity	5 rds.	5 rds.	5 rds.	3 rds.	5 rds.	3 rds.
Barrel Length	24"	24"	24"	24"	24"	24"
Rifling	1-10"	1-10"	1-10"	1-10"	1-10"	1-10"
Sights	Scope or iron sights at extra cost.					
Stocks	American Walnut, 13½" pull, fore-end tip & pistol grip cap					
Action	Vanguard action of the improved Mauser type					
Safety	Side operated, forward moving release, accessible & positive					
Scope Mounts	The Vanguard accepts any Mark V scope mount					

MARK XXII
22 LR SEMIAUTOMATIC CLIP-FED
$279.95 (with open sights)

Also available with 15-shot tubular magazine (not illus.), with open sights **$289.95**

MARK XXII RIMFIRE RIFLE—Caliber: 22 Long Rifle Rimfire. **Action:** semiautomatic, clip magazine (5 and 10 shot). Single shot selector. Bolt stays open after last shot. Shotgun-type tang safety. Receiver grooves for scope mounting. **Sights:** folding rear leaf and ramp front sight. **Stock:** Monte Carlo with cheek piece and hand checkering. Rosewood pistol grip cap and fore-end tip, and a "non-skid" rubber butt plate. Sling swivels. **Overall length:** 42¼ inches. **Weight:** approximately 6 lbs.

WINCHESTER RIFLES

MODEL 70XTR Sporter

MODEL 70® XTR SPORTER Magnum
375 H&H Magnum

Calibers: 264 Win. Mag., 7mm Rem. Mag.,
300 Win. Mag., 338 Win. Mag.

Model 70® XTR® Sporter

Model 70 XTR advantages: Versatility and broad selection of calibers. Inherent accuracy due to barrel construction and precise chambering. High strength and durability from machined steel components. Dependable, smooth operation because of anti-bind bolt; fully machined and polished internal surfaces. Three-position safety; easy removal of firing pin assembly from bolt.

Features include: Monte Carlo stock of American walnut with cheek piece; Fine cut checkering; Tough satin finish on wood; Contoured rubber butt pad; Hooded ramp front sight—new adjustable rear sight; Receiver drilled and tapped for scope; High polish and blueing; Engine-turned bolt; Detachable sling swivels; Hinged floor plate for fast unloading; Crisp trigger pull; Swaged rifling for accuracy.

Sets the standard for accuracy, ruggedness and dependability for hunters.

24 in. barrel, right hand twist, 1 turn in 10 in., and 30.06 Springfield and 270 Win.

Hooded front bead and adjustable rear sights. **Stock dimensions:** length of pull 13½ in., drop at comb 1¾ in., drop at heel 2⁷/₁₆ in., drop at Monte Carlo 1⅞ in., with cheek piece. Magazine holds 5 cartridges plus 1 in chamber.

MODEL 70 XTR SPORTER VARMINT
Calibers: 223 Rem., 22-250 Rem. & 243 Win.

Model 70 Sporter Varmint. Potent performance in an accurate, flat-shooting rifle chambered for varmint loads. 24'' Winchester Proof-Steel barrel. Blocks for scope mounts. Mirror-blue finish on receiver. In 243 Winchester, 22-250, and 223 Rem. calibers.

MODEL 70 XTR BOLT-ACTION FEATHERWEIGHT
Calibers: 243, 270 and 308 Win., 30-06 Spr., 257 Roberts & 7mm Mauser

The Model 70 XTR Featherweight features special tapered 22'' cold-formed barrel of Winchester-proof steel. Receiver drilled and tapped for scope mounting. Barrel and all external metal surfaces polished to a richly blued XTR finish. Stainless steel magazine follower. Three-position safety and detachable sling swivels. Stock is schnabel-style, satin-finished American walnut with straight comb and new red buttpad with black spacer. Approx. wt.: 6¾ lbs.

Model	Caliber	Magazine Capacity (a)	Barrel Length	Overall Length	Nominal Length of Pull	Nominal Drop at Comb	Heel	MC	Nominal Weight (lbs.)	Rate of Twist (R.H.) 1 Turn in	Sights
70 XTR	22-250 Rem.	5	24"	44½"	13½"	*½"	*1⁵/₁₆"	*¾"	7¾	14"	—
Sporter Varmint	223 Rem.	5	24"	44½"	13½"	*½"	*1⁵/₁₆"	*¾"	7¾	12"	—
	243 Win.	5	24"	44½"	13½"	*½"	*1⁵/₁₆"	*¾"	7¾	10"	—

WINCHESTER RIFLES

NEW Model 70 XTR Super Express™ Magnum Bolt-Action Centerfire Rifles

Go after the biggest game in true Sporter style with these new Model 70 XTR Super Express Magnum rifles. Their high performance and dependability stem from the proven Model 70 African™ ... now improved and up-graded with XTR styling and convenience features. This big game pair of rifles boasts all the Sporter Magnum features in 375 H&H and 458 Winchester Magnum calibers. The crisply styled Sporter stock design has the same innovative cheekpiece for shooter comfort, but is reinforced with two steel crossbolts for added strength.

The forward sling swivel is mounted directly on the rifle barrel for improved carrying balance and strength. Magazine capacity is three Magnum cartridges.

The new Monte Carlo stock with innovative sculpted cheekpiece on Model 70 XTR Sporter Magnum and Super Express Magnum rifles is shown in the photo above.

XTR elegance checkering is custom-patterned at 18 lines per inch; wraps around forend for improved handling, gripping and appearance.

RIFLES

MODEL 70 WESTERNER

Specifications

Model	Price	Caliber	Magazine Capacity (a)	Barrel Length	Overall Length	Nominal Length of Pull	Nominal Drop at			Nominal Weight (lbs.)	Rate of Twist (R.H.) 1 Turn in	Sights
							Comb	Heel	MC			
70 XTR Sporter	$460	270 Win.	5	24"	44½"	13½"	1¹¹/₁₆"	2⁷/₁₆"	1⁷/₈"	7¾	10"	RT
		30-06 Springfield	5	24"	44½"	13½"	1¹¹/₁₆"	2⁷/₁₆"	1⁷/₈"	7¾	10"	RT
70 XTR Sporter Magnum	$460	264 Win. Mag.	3	24"	44½"	13½"	1¹¹/₁₆"	2⁷/₁₆"	1⁷/₈"	7¾	9"	RT
		7mm Rem. Mag.	3	24"	44½"	13½"	1¹¹/₁₆"	2⁷/₁₆"	1⁷/₈"	7¾	9½"	RT
		300 Win. Mag.	3	24"	44½"	13½"	1¹¹/₁₆"	2⁷/₁₆"	1⁷/₈"	7¾	10"	RT
		338 Win. Mag.	3	24"	44½"	13½"	1¹¹/₁₆"	2⁷/₁₆"	1⁷/₈"	7¾	10"	RT
70 XTR Sporter Varmint	$460	22-250 Rem.	5	24"	44½"	13½"	*½"	*1⁵/₁₆"	*¾"	7¾	14"	—
		223 Rem.	5	24"	44½"	13½"	*½"	*1⁵/₁₆"	*¾"	7¾	12"	—
		243 Win.	5	24"	44½"	13½"	*½"	*1⁵/₁₆"	*¾"	7¾	10"	—
70 XTR Super Express Magnum	$700 / 750	375 H & H Mag.	3	24"	44½"	13½"	1⁷/₁₆"	2³/₁₆"	1⁵/₈"	8½	12"	RT
		458 Win. Mag.	3	22"	42½"	13½"	1⁷/₁₆"	2³/₁₆"	1⁵/₈"	8½	14"	RT

Model		Caliber	Magazine Capacity (a)	Barrel Length	Overall Length	Nominal Length of Pull	Nominal Drop at		Nominal Weight (lbs.)	Rate of Twist (R.H.) 1 Turn in	Sights
							Comb	Heel			
70 XTR Featherweight		243 Win.	5	22"	42½"	13½"	1⁵/₁₆"	1⁵/₈"	6¾	10"	RTO
		257 Roberts	5	22"	42½"	13½"	1⁵/₁₆"	1⁵/₈"	6¾	10"	RTO
		270 Win.	5	22"	42½"	13½"	1⁵/₁₆"	1⁵/₈"	6¾	10"	RTO
	$500	7mm Mauser (7X57)	5	22"	42½"	13½"	1⁵/₁₆"	1⁵/₈"	6¾	8¼"	RTO
		30-06 Springfield	5	22"	42½"	13½"	1⁵/₁₆"	1⁵/₈"	6¾	10"	RTO
		308 Win.	5	22"	42½"	13½"	1⁵/₁₆"	1⁵/₈"	6¾	12"	RTO
70 Westerner (4X Scope optional)		223 Rem.	4	22"	42½"	13½"	1⁵/₈"	2¹/₈"	7½	12"	RT-SO
		243 Win.	4	22"	42½"	13½"	1⁵/₈"	2¹/₈"	7⅛	10"	RT-SO
		270 Win.	4	22"	42½"	13½"	1⁵/₈"	2¹/₈"	7⅛	10"	RT-SO
	$370	30-06 Springfield	4	22"	42½"	13½"	1⁵/₈"	2¹/₈"	7⅛	10"	RT-SO
		308 Win.	4	22"	42½"	13½"	1⁵/₈"	2¹/₈"	7⅛	12"	RT-SO
		7mm Rem. Mag.	3	24"	44½"	13½"	1⁵/₈"	2¹/₈"	7½	9½"	RT-SO
		300 Win. Mag.	3	24"	44½"	13½"	1⁵/₈"	2¹/₈"	7½	10"	RT-SO

(a) For additional capacity, add one round in chamber when ready to fire. MC—Monte Carlo Stock RT—Rifle Type Front and Rear S—Short L—Long LR—Long Rifle WMR—Winchester Magnum Rimfire S—4XScope O—Optional *From center line of bore; all others from line of sight.

WINCHESTER RIFLES

NEW Model 70 XTR Sporter™ Magnum
Bolt-Action Centerfire Rifles

These new Model 70 XTR Sporter Magnum rifles bring an entirely new look and feel to big game hunting. Four hard-hitting Magnum calibers give them the power to match their proud appearance in 264, 300 and 338 Winchester Magnum and 7mm Rem. Magnum.

True Sporter styling starts with the totally new Monte Carlo stock. Its custom-like design is crisp and sharp with excellent definition throughout. The innovative undercut cheekpiece enhances shooter comfort and positioning with a new sculpted shape. The one-piece stock design ends in a gradually tapered forend. XTR elegance checkering in an intricate 18-line-per-inch pattern adds to

the beauty and handling ease. XTR protective satin finish on American walnut and polished, deep blueing on metal highlight the crisp styling.

Every Model 70 XTR convenience feature is built into this Sporter Magnum: exclusive three-position safety, chromium molybdenum 24-inch barrel, hooded ramp front sight, adjustable folding leaf rear sight, detachable sling swivels, stainless steel magazine follower, contoured rubber butt pad. The Model 70 XTR Sporter has it all, including consistent accuracy assured by the epoxy-bedded receiver recoil lug. Exceptional styling and handling make this the big game rifle you've been hunting for.

Model 9422 XTR
Lever-Action Rimfire Rifles

These Model 9422 XTR rimfire rifles combine classic 94 styling and handling in ultra-modern lever action 22s of superb craftsmanship. Handling and shooting characteristics are superior because of their carbine-like size.

Positive lever action and bolt design ensure feeding and chambering from any shooting position. The bolt face is T-slotted to guide the cartridge with complete control from magazine to chamber. A color-coded magazine follower shows when the brass magazine tube is empty. Receivers

are grooved for scope mounting. Other functional features include exposed hammer with half-cock safety, hooded bead front sight, semi-buckhorn rear sight and side ejection of spent cartridges.

Stock and forearm are American walnut with XTR checkering, high-luster finish, and straight-grip design. Internal parts are carefully finished for smoothness of action.

Model 9422 XTR Standard is considered one of the world's finest production sporting arms. It holds 21 Short, 17 Long or 15 Long Rifle cartridges.

Model 9422 XTR Magnum gives exceptional accuracy at longer ranges than conventional 22 rifles. It is designed specifically for the 22 Winchester Magnum Rimfire cartridge and holds eleven cartridges.

WINCHESTER RIFLES

Model 94™
Lever-Action Centerfire Carbines

Modern Model 94 carbines have been developed and refined through almost a century of sporting use and technological advancement. Major components are of machined steel. Chromium molybdenum barrels assure long-lasting strength. Chamber and rifling are cold-forged in a single operation for precise alignment and accuracy. All versions feature the exposed hammer, stock and forearm of American walnut, and steel barrel bands. Receivers accept a variety of scope mounts. The original design permits easy visual inspection of magazine and chamber through the top of the receiver with the action open. The balance, reliability, and ease of handling of these carbines make them favorites with modern sportsmen.

NEW Model 94 Wrangler® is compact and lightweight . . . ideal for hunting in thick brush. Weighing only 6⅛ pounds and just 33¾'' long, it is a fine saddle or brush gun. It is chambered for 32 Winchester Special caliber . . . and excellent choice for deer and other North American game in tough country. The 94 Wrangler's outstanding features are its hoop type finger lever and short 16'' barrel. The overside hoop finger lever fits larger hands and makes for easier handling and levering. The receiver is roll-engraved with Western scenes. The barrel bears a decorative roll-engraved Wrangler logo and has a dovetailed blade front sight. The Model 94 Wrangler brings a new look and handling quickness to the Western carbine.

Model 94 XTR is top choice for lever action styling and craftsmanship. Metal surfaces are highly polished and blued. American walnut stock and forearm have a protective satin finish with precise-cut XTR wrap-around checkering. It has a 20'' barrel with hooded blade front sight and semi-buckhorn rear sight. Available in 30-30 Winchester caliber.

Model 94 Trapper® is a 16'' short-barrel lever action with straightforward styling. Compact and fast-handling in dense cover, it has a magazine capacity of five shots. Available in 30-30 Winchester caliber.

Model 94 Standard is an economical version of the 94 XTR. Lever action is smooth and reliable. In 30-30 Winchester, the rapid-firing six-shot magazine capacity provides two more shots than most centerfire hunting rifles.

Model 94 Antique offers a special ''vintage'' appearance with decorative color-case-hardened receiver, scrollwork, brass-plated loading gate, and classic saddle ring.

Specifications:

Model	Caliber	Magazine Capacity (a)	Barrel Length	Overall Length	Nominal Length of Pull	Nominal Drop at Comb	Heel	MC	Nominal Weight (lbs.)	Rate of Twist (R.H.) 1 Turn in	Sights
94 XTR Angle Eject	375 Win.	6	20''	38⅝''	13⅝''	1⅝''	1¾''	1⁹/₁₆''	7	12''	RT
	356 Win.	6	20''	38⅝''	13⅝''	1⅝''	1¾''	1⁹/₁₆''	7	12''	RT
	307 Win.	6	20''	38⅝''	13⅝''	1⅝''	1¾''	1⁹/₁₆''	7	12''	RT

(a) For additional capacity, add one round in chamber when ready to fire.   MC—Monte Carlo Stock   RT—Rifle Type Front and Rear

WINCHESTER RIFLES

CHIEF CRAZY HORSE® WINCHESTER MODEL 94 COMMEMORATIVE LEVER ACTION CENTERFIRE RIFLE®

This Commemorative Model 94 rifle is a very special tribute to Chief Crazy Horse and the Sioux. Its Indian decorations are genuine and full of meaning. The brass tacks in a teepee shape on the stock signify the white man's rifle. Tacks on the forearm are arranged to form an individual mark of ownership. The medallion in the stock is the symbol of The United Sioux Tribes. The names of the Sioux tribes are engraved on the receiver in both Lakota Sioux and English.

All decorations are authenticated by the United Sioux Tribes of South Dakota . . . and issue of the Chief Crazy Horse Commemorative 94 rifle was approved unanimously by tribal chairmen of all eleven tribes with royalties from sales of this rifle benefitting the Sioux people.

This rifle has all the modern features of the Model 94 . . . for high accuracy and reliable performance. Smooth, strong lever action; machined steel components; dovetailed blade front and adjustable buckhorn rear sights. Stock and forearm are of American walnut with satin luster protective finish. The gold-filled receiver is engraved with a portrait and a buffalo hunting scene. The traditional crescent butt plate has a high-luster blued finish. Receiver and forearm cap feature a new fiery case-hardened antique finish . . . the first to appear on a Winchester Commemorative firearm. The barrel is inscribed with the legend "Chief Crazy Horse". All other exterior metal surfaces are highly polished and blued.

The Chief Crazy Horse Commemorative is issued in a limited edition of 19,999 rifles, numbered CCH1 through CCH19999. It is chambered for the classic 38-55 Winchester cartridge.

SPECIFICATIONS:

Model	Caliber	Magazine Capacity	Barrel Length	Overall Length	Nominal Length of Pull	Nominal Drop at Comb	Nominal Drop at Heel	Nominal Weight (lbs.)	Rate of Twist(R.H.) 1 Turn in	Sights	Price
9422 Annie Oakley Comm.	22	21S,17L,15LR	20½ in.	37⅛ in.	13½ in.	1¾ in.	2½ in.	6¼	16 in.	RT	
9422 XTR Standard	22	21S,17L,15LR	20½ in.	37⅛ in.	13½ in.	1¾ in.	2½ in.	6¼	16 in.	RT	$699
9422 XTR Magnum	22 WMR	11 WMR	20½ in.	37⅛ in.	13½ in.	1¾ in.	2½ in.	6¼	16 in.	RT	

RT—Rifle Type Front and Rear   S—Short   L—Long   LR—Long Rifle   WMR—Winchester Magnum Rimfire

Model	Caliber	Magazine Capacity	Barrel Length	Overall Length	Nominal Length of Pull	Nominal Drop at Comb	Nominal Drop at Heel	Nominal Weight (lbs.)	Rate of Twist(R.H.) 1 Turn in	Sights	Price
94 Chief Crazy Horse Commemorative	38-55 Win.	7	24 in.	41¾ in.	13 in.	1¾ in.	2½ in.	6¾	18 in.	RT	$600

(a) For additional capacity, add one round in chamber when ready to fire.   RT—Rifle Type Front and Rear.

Model	Caliber	Magazine Capacity	Barrel Length	Overall Length	Nominal Length of Pull	Nominal Drop at Comb	Nominal Drop at Heel	Nominal Weight (lbs.)	Rate of Twist(R.H.) 1 Turn in	Sights	Price
94 XTR, Standard and Antique	30-30 Win.	6	20 in.	37¾ in.	13 in.	1¾ in.	2½ in.	6½	6½	RT	250.00 220.00/240.00
*94 Trapper	30-30 Win.	5	16 in.	33¾ in.	13 in.	1¾ in.	2½ in.	6⅛	12 in.	RT	220.00
*94 Wrangler	32 Win. Spec.	5	16 in.	33¾ in.	13 in.	1¾ in.	2½ in.	6¼	16 in.	RT	249.95
9422 XTR Standard	22	21S,17L,15LR	20½ in.	37⅛ in.	13½ in.	1¾ in.	2½ in.	6¼	16 in.	RT	300.00
9422 XTR Magnum	22WMR	11	20½ in.	37⅛ in.	13½ in.	1¾ in.	2½ in.	6¼	16 in.	RT	300.00

ANNIE OAKLEY® COMMEMORATIVE MODEL 9422

ANNIE OAKLEY® COMMEMORATIVE

The Annie Oakley® Commemorative Model 9422 is a highly decorative lever action 22 . . . the first Winchester commemorative rifle to honor an American heroine. Finger lever, receiver, and barrel bands are antique gold-plated. The receiver is roll-engraved with her portrait and a show scene. The barrel is inscribed in gold "Annie Oakley Commemorative". Stock and forearm are American walnut with a protective high-luster finish. Features are the same as those of the standard Model 9422 XTR.

The Annie Oakley Commemorative 9422 is offered in a limited issue of six thousand rifles, bearing serial numer AOK1 through AOK6000.

WINSLOW RIFLES

STANDARD SPECIFICATIONS FOR ALL WINSLOW RIFLES

Stock: Hand rubbed black walnut. Length of pull—13½ inches. Plainsmaster ⅜ inch castoff. Bushmaster 3/16 inch castoff. All rifles are drilled and tapped to incorporate the use of telescopic sights. Rifles with receiver or open sights are available on special order. All rifles are equipped with quick detachable sling swivel studs and white line recoil pad. Choice of two standard stock models; Plainsmaster stock, and Bushmaster stock. **Magazine:** Staggered box type, four shot. (Blind in the stock has no floor plate). **Action:** Mauser Mark x Action. **Overall Length:** 43 inches (Standard Model); 45 inches (Magnum). All Winslow rifles have company name and serial number and grade engraved on the action and caliber engraved on barrel. **Barrel:** Douglas barrel premium grade, chrome moly-type steel. All barrels 20 caliber through 35 caliber have six lands and grooves. All barrels larger than 35 caliber have eight lands and grooves.

All barrels are finished to (.2 to .4) micro inches inside the lands and grooves. **Total Weight (without scope):** 24 inch barrel—Standard calibers 243, 308, 270, etc. 7 to 7½ lbs. 26 inch barrel—Magnum calibers 264 Win., 300 Wby., 458 Win., etc. 8 to 9 lbs.

Winslow rifles are made in the following calibers:

Standard cartridges—22-250, 243 Win., 244 Rem., 257 Roberts, 308 Win., 30-06, 280 Rem., 270 Win., 25-06, 284 Win., 358 Win. and 7mm (7x57).

Magnum Cartridges—300 Weatherby, 300 Win., 338 Win., 358 Norma, 375 H.H., 458 Win., 257 Weatherby, 264 Win., 270 Weatherby, 7mm Weatherby, 7mm Rem., 300 H.H., 308 Norma.

Left-handed models available in most calibers.

The Winslow rifle can be fitted to suit your needs through choice of two models of stock. The Plainsmaster—Pinpoint accuracy in open country with full curl pistol grip and flat forearm. The Bushmaster—Lighter weight for bush country. Slender pistol with palm swell. Beavertail forend for light hand comfort.

All Winslow stocks incorporate a slight castoff to deflect recoil, minimizing flinch and muzzle jump.

WINSLOW BASIC RIFLE

The Basic Rifle, available in the Bushmaster stock, features one ivory diamond inlay in a rose-wood grip cap and ivory trademark in bottom of forearm. Grade 'A' walnut jewelled bolt and follower **$1265.00**. Plainsmaster stock **$100.00** extra. **Left-hand** model **$1375.00**

WINSLOW GRADE CROWN

In addition to the foregoing features, the Crown includes basket weave carving, both sides and under forearm, also on each side of and to the rear of pistol grip. It also includes two eightpoint ivory and ebony inlays, one on each side of the magazine box, two large triangle ivory and ebony inlays, one on each side of the buttstock. **Price upon request**

WINSLOW VARMINT

This 17 caliber is available in the Bushmaster stock and the Plainsmaster stock, which is a miniature of the original high roll-over cheek piece and a round leading edge on the forearm, modified spoon billed pistol grip. Available in 17/222, 17/222 mag. 17/233, 222 Rem. and 223. Regent grade shown. **Price upon request**

WINSLOW RIFLES

WINSLOW GRADE ROYAL

In addition to foregoing features, the Winslow Royal includes carving under forearm tip, carving on each side of magazine box, carving grip cap, carving belly behind pistol grip, carving in front of and in back of cheek piece, carving on each side of buttstock. **Price upon request.**

WINSLOW GRADE IMPERIAL

In addition to foregoing features, the Winslow Imperial includes barrel engraved from receiver to point eleven inches forward of receiver, engraving on the forward receiver ring, engraving on rear receiver ring, engraving on bolt handle and trigger guard, engraving on scope mounts and rings. **Price upon request.**

WINSLOW GRADE EMPEROR

In addition to the foregoing features, the Winslow Emperor is engraved in gold raised relief from receiver to point six inches forward of receiver and on tip of barrel, 1 animal on each side of front receiver, 1 animal on rear receiver, 1 animal head top each scope ring, 1 animal head on bolt handle and 1 animal head on trigger guard. **Price upon request.**

Shotguns

ARMSPORT SHOTGUNS

Holland & Holland Type Side Lock Double Barrel

The new Armsport side lock Holland & Holland type side by side shotgun with automatic ejectors is handcrafted in Italy. Its beautiful grained English style walnut stock and finely checkered butt, pistol grip and forend, enhance the graceful silver colored hand-engraved receiver and highly polished steel barrels.

Holland & Holland Type Shotgun

4031	12 Gauge	Modified and Full Choke	$3,950.00

Premier Mono Trap and Set

Armsport's new Premier Mono Trap and Trap Set designed for competitive trap shooting is manufactured to give perfect service and performance for the competitive trap shooter. The special steel beautifully hand-engraved receiver and highly polished barrels are manufactured to insure continuous trouble free shooting. Its ease of handling places this gun among the tops in its class in competitive trap shooting.

Premier Mono Trap and Set

Model No.	Description	Gauge	Barrel Length	
4032	Mono Trap	12	32"	$2,075.00
4033	Mono Trap	12	34"	2,075.00
4034	Mono Trap Set	12	32" Single 30" Over & Under	2,950.00
4035	Mono Trap Set	12	34" Single 32" Over & Under	2,950.00
			Auto Ejection	

PREMIER SLUG SIDE BY SIDE SHOTGUN AND SET

Armsport's special side by side slug shotgun and set, excellent for wild boar and other specialized hunting, has a new type rib with leaf rear sight and blade front sight. With a handsomely hand relief-engraved receiver and finely grained walnut stock, along with its fine hand-checkered half pistol grip stock and beavertail forend, it is not only a beautiful, strong, light and compact shotgun, but combines remarkable power and accuracy. The extra set of 28" 12 Gauge barrels is a perfect match for open field hunting.

PREMIER SLUG SIDE BY SIDE 1,325.00

4040	Side by side Slug special	12 Gauge	23" Barrel	Cyl/Imp Cyl.
4041	Slug set	12 Gauge	23" & 28"	23" Cyl/Imp Cyl. 28" Mod/Full

OVER AND UNDER SHOTGUNS
SINGLE SELECTIVE TRIGGER, VENTILATED RIB

Handcrafted in Italy, superbly designed and engineered for generations of shooting, this shotgun combines ruggedness, strength and beauty. Close grained European walnut stock and forend are excellently fitted and hand checkered. Handsomely engraved receiver and hand fitted ventilated rib add beauty to this gun of excellent balance. The single selective trigger allows you to fire either barrel at will by a simple movement of the selector lever. Available in 12 and 20 gauge. Chambered for 3 inch shells.

SINGLE SELECTIVE TRIGGER, Ventilated Rib $495.00

1626	12 Gauge	26" Barrel	Improved & Modified Choke
1628	12 Gauge	28" Barrel	Modified & Full
1726	20 Gauge	26" Barrel	Improved & Modified
1728	20 Gauge	28" Barrel	Modified & Full

SINGLE SELECTIVE TRIGGER, AUTOMATIC EJECTORS

This is a superbly designed, handsomely engraved over and under shotgun with ventilated rib. The single selective trigger allows you to fire either barrel at will by a single movement of the selector lever. It has exceptionally fine hand picked walnut stock and forend, hand crafted and fitted for generations of fine shooting.

SINGLE SELECTIVE TRIGGER, Automatic Ejectors 595.00

2526	12 Gauge	26" Barrel	Improved & Modified Choke
2528	12 Gauge	28" Barrel	Modified & Full
2626	20 Gauge	26" Barrel	Improved & Modified
2628	20 Gauge	28" Barrel	Modified & Full

PREMIER COMPETITION SKEET GUN

The "Armsport-Zoli" Premier Competition Skeet Gun is made to meet the shooter's demand for a rugged, strong and reliable gun at an affordable price. Its exceptional balance, sight plane, and ease of pointing give the shooter the true performance constantly necessary for skeet shooting. Add to this the fine select grained European walnut stock with swell pistol grip and the attractively engraved action to make this a skeet gun to own and shoot with pride.

PREMIER COMPETITION SKEET GUN 2,000.00

4055	12 Gauge	26" Barrel
4056	12 Gauge	28" Barrel

ARMSPORT SHOTGUNS

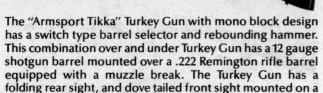

Deluxe Turkey Gun

The "Armsport Tikka" Turkey Gun with mono block design has a switch type barrel selector and rebounding hammer. This combination over and under Turkey Gun has a 12 gauge shotgun barrel mounted over a .222 Remington rifle barrel equipped with a muzzle break. The Turkey Gun has a folding rear sight, and dove tailed front sight mounted on a ventilated rib. Sling swivels are packed with each gun.

Deluxe Turkey Gun $750.00

4651	12 Gauge	3" .222 Rem.

Armsport Side by Side Shotgun

Armsport's new hammerless side by side shotguns are beautifully crafted. All special steel is brightly blued to blend with the highly grained opaqued oil finished walnut stock and forend. The hand engraved receiver and hand checkering add to its beauty.

Armsport Side by Side Shotgun

1040	12 Gauge 26" Barrels	Improved & Mod. Choke
1041	12 Gauge 28" Barrels	Modified & Full $450.00
1042	20 Gauge 26" Barrels	Improved & Modified 450.00
1043	20 Gauge 28" Barrels	Modified & Full

Armsport Deluxe Goose Gun

This beautifully crafted 10 gauge 3½" mag. double barrel Goose Gun features a handsome select grained walnut stock and full beavertail forend. The hand-engraved receiver enhances the beauty of the combined bright blued barrels and stock.

Armsport Deluxe Goose Gun $495.00

1032Z	10 Gauge 3½" mag. 32" Barrel	Full & Full Choke

Armsport Western Double with Outside Hammers

This outside hammered double barreled shotgun with its handsomely hand-engraved action, hand-picked finely-grained walnut stock and beautifully-tapered forend gives the shooter beauty, reliability and ruggedness from the butt pad to the muzzle of its bright blued 20" barrels.

Armsport Western Double 450.00

1212	12 Gauge	20" Barrel

ASTRA SHOTGUNS

MODEL 750E
$733.00

Model No.	650	650E	750	750E	750 Skeet Skeet	750 Trap
Gauge	12	12	12	12	12	12
Barrel length	28 in.	28 in.	28 in.	28 in.	28 in.	30 in.
Chokes	MF	MF	MF	MF	SS	MF
Stock	walnut: plastic butt	walnut: plastic butt	walnut: plastic butt	walnut: plastic butt	walnut: Monte Carlo*	walnut: Monte Carlo*
Extractors	yes	no	yes	no	no	no
Selective ejectors	no	yes	no	yes	yes	yes
Triggers	2	2	1	1	1	1
Price	$493.00	$630.00	$600.00	$733.00	$850.00	$850.00

*With rubber recoil pad

BERETTA SHOTGUNS

MODEL 424
SIDE-BY-SIDE SHOTGUNS

The action body, made of solid forged alloy steel, is of Boxlock design (Beretta patent) with coil springs throughout, and is nicely finished with light border engraving on rust-resistant, satin-chrome frame. Lockup is by means of double underlugs and bolts.

Barrels of steel "S" (chrome-moly) are joined on the "Mono Bloc" system giving alignment and rigidity. They are finished in a rich blue-black and are chrome lined. A hollow, matted rib is fitted to the barrels.

Model 424 shotguns are equipped with double triggers (front trigger hinged), automatic safety and plain, positive extractors.

Stocks are made of the "English" straight grip type, forends and stocks are made of fine, seasoned European walnut and hand-checkered.

STANDARD DIMENSIONS

Length of Pull:	14⅛ inches (358 mm)
Drop at Comb:	1-9/16 inches (40mm)
Drop at Heel:	2-9/16 inches (65mm)

Note: Gun weights may vary due to different stock wood densities, etc. Model 424 (12 & 20 ga.) $900.00

Ga.	Length	Chamber	Description	Approx. Weight
12	26 in.	2¾ in.	Imp Cyl./Mod.	6 lbs. 10 oz.
12	28 in.	2¾ in.	Mod./Full	6 lbs. 10 oz.
20	26 in.	3 in.	Imp. Cyl./Mod.	5 lbs. 14 oz.
20	28 in.	3 in.	Mod./Full	5 lbs. 14 oz.

MODEL 426
SIDE-BY-SIDE SHOTGUNS

The 426 is basically the same as the 424, with the following added features:

The action body is decorated with fine engraving. A silver pigeon is inlaid into the top lever. The action is fitted with a selective single trigger (selector button on safety slide) and the gun has selective automatic ejectors. A hollow matted rib is joined to the barrels. The pistol-grip style stock and forend are of select European walnut, hand-checkered and richly finished.

Standard Dimensions	Length of Pull:	14⅛ inches (358mm)
Drop at Comb.:		1-9/16 inches (40mm)
Drop at Heel:		2-9/16 inches (65mm)

Note: Gun weights may vary due to different stock wood densities, etc.

Model 426 (12 & 20 ga.) $1115.00

STANDARD DIMENSIONS

Ga.	Length	Chamber	Description	Approx. Weight
12	26 in.	2¾ in.	Imp. Cyl./Mod.	6 lbs. 10 oz.
12	28 in.	2¾ in.	Mod./Full	6 lbs. 10 oz.
20	26 in.	3 in.	Imp. Cyl./Mod.	5 lbs. 14 oz.
20	28 in.	3 in.	Mod./Full	5 lbs. 14 oz.

A302
Mag-Action™ Autoloaders

Beretta technology at its finest: one tough, machined action handles both 2¾- and 3-inch magnum chambered barrels, easily interchanged on the same gun without any special tools or adjustment. Fully interchangeable barrels give maximum field flexibility and fast barrel changes, so you can mix up your bag of game at whim. And the A302's magazine cut-off lever lets you load automatically, or hand chamber different loads for different game.

On its fast-swinging frame, Beretta designs state-of-the-field features into all A302's; hard-chrome-lined nickel-chrome-moly steel barrels shrug off barrel-punishing steel shot and mag load forces ... receivers forged and machined from solid blocks of lightweight, top-quality alloy ... gas-operated action with no washers, no rings, supremely reliable yet simple for field stripping ... very low recoil ... plus every safety feature possible in a shotgun, topped off with the rich touch of Beretta quality.

BERETTA SHOTGUNS

New A302 Multichoke

"The Total Gun", a unique, year-long adaptability for all shooting: screw-in interchangeable choke tubes customize your hunting with Full, Improved Modified, Modified and Improved Cylinder ability. Available in 12 GA 28-inch barrels with either 2¾- or 3-inch Magnum chamber.

New A302 Slug

Lightweight, accurate, quick to sight on American big game where rifled slugs are a must. Adjustable front sight, folding leaf rear sight. Brush-ready 22-inch barrel. Available in 12 GA or 20 GA.

New A302 Super Lusso

The ultimate automatic for the collector and fine shotgun fancier. Richly hand-engraved receiver accented by gold-plated trigger and safety, magazine cut-off and action button. Stocked in burly, presentation-grade walnut with fine line hand checkering. Plus all the functional features of the A302 Mag-Action™.

New A302 Mag-Action™ 20 Gauge

Slightly smaller but all the big advantages of Beretta's Big Brother 12's: same quality features, but designed to make the most of the 20's potential, and for smaller hunters and shooters.

A302 Competition Trap

A hard-hitting clay buster with a gas-operated system to take the punch out of recoil. Wide floating vent rib with fluorescent front and mid-rib sight beads. Handsome walnut Monte Carlo stock, fitted with a competition recoil pad. See specifications table for barrel/choke combinations.

A302 Competition Skeet

At home in the fast track of skeet where strong action, fast swing, pointability all become part of the skeet shooter's instinctive technique when averages are on the line. Recoil-absorbing gas-actuated autoloading to cushion the shoulder ... with the added reliability and strength of Beretta's tough, beefed-up Mag-Action™ design. Wide vent rib ... interchangeable barrels ... select walnut, beautifully finished with hand-checkered pistol grip and forend ... gold-plated trigger and safety complete the premium-like touches to this fine skeeter.

NEW MAG-ACTION SYSTEM
MODEL A302 SEMI-AUTO SHOTGUN

(ONE COMPLETE ACTION WILL HANDLE 2¾- or 3-inch INTERCHANGEABLE BARRELS)

MODEL NO.	DESCRIPTION	PRICE
A302	12GA (2¼ in.) 26 in. Improved Cyl.	$565.00
A302	12GA (2¾ in.) 28 in. Modified	565.00
A302	12GA (2¾ in.) 28 in. Full	565.00
A302	12GA (2¾ in.) 30 in. Full	565.00
A302	12GA (2¾ in.) 28 in. Multi-choke (4 tubes)	650.00
A302	12GA (2¾ in.) 22 in. SLUG	580.00
A302	12GA (2¾ in.) 30 in. Full-Trap w/Monte Carlo	590.00
A302	12GA (2¾ in.) 26 in. SKEET	580.00
A302	12GA (3 in. Mag.) 28 in. Modified	565.00
A302	12GA (3 in. Mag.) 30 in. Full	565.00
A302	12GA (3 in. Mag.) 28 in. Multi-choke (4 tubes)	650.00
A302	20GA (2¾ in.) 26 in. Improved Cyl.	565.00
A302	20GA (2¾ in.) 28 in. Modified	565.00
A302	20GA (2¾ in.) 28 in. Full	565.00
A302	20GA (2¾ in.) SLUG	580.00
A302	20GA (2¾ in.) 26 in. SKEET	580.00
A302	20GA (3 in. Mag.) 26 in. Improved Cyl.	565.00
A302	20GA (3 in. Mag.) 28 in. Modified	565.00
A302	20GA (3 in. Mag.) 28 in. Full	565.00

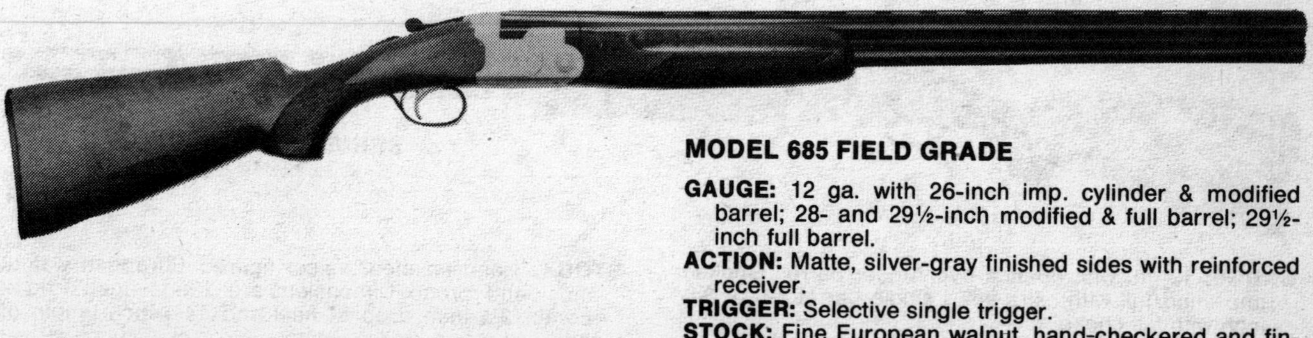

SHOTGUNS

MODEL 685 FIELD GRADE

GAUGE: 12 ga. with 26-inch imp. cylinder & modified barrel; 28- and 29½-inch modified & full barrel; 29½-inch full barrel.

ACTION: Matte, silver-gray finished sides with reinforced receiver.

TRIGGER: Selective single trigger.

STOCK: Fine European walnut, hand-checkered and finished.

WEIGHT: 7 lbs. 2 oz.

PRICE: $820.00

BERETTA SHOTGUNS

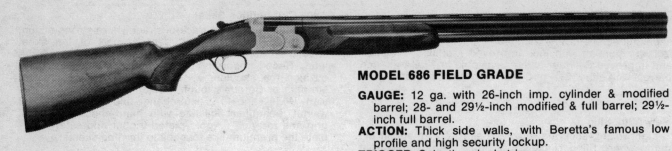

MODEL 686 FIELD GRADE

GAUGE: 12 ga. with 26-inch imp. cylinder & modified barrel; 28- and 29½-inch modified & full barrel; 29½-inch full barrel.
ACTION: Thick side walls, with Beretta's famous low profile and high security lockup.
TRIGGER: Selective single trigger.
STOCK: Choice European walnut, hand checkered and hand finished with a tough gloss finish.
WEIGHT: 7 lbs. 2 oz.
PRICE: $980.00

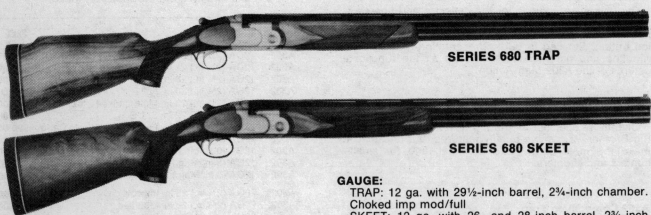

SERIES 680 TRAP

SERIES 680 SKEET

Beretta makes the 680 Series Trap and Skeet guns with competition features such as true box-locks and a patented firing mechanism to give the shortest possible firing time. A specially designed trigger prevents slipping. The finely sculpted receiver is reinforced with thick walls and a high security lockup. The low-profile design of the 680 makes recoil much more controllable. The technology and quality of the Beretta 680 Series makes for an ideal competition shotgun.

GAUGE:
TRAP: 12 ga. with 29½-inch barrel, 2¾-inch chamber. Choked imp mod/full
SKEET: 12 ga. with 26- and 28-inch barrel, 2¾-inch chamber. Choked skeet/skeet
ACTION: Thick walled and heat treated for durability and strength, with Beretta's low profile
TRIGGER: Selective gold-plated trigger
STOCK: Hand-finished select figured European walnut. Dimensions are: 1¼-1½-inch drop at comb. 2⅛-inch drop at heel and 14⅜-inch length of pull
WEIGHT: TRAP: 8⅛ lbs.
SKEET: 8 lbs.
PRICE: $1580.00

SERIES 680 COMBO

GAUGE: 12 ga. with 30-inch over/under barrel. Choked imp. mod/full with extra fitted single barrel 32- or 34-inch with full choke
ACTION: Thick walled and heat treated for durability and strength, with Beretta's low profile
TRIGGER: Single selector, gold plated

STOCK: Hand-finished, select figured European walnut stock and forend. Dimensions are: 1¼-1½-inch drop at comb, 2⅛-inch drop at heel and 14⅜-inch length of pull
WEIGHT: 8½ lbs.
PRICE: $2200.00

BROWNING PRESENTATION SUPERPOSED SHOTGUNS

OVER/UNDER SUPERPOSED SPECIFICATIONS

STOCK—

	12 Gauge Hunting	20, 28 and .410 Gauge Hunting
Length of Pull	14¼ in.	14¼ in.
Drop at Comb	1⅝ in.	1½ in.
Drop at Heel	2½ in.	2⅜ in.

EXTRA SET OF BARRELS — Presentation Series Superposed in any of the specifications listed below are available in gauge combinations of 12 & 12, 12 & 20, 20 & 20, 20 & 28, and/or .410, 28 & .410. A choice of either Hunting, Skeet or Trap stock.

SIGHTS — Medium raised steel bead. Trap and Skeet models: Ivory Front and Center sights.

CHOKE — On all models any combination of Full — Improved-Modified — Modified — Improved-Cylinder — Skeet — Cylinder.

TRIGGER — Gold-plated on all models except the Super Light. Fast, crisp, positive.

Model and Gauge HUNTING	Barrel Length	Average Weight (1)	Rib
Lightning 12	28″	7 lbs. 8 oz.	⁵⁄₁₆″ Vent
Lightning 12	26½″	7 lbs. 6 oz.	⁵⁄₁₆″ Vent
Super Light 12	26½″	6 lbs. 8 oz.	⁵⁄₁₆″ Vent
Magnum 12 (2)	30″	8 lbs. 1 oz.	⁵⁄₁₆″ Vent
Magnum 12 (2)	28″	7 lbs. 15 oz.	⁵⁄₁₆″ Vent
Lightning 20	28″	6 lbs. 6 oz.	¼″ Vent
Lightning 20	26½″	6 lbs. 4 oz.	¼″ Vent
Super Light 20	26½″	6 lbs.	¼″ Vent
Lightning 28	28″	6 lbs. 10 oz.	¼″ Vent
Lightning 28	26½″	6 lbs. 7 oz.	¼″ Vent
Lightning .410	28″	6 lbs. 14 oz.	¼″ Vent
Lightning .410	26½″	6 lbs. 10 oz.	¼″ Vent

TARGET GUN SPECIFICATIONS

SKEET MODELS

SUPERPOSED	Barrel Length (in.)	Approx. Weight (lbs.-oz.)	Vent. Rib (width, in.)	Length of Pull (in.)	Drop at Comb (in.)	Drop at Heel (in.)	Chokes	Grades Available
Lightning 12	26½	7 lbs. 9 oz.	⁵⁄₁₆	14⅜	1½	2	S-S	All
Lightning 12	28	7 lbs. 11 oz.	⁵⁄₁₆	14⅜	1½	2	S-S	All
Lightning 20	26½	6 lbs. 8 oz.	¼	14⅜	1½	2	S-S	All
Lightning 20	28	6 lbs. 12 oz.	¼	14⅜	1½	2	S-S	All
Lightning 28	26½	6 lbs. 11 oz.	¼	14⅜	1½	2	S-S	All
Lightning 28	28	6 lbs. 14 oz.	¼	14⅜	1½	2	S-S	All
Lightning .410	26½	6 lbs. 13 oz.	¼	14⅜	1½	2	S-S	All
Lightning .410	28	7 lbs.	¼	14⅜	1½	2	S-S	All
Skeet Set 12, 20, 28, .410	26½	7 lbs. 10 oz.	¼	14⅜	1½	2	S-S	All
Skeet Set 12, 20, 28, .410	28	7 lbs. 12 oz.	¼	14⅜	1½	2	S-S	All

TRAP MODELS

SUPERPOSED	Barrel Length (in.)	Approx. Weight (lbs.-oz.)	Vent. Rib (width, in.)	Length of Pull (in.)	Drop at Comb (in.)	Drop at Monté Carlo (in.)	Drop at Heel (in.)	Chokes	Grades Available
Lightning 12*	30	7 lbs. 13 oz.	⁵⁄₁₆	14⅜	1⁷⁄₁₆		1⅝	F-F,IM-F, M-F	All
Broadway 12*	30	7 lbs. 15 oz.	⅝	14⅜	1⁷⁄₁₆		1⅝	F-F,IM-F, M-F	All
Broadway 12*	32	8 lbs.	⅝	14⅜	1⁷⁄₁₆		1⅝	F-F,IM-F, M-F	All
*These models also available with Monte Carlo comb				14⅜	1⅜	1⅜	2		

BROWNING PRESENTATION SUPERPOSED SHOTGUNS

HUNTING MODELS

Lightning 12 and 20, 3-inch Magnum 12 gauges

Presentation 1 Engraved	$ 4500.00
Presentation 1 Gold Inlay	5110.00
Presentation 2 Engraved	5480.00
Presentation 2 Gold Inlay	6580.00
Presentation 3 Gold Inlay	8040.00
Presentation 4 Engraved	9240.00
Presentation 4 Gold Inlay	10,470.00

Super-Light 12 and 20 gauges

Presentation 1 Engraved	4560.00
Presentation 1 Gold Inlay	5170.00
Presentation 2 Engraved	5540.00
Presentation 2 Gold Inlay	6640.00
Presentation 3 Gold Inlay	8090.00
Presentation 4 Engraved	9300.00
Presentation 4 Gold Inlay	10,530.00

Lightning 28 gauge and .410 bore

Presentation 1 Engraved	4620.00
Presentation 1 Gold Inlay	5230.00
Presentation 2 Engraved	5600.00
Presentation 2 Gold Inlay	6690.00
Presentation 3 Gold Inlay	8160.00
Presentation 4 Engraved	9350.00
Presentation 4 Gold Inlay	10,600.00

TRAP MODELS

Lightning 12 gauge

Presentation 1 Engraved	4570.00
Presentation 1 Gold Inlay	5180.00
Presentation 2 Engraved	5550.00

Presentation 2 Gold Inlay	$ 6650.00
Presentation 3 Gold Inlay	8100.00
Presentation 4 Engraved	9310.00
Presentation 4 Gold Inlay	10,550.00

BROADway 12 gauge

Presentation 1 Engraved	4680.00
Presentation 1 Gold Inlay	5290.00
Presentation 2 Engraved	5660.00
Presentation 2 Gold Inlay	6760.00
Presentation 3 Gold Inlay	8210.00
Presentation 4 Engraved	9420.00
Presentation 4 Gold Inlay	10,660.00

SKEET MODELS

Lightning 12 and 20 gauges

Presentation 1 Engraved	4570.00
Presentation 1 Gold Inlay	5180.00
Presentation 2 Engraved	5550.00
Presentation 2 Gold Inlay	6650.00
Presentation 3 Gold Inlay	8100.00
Presentation 4 Engraved	9310.00
Presentation 4 Gold Inlay	10,550.00

Lightning 28 gauge and .410 bore

Presentation 1 Engraved	4690.00
Presentation 1 Gold Inlay	5300.00
Presentation 2 Engraved	5670.00
Presentation 2 Gold Inlay	6770.00
Presentation 3 Gold Inlay	8220.00
Presentation 4 Engraved	9430.00
Presentation 4 Gold Inlay	10,660.00

LIMITED EDITION WATERFOWL SUPERPOSED

GAUGE: 12 gauge
BARREL: 28 inches
Choke is Modified/full

RECEIVER: Gold inlaid and engraved gray steel.
STOCK AND FOREARM: Hand-oiled, high-grade select walnut. Hand-checkered forearm and checkered butt.

Limited to 500 guns

BLACK DUCK ISSUE
$8000.00

LIMITED EDITION WATERFOWL SUPERPOSED

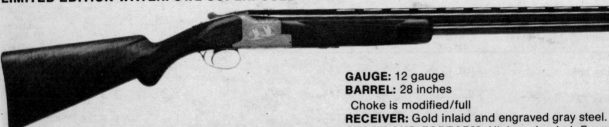

Limited to 500 Belgian-made guns. Each gun comes with a form-fitted, velvet-lined, handcrafted black walnut case.

GAUGE: 12 gauge
BARREL: 28 inches
Choke is modified/full
RECEIVER: Gold inlaid and engraved gray steel.
STOCK AND FOREARM: Highgrade, dark French walnut with hand-oiled finished stock. Hand-checkered forearm; rounded pistol grip and checkered butt.

BROWNING SHOTGUNS

SUPERPOSED CONTINENTAL
20 GAUGE $6000.00

ACTION: Superposed 20 gauge action, engineered to function with extra set of 30-06 Sprg. over and under rifle barrels.

SHOTGUN BARRELS: 20 gauge, 26½ inches. Choked, modified and full with 3-inch chambers. Engine turned ventilated rib with medium raised German nickel silver sight bead.

RIFLE BARRELS: 30-06 Springfield caliber, 24 inches. Right-hand rifling twist, 1 turn in 10 inches. Crowned muzzles. Folding leaf rear sight finely calibrated for elevation. Flat face gold bead front sight mounted on matted ramp. Sight radius—16-15/16 inches. Maximum distance between centers of impact of a 2 shot group from each barrel, using commercially available 150 grain 30-06 ammunition, is 1½ inches at 100 yards.

TRIGGER: Single, selective, inertia. Gold plated, fast and crisp. Let off approximately 4½ lbs.

AUTOMATIC SELECTIVE EJECTORS: Fired shells ejected from chambers upon opening of action. Unfired shells elevated for easy removal.

SAFETY: Manual thumb safety on top tang incorporated with barrel selector mechanism. Either over or under barrel can be selected to fire first.

STOCK AND FOREARM: Select high grade American walnut with deluxe oil finish. Straight grip stock and Schnabel forearm with 25 line hand checkering.

	With Shotgun Barrels Installed	With Rifle Barrels Installed
Length of pull	14¼ in.	14¼ in.
Drop at comb	1½ in.	1-11/16 in.
Drop at heel	2-7/32 in.	2½ in.

OVERALL LENGTH: With 20-gauge shotgun barrels 43½ inches. With 30-06 rifle barrels 41 inches.

APPROXIMATE WEIGHT: With 20-gauge shotgun barrels 5 lbs. 14 oz. With 30-06 rifle barrels 6 lbs. 14 oz.

SUPERPOSED CONTINENTAL MODEL: 20-Gauge Over/Under Shotgun with extra set of 30-06 Over/Under Rifle barrels, including fitted luggage.

BPS PUMP SHOTGUN
12 GAUGE

GAUGE: 12 and 20 gauge.

BARRELS: Choice of 26-, 28- or 30-inches with high post ventilated rib. Trap model has front and center ivory sight beads. Hunting model has German nickel sight bead.

ACTION: Pump action with double-action bars. Bottom loading and ejection. Magazine cut-off to switch loads in chamber without disturbing shells in magazine and to convert gun from repeating to single shot operation.

CHOKE: Your choice of full, modified or improved cylinder.

TRIGGER: Crisp and positive.

CHAMBER: Hunting model: All 2¾-, 2¾-inch magnum and 3-inch magnum shells. Target models: 2¾-inch shells only.

SAFETY: Convenient top receiver safety. Slide forward to shoot.

APPROXIMATE WEIGHT: 28-inch barrel model weighs 7 lbs. 12 oz.

OVERALL LENGTH: 26-inch barrel 46¾ inches. 28-inch barrel 48¾ inches. 30-inch barrel 50¾ inches.

STOCK AND FOREARM: Select walnut, weather-resistant finish, sharp 20-line checkering. Full pistol grip. Semi-beavertail forearm with finger grooves. Length of pull—14¼ inches. Drop at comb—1½ inches. Drop at heel—2½ inches.

Grade I, Hunting, 12 and 20 ga., Ventilated Rib $374.95
Grade I, Trap, 12 ga., Ventilated Rib 394.95
Grade I, Buck Special, 12 and 20 ga., no accessories 399.95
Grade I, Buck Special, 12 and 20 ga., with accessories 419.95
Grade I, Hunting with invector, 12 ga. V.R. 394.95
Grade I, Trap with invector, 12 ga. V.R. 414.95

BROWNING AUTOMATIC SHOTGUNS

AUTO-5 MODELS—The Browning Auto-5 Shotgun is offered in an unusually wide variety of models and specifications. The Browning 12-gauge 3-inch Magnum accepts up to and including the 3-inch, 1⅛ ounce, 12-gauge Magnum load, which contains only ⅛ ounces of shot less than the maximum 3½-inch 10-gauge load. The 2¾-inch Magnums and 2¾-inch high velocity shells may be used with equal pattern efficiency. Standard features include a special shock absorber and a hunting-style recoil pad. The kick is not unpleasant with even the heaviest 3-inch loads.

Browning also offers the 20 gauge in a 3-inch Magnum model. This powerful, light heavyweight offers maximum versatility to 20-gauge advocates. It handles the 20-gauge, 2¾-inch high velocity and Magnums, but it literally thrives on the 3-inch, 1¼ ounce load which delivers real 12-gauge performance in a 20-gauge package.

The 12-gauge Auto-5, chambered for regular 2¾-inch shells handles all 12-gauge, 2¾-inch shells, from the very lightest 1 ounce field load to the heavy 1½ ounce Magnums. The Browning 20-gauge Auto-5 is lightweight

and a top performer for the upland hunter. Yet, with 2¾-inch high velocity or 2¾-inch Magnums, it does a fine job in the duck blind.

All models and gauges of the Automatic-5 are available in the Buck Special version, which is designed to accurately fire the rifled slug or buckshot loads. In addition its specially bored 24-inch barrel will deliver nice open patterns with standard field loads.

SKEET MODELS—Special 26-inch skeet barrels fit all Browning Automatic-5's of like gauge and model so an owner may easily convert his favorite hunting gun to a skeet gun by a quick change of barrels. **$559.95**

HUNTING MODELS—

Light 12, and Light 20 gauge **$559.95**
3-inch magnum 12 gauge and magnum 20 gauge 569.95
Buck Special without accessories
Light 12, and Light 20 gauge 569.95
3-inch magnum 12 gauge and magnum 20 gauge 584.95
Buck Special with accessories
Light 12, and Light 20 gauge **$589.95**
3-inch magnum 12 gauge and magnum 20 gauge 604.95

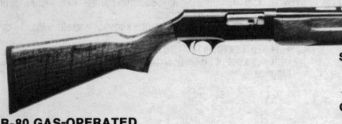

B-80 GAS-OPERATED, SEMI-AUTOMATIC SHOTGUN

Browning's new 12 gauge Super-light B-80 with a 26-inch barrel weighs only 6 pounds 8 ounces and gives the upland hunter everything he could ask for in a gas operated shotgun. The Superlight B-80 is the perfect combination of light weight and reliable firepower. The 12 and 20 gauge Hunting models and the new Superlight model B-80s feature a reliable 10 seal gas system for optimum performance and a choice of interchangeable 2¾- or 3-inch barrels with chrome-lined bores that shrug off the wearing effect of steel shot. B-80s feature the eye catching traditional Browning squared receiver that puts you on target faster.

B-80 SPECIFICATIONS

Trigger: Crisp and positive

Chamber: Both 12 and 20 gauge barrels with 2¾inch chambers will accept 2¾-inch standard and 2¾-inch magnum loads. Models with 3-inch magnum chambers will function properly with 3-inch magnums only.

Safety: Cross bolt. Red warning band visible when in fire position.

Receiver: Cold forged and machined from high grade steel on all models except Superlight. Superlight receiver is anodized aluminum alloy.

Stock and Forearm: Walnut skillfully cut checkered. Full pistol grip. Length of pull: 14¼ inches; Drop at Comb: 1⅝ inches; Drop at heel: 2½ inches. A field recoil pad is fitted.

Gauge: 12 and 20 gauge. Superlight available in 12 gauge only.

Barrels: 12 and 20 gauge interchangeable spare barrels available with either 2¾ or 3 inch chambers. Barrels are equipped with ventilated ribs except Buck Special barrels which have adjustable rifle sights. Barrels of the same gauge are interchangeable.

Magazine Capacity: Three 2¾- or 3-inch loads; or two 2¾- or 3-inch loads with the magazine plug installed. Each gun comes with the magazine plug in place.

HUNTING MODELS	PRICE
Superlight 12 Gauge Ventilated Rib	$549.95
Light 12 and Light 20 Gauge Ventilated Rib	549.95
Magnum 12 and Magnum 20 Gauge Ventilated Rib	549.95
Buck Special Without Accessories	559.95
Buck Special With Accessories	579.95

EXTRA BARRELS

HUNTING BARRELS	
Superlight 12, Light 12, Light 20 Gauge Ventilated Rib	179.95
Magnum 12 and Magnum 20 Gauge Ventilated Rib	179.95
Buck Special Barrel with Rifle Sights	189.95

BROWNING SHOTGUNS

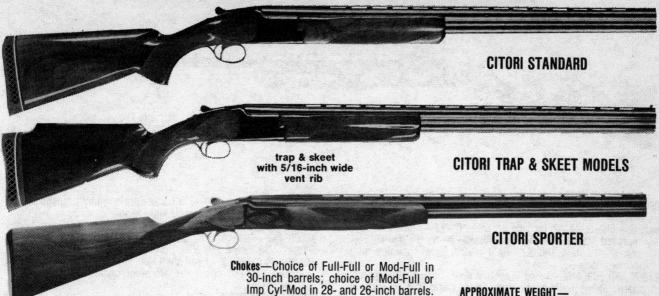

CITORI STANDARD

trap & skeet
with 5/16-inch wide
vent rib

CITORI TRAP & SKEET MODELS

CITORI SPORTER

FIELD GRADE

Gauge—12, 20, 28 and 410 gauge.

Barrels—Choice of 30-, 28- or 26-inch in 12 gauge. 28- or 26-inch in 20 gauge. Ventilated rib with matted sighting plane. Medium raised German nickel silver sight bead. 26 or 28-inch in 28 gauge. 26- or 28-inch in 410 gauge.

Overall Length—12, 20, 28 and 410 gauge.
With 26-inch barrels—43 inches
With 28-inch barrels—45 inches
With 30-inch barrels—47 inches

Chokes—Choice of Full-Full or Mod-Full in 30-inch barrels; choice of Mod-Full or Imp Cyl-Mod in 28- and 26-inch barrels.

Trigger—Single selective. Gold-plated. Fast and crisp.

Chamber—All 20-gauge Field models and all 12-gauge Field models accept all 3-inch magnum loads, as well as 2¾-inch loads. 28 gauge accepts 2¾-inch loads. 410 gauge accepts 2½-, 3 or 3-inch mag. loads.

Safety—Manual thumb safety. Combined with barrel selector mechanism.

Automatic Ejectors—Fired shells thrown out of gun; unfired shells are elevated for easy removal.

APPROXIMATE WEIGHT—

	12 gauge	20 gauge
26 in. barrels	7 lbs. 9 oz.	6 lbs. 11 oz.
28 in. barrels	7 lbs. 11 oz.	6 lbs. 13 oz.
30 in. barrels	7 lbs. 13 oz.	

Stock and Forearm—Dense walnut. Skillfully checkered. Full pistol grip. Hunting Beavertail forearm. Field type recoil pad installed on 12 gauge models.

	12 gauge	20 gauge
Length of pull	14¼ in.	14¼ in.
Drop at comb	1⅝ in.	1½ in.
Drop at heel	2½ in.	2⅜ in.

HUNTING, SUPERLIGHT, AND SPORTER MODELS

MAGNUM 12 and 20 GAUGE

	PRICE
Grade I Invector (12 Gauge)	$ 802.00
Grade I	775.00
Grade V (New engraving styles)	1960.00
Grade VI	2050.00

SUPERLIGHT 12 and 20 GAUGE

Grade I Invector	827.00
Grade I	800.00
Grade V (New engraving style	1960.00
Grade VI	2050.00

Sideplate 20 Gauge

Grade V	1960.00

HUNTING 28 Gauge and .410 Bore

Grade I	800.00
Grade V (New engraving style)	1960.00
Grade VI	2050.00

SUPERLIGHT 28 Gauge and .410 BORE

Grade I	800.00
Grade V (New engraving style)	1960.00
Grade VI	2050.00

TRAP MODELS

Standard 12 Gauge

Grade I Invector (High Post Target Rib)	892.00
Grade I (High Post Target Rib)	865.00
Grade V (New engraving style) (High Post Target Rib)	2095.00
Grade VI (High Post Target Rib)	2150.00

SKEET MODELS

Standard 12 and 20 Gauge

Grade I (High Post Target Rib)	865.00
Grade V (New engraving style) (High Post Target Rib)	2095.00
Grade VI (High Post Target Rib)	2150.00

Standard 28 Gauge and .410 Bore

Grade I (High Post Target Rib)	900.00
Grade V (New engraving style) (High Post Target Rib)	2095.00
Grade VI (High Post Target Rib)	2150.00

COMBO TRAP SET

**Standard 12 Gauge with 32 in. Over/Under barrels and 34 in. single barrel.
One removable forearm and adjustable balance weight supplied.**
(Furnished with fitted luggage case for gun and extra barrel.)

Grade I (High Post Target Rib)	1450.00

4 BARREL SKEET SET

12 Gauge with one removable forearm and four sets of barrels, 12, 20, 28, and .410 gauges.
(Furnished with fitted luggage case for gun and extra barrels.)

Grade 1 (High Post Target Rib)	2900.00

SHOTGUNS

BROWNING SHOTGUNS

**BT-99
BROWNING TRAP SPECIAL**

RECEIVER—Machined steel, tastefully hand-engraved and richly blued.
BARREL—Choice of 32 inch or 34 inch. **CHOKE**—Choice of Full, Improved Modified or Modified. **CHAMBER**—for 12 gauge, 2¾-inch shells only. **TRIGGER**—Gold plated, crisp, positive, pull approximately 3½ pounds.
STOCK AND FOREARM—Select French walnut, hand-rubbed finish, sharp 20-line hand-checkering. Monte Carlo or Conventional stock available.
Stock: Full pistol grip; **Length of Pull:** 14⅜ inches; **Drop at Comb:** 1⅜ inches; **Drop at Heel:** 2 inches; **Forearm:** Full beavertail.

SAFETY—No manual safety, a feature preferred by trap shooters.
SIGHTS—Ivory front and center sight beads.
RIB—High post, ventilated, full floating, matted, 11/32 inch wide.
RECOIL PAD—Deluxe, contoured trap style.
WEIGHT—32 inch barrel 8 lbs., 34 inch barrel 8 lbs. 3 oz.
AUTOMATIC EJECTION—Fired shell ejected automatically on opening action, unfired shell elevated from chamber for convenient removal.

GRADE I COMPETITION: 32- & 34-inch barrel	$ 724.95
With extra barrel (includes case)	1030.00
PIGEON GRADE COMPETITION	1650.00
GRADE I INVECTOR	744.95

SIDE-BY-SIDE SHOTGUN

**BROWNING "B-SS"
SIDE-BY-SIDE SHOTGUN
12 & 20 GAUGE**

STOCK AND FOREARM: Select walnut, hand-rubbed finish, sharp 20-line hand checkering. Full pistol grip. Full grip beavertail forearm.
Length of pull: 14¼ inches
Drop at comb: 1⅝ inches
Drop at heel: 2½ inches

The Browning Side by Side has a "mechanical" trigger which differs from the "inertia" trigger found on many two barreled guns in that the recoil of the first shot is not used to set up the mechanism for the second shot. The first pull of the trigger fires the right barrel. The next pull fires the left barrel. The positive linkage of the B-SS mechanical trigger prevents doubling (both barrels firing at the same instant) or balking. The chromed trigger lets off crisply at about 4½ pounds.

Grade I Standard 12 & 20 ga. with Barrel Selector	$ 760.00
Grade II Standard 12 & 20 ga. with Barrel Selector	1275.00
Grade I Sporter 12 & 20 ga. with Barrel Selector	760.00
Grade II Sporter 12 & 20 ga. with Barrel Selector	1275.00

B-SS with Side Lock (12 Ga. ONLY)

BARREL: 26- or 28-inches
CHAMBER: 2¾ or 2¾ Mag. only
WEIGHT: 28-in. - 6 lbs. 11 oz.
28-in. - 6 lbs. 11 oz.
26-in. - 6 lbs. 9 oz.

B-SS SPECIFICATIONS:

BARRELS: Choice of 26-, 28- or 30-inch barrels. Solid rib with matted top. Sight bead is German nickel silver.
CHOKE: 30-inch barrels choked full or modified and full. 28-inch barrel model choked modified and full. 26-inch barrels choked, modified and full, or improved cylinder and modified.
TRIGGER: Single mechanical trigger fires right barrel first (the more open choke). Gold plated on all models.
CHAMBER: 2¾-, 2¾-inch Mag. and 3-inch mag. shells.
AUTOMATIC SAFETY: Goes on safe when breech is opened and remains there until manually moved to off safe.
AUTOMATIC EJECTORS: Fired shells are thrown out of gun. Unfired shells are elevated for easy removal.
WEIGHT: With 30-inch barrels approx. 7 lbs. 7 oz., with 26-inch barrels approx. 7 lbs. 3 oz., with 28-inch barrels approx. 7 lbs. 5 oz.
OVERALL LENGTH: 26-inch barrels 43 inches. 28-inch barrels 45 inches. 30-inch barrels 47 inches.

FRANCHI SHOTGUNS

**STANDARD AUTOMATIC SHOTGUN
WITH VENT RIB
ALSO AVAILABLE WITH 22-INCH SLUG BBL.**

**MAGNUM AUTOMATIC
WITH VENT RIB**

SPECIFICATIONS

GAUGES: 12 and 20 (Standard models chambered for all 2¾-inch shells; Magnum models chambered for all 3-inch shells.)

BARRELS: Standard models: 24-, 26- and 28-inch. Standard 12 gauge only, 30 inches. Magnum 12 gauge, 32 inches; Magnum 20 gauge, 28 inches.

CHOKES: Standard models: cylinder, improved cylinder, modified and full. Magnum models, full.

SAFETIES: Lateral push-button safety. Removal of two lateral pins, located through the receiver permits the trigger-safety lifter mechanism to be removed as a single unit.

STOCKS: Stock and forend with fully machine cut checkered pistol grip and foregrip. Magnum models equipped with factory-fitted recoil pad (optional on other 12-gauge models).

WEIGHTS: Standard 12 gauge, 6 lbs. 4 oz.; Standard 20 gauge, 5 lbs. 2 oz.; Magnum 12 gauge, 8 lbs. 4 oz.; 20 gauge Magnum, 6 lbs.

OVERALL LENGTH: 47½ inches with 28-inch barrel

**HUNTER MODEL
12 or 20 GAUGE WITH VENT RIB**

Franchi Hunter features include: specially selected European stock, forend; fully engraved million-dollar light-weight receiver covered by a lifetime guarantee; the automatic safety, which securely locks the hammer, is silent and positive; hand safety can be reversed for left-handed shooters; chrome-lined barrel for light weight and maximum strength; checkered pistol grip; reliable recoil action requiring no maintenance and no cleaning. Chambered for 2¾ shells.

MODEL	DESCRIPTION	Price
FRANCHI AUTOLOADING SHOTGUNS		
Standard	12 Ga. (48/AL12) or 20 Ga. (48/AL20)	$394.95
Hunter	12 Ga. (48/AH12) or 20 Ga. (48/AH20)	419.95
Magnum	12 Ga., 3 in. (48/AM12)	419.95
Spas-12	12 Ga. Weapon System	559.95
OVER-AND-UNDER MODELS		
Alcione SL	12 Ga. (28-inch M/F) or (27-inch I.C./I.M.) with Luggage Case	$1595.00
Falconet S	12 Ga. (28-inch M/F) or (27-inch I.C./I.M.)	1015.00
Diamond	12 Ga. (28-inch M/F)	850.00

BARREL LENGTHS & CHOKES:	22 in. Slug	24 in. Cyl.	26 in. I.C.	26 in. Mod.	28 in. Mod.	28 in. Full	30 in. Full	32 in. Full
Standard or Hunter 12 Ga.	X	X	X		X		X	
Standard or Hunter 20 Ga.	X	X	X	X	X	X		
Magnum 12								X

GARBI SHOTGUNS

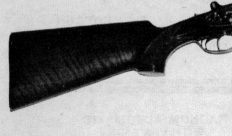

MODEL 51 $515.00
Gauges: 12, 16 and 20
Chokes: Modified and full
Action: Box-lock
Stock: Hand-checkered stock and forend
Features: Double trigger and extractors; hand-engraved receiver

MODEL 51B $890.00
WITH EJECTORS

MODEL 60-A 12 Ga. only
WITH EXTRACTORS $830.00 (shown)
MODEL 60-B Gauges: 12, 16 and 20. **WITH EJECTORS $1139.00**

Gauges: 12, 16 and 20
Action: Sidelock with Purdey locking system
Stock: Select walnut with hand checkering
Barrel Lengths: 26-, 28- or 30 inches
Features: Several choke options; extensive scroll engraving on receiver; double triggers and extractors; made to customer's dimensions

MODEL 62-A 12 Ga. only
WITH EXTRACTORS $830.00
MODEL 62-B Gauges: 12, 16 and 20. **WITH EJECTORS $1115.00**

Gauges: 12, 16 and 20
Stock: Select walnut with hand-checkering
Barrel Lengths: 26-, 28- or 30 inches
Barrels are special steel demi-bloc
Features: Several choke options; jointed trigger (double trigger); plain receiver with engraved border; gas exhaust valves; made to customer's dimensions

H&R SINGLE BARREL SHOTGUNS

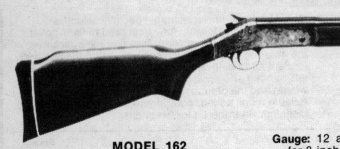

MODEL 162
12/24-inch Cyl. Bore and
20/24-inch Cyl. Bore
$100.50

Gauge: 12 and 20 chambered for 3-inch shells
Capacity: Single shot
Stock: Walnut finished American hardwood

Overall Length: 40 inches
Weight: 5½ lbs.
Barrel Length: 24 inches with fully adjustable rear sight and dovetail front sight

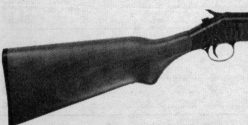

H&R MODEL 088 and 088JR
$75.50

12 ga. 30- and 32-inch $80.00
12 ga. 36-inch bbl. $82.00

Gauge: Model 088 available in 12, 16, 20, and .410; Model 088JR available in 20 and .410
Capacity: Single shot
Stock: Semi-pistol grip walnut finished. Semi-beavertail forend

Overall Length: 40- to 47 inches
Weight: 5 to 6½ lbs.
Barrel Lengths: 12 ga.—28-, 30-, 32-inches; 16 ga.—28 inches; 20 ga.—26 inches; 410 ga.—25 inches; 20 ga. JR—25 inches; 410 ga. JR—25 inches

H&R SINGLE BARREL SHOTGUNS

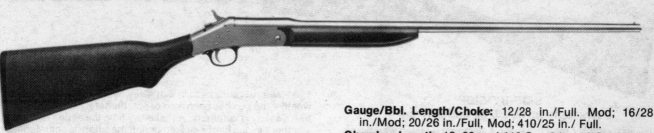

MODEL 099 DELUXE $95.00

Average Weight: 5 to 6 pounds
Sights: Bead front sight
O/A Length: 40 in. to 43 in.

Gauge/Bbl. Length/Choke: 12/28 in./Full. Mod; 16/28 in./Mod; 20/26 in./Full, Mod; 410/25 in./ Full.
Chamber Length: 12, 20 and .410 Ga., 3 in.; 16 Ga. 2¾ in.
Stock: Semi-pistol grip walnut-finished American hardwood. Semi-beavertail fore-end.
Metal Finish: H&R Hard-Guard electro-less matte nickel process, inside and out.
Stock Dimensions: Length 13¾ in. drop at comb 1½ in., drop at heel 2½ in.

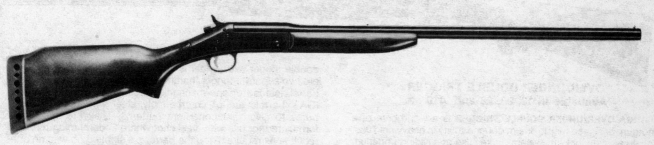

MODEL 490 $84.50

Gauge: 20 gauge, modified, 3-inch chamber; .410 gauge, full, 3-inch chamber; 28 gauge, modified, 2¾-inch chamber
Capacity: Single shot

Stock: Walnut finished American hardwood with recoil pad
Overall Length: 40 inches
Weight: 5 lbs.
Barrel Length: 26-inch barrel
Greenwing: $95.00

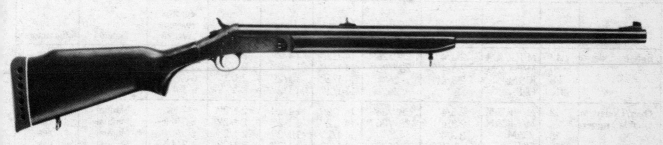

MODEL 176 10 Gauge

Gauge: 10 full
Chamber: 10 Ga., 3½-inch Magnum
Stock: Walnut-finished hardwood with recoil pad
Metal Finish: Blue-black barrel. Color cased frame
Stock Dimensions: Length 13¼ inches; Drop at comb 1½ inches; Drop at heel 2½ inches

Sights: Brass bead front
Overall Length: 47-51 in.
Weight & Price:
10 ga. 36-inch bbl. 10 lbs. $105.50
10 ga. 32-inch bbl. 9½ lbs....................................105.50
Also available: Model 176 slug gun 10 ga., 28-inch bbl., cyl: bore 122.00

IGA SHOTGUNS

SIDE-BY-SIDE
Available in 12, 20, 28 and .410 ga.

The **IGA SIDE-BY-SIDE** is a rugged, endurance-tested workhorse of a shotgun, designed from the ground up to give you years and years of trouble-free service. A vise-tight, super-safe locking system is provided by two massive underlugs for lasting strength and durability. Two design features which make the IGA a standout for reliability are its positive mechanical extraction of spent shells and its traditional double trigger mechanism. The

IGA's safety is automatic in that every time the action is opened, whether the gun has been fired or not, the safety is actuated. The IGA's safety is automatic in that every time the action is opened, whether the gun has been fired or not, the safety is actuated. The IGA's polish and blue is deep and rich. The solid sighting rib carries a machined-in matte finish for glare-free sighting. Barrels are of chrome-moly steel with micro-polished bores to give dense, consistent patterns. The stock and forend are of classic design in durable hardwood . . . oil finished, hand-rubbed and hand-checkered.

OVER/UNDER DOUBLE TRIGGER
Available in 12, 20, 28 and .410 ga.

The **IGA OVER/UNDER DOUBLE TRIGGER** is a workhorse of a shotgun, designed for maximum dependability in heavy field use. The super-safe lock-up system makes use of a sliding underlug, the best system for over/under shotguns. A massive monoblock joins the barrel in a solid one-piece assembly at the breech end. Reliability is assured, thanks to the mechanical extraction system. Upon opening the breech, the spent shells are partially lifted from the chamber, allowing easy removal by hand. The

double trigger over/under is durable and dependable, as there are two separate trigger/hammer mechanisms . . . one for each barrel, instead of one mechanism doing the work of two. The IGA's barrels are of chrome-moly steel with micro-polished bores to give tight consistent patterns. They are specifically formulated for use with steel shot where Federal migratory bird regulations require. Atop the barrel is a sighting rib with an anti-glare surface. The buttstock and forend are of durable hardwood, hand-checkered and finished with an oil-based formula that takes dents and scratches in stride.

The IGA over/under shotgun is also available in a single trigger model.

I.G.A. Specifications

Model	Gauge	Chokes	Chamber	Barrel Length	Length of Pull	Drop at Comb	Drop at Heel	Approx. Average Weight	Safety	Extractors
Side-by-Side	12	M/F IC&M	2-3/4''	28''/26''	14-1/2''	1-1/2''	2-1/2''	7 lbs.	Automatic	Yes
	20	M/F IC&M	2-3/4''	28''/26''	14-1/2''	1-1/2''	2-1/2''	6-3/4 lbs.	Automatic	Yes
	28	IC&M	2-3/4''	26''	14-1/2''	1-1/2''	2-1/2''	6-3/4 lbs.	Automatic	Yes
	.410	F&F	3''	26''	14-1/2''	1-1/2''	2-1/2''	6-3/4 lbs.	Automatic	Yes
Over/Under Double Trigger	12	M/F IC&M	2-3/4''	28''/26''	14-1/2''	1-1/2''	2-1/2''	7 lbs.	Manual	Yes
	20	M/F IC&M	2-3/4''	28''/26''	14-1/2''	1-1/2''	2-1/2''	6-3/4 lbs.	Manual	Yes
	28	IC&M	2-3/4''	26''	14-1/2''	1-1/2''	2-1/2''	6-3/4 lbs.	Manual	Yes
	.410	F&F	3''	26''	14-1/2''	1-1/2''	2-1/2''	6-3/4 lbs.	Manual	Yes
Over/Under Single Trigger	12	M/F IC&M	2-3/4''	28''/26''	14-1/2''	1-1/2''	2-1/2''	7 lbs.	Manual	Yes
	20	M/F IC&M	2-3/4''	28''/26''	14-1/2''	1-1/2''	2-1/2''	6-3/4 lbs.	Manual	Yes
	28	IC&M	2-3/4''	26''	14-1/2''	1-1/2''	2-1/2''	6-3/4 lbs.	Manual	Yes
	.410	F&F	3''	26''	14-1/2''	1-1/2''	2-1/2''	6-3/4 lbs.	Manual	Yes
Coach Gun	12	IC&M	2-3/4''	20''	14-1/2''	1-1/2''	2-1/2''	6-1/2 lbs.	Automatic	Yes
	20	IC&M	2-3/4''	20''	14-1/2''	1-1/2''	2-1/2''	6-1/2 lbs.	Automatic	Yes

IGA SHOTGUNS

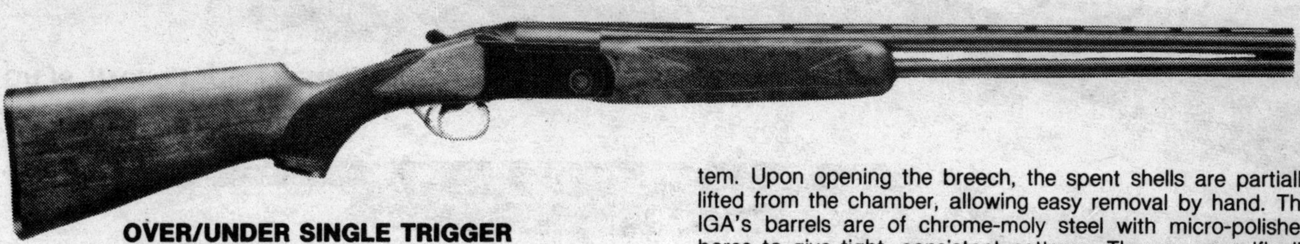

OVER/UNDER SINGLE TRIGGER
Available in 12, 20, 28 and .410 ga.

The **IGA OVER/UNDER SINGLE TRIGGER** is a workhorse of a shotgun, designed for maximum dependability in heavy field use. The super-safe lock-up system makes use of a sliding underlug, the best system for over/under shotguns. A massive monoblock joins the barrel in a solid one-piece assembly at the breech end. Reliability is assured, thanks to the mechanical extraction sys-tem. Upon opening the breech, the spent shells are partially lifted from the chamber, allowing easy removal by hand. The IGA's barrels are of chrome-moly steel with micro-polished bores to give tight, consistent patterns. They are specifically formulated for use with steel shot where Federal migratory bird regulations require. Atop the barrel is a sighting rib with an anti-glare surface. The buttstock and forend are of durable hard-wood, hand-checkered and finished with an oil-based formula that takes dents and scratches in stride.

The IGA over/under shotgun is also available in a double-trigger model.

COACH GUN
Available in 12 and 20 ga.

The **IGA CLASSIC SIDE-BY-SIDE COACH GUN** sports a 20" barrel. Lightning fast, it is the perfect shotgun for hunting upland game in dense brush or close quarters. This endurance-tested workhorse of a gun is designed from the ground up to give you years and years of trouble-free service. Two massive underlugs provide a super-safe, vice-tight locking system for lasting strength and durability. The IGA's mechanical extraction of spent shells and double trigger mechanism assure reliability. The automatic safety is actuated whenever the action is opened, whether or not the gun has been fired. The IGA's polish and blue is deep and rich, and the solid sighting rib is matte-finished for glare-free sighting. Chrome-moly steel barrels with micro-polished bores gives dense, consistent patterns. The classic stock and forend are of durable hardwood . . . oil finished, hand-rubbed and hand-checkered.

Improved cylinder/modified choking and its short barrel make the IGA coach gun the ideal choice for hunting in close quarters, security and police work.

I.G.A.

Code #	Model	Chamber	Retail
IG5000000	IGA Side by Side 12/26 IC&M	2¾ in.	$325.00
IG5001000	IGA Side by Side 12/28 M&F	2¾ in.	325.00
IG5002000	IGA Side by Side 20/26 IC&M	2¾ in.	325.00
IG5003000	IGA Side by Side 20/28 M&F	2¾ in.	325.00
IG5004000	IGA Side by Side 28/26 IC&M	2¾ in.	325.00
IG5005000	IGA Side by Side 410/26 F&F	3 in.	325.00
IG5010000	IGA O/U (Single Trigger) 12/26 IC&M	2¾ in.	499.95
IG5011000	IGA O/U (Single Trigger) 12/28 M&F	2¾ in.	499.95
IG5012000	IGA O/U (Single Trigger) 20/26 IC&M	2¾ in.	499.95
IG5013000	IGA O/U (Single Trigger) 20/28 M&F	2¾ in.	499.95
IG5014000	IGA O/U (Single Trigger) 28/26 IC&M	2¾ in.	499.95
IG5015000	IGA O/U (Single Trigger) 410/26 F&F	3 in.	499.95
IG5020000	IGA O/U (Double Trigger) 12/26 IC&M	2¾ in.	417.00
IG5021000	IGA O/U (Double Trigger) 12/28 M&F	2¾ in.	417.00
IG5022000	IGA O/U (Double Trigger) 20/26 IC&M	2¾ in.	417.00
IG5023000	IGA O/U (Double Trigger) 20/28 M&F	2¾ in.	417.00
IG5024000	IGA O/U (Double Trigger) 28/26 IC&M	2¾ in.	417.00
IG5025000	IGA O/U (Double Trigger) 410/26 F&F	3 in.	417.00
IG5030000	IGA Coach Gun 12/20 IC&M	2¾ in.	283.95
IG5031000	IGA Coach Gun 20/20 IC&M	2¾ in.	283.85

HECKLER & KOCH BENELLI SHOTGUNS

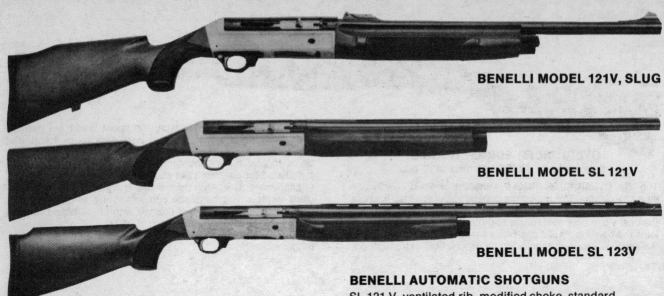

BENELLI MODEL 121V, SLUG

BENELLI MODEL SL 121V

BENELLI MODEL SL 123V

BENELLI MODEL SL 121V

Gauge: 12 (5 shot); 3-shot plug furnished
Action: Tubular steel receiver, bolt group and alloy trigger group
Barrel length: 26- or 28-inch
Stock: Walnut; hand-checkered pistol grip and forearm
Weight: 6¾ lbs.
121V, SLUG **$492.00**

BENELLI AUTOMATIC SHOTGUNS

SL 121 V, ventilated rib, modified choke, standard
model **449.00**
SL 123V, 12 gauge, ventilated rib, modified choke,
deluxe model, engraved receiver **$525.00**
Also available:
SL 123 V with full choke **525.00**
SL 201, 20 gauge, ventilated rib, 26-inch barrel,
improved modified choke **453.00**
Benelli spare barrels **236.00**
121-MI Police/Military **499.00**

ITHACA SHOTGUNS

**MODEL 37 ULTRALITE™
PUMP SHOTGUN $435.00**

SPECIFICATIONS:
Gauge: 12, 20
Chamber length: 2¾ inches
Barrel length: 25 inches (20 ga.), 26 inches (12 ga.)
Choke: Full, Modified, Imp. Cyl.
Length of pull: 14 inches
Drop at comb: 1½ inches
Drop at heel: 2¼ inches
Weight: 5 lbs. (20), 5¾ lbs. (12)

The Ultralite™ features bottom ejection, which puts empties conveniently at your feet for easy recovery. The gun may be fired right- or left-handed with no worry about shells ejecting across your line of sight.

Orange iridescent Raybar™ sight points out game even against dense foilage and in poor light conditions. The Ultralite™ also features high-gloss American walnut stock, streamlined forend, gold trigger, Sid Bell grip cap and ventilated rib.

**MODEL 37 STANDARD
WITH VENTILATED RIB $396.00**

A versatile gun that shoots squirrel, rabbit, duck, geese, even waterfowl. The Model 37 is suitable for both right-

and left-handed shooters, with left-handed safety available. Pumping the action requires only a slight movement of your arm. With the ejection port on the bottom of the gun instead of on the side, rain, dirt and debris stay outside of the Model 37's Featherlight™ action.

ITHACA SHOTGUNS

Model	Grade	Gauge	Chamber Length	Barrel Length	Choke	Length of Pull	Drop at Comb	Drop at Heel	Weight (lbs.)	Price
37	Standard, Standard Vent, or Deluxe Vent	12	2¾ in.	30 in.	Full	14 in.	1½ in.	2¼ in.	6¾	Standard $345.00
		12	2¾ in.	28 in.	Mod.	14 in.	1½ in.	2¼ in.	6¾	Standard Vent $396.00
		12	2¾ in.	26 in.	Imp. Cyl.	14 in.	1½ in.	2¼ in.	6¾	
		20	2¾ in.	28 in.	Full or Mod.	14 in.	1½ in.	2¼ in.	6¼	Deluxe Vent $414.00
		20	2¾ in.	26 in.	Imp. Cyl.	14 in.	1¼ in.	2¼ in.	6¼	

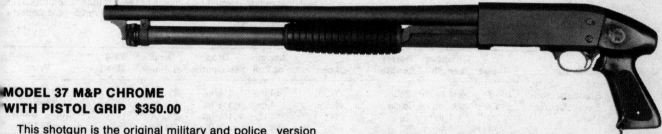

MODEL 37 M&P CHROME WITH PISTOL GRIP $350.00

This shotgun is the original military and police version of the Model 37. Its bottom ejection makes it possible to fire from either the left or right shoulder without the possible distraction of shells ejected across the shooter's field of vision. Metal parts are either Parkerized or matte-chrome finished. Wood has a non-glare, maintenance-free tung oil finish.

Model	Gauge	Chamber Length	Barrel Length	Choke	Length of pull	Drop at comb	Drop at heel	Weight (lbs.)	Finish	Price
M37 M&P 5-shot	12	2¾"	18½"	Cyl.	14"	1½"	2¼"	6½	Parkerized	$363.50
M37 M&P 5-shot	12	2¾"	20"	Cyl.	14"	1½"	2¼"	6½	Parkerized	$363.50
M37 M&P 5-shot	12	2¾"	20"	Full	14"	1½"	2¼"	6½	Parkerized	$363.50
M37 M&P 8-shot	12	2¾"	20"	Cyl.	14"	1½"	2¼"	6¾	Parkerized	$378.50
M37 M&P 8-shot	12	2¾"	20"	Full	14"	1½"	2¼"	6¾	Parkerized	$378.50
M37 M&P 8-shot	12	2¾"	20"	Cyl.	14"	1½"	2¼"	6¾	Chrome	$418.50

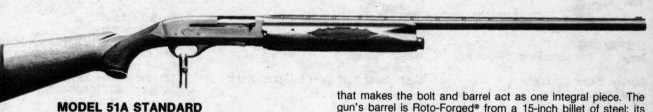

MODEL 51A STANDARD WITH VENTILATED RIB $477.00

The Model 51A is a gas-operated, semiautomatic shotgun featuring a machines, solid-steel receiver and a triple-lug lock-up that makes the bolt and barrel act as one integral piece. The gun's barrel is Roto-Forged® from a 15-inch billet of steel; its stock is solid American walnut.

Model 51A Deluxe target gun has full-fancy hand-checkered wood and target-grade barrel. Model 51A Standard comes with a plain or vent-rib barrel, or 3-inch Magnum version.

Model	Grade	Gauge	Chamber Length	Barrel Length	Choke	Length of Pull	Drop at Comb	Drop at Heel	Weight (lbs.)	Price
51A	Standard Vent	12	2¾ in.	30 in.	Full	14 in.	1½ in.	2¼ in.	7½	
		12	2¾ in.	28 in.	Full or Mod.	14 in.	1½ in.	2¼ in.	7½	$477.00
		12	2¾ in.	26 in.	Imp. Cyl.	14 in.	1½ in.	2¼ in.	7½	
		20	2¾ in.	28 in.	Full or Mod.	14 in.	1½ in.	2¼ in.	7¼	
		20	2¾ in.	26 in.	Imp. Cyl.	14 in.	1½ in.	2¼ in.	7¼	
51A	Vent Magnum	12	3 in.	30 in.	Full	14 in.	1½ in.	2¼ in.	8	477.00
		20	3 in.	28 in.	Full	14 in.	1½ in.	2¼ in.	7¾	
51A	Deluxe Trap	12	2¾ in.	30 in.	Full	14½ in.	1-5/16 in.	1-7/16 in.	8	614.00
51A	Deluxe Trap M.C.	12	2¾ in.	30 in.	Full	14½ in.	1½ in.	1½ -2 in.	8	650.00
51A	Deluxe Skeet	12	2¾ in.	26 in.	SKT	14 in.	1½ in.	2¼ in.	7½	604.00
		20	2¾ in.	26 in.	SKT	14 in.	1½ in.	2¼ in.	7½	

ITHACA SHOTGUNS

MODEL 37 & 51 DEERSLAYERS®

Ithaca now has four Deerslayer® models for firing rifled slugs with famous Deerslayer® accuracy. You'll bring home Whitetails with this gun that you'd be lucky to get with regular shotguns. With shotshells, these barrels also provide effective 35-yard patterns on upland game.

Model	Grade	Gauge	Chamber Length	Barrel Length	Choke	Length of Pull	Drop at Comb	Drop at Heel	Weight (lbs.)	Price
37	Standard and	12	2¾ in.	26 in.	RS	14 in.	1½ in.	2¼ in.	6¾	Standard
	Super Deluxe	12	2¾ in.	20 in.	RS	14 in.	1½ in.	2¼ in.	6½	**$385.00**
		20	2¾ in.	26 in.	RS	14 in.	1½ in.	2¼ in.	6¼	Super Deluxe
		20	2¾ in.	20 in.	RS	14 in.	1½ in.	2¼ in.	6	**435.00**
37	Ultra-Deerslayer	20	2¾ in.	20 in.	RS	14 in.	1½ in.	2¼ in.	5	**414.00**
51	Deerslayer	12	2¾ in.	24 in.	RS	14 in.	1½ in.	2¼ in.	7½	**477.00**

MARLIN SHOTGUNS

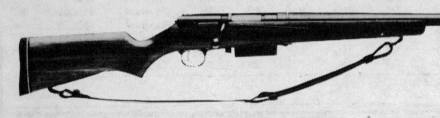

MARLIN SUPERGOOSE 10
$263.95

Action: Bolt action
Safety: Positive thumb
Stock: Extra-long walnut-finish hardwood with pistol grip and Pachmayr® ventilated recoil pad; quick-detachable steel swivels and deluxe leather carrying strap; Mar-Shield® finish.

SPECIFICATIONS:
Gauge: 10, 3½- Magnum or 2⅞-inch reg. shells
Capacity: 2-shot clip magazine
Barrel length: 34 inches

Weight: 10½ lbs.
Overall length: 55½ inches
Sights: Bead front sight & U-groove rear sight

ORIGINAL GOOSE GUN 12 GAUGE 3-INCH MAGNUM— 36-INCH BARREL (FULL CHOKE ONLY)
$160.95

High-flying ducks and geese are the Goose Gun's specialty. The Marlin Goose Gun has an extra-long 36-inch full-choked barrel and Magnum capability, making it the perfect choice for tough shots at wary waterfowl. It also features a quick-loading 2-shot clip magazine, a convenient leather carrying strap and a quality ventilated recoil pad.

SPECIFICATIONS:
Gauge: 12 gauge: 2¾-inch Magnum 3-inch Magnum or 2¾-inch Regular shells
Choke: Full
Capacity: 2-shot clip magazine
Action: Bolt action; positive thumb safety; red cocking indicator.

Stock: Walnut-finish hardwood with pistol grip and ventilated recoil pad; swivels and leather carrying strap; tough Mar-Shield® finish.
Barrel: 36 inches with bead front sight & U-groove rear sight
Overall length: 56¾ inches
Weight: About 8 lbs.

MARLIN SHOTGUNS
MARLIN MODEL 120 12-GAUGE MAGNUM PUMP-ACTION SHOTGUN

**MARLIN 120 MAGNUM PUMP SHOTGUN
WITH VENTILATED RIB
$355.95**

After years of design study, Marlin has introduced a pump action shotgun that is designed to fill the demand for a solid, reliable, pump action gun. An all-steel receiver is made from a solid block of high tensile steel. New-design, exclusive slide lock release lets you open the action to remove unfired shells even with gloved hands. All-steel floating concave ventilated rib, serrated on top, provides clean sighting, reduces mirage when trap and skeet shooting. Front and middle sights help the eye align barrel and target. Handsomely engine turned bolt, shell carrier and bolt slide add elegance and double action bars provide smoothest possible operation with no binding or twisting. Matte finish, grooved receiver top eliminates glare, aids natural gun pointing and sighting. Big reversible safety button—serrated and located where it belongs, in front of the trigger—operates the cross-bolt safety that positively blocks the trigger. Choice of barrels—26-inch improved cylinder choke, 28-inch modified choke, 30-inch full choke, 20-inch slug barrel (with rifle

sights), and 38-inch full choke barrel. Select the length and boring of your choice. Extra barrels are completely interchangeable. 5-shot magazine capacity (4 with 3-inch shells) 3-shot plug furnished. Stainless steel, non-jamming shell follower. The 120 Magnum has a genuine American walnut stock and forend. The buttstock design is made to fit American shooters with its full dimensions. Semi-beavertail forend is full and fits a full range of hands. Both stock and forend are hand-checkered with a handsome pattern and feature Mar-Shield® finish. Deluxe recoil pad is standard.

MARLIN 120 MAGNUM SPECIFICATIONS: 12 gauge, 2¾- or 3-inch Magnum or regular shells interchange   ; 5 shots in magazine (4 with 3-inch shells), 3-shot plug furnished; approx. 7¾-inch #; 20-, 26-, 28- or 30-inch barrels with steel ventilated ribs, front and middle sights; recoil pad; grip cap; white butt and grip spacers; stock dimensions: 14-inch long including recoil pad, 1½-inch drop at comb, 2⅜-inch drop at heel; genuine American walnut stock and forend are finely hand-checkered and Mar-Shield® finished; all-steel receiver; cross bolt safety.

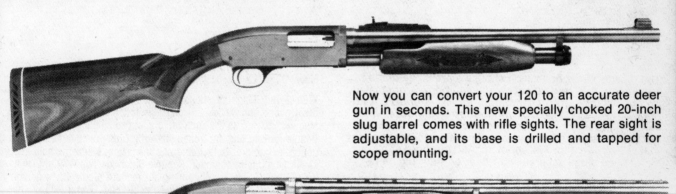

Now you can convert your 120 to an accurate deer gun in seconds. This new specially choked 20-inch slug barrel comes with rifle sights. The rear sight is adjustable, and its base is drilled and tapped for scope mounting.

**MARLIN 778
12 GAUGE PUMP
Plain $244.95 Vent. Rib $277.95**

778 SPECIFICATIONS:
Gauge: 12 gauge; handles 2¾-inch Magnum, 3-inch Magnum, or 2¾-inch Regular shells interchangeably
Choke: Modified
Capacity: 5-shot rubular magazine (4-shot with 3-inch shells); 3-shot plug furnished

Stock: Two-piece walnut finish hardwood with full pistol grip; semi-beavertail forend.   Ventilated recoil pad; checkering on pistol grip
Action: Pump; engine-turned bolt, shell carrier and bolt slide; double action bars; slide lock release; stainless steel shell follower; reversible crossbolt

safety; blued steel trigger; deeply blued metal surfaces.
Barrel: 26-inch Improved Cylinder, with or without vent rib. 28-inch Modified Choke, with or without vent rib. 30-inch Full Choke, with or without vent rib. 38-inch MXR, Full Choke, without rib. 20-inch Slug Barrel (Improved Cylinder) with semi-buckhorn rear, ramp front sight with brass bead and Wide-Scan™ hood. Drilled and tapped for scope mount.
Approx. Weight: 7¾ lbs.

MOSSBERG SHOTGUNS

**BOLT-ACTION SHOTGUNS
VENTILATED RIB**

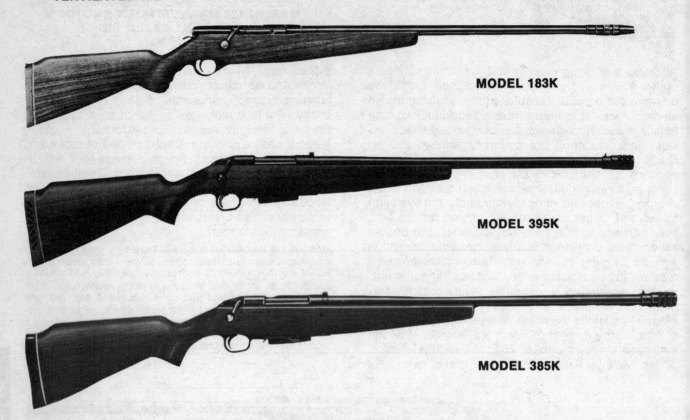

MODEL 183K

MODEL 395K

MODEL 385K

The most popular bolt-action shotguns are those made by Mossberg, in 12 and 20 gauge and .410 bore. Proof-tested in our factory and chambered for all standard and Magnum factory loads. A modern streamline designed self-cocking action with **positive safety on top—right under your thumb.** The design and dimensions of these guns make them ideal for fast shooting. All Mossberg shotguns shoot rifled slugs accurately for deer or other big game.

Model 183K .410 bore bolt-action with C-LECT CHOKE

The only .410 bore shotgun that gives you the advantage of finger-operated adjustable choke. **Action**—Fixed-type top loading magazine holds two shells, plus one in chamber. Chambered for all 2½- and 3-inch factory loaded shells. Convenient thumb-operated safety.
Stock—Walnut finish Monte Carlo design. Rubber recoil pad with white liner. Molded trigger guard. **Barrel**—25-inch tapered blued steel barrel, including C-LECT-CHOKE. Mossberg's exclusive factory installed adjustable choke lets you instantly choose Full Choke, Modified Choke, Improved Cylinder Bore or points in between. Gold bead front sight.
Weight—About 5¾ lbs. Length overall 45¼ inches.

Model 395K 12 ga. bolt-action with C-LECT-CHOKE

With 3-inch Magnum shells and number 2 shot this becomes a great goose gun. **Action**—Strong bolt action chambered for 3-inch Magnum as well as 2¾-inch factory loaded shells.
Double locking lugs for added strength. Quick removable bolt with double extractors. Detachable clip magazine. Magazine holds two shells plus one in chamber. Positive Safety on Top—"Right Under Your Thumb". **Stock**—Walnut finish, modern Monte Carlo design, pistol grip and cushion rubber recoil pad. **Barrel**—28 inches including C-LECT-CHOKE. **Sights**—Grooved rear sight for accurate alignment. Shotgun bead front. **Weight**—About 7½ lbs. Length overall 45¾ inches.

Model 385K 20 ga. bolt action with C-LECT-CHOKE

Identical to Model 395K except that it is a 20-gauge shotgun with 28-inch barrel, including C-LECT-CHOKE. Chambered for 3-inch Magnum as well as 2¾-inch factory loaded shells. **Weight**—About 6⅜ lbs. Length overall 45¾ inches.

Model 395SPL 12 ga. repeater, detachable magazine with 38-inch barrel. Full choke.

MANUFACTURER DOES NOT LIST SUGGESTED RETAIL PRICES

MOSSBERG SHOTGUNS

SLIDE-ACTION SHOTGUNS PLAIN BARRELS AND VENTILATED RIB

MODEL 500 AKT

MODEL 500 SLUGSTER

Slide Action 500 "T" offers a lightweight action, high tensile strength alloy. It also features the famous Mossberg "Safety on Top" and a full range of interchangeable barrels. The stock is walnut-finished birch with serrated buttplate and has a fluted comb and grooved beavertail forend.

Model 500 AT: 12 ga. Std. grade, 30-inch full or 28-inch mod., plain barrel. 26-inch Imp. Cyl.

Model 500 CT: 20 ga. Std. grade, 28-inch full or 28-inch mod., plain barrel. 26-inch Imp. Cyl.

Model 500 ET: .410 Std. grade, 26-inch full, plain barrel.

Model 500 ATV: 12 ga. Std. grade, 30-inch full or 28-inch mod., vent. rib barrel. 26-inch Imp. Cyl.

Model 500 CGV: 20 ga. Std. grade, 28-inch full or 28-inch mod., vent. rib barrel. 26-inch Imp. Cyl.

Model 500 Youth: 20 ga., 25-inch Mod. vent or plain, 13-inch stock.

Model 500 GV: .410 Bore, Std. grade, 26-inch Full, vent. rib barrel.

Model 500 AGT: 12 ga. Std. grade, 28-inch C-LECT-CHOKE, plain barrel.

Model 500 CKG: 20 ga. Std. grade, 28-inch C-LECT-CHOKE, plain barrel

Model 500 AKGY: 12 ga. Std. grade, 28-inch C-LECT-CHOKE, vent. rib barrel

Model 500 CETV: 20 ga. Std. grade, 28-inch C-LECT-CHOKE, vent. rib barrel.

Model 500 SLUGSTER: 12 ga. Std. grade, 28-inch Slugster barrel with rifle sights.

MODEL 500 AGVD

MODEL 500 SPECIFICATIONS:

Action—Positive slide-action. **Barrel**—12 or 20 gauge with free-floating vent. rib. ACCU-CHOKE interchangeable choke tubes. Chambered for 2¾-inch standard and Magnum and 3-inch Magnum shells. **Receiver**—Aluminum alloy, deep blue/black finish. Ordnance steel bolt locks in barrel extension for solid "steel-to-steel" lockup. **Capacity**—6-shot (one less when using 3-inch Magnum shells). Plug for 3-shot capacity included. **Safety**—Top tank, thumb-operated. Disconnecting trigger. **Stock & Forend**—Walnut-finished American hardwood with checkering. Both models with rubber recoil pad. **Standard Stock Dimensions**—14-inch length of pull; 2½-inch drop at heel; 1½-inch drop at comb. **Sights**—Metal bead front. **Overall Length**—48 inches with 28-inch barrel. **Weight**—12 ga. 7¼ lbs.; 20 ga. 6¾ lbs. (Varies slightly due to wood density.).

500 Hi-RIB TRAP

Model 500-AHTD 12 ga. 28-inch and 30-inch ACCU-CHOKE w/Imp., Mod., Mod. & Full choke tubes

Model 500-AHT 12 ga. 30-inch Full choke

500-COMBO PACK w/EXTRA SLUGSTER BAR

Model 500 AGVDX 12 ga. 28-inch ACCU-CHOKE, Vent. rib & 24-inch Slugster

500-VENT. RIB

Model 500ALDR 12 ga. w/Vent. Rib. 3 interchangeable choke tubes: full; modified; improved cylinder. Chambered for 2¾- and 3-inch factory loaded shells. Barrel length—28 inches. Overall length—48 inches. Weight—7¼ lbs.

Model 500CLDR 20 ga. Same as model 500ALDR. Weight—6¾ lbs.

MANUFACTURER DOES NOT LIST SUGGESTED RETAIL PRICES

MOSSBERG SHOTGUNS

LAW ENFORCEMENT SHOTGUNS:

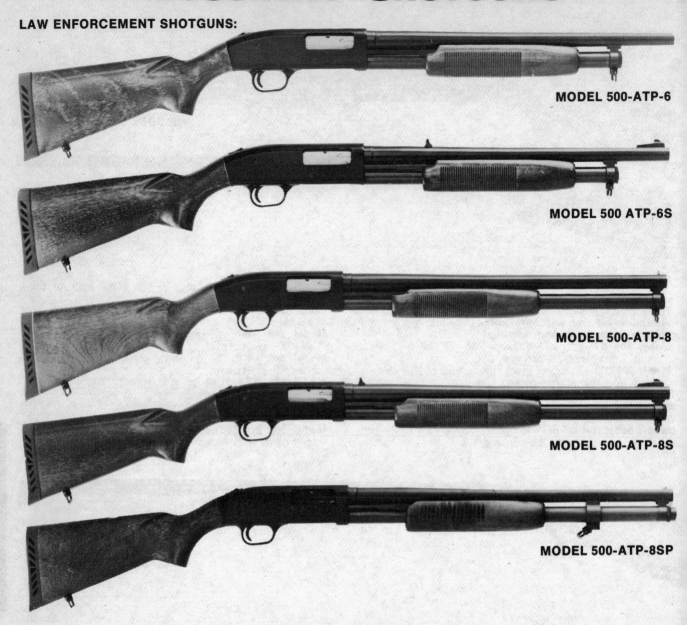

MODEL 500-ATP-6

MODEL 500 ATP-6S

MODEL 500-ATP-8

MODEL 500-ATP-8S

MODEL 500-ATP-8SP

Model 500 ATP-8 8-shot 20-inch barrel
Model 500 ATP-8S 8-shot 20-inch barrel w/sights

Special firepower, 12 gauge, 8-shot, pump-action shotgun in Cylinder Bore. 20-inch Barrel. Magazine tubes hold seven standard 2¾-inch shells, plus one in the chamber for 8-shot capacity (capacity is one less with 3-inch mag.). Lustre-deep bluing. Walnut stained stock and forearm. Deluxe recoil pad. Drilled and tapped for scope and factory installed sling swivels.

Model 500 ATP-6 6-shot 18½-inch barrel
Model 500 ATP-6S 6-shot 18½-inch barrel
Special 12 gauge, 6-shot pump-action shotgun in Cylinder

Bore. 18½-inch barrel. Magazine tube holds five standard 2¾-inch shells, plus one in the chamber for 6-shot capacity. (Capacity is one less with 3-inch mag.). Lustre-deep bluing. Walnut-stained stock and forearm. Deluxe recoil pad.

Model 500 ATP-8SP 8-shot 20-inch barrel Special Defense/Enforcement Shotgun

Special 12 gauge, 8-shot pump-action shotgun in Cylinder Bore Choke. 20-inch Barrel. Magazine tube holds seven standard 2¾-inch shells, plus one in the chamber (capacity is one less with 3-inch mag.) non-glare, military-style metal finish. Stock and forearm oil finished. Equipped with bayonet lug for U.S. M-7 Bayonet.

MANUFACTURER DOES NOT LIST SUGGESTED RETAIL PRICES

REMINGTON AUTOLOADING SHOTGUNS

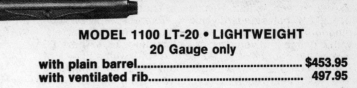

MODEL 1100 LT-20 • LIGHTWEIGHT
20 Gauge only

with plain barrel.. $453.95
with ventilated rib.. 497.95

Barrel length and choke combinations for the Model 1100 lightweight in 20 gauge; 28-inch full; 28-inch modified; and 26-inch improved Cylinder. Weight, 6½ pounds.

Model 1100 SA Skeet 20 gauge lightweight LT-20, with ventilated rib barrel. **$513.95**

MODEL 1100 • SMALL GAUGES
28 & .410 Gauges, 25-inch Barrel

with ventilated rib.. $509.95
SA Skeet Ventilated Rib,
   28 & .410 ga., 25-inch skeet bbl.................. 525.95
Tournament Skeet Vent. Rib............................. 620.95

The Remington Model 1100 Autoloading shotguns in 28 and .410 gauges are scaled-down models of the 12 gauge version. Built on its own receiver and frame, these small gauge shotguns are available in a wide selection of chokes with either plain or ventilated rib barrels. The .410 bore field grade will handle 2½-inch and 3-inch shotgun shells, while the .410 Skeet gun is supplied with a 2½-inch

chambered barrel. Extra barrels are interchangeable within gauge regardless of chamber length of original barrel. Bore .410 guns are designed for the exclusive use of plastic shells. The Model 1100 field grade 28 and .410 gauge guns are equipped with American walnut stocks and forends and feature a scratch resistant RK-W wood finish.

MODEL 1100 SPECIFICATIONS: STYLE—Gas-operated. 5 shot capacity with 28 ga. shells—4 shot capacity with 3-inch-410 ga. shells. 3 shot plug furnished. **BARREL**—Special Remington ordnance steel. Extra barrels interchangeable within gauge. **CHAMBER**—2½-inch in .410 ga. skeet; 3-inch in field grades; 2¾-inch in 28 ga. field and skeet models. **OVERALL LENGTH**—45½ inches. **SAFETY**—Convenient cross-bolt type. **RECEIVER**—Made from solid steel, top matted, scroll work on bolt and both sides of receiver. **STOCK DIMENSIONS**—walnut in .410, 28 ga., and 20 ga.—14 inches long, 2½-inch drop at heel, 1½-inch drop at comb. **AVERAGE WEIGHT**—28 ga. skeet-6¾ lbs.; .410 ga. skeet-7¼ lbs.; 28 ga. plain barrel-6¼ lbs.; .410 ga. plain barrel-6¾ lbs.; 28 ga. vent. rib-6½ lbs.; .410 ga. vent. rib-7 lbs.

MODEL 1100
28 & .410 GAUGES
BARREL LENGTH
& CHOKE COMBINATIONS

25-inch Full Choke
25-inch Modified Choke
25-inch Imp. Cyl. Choke

MODEL 1100 LT-20 LIMITED • LIGHTWEIGHT
20 Gauge only

with ventilated rib, 12½-inch stock,
23½-inch bbl. $497.95

The Model 1100 LT-20 Limited autoloading shotgun is the same as the Model 1100 except it is 4½ inches shorter overall.

REMINGTON AUTOLOADING SHOTGUNS

The Remington Model 1100 is a 5-shot gas operated autoloading shotgun with a gas metering system designed to reduce recoil-effect. This design enables the shooter to use all 2¾-inch standard velocity, "Express," and 2¾-inch magnum loads without any gun adjustments. Barrels, within gauge and versions, are interchangeable. The 1100 is made in gauges of 12, 20, 28 and .410, with a choice of different chokes, barrel lengths and gauge combinations. The solid-steel receiver features decorative scroll work. Stocks come with fine-line checkering in a fleur-de-lis design combined with American walnut and a scratch-resistant finish developed by Du Pont called RK-W. Features include decorative receiver scrolls, white-diamond inlay in pistol-grip cap, white-line spacers, full beavertail forend, fluted-comb cuts and chrome-plated bolt.

Model 1100 D Tournament with vent. rib barrel	**$2000.00**
Model 1100 F Premier vent. rib barrel	**4000.00**
Model 1100 F Premier with gold inlay	**6000.00**

MODEL 1100 FIELD GUN
12 Gauge

with plain barrel	**$453.95**
with ventilated rib	**497.95**
Model 1100 Special Field 12 & 20 gauge	**524.95**

REMINGTON MODEL 1100 LEFT HAND ACTION—12 GAUGE

MODEL 1100 LEFT HAND

A complete mirror image of the regular Model 1100, these left-hand shotguns put an end to the bothersome flying hulls that left-handed shooters had to face. Ejection is on the left side—all other specifications are the same as the regular Model 1100, 12 gauge. Left-hand Monte Carlo stock available on trap model.

Model	Barrel length, in.	Choke	Price
1100LH with Vent. Rib Barrel	30 28 26	Full Mod. I.C.	$528.95
1100LH Mag. with Vent. Rib Barrel	30	Full	$573.95
1100LH SA Skeet with Vent. Rib Barrel	26	Skeet	$544.95

Model	Barrel length, in.	Choke	Price
1100 LH TA Trap	30	Full	$555.95
1100 LH TA Trap Monte Carlo	30	Full	$565.95
Deer Gun with Rifle Sights	22	I.C.	$528.95

12 & Lightweight-20 Gauges
For 3-inch & 2¾-inch Magnum Shells Only

MODEL 1100 MAGNUM

with plain barrel	**$497.95**
with ventilated rib	**542.95**

Designed for 3-inch and 2¾-inch Magnum shells but accepts and functions with any 1100 standard 2¾-inch chambered barrel. Available in 12 gauge 30-inch full or 28-inch modified choke, plain or ventilated rib and 28-inch full or modified choke in 20 gauge, plain or ventilated rib barrels. Stock dimensions: 14 inches long including pad, 1½-inch drop at comb. Furnished with recoil pad. Weight: about 8 lbs.

MODEL 1100 DEER GUN
12 & Lightweight-20 Gauges

22-inch barrel, improved cylinder choke. Rifle sights adjustable for windage and elevation. Recoil pad. Weight: about 7¼ lbs. Choked for both rifled slugs and buck shot. **$497.95**

REMINGTON AUTOLOADING SHOTGUNS

**"THE MISSISSIPPI"
REMINGTON
MODEL 1100 MAGNUM
1983 D.U. EDITION**

$453.95

This special edition 12 gauge Model 1100 Magnum shotgun features a unique 32-inch full choke barrel and will be produced only in 1983. It is the second in a series of four guns, designed by Remington in cooperation with Ducks Unlimited and dedicated to each of the four major waterfowl flyways: The Atlantic, The Mississippi, The Central and The Pacific.

REMINGTON O&U SHOTGUNS

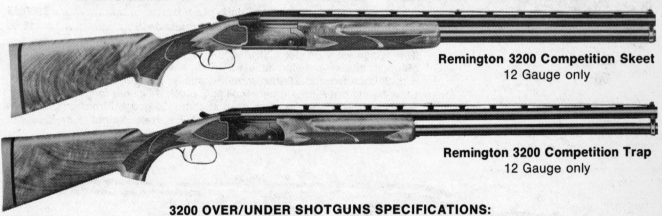

Remington 3200 Competition Skeet
12 Gauge only

Remington 3200 Competition Trap
12 Gauge only

3200 OVER/UNDER SHOTGUNS SPECIFICATIONS:

Stock and Forend: Specially selected fancy walnut stock and forend. (Special Trap select but not fancy grade.) Cut checkering, 20 lines to the inch. Full beavertail forend. Satin finish standard on Competition grade guns. Optional 1⅜ or 1½-inch drop on Monte Carlo stocks in Competition grade guns. All with recoil pad.
Frame: Machined steel with sliding top lock. Shield-covered breech. Hammers cock on opening. Sides richly embellished.

Ejection: Automatic. Fired shells eject on opening. Unfired shells remain in chamber but are raised above chamber level for easy manual extraction.
Safety and Barrel Selector: Combination manual safety and barrel selector mounted on top tang. Left for bottom barrel; right for top barrel; middle position for safety on.
Trigger: Single selective. 5/16 inches wide. Crisp with extra-fast lock time.
Sights: Ivory bead front, white-metal middle.

3200 Trap

Nominal Stock Dimensions: 14⅜ inches long. 2-inch drop at heel. 1½-inch drop at comb. 1⅜-inch drop at comb.
Overall Length: 48 inches with 30-inch barrels and recoil pad.
Average Weight: 8¼ lbs. for guns with 30-inch barrels.

3200 Skeet

Nominal Stock Dimensions: 14 inches long, 2⅛-inch drop at heel. 1½-inch drop at comb.
Over-all Length: Skeet—44¼ inches with 26-inch barrels. Competition Skeet—43 inches with 26-inch barrels.
Average Weight: 7¾ lbs. with 26-inch barrels.
3200 Skeet Gun Set Limited-Edition "Competition"
Contains the Model 3237, 12 ga., 28 in. barrel skeet gun with new small-gauge barrel set—20 ga., 28 ga. and .410 —complete in case.

3200 Models	Barrel Length	Type of Choke	Price
Competition Skeet	28 in.	Skeet & Skeet	$1925.00
	26 in.	Skeet & Skeet	1925.00
Competition Trap	32 in.	Imp. Modified & Full	1925.00
	30 in.	Full & Full	1925.00
	30 in.	Imp. Modified & Full	1925.00
Competition Trap with Monte Carlo Stock	32 in.	Imp. Modified & Full	1925.00
	32 in.	Imp. Modified & Full	1925.00
	30 in.	Full & Full	1925.00
	30 in.	Imp. Modified & Full	1925.00
	30 in.	Imp. Modified & Full	1925.00
Live Bird	28 in.	Imp. Modified & Full	1925.00
Skeet Set	28 in.	Skeet & Skeet	4950.00

REMINGTON PUMP SHOTGUNS

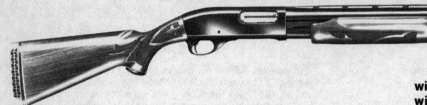

Shown with ventilated rib

STANDARD MODEL 870
12 & 20 Gauges
with plain barrel $342.95
with ventilated rib 386.95

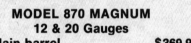

Shown with ventilated rib

MODEL 870 MAGNUM
12 & 20 Gauges
with plain barrel $369.95
with ventilated rib 413.95

The Wingmaster Model 870 Magnum is a 5 shot; chambered for 3-inch Magnum shells—will also handle 2¾-inch shells with 3-shot plug. 12 gauge with 30-inch full and 28-inch modified choke, plain or ventilated rib barrel. Steel-bead front sight, rubber recoil pad. Stock: 14 inches long including pad, 2½-inch drop at heel, 1⅝-inch drop at comb. 20 gauge furnished in 28-inch full or modified choke ventilated rib and plain barrels. Weight 12 gauge about 8 lbs., 20 gauge about 7 lbs.

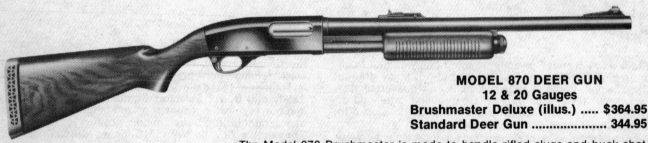

Shown with rifle sight barrel

MODEL 870 DEER GUN
12 & 20 Gauges
Brushmaster Deluxe (illus.) $364.95
Standard Deer Gun 344.95

The Model 870 Brushmaster is made to handle rifled slugs and buck shot. With 20-inch barrel and fully adjustable rifle-type sights. Stock fitted with rubber recoil pad and white-line spacer. Other specifications same as standard 870. Also available in standard model. Same as Deluxe Brushmaster above, but with lacquer finish; no checkering, recoil pad, grip cap; special handy short forend.

MODEL 870
12 & 20 GAUGE
BARREL LENGTH
& CHOKE COMBINATIONS

30 in.	**Full Choke**
28 in.	**Full Choke**
28 in.	**Modified Choke**
26 in.	**Imp. Cyl. Choke**
Deer Gun 20-inch Imp. Cyl.	

MODEL 870

SPECIFICATIONS: STYLE— 5-shot pump-action shotgun. Take down. 3-shot plug furnished. **GAUGES**—12 and 20. **BARREL**—Special Remington ordnance steel. Extra barrel is interchangeable within gauge: **OVERALL LENGTH**—48½ inches with 28-inch barrel. **SAFETY**— Convenient cross-bolt type, positive. **RECEIVER**—Made from solid steel, top matted. **STANDARD STOCK DIMENSIONS**— Stock and forend rich American walnut; beautiful checkering. 14 inches long, 2½-inch drop at heel 1⅝-inch drop at comb. Trap reg.—14⅜ inches long, 1⅞-inch drop at heel, 1½-inch drop at comb. Monte Carlo—14⅜ inches long, 1⅞-inch drop at heel, 1⅜-inch drop at comb, 1⅜-inch drop at M.C. **AVERAGE WEIGHT**—12 ga.-7 lbs.; 20 ga.-6½ lbs.

REMINGTON PUMP SHOTGUNS

MODEL 870 TA • Trap Gun 12 GAUGE ONLY

SPECIFICATIONS:

TA Trap Ventilated Rib 30-inch barrel Full	**$396.95**
TA Trap with Monte Carlo 30-inch barrel Full	**406.95**

REMINGTON MODEL 870 "COMPETITION" TRAP

The 870 "Competition" is a single-shot trap gun which features a unique gas-assisted recoil-reducing system, a completely new choke design, a high step-up ventilated rib and a redesigned stock and fore-end with cut checkering and a satin finish. Length of pull 14⅜ in., drop at heel 1⅞ in., drop at comb 1⅜ in. Weight 8½ lbs. Barrel 30 in. **$624.95**

MODEL 870 HIGH GRADE

D Tournament Ventilated Rib, all gauges and versions	**$2000.00**
F Premier Ventilated Rib, all gauges and versions	**4000.00**
F Premier Ventilated Rib with Gold Inlay, all gauges and versions	**6000.00**

MODEL 870 • 28 & .410 Gauges

These small gauges are scale models of the famous Model 870 "Wingmaster" in the larger gauges. Built on their own receiver and frame, they give the shooter unique handling and pointing characteristics. Beautiful fleur-de-lis fine-line checkering, white-line spacers at butt plate and grip cap, chrome plated bolt, and steel bead front sight are bonus features. American walnut stock and forend.

Model 870 with Vent. Rib Barrel

Barrel length in.	Choke	Price
25	Full	
25	Modified	**$398.95**
25	Imported Cylinder	

REMINGTON PUMP SHOTGUNS

MODEL 870 LEFT HAND • Field Gun "WINGMASTER" 12 and 20 Gauges

A complete mirror image of the regular Model 870, these left-hand shotguns put an end to the bothersome flying hulls that left-handed shooters had to face. Ejection is on the left side—all other specifications are the same as the regular Model 870, 12 and 20 gauge. Left-hand Monte Carlo stock available on trap model.

Model	Barrel length, in.	Choke	Price
870LH With Vent. Rib Barrel	30 28 26	Full Mod. I.C.	$412.95
870LH Mag. with Vent. Rib Barrel	30	Full	$439.95

STYLE	5-shot pump-action shotgun
GAUGES	12 and 20
BARREL	Special Remington proof steel. Extra barrels are interchangeable within version (reg. or left hand) and gauge without fitting.
OVER-ALL LENGTH	48½ inches with 28-inch barrel
SAFETY	Convenient positive cross-bolt type. Reversed on left hand models.
RECEIVER	Made from solid ordance quality steel, top matted
STANDARD STOCK DIMENSIONS	Stock and fore-end. Rich American walnut. Beautiful checkering. 14 inches long including recoil pad, 2½-inch drop at heel, 1⅝-drop at comb.
AVERAGE WEIGHT	20 ga.-6½ lbs.; 12 ga.-7 lbs.

MODEL 870 • 20 Gauge Lightweight (shown)
MODEL 870 • 20 Gauge Lightweight Magnum

20-Gauge Lightweight
20-Gauge Lightweight 3-inch Magnum

This is the pump action designed for the upland game hunter who wants enough power to stop fast flying game birds but light enough to be comfortable on all day hunting. The 20-gauge Lightweight handles all 20-gauge 2¾ in. shells. The magnum version handles all 20-gauge shells including the powerful 3 in. shells. American walnut stock and forend.

Model	Barrel length, in.	Choke	Price
870L.W. With Plain Barrel	28 28 26	Full Mod. I.C.	$342.95
870L.W. With Vent. Rib Barrel	28 28 26	Full Mod. I.C.	$386.95
870L.W. Mag. With Plain Barrel	28	Full	$369.95
870L.W. Mag. With Vent. Rib Barrel	28	Full	$413.95

REMINGTON TRAP & SKEET GUNS

BARREL LENGTH & CHOKE COMBINATIONS

26 in.	Rem. Skeet 12/20
25 in.	Rem. Skeet 28/410

Model 1100SA Skeet Gun is made in 12, 20, LT-20, 28 gauge and .410 bore. It comes with 26-inch barrel, skeet boring, ventilated rib, ivory bead front sight and white metal rear sight. Stock dimensions are 14 inches long, 2½-inch drop at heel, 1½-inch drop at comb. Weight, about 7½ lbs.

Model 1100 SA Skeet, with ventilated rib barrel... $513.95
Model 1100 Tournament Skeet 12 and LT-20 gauge..................................... 608.95
Model 1100 Tournament Skeet small bore version .410 and 28 gauge........... 620.95

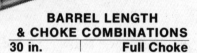

BARREL LENGTH & CHOKE COMBINATIONS

30 in.	Full Choke

Model 1100TA Trap Gun is made in 12 gauge only and is equipped with rubber recoil pad and ventilated rib barrel. Stock is of selected grade wood and features fine-line fleur-de-lis design checkering and white spacers on butt plate and grip cap. Forend has swept back design and fluting to give secure gripping area. Trap stock dimensions are: 14⅜ inches long including recoil pad, 1¾-inch drop at heel, 1⅜-inch drop at comb. Weight: about 8 lbs. Available in 30-inch full choke only. Ivory bead front sight, white metal rear sight. Also available with Monte Carlo stock $10.00 extra.

Model 1100 TA Trap, w/vent rib barrel...$524.95
Model 1100 TA Trap, w/vent rib & Monte Carlo Stock................................... 534.95
Model 1100 Tournament Trap 30-inch barrel Full... 619.95
Model 100 Tournament Trap 30-inch barrel Monte Carlo stock Full............... 629.95

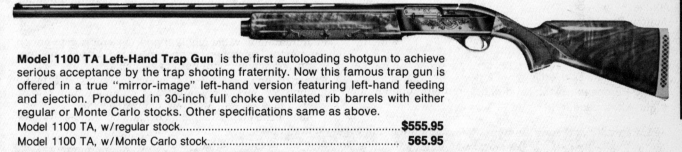

Model 1100 TA Left-Hand Trap Gun is the first autoloading shotgun to achieve serious acceptance by the trap shooting fraternity. Now this famous trap gun is offered in a true "mirror-image" left-hand version featuring left-hand feeding and ejection. Produced in 30-inch full choke ventilated rib barrels with either regular or Monte Carlo stocks. Other specifications same as above.

Model 1100 TA, w/regular stock..$555.95
Model 1100 TA, w/Monte Carlo stock.. 565.95

SPECIFICATIONS: STYLE—5 shot gas operated shotgun. 3 shot plug furnished. GAUGE—Made in 12 and 20 gauge. BARREL—Special Remington ordnance steel. Extra barrel is interchangeable within gauge. OVERALL LENGTH—48 inches (with 28-inch barrel). SAFETY—Convenient cross-bolt type. RECEIVER—Made from solid steel, top matted, scroll work on bolt and both sides of receiver. STANDARD STOCK DIMENSIONS—Stock and forend; rich American walnut. 14 inches long 2½-inch drop at heel, 1½-inch drop at comb. Trap reg., 14⅜ inches long, 1¾-inch drop at heel, 1⅜-inch drop at comb. Monte Carlo, 14⅜ inches long, 1¾-inch drop at heel, 1¼-inch drop at comb, 1¼-inch drop at M.C. AVERAGE WEIGHT—12 ga.-7½ lbs., 20 ga.-6½ lbs.

MODEL 1100 12 & LT-20 Gauges BARREL LENGTH & CHOKE COMBINATIONS

30 in.	Full Choke
28 in.	Full Choke
28 in.	Modified Choke
26 in.	Imp. Cyl. Choke

Note: 20 gauge model is not available in 30-inch barrel length.

ROSSI SHOTGUNS

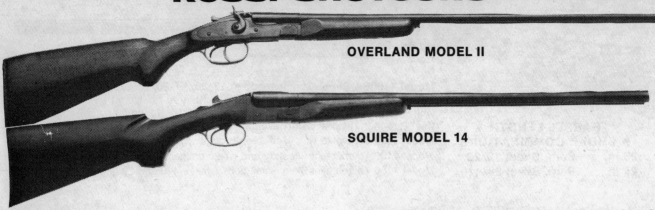

OVERLAND MODEL II

SQUIRE MODEL 14

OVERLAND MODEL II. Available in a .410 bore and 12 or 20 gauge for both standard 2¾-inch shells or 3-inch magnum. The 12 and 20 gauges are offered in the Coach Gun version with abbreviated 20-inch barrels with improved and modified chokes. Overlands feature a raised rib with matted sight surface, hardwood stocks, rounded semi-pistol grips, color case-hardened hammers, triggers and locking lever.

Gauge	Barrel Length	Choke	Price
12	20 in. 28 in.	IC&M M&F	$270.00
20	20 in. 26 in.	IC&M	270.00
.410	26 in.	F&F	285.00

SQUIRE MODEL 14. Available in 410 bore or 12 or 20 gauge, the Squire has 3-inch chambers to handle the full range of shotgun loads. Features double triggers, raised matted rib, beavertail forend and pistol grip. Twin underlugs mesh with synchronized sliding bolts for double-safe solid lockup.

Gauge	Barrel Length	Choke	Price
20	26 in.	IC&M	$285.00
.410	26 in.	F&F	300.00

ROTTWEIL SHOTGUNS

Rottweil Supreme Field Over/Under Shotgun

SPECIFICATIONS:

Gauge: 12 ga. only

Action: Boxlock

Barrel: 28-inch (Mod. & Full, Imp. Cyl. & Imp. Mod. & Full), vent rib.

Weight: 7¼ lbs.

Length: 47 inches overall

Stock: European walnut, hand-checkered and rubbed

Sight: Metal bead front

Features: Removable single trigger assembly with button selector; retracting spring mounted firing pins; engraved action. Extra barrels available.

Price: 28-inch Mod. & Full $2145.00
28-inch Imp. Cyl. & Imp. Mod. 2145.00
28-inch Live Pigeon, Mod. & Full, overall length 45½ inches 2145.00

SPECIFICATIONS:

Gauge: 12 ga.

Action: Boxlock, Skeet and Skeet choke

Barrel: 27-inch Skeet and Skeet, vent rib

Weight: 7½ lbs.

Length: 44½ inches overall

Stock: Selected European walnut, hand-checkered, modified forend

**Rottweil American Skeet
(designed for tube sets) $2395.00**

Sights: Plastic front housed in metallic sleeve with additional center bead.

Features: Interchangeable inertia-type trigger group. Receiver milled from solid block of special gun steel. Retracting firing pins are spring mounted. All coil springs. This was the first shotgun specially designed for tube sets.

ROTTWEIL SHOTGUNS

Rottweil Montreal Trap $2145.00

SPECIFICATIONS:
Gauge: 12 ga. only
Action: Boxlock
Barrel: 30-inch Imp. Mod. & Full
Weight: 8 lbs.
Length: 48½ inches overall

Stock: European walnut, hand-checkered
Sights: Metal bead front
Features: Inertia-type trigger, interchangeable for any system. Frame and lock milled from solid-steel block. Retracting firing pins are spring mounted. All coil springs. Selective single trigger. Action engraved. Extra barrels available.

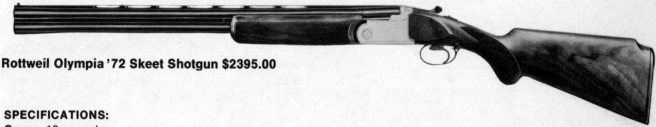

Rottweil Olympia '72 Skeet Shotgun $2395.00

SPECIFICATIONS:
Gauge: 12 ga. only
Action: Boxlock
Barrel: 27-inch (special skeet choke), vent. rib.
Weight: 7¼ lbs.
Length: 44½ inches overall
Stock: European walnut, hand-checkered, modified beavertail forend.

Sights: Metal bead front
Features: Inertia-type trigger, interchangeable for any system. Frame and lock milled from solid-steel block. Retracting firing pins are spring mounted. All coil springs. Selective single trigger. Action engraved. Extra barrels available.

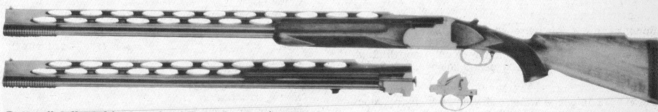

Rottweil Adjustable American Trap Combo $2795.00
single barrel only **2145.00**
double barrel only **2145.00**

SPECIFICATIONS:
Gauge: 12 ga.
Action: Rebounding lock, ejector
Barrels: Double barrel, 12 ga., length 32 inches, improved modified and full choke, exposed lower barrel, muzzle-collar-fitted
Weight: 8½ lbs.
Stock: European Walnut, hand-checkered and rubbed

Sights: Plastic front housed in mettalic sleeve with additional center bead
Features: The trap shooter adjusts the point of impact of the barrel with an L-wrench. Solid-block, special gun steel receiver. Recessed barrel-locking lugs. Interchangeable stocks, firing pins and bolts. Double-vented recoil pad. Sand-blasted receiver.

RUGER SHOTGUNS

RUGER OVER AND UNDER SHOTGUN
$798.00

Hardened 4140 chrome molybdenum and other alloy steels and music wire coil springs are used throughout the frame. Single selective trigger. Automatic top safety serves as the selector that determines which of the two barrels will be fired first. Standard gold bead front sight. Stock and semi-beavertail forearm are shaped from American walnut with hand cut checkering. Pistol grip cap and rubber recoil pad are standard and all wood surfaces are polished and weatherproof-sealed.

SPECIFICATIONS:

Gauge	20
Chambers	3 in.
Barrel Lengths	26 in., 28 in.
Overall Length (26 in. Barrels)	43 in.
Chokes . . . Skeet & Skeet, Improved Cylinder & Modified, Full & Modified	
Length of Pull	14 in.
Drop at Comb	1½ in.
Drop at Heel	2½ in.
Weight	Approximately 7 lbs.

SAVAGE & STEVENS SHOTGUNS

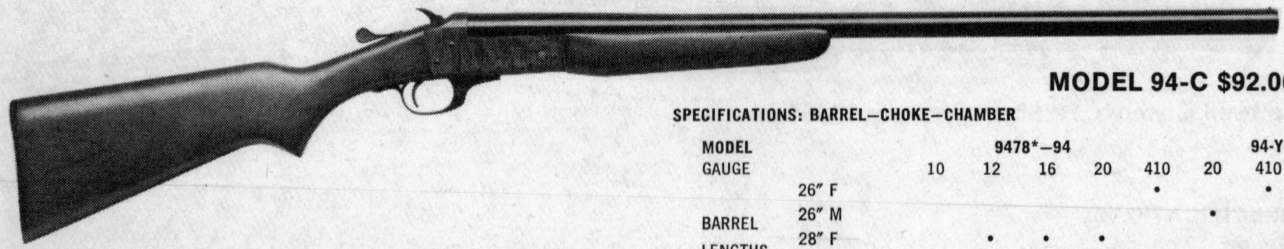

Stevens 94: Single barrel shotgun with hammer style action. Opening lever on top tang swings either way, automatic ejectors, checkered walnut finished hardwood stock and forend. Available with 36-inch "Long Tom" barrel in 12 gauge **$98.50**

94-Y Youth Model: 20 & .410 gauges, top lever opening. Has shooter stock with rubber recoil pad, 26-inch barrel. **$98.50**

Model 9478: A single barrel shotgun in 10, 12, 20, or .410 gauges. Features manual cocking, visible hammer, unbreakable coil springs. Automatic ejection and bottom-opening lever. Color, case-hardened finish **$84.50**

Model 9478 10 gauge Waterfowl: With 36-in. barrel, stock is fitted with rubber recoil pad, and grooved forend. **$116.50**

MODEL 94-C $92.00

SPECIFICATIONS: BARREL—CHOKE—CHAMBER

MODEL		9478*—94					94-Y	
GAUGE		10	12	16	20	410	20	410
BARREL LENGTHS & CHOKES	26" F					•		•
	26" M						•	
	28" F		•	•	•			
	30" F		•					
	32" F		•					
	36" F	•	•					
CHAMBERED FOR		2⅞" &3½"	2¾" &3"	2¾"	2¾" &3"	2½" &3"	2¾" &3"	2½" &3"
OVERALL LENGTHS	OVERALL		42"—52"				40½"	
LENGTH	TAKEN DOWN		26"—36"				26"	
	STOCK		14"				12½"	
DROP AT	COMB		1½"				1½"	
	HEEL		2½"				2½"	
AVERAGE WEIGHT (LBS.)		8½	6—6¼				5½	

*MODEL 9478 NOT AVAILABLE IN 16 GAUGE OR 12 GAUGE 32" F

FEATURES

MODEL	94-C—94-Y	9478—9478-Y
2-WAY TOP LEVER OPENING	•	
BOTTOM OPENING LEVER		•
AUTO EJECTOR	•	•
POSITIVE EXTRACTION	•	•
STOCK WAL. FIN. HARDWOOD	•	•
FOREND WAL. FIN. HARDWOOD	•	•

MODEL 24-V $225.50

24-V Combinations: 30-30 Win./20ga.; 222 Rem./20 ga.; 223 Rem./20 ga.; 357 Rem. Mag./20 ga.; 22 Hornet/20 ga. Takes regular 3-inch Magnum shells for small game, use a 20-gauge slug for larger game.

STEVENS & FOX SHOTGUNS

STEVENS MODEL 311
12, 20 & .410 Gauges
$229.50

This double barrel shotgun has many refinements usually found only in higher priced guns. It offers sturdy construction, solid lockup, excellent balance and superior shooting qualities. Three-inch Magnum available in 12 and 20 gauges.

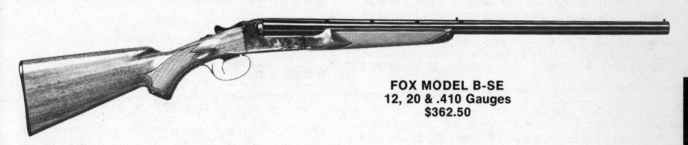

FOX MODEL B-SE
12, 20 & .410 Gauges
$362.50

Fox B-SE Gauges 12, 20 and .410. Automatic ejectors are standard equipment on the Fox B-SE. Other fine gun features are the single trigger and ventilated rib. The B-SE has the lines found only in a double gun, enriched with materials and finishes typical of expensive custom guns.

Its selected walnut stock has a deeply fluted comb and checkering on pistol grip. The gracefully tapered beavertail forend is also attractively checkered. The frame has color case hardened finish with decoration on bottom. Convenient top tang safety.

SPECIFICATIONS — FEATURES

MODEL	Vent Rib	Solid Rib	Bead Sights	Automatic Top Tang Safety	Extractors	Selective Ejectors	Trigger Single	Trigger Double	Frame Case Hardened	Frame Coil Springs	White Line Butt Plate	Average Weight (Lbs.)
B-SE	X		2	X		X	X		X	X		7–8
311		X	1	X	X			X	X	X	X	7¼–8

ALL MODELS Stock: Length 14"; drop 1½" at comb, 2½" at heel.
Length overall 41¾"-45", take down 26"-30". All Models proof tested.

SAVAGE RIFLE/SHOTGUNS

MODEL 24-D

MODEL 24 FIELD GRADE

24 Field Grade Combinations: 22 long rifle/20 or .410 gauge; 22 magnum/20. A combination gun at a field grade price makes this model an ideal first gun—combines the ever popular 22 cartridge with either of two popular shotgun gauges. Walnut finished hardwood stock and forend are coated with sturdy electro-cote. **$158.00**

24-C Campers Companion Combination: 22 long rifle/20 gauge. At 5¾ pounds, it's a pound lighter and five inches shorter than other 24's. When stored in special case, it measures just 5 in. x 22 in. The case has handles for carrying, thongs for tying to pack or saddle. Recess in stock holds extra shells. **$177.50**

24-D Deluxe Combinations: 22 long rifle/20 or .410 gauge; 22 magnum/20 gauge. A breech and separated barrels on this handsome deluxe model mean lighter weight and better balance. Two-way top opening lever swings either way for right- or left-hand use. The walnut stock and forend are protected for lasting beauty with electro-cote finish. The decorated receiver adds a final deluxe touch. This combination gun is ideal for small game, pests and varmints as well as plinking. A 20-gauge slug can be used for larger game; the 22 magnum adds extra power and range for bobcat, fox, turkey **$195.50**

MODEL	Caliber Gauge	Barrel 24 in. F	20 in. C	Chambered For
	223,20	X		2¾ in. & 3 in.
	357 Rem. Mag., 20	X		2¾ in. & 3 in.
	30-30, 20	X		2¾ in. & 3 in.
24-V	22 Hornet, 20	X		2¾ in. & 3 in.
	222, 20	X		2¾ in. & 3 in.
24-D	22 L.R., 20	X		2¾ in. & 3 in.
	22 L.R., 410	X		2½ in. & 3 in.
	22 Mag., 20	X		2¾ in. & 3 in.
24-F.G.	22 L.R., 20	X		2¾ in. & 3 in.
	22 L.R., 410	X		2½ in. & 3 in.
	22 Mag., 20	X		2¾ in. & 3 in.
24-C	22 L.R., 20		X	2¾ in.

F—Full   C—Cylinder

SPECIFICATIONS—FEATURES

MODELS	Barrels Length	Scope Mounting	Grooved For Scope	Sights Front	Sights Rear	Color Case Hardened Frame	Rebounding Hammer	Hammer Selector	Top Lever Opening	Takedown	Stock Select Walnut	Stock Walnut Finished Hardwood	Checkered Stock	Monte Carlo	White Line Butt Plate	White Line Grip Cap	Length Over-all	Avg. Wgt. (Lbs.)
24-V	24″	Tapped		Ramp	Folding Leaf	X	X	X	X	X	X			X			40″	6¾–7½
24-D	24″		X	Ramp	Sporting	X	X	X		X	X			X			40″	7½
24-F.G.	24″		X	Ramp	Sporting	X	X	X		X		X					40″	6½
24-C	20″		X	Ramp	Sporting	X	X	X		X		X					36½″	5¾

MODELS 24-V, 24-D Stock: Length 14″; drop 2″ at comb, 1¾″ at Monte Carlo, 2⅝″ at heel; taken down 24″.
24-C Stock: Length 14″; drop 1¾″ at comb, 2¾″ at heel; taken down 20″.
24-F.G. Stock: Length 14″; drop 1¾″ at comb, 2¾″ at heel; taken down 24″.

RATE OF TWIST (R.H.) 1 turn in 12″ for 30-30, 357 Mag.; 14″ for 222, 223; 16″ for 22 Mag., 22 L.R., 22 Hornet.

SHOTGUNS OF ULM

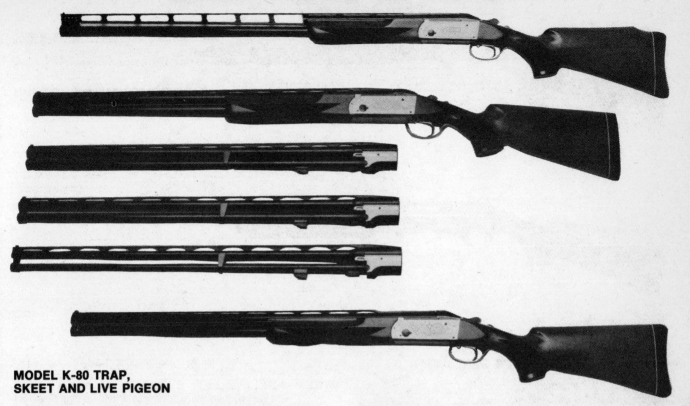

MODEL K-80 TRAP, SKEET AND LIVE PIGEON

BARRELS: Made of Boehler steel; free-floating bottom barrel with adjustable point of impact; standard rib is non-tapered 12mm wide. Tapered 12mm rib or straight rib available on special order. Trap, Skeet, Live Pigeon and International barrels all interchangeable.

RECEIVERS: Hard satin-nickel finish; blue finish available as special order

TRIGGERS: Wide profile, quick-set adjustable

EJECTORS: Selective automatic

SIGHTS: Strong metal front sight with insert and metal center bead

STOCKS: Hand-checkered and oil-finished select walnut stock and forearm; silver soldered metal-to-metal assemblies. Removable palm swell stocks available in five different engraving patterns.

MODEL	DESCRIPTION	BBL LENGTH	CHOKE	STANDARD	BAVARIA	DANUBE	GOLD TARGET	EXTRA BARRELS
TRAP:	(12 mm, Parallel step rib)							
	K-80 Over & Under	30 in. or 32 in.	IM/F	$3,380.	$5,500.	$ 6,860.	$8,870.	$ 995.
	K-80 Unsingle	32 in. or 34 in.	Full	3,990.	6,175.	7,555.	9,595.	1,855.
	K-80 Combo	30 in. + 32 in.						
		30 in. + 34 in.	IM/F+F	5,150.	7,215.	8,580.	11,000.	
		32 in. + 34 in.						
	OPTIONAL FEATURES							
	Tapered step rib (ea. barrel)	**$125.**						
	Single factory release	**150.**						
	Double factory release	**275.**						
SKEET:	K-80 4-Barrel Set	28 in. 12 ga.	Tula	$7,150.	$9,230.	$10,595.	$13,975.	$1,070.
	(8mm rib)	28 in. 20 ga.	Skeet					1,140.
		28 in. 28 ga.	Skeet					1,140.
		28 in. .410 ga.	Skeet					1,140.
	K-80 Lightweight	28 in. 12 ga.	Skeet	2,950.	5,100.	6,450.	8,450.	930.
	(8 mm rib)							
	K-80 International	28 in. 12 ga.	Tula	3,495.	5,580.	7,000.	9,000.	2,070.
	(12 mm rib)							
PIGEON:	(Standard: Tapered step rib)							
	K-80 Pigeon	28 in.	IM/SF	3,495.	5,580.	7,000.	9,000.	1,120.
		29 in.	IM/SF	"	"	"	"	"
		30 in.	IM/SF	"	"	"	"	"

ALL K-80's come cased. CUSTOM grade guns P.O.R.

SMITH & WESSON SHOTGUNS

MODEL 1000 AUTO SHOTGUN

MODEL 3000 PUMP SHOTGUN

MODEL 3000 PUMP SHOTGUN SPECIFICATIONS

STYLE: 5-Shot Pump Action
GAUGE: 12,20 (3-inch Chamber)
BARREL: Cold hammer forged Molybdenum Steel. Optional extra 22-inch Cylinder Bore Slug barrel with fully adjustable rifle sights.
RECEIVER: Machined steel
LENGTH: 48½ inches with 28-inch barrel
SAFETY: Cross Bolt safety. Interchangeable left or right hand.
STOCK: American walnut stock and forend; hand-cut checkering; hand-rubbed and lacquered finish. Length of Pull 14 inches, Drop at Comb 1⅜ inches, Drop at Heel 2¼ inches.
WEIGHT: 7 lbs. 7 oz. with 28-inch barrel
PRICE: For vent. rib **$378.95**; for slug gun **$347.95**. Extra barrel for vent. rib **$125.95**. Slug barrel **$102.95**. Multi-choke **$152.95**

26 in.	Improved Cylinder	with Plain or
28 in.	Modified	Vent. Rib and 3–in.
30 in.	Full	Chamber

MODEL 1000 SPECIFICATIONS

STYLE: 4-Shot (Plugged for 2 Shots) Autoloading gas-operated shotgun with pressure compensator and floating piston for light recoil
GAUGE: 12 and 20 2¾-inch Chamber and 3-inch Magnum Chamber
BARREL: Smith & Wesson Proof-Tested Chrome Molybdenum Steel
RECEIVER: Light Weight High Tensile Strength Alloy, Scroll Engraved both sides; 12 gauge 3-inch magnum has steel receiver.
LENGTH: 48 inches with 28-inch Barrel
SAFETY: Positive Cross-Bolt Type, Interchangeable left or right hand
STOCK: Selected American Walnut; Length of Pull 14 inches, Drop at Comb 1½ inches, Drop at Heel 2⅜ inches.
WEIGHT: 7½ lbs. with 28-inch barrel (12 gauge, 2¾-inch chamber); 6½ lbs. with 28-inch barrel (20 gauge, 2¾-inch chamber); 8 lbs. with 30-inch barrel (12 gauge, 3-inch chamber).
PRICE: 12 and 20 ga. w/vent. rib & 3-inch Magnum chamber **$511.95**.
12 and 20 ga., w/vent rib & 2¾-inch chamber **$469.95**.

26 in.	Skeet	with
26 in.	Improved Cylinder	Vent. Rib and 2¾-inch
28 in.	Modified	Chamber
28 in.	Full	
30 in.	Full	
30 in.	Modified	with Vent. Rib and 3-inch
30 in.	Full	Chamber

VALMET SHOTGUNS

412 K & 412 KE

The heart of the Valmet line, these O/U shotguns feature free interchangeability of barrels, stocks, and forearms into the 412 K and KE series in all gauges. Also features simple barrel positioning adjustment, two piece firing pin, monobloc locking shield for extra strength in protecting barrel shift, positive and automatic extraction models, top auto safety, trigger-located barrel selector and barrel indicators.

412 K Series Specifications (Extractor Model) Price: $749.00

Model	Gauge	Chamber	Barrel Length	Choke	Stock	Pad
40266	12	3	36	Full/Full	Monte Carlo	Recoil

412 KE Series Specifications (Automatic Ejection Model) 759.00

Model	Gauge	Chamber	Barrel Length	Choke	Stock	Pad
41261	12	2¾	26	Imp Cyl/Mod	Monte Carlo	Recoil
41282	12	2¾	28	Mod/Full	Monte Carlo	Recoil
41202	12	3	30	Mod/Full	Monte Carlo	Recoil
41061	20	3	26	Imp Cyl/Mod	Monte Carlo	Recoil
41082	20	3	28	Mod/Full	Monte Carlo	Recoil

412 KE Target Series

Trap

The 412 KE Trap confidently swings and molds to your shoulder to provide instant sighting with its centerline groove and wide broadway rib.

This piece has an American walnut trap stock that is combed for pure trap shooting.

The choice set of 30″ barrels are coldhammered of select chrome alloyed steel.

The trigger-located barrel selector offers the trap shooter distinct advantages and can be easily operated even when wearing gloves.

Skeet

The 412 KE Skeet is designed and crafted in American walnut. Its Monte Carlo style stock and drop characteristics are an integral part of the quick sight system which includes a centerline groove and wide broadway rib. Every time you snap this finely balanced piece to your shoulder, the twin beaded sights fall into place.

Valmet offers the non-automatic safety feature preferred by most trap and skeet shooters. However, if desired, its center screw can be loosened to provide automatic safety.

412 KE Target Series Specifications   Price: $ 754.00

Model	Gauge	Chamber	Barrel Length	Choke	Stock	Pad
Trap						
42204	12	2¾	30	Imp/Mod	Trap	Recoil
Skeet						
43265	12	2¾	26	C/IC	Skeet	Butt
43285	12	2¾	28	Sk/Sk	Skeet	Butt
43065	20	2¾	26	Sk/Sk	Skeet	Butt

412 K Combination Shotgun/Rifle

All of the fine quality features of the 412 Series apply to these models as well.

In addition to being durable these handsome barrels boast the deep blue lustre shared with all other Valmet guns.

Finnish craftsmanship and attention to detail—hand checkering, trigger located barrel selector, coldhammered barrels and high-gloss American walnut stock—make this gun a fine addition to any collection. 12 gauge barrel is chambered 3″ in all models.

Combination Shotgun/Rifle Specifications Price: $834.00

Model	Gauge	Calibre	Barrel Length	Choke	Stock	Pad
44222	12	.222	24	Imp Mod	Monte Carlo	Recoil
44223	12	.223	24	Imp Mod	Monte Carlo	Recoil
44243	12	.243	24	Imp Mod	Monte Carlo	Recoil
44308	12	.308	24	Imp Mod	Monte Carlo	Recoil
44306	12	30.06	24	Imp Mod	Monte Carlo	Recoil

SHOTGUNS

VENTURA SHOTGUNS

VENTURA MODEL 66/66 XXV-SL, SIDE BY SIDE DOUBLES

GAUGE: 12 ga. (2¾-inch), 20 ga. (3-inch), 28 ga. (2¾-inch)

ACTION: Holland and Holland sidelock, with double underlugs.

BARRELS: 25-inch, 27½-inch, 30-inch (12 gal. only), with chokes according to use.

FEATURES: Single selective trigger or double triggers, automatic ejectors, gas escape valves and intercepting safeties. Extensive hand-engraving and finishing. Can be made to customers' measurements. Options: Extra barrel sets, leather trunk cases, wood cleaning rods and brass snap caps.

PRICE: From .... $1260.00 to $1496.00

VENTURA MODEL 53/53 XXV-BL, SIDE BY SIDE DOUBLES

GAUGE: 12 ga. (2¾-inch), 20 ga. (3-inch) 28 ga. (2¾-inch), .410 ga. (3-inch)

ACTION: Anson and Deeley, with double underlugs.

BARRELS: 25-inch, 27½-inch, 30-inch (12 ga. only), with chokes according to use.

STOCK: Select French walnut, hand-checkered pistol grip stock with slender beavertail forend.

FEATURES: Single selective trigger or double triggers, automatic ejectors, hand-engraved scalloped frames. Options: leather trunk cases, wood cleaning rods and brass snap caps.

PRICE: From .... $776.00 to $976.00

VENTURA MODEL 51, SIDE BY SIDE DOUBLE

GAUGE: 12 ga. (2¾-inch), 20 ga. (3-inch)

ACTION: Anson and Deeley, with double underlugs.

BARRELS: 27½-inch, 30-inches (12 ga. only), with chokes according to use.

WEIGHT: With 27½-inch bbls., 12 ga. - 6½ lbs.; 20 ga. - 6 lbs.

STOCK: Select French walnut, hand-checkered pistol grip stock with slender beavertail forend.

FEATURES: Single selective trigger, automatic ejectors, hand-engraved action. Options: leather trunk cases, wood cleaning rods and brass snap caps.

PRICE: $724.00

WEATHERBY SHOTGUNS

WEATHERBY EIGHTY-TWO AUTOMATIC
12 GAUGE ONLY
Field Model $439.95   Trap Model $469.95
Multi-choke Models $459.95   Trap Grade $489.95

Buckmaster Slug Model $459.95

WEATHERBY NINETY-TWO PUMP
12 GAUGE ONLY
Field Model $399.95   Trap Model $429.95
Buckmaster Slug Model $419.95

WEATHERBY EIGHTY-TWO AUTOMATIC

Gas operated means no friction rings and collars to adjust for different loads. The barrel holds stationary instead of plunging backward with every shot.

To these natural advantages of the gas-operated, automatic, Weatherby has added revolutionary "Floating Piston" action. In the Weatherby Eighty-two, the piston "floats" freely on the magazine tube completely independent of every other part of the action. Nothing to get out of alignment. Nothing to cause drag or friction.

WEATHERBY NINETY-TWO PUMP

The super-fast slide action operates on double rails for precision and reliability. No twists, no binds, no hang-ups.

To remove a loaded round, push the gold-plated forearm release lever to its forward position. Now the forearm is unlocked and the action can be opened.

Also available in multi-choke barrels with two interchangeable choke tubes. (Pump auto only)

SPECIFICATIONS FOR
EIGHTY-TWO and NINETY-TWO SHOTGUNS

Gauges:	12 ga. only
Chamber length:	2¾" chamber and 3" Mag.
Barrel lengths & chokes:	30" Full 28" Mod 26" Imp Cyl 30" Full 3" Mag
	28" Full 26" Mod 26" Skeet 30" Full Trap

Stock dimensions	Field	Trap
Length of pull:	14¼"	14¾"
Drop at comb:	1⅜"	1⅜"
Drop at heel:	2¼"	1¾"

Approx. weight:	
Ninety-two pump shotguns:	30" bbl — 7 lb. 9 oz.
	28" bbl — 7 lb. 7 oz.
	26" bbl — 7 lb. 5¼ oz.
Eighty-two auto shotguns:	30" bbl — 7 lb. 11¾ oz.
	28" bbl — 7 lb. 10½ oz.
	26" bbl — 7 lb. 9¼ oz.
Safety:	Cross bolt type, right or left hand
Stock:	Figured American walnut, fine line hand checkering.
Interchangeable barrels:	Available in above lenghts and chokes.
Price of extra barrels:	Eighty-two—$164.95
	Ninety-two— 179.95

WEATHERBY ATHENA SHOTGUN

12 & 20 GA. FIELD	$1099.95
12 GA. TRAP	1109.95
12 & 20 GA. SKEET	1119.95

RECEIVER . . . The Athena receiver houses a strong, reliable box lock action, yet it features side lock type plates to carry through the fine floral engraving. The hinge pivots, are made of a special high strength steel alloy. The locking system employs the time-tested Greener cross-bolt design.

SINGLE SELECTIVE TRIGGER . . . It is mechanically rather than recoil operated. This provides a fully automatic switch-over, allowing the second barrel to be fired on a subsequent trigger pull, even in the event of a misfire.

The Athena trigger is selective as well. A flick of the trigger finger and the selector lever, located just in front of the trigger, is all the way to the left enabling you to fire the lower barrel first, or to the right for the upper barrel.

SELECTIVE AUTOMATIC EJECTORS . . . The Athena contains ejectors that are fully automatic both in selection and action. **SLIDE SAFETY** . . . The safety is the traditional slide type located conveniently on the upper tang on top of the pistol grip. **BARRELS** . . . The breech block is hand fitted to the receiver, providing closest possible tolerances. Every Athena is equipped with a matted, ventilated rib and bead front sight.

ATHENA SHOTGUN SPECIFICATIONS

	Field and Skeet Models		Trap Models
Gauges	12 ga.	20 ga.	12 ga. (20 ga. not avail.)
Chamber Length	3" chamber	3" chamber	2¾" chamber
Barrel Lengths & Chokes	26" M/IC. S/S	26" M/IC. S/S	30" F/F. F/IM. F/M
	28" F/M. M/IC. S/S	28" F/M M/IC. S/S	32" F/F. F/IM. F/M
	30" F/M		
Stock Dimensions			
Length of pull	14¼"	14¼"	14⅜"
Drop at comb	1½"	1½"	1⅜"
Drop at heel	2½"	2½"	1⅞"
Approx. Weight	26" 7 lbs. 3 oz.	26" 6 lbs. 11 oz.	30" 7 lbs. 12 oz.
	28" 7 lbs. 6 oz.	28" 6 lbs. 14 oz.	32" 8 lbs.
	30" 7 lbs. 9 oz.		

Safety on all models—Slide operated rear tang
Stock on all models—Select American Walnut

WEATHERBY SHOTGUNS

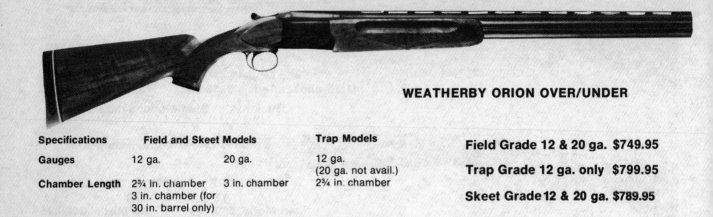

WEATHERBY ORION OVER/UNDER

Specifications	Field and Skeet Models		Trap Models
Gauges	12 ga.	20 ga.	12 ga. (20 ga. not avail.) 2¾ in. chamber
Chamber Length	2¾ in. chamber 3 in. chamber (for 30 in. barrel only)	3 in. chamber	
Barrel Lengths & Chokes	30 in. F/M 28 in. F/M, M/IC, S/S 26 in. M/IC, S/S	28 in. F/M, M/IC, S/S 26 in. F/M, M/IC, S/S	32 in. F/M, F/M 30 in. F/M, F/IM
Stock Dimensions			
Length of pull	14-13/16 in.	14 in.	14⅜ in.
Drop at Comb	1½ in.	1½ in.	1-7/16 in.
Drop at heel (Monte Carlo)*	2½ in.	2½ in.	1-15/16 in. 1-11/16 in.
Approx. Weight	28 in. 7 lbs. 12 oz. 26 in. 7 lbs. 8 oz.	28 in. 7 lbs. 1 oz. 26 in. 6 lbs. 14 oz.	30 in. 8 lbs.

Field Grade 12 & 20 ga. $749.95

Trap Grade 12 ga. only $799.95

Skeet Grade 12 & 20 ga. $789.95

Safety on all models—Tang thumb operated and combined with automatic barrel selector.

Stocks on all models—American Walnut.

*Trap models only.

WINCHESTER SHOTGUNS

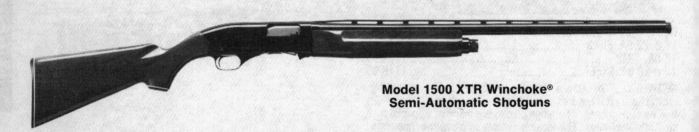

Model 1500 XTR Winchoke®
Semi-Automatic Shotguns

Model 1500 XTR shotguns combine all the advantages of the semi-automatic ... fast-shooting second and third shots with minimal recoil ... and the versatility of the Winchoke interchangeable choke system. The gas-operated action handles high or low brass loads interchangeably. Available in 12 and 20 gauge versions, these shotguns are chambered for 2¾-inch standard of 2¾-inch Magnum shotshells. The Model 1500 XTR is light weight, smooth swinging, fast pointing and highly reliable.

Winchester XTR styling points match its performance. The American walnut stock and forearm gleam with a protective high-luster finish. XTR deep-cut checkering adds up to great handling and handsome appearance. Finger grooves on the forearm, a black serrated butt plate, the nickel-plated carrier and engine-turned bolt are finish-ing touches. Metal surfaces are highly polished and deeply blued.

Model 1500 XTR shotguns come with a 28-inch ventilated rib or plain barrel specially adapted for the Winchoke system. The floating ventilated rib allows the barrel to expand independently, eliminating changes in point-of-impact due to heat during prolonged firing. Full, Modified and Improved Cylinder Winchoke tubes and wrench are furnished with the gun. Extra barrel and Winchoke options make the 1500 XTR even more versatile.

Other features include cross-bolt safety with red indicator, convenient push-button carrier release, and the unique front-locking, rotating bolt for ultimate single-unit strength and security.

WINCHESTER SHOTGUNS

Model 1300 XTR Winchoke
Slide Action Shotguns

The Model 1300 XTR is one of the fastest, surest slide action shotguns ever made. . .with perfected pump action, light weight and high strength. The Winchoke system and extra barrel options give this field gun unbeatable versatility. It is light carrying and lightning fast for superquick follow-up shots.

Available in 12 and 20 gauge, all Model 1300 XTR shotguns handle 3-inch Magnum, 2¾-inch Magnum, and standard 2¾-inch shotshells interchangeably. In combination with the Winchoke system, this capability increases the gun's all-around utility and eliminates the need to buy separate shotguns for different game. The 1300 XTR displays superb XTR styling features and finishes with fine cut checkering. The forearm is a shortened, contoured design promoting handling ease.

Twin action slide bars guide the action without binding. The 28-inch plain or ventilated rib barrel is specially adapted for the Winchoke system. The floating ventilated rib helps maintain correct point-of-impact, shot after shot. The front-locking, rotating bolt is ultra-strong and secure. Cross-bolt safety with red indicator, metal bead front sight, nickel-plated carrier, and rubber butt pad ... everything you want in a slide action shotgun is engineered into the 1300 XTR.

Model 1300 XTR Deer Gun is available in 12 gauge with 24⅛-inch barrel, rifle type sights, sling swivels and recoil pad.

Model 1300 XTR Waterfowl comes with a special 30-inch ventilated rib Winchoke barrel and three Winchoke tubes: Extra Full, Full and Modified. This 12-gauge shotgun is expressly designed for high-flying ducks and geese.

Model 1200 Defender, Police and
Marine Slide Action Security Shotguns

This trio of tough 12-gauge shotguns provides backup strength for security and police work as well as all-around utility. The Model 1200 action is one of the fastest second-shot pumps made. It features a front-locking rotating bolt for strength and secure, single-unit lock-up into the barrel. Twin action slide bars prevent binding.

All three guns are chambered for 3-inch shotshells. They handle 3-inch Magnum, 2¾-inch Magnum and standard 2¾-inch shotshells interchangeably. They have cross-bolt safety, walnut-finished hardwood stock and forearm, black rubber butt pad and plain 18-inch barrel with Cylinder Bore choke. All are ultra-reliable and easy handling.

Special chrome finishes on Police and Marine guns are actually triple-plated: first with copper for adherence, then with nickel for rust protection, and finally with chrome for a hard finish. This triple-plating assures durability and quality. Both guns have a forend cap with swivel to accommodate sling.

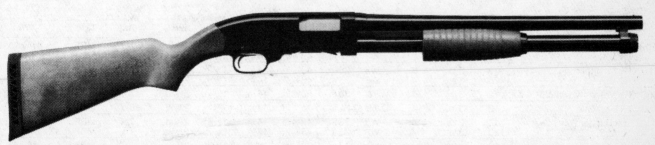

Model 1200 Defender™ is ideal for home security use. The compact 35⅝-inch overall length handles and stores easily. The Defender has a deep blued finish on metal surfaces and features a traditional ribbed forearm for sure pumping grip. It has a metal bead front sight. The magazine holds seven 12-gauge 2¾-inch shells.

Model 1200 Police™ is designed for police and security force work. It features an 18-inch ordnance stainless steel barrel and a satin chrome finish on all external metal parts. The distinctive satin chrome finish diffuses light and resists corrosion. The magazine has a capacity of six 2¾-inch shotshells, plus one shell in the chamber. Optional metal bead front sight or rifle-type front and rear sights.

WINCHESTER SHOTGUNS

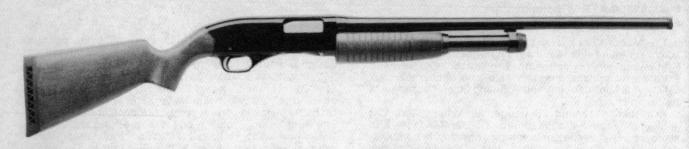

WINCHESTER RANGER YOUTH SLIDE ACTION SHOTGUN

Gauge: 20 gauge only, 3'' chamber, 5-shot magazine
Barrel: 22'' plain barrel, Winchoke (Full, Modified, Improved Cylinder)
Weight: 6½ lbs.
Length: 41⅝'' overall
Stock: Walnut-finished hardwood with ribbed fore-end

Sights: Metal Bead Front
Features: Cross-bolt safety, black rubber butt pad, twin action slide bars, front locking rotating bolt, removable segmented magazine plug to limit shotshell capacity for training purposes; discount certificate for full-size adult stock. Made under license by U.S. Repeating Arms Company.
Price: Plain barrel, Winchoke **$179.95**
Price: Plain barrel, Modified **164.95**

WINCHESTER RANGER SEMI-AUTOMATIC SHOTGUN

Gauge: 12 and 20, 2¾'' Chamber, 3 Shot Magazine
Barrel: 28'' Vent Rib with Full, Modified and Improved Cylinder Winchoke Tubes . . . or . . . 28'' Plain Barrel Modified
Weight: 7 to 7¼ pounds
Length: 48⅝'' overall

Stock: Walnut-finished hardwood with ribbed fore-end
Sights: Metal Bead Front
Features: Cross-bolt safety, front-locking rotating bolt, black serrated butt plate, gas-operated action. Made under License by U.S. Repeating Arms Company.
Price: Vent Rib with Winchoke **$279.95**
Price: Plain Barrel **259.95**

Shotguns Model	Gauge	Chamber	Magazine Capacity(a)	Choke	Barrel Length	Overall Length	Nominal Length of Pull	Nominal Drop at Comb	Nominal Drop at Heel	Nominal Weight (lbs.)	Sights	Price
1500XTR Winchoke	12	2¾ in.	2	W3	28 in.	48⅝ in.	14 in.	1½ in.	2½ in.	7¼	MBF	$449.95
with V.R.	20	2¾ in.	2	W3	28 in.	48⅝ in.	14 in.	1½ in.	2½ in.	7¼	MBF	
1300 XTR Winchoke	12	3 in.	4	W3	28 in.	48⅝ in.	14 in.	1½ in.	2½ in.	7¼	MBF	359.95
with V.R.	20	3 in.	4	W3	28 in.	48⅝ in.	14 in.	1½ in.	2½ in.	7¼	MBF	
1300 XTR Waterfowl with V.R.	12	3 in.	4	W3W	30 in.	50⅝ in.	14 in.	1½ in.	2½ in.	7½	MBF	359.95
1300 XTR Deer Gun	12	3 in.	4	Cyl.B	24⅛ in.	44¾ in.	14 in.	1½ in.	2⅜ in.	6½	RT	339.95
Winchester Ranger Winchoke	12	3 in.	4	W3	28 in.	48⅝ in.	14 in.	1½ in.	2½ in.	7¼	MBF	279.95
with V.R.	20	3 in.	4	W3	28 in.	48⅝ in.	14 in.	1½ in.	2½ in.	7¼	MBF	
1200 Defender	12	3 in.	7(b)	Cyl.B	18 in.	38⅝ in.	14 in.	1½ in.	2½ in.	7	MBF	189.95
Stainless Police	12	3 in.	6(b)	Cyl.B	18 in.	38⅝ in.	14 in.	1½ in.	2½ in.	7	MBFO or RT	339.95 354.95
Stainless Marine	12	3 in.	6(b)	Cyl.B	18 in.	38⅝ in.	14 in.	1½ in.	2½ in.	7	RT	354.95

(a) For additional capacity, add one shotshell in chamber when ready to fire. V.R. - Ventilated Rib MBF - Metal Bead Front Cyl.B - Cylinder Bore RT - Rifle Type Front and Rear O Optional W3 - Comes with Winchoke set including Full, Modified and Improved Cylinder tubes with wrench. W3W Comes with Winchoke Set including Extra Full, Full and Modified tubes with wrench. Models 1300 XTR and Ranger by Winchester have factory-installed magazine plug which limits capacity to two shells.
(b) One less for 3-inch shells.

Paramilitary

AKM

STEYR
AKM
SEMI-AUTOMATIC RIFLE

THE AKM (SEMI-AUTOMATIC)
(KALASHNIKOV)

No automatic rifle has created more interest or curiosity among collectors and shooters for its rigid reliability and versatility as the AKM, which came upon the international firearms scene thirty years ago. Admired by designers as well as astute military authorities for its ease of operation, simplicity of design and absolute reliability.

No automatic rifle has ever been made in such great quantities as the AKM - more than thirty million have been manufactured since its concept. It is now being manufactured commercially in this semi-automatic version. It fires the reliable 7.62x39mm workhorse cartridge.

The AKM is one of the only weapons in the entire world that will function under the most adverse environmental conditions found anywhere in the world from steaming jungle to blistering deserts to the Arctic circle.

SPECIFICATIONS

Caliber: 7.62x39mm
Overall Length: 34.65 inches
Barrel Length: 16.33 inches
Rifling: 4 grooves, right-hand twist

Weight: 6.4 lbs.
Sights: Front: Protected post **Rear:** U-notch, zero to 1000m
Maximum Range: 1500 meters
Magazine Capacity: 30 rounds (where permitted)
Extra Accessories include: military sling, oiler, extra magazine, cleaning kit and bayonet with scabbard.

Maadi AKM	Price:
Semi-Automatic Rifle	$ 995.00
Caliber: 7.62x39mm	
AKM Accessories:	
30-round magazine	29.55
Cleaning kit	25.00
Sling	15.00

AUG

STEYR AUG
SEMI-AUTOMATIC RIFLE
5.56mm (.223 Rem.)

The AUG round is the hard-hitting .223 Remington, and the quickly detachable magazine holds 30 rounds. A 1.5-power optical sight, with both windage and elevation settings, forms the carrying grip above the receiver. You'll find no cosmetic frills, no unneeded extras. If it doesn't serve a useful purpose, it isn't on the AUG.

Versatility is the AUG's middle name. For right-handed or left-handed shooters, the bolt is replaceable and the cartridge ejector port may be moved to either side. For carrying purposes, the rear sling swivel is movable from side to side, as well.

Field stripping is hardly ever necessary, except for routine cleaning. When it is necessary, the AUG breaks down into only six integral components—all in a matter of seconds.

The AUG's unique transparent magazine never leaves any doubt as to the number of rounds you have left. Because of its gas blowback system of operation, recoil is kept to a minimum. In addition, the rock-solid vertical grips and the sturdy stock make the AUG an unusually firm-shooting gun.

You'd be wise to investigate the versatility and the advantages of the AUG. It can truly be said without exaggeration that no finer semi-automatic rifle is available anywhere today.

AUG

SPECIFICATIONS

Type: Compact semi-automatic rifle, with interchangeable barrel systems

Caliber: 5.56mm (.223 Rem.)

Magazine Capacity: 30 rounds; 40 rounds (optional)

Action: Gas-operated. Gas-pressure adapter (with shut-off valve on the barrel) with two action settings for firing under normal and adverse weather conditions

Stock: Synthetic, green. One-piece molding houses receiver group, hammer mechanism and magazine

Hammer Mechanism: Synthetic (except for wire springs and steel bearing pins)

Magazine: Detachable. Synthetic (transparent) staggered magazine feeds from below

Safety: Lateral push-through type locks trigger movement

Bolt: Fixed locking turnbolt type, with eight locking lugs

Barrel Groups: Interchangeable; 16-, 20- and 24-inch, with gas pressure adapter and swing/pivot type barrel grip. Cold hammer-forged. Chrome-lined bores. Barrel locks into receiver body by rotating it one-eighth turn

Rifling: Six lands and grooves, right-hand twist, one turn in 9 inches

Weight (Empty): w/16 in. bbl.: 7.2 lbs.; w/20 in. bbl.; 7.9 lbs.; w/24 in. bbl.; 8.6 lbs.

Magazine Weight (Empty): 5 ozs.

Overall Length: w/16 in. bbl., 27 in.; w/20 in. bbl., 31 in.; w/24 in. bbl., 35 in.

Overall Height: 11 inches

STEYR AUG

Semi-Automatic Rifle w/std. 20-in. bbl.	1175.00
Caliber: 5.56mm (.223 Rem.)	
AUG Accessories:	
30-round magazine	24.50
40-round magazine	34.25
16-in. or 20-in. barrel	185.00
24-in. barrel w/telescopic bi-pod	425.00
Left-handed bolt	75.00
Sling	14.00

AUTO - ORDNANCE

**THOMPSON
MODEL 27A-1
SEMI-AUTOMATIC
STANDARD**

Auto Ordnance Corporation is proud to re-introduce their famous Model 27 A-1 semi-automatic version of the Thompson Machine Gun. Great attention has been paid even to the finest detail, including the original roll stampings and the famous Thompson bullet logo. The only major change is that the barrel has been increased from the original 11¼ inches without compensator attached, to 16 inches. Although the Model 27 A-1 captures all of the nostalgia of the famous family of Thompson Guns (of which 2½ million have been sold), the internal mechanism has been adapted so that the gun does not have automatic firing capability. Over a year has been spent on this feature, with many prototypes being discarded because of their automaic adaptability. However, this final version is, and can only be, a semi-automatic .45 caliber rifle.

STANDARD

The Standard Model features the same careful attention to pride and craftsmanship and is manufactured from solid milled steel, same as our Deluxe Model. Actually, the differences are in appearance, not operation. The Standard Model has a plain barrel with standard military sights without the compensator. It also has a standard military forearm made popular by the famous WWII version carried by allied forces all over the world. There is a deep rich blue on all metal parts, which is complemented by the rich walnut stocks and handgrips. It will be supplied with a 30-shot magazine. All of the available accessories which include a complete selection of magazines, XL drum and the deluxe forearm stock will also fit this Standard Model.

**MODEL
27A-3
22 Caliber**

AUTO-ORDNANCE

**THOMPSON
MODEL 27A-1
SEMI-AUTOMATIC
DELUXE**

DELUXE

The Deluxe Model features a vertical foregrip, finned barrel, deluxe rear sight and a compensator. There is a deep rich blue on all metal parts which is complemented by the rich walnut stocks and handgrips. It will be supplied with a 30-shot magazine and pistol grip front stock. Additional accessories which include a complete selection of magazines, XL drum magazine and forearm stocks are available.

**THOMPSON
MODEL 27A-1
SEMI-AUTOMATIC PISTOL**

THOMPSON MODEL 27A-1 SEMI-AUTOMATIC PISTOL

Auto Ordnance has re-designed the famous Model 1928 A into a lightweight semi-automatic handgun. The pistol actually duplicates the famous 28 configuration without a detachable stock. It features the use of some lightweight space age alloys making for great shooting balance with a weight of under seven pounds. The overall length is 26 inches with a precision-rifled and finned 13 inch barrel. It is in the very popular .45 caliber and will accept all the additional accessories that can be used in our ever so famous Model 27 A-1 such as our XL drum and the 5-shot, 15-shot, 20-shot and 30-shot magazines. A limited production gun destined to be of extreme historical significance.

THE NEW LIGHTWEIGHT

By popular demand, Auto Ordnance announces a new lightweight version of the .45 cal. 27 A-1 Deluxe. This is the same gun as the Deluxe Model, only it's about 20% lighter! Manufactured in a lightweight alloy that decreases the weight, but not the performance. Comes supplied with a 30-shot magazine.

T1	1927A1 Thompson Deluxe Semi-Automatic Carbine .45 Cal.	**$498.50**
T2	1927A1 Thompson Standard Semi-Automatic Carbine .45 Cal.	**479.95**
T3	1927A5 Thompson Pistol Semi-Automatic .45 Cal.	**469.95**
T4	1927A3 Thompson Semi-Automatic Carbine .22 Cal.	**449.95**
T5	1927A1C New Lightweight Thompson Semi-Automatic Deluxe .45 Cal.	**489.95**
T6	Transportation Case	**79.95**
T7	Thompson Hard Case	**129.75**
T8	Horizontal Foregrip	**8.95**
T9	Vertical Foregrip	**14.95**
T10	5-, 15- & 20-Shot Magazines .45 Cal.	**9.75**
T11	30-Shot Magazine .45 Cal.	**11.50**
T12	XL Drum Magazine .45 Cal.	**69.95**
T13	Web Set w/3 pocket 30 rd. pouch	**33.95**
	a) belt alone	**15.50**
	b) Drum pouch alone	**9.95**
	c) 30 rd. clip pouch	**11.45**
T14	1923 & 1936 Catalogs (Per Set)	**3.50**
T15	Cleaning Rod .45 Cal.	**4.95**

COLT RIFLES

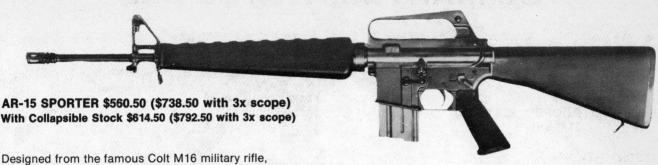

AR-15 SPORTER $560.50 ($738.50 with 3x scope)
With Collapsible Stock $614.50 ($792.50 with 3x scope)

Designed from the famous Colt M16 military rifle,
the Colt AR-15 is lightweight, with simple maintenance,
easy handling and extreme accuracy. Semiautomatic 223
(5.56 mm) with 5-round magazine capacity. Front sight post adjustable
for elevation. Quick flip rear sight assembly with short-range and long-range
tangs, adjustable for windage. Weight: 7½ lbs. Overall Length: 39 inches
Barrel Length: 20 inches; with collapsible stock 16 inches

FABRIQUE NATIONALE
SEMI AUTOMATIC RIFLES

F.N.-LAR COMPETITION (308 MATCH)
$1659.00

The F.N.-LAR Competition 308 Win. Match gas-operated
semiautomatic has a rifled bore with 4-lands and
grooves, plus right-hand twist, one turn in 12 inches. The
rear sight is adjustable from 200 to 600 yards in 100 yard
increments. Sight radius is 21¾ inches. Synthetic stock
with ventilated forend. **Weight** (without magazine): 9 lbs.
7 oz. **Overall Length:** 44½ inches. **Barrel Length:** 21
inches (24½ inches with flash hider).

F.N.-LAR PARATROPPER (308 MATCH)
$1754.00

F.N.-LAR H.B. (Heavy Barrel) (308 MATCH)
With wood stock & metal bipod $2198.00
With synthetic stock $2030.00

FABRIQUE NATIONALE SEMIAUTOMATIC RIFLES

FNC PARATROOPER (223 REM.)
$1438.40

SPECIFICATIONS:
Caliber: 223 Rem. (5.56mm)
Capacity: 30-round magazine
Action: Gas-operated, semiautomatic
Barrel Length: 18 inches
Weight: 9.61 lbs. with magazine
Rifling: 6 lands and grooves with right-hand twist

HECKLER & KOCH SEMIAUTOMATIC RIFLES

HK93 SEMIAUTOMATIC RIFLE
223 Caliber

HK93 SPECIFICATIONS:	A-2	A-3
Length of rifle:	37.0 in.	29.92 in.
Length of barrel:	16.14 in.	16.14 in.
Sight radius:	19.09 in.	19.09 in.
Weight of rifle without magazine:	7.94 lbs.	8.60 lbs.
Weight of 40 round magazine, empty:	11 oz.	
Weight of 25 round magazine, empty:	8.84 oz.	

Weight of 5-round magazine, empty:	2.11 oz.
Sight adjustments:	200, 300, 400 m and V-notch rear
Telescopic sight mount:	HK clamp mount ($180.00)

Model HK93 (w/25-round magazine & sling) $640.00
With retractable metal stock 699.00

HK91 SEMIAUTOMATIC RIFLES
308 Caliber

HK91 SPECIFICATIONS:	A-2	A-3
Length of rifle:	40.35 in.	33.07 in.
Length of barrel:	17.71 in.	17.71 in.
Sight radius:	22.44 in.	22.44 in.
Weight of rifle without magazine:	9.70 lbs.	10.56 lbs.
Weight of 20 round magazine, empty:	9.88 oz.	

Weight of 5-round magazine, empty	3.17 oz.
Sight adjustments:	200, 300, 400mm and V-notch rear
Telescopic sight mount	HK clamp mount ($180.00)

Model HK91 (w/20-round magazine & sling) $640.00
With retractable metal stock 699.00

IVER JOHNSON CARBINES

PLAINFIELD MODEL M-1 CARBINES
PM 30P $260.00
PM 30 PS (stainless steel) $330.00

Sights: Adjustable
Finish: Blue
Stock: Telescoping American walnut permits packing in backpack or saddlebag for campers and hunters
PM 30G & PM 30S, new military and military sporter versions of PM 30P **$221.76**

SPECIFICATIONS:
Caliber: 30
Weight: 5½ lbs.
Magazine: 15 and 30 rounds
Barrel Lengths: 12 inches and 18 inches

PP 30 SUPER ENFORCER $260.00
PP 30S (stainless steel) $320.00

SPECIFICATIONS:
Caliber: 30
Weight: 4 lbs.
Magazine: 15 and 30 rounds
Action: Based on carbine action
Barrel Length: 9½ inches
Sights: Adjustable
Stock: American walnut

MODEL PM30G M1 CARBINE $235.00
PM5.7 230.00
SPECIFICATIONS:
Caliber: 30 U.S. Carbine or 5.7mm
Weights: unloaded 15 round mag, 5.50 lbs.
  loaded 15 round mag with sling, 6.10 lbs.
  unloaded 30 round mag, 5.53 lbs.
  loaded 30 round mag with sling, 6.60 lbs.

Lengths: overall, 35.6 in., with bayonet, 42.3 in.
Barrel: length, 18 in., normal chamber PSI, 40,000 lbs.
Trigger pull: minimum, 5 lbs., maximum, 7 lbs.
Range: effective, 300 yds. +, maximum, 2,200 yds.
Muzzle velocity: 1970 FPS
Stock: American Walnut

SPRINGFIELD ARMORY

Prices not set

M1 Garand Standard Model

Also available:
National Match Model
Ultra-Match Model

SPECIFICATIONS:
Gas-operated, semiautomatic, clip-fed. **Grade:** Standard "Issue-Grade" w/walnut stock. **Caliber:** 30M2 (30-06) and 308 (7.62mm) **Weight:** 9 lbs. 8 ozs. **Barrel Length:** 24 inches. **Overall Length:** 43½ inches. **Magazine Capacity:** 8 rounds. **Stock Dimensions:** Length of pull, 13 inches; drop at comb, 2 inches; drop at heel, 2½ inches. **Sights:** Front, military square blade; rear, full click-adjustable aperture.

M1A Standard Model

Also available:
National Match Model
Super Match Model
M1A-A1 Assault Model

SPECIFICATIONS:
Gas-operated, semiautomatic, clip-loaded, detachable box magazine. **Caliber:** 7.62mm NATO (308 Winchester). **Weight:** 9 lbs., 14 oz. **Barrel Length:** 19-7/16 inches. **Overall Length:** 43-11/16 inches. **Magazine Capacity:** 20 rounds. **Sights:** Military; square blade front; full-click adjustable aperture rear. **Sight Radius:** 21⅜ inches. **Accessories:** Combination muzzle brakeflash suppressor-grenade launcher; bipod, grenade launcher-winter trigger, grenade launcher sight, bayonet, field oiling & cleaning equipment.

BN58 Standard Ital Model

Also available:
Ital-Alpine Model
Alpine Paratrooper Model
Nigerian Mark IV Model

SPECIFICATIONS:
Gas-operated, semiautomatic, clip-loaded, detachable box magazine. **Grade:** Standard "Issue-Grade" w/walnut stock. **Caliber:** 7.62 mm. NATO (308 Winchester). **Weight:** 8 lbs. 15 ozs. **Barrel Length:** 25-1/16 inches w/flash suppressor. **Overall Length:** 44¼ inches. **Magazine Capacity:** 20 rounds. **Stock Dimensions:** Length of pull, 13¼ inches; drop at comb, 2⅜ inches; drop at heel, 2¾ inches. **Sights:** Military; square blade front; full click-adjustable aperture rear. **Sight Radius:** 26-1/16 inches. **Accessories:** 1 magazine.

UZI
SEMIAUTOMATIC CARBINES

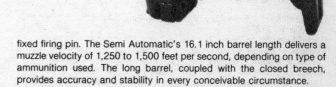

UZI SEMIAUTOMATIC CARBINE

A masterful adaptation of the internationally acclaimed UZI 9mm submachine gun, the UZI Semi Automatic Carbine is now being distributed throughout the United States.

It is providing collectors, sportsmen and gun enthusiasts of every description with understandable pride in owning one of the finest firearms ever manufactured. And it is also providing them with an unprecedented sense of security with the knowledge that their UZI is one of the safest, simplest and surest semiautomatics available in the world today.

First introduced in 1954, the UZI submachine gun established standards of precision and perfection that resulted in its unrivaled reputation.

Designed by Col. Uzi Gal (Ret.), an officer of the Israeli Army, the UZI won fame in Israel's historic six-day war. It soon became the choice of the NATO alliance and was adopted for use in armies of major western and third world countries. It is also used extensively by security personnel protecting leaders of the free world. The UZI has earned lavish praise in the pages of such authoritative publications as *Small Arms of the World, Jane's Small Arms, The World's Submachine Guns,* and many others.

Everywhere the judgement is the same: the UZI is the finest submachine gun ever designed.

Action Arms' UZI Semi Automatic Carbine, designed by Col. Uzi Gal, incorporates modifications of his submachine gun so that it meets the requirements of U.S. Federal regulations.

In appearance the UZI Semi Automatic is virtually identical to the submachine gun, except for a longer barrel. A principal difference between the two is that the Semi Automatic works from a closed breech with floating firing pin while the submachine gun has an open breech with

fixed firing pin. The Semi Automatic's 16.1 inch barrel length delivers a muzzle velocity of 1,250 to 1,500 feet per second, depending on type of ammunition used. The long barrel, coupled with the closed breech, provides accuracy and stability in every conceivable circumstance.

This is UZI. An authentic small-arms masterpiece. A gun that you can fire accurately and dependably every time.

The UZI owner quickly recognizes the outstanding qualities of his semiautomatic: stability, safety, compactness, reliability, a center of gravity that provides excellent balance and comfortable handling, ease of cleaning and maintenance. An extremely low recoil and perfect balance permit accurate firepower even when held in only one hand.

The UZI Semi Automatic is manufactured by Israel Military Industries, as is the submachine gun. Each Semi-Automatic is subjected to IMI's rigid inspection procedures–the most stringent in the industry. Each is 100% tested. It is this strict adherence to UZI standards of design and manufacture which make the UZI a pleasure to own and use.

UZI CARRYING CASE
(at left)

- **UZI SEMIAUTOMATIC**
- **Three or 32-round magazines**
- **Front Sight Adjustment Tool**
- **Magazine Loading & Unloading Tool**

UZI SWAT CASE

- **UZI SEMIAUTOMATIC**
- **Three 25- or 32-round magazines**

UZI
SEMIAUTOMATIC CARBINES

Type: Semi Automatic Carbine
Designation: UZI
Manufacturer: Israel Military Industries
Caliber: 9mm Parabellum
Operation Principle: Blowback, closed breech with floating firing pin
Type of Fire: Semi-automatic only
Magazine: Staggered box type holding 25 or 32 rounds
Safety Systems: (1.) Fire selector in position "S" (2.) Pistol grip safety
Sights: Front: "Post" type **Rear:** L flip type adjustable for 100m (330 ft) and 200m (660 ft)
Stock: Folding metal stock
Weight: Empty Magazine: 25 round-200 g (7.0 oz); 32 round-220 g (7.8 oz)
Length: (Metal stock folded) 620mm (24.4 in); (Metal stock extended) 800mm (31.5 in)
Barrel Length: 410mm (16.1 in)
Number of Lands & Grooves: 4–(Right hand twist) 1 turn in 10 inches
*__Approx. Muzzle Velocity:__ 380-460 m/sec (1250-1500 ft/sec)
*__Maximum Range:__ Up to 2000m (2200 yd) at 30° elevation
*Depending upon type of ammunition used. Specifications subject to change without notice

UZI SEMIAUTOMATIC CARBINE ....**$ 627.00**
MODEL A 9mm
INCLUDING: Molded Styrofoam Case, 25 Round Magazine, Carrying Sling, 16.1 inch Barrel, Short Display Barrel, Detailed Owner's Manual.

ACCESSORIES

1720000	32 Round Magazine	$ 30.00
1710000	25 Round Magazine	$ 22.00

1931200	Magazine Loading Tool	$ 20.00
1950910	Magazine Clip	$ 2.25
1940800	Front Sight Adjustment Tool	$ 24.00
1927000	Carry Sling	$ 18.00
2009125	Display Barrel	$ 13.00
9311000	Bayonet	$ 88.00
9720000	Spotting Light	$140.00
2009002	Pouch for 3 - 25 Round Magazines ..	$ 16.00
2009001	Pouch for 2 - 25 Round Magazines ..	$ 14.25
2009006	Pouch for 3 - 32 Round Magazines ..	$ 18.50
2009005	Pouch for 2 - 32 Round Magazines ..	$ 16.50
0940500	Wood Stock	$ 87.50
2009100	Carrying Case	$ 34.50
2009105	Swat Case	$ 34.50
2009115	Scope Mount	$ 70.00

VALMET
SEMIAUTOMATIC RIFLES

M76 with wooden stock

VALMET M76
SEMIAUTOMATIC RIFLE

Based on their famous assult rifle, Valmet offers this Finnish-made semiautomatic version with a choice of either the wooden or folding-steel stock.

The M76 is a lightweight infantry-based .223 caliber weapon built to withstand rough handling, high firing loads, and all kinds of terrain and climate. It can be field-stripped without tools.

The weapon is gas-operated and automatically ejects spent cartridges. The firing rate is 20 to 30 rounds per minute.

External moving parts, besides the trigger and bolt, include the cocking handle and the selector lever, both on the right side.

M76 with folding steel stock

The rear leaf peep-sight has a range adjustment and, when flipped forward, becomes a night sight with a luminous dot on either side of a V-notch. The adjustable front tunnel-guard post sight also turns to convert to a night sight with a luminous aiming dot.

The M76 is equipped with sling loops, a bayonet mount on the flash suppressor, a 15-round magazine, and comes with a cleaning kit. An optional adapter cover, to replace the standard leaf-sight cover, is available to accept any one-inch scope.

	Price
M76 with wooden stock	$686.00
M76 with folding stock	873.00
15-round .223 magazine	26.00
30-round .223 magazine	31.00
Knife bayonet	64.00
Bayonet scabbard	**Sold as set only**
Extra cleaning kit	21.00
Scope adapter cover	54.00

Black Powder Guns

COLT

1847 WALKER

SPECIFICATIONS:
Caliber: 44
Barrel: 9 inches, 7 groove, right-hand twist
Weight: 73 oz.
Cylinder: 6 chambers, 1 safety lock pin, scene of soldiers fighting Indians.
Sight: German silver
Finish: Color case-hardened frame, hammer, loading lever and plunger. Blue barrel, cylinder, backstrap, trigger and wedge. Polished-brass trigger guard and oil finish grip.
Price: $449.50

1ST MODEL DRAGOON

SPECIFICATIONS:
Caliber: 44
Barrel: 7½ inches, part round, part octagonal, 7 grooves, left-hand twist
Weight: 66 oz.
Cylinder: 6 Chambers, ranger-Indian scene
Sights: German silver
Finish: Color case-hardened frame, loading lever, plunger; blue barrel, cylinder, trigger and wedge. Polished-brass backstrap and trigger guard; one-piece oil finish walnut stocks.
Price: 1st, 2nd and 3rd Model Dragoons **$447.95** each.

BABY DRAGOON

SPECIFICATIONS:
Caliber: 31
Barrel: 4 inches, 7 groove, right-hand twist
Cylinder: 5-shot unfluted, straight with ranger and Indian scene, oval bolt cuts
Sight: Brass pin
Finish: Color case-hardened frame and hammer, blue barrel, trigger, wedge, cylinder and screws; silver backstrap and trigger guard and varnished grips.
Price: $324.50

1862 POCKET POLICE

SPECIFICATIONS:
Caliber: 36
Barrel: 5½ inches round, 7 groove, left-hand twist
Weight: 25 oz.
Cylinder: 5 chambers, rebated, fluted

Sights: Brass front
Finish: Color case-hardened frame, hammer, loading lever, plunger and latch. Blue barrel, wedge, cylinder, trigger and screws. Silver-plated trigger guard and backstrap. Varnished one-piece walnut grips.
Price: $315.50

COLT

1851 NAVY REVOLVER

SPECIFICATIONS:
Caliber: 36
Barrel: 7½ inches, 7 groove, left-hand twist
Weight: 42 oz.
Cylinder: 6 chambers with Naval scene
Sights: Brass front sight
Finish: Color case-hardened frame, loading lever, plunger, hammer and latch. Blue cylinder, trigger, barrel, screws and wedge. Silver-plated trigger guard and backstrap.
Price: $335.95

1861 NAVY REVOLVER

SPECIFICATIONS:
Same as 1851 Navy Revolver except:
Sights: German silver front
Price: $335.95

1860 ARMY REVOLVER

SPECIFICATIONS:
Caliber: 44
Barrel: 8 inches, 7 groove, left-hand twist
Overall Length: 13¾ inches
Weight: 42 oz.
Sights: German silver; radius—10½ inches
Finish: Colt blue, color case-hardened frame, hammer loading lever, plunger; one-piece walnut grip.
Price: $344.50
　　　364.50 (fluted)

COLT

1862 POCKET NAVY REVOLVER

SPECIFICATIONS:
Caliber: 36
Barrel: 5½ inches, octagonal, 7 groove, left-hand twist
Weight: 27 oz.

Cylinder: 5 chambers, round-rebated with stagecoach scene, 1-3/16 inches overall, rebated 9/16 inch
Sights: Brass pin front
Finish: Color case-hardened frame, hammer loading lever, plunger and latch; blue barrel, wedge, cylinder, trigger guard and backstrap. Varnished one-piece walnut grips.
Price: $315.50

CVA

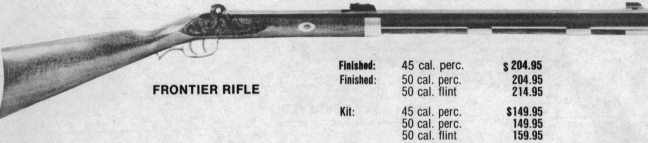

FRONTIER RIFLE

Finished:	45 cal. perc.	$ 204.95
Finished:	50 cal. perc.	204.95
	50 cal. flint	214.95
Kit:	45 cal. perc.	$149.95
	50 cal. perc.	149.95
	50 cal. flint	159.95

Stock: Select hardwood.
Triggers: Double set will fire set and unset.
Sights: Brass blade front sight; fully adjustable, open hunting-style rear.
Finish: Blue steel; brass wedge plates; brass nose cap; trigger guard and butt plate.
Accessories: Stainless steel nipple, hardwood ramrod with brass tips, cleaning jag; kits available.
Price: $315.50

Lock: Color case-hardened, engraved percussion-style, bridle with fly and tumbler; screw-adjustable, sear engagement; authentic V-type mainspring.
Barrel: 28 inches octagon, 15/16 inch across the flats; barrel tenon, hooked breech, round brass thimbles, deep-grooved.
Overall Length: 44 inches.
Caliber: 45 and 50 percussion and 50 cal. flint.
Weight: 6 lbs. 14 oz.

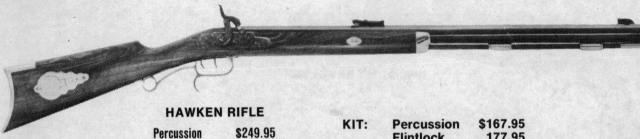

HAWKEN RIFLE

Percussion	$249.95
Flintlock	259.95

KIT:	Percussion	$167.95
	Flintlock	177.95

Caliber: 50 and 54 percussion or flintlock.
Ignition: Color case-hardened; bridle, fly, screw adjustable sear engagement and authentic V-type mainspring; two lock screws.
Barrel: 28 inches octagon rifled one turn in 66 inches; 1 inch across the flats, barrel tenon, hooked breech.
Overall Length: 44 inches
Weight: 7 lbs. 15 oz.

Finish: Solid brass patchbox, wedge plates, nose cap, ramrod thimbles, trigger guard and butt plate; blued steel finish.
Triggers: Double set, with fire set and unset; fully adjustable for trigger pull.
Sights: Dovetail, beaded blade front sight; fully adjustable, dovetail; open hunting rear sight.
Stock: Select walnut with fully formed beavertail cheekpiece.
Accessories: Stainless steel nipple or flash hole liner; hardwood ramrod with brass tips and cleaning jag; kits available.

CVA

KENTUCKY RIFLE   **Percussion**   **$184.95**
                         Flintlock   194.95

Ignition: Engraved color case hardened V-type mainspring.
Caliber: 45 percussion or flintlock.
Barrel: 33½ inches, rifled, octagon.
Overall Length: 48 inches.

Weight: 7 lbs. 4 oz.
Finish: Deep-luster blue, polished brass hardware.
Sights: Kentucky-style front and rear.
Stock: Dark, walnut tone.
Accessories: Brass-tipped, hardwood ramrod, stainless steel nipple; kits available.

KENTUCKY RIFLE KIT: **Percussion**   **$109.95**
                                   Flintlock   117.95

MOUNTAIN RIFLE   **Percussion**   **$284.95**
                           Flintlock   294.95

Ignition: Engraved percussion color case-hardened lock with adjustable sear engagement, fly and bridle, authentic V-type mainspring.
Caliber: 45 and 50 percussion or flintlock.
Barrel: 32 inches, custom rifled, octagon, 15/16 inches across the flats, hooked breech with two barrel tenons.
Overall Length: 48 inches.

Weight: 7 lbs. 14 oz.
Finish: Brown steel, German silver patch box and wedge plates, pewter-type nose cap.
Triggers: Double set, will fire both set and unset.
Sights: German silver blade front, screw adjustable dovetail rear.
Stock: Select hardwood with fully formed cheekpiece.
Accessories: Stainless steel nipple, hardwood ramrod, cleaning jag; kits available.

MOUNTAIN RIFLE KIT: **Percussion**   **$189.95**
                               Flintlock   199.95

"BIG BORE" MOUNTAIN RIFLE $294.95

Overall Length: 48 inches
Weight: 8 lbs. 2 oz.
Triggers: Double set, will fire set and unset.
Stock: Select hardwood with fully-formed cheekpiece.
Sights: German silver front sight; screw-adjustable dovetail rear.
Finish: Rich browned steel and wedge plates; authentic pewter-type nose cap.
Accessories: Stainless-steel nipple; hardwood ramrod with brass-tips; cleaning jag.

Big Bore Mountain Rifle Kit $209.95

Caliber: 54 and 58 percussion in kit only.
Lock: Color case-hardened, engraved percussion and flint lock style; adjustable sear engagement; bridle and fly in tumbler; authentic V-type mainspring.
Barrel: 32 inches octagon; 1 inch across the flats; hooked breech with two barrel tenons; 54 caliber is rifled 1 turn 66 inches for patch ball accuracy; 58 caliber is rifled 1 turn in 72 inches. Authentic round thimbles; especially smooth rifling for fast break-in.

CVA

MOUNTAIN PISTOL

MOUNTAIN PISTOL $124.95

Ignition: Engraved percussion color case-hardened lock with adjustable sear engagement, fly and bridle.
Caliber: 45 or 50 percussion kit and 50 cal. perc. finish only.
Barrel: 9 inches octagon, 15/16 inch across the flats, hooked breech, custom rifling.
Overall Length: 14 inches.
Weight: 40 oz.
Finish: Brown steel, German silver wedge plates.
Trigger: Early style.
Sights: German silver blade front, fixed primitive rear.
Stock: American maple.
Accessories: Stainless steel nipple, hardwood ramrod, belt hook optional; kits available.

MOUNTAIN PISTOL KIT: $109.95

KENTUCKY PISTOL $89.95

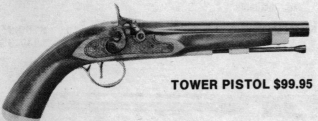

TOWER PISTOL $99.95

Ignition: Engraved lock, screw adjustable sear engagement, V-type mainspring.
Caliber: 45 (451 bore) percussion.
Barrel: 9 inches, octagon at breech, tapers to round at muzzle.
Overall Length: 15¼ inches
Weight: 36 oz.
Finish: Case-hardened lock, blued barrel, brass hardware.
Stock: Dark-grained walnut tone.
Accessories: Steel ramrod, stainless steel nipple; kits available for percussion and flintlock.

TOWER PISTOL KIT:		
	Percussion	$69.95
	Flint	79.95

Ignition: Engraved percussion lock on finished pistol, adjustable sear.
Caliber: 45 (451 bore) percussion.
Barrel: 10¼ inches, rifled, octagon.
Overall Length: 15¼ inches.
Weight: 40 oz.
Finish: Case-hardened lock, blued barrel, brass hardware.
Sights: Dovetailed Kentucky front and rear.
Accessories: Brass-tipped, hardwood ramrod; kits available for percussion and flintlock.

KENTUCKY PISTOL KIT:		
	Percussion	$59.95
	Flint	69.95

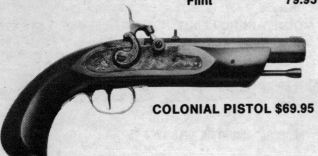

COLONIAL PISTOL $69.95

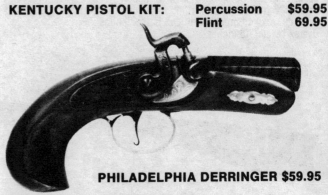

PHILADELPHIA DERRINGER $59.95

Ignition: Engraved lock.
Caliber: 45 (451 bore) percussion.
Barrel: 6¾ inches, rifled, octagon.
Overall Length: 12¾ inches
Weight: 31 oz.
Finish: Case-hardened lock, blued barrel, brass hardware.
Sights: Dovetail rear, brass blade front.
Stock: Dark, walnut tone.
Accessories: Steel ramrod, stainless steel nipple; kits available for percussion and flintlock.

COLONIAL PISTOL KIT:		
	Percussion	$49.95
	Flint	59.95

Ignition: Percussion, coil-spring back-action lock.
Caliber: 45 percussion.
Barrel: 3¼ inches, rifled.
Overall Length: 7⅛ inches.
Weight: 16 oz.
Finish: Case hardened with brass hardware, blued barrel.
Stock: Walnut toned.
Accessories: Stainless steel nipple; kit available.

PHILADELPHIA DERRINGER KIT $39.95

CVA

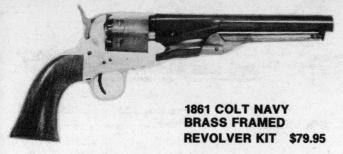

**1861 COLT NAVY
BRASS FRAMED
REVOLVER KIT $79.95**

1861 COLT NAVY
BRASS FRAMED REVOLVER $99.95

Caliber: 44
Barrel: 7½-inch rounded; creeping style.
Weight: 44 oz.
Cylinder: 6-shot, engraved.
Sights: Blade front; Hammer notch rear.
Finish: Solid brass frame, trigger guard and backstrap; blued barrel and cylinder.
Grip: One-piece walnut

**1851 COLT NAVY
REVOLVER KIT $78.95**

1851 COLT NAVY
REVOLVER $97.95

Caliber: 36
Barrel: 7½-inch octagonal; hinged-style loading lever
Length: 13 inch overall
Weight: 44 oz.
Cylinder: 6-shot, engraved
Sights: Post front; hammer notch rear.
Grip: One-piece walnut.
Finish: Solid brass frame, trigger guard and backtrap; blued barrel and cylinder; color case-hardened loading lever and hammer.

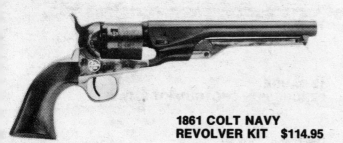

**1861 COLT NAVY
REVOLVER KIT $114.95**

1861 COLT NAVY
REVOLVER $155.95

Caliber: 36
Barrel: 7½-inch rounded; creeping style loading lever
Length: 13 inch overall.
Weight: 44 oz.
Cylinder: 6-shot, engraved
Sights: Blade front; hammer notch rear.
Grip: One-piece walnut.
Finish: Solid brass trigger guard and backstrap; blued barrel and cylinder; color case-hardened loading lever, hammer and frame.

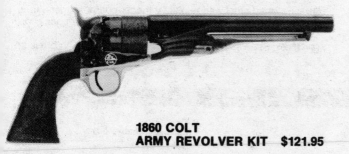

**1860 COLT
ARMY REVOLVER KIT $121.95**

1860 COLT
ARMY REVOLVER $157.95

Caliber: 44
Length: 13½-inch overall.
Weight: 44 oz.
Cylinder: 6-shot, engraved and rebated.
Sights: Blade front; hammer notch rear.
Grip: One-piece walnut
Finish: Solid brass trigger guard; blued barrel and cylinder with color case-hardened loading lever, hammer and frame.

**1858 REMINGTON
ARMY REVOLVER KIT $123.95**

1858 REMINGTON
ARMY REVOLVER $163.95

Caliber: 44
Barrel: 8 inch octagonal.
Length: 13½-inch overall.
Weight: 38 oz.
Cylinder: 6-shot
Sights: Blade front; groove rear.
Grip: Two-piece walnut.
Finish: Solid brass trigger guard; blued barrel, cylinder; frame and loading lever and hammer color case-hardened.

CVA

Percussion.............................. $149.95

SQUIRREL RIFLE KIT Flintlock................................ 159.95

Barrel: 25'' octagonal, 11/16'' across flats, hooked breech for easy take down and cleaning; Rifling, one turn in 48'', eight lands, deep grooves. Blued steel.
Length: 40¾'' overall
Weight: 5 lbs. 12 oz.
Trigger: Double set (will fire set or unset).
Front Sight: Dovetail, beaded blade
Rear Sight: Fully adjustable, open hunting-style dovetail
Finish: Solid brass butt plate, trigger guard, wedge plates and thimbles
Accessories: Stainless steel nipple or flash hole liner; aluminum ramrod with brass tips, cleaning jag

Percussion.. $207.95

SQUIRREL RIFLE Flintlock.. 217.95

Ignition: Color case-hardened and engraved lockplate. Internal features: bridle, fly, screw-adjustable sear engagement authentic v-type mainspring.
Caliber: 32 percussion or flintlock.
Stock: Select hardwood

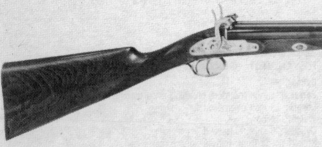

12 GAUGE PERCUSSION SHOTGUN $279.95

Ignition: Polished steel and engraved lock plate. Internal features: bridle, fly, screw-adjustable sear engagement, authentic v-type mainspring.
Gauge: 12
Stock: Select hardwood, checkered. (Kits not checkered.)
Barrel: 28'' round, double barrel, smoothbore. Blued steel.

12 GAUGE
PERCUSSION SHOTGUN KIT $219.95

Length: 44¼'' overall
Weight: 6 lbs. 10 oz.
Triggers: Double
Front Sight: Brass bead
Finish: Polished steel wedge plates, trigger guard, triggers, tang, lock and hammers. Lock, hammers, tang and trigger guard engraved.
Accessories: Stainless steel nipple, wooden ramrod with brass tip

(Flintlock Illustrated)

Percussion..... $279.95

PENNSYLVANIA LONG RIFLE KIT Flintlock........ 289.95

Length: 55¾'' overall
Weight: 8 lbs. 3 oz.
Trigger: Double set (will fire set or unset).
Rear Sight: Fixed semi-buckhorn, dovetail
Finish: Brass butt plate, patchbox, trigger guard, thimbles and nose cap
Accessories: Stainless steel nipple or flash hole liner; hardwood ramrod and brass tips

Percussion.............. $349.95

PENNSYLVANIA LONG RIFLE Flintlock.................. 359.95

Ignition: Color case-hardened and engraved lockplate. Internal features: bridle, fly, screw-adjustable sear engagement authentic v-type mainspring.
Caliber: 50 percussion or flintlock.
Stock: Select walnut
Barrel: 40'' octagonal, ⅞'' across flats; Rifling eight lands, deep grooves

DIXIE

DIXIE NAVY REVOLVER
Plain Model $78.95
Engraved Model   92.50

This 36-caliber revolver was a favorite of the officers of the Civil War. Although called a navy type, it is somewhat misnamed since many more of the army personnel used it. Made in Italy. Use .376 mold or ball to fit. Use number 11 caps. Blued steel barrel and cylinder with brass frame.

SPILLER & BURR 36 CALIBER BRASS FRAME REVOLVER
$79.95

The 36 caliber octagon barrel on this revolver is 7 inches long. The cylinder chambers mike .378. The cylinder is a six shot and the hammer engages a slot between the nipples on the cylinder as an added safety device. It has a solid brass trigger guard and frame with backstrap cast integral with the frame, two-piece walnut grips and Whitney-type case-hardened loading lever.

DIXIE KENTUCKY PISTOL
$89.95

This is the first reproduction black powder pistol and an authentic replica of a typical Kentucky pistol. Features Kentucky-type rifling and sights, brass furniture, dark cherry-stained maple stocks. Barrel length: 9 inches, 13/16 inch across the flats. Caliber: 45. Recommended ball size: .445.

THE TROPHY WINNER 44 SINGLE SHOT PISTOL
$125.00

The Trophy Winner 44 has a smooth bore shotgun pistol barrel that will interchange with the rifle barrel that is on the pistol. The gun is equipped with a 10-inch blued octagon barrel and has 7 grooves and 7 lands of equal width. Groove to groove diameter mikes .445, land to land diameter mikes .442. It has a fixed ramp front sight and adjustable rear sight. Overall length 12¾ inches. Weight 42 oz.
SHOTGUN PISTOL BARREL: 28-gauge blued octagon smooth bore barrel, 10 inches long, brass front sight.
.... **$19.95**

DIXIE 1860 ARMY REVOLVER
$130.00

The Dixie 1860 Army has a half-fluted cylinder and its chamber diameter is .447. Use .451 round ball mold to fit this 8-inch barrel revolver. Cut for shoulder stock.

"WYATT EARP" REVOLVER
$85.00

12-inch octagon rifled barrel; cylinder is rebated and is 44 caliber. Highly polished brass frame, backstrap and trigger guard. The barrel and cylinder have a deep blue lustre finish. Hammer, trigger, and loading lever are case-hardened. Walnut grips. Recommended ball size is .451.

Shoulder stock for Dixie's "Wyatt Earp" Revolver .. **$45.00**

DIXIE

**DW-105
WALKER REVOLVER**

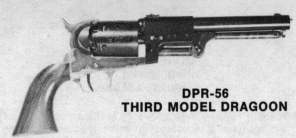

**DPR-56
THIRD MODEL DRAGOON**

DSB-58 SCREW BARREL DERRINGER
$69.95

Overall length 6½ inches; unique loading system; sheath trigger, color case-hardened frame, trigger and center-mounted hammer; European walnut, one-piece, "bag"-type grip. Uses #11 percussion caps.

DW-105 WALKER REVOLVER
$125.00

This 4½-pound, 44 caliber pistol is the largest ever made; back strap and guard are brass with Walker-type rounded-to-frame walnut grips; all other parts are blued; chambers measure .445 and take a .450 ball slightly smaller than the originals.

DPR-56 THIRD MODEL DRAGOON
$140.00

This engraved-cylinder, 4-and-a-half pounder is a reproduction of the last model of Colt's 44 caliber "horse" revolvers. Barrel measures 7⅜ inches, ⅛ inch shorter than the original; color case-hardened steel frame, one-piece walnut grips. Recommended ball size: .454.

DIXIE PENNSYLVANIA PISTOL
Percussion $95.00
Flintlock 110.00

Available in percussion or flint. Barrels have a bright lustre blue finish, ⅞ inch octagon, rifled, 44 caliber, brass front and rear sight, 10 inches length and takes a .430 ball. The barrel is held in place with a steel wedge and tang screw. The brass trigger guard, thimbles, nosecap, wedge plates and side plates are highly polished. Locks are fine quality with early styling. Plates measure 4¾ inches x ⅞ inch. Percussion hammer is engraved and both plates are left in the white. Flint is an excellent style lock with the gooseneck hammer having an early wide thumb piece. Stock is walnut stained and has a wide bird-head-type grip.

MX 3 OVERCOAT PISTOL
$26.95

39 caliber with 4-inch smooth bore barrel. The breech plug and engraved lock have a burnished-steel finish and the octagon barrel and guard are blued.

MX 3S OVERCOAT PISTOL

Same as MX 3 but with engraved barrel, lock, trigger guard and breech plug. **$34.50**

DCW-712 FRENCH CHARLEVILLE FLINT PISTOL
$125.00

Reproduction of the Model 1777 Cavalry, Revolutionary War-era pistol. Has reversed frizzen spring; forend and lock housing are all in one; case-hardened, round-faced, double-throated hammer; walnut stock; case-hardened frizzen and trigger; shoots .680 round ball loaded with about 40 grains ffg black powder.

LINCOLN DERRINGER
$144.95

41 caliber, 2-inch browned barrel with 8 lands and 8 grooves and will shoot a .400 patch ball.

DIXIE BRASS FRAMED "HIDEOUT" DERRINGER
Plain $43.95
Engraved 54.95

Made with brass frame and walnut grips and fires a .395 round ball.

ABILENE DERRINGER
$49.95

This gun is an all-steel version of Dixie's brass-framed derringers. The 2½-inch, 41-caliber barrel is finished in a deep blue black; frame and hammer are case-hardened. Bore is rifled with six lands and grooves. Uses a tightly patched .395 round ball and 15 or 20 grains of FFFg powder. Walnut grips. Comes with wood presentation case.

DIXIE

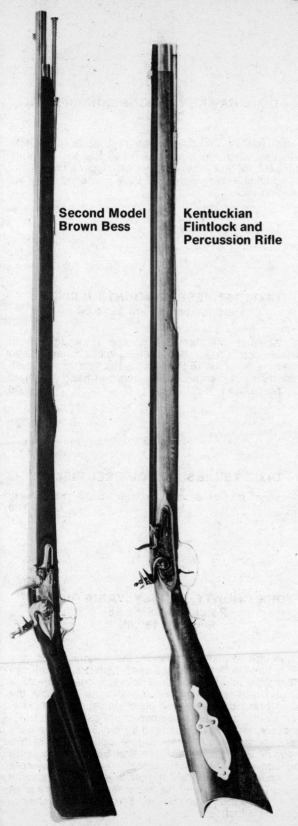

**Second Model
Brown Bess**

**Kentuckian
Flintlock and
Percussion Rifle**

SECOND MODEL BROWN BESS MUSKET
$275.00

74 caliber with a 41¾-inch smooth bore barrel which takes a .715 round ball. In keeping with the traditional musket it has brass furniture on a walnut-stained stock. The lock is marked "Tower" and has the crown with the "GR" underneath. Barrel, lock and ramrod are left bright.

THE KENTUCKIAN FLINTLOCK AND
PERCUSSION RIFLE
Flintlock $175.00
Percussion 165.00

This rifle has a 33½-inch octagon blued barrel which is 13/16 inch across the flats. The rifle comes in 45 caliber only. The bore is rifled with 6 lands and grooves of equal width and about .006 inch deep. Land to land diameter is .453 and groove to groove diameter is .465. You will need a ball size .445 to .448. The rifle has a brass blade front sight and a steel open rear sight. Overall length of the rifle is 48 inches. The Kentuckian is furnished with brass butt plate, trigger guard, patch box, side plate, thimbles and nose cap. It has a case-hardened and engraved lock plate. Weight is about 6¼ pounds. Has a highly polished and finely finished stock in European walnut.

KENTUCKIAN FLINTLOCK AND
PERCUSSION CARBINE
Flintlock $175.00
Percussion 165.00

This carbine is made exactly like the Kentuckian Rifle with the exception that it has a 27½-inch long barrel and the gun is 43 inches in length overall. Land-to-land diameter is .453 and groove-to-groove diameter is .465; will take a .445 to .488 ball. **Caliber:** 45 only. **Weight:** 5½ lbs.

DIXIE DOUBLE BARREL
MUZZLE LOADING SHOTGUN
$260.00

A full 12-gauge, high-quality, double-barrelled percussion shotgun with browned barrels that are 30 inches long. Will take the plastic shot cups for better patterns. Bores are choked modified and full. Lock, barrel tang and trigger are case-hardened in a light gray color and are nicely engraved. Also available: 10-gauge, double-barrel-choke cylinder bored, otherwise same specs as above .. **$315.00**

DIXIE

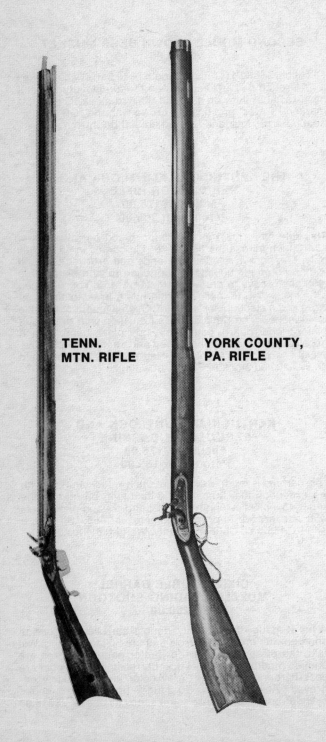

TENN. MTN. RIFLE

YORK COUNTY, PA. RIFLE

DIXIE HAWKEN PERCUSSION RIFLE
$189.95

45 and 50 caliber with 28-inch blued barrel. Overall length 45½ inches. Recommended round ball size is .445 for 45 caliber, .495 for 50 caliber. Double set triggers, blade front sight, adjustable rear sight and case-hardened bar-style percussion lock.

DIXIE TENNESSEE MOUNTAIN RIFLE
Percussion or Flint $225.00

This 50-caliber rifle features double set triggers with adjustable set screw, bore rifled with six lands and grooves, barrel of 15/16 inch across the flats, brown finish and cherry stock. Length: 41½ inches Left-hand version in flint or percussion.   **$245.00**

DIXIE TENNESSEE SQUIRREL RIFLE

In 32 caliber flint or percussion, right hand only, cherry stock   **$295.00**
$255.00 Kit

YORK COUNTY, PENNSYLVANIA RIFLE
Percussion $152.95
Flintlock 162.95

A lightweight at just 7½ pounds, the 36-inch blued rifle barrel is fitted with a standard open-type brass Kentucky rifle rear sight and front blade. The maple one-piece stock is stained a medium darkness that contrasts with the polished brass butt plate, toe plate, patchbox, side plate, trigger guard, thimbles and nose cap. Featuring double-set triggers, the rifle can be fired by pulling only the front trigger, which has a normal trigger pull of four to five pounds; or the rear trigger can first be pulled to set a spring loaded mechanism that greatly reduces the amount of pull needed for the front trigger to kick off the sear in the lock. The land-to-land measurement of the bore is an exact .450 and the recommended ball size is .445. Overall length is 51½ inches.

DIXIE

MMR-7 MISSISSIPPI RIFLE
$225.00

Commonly called the U.S. Rifle Model 1841. This Italian-made replica is rifled in a 58 caliber to use a round ball or a Minie ball; 3 grooves and regulation sights; solid brass furniture; case-hardened lock.

WINCHESTER '73 CARBINE
$450.00
ENGRAVED WINCHESTER '73 RIFLE
$499.00

44-40 caliber which may use modern or black powder cartridges. Overall length is 39 inches with the round barrel being 20 inches long. Its full tubular magazine will hold 11 shots. The walnut forearm and buttstock complement the high-lustre bluing of the all steel parts such as the frame, barrel, magazine, loading lever and butt plate. Comes with the trap door in the butt for the cleaning rod. It comes with the leaf rear sight and blade front sight. This carbine is marked "Model 1873" on the tang and caliber "44-40" on the brass carrier block.

BUFFALO HUNTER
$215.00

This sporterized version of Dixie's Italian-made Zouave uses a .570 ball or bullet and has the same 58 caliber rifled bore. Features walnut half-stock, checkering around the wrist, case-hardened lock, fine blued barrel and brass patchbox.

ZOUAVE CARBINE
$215.00

Same as the regular Zouave rifle, but with a short 20-inch steel barrel. This carbine takes a .570 ball or .575 bullet.

ZOUAVE, MODEL 1863, 58 CAL. RIFLE
$250.00

The Zouave is a copy of an original Remington Zouave rifle which saw service in the Civil War and was acknowledged to be the most accurate military rifle of its day. In the hands of many a Civil War veteran, it helped open the West and furnished necessary food and protection. With its walnut stock, blued barrel, brass fittings and case-hardened lock, it is the most colorful rifle of its day 58 caliber, rifled barrel. Use .570 ball or .575 Minie bullet.

EUROARMS OF AMERICA

MODEL 1005

ROGERS & SPENCER ARMY REVOLVER
MODEL 1006, TARGET $200.00

Caliber: 44; takes .451 round or conical lead balls; #11 percussion cap
Weight: 47 ounces
Barrel Length: 7½ inches
Overall Length: 13¾ inches
Finish: High-gloss blue, walnut grip, solid-frame design, precision rifled barrel
Sights: Rear fully adjustable for windage and elevation; ramp front sight

ROGERS & SPENCER REVOLVER
MODEL 1007, LONDON GRAY $186.00

Revolver is the same as Model 1005, except for London Gray finish, which is heat treated and buffed for rust resistance; same recommended ball size and percussion caps.

NEW MODEL ARMY REVOLVER
MODEL 1020 $155.00

This model is equipped with blued steel frame, brass trigger guard in 44 caliber.
Weight: 40 oz.
Barrel Length: 8 inches
Overall Length: 14¾ inches
Finish: Deep luster blue rifled barrel, polished walnut stock, brass trigger guard

NEW MODEL NAVY REVOLVER
MODEL 1010 $155.00

Same as Model 1020 except with 6½-inch barrel and 36 caliber.

NEW MODEL ARMY (TARGET)
MODEL 1030 $186.00

Caliber: 44
Weight: 41 oz.
Barrel: 8 inches; octagonal, blued, rifled
Overall Length: 14¾ inches
Sights: Rear sight adjustable for windage and elevation; ramp front sight.
Finish: Deep luster blue, rifled barrel, polished walnut stock, brass trigger guard.

ROGERS & SPENCER REVOLVER
MODEL 1005 $160.00

Caliber: 44 Percussion; #11 percussion cap
Barrel Length: 7½ inches
Sights: Integral rear sight notch groove in frame, truncated cone front sight of brass
Overall Length: 13¾ inches
Weight: 47 ounces
Finish: High-gloss blue, walnut grip, solid-frame design, precision rifled barrel.
Recommended Ball Diameter: 451 round on conical, pure lead.

MODEL 1006

ROGERS & SPENCER REVOLVER
MODEL 1008, ENGRAVED $232.00

Revolver is the same as Model 1007, except for engraving.

NEW MODEL ARMY (1020)

NEW MODEL ARMY ENGRAVED
MODEL 1040 $228.00

Classical 19th-century style scroll engraving on this 1858 Remington New Model revolver.
Caliber: 44 Percussion; #11 cap
Barrel Length: 8 inches
Overall Length: 14¾ inches
Weight: 41 ounches
Sights: Integral rear sight notch groove in frame, blade front sight
Recommended Ball Diameter: .451 round or conical, pure lead

EUROARMS OF AMERICA

NEW MODEL ARMY TARGET
MODEL 1045 $233.00

Caliber: 44 Percussion: #11 cap
Barrel Length: 8 inches, precision rifled
Overall Length: 14¾ inches
Weight: 41 ounces
Sights: Integral rear sight notch groove in frame; dove-tailed stainless steel front sight adjustable for windage
Finish: Stainless steel; polished yellow brass trigger guard; walnut grips
Recommended Ball Diameter: .451 round or conical, pure lead

**NEW MODEL
ARMY TARGET (1045)**

REMINGTON 1858 NEW MODEL
ARMY REVOLVER MODEL 1046 $200.00

Caliber: 36
Weight: 41 oz.
Barrel Length: 6½ in.
Overall Length: 13¼ in.
Finish: Stainless steel with polished walnut stock, polished brass trigger guard.
MODEL 1047: 44 Cal., 6½-inch barrel   **$200.00**
MODEL 1048: 44 Cal., 8-inch barrel   **$200.00**

**1858 NEW MODEL
ARMY REVOLVER (1046)**

1851 COLT NAVY SHERIFF (1080)

1851 COLT NAVY SHERIFF
MODEL 1080 $95.00

Caliber: 36 Percussion; #11 cap
Barrel Length: 5 inches
Overall Length: 11½ inches
Weight: 38 ounces
Sights: Rear sight is traditional 'V' notch groove in hammer, truncated cone front sight of brass
Finish: High-gloss blue on barrel and cylinder; backstrap frame and trigger guard polished yellow brass; walnut grips; hammer and loading lever color case-hardened
Recommended Ball Diameter: .375 round or conical, pure lead

1851 COLT NAVY SHERIFF
MODEL 1090 $99.00
Same as Model 1080 except in 44 caliber, with .451 round or conical ball diameter

1851 COLT NAVY CONFEDERATE (1100)

1851 COLT NAVY CONFEDERATE BRASS FRAME
MODEL 1100 $95.00

Caliber: 36 Percussion; #11 cap
Barrel: 7½ inches; octagonal to round, precision rifled
Overall Length: 13 inches
Weight: 41 ounces
Sights: Rear sight is traditional 'V' notch groove in hammer, truncated cone front sight of brass
Recommended Ball Diameter: .375 round or conical, pure lead
Finish: Blued barrel and cylinder; frame, backstrap and trigger guard are polished yellow brass; color case-hardened hammer and loading lever; walnut grips

1851 COLT NAVY CONFEDERATE BRASS FRAME
MODEL 1110 $99.00
Same as Model 1100 except in 44 caliber, with recommended ball diameter of .451 round or conical, pure lead

EUROARMS OF AMERICA

1851 COLT NAVY REVOLVER
MODEL 1200 $150.00

Same as Model 1190 except with 7½-inches octagonal barrel.
Weight: 41 oz.
Barrel Length: 7½ inches
Overall Length: 13 inches

ARMY 1860 REVOLVER
44 CALIBER MODEL 1210 $145.00

The historic Army Model 1860 needs no introduction to shooter and collector. The cylinder is authentically roll engraved with a highly polished brass trigger guard and steel frame cut for shoulder stock. The frame, loading lever and hammer are beautifully finished in color case hardening.
Weight: 41 oz.
Barrel Length: 8 inches, streamlined barrel.
Overall Length: 13⅝ inches
Caliber: 44
Finish: Brass trigger guard and backstrap, steel frame, round barrel, rebated cylinder engraved battle scene. Frame cut for shoulder stock.

44 CALIBER MODEL 1220
  (with 5" barrel) $145.00
44 CALIBER MODEL 1215
  (in stainless steel) 194.00
44 CALIBER MODEL 1236
  Same as Model 1210 except with brass
  frame 99.00

1862 POLICE REVOLVER
MODEL 1250 $160.00

Police revolver with a steel frame, fluted cylinder and 7½-inch barrel in 36 caliber, lanyard ring in butt of revolver.
Weight: 40 oz.
Barrel: 7½ inches
Overall Length: 13 inches
Finish: Deep luster blue rifled round barrel

1860 ENGRAVED COLT ARMY
MODEL 1230 $198.00

Caliber: 44 Percussion: #11 cap
Barrel Length: 8 inches, streamlined round barrel
Overall Length: 13-5/6 inches
Weight: 41 ounces
Sights: Rear sight is traditional 'V' notch in hammer, blade front sight of brass
Recommended Ball Diameter: .451 round or conical, pure lead
Finish: Engraved with a beautiful 19th-century scroll pattern; engraved backstrap and trigger guard are of polished yellow brass; walnut grips

1861 COLT NAVY REVOLVER
MODEL 1240 $160.00

This is Sam Colt's modernized version of the popular Navy Model, with round barrel and the creeping loading lever "borrowed" from the 1860 Army model.
Caliber: 36
Weight: 41 oz.
Barrel Length: 7½ inches
Overall Length: 13 inches
Finish: Blue with polished brass backstrap and guard; color case-hardened hammer, frame and loading lever; one-piece walnut grip; engraved cylinder with naval battle scene.

1862 POLICE REVOLVER

SCHNEIDER & GLASSICK
CONFEDERATE REVOLVER
36 CALIBER MODEL 1050 $95.00
44 CALIBER MODEL 1060   99.00

A modern replica of a Confederate Percussion Army Revolver. Polished brass frame, rifled high-luster blued octagonal barrel and polished walnut grips.
Weight: 40 oz.
Barrel Length: 7½ inches
Overall Length: 13 inches
Finish: Brass frame, backstrap and trigger guard, blued rifled barrel, case-hardened hammer and loading lever, engraved cylinder with naval battle scene.

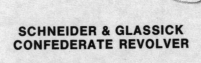

**SCHNEIDER & GLASSICK
CONFEDERATE REVOLVER**

EUROARMS OF AMERICA

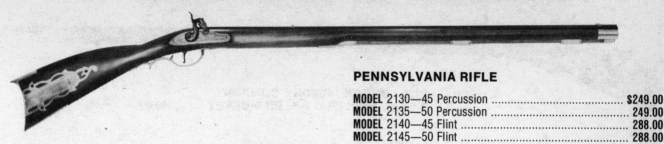

PENNSYLVANIA RIFLE

MODEL 2130—45 Percussion $249.00
MODEL 2135—50 Percussion 249.00
MODEL 2140—45 Flint 288.00
MODEL 2145—50 Flint 288.00

SPECIFICATIONS:

Caliber: 45 (actual bore size .450″) 50 (actual bore size .500″)
Barrel: Octagonal 13/16 inches across flats, length of barrel 36 inches.
Lock Plate: Flint or Percussion. Case-hardened with flash shield on percussion guns.
Stock: Full-length one-piece walnut stock.
Ramrod: Made in a single piece, brass tipped at both ends and threaded at bottom end.
Mountings: Polished brass, including a large original-type patch box. Light engraving on lock plate.
Overall Length: 50 inches.
Weight: 6½ to 7 lbs., depending on density of walnut stock.

HAWKEN RIFLE
MODEL 2210A $186.00

Traditional styling based on the original St. Louis rifle of Sam and Jake Hawken with hooked breech system.

Caliber: 50-caliber percussion
Barrel: 28 inches long; blued precision rifled, octagonal
Weight: 9½-9¾ lbs., depending on density of wood
Stock: Solid one-piece walnut
Ramrod: Wooden, with brass tips threaded for cleaning jay, worm or ball puller.
Sights: Target rear sight adjustable for windage and elevation. Front sight dovetail cut.
Triggers: Double set triggers adjustable for hair trigger, if desired
Furniture: Polished brass mountings, barrel key

REMINGTON 1862 RIFLE
MODEL 2255 $250.00

SPECIFICATIONS:

Caliber: 58
Ignition: Case-hardened percussion lock
Barrel: 32½ inches rifled
Overall Length: 48½ inches
Weight: 9½ lbs.
Finish: High-polished round barrel, polished brass mountings and cap box, walnut stock.
Sights: Original 3-leaf rear sight, blade front sight
Ramrod: Heavy one-piece steel

EUROARMS OF AMERICA

2260 LONDON ARMORY COMPANY 3-BAND ENDFIELD RIFLED MUSKET $340.00

Caliber: 58
Barrel Length: 39 inches, blued and rifled
Overall Length: 54 inches
Weight: 9½-9¾ lbs., depending on wood density.
Stock: One-piece walnut. Polished "bright" brass butt plate, trigger guard and nose cap, blued barrel bands.
Ramrod: Steel. Threaded end for accessories.
Sights: Traditional Enfield folding ladder rear sight. Inverted "V" front sight.

2270 LONDON ARMORY COMPANY 2-BAND RIFLE MUSKET $328.00

Caliber: 58
Barrel Length: 33 inches, blued and rifled
Overall Length: 49 inches
Weight: 8½-8¾ lbs., depending on wood density
Stock: One-piece walnut. Polished "bright" brass butt plate, trigger guard and nose cap. Blued barrel bands.
Sights: Inverted 'V' front sight; Enfield folding ladder rear.
Ramrod: Steel.

LONDON ARMORY COMPANY ENFIELD MUSKETOON MODEL 2280 $280.00

Caliber: 58. Minie ball.
Barrel Length: 24 inches
Overall Length: 40½ inches.
Weight: 7 to 7½ lbs., depending on density of wood.
Barrel: Round high-luster blue barrel.
Stock: Seasoned walnut stock, with sling swivels.
Ramrod: Steel.
Ignition: Heavy-duty percussion lock.
Sights: Graduated military-leaf sight.
Furniture: Brass trigger guard, nose cap and butt plate. Blued barrel bands and lock plate, and swivels.

EUROARMS OF AMERICA

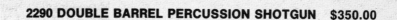

2290 DOUBLE BARREL PERCUSSION SHOTGUN $350.00

A beautifully designed 12-gauge double barrel percussion muzzle-loading shotgun with modified and full choke. Tastefully engraved side locks and blue barrels. A wooden ramrod, brass tipped, capable of taking a brush or worm. Checkered English-style walnut stock. The weight is approximately 6 lbs. making it an easy-to-handle lightweight field gun.

2295 SINGLE-BARRELED MAGNUM CAPE GUN $295.00

Euroarms of America offers a beautiful reproduction of a classic English-styled 12-gauge single barreled shotgun. It is a true 12 gauge with a 32-inch open choked barrel. Although the single barrel muzzleloader weighs only 7½ pounds, the English-styled stock is well proportioned and recoil with even relatively heavy powder charges is moderate. The stock is of European walnut with a satin oil finish. The barrel, underrib, thimbles, nose cap, trigger guard and butt plate are finished with EOA deep, rich blue. The lock is left in the white and displays a scroll engraving, as does the bow of the trigger guard. Overall length of the single barreled shotgun is 47½ inches. Uses #11 percussion caps and recommended wads are felt overpowder and cardboard overshot.

COOK & BROTHER CONFEDERATE CARBINE
MODEL 2300 $280.00

Classic re-creation of the rare 1861, New Orleans-made Artillery Carbine. Lockplate is marked "Cook & Brother N.O. 1861" and is stamped with a Confederate flag at rear of hammer.

Caliber: 58
Barrel Length: 24 inches
Overall Length: 40⅓ inches
Weight: 7½ lbs.
Sights: Adjustable dovetailed front and rear sights
Ramrod: Steel.
Finish: Barrel is antique brown; buttplate, trigger guard, barrel bands, sling swivels and nosecap are polished brass; stock is walnut.
Recommended Ball Sizes: .575 r.b., .577 Minie and .580 maxi. Uses musket caps.

FIE

Kentucky Rifle

Cavalry Carbine
Remington Cavalry Carbine replica 58 cal. rifled barrel, case-hardened hammer and lock, polished brass fittings. Weight 7 lbs. **$159.95**

Berdan Rifle w/Brass Breech
Muzzle-loading 45 cal. percussion rifle. Adjustable sights, double-set adjustable trigger, solid brass patch box and fittings. Overall length: 42¾ inches. Weight: 7 lbs. **$154.95**

Deluxe Kentucky Rifle
Muzzle-loading Kentucky rifle, 45 cal. rifled 35-inch octagonal barrel—polished solid-brass patch box, trigger guard, butt plate and stock fittings. Weight 7 lbs. **$149.95**
Flintlock model **179.95**

Colt Navy Revolver
1851 Model Colt Navy 36-cal. cap and ball revolver, 7½ inches octagonal barrel, polished-brass frame, one-piece walnut grip. Weight 40 oz. **$79.95**

Baby Dragoon Revolver
Baby Dragoon 31 cal. revolver replica engraved cylinder 4- or 6-inch octagonal barrel, polished-brass frame, square back trigger guard, one-piece walnut grip. Weight 23 oz.—4 inches; 26 oz.—6 inches **$84.95**
Also available in engraved model **94.95**

Colt Navy Revolver
1851 Model Colt Navy 44 cal. cap and ball revolver, 7½ inches octagonal barrel, polished-brass frame, one-piece walnut grip. Weight 40 oz. .... **$ 79.95**
Full steel model **109.95**

Remington New Army Revolver
New Army Remington replica 44 cal. Revolver model 1858 with polished-brass frame, 7½ inches blued octagonal barrel, walnut grips. Weight 42 oz. .... **$ 89.95**
Full steel model 44 caliber **119.95**
Also available in 36 caliber **89.95**

Tower Flintlock Pistol
Tower Flintlock pistol 69 cal. smooth bore, cherrywood stock with solid-brass trim, ramrod 9-inch barrel, 15½ inches long. Weight 48 oz. **$59.95**

Model HAW50 Hawken
50 caliber percussion or flintlock. Oil finished European walnut stock. Highly polished brass furniture, double triggers, sights fully adjustable for windage and elevation.
Percussion model **$219.95**
Flintlock model **269.95**

HOPKINS & ALLEN ARMS

THE MINUTEMAN RIFLE
Flint $129.95
Percussion $139.95

(Available in Kit only)

Caliber: 45
Lock Mechanism: Exactly like that of the Minuteman era, in flintlock or percussion.
Stock: In the classic Kentucky style, figured maple stock is 55 inches long with rich oil finish.
Furniture: Brass patch box, butt plate and trigger guard.
Barrel: 39-inch octagonal barrel; 15/16 inch across the flats.
Sights: Precision "Silver Blade" front sight; notched "Kentucky" rear sight.
Weight: 9 lbs.

KENTUCKY PISTOL MODEL 10

This 44-caliber pistol has a 15/16-inch x 10-inch rifled barrel and features a convertible ignition system, heavy-duty ramrod and special Hopkins & Allen breech and tang.

Overall Length: 15½ inches. **Weight:** 3 lbs.

Percussion $104.05 Flint $92.95

BOOT PISTOL
$71.50

The Boot Pistol is available in 45 caliber and comes with a sculptured walnut pistol grip and a full 6-inch octagonal barrel. It measures 13 inches overall in length. The 15/16-inch octagon barrel is fitted with open sights—post type front sight and open rear sight with step elevator. The H&A Boot Pistol features a rich blueblack finish and is equipped with a match trigger.

BRUSH RIFLE

Caliber: 45 and 36
Barrel: 25'' Octagon 15/16 across flats
Weight: 7 lbs.

Stock: Selected hardwood
Sights: Notched rear-Silver blade front
Features: Compact, light, quick pointing rifle. Convertible ignition.

Kit..$ 99.50 Perc.	$110.60 Flint
Pre-Assembled Kit.................. 129.00 Perc.	140.10 Flint
Assembled.............................. 189.00 Perc.	200.10 Flint

KENTUCKY RIFLE KIT MODEL 34

Flint $89.95 (Shown)
Percussion 53.10

Caliber: 45
Lock Mechanism: Flintlock or percussion
Barrel: 34 inches octagonal; 15/16 inch across the flats
Overall Length: 50 inches
Weight: 8½ lbs.
Special Features: Convertible ignition system; heavy-duty ramrod

HOPKINS & ALLEN ARMS

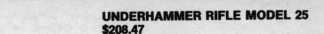

UNDERHAMMER RIFLE MODEL 25
$208.47

Calibers: 36 and 45
Stock: American walnut with cap box and walnut forend
Barrel: octagonal; avail. in lengths of 20, 25, or 32 inches; 15/16 inch across the flats; rifled with uniform round ball twist
Special Features: Only three moving parts in the action give the shooter years of trouble-free performance; uninterrupted sighting plane; target trigger; positive ignition

PENNSYLVANIA HAWKEN RIFLE MODEL 29

Flint	**$210.60**
Percussion	**199.50 (shown)**

Caliber: 50
Lock Mechanism: Flintlock or percussion
Barrel: 29 in. long; octagonal; 15/16 inch across the flats; rifled with round ball twist
Overall Length: 44 inches
Weight: 7¼ lbs.
Stock: Walnut with cheekpiece and dual barrel wedges for added strength
Furniture: Brass fixtures, incl. patch box
Special Feature: Convertible ignition system

KASSNAR

HAWKEN
$249.95

"The Hawken," a favorite for nearly half of the nineteenth century, as well as playing an important part in the shaping of American history, has once again emerged as a favorite among muzzle-loading enthusiasts. Available in 45, 50, 54 and 58 caliber in flintlock or percussion. Also available in left-hand version in percussion or flintlock **$299.95**

LYMAN REVOLVERS

NEW MODEL ARMY 44
$169.95

This rugged replica of Remington's 1858 New Model Army 44 has been the favorite of target shooters and other experienced muzzle loaders. The sturdy top strap, besides strengthening the basic frame design, provides an excellent platform for installation of an adjustable rear sight. Features include a deep-blue finish on the machined steel frame, barrel, cylinder and loading lever. The trigger and hammer are color case-hardened. The trigger guard is polished brass and the two-piece grips are well-finished European walnut. Available in 44 caliber; barrel length: 8 inches; overall length: 13½ inches; weight: 2 lbs. 9 oz.

1860 ARMY 44
$169.95

This revolver was the most widely used sidearm during the Civil War. Both sides prized the 1860 for its reliability and advanced features such as the "creeping" loading lever system. This, the last U.S. military percussion revolver, was the most advanced of the open-top revolvers. After the War, this gun went West and helped the pioneers survive and settle. Lyman's 1860 Army 44 is patterned exactly after the original and features one-piece walnut grips, color case-hardened frame, hammer and loading lever. The barrel and rebated engraved cylinder are polished blued steel while the backstrap and trigger guard are nickel-plated brass. The four-screw frame is cut for a shoulder stock. Available in 44 caliber; barrel length: 8 inches; overall length; 13⅝ inches; weight 2 lbs. 9 oz.

1851 SQUAREBACK NAVY 36
$154.95

This 36 caliber replica is patterned after what may be the most famous percussion revolver ever made. Its classic lines and historic appeal make it as popular today as it was when Sam Colt was turning out the originals. Like the Remingtons, this replica of the second model 1851 (about 5,000 made) is made of quality material. The revolver features a color case-hardened steel frame, hammer and loading lever. The blued cylinder is engraved with the same naval battle scene as were the originals. The nickel-plated backstrap, square-back trigger guard and one-piece walnut grips combine to make Lyman's 1851 a real classic. Available in 36 caliber; barrel length: 7½ inches; overall length: 13 inches; weight: 2 lbs. 9 oz.

LYMAN

LYMAN PLAINS PISTOL
$159.95

This replica of the pistol carried by the Western pioneers of the 1830s features a pistol-sized Hawken lock with dependable coil spring and authentic rib and thimble styling. It has a richly stained walnut stock, blackened iron furniture and polished brass trigger guard and ramrod tips. Equipped with a spring-loaded target trigger and a fast twist barrel for target accuracy, the Plains Pistol is available in 50 or 54 caliber.

GREAT PLAINS RIFLE
Percussion $369.95
Flintlock   379.95

The Great Plains Rifle has a 32-inch deep-grooved barrel and 1 in 66-inch twist to shoot patched round balls. Browned steel furniture including the thick steel wedge plates and steel toe plate; correct lock and hammer styling with coil spring dependability; and a walnut stock without a patch box. A Hawken-style trigger guard protects double set triggers. Steel front sight and authentic buckhorn styling in an adjustable rear sight. Available in 50 or 54 caliber.

LYMAN TRADE RIFLE
Percussion $269.95
Flintlock   279.95

The Lyman Trade Rifle features a 28-inch octagonal barrel, rifled one turn at 48 inches, designed to fire both patched round balls and the popular maxistyle conical bullets; overall length 45 inches; polished brass furniture with blued finish on steel parts; walnut stock; hook breech; single trigger, spring-loaded; coil-spring percussion lock; fixed steel sights; steel barrel rib and ramrod ferrules; available in 50 or 54 caliber percussion only.

NAVY ARMS

SPILLER & BURR REVOLVER

A brass-frame copy of the Whitney revolvers made in the Confederacy. Available in 36 caliber only with 7-inch full-octagon barrel. Weight: 2½ lbs., overall length 12½ inches.

SPILLER & BURR
$109.00

36 CALIBER 1861 NAVY

The Officer model 1861 Navy Replica comes in 36 caliber with a 7½-inch barrel and may be had with a 6-shot round or fluted cylinder and choice of brass or iron straps. The model with iron straps is also available with a square back guard. Features include: case-hardened frame, lever, and hammer; balance of gun is blued. The 1861 Navy comes cut for a shoulder stock.

Shoulder Stock	$ 50.00
Single Cased Set	230.00
Double Cased Set	386.50

1861 NAVY
$142.00

COLT WALKER 1847

The 1847 Walker replica comes in 44 caliber with a 9-inch barrel. The full size Walker 44 weighs 4 lbs. 8 oz. and is well suited for the collector as well as the black powder shooter. Features include: rolled cylinder scene; blue and case-hardened finish; and brass guard. Proof tested.

COLT WALKER 1847
$195.00

1862 POLICE MODEL

4½-, 5½- and 6½-inch barrel—This is the last gun manufactured by the Colt Plant in the percussion era. It encompassed all the modifications of each gun starting from the early Paterson to the 1861 Navy. It was favored by the New York Police Dept. for many years. One-half fluted and rebated cylinder, 36 cal., 5 shot, **.375** dia. ball, 18 grains of black powder, brass trigger guard and backstrap. Case-hardened frame, loading lever and hammer—balance blue.

5½-inch barrel in presentation case.............$180.00

1862 POLICE
$137.00

NAVY ARMS

REB MODEL 1860
$93.00

A modern replica of the confederate Griswold & Gunnison percussion Army revolver. Rendered with a polished brass frame and a rifled steel barrel finished in a high-luster blue with genuine walnut grips. **All Army Model 60's** are completely proof-tested by the Italian government to the most exacting standards. **Calibers:** 36 and 44. **Barrel Length:** 7¼ inches. **Overall Length:** 13 inches. **Weight:** 2 lbs. 10 oz.-11-oz. **Finish:** Brass frame, backstrap and trigger guard, round barrel hinged rammer on the 44 cal. rebated cylinder.

Matching Shoulder Stock.......................................$45.00
Single Cased Set...180.00
Double Cased Set...288.00

ARMY 1860
$131.50

These guns from the Colt line are 44 caliber and all six shot. The cylinder was authentically roll engraved with a polished brass trigger guard and steel strap cut for shoulder stock. The frame, loading lever and hammer are finished in high-luster color case-hardening. Walnut grips. **Weight:** 2 lbs. 9 oz. **Barrel Length:** 8 inches. **Overall Length:** 13⅝ inches. **Caliber:** 44. **Finish:** Brass trigger guard, steel back strap, round barrel creeping cylinder, rebated cylinder engraved. Navy scene. Frame cut for s/stock (4 screw).

Shoulder Stock..$50.00
Single Cased Set...220.00
Double Cased Set...365.00
Kit...93.00

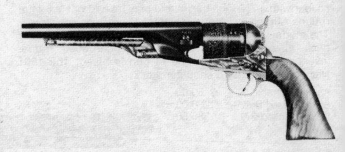

LEECH & RIGDON
$136.50

A modern version of the famous Leech & Rigdon Army Revolver. Manufactured during the Civil War in Augusta, Georgia, and furnished to many of the Georgia Cavalry units. It is basically a copy of the Colt Navy Revolver, but with a round Dragoon-type barrel. **Weight:** 2 lbs. 10 oz. **Barrel Length:** 7¼ inches. **Overall Length:** 13 inches. **Caliber:** 36. **Finish:** Steel case-hardened frame. Round barrel, hinged rammer.

ROGERS & SPENCER NAVY REVOLVER
$160.00

This revolver features a six-shot cylinder, octagonal barrel, hinged-type loading lever assembly, two-piece walnut grips, blued finish and case-hardened hammer and lever. **Caliber:** 44. **Barrel Length:** 7½ in. **Overall Length:** 13¾ in. **Weight:** 3 lbs.

NAVY ARMS

TARGET MODEL REMINGTON REVOLVER
$149.00

With its top strap and frame, the Remington Percussion Revolver is considered the magnum of Civil War revolvers and is ideally suited for the heavy 44 caliber charges. Based on the Army Model, the target gun has target sights for controlled accuracy. Ruggedly built from modern steel and proof tested. Also available in 36 caliber.

ARMY 60 SHERIFF'S MODEL $125.00

A shortened version of the Army Model 60 Revolver. The Sheriff's model version became popular because the shortened barrel was fast out of the leather. This is actually the original snub nose. The predecessor of the detective specials or belly guns designed for quick-draw use. A piece of traditional Americana, the Sheriff's model was adopted by many local police departments. Available in 36 and 44 calibers.

"YANK" REVOLVER $113.00

One of the most famous guns in all American history. During the Civil War it served both the North and South. Later, when the rush to open the west began, it became "standard equipment" for every man who ventured on a horse or rode a covered wagon to the virgin lands of wheat, cattle and gold. Due to its light recoil and lightning-fast action, it is still selected by many quick draw artists as the fastest single-action revolver in the world. Cylinder roll engraved with classic naval battle scene. Backstrap and trigger guard are polished brass. Case-hardened frame, hammer and loading lever. **Caliber:** 36. **Barrel Length:** 7½ inches. **Overall Length:** 13 inches **Weight:** 2 lbs. 9 oz.

Shoulder Stock	$45.00
Single Cased Set	207.00
Double Cased Set	339.75
Kit	87.75

REMINGTON NEW MODEL ARMY REVOLVER
Blue $137.00
Nickel 152.75

The most advanced design of the time, the Remington was considered the most accurate cap & ball revolver. A rugged, dependable, battle-proven Civil War veteran. With its top strap and rugged frame these guns are considered the magnum of C.W. revolvers and are ideally suited for the heavy 44 charges. Nickel finish in 44 cal. only. **Calibers:** 36, 44. **Barrel Length:** 8 inches **Overall Length:** 13½ inches **Weight:** 2 lbs. 9 oz.

Single cased set, blue	$225.00
Single cased set, nickel	240.00
Double cased set, blue 375.00 **Double cased set, nickel**	400.00

CIVILIAN MODEL "YANK" NAVY. 36 cal., cylinder roll engraved with classic naval battle scene. Backstrap and trigger guard silver plated. $118.00

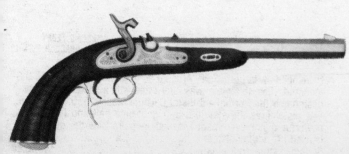

LE PAGE DUELING PISTOL $250.00

This replica of a French percussion pistol has an octagonal barrel, single-set trigger and adjustable rear sight. The buttstock is made of European walnut. **Caliber:** 44. **Barrel Length:** 9 in. **Overall Length:** 15 in. **Weight:** 2 lbs. 2 oz.

Single cased set	$400.00
Double cased set	700.00

NAVY ARMS

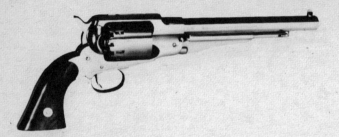

STAINLESS STEEL 1858 REMINGTON $210.00

Exactly like the standard 1858 Remington except that every part with the exception of the grips and trigger guard is manufactured from corrosion-resistant stainless steel. This gun has all the style and feel of its ancestor with all of the conveniences of stainless steel. 44 Caliber.

KENTUCKY PISTOLS

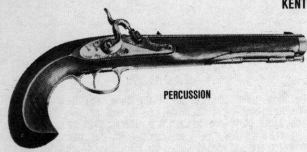

PERCUSSION

FLINTLOCK

Flint	**$136.75**
Flint Brass-barrel model	**153.00**
Single Cased Set—Flint	**225.00**
Single Cased Set—Flint Brass Barrel	**240.00**
Percussion	**$120.00**
Percussion Brass-barrel model	**136.75**
Single Cased Set—Percussion	**208.00**
Single Cased Set—Percussion Brass Barrel	**225.00**
Double Cased Set, Flint	**$370.00**
Double Cased Set, Flint, Brass bbl.	**400.00**
Double Cased Set, Perc.	**335.00**
Double Cased Set, Perc., Brass bbl.	**370.00**

The Kentucky Pistol is truly a historical American gun . . . carried during the Revolution by the Minutemen . . . the sidearm of "Andy" Jackson in the Battle of New Orleans. Now Navy Arms Company has gone through great research to manufacture a pistol truly representative of its kind and with the balance and handle of the original for which it became famous.

HARPER'S FERRY PISTOLS

FLINTLOCK

HARPER'S FERRY

Of all the early American martial pistols, Harper's Ferry is one of the best known. They were carried by both the Army and the Navy. **NAVY ARMS COMPANY** has authentically reproduced the Harper's Ferry to the last minute detail. Well balanced and well made. **$165.00**

SPECIFICATIONS:
Weight: 2 lb. 9 oz. **Barrel Length:** 10 inches. **Overall Length:** 16 inches. **Caliber:** 58 smoothbore. **Finish:** Walnut stock, case-hardened lock, brass mounted browned barrel.

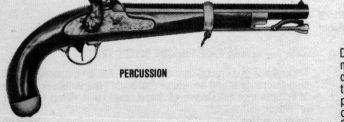

PERCUSSION

HARPER'S FERRY
MODEL 1855 DRAGOON PISTOL

Developed at Harper's Ferry Arsenal as a holster pistol for the U.S. mounted rifles, this pistol was later fitted with a shoulder stock and designated the Springfield Pistol Carbine Model 1855. In 58 cal., this pistol fires the standard 500 gr. Minie ball and is the most powerful pistol ever made. Issued in pairs and designed to be carried in saddle holsters **$218.50**
Shoulder stock (not illus.) **45.00**

NAVY ARMS

HENRY CARBINE

This arm first utilized by the Kentucky Cavalry. Available in either original 44 rimfire caliber or in 44/40 caliber. Oil stained American walnut stock, blued finish with brass frame. Also available in a limited deluxe edition of only 50 engraved models complete with deluxe American walnut stock, original styled engraving and silver plated frames.
Specifications: Caliber: 44 rimfire & 44/40 Barrel Length: 23⅝ inches Overall Length: 45 inches. **$500.00**
Engraved Model **1500.00**

J.P. MURRAY ARTILLERY CARBINE $263.00

Copy of the carbine used by the Southern artillery units during the Civil War. This carbine has been carefully reproduced with a browned, 23½-inch barrel in 58 cal.

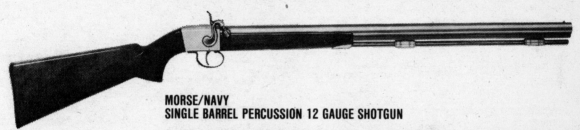

MORSE/NAVY
SINGLE BARREL PERCUSSION 12 GAUGE SHOTGUN

The Morse/Navy single barrel 12-gauge Muzzle-loading Shotgun is a well-balanced, American-made replica featuring a highly polished brass receiver with select American walnut stock. Navy Arms has improved upon the old Morse design to modernize this into a contemporary and exciting muzzle-loading configuration. **$167.00**

KENTUCKY RIFLE—45 or 50 CALIBER PERCUSSION $246.00   FLINT $273.50

No weapon, before or since, has been so imbued with Americana as the Kentucky Rifle. The Kentucky was the wilderness weapon, Pennsylvania-born and universally used along the frontier. First called simply the long rifle, it was designated "the Kentucky" by gun lovers after the Civil War because Daniel Boone used it most effectively in opening up the Kentucky territory. In the hands of those who know how to use it, the Kentucky still can give many modern rifles a run for the money. The frontiersman could, with ease, pot a squirrel high in an oak tree or drop a deer at 100 yards. Barrel length is 35 inches. Available in flint or percussion.

MORSE MUZZLE-LOADING RIFLE

Improved production techniques and modern engineering have produced this traditionally styled, muzzle-loading rifle. Quality plus custom craftsmanship is evident throughout this rifle with careful attention being paid to the most minute detail. It features Navy Arms "pre-straightened" precision rifled ordnance steel barrel. 45, 50 or 58 caliber **$167.00**
Also available in 12-gauge. **167.00**

NAVY ARMS

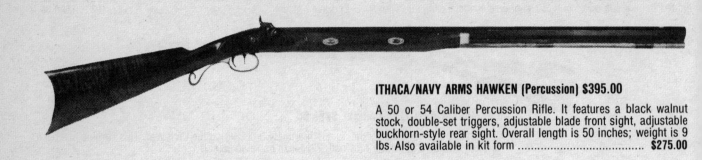

ITHACA/NAVY ARMS HAWKEN (Percussion) $395.00

A 50 or 54 Caliber Percussion Rifle. It features a black walnut stock, double-set triggers, adjustable blade front sight, adjustable buckhorn-style rear sight. Overall length is 50 inches; weight is 9 lbs. Also available in kit form **$275.00**

ITHACA/NAVY ARMS HAWKEN (Flintlock) $425.00

A 50 or 54 caliber rifle, the Ithaca/Navy Arms Hawken flintlock features Hawken-style furniture, octagonal 32-inch barrel, double set triggers, buckhorn-style rear sight and Hawken-style toe and butt plates. Weight approx. 9 lbs.

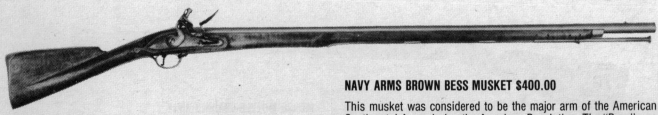

NAVY ARMS BROWN BESS MUSKET $400.00

This musket was considered to be the major arm of the American Continental Army during the American Revolution. The "Bess" was derived from Queen Elizabeth I and "Brown" came from the barrel's finish. This carefully reproduced replica carries the Colonial Williamsburg mark of authenticity and features a polished barrel and lock with brass trigger guard and buttplate. **Caliber:** 75. **Barrel Length:** 42 inches **Overall Length:** 59 inches **Weight:** 9½ lbs.

NAVY ARMS

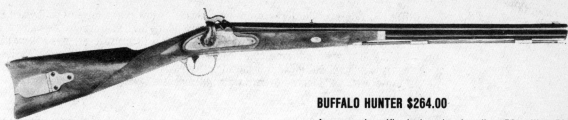

BUFFALO HUNTER $264.00

A percussion rifle designed to handle a 58-caliber 500-grain slug, it comes with a walnut-colored wood stock and features a color case-hardened lock and hammer. Barrel is precision rifled of ordnance steel.

Also available in kit form $310.00

1863 SPRINGFIELD RIFLE $380.00

An authentically reproduced replica of one of America's most historical firearms, the 1863 Springfield rifle features a full-size, three-band musket and precision-rifled barrel. **Caliber:** 58. **Barrel Length:** 40 inches **Overall Length:** 56 inches **Weight:** 9½ lbs. **Finish:** Walnut stock with polished metal lock and stock fittings.
Springfield Bayonet and Scabbard..$30.00

Also available in kit form $265.00

ZOUAVE RIFLE $263.00   DELUXE $355.00

A 58 caliber military percussion, it features a walnut-toned stock, deep-blued barrel, case-hardened lock, brass fitting and patch box. The precision rifled barrel is 32½ inches with an overall length of 48½ inches.

12-GA. CLASSIC SIDE-BY-SIDE SHOTGUN PERCUSSION $342.00

This 12-gauge shotgun features a color case-hardened lock, plates and hammers. All internal parts are steel. The walnut stock is hand checkered. The 28-inch barrels are blued. The shotgun will shoot all 12, 10 and light 8 gauge equivalent percussion loads. Muzzle loader choked cylinder and cylinder. **Weight:** 7 lbs. 12 oz.

NAVY ARMS

MISSISSIPPI RIFLE MODEL 1841 $263.00

The historic percussion lock weapon that gained its name as a result of its performance in the hands of Jefferson Davis' Mississippi Regiment during the heroic stand at the battle of Buena Vista. Also known as the "Yager" (a misspelling of the German Jaeger), this was the last rifle adopted by Army Ordnance to fire the traditional round ball. In 58 caliber, the Mississippi is handsomely furnished in brass, including patch box for tools and spare parts. **Weight:** 9½ lbs.; **Barrel Length:** 32½ inches; **Overall Length:** 48½ inches; **Caliber:** 58; **Finish:** Walnut finish stock, brass mounted.

HARPER'S FERRY RIFLE $316.00

Navy Arms is proud to offer the ever-popular and most-sought-after Harper's Ferry Rifle, the most authentic replica rendition ever offered to the American shooter. Available in limited quantities. A historically significant weapon complete with precision rifled 58 caliber browned barrel with attractive highly polished brass furniture.

1853 ENFIELD RIFLE MUSKET $315.00

The Enfield Rifle Musket marked the zenith in design and manufacture of the military percussion rifle and this perfection has been reproduced by Navy Arms Company. This and the other Enfield muzzle loaders reproduced by Navy Arms were the most coveted rifles of the Civil War, treasured by Union and Confederate troops alike for their fine quality and deadly accuracy. **Caliber:** 557; **Barrel Length(s):** 39 inches; **Weight:** 9 lbs.; **Overall Length:** 55 inches; **Sights:** Fixed front, graduated rear; **Rifling:** 3 groove, cold forged; **Stock:** Seasoned walnut with solid brass furniture.

1858 ENFIELD RIFLE $305.00

In the late 1850s the British Admiralty, after extensive experiments, settled on a pattern of rifle which had a 5-groove barrel of heavy construction, sighted to 1100 yards, and this was designated the Naval rifle, Pattern 1858. In the recreation of this famous rifle Navy Arms has referred to the original 1858 Enfield Rifle in the Tower of London and has closely followed the specification even to the progressive depth rifling. **Caliber:** 557; **Barrel length(s):** 33 inches; **Weight:** 8 lbs. 8 oz.; **Overall Length:** 48.5 inches; **Sights:** Fixed front, graduated rear; **Rifling:** 5 groove; cold forged; **Stock:** Seasoned walnut with solid brass furniture.

1861 ENFIELD MUSKETOON $290.00

The 1861 Enfield Musketoon is a Limited Collector's edition, individually serial numbered with certificate of authenticity. **Caliber:** 557; **Barrel length(s):** 24 inches; **Weight:** 7 lbs. 8 oz.; **Overall length:** 40.25 inches; **Sights:** Fixed front, graduated rear; **Rifling:** 5-groove; cold forged; **Stock:** Seasoned walnut with solid brass furniture.

Also available in kit form..$185.00

NAVY ARMS

WHITWORTH MILITARY TARGET RIFLE

Recreation of Sir Joseph Whitworth's deadly and successful sniper and target weapon of the mid-1800s. Devised with a hexagonal bore with a pitch of 1 turn in 20 inches. Barrel is cold forged from ordnance steel, reducing the build-up of black powder fouling. Globe front sight; open military target rifle rear sight has interchangeable blades of different heights. Walnut stock is hand checkered. Caliber: 451; Barrel length: 36 inches; Weight: 9½ lbs. Price includes kit of accessories $575.00

PARKER-HALE 2 BAND MUSKET—MODEL 1858
Barrel: 33 inches, Overall length: 48½ inches,
   Weight: 8½ lbs. $370.00

PARKER-HALE MUSKETOON—MODEL 1861
Barrel: 24 inches, Overall length: 40¼ inches,
   Weight: 7½ lbs. $300.00

PARKER-HALE 3 BAND MUSKET—MODEL 1853
Barrel: 39 inches, Overall length: 55 inches,
   Weight: 9 lbs. $400.00

PARKER-HALE 451 VOLUNTEER RIFLE

Originally designed by Irish gunmaker, William John Rigby, this relatively small-caliber rifle was issued to volunteer regiments during the 1860s. Today it is rifled by the cold-forged method, making one turn in 20 inches. Sights are adjustable: globe front and ladder-type rear with interchangeable leaves; hand-checkered walnut stock; weight 9½ lbs. Price includes comprehensive kit of accessories. $575.00

RUGER BLACK POWDER REVOLVER

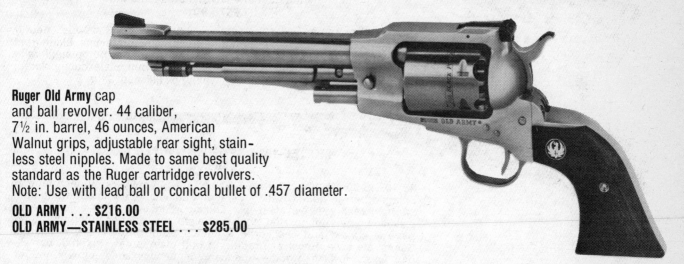

Ruger Old Army cap and ball revolver. 44 caliber, 7½ in. barrel, 46 ounces, American Walnut grips, adjustable rear sight, stainless steel nipples. Made to same best quality standard as the Ruger cartridge revolvers. Note: Use with lead ball or conical bullet of .457 diameter.

OLD ARMY . . . $216.00
OLD ARMY—STAINLESS STEEL . . . $285.00

SPECIFICATIONS of the OLD ARMY

Frame, Cylinder and other **Working Components** are of heat-treated chromemoly steel.
Caliber: 44. Bore .443 in., groove .451 inch
Weight: 2 pounds 14 ounces (46 ounces).
Barrel: 7½ in. Six grooves, right twist, 1 in 16 inches.
Sights: Target rear (adjustable for elevation and windage) and ramp front.
Nipples: Stainless steel for standard caps.
Grips: American Walnut.
Finish: Polished all over; blued and anodized.
The Lockwork is the same as that in the original Ruger Super Blackhawk. All Springs are coil, made from the highest quality steel music wire.

SHILOH
"Sharps Old Reliable" Metallic Cartridge Rifles

MODEL 1874 MILITARY RIFLE
$630.00

45-70 and 50-70 calibers. 30-inch round barrel. Blade front and Lawrence-style sights. Military style forend with 3 barrel bands and 1¼-inch swivels. Receiver group, butt plate and barrel bands case-colored, barrel—dark blue, wood—oil finish. 8 lbs. 12 oz.

MODEL 1874 CARBINE
$499.00

45-70 and 45-90 calibers. 24-inch round barrel, single trigger, blade front and sporting rear sight, butt stock straight grip, steel rifle butt plate, forend sporting Schnabble style. Case-colored receiver group and butt plate; barrel—dark blue; wood—oil finish; 8 lbs. 4 oz.

MODEL 1874 BUSINESS RIFLE
$575.00

45-70, 45-90, 45-120, 50-70, 50-90 and 50-140 calibers. 28-inch heavy-tapered round barrel, double set triggers adjustable set, sights, blade front and sporting rear with leaf. Butt stock is straight grip rifle butt plate, forend sporting Schnabble style. Receiver group and butt plate case-colored, barrel—dark blue, wood—American Walnut oil finished. 9 lbs. 8 oz.

MODEL 1874 SPORTING RIFLE NO. 3
$599.00

45-70, 45-90, 45-120, 50-70, 50-90 and 50-140 calibers. 30-inch tapered octagon barrel, double set triggers with adjustable set, blade front sight, sporting rear with elevation leaf and sporting tang sight adjustable for elevation and windage. Butt stock is straight grip with rifle butt plate, trigger plate is curved and checkered to match pistol grip. Forend is sporting Schnabble style. Receiver group and butt plate is case colored, barrel—high finish blu-black wood—American Walnut oil finished. 9 lbs. 12 oz.

MODEL 1874 SPORTING RIFLE NO. 1
$699.00

45-70, 45-90, 45-120, 50-70, 50-90 and 50-140 calibers. 28 or 30-inch tapered octagon barrel. Double-set triggers with adjustable set, blade front sight, sporting rear with elevation leaf and sporting tang sight adjustable for elevation and windage. Butt stock is pistol grip, shotgun butt, sporting forend Schnabble style. Receiver group and butt plate case colored barrel—high finish blu-black, wood—American Walnut oil finish. 9 lbs. 8 oz.

SHILOH

MODEL 1874 LONG-RANGE EXPRESS SPORTING RIFLE
$749.00

Calibers: 45-70-2 1/10 inch, 45-90-2 4/10 inch, 45-100-2 6/10 inch, 45-110-2⅞ inches, 45-120-3¼ inches, 50-110-2½ inches and 50-140-3¼ inches. 34-inch medium-weight tapered octagon barrel, globe front sight, sporting Tang sight, double set triggers with adjustable set; shotgun-style butt stock, pistol grip and traditional cheek rest with accent line; forend is tapered with Schnabble tip; stock is American black walnut oil finished; overall length—51 inches; 10 lbs. 8 oz.

Breech-loading Percussion Rifles

NEW MODEL 1863 CAVALRY CARBINE
$499.00

54 caliber (Calibers 45 and 50—Special Order). 22-inch round barrel with blade front and Lawrence rear sight with elevation leaf. Military forend with barrel band butt stock Military-style straight grip. Walnut finish. 8 lbs. 12 oz.

NEW MODEL 1863 MILITARY RIFLE
$630.00

54 caliber (Calibers 45 and 50—Special Order). 30-inch round barrel with blade front sight. Lawrence rear sight with elevation leaf. Forend 24 inches in length with steel nose cap, 3 barrel bands, 1¼-inch sling swivels. Butt stock straight grip Military-style, steel butt plate and patch box. 8 lbs. 12 oz.

MODEL 1863 SPORTING RIFLE
$599.00

54 caliber. 30-inch tapered octagon barrel, blade front sight, sporting rear with elevation leaf, double set triggers with adjustable set; curved trigger plate, pistol grip butt stock with steel butt plate, forend Schnabble style; optional Tang sight; 9 lbs.

THOMPSON/CENTER

THE PATRIOT
45 caliber

Featuring a hooked breech, double-set triggers, first-grade American walnut stock, adjustable (patridge-type) target sights, solid-brass trim, beautifully decorated and color case-hardened lock with a small dolphin-shaped hammer, the Patriot weighs approximately 36 ounces. Inspired by traditional gallery and dueling-type pistols, its carefully selected features retain the full flavor of antiquity, yet modern metals and manufacturing methods have been used to ensure its shooting qualities.

Patriot Pistol 36 caliber $185.00
45 caliber 185.00

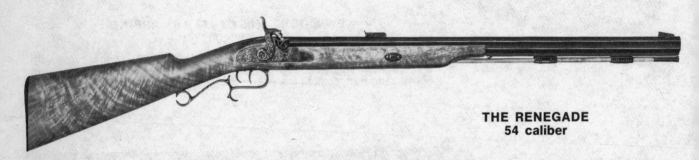

THE RENEGADE
54 caliber

Available in 50, 54 or 56 caliber percussion, the Renegade was designed to provide maximum accuracy and maximum shocking power. Constructed from superior modern steel with investment cast parts carefully fitted to an American walnut stock, the rifle features a precision-rifled (26-inch carbine-type) octagon barrel, hooked-breech system, coil spring lock, double-set triggers, adjustable hunting sights and steel trim.

Renegade 50 and 54 caliber Caplock and 56 caliber smoothbore $215.00
Renegade 50 and 54 caliber Flintlock 227.50

THE SENECA
36 & 45 caliber

Available in either 36 or 45 caliber percussion, the Seneca rifle is patterned on the style of an early New England hunting rifle. Six pounds light, this graceful little half-stock features a hooked breech, double-set triggers, first grade American walnut, adjustable hunting sights, solid-brass trim, coil mainspring and finely patterned color case-hardened lock.
Seneca 36 or 45 caliber Caplock $270.00

THE HAWKEN
45, 50 and 54 caliber

Similar to the famous Rocky Mountain rifles made during the early eighteen hundreds, the Hawken is intended for serious shooting. Button-rifled for ultimate precision, the Hawken is available in 45 or 50 caliber, flint or percussion. Featuring a hooked breech, double-set triggers, first-grade American walnut, adjustable hunting sights, solid-brass trim, beautifully decorated and color case-hardened lock.
Hawken 45, 50 or 54 caliber Caplock $270.00
Hawken 45, 50 or 54 caliber Flintlock 282.50

Air Guns

ANSCHUTZ

MODEL 335—MAGNUM .177 PELLET
$171.50

MODEL 335—.177 PELLET
$161.50

The Model 335 is a superbly designed & manufactured air rifle, specially designed for 10 meter "Novice Expert" competition shooters.

Incredibly accurate in the Anschutz tradition, this fine rifle has many features found on the famous .22 small bore match rifles. The rugged stock is made of selected European hardwood with checkered pistol grip and white line rubber butt plate. Shoots 4.5 mm (.177) pellets. Two stage trigger can be externally adjusted for both travel and weight of pull. Shown with Anschutz front globe and Williams peep receiver sights which are available separately.

Automatic safety lever prevents discharge during cocking. Special barrel cocking mechanism insures consistent straight sight alignment.

Technical Description	335 Magnum	335
Caliber	.177	.177
Precision adjusted two stage trigger, factory set to about	3.75 lbs.	3.75 lbs.
Barrel length	18½ in.	18½ in.
Length overall	43¼ in.	43¼ in.
Total weight (w/o sights)	7¼ lbs.	7¼ lbs.
Rate of twist	One in 14 in.	One in 14 in.

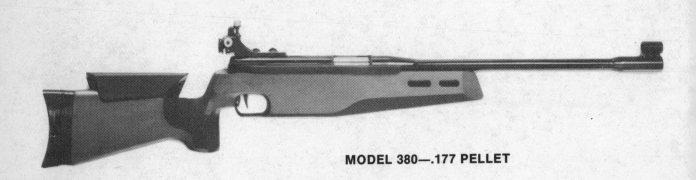

MODEL 380—.177 PELLET

MODEL 380—.177 PELLET
$886.00

A new concept incorporating state of the art design and manufacturing. The easy pull cocking lever assures effortless cocking. The unbelievably superb engineering of this latest Anschutz development makes this rifle absolutely recoilless and vibration free. Sights are motionless during firing. Match two-stage trigger can be adjusted from outside. Cheek piece is removable. Intermediate plates may be added to adapt to individual shooter's stature.

Certified actual 10-shot test target supplied with each rifle. Dated and signed by shooter giving range and brand of ammunition used.

Technical description—Air Rifle Model 380	
Caliber	177
Precision adjusted Match two-stage trigger, factory adjusted to about	3.5 oz.
Sight set	6723
Barrel	12 grooves
Barrel length	20¼ in.
Length overall	42⅛ in.
Total weight including sights 6723	10.8 lbs.

BSA AIR GUNS

SPECIFICATIONS:
Caliber: 177
Barrel Length: 7⅞ inches
Weight: 3.6 lbs.
Overall Length: 15¾ inches
Safety: Safety catch is automatically applied on loading.
Sights: Extra-long sight base; rear sight fully adjustable for windage and elevation.
Features: Precision-bored, all-steel barrel with mirror finish; hammer release system with independent sear for light consistent let-off; trigger weight is externally adjustable.
MK8 Pistolscope, designed for use with
Scorpion Pistol **$59.95**

BSA SCORPION
$139.95

SPECIFICATIONS:
Calibers: 177 and 22
Barrel Length: 19.5 inches
Weight: 8 lbs.
Overall Length: 44.7 inches
Sights: Open; ramp foresight with reversible bead/blade element adjustable for height
Stock: Oil-finished French walnut with high comb Monte Carlo cheekpiece; checkered pistol grip and forend; ventilated recoil pad
Features: Positive underlever action; precision-engineered breech plug; heavy barrel with cold-formed rifling

BSA AIRSPORTER SUPER
$399.95

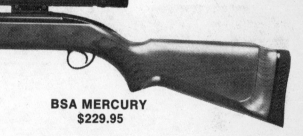

SPECIFICATIONS:
Calibers: 177 and 22
Barrel Length: 18.5 inches
Weight: 7 lbs.
Overall Length: 43.5 inches
Sights: Adjustable bead/blade foresight and tangent rear sight with click adjustment for windage and elevation; reversible "V" and "U" elements
Stock: Polished hardwood with broad forend; Monte Carlo cheekpiece; ventilated rubber recoil pad
Features: High pressure "power seal" unit; match-type, single-stage trigger mechanism

BSA MERCURY
$229.95

BSA MERCURY SUPER
$289.95

BSA METEOR
$149.95

SPECIFICATIONS:
Calibers: 177 and 22
Barrel Length: 18.5 inches
Weight: 6 lbs.
Overall Length: 42 inches
Sights: Adjustable bead/blade foresight; tangent rear sight with click adjustment for windage and elevation; reversible "V" and "U" elements
Stock: Polished hardwood; **Meteor Super** features sculptured Monte Carlo cheekpiece and ventilated rubber recoil pad

BSA METEOR SUPER
$169.95

BEEMAN AIR RIFLES

BEEMAN FEINWERKBAU 124/127
MAGNUM SPORTER $269.00-$319.00

Available in two calibers—.177 cal. (124) and .22 cal. (127) this extra high velocity, barrel cocking sporter features twelve groove precision rifling for minimum pellet distortion and long range accuracy. Non-drying, nylon piston and breech seals are easily replaceable with just a screwdriver after gun disassembly. All steel safety, precision forged receiver. Standard or Deluxe (shown) models. Velocity: 800-830+ fps. (.177 cal.), 680+ fps. (.22 cal.); Barrel length: 18.3 inches; Weight: 6.9 lbs.; Cocking force only 18 lbs.

BEEMAN FEINWERKBAU 300S MATCH
$649.00-$785.00

This .177 caliber rifle is available in several versions, running from the Mini-300 with 17.2-inch barrel to the Match version with 19.9-inch barrels. All have five way adjustable match triggers and ultra-precision aperture rear sights with interchangeable inserts. All are recoilless. Construction emphasizes precision milling rather than stamped parts. Right and left hand models. Weight: 8.8-10.8 lbs.; Velocity: 640 fps. Only 9 lbs. cocking effort.

BEEMAN CARBINE MODEL C1
$149.50

The ONLY mini-magnum air rifle. Velocity: 830 fps. Weighs only 6¼ lbs.; overall length: 38 inches. Accuracy: .20-inch ctc at 25 feet. Single shot, barrel-cocking, spring piston powered. 12-groove rifled, ordnance steel barrel. Single stage trigger adjustable from 2½ to 5½ lbs. Synthetic piston and breech seals. Grooved for scopes. Rear sight click adjustable for windage and elevation.

(shown with optional BEEMAN SS-1 Scope)

BEEMAN AIR RIFLES

BEEMAN/FEINWERKBAU 300S RUNNING BOAR TH
$699.00

The 177-caliber "Running Boar" will aid every stalking hunter with its vibration-free action; grooved for scope only; sidelever cocking; single-stage tripper; spring piston; adjustable walnut comb, thumbhole grip; contoured adjustable buttplate. Barrel length: 19.9 inches; weight: 10.9 lbs.; 640 fps velocity; **$760.00** (left hand).

BEEMAN/FEINWERKBAU 300S UNIVERSAL
$789.50

Extremely versatile, this 177-caliber, spring-piston powered rifle has two detachable front sights, two interchangeable cheekpieces and a special riser rail to raise the scope to higher cheekpiece levels. Barrel length: 19.9 inches; weight: 10.2 lbs. (**$850.00** for left-handed).

BEEMAN/WEBLEY VULCAN II
$189.50

Magnum power and precision at economy price. Incredibly efficient "power intensification". Only regular size adult air rifle under $200 that breaks the 800 fps. velocity barrier. Nice size, lifetime durability, and excellent accuracy make this a top buy for field use. Adjustable trigger, manual safety. Non-drying synthetic piston and breech seals. Scope grooves. Monte Carlo comb stock with white line spacers, rubber buttpad. **Deluxe** version has cut-checkering, genuine solid walnut stock. Vel. 830 fps. in .177 cal., 675 fps. in .22 cal. Accuracy at 25 foot ¼-inch. Wgt. 7½ lbs. Length 43.7-inch. Cocking force 26 lbs. **Cat. No. 1273**—Standard .177 cal., **Cat. No. 1276**—Standard .22 cal. **Cat. No. 1274**—Deluxe .177 cal.

BEEMAN R7
$170.00

Designed in 1982, this 177-caliber rifle features nylon spring piston and breech seals for long life and maximum power. Also has double jointed cocking lever; spring piston power; match grade trigger block; solid metal grooved trigger and micro-adjustable rear sight. Velocity: 680 fps; Barrel length: 17 inches; Weight: 5.8 lbs.

BEEMAN AIR PISTOLS

BEEMAN FEINWERKBAU MODEL 65 MK II
$495.00-$585.00

This new short barrel version of the world's top winning air pistol features two mainsprings for more power and smoothness. New short barrel (now 6.1 inches long) provides better balance and handling characteristics. Also recoilless action and spring piston power with steel piston ring. Side lever cocking, requires only 16 lbs. effort. Only recoilless pistol that is instantly convertible to firearm recoil and trigger action. Velocity: 450-525 fps. Available with standard and adjustable match grips (shown).

BEEMAN FEINWERKBAU MODEL 80
$595.00 ($625.00 for left handers)

177 caliber spring-piston powered pistol with metal piston ring and dual mainsprings. Single stroke side-lever cocking arm requires only 17 lbs. effort. Fixed barrel and straight line breech block seating mean maximum accuracy. Features balance-adjustable weights which do not touch barrel and special 4-way adjustable match trigger. Adjustable grip. Match sights fully adjustable, including notch width. Weight: 2.8-3.2 lbs.; Barrel: 7.5 inches, 12 groove rifling; Length: 16.4 inches overall.

BEEMAN/FEINWERKBAU 90
$625.00-$655.00

Boasts an incredible electronic trigger. Trigger action at any given setting is absolutely constant, and this mechanism may be dry-fired for practice sessions. Other features the same as the Beeman/FWB 80, but without balance adjustment weights. Wgt. 3.0 lbs.; Lgth. 16.4 inches. **Cat. No. 2151.**

BEEMAN/WEBLEY HURRICANE
$129.95

Available in 177 and 22 calibers. Rearward recoil like firearm pistol. Features adjustable rear sight and trigger pull, manual safety, and detachable scope mount. Steel piston and steel cylinder. Weight: 2.4 lbs.; Length: 11½ inches overall; Barrel length: 8 inches; Velocity: 470 fps. (177).

BENJAMIN AIR RIFLE

MODELS 3100, 3120: Benjamin Super Repeater Air Rifles with Monte Carlo stock. Cal. BB or 22 . **$96.20**

MODELS NO. 340, 342, 347: Benjamin Super Single Shot Air Rifle with Monte Carlo stock. Cal. BB or 177 or 22 has new rugged square top ramp-type front sight **$96.20**

No. 273 Detachable Rear Peep

Sight. Adjustable. For Models 340 - 342 - 347 - 310 - 312 - 317 - 720 - BENJAMIN AIR RIFLES. Advise Model.
Each **$6.50**
Extra Discs, Small, Medium, Large. Each **$3.30**

BAR-O Detachable Rear Peep

Sight. Adjustable. For all Models Benjamin Rifles with BAR-V Sight. Advise Model.
Each **$2.90**
Extra Discs, Small, Medium, Large. Each **$1.45**

Benjamin BAR-V Rear

Sight. It Rotates! Provides Quick, Sensitive Adjustment of Elevation and Windage.
Each **$2.90**

BENJAMIN H-C LEAD PELLETS
"Sized and Lubricated"

	Per Can
Benjamin H-C Lead Pellets Cal. 177 (250)	**$2.00**
Benjamin H-C Lead Pellets Cal. 177 (500)	**3.70**
Benjamin H-C Lead Pellets Cal. 22 (250)	**2.60**
Benjamin H-C Lead Pellets Cal. 22 (500)	**4.75**

BENJAMIN ROUND BALL SHOT

Benjamin Steel Air Rifle Shot—BB 500	**$1.25**
Benjamin Steel Air Rifle Shot—BB 1 lb.	**2.55**
Benjamin Lead Air Rifle Shot—BB 500	**3.90**
Benjamin Lead Air Rifle Shot—BB—4.5mm 1 lb.	**6.00**
Benjamin Round Lead Shot—Cal. 22—5.5 mm. 1 lb.	**6.00**

MODELS 130, 132, 137 Single Shot Air Pistol Cal. BB or 177 or 22 $78.10

STANDARD SIZE JET KING CO$_2$ CARTRIDGE

For use in Benjamin Super Gas Rifles and Pistols. 10 in a box. **$4.95**
Size 2⅝ in. x 47/64 in. 8.5 Gram.

CROSMAN AIR & GAS PISTOLS

MODEL 454
SEMI-AUTO BB MATIC
$29.95

Positive force feed magazine holds 16 Super BBs • Contoured grips with thumbrest for left- or right-handed shooters • Over 80 shots per CO_2 Power-let • Average muzzle velocity— 375 f.p.s. • Positive slide-action safety • Rear sights adjustable for windage and elevation • Barrel length 7¾ inches • Overall length—11⅜ inches • Weight—29 Oz.

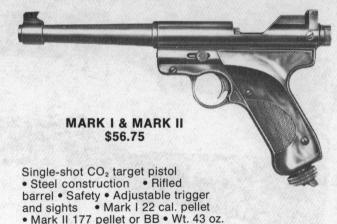

MARK I & MARK II
$56.75

Single-shot CO_2 target pistol • Steel construction • Rifled barrel • Safety • Adjustable trigger and sights • Mark I 22 cal. pellet • Mark II 177 pellet or BB • Wt. 43 oz. • Length 11⅛ inches. (Left-hand grips available).

MODELS 1322 & 1377
$47.50

MODEL 1322: Single-shot 22 caliber pump pistol. Heavy duty pump link with sure grip checkered forearm. Selective pump power. Fully adjustable sights. Cross-bolt safety. Button rifled solid steel barrel. Gun blued steel parts.

MODEL 1377: Single-shot 177 caliber pump pistol. Heavy duty pump link with sure grip checkered forearm. Selective pump power. Fully adjustable sights. Cross-bolt safety. Button rifled, solid steel barrel. Gun blued steel parts.

MODEL 38-T
$41.25

MODEL 38-C: Combat. CO_2 177 Pellet Revolver. Holds six 177 caliber Pells. Single and Double action and revolving cylinder. Length 9½ inches. Weight 46 ozs. 10 lands R.H. twist. 3¼-inch barrel. **$41.95**

MODEL 38-T: CO_2 177 Pellet Revolver. For Target shooting. Length 11¾ inches. Weight 46 ozs. Rifling: 10 lands R.H. twist, 1 turn in 16 inches, button rifled. 6-inch barrel. **$41.95**

MODEL 1861 SHILOH
$31.25

Six-shot CO_2– powered pistol • Shoots BBs and 177 caliber pellets • Features cross-bolt safety, wood styled grips and 6¾-inch rifled steel barrel • Length 12¾ inches.

MODEL 1600 POWERMATIC
$29.50

MODEL 1600 POWERMATIC

Automatic firing 16-shot BB repeater • Leakproof CO_2 powered • Length 11⅜ inches • Weight 29 oz.

CROSMAN AIR & GAS RIFLES

MODEL 1: 22 caliber pneumatic air rifle. Micrometer adjustable rear sights. Single-shot bolt action. Grooved metal receiver for scope mounting. Features an American hardwood stock and forearm. Rifled brass barrel for maximum accuracy. Length: 39 inches; weight: 5 lbs. 1 oz. **$86.75**

MODEL 73: 16-shot BB repeater. CO_2 powered. Solid steel barrel. Positive lever safety. Also shoots 177 caliber pellets. Length: 34¾ inches; weight: 3 lbs. 4 oz. Average muzzle velocity: BB—425 fps; Pellet—435 fps. **$30.00**

MODEL 760: 180-shot BB repeater, pump action. Shoots 177 or BB caliber. BB's from storage chamber are metered into visual loading magazine. **$37.50**

MODEL 788 BB SCOUT: Starter gun with selective pump-up power and gravity-feed magazine, open rear sights adjustable for windage and elevation, positive bolt action, butt plate on stock and a solid-steel barrel and cross-bolt safety. Magazine holds 20 BBs and one BB in chamber. Overall length is 31 inches. **$25.95**

CROSMAN RIFLES & ACCESSORIES

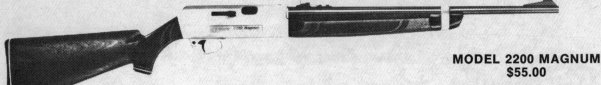

MODEL 2200 MAGNUM
$55.00

Bolt action, single shot 22 caliber pellet pneumatic rifle with a contoured pistol-grip stock, pumping mechanism with selective power; fixed blade front sight; butt plate with white line spacer and metal rear sights that are adjustable for windage and elevation. Weight is 4 lbs. 12 oz. Overall length is 39¾ inches.

MODEL 766 $47.95

American Classic Model 766 features rifled barrel, bolt action receiver and a positive cross-bolt safety. 177 caliber, single-shot pneumatic rifle. Rear sight adjustable for windage and elevation with a fixed blade front sight. Weight 4 lbs. 14 oz. Length 39¾ inches.

CROSMAN COPPERHEAD™ BBs

Perfectly round copper-plated steel shots assure greatest accuracy and in-flight stability; waisted diabolo design assures maximum weight distribution from head to skirt.

Model 617—200 BBs (bag) .... $ .25
Model 627—400 BBs (bag) .... .49
Model 737—1500 BBs (carton) 1.49
Model 747—2500 BBs (carton) 2.49
Model 757—5000 BBs (carton) 4.69

CROSMAN COPPERHEAD™ CO POWERLETS®

These CO_2 Powerlets® are leakproof, corrosion-resistant and uniform in pressure. 5 Powerlets® to a pack $1.99

DAISY AIR GUNS

Daisy 179 SIX GUN
$28.00

The "Spittin' Image" of the famed Colt Peacemaker in style and action. Forced-feed, 12-shot repeating action. Single-action cocking hammer. Blued barrel, receiver; wood-grained molded grips. 11½ inches length.

MODEL 188 B-B/PELLET PISTOL
$22.30

• **SPRING ACTION AIR PISTOL. CALIBER:** 177 cal. **OVERALL LENGTH:** 12 inches. **MUZZLE VELOCITY:** B •B's, 215 feet-per-second (65.5 mps); pellets, 180 feet-per-second (55 mps). **ACTION:** Under barrel cocking lever. **SIGHTS:** Blade and ramp front, notched rear. **GRIPS:** Checkered and contoured with thumbrest. **FEED:** Gravity, easy-loading port, 24 B•B shot capacity or single shot pellet.

MODEL 1188 B-B PISTOL
$22.30

A new concept in controlled velocity, spring-action air pistols. **GRIP & RECEIVER:** Black, die-cast metal, contoured grip with thumbrest, checkering. **BARREL:** Smooth bore steel. **ACTION:** Under-barrel cocking lever. **SIGHTS:** Blade and ramp front, notched rear. **FEED:** Gravity, easy-loading port, 24 B•B shot repeater. **SAFETY:** Manual. **MUZZLE VELOCITY:** 215 fps (65.5 mps). **LENGTH:** 12 inches (30.4 cm). Boxed.

MODELS 717
$68.00

• **MATCH QUALITY PNEUMATIC AIR PELLET PISTOLS. CALIBER:** Model 717, 177 cal.; **OVERALL LENGTH:** 13½ inches. **ACTION:** Single pump pneumatic, side-operating pump lever. **MUZZLE VELOCITY:** Model 717, 360 feet-per-second (109.7 mps). **SIGHTS:** Blade and front ramp, match grade fully adjustable notch rear with micrometer adjustments. **GRIPS:** Super-strength molded, woodgraining and checkering; contoured with thumbrest. Left-hand grips available.

DAISY AIR GUNS

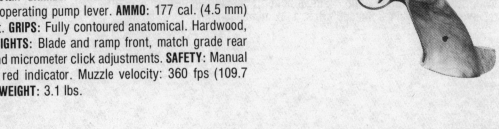

POWER LINE 777
$240.00

RECEIVER: Black, die-cast metal. **BARREL:** Rifled steel. **ACTION:** Recoilless, single pump pneumatic. Side operating pump lever. **AMMO:** 177 cal. (4.5 mm) lead pellets. **FEED:** Single shot. **GRIPS:** Fully contoured anatomical. Hardwood, available right or left hand. **SIGHTS:** Blade and ramp front, match grade rear with adjustable width notch and micrometer click adjustments. **SAFETY:** Manual cross-bolt trigger block with red indicator. Muzzle velocity: 360 fps (109.7 mps). **LENGTH:** 13½ inches". **WEIGHT:** 3.1 lbs.

POWER LINE 790*
$68.00

RECEIVER: Black, die-cast metal. **BARREL:** Rifled steel. **ACTION:** CO_2 gas operated, manual cocking. **FEED:** Single shot. **AMMO:** Model 790, 177 cal. lead pellets. **LENGTH:** 11.3 inches **GRIPS:** Super-strength molded, woodgrained and checkered, contoured to fit right or left hand. **SIGHTS:** Blade and ramp front, fully adjustable notch rear. **SAFETY:** Manual cross-bolt trigger block. Muzzle velocity; Model 790, 355-425 fps.

*Model 790 formerly Smith & Wesson model 796.

MODEL 1200 CUSTOM CO₂ B•B PISTOL
$35.70

GRIP: Contoured, checkered, molded wood grained. **BARREL:** Smoothbore, heavy wall, seamless. **ACTION:** CO gas operated. **SIGHTS:** Blade and ramp front, fully adjustable square notch rear. **CALIBER:** 177 B•B repeater, 60 B•B shot reservoir. **VELOCITY:** 420/450 fps. **LENGTH:** 12⅛ inches.

DAISY MODEL 840
$35.70

DAISY MODEL 840. Single pump pneumatic rifle with straight pull bolt action. Single shot .155 caliber pellet or 350-shot B•B repeater. Rifled barrel. Molded wood-grained stock and forearm; steel butt plate. Forearm forms pump lever. Adjustable open rear sight, ramp front. Cross bolt trigger safety. Muzzle velocity: B•Bs 310 fps; pellets 270 fps.

DAISY AIR GUNS

POWER LINE MODEL 850 $64.60

POWER LINE MODEL 850 SINGLE PUMP PNEUMATIC B•B/ PELLET RIFLE. Magazine: 100-shot B•B reservoir; **Ammo:** 177 cal. Daisy pellets, Daisy Bullseye® B•Bs; **Barrel:** Rifled steel. **Stock/Forearm:** Full length molded. Sporter styling with hand-wiped checkered wood-grain finish. Separate butt plate; **Receiver:** Black die cast metal. Dovetail scope mount; **Safety:** Manual cross-bolt trigger block with red indicator; **Sights:** Ramp front, fully adjustable open rear; **Weight:** 4.3 lbs.; **Overall Length:** 38⅜ inches; Muzzle velocity: 177 cal. pellets, 480 fps.; B•Bs, 520 fps.

MODEL 851: Same as Model 850, with select hardwood stock and forearm.$86.00

POWER LINE MODEL 880 $53.20

POWER LINE MODEL 880 PUMP-UP B•B REPEATER AND SINGLE SHOT PELLET GUN IN ONE. Great for shooters 14 and over. Pneumatic pump-up for variable power (velocity and range) increasing with pump strokes. Only 10 strokes required for maximum power. 100-shot capacity B•B magazine. Single-shot 177 caliber pellets. Ramp front and open rear sights. Scope mount. Monte Carlo design, molded stock with cheekpiece and molded forearm. Cross-bolt safety with red indicator and positive cocking valve safety prevents hang-fires. Length: 37¾ inches.

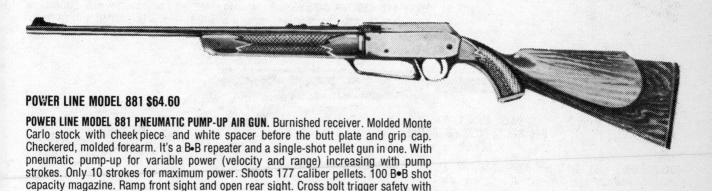

POWER LINE MODEL 881 $64.60

POWER LINE MODEL 881 PNEUMATIC PUMP-UP AIR GUN. Burnished receiver. Molded Monte Carlo stock with cheekpiece and white spacer before the butt plate and grip cap. Checkered, molded forearm. It's a B•B repeater and a single-shot pellet gun in one. With pneumatic pump-up for variable power (velocity and range) increasing with pump strokes. Only 10 strokes for maximum power. Shoots 177 caliber pellets. 100 B•B shot capacity magazine. Ramp front sight and open rear sight. Cross bolt trigger safety with red indicator and positive cocking valve. Length: 37¾ inches.

DAISY MODEL 95 $32.75

DAISY 95 WOODSTOCK. Modern sporter style with real gun heft and feel. Full seasoned wood stock, sporter forearm. Gravity-feed 700-shot repeating action. Controlled velocity. Ramp front, adjustable "V" slot rear sights. Length: 35 inches.

DAISY AIR GUNS

POWR LINE MODEL 922
$70.90

Action: Pneumatic pump-up clip-fed pellet repeater. Straight pull bolt; **Feed System:** 5-shot positive index clip. Single shot adapter included; **Ammo:** Daisy Match pellets. 922: .22 cal. (5.5 mm). 917: .177 cal. (4.5 mm); **Barrel:** 20.8 inches (52.8 cm) Decagon rifled brass. Twist 1 turn in 16 inches (40.6 cm); **Barrel Shroud:** Tapered steel; **Stock/Forearm:** Monte Carlo stock, super-strength molded, hand-wiped finish, wood-graining, checkering, thumb grooves, separate butt plate and grip cap, white spacers, checkered forearm, diamond inlay; **Receiver:** Engraved gold tone filled; black finish. Dove-tail scope mount; **Safety:** Manual cross bolt trigger block. Red indicator and open bolt; **Trigger Pull Weight:** 5 lbs. (2.3 kg); **Sights:** Ramp front, fully adjustable open rear, dovetail on receiver; **Weight:** 5 lbs. (2.2 kg); **Overall Length:** 37¾ inches (95.8 cm); **Pumping Effort:** 4 to 18.5 lbs., 1 to 10 pumps.

DAISY MODEL 105
$22.00

DAISY 105 PAL. Lever action with automatic trigger block safety. Post front sight, open rear sight. Extra strength molded stock. Gravity feed, 350 shot. 260′ controlled velocity. Length: 30½ inches.

DAISY MODEL 111
$29.00

DAISY 111 WESTERN CARBINE. Lever-cocking western carbine style with underbarrel rapid-loading port. Famed Daisy gravity-feed 700-shot repeating action with controlled velocity. Post front, adjustable "V" slot rear sights. Simulated gold receiver engraving. Length 35 inches.

DAISY MODEL 1938
RED RYDER COMMEMORATIVE
$42.50

DAISY MODEL 1938 RED RYDER COMMEMORATIVE. The B•B gun Dads remember. Wood stock burned with Red Ryder lariat signature, wood forearm, saddle ring with leather thong. Lever cocking 700-shot repeating action. Post front, adjustable V-slot, rear sights. Length: 35 inches.

DAISY MODEL 1894
$42.50

DAISY 1894 SPITTIN' IMAGE B•B GUN. The "Spittin' Image" of the famed "carbine that won the West." 2-way lever cocking, side-loading port. 40-shot controlled-velocity repeated. 38 inches.

GAMO AIR RIFLES

CADET $94.00
177 Caliber

The Gamo Cadet is specifically scaled to the young shooter but has the heft, feel and look of an adult air rifle. Features an automatic trigger block safety, which must be moved before firing; an all-steel precision-rifled barrel; micro-adjustable 2-way click rear sight and grooved receiver for mounting scopes using 11mm bases. Stock is lacquered hard beechwood. One cocking stroke provides 570 fps muzzle velocity. The Cadet carries a one-year warranty.

EXPO $110.00
177 and 22 Calibers

The Gamo Expo target rifle has a 12-grooved, precision-rifled barrel with fully adjustable sights. Trigger tension is externally adjustable for a smooth, crisp pull; barrel is all steel and precision rifled for maximum rigidity and accuracy. The Expo also features a single cocking stroke to expose the breech for manual loading and provide a full 600 fps velocity. A year's warranty is provided.

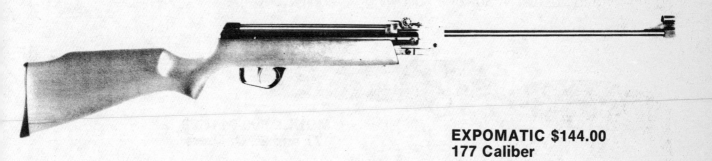

EXPOMATIC $144.00
177 Caliber

The Gamo Expomatic, a high-performance target rifle, features a 25-pellet and spring-loaded tubular magazine. As the barrel is cocked, a pellet is automatically fed into the chamber, so reloading is fast and rapid-fire action is easy and accurate. This air gun also features an all-steel barrel in a heavy-weight contour; adjustable trigger; micro-adjustable rear sight and hooded front sight and lacquered beechwood stock. One-year warranty. Velocity: 600 fps.

GAMO AIR RIFLES

GAMO 68 $144.00
177 and 22 Calibers

The Gamo 68 features an aluminum butt-stock with a polymer forestock in grip, micro-adjustable sights and a precision-rifled barrel that provides exceptional accuracy. Because the Gamo 68 pistol grip is usually held during the cocking operation, a special safety device blocks the trigger until the barrel is fully locked. The trigger is externally adjustable for weight of pull. A single cocking stroke provides 600 fps muzzle velocity. One-year warranty.

GAMATIC $178.00
177 Caliber

The Gamatic, available in 177 caliber only, offers the same quality features as the Gamo 68 but also boasts a 25-pellet, spring-loaded tubular magazine, allowing rapid fire action. When the barrel is cocked, a pellet is automatically fed into the chamber, making reloading fast and effortless. A year's warranty accompanies the gun. Velocity: 600 fps.

MODEL 600 $144.00
177 and 22 Calibers

The Model 600 is an adult-size gun with all the performance needed for plinking and target shooting. A precision-rifled, target-quality barrel delivers quarter-inch groups at 25 feet; trigger is fully adjustable for crisp release; rear sight is micro-adjustable for windage and elevation; receiver is grooved to accept 11 millimeter scope mounts; stock is lacquered beechwood. One cocking stroke provides 660 fps muzzle velocity. The Model 600 carries a year's warranty.

GAMO AIR GUNS & ACCESSORIES

CENTER PISTOL
177 Caliber $110.00

The Center Pistol is equipped with a precision-broad, fixed barrel and underbarrel lever cocking spring; swing-out breech for easy loading; 14-inch sight radius with fully adjustable target sights and fully adjustable trigger. Anatomically designed competition-style grip is adjustable to suit individual shooter's preference. The Center Pistol carries a one-year warranty.

GAMO PISTOL
177 Caliber $60.00

NEW GAMO AIR PISTOL POWER, PERFORMANCE AND ACCURACY COMBINED WITH QUALITY YOU WON'T BELIEVE. VELOCITY: 435 FPS.

PRECISION PELLETS

	Caliber	Price Per Can
Diabolo Pellets (500 in Can)	177	**$2.70**
Diabolo Pellets (250 in Can)	177	1.90
Diabolo Pellets (250 in Can)	22	2.70

ACCESSORIES

	Price
Catch Pellet	**$15.00**
Catch Pellet Rocker	50.00
Bullet Trap	30.00
Target Transport Device	100.00
Flat Catch Pellet	10.00

MARKSMAN AIR GUNS & ACCESSORIES

MODEL 1740
177 caliber
$35.00

SPECIFICATIONS:
Caliber: 177 BB's, pellets, darts
Capacity: 100 rds.
Barrel Length: 15½ inches
Weight: 5.08 lbs.
Action: Spring, break action
Safety: Automatic safety sets after each firing
Finish: One-piece walnut finished stock

PLAINSMAN MODEL 1049
CO₂ AIR PISTOL
$35.00

SPECIFICATIONS:
Caliber: 177 BB shot
Capacity: 100 rds.
Barrel Length: 5⅞ inches
Weight: 1¾ lbs.
Sights: Sport blade front; fixed notched rear
Action: Double-action trigger pull
Safety: Thumb
Finish: Durable black epoxy with walnut wood-grain plastic grips

SPECIFICATIONS:
Caliber: 177 BB's, pellets, darts
Capacity: 20 rounds
Barrel Length: 2½ inches
Weight: 1 lb. 8 oz.
Sights: Sport blade front; fixed notch rear
Action: Spring
Safety: Thumb
Finish: Durable black epoxy frame
MODEL 1020 AIR PISTOL: Same as Model 1010, except shoots BB's only.

MARKSMAN 1010 AIR PISTOL
$14.00

MARKSMAN AIR GUN PELLETS

For all makes of air pistols and air rifles. These "waisted design" lead pellets ensure positive grip on rifling and expansion on targets. Produced to close size and weight tolerances.

177 caliber (4.5mm) lead pellets:		22 Caliber (5.5mm) lead pellets:	
No. 1212 (200 pellets)	**$1.50**	No. 1222 (200 pellets)	**$1.50**
No. 1215 (500 pellets)	2.75	No. 1225 (500 pellets)	2.75

PRECISE AIR GUNS

SPECIFICATIONS:
Caliber: 177
Capacity: Single shot
Barrel Length: 6 inches
Weight: 2 lbs. 3 oz.
Sights: Four interchangeable front sights; four rotating rear sights, micro-adjustable for windage and elevation
Action: Break action, barrel cocking
Muzzle Velocity: 310 fps

RO-72 AIR PISTOL
$40.00

Caliber: .177
Capacity: Single Shot
Overall Length: 43 inches
Barrel Length: 19 inches (rifled)
Weight: 5 lbs. 8 oz.
Sights: Hooded front sight; ratchet-adjustable rear
Action: Spring; barrel cocking
Finish: Hardwood stock, hardware mounted to stock for attaching sling, barrel lock/release to ease cocking.
Muzzle Velocity: 785 f.p.s.

PRECISE MINUTEMAN® MEDALIST
$65.00

SPECIFICATIONS:
Caliber: 177
Capacity: Single shot
Barrel Length: 19.4 inches
Weight: 7 lbs. 4 oz.
Sights: Hooded front sight; micrometer adjustable rear
Action: Spring; underlever cocking
Finish: Dark hardwood Monte Carlo stock with raised cheekpiece and buttplate; receiver grooved for mounting scope
Muzzle Velocity: 575 fps

PRECISE MINUTEMAN® MAGNUM
$100.00

SHERIDAN AIR GUNS

MODEL HB
$80.40

Sheridan's pneumatic Model HB Pistol has the same dependability, durability, and accuracy associated with all Sheridan Products. This new Pistol offers Sheridan's "Controlled-Power®" with a range of three to ten pumps. The new Model HB gives you a velocity of 400 ft./sec. with ten pumps.

SPECIFICATIONS:
Action: Turn bolt-single shot
Caliber: Sheridan 5mm
Barrel: 9⅜-inch rifled and rust proof
Sights: Blade front — fully adjustable rear

Length: 12 inches overall
Safety: Cross bolt
Finish: Blue
Weight: 36 oz.

MODEL EB-CO₂ PISTOL
$60.35 (not illus.)

SPECIFICATIONS:
Caliber: 20, 5mm
Barrel Length: 6½ inches
Weight: 27 oz.
Sights: Blade front sight; fully adjustable rear

Power: 12 gram CO_2 cylinders
Action: Turn bolt, single action
Finish: Durable blue with checkered simulated walnut grips

SHERIDAN AIR GUNS

PNEUMATIC RIFLES

Blue Streak Model CB **Single Shot: 5MM.**

Silver Streak Model C

A rifle for target or small-game shooters. Full-length Mannlicher stock is made of genuine hand rubbed walnut. All working parts are precision engineered to assure accuracy and dependability.

- Controlled velocity. Pump action permits the shooter to determine the exact amount of velocity required for each shot. Improved valving mechanism assures long, trouble-free, high-quality performance.
- "Over and under" design with precision-rifled rigid mount barrel
- Take-down walnut stock is readily removable
- Single shot, bolt action design
- Manual safety, mounted for easy thumb control
- Choice of blue (BLUE STREAK) or satin-silver (SILVER STREAK) finish.
- Overall length: 37 in. Weight: 5¼ lbs.

MODELS AVAILABLE

MODEL	DESCRIPTION	PRICE
	With Standard Open Sight	
CB	Blue Streak	$101.55
C	Silver Streak	105.40
	With Receiver Sight	
CBW	Blue Streak	118.15
CW	Silver Streak	121.95
	With Scope Sight	
CBS	Blue Streak	134.15
CS	Silver Streak	138.00

GAS POWERED CO$_2$ RIFLES

Blue Streak Model FB **Single Shot: 5MM**

35 Power Packed Shots

Silver Streak Model F

The Gas-Powered CO$_2$ Rifle is a companion line to the Pneumatics for those who enjoy or need faster shooting or who can't or just don't like to pump an air rifle

- Blade type front sight
- 5mm (20 cal.) precision-rifled rust proof barrel
- Lightweight (6 lbs.)
- Compact length (37 in.).
- Over and under type construction with rigid mount barrel
- Open sight easily adjustable for windage and elevation
- Choice of blue or durable silver-satin plated finish
- Bolt action (single shot)
- "Fireproof" safety
- Sturdy valving mechanism with "locked in" charge
- Easy takedown design
- Full sporter length walnut stock

Note—All rifles listed on this page are available in left-hand versions at the same price.

MODELS AVAILABLE

MODEL	DESCRIPTION	PRICE
	With Standard Open Sight	
FB	Blue Streak	$101.55
F	Silver Streak	105.40
	With Receiver Sight	
FBW	Blue Streak	118.15
FW	Silver Streak	121.95
	With Scope Sight	
FBS	Blue Streak	134.15
FS	Silver Streak	138.00

SHERIDAN ACCESSORIES

SHERIDAN INTERMOUNT

The Sheridan Intermount will accept any scope and mount made to fit the ⅜ in. standard dove tail. We can of course also furnish an excellent low-priced scope sight that we feel best suited to the needs of Sheridan owners. Prices are shown below.

No. 61—Wt. each 3 oz. **$12.65**

SHERIDAN INTERMOUNT AND SCOPE
Supplied with Weaver 4x scope.

No. 62—Wt. each 2 lbs. **$30.60**

LOW COST SHERIDAN AMMUNITION

The 5mm (20 caliber) ammo is solid-nosed, bullet-shaped, super-penetrating, matched to the precision-rifled Sheridan barrels for proper sectional density and best ballistic coefficient. New plastic, reusable pellet box holds 500 rounds. Inset, hinged dispenser permits removal of pellets, one at a time.

No. 50—500 in a box **$5.80**

No. 51—500 in a box **$5.80**

PELLETRAP

Sheridan's Pelletrap is a compact, inexpensive, versatile target holder and backstop for air rifle practice. Wall hanger and flat base permit use most anywhere, indoors or out.

Weight each 6 lbs. **$19.00**

No. 24—Pelletrap Target Faces per 100 .... **$2.55**

SHERIDAN CO₂ CARTRIDGES

Standard 12.5 gram size and may be used in any CO_2 rifle or pistol calling for a 12.5 gram cartridge.

No. 63—5 in a box .... **$3.60** per box

Genuine leather holster for Sheridan CO_2 pistol. Features snap buttons on belt loop and safety snap.

No. 66 .... **$15.90**

Cleaning rod for Sheridan products.

No. 41 .... **$5.10**

SIG-HAMMERLI AIR GUNS

403 MATCH-SPORTER RIFLE $395.00
(without receiver sight)
Caliber: 177
Weight: 9 lbs. 4 ozs.
Overall Length: 45 inches
Sights: Front sight is globe tunnel with interchangeable sight inserts; rear sight is adjustable match-micrometer type.
Stock: Beechwood
Muzzle Velocity: 700-740 fps
Features: Raised cheekpiece; oversized rubber recoil pad; side-lever cocking; square forends.

MILITARY LOOK 420 $295.00
(without scope)
Calibers: 177 or 22
Barrel Length: 19 inches
Weight: 7½ lbs.
Overall Length: 43 inches
Sights: Front sight is globe tunnel with interchangeable sight inserts; rear sight is open and adjustable for windage.
Stock: Dark green, high-impact plastic.
Muzzle Velocity: 700-740 fps

WALTHER AIR GUNS

SPECIFICATIONS:
Caliber: 177
Capacity: Single shot
Barrel Length(s): 9⅜ inches
Weight: 45.8 oz.
Overall Length: 13-3/16 inches
Sights: Micro-click rear sight, adjustable for windage and elevation
Action: Lever
Features: Power is compressed air. Recoilless operation, cocking in grip frame. 4-way adjustable trigger. Plastic thumbrest grips

WALTHER MODEL LP3
$385.00

WALTHER MODEL LP3 MATCH $465.00
SPECIFICATIONS:
Same as Model LP3 except with improved target grips with adjustable hand shelf

WALTHER MODEL LP53 $215.00
SPECIFICATIONS:
Caliber: 177
Capacity: Single shot
Barrel Length(s): 9⅜ inches
Weight: 40.5 oz.
Overall Length: 12⅜ inches
Sights: Micrometer rear sight; interchangeable rear sight blades
Features: Power is spring air. Target grips. Optional equipment includes barrel weight for improved balance.

WALTHER LGR MATCH AIR RIFLE
$750.00

SPECIFICATIONS:
Caliber: 4.5mm (177)
Barrel Length: 19½
Overall Length: 44¼ inches
Weight: 10 lbs. 2 oz.
Stock: Same as LGR Air with exception of a high comb stock.
Sights: Same as LGR Air with the exception that sights are mounted on riser blocks.
Features: Same as LGR Air Rifle.

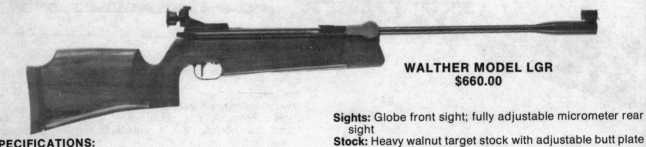

WALTHER MODEL LGR
$660.00

Sights: Globe front sight; fully adjustable micrometer rear sight
Stock: Heavy walnut target stock with adjustable butt plate and adjustable muzzle weight
Features: Lever cocking, static pressure system provides constant velocity, shot after shot. Recoilless and vibration free. Adjustable trigger

SPECIFICATIONS:
Caliber: 4.5mm (177)
Barrel Length(s): 19½ inches
Weight: 10 lbs. 2 oz.
Overall Length: 44¼ inches

WALTHER MODEL LGV SPECIAL
$550.00

SPECIFICATIONS:
Caliber: 4.5 mm (177)
Capaicty: Single shot
Barrel Length(s): 16 inches
Weight: 10 lbs. 4 oz.
Overall Length: 41⅜ inches

Sights: Globe front sight; micrometer adjustable rear sight
Trigger: Adjustable
Stock: Heavy walnut target stock matches styling and weight of the Walther small-bore target rifles, with fully adjustable butt plate

Sights, Scopes & Mounts

BUEHLER SAFETY & GUN SCREWS

BUEHLER LOW-SCOPE SAFETY

The Buehler Safety operates on the same mechanical principles as the manufacturer's original safety. In the "ON" position, pressure of the striker spring locks it securely. It will not cam over into firing position. Safety holds BOTH BOLT and STRIKER in locked position.

This safety operates on the right side of the action, rotating through an arc of 70 degrees with definite stops in the OFF and ON positions. It can be used equally well with or without a scope, and will be found to be faster and more convenient than the original safety. Complete with instructions for installation.

For following models:
MAUSER (M98, F.N.), KRAG, SPRINGFIELD
WINCHESTER M54, 1891 ARGENTINE
MAUSER

FILLISTER HEAD & PLUG SCREWS

		Prices
6x48 SCREWS (⅛, ¼, 5/16, ½" Mixed)		12-$2.00
6x48 PLUG SCREWS 3/32"		12- 2.00
8x40 SCREWS (¼ & ⅜" Mixed)		12- 2.00
8x40 PLUG SCREWS 3/32".		12- 2.00
10x32 PLUG SCREWS 3/32".		12- 2.00

GUARD SCREWS: Prices
UNIVERSAL .... $1.85 Ea.
ENFIELD GUARD SCREW
  SCREWS UNIVERSAL ....1.85 Ea.
SPRINGFIELD (KRAG) GD.
MAUSER GUARD SCREWS 4.60 Set

BUEHLER SCOPE MOUNTS

BUEHLER TELESCOPIC SIGHT MOUNTS: By using one of the five basic styles of mount bases, you may position the scope of your choice in the best possible location. The best location is the one that positions the scope in such a way as to give a full field of view when the shooter's face is nestled in a comfortable, natural position against the stock. Scopes vary in eye relief from 3 to 5 inches. Sight adjustment turrets are in different locations. The amount of space available on the scope for the mount varies. Most important of all is the difference in shooters and in the way each one holds a rifle. One of the five styles of mounts will locate your scope in the best position for you. A good gunsmith or experienced sporting goods dealer is a great help in making this choice. All Buehler mount rings fit and are interchangeable with all Buehler bases.

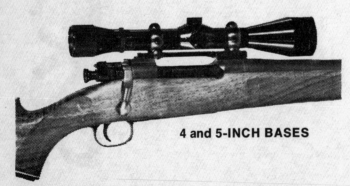

4 and 5-INCH BASES

SHORT ONE-PIECE BASES

The short one-piece base locates the front ring over the top of the receiver ring about 1 inch aft of the long one-piece base. The rear ring is in about the same location. Thus, ring spacing averages 4 inches. The short base is recommended for shorter scopes, scopes with large and long objective bells, and scopes with turrets near the center of the tube.

LONG ONE-PIECE BASES

This base is made to fit most of the rifles in common use. In most models it has the rings, spaced about 5 inches apart.
One Piece Scope Mount base, 4" or 5" $24.75

TWO-PIECE BASE

Two-piece bases locate the front ring over the receiver ring in the same place as the short one-piece base. The rear ring, however, is over the bridge on bolt action rifles, not ahead of it as is the case with the one-piece bases. The ring spacing averages 4½ inches. Will accommodate scopes described under the *short* one-piece bases. The eye relief is shorter than either one-piece base but adequate for the average installation.
Two-Piece Scope Mount Base $24.75

BUEHLER RINGS FOR BOTH ONE AND TWO-PIECE MOUNTS

SPLIT RINGS

A double split type ring with the added beauty of a smoothly rounded "ball turret top." The steel spacer at the top of each ring not only fills up an unsightly gap, but is made of 16 laminations .002 thick which may be peeled off one or more at a time, thus accurately fitting all scopes up to .010 smaller in size than the normal dimension of the ring.

BUEHLER SCOPE MOUNTS

SOLID & DOUBLE RING

Solid rings, per set **$15.00**
Double split rings, codes 6, 7 & 8 .... **31.00**
Double split rings, codes 5, 10 and 11 .... **36.00**

ENGRAVED SPLIT RINGS
Beautiful fully engraved
one-inch Split Rings.
Available in Codes 6, 7, 8.
Per Set **$80.25**

MICRO DIAL MOUNT

Both windage and elevation features are built in. A twist of the fingers dials the elevation desired on a dial clearly marked in minutes (one inch at 100 yards). With ¼ minute clicks. Another twist on the lock wheel directly below the dial securely locks the setting. The windage screws also are calibrated in minutes on both sides. The Micro Dial is designed primarily for all scopes with internal adjustments, such as the Balvar 2½ to 8 (use Code 7 Rings for Balvar), but can be used to advantage with many other scopes—the reticule can always be perfectly centered. The Micro Dial also makes it possible to switch scopes between rifles. The ring spacing is 4 inches.

Micro-Dial Base, Ruger Mini 14, Sako .. **$38.25**

Mount Bases, Pistol **24.75**

Mount Bases, Stainless Steel, pistol **31.25**

Split Rings Only, per set,
   codes 6, 7 & 8 .... **32.50**

Special Rings Only, per set,
   codes 10 and 11 .... **41.25**

BURRIS SCOPES

3X-9X FULLFIELD

A versatile scope for big game and varmint hunting. The most popular variable power scope because it fulfills a variety of purposes from long-range varmint shooting to shorter ranges of heavy brush shooting. A rugged, factory sealed hunting scope with a big 15 foot field of view at 9X and a 40 foot field at 3X.

3X-9X FULLFIELD

Plex	**$231.95**
Post Crosshair	**236.95**
1 in.-3 in. Dot	**238.95**

2X-7X FULLFIELD (not illus.)
Field of view: at 7X, 19 ft.; at 2X 50 ft.

Plex	**$220.95**
Post Crosshair	**226.95**
1 in.-3 in. Dot	**228.95**

1¾ X-5X FULLFIELD (not illus.)
Field of view: at 5X, 27 ft.; at 1¾ X, 70 ft.

Plex	**$194.95**
Post Crosshair	**199.95**
1 in.-3 in. Dot	**201.95**

3X-9X and 2X-7X available with Safari Finish, a Burris-developed low-lustre, high-performance finish. $10.00 extra.
Storm Queen Lens Cover for all three scopes, $6.95.

BURRIS SCOPES

4X-12X

6X-18X

4X-12X FULLFIELD

The ideal scope for long range varmint hunting and testing hand loads. Can also be used for big game hunting.

Crisp resolution, accurate parallax settings and a big field of view are some of the features of this scope. Friction type parallax settings from 50 yards to infinity with positive stop to prevent overturning. Fully sealed to withstand the worst field conditions and designed to deliver years of excellent service.

6X-18X FULLFIELD

This is a versatile scope that can be used for hunting, testing hand loads or shooting bench rest.

This high magnification variable scope features excellent optics, a precise parallax adjustment from 50 yards to infinity, accurate internal adjustments and a rugged, reliable merchanical design that will give years of dependable service.

Fully sealed against moisture and dust.

4X-12X FULLFIELD

Plex	$272.95
Fine Crosshair	272.95
.7 in.-2 in. Dot	279.95
Storm Queen Lens Cover	6.95

6X-18X FULLFIELD

Plex	$277.95
Fine Crosshair	277.95
.7 in.-2 in. Dot	284.95
Storm Queen Lens Cover	6.95

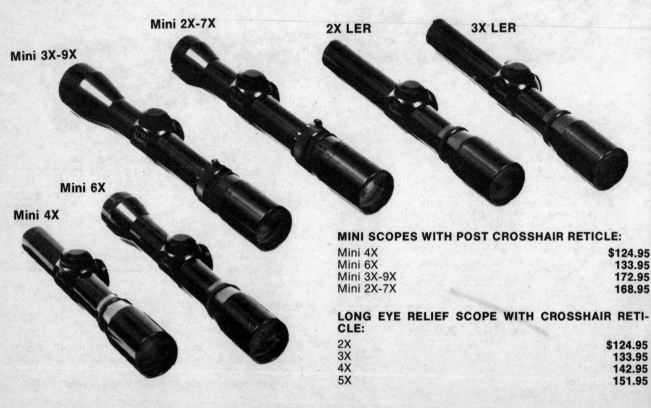

Mini 2X-7X   **2X LER**   **3X LER**

Mini 3X-9X

Mini 6X

Mini 4X

MINI SCOPES WITH POST CROSSHAIR RETICLE:

Mini 4X	$124.95
Mini 6X	133.95
Mini 3X-9X	172.95
Mini 2X-7X	168.95

LONG EYE RELIEF SCOPE WITH CROSSHAIR RETICLE:

2X	$124.95
3X	133.95
4X	142.95
5X	151.95

BURRIS RINGS, BASES AND MOUNTS

SIGHT-THRU MOUNT
$18.95

MEDIUM RINGS,
UNIVERSAL DOVETAIL
$25.95

SUPREME BASE,
UNIVERSAL DOVETAIL
$18.95

MEDIUM EXTENSION FRONT RING,
STANDARD REAR RING,
UNIVERSAL DOVETAIL
$29.95

LONG EYE RELIEF
UNIVERSAL BASE (LU)
$16.95

TRUMOUNT BASE,
UNIVERSAL DOVETAIL
$16.95

BUSHNELL RIFLE SCOPES

1.3X BUSHNELL
MAGNUM PHANTOM®

The Phanthom increases clarity of sight picture and permits accurate holding on the target because the crosshair and target are on the same plane. The scope has micrometer reticle adjustments, and is made in crosshair reticle only.

This scope was designed specifically for handguns, and has an eye-relief of 7″ thru 21″ which takes the shooter easily from "two hand" varmint to "arms length," target position. All optics are hand coated.

1.3x all purpose game & target **$71.95**
2.5x varmint & long range **79.95**

BUSHNELL RIFLE SCOPES

BANNER RIFLESCOPES

Banner riflescopes feature the Multi-X® reticle and are available with the Bullet Drop Compensator. The neoprene eye guard combines with the long eye relief to give that extra margin of safety (except in wide angles).

2 Fixed Powers

BANNER 10X 40mm Long Range
BDC $150.95

BANNER 6X 40mm Open Country
(MX) $98.95

BANNER 4 X 40mm Wide Angle General-purpose
(MX) $111.95
w/BDC   118.95

BANNER 4X 32mm General-purpose
(MX) $83.95
w/BDC   90.95

BANNER 2.5X Short Range
(MX) $78.95

BUSHNELL RIFLE SCOPES

Variable Power

BANNER 4X-12X 40mm Medium to Long Range
w/BDC $147.95
w/BDC and PRF   169.95

BANNER 3X-9X 40mm All-purpose
(MX) $132.95
w/BDC   139.95
w/BDC and PRF   162.95

BANNER 3X-9X 38mm Wide Angle All-purpose
w/BDC $151.95
w/BDC and PRF   174.95

BANNER 3X-9X 32mm All-purpose
(MX) $116.95
w/BDC   123.95

BANNER 1.75X-4.5X 21mm Wide Angle Close Medium Range
w/BDC $129.95
(MX)   122.95

BANNER 1.5X-4X 21mm Close-in Medium Range
(MX) $111.95

BUSHNELL RIFLE SCOPES

CUSTOM 22

4X All Purpose $41.95
w/BD 49.95

3X-7X All Purpose . $51.95
w/BDC 59.95

Custom 3x-7x 22 Variable

Magnifications:	3x	4x	5x	6x	7x
Field at 100 yards (ft.):	33	23	17	15	13.6
Exit pupil (mm):	6	4.5	3.6	3	2.6

Overall length: 10"; overall weight: 6½ oz.; clear aperture of objective lens: 18mm; outside diameter, eyepiece end: 1⅛"; outside diameter, objective end: ⅞"; eye relief: 2¼"-2½"; adjustment scale graduations equal: 1" at 100 yds.

Custom 4x 22

Field at 100 yards (ft.): 28.4; exit pupil:4.5mm overall length: 10 5/16"; overall weight: 5¼ oz.; clear aperture of objective lens: 18mm; outside diameter, eyepiece end: 1"; outside diameter, objective end: ⅞"; eye relief: 2½"; adjustment scale graduations equals: 1" at 100 yds.

The ScopeChief VI Riflescope also comes with the Bullet Drop Compensator feature (BDC) and provides two scopes in one. BDC's whole purpose is to take the guesswork out of hold-over. Range still has to be estimated as it would with any scope. But BDC gives the hunter a choice: he can simply dial the estimated distance to the target and aim dead-on. Or he can preset it at the distance at which he zeroed in and allow for hold-over as he would with a regular scope. Scopes equipped with BDC come with three calibrated dials to cover normal factory loads. Additionally, there's a fourth dial for wildcat loads.

SCOPECHIEF VI

®

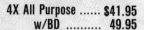

(MX) **SCOPECHIEF® VI WITH MULTI-X® RETICLE**

With its MULTI-X RETICLE, Bushnell brings to the shooter **in one reticle** the advantage of the popular crosshairs, **plus** — post and crosshair, and rangefinding reticles.

The heavier portions of the new reticle lead the eye to the center aiming point providing improved accuracy under dawn and dusk shooting conditions. At the same time, the crosshairs at the center offer superior accuracy under normal shooting conditions for even the small target.

SCOPECHIEF VI
1.5x-4.5x $159.95

SCOPECHIEF VI 2.5x-8x $161.95
w/BDC $169.95

SCOPECHIEF VI 3x-9x . $191.95
w/BDC 199.95
wide angle
w/BDC and PRF 239.95

SCOPECHIEF VI SPECIFICATION CHART

	VARIABLE POWERS			FIXED POWER
Magnification	3x-9x	2.5x-8x	1.5x-4.5x	4x
Objective Lens Aperture (mm)	40	32	20	32
Field of View @ 100 yards (ft)	3x-35 9x-12.6	2.5x-45 8x-14	1.5x-73.7 4.5x-24.5	29
Weight (oz)	14.3	12.1	9.5	9.3
Length (in)	12.6	11.2	9.6	12
Eye Relief (in)	3x-3.5 9x-3.3	2.5x-3.7 8x-3.3	1.5x-3.5 4.5x-3.5	3.5
Exit Pupil (mm)	3x-13.3 9x-4.4	2.5x-12.8 8x-4	15x-13.3 4.5x-4.4	8
Relative Light Efficiency	3x-267 9x-30	2.5x-247 8x-96	1.5x-267 4.5x-30	96
MX Center CH Width @ 100 yards	3x-.67 9x-.22	2.5x-.8 8x-.25	1.5x-1.3 4.5x-.44	.5
MX Distance Post Tip to Post Tip (in) @ 100 yards	3x-24 9x-8	2.5x-28.8 8x-9	1.5x-48 4.5x-16	18
100 yards (in)	.5			

SCOPECHIEF VI 4x $119.95
wide angle
w/BDC 159.95

BUSHNELL RIFLE SCOPES

BANNER RIFLESCOPE SPECIFICATION CHART

Magnification	BULLET DROP COMPEN-SATOR	Field of view at 100 yds. (ft.)	Weight (oz.)	Length (inches)	Eye distance (inches)	Entrance pupil (mm)	Exit pupil (mm)	Relative Light Efficiency	MX center CH width at 100 yds. (inches)	MX distance post tip to post tip (inches)	Graduation at 100 yds. (inches)
4x-12x 40mm	BDC	29 at 4x 10 at 12x	15.5	13.5	3.2	40	10 at 4x 3.3 at 12x	150 17	0.5 .17	18 6	.75
3x-9x 40mm	BDC	35 at 3x 12.6 at 9x	13	13	3.5	40	13.3 at 3x 4.4 at 9x	267 30	.66 .22	24 8	.75
3x-9x 38mm	BDC	43 at 3x WIDE ANGLE 14.6 at 9x	14	12.1	3	38	12.7 at 3x 4.2 at 9x	241 26.5	.66 .22	24 8	1.0
3x-9x 32mm	BDC	39 at 3x 13 at 9x	11	11.5	3.5	32	10.7 at 3x 3.6 at 9x	171 19	.66 .22	24 8	1.0
1.75x-4.5x 21mm	BDC	71 at 1.75x WIDE ANGLE 27 at 4.5x	11.5	10.2	2.9	21	12 at 1.75x 4.7 at 4.5x	216 33	1.18 .44	45.7 17.8	1.5
1.5x-4x 21mm		63 at 1.5x 28 at 4x	10.3	10.5	3.5	21	14 at 1.5x 5 at 4x	294 41	1.3 0.5	48 18	1.5
10x 40mm	BDC	12	14.0	14.5	3	40	4	24	0.2	7.2	.66
6x 40mm	BDC	19.5	11.5	13.5	3	40	6.7	67	0.3	12	.75
4x 40mm	BDC	37.3 WIDE ANGLE	12	12.3	3	40	10	150	0.6	21	1.0
4x 32mm	BDC	29	10	12.0	3.5	32	8	96	0.5	18	1.0
2.5x 20mm		45	8	10.9	3.5	20	8	96	0.8	28.8	1.5

BUSHNELL 45 SPACEMASTER®

60mm Prismatic telescope, without eyepiece, 20-year limited warranty, Model 78-2300 .... **$319.95**

TRUSCOPE® POCKET BORE SIGHTER

This pocket-size bore sighter gives you the flexibility to carry it in your shirt or hunting jacket pocket. Rugged plastic case; comes complete with weatherproof cap and adjustable arbor. Fits any bore from 243 to 308 caliber.

TruScope will work on all scopes and most rifles, excluding rifles with tubular magazines, full stocks or extra wide barrels (bull barrels). Color—gray; weight 3.6 oz.; size 3½ in. x 2¾ in. x 1⅛ in. **$24.95**

BUSHNELL ARMORED SPORTVIEW® BINOCULARS

Model 13-8330, 8 x 30 wide-angle center focus, one-year limited warranty **$96.95**

GRIFFIN & HOWE

FRONT SIGHT
$200.00-255.00

The Griffin & Howe type matted ramp front sight is hand-fitted to the barrel by means of a band. When fitted with a gold or ivory bead front sight and removable front sight cover, this sight gives a pleasing appearance and maximum efficiency. Available only on an installed basis.

BARREL BAND
$85.00

The forward swing swivel may be attached by a barrel band in front of the forearm or a barrel band through the forearm. Available only on an installed basis.

QUARTER RIB EXPRESS SIGHT
$575.00 and up

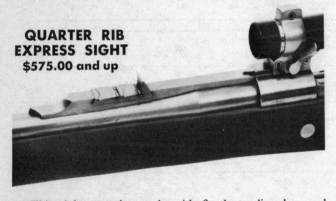

This sight may be made with fixed standing bar and folding leaves sighted in for any range desired. All leaves are marked for distance; the surface is matted with a gold directional line extending down from a wide V. Available only on an installed basis.

Top Ejection Mount   Standard Double-Lever Side Mount

TELESCOPE MOUNT

This mount has a locking cam action and is available for all models of rifles and is obtainable with 1″ or 26mm brackets, there are models to fit both domestic and imported telescopes. The mount holds the scope immovable in its split ring brackets. It can be mounted either low or high enough to enable using the iron sights when the telescope is mounted. It is readily detachable and, when replaced, it will always return to its original position with no scope mount adjustment necessary. It comes in the following models:

Side Mount $110.00

Side Mount, installed 200.00

Top Mount* .... 275.00 and up

*Available only on an installed basis.

Standard double-lever side mount with split rings, for telescopes with built in elevation and windage adjustment; Top ejection mount, for rifles similar to the Winchester 94, where the fired cases extract upwards. This mount, of necessity, has to be fitted in the off-set position; Garand mount, designed for use on the Garand military rifle, is mounted on the left side of the receiver to permit clip loading and top ejection.

JAEGER MOUNTS & ACCESSORIES

JAEGER QUICK DETACHABLE SIDE MOUNT $150.00

The Jaeger mount permits removing and attaching scope within a few seconds without the use of any coins or tools. The construction combines light weight with great rigidity. The unique clamping device locks the slide to the base securely, and insures return to zero. All mounts have windage adjustment at the rear ring.

Made for most bolt action rifles as well as Remington 740 & 760, Savage 99, Winchester 88 and other lever action rifles.

Especially well suited for Mannlicher Schoenauer rifles.

All mounts have split rings and are made in the following ring sizes and heights:

Mod. 20—1 in. low
Mod. 21—1 in. medium
Mod. 22—1 in. high

Low rings for most scopes in low position, medium height rings for large objective scopes in low position, high rings for use of iron sights below scope.

JAEGER M2 SAFETY $14.50

For low mounted scope. Available in two models: For Springfield and Mauser.

KAHLES OF AMERICA SCOPES

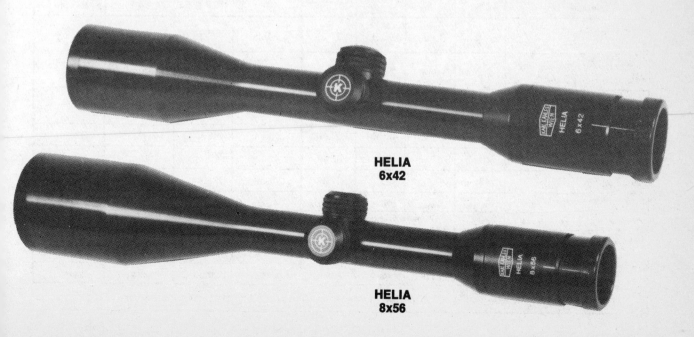

HELIA 6x42

HELIA 8x56

KAHLES OF AMERICA SCOPES

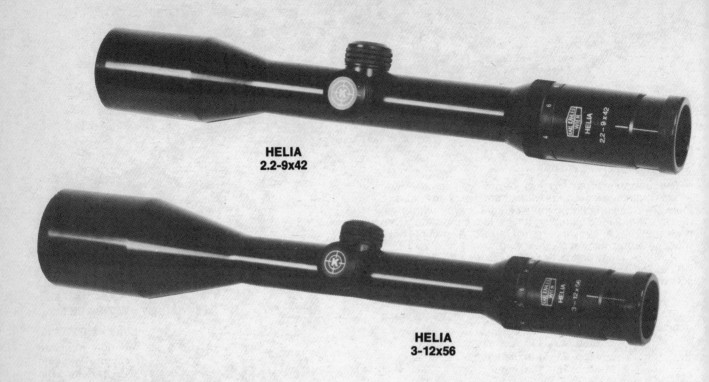

HELIA 2.2-9x42

HELIA 3-12x56

SPECIFICATIONS:	2.5x20	4x32	6x42	8x56	1.1-4.5x20	1.5-6x42	2.2-9x42	3-12x56
Magnification	2.5x	4x	6x	8x	1.1-4.5x	1.5-6x	2.2-9x	3-12x
Max. effective objective dia.	20mm	32mm	42mm	56mm	20mm	42mm	42mm	56mm
Exit pupil diameter	8mm	8mm	7mm	7mm	14.3-4.4mm	14.3-7mm	14.3-4.7mm	14.3-4.7mm
Field of view at 100m	16.5m	10m	7m	5.2m	24-9m	18.5-6.5m	12-4.5m	9-3.3m
Twilight eff. factor (DIN 58388)	7.1	11.3	15.9	21.1	3.1-9.5	4.2-15.9	6.2-19.1	8.5-25.9
Intermediate tube diameter Standard Helia S and L	26mm	26mm	26mm	26mm	30mm	30mm	30mm	30mm
Intermediate tube diameter Special (1 inch) Helia S	25.4mm	25.4mm	25.4mm	25.4mm				
Objective tube diameter	26mm	38mm	48mm	62mm	30mm	48mm	48mm	62mm
Ocular tube diameter	40mm	40mm	40mm	40mm	40mm	40mm	40mm	40mm
Scope length	247mm	290mm	322mm	370mm	270mm	322mm	342mm	391mm
Weight (approx.) Helia S	360g	430g	500g	660g	430g	570g	580g	710g
Helia L	290g	320g	370g	460g	360g	430g	440g	510g
A change of the impact point per click in mm/100m	12	7	6	4	12	9	6	4
PRICES	$279	$319	$349	$389	$369	$399	$449	$449

Conversions: 10mm = 0.39 inch   1m = 3.28 ft.   100m = 109 yards   100g = 3.52 oz.   S = steel forged tube   L = light alloy forged tube

LEUPOLD RIFLE SCOPES

Many hunters prefer the classic simplicity of a fixed-power scope.

M8-2X EXTENDED EYE RELIEF

With an eye relief of 10″ to 24″, this scope has proved popular on rifles where forward mounting is desirable. Handgunners have found its compact size and non-critical eye relief make it an excellent choice for a variety of pistols and revolvers. (Also available in silver finish for mounting on stainless steel or nickel plated handguns). **$150.55**

M8-4X EXTENDED EYE RELIEF

Now you can put this popular magnification on rifles with top ejection or any other arm where forward mounting is desirable — and on handguns. The M8-4X E.E.R. is also available in a "Silhouette Model" with a target style click adjustment for elevation only. **$183.75**

M8-2.5X COMPACT

Weighing just 7½ oz. and only 8½″ long, this scope truly is a lightweight compact. But, in performance terms, it is a giant. Its optical system equals or surpasses other scopes in its power class. **$160.95**

M8-4X COMPACT

This compact 4X is dramatically smaller than our regular 4X. It would be equally at home on a .22 Rimfire, a .458 Winchester Magnum, an ultra-light sporter or any other compact weapon were a light, small-size scope is desirable. **$183.75**

M8-4X

Without question, this magnification is one of the most popular of all. In fact, many hunters using variable-powers set them at 4X and only occasionally go beyond. This scope is excellent for most big game hunting, from relatively short to moderately-long ranges. **$183.75**

M8-6X

Many shooters are beginning to choose this power over the 4X because it allows big game hunting up to longer ranges. Its ample resolution also makes it an effective sight for light varmint calibers. Very compact, it is almost as small as many 4-powers. **$195.25**

M8-8X*

This scope has abundant power for most varmint hunting, including ground squirrels and prairie dogs, at quite long ranges. Its sharp resolution, contrast and accuracy also make it effective for some types of target shooting. **$261.60**

M8-12X*

This model offers superlative optical qualities and outstanding resolution. Its magnification makes it a natural for all kinds of varmint hunting at the longest ranges. This new redesigned 12X is 1.3″ shorter and .9 oz. lighter than our previous model **$265.10**

M8-12X Silhouette*

A 1982 introduction, the 12X Silhouette has the magnification and clear, sharp-contrast sight picture that silhouette target shooters need. To increase its versatility, two types of redesigned windage/elevation adjustment knobs are included. **$297.25**

M8-24X*

Any competitive shooter who liked the 15.2″ length and 16-oz. weight of our previous 24X will be impressed by our redesigned 24X. The new model is 1.6″ shorter and 1.5-oz. lighter — with no sacrifice of optical quality. **$369.30**

M8-36X*

This 36X gives the kind of performance Leupold likes to offer... 50% more magnification than a 24X, yet shorter an lighter than most other scopes in this power range. Its optical system delivers a full 36-power resolution and it is sharp over the entire field. **$369.30**

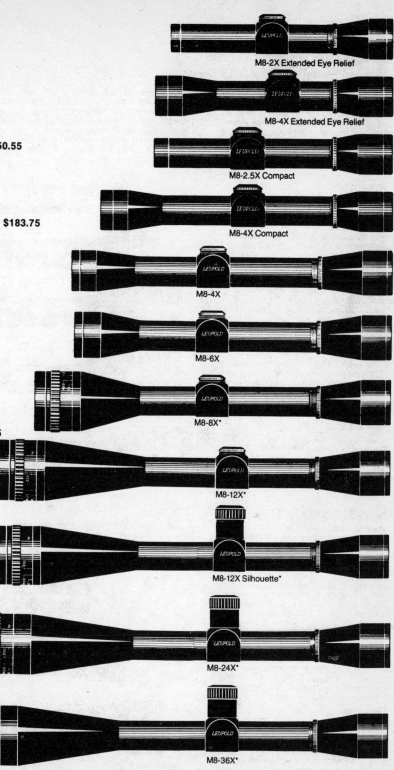

M8-2X Extended Eye Relief

M8-4X Extended Eye Relief

M8-2.5X Compact

M8-4X Compact

M8-4X

M8-6X

M8-8X*

M8-12X*

M8-12X Silhouette*

M8-24X*

M8-36X*

*With adjustable objective

LEUPOLD RIFLE SCOPES

Variable-Power Scopes
The "Gold Medallion" Vari-X III Series

The introduction of Leupold's newest series, the Vari-X III scopes, advances the state-of-the-art of scope technology another step. In scientific terms, these scopes feature a new "Anastigmat" power-changing system that is similar to the sophisticated lens systems in today's finest cameras. Some of the improvements are subtle, such as the extremely accurate internal control system which is the result of both design and time-consuming hand matching of critical mating parts. Others —the sharp, superb-contrast sight picture and the "flatness" of field—are obvious. The total result is a series of tough, dependable scopes that is superior in optical and mechanical quality . . . particularly pleasing to the discriminating sportsman who really appreciates the true value of such quality. Reticles are same apparent size throughout power range, stay centered during elevation/windage adjustments. Eyepieces adjustable. Fog-free, of course.

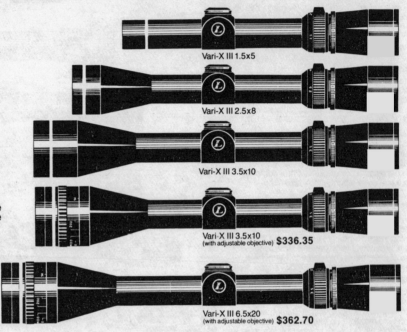

VARI-X III 1.5x5
Here's a fine selection of hunting powers for ranges varying from very short to those at which big game is normally taken. The exceptional field at 1.5X lets you get on a fast-moving animal quickly. With the generous magnification at 5X, you can hunt medium and big game around the world, at all but the longest ranges. **$259.55**

VARI-X III 2.5x8
This is an excellent range of powers for almost any kind of game, including varmints. In fact, it possibly is the best all-around variable going today. The top magnification provides plenty of resolution for practically any situation. **$292.95**

VARI-X III 3.5x10 (2 Models)*
The extra power range makes these scopes the optimum choice for year-around big game and varmint hunting. The adjustable objective model, with its precise focusing at any range beyond 50 yards, also is an excellent choice for some forms of target shooting. **$306.25**

VARI-X III 6.5x20
This scope has the widest range of power settings in our variable line, with magnifications that are especially useful to hunters of all types of varmints. In addition, it can be used for any kind of big game hunting where higher magnifications are an aid.

Vari-X III 1.5x5

Vari-X III 2.5x8

Vari-X III 3.5x10

Vari-X III 3.5x10
(with adjustable objective) **$336.35**

Vari-X III 6.5x20
(with adjustable objective) **$362.70**

The PERFORMANCE-PROVED Vari-X II Series

Since their introduction, Leupold's Vari-X II scopes have earned the highest reputation among knowledgeable shooters, gunsmiths and dealers. Compare them with any brand you wish—in *any* price range. Be critical. We believe you'll agree that these Leupold scopes offer more value in both optical and mechanical quality. Reticles are same apparent size throughout power range, stay centered during elevation and windage adjustments. Eyepieces are adjustable. Fog-free, of course.

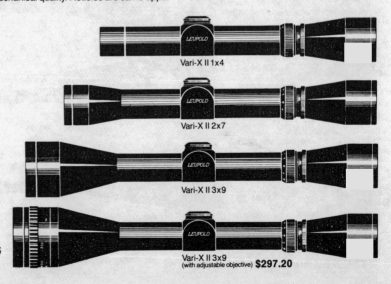

VARI-X II 1x4
This is a good magnification range for a variety of hunting. At the low end, the larger field of view makes it easier to make close-in shots on fast-moving game. At the high end, many hunters feel the 4X power is the optimum magnification for big-game hunting. **$225.05**

VARI-X II 2x7
A compact scope, no larger than the Leupold M8-4X, offering a wide range of power. It can be set at 2X for close ranges in heavy cover or zoomed to maximum power for shooting or identifying game at longer ranges. **$245.70**

VARI-X II 3x9 (2 Models)*
A wide selection of powers lets you choose the right combination of field of view and magnification to fit the particular conditions you are hunting at the time. Many hunters use the 3X or 4X setting most of the time, cranking up to 9X for positive identification of game or for extremely long shots. The adjustable objective eliminates parallax and permits precise focusing on any object from less than 50 yards to infinity for extra-sharp definition. **$263.95**

*Available with or without adjustable objective

Vari-X II 1x4

Vari-X II 2x7

Vari-X II 3x9

Vari-X II 3x9
(with adjustable objective) **$297.20**

LEUPOLD SCOPE SPECIFICATIONS

Scope	Ext. E.R.		Compact		Standard Fixed Power							Vari-X II						Vari-X III							
	2X	4X	2.5X	4X	4X	6X	8X¹	12X¹	12X Sil.²	24X²	36X²	1X	4X	2X	7X	3X	9X	1.5X	5X	2.5X	8X	3.5X	10X	6.5X	20X
Actual Magnification	1.8	3.5	2.3	3.6	4.1	5.9	7.8	11.6	11.6	24.0	36.0	1.6	4.2	2.5	6.6	3.5	9.0	1.5	4.6	2.7	7.9	3.4	9.9	6.5	19.2
Field @ 100 Yards (feet)	22.0	9.5	42	26.5	28	18.0	14.5	9.2	9.2	4.7	3.2	70.5	28.5	44.0	19.0	32.0	13.5	66.0	24.0	38.0	14.0	29.5	10.5	14.8	5.7
Field @ 100 Meters (meter)	7.3	3.2	14	8.83	9.3	6.0	4.8	3.1	3.1	1.6	1.1	24.3	9.5	14.7	6.3	10.7	4.5	22.0	8.0	12.7	4.7	9.8	3.5	4.9	1.9
Optimum Eye Relief (inch)	12–24		4.3	4.1	4.4	4.3	4.0	4.2	4.2	3.2	3.4	4.1	3.8	4.1	3.7	4.1	3.7	4.7	3.5	3.4	4.6	4.6	3.6	5.3	3.7
Optimum Eye Relief (mm)	254–610		109	104	111	108	100	106	106	82	86	109	97	104	94	104	94	119	89	107	86	116	93	135	95
Unrestricted Obj. Lens Diam. (inch)	.75	1.1	.75	1.1	1.1	1.4	1.6	1.6	1.6	1.6	1.6	.75		1.1		1.6		.75		1.4		1.6		1.6	
Unrestricted Obj. Lens Diam. (mm)	19	28	19	28	28	36	41	41	41	41	41	19		28		41		19		36		41		41	
Unrestricted Eye Lens Diam. (inch)	1.1	1.1	1.1	1.1	1.4	1.4	1.4	1.4	1.4	1.4	1.4	1.4		1.4		1.4		1.4		1.4		1.4		1.4	
Unrestricted Eye Lens Diam. (mm)	28	28	28	28	36	36	36	36	36	36	36	36		36		36		36		36		36		36	
Objective O.D. Diameter (inch)	1.0	1.4	1.0	1.4	1.4	1.7	2.0	2.0	2.0	2.0	2.0	1.0		1.4		1.8 / 2.0		1.0		1.6		1.8 / 2.0		2.0	
Objective O.D. Diameter (mm)	25	36	25	36	36	42	51	51	51	51	51	25		36		47 / 51		25		39		47 / 51		51	
Eyepiece O.D. Diameter (inch)	1.4	1.4	1.4	1.4	1.6	1.6	1.6	1.6	1.6	1.6	1.6	1.6		1.6		1.6		1.6		1.6		1.6		1.6	
Eyepiece O.D. Diameter (mm)	36	36	36	36	39	39	39	39	39	39	39	39		39		39		39		39		39		39	
Tube Diameter (inch)	1.0	1.0	1.0	1.0	1.0	1.0	1.0	1.0	1.0	1.0	1.0	1.0		1.0		1.0		1.0		1.0		1.0		1.0	
Tube Diameter (mm)	25	25	25	25	25	25	25	25	25	25	25	25		25		25		25		25		25		25	
Length (inch)	8.1	8.4	8.5	10.3	11.4	11.4	12.5	13.0	13.0	13.6	13.9	9.2		10.7		12.3		9.4		11.3		12.4		14.2	
Length (mm)	206	213	216	262	291	290	317	330	330	345	353	234		271		313		239		287		315		361	
Weight (oz.)	6.8	7.6	7.4	8.5	8.8	9.9	13.0	13.5	14.5	14.5	15.5	9.0		10.4		13.1 / 14.5		9.3		11.0		13.0 / 14.4		16	
Weight (gram)	193	215	210	241	249	281	368	383	411	411	440	255		295		371 / 411		264		312		368 / 408		454	
Adj. Scale Div. Equal To: (min. of angle)	1	1	1	1	1	1	½	½	1²	1²	1²	1		½		½		1		1		½		½	
Max Adj. Elev. & Windage @ 100 Yards (inch)	100	75	100	100	80	70	68	52	62	52	46	50		36		26		80		60		44		40	
Max Adj. Elev. & Windage @ 100 Meters (cm)	276	208	278	278	222	194	189	144	172	144	128	139		100		72		222		167		122		111	

Available with these reticles.

	2X	4X	2.5X	4X	4X	6X	8X	12X	12X Sil.	24X	36X	1x4	2x7	3x9	1.5x5	2.5x8	3.5x10	6.5x20
Duplex	✔	✔	✔	✔	✔	✔	✔	✔	—	—	—	✔	✔	✔	✔	✔	✔	✔
CPC	—	—	—	—	✔	✔	✔	✔	—	—	—	✔	✔	✔	✔	✔	✔	✔
Crosshair	—	—	—	—	—	—	—	—	✔	✔	✔	—	—	—	—	—	—	—
Dot	—	—	—	—	—	—	—	✔	✔	3	3	—	—	—	—	—	—	—

(1) With adjustable objective
(2) Silhouette/Target scopes have 1-Min divisions, with ¼-Min. "clicks," and adjustable objectives
(3) Target Dot ⅛-Min.

We reserve the right to make design modifications and other improvements without prior notice. Leupold Scopes are manufactured under one or more of the following patents: No. 3,058,391; No. 3,161,716; No. 3,286,352; No. 3,297,389; No. 3,918,791 (Foreign Patents Pending).

Leupold "STD" Standard Mount

... the perfect companion to your Leupold "Golden Ring"® Scope

The Leupold "STD" Mount is carefully machined from cold-rolled bar-stock steel to provide the ultimate in strength and rugged dependability. Featuring generous windage adjustments, precision-fitted dovetail and handsome, streamlined rings, the "STD" offer a firm, slip-free mount for any 1"-tube-diameter scope. Permits quick removal and return of scope. Available for the majority of popular rifles. *Note:* "STD" Mount Bases and Rings interchange with Redfield "JR" and "SR" components.

CHOICE OF 3 RING HEIGHTS —

TWO SIZES: 1 in. or 26mm.**

.900"
1" HIGH

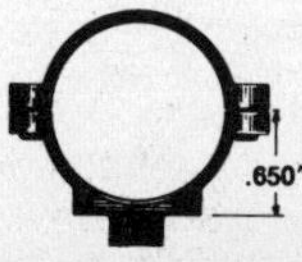

.650"
1" LOW $27.00

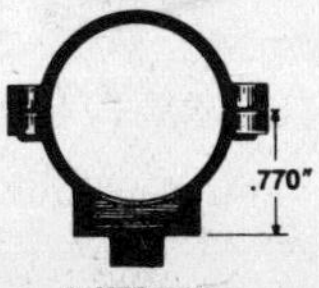

.770"
1" MEDIUM 26mm MEDIUM $29.50

**26mm Rings available in medium height only.

Leupold "STD" Mount Bases fit these popular models:

For Rifles — Base only $18.70

Model	Firearm Model
STD BA	Browning Automatic Rifle (all calibers)
STD BLA	Browning Lever Rifle (all calibers)
STD HC	Smith & Wesson, J.C. Higgins (after 1955), Husqvarna Crown Grade, HVA-Carl Gustaf
STD 336R	Marlin 36/336, Western Field M/740
STD M	Mauser 95/98*
STD FN	FN Mauser, Mauser Mark 10, Browning (.264 thru .458 FN action), Weatherby FN, Weatherby .224 Varmintmaster, Weatherby .22/250, Marlin 455, Parker Hale 1000/1100/1200, Sako (round receiver)
STD 700RH-LA	Remington 700/721/725, Remington 40X, Ruger M77 (round receiver), Weatherby Mark V & Vanguard, BSA Monarch — (all right hand, long action)
STD 700LH-LA	Remington 700 (left hand, long action), Weatherby Mark V (left hand)
STD 700RH-SA	Remington 700/722/725, Remington 40X BSA Monarch — (all short action)
STD 700SA-Spec	Remington 700 (Special long base for short actions)
STD 760	Remington 740/742/760
STD 788	Remington 788 (long/extra-long actions)
STD 7400	Remington 7400 Auto/7600 Pump Action, Remington Model Four & Model Six
STD RM14	Ruger Mini-14*
STD R77	Ruger M77 (short & long actions w/dovetail receiver)*
STD R1022	Ruger 10/22 Carbine (rimfire)
STD 99R	Savage 99 Lever Action
STD 110RL	Savage 110/110C/110E/111 (long action)
STD S	Springfield 1903*
STD S-Spec	Springfield 1903A3*
STD T/C-H	Thompson/Center Hawken Rifle
STD 70A	Winchester Model 70 (Ser. No. higher than 66,360 — not including .300 H&H and .375 H&H Magnums)
STD W94	Winchester Model 94 Carbine*

For Handguns — Base & 2 Rings $47.80

Model	Firearm Model
STD RBH	Ruger Blackhawk & other Ruger revolvers with adjustable sights*
STD T/C-C	Thompson/Center Contender
STD S&W-K	Smith & Wesson K&N Frame Revolvers*

*Drilling & tapping required

Leupold Extension Ring Sets

Reversible extended front ring, regular rear ring, in 1" LOW or MEDIUM heights. $37.40

Leupold Reticles

Chart above shows reticles available in each Leupold scope.

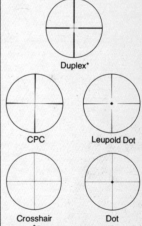

Duplex*

CPC   Leupold Dot

Crosshair   Dot

*Our most popular reticle by far.

Accessories

50-Ft. Focus Adapter

Allows sharp focusing for 50-foot gallery target shooting. $37.50

Sunshade

2½" long. Also acts as support for improvised "mirage tube." $10.65

LONDON GUN SIGHTS

DOVETAIL BASE FOR EXPRESS SIGHT

Available in large and small sizes. **$20.00**

BRITISH STYLE EXPRESS SIGHT

Features one standing sight with three folding leaves. Made of steel. **$60.00**

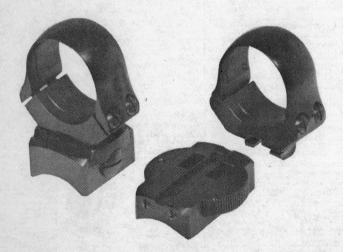

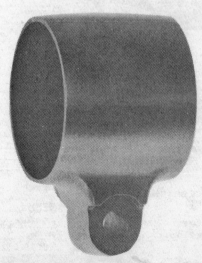

SCOPE MOUNT

Quick-detachable claw-style scope mount for Mauser 98 with 1-inch rings. Scope pivots to rear to detach. **$150.00**

BARREL BAND FOR QUICK-DETACHABLE SWIVELS

Available in two styles: standard quick-detachable swivels (SD) & old-style Winchester quick-detachable swivels (W). Twelve sizes available from .630 through .905; all made of steel. SD & W **$16.00**

LYMAN RIFLE SCOPES

BENCH REST SCOPES

20X BENCH REST SCOPE

The Bench Rest series rifle scopes have been designed to fulfill the demanding needs of today's benchrest, high-power, and small-bore rifleman. They are hand-assembled for dependable performance on the range.

LYMAN 3-9X VARIABLE SCOPE $179.95

HUNTING SCOPES

• Full magnification at all power settings. • Full field of view. • Non-magnifying, constantly centered reticle • Finest quality, fully coated optical system to provide top light transmission. • Ultra durable anodized exterior surface. • Matted interior surfaces to reduce stray light reflection. • Smooth control power ring, free of projections which could snag on clothing or straps.

SILHOUETTE SCOPES

These scopes are designed for metallic silhouette competition and have been carefully constructed to withstand the punishment of adverse hunting conditions, while delivering the unexcelled performance inherent in Lyman's LWBR Target Rifle Scopes. They feature Lyman's exclusive hand-fit optical mechanical system, parallax-adjustable objective lens with positive recoil-proof locking, Lyman hand-lapped, zero-repeat, windage and elevation systems, and external adjustment controls with zero reset, a feature allowing each user to preselect the zero reference point for his guns and loads.

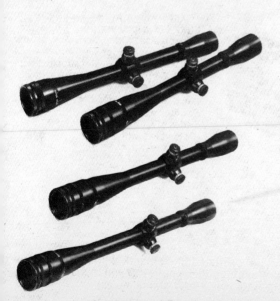

SILHOUETTE SCOPES

Hunting Scopes

2-7X Var. Price: **$169.95**
3-9X Var. Price: **$179.95**
4X Price: **$149.95**
(All Center Range Reticle)

Silhouette Scopes

6X-SL Price: **$249.95**
8X-SL Price: **$259.95**
10X-SL Price: **$269.95**

Bench Rest Scopes

20X Price: **$339.95**
25X Price: **$369.95**
35X Price: **$399.95**

Standard Bench Rest reticles available:

	Standard Fine Crosswire	Extra Fine Crosswire	¼ Minute Dot	⅛ Minute Dot
	(.0005) Center Covers	(.0003) Center Covers	Dot Covers	Dot Covers
20X	.063" at 100 yds.	.038" at 100 yds.	¼" at 100 yds.	⅛" at 100 yds.
25X	.054" at 100 yds.	.032" at 100 yds.	¼" at 100 yds.	⅛" at 100 yds.
35X	.042" at 100 yds.	.025" at 100 yds.	¼" at 100 yds.	⅛" at 100 yds.

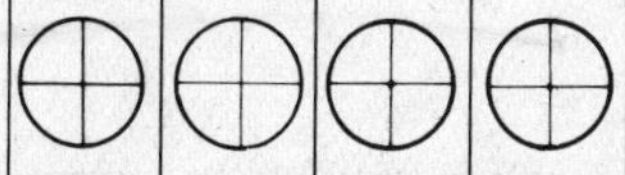

Standard Silhouette reticles available:

	#7 Standard Crosswire	#4 Center Range	1 Minute Dot	½ Minute Dot
	Center Covers	Center Wire Covers	Dot Covers	Dot Covers
6X-SL	1.1" at 200 m.	1.8" at 200 m.	2.2" at 200 m.	1.1" at 200 m.
8X-SL	.65" at 200 m.	.54" at 200 m.	2.2" at 200 m.	1.1" at 200 m.
10X-SL	.54" at 200 m.	.54" at 200 m.	2.2" at 200 m.	1.1" at 200 m.

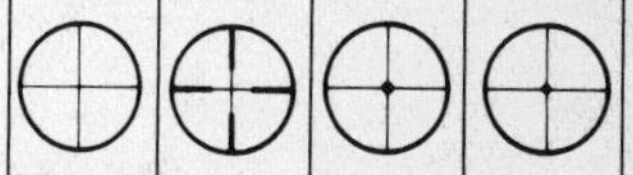

LYMAN RECEIVER SIGHTS

NO. 57 SIGHT

LYMAN 57 RECEIVER SIGHT: An unobtrusive micrometer receiver sight for hunting or target shooting with sporter, target or military rifle. This sight is equipped with a push-button quick-release slide that makes it ideal for alternating use on a scope-equipped rifle.

Fully adjustable with audible ¼-minute clicks for windage and elevation. Choice of coin-slotted stayset knobs for hunting or finger operated target knobs.

Slide adjustments are equipped with precision scales to aid in pre-setting sights for specific ranges or wind conditions. Slide furnished with elevation stop screw that facilitates return to "zero" if removed and re-attached.

Slide operates in dovetail channel.

No.57 Receiver Sight, complete **$44.95**

LYMAN 66 RECEIVER SIGHT: Similar in design and construction to the No. 57 receiver sight, the model 66 was designed specifically for autoloading, pump-action and lever-action rifles. Ideally suited for use on the new Ruger 44 Carbine. Features include ¼-minute click adjustments for windage and elevation, quick release slide, and elevation stop screw for return to "zero" if detached.

Push button release features of slide facilitates speedy removal and reattachment.

May be had with choice of coin-slotted stayset hunting knobs or target knobs.

Like the model 48 and 57 this sight is furnished with settings scales for easy reference.

No. 66 Receiver Sight, complete **$44.95**

NO. 66 SIGHT

TARGET FRONT SIGHTS

SIGHT HEIGHT*

17AHB ..... .360 in. 17AMI .... .445 in. 17AUG ... .532 in.

*From bottom of dovetail to center of aperture.

SERIES 17A TARGET FRONTS

Teamed with a Lyman receiver sight, these low silhouette front sights provide precise, x-ring accuracy on the range. Designed for use with dovetail slot mounting, they are supplied with seven interchangeable inserts (see descriptions below) that are locked into place with a threaded cap.

Price:

Series 17A Target Front Sight
  Complete with Inserts **$19.95**

INSERTS FOR USE WITH SERIES 17A SIGHTS

Set includes: two post type inserts (.100-inch and .050-inch wide) five aperture-type inserts (1 plastic .120-inch hole insert and four steel inserts with .070-inch, .093-inch, .110-inch, and .120-inch holes).

Price: Complete Set of Inserts for Series 17Z or 77 Sights **$7.95**

LYMAN HUNTING FRONT SIGHTS

Despite the exceptionally sharp definition provided by a fine aperture receiver sight, an equally fine front sight is necessary for consistently accurate shooting, particularly in extreme glare and overcast in the field. Lyman ivory bead front sights are the ideal field front sights. They present a flat optical surface that's equally illuminated by bright or dull light, and they keep their "color" under all light conditions. The Lyman ivory bead front sight is the perfect teammate for your favorite Lyman receiver sight, and will give you a reliable, sharply defined, glareless aiming surface, even under the worst conditions. You can fit a ready adaptable Lyman bead fron sight to your rifle in minutes.

A—WIDTH   F—WIDTH

These illustrations show the size and appearance difference between the two standard base widths. In general, the outside diameter of the barrel determines the width of the base to be used. "A" width is used with most ramps.

DOVETAIL TYPE FRONT SIGHTS (first letter following number of sight gives the height, the second letter the width)

SIGHT SELECTION CHART

MODELS SUPPLIED 1/16″ bead	Height Inches	Width Inches
31BA	.240	1 1/32
31CA	.290	1 1/32
3CF	.290	1 7/32
31FA	.330	1 1/32
3FF	.330	1 7/32
31GA	.345	1 1/32
3GF	.345	1 7/32
31HA	.360	1 1/32
3HF	.360	1 7/32
31JA	.390	1 1/32
3JF	.390	1 7/32
31KA	.410	1 1/32
3KF	.410	1 7/32
31MA	.445	1 1/32
3MF	.445	1 7/32
31SA	.500	1 1/32
3SF	.500	1 7/32
31VA	.560	1 1/32
3VF	.560	1 7/32

No. 31

○ 1/16-inch BEAD

NO. 31 FRONT SIGHT ... This sight is designed to be used on ramps. Standard 3/8 inch dovetail. Ivory bead. See Sight Selection Chart.

Price: No. 31 Front Sight **$6.95**

No. 3

○ 1/16-inch BEAD

NO. 3 FRONT SIGHT ... This sight is mounted directly in the barrel dovetail. 3/8 inch dovetail is standard. Ivory bead. See Sight Selection Chart.

Price: No. 3 Front Sight **$6.95**

RAMP FRONT SIGHTS

18E

18A   18C

NO. 18 SCREW-ON TYPE RAMP ... The screw-on ramp is designed to be secured with a heavy 8-40 screw (it may be brazed on if desired). Screw-on ramps are ruggedly built and extremely versatile. They use A width front sights, and are available in the following heights:

18A—Low Ramp: .100-inch from top of barrel to bottom of dovetail.

18C—Medium Ramp: .250-inch from top of barrel to bottom of dovetail.

18E—High Ramp: .350-inch from top of barrel to bottom of dovetail.

No. 18 Screw-On Ramp Less Sight . **$11.95**

LYMAN SIGHTS

LEAF SIGHTS

NO. 16 FOLDING LEAF SIGHT... Designed primarily as open rear sights with adjustable elevation, leaf sights make excellent auxiliary sights for scope-mounted rifles. They fold close to the barrel when not in use, and they can be installed and left on the rifle without interfering with scope or mount. Two lock screws hold the elevation blade adjustments firmly in place. A sight of this type could save the day if the scope becomes damaged through rough handling. Leaf sights are available in the following heights:

16A —.400″ high; elevates to .500″.
16B —.345″ high; elevates to .445″.
16C —.500″ high; elevates to .600″.

For installation on rifles without a dovetail slot, use Lyman No. 25 Base.

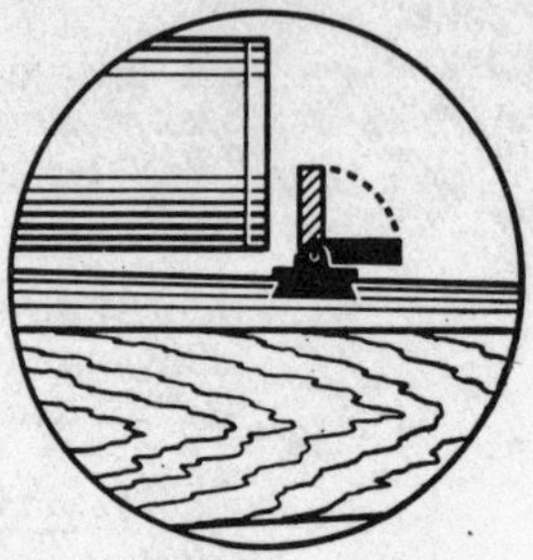

SIGHT FOLDS TO CLEAR SCOPE

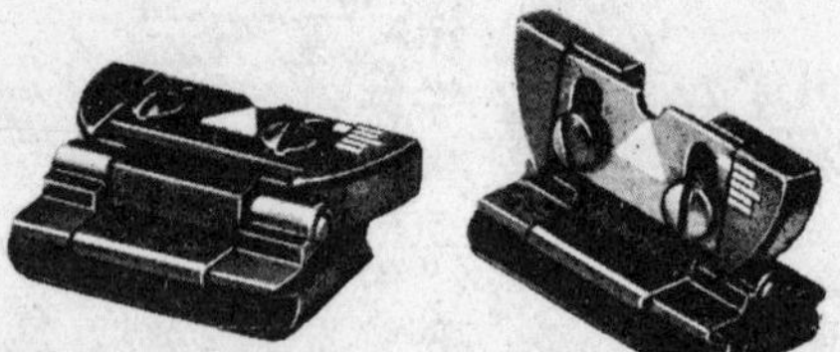

GRADUATED BLADE ELEVATES BY SLIDING IN ELONGATED SCREW HOLES

A "Patridge" type blade for the No. 16A Folding Leaf Sight is offered as an auxiliary blade.

Price:
No. 16 Folding Leaf Sight...... **$9.95**

BASES

NO. 25 BASES

Permit the installation of dovetail rear sights such as Lyman 16 leaf sight on rifles that do not have dovetail cut in barrel. They also supply a higher line of sight when needed. The No. 25 Base is mounted by drilling and tapping the barrel for two 6-48 screws. Screws are supplied with base.

Price: No. 25 Base **$6.95**

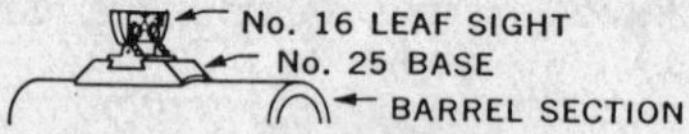

STANDARD BASES	HEIGHT FROM TOP OF BARREL to BOTTOM of DOVETAIL	BARREL RADIUS
25A-Base (Low)	.025—	.875 or larger
25C-Base (High)	.125—	.875 or larger
SPECIAL BASES		
25B-Base Fits factory screw holes on Remington 740, 742, 760, 725 & replaces factory rear	.125—	.875 or larger
25D-Base For small diameter barrels, Note Radius	.025—	For Barrels under .875 dia.

NOTE: For gunsmith use — 25A, C and D bases are also available in the white (unblued), and without screw holes. Heights and radii as above. **Price: $1.25**

NO. 12 SLOT BLANKS

These Blanks fill the standard ⅜″ rear barrel dovetail when a receiver sight is installed. They are also available for front sight dovetails and ramps when a scope is being used. Three lengths are available, all fit standard ⅜″ dovetails.

No. 12S (⅜″ x ⅝″ long) for standard rear barrel slots.

No. 12SS (⅜″ x 9/16″ long) for standard front sight slots and some rear slots in narrow barrels.

No. 12SF (⅜″ x 11/32″ long) this blank has square ends and is intended for use in ramps.

Price: (all sizes) **$2.95**

SHOTGUN SIGHTS

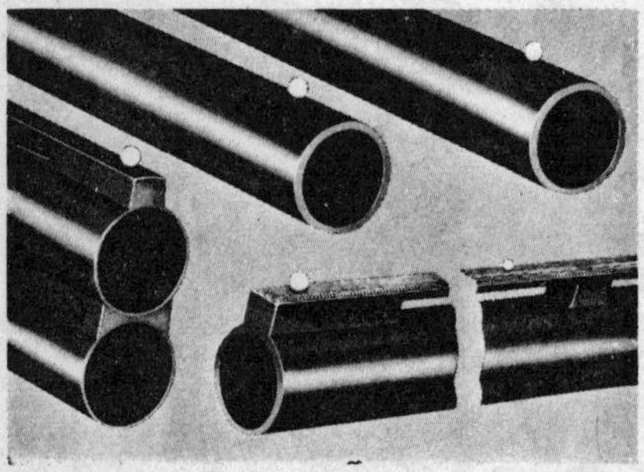

SHOTGUN SIGHTS . . . . . . Lyman shotgun sights are available for all shotguns. Equipped with oversized ivory beads that give perfect definition on either bright, or dull days, they are easy to see under any light conditions. They quickly catch your eye on fast upland targets, and point out the lead on long passing shots. Lyman shotgun sights are available with WHITE or RED bead, and can be fitted to your gun in minutes.

NO. 10 FRONT SIGHT (Press Fit) for use on double barrel, or ribbed single barrel guns. Sight **$3.50**

NO. 10D FRONT SIGHT (Screw Fit) for use on non-ribbed single barrel guns. These sights are supplied with a wrench. Sight & Wrench **4.50**

NO. 11 MIDDLE SIGHT (Press Fit) This small middle sight is intended for use on double barrel and ribbed single barrel guns. Sight **3.50**

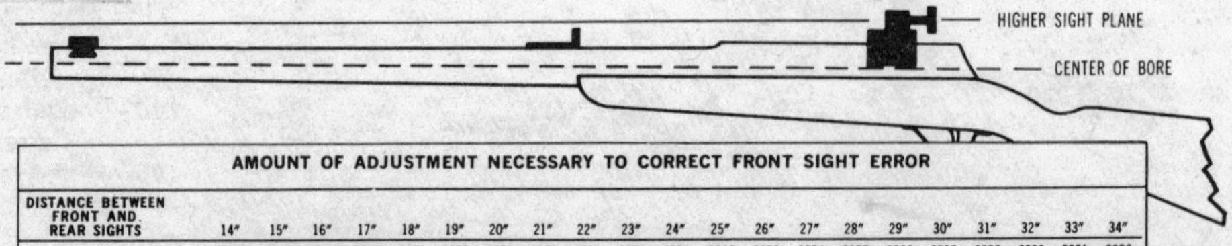

When you replace an open rear sight with a receiver sight, it is usually necessary to install a higher front sight, to compensate for the higher plane of the new receiver sight. The table below shows the increase in front sight height that's required to compensate for a given error at 100 yards.

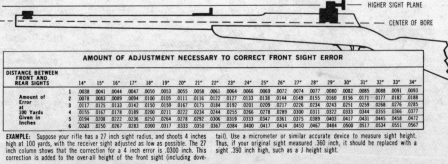

AMOUNT OF ADJUSTMENT NECESSARY TO CORRECT FRONT SIGHT ERROR

DISTANCE BETWEEN FRONT AND REAR SIGHTS		14″	15″	16″	17″	18″	19″	20″	21″	22″	23″	24″	25″	26″	27″	28″	29″	30″	31″	32″	33″	34″
Amount of Error at 100 Yards Given in Inches	1	.0038	.0041	.0044	.0047	.0050	.0053	.0055	.0058	.0061	.0064	.0066	.0069	.0072	.0074	.0077	.0080	.0082	.0085	.0088	.0091	.0093
	2	.0078	.0083	.0089	.0094	.0100	.0105	.0111	.0116	.0122	.0127	.0133	.0138	.0144	.0149	.0155	.0160	.0156	.0171	.0177	.0182	.0188
	3	.0117	.0125	.0133	.0142	.0150	.0159	.0167	.0175	.0184	.0192	.0201	.0209	.0217	.0226	.0234	.0243	.0251	.0259	.0268	.0276	.0285
	4	.0155	.0167	.0178	.0189	.0200	.0211	.0222	.0234	.0244	.0255	.0266	.0278	.0289	.0300	.0311	.0322	.0333	.0344	.0355	.0366	.0377
	5	.0194	.0208	.0222	.0236	.0250	.0264	.0278	.0292	.0306	.0319	.0333	.0347	.0361	.0375	.0389	.0403	.0417	.0431	.0445	.0458	.0472
	6	.0233	.0250	.0267	.0283	.0300	.0317	.0333	.0350	.0367	.0384	.0400	.0417	.0434	.0450	.0467	.0484	.0500	.0517	.0534	.0551	.0567

EXAMPLE: Suppose your rifle has a 27 inch sight radius, and shoots 4 inches high at 100 yards, with the receiver sight adjusted as low as possible. The 27 inch column shows that the correction for a 4 inch error is .0300 inch. This correction is added to the over-all height of the front sight (including dovetail). Use a micrometer or similar accurate device to measure sight height. Thus, if your original sight measured .360 inch, it should be replaced with a sight .390 inch high, such as a J height sight.

MERIT SHOOTING AIDS

MERIT IRIS SHUTTER DELUX MASTER TARGET DISC

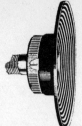

PATENT PENDING

WITH
FLEXIBLE NEOPRENE LIGHT SHIELD

May be cut to size

Particularly adapted for use with extension, telescope height and tang sights . . .

• The 1½" in diameter flexible neoprene light shield is permanently attached to the eye cup which is replacable by removing three screws. The shield is concentrically ribbed on its concave face for cutting to suitable size. It is more advantageous than a large metal disc since it protects the sighting equipment in case the disc is accidentally bumped.

• The Master Target Disc may be used on all sights having clearance for a disc 7/16" thick and 3/4" or larger in diameter.

MERIT DELUX Master Disc . . .	$ 54.30
Replacement Shield	8.25
Delux Replacement Shield and Steel Cup	9.30

THE MERIT DELUX LENS DISC is made with any of the No. 3 Series shanks. The body of the Delux Lens Disc is 7/16-inch thick . . . the Master Target Lens Disc is ¾-inch thick . . . Outside diameters are the same as shown for No. 3 Series and Master Target Discs.
The Merit Lens Disc is properly cushioned to absorb recoil shock.

MERIT DELUX No. 3 Lens Disc	$57.75
MERIT DELUX Master Lens Disc	67.50

MERIT No. 4SS—Outside diameter of disc ½". Shank 5/16" long. Disc thickness ¼".	$37.50
MERIT No. 4LS—Outside diameter of disc ½". Shank 11/32" long. Disc thickness ¼".	37.50
MERIT No. 4ELS—Outside diameter of disc ½". Shank ½" long. Disc thickness ¼".	37.50

SIGHT CHART

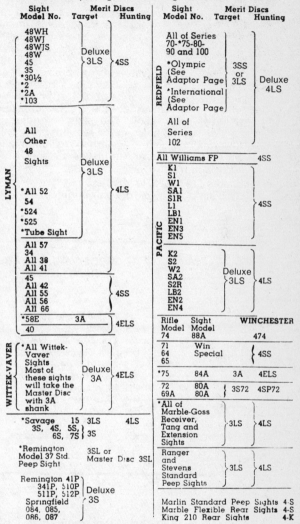

Popular Peep Sights and the proper Merit Discs to fit them. The Merit Master Target Disc may be had with any of the No. 3 series shanks. All of the sights marked ★ will take the Master Disc depending on the front sight used. See chart below:

LYMAN

Sight Model No.	Merit Discs Target	Hunting
48WH, 48WJ, 48WJS, 48W, 45, 35, *30½, *2, *2A, *103	Deluxe 3LS	4SS
All Other 48 Sights	Deluxe 3LS	
*All 52, 54, *524, *525, *Tube Sight		4LS
All 57, 34, All 38, All 41		
45, All 42, All 55, All 56, All 66		4SS
*58E	3A	4ELS
40		

WITTEK-VAVER

Sight Model No.	Merit Discs Target	Hunting
*All Wittek-Vaver Sights. Most of these sights will take the Master Disc with 3A shank	Deluxe 3A	4ELS
*Savage 15, 3S, 4S, 5S, 6S, 7S	3LS / 3S	4LS
*Remington Model 37 Std. Peep Sight	3SL or Master Disc 3SL	
Remington 41P, 341P, 510P, 511P, 512P, Springfield 084, 085, 086, 087	Deluxe 3S	

REDFIELD

Sight Model No.	Merit Discs Target	Hunting
All of Series 70-*75-80-90 and 100, *Olympic (See Adaptor Page), *International (See Adaptor Page)	3SS or 3LS	Deluxe 4LS
All of Series 102		
All Williams FP		4SS

PACIFIC

Sight Model No.	Merit Discs Target	Hunting
K1, S1, W1, SA1, S1R, L1, LB1, EN1, EN3, EN5		4SS
K2, S2, W2, SA2, S2R, LB2, EN2, EN4	Deluxe 3LS	4LS

WINCHESTER

Rifle Model	Sight Model	
74	88A	474
71, 64, 65	Win Special	4SS
*75	84A	3A 4ELS
72, 69A	80A	3S72 4SP72
*All of Marble-Goss Receiver, Tang and Extension Sights	3LS	4LS
Ranger and Stevens Standard Peep Sights	3LS	4LS

Marlin Standard Peep Sights 4-S
Marble Flexible Rear Sights 4-S
King 210 Rear Sights 4-K

THE MERIT OPTICAL ATTACHMENT WITH APERTURE IS THE ANSWER TO A SHOOTER'S PROBLEM WHEN THE EYESIGHT IS IMPAIRED.

(1) concentrates and sharpens the vision by increasing the focal depth of the eye, making pistol or rifle sights stand out sharp and clear; (2) Cuts out objectionable side lights; (3) Helps the shooter to take the same position for each shot. (This is a very vital factor in accurate shooting;) (4) Gives instant and easy choice of just the right aperture suiting your own eye and particular conditions at time of shooting.

Delux Optical Attachment Price: **$54.75**
The Delux model has swinging arm feature so that the shooter can swing the aperture from the line of vision when not shooting.
Replacement suction cup—Price 7.50

MICRO SIGHTS FOR HANDGUNS

The Micro Sight is small and compact. The sight is attached to models with dovetail slot for rear and removable front sights in the same manner as the factory sight. The rear sight has positive self-locking click adjustments in both windage and elevation. Each click changes point of impact ½-in. at twenty-five yards. Once set—the sight is constant and will not move from recoil. The sighting radius is raised, allowing for a deep notch in the rear aperture. This added depth gives the shooter sharper definition and eliminates glare. It is necessary to install a higher front sight to conform with the rear.

Front sight blades are available in: ⅛-in.
The styles are plain post, quick-draw or undercut.

ADJUSTABLE REAR SIGHTS, with BLADE FRONT SIGHTS for the following:

1P	Colt 45 Govt/Cmdr/MK IV (STD MOUNT)	
1P	Star Model B 9MM	
2P	Colt 38 Sup/9MM-38 Cmdr (STD MOUNT)	
2P	Colt MK IV 38 Sup-9MM (STD MOUNT)	
*3P	Colt 45 Govt/Cmdr/MK IV (LOW MOUNT)	
*4P	Colt 38 Sup/9MM-38 Cmdr (LOW MOUNT)	
*4P	Colt MK IV 38 Sup. 9MM (LOW MOUNT)	
5P	Colt 22 Ace/22-45 Conv (LOW MOUNT)	
15P	Colt MT Woodsman Postwar	
16P	Colt Target Woodsman Postwar	
17P	Colt MT Woodsman Prewar	
19P	Colt 22 OM Match/OM Special	
20P	Colt 38 OM Match/OM Special	
23P	Ruger 22 Standard Auto	
*27P	Browning 9MM HP (LOW MOUNT)	

$35.00

MICRO ADJUSTABLE REAR SIGHT w/RAMP FRONT $43.00

(fit the following)

AR	Ruger Single Six	LR	Great Western SA 22
BR	S&W 38 M&P	MR	Great Western SA 38/357
CR	Colt Official Police 38	NR	Great Western SA 45
DR	Colt Official Police 22	PR	Colt New Service 45
ER	S&W 1917 45-455 Revolver	QR	Colt Challenger 22
FR	S&W 38/44 Heavy Duty	RR	Colt Sport Woodsman Prewar
GR	S&W 44 Special	ZR	Colt Scout 22
HR	S&W 1950 45 Army	3R	Colt Huntsman
IR	Colt SAA 22	4R	Colt Targetsman
JR	Colt SAA 38/357	7R	Navy Arms 44 Rem Cap & Ball
KR	Colt SAA 45/44 Special	8R	Hy Hunter Six Shooter 357

24P	MICRO FIXED Rear w/Blade Front for 45 Govt	**$15.00**
	MICRO FIXED rear only	9.00
	MICRO front blade only for 24P fixed rear	8.00
	MICRO adjustable rear only	**$29.50**
	MICRO front blade only	8.00
	MICRO front ramp - less blade	11.00
	MICRO blade only for front ramp	8.00
	MICRO front blade for Colt Python ⅛-in Plain Post only	9.00

MICRO insert only for rear sight	2.00
MICRO insert only for rear sight w/white outline	6.50
MICRO-TITE barrel brushing for Colt 45 Govt	10.00
MICRO barrel brushing wrench	2.00
MICRO blank rear inserts (std, .210, .270 height)	5.00
MICRO elevation and windage screws	1.00
MICRO elevation and windage springs	.50

MR-35 ALL-STEEL REPLACEMENT REAR SIGHT for Ruger Blackhawk first model in .357 and .44 calibers (not the Super Blackhawks) with the round front end of the sight leaf 18.00

MR-44 ALL-STEEL REPLACEMENT REAR SIGHT for Ruger SA & DA revolvers. To replace factory sight with square front end of the sight leaf. Will not fit newest sight with swell on underside front of leaf 18.00

*LOW MOUNT requires special milling of slide . . . gives lowest profile. Not possible for older model Browning 9MM HP where extractor extends to rear of slide.

PACHMAYR SCOPE MOUNTS

LO-SWING® TOP MOUNTS $65.00

The swing-aside feature of the Lo-Swing® Top Mount provides a more natural sighting position due to the low positioning of the scope on the receiver as opposed to the "see through" type where the scope is mounted in a fixed position high on the receiver so that the iron sight can be viewed underneath the scope. The swing-aside feature provides for instant use of the scope or iron sights. Zero alignment is guaranteed no matter how many times the scope is rotated back and forth. Mounts are available for most of the popular rifles. See the chart below for ordering information.

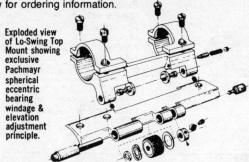

Exploded view of Lo-Swing Top Mount showing exclusive Pachmayr spherical eccentric bearing windage & elevation adjustment principle.

TOP MOUNTS $65.00

MAKE OF GUN	GUN MODELS	MOUNT NO.
Remington	700,721,725 (long action)	R700 RT
	700, 722, 725 (short action)	R700ST
	700 L.H. (long action)	R700 L.H.RT
	700 L.H. (short action)	R700 L.H.ST
	720, 30	R30T
	600	R600T
	(**660)	R600T
	740	R740T
	742 Ser. 184, 499 and below	R7 40T
	742 Ser. 184, 500 and up	R742BDLT
	760 Ser. 443, 499 and below	R740T
	760 Ser. 443, 500 and up	R742BDLT
	788 short action	R788S-T
	788 long action	R788L-T
	788 extra long action	R788X-T
	7400	R7400T
	Four	R7400T
	7600	R7400T
	Six	R7400T
Winchester	Win. 70-670, 770 All cals., except .300 & .375 H&H Mag. above Serial No. 66,350	W70T
	Win. 70 .300 / .375 H&H Mag., above Serial No. 700,000	W70MT
	Win. 70 Target	W70TGT
	Win. 70 .300 & .375 H&H Mag. between Serial Nos. 66,350 and 700,000	W70TGT
	Win. 70 All cals. except .300 & .375 H&H Mag. below Serial No. 66,350	W70T
	Win. 70 .300 & .375 H&H Mag. below Serial No. 66,350	W70TGT
	88 and 100	W-88T
Savage	99	S-99T
	110 R.H. Long Action	S-110RHT
	110 L.H. Long Action	S-110LHT
	110 Short Action R.H.	S-110RHST
	110 Short Action L.H.	S-110LHST
Sako	Finnbear	SK-FIT
	Forester	SK-FOT
	Vixen	SK-VT
Marlin	**336, 1895, 44	M-336T
	**1894	M-1894T
Mauser	98 (large ring, long action)	MR-T
	Yugoslav 1924 (lg. Rr. sht. act.)	YU-T
	Kar 98 (small ring, long action)	KA-T
	Mexican (small ring, short action)	Mex-T
	FN (std. FN action)	FN-T
	Santa Fe (FN action spec. hole spacing)	MSF-T
	66 (dovetail receiver)	MR66T
	2000	MR2000T
	4000	M-4000T
Mossberg	800	MO-800T
	810	MO-810T
	472	MO-472T

Husqvarne	Short action (small ring)	HV-SRT
	Long action (large ring)	HV-T
Springfield	03-06	SPR-03T
	03/A3	SPR-A3T
Enfield	Eddystone	EN-T
Schultz	Regular	SLR-T
& Larsen	Magnum	SLM-T
Ruger	44	R-44T
	10/22	R-22T
	M-77 RS long (dovetail)	R77-RS-LT
	M-77 RS short (dovetail)	R77-RS-ST
	M-77 ST long (round)	R77-ST-LT
	No. 1 Light Sporter/Standard Rifle	R No. 1T
Browning Sako	222, 222 Magnum	B469-T
	243, 308, 22-250	B479-T
Browning	Safari	FN-T
	Short Action	BRO-S-T
	Semi-auto rifle	BRO-SAT
	Lever action	BRO-LAT
	BBR Rifle	BBR
BSA Monarch	Dovetail rec. long action	BSA-TR
	Dovetail rec. short action	BSA-TS
	Round Receiver Long Action	R 700 RT
	Round Receiver Short Action	R 700 ST
Weatherby	Mark V, left hand Vangard, LH	WLH-T
	Mark V, Vangard, RH Long Action	R700 RT
Parker Hale	1200 and P1200	FN-T
Harrington Richardson	300 and 301	FN-T
Smith & Wesson	A, B, C, D, E	HV-SRT
Ranger Arms	Texas Maverick	RA-TMV
	Texas Magnum 458	RA-458-T
	Texas Magnum 375	RA-375-T
Interarms	Mark X	FN-T
Votre Shikar		VST
Colt Sauer	.300 Win. Mag. 300 Weatherby Mag. 7 mm Remington Mag. only	CS-M

**Due to special stop pin lengths, these bases should be ordered only with machine loops.

SIDE MOUNTS $65.00

MAKE OF GUN	GUN MODELS	MOUNT NO.
Winchester	54, 70	** W-70
	64, 94, Rem. 121, 241	** W-94
	Model 12 Shotgun	W-12
	88, 100	W-88
Remington	Enfield 30S, R720	** Enf.
	8, 81	** R-81
	141, 14	** R-14
	721, 722, 725 and 700 series	** R-721
	740, 760, 742	R-740
	Shotgun 1100	R-1100
	870	R-1100
Savage	40, 45 and Ariska, Husquvarna Cr. Swedish Mauser	S-40
	20, Japanese 25	S-20
	99	S-99
	340, 342, Sako .222	S-340
Springfield	1903, A3, 1922, Sedley-Newton	** Spr.
Marlin	36A, 336	M-36
	39A	** M-39
Mauser	93	S-40
	98	** MR
	All FN Bolt Actions	** MR
Mauser Carbine	Carbine Brno	MC
Mannlicher-Schoenauer	1950 or later	MS
Krag		** K
Garand Brng. Std.	Military auto 30/06, 308	M-1
Rem. 11	Shotguns	B-R
Military	* Carbine 30M1	M-1 Carbine
Lee Enfield	SMLE No. 1, Mk. 1, 2, 3	L-Enf A
	SMLE No. 4, Mk. 1	L-Enf. B
Ithica	37	W-12
Ruger	Mini 14 Serial No. Prefix 180 or 190	** RU-14-180 190
	Mini 14 Serial No. Prefix 181 or 191	** RU-14-181 191

* Due to near vertical shell ejection, it is recommended that these bases be used with a left hand loop and a crosshair reticle scope.

REDFIELD SCOPES

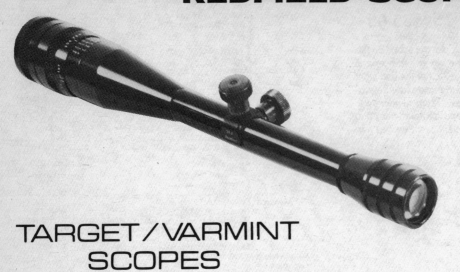

TARGET/VARMINT SCOPES

TARGET/VARMINT SCOPES

Item No.	Power	Reticle	Item No.	Power	Reticle	Item No.	Power	Reticle
Metallic Silhouette			**6400**			**Running Boar Scope***		
137156	8X	4 Plex	128111	16X 1/4 MOA	FCH	123102	3X-9X 10m	N/A
133156	10X	4 Plex	128121	20X 1/4 MOA	FCH	123103	3X-9X 50m	N/A
134156	12X	4 Plex	128131	24X 1/4 MOA	FCH	119003	4X-12X 50m	N/A
			128611	16X 1/8 MOA	FCH	120009	6X-18X 50m	N/A
			128621	20X 1/8 MOA	FCH			
			128631	24X 1/8 MOA	FCH			

*Reticles feature a lead dot positioned on each side of the crosshair intersection. See diagram on page 18. These special lead dot reticles fit criteria established by U.S.A.M.U.

THE ILLUMINATOR

Introducing the state of the art in hunting scopes

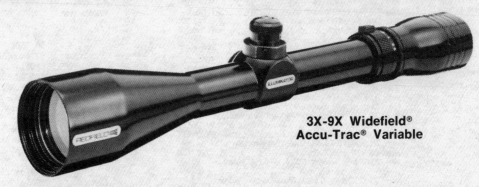

3X-9X Widefield® Accu-Trac® Variable

Every sportsman knows that dawn and dusk are the most productive times to hunt. Game uses the cover of darkness for security while feeding, blending in easily with the greens, grays and browns of the outdoors during dim light conditions.

With our new Illuminator series, you can add precious minutes to morning and evening hunting. These scopes actually compensate for the low light, letting you "see" contrasts between field and game.

Optimum resolution, contrast, color correction, flatness of field, edge to edge sharpness and absolute fidelity are improved by the unique air-spaced, triplet objective, and the advanced 5-element erector lens system.

And, brightness is only the beginning. The Illuminators also feature a zero tolerance nylon cam follower and thrust washers to provide absolute point of impact hold through all power ranges. The one piece tube construction is virtually indestructible, tested at 1200g acceleration forces, and fog-free through the elimination of potential leak paths.

The brightest optics ever developed and the strong, magnum proof engineering make the Illuminators the toughest, finest all around scopes ever made. Offered in both the Traditional and Widefield® variable power configurations, the Illuminator is also available with the Accu-Trac® feature.

ILLUMINATOR SCOPES

3x-9x Traditional Variable Power
123906 3x-9x 4 Plex $348.50

3x-9x Widefield Variable Power
112906 3x-9x 4 Plex   384.25

3x-9x Widefield Accu-Trac Variable Power
112910 3x-9x 4 Plex   428.95

REDFIELD SCOPES

THE TRACKER

The addition this year of the Tracker line of scopes has enabled Redfield to bridge the gap between performance and price. For the first time young or beginning shooters can have the same precision that all Redfield scopes provide at a price that's affordable. This ensures that newcomers to the sport get started with the proper scope, eliminating the frustration and poor performance that can result from inferior equipment.

TRACKER SCOPES	
2x-7x Tracker Variable Power	
122300 2x-7x 4 Plex	$142.95
3x-9x Tracker Variable Power	
123300 3x-9x 4 Plex	160.80
4x Tracker Fixed Power	
135300 4x 4 Plex	107.15

Traditional

Exceptional brilliance and precision in conventional scopes.

Our reputation for exceptional optical brilliance and mechanical precision was originally established with our trendsetting, conventionally designed scopes. These instruments became known as our Traditional Scopes and have undergone continuous improvements year after year to make them the finest value on the market today.

Redfield offers you a wide choice of Traditional Scope models including: fixed powers from 2-1/2X to 6X and variable powers from 2X-7X to 6X-18X. All variables are available with Accu-Trac®. Naturally, each scope is engineered with all the dependable high quality and innovative technology you'd expect from Redfield. Choose the one that's perfect for your needs.

Variable Power

2x-7x

3x-9x

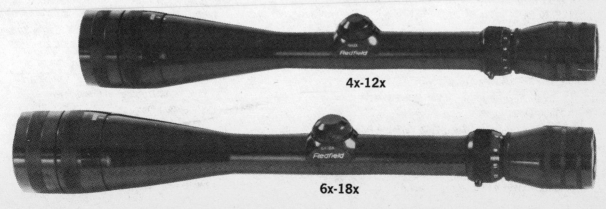

4x-12x

6x-18x

REDFIELD SCOPES

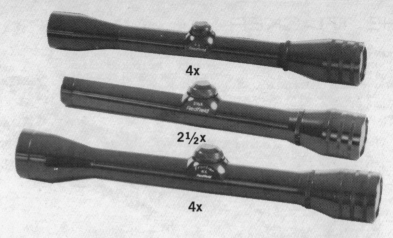

Traditional

Fixed Power

4x

2½x

4x

6x

8x MS
10x MS
12x MS

TRADITIONAL SCOPES

Item No.	Description	List
2x-7x Traditional Variable Power		
122106	2x-7x 4 Plex	$ 210.65
2x-7x Traditional Accu-Trac Variable Power		
122710	2x-7x 4 Plex AT	251.75
3x-9x Traditional Variable Power		
123106	3x-9x 4 Plex	$ 232.10
3x-9x Traditional Accu-Trac Variable Power		
123710	3x-9x 4 Plex AT	273.15
3x-9x Royal Traditional Variable Power		
123206	3x-9x 4 Plex	267.80
3x-9x Royal Traditional Accu-Trac Variable Power		
123210	3x-9x 4 Plex AT	308.90
4x-12x Traditional Variable Power		
119000	4x-12x CH	321.40
119006	4x-12x 4 Plex	321.40
4x-12x Traditional Accu-Trac Variable Power		
119710	4x-12x 4 Plex AT	$ 362.45
6x-18x Traditional Variable Power		
120000	6x-18x CH	357.10
120003	6x-18x 4 Plex	357.10
6x-18x Traditional Accu-Trac Variable Power		
120710	6x-18x 4 Plex AT	398.20
2½x Traditional Fixed Power		
132106	2½x 4 Plex	135.65
4x Traditional Fixed Power		
135006	4x 4 Plex	153.50
6x Traditional Fixed Power		
136106	6x 4 Plex	178.50
4x ¾″ Tube Traditional Fixed Power		
138006	¾T 4x 4 Plex	98.15
138010	¾T 4x 4 Plex 10m	98.15

REDFIELD SCOPES

Variable Power

Low Profile Widefield
2X-7X Variable

Low Profile Widefield
3X-9X Variable

3X-9X Accu-Trac

LOW PROFILE
widefield

4-PLEX

The Low Profile Widefield® with 25% more field of view

In heavy cover, game may jump out of the brush 10 feet away or appear in a clearing several hundred yards off, either standing or on the move.

The Widefield®, with 25% more field of view than conventional scopes, lets you spot game quicker, stay with it and see other animals that might be missed.

The patented Low Profile design means a low mounting on the receiver, allowing you to keep your cheek tight on the stock for a more natural and accurate shooting stance, especially when swinging on running game.

The one piece, fog proof tube is machined with high tensile strength aluminum alloy and is anodized to a lustrous finish that's absolutely rust free and virtually scratch-proof.

Because of its broad appeal, the versatile Widefield® is available in seven models. One is sure to fit your requirements.

Item No.	Description	List
WIDEFIELD LOW PROFILE SCOPES		
1¾x-5x Low Profile Variable Power		
113606	1¾x-5x 4 Plex	$248.40
2x-7x Low Profile Variable Power		
111606	2x-7x 4 Plex	255.55
2x-7x Low Profile Accu-Trac Variable Power		
111710	2x-7x 4 Plex AT	300.25
3x-9x Low Profile Variable Power		
112606	3x-9x 4 Plex	282.35
3x-9x Low Profile Accu-Trac Variable Power		
112710	3x-9x 4 Plex AT	327.05
2¾x Low Profile Fixed Power		
141007	2¾x 4 Plex	178.70
4x Low Profile Fixed Power		
143606	4x 4 Plex	198.35
6x Low Profile Fixed Power		
146606	6x 4 Plex	218.00

REDFIELD SCOPES

Fixed Power

widefield

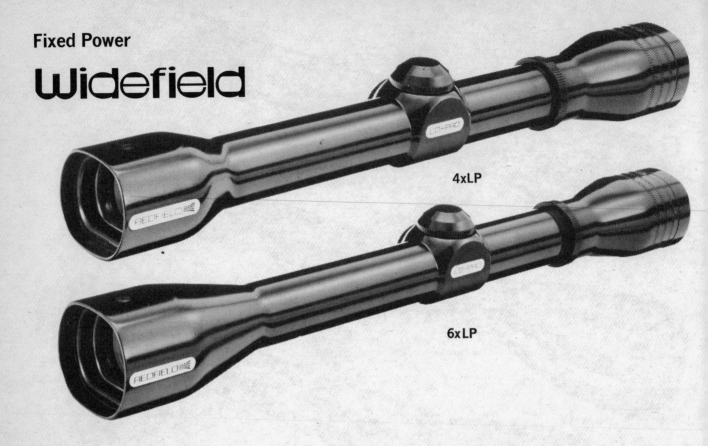

4xLP

6xLP

PISTOL SCOPES

Absolutely magnum proof for dependable performance

Tests show Redfield pistol scopes can shrug off thousands of magnum rounds with absolutely no malfunctions or changes in accuracy.

The reason? Instead of simply lengthening the eye relief of our rifle scopes, we went back to the drawing board. We designed our magnum proof pistol scope system to take the hard, sharp recoil of todays magnum handguns. To achieve this result we developed a new internal lens assembly, mounted on a non-rotating ball pivot system that's integral with the outer tube. This gives strength to the scope at its greatest stress points. Then, we designed an exclusive double rotary dovetail mount to assure positive holding power under heavy recoil.

High quality, innovative Redfield pistol scopes and mounting systems are designed for most popular handguns and octagon barrel, black powder rifles. They're also excellent for metallic silhouette competition.

4-Power Pistol Scope

PISTOL SCOPES		
148005	1½x 4 Plex	$128.50
148006	2½x4 Plex	135.65
148007	4x 4 Plex	160.80

SAKO SCOPE MOUNTS

The scope mounting system on Sako Scopes is among the strongest in the world. Instead of using separate bases, a tapered dovetail is milled right into the reciever, to which the scope rings are mounted. A beautifully simple system that's been proven by over twenty years of use. Available in low (2½- 3-power); medium (4-power), and high (6-power). One-inch rings only.

Low	$82.00
Medium	82.00
High	82.00

TASCO SCOPES

TASCO QUALITY OPTICS
All Tasco scopes feature a
LIFETIME WARRANTY

MODEL RC39X40WA
3-9 x 40
WIDE ANGLE RUBBER COVERED
RIFLE SCOPE

MODEL NO.	DESCRIPTION	RETICLE	Price
New Rubber Covered			
RC4x40WA	4x40 Rubber Covered	30/30	$159.95
RC39x40WA	3-9x40 Rubber Covered	30/30	179.95
Pistol Scopes			
P1.5x20	1.5x20 Long Eye Relief	30/30	89.95
P2x20	2x20 Long Eye Relief	30/30	99.95
BA2x20	2x20 Long Eye Relief Brushed Alum.	30/30	99.95
P3x20	3x20 Long Eye Relief	30/30	99.95
S3x20	3x20 Silhouette	30/30	109.95
S1.5x20	1.5x20 Silhouette	30/30	99.95
TASCOrama Battery Dot & New Sure-Point			
BD1XCF	1Xw/rings-Fits standard bases		239.95
BD1XCFV	1Xw/rings-Fits .22 grooved rec.		239.95
SP1XCF	1Xw/rings-Fits standard bases		79.95
SP1SRF	1Xw/rings-Fits .22 grooved rec.		79.95

TASCO SCOPES

MODEL RF 4x15
4 x 15
RIFLESCOPE FOR .22's

MODEL RF 4x15 TVC
4 x 15
RIFLESCOPE
FOR .22's

MODEL NO.	DESCRIPTION	RETICLE		Price
Riflescopes for .22's w/.22 ring mounts				
RF4x15	4x15	¾ in.	Cross	$14.95
RF4x15TVC	4x15	¾ in. TV	Cross	16.95
*RF4x20DF	4x20	¾ in. TV	30/30	20.95
*DR4x20	4x20	⅞ in.	30/30	49.95
RF37x20DF	3-7x20	¾ in. TV	30/30	46.95
RF4x32	4x32	1 in. w/.22 mts	30/30	74.95
DF37x20	3-7x20	⅞ in.	30/30	63.95

*New

WIDE ANGLE VARIABLE 200M RIFLESCOPE

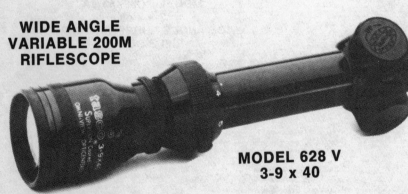

MODEL 628 V
3-9 x 40

- 25% larger field of view
- Exceptional optics
- Fully coated for maximum light transmission
- Waterproof, shockproof, fogproof
- Non-removable eye bell
- Free haze filter lens caps
- Tasco's unique Lifetime Warranty!

Wide Angle Variable Zoom Riflescopes (All Waterproof)

WA2.5x32	2.5x32	Wide Angle	30/30	$109.95
WA4x32	4x32	Wide Angle	30/30	109.95
WA4x40	4x40	Wide Angle	30/30	114.95
WA1.75x20	1.75x20	Wide Angle	30/30	119.95
WA27x32	2-7x32	Wide Angle	30/30	134.95
WA39x32	3-9x32	Wide Angle	30/30	129.95
WA39x40	3-9x40	Wide Angle	30/30	139.95

TASCO SCOPES

MODEL TR 39x40

TRAJECTORY RANGE FINDER
SYSTEM RIFLESCOPES

MODEL NO.	DESCRIPTION	RETICLE	PRICE
TR39x32	3-9x32	30/30 RF	$124.95
TR39x40	3-9x40WA	30/30 RF	179.95
TR27x32	2-7x32WA	30/30 RF	149.95
TR412x40	4-12x40	30/30 RF	169.95
TR618x40	6-18x40	30/30 RF	189.95

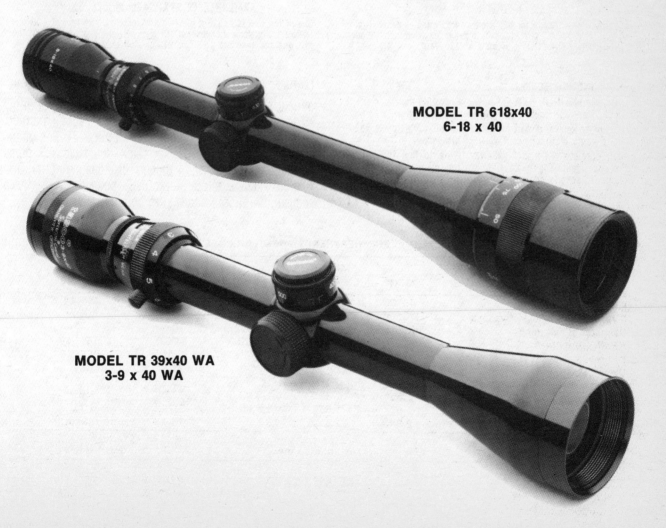

MODEL TR 618x40
6-18 x 40

MODEL TR 39x40 WA
3-9 x 40 WA

WEATHERBY PREMIER SCOPES

CHOICE OF RETICLES

Standard Model

"LUMI-PLEX" with luminous reticle	Open Dot	Cross Hair	Tapered Post and Cross Hair

Not Available In Wide angle Model

Wide Angle Model

3 TO 9 POWER

The most desirable variable for every kind of shooting from target to long range big game. Outstanding light-gathering power. Fast, convenient focusing adjustment.

4 POWER

This is a fixed power scope for big game and varmint hunting. Bright, clear image. "Never-wear" coated lenses for maximum luminosity under adverse conditions. 31-foot field of view at 100 yards.

2¾ POWER—
AVAILABLE IN STANDARD MODEL ONLY

One of the widest fields of view on any scope . . . 45 feet at 100 yards. Ideal for big game because of its clear, bright image. Ruggedly built to withstand even the pounding of our .460 Magnum.

WEATHERBY PREMIER SCOPES

WIDE ANGLE FIELD OF VIEW. Now, a twenty-five per cent wider field! Great for holding running game in full view.

As every hunter knows, one of his most difficult problems is keeping running game in the field of view of his scope.

Once lost, precious seconds fade away trying to find the animal in the scope again. Too much time wasted means the ultimate frustration. No second shot. Or no shot at all.

The Weatherby Wide Angle helps you surmount the problem by increasing your field of view by a full 25%!

FEATURES

OPTICAL EXCELLENCE—NOW PROTECTED WITH NEW "NEVER-WEAR" ANTI-GLARE COATING. • FOG FREE AND WATERPROOF CONSTRUCTION. • CONSTANTLY SELF CENTERED RETICLES. • NON-MAGNIFYING RETICLE. • FINGER TIP ¼" CLICK ADJUSTMENTS. • QUICK VARIABLE POWER CHANGE. • UNIQUE LUMINOUS RETICLE. • LIFETIME NEOPRENE EYEPIECE. • EXCLUSIVE BINOCULAR TYPE SPEED FOCUSING. • RUGGED SCORE TUBE CONSTRUCTION.

SPECIFICATIONS FOR WEATHERBY PREMIER SCOPES

	STANDARD LENS			WIDE ANGLE LENS	
	2¾X40	4X40	3X - 9X40	4X40	3X - 9X40
Field of view	45' 0"	31' 0"	40' - 12'	35' 8"	43' 7" - 14' 8"
Clear aperture of objective lens	40mm	40mm	40mm	40mm	40mm
Diameter of exit pupil	14.56mm	10.0mm	13.3 - 4.4mm	10mm	13.3 - 4.4mm
Relative brightness	211.99	100.0	176.9 - 19.3	100.0	176.9 - 19.3
Eye relief	3.5"	3.5"	3.5"	3.0"	3.4" - 3.0"
Overall length	11.8"	12.7"	12.2"	11.8"	12.1"
Diameter of tube	1"	1"	1"	1"	1"
O.D. of objective end	1.85"	1.85"	1.85"	1.85"	1.85"
O.D. of ocular end	1.53"	1:53"	1.53"	1.71"	1.71"
Weight	12.3 oz.	12.3 oz.	13.7 oz.	14.1 oz.	14.8 oz.
Internal adjustment graduation	¼" clicks 1" calibration marks			¼" clicks 1" calibration marks	
Price and reticle:					
CH or TP&CH		$154.95	$164.95	$174.95	$179.95
Lumi-Plex	$149.95	159.95	169.95	179.95	189.95
TRA-COM Lumi Plex					199.95

WEAVER K & V MODEL SCOPES

Weaver Steel-Lite II scopes feature seven Wider-View models, including the V9W (without Range Focus).

A rectangular-shaped eyepiece gives a wider view than a standard scope of the same power—as much as 40% wider on the K3W. And there's no sacrifice in superior quality and outstanding performance.

Wider-View is designed by Weaver engineers to include all the proven features that have made K and V Models America's leading scopes: One-piece, machine-tooled steel tube. The patented Micro-Trac adjustment system. Vacuumized, nitrogen-processed, and super-sealed for absolute fogproofing. Bright, crisp, distortion-free optics. Long, safe eye relief. And SL-II finish to match the receivers and barrels of the finest rifles.

Range Focus now offered on the V9WF. Five most popular reticle styles are offered.

	K3W		K4W		K6W		V4.5W		V7W		V9W		V9WF	
Actual Magnification	2.9	2.9	3.7	3.7	6.0	6.0	1.6-4.2	1.6-4.2	2.6-6.9	2.6-6.9	3.3-8.8	3.3-8.8	3.3-8.8	3.3-8.8
Field of View at 100 yds (ft) at 100 m (m)	48	16	38	12.7	24	8	74-27	24.6-9	43-17	14.3-5.7	35-13	11.7-4.3	35-13	11.7-4.3
Eye Distance (inches) (mm)	3.5	89	3.7	92	3.5	89	4.3-3.8	108-95	3.7-3.8	92-95	3.7-3.7	92-92	3.7-3.7	92-92
Tube Diameter (inches) (mm)	1.000	25.4	1.000	25.4	1.000	25.4	1.000	25.4	1.000	25.4	1.000	25.4	1.000	25.4
Eyepiece Diameter (inches) (mm)	1.710	43.4	1.710	43.4	1.710	43.4	1.710	43.4	1.710	43.4	1.710	43.4	1.710	43.4
	x1.425	x36.2	x1.425	x36.2	x1.425	x36.2	x1.425	x36.2	x1.425	x36.2	x1.425	x36.2	x1.425	x36.2
Front End Diameter (inches) (mm)	1.000	25.4	1.550	39.4	1.725	43.8	1.000	25.4	1.550	39.4	1.875	47.6	2.020	51.3
Length (inches) (mm)	11	279	11.9	300	13.3	337	10.4	264	12.4	314	14.2	359	14	356
Weight (ounces) (grams)	11	312	13	368	14.5	410	14.2	404	15.2	432	18.2	517	18.2	517
Graduated Adjustments (change in inches at 100 yards, or minute of angle)	.5	.5	.25	.25	.25	.25	.5	.5	.25	.25	.25	.25	.25	.25
Reticles* Available	1,2,4,5,6	1,2,4,5,6	1,2,4,5,6	1,2,4,5,6	1,2,4,5,6	1,2,4,5,6	1,2,4,5,6	1,2,4,5,6	1,2,4,5,6	1,2,4,5,6	1,2,4,5,6	1,2,4,5,6	1,2,4,5,6	1,2,4,5,6

***RETICLES 1** Dual X **2** Crosshair **4** Post and Crosshair **5** Dot **6** German Post
Reticles available as indicated: 1 standard; 2, 4, 5, 6 on special order at extra cost.

FOCUS Eyepiece of all scopes adjusts to user's vision.

1. DUAL X®   2. CROSSHAIR   4. POST AND CROSSHAIR
ON VW Models, post does not extend above crosshair.   5. DOT   6. GERMAN POST

WEAVER "22" MODEL SCOPES

Advanced D Models and V22® variable have outstanding features usually found only in more expensive scopes: large 7/8″ tubes, matching turret of modern design, improved optics with larger eyepiece. Stronger than ever, they are made of finest materials by skilled American craftsmen.

Weaver's constantly-centered reticle permits unusual speed and ease of aim. Use is limited to light recoil rifles only because of relatively short eye relief.

Factory-equipped with Tip-Off® Mount at no extra cost.

Choice of Dual X® or Crosshair Reticle in all three models.

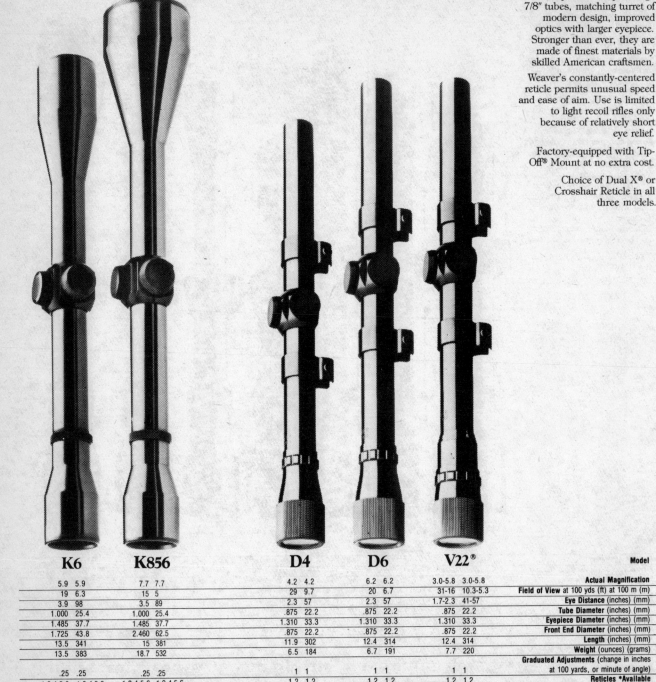

K6		K856		D4		D6		V22®		Model
5.9	5.9	7.7	7.7	4.2	4.2	6.2	6.2	3.0-5.8	3.0-5.8	**Actual Magnification**
19	6.3	15	5	29	9.7	20	6.7	31-16	10.3-5.3	**Field of View** at 100 yds (ft) at 100 m (m)
3.9	98	3.5	89	2.3	57	2.3	57	1.7-2.3	41-57	**Eye Distance** (inches) (mm)
1.000	25.4	1.000	25.4	.875	22.2	.875	22.2	.875	22.2	**Tube Diameter** (inches) (mm)
1.485	37.7	1.485	37.7	1.310	33.3	1.310	33.3	1.310	33.3	**Eyepiece Diameter** (inches) (mm)
1.725	43.8	2.460	62.5	.875	22.2	.875	22.2	.875	22.2	**Front End Diameter** (inches) (mm)
13.5	341	15	381	11.9	302	12.4	314	12.4	314	**Length** (inches) (mm)
13.5	383	18.7	532	6.5	184	6.7	191	7.7	220	**Weight** (ounces) (grams)
										Graduated Adjustments (change in inches
.25	.25	.25	.25	1	1	1	1	1	1	at 100 yards, or minute of angle)
1,2,4,5,6	1,2,4,5,6	1,2,4,5,6	1,2,4,5,6	1,2	1,2	1,2	1,2	1,2	1,2	**Reticles *Available**

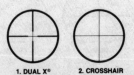

1. DUAL X®   2. CROSSHAIR

*RETICLES 1 Dual X **2** Crosshair
FOCUS Eyepiece of all scopes adjusts to user's vision.

WEAVER "V" MODEL SCOPES

V856 . . . THE ALL-NEW LOW-LIGHT VARIABLE

Following the success of our K856, we're introducing the new 3- to 8-power variable model V856. This scope gets its name from our variable-power line of scopes, the V Models, from its maximum power, 8, and from the diameter of its objective, 56mm. Extra large exit pupil allows the maximum amount of light to enter the eye. So even in low-light hunting conditions, shooters will get maximum brightness.

Available for shipment mid-1983.

More and more hunters find that only a Weaver V Model offers all the flexibility and versatility they need—plus the sure year-after-year dependability of the sturdiest fixed-power scopes. An easy turn of the power change ring supplies the magnification that's just right for 'most any hunting situation.

All-new V856, the 3- to 8-power variable for inclement hunting conditions, is described to the left. The new V9M with Matte Finish is shown on page 9.

Seven great V Models. include the 3- to 9-power (without focusing objective) V9. All Weaver Variable models offer a continuous and smooth power change; improved sealing and fog-proofing; the Micro-Trac Adjustment System for super-accuracy; and Steel-Lite II construction for a new dimension in lightness, toughness, and dependability.

Focus and point of impact are the same at all powers. Reticle remains constantly centered.

Precision optics are magnesium fluoride coated. Long eye relief is safe at all magnifications. Models V9F and V12F have Range-Focus. Five most popular reticle styles are offered.

V4.5		V7		V856		V9		V9F		V12F		Model
1.6-4.3	1.6-4.3	2.5-6.7	2.5-6.7	3.08-8.33	3.08-8.33	3.3-8.8	3.3-8.8	3.3-8.8	3.3-8.8	4.4-11.8	4.4-11.8	**Actual Magnification**
63-24	21-8	40-15	13.3-5	35-13	11.7-4.33	31-12	10.3-4	31-12	10.3-4	23-9	7.7-3	**Field of View** at 100 yds (ft) at 100 m (m)
4.4-3.9	111-98	4-3.9	102-98	3.8-3.8	95-95	3.8-3.8	95-95	3.8-3.8	95-95	3.9-4.3	98-108	**Eye Distance** (inches) (mm)
1.000	25.4	1.000	25.4	1.000	25.4	1.000	25.4	1.000	25.4	1.000	25.4	**Tube Diameter** (inches) (mm)
1.485	37.7	1.485	37.7	1.485	37.7	1.485	37.7	1.485	37.7	1.485	37.7	**Eyepiece Diameter** (inches) (mm)
1.000	25.4	1.550	39.4	2.460	62.5	1.875	47.6	2.020	51.3	2.020	51.3	**Front End Diameter** (inches) (mm)
10.4	264	12.4	314	14.3	362	14.2	359	14	356	14	356	**Length** (inches) (mm)
12.1	343	14.5	410	21.5	609	17.5	496	17.5	496	17.5	496	**Weight** (ounces) (grams)
												Graduated Adjustments (change in inches at 100 yards, or minute of angle)
.5	.5	.25	.25	.25	.25	.25	.25	.25	.25	.25	.25	
1,2,4,5,6	1,2,4,5,6	1,2,4,5,6	1,2,4,5,6	1	1	1,2,4,5,6	1,2,4,5,6	1,2,4,5,6	1,2,4,5,6	1,2,4,5,6	1,2,4,5,6	**Reticles * Available**

*RETICLES 1 Dual X 2 Crosshair 4 Post and Crosshair 5 Dot 6 German Post
Reticles available as indicated: 1 standard; 2, 4, 5, 6 on special order.

FOCUS Eyepiece of all scopes adjusts to user's vision.

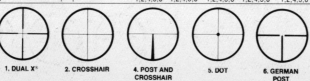

1. DUAL X* 2. CROSSHAIR 4. POST AND CROSSHAIR 5. DOT 6. GERMAN POST

WEAVER "T" MODEL SCOPES

You'll find a lot of T Model Weaver scopes on the target and silhouette range, and you'll find a lot of satisfied Weaver customers that will swear by them. In their first years on the market, the T's made their mark by consistently dominating both winners and line count at major silhouette events.

Three varmint scopes — the KT6, KT10, and KT16 feature a fast-focus front end and smaller, covered adjustment knobs.

Thanks to Weaver's exclusive Micro-Trac adjustment system, the shooter can count on superior repeatability and precise adjustment with virtually no wear on the mechanism. Micrometer adjustments on the focusing objective allow parallax-free settings to be established for varying distances, and the easy-to-read elevation adjustment lets the shooter go from 200 to 500 meters in a single rotation. T Models have enough windage and elevation capability to encompass virtually all shooting sports, and the zero-set feature allows the shooter to set each knob to zero as a reference point, once the sighting-in is completed.

	T6		KT6		T10		KT10		T16		KT16	
Model												
Actual Magnification	6	6	6	6	10	10	10	10	16	16	16	16
Field of View at 100 yds (ft) at 100 m (m)	19	6.3	17	5.7	11	3.7	11	3.7	7	2.3	6.4	2.1
Eye Distance (inches) (mm)	3.5	89	3.7	92	3.5	89	3.1	78	3.7	92	3.5	89
Tube Diameter (inches) (mm)	1.000	25.4	1.000	25.4	1.000	25.4	1.000	25.4	1.000	25.4	1.000	25.4
Eyepiece Diameter (inches) (mm)	1.485	37.7	1.485	37.7	1.485	37.7	1.485	37.7	1.485	37.7	1.485	37.7
Front End Diameter (inches) (mm)	2.020	51.3	2.020	51.3	2.020	51.3	2.020	51.3	2.020	51.3	2.020	51.3
Length (inches) (mm)	14.3	362	13.75	349	15	381	14.3	362	15.8	400	15.125	384
Weight (ounces) (grams)	17.7	503	16.5	468	18	510	17	482	18.7	532	17.5	496
Graduated Adjustments (change in inches at 100 yards, or minute of angle)	.25	.25	.25	.25	.25	.25	.25	.25	.25	.25	.25	.25
Reticles* Available	1,2,3,5	1,2,3,5	1,2,3,5	1,2,3,5	1,2,3,5	1,2,3,5	1,2,3,5	1,2,3,5	1,2,3,5	1,2,3,5	1,2,3,5	1,2,3,5

*RETICLES **1** Dual X **2** Crosshair
3 Fine Crosshair **5** Dot
FOCUS Eyepiece of all scopes adjusts to user's vision.

1. DUAL X®.   2. CROSSHAIR   3. FINE CROSSHAIR   5. DOT

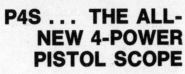

New Stainless-Steel Pistol Scope

P4S ... THE ALL-NEW 4-POWER PISTOL SCOPE

This year we're adding the 4-power, Stainless-Steel P4S to our line of pistol scopes. And we think a lot of shooters are going to find it to their liking. The P4S features precise Weaver built optics, superior weatherproofing, and the patented Micro-Trac® adjustment system. Shooters will get more than adequate eye relief of 10 inches to 24 inches. And a field of view of 7 feet at 100 yards.

Available for shipment mid-1983

Weaver introduced the industry's first no-drill, no-tap Pistol Mount Base System — a big breakthrough for the handgun enthusiast. Last year, we introduced a brand-new, 2-power, stainless-steel Weaver pistol scope, the P2S. And for 1983, Weaver offers the 4-power P4S. It's another quality stainless-steel scope that will look great on stainless-steel handguns.

Like all Weaver scopes, the P2S and P4S feature precise, Weaver-built optics, superior weatherproofing, and the patented Micro-Trac® adjustment system. Shooters get more-than-adequate eye relief of 10 inches to 24 inches.

The durable, rustproof qualities of stainless steel not only make the Weaver pistol scopes impervious to the elements, but also give them a look that will really be impressive when matched with the stainless-steel barrels and receivers of some of the world's finest pistols. And anyone can mount the P2S and P4S with no drilling or tapping.

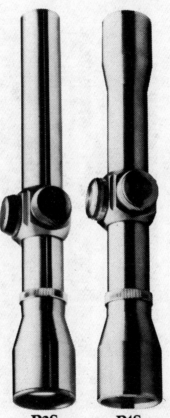

T25		P2S		P4S		Model
25	25	1.9	1.9	4.0	4.0	**Actual Magnification**
4.2	1.4	14	4.7	7	2.3	**Field of View** at 100 yds (ft) at 100 m (m)
3.8	95	13-24	330-610	12-20	305-508	**Eye Distance** (inches) (mm)
1.000	25.4	1.000	25.4	1.000	25.4	**Tube Diameter** (inches) (mm)
1.485	37.7	1.485	37.7	1.485	37.7	**Eyepiece Diameter** (inches) (mm)
2.020	51.3	1.000	25.4	1.250	31.7	**Front End Diameter** (inches) (mm)
19.2	486	10	254	9.9	251	**Length** (inches) (mm)
20	568	12	340	12.5	354	**Weight** (ounces) (grams)
						Graduated Adjustments (change in inches at 100 yards, or minute of angle)
.25	.25	.5	.5	.5	.5	
1,2,3,5	1,2,3,5	1	1	1	1	**Reticles * Available**

1. DUAL X®

*RETICLE 1 Dual X

FOCUS Eyepiece of all scopes adjust to user's vision.

WEAVER "K" MODEL SCOPES

Weaver K Models, pacesetters for 30 years, continue to set new high standards in scope design and performance with the introduction of Steel-Lite II® models.

Unique, one-piece steel tube. The sharp, clean-cut shape is machine-tooled and hand-polished to a new and deeper SL-II™ finish. It's a beautiful match to the finest rifles, and highest quality steel provides the best possible protection for the superior optics.

The K Models feature Weaver's Micro-Trac® Adjustment System for super-accurate windage and elevation settings. They're vacuumized, filled with dry nitrogen gas, and super sealed. They're the most dependable, most fogproofed scopes we've ever designed.

Weaver's most popular hunting scope, the K4, is offered in 1983 in four versions. The 50th Anniversary K4·50, as described to the right; the new K4M in Matte Finish, as shown on page 9; the bright new Stainless-Steel K4S; and the K4 in SL-II finish.

The new K856 is the hunting scope made for inclement weather and low-light conditions. 8-power magnification, 56mm objective lens, 7mm exit pupil.

Five reticle styles, including the new German Post, are available in all K Models except K4·50 and K4M.

K4·50 ... WEAVER'S 50TH ANNIVERSARY MODEL

In celebration of our 50th year of quality scope leadership we proudly offer the K4·50. This limited edition, commemorative version of our K4 scope is as beautiful as it is functional. Gold rings on both the ocular and objective ends complement the scroll engravings. Turret cap medallions are sure to make this scope a showpiece among collectors and shooters alike. Also included are a special set of engraved mount rings.

Available for shipment mid-1983.

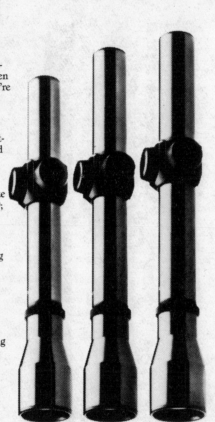
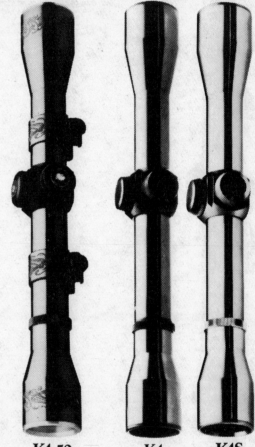

Model	K1.5		K2.5		K3		K4·50		K4		K4S	
Actual Magnification	1.5	1.5	2.6	2.6	3.2	3.2	4.1	4.1	4.1	4.1	4.1	4.1
Field of View at 100 yds (ft) at 100 m (m)	55	18.3	38	12.7	34	11.3	27	9	27	9	27	9
Eye Distance (inches) (mm)	5.3	133	4.5	114	4	102	4	102	4	102	4	102
Tube Diameter (inches) (mm)	1.000	25.4	1.000	25.4	1.000	25.4	1.000	25.4	1.000	25.4	1.000	25.4
Eyepiece Diameter (inches) (mm)	1.485	37.7	1.485	37.7	1.485	37.7	1.485	37.7	1.485	37.7	1.485	37.7
Front End Diameter (inches) (mm)	1.000	25.4	1.000	25.4	1.000	25.4	1.550	39.4	1.550	39.4	1.550	39.4
Length (inches) (mm)	9.4	238	10.4	264	10.7	270	11.8	299	11.8	299	11.8	299
Weight (ounces) (grams)	9.7	276	10.2	291	10.2	291	12	340	12	340	13.3	377
Graduated Adjustments (change in inches at 100 yards, or minute of angle)	.5	.5	.5	.5	.5	.5	.25	.25	.25	.25	.25	.25
Reticles* Available	1,2,4,5,6	1,2,4,5,6	1,2,4,5,6	1,2,4,5,6	1,2,4,5,6	1,2,4,5,6	1	1	1,2,4,5,6	1,2,4,5,6	1,2,4,5,6	1,2,4,5,6

*RETICLES 1 Dual X 2 Crosshair 4 Post and Crosshair 5 Dot 6 German Post
Reticles available as indicated: 1 standard; 2, 4, 5, 6 on special order.

FOCUS Eyepiece of all scopes adjusts to user's vision.

1. DUAL X®   2. CROSSHAIR   4. POST AND CROSSHAIR   5. DOT   6. GERMAN POST

WEAVER MOUNTS AND BASES

Weaver makes the industry's finest no-drill, no-tap mount bases for many of the world's most popular handguns.

Weaver P2S with Mount Base System 301 on Ruger® Blackhawk® 357 Magnum

New Weaver P4S with Mount Base System 308S on Ruger® Redhawk® 44 Magnum

Weaver Mount Base Systems make it easier than ever to mount a scope to many of America's most popular handguns, as well as Ruger's popular Mini-14... with no drilling or tapping.

Attractive new Stainless-Steel Systems are now available for Ruger handguns, Ruger Mini-14, and Smith & Wesson pistols, as listed below.

Many gunsmiths and manufacturers are reluctant to recommend drilling or tapping of a handgun, but there were few alternatives. Now the Weaver no-drill, no-tap Pistol Mount Systems are available.

Mount Base Systems install in minutes. You can do it yourself with just a standard Allen Wrench (which we provide) and a screwdriver. Simply remove the rear sight, slip on the barrel yoke, and the mount attaches easily with two screws. They're lighter than many competitive mounts. And each system comes complete with two Detachable Top Mount Rings.

Like all Weaver Mounts, these new Mount Base Systems are compact and lightweight. Their SL-II finish or Stainless Steel match the barrels and receivers of the finest pistols. The Weaver-designed locating and holding principle is widely known for its accuracy.

Mount Base attaches with no drilling or tapping.

So these new Mount Systems can be used with complete assurance, even on pistols of the heaviest recoil. You can be confident of rigid support, accurate alignment, and shockproof performance through years and years of shooting.

Here's what you get with the Weaver® Mount Base System.

Two Weaver Detachable Top Mount Rings

Mount Base

Barrel Yoke

Barrel Yoke Screw

Receiver Screw

Allen Wrench

Every Weaver Pistol Mount System comes complete with all you need to mount it yourself.

Ruger® Mini-14® with Weaver® Mini-14® Mount Base System and K4S Scope.

WEAVER® MOUNT BASE SYSTEMS: NO DRILLING, NO TAPPING

MAKE, MODEL OF GUN	MOUNT BASE SYSTEM
COLT Python, Trooper MKIII, Trooper MKV	304
Colt Trooper, Colt .357, Colt Officer's Model Match 1953 through 1970 only	303
RUGER® Blackhawk®, Super Blackhawk® Handguns	301, 301S
Mini-14® series 181, 182, 183 (will not fit series 180 or Ranch Rifle)	302, 302S
Security Six®	305
22 Automatic Pistols	306
Redhawk®	308S
SMITH & WESSON L and current K Frames with adjustable rear sight	307, 307S
N Frames	309, 309S

WEAVER

Spotting Scopes

The TS4 and TS6 spotting scopes are two of the latest examples of Weaver quality.

From the bright, crisp, distortion-free optics to the rugged non-glare finish, these scopes consistently deliver superior resolution and brightness, under a variety of hunting and shooting conditions.

The TS6 is ideal for hunting trips and for general field use. Straight-through viewing helps the shooter pick out game in heavy brush or at long distances. Eyepieces provide 15 power, 20 power, 25 power, and 40 power.

The TS4 features a 45° sighting angle. This makes it easy for the target shooter to get a really close-up view of the target — without having to move from his firing position. Reflected light is effectively eliminated by a telescoping sunshade. Magnifications available from the four interchangeable eyepieces are 12, 16, 20, and 32.

Four interchangeable eyepieces, sold separately and not included in the price of the scopes, offer most-used magnifications for each of the Weaver spotting scopes.

Adjustable stand also available.

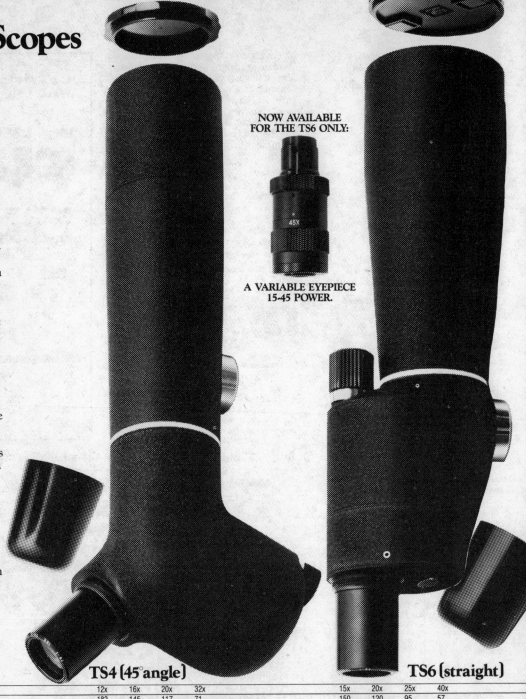

NOW AVAILABLE FOR THE TS6 ONLY:

A VARIABLE EYEPIECE 15-45 POWER.

Model	TS4 (45° angle)					TS6 (straight)			
Power (determined by eyepiece)	12x	16x	20x	32x		15x	20x	25x	40x
Field of View at 1000 yards (feet)	182	145	117	71		150	120	95	57
Field of View at 1000 meters (m)	60.67	48.33	39	23.67		50	40	31.67	19
Eye Relief (inches)	.966	.792	.699	.209		.966	.792	.699	.209
Eye Relief (mm)	24.54	20.12	17.76	5.31		24.54	20.12	17.76	5.31
Exit Pupil Diameter (inches)	.164	.123	.098	.062		.157	.118	.094	.059
Exit Pupil Diameter (mm)	4.17	3.13	2.50	1.56		4.00	3.00	2.40	1.50
Objective Diameter (inches)	1.970	1.970	1.970	1.970		2.36	2.36	2.36	2.36
Objective Diameter (mm)	50	50	50	50		60	60	60	60
Length (inches)	12.6	12.6	12.6	12.6		12.4	12.4	12.4	12.4
Length (mm)	320	320	320	320		314	314	314	314
Weight (ounces)	37.4	37.4	37.4	37.4		37.4	37.4	37.4	37.4
Weight (grams)	1060	1060	1060	1060		1060	1060	1060	1060

WILLIAMS TWILIGHT SCOPES

$109.95
2½x

$118.50
4x

$161.15
2x-6x

$169.15
3x-9x

The 'Twilight' series of scopes was introduced to accommodate those shooters who want a high quality scope in the medium priced field. The 'Twilight' scopes are the best value on the market. They are waterproof and shockproof, have coated lenses and are nitrogen filled. Resolution is sharp and clear — actually much superior to the optics of several other more expensive makes. All 'Twilight' scopes have a highly polished, rich black, hard anodized finish.

There are four models available — the 2-1/2X, the 4X, the 2X-6X, and the 3X-9X. They are available in T-N-T reticle only (which stands for thick and thin.)

Williams Gun Sight Company is one of the oldest firms in the sight business, first starting business at their present location in 1926. They have built an international reputation for producing quality equipment — backed by service.

Williams Twilight Scopes Are Available In The Popular T.N.T. Reticle Only.

TWILIGHT SPECIFICATIONS

OPTICAL SPECIFICATIONS	2.5X	4X	2X-6X At 2X	At 6X	3X-9X At 3X	At 9X
Clear aperture of objective lens	20mm	32mm	32mm	Same	38mm	Same
Clear aperture of ocular lens	32mm	32mm	32mm	Same	32mm	Same
Exit Pupil	8mm	8mm	16mm	5.3mm	12.7mm	4.2mm
Relative Brightness	64	64	256	28	161.2	17.6
Field of view (degree of angle)	12°20'	5°30'	8°30'	3°10'	7°	2°20'
Field of view at 100 yards	32'	29'	45½'	16¾'	36½'	12¾'
Eye Relief	3.7"	3.6"	3"	3"	3.1"	2.9"
Parallax Correction (at)	50 yds.	100 yds.	100 yds.	Same	100 yds.	Same
Lens Construction	9	9	11	Same	11	Same
MECHANICAL SPECIFICATIONS						
Outside diameter of objective end	1.00"	1.525"	1.525"	Same	1.850"	1.850"
Outside diameter of ocular end	1.455"	1.455"	1.455"	Same	1.455"	Same
Outside diameter of tube	1"	1"	1"	Same	1"	Same
Internal adjustment graduation	½ min.	½ min.	½ min.	Same	½ min.	Same
Minimum internal adjustment	75 min.	75 min.	75 min.	Same	60 min.	Same
Finish	Glossy Hard Black Anodized					
Length	10"	11¾"	11½"	11½"	12¾"	12¾"
Weight	8½ oz.	9½ oz.	11½ oz.	Same	13½ oz.	Same

WILLIAMS SCOPE MOUNTS

Shown on Model 70A Winchester

MODELS	Front	Rear
Remington Models 760-740-742, and Savage Model 170	1	2
Winchester Models 70 Standard, 670 and 770; Browning BBR Bolt	4	3
* 1917 Enfield	4	4
Remington Models 700-721-722-725, Remington 700 L.H. and Remington 40X; BSA; Weatherby MK-V & Vanguard; Ruger 77ST; and S&W 1500 . .	4	5
Savage Models 110, 111 and 112V	4	16
Winchester Models 88 and 100	6	6
Browning BAR Auto and BLR Lever	7	7
Marlin Models 336, 1894 & 1894C	8	8
Remington Model 788	9	9
Thompson/Center .45 & .50 Cal. Hawken and .54 Cal. Renegade	10**	10**
Remington 541-S. Also, Remington Models 580-581-582 (require drilling & tapping)	11	11
Ruger Model 44	11	12
Ruger Model 10/22	13	12
Browning Safari Bolt and Mark X	14	15
Ithaca LSA-55 and LSA-65 Bolt	16	16
Rem. Models Four, Six, 7400 and 7600	17	18

* With the rear receiver radiused the same diameter as the front receiver ring.

** Require Sub Block

STREAMLINE TOP MOUNT

The new Williams "Streamline" top mount is a revolutionary concept in two-piece mount design. It's solid ring-base construction allows the strongest possible installation of scope to rifle.

Because the bases are the rings, there can be no movement between the rings and bases as on other two piece mounts.

By design, the "Streamline" mount eliminates the need for extension rings as the mounts can be reversed allowing for installation of virtually all 1" scopes.

Simplicity of installation — solid construction — and versatility make it the most unique and most rigid two-piece mount on the market.

- **AVAILABLE FOR WIDE ASSORTMENT OF FACTORY DRILLED RIFLES**
- **PRECISION MACHINED — LIGHTWEIGHT**
- **SOLID CONSTRUCTION**
- **ELIMINATES NEED FOR EXTENSION RINGS— ALLOWS USE OF VIRTUALLY ALL 1" SCOPES**
- **THE BASES ARE THE RINGS**
- **HARD BLACK ANODIZED FINISH**

Shown on Thompson/Center Renegade w/Sub Blocks

Williams 'Streamline' Two-Piece Top Mount Complete $17.75
Williams 'Streamline' Front or Rear Base Only. 8.88
Williams 'Streamline' Two-Piece Top Mount with Sub-Blocks for Hawken M/L 24.20
Williams 'Streamline' Sub-Blocks for Hawken M/L . . . . (Per Pair) 6.45

WILLIAMS SIGHT CHART

AMOUNT OF ADJUSTMENT NECESSARY TO CORRECT FRONT SIGHT ERROR

DISTANCE BETWEEN FRONT AND REAR SIGHTS	14"	15"	16"	17"	18"	19"	20"	21"	22"	23"	24"	25"	26"	27"	28"	29"	30"	31"	32"	33"	34"
Amount of Error at 100 Yards Given in Inches — 1	.0038	.0041	.0044	.0047	.0050	.0053	.0055	.0058	.0061	.0064	.0066	.0069	.0072	.0074	.0077	.0080	.0082	.0085	.0088	.0091	.0093
2	.0078	.0083	.0089	.0094	.0100	.0105	.0111	.0116	.0122	.0127	.0133	.0138	.0144	.0149	.0155	.0160	.0156	.0171	.0177	.0182	.0188
3	.0117	.0125	.0133	.0142	.0150	.0159	.0167	.0175	.0184	.0192	.0201	.0209	.0217	.0226	.0234	.0243	.0251	.0259	.0268	.0276	.0285
4	.0155	.0167	.0178	.0189	.0200	.0211	.0222	.0234	.0244	.0255	.0266	.0278	.0289	.0300	.0311	.0322	.0333	.0344	.0355	.0366	.0377
5	.0194	.0208	.0222	.0236	.0250	.0264	.0278	.0292	.0306	.0319	.0333	.0347	.0361	.0375	.0389	.0403	.0417	.0431	.0445	.0458	.0472
6	.0233	.0250	.0267	.0283	.0300	.0317	.0333	.0350	.0367	.0384	.0400	.0417	.0434	.0450	.0467	.0484	.0500	.0517	.0534	.0551	.0567

When you replace an open rear sight with a receiver sight, it is usually necessary to install a higher front sight, to compensate for the higher plane of the new receiver sight. The table above shows the increase in front sight height that's required to compensate for a given error at 100 yards. Suppose your rifle has a 19 inch sight radius, and shoots 6 inches high at 100 yards, with the receiver sight adjusted as low as possible. The 19 inch column shows that the correction for a 6 inch error is .0317 inch. This correction is added to the over-all height of the front sight (including dovetail). Use a micrometer or similar accurate device to measure sight height. Thus, if your original sight measured .250 inch, it should be replaced with a sight .290 inch high.

WILLIAMS SIGHT-THRU MOUNTS

INSTANT DUAL SIGHTING — SCOPE ABOVE, IRON SIGHTS BELOW

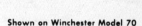

Shown on Remington Model 742

Shown on Winchester Model 70

- One-piece construction
- Large field of view for Iron Sights right under the scope
- Available for a wide assortment of factory drilled rifles
- All parts are precision machined
- Lightweight
- Hard black anodized finish
- Fast accurate sighting under all field conditions

The Williams Sight-Thru Mount provides instant use of scope, above, or iron sights below. Easily installed. Uses existing holes on top of receiver. No drilling or tapping necessary. The Sight-Thru is compact and lightweight — will not alter balance of the rifle. The high tensile strength alloy will never rust. All parts are precision machined. Completely rigid. Shockproof. The attractive streamlined appearance is further enhanced by a beautiful, hard black anodized finish.

Rings are 1" in size
⅞" Sleeves available
*Patent Pending

Williams 'Sight-Thru' Mount Complete	$17.75
Williams 'Sight-Thru' Base and Ring	8.88
Williams Sub-Block for 'Sight-Thru'	2.00
Williams 'Sight-Thru' D-22 Mount — 3/4"	7.50
Williams 'Sight-Thru' D-22 Mount — 7/8"	8.15

MODELS	Front	Rear
Winchester Models 88 and 100; Sako Finnwolf; Ithaca 37 †	A	A
Remington Models 760-740-742 and Savage Model 170	A	B
Winchester Models 70 Standard, 670 and 770; Browning BBR	D	C
Remington Models 700 R.H. and L.H., 721, 722, 725; Weatherby MK-V and Vanguard; BSA round top receivers; Ruger 77ST; Smith & Wesson Model 1500	D	E
Savage Models 110, 111 and 112V	D	F
Browning BLR Lever Action	O	O
Browning BAR High Power Auto; Mossberg 800; Remington 541S †. Will also fit Ward's Western Field Model 72 and Mossberg Model 472 lever action. *See note below	G	G
Late models Marlin 336, 1894 and 1894C	H	H
FN Mauser; Browning Bolt Action; J. C. Higgins 50-51; Interarms Mark X Mauser	D	I
Savage 99 (New Style)	J	K**
Schultz & Larsen	A	G
1917 Enfield	J	J
Ruger 10/22	L	M
Ruger 44	O	M
Ruger 77R and RS Series †	H	P
Remington Models 4, 7400, 6, and 7600	R	S

*When ordering 'G' bases for Western Field Model 72 and Mossberg Model 472, please specify that .360 screws must be furnished.

** Requires Sub Block   † Drilling and Tapping Required

SIGHT-THRU MOUNT FOR 22s

These new mounts are precision made. They are designed to fasten on the dovetails of all current .22's. For those .22's not having dovetails, there are mounting plates available to attach to receiver that creates the dovetails. Base of mount can be installed in a very low position with an unobstructed, clear view right down to the top of receiver — yet scope can still be elevated approximately ¼" additional.

These WST-D22 Sight-Thru mounts are recommended for .22's only and are available in 3/4" or 7/8" tube diameters. Specify tube diameter when ordering —

WST-D22 — 3/4"   **WST-D22 — 7/8"**

WILLIAMS
QUICK CONVERTIBLE TOP MOUNTS

TM-70 on Winchester Model 70

In spite of the sales appeal for our 'Sight-Thru' mount and all other mounts that will permit the use of iron as well as optical sights, the Q.C. Low Central Overbore is still the strongest and most positive mount on the market.

Williams Q.C. Top Mount Base (Except TM-AR-15) . . . $21.75
Williams Q.C. Top Mount Complete with Rings 38.60
Williams Q.C. Top Mount Base for AR-15 . . . . 33.25
Williams Q.C. Top Mount Complete with Rings for AR-15 50.10

TM-AR-15 on Colt AR-15

*TM-03	For 03 Springfield.
*TM-03/A3	For 03/A3 Springfield.
*TM-7x61 (54)	For Sharpe & Hart 7x61, 54 bolt action.
*TM-7x61 (60)	For Sharpe & Hart 7x61, 60 bolt action.
*TM-14	For Remington Model 14 slide action.
*TM-17	For 1917 Enfield and 30 Express and 720 Remingtons. On the Enfield grind the receiver to the same height and radius in the rear as in the front.
*TM-17 Special	For 1917 Enfield. There is enough stock left at the rear of mount base so the Model 17's not cut to standard specifications may be fitted.
*TM-22RU	For Ruger 10/22 Auto Rifle.
*TM-30	For J. C. Higgins Model 30.
*TM-43N	For new Model 43 factory drilled and tapped.
*TM-50	For early versions of J. C. Higgins Model 50.
*TM-52	Fits late Winchester Model 52 Sporter and Target. (Older models are not drilled and tapped.)
*TM-70	For all factory drilled 70's and 670's, 770's except 300 H&H and 375 H&H. Rear hole spacing—center to center—.860.
*TM-77	For Winchester 77 .22 Auto.
*TM-88	For Winchester 88 lever action, fitting factory drilling and tapping.
*TM-98	For 98 Mauser and standard Husqvarna. It is necessary to flatten the top of receiver where the 5-shot clip enters receiver if the gun is not going to be reblued. If it is to be reblued, grind this lobe off.
*TM-99	For all 99's without tang safety.
*TM-99S	For the 99 Savage 99DL and F models with tang type safety.
*TM-100	For Model 100 Winchester Auto; Sako Finnwolf.
*TM-110-LS	For Savage left hand, short actions, .243 and .308.
*TM-110-S	For Savage Model 110, .243 and .308 short actions.
*TM-336N	Fits late 336 Marlins that are factory drilled and tapped. Mounting screw holes are 8-40. Earlier models must be drilled and tapped. Includes the 444's.
*TM-600	For Rem. 600, 660 bolt action, 40X and XP100 pistol.

*TM-721-MK5	For factory drilled and tapped 721, 725, 700 (long action) Remingtons; Weatherby Mark 5; BSA; and Smith & Wesson Model 1500.
*TM-722	Fits factory drilled and tapped 722 and 700 short action Remingtons.
*TM-760	Fits 760, 740, 742 Remingtons. Most of these rifles are drilled and tapped on top for this mount. Also fits Savage 170.
*TM-800	For Mossberg 800.
*TM-AR-15	For Colt AR-15 .223 (Also M-16).
*TM-B22-241	For Browning .22 Auto and Rem. 241 with mount fastening on barrel and extending back over receiver.
*TM-BAR	For Browning High Power Auto rifle and lever action.
*TM-BRS	For short action 243 Browning, FN Browning short action.
*TM-CGH	For Crown Grade Husqvarna. Fits factory drilling and tapping. Also for Smith & Wesson Model 125 rifle.
*TM-FNA	For FN actions. Fits FN actions, Weatherby, and late J. C. Higgins Models 50 and 51, Browning High Power rifles. (Except short FN actions.)
*TM-L-57	For Sako medium action .243, .308, etc. Necessary to drill and tap.
*TM-MK5-LH	For Weatherby Mark V L.H. & Rem. 700 L.H.
*TM-RU	For Ruger .44 Magnum carbine. Fits old style factory drilling and tapping with all 4 holes on receiver.
*TM-SW Mauser	For Mauser Mark X.
*TM-VOERE	For Voere Mauser.
*TM-WBY-VM	Varmint Master, Weatherby .224 and .22/250 calibers.

* DISCONTINUED — SUBJECT TO STOCK ON HAND.

WILLIAMS SCOPE MOUNTS

SM-Mini 14 with H.C.O. Rings
on Ruger Mini-14

QUICK CONVERTIBLE SIDE MOUNTS

SM WITH REGULAR
RINGS

SM WITH HCO
RINGS

The Williams QC Side Mount permit the shooter to have both scope and iron sight always available for instant use. From the same base, shooter has his choice of rings that place scope directly over the bore or in the offset position. These sighting combinations are becoming more and more popular every day with shooters all over' the world.

Williams Side Mounts have positive locks. Using these locks, the mount becomes a "one piece" mount. Used optionally, the mount is quickly detached. The eccentric bushing in the base of the Williams QC Mount provides a limited amount of windage adjustment to insure a good mounting job.

Williams Q.C. Side Mount Base $21.75
Williams Q.C. Side Mount Complete with Split or Extension Rings . 38.60
Williams Q.C. Side Mount with H.C.O. Rings 47.05

NEW SM94 - 36 SIDE MOUNT ON THE 94

This new QC side mount requires no drilling or tapping for the 64, 65, 66 and 94 Winchesters. On the 36 and 336 Marlins, drill and tap just one hole.

SM-70	Fits 70, 770, 670, 54 Winchesters; 600, 660, 700 R.H. and L.H., 721, 722 Remingtons; Mossberg 800 and 3000; Weatherby; Mauser; Enfield; Springfield; Jap; Smith & Wesson Model 1500 rifles; Interarms Mark X rifles; round receivered SMLE's; Husqvarna; 7x61 S&H; Swiss 1911; 7.5; BSA; Savage 110 R.H.; and 91-93-95 small ring Mausers. (Also fits 98 Mauser large ring and 1917 Enfield large ring--request shim packs with mount.)
SM-71	Fits Marlin Models 36, 336, 93, 444, 1894, 1894C, and 95; 71* and 86* Winchesters; Remington 14 and 141; 7.62 Russian; and flat receivered SMLE's.
SM-88	Fits 88 and 100 Winchesters; Ruger 44 and 10/22; Winchester 150, 190, 250, 270, and 290; Weatherby 22; Browning lever action; and Sako Finnwolf.
SM-94/36	Fits 64, 65, 66, and 94 Winchesters. No drilling or tapping. On 36 and 336 Marlins drill and tap just one hole. NOTE: If mount is to be used with FP or 5D receiver sight, then use the SM-71 mount equipped with proper 94 screws.
SM-94/375	Fits Winchester 94 Big Bore .375.
SM-99	Fits 99 Savage.
SM-110LH	For the Savage 110 left hand model (fastens on right side of receiver) and fits both short or long actions; and Weatherby Mark 5 L.H.
SM-340	Fits Savage 340 factory drilling and tapping. Also fits old 322-325 and 340-343 (drilling and tapping necessary).
SM-760/40/42	For 760-740-742 Remingtons. Regular mount base with four mounting holes. Also fits 30-M1 Garand and Carbine with mounting plate; Browning A.R.; Winchester 1200 and 1400; flat receivered shotguns such as Model 12; and flat receivered .22's such as 572 and 552.
SM-MS-52/56	For Mannlicher-Schoenauer of the modified version imported by Stoeger in 1952 and altered in 1956. Also for 1903 Greek Mannlicher modified receiver, like the 52-56. Will also fit Ithaca Model 37 as well as the Winchester 05-07-09 with no mounting plate necessary.
SM-Krag	For Krag* and Remington 788 right and left hand. Also for Rem. 870 and 1100 (12 ga. only) and Rem. 8-81.
SM-Mini-14	Fits Ruger Mini-14 .223 rifle with new style receiver (181 series). This is also available with a clear anodized finish for the stainless steel guns.

Mounting Plate for 30-M1 Carbine:- $9.20
(Attach with 8-40 fillister screws.) Use the Williams SM-740 side mount base with this mounting plate. Scope can be offset or high overbore.

Mounting Plate for SMLE No. 1:- $5.95
(Attach with 8-40 fillister head mounting screws.) This mounting plate is supplied with long 8-40 fillister head screws to replace SM-70 short screws. Use the SM-70 base. Mount can be installed offset or central overbore.

Mounting Plate for M1 Garand Rifle:- $9.20
The mounting screws for this mounting plate are 8-40 x .475 fillister head. Use the Williams SM-740 (4 holes) side mount with this mounting plate.

* Will not accommodate central overbore rings.

WILLIAMS SIGHTS

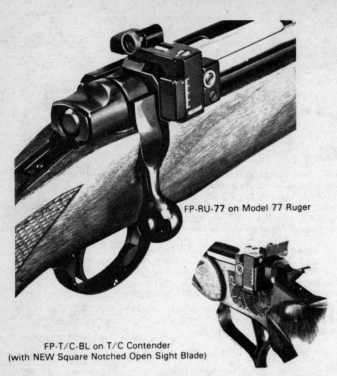

FP-RU-77 on Model 77 Ruger

FP-T/C-BL on T/C Contender
(with NEW Square Notched Open Sight Blade)

FP RECEIVER SIGHTS

Internal micrometer adjustments have positive internal locks. The FP is strong, rugged, dependable. The alloy used to manufacture this sight has a tensile strength of 85,000 pounds. Yet, the FP is light and compact, weighing only 1½ ounces.

For big game hunting, the FP will outsell all other makes and models of receiver sights put together.

Most rifles are now being drilled and tapped at the factory for installation of the FP.

New target knobs are now available on all models of the FP receiver sight if desired.

Williams FP Receiver Sight (Except FP-Hawken) . . . $34.75
Williams FP-Hawken Receiver Sight 37.20

FP-T/C-TK on T/C Contender

These Models Fit More Than 100 Guns

FP-12/37	For Winchester 12, 1200, 1400, 150, 190, 250, 255, 270, 275 and 290; Ithaca 37; Remington Sportsman 48, 58, 11-48, 1100, 870* and most flat receivered pumps and autoloaders.
FP-14	For Remington 14 and 141.
FP-17	For Enfield, Remington Express and British Pattern 14.
FP-30 Car.	For Government 30 Carbine.
FP-39	For Marlin 39A lever action.
FP-70	For 70 and 54 Winchesters; 721, 722, 725 Remingtons; Mossberg 800.
FP-70AP	For new Model 70, 670 and 770 with high sight line; Remington 700; Mossberg 800 and 3000; BSA; and Smith & Wesson Model 1500.
FP-71	For Winchester 71, 86, 05, 07 and 10. Also for Model 95 Winchester lever action.
FP-88/100	For Win. 88 lever action; Win. 100 auto; Marlin 56, 57, 62, 99 auto-loading; and Sako Finnwolf.
FP-94/36	For Winchester Models 94, 55, 63, 64, 65, and 9422; Marlin Models 36, 336, 444, 44 Magnum, and 93; Sears and Browning centerfire lever actions.
FP-94/375	For Winchester 94 Big Bore .375.
FP-98	For military Mauser, Husqvarna, Weatherby Mark V, right and left, and BRNO without dovetailed receiver.
FP-98AP	For Browning high power bolt with high line of sights; also for Rem. 700 left hand.
FP-99S	For late Savage 99 with top tang safety. Will fit old 99, but it will be necessary to drill and tap.
FP-110	For Savage 110 bolt action, right and left.
FP-121	For Remington 12 and 121.

NOTE: Add 'TK' to model number if target knobs are desired.
Add 'BL' to model number if square notched blade is desired.

FP-340	For 322-325-340-342 Stevens-Savage.
FP-600	For Remington 600, 660 bolt action & XP-100. If you specify TK for target knobs, they are furnished for elevation only (not for windage).
FP-740AP	For all 742 Remingtons and for the late 760-740 Remingtons with high comb (all purpose stock) and high iron sights. Also for the higher sight models of the 740 in the 30-06 and 280 calibers above serial number 207,200, and the 308 caliber above serial number 200,000. Also for Remington 572BDL and 552BDL and Savage 170. Will also fit new Remington models 4, 7400, 6, and 7600.
FP-788	For Remington 788 bolt action.
FP-788LH	For Remington 788 left hand action.
FP-A3	For 03/A3 and 03 Springfields.
FP-BAR	For Browning auto-loading high power rifle.
FP-CGH	For Crown Grade Husqvarna and S&W rifle.
FP-FN	For factory drilled and tapped FN and Dumoulin, Mark X, Daisy 99 and 299.
FP-Hawken	For Thompson/Center Hawken and Renegade M/L rifles. This sight fitted with sub-block to eliminate drilling and tapping.
FP-JAP	For Jap .25 and .31 caliber rifles.
FP-Krag	For American Krag and Norwegian Krag.
FP-RU	For 44 Mag. Ruger carbine and .22 L.R. 10/22 all models.
FP-RU-77	For Ruger Model 77 bolt action.
FP-S&L	For Schultz & Larsen 54J, Model 60 and 65DL.
FP-SMLE	For British Short Magazine Lee Enfields.
FP-SSM	For square sterned auto shotguns. Also fits 8-81 Rem.
FP-SW	For 1911, Swiss 7.5.
FP-T/C	For Thompson/Center Contender Pistol.

Ammunition

CCI AMMUNITION

22 RIMFIRE

0030
Mini-Mag Long Rifle $4.77*

0034
Mini-Mag Long Rifle
50 pack paper $238

0031
Mini-Mag Long Rifle
Hollow Point $5.27*

0032
Mini-Group Long Rifle
$4.77*

0029
Mini-Mag Long $4.47*

0027
Mini-Mag Short $4.20*

0028
Mini-Mag Short
Hollow Point $4.47*

0037
Mini-Group
Short Target $4.55*

0038
Mini-Mag CB Long $4.25*

0026
Mini-Cap CB $4.25*

0039
Mini-Mag Shotshell $2.43*
20/Box

0050
Stinger, Long Rifle $3.18
Hollow Point 50/Box

0023
Maxi-Mag WMR
Solid $6.43 50/Box

0024
Maxi-Mag WMR
Hollow Point $6.43 50/Box

0025
Maxi-Mag WMR
Shotshell $3.95 20/Box

380 AUTO

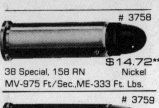

#3605
$15.95**
380 88JHP
MV1000Ft/Sec.   ME-195 Ft. Lbs

9mm LUGER

3610
$19.38**
9mm Luger,100 JHP   Brass
MV-1315 Ft/Sec. ME-384 Ft. Lbs.

3620
$19.38**
9mm Luger, 125 JSP   Brass
MV-1120Ft/Sec., ME-348 Ft. Lbs.

38 SPECIAL

3710
$18.68**
38 Special, 110 JHP   Nickel
MV-1245 Ft/Sec., ME-378 Ft. Lbs.

3720
$18.68**
38 Special, 125 JHP   Nickel +P
MV-1425 Ft/Sec., ME-563 Ft. Lbs.

3725
$18.68**
38 Special, 125 JSP   Nickel +P
MV-1425 Ft/Sec.,ME-563 Ft. Lbs.

3740
$18.68**
38 Special, 140 JHP   Nickel +P
MV-1200 Ft/Sec., ME-447 Ft.Lbs.

3748
$15.33**
38 Special,148 HBWC   Brass
MV-825 Ft/Sec.,ME-223 Ft. Lbs.

3752
$15.08**
38 Special, 158 SWC   Nickel
MV—975 Ft/Sec.,ME-333 Ft. Lbs.

3758
$14.72**
38 Special, 158 RN   Nickel
MV-975 Ft/Sec.,ME-333 Ft. Lbs.

3759
$18.68**
38 Special, 158 JSP   Nickel +P
MV-1025 Ft/Sec., ME-368 Ft. Lbs.

3760
$18.68**
38 Special, 158 JHP   Nickel+P
MV-1025 Ft/Sec.,ME-368 Ft. Lbs.

$19.73   # 3708
38/357 Shotshell   Neckel
#9 Shot 50/Box

3709
38/357 Shotshell   Nickel
#9 shot 10/Box $4.82
MV-1150 Ft/Sec.,ME-308 Ft. Lbs.

357 MAGNUM

3910
$20.48**
357 Magnum, 110 JHP   Nickel
MV-1700 Ft/Sec., ME-705 Ft. Lbs.

3920
$20.48**
357 Magnum, 125 JHP   Nickel
MV-1900 Ft/Sec. ME-1001 Ft. Lbs.

3925
$20.48**
357 Magnum, 125 JSP   Nickel
MV-1900 Ft/Sec.,ME-1001 Ft. Lbs.

3940
$20.48**
357 Magnum, 140 JHP   Nickel
MV-1780 Ft/Sec. ME-984 Ft. Lbs.

3959
$20.48**
357 Magnum, 158 JSP   Nickel
MV-1625 Ft/Sec.,ME-926 Ft. Lbs.

3960
$20.48**
357 Magnum, JHP   Nickel
MV-1625 Ft/Sec., ME-926 Ft. Lbs.

44 MAGNUM

$13.36**   # 3972

44 Magnum, 200 JHP   Brass
25/Box
MV-1675 Ft/Sec.,ME-1246 Ft. Lbs.

$13.36***   # 3974

44 Magnum, 240 JSP   Brass
25/Box
MV-1650 Ft/Sec. ME-1450 Ft. Lbs.

10/Box $6.44

44 Magnum Shotshell   # 3978
#9 shot 25/Box   Brass

44 Magnum Shotshell   # 3979
#9 Shot 10/Box   Brass
MV-1200 Ft/Sec., ME-494 Ft. Lbs.

45 AUTO

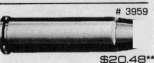

3965
$11.04***
45 Auto, 200 JHP   Brass
MV-1025 Ft/Sec.,ME-466 Ft.Lbs.

BLAZER CENTERFIRE

50 Pak		
25 AUTO		
# 3501	25 Auto-50-FMJ	8.67
9mm		
# 3509	9mm-115-FMJ	12.33
38 SPECIAL		
# 3514	38 + P-125-JHP	12.08
# 3517	38-148-HBWC	10.00
# 3519	38 + P-150-FMJ	12.08
# 3522	38-158-RNL	10.00
# 3523	38 + P-158-SWC HP	10.00
# 3526	38 + P-158-JHP	12.08
357 MAGNUM		
# 3532	357-125-JHP	13.33
# 3542	357-158-JHP	13.33

*100 PAK   ** 50 PAK   *** 25 PAK

FEDERAL CENTERFIRE AMMUNITION

RIFLE CARTRIDGES

NO.	CALIBER	WT. GRS.	BULLET STYLE	FACTORY PRIMER NO.	BOX OF 20
222A	222 Remington	50	Soft Point	205	$ 9.95
222B	222 Remington	55	Metal Case Boat-tail	205	9.95
22250A	22-250 Remington	55	Soft Point	210	10.90
223A	223 Remington (5.56mm)	55	Soft Point	205	10.90
223B	223 Remington (5.56mm)	55	Metal Case Boat-tail	205	10.90
6A	6mm Remington	80	Soft Point	210	13.60
6B	6mm Remington	100	Hi-Shok Soft Point	210	13.60
243A	243 Winchester	80	Soft Point	210	13.60
243B	243 Winchester	100	Hi-Shok Soft Point	210	13.60
2506A	25-06 Remington	90	Hollow Point	210	14.80
2506B	25-06 Remington	117	Hi-Shok Soft Point	210	14.80
270A	270 Winchester	130	Hi-Shok Soft Point	210	14.80
270B	270 Winchester	150	Hi-Shok Soft Point	210	14.80
7A	7mm Mauser	175	Hi-Shok Soft Point	210	15.05
7RA	7mm Remington Magnum	150	Hi-Shok Soft Point	215	18.30
7RB	7mm Remington Magnum	175	Hi-Shok Soft Point	215	18.30
30CA	30 Carbine	110	Soft Point	205	9.50
30CB	30 Carbine	110	Metal Case	205	9.50
3030A	30-30 Winchester	150	Hi-Shok Soft Point	210	11.60
3030B	30-30 Winchester	170	Hi-Shok Soft Point	210	11.60
3006A	30-06 Springfield	150	Hi-Shok Soft Point	210	14.80
3006B	30-06 Springfield	180	Hi-Shok Soft Point	210	14.80
3006C	30-06 Springfield	125	Soft Point	210	14.80
3006D	30-06 Springfield	165	Soft Point Boat-tail	210	15.35
3006E	30-06 Springfield	200	Soft Point Boat-tail	210	15.35
300A	300 Savage	150	Hi-Shok Soft Point	210	14.95
300B	300 Savage	180	Hi-Shok Soft Point	210	14.95
300WB	300 Winchester Magnum	180	Hi-Shok Soft Point	215	19.35
308A	308 Winchester	150	Hi-Shok Soft Point	210	14.80
308B	308 Winchester	180	Hi-Shok Soft Point	210	14.80
8A	8mm Mauser	170	Hi-Shok Soft Point	210	15.25
32A	32 Winchester Special	170	Hi-Shok Soft Point	210	12.40
35A	35 Remington	200	Hi-Shok Soft Point	210	13.65
44A	44 Remington Magnum	240	Hollow Soft Point	150	11.35
4570A	45-70 Government	300	Hollow Soft Point	210	16.80
3030C	30-30 Winchester	125	Hollow Point	210	11.60

PISTOL CARTRIDGES

NO.	CALIBER	WT. GRS.	BULLET STYLE	PRIMER NO.	BOX OF 50
25 AP	25 Auto Pistol (6.35mm)	50	Metal Case	100	$14.40
32AP	32 Auto Pistol (7.65mm)	71	Metal Case	100	16.50
380AP	380 Auto Pistol	95	Metal Case	100	16.90
380BP	380 Auto Pistol	90	Jacketed Hollow Point	100	16.90
9AP	9mm Luger Auto Pistol	123	Metal Case	100	20.50
9BP	9mm Luger Auto Pistol	115	Jacketed Hollow Point	100	20.50
38A	38 Special (Match)	148	Lead Wadcutter	100	16.25
38B	38 Special	158	Lead Round Nose	100	15.60
38C	38 Special	158	Lead Semi-Wadcutter	100	16.75
38D	38 Special (High Vel + P)	158	Lead Round Nose	200	17.30
38E	38 Special (High Vel + P)	125	Jacketed Hollow Point	200	19.80
38F	38 Special (High Vel + P)	110	Jacketed Hollow Point	200	19.80
38G	38 Special (High Vel + P)	158	Lead Semi-Wad Cutter Hollow Point	200	16.95
38J	38 Special (High Vel + P)	125	Jacketed Soft Point	200	19.80
38H	38 Special (High Vel + P)	158	Lead Semi-Wadcutter	200	15.90
357A	357 Magnum	158	Jacketed Soft Point	200	21.70
357B	357 Magnum	125	Jacketed Hollow Point	200	21.70
357C	357 Magnum	158	Lead Semi-Wadcutter	200	18.35
357D	357 Magnum	110	Jacketed Hollow Point	200	21.70
357E	357 Magnum	158	Jacketed Hollow Point	200	21.70
44SA	S & W Special	200	Semi-Wadcutter Hollow Point	150	21.80
44B	44 Remington Magnum		Jacketed Hollow Point	150	25.80
45A	45 Automatic (Match)	230	Metal Case	150	22.60
45B	45 Automatic (Match)	185	Metal Case S.W.C.	150	23.70
45C	45 Automatic	185	Jacketed Hollow Point	150	23.70
45LCA	45 Colt	225	Lead Semi-Wad Cutter Hollow Point	150	20.85

FEDERAL RIMFIRE AMMUNITION

HI-POWER 22's with copper-plated bullets. A high velocity load for that extra-hard blow you need when hunting small game or pests. Their flat trajectory and accuracy provide an advantage at normal ranges. All have a non-corrosive, non-mercuric priming mixture that has long-term stability and will not cause barrel rust. Packed 50 per box except where noted.

NO.	CALIBER	WT. GRS.	BULLET STYLE	PER BOX
701	22 Short Hi-Power	29	Lead, Solid	$2.15
703	22 Short Hi-Power Hollow Point	29	Lead, HP	2.30
706	22 Long Hi-Power	29	Lead, Solid	2.30
710	22 Long Rifle Hi-Power	40	Lead, Solid	2.45
712	22 Long Rifle Hi-Power Hollow Point	38	Lead, HP	2.70
716	22 Long Rifle Hi-Power Shot	25	No. 12 Shot	5.00
810	22 Long Rifle Hi-Power (100 pack)	40	Lead, Solid	4.90
812	22 Long Rifle Hi-Power Hollow Point (100 pack)	38	Lead, HP	5.45

CHAMPION standard velocity 22's. A standard velocity load with a lubricated lead bullet for plinking, short range hunting, and informal target shooting where consistent accuracy is needed. All have non-corrosive, non-mercuric priming mixture which will not cause barrel rust. Packed 50 per box except where noted.

NO.	CALIBER	WT. GRS.	BULLET STYLE	PER BOX
711	22 Long Rifle	40	Lead, Solid	$2.45
811	22 Long Rifle (100 pack)	40	Lead, Solid	4.00

FEDERAL SHOTSHELLS

Gauge	Load No.	Shell Length Inches	Dram Equiv.	Shot Charge Oz.	Shot Sizes	Price Per Box
SUPER MAGNUM LOADS						
▲10	F103	3½	4¼	2	BB,2,4	$26.40
▲12	F131	3	4	1⅞	BB,2,4	17.70
▲12	F129	3	4	1⅝	2,4,6	16.35
▲12	F130	2¾	3¾	1½	BB,2,4,5,6	14.80
▲16	F165	2¾	3¼	1¼	2,4,6	14.55
▲20	F207	3	3	1¼	2,4,6;7½	13.70
▲20	F205	2¾	2¾	1⅛	4,6,7½	12.15
HI-POWER LOADS						
12	F127	2¾	3¾	1¼	BB,2,4,5,6,7½,8,9	11.40
16	F164	2¾	3¼	1⅛	4,5,6,7½	10.90
20	F203	2¾	2¾	1	4,5,6,7½,8,9	10.00
28	F283	2¾	2¼	¾	6,7½,8	10.10
.410	F413	3	Max.	¹¹⁄₁₆	4,5,6,7½,8	9.40
.410	F412	2½	Max.	½	6,7½	7.95
WATERFOWL STEEL SHOT LOADS						
12	W147	2¾	3¾	1⅛	1,2,4 Steel	$14.25
▲12	W148	2¾	3¾	1¼	BB1,2,4 Steel	15.60
▲12	W149	3	3½	1⅜	BB1,2,4 Steel	19.10
▲10	W104	3½	4¼	1⅝	BB2 Steel	23.95
▲20	W209	3	3¼	1	4 Steel	13.65
FIELD LOADS						
12	F125	2¾	3¼	1¼	7½,8	$10.70
12	F124	2¾	3¼	1¼	7½,8,9	10.05
12	F123	2¾	3¼	1⅛	4,5,6,7½,8,9	9.75
16	F162	2¾	2¾	1⅛	4,6,7½,8	9.70
20	F202	2¾	2½	1	4,5,6,7½,8,9	8.85
GAME LOADS						
12	F121	2¾	3¾	1	6,7½,8	
16	F160	2¾	2½	1	6,7½,8	
20	F200	2¾	2½	⅞	6,7½,8	
DUCK & PHEASANT LOADS						
12	F126	2¾	3¾	1¼	4,5,6,7½	
16	F163	2¾	3¼	1⅛	4,6,7½	
20	F204	2¾	2¾	1	4,6,7½	

Gauge	Load No.	Shell Length Inches	Dram Equiv.	Shot Charge Oz.	Shot Sizes	Price Per Box
RIFLED SLUG LOADS						
12	F127	2¾	Max.	1	Rifled Slug	$3.70
16	F164	2¾	Max.	⅘	Rifled Slug	3.70
20	F203	2¾	Max.	⅝	Rifled Slug	3.40
.410	F412	2½	Max.	⅕	Rifled Slug	3.20
TARGET LOADS						
12	F115	2¾	2¾	1⅛	7½,8,9	$7.85
12	F116	2¾	3	1⅛	7½,8,9	7.85
12	C117	2¾	2¾	1⅛	7½,8,8½,9	7.65
12	C118	2¾	3	1⅛	7½,8,9	7.65
12	T122	2¾	3	1⅛	9	8.10
20	F206	2¾	2½	⅞	8,9	7.35
20	S206	2¾	2½	⅞	9	7.35
28	F280	2¾	2	¾	9	8.65
.410	F412	2½	Max.	½	9	7.15
HI-POWER® BUCKSHOT LOADS						
10	G108	3½	Mag.		4 Buck—54 Pellets	$ 5.40
12	F131	3	Mag.		000 Buck—10 Pellets	4.10
12	F131	3	Mag.		00 Buck—15 Pellets	4.10
12	F131	3	Mag.		1 Buck—24 Pellets	4.10
12	F131	3	Mag.		4 Buck—41 Pellets	4.10
▲12	A131	3	Mag.		4 Buck—41 Pellets	20.50
12	F130	2¾	Mag.		00 Buck—12 Pellets	3.55
12	F130	2¾	Mag.		1 Buck—20 Pellets	3.55
12	F130	2¾	Mag.		4 Buck—34 Pellets	3.55
▲12	A130	2¾	Mag.		4 Buck—34 Pellets	20.50
12	F127	2¾	Max.		000 Buck— 8 Pellets	17.75
12	G127	2¾	Max.		00 Buck— 9 Pellets	3.20
12	F127	2¾	Max.		00 Buck— 9 Pellets	3.20
12	F127	2¾	Max.		0 Buck—12 Pellets	3.20
12	F127	2¾	Max.		1 Buck—16 Pellets	3.20
12	F127	2¾	Max.		4 Buck—27 Pellets	3.20
▲12	A127	2¾	Max.		4 Buck—27 Pellets	3.20
16	F164	2¾	Max.		1 Buck—12 Pellets	3.20
20	F207	3	Mag.		2 Buck—18 Pellets	3.55
20	F203	2¾	Max.		3 Buck—20 Pellets	3.20

Buckshot and rifled slugs packed 5 rounds per box, except ▲ 25 rounds per box. All other shotshells packed 25 rounds per box.

HORNADY FRONTIER CARTRIDGES

RIFLE AMMUNITION

PER BOX

222 REM.
50 gr. SX	#8010	$ 9.50
55 gr. SX	#8015	$ 9.50

223 REM.
55 gr. SP	#8025	$10.50
55 gr. FMJ	#8027	$10.50

22-250 REM.
53 gr. HP	#8030	$10.50
55 gr. SP	#8035	$10.50
55 gr. FMJ	#8037	$10.50

220 SWIFT
55 gr. SP	#8120	$14.70
60 gr. HP	#8122	$14.70

243 WIN.
75 gr. HP	#8040	$13.00
80 gr. FMJ	#8043	$13.00
100 gr. SP	#8045	$13.00

270 WIN.
110 gr. HP	#8050	$14.15
130 gr. SP	#8055	$14.15
140 gr. BTSP	#8056	$14.35
150 gr. SP	#8058	$14.15

7mm REM. MAG.
154 gr. SP	#8060	$17.60
175 gr. SP	#8065	$17.60

30 M1 CARBINE
*110 gr. RN	#8070	$22.80
*110 gr. FM	#8077	$22.80

30-30 WIN.
150 gr. RN	#8080	$11.15
170 gr. FP	#8085	$11.15

308 WIN.
150 gr. SP	#8090	$14.15
165 gr. SP	#8095	$14.15
165 gr. BTSP	#8098	$14.70
168 gr. BTHP (Match)	#8097	$16.55

PER BOX

30-06 SPRINGFIELD
150 gr. SP	#8110	$14.15
165 gr. BTSP	#8115	$14.70
168 gr. BTHP (Match)	#8117	$16.55
180 gr. SP	#8118	$14.15

300 WIN. MAG.
180 gr. SP	#8200	$18.55

PISTOL AMMUNITION

25 AUTO
*50 gr. FMJ-RN	#9000	$13.75

380 AUTO
*90 gr. JHP	#9010	$16.10
*100 gr. FMJ	#9015	$16.10

9MM LUGER
*90 gr. JHP	#9020	$19.60
*100 gr. FMJ	#9023	$19.60
*115 gr. JHP	#9025	$19.60
*124 gr. FMJ-FP	#9027	$19.60

38 SPECIAL
*110 gr. JHP	#9030	$18.55
*125 gr. JHP	#9032	$18.55
*125 gr. JFP	#9033	$18.55
*148 gr. HBWC (Match)	#9043	$15.90
*158 gr. JHP	#9036	$18.55
*158 gr. JFP	#9038	$18.55
*158 gr. LRN	#9045	$15.15
*158 gr. SWC	#9046	$15.15

357 MAG.
*125 gr. JHP	#9050	$20.70
*125 gr. JFP	#9053	$20.70
*158 gr. JHP	#9056	$20.70
*158 gr. JFP	#9058	$20.70
*158 gr. SWC	#9065	$17.55

44 REM. MAG.
200 gr. JHP	#9080	$10.75
240 gr. JHP	#9085	$10.75
240 gr. SWC	#9087	$ 9.15

45 ACP
185 gr. JHP	#9090	$ 9.15
185 gr. Target SWC	#9095	$ 9.90
200 gr. SWC	#9110	$ 8.45
200 gr. FMJ-C/T (Match)	#9111	$10.00
230 gr. FMJ-RN	#9097	$ 9.15
230 gr. FMJ-FP	#9098	$ 9.15

*Packed 50 per box. All others packed 20 per box.

NORMA CENTERFIRE RIFLE AMMO

NO.	WT. GRAINS	BULLET STYLE	PER BOX OF 20
220 SWIFT:			
15701	50	Soft Point Semi Pointed	$15.85
222 REMINGTON:			
15711	50	Soft Point Semi Pointed	10.85
15712	**50**	**Full Jacket**	**10.85**
15714	53	Soft Point Semi Pointed Match Spitzer	10.85
22-250			
15733	53	Soft Point Semi Pointed Match Spitzer	11.05
22 SAVAGE HIGH POWER: (5.6x52 R):			
15604	71	Soft Point Semi Pointed	21.00
15605	71	Full Jacketed Semi Pointed	NA
243 WINCHESTER:			
16002	100	Full Jacketed Semi Pointed	13.60
16003	100	Soft Point Semi Pointed	13.60
6.5 JAP:			
16531	139	Soft Point Semi Pointed Boat Tail	21.00
16532	156	Soft Point Round Nose	21.00
6.5 x 55:			
16550	77	Soft Point Semi Pointed	NA
16557	139	Plastic Pointed "Dual-Core"	21.95
16552	156	Soft Point Round Nose	21.00
6.5 CARCANO:			
16535	156	Soft Point Round Nose	21.00
16536	139	Plastic Pointed "Dual-Core"	21.95
270 WINCHESTER:			
16902	130	Soft Point Semi Pointed Boat Tail	14.75
16903	150	Soft Point Semi Pointed Boat Tail	14.75
7 x 57 (7MM MAUSER):			
17002	150	Soft Point Semi Pointed Boat Tail	19.45
7 x 57 R:			
17005	150	Soft Point Semi Pointed Boat Tail	NA
17006	150	Full Jacketed Pointed Boat Tail	NA
7MM REM. MAGNUM:			
17021	150	Soft Point Semi Pointed Boat Tail	18.10
7 x 64:			
17013	150	Soft Point Semi Pointed Boat Tail	NA
17015	175	Soft Point Nosler	NA

NO.	WT. GRAINS	BULLET STYLE	PER BOX OF 20
280 REMINGTON (7MM EXPRESS):			
17050	150	Soft Point Semi Pointed Boat Tail	NA
7.5 x 55 SWISS:			
17511	180	Soft Point Semi Pointed Boat Tail	$22.00
30 U.S. CARBINE:			
17621	110	Soft Point Round Nose	9.50
7.62 x 39 SHORT RUSSIAN:			
17672	125	Soft Point	18.95
7.62 RUSSIAN:			
17634	180	Soft Point Semi Pointed Boat Tail	22.35
30-06 SPRINGFIELD:			
17640	130	Soft Point Semi Pointed Boat Tail	14.75
17643	150	Soft Point Semi Pointed Boat Tail	18.95
17648	180	Soft Point Round Nose	14.75
17653	180	Plastic Pointed "Dual-Core"	16.95
17656	**180**	**Plastic Pointed "Dual-Core"**	7.10 (10 pack)
30-30 WINCHESTER:			
17630	150	Soft Point Flat Nose	11.00
17631	170	Soft Point Flat Nose	11.00
308 WINCHESTER:			
17623	130	Soft Point Semi Pointed Boat Tail	14.75
17624	150	Soft Point Semi Pointed Boat Tail	14.75
17628	180	Plastic Pointed "Dual-Core"	15.85
308 NORMA MAGNUM:			
17638	180	Plastic Pointed "Dual-Core"	27.90
7.65 ARGENTINE:			
17701	150	Soft Point Semi Pointed	21.95
303 BRITISH:			
17712	150	Soft Point Semi Pointed	15.50
17713	180	Soft Point Semi Pointed Boat Tail	15.50
7.7 JAP:			
17721	130	Soft Point Semi Pointed	22.50
17722	180	Soft Point Semi Pointed Boat Tail	22.50
8 x 57 J (.318"):			
17901	196	Plastic Pointed "Dual-Core"	NA
8 x 57 JS (8 MM MAUSER):			
18003	196	Soft Point Round Nose	19.65
358 NORMA MAGNUM:			
19001	250	Soft Point	NA
9.3 x 57:			
19302	286	Plastic Pointed "Dual-Core"	NA
9.3 x 62:			
19314	286	Plastic Pointed "Dual-Core"	NA

NORMA CENTERFIRE PISTOL AMMUNITION

NO.	WT. GRAINS	BULLET STYLE	PER BOX OF 50
30 LUGER:			
17612	93	Full Jacketed Round Nose	$26.35
32 ACP:			
17614	77	Full Jacketed Round Nose	16.50
9MM LUGER:			
19021	115	Hollow Point	23.50
19022	116	Full Jacketed Round Nose	NA
19026	116	Soft Point Flat Nose	22.00
38 SPECIAL:			
19114	158	Full Jacketed Semi-Wad Cutter	22.95
19119	110	Jacketed Hollow Point Magnum	23.25
19110	148	Lead Wad Cutter	15.95
19112	158	Lead Round Nose	15.95

NO.	WT. GRAINS	BULLET STYLE	PER BOX OF 50
38 SPECIAL:			
19124	158	Soft Point Flat Nose	$21.85
19125	158	Hollow Point	21.85
357 MAGNUM:			
19101	158	Hollow Point	21.85
19106	158	Full Jacketed Semi-Wad Cutter	27.35
19107	158	Soft Point Flat Nose	21.85
44 MAGNUM:			
11103	240	Power Cavity (Box of 20)	11.20
44 AUTO MAGNUM:			
11105	240	Flat Point	NA

REMINGTON CENTERFIRE PISTOL & REVOLVER CARTRIDGES
with "KLEANBORE" PRIMING

22 Remington "Jet" Magnum

No.	Bullet weight	Bullet style	Wt. case, lbs.	Per box
R22JET	40 gr.	Soft Point	12	$27.05

50 in a box, 500 in a case.

32 Short Colt

No.	Bullet weight	Bullet style	Wt. case, lbs.	Per box
R32SC	80 gr.	Lead	10	$13.85

50 in a box, 500 in a case.

221 Remington "Fire Ball"

No.	Bullet weight	Bullet style	Wt. case, lbs.	Per box
R221F	50 gr.	PTd. Soft Point	12	$11.50

20 in a box, 500 in a case.

32 Long Colt

No.	Bullet weight	Bullet style	Wt. case, lbs.	Per box
R32LC	82 gr.	Lead	10	$14.40

50 in a box, 500 in a case.

25 (6.35mm) Auto. Pistol

No.	Bullet weight	Bullet style	Wt. case, lbs.	Per box
R25AP	50 gr.	Metal Case	28	$14.40

50 in a box, 2,000 in a case.

32 (7.65mm) Auto. Pistol

No.	Bullet weight	Bullet style	Wt. case, lbs.	Per box
R32AP	71 gr.	Metal Case	36	$16.55

50 in a box, 2,000 in a case.

REMINGTON CENTERFIRE PISTOL AND REVOLVER CARTRIDGES

32 S & W

No.	Bullet weight	Bullet style	Wt. case, lbs.	Per box
R32SW	88 gr.	Lead	41	$13.90

50 in a box, 2,000 in a case.

32 S & W Long

No.	Bullet weight	Bullet style	Wt. case, lbs.	Per box
R32SWL	98 gr.	Lead	46	$14.40

50 in a box, 2,000 in a case.

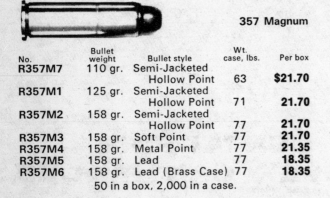

357 Magnum

No.	Bullet weight	Bullet style	Wt. case, lbs.	Per box
R357M7	110 gr.	Semi-Jacketed Hollow Point	63	$21.70
R357M1	125 gr.	Semi-Jacketed Hollow Point	71	21.70
R357M2	158 gr.	Semi-Jacketed Hollow Point	77	21.70
R357M3	158 gr.	Soft Point	77	21.70
R357M4	158 gr.	Metal Point	77	21.35
R357M5	158 gr.	Lead	77	18.35
R357M6	158 gr.	Lead (Brass Case)	77	18.35

50 in a box, 2,000 in a case.

9mm Luger Auto. Pistol

No.	Bullet weight	Bullet style	Wt. case, lbs.	Per box
R9MM1	115 gr.	Jacketed Hollow Point	54	$20.50
R9MM2	124 gr.	Metal Case	56	20.50

50 in a box, 2,000 in a case.

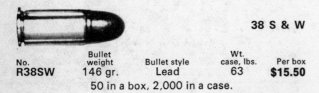

38 S & W

No.	Bullet weight	Bullet style	Wt. case, lbs.	Per box
R38SW	146 gr.	Lead	63	$15.50

50 in a box, 2,000 in a case.

(+P) Ammunition with (+P) on the case headstamp is loaded to higher pressure. Use only in firearms designated for this cartridge and so recommended by the gun manufacturer.

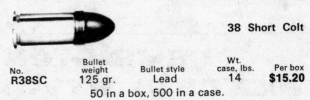

38 Special

No.	Bullet weight	Bullet style	Wt. case, lbs.	Per box
R38S1	95 gr.	Semi-Jacketed Hollow Point (+P)	52	$20.75
R38S10	110 gr.	Semi-Jacketed Hollow Point (+P)	56	19.80
R38S2	125 gr.	Semi-Jacketed Hollow Point (+P)	65	19.80
R38S3	148 gr.	Targetmaster Lead Wadcutter	66	16.25
R38S4	158 gr.	Targetmaster Lead Round Nose	70	16.25
R38S5	158 gr.	Lead	70	15.60
R38S6	158 gr.	Lead Semi-Wadcutter	70	16.75
R38S7	158 gr.	Metal Point	70	19.80
R38S8	158 gr.	Lead (+P)	70	17.30
R38S12	158 gr.	Lead Hollow Point (+P)	69	16.95
R38S9	200 gr.	Lead	82	16.65

50 in a box, 2,000 in a case.

38 Short Colt

No.	Bullet weight	Bullet style	Wt. case, lbs.	Per box
R38SC	125 gr.	Lead	14	$15.20

50 in a box, 500 in a case.

38 Super Auto. Colt Pistol

Adapted only for 38 Colt Super and Colt Commander Automatic Pistols.

No.	Bullet weight	Bullet style	Wt. case, lbs.	Per box
R38SUI	115 gr.	Jacketed Hollow Point (+P)	56	$20.80
R38SUP	130 gr.	Metal Case (+P)	62	17.85

50 in a box, 2,000 in a case.

38 Auto. Colt Pistol

Adapted only for 38 Colt Sporting, Military and Pocket Model Automatic Pistols.

No.	Bullet weight	Bullet style	Wt. case, lbs.	Per box
R38ACP	130 gr.	Metal Case	62	$18.40

50 in a box, 2,000 in a case.

REMINGTON CENTERFIRE CARTRIDGES
PISTOL/REVOLVER

380 Auto. Pistol

No.	Bullet weight	Bullet style	Wt. case, lbs.	Per box
R380A1	88 gr.	Jacketed Hollow Point	45	**$16.90**
R380AP	95 gr.	Metal Case	45	**16.90**

50 in a box, 2,000 in a case.

41 Magnum

No.	Bullet weight	Bullet style	Wt. case, lbs.	Per box
R41MG1	210 gr.	Soft Point	52	**$28.50**
R41MG2	210 gr.	Lead	49	**24.35**

50 in a box, 1,000 in a case.

44 S&W Special

No.	Bullet weight	Bullet style	Wt. case, lbs.	Per box
R44SW	246 gr.	Lead	25	**$21.80**

50 in a box, 500 in a case.

44 Remington Magnum

No.	Bullet weight	Bullet style	Wt. case, lbs.	Per box
R44MG1	240 gr.	Lead, Gas-Check	57	**$27.70**
R44MG4	240 gr.	Lead	57	**23.65**

50 in a box, 1,000 in a case.

No.	Bullet weight	Bullet style	Wt. case, lbs.	Per box
R44MG2	240 gr.	Soft Point	29	**$11.35**
R44MG3	240 gr.	Semi-Jacketed Hollow Point	29	**11.35**
R44MG5	180 gr.	Semi-Jacketed Hollow Point	29	**10.35**

20 in a box, 500 in a case.

45 Colt

No.	Bullet weight	Bullet style	Wt. case, lbs.	Per box
R45C	250 gr.	Lead	26	**$22.15**

50 in a box, 500 in a case.

45 Auto.

No.	Bullet weight	Bullet style	Wt. case, lbs.	Per box
R45AP1	185 gr.	Targetmaster Metal Case Wadcutter	43	**$23.70**
R45AP2	185 gr.	Jacketed Hollow Point	43	**23.70**
R45AP4	230 gr.	Metal Case	49	**22.60**

50 in a box, 1,000 in a case.

45 Auto. Rim

No.	Bullet weight	Bullet style	Wt. case, lbs.	Per box
R45AR	230 gr.	Lead	27	**$24.00**

50 in a box, 500 in a case.

REMINGTON CENTER FIRE BLANK

No.	Caliber	No. in case	Wt. case, lbs.	Per box
R32BLNK	32 S & W	5,000	37	**$13.75**
R38SWBL	38 S & W	2,000	25	**16.65**
R38BLNK	38 Special	2,000	28	**16.75**

50 in a box.

RIFLE

17 Remington

No.	Bullet weight	Bullet style	Wt. case, lbs.	Per box
R17REM	25 gr.	Hollow Point "Power-Lokt"	12	**$12.65**

20 in a box, 500 in a case.

22 Hornet

No.	Bullet weight	Bullet style	Wt. case, lbs.	Per box
R22HN1	45 gr.	Pointed Soft Point	9	**$23.35**
R22HN2	45 gr.	Hollow Point	9	**23.35**

50 in a box, 500 in a case.

222 Remington

No.	Bullet weight	Bullet style	Wt. case, lbs.	Per box
R222R1	50 gr.	Pointed Soft Point	27	**$ 9.95**
R222R4	55 gr.	Metal Case	27	**9.95**
R222R3	50 gr.	Hollow Point "Power-Lokt"	27	**10.90**

20 in a box, 1,000 in a case.

222 Remington Magnum

No.	Bullet weight	Bullet style	Wt. case, lbs.	Per box
R222M1	55 gr.	Pointed Soft Point	15	**$11.35**
R222M2	55 gr.	Hollow Point "Power-Lokt"	15	**12.10**

20 in a box, 500 in a case.

22-250 Remington

No.	Bullet weight	Bullet style	Wt. case, lbs.	Per box
R22501	55 gr.	Pointed Soft Point	42	**$10.90**
R22502	55 gr.	Hollow Point "Power-Lokt"	42	**11.75**

20 in a box, 1,000 in a case.

(*) May be used in rifles chambered for .244 Remington.

REMINGTON CENTERFIRE RIFLE CARTRIDGES

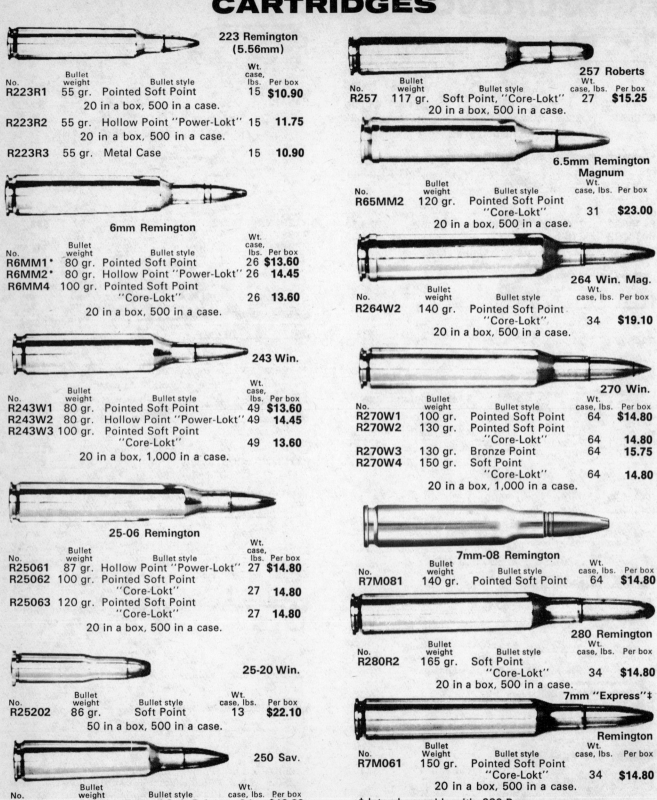

223 Remington (5.56mm)

No.	Bullet weight	Bullet style	Wt. case, lbs.	Per box
R223R1	55 gr.	Pointed Soft Point	15	$10.90

20 in a box, 500 in a case.

No.	Bullet weight	Bullet style	Wt. case, lbs.	Per box
R223R2	55 gr.	Hollow Point "Power-Lokt"	15	11.75

20 in a box, 500 in a case.

No.	Bullet weight	Bullet style	Wt. case, lbs.	Per box
R223R3	55 gr.	Metal Case	15	10.90

6mm Remington

No.	Bullet weight	Bullet style	Wt. case, lbs.	Per box
R6MM1*	80 gr.	Pointed Soft Point	26	$13.60
R6MM2*	80 gr.	Hollow Point "Power-Lokt"	26	14.45
R6MM4	100 gr.	Pointed Soft Point "Core-Lokt"	26	13.60

20 in a box, 500 in a case.

243 Win.

No.	Bullet weight	Bullet style	Wt. case, lbs.	Per box
R243W1	80 gr.	Pointed Soft Point	49	$13.60
R243W2	80 gr.	Hollow Point "Power-Lokt"	49	14.45
R243W3	100 gr.	Pointed Soft Point "Core-Lokt"	49	13.60

20 in a box, 1,000 in a case.

25-06 Remington

No.	Bullet weight	Bullet style	Wt. case, lbs.	Per box
R25061	87 gr.	Hollow Point "Power-Lokt"	27	$14.80
R25062	100 gr.	Pointed Soft Point "Core-Lokt"	27	14.80
R25063	120 gr.	Pointed Soft Point "Core-Lokt"	27	14.80

20 in a box, 500 in a case.

25-20 Win.

No.	Bullet weight	Bullet style	Wt. case, lbs.	Per box
R25202	86 gr.	Soft Point	13	$22.10

50 in a box, 500 in a case.

250 Sav.

No.	Bullet weight	Bullet style	Wt. case, lbs.	Per box
R250SV	100 gr.	Pointed Soft-Point	24	$13.80

20 in a box, 500 in a case.

257 Roberts

No.	Bullet weight	Bullet style	Wt. case, lbs.	Per box
R257	117 gr.	Soft Point, "Core-Lokt"	27	$15.25

20 in a box, 500 in a case.

6.5mm Remington Magnum

No.	Bullet weight	Bullet style	Wt. case, lbs.	Per box
R65MM2	120 gr.	Pointed Soft Point "Core-Lokt"	31	$23.00

20 in a box, 500 in a case.

264 Win. Mag.

No.	Bullet weight	Bullet style	Wt. case, lbs.	Per box
R264W2	140 gr.	Pointed Soft Point "Core-Lokt"	34	$19.10

20 in a box, 500 in a case.

270 Win.

No.	Bullet weight	Bullet style	Wt. case, lbs.	Per box
R270W1	100 gr.	Pointed Soft Point	64	$14.80
R270W2	130 gr.	Pointed Soft Point "Core-Lokt"	64	14.80
R270W3	130 gr.	Bronze Point	64	15.75
R270W4	150 gr.	Soft Point "Core-Lokt"	64	14.80

20 in a box, 1,000 in a case.

7mm-08 Remington

No.	Bullet weight	Bullet style	Wt. case, lbs.	Per box
R7M081	140 gr.	Pointed Soft Point	64	$14.80

280 Remington

No.	Bullet weight	Bullet style	Wt. case, lbs.	Per box
R280R2	165 gr.	Soft Point "Core-Lokt"	34	$14.80

20 in a box, 500 in a case.

7mm "Express"‡ Remington

No.	Bullet Weight	Bullet style	Wt. case, lbs.	Per box
R7M061	150 gr.	Pointed Soft Point "Core-Lokt"	34	$14.80

20 in a box, 500 in a case.

‡ Interchangeable with .280 Rem.

REMINGTON CENTERFIRE RIFLE CARTRIDGES

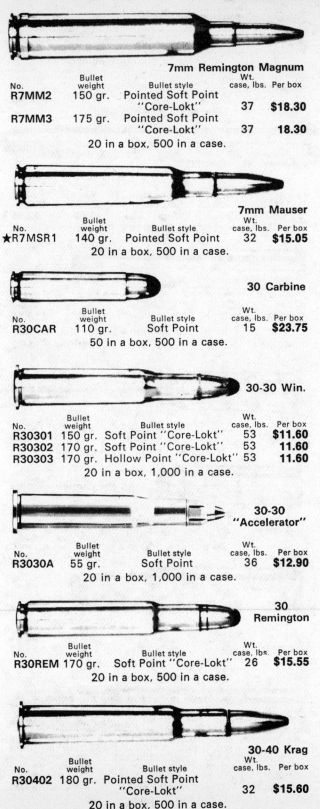

7mm Remington Magnum

No.	Bullet weight	Bullet style	Wt. case, lbs.	Per box
R7MM2	150 gr.	Pointed Soft Point "Core-Lokt"	37	$18.30
R7MM3	175 gr.	Pointed Soft Point "Core-Lokt"	37	18.30

20 in a box, 500 in a case.

7mm Mauser

No.	Bullet weight	Bullet style	Wt. case, lbs.	Per box
★R7MSR1	140 gr.	Pointed Soft Point	32	$15.05

20 in a box, 500 in a case.

30 Carbine

No.	Bullet weight	Bullet style	Wt. case, lbs.	Per box
R30CAR	110 gr.	Soft Point	15	$23.75

50 in a box, 500 in a case.

30-30 Win.

No.	Bullet weight	Bullet style	Wt. case, lbs.	Per box
R30301	150 gr.	Soft Point "Core-Lokt"	53	$11.60
R30302	170 gr.	Soft Point "Core-Lokt"	53	11.60
R30303	170 gr.	Hollow Point "Core-Lokt"	53	11.60

20 in a box, 1,000 in a case.

30-30 "Accelerator"

No.	Bullet weight	Bullet style	Wt. case, lbs.	Per box
R3030A	55 gr.	Soft Point	36	$12.90

20 in a box, 1,000 in a case.

30 Remington

No.	Bullet weight	Bullet style	Wt. case, lbs.	Per box
R30REM	170 gr.	Soft Point "Core-Lokt"	26	$15.55

20 in a box, 500 in a case.

30-40 Krag

No.	Bullet weight	Bullet style	Wt. case, lbs.	Per box
R30402	180 gr.	Pointed Soft Point "Core-Lokt"	32	$15.60

20 in a box, 500 in a case.

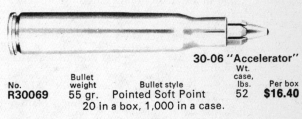

30-06 Spfd.

No.	Bullet weight	Bullet style	Wt. case, lbs.	Per box
R30061	125 gr.	Pointed Soft Point	69	$14.80
R30062	150 gr.	Pointed Soft Point "Core-Lokt"	69	14.80
R30063	150 gr.	Bronze Point	69	15.75
R30068	165 gr.	Pointed Soft Point	62	14.80
R30064	180 gr.	Soft Point "Core-Lokt"	69	14.80
R30065	180 gr.	Pointed Soft Point "Core-Lokt"	69	14.80
R30066	180 gr.	Bronze Point	69	15.75
R30067	220 gr.	Soft Point "Core-Lokt"	69	14.80

20 in a box, 1,000 in a case.

30-06 "Accelerator"

No.	Bullet weight	Bullet style	Wt. case, lbs.	Per box
R30069	55 gr.	Pointed Soft Point	52	$16.40

20 in a box, 1,000 in a case.

300 Sav.

No.	Bullet weight	Bullet style	Wt. case, lbs.	Per box
R30SV3	180 gr.	Soft Point "Core-Lokt"	58	$14.95
R30SV4	180 gr.	Pointed Soft Point "Core-Lokt"	58	14.95

20 in a box, 1,000 in a case.

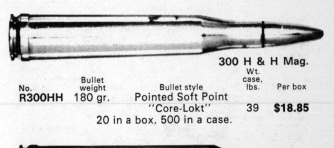

300 H & H Mag.

No.	Bullet weight	Bullet style	Wt. case, lbs.	Per box
R300HH	180 gr.	Pointed Soft Point "Core-Lokt"	39	$18.85

20 in a box, 500 in a case.

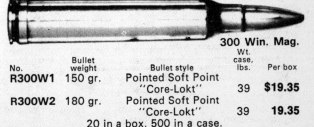

300 Win. Mag.

No.	Bullet weight	Bullet style	Wt. case, lbs.	Per box
R300W1	150 gr.	Pointed Soft Point "Core-Lokt"	39	$19.35
R300W2	180 gr.	Pointed Soft Point "Core-Lokt"	39	19.35

20 in a box, 500 in a case.

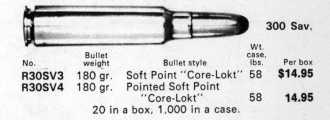

REMINGTON CENTERFIRE RIFLE CARTRIDGES

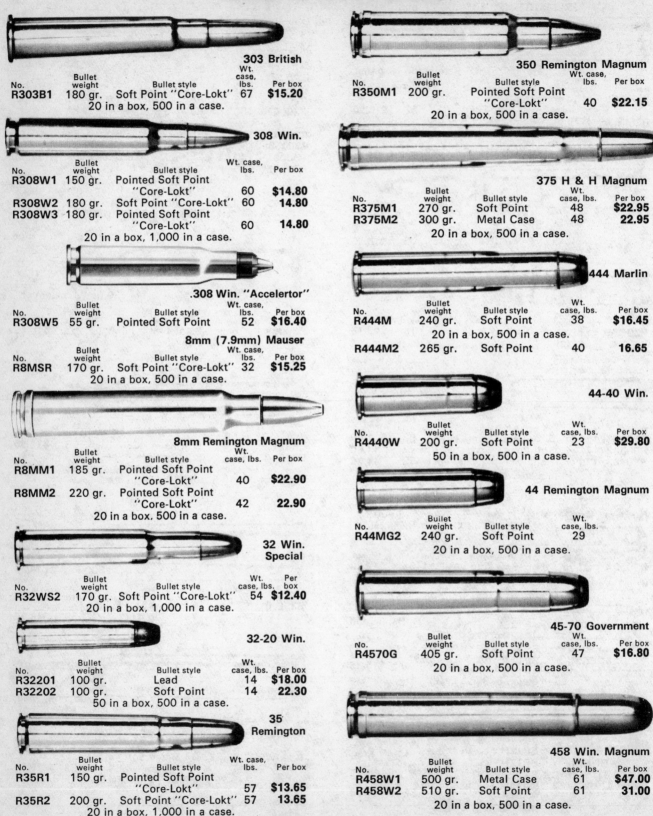

303 British

No.	Bullet weight	Bullet style	Wt. case, lbs.	Per box
R303B1	180 gr.	Soft Point "Core-Lokt"	67	$15.20

20 in a box, 500 in a case.

308 Win.

No.	Bullet weight	Bullet style	Wt. case, lbs.	Per box
R308W1	150 gr.	Pointed Soft Point "Core-Lokt"	60	$14.80
R308W2	180 gr.	Soft Point "Core-Lokt"	60	14.80
R308W3	180 gr.	Pointed Soft Point "Core-Lokt"	60	14.80

20 in a box, 1,000 in a case.

.308 Win. "Accelertor"

No.	Bullet weight	Bullet style	Wt. case, lbs.	Per box
R308W5	55 gr.	Pointed Soft Point	52	$16.40

8mm (7.9mm) Mauser

No.	Bullet weight	Bullet style	Wt. case, lbs.	Per box
R8MSR	170 gr.	Soft Point "Core-Lokt"	32	$15.25

20 in a box, 500 in a case.

8mm Remington Magnum

No.	Bullet weight	Bullet style	Wt. case, lbs.	Per box
R8MM1	185 gr.	Pointed Soft Point "Core-Lokt"	40	$22.90
R8MM2	220 gr.	Pointed Soft Point "Core-Lokt"	42	22.90

20 in a box, 500 in a case.

32 Win. Special

No.	Bullet weight	Bullet style	Wt. case, lbs.	Per box
R32WS2	170 gr.	Soft Point "Core-Lokt"	54	$12.40

20 in a box, 1,000 in a case.

32-20 Win.

No.	Bullet weight	Bullet style	Wt. case, lbs.	Per box
R32201	100 gr.	Lead	14	$18.00
R32202	100 gr.	Soft Point	14	22.30

50 in a box, 500 in a case.

35 Remington

No.	Bullet weight	Bullet style	Wt. case, lbs.	Per box
R35R1	150 gr.	Pointed Soft Point "Core-Lokt"	57	$13.65
R35R2	200 gr.	Soft Point "Core-Lokt"	57	13.65

20 in a box, 1,000 in a case.

350 Remington Magnum

No.	Bullet weight	Bullet style	Wt. case, lbs.	Per box
R350M1	200 gr.	Pointed Soft Point "Core-Lokt"	40	$22.15

20 in a box, 500 in a case.

375 H & H Magnum

No.	Bullet weight	Bullet style	Wt. case, lbs.	Per box
R375M1	270 gr.	Soft Point	48	$22.95
R375M2	300 gr.	Metal Case	48	22.95

20 in a box, 500 in a case.

444 Marlin

No.	Bullet weight	Bullet style	Wt. case, lbs.	Per box
R444M	240 gr.	Soft Point	38	$16.45

20 in a box, 500 in a case.

R444M2	265 gr.	Soft Point	40	16.65

44-40 Win.

No.	Bullet weight	Bullet style	Wt. case, lbs.	Per box
R4440W	200 gr.	Soft Point	23	$29.80

50 in a box, 500 in a case.

44 Remington Magnum

No.	Bullet weight	Bullet style	Wt. case, lbs.	Per box
R44MG2	240 gr.	Soft Point	29	

20 in a box, 500 in a case.

45-70 Government

No.	Bullet weight	Bullet style	Wt. case, lbs.	Per box
R4570G	405 gr.	Soft Point	47	$16.80

20 in a box, 500 in a case.

458 Win. Magnum

No.	Bullet weight	Bullet style	Wt. case, lbs.	Per box
R458W1	500 gr.	Metal Case	61	$47.00
R458W2	510 gr.	Soft Point	61	31.00

20 in a box, 500 in a case.

REMINGTON PLASTIC SHOTSHELLS
SHOTGUN SHELLS
REMINGTON "EXPRESS" and "NITRO MAG" HIGH BASE PLASTIC SHELLS
with "POWER-PISTON" WADS and "KLEANBORE" PRIMING

	No.	Gauge	Length shell, in.	Powder equiv. drams	Shot, oz.	Size shot	Wt. case, lbs.	Per box
"EXPRESS" LONG RANGE LOADS	SP10	10	2⅞	4¾	1⅝	4	74	**$16.35**
	SP12	12	2¾	3¾	1¼	BB 2 4 5 6 7½ 9	58	**11.40**
	SP16	16	2¾	3¼	1⅛	4 5 6 7½ 9	52	**10.90**
	SP20	20	2¾	2¾	1	4 5 6 7½ 9	47	**10.05**
	SP28	28	2¾	2¼	¾	6 7½	36	**10.10**
	SP410	410	2½	Max.	½	4 6 7½	23	**7.95**
	SP4103	410	3	Max.	11⁄16	4 5 6 7½ 9	31	**9.40**

‡ 28 ga. and 2½", 410 bore No. 9 shot marked "Skeet Load."

	No.	Gauge	Length shell, in.	Powder equiv. drams	Shot, oz.	Size shot	Wt. case, lbs.	Per box
"NITRO MAG" HIGH PERFORMANCE MAGNUM LOADS BUFFERED SHOT	SP12SNM	12	2¾	Max.	1½	2 4	68	**$14.80**
	SP12NM	12	3	4	1⅝	2 4	70	**16.35**

	No.	Gauge	Length shell, in.	Powder equiv. drams	Shot, oz.	Size shot	Wt. case, lbs.	Per box
"EXPRESS" MAGNUM LOADS	SP10Mag●	10	3½	Max.	2	BB 2 4 (Mag.)	45	**$25.50**
	SP12Mag●	12	3	4	1⅝	2 4 6 (Mag.)	37	
	SP12SMag●	12	2¾	Max.	1½	2 4 5 6 (Mag.)	34	
	SP12HMag●	12	3	Max.	1⅞	BB 2 4 (Mag.)	41	
	SP16CMag●	16	2¾	Max.	1¼	2 4 6 (Mag.)	29	**14.05**
	SP20SMag●	20	2¾	Max.	1⅛	4 6 7½ (Mag.)	28	
	SP20HMag●	20	3	Max.	1¼	2 4 6 7½ (Mag.)	30	

	No.	Gauge	Length shell, in.	Powder equiv. drams	Shot, oz.	Size shot	Wt. case, lbs.	Per box
STEEL SHOT WATER FOWL LOADS	STL12	12	2¾	Max.	1⅛	1 2 4	55	**$15.60**
	STL12Mag	12	3	Max.	1¼	1 2 4	60	**18.85**

	No.	Gauge	Length shell, in.	Powder equiv. drams	Shot, oz.	Size shot	Wt. case, lbs.	Per box
"SLUGGER" RIFLED SLUG LOADS	SP12RS-5PK●	12	2¾	3¾	1	Rifled Slug H.P.	26	**$3.70**
	SP16RS-5PK●	16	2¾	3	⅘	Rifled Slug H.P.	24	**3.70**
	SP20RS-5PK●	20	2¾	2¾	⅝	Rifled Slug H.P.	19	**3.40**
	SP41RS-5PK●	410	2½	Max.	⅕	Rifled Slug	8	**3.20**

	No.	Gauge	Length shell, in.	Powder equiv. drams	Shot, oz.	Size shot	Wt. case, lbs.	Per box
"Power Pakt" "EXPRESS" BUCKSHOT LOADS	SP12BK-5PK●	12	2¾	3¾	...	000 Buck— 8 Pellets	31	**$3.20**
	SP12BK-5PK●	12	2¾	3¾	...	00 Buck— 9 Pellets	29	**3.20**
	SP12BK-5PK●	12	2¾	3¾	...	0 Buck—12 Pellets	32	**3.20**
	SP12BK-5PK●	12	2¾	3¾	...	1 Buck—16 Pellets	32	**3.20**
	SP12BK-5PK●	12	2¾	3¾	...	4 Buck—27 Pellets	31	**3.20**
	SP16BK-5PK●	16	2¾	3	...	1 Buck—12 Pellets	26	**3.20**
	SP20BK-5PK●	20	2¾	2¾	...	3 Buck—20 Pellets	24	**3.20**

	No.	Gauge	Length shell, in.	Powder equiv. drams	Shot, oz.	Size shot	Wt. case, lbs.	Per box
"Power Pakt" "EXPRESS" MAGNUM BUCKSHOT LOADS	SP12SMagBK-5PK●	12	2¾	4	...	00 Buck—12 Pellets	34	**$3.55**
	SP12SMagBK-5PK●	12	2¾	4	...	1 Buck—20 Pellets	34	**3.55**
	SP12HMagBK-5PK●	12	3	4	...	000 Buck—10 Pellets	40	**4.10**
	SP12HMagBK-5PK●	12	3	4	...	00 Buck—15 Pellets	40	**4.10**
	SP12HMagBK-5PK●	12	3	4	...	1 Buck—24 Pellets	40	**4.10**
	SP12HMagBK-5PK●	12	3	4	...	4 Buck—41 Pellets	42	**4.10**

● Packed 250 per case. 25 in a box, 500 in a case.   H.P. = Hollow Point

REMINGTON PLASTIC SHOTSHELLS
SHOTGUN SHELLS
**REMINGTON "SHURSHOT" LOW BASE PLASTIC SHELLS AND REMINGTON TARGET LOADS
with "POWER-PISTON" WADS and "KLEANBORE" PRIMING**

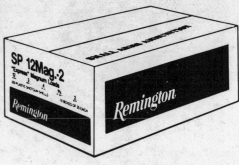

NEW! 250 RD. CASE   NEW! 250 RD. CASE

REMINGTON FIELD LOADS

	No.	Gauge	Length shell, in.	Powder equiv. drams	Payload size, oz.	Size shot	Wt. case, lbs.	Per box
"SHUR SHOT" PLASTIC FIELD LOADS With "Power Piston" Wad	★R12H250SC•	12	2¾	3¼	1⅛	7½ 8	29	$9.80
	R12H	12	2¾	3¼	1⅛	4 5 6 9	51	9.80
	RP12H▲	12	2¾	3¼	1¼	7½ 8	58	9.60
	R16H	16	2¾	2¾	1⅛	4 6 7½ 8 9	51	9.70
	R20M	20	2¾	2½	1	4 5 6 9	45	8.85
	★R20M250CS•	20	2¾	2½	1	7½ 8	23	8.85

▲ Contains Extra Hard Shot
● Packed 250 per case.

Index No.	Gauge	Shell Length (Inches)	Powder Equiv. (Drams)	Ozs. of Shot	SHOT SIZE	Avg. Wgt. Per Case (lbs.)	Per Box
PREMIER® EXTENDED RANGE MAGNUM LOADS Copper-Lokt® Shot, Patented Power Piston Wad, Granulated plastic buffering for extra dense patterns at extended ranges. (25 Rounds per box, 250 Rounds per case).							
PR12SMag.	12	2¾	Max.	1½	BB,2,4, 6	34	16.80
PR12Mag.	12	3	4	1⅝	4, 6	37	17.70
PR12HMag.	12	3	Max.	1⅞	BB,2,4	41	18.95
PR20SMag.	20	2¾	Max.	1⅛	4,6	26	14.30
PR20HMag.	20	3	Max.	1¼	2,4,6	30	15.05
PREMIER® EXTRA LONG RANGE LOADS High base with Copper-Lokt® Shot and Patented Power Piston Wad. (25 Rounds per box, 250 Rounds per case).							
PR12	12	2¾		1¼	2,4,6,7½	29	12.25
PR20	20	2¾		1	4,6	24	10.75
PREMIER® POWER-PATTERN® FIELD LOADS Low Base with Copper-Lokt® Shot and Patented Power Piston Wad. (25 Rounds per box, 250 Rounds per case).							
PR12F	12	2¾	3¼	1	7½,8	29	10.50
PR12HF	12	2¾	3¼	1¼	7½,8	29	10.90
PR20F	20	2¾	2½	1	7½,8	23	9.50

REMINGTON RIMFIRE CARTRIDGES

"HIGH VELOCITY" CARTRIDGES
with "Golden" Bullets

22 Short

No.	Bullet weight and style	Wt. case, lbs.	Per box
1022	29 gr., Lead	29	$2.17
1122	27 gr., Lead, Hollow Point	28	2.30

50 in a box, 5,000 in a case.

22 Long

No.	Bullet weight and style	Wt. case, lbs.	Per box
1322	29 gr., Lead	31	$2.30

50 in a box, 5,000 in a case.

"VIPER" CARTRIDGES
Hyper-Velocity

22 Long Rifle

No.	Bullet weight and style	Wt. case, lbs.	Per box
1922	36 gr. Truncated Cone, Solid Point, Copper Plated	38	$2.67

50 in a box, 5,000 in a case.

"TARGET" STANDARD VELOCITY CARTRIDGES

22 Short

No.	Bullet weight and style	Wt. case, lbs.	Per box
5522	29 gr., Lead	29	$2.17

50 in a box, 5,000 in a case.

22 Long Rifle

No.	Bullet weight and style	Wt. case, lbs.	Per box
6122	40 gr., Lead	40	$2.46

50 in a box, 5,000 in a case.

.22 Long Rifle, Target
100 pack.

No.	Bullet weight and style	Wt. case, lbs.	Per box
6100	40 gr., Lead	40	$4.91

100 in a box, 5,000 in a case.

"YELLOW JACKET" CARTRIDGES
Hyper-Velocity

22 Long Rifle

No.	Bullet weight and style	Wt. case, lbs.	Per box
1722	33 gr. Truncated Cone, Hollow Point	36	$3.08

50 in a box, 5,000 in a case.

"HIGH VELOCITY" CARTRIDGES
with "Golden" Bullets

22 Long Rifle

No.	Bullet weight and style	Wt. case, lbs.	Per box
1522	40 gr., Lead	40	$2.46
1622	36 gr., Lead, Hollow Point	38	2.74

50 in a box, 5,000 in a case.

100 Pack

No.	Bullet weight and style	Wt. case, lbs.	Per box
1500	40 gr., Lead	40	$4.91
1600	36 gr., Lead, Hollow Point	38	5.45

100 in a box, 5,000 in a case.

WEATHERBY CENTERFIRE RIFLE CARTRIDGES

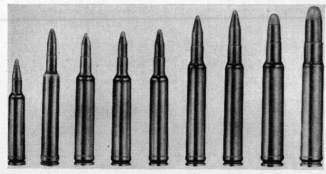

Weatherby Magnum Cartridges: Left to Right—.224 W.M., .240 W.M., .257 W.M., .270 W.M., 7mm W.M., .300 W.M., .340 W.M., .378 W.M., and .460 W.M.

Cartridge	Ammunition 20 per box	Unprimed Cases 20 per box
224—50 or 55 gr.	$22.95	$13.85
240—70, 87 or 100 gr.	22.95	13.85
—100 gr. Nosler	30.95	
257—87, 100 or 117 gr.	23.95	13.85
—100 or 117 gr. Nosler	32.95	
270—100, 130 or 150 gr.	23.95	13.85
—130 or 150 gr. Nosler	32.95	
7mm—139.154 or 175 gr.	23.95	13.85
—140 or 160 gr. Nosler	32.95	
300—110, 150, 180 or 220 gr.	23.95	13.85
—150, 180 or 200 gr. Nosler	32.95	
340—200 or 250 gr.	25.95	14.25
—210 or 250 gr. Nosler	40.65	
378—270, or 300 RN	40.95	23.95
—300 gr. FMJ	46.95	
460—500 RN	44.95	26.95
—500 RMJ	51.95	

WINCHESTER-WESTERN CENTERFIRE RIFLE/ PISTOL/REVOLVER CARTRIDGES

CENTERFIRE RIFLE

Symbol No.	Cartridge	Wt. Grs.	Type of Bullet	Suggested Retail Per Box
•X218B	218 Bee	46	HP	$35.20
•X22H1	22 Hornet	45	SP	23.35
•X22H2	22 Hornet	46	HP	23.35
X222501	22-250 Remington	55	PSP	10.90
X222R	222 Remington	50	PSP	10.00
X222R1	222 Remington	55	FMC	10.00
X223R	223 Remington	55	PSP	10.90
X223R1	223 Remington	55	FMC	10.90
X2251	225 Winchester	55	PSP	12.10
X2431	243 Win. (6mm)	80	PSP	13.60
X2432	243 Win. (6mm)	100	PP (SP)	13.60
X6MMR1	6 mm Remington	80	PSP	13.60
X6MMR2	6 mm Remington	100	PSP	13.60
X25061	25-06 Remington	90	PEP	14.80
X25062	25-06 Remington	120	PEP	14.80
•X25202	25-20 Winchester	86	SP	22.10
X2535	25-35 Winchester	117	SP	15.45
X2501	250 Savage	87	PSP	13.80
X2503	250 Savage	100	ST Exp	13.80
•X2561P	256 Win. Magnum	60	HP	28.45
X2572	257 Roberts	100	ST Exp	15.25
X2573	257 Roberts	117	PP (SP)	15.25
X257P2	257 Roberts + P new	100	ST Exp	15.25
X257P3	257 Roberts + P new	117	PP (SP)	15.25
X2641	264 Win. Magnum	100	PSP	19.10
X2642	264 Win. Magnum	140	PP (SP)	19.10
X2701	270 Winchester	100	PSP	14.80
X2705	270 Winchester	130	PP (SP)	14.80
X2703	270 Winchester	130	ST Exp	14.80
X2704	270 Winchester	150	PP (SP)	14.80
X2842	284 Winchester	150	PP (SP)	17.45
X7MM	7 mm Maus.(7x57)	175	SP	15.05
X7MMR1	7 mm Rem. Mag.	150	PP (SP)	18.35
X7MMR2	7 mm Rem. Mag.	175	PP (SP)	18.35
X7MMR3	7 mm Rem. Mag.	125	PP (SP)	18.35
•X30M1	30 Carbine	110	HSP	23.75
•X30M2	30 Carbine	110	FMC	23.75
X30301	30-30 Winchester	150	HP	11.60
X30306	30-30 Winchester	150	PP (SP)	11.60
X30302	30-30 Winchester	150	ST Exp	11.60
X30303	30-30 Winchester	170	PP (SP)	11.60
X30304	30-30 Winchester	170	ST Exp	11.60
X30060	30-06 Springfield	110	PSP	14.80
X30062	30-06 Springfield	125	PSP	14.80
X30061	30-06 Springfield	150	PP (SP)	14.80
X30063	30-06 Springfield	150	ST Exp	14.80
X30064	30-06 Springfield	180	PP (SP)	14.80
X30066	30-06 Springfield	180	ST Exp	14.80
X30068	30-06 Springfield	220	PP (SP)	14.80
X30069	30-06 Springfield	220	ST Exp	14.80
X30401	30-40 Krag	180	PP (SP)	15.60
X30403	30-40 Krag	180	ST Exp	15.60
X30WM1	300 Win. Magnum	150	PP (SP)	19.35
X30WM2	300 Win. Magnum	180	PP (SP)	19.35
X30WM3	300 Win. Magnum	220	ST Exp	19.35
X300H2	300 H & H Mag.	180	ST Exp	18.85
X3001	300 Savage	150	PP (SP)	14.95
X3003	300 Savage	150	ST Exp	14.95

CENTERFIRE RIFLE [Continued]

Symbol No.	Cartridge	Wt. Grs.	Type of Bullet	Suggested Retail Per Box
X3004	300 Savage	180	PP (SP)	14.95
X3005	300 Savage	180	ST Exp	14.95
X3032	303 Savage	190	ST Exp	17.05
X303B1	303 British	180	PP (SP)	15.20
X3075	307 Win. New	150	PP (SP)	14.80
X3076	307 Win. New	180	PP (SP)	14.80
X3081	308 Winchester	110	PSP	14.80
X3087	308 Winchester	125	PSP	14.80
X3085	308 Winchester	150	PP (SP)	14.80
X3082	308 Winchester	150	ST Exp	14.80
X3086	308 Winchester	180	PP (SP)	14.80
X3083	308 Winchester	180	ST Exp	14.80
X3084	308 Winchester	200	ST Exp	14.80
X32WS2	32 Win. Special	170	PP (SP)	12.40
X32WS3	32 Win. Special	170	ST Exp	12.40
•X32201	32-20 Winchester	100	L	18.00
•X32202	32-20 Winchester	100	SP	22.30
W3240JW	32-40 Winchester	165	SP	15.50
	John Wayne Commemorative			
X8MM	8 mm Mauser (8x57, 7.9)	170	PP (SP)	15.25
X3381	338 Win. Magnum	200	PP (SP)	23.10
X3383	338 Win. Magnum	225	SP	23.10
X3482	348 Winchester	200	ST Exp	27.20
X35R1	35 Remington	200	PP (SP)	13.65
X35R3	35 Remington	200	ST Exp	13.65
•X351SL2	351 Win. S.L.	180	SP	38.60
X3561	356 Win. new	200	PP (SP)	20.90
X3563	356 Win. new	250	PP (SP)	20.90
X3581	358 Win. (8.8mm)	200	ST Exp	20.90
X375W	375 Winchester	200	PP (SP)	18.00
X375W1	375 Winchester	250	PP (SP)	18.00
X375H1	375 H & H Mag.	270	PP (SP)	23.00
X375H2	375 H & H Mag.	300	ST Exp	23.00
X375H3	375 H & H Mag.	300	FMC	23.00
•X3840	38-40 Winchester	180	SP	28.80
X3855	38-55 Winchester	255	SP	16.75
•X44MP	44 Rem. Mag. SX	240	L (GC)	27.70
X44MHSP	44 Rem. Mag. SX	240	HSP	11.35
•X4440	44-40 Winchester	200	SP	29.80
X4570H	45-70 Govt.	300	JHP	16.85
X4580	458 Win. Magnum	500	FMC	47.05
X4581	458 Win. Magnum	510	SP	31.00

CENTERFIRE PISTOL & REVOLVER

Symbol No.	Cartridge	Wt. Grs.	Type of Bullet	Suggested Retail Per Box
•X25AXP	25 Auto (6.35mm)	45	EP	15.45
•X25AP	25 Auto (6.35mm)	50	FMC	14.45
•X2561P	256 Win. Magnum	60	HP	28.45
•X30LP	30 Luger (7.65mm)	93	FMC	23.65
•X32ASHP	32 Automatic	60	STHP	17.85
•X32AP	32 Automatic	71	FMC	16.55
•X32SWP	32 S & W	85	L	13.95
•X32SWLP	32 Smith & Wesson (Colt New Police) Long	98	L	14.70
•X32SCP	32 Short Colt	80	L	13.85
•X32LCP	32 Long Colt	82	L	14.45
	32 Colt New Police - See 32 S & W Long			
•X32201	32-20 Winchester	100	L	18.00
•X32202	32-20 Winchester	100	SP	22.30

CENTERFIRE PISTOL & REVOLVER [Continued]

Symbol No.	Cartridge	Wt. Grs.	Type of Bullet	Suggested Retail Per Box
•X3573P	357 Magnum SX	110	JHP	21.70
•X3576P	357 Magnum SX	125	JHP	21.70
•X357SHP	357 Magnum	145	STHP	22.80
•X3571P	357 Magnum SX	158	L	18.35
•X3574P	357 Magnum SX	158	JHP	21.70
•X3575P	357 Magnum SX	158	JSP	21.70
•X9MMJSP	9mmLuger(Par) + P	95	JSP	20.50
•X9LP	9mm Luger (Par)	115	FMC	20.50
•X9MMSHP	9mm Luger (Par)	115	STHP	21.55
•X38SWP	38 S & W	145	L	15.50
•X38WCPSV	38 Special	158	SWC	16.75
•X38S1P	38 Special	158	L	15.60
•X38S2P	38 Special	158	MP	19.80
•38S3P	38 Special	200	L	16.70
•X38SSHP	38 Spec. SX + P	95	STHP	20.80
•X38S6PH	38 Spec. SX + P	110	JHP	19.80
•X38S7PH	38 Spec. SX + P	125	JHP	19.80
•38SPD	38 Spec. SX + P	158	HP	16.95
•X38WCP	38 Spec. SX + P	158	SWC	15.90
•X38S4P	38 Special	150	L	17.30
•X38SMRP	38 Special Mid-Range	148	(Sharp Corner) Match	16.25
•X38SMP	38 Special SM	158	L	16.25
•X38SCP	38 Short Colt	130	L	15.25
•X38LCP	38 Long Colt	150	L	23.35
•X38ASHP	38 Automatic SX (For use only in 38 Colt Super and Colt Commander Automatic Pistols) + P	125	STHP	20.80
•X38A1P	38 Automatic SX (For use only in 38 Colt Super and Colt Commander Automatic Pistols) + P	130	FMC	17.85
•X38A2P	38 Automatic (For all 38 Colt Automatic Pistols)	130	FMC	'18.45
•X380ASHP	380 Automatic	85	STHP	17.65
•X380AP	380 Automatic	95	FMC	16.90
•X3840	38-40 Winchester	180	SP	28.80
•X41MP	41 Rem. Mag. SX	210	L	24.35
•X41MJSP	41 Rem. Mag. SX	210	JSP	28.55
•X41MHP	41 Rem. Mag. SX	210	JHP	28.55
•X44SP	44 S & W Special	246	L	21.85
•X44STHPS	44 S&W Spec. new	200	STHP	22.95
•X44MP	44 Rem. Mag. SX	240	L (GC)	27.70
X44MHSP	44 Rem. Mag. SX	240	HSP	11.35
•X4440	44-40 Winchester	200	SP	29.80
•X45CSHP	45 Colt	225	STHP	9.30
•X45CP	45 Colt	255	L	22.15
•X45A1P	45 Automatic	230	FMC	22.60
•X45ASHP	45 Automatic	185	STHP	9.50
•X45AWCP	45 Automatic SM Clean Cutting	185	FMC	23.75
•X45WM	45 Win. Mag. SX Not for arms chambered for standard 45 Automatic	230	FMC	24.65

CENTERFIRE BLANK CARTRIDGES

Symbol No.	Cartridge	Wt. Grs.	Type of Bullet	Suggested Retail Per Box
•32BL1P	32 S & W (No Bullet) Smokeless			13.75
•32BL2P	32 S & W (No Bullet) Black Powder			13.75
•38BLP	38 S & W (No Bullet) Smokeless			16.70
•38SBLP	38 Special (No Bullet) Smokeless			16.75

+ P = Ammunition with a (+ P) on the case head stamp is loaded to higher pressure. Use only in firearms designated for this cartridge and so recommended by the gun manufacturer.

•Packed 50 in a box, all others 20 in a box.

EP—Expanded Point
FMC—Full Metal Case
GC—Gas Check
HV—High Velocity
HP—Hollow Point
HSP—Hollow Soft Point
JSP—Jacketed Soft Point

JHP—Jacketed Hollow Point
L—Lead
Mag.—Magnum
Met. Pierc.—Metal Piercing
MP—Metal Point
MR—Mid-Range
OPE—Open Point Expanding

PEP—Positive Expanding Point
PP—Power-Point
Rem.—Remington
SL—Self-Loading
ST Exp—Silvertip Expanding
SP—Soft Point
PSP—Pointed Soft Point

Spgfld.—Springfield
SM—Super-Match
STHP—Silvertip Hollow Point
SWC—Semi-Wad Cutter
SX—Super-X
Win.—Winchester

WINCHESTER-WESTERN RIMFIRE AMMUNITION

WINCHESTER SYMBOL	CARTRIDGE	BULLET OR SHOT WT. GRS.	BULLET TYPE	CAR-TRIDGES PER BOX	CASE WT. LBS.	CASES PER PALLET	PRICE PER BOX
Super-X 22 Rimfire Cartridges—High Velocity							
X22S	22 Short, Super-X	29	L	50	29	120	$ 2.17
X22SH	22 Short, H.P., Super-X .	27	L	50	28	120	2.31
X22L	22 Long, Super-X	29	L	50	32	120	2.31
X22LR	22 L.R., Super-X	40	L	50	40	80	2.47
X22LR1	22 L.R., Super-X	40	L	100	46	65	4.92
X22LRD	22 L.R. DYNAPOINT Super-X (Semi-H.P.) . . .	40	L	50	40	80	2.73
X22LRH	22 L.R., H.P., Super-X . . .	37	L	50	38	100	2.73
X22LRH1	22 L.R., H.P., Super-X . . .	37	L	100	45	65	5.45
X22LRS	22 L.R. Shot, Super-X . .	25	No. 12 Shot	50	32	120	5.04
—New | XS22LR1	22 L.R. Silhouette | 42 | Lead | 5.47			*Packed 100 per Box—all others 50			

L = Lubaloy   H.P. = Hollow Point   L.R. = Long Rifle

WINCHESTER SYMBOL	CARTRIDGE	BULLET OR SHOT WT. GRS.	BULLET TYPE	CAR-TRIDGES PER BOX	CASE WT. LBS.	CASES PER PALLET	PRICE PER BOX
Super-X 22 Winchester Magnum Rimfire Cartridges							
X22WMR	22 Win. Mag., Super-X . .	40	J.H.P.	50	50	64	6.44
X22MR1	22 Win. Mag., Super-X . .	40	F.M.C.	50	50	64	6.44

J.H.P. = Jacketed Hollow Point   F.M.C. = Full Metal Case

WINCHESTER SYMBOL	CARTRIDGE	BULLET OR SHOT WT. GRS.	BULLET TYPE	CAR-TRIDGES PER BOX	CASE WT. LBS.	CASES PER PALLET	PRICE PER BOX
T22 Rimfire Cartridges—Standard Velocity Target and Sporting							
XT22S	22 Short	29	Lead	50	29	120	2.17
XT22LR	22 L.R.	40	Lead	50	39	80	2.47
XT22LR1	22 L.R.—New | 40 | Lead | 4.92						

WINCHESTER SYMBOL	CARTRIDGE	BULLET OR SHOT WT. GRS.	BULLET TYPE	CAR-TRIDGES PER BOX	CASE WT. LBS.	CASES PER PALLET	PRICE PER BOX
Super-Match Rimfire Cartridges							
SM22LR4	22 L.R. SUPER-MATCH MARK IV Pistol	40	Lead	50	39	80	5.40

SUPER-MATCH cartridges are especially recommended for the highest degree of match shooting with pistols.

WINCHESTER SYMBOL	CARTRIDGE	BULLET OR SHOT WT. GRS.	BULLET TYPE	CAR-TRIDGES PER BOX	CASE WT. LBS.	CASES PER PALLET	PRICE PER BOX
Other Winchester Rimfire Cartridges							
22BL	22 Short Blank	—	—	50	10	180	2.87
WW22CBS2	22 Short C.B.	29	Lead	250	29	126	11.01

WINCHESTER-WESTERN SHOTSHELLS

SUPER-X HOLLOW POINT RIFLED SLUG LOADS—5 ROUND PACK

X12RS15	☐12	2¾	Max.	1	Rifled Slug	3.70
X16RS5	☐16	2¾	Max.	4/5	Rifled Slug	3.70
X20RSM5	☐20	2¾	Max.	¾	Rifled Slug	3.40
X41RS5	☐410	2½	Max.	1/5	Rifled Slug	3.20

UPLAND FIELD LOADS

Symbol No.	Gauge	Length of Shell Inches	Powder Dram Equiv.	Oz. Shot	Shot Sizes	Suggested Retail Per Box
UW10BL	10	2-7/8	8	—	‡Blank	$20.85
UW12H	12	2¾	3¼	1-1/8	4,5,6,7½,8,9	9.80
UW12P	12	2¾	3¼	1¼	6,7½,8	10.10
UW12BL	12	2¾	6	—	‡Blank	16.90
UW16H	#△16	2¾	2¾	1-1/8	4,5,6,7½,8,9	9.75
UW20H	△20	2¾	2½	1	4,5,6,7½,8,9	8.85

WINCHESTER FIELD TRIAL POPPER LOAD

XP12FBL	12	2¾	—	—	Blank	7.35

AA PLUS[tm] TRAP LOADS

WW12LAAP	12	2¾	2¾	1	8	7.40
WW12AAP	12	2¾	2¾	1-1/8	7½,8	7.85
WW12MAAP	12	2¾	3	1-1/8	7½,8	7.85

DOUBLE A INTERNATIONAL TRAP LOADS

WWIN12AH	12	2¾	3¼	1-1/8	7½,8 (Nic. Pl. Shot)	10.90
WWIN12A	12	2¾	3¼	1-1/8	7½,8	10.50

DOUBLE A INTERNATIONAL SKEET LOAD [No shot protectors]

WWAA12IS	12	2¾	3½	1-1/8	9	10.50

AA PLUS SKEET LOADS

WW12LAAP	12	2¾	2¾	1	9	7.40
WW12AAP	12	2¾	2¾	1-1/8	9	7.85
WW12MAAP	12	2¾	3	1-1/8	9	7.85
WW20AAP	20	2¾	2½	7/8	9	7.35
WW28AAP	28	2¾	2	¾	9	8.65
WW41AAP	410	2½	Max.	½	9	7.15

SUPER PIGEON TARGET LOADS

WW12SP	12	2¾	3¼	1¼	7½,8	11.70

Staynless Non-Corrosive Priming. Packed 25 per Box, 500 per Case unless otherwise noted.

WINCHESTER SYMBOL	GAUGE	LENGTH OF SHELL INCHES	POWDER DRAM EQUIV.	OZ. SHOT	SHOT SIZES	CASE WT. LBS.	CASES PER PALLET	NET WEIGHT PER PALLET	PRICE PER BOX
Super-X—Long Range									
X10	□10	2⅞	Max.	1⅝	4	36	48	1728	$16.35
X12	12	2¾	3¾	1¼	BB,2,4,5,6,7½,9 . . .	56	60	3360	11.40
X16H	16	2¾	3¼	1⅛	4,5,6,7½,9	49	64	3136	10.95
X20	20	2¾	2¾	1	4,5,6,7½,9	44	80	3520	10.05
X28	28	2¾	2¼	¾	6,7½	35	90	3150	10.10
X41	410	2½	Max.	½	4,6,7½	23	161	3703	8.00
X413	410	3	Max.	¹¹⁄₁₆	4,5,6,7½,9	29	108	3132	9.40
Super-X—Long Range—Magnum Buffered Loads—NEW									
X10MG	□10	3½ Mag.	4¼	2	2	43	40	1720	26.45
X12HG	□12	2¾ Mag.	Max.	1½	2,4,5,6	32	105	3360	14.80
X12MG	□12	3 Mag.	4	1⅝	2,4,6	34	84	2856	16.40
X123G	□12	3 Mag.	4	1⅞	BB,2,4	39	84	3276	17.70
X16MG	□16	2¾ Mag.	3¼	1¼	2,4,6	27	112	3024	14.55
X20HG	□20	2¾ Mag.	2¾	1⅛	4,6,7½	24	112	2688	12.15
X20MG	□20	3 Mag.	3	1¼	4,6,7½	26	84	2184	13.70
Super Double X—NEW with copper-plated buffered shot									
X103XC	□10	3½ Mag.	4½	2¼	BB,2,4	47	40	1880	28.35
X12XC	□12	2¾ Mag.	Max.	1½	BB,2,4,6	32	105	3360	16.85
X12MXC	□12	3 Mag.	4	1⅝	4,6	34	84	2856	17.75
X123XC	□12	3 Mag.	4	1⅞	BB,2,4,6	39	84	3276	18.95
X203XC	□20	3 Mag.	3	1¼	2,4,6	26	84	2184	15.05
Steel Shot—Super-X									
X10SSM	□10	3½ Mag.	Max.	1¾	BB,2	39	40	1560	24.00
X12SSF	12	2¾ Mag.	Max.	1¼	BB,1,2,4	58	60	3480	15.60
X12SSM	□12	3 Mag.	Max.	1½	BB,1,2,4	31	84	2604	18.90
X20SSM new	20	3 Mag.	Max.	1	4			13.70	

BUCKSHOT LOADS

Super-X Super Buckshot Loads—25 Round Box

X12RB	12	2¾			9 Pellets 00 Buck	52	60	3120	16.10
X124B	12	2¾			27 Pellets 4 Buck	56	60	3360	16.10

Super-X Super Buckshot Loads—5 Round Pack—Packed 250 Rounds per Case

X12000B5	12	2¾			8 Pellets 000 Buck	32	54	1728	3.20
X12RB5	12	2¾			9 Pellets 00 Buck	27	63	1701	3.20
X120B5	12	2¾			12 Pellets 0 Buck	32	54	1728	3.20
X121B5	12	2¾			16 Pellets 1 Buck	33	54	1782	3.20
X124B5	12	2¾			27 Pellets 4 Buck	29	54	1566	3.20
X16B5	16	2¾			12 Pellets 1 Buck	26	91	2366	3.20
X20B5	20	2¾			20 Pellets 3 Buck	24	104	2496	3.20

Super-X Magnum Super Buckshot Loads—5 Round Pack—Packed 250 Rounds per Case

X104B5	10	3½ Mag.			54 Pellets 4 Buck	51	40	2040	5.40
X123000B5	12	3 Mag.			10 Pellets 000 Buck	35	45	1575	4.10
X12B5	12	2¾ Mag.			12 Pellets 00 Buck	33	54	1782	3.55
X123B5	12	3 Mag.			15 Pellets 00 Buck	39	45	1755	4.10
X12M1B5	12	2¾ Mag.			20 Pellets 1 Buck	38	45	1710	3.55
X1231B5	12	3 Mag.			24 Pellets 1 Buck	44	45	1980	4.10
X12MB5	12	3 Mag.			41 Pellets 4 Buck	39	45	1755	4.10

□ Packed 25 Rounds per Carton, 250 Rounds per Case

Ballistics

Shooter's Bible
Conversion Factors and Tables

Common inch calibers converted to metric

.25   inch = 6.35mm
.256 inch = 6.5mm
.270 inch = 6.858mm
.280 inch = 7.11mm
.297 inch = 7.54mm
.300 inch = 7.62mm
.301 inch = 7.62mm
.303 inch = 7.696mm
.308 inch = 7.82mm
.311 inch = 7.899mm
.312 inch = 7.925mm
.380 inch = 9.65mm
.400 inch = 10.16mm
.402 inch = 10.21mm
.450 inch = 11.43mm
.455 inch = 11.557mm
.500 inch = 12.7mm
.550 inch = 13.97mm
.577 inch = 14.65mm
.600 inch = 15.24mm
.661 inch = 16.79mm

Pressure

1 kg per sq cm = 14.223 lb per sq inch
1 kg per sq cm =   0.0063493 tons per sq inch
1 kg per sq cm =   0.968 Atmospheres
1 Atmosphere = 14.7 lb. per sq inch
1 Atmosphere =   0.00655 tons per sq inch

1 ton per sq inch = 152.0 Atmospheres
1 lb per sq inch =   0.0680 Atmospheres
1 Atmosphere   =   1.03 kg per sq cm
1 lb per sq inch =   0.070309 kg per sq cm
1 ton per sq inch = 157.49 kg per sq cm

Energy

1 m.kg = 7.2331 foot lb
1 foot lb = 0.13825 m.kg

Velocity

1 metre per second = 3.2809 feet per second
1 foot   per second = 0.30479 meters per second

Weight

1 gram = 15.432 grains
1 grain = 0.648 grams
1 oz   = 28.349 grams

Linear

1 metre = 1.0936 yards
1 metre = 3.2808 feet
1 yard = 0.91438 meters
1 foot = 0.30479 meters
1 inch = 25.4mm
¼ inch =   6.35mm
½ inch = 12.7mm
¾ inch = 19.05mm
⅛ inch =   3.175mm
⅜ inch =   9.525mm
⅝ inch = 15.875mm
⅞ inch = 22.225mm
  1/16 inch =   1.5875mm
  3/16 inch =   4.7625mm
  5/16 inch =   7.9375mm
  7/16 inch = 11.1125mm
  9/16 inch = 14.2875mm
11/16 inch = 17.4625mm
13/16 inch = 20.6375mm
15/16 inch = 23.8125mm

FEDERAL BALLISTICS

25AP	32AP	380AP	9AP	9BP	38B 38D	38C 38G 38H	38E 38F 38J

357A 357B 357D 357E   44SA   45A   45B

Automatic Pistol Ballistics (Approximate)

Federal Load No.	Caliber	Bullet Style	Bullet Weight in Grains	Velocity in Feet Per Second		Energy in Foot/Lbs.		Mid-range Trajectory 50 yds.	Test Barrel Length
				Muzzle	50 yds.	Muzzle	50 yds.		
25AP	25 Auto Pistol (6.35mm)	Metal Case	50	810	775	73	63	1.8″	2″
32AP	32 Auto Pistol (7.65mm)	Metal Case	71	905	855	129	115	1.4″	4″
380AP	380 Auto Pistol	Metal Case	95	955	865	190	160	1.4″	3¾″
380BP	380 Auto Pistol	Jacketed Hollow Point	90	1000	890	200	160	1.4″	3¾″
9AP	9mm Luger Auto Pistol	Metal Case	123	1120	1030	345	290	1.0″	4″
9BP	9mm Luger Auto Pistol	Jacketed Hollow Point	115	1160	1060	345	285	0.9″	4″
45A	45 Automatic (Match)	Metal Case	230	850	810	370	335	1.6″	5″
45B	45 Automatic (Match)	Metal Case, S.W.C.	185	775	695	247	200	2.0″	5″
45C	45 Automatic	Jacketed Hollow Point	185	950	900	370	335	1.3″	5″

Revolver Ballistics—Vented Barrel* (Approximate)

Federal Load No.	Caliber	Bullet Style	Bullet Weight in Grains	Velocity in Feet Per Second		Energy in ft./Lbs.		Mid-range Trajectory 50 yds.	Test Barrel Length
				Muzzle	50 yds.	Muzzle	50 yds.		
38A	38 Special (Match)	Lead Wadcutter	148	710	634	166	132	2.4″	4″
38B	38 Special	Lead Round Nose	158	755	723	200	183	2.0″	4″
38C	38 Special	Lead Semi-Wadcutter	158	755	723	200	183	2.0″	4″
▲ 38D	38 Special (High Velocity + P)	Lead Round Nose	158	915	878	294	270	1.4″	4″
▲ 38E	38 Special (High Velocity + P)	Jacketed Hollow Point	125	945	898	248	224	1.3″	4″
▲ 38F	38 Special (High Velocity + P)	Jacketed Hollow Point	110	1020	945	254	218	1.1″	4″
▲ 38G	38 Special (High Velocity + P)	Lead, Semi-Wadcutter Hollow Point	158	915	878	294	270	1.4″	4″
▲ 38H	38 Special (High Velocity + P)	Lead Semi-Wadcutter	158	915	878	294	270	1.4″	4″
▲ 38J	38 Special (High Velocity + P)	Jacketed Soft Point	125	945	898	248	224	1.3″	4″
357A	357 Magnum	Jacketed Soft Point	158	1235	1104	535	428	0.8″	4″
357B	357 Magnum	Jacketed Hollow Point	125	1450	1240	583	427	0.6″	4″
357C	357 Magnum	Lead Semi-Wadcutter	158	1235	1104	535	428	0.8″	4″
357D	357 Magnum	Jacketed Hollow Point	110	1295	1094	410	292	0.8″	4″
357E	357 Magnum	Jacketed Hollow Point	158	1235	1104	535	428	0.8″	4″
NEW 44SA	44 S&W Special	Semi-Wadcutter Hollow Point	200	900	830	360	305	1.4″	6½″
** 44A	44 Rem. Magnum	Jacketed Hollow Point	240	1180	1081	741	623	0.9″	4″
** 44B	44 Rem. Magnum	Jacketed Hollow Point	180	1610	1365	1045	750	0.5″	4″
.45LCA	45 Colt	Semi-Wadcutter Hollow Point	225	900	860	405	369	1.6″	5½″

*To simulate service conditions, these figures were obtained from a 4″ length vented test barrel with a .008″ cylinder gap and with the powder positioned horizontally inside the cartridge case. 44SA and 45LCA data from revolvers of indicated barrel length.
**Both 44A and 44B can be used in either pistols or rifles of this caliber. However, the 44B is accurate only in pistols.

▲This ammunition is loaded to a higher pressure, as indicated by the "+P" marking on the case headstamp, to achieve higher velocity. Use only in firearms especially designed for this cartridge and so recommended by the manufacturer.

22 Caliber Rimfire Cartridges

	Federal Load Number	Cartridges Per Box	Cartridge	Bullet Type	Bullet Wt. in Grains	Velocity in Ft. Per Sec.		Energy in Foot/lbs.		Bullet Drop In Inches at 100 yds	Drift In 10 mph Cross-wind 100 yds	Height of Trajectory					
						Muzzle	100 yds	Muzzle	100 yds			Inches above line of sight if sighted in at ⊕ yardage. Sight .9″ above bore.					
												50 yds	100 yds	150 yds	50 yds	100 yds	150 yds
HI Power	701	50	22 Short	Solid	29	1095	905	77	53	16.8	5.3″	⊕	−8.0	−26.8	+4.0	⊕	−14.7
	703	50	22 Short	Hollow Point	29	1120	905	81	53	16.4	5.9″	⊕	−7.9	−26.4	+3.9	⊕	−14.6
	706	50	22 Long	Solid	29	1240	960	99	60	14.1	6.9″	⊕	−6.8	−23.0	+3.4	⊕	−12.8
	710	50	22 Long Rifle	Solid	40	1255	1015	140	92	13.2	5.5″	⊕	−6.2	−20.8	+3.1	⊕	−11.5
	712	50	22 Long Rifle	Hollow Point	38	1280	1020	138	88	12.9	5.9″	⊕	−6.1	−20.6	+3.1	⊕	−11.4
	716	50	22 Long Rifle	No. 12 Shot	25	—	—	—	—	—	—	—	—	—	—	—	—
100 Pack	810	100	22 Long Rifle	Solid	40	1255	1015	140	92	13.2	5.5″	⊕	−6.2	−20.8	+3.1	⊕	−11.5
	812	100	22 Long Rifle	Hollow Point	38	1280	1020	138	88	12.9	5.9″	⊕	−6.1	−20.6	+3.1	⊕	−11.4
Champion Standard Velocity	711	50	22 Long Rifle	Solid	40	1150	975	117	85	15.0	4.4″	⊕	−7.0	−23.2	+3.5	⊕	−12.6
	811	100	22 Long Rifle	Solid	40	1150	975	117	85	15.0	4.4″	⊕	−7.0	−23.2	+3.5	⊕	−12.6

Unless otherwise noted, these ballistic specifications were derived from test barrels 24 inches in length.
All specifications are nominal; individual guns may vary from test barrel figures.

FEDERAL BALLISTICS

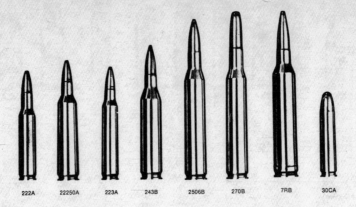

222A   22250A   223A   243B   2506B   270B   7RB   30CA

Centerfire Rifle Cartridge Ballistics

Federal Load No.	Caliber	Bullet Weight in Grains	Bullet Style	Factory Primer	Velocity In Feet Per Second						Energy In Foot Pounds					
					Muzzle	100 yds	200 yds	300 yds	400 yds	500 yds	Muzzle	100 yds	200 yds	300 yds	400 yds	500 yds
222A	222 Remington	50	Soft Point	205	3140	2600	2120	1700	1350	1110	1090	750	500	320	200	135
222B	222 Remington	55	Metal Cs. Boat-T.	205	3020	2740	2480	2230	1990	1780	1115	915	750	610	485	385
22250A	22-250 Remington	55	Soft Point	210	3730	3180	2700	2260	1860	1520	1700	1240	885	620	425	280
223A	223 Remington	55	Soft Point	205	3240	2750	2300	1910	1550	1270	1280	920	650	445	295	195
223B	223 Remington	55	Metal Cs. Boat-T.	205	3240	2880	2540	2230	1940	1680	1280	1010	790	610	460	340
6A	6mm Remington	80	Soft Point	210	3470	3060	2690	2350	2040	1750	2140	1670	1290	980	740	540
6B		100	Hi-Shok S.P.	210	3130	2860	2600	2360	2130	1910	2180	1810	1500	1230	1000	810
243A	243 Winchester	80	Soft Point	210	3350	2955	2595	2260	1950	1670	1995	1550	1195	905	675	495
243B		100	Hi-Shok S.P.	210	2960	2700	2450	2220	1990	1790	1950	1620	1330	1090	880	710
2506A	25-'06 Remington	90	Hollow Point	210	3440	3040	2680	2340	2030	1750	2360	1850	1440	1100	825	610
2506B		117	Hi-Shok S.P.	210	3060	2790	2530	2280	2050	1840	2430	2020	1660	1360	1100	875
270A	270 Winchester	130	Hi-Shok S.P.	210	3110	2850	2600	2370	2150	1940	2790	2340	1960	1620	1330	1090
270B		150	Hi-Shok S.P.	210	2900	2550	2230	1930	1650	1420	2800	2170	1650	1240	910	665
7A	7mm Mauser	175	Hi-Shok S.P.	210	2470	2170	1880	1630	1400	1220	2370	1820	1380	1030	765	575
7RA	7mm Remington Magnum	150	Hi-Shok S.P.	215	3110	2830	2570	2320	2090	1870	3220	2670	2200	1790	1450	1160
7RB		175	Hi-Shok S.P.	215	2860	2650	2440	2240	2060	1880	3180	2720	2310	1960	1640	1370
*†30CA	30 Carbine	110	Soft Point	205	1990	1570	1240	1040	920	840	965	600	375	260	210	175
*†30CB	30 Carbine	110	Metal Case	205	1990	1600	1280	1070	950	870	970	620	400	280	220	190
3030A	30-30 Winchester	150	Hi-Shok S.P.	210	2390	2020	1680	1400	1180	1040	1900	1360	945	650	460	355
3030B		170	Hi-Shok S.P.	210	2200	1900	1620	1380	1190	1060	1830	1360	990	720	535	425
3030C		125	Hollow Point	210	2570	2090	1660	1320	1080	960	1830	1210	770	480	320	260
3006A	30-'06 Springfield	150	Hi-Shok S.P.	210	2910	2620	2340	2080	1840	1620	2820	2280	1830	1450	1130	875
3006B		180	Hi-Shok S.P.	210	2700	2470	2250	2040	1850	1660	2910	2440	2020	1670	1360	1110
3006C		125	Soft Point	210	3140	2780	2450	2140	1850	1600	2740	2150	1660	1270	955	705
3006D		165	Boat Tail S.P.	210	2800	2610	2420	2240	2070	1910	2870	2490	2150	1840	1580	1340
3006E		200	Boat Tail S.P.	210	2550	2400	2260	2120	1990	1860	2890	2560	2270	2000	1760	1540
300WB	300 Winchester Magnum	180	Hi-Shok S.P.	215	2960	2745	2540	2345	2155	1980	3500		2580	2195	1860	1565
300A	300 Savage	150	Hi-Shok S.P.	210	2630	2350	2100	1850	1630	1430	2300	1850	1460	1140	885	685
300B		180	Hi-Shok S.P.	210	2350	2140	1940	1750	1570	1410	2210	1830	1500	1220	985	800
308A	308 Winchester	150	Hi-Shok S.P.	210	2820	2530	2260	2010	1770	1560	2650	2140	1710	1340	1050	810
308B		180	Hi-Shok S.P.	210	2620	2390	2180	1970	1780	1600	2740	2290	1900	1560	1270	1030
**8A	8mm Mauser	170	Hi-Shok S.P.	210	2510	2110	1740	1430	1190	1040	2380	1670	1140	770	530	400
32A	32 Winchester Special	170	Hi-Shok S.P.	210	2250	1920	1630	1370	1170	1040	1910	1390	1000	710	520	410
35A	35 Remington	200	Hi-Shok S.P.	210	2080	1700	1380	1140	1000	910	1920	1280	840	575	445	370
*†44A	44 Remington Magnum	240	Hollow S.P.	150	1760	1380	1090	950	860	790	1650	1015	640	485	395	330
*4570A	45-'70 Government	300	Hollow S.P.	210	1880	1650	1425	1235	1105	1010	2355	1815	1355	1015	810	680

Unless otherwise noted, ballistic specifications were derived from test barrels 24 inches in length.
†Test Barrel Length 20 Inches.   *Without Cartridge Carrier.
**Only for use in barrels intended for .323 inch diameter bullets. Do not use in 8mm Commission Rifles (M1888) or sporting arms of similar bore diameter.

FEDERAL BALLISTICS

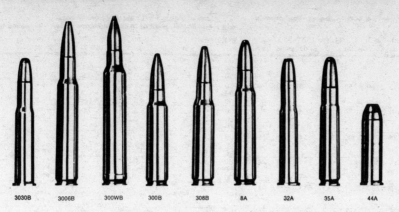

3030B 3006B 300WB 300B 308B 8A 32A 35A 44A

Centerfire Rifle Cartridge Ballistics

Bullet Drop — In Inches From Bore Line
Drift — In Inches In 10 mph Crosswind
Height of Trajectory — Inches above line of sight if sighted in at ⊕ yards. For sights .9″ above bore.
Trajectory figures show the height of bullet impact above or below the line of sight at the indicated yardages. Aim low indicated amount for + figures and high for − figures. Zero ranges indicated by circled crosses.

BD 100	BD 200	BD 300	BD 400	BD 500	Dr 100	Dr 200	Dr 300	Dr 400	Dr 500	HT 50	HT 100	HT 150	HT 200	HT 250	HT 300	HT 100	HT 150	HT 200	HT 250	HT 300	HT 400	HT 500
2.0	9.2	24.3	51.6	98.2	1.7	7.3	18.3	36.4	63.1	+0.5	+0.9	⊕	−2.5	−6.9	−13.7	+2.2	+1.9	⊕	−3.8	−10.0	−32.3	−73.8
2.0	8.6	21.0	40.8	68.2	0.9	3.4	8.5	16.8	26.3	+0.5	+0.8	⊕	−2.1	−5.4	−10.8	+1.9	+1.6	⊕	−2.8	−7.7	−22.7	−45.3
1.4	6.2	16.0	32.6	59.4	1.2	5.1	12.3	23.9	41.2	+0.2	+0.5	⊕	−1.5	−4.3	−8.4	+2.2	+2.6	+1.9	⊕	−3.3	−15.4	−37.7
1.8	8.4	21.5	44.4	81.8	1.4	6.1	15.0	29.4	50.8	+0.4	+0.8	⊕	−2.2	−6.0	−11.8	+1.9	+1.6	⊕	−3.3	−8.5	−26.7	−59.6
1.8	7.8	19.2	37.7	65.4	1.0	4.2	10.1	19.2	32.1	+0.4	+0.7	⊕	−1.9	−5.1	−9.9	+1.7	+1.4	⊕	−2.8	−7.1	−21.2	−44.6
1.6	6.9	17.0	33.4	58.3	1.0	4.1	9.9	18.8	31.6	+0.3	+0.6	⊕	−1.6	−4.5	−8.7	+2.4	+2.7	+1.9	⊕	−3.3	−14.9	−35.0
1.9	8.0	19.4	37.0	62.3	0.8	3.3	7.8	14.5	23.8	+0.4	+0.7	⊕	−1.9	−5.1	−9.7	+1.7	+1.4	⊕	−2.7	−6.8	−20.0	−40.8
1.7	7.4	18.3	36.0	63.0	1.0	4.3	10.4	19.8	33.3	+0.3	+0.7	⊕	−1.8	−4.9	−9.4	+2.6	+2.9	+2.1	⊕	−3.6	−16.2	−37.9
2.1	9.0	21.7	41.6	70.2	0.9	3.6	8.4	15.7	25.8	+0.5	+0.9	⊕	−2.2	−5.8	−11.0	+1.9	+1.6	⊕	−3.1	−7.8	−22.6	−46.3
1.6	7.0	17.2	33.8	58.9	1.0	4.1	9.8	18.7	31.3	+0.3	+0.6	⊕	−1.7	−4.5	−8.8	+2.4	+2.7	+2.0	⊕	−3.4	−15.0	−35.2
2.0	8.4	20.4	39.0	65.9	0.8	3.5	8.2	15.3	25.2	+0.5	+0.8	⊕	−2.0	−5.4	−10.3	+1.8	+1.5	⊕	−2.9	−7.3	−21.2	−43.4
1.9	8.1	19.4	37.0	62.1	0.8	3.2	7.4	13.9	22.7	+0.4	+0.7	⊕	−1.9	−5.1	−9.7	+1.7	+1.4	⊕	−2.7	−6.8	−19.9	−40.5
2.2	9.9	24.6	48.8	85.4	1.2	5.2	12.5	23.9	40.2	+0.6	+1.0	⊕	−2.5	−6.8	−13.1	+2.2	+1.9	⊕	−3.6	−9.3	−28.1	−59.7
3.1	13.7	34.1	67.8	119.3	1.5	6.2	15.0	28.7	47.8	+0.4	⊕	−2.2	−6.6	−13.4	−23.0	+1.5	⊕	−3.6	−9.7	−18.6	−46.8	−92.8
1.9	8.2	19.7	37.8	63.9	0.8	3.4	8.1	15.1	24.9	+0.4	+0.8	⊕	−1.9	−5.2	−9.9	+1.7	+1.5	⊕	−2.8	−7.0	−20.5	−42.1
2.2	9.5	22.5	42.5	70.8	0.7	3.1	7.2	13.3	21.7	+0.6	+0.9	⊕	−2.3	−6.0	−11.3	+2.0	+1.7	⊕	−3.2	−7.9	−22.7	−45.8
5.2	24.8	67.2	142.0	257.6	3.4	15.0	35.5	63.2	96.7	+0.9	⊕	−4.5	−13.5	−28.3	−49.9	⊕	−4.5	−13.5	−28.3	−49.9	−118.6	−228.1
5.1	24.1	64.5	135.1	244.1	3.1	13.7	32.6	58.7	90.3	+0.9	⊕	−4.3	−13.0	−26.9	−47.4	+2.9	⊕	−7.2	−19.7	−38.7	−100.4	−200.5
3.4	15.4	39.9	82.3	149.8	2.0	8.5	20.9	40.1	66.1	+0.5	⊕	−2.6	−7.7	−16.0	−27.9	+1.7	⊕	−4.3	−11.6	−22.7	−59.1	−120.5
4.0	17.7	44.8	90.3	160.2	1.9	8.0	19.4	36.7	59.8	+0.6	⊕	−3.0	−8.9	−18.0	−31.1	+2.0	⊕	−4.8	−13.0	−25.1	−63.6	−126.7
3.0	14.2	38.0	81.0	148.7	2.2	10.1	25.4	49.4	81.6	+0.1	⊕	−2.0	−7.3	−15.8	−28.1	+3.2	+2.4	⊕	−5.5	−15.8	−51.7	−112.3
2.2	9.5	23.2	44.9	76.9	1.0	4.2	9.9	18.7	31.2	+0.6	+0.9	⊕	−2.3	−6.3	−12.0	+2.1	+1.8	⊕	−3.3	−8.5	−25.0	−51.8
2.5	10.8	25.9	49.4	83.2	0.9	3.7	8.8	16.5	27.1	+0.2	⊕	−1.6	−4.8	−9.7	−16.5	+2.4	+2.0	⊕	−3.7	−9.3	−27.0	−54.9
1.9	8.3	20.6	40.6	70.7	1.1	4.5	10.8	20.5	34.4	+0.4	+0.8	⊕	−2.1	−5.6	−10.7	+1.8	+1.5	⊕	−3.0	−7.7	−23.0	−48.5
2.2	9.5	22.7	42.8	71.0	0.7	2.8	6.6	12.3	19.9	+0.5	⊕	−1.1	−4.2	−8.8	−14.3	+2.1	+1.8	⊕	−3.0	−8.0	−22.9	−45.9
2.6	11.2	26.6	59.7	81.6	0.6	2.6	6.0	11.0	17.7	+0.6	⊕	−2.7	−6.0	−12.4	−18.8	+2.3	+1.8	⊕	−4.1	−9.0	−25.8	−51.3
2.1	8.8	20.9	39.4	65.3	0.7	2.8	6.6	12.3	20.0	+0.5	+0.8	⊕	−2.1	−5.5	−10.4	+1.9	+1.6	⊕	−2.9	−7.3	−20.9	−41.9
2.7	11.7	28.7	55.8	96.1	1.1	4.8	11.6	21.9	36.3	+0.3	⊕	−1.8	−5.4	−11.0	−18.8	+2.7	+2.2	⊕	−4.2	−10.7	−31.5	−65.5
3.4	14.3	34.7	66.4	112.3	1.1	4.6	10.9	20.3	33.3	+0.4	⊕	−2.3	−6.7	−13.5	−22.8	+1.5	⊕	−3.6	−9.6	−18.2	−44.1	−84.2
2.3	10.1	24.8	48.0	82.4	1.0	4.4	10.4	19.7	32.7	+0.2	⊕	−1.5	−4.5	−9.3	−15.9	+2.3	+1.9	⊕	−3.6	−9.1	−26.9	−55.7
2.7	11.5	27.6	52.7	88.8	0.9	3.9	9.2	17.2	28.3	+0.2	⊕	−1.8	−5.2	−10.4	−17.7	+2.6	+2.1	⊕	−4.0	−9.9	−28.9	−58.8
3.1	14.2	36.8	76.7	141.2	1.9	8.5	21.0	40.6	67.5	+0.4	⊕	−2.3	−7.0	−14.6	−25.7	+1.6	⊕	−3.9	−10.7	−21.0	−55.4	−114.3
3.8	17.1	43.7	88.9	159.3	1.9	8.4	20.3	38.6	63.0	+0.6	⊕	−2.9	−8.6	−17.6	−30.5	+1.9	⊕	−4.7	−12.7	−24.7	−63.2	−126.9
4.6	21.5	56.9	118.9	215.6	2.7	12.0	29.0	53.3	83.3	+0.8	⊕	−3.8	−11.3	−23.5	−41.2	+2.5	⊕	−6.3	−17.1	−33.6	−87.7	−176.3
6.7	32.4	87.0	179.8	319.6	4.2	17.8	39.8	68.3	102.5	⊕	−2.7	−10.2	−23.6	−44.2	−73.3	⊕	−6.1	−18.1	−37.4	−65.1	−150.3	−282.5
4.3	21.5	57.2	112.8	NA	1.7	7.6	18.6	35.7	NA	⊕	−2.4	−8.2	−17.6	−31.4	−51.5	⊕	−4.6	−12.8	−25.4	−44.3	−95.5	NA

NOTE: These trajectory tables were calculated by computer and are given here unaltered. The computer used a standard modern scientific technique to predict trajectories from the best available data for each round. Each trajectory is expected to be reasonably representative of the behavior of the ammunition at sea level conditions, but the shooter is cautioned that trajectories differ because of variations in ammunition, rifles, and atmospheric conditions.

NORMA BALLISTICS

Caliber / Bullet weight / Prod.no	Velocity – Feet per sec. Muzzle	100 yards	200 yards	300 yards	Energy–Foot pounds Muzzle	100 yards	200 yards	300 yards	Sight at yards	25 yards	50 yards	100 yards	150 yards	200 yards	300 yards
220 Swift 50 gr/3.2 g 15701	4110	3611	3133	2681	1877	1448	1090	799	100	−0.9	−0.5	0	−0.2	−1.2	−5.9
									180	−0.8	−0.3	+0.4	+0.4	−0.4	−4.7
									200	−0.8	−0.2	+0.6	+0.7	0	−4.1
222 Rem. 50 gr/3.2 g 15711	3200	2650	2170	1750	1137	780	520	340	100	−0.8	−0.3	0	−0.9	−3.2	−12.9
									180	−0.5	+0.3	+1.2	+0.8	−0.9	−9.4
									200	−0.4	+0.5	+1.6	+1.5	0	−8.2
222 Rem. 50 gr/3.2 g 157:2	3200	2610	2080	1630	1137	756	480	295	100	−0.7	−0.2	0	−1.1	−3.7	−15.7
									180	−0.4	+0.5	+1.4	+1.0	−1.0	−11.6
									200	−0.3	+0.7	+1.9	+1.7	0	−10.1
222 Rem. 50 gr/3.2 g 15713	2790	2235	1755	1390	863	554	341	214	100	−0.6	±0.0	0	−1.7	−5.8	−23.4
									180	−0.1	+1.0	+2.1	+1.5	−1.5	−17.1
									200	+0.1	+1.4	+2.9	+2.6	0	−14.8
222 Rem. 50 gr/3.2 g 15715	3200	2610	2080	1630	1137	756	480	295	100	−0.7	−0.2	0	−1.1	−3.7	−15.7
									180	−0.4	+0.5	+1.4	+1.0	−1.0	−11.6
									200	−0.3	+.07	+1.9	+1.7	0	−10.1
222 Rem. 53 gr/3.4 g 15714	3117	2670	2267	1901	1142	838	604	425	100	−0.7	−0.2	0	−1.0	−3.5	−14.0
									180	−0.4	+0.4	+1.3	+0.9	−0.9	−10.1
									200	−0.3	+0.6	+1.7	+1.6	0	−8.7
22–250 53 gr/3.4 g 15733	3707	3192	2741	2332	1616	1198	883	639	100	−0.9	−0.4	0	−0.5	−1.9	−8.6
									180	−0.7	−0.1	+0.7	+0.5	−0.6	−6.6
									200	−0.6	+0.1	+1.0	+1.0	0	−5.7
5.6x52 R 71 gr/4.6 g 15604	2790	2296	1886	1558	1226	831	561	383	100	−0.6	−0.1	0	−1.5	−4.8	−18.6
									180	−0.2	+0.8	+1.8	+1.2	−1.2	−13.2
									200	0	+1.1	+2.4	+2.1	0	−11.4
5.6x52 R 71 gr/4.6 g 15605	2790	2296	1886	1558	1226	831	561	383	100	−0.6	−0.1	0	−1.5	−4.8	−18.6
									180	−0.2	+0.8	+1.8	+1.2	−1.2	−13.2
									200	0	+1.1	+2.4	+2.1	0	−11.4
243 Win. 100 gr/6.5 g 16002	3070	2790	2540	2320	2090	1730	1430	1190	100	−0.7	−0.2	0	−0.9	−2.9	−10.6
									180	−0.5	+0.3	+1.1	+0.7	−0.7	−7.4
									200	−0.4	+0.5	+1.4	+1.3	0	−6.3
243 Win. 100 gr/6.5 g 16003	3070	2790	2540	2320	2090	1730	1430	1190	100	−0.7	−0.2	0	−0.9	−2.9	−10.6
									180	−0.5	+0.3	+1.1	+0.7	−0.7	−7.4
									200	−0.4	+0.5	+1.4	+1.3	0	−6.3
6.5 Jap. 139 gr/9.0 g 16531	2430	2280	2130	1990	1820	1605	1401	1223	100	−0.5	±0.0	0	−1.8	−5.4	−18.8
									130	−0.4	+0.4	+0.6	−0.8	−4.1	−16.9
									200	+0.1	+1.4	+2.7	+2.3	0	−10.8
6.5 Jap. 156 gr/10.1 g 16532	2065	1871	1692	1529	1481	1213	992	810	100	−0.3	+0.4	0	−2.9	−8.5	−29.2
									130	±0.0	+0.9	+1.1	−1.2	−6.3	−26.0
									200	+0.8	+2.5	+4.3	+3.5	0	−16.4
6.5 Carcano 139 gr/9 g 16536	2576	2379	2192	2012	2046	1745	1481	1249	100	−0.6	±0.0	0	−1.5	−4.7	−16.6
									180	−0.1	+0.9	+1.8	+1.1	−1.1	−11.3
									200	±0.0	+1.2	+2.3	+2.0	0	−9.6
6.5 Carcano 156 gr/10.1 g 16535	2430	2208	2000	1800	2046	1689	1386	1123	100	−0.5	+0.1	0	−1.9	−5.7	−20.2
									180	±0.0	+1.2	+2.2	+1.4	−1.3	−13.7
									200	+0.2	+1.5	+2.9	+2.4	0	−11.7
6.5x55 77 gr/5.0 g 16550	2725	2362	2030	1811	1271	956	706	562	100	−0.6	−0.1	0	−1.5	−4.8	−18.1
									180	−0.2	+0.8	+1.8	+1.2	−1.2	−12.7
									200	±0.0	+1.1	+2.4	+2.1	0	−10.9
6.5x55 80 gr/5.2 g 16528	3002	2398	1886	1499	1604	1023	633	400	100	−0.7	−0.2	0	−1.4	−4.7	−19.3
									180	−0.3	+0.7	+1.7	+1.2	−1.2	−14.2
									200	±0.0	+1.0	+2.3	+2.1	0	−12.3
6.5x55 139 gr/9.0 g 16551	2854	2691	2533	2370	2512	2233	1978	1732	100	−0.7	−0.2	0	−1.0	−2.3	−12.3
									180	−0.6	+0.4	+1.3	+0.8	−0.8	−8.6
									200	−0.2	+0.5	+1.7	+1.5	0	−7.4
6.5x55 139 gr/9.0 g 16557	2790	2630	2470	2320	2402	2136	1883	1662	100	−0.7	−0.2	0	−1.1	−3.7	−13.3
									180	−0.3	+0.5	+1.4	+0.9	−0.9	−9.2
									200	−0.2	+0.8	+1.8	+1.6	0	−7.8
6.5x55 156 gr/10.1 g 16552	2495	2271	2062	1867	2153	1787	1473	1208	100	−0.6	+0.2	0	−1.7	−5.3	−18.8
									180	±0.0	+1.0	+2.0	+1.3	−1.3	−12.7
									200	+0.1	+1.3	+2.6	+2.2	0	−10.9
270 Win. 130 gr/8.4 g 16902	3140	2884	2639	2404	2847	2401	2011	1669	100	−0.8	−0.3	0	−0.8	−4.1	−10.7
									180	−0.5	+0.2	+1.0	+0.7	−0.7	−7.7
									200	−0.4	+0.4	+1.4	+1.3	0	−6.6
270 Win. 150 gr/9.7 g 16903	2800	2616	2436	2262	2616	2280	1977	1705	100	−0.7	−0.2	0	−1.1	−3.6	−13.1
									180	−0.3	+0.5	+1.4	+0.9	−0.9	−9.0
									200	−0.2	+0.7	+1.8	+1.6	0	−7.7
7x57 150 gr/9.7 g 17002	2755	2539	2331	2133	2530	2148	1810	1516	100	−0.7	−0.1	0	−1.2	−3.9	−14.3
									180	−0.3	+0.6	+1.5	+1.0	−1.0	−9.8
									200	−0.2	+0.9	+2.0	+1.7	0	−8.4
7x57 R 150 gr/9.7 g 17005	2690	2476	2270	2077	2411	2042	1717	1437	100	−0.6	−0.1	0	−1.3	−4.2	−15.2
									180	−0.2	+0.7	+1.6	+1.1	−1.0	−10.4
									200	−0.1	+1.0	+2.1	+1.8	0	−8.9
7x57 R 150 gr/9.7 g 17006	2690	2476	2270	2077	2411	2042	1717	1437	100	−0.6	−0.1	0	−1.3	−4.2	−15.2
									180	−0.2	+0.7	+1.6	+1.1	−1.0	−10.4
									200	−0.1	+1.0	+2.1	+1.8	0	−8.9
7 mm Rem. M 150 gr/9.7 g 17021	3250	2960	2638	2440	3519	2919	2318	1983	100	−0.8	−0.3	0	−0.7	−2.4	−9.5
									180	−0.6	+0.1	+0.9	+0.6	+0.6	−6.8
									200	−0.5	+0.3	+1.2	+1.1	0	−5.8
7x64 150 gr/9.7 g 17013	2890	2598	2329	2113	2779	2449	1807	1487	100	−0.7	−0.2	0	−1.0	−3.3	−12.5
									180	−0.4	+0.4	+1.2	+0.9	−0.8	−8.8
									200	−0.3	+0.6	+1.7	+1.5	0	−7.5
7x64 175 gr/11.3 g 17015	2725	2516	2339	2198	2884	2460	2126	1878	100	−0.7	−0.1	0	−1.2	−3.6	−12.7
									180	−0.3	+0.6	+1.4	+0.9	−0.9	−8.5
									200	−0.2	+0.8	+1.8	+1.6	0	−7.2
280 Rem. 150 gr/9.7 g 17050	2900	2683	2475	2277	2802	2398	2041	1727	100	−0.7	−0.2	0	−1.0	−3.4	−12.4
									180	−0.4	+0.4	+1.2	+1.1	−0.8	−8.6
									200	−0.3	+0.7	+1.7	+1.5	0	−7.4
7.5x55 Swiss 180 gr/11.0 g 17511	2650	2441	2248	2056	2792	2380	2020	1690	100	−0.6	−0.1	0	−1.4	−4.3	−15.3
									180	−0.2	+0.7	+1.6	+1.1	−1.0	−10.4
									200	−0.1	+1.0	+2.1	+1.8	0	−8.9

	Muzzle	100 yards	200 yards	300 yards	Muzzle	100 yards	200 yards	300 yards		25 yards	50 yards	100 yards	150 yards	200 yards	300 yards
30 US Carbine 110 gr/7.1 g 17621	1970	1595	1300	1090	948	622	413	290	100	−0.1	+0.6	0	−4.1	−12.4	−45.7
									130	+0.3	+1.4	+1.5	−1.8	−9.3	−41.1
									200	+1.4	+3.7	+6.2	+5.2	0	−27.0
7.62 Russian 180 gr/11.6 g 17634	2625	2415	2222	2030	2749	2326	1970	1644	100	−0.6	−0.1	0	−1.4	−4.4	−15.7
									180	−0.2	+0.8	+1.7	+1.1	−1.1	−10.7
									200	−0.1	+1.0	+2.2	+1.9	0	−9.1
30−06 130 gr/8.4 g 17640	3205	2876	2561	2263	2966	2388	1894	1479	100	−0.8	−0.3	0	−0.8	−2.7	−10.8
									180	−0.5	+0.2	+1.0	+0.7	−0.7	−7.8
									200	−0.4	+0.4	+1.4	+1.3	0	−6.7
30−06 146 gr/9.5 g 17651	2772	2549	2336	2133	2485	2102	1765	1472	100	−0.7	−0.1	0	−1.2	−3.9	−14.3
									180	−0.3	+0.6	+1.5	+1.0	−1.0	−9.9
									200	−0.2	+0.8	+2.0	+1.7	0	−8.4
30−06 150 gr/9.7 g 17643	2970	2680	2402	2141	2943	2393	1922	1527	100	−0.7	−0.2	0	−1.0	−3.4	−12.9
									180	−0.4	+0.4	+1.3	+0.9	−0.9	−9.1
									200	−0.3	+0.6	+1.7	+1.5	0	−7.8
30−06 180 gr/11.6 g 17648	2700	2477	2261	2070	2914	2430	2025	1713	100	−0.6	−0.1	0	−1.3	−4.1	−14.9
									180	−0.3	+0.7	+1.6	+1.0	−1.7	−10.2
									200	−0.1	+0.9	+2.1	+1.8	0	−8.7
30−06 180 gr/11.6 g 17649	2700	2494	2296	2109	2914	2487	2107	1778	100	−0.6	−0.1	0	−1.3	−4.1	−14.8
									180	−0.3	+0.7	+1.5	+1.0	−1.0	−10.2
									200	−0.1	+0.9	+2.0	+1.8	0	−8.7
30−06 180 gr/11.6 g 17653	2700	2494	2296	2109	2914	2487	2107	1778	100	−0.6	−0.1	0	−1.3	−4.1	−14.8
									180	−0.3	+0.7	+1.5	+1.0	−1.0	−10.2
									200	−0.1	+0.9	+2.0	+1.8	0	−8.7
30−30 Win. 150 gr/9.7 g 17630	2410	2075	1790	1550	1934	1433	1066	799	100	−0.5	+0.1	0	−2.2	−7.0	−26.1
									130	−0.3	+0.6	+0.8	−1.0	−5.4	−23.6
									200	+0.4	+1.9	+3.5	+3.0	0	−15.6
30−30 Win. 170 gr/11.0 g 17631	2220	1890	1630	1410	1860	1350	1000	750	100	−0.4	+0.3	0	−2.7	−8.1	−29.2
									130	−0.1	+0.8	+1.0	−1.2	−6.1	−26.3
									200	+0.6	+2.3	+4.0	+3.4	0	−17.1
308 Win. 130 gr/8.4 g 17623	2900	2590	2300	2030	2428	1937	1527	1190	100	−0.7	−0.2	0	−1.1	−3.7	−14.2
									180	−0.4	+0.5	+1.4	+1.0	−0.9	−10.0
									200	−0.2	+0.8	+1.9	+1.7	0	−8.6
308 Win. 146 gr/9.5 g 17622	2812	2589	2375	2172	2558	2168	1824	1526	100	−0.7	−0.1	0	−1.3	−4.1	−15.6
									180	−0.3	+0.6	+1.5	+1.1	−1.0	−11.0
									200	−0.2	+0.9	+2.1	+1.8	0	−9.4
308 Win. 150 gr/9.7 g 17624	2860	2570	2300	2050	2725	2200	1760	1400	100	−0.7	−0.2	0	−1.2	−3.8	−14.2
									180	−0.3	+0.6	+1.4	+1.0	−1.0	−10.0
									200	−0.2	+0.8	+1.9	+1.7	0	−8.5
308 Win. 180 gr/11.6 g 17628	2610	2400	2210	2020	2725	2303	1952	1631	100	−0.6	−0.1	0	−1.4	−4.5	−16.2
									180	−0.2	+0.8	+1.7	+1.1	−1.1	−11.0
									200	±0.0	+1.1	+2.3	+1.9	0	−9.4
308 Win. 180 gr/11.6 g 17635	2610	2400	2210	2020	2725	2303	1952	1631	100	−0.6	−0.1	0	−1.4	−4.5	−16.2
									180	−0.2	+0.8	+1.7	+1.1	−1.1	−11.0
									200	±0.0	+1.1	+2.3	+1.9	0	−9.4
308 Win. 180 gr/11.6 g 17636	2610	2393	2185	1988	2724	2287	1906	1578	100	−0.6	±0.0	0	−1.5	−4.6	−16.5
									180	−0.2	+0.8	+1.7	+1.1	−1.1	−11.3
									200	±0.0	+1.1	+2.3	+2.0	0	−9.6
308 Norma M 180 gr/11.6 g 17638	3020	2798	2585	2382	3646	3130	2671	2268	100	−0.8	−0.3	0	−0.8	−2.6	−10.1
									180	−0.5	+0.2	+1.0	+0.7	−0.7	−7.1
									200	−0.4	+0.4	+1.3	+1.2	0	−6.1
7.65 Argentine 150 gr/9.7 g 17701	2920	2630	2355	2105	2841	2304	1848	1476	100	−0.7	−0.2	0	−1.0	−3.6	−12.9
									180	−0.4	+0.5	+1.3	+0.9	−0.9	−9.1
									200	−0.3	+0.7	+1.7	+1.5	0	−7.8
303 British 150 gr/9.7 g 17712	2720	2440	2170	1930	2465	1983	1569	1241	100	−0.6	−0.1	0	−1.4	−4.4	−16.3
									180	−0.2	+0.7	+1.7	+1.1	−1.1	−11.3
									200	−0.1	+1.0	+2.2	+1.9	0	−9.7
303 British 180 gr/11.6 g 17713	2540	2340	2147	1965	2579	2189	1843	1544	100	−0.6	±0.0	0	−1.6	−4.9	−17.3
									130	−0.4	+0.3	+0.6	−0.7	−3.7	−15.6
									200	±0.0	+1.2	+2.4	+2.1	0	−10.0
7.7 Jap. 130 gr/8.4 g 17721	2950	2635	2340	2065	2513	2004	1581	1231	100	−0.7	−0.2	0	−1.1	−3.5	−13.5
									180	−0.4	+0.5	+1.3	+0.9	−0.9	−9.5
									200	−0.3	+0.7	+1.8	+1.6	0	−8.2
7.7 Jap. 180 gr/11.6 g 17722	2495	2292	2101	1922	2484	2100	1765	1477	100	−0.6	±0.0	0	−1.7	−5.2	−18.1
									130	−0.4	+0.3	+0.6	−0.8	−3.9	−16.3
									200	+0.1	+1.3	+2.6	+2.2	0	−10.4
8x57 J 196 gr/12.7 g 17901	2525	2195	1894	1627	2778	2097	1562	1152	100	−0.6	±0.0	0	−1.8	−5.8	−21.4
									130	−0.4	+0.4	+0.7	−0.8	−4.4	−19.3
									200	+0.2	+1.5	+2.9	+2.5	0	−12.7
8x57 JS 108 gr/7.0 g 18009	2976	2178	1562	1129	2122	1137	585	305	100	−0.6	−0.1	0	−1.8	−6.1	−27.1
									150	−0.4	+0.5	+1.2	0	−3.8	−23.5
									200	−0.1	+1.5	+3.1	+4.0	0	−17.9
8x57 JS 196 gr/12.7 g 18003	2525	2195	1894	1627	2778	2097	1562	1152	100	−0.6	±0.0	0	−1.8	−5.8	−21.4
									130	−0.4	+0.4	+0.7	−0.8	−4.4	−19.3
									200	+0.2	+1.5	+2.9	+2.5	0	−12.7
8x57 JS 196 gr/12.7 g 18007	2525	2195	1894	1627	2778	2097	1562	1152	100	−0.6	±0.0	0	−1.8	−5.8	−21.4
									130	−0.4	+0.4	+0.7	−0.8	−4.4	−19.3
									200	+0.2	+1.5	+2.9	+2.5	0	−12.7
358 Norma M 250 gr/16.2 g 19001	2800	2493	2231	2001	4322	3451	2764	2223	100	−0.7	−0.1	0	−1.2	−4.0	−14.3
									180	−0.3	+0.6	+1.5	+1.0	−1.0	−9.8
									200	−0.2	+0.9	+2.0	+1.7	0	−8.3
9.3x57 286 gr/18.5 g 19302	2065	1818	1595	1404	2714	2099	1616	1252	100	−0.3	+0.4	0	−3.1	−9.1	−32.0
									130	±0.0	+1.0	+1.1	−1.3	−6.8	−28.5
									200	+0.9	+2.7	+4.6	+3.8	0	−18.3
9.3x57 286 gr/18.5 g 19303	2065	1818	1595	1404	2714	2099	1616	1252	100	−0.3	+0.4	0	−3.1	−9.1	−32.0
									130	±0.0	+1.0	+1.1	−1.3	−6.8	−28.5
									200	+0.9	+2.7	+4.6	+3.8	0	−18.3
9.3x62 286 gr/18.5 g 19314	2360	2088	1815	1592	3544	2769	2092	1700	100	−0.5	+0.1	0	−2.1	−6.5	−23.5
									180	+0.1	+1.4	+2.5	+1.6	−1.6	−16.0
									200	+0.3	+1.8	+3.3	+2.8	0	−13.7
9.3x62 286 gr/18.5 g 19315	2360	2088	1815	1592	3544	2769	2092	1700	100	−0.5	+0.1	0	−2.1	−6.5	−23.5
									180	+0.1	+1.4	+2.5	+1.6	−1.6	−16.0
									200	+0.3	+1.8	+3.3	+2.8	0	−13.7

REMINGTON CENTERFIRE RIFLE BALLISTICS

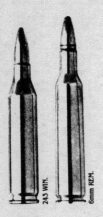
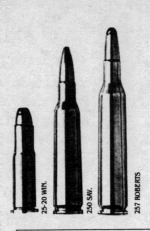
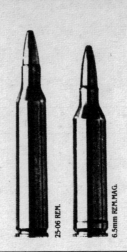
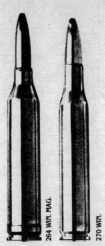

243 WIN.   6mm REM.   25-20 WIN.   250 SAV.   257 ROBERTS   25-06 REM.   6.5mm REM. MAG.   264 WIN. MAG.   270 WIN.

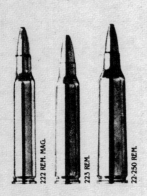

222 REM. MAG.   223 REM.   22-250 REM.

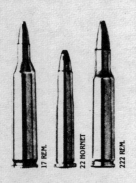

17 REM.   22 HORNET   222 REM.

†† 280 Rem. and 7mm Express Rem. are interchangeable.
† Subject to stock on hand.
* Illustrated.
** Interchangeable in 244 Rem.
‡ Inches above or below line of sight. Hold low for positive numbers, high for negative numbers.

Cartridges not shown in actual size.
Specifications are nominal.
Ballistics figures established in test barrels.
Individual rifles may vary from test-barrel specifications.

Remington Ballistics

CALIBERS	REMINGTON Order No.	BULLET Wt.-Grs.	BULLET Style	Primer No.
17 REM.	R17REM	25*	Hollow Point Power-Lokt*	7½
22 HORNET	R22HN1	45*	Pointed Soft Point	6½
	R22HN2	45	Hollow Point	6½
222 REM.	R222R1	50	Pointed Soft Point	7½
	R222R3	50*	Hollow Point Power-Lokt	7½
	R222R4	55	Metal Case	7½
222 REM. MAG.	R222M1	55*	Pointed Soft Point	7½
	R222M2	55	Hollow Point Power-Lokt	7½
223 REM.	R223R1	55	Pointed Soft Point	7½
	R223R2	55*	Hollow Point Power-Lokt	7½
	R223R3	55	Metal Case	7½
22-250 REM.	R22501	55*	Pointed Soft Point	9½
	R22502	55	Hollow Point Power-Lokt	9½
243 WIN.	R243W1	80	Pointed Soft Point	9½
	R243W2	80*	Hollow Point Power-Lokt	9½
	R243W3	100	Pointed Soft Point Core-Lokt*	9½
6mm REM.	R6MM1	80**	Pointed Soft Point	9½
	R6MM2	80**	Hollow Point Power-Lokt	9½
	R6MM4	100*	Pointed Soft Point Core-Lokt	9½
25-20 WIN.	R25202	86*	Soft Point	6½
250 SAV.	R250SV	100*	Pointed Soft Point	9½
257 ROBERTS	R257	117*	Soft Point Core-Lokt	9½
25-06 REM.	R25061	87	Hollow Point Power-Lokt	9½
	R25062	100*	Pointed Soft Point Core-Lokt	9½
	R25063	120	Pointed Soft Point Core-Lokt	9½
6.5mm REM. MAG.	R65MM2	120*	Pointed Soft Point Core-Lokt	9½M
264 WIN. MAG.	R264W2	140*	Pointed Soft Point Core-Lokt	9½M
270 WIN.	R270W1	100	Pointed Soft Point	9½
	R270W2	130*	Pointed Soft Point Core-Lokt	9½
	R270W3	130	Bronze Point	9½
	R270W4	150	Soft Point Core-Lokt	9½
7mm MAUSER	R7MSR1	140*	Pointed Soft Point	9½
7mm-08 REM.	R7M081	140*	Pointed Soft Point	9½
280 REM.††	R280R2	165*	Soft Point Core-Lokt	9½
7mm EXPRESS REM.††	R7M061	150*	Pointed Soft Point Core-Lokt	9½
7mm REM. MAG.	R7MM2	150*	Pointed Soft Point Core-Lokt	9½M
	R7MM3	175	Pointed Soft Point Core-Lokt	9½M
30 CARBINE	R30CAR	110*	Soft Point	6½
30 REM.	R30REM	170*	Soft Point Core-Lokt	9½
30-30 WIN. "ACCELERATOR"	R3030A	55*	Soft Point	9½
30-30 WIN.	R30301	150*	Soft Point Core-Lokt	9½
	R30302	170	Soft Point Core-Lokt	9½
	R30303	170	Hollow Point Core-Lokt	9½

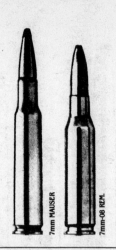

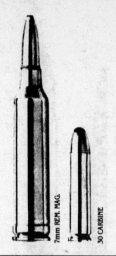
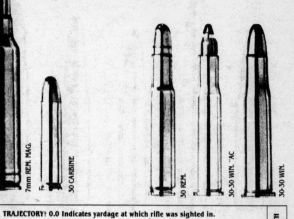

7mm MAUSER • 7mm-08 REM. • 280 REM. • 7mm EXPRESS REM. • 7mm REM. MAG. • 30 CARBINE • 30 REM. • 30-30 WIN. "AC" • 30-30 WIN.

TRAJECTORY† 0.0 indicates yardage at which rifle was sighted in.

SHORT RANGE — Bullet does not rise more than one inch above line of sight from muzzle to sighting-in range.

LONG RANGE — Bullet does not rise more than three inches above line of sight from muzzle to sighting-in range.

VELOCITY FEET PER SECOND						ENERGY FOOT-POUNDS						SHORT RANGE						LONG RANGE							BARREL LENGTH
Muzzle	100 Yds.	200 Yds.	300 Yds.	400 Yds.	500 Yds.	Muzzle	100 Yds.	200 Yds.	300 Yds.	400 Yds.	500 Yds.	50 Yds.	100 Yds.	150 Yds.	200 Yds.	250 Yds.	300 Yds.	100 Yds.	150 Yds.	200 Yds.	250 Yds.	300 Yds.	400 Yds.	500 Yds.	
4040	3284	2644	2086	1606	1235	906	599	388	242	143	85	0.1	0.5	0.0	-1.5	-4.2	-8.5	2.1	2.5	1.9	0.0	-3.4	-17.0	-44.3	24"
2690	2042	1502	1128	948	840	723	417	225	127	90	70	0.3	0.0	-2.4	-7.7	-16.9	-31.3	1.6	0.0	-4.5	-12.8	-26.4	-75.6	-163.4	24"
2690	2042	1502	1128	948	840	723	417	225	127	90	70	0.3	0.0	-2.4	-7.7	-16.9	-31.3	1.6	0.0	-4.5	-12.8	-26.4	-75.6	-163.4	24"
3140	2602	2123	1700	1350	1107	1094	752	500	321	202	136	0.5	0.9	0.0	-2.5	-6.9	-13.7	2.2	1.9	0.0	-3.8	-10.0	-32.3	-73.8	
3140	2635	2182	1777	1432	1172	1094	771	529	351	228	152	0.5	0.9	0.0	-2.4	-6.6	-13.1	2.1	1.8	0.0	-3.6	-9.5	-30.2	-68.1	
3020	2562	2147	1773	1451	1201	1114	801	563	384	257	176	0.6	1.0	0.0	-2.5	-7.0	-13.7	2.2	1.9	0.0	-3.8	-9.9	-31.0	-68.7	24"
3240	2748	2305	1906	1556	1272	1282	922	649	444	296	198	0.4	0.8	0.0	-2.2	-6.0	-11.8	1.9	1.6	0.0	-3.3	-8.5	-26.7	-59.5	
3240	2773	2352	1969	1627	1341	1282	939	675	473	323	220	0.4	0.8	0.0	-2.1	-5.8	-11.4	1.8	1.6	0.0	-3.2	-8.2	-25.5	-56.0	24"
3240	2747	2304	1905	1554	1270	1282	921	648	443	295	197	0.4	0.8	0.0	-2.2	-6.0	-11.8	1.9	1.6	0.0	-3.3	-8.5	-26.7	-59.6	
3240	2773	2352	1969	1627	1341	1282	939	675	473	323	220	0.4	0.8	0.0	-2.1	-5.8	-11.4	1.8	1.6	0.0	-3.2	-8.2	-25.5	-56.0	
3240	2759	2326	1933	1587	1301	1282	929	660	456	307	207	0.4	0.8	0.0	-2.1	-5.9	-11.6	1.9	1.6	0.0	-3.2	-8.4	-26.2	-57.9	24"
3730	3180	2695	2257	1863	1519	1699	1235	887	622	424	282	0.2	0.5	0.0	-1.5	-4.3	-8.4	2.2	2.6	1.9	0.0	-3.3	-15.4	-37.7	
3730	3253	2826	2436	2079	1755	1699	1292	975	725	528	376	0.2	0.5	0.0	-1.4	-4.0	-7.7	2.1	2.4	1.7	0.0	-3.0	-13.4	-32.4	24"
3350	2955	2593	2259	1951	1670	1993	1551	1194	906	676	495	0.3	0.7	0.0	-1.8	-4.9	-9.4	2.6	2.9	2.1	0.0	-3.6	-16.2	-37.9	
3350	2955	2593	2259	1951	1670	1993	1551	1194	906	676	495	0.3	0.7	0.0	-1.8	-4.9	-9.4	2.6	2.9	2.1	0.0	-3.6	-16.2	-37.9	
2960	2697	2449	2215	1993	1786	1945	1615	1332	1089	882	708	0.5	0.9	0.0	-2.2	-5.8	-11.0	1.9	1.6	0.0	-3.1	-7.8	-22.6	-46.3	24"
3470	3064	2694	2352	2036	1747	2139	1667	1289	982	736	542	0.3	0.6	0.0	-1.6	-4.5	-8.7	2.4	2.7	1.9	0.0	-3.3	-14.9	-35.0	
3470	3064	2694	2352	2036	1747	2139	1667	1289	982	736	542	0.3	0.6	0.0	-1.6	-4.5	-8.7	2.4	2.7	1.9	0.0	-3.3	-14.9	-35.0	
3130	2857	2600	2357	2127	1911	2175	1812	1501	1233	1004	811	0.4	0.7	0.0	-1.9	-5.1	-9.7	1.7	1.4	0.0	-2.7	-6.8	-20.0	-40.8	24"
1460	1194	1030	931	858	797	407	272	203	165	141	121	0.0	-4.1	-14.4	-31.8	-57.3	-92.0	0.0	-8.2	-23.5	-47.0	-79.6	-175.9	-319.4	24"
2820	2504	2210	1936	1684	1461	1765	1392	1084	832	630	474	0.2	0.0	-1.6	-4.7	-9.6	-16.5	2.3	2.0	0.0	-3.7	-9.5	-28.3	-59.5	24"
2650	2291	1961	1663	1404	1199	1824	1363	999	718	512	373	0.3	0.0	-1.9	-5.8	-11.9	-20.7	2.9	2.4	0.0	-4.7	-12.0	-36.7	-79.2	24"
3440	2995	2591	2222	1884	1583	2286	1733	1297	954	686	484	0.3	0.6	0.0	-1.7	-4.8	-9.3	2.5	2.9	2.1	0.0	-3.6	-16.4	-39.1	
3230	2893	2580	2287	2014	1762	2316	1858	1478	1161	901	689	0.4	0.7	0.0	-1.9	-5.0	-9.7	1.6	1.4	0.0	-2.7	-6.9	-20.5	-42.7	
3010	2749	2502	2269	2048	1840	2414	2013	1668	1372	1117	902	0.5	0.8	0.0	-2.1	-5.5	-10.5	1.9	1.6	0.0	-2.9	-7.4	-21.6	-44.2	24"
3210	2905	2621	2353	2102	1867	2745	2248	1830	1475	1177	929	0.4	0.7	0.0	-1.8	-4.9	-9.5	2.7	3.0	2.1	0.0	-3.5	-15.5	-35.3	24"
3030	2782	2548	2326	2114	1914	2854	2406	2018	1682	1389	1139	0.5	0.8	0.0	-2.0	-5.4	-10.2	1.8	1.5	0.0	-2.9	-7.2	-20.8	-42.2	24"
3480	3067	2690	2343	2023	1730	2689	2088	1606	1219	909	664	0.3	0.6	0.0	-1.6	-4.5	-8.7	2.4	2.7	1.9	0.0	-3.3	-15.0	-35.2	
3110	2823	2554	2300	2061	1837	2791	2300	1883	1527	1226	974	0.4	0.8	0.0	-2.0	-5.3	-10.0	1.7	1.5	0.0	-2.8	-7.1	-20.8	-42.7	
3110	2849	2604	2371	2150	1941	2791	2343	1957	1622	1334	1087	0.4	0.7	0.0	-1.9	-5.1	-9.7	1.7	1.4	0.0	-2.7	-6.8	-19.9	-40.5	
2900	2550	2225	1926	1653	1415	2801	2165	1649	1235	910	667	0.6	1.0	0.0	-2.5	-6.8	-13.1	2.2	1.9	0.0	-3.6	-9.3	-28.1	-59.7	24"
2660	2435	2221	2018	1827	1648	2199	1843	1533	1266	1037	844	0.2	0.0	-1.7	-5.0	-10.0	-17.0	2.5	2.0	0.0	-3.8	-9.6	-27.7	-56.3	24"
2860	2625	2402	2189	1988	1798	2542	2142	1793	1490	1228	1005	0.6	0.9	0.0	-2.3	-6.11	-11.6	2.1	1.7	0.0	-3.2	-8.1	-23.5	-47.7	24"
2820	2510	2220	1950	1701	1479	2913	2308	1805	1393	1060	801	0.2	0.0	-1.5	-4.6	-9.5	-16.4	2.3	1.9	0.0	-3.7	-9.4	-28.1	-58.8	24"
2970	2699	2444	2203	1975	1763	2937	2426	1989	1616	1299	1035	0.5	0.9	0.0	-2.2	-5.8	-11.0	1.9	1.6	0.0	-3.1	-7.8	-22.8	-46.7	24"
3110	2830	2568	2320	2085	1866	3221	2667	2196	1792	1448	1160	0.4	0.8	0.0	-1.9	-5.2	-9.9	1.7	1.5	0.0	-2.8	-7.0	-20.5	-42.1	
2860	2645	2440	2244	2057	1879	3178	2718	2313	1956	1644	1372	0.6	0.9	0.0	-2.3	-6.0	-11.3	2.0	1.7	0.0	-3.2	-7.9	-22.7	-45.8	24"
1990	1567	1236	1035	923	842	967	600	373	262	208	173	0.9	0.0	-4.5	-13.5	-28.3	-49.9	0.0	-4.5	-13.5	-28.3	-49.9	-118.6	-228.2	20"
2120	1822	1555	1328	1153	1036	1696	1253	913	666	502	405	0.7	0.0	-3.3	-9.7	-19.6	-33.8	2.2	0.0	-5.3	-14.1	-27.2	-69.0	-136.9	24"
3400	2693	2085	1570	1187	986	1412	886	521	301	172	119							2.0	1.8	0.0	-3.8	-10.0	-35.0	-84.4	24"
2390	1973	1605	1303	1095	974	1902	1296	858	565	399	316	0.5	0.0	-2.7	-8.2	-17.0	-30.0	1.8	0.0	-4.6	-12.5	-24.6	-65.3	-134.9	24"
2200	1895	1619	1381	1191	1061	1827	1355	989	720	535	425	0.6	0.0	-3.0	-8.9	-18.0	-31.1	2.0	0.0	-4.8	-13.0	-25.1	-63.6	-126.7	24"
2200	1895	1619	1381	1191	1061	1827	1355	989	720	535	425	0.6	0.0	-3.0	-8.9	-18.0	-31.1	2.0	0.0	-4.8	-13.0	-25.1	-63.6	-126.7	24"

REMINGTON CENTERFIRE RIFLE BALLISTICS

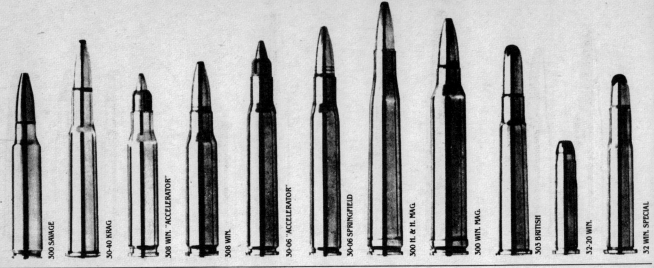

300 SAVAGE   30-40 KRAG   308 WIN. "ACCELERATOR"   308 WIN.   30-06 "ACCELERATOR"   30-06 SPRINGFIELD   300 H. & H. MAG.   300 WIN. MAG.   303 BRITISH   32-20 WIN.   32 WIN. SPECIAL

Remington Ballistics

CALIBERS	REMINGTON Order No.	BULLET Wt.-Grs.	BULLET Style	Primer No.	Muzzle	100 Yds.	200 Yds.	300 Yds.	400 Yds.	500 Yds.
300 SAVAGE	R30SV1	150	Soft Point Core-Lokt	9½	2630	2247	1897	1585	1324	1131
	R30SV3	180	Soft Point Core-Lokt	9½	2350	2025	1728	1467	1252	1098
	R30SV4	180*	Pointed Soft Point Core-Lokt	9½	2350	2137	1935	1745	1570	1413
30-40 KRAG	R30402	180*	Pointed Soft Point Core-Lokt	9½	2430	2213	2007	1813	1632	1468
308 WIN. "ACCELERATOR"	R308W5	55*	Pointed Soft Point	9½	3770	3215	2726	2286	1888	1541
308 WIN.	R308W1	150*	Pointed Soft Point Core-Lokt	9½	2820	2533	2263	2009	1774	1560
	R308W2	180	Soft Point Core-Lokt	9½	2620	2274	1955	1666	1414	1212
	R308W3	180	Pointed Soft Point Core-Lokt	9½	2620	2393	2178	1974	1782	1604
30-06 "ACCELERATOR"	R30069	55*	Pointed Soft Point	9½	4080	3485	2965	2502	2083	1709
30-06 SPRINGFIELD	R30061	125	Pointed Soft Point	9½	3140	2780	2447	2138	1853	1595
	R30062	150	Pointed Soft Point Core-Lokt	9½	2910	2617	2342	2083	1843	1622
	R30063	150	Bronze Point	9½	2910	2656	2416	2189	1974	1773
	R3006B	165*	Pointed Soft Point Core-Lokt	9½	2800	2534	2283	2047	1825	1621
	R30064	180	Soft Point Core-Lokt	9½	2700	2348	2023	1727	1466	1251
	R30065	180	Pointed Soft Point Core-Lokt	9½	2700	2469	2250	2042	1846	1663
	R30066	180	Bronze Point	9½	2700	2485	2280	2084	1899	1725
	R30067	220	Soft Point Core-Lokt	9½	2410	2130	1870	1632	1422	1246
300 H. & H. MAG.	R300HH	180*	Pointed Soft Point Core-Lokt	9½M	2880	2640	2412	2196	1990	1798
300 WIN. MAG.	R300W1	150	Pointed Soft Point Core-Lokt	9½M	3290	2951	2636	2342	2068	1813
	R300W2	180*	Pointed Soft Point Core-Lokt	9½M	2960	2745	2540	2344	2157	1979
303 BRITISH	R303B1	180*	Soft Point Core-Lokt	9½	2460	2124	1817	1542	1311	1137
32-20 WIN.	R32201	100	Lead	6½	1210	1021	913	834	769	712
	R32202	100*	Soft Point	6½	1210	1021	913	834	769	712
32 WIN. SPECIAL	R32WS2	170*	Soft Point Core-Lokt	9½	2250	1921	1626	1372	1175	1044
8mm MAUSER	R8MSR	170*	Soft Point Core-Lokt	9½	2360	1969	1622	1333	1123	997
8mm REM. MAG.	R8MM1	185*	Pointed Soft Point Core-Lokt	9½M	3080	2761	2464	2186	1927	1688
	R8MM2	220	Pointed Soft Point Core-Lokt	9½M	2830	2581	2346	2123	1913	1716
35 REM.	R35R1	150	Pointed Soft Point Core-Lokt	9½	2300	1874	1506	1218	1039	934
	R35R2	200*	Soft Point Core-Lokt	9½	2080	1698	1376	1140	1001	911
350 REM. MAG.	R350M1	200*	Pointed Soft Point Core-Lokt	9½M	2710	2410	2130	1870	1631	1421
375 H. & H. MAG.	R375M1	270*	Soft Point	9½M	2690	2420	2166	1928	1707	1507
	R375M2	300	Metal Case	9½M	2530	2171	1843	1551	1307	1126
44-40 WIN.	R4440W	200*	Soft Point	2½	1190	1006	900	822	756	699
44 REM. MAG.	R44MG2	240	Soft Point	2½	1760	1380	1114	970	878	806
	R44MG3	240	Semi-Jacketed Hollow Point	2½	1760	1380	1114	970	878	806
444 MAR.	R444M	240	Soft Point	9½	2350	1815	1377	1087	941	846
	R444M2	265*	Soft Point	9½	2120	1733	1405	1160	1012	920
45-70 GOVERNMENT	R4570G	405*	Soft Point	9½	1330	1168	1055	977	918	869
458 WIN. MAG.	R458W1	500	Metal Case	9½M	2040	1823	1623	1442	1237	1161
	R458W2	510*	Soft Point	9½M	2040	1770	1527	1319	1157	1046

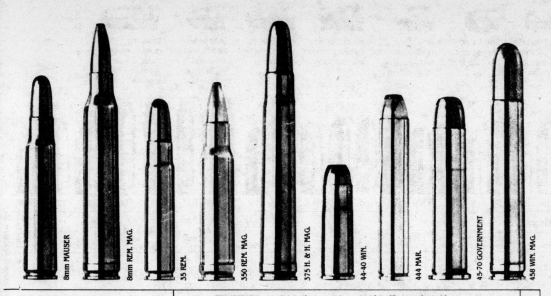

8mm MAUSER · 8mm REM. MAG. · 35 REM. · 350 REM. MAG. · 375 H. & H. MAG. · 44-40 WIN. · 444 MAR. · 45-70 GOVERNMENT · 458 WIN. MAG.

TRAJECTORY† 0.0 Indicates yardage at which rifle was sighted in.

ENERGY FOOT-POUNDS						SHORT RANGE — Bullet does not rise more than one inch above line of sight from muzzle to sighting-in range.						LONG RANGE — Bullet does not rise more than three inches above line of sight from muzzle to sighting-in range.							BARREL LENGTH
Muzzle	100 Yds.	200 Yds.	300 Yds.	400 Yds.	500 Yds.	50 Yds.	100 Yds.	150 Yds.	200 Yds.	250 Yds.	300 Yds.	100 Yds.	150 Yds.	200 Yds.	250 Yds.	300 Yds.	400 Yds.	500 Yds.	
2303	1681	1198	837	584	426	0.3	0.0	-2.0	-6.1	-12.5	-21.9	1.3	0.0	-3.4	-9.2	-17.9	-46.3	-94.8	24"
2207	1639	1193	860	626	482	0.5	0.0	-2.6	-7.7	-15.6	-27.1	1.7	0.0	-4.2	-11.3	-21.9	-55.8	-112.0	
2207	1825	1496	1217	985	798	0.4	0.0	-2.3	-6.7	-13.5	-22.8	1.5	0.0	-3.6	-9.6	-18.2	-44.1	-84.2	24"
2360	1957	1610	1314	1064	861	0.4	0.0	-2.1	-6.2	-12.5	-21.1	1.4	0.0	-3.4	-8.9	-16.8	-40.9	-78.1	24"
1735	1262	907	638	435	290	0.2	0.5	0.0	-1.5	-4.2	-8.2	2.2	2.5	1.8	0.0	-3.2	-15.0	-36.7	24"
2648	2137	1705	1344	1048	810	0.2	0.0	-1.5	-4.5	-9.3	-15.9	2.3	1.9	0.0	-3.6	-9.1	-26.9	-55.7	
2743	2066	1527	1109	799	587	0.3	0.0	-2.0	-5.9	-12.1	-20.9	2.9	2.4	0.0	-4.7	-12.1	-36.9	-79.1	24"
2743	2288	1896	1557	1269	1028	0.2	0.0	-1.8	-5.2	-10.4	-17.7	2.6	2.1	0.0	-4.0	-9.9	-28.9	-58.8	
2033	1483	1074	764	530	356	0.4	1.0	0.9	0.0	-1.9	-5.0	1.8	2.1	1.5	0.0	-2.7	-12.5	-30.5	24"
2736	2145	1662	1269	953	706	0.4	0.8	0.0	-2.1	-5.6	-10.7	1.8	1.5	0.0	-3.0	-7.7	-23.0	-48.5	
2820	2281	1827	1445	1131	876	0.6	0.9	0.0	-2.3	-6.3	-12.0	2.1	1.8	0.0	-3.3	-8.5	-25.0	-51.8	
2820	2349	1944	1596	1298	1047	0.6	0.9	0.0	-2.2	-6.0	-11.4	2.0	1.7	0.0	-3.2	-8.0	-23.3	-47.5	
2872	2352	1909	1534	1220	963	0.7	1.0	0.0	-2.5	-6.7	-12.7	2.3	1.9	0.0	-3.6	-9.0	-26.3	-54.1	24"
2913	2203	1635	1192	859	625	0.2	0.0	-1.8	-5.5	-11.2	-19.5	2.7	2.3	0.0	-4.4	-11.3	-34.4	-73.7	
2913	2436	2023	1666	1362	1105	0.2	0.0	-1.6	-4.8	-9.7	-16.5	2.4	2.0	0.0	-3.7	-9.3	-27.0	-54.9	
2913	2468	2077	1736	1441	1189	0.2	0.0	-1.6	-4.7	-9.6	-16.2	2.4	2.0	0.0	-3.6	-9.1	-26.2	-53.0	
2837	2216	1708	1301	988	758	0.4	0.0	-2.3	-6.8	-13.8	-23.6	1.5	0.0	-3.7	-9.9	-19.0	-47.4	-93.1	
3315	2785	2325	1927	1583	1292	0.6	0.9	0.0	-2.3	-6.0	-11.5	2.1	1.7	0.0	-3.2	-8.0	-23.3	-47.4	24"
3605	2900	2314	1827	1424	1095	0.3	0.7	0.0	-1.8	-4.8	-9.3	2.6	2.9	2.1	0.0	-3.5	-15.4	-35.5	24"
3501	3011	2578	2196	1859	1565	0.5	0.8	0.0	-2.1	-5.5	-10.4	1.9	1.6	0.0	-2.9	-7.3	-20.9	-41.9	
2418	1803	1319	950	687	517	0.4	0.0	-2.3	-6.9	-14.1	-24.4	1.5	0.0	-3.8	-10.2	-19.8	-50.5	-101.5	24"
325	231	185	154	131	113	0.0	-6.3	-20.9	-44.9	-79.3	-125.1	0.0	-11.5	-32.3	-63.8	-106.3	-230.3	-413.3	24"
325	231	185	154	131	113	0.0	-6.3	-20.9	-44.9	-79.3	-125.1	0.0	-11.5	-32.3	-63.6	-106.3	-230.3	-413.3	24"
1911	1393	998	710	521	411	0.6	0.0	-2.9	-8.6	-17.6	-30.5	1.9	0.0	-4.7	-12.7	-24.7	-63.2	-126.9	24"
2102	1463	993	671	476	375	0.5	0.0	-2.7	-8.2	-17.0	-29.8	1.8	0.0	-4.5	-12.4	-24.3	-63.8	-130.7	24"
3896	3131	2494	1963	1525	1170	0.5	0.8	0.0	-2.1	-5.6	-10.7	1.8	1.6	0.0	-3.0	-7.6	-22.5	-46.8	24"
3912	3254	2688	2201	1787	1438	0.6	1.0	0.0	-2.4	-6.4	-12.1	2.2	1.8	0.0	-3.4	-8.5	-24.7	-50.5	
1762	1169	755	494	359	291	0.6	0.0	-3.0	-9.2	-19.1	-33.9	2.0	0.0	-5.1	-14.1	-27.8	-74.0	-152.3	24"
1921	1280	841	577	445	369	0.8	0.0	-3.8	-11.3	-23.5	-41.2	2.5	0.0	-6.3	-17.1	-33.6	-87.7	-176.4	
3261	2579	2014	1553	1181	897	0.2	0.0	-1.7	-5.1	-10.4	-17.9	2.6	2.1	0.0	-4.0	-10.3	-30.5	-64.0	20"
4337	3510	2812	2228	1747	1361	0.2	0.0	-1.7	-5.1	-10.3	-17.6	2.5	2.1	0.0	-3.9	-10.0	-29.4	-60.7	24"
4263	3139	2262	1602	1138	844	0.3	0.0	-2.2	-6.5	-13.5	-23.4	1.5	0.0	-3.6	-9.8	-19.1	-49.1	-99.5	
629	449	360	300	254	217	0.0	-6.5	-21.6	-46.3	-81.8	-129.1	0.0	-11.8	-33.3	-65.5	-109.5	-237.4	-426.2	24"
1650	1015	661	501	411	346	0.0	-2.7	-10.0	-23.0	-43.0	-71.2	0.0	-5.9	-17.6	-36.3	-63.1	-145.5	-273.0	24"
1650	1015	661	501	411	346	0.0	-2.7	-10.0	-23.0	-43.0	-71.2	0.0	-5.9	-17.6	-36.3	-63.1	-145.5	-273.0	20"
2942	1755	1010	630	472	381	0.6	0.0	-3.2	-9.9	-21.3	-38.5	2.1	0.0	-5.6	-15.9	-32.1	-87.8	-182.7	24"
2644	1768	1162	791	603	498	0.7	0.0	-3.6	-10.8	-22.5	-39.5	2.4	0.0	-6.0	-16.4	-32.2	-84.3	-170.2	
1590	1227	1001	858	758	679	0.0	-4.7	-15.8	-34.0	-60.0	-94.5	0.0	-8.7	-24.6	-48.2	-80.3	-172.4	-305.9	24"
4620	3689	2924	2308	1839	1469	0.7	0.0	-3.3	-9.6	-19.2	-32.5	2.2	0.0	-5.2	-13.6	-25.8	-63.2	-121.7	24"
4712	3547	2640	1970	1516	1239	0.8	0.0	-3.5	-10.3	-20.8	-35.6	2.4	0.0	-5.6	-14.9	-28.5	-71.5	-140.4	

† Subject to stock on hand.
* Illustrated.
† Inches above or below line of sight.
Hold low for positive numbers, high for negative numbers.

Cartridges not shown in actual size.
Specifications are nominal.
Ballistics figures established in test barrels.
Individual rifles may vary from test-barrel specifications.

REMINGTON BALLISTICS

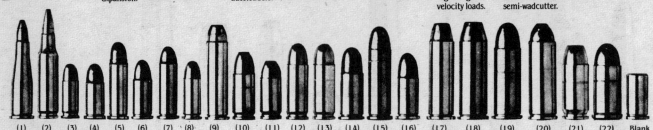

Semi-Jacketed Hollow Point, for maximum expansion.

Soft Point, for deeper penetration than SJHP.

Metal Case ensures positive functioning in autoloaders.

Wadcutter, solid lead for precision target shooting.

Metal Point, jacketed for best penetration.

Lead Gas-Check, minimizes lead fouling in higher-velocity loads.

Lead, our general-purpose bullet, in both round nose and semi-wadcutter.

(1) (2) (3) (4) (5) (6) (7) (8) (9) (10) (11) (12) (13) (14) (15) (16) (17) (18) (19) (20) (21) (22) Blank

Remington Ballistics

CALIBER	REMINGTON Order No.	Primer No.	Wt.-Grs.	Style	VELOCITY (FPS) Muzzle	50 Yds.	100 Yds.	ENERGY (FT LB) Muzzle	50 Yds.	100 Yds.	TRAJECTORY 50 Yds.	100 Yds.	BARREL LENGTH
(1) 22 REM. "JET" MAG.	R22JET	6½	40*	Soft Point	2100	1790	1510	390	285	200	0.3"	1.4"	8⅜"
(2) 221 REM. "FIRE BALL"	R221F	7½	50*	Pointed Soft Point	2650	2380	2130	780	630	505	0.2"	0.8"	10½"
(3) 25 (6.35mm) AUTO. PISTOL	R25AP	1½	50*	Metal Case	810	755	700	73	63	54	1.8"	7.7"	2"
(4) 32 S. & W.	R32SW	5½	88*	Lead	680	645	610	90	81	73	2.5"	10.5"	3"
(5) 32 S. & W. LONG	R32SWL	1½	98*	Lead	705	670	635	115	98	88	2.3"	10.5"	4"
(6) 32 SHORT COLT	R32SC	1½	80*	Lead	745	665	590	100	79	62	2.2"	9.9"	4"
(7) 32 LONG COLT	R32LC	1½	82*	Lead	755	715	675	100	93	83	2.0"	8.7"	4"
(8) 32 (7.65mm) AUTO. PISTOL	R32AP	1½	71*	Metal Case	905	855	810	129	115	97	1.4"	5.8"	4"
(9) 357 MAG. Vented Barrel	R357M7	5½	110	Semi-Jacketed H.P.	1295	1094	975	410	292	232	0.8"	3.5"	4"
	R357M1	5½	125	Semi-Jacketed H.P.	1450	1240	1090	583	427	330	0.6"	2.8"	4"
	R357M2	5½	158*	Semi-Jacketed H.P.	1235	1104	1015	535	428	361	0.8"	3.5"	4"
	R357M3	5½	158	Soft Point	1235	1104	1015	535	428	361	0.8"	3.5"	4"
	R357M4	5½	158	Metal Point	1235	1104	1015	535	428	361	0.8"	3.5"	4"
	R357M5	5½	158	Lead	1235	1104	1015	535	428	361	0.8"	3.5"	4"
	R357M6	5½	158	Lead (Brass Case)	1235	1104	1015	535	428	361	0.8"	3.5"	4"
(10) 9mm LUGER AUTO. PISTOL	R9MM1	1½	115*	Jacketed H.P.	1110	1030	971	339	292	259	1.0"	4.1"	4"
	R9MM2	1½	124	Metal Case	1115	1047	971	341	2	241	0.9"	3.9"	4"
(11) 380 AUTO. PISTOL	R380AP	1½	95	Metal Case	955	865	785	190	160	130	1.4"	5.9"	4"
	R380A1	1½	88*	Jacketed H.P.	990	920	868	191	165	146	1.2"	5.1"	4"
(12) 38 AUTO. COLT PISTOL	R38ACP	1½	130*	Metal Case	1040	980	925	310	275	245	1.0"	4.7"	4½"
(13) 38 SUPER AUTO. COLT PISTOL	R38SU1	1½	115*	Jacketed H.P. (+P)†	1300	1147	1041	431	336	277	0.7"	3.3"	5"
	R38SUP	1½	130	Metal Case (+P)†	1280	1140	1050	475	375	320	0.8"	3.4"	5"
(14) 38 S. & W.	R38SW	1½	146*	Lead	685	650	620	150	135	125	2.4"	10.0"	4"
(15) 38 SPECIAL Vented Barrel	R38S1	1½	95	Semi-Jacketed H.P. (+P)†	1175	1044	959	291	230	194	0.9"	3.9"	4"
	R38S10	1½	110	Semi-Jacketed H.P. (+P)†	1020	945	887	254	218	192	1.1"	4.9"	4"
	R38S2	1½	125	Semi-Jacketed H.P. (+P)†	945	898	858	248	224	204	1.3"	5.4"	4"
	R38S3	1½	148	"Targetmaster" Lead W.C.	710	634	566	166	132	105	2.4"	10.8"	4"
	R38S4	1½	158	"Targetmaster" Lead	755	723	692	200	183	168	2.0"	8.3"	4"
	R38S5	1½	158*	Lead (Round Nose)	755	723	692	200	183	168	2.0"	8.3"	4"
	R38S6	1½	158	Semi-Wadcutter	755	723	692	200	183	168	2.0"	8.3"	4"
	R38S7	1½	158	Metal Point	755	723	692	200	183	168	2.0"	8.3"	4"
	R38S8	1½	158	Lead (+P)†	915	878	844	294	270	250	1.4"	5.6"	4"
	R38S12	1½	158	Lead H.P. (+ P)†	915	878	844	294	270	250	1.4"	5.6"	4"
	R38S9	1½	200	Lead	635	614	594	179	168	157	2.8"	11.5"	4"
(16) 38 SHORT COLT	R38SC	1½	125*	Lead	730	685	645	150	130	115	2.2"	9.4"	6"
(17) 41 REM. MAG. Vented Barrel	R41MG1	2½	210*	Soft Point	1300	1162	1062	788	630	526	0.7"	3.2"	4"
	R41MG2	2½	210	Lead	965	898	842	434	376	331	1.3"	5.4"	4"
(18) 44 REM. MAG. Vented Barrel	R44MG5	2½	180*	Semi-Jacketed H.P.	1610	1365	1175	1036	745	551	0.5"	2.3"	6"
	R44MG1	2½	240	Lead Gas Check	1350	1186	1069	971	749	608	0.7"	3.1"	4½"
	R44MG2	2½	240	Soft Point	1180	1081	1010	741	623	543	0.9"	3.7"	4½"
	R44MG3	2½	240	Semi-Jacketed H.P.	1180	1081	1010	741	623	543	0.9"	3.7"	4½"
	R44MG4	2½	240	Lead (Med. Vel.)	1000	947	902	533	477	433	1.1"	4.8"	4½"
(19) 44 S. & W. SPECIAL	R44SW	2½	246*	Lead	755	725	695	310	285	265	2.0"	8.3"	6½"
(20) 45 COLT	R45C	2½	250*	Lead	860	820	780	410	375	340	1.6"	6.6"	5½"
(21) 45 AUTO.	R45AP1	2½	185	Metal Case Wadcutter	770	707	650	244	205	174	2.0"	8.7"	5"
	R45AP2	2½	185*	Jacketed H.P.	940	890	846	363	325	294	1.3"	5.5"	5"
	R45AP4	2½	230	Metal Case	810	776	745	335	308	284	1.7"	7.2"	5"
(22) 45 AUTO. RIM	R45AR	2½	230*	Lead	810	770	730	335	305	270	1.8"	7.4"	5½"
Blank 38 S. & W.	R38SWBL	1½	– *	Blank	–	–	–	–	–	–	–	–	–
32 S. & W.	R32BLNK	5½	–	Blank	–	–	–	–	–	–	–	–	–
38 SPECIAL	R38BLNK	1½	–	Blank	–	–	–	–	–	–	–	–	–

†Ammunition with (+P) on the case headstamp is loaded to higher pressure. Use only in firearms designated for this cartridge and so recommended by the gun manufacturer.
*Illustrated (not shown in actual size).

REMINGTON RIMFIRE BALLISTICS

	Remington Order No.	Wt. Grs.	Bullet Style	Velocity—Ft. Per Second Muzzle	100 Yds.	Energy—Foot-Pounds Muzzle	100 Yds.	Mid-Range Trajectory 100 Yds. inches
"HYPER VELOCITY" 22 CARTRIDGES								
22 Long Rifle "Viper"	1922	36	Truncated Cone, Solid	1410	1056	159	89	3.1
22 Long Rifle "Yellow Jacket"	1722	33	Truncated Cone, Hollow Point	1500	1075	165	85	2.8
"HIGH VELOCITY" 22 CARTRIDGES								
22 Long Rifle	1522 1500†	40	Lead	1255	1017	140	92	3.6
	1622 1600†	36	Hollow Point	1280	1010	131	82	3.5
22 Long	1322	29	Lead	1240	962	99	60	3.9
22 Short	1022	29	Lead	1095	903	77	52	4.5
	1122	27	Hollow Point	1120	904	75	49	4.4
"TARGET" STANDARD VELOCITY 22 CARTRIDGES								
22 Long Rifle	6122 6100†	40	Lead	1150	976	117	85	4.0
22 Short	5522	29	Lead	1045	872	70	49	4.8

WEATHERBY BALLISTICS

Note: Any load having an average breech pressure of over 55,000 p.s.i. should not be used, and is shown for reference only. All ballistic data were compiled using Weatherby cartridge cases, Hornady or Nosler bullets and powder and primers as indicated. Loads shown with Norma powder are factory-equivalent loads. Other powders shown are DuPont IMR 3031, 4350 and 4064, and Hodgdon 4831. Velocities from 24" barrels for all calibers are approximately 90 fps less than those listed.

.224 WEATHERBY MAGNUM VARMINTMASTER

Primer: Federal #215   Overall cartridge length: 2⁵/₁₆"

Charge	Powder	Bullet	Muzzle Velocity in 26" Barrel	Avg. Breech Pressure	Muzzle Energy in Foot-Pounds
29.5 grs	3031	50 gr	3500-FPS	45,700-PSI	1360
30.0 grs	3031	50 gr	3560	47,500	1410
30.5 grs	3031	50 gr	3620	50,000	1455
31.0 grs	3031	50 gr	3670	52,000	1495
31.5 grs	3031	50 gr	3695	52,600	1515
32.0 grs	3031	50 gr	3740	55,200	1550
29.0 grs	3031	55 gr	3390	46,700	1405
29.5 grs	3031	55 gr	3450	48,000	1455
30.0 grs	3031	55 gr	3470	49,100	1470
30.5 grs	3031	55 gr	3525	53,200	1520
31.0 grs	3031	55 gr	3580	56,200	1570

WEATHERBY BALLISTICS

.240 WEATHERBY MAGNUM

Primer: Federal #215   Overall cartridge length: 3¹/₁₆″

Charge	Powder	Bullet	Muzzle Velocity in 26″ Barrel	Avg. Breech Pressure	Muzzle Energy in Foot-Pounds
53 grs	4350	70 gr	3684	48,530	2110
54 grs	4350	70 gr	3732	50,440	2163
55 grs	4350	70 gr	3780	52,270	2221
56 grs	4350	70 gr	3842	54,840	2293
55 grs	4831	70 grs	3533	44,680	1937
56 grs	4831	70 gr	3598	47,630	2011
57 grs	4831	70 gr	3708	52,070	2136
58.3 grs	Norma MRP	70 gr	3850	53,790	2304
54.1 grs	Norma MRP	87 gr	3500	53,420	2366
50 grs	4350	90 gr	3356	48,970	2246
51 grs	4350	90 gr	3424	51,270	2340
52 grs	4350	90 gr	3507	54,970	2453
53 grs	4831	90 gr	3325	48,630	2205
54 grs	4831	90 gr	3395	50,860	2299
55 grs	4831	90 gr	3451	52,410	2374
54.0 grs	Norma MRP	100 gr	3395	52,900	2560
49 grs	4350	100 gr	3223	50,680	2302
50 grs	4350	100 gr	3308	53,400	2425
51 grs	4350	100 gr	3367	56,190	2512
51 grs	4831	100 gr	3157	48,850	2208
52 grs	4831	100 gr	3222	50,950	2297
53 grs	4831	100 gr	3268	51,760	2370
54 grs	4831	100 gr	3362	54,740	2502

.257 WEATHERBY MAGNUM

Primer: Federal #215   Overall cartridge length: 3¹/₄″

Charge	Powder	Bullet	Muzzle Velocity in 26″ barrel	Avg. Breech Pressure	Muzzle Energy in Foot-Pounds
68 grs	4350	87 gr	3698	51,790	2644
69 grs	4350	87 gr	3715	53,270	2666
70 grs	4350	87 gr	3831	56,120	2835
69 grs	4831	87 gr	3521	44,750	2390
71 grs	4831	87 gr	3617	48,140	2532
73 grs	4831	87 gr	3751	52,470	2717
75 grs	4831	87 gr	3876	57,910	2901
74.1 grs	Norma MRP	87 gr	3825	50,700	2825
65 grs	4350	100 gr	3450	52,860	2638
66 grs	4350	100 gr	3520	54,860	2747
67 grs	4350	100 gr	3588	57,130	2857
66 grs	4831	100 gr	3315	43,640	2435
68 grs	4831	100 gr	3418	48,190	2593
70 grs	4831	100 gr	3543	53,410	2786
71 grs	4831	100 gr	3573	55,690	2833
71.3 grs	Norma MRP	100 gr	3555	51,730	2806
62 grs	4350	117 gr	3152	50,020	2573
64 grs	4350	117 gr	3262	54,860	2755
63 grs	4831	117 gr	3152	46,650	2573
65 grs	4831	117 gr	3213	48,520	2679
67 grs	4831	117 gr	3326	53,930	2867
67.1 grs	Norma MRP	117 gr	3300	53,050	2830

WEATHERBY BALLISTICS

.270 WEATHERBY MAGNUM

Primer: Federal #215   Overall cartridge length: 3¼"

Charge	Powder	Bullet	Muzzle Velocity in 26" Barrel	Avg. Breech Pressure	Muzzle Energy in Foot-Pounds
70 grs	4350	100 gr	3636	49,550	2934
72 grs	4350	100 gr	3764	54,540	3148
74 grs	4350	100 gr	3885	58,200	3353
74 grs	4831	100 gr	3492	43,800	2700
76 grs	4831	100 gr	3594	47,790	2865
77 grs	4831	100 gr	3654	50,940	2966
78 grs	4831	100 gr	3705	52,890	3048
77.2 grs	Norma MRP	100 gr	3760	51,400	3139
65 grs	4350	130 gr	3184	46,780	2922
66 grs	4350	130 gr	3228	49,130	3006
67 grs	4350	130 gr	3286	52,120	3108
68 grs	4350	130 gr	3345	55,210	3224
68 grs	4831	130 gr	3076	43,320	2730
70 grs	4831	130 gr	3178	47,600	2913
71 grs	4831	130 gr	3242	51,150	3024
72 grs	4831	130 gr	3301	52,980	3138
73 grs	4831	130 gr	3335	54,350	3206
74 grs	4831	130 gr	3375	56,520	3283
73.3 grs	Norma MRP	130 gr	3375	50,260	3285
65 grs	4350	150 gr	3085	52,120	3167
67 grs	4350	150 gr	3150	57,560	3299
66 grs	4831	150 gr	2920	46,470	2840
67 grs	4831	150 gr	2971	48,380	2939
68 grs	4831	150 gr	3014	50,580	3027
69 grs	4831	150 gr	3069	53,720	3140
70 grs	4831	150 gr	3124	56,960	3246
68.5 grs	Norma MRP	150 gr	3245	51,800	3508

7MM WEATHERBY MAGNUM

Primer: Federal #215   Overall cartridge length: 3¼"

Charge	Powder	Bullet	Muzzle Velocity in 26" Barrel	Avg. Breech Pressure	Muzzle Energy in Foot-Pounds
68 grs	4350	139 gr	3250	51,930	3254
69 grs	4350	139 gr	3308	54,310	3375
70 grs	4350	139 gr	3373	57,960	3500
72 grs	4831	139 gr	3147	45,990	3047
73 grs	4831	139 gr	3233	49,700	3223
74 grs	4831	139 gr	3291	52,570	3335
75 grs	4831	139 gr	3328	54,520	3417
74.1 grs	Norma MRP	139 gr	3300	50,300	3360
66 grs	4350	154 gr	3055	49,960	3191
67 grs	4350	154 gr	3141	54,500	3365
68 grs	4350	154 gr	3175	55,210	3439
70 grs	4831	154 gr	3013	46,940	3109
71 grs	4831	154 gr	3066	49,160	3212
72 grs	4831	154 gr	3151	53,010	3387
73 grs	4831	154 gr	3183	53,520	3462
71.0 grs	Norma MRP	154 gr	3160	51,250	3414
71.8 grs	Norma MRP	160 gr Nosler	3150	53,700	3525
71.0 grs	Norma MRP	*175 gr	3070	53,350	3662
63 grs	4350	*175 gr	2828	46,900	3112
65 grs	4350	*175 gr	2946	53,830	3369
68 grs	4831	*175 gr	2852	49,470	3157
69 grs	4831	*175 gr	2885	49,930	3234
70 grs	4831	*175 gr	2924	52,680	3323
71 grs	4831	*175 gr	2975	55,800	3439

*The 175 grain bullet is recommended for use only in 7mm W.M. rifles having 1 in 10" twist barrels.

WEATHERBY BALLISTICS

.300 WEATHERBY MAGNUM

Primer: Federal #215   Overall cartridge length: 3-9/16″

Charge	Powder	Bullet	Muzzle Velocity in 26″ Barrel	Avg. Breech Pressure	Muzzle Energy in Foot-Pounds
86 grs	4350	110 gr	3726	48,950	3390
88 grs	4350	110 gr	3798	51,180	3528
90 grs	4350	110 gr	3863	53,460	3649
81.0 grs	Norma 203	110 gr	3900	53,050	3714
82 grs	4350	130 gr	3488	49,540	3510
84 grs	4350	130 gr	3567	52,570	3663
86 grs	4350	130 gr	3627	54,730	3793
80 grs	4350	150 gr	3343	48,000	3710
82 grs	4350	150 gr	3458	52,380	3981
84 grs	4350	150 gr	3538	56,230	4167
84 grs	4831	150 gr	3305	47,620	3632
86 grs	4831	150 gr	3394	51,990	3831
88 grs	4831	150 gr	3470	54,570	4004
88.0 grs	Norma MRP	150 gr	3545	53,490	4185
77 grs	4350	180 gr	3066	50,830	3755
78 grs	4350	180 gr	3110	53,130	3857
79 grs	4350	180 gr	3145	53,610	3946
80 grs	4831	180 gr	3060	50,240	3742
82 grs	4831	180 gr	3145	54,310	3946
84 grs	4831	180 gr	3223	57,370	4147
81.8 grs	Norma MRP	180 gr	3245	51,800	4208
77.2 grs	Norma MRP	200 gr Nosler	3000	49,000	3996
76 grs	4831	200 gr Nosler	2858	46,480	3632
78 grs	4831	200 gr Nosler	2926	50,620	3800
80 grs	4831	200 gr Nosler	3029	54,690	4078
73 grs	4350	220 gr	2878	54,890	4052
75 grs	4350	220 gr	2926	56,510	4180
74 grs	4831	220 gr	2740	47,920	3667
76 grs	4831	220 gr	2800	51,060	3830
78 grs	4831	220 gr	2881	55,760	4052
77.2 grs	Norma MRP	220 gr	2905	52,850	4122

WEATHERBY BALLISTICS

.340 WEATHERBY MAGNUM

Primer: Federal #215   Overall cartridge length: 3-9/16"

Charge	Powder	Bullet	Muzzle Velocity in 26" Barrel	Avg. Breech Pressures	Muzzle Energy in Foot-Pounds
80 grs	4350	200 gr	3075	48,290	4200
82 grs	4350	200 gr	3151	53,180	4398
84 grs	4350	200 gr	3210	54,970	4566
84 grs	4831	200 gr	2933	43,240	3824
86 grs	4831	200 gr	3004	45,940	4012
88 grs	4831	200 gr	3066	48,400	4172
90 grs	4831	200 gr	3137	52,730	4356
91.0 grs	Norma MRP	200 gr	3210	50,185	4575
92.0 grs	Norma MRP	210 gr Nosler	3180	51,290	4714
84 grs	4350	210 gr Nosler	3115	51,450	4515
85 grs	4350	210 gr Nosler	3148	53,300	4618
86 grs	4350	210 gr Nosler	3172	54,960	4675
74 grs	4350	250 gr	2741	49,240	4168
76 grs	4350	250 gr	2800	51,370	4353
78 grs	4350	250 gr	2862	55,490	4540
80 grs	4831	250 gr	2686	44,970	4005
82 grs	4831	250 gr	2764	49,180	4243
84 grs	4831	250 gr	2835	53,370	4460
85 grs	4831	250 gr	2860	54,400	4540
86 grs	4831	250 gr	2879	55,500	4605
87 grs	4831	250 gr	2886	56,270	4623
84.9 grs	Norma MRP	250 gr	2850	49,600	4508

.378 WEATHERBY MAGNUM

Primer: Federal #215   Overall cartridge length: 3-11/16"

Caution: Use only the #215 primer in reloading the .378 W. M.

Charge	Powder	Bullet	Muzzle Velocity in 26" Barrel	Avg. Breech Pressure	Muzzle Energy in Foot-Pounds
106 grs	4350	270 gr	3015	44,800	5446
107 grs	4350	270 gr	3015	49,700	5713
108 grs	4350	270 gr	3112	54,620	5786
116 grs	4831	270 gr	3080	50,190	5689
117 grs	4831	270 gr	3102	50,930	5748
118 grs	4831	270 gr	3128	51,930	5862
101 grs	4350	300 gr	2831	49,500	5334
103 grs	4350	300 gr	2922	54,300	5679
110 grs	4831	300 gr	2897	51,050	5583
111 grs	4831	300 gr	2933	52,270	5736
112 grs	4831	300 gr	2958	53,410	5835

.460 WEATHERBY MAGNUM

Primer: Federal #215   Overall cartridge length: 3¾"

Caution: Use only the #215 primer in reloading the .460 W. M.

Charge	Powder	Bullet	Muzzle Velocity in 26" Barrel	Avg. Breech Pressure	Muzzle Energy in Foot-Pounds
115 grs	4350	500 gr	2513	44,400	6995
118 grs	4350	500 gr	2577	47,460	7390
120 grs	4350	500 gr	2601	48,330	7505
122 grs	4350	500 gr	2632	50,370	7680
124 grs	4350	500 gr	2678	52,980	7980
126 grs	4350	500 gr	2707	55,130	8155
102 grs	4064	500 gr	2486	49,000	6860
104 grs	4064	500 gr	2521	51,340	7050
106 grs	4064	500 gr	2552	53,280	7220
92 grs	3031	500 gr	2405	49,530	6420
94 grs	3031	500 gr	2426	50,170	6525
96 grs	3031	500 gr	2470	53,560	6775

WI. CHESTER-WESTER. CENTERFIRE PISTOL & REVOLVER BALLISTICS

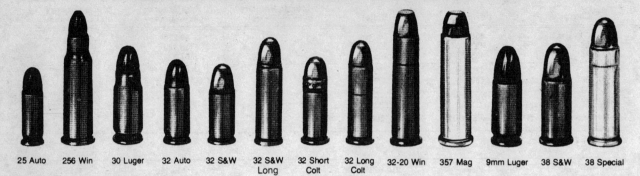

| 25 Auto | 256 Win | 30 Luger | 32 Auto | 32 S&W | 32 S&W Long | 32 Short Colt | 32 Long Colt | 32-20 Win | 357 Mag | 9mm Luger | 38 S&W | 38 Special |

CALIBER	BULLET WT. GRS.	TYPE	SYMBOL	PRIMER
25 Automatic (6.35mm)	50	FMC	X25AP	1½-108
256 Winchester Magnum Super-X	60	OPE(HP)	X2561P	6½-116
30 Luger (7.65mm)	93	FMC	X30LP	1½-108
32 Automatic	71	FMC	X32AP	1½-108
32 Automatic	60	STHP	X32ASHP	1½-108
32 Smith & Wesson (inside lubricated)	85	Lead	X32SWP	1½-108
32 Smith & Wesson Long (inside lubricated)	98	Lead	X32SWLP	1½-108
32 Short Colt (greased)	80	Lead	X32SCP	1½-108
32 Long Colt (inside lubricated)	82	Lead	X32LCP	1½-108
357 Magnum Jacketed Hollow Point Super-X	110	JHP	X3573P	1½-108
357 Magnum Jacketed Hollow Point Super-X	125	JHP	X3576P	1½-108
357 Magnum Super-X (inside lubricated)	158	Lead	X3571P	1½-108
357 Magnum Jacketed Hollow Point Super-X	158	JHP	X3574P	1½-108
357 Magnum Jacketed Soft Point Super-X	158	JSP	X3575P	1½-108
357 Magnum Metal Piercing Super-X (inside lubricated, lead bearing)	158	Met. Pierc.	X3572P	1½-108
9 mm Luger (Parabellum)	95	JSP	X9MMJSP	1½-108
9 mm Luger (Parabellum)	100	JHP	X9MMJHP	1½-108
9 mm Luger (Parabellum)	115	FMC	X9LP	1½-108
9 mm Luger (Parabellum)	115	STHP	X9MMSHP	1½-108
9 mm Winchester Magnum Super-X	115	FMC	X9MMWM	1½-108
38 Smith & Wesson (inside lubricated)	145	Lead	X38SWP	1½-108
38 Special (inside lubricated)	158	Lead	X38S1P	1½-108
38 Special Metal Point (inside lubricated, lead bearing)	158	Met. Pt.	X38S2P	1½-108
38 Special Super Police (inside lubricated)	200	Lead	X38S3P	1½-108
38 Special Super-X Jacketed Hollow Point +P	110	JHP	X38S6PH	1½-108
38 Special Super-X Jacketed Hollow Point +P	125	JHP	X38S7PH	1½-108
38 Special Super-X+P	95	STHP	X38SSHP	1½-108
38 Special Super-X (inside lubricated)+P	150	Lead	X38S4P	1½-108
38 Special Metal Piercing Super-X (inside lubricated, lead bearing) +P	150	Met. Pierc.	X38S5P	1½-108
38 Special Super-X (inside lubricated)+P	158	Lead-HP	X38SPD	1½-108
38 Special Super-X Semi-Wad Cutter (inside lubricated) +P	158	Lead-SWC	X38WCP	1½-108
38 Special Super-Match and Match Mid-Range Clean Cutting (inside lubricated)	148	Lead-WC	X38SMRP	1½-108
38 Special Super Match (inside lubricated)	158	Lead	X38SMP	1½-108
38 Short Colt (greased)	130	Lead	X38SCP	1½-108
38 Long Colt (inside lubricated)	150	Lead	X38LCP	1½-108
38 Automatic Super-X (For use only in 38 Colt Super and Colt Commander Automatic Pistols)	125	JHP	X38A3P	1½-108
38 Automatic Super-X +P (For use only in 38 Colt Super and Colt Commander Automatic Pistols)	130	FMC	X38A1P	1½-108
38 Automatic (For all 38 Colt Automatic Pistols)	130	FMC	X38A2P	1½-108
380 Automatic	95	FMC	X380AP	1½-108
380 Automatic	85	STHP	X380ASHP	1½-108
41 Remington Magnum Super-X (inside lubricated)	210	Lead	X41MP	7-111F
41 Remington Magnum Super-X Jacketed Soft Point	210	JSP	X41MJSP	7-111F
44 Smith & Wesson Special (inside lubricated)	246	Lead	X44SP	7-111
44 Remington Magnum Super-X (Gas Check) (inside lubricated)	240	Lead	X44MP	7-111F
45 Colt (inside lubricated)	255	Lead	X45CP	7-111
45 Automatic	185	STHP	X45ASHP	7-111
45 Automatic	230	FMC	X45A1P	7-111
45 Automatic Super-Match Clean Cutting	185	FMC-WC	X45AWCP	7-111
45 Winchester Magnum Super-X	230	FMC	X45WM	7-111

Met. Pierc.-Metal Piercing FMC-Full Metal Case SP-Soft Point JHP-Jacketed Hollow Point JSP-Jacketed Soft Point Met. Pt.-Metal Point
OPE-Open Point Expanding HP-Hollow Point PP-Power Point WC-Wad Cutter SWC-Semi Wad Cutter STHP-Silvertip Hollow Point
Specifications are nominal. Test barrels are used to determine ballistics figures. Individual firearms may differ from these test barrel statistics.

WINCHESTER-WESTERN CENTERFIRE PISTOL & REVOLVER BALLISTICS

38 Special S.M.   38 Short Colt   38 Long Colt   38 Auto   380 Auto   38-40 Win   41 Rem Mag.   44 S&W   44 Rem Mag.   44-40 Win   45 Colt   45 Auto   45 Auto S.M.

| VELOCITY-FPS | | | ENERGY FT-LBS. | | | MID-RANGE TRAJECTORY INCHES | | BARREL LENGTH INCHES |
MUZZLE	50 YDS.	100 YDS.	MUZZLE	50 YDS.	100 YDS.	50 YDS.	100 YDS.	
810	755	700	73	63	54	1.8	7.7	2
2350	2030	1760	735	550	415	0.3	1.1	8½
1220	1110	1040	305	255	225	0.9	3.5	4½
905	855	810	129	115	97	1.4	5.8	4
970	895	835	125	107	93	1.3	5.4	4
680	645	610	90	81	73	2.5	10.5	3
705	670	635	115	98	88	2.3	10.5	4
745	665	590	100	79	62	2.2	9.9	4
755	715	675	100	93	83	2.0	8.7	4
1295	1094	975	410	292	232	0.8	3.5	4 V
1450	1240	1090	583	427	330	0.6	2.8	4 V
1235	1104	1015	535	428	361	0.8	3.5	4 V
1235	1104	1015	535	428	361	0.8	3.5	4 V
1235	1104	1015	535	428	361	0.8	3.5	4 V
1235	1104	1015	535	428	361	0.8	3.5	4 V
1355	1140	1008	387	274	214	0.7	3.3	4
1320	1114	991	387	275	218	0.7	3.4	4
1155	1047	971	341	280	241	0.9	3.9	4
1225	1095	1007	383	306	259	0.8	3.6	4
1475	1264	1109	556	408	314	0.6	2.7	5
685	650	620	150	135	125	2.4	10.0	4
755	723	693	200	183	168	2.0	8.3	4 V
755	723	693	200	183	168	2.0	8.3	4 V
635	614	594	179	168	157	2.8	11.5	4 V
1020	945	887	254	218	192	1.1	4.8	4 V
945	898	858	248	224	204	1.3	5.4	4 V
1100	1002	932	255	212	183	1.0	4.3	4 V
910	870	835	276	252	232	1.4	5.7	4 V
910	870	835	276	252	232	1.4	5.7	4 V
915	878	844	294	270	250	1.4	5.6	4 V
915	878	844	294	270	250	1.4	5.6	4 V
710	634	566	166	132	105	2.4	10.8	4 V
755	723	693	200	183	168	2.0	8.3	4 V
730	685	645	150	130	115	2.2	9.4	6
730	700	670	175	165	150	2.1	8.8	6
1245	1105	1010	430	340	285	0.8	3.6	5
1280	1140	1050	475	375	320	0.8	3.4	5
1040	980	925	310	275	245	1.0	4.7	4½
955	865	785	190	160	130	1.4	5.9	3¾
1000	921	860	189	160	140	1.2	5.1	3¾
965	898	842	434	376	331	1.3	5.4	4 V
1300	1162	1062	788	630	526	0.7	3.2	4 V
755	725	695	310	285	265	2.0	8.3	6½
1350	1186	1069	971	749	608	0.7	3.1	4 V
860	820	780	420	380	345	1.5	6.1	5½
1000	938	888	411	362	324	1.2	4.9	5
810	776	745	335	308	284	1.7	7.2	5
770	707	650	244	205	174	2.0	8.7	5
1400	1232	1107	1001	775	636	0.6	2.8	5

+P Ammunition with (+P) on the case head stamp is loaded to higher pressure. Use only in firearms designated for this cartridge and so recommended by the gun manufacturer.

V-Data is based on velocity obtained from 4″ vented barrels for revolver cartridges (38 Special, 357 Magnum, 41 Rem. Mag. and 44 Rem. Mag.) and unvented (solid) test barrels of the length specified for 9mm and 45 auto pistols.

WINCHESTER-WESTERN CENTERFIRE RIFLE BALLISTICS

218 Bee 22 Hornet 22-250 Rem 222 Rem 223 Rem 225 Win 243 Win 6 MM Rem 25-06 Rem 25-20 Win 25-35 Win 250 Savage

WINCHESTER FIREARM SELECTOR	CARTRIDGE	GAME SELECTOR GUIDE	BULLET WT. GRS.	BULLET TYPE	SYMBOL	PRIMER	BARREL LENGTH INCHES	MUZZLE	VELOCITY IN FEET PER SECOND 100	200	300 YARDS	400	500
	218 Bee Super-X	S	46	OPE(HP)	X218B	6½-116	24	2760	2102	1550	1155	961	850
	22 Hornet Super-X	S	45	SP	X22H1	6½-116	24	2690	2042	1502	1128	948	840
	22 Hornet Super-X	S	46	OPE(HP)	X22H2	6½-116	24	2690	2042	1502	1128	948	841
■□	22-250 Remington Super-X	S	55	PSP	X222501	8½-120	24	3730	3180	2695	2257	1863	1519
■□	222 Remington Super-X	S	50	PSP	X222R	6½-116	24	3140	2602	2123	1700	1350	1107
■□	222 Remington Super-X	S	55	FMC	X222R1	6½-116	24	3020	2675	2355	2057	1783	1537
	223 Remington Super-X	S	55	PSP	X223R	6½-116	24	3240	2747	2304	1905	1554	1270
	223 Remington Super-X	S	55	FMC	X223R1	6½-116	24	3240	2877	2543	2232	1943	1679
	225 Winchester Super-X	S	55	PSP	X2251	8½-120	24	3570	3066	2616	2208	1838	1514
■□	243 Winchester Super-X	S	80	PSP	X2431	8½-120	24	3350	2955	2593	2259	1951	1670
■□	243 Winchester Super-X	D,O/P	100	PP(SP)	X2432	8½-120	24	2960	2697	2449	2215	1993	1786
	6 MM Remington Super-X	S	80	PSP	X6MMR1	8½-120	24	3470	3064	2694	2352	2036	1747
	6 MM Remington Super-X	D,O/P	100	PP(SP)	X6MMR2	8½-120	24	3130	2857	2600	2357	2127	1911
■	25-06 Remington Super-X	S	90	PEP	X25061	8½-120	24	3440	3043	2680	2344	2034	1749
■	25-06 Remington Super-X	D,O/P	120	PEP	X25062	8½-120	24	3010	2749	2502	2269	2048	1840
	25-20 Winchester	S	86	SP	X25202	6½-116	24	1460	1194	1030	931	858	798
	25-20 Winchester	S	86	Lead	X25201	6½-116	24	1460	1194	1030	931	858	798
	25-35 Winchester Super-X	D	117	SP	X2535	8½-120	24	2230	1866	1545	1282	1097	984
	250 Savage Super-X	S	87	PSP	X2501	8½-120	24	3030	2673	2342	2036	1755	1504
	250 Savage Super-X	D,O/P	100	ST	X2503	8½-120	24	2820	2467	2140	1839	1569	1339
	256 Winchester Mag. Super-X	S	60	OPE(HP)	X2561P	6½-116	24	2760	2097	1542	1149	957	846
	257 Roberts Super-X	S	87	PSP	X2571	8½-120	24	3170	2802	2462	2147	1857	1594
	257 Roberts Super-X	D,O/P	100	ST	X2572	8½-120	24	2900	2541	2210	1904	1627	1387
	257 Roberts Super-X	D,O/P	117	PP(SP)	X2573	8½-120	24	2650	2291	1961	1663	1404	1199
•	264 Winchester Mag. Super-X	S	100	PSP	X2641	8½-120	24	3320	2926	2565	2231	1923	1644
•	264 Winchester Mag. Super-X	D,O/P	140	PP(SP)	X2642	8½-120	24	3030	2782	2548	2326	2114	1914
■	270 Winchester Super-X	S	100	PSP	X2701	8½-120	24	3480	3067	2690	2343	2023	1730
■	270 Winchester Super-X	D,O/P	130	PP(SP)	X2705	8½-120	24	3110	2849	2604	2371	2150	1941
■	270 Winchester Super-X	D,O/P	130	ST	X2703	8½-120	24	3110	2823	2554	2300	2061	1837
	270 Winchester Super-X	D,L	150	PP(SP)	X2704	8½-120	24	2900	2632	2380	2142	1918	1709
	284 Winchester Super-X	D,O/P	125	PP(SP)	X2841	8½-120	24	3140	2829	2538	2265	2010	1772
	284 Winchester Super-X	D,O/P,L	150	PP(SP)	X2842	8½-120	24	2860	2595	2344	2108	1886	1680
	7 MM Mauser (7x57) Super-X	D	175	SP	X7MM	8½-120	24	2440	2137	1857	1603	1382	1204
•	7 MM Remington Mag. Super-X	D,O/P	125	PP(SP)	X7MMR3	8½-120	24	3310	2976	2666	2376	2105	1852
•	7 MM Remington Mag. Super-X	D,O/P	150	PP(SP)	X7MMR1	8½-120	24	3110	2830	2568	2320	2085	1866
•	7 MM Remington Mag. Super-X	D,O/P,L	175	PP(SP)	X7MMR2	8½-120	24	2860	2645	2440	2244	2057	1879
	30 Carbine	S	110	HSP	X30M1	6½-116	20	1990	1567	1236	1035	923	842
	30 Carbine	S	110	FMC	X30M2	6½-116	20	1990	1596	1278	1070	952	870
★	30-30 Winchester Super-X	D	150	OPE	X30301	8½-120	24	2390	2018	1684	1398	1177	1036
★	30-30 Winchester Super-X	D	150	PP(SP)	X30306	8½-120	24	2390	2018	1684	1398	1177	1036
★	30-30 Winchester Super-X	D	150	ST	X30302	8½-120	24	2390	2018	1684	1398	1177	1036
★	30-30 Winchester Super-X	D	170	PP(SP)	X30303	8½-120	24	2200	1895	1619	1381	1191	1061
★	30-30 Winchester Super-X	D	170	ST	X30304	8½-120	24	2200	1895	1619	1381	1191	1061
	30 Remington Super-X	D	170	ST	X30R2	8½-120	24	2120	1822	1555	1328	1153	1036
■	30-06 Springfield Super-X	S	110	PSP	X30060	8½-120	24	3380	2843	2365	1936	1561	1261
■	30-06 Springfield Super-X	S	125	PSP	X30062	8½-120	24	3140	2780	2447	2138	1853	1595
■	30-06 Springfield Super-X	D,O/P	150	PP(SP)	X30061	8½-120	24	2920	2580	2265	1972	1704	1466
■	30-06 Springfield Super-X	D,O/P	150	ST	X30063	8½-120	24	2910	2617	2342	2083	1843	1622
■	30-06 Springfield Super-X	D,O/P,L	180	PP(SP)	X30064	8½-120	24	2700	2348	2023	1727	1466	1251
■	30-06 Springfield Super-X	D,O/P,L	180	ST	X30066	8½-120	24	2700	2469	2250	2042	1846	1663
■	30-06 Springfield Super-X	L	220	PP(SP)	X30068	8½-120	24	2410	2130	1870	1632	1422	1246
■	30-06 Springfield Super-X	L	220	ST	X30069	8½-120	24	2410	2192	1985	1791	1611	1448

WINCHESTER FIREARMS SELECTOR CODE

■ = Models 70 XTR & 70A XTR   • = Models 70 XTR Magnum   ★ = Model 94   S = Small game

□ = Model 70 XTR Varmint   o = Model 70A XTR Magnum   D = Deer

GAME SELECTOR CODE

O/P = Open or Plains shooting (i.e. Antelope, Deer)

L = Large game (i.e. Moose, Elk)

XL = Extra Large game (i.e. Kodiak bear)

WINCHESTER-WESTERN CENTERFIRE RIFLE BALLISTICS

256 Win 257 Roberts 264 Win 270 Win 284 Win 7 MM Mauser 7 MM Rem Mag. 30 Carbine 30-30 Win 30 Rem 30-06 Springfield

TRAJECTORY Inches above (+) or below (-) line of sight 0 = Indicates yardage at which rifle is sighted in.

| ENERGY IN FOOT POUNDS | | | | | | SHORT RANGE | | | | | | LONG RANGE | | | | | | |
MUZZLE	100	200	300 YARDS	400	500	50	100	150	200 YARDS	250	300	100	150	200	250 YARDS	300	400	500
778	451	245	136	94	74	0.3	0	-2.3	-7.2	-15.8	-29.4	1.5	0	-4.2	-12.0	-24.8	-71.4	-155.6
723	417	225	127	90	70	0.3	0	-2.4	-7.7	-16.9	-31.3	1.6	0	-4.5	-12.8	-26.4	-75.6	-163.4
739	426	230	130	92	72	0.3	0	-2.4	-7.7	-16.9	-31.3	1.6	0	-4.5	-12.8	-26.4	-75.5	-163.3
1699	1235	887	622	424	282	0.2	0.5	0	-1.5	-4.3	-8.4	2.2	2.6	1.9	0	-3.3	-15.4	-37.7
1094	752	500	321	202	136	0.5	0.9	0	-2.5	-6.9	-13.7	2.2	1.9	0	-3.8	-10.0	-32.3	-73.8
1114	874	677	517	388	288	0.5	0.9	0	-2.2	-6.1	-11.7	2.0	1.7	0	-3.3	-8.3	-24.9	-52.5
1282	921	648	443	295	197	0.4	0.8	0	-2.2	-6.0	-11.8	1.9	1.6	0	-3.3	-8.5	-26.7	-59.6
1282	1011	790	608	461	344	0.4	0.7	0	-1.9	-5.1	-9.9	1.7	1.4	0	-2.8	-7.1	-21.2	-44.6
1556	1148	836	595	412	280	0.2	0.6	0	-1.7	-4.6	-9.0	2.4	2.8	2.0	0	-3.5	-16.3	-39.5
1993	1551	1194	906	676	495	0.3	0.7	0	-1.8	-4.9	-9.4	2.6	2.9	2.1	0	-3.6	-16.2	-37.9
1945	1615	1332	1089	882	708	0.5	0.9	0	-2.2	-5.8	-11.0	1.9	1.6	0	-3.1	-7.8	-22.6	-46.3
2139	1667	1289	982	736	542	0.3	0.6	0	-1.6	-4.5	-8.7	2.4	2.7	1.9	0	-3.3	-14.9	-35.0
2175	1812	1501	1233	1004	811	0.4	0.7	0	-1.9	-5.1	-9.7	1.7	1.4	0	-2.7	-6.8	-20.0	-40.8
2364	1850	1435	1098	827	611	0.3	0.6	0	-1.7	-4.5	-8.8	2.4	2.7	2.0	0	-3.4	-15.0	-35.2
2414	2013	1668	1372	1117	902	0.5	0.8	0	-2.1	-5.5	-10.5	1.9	1.6	0	-2.9	-7.4	-21.6	-44.2
407	272	203	165	141	122	0	-4.1	-14.4	-31.8	-57.3	-92.0	0	-8.2	-23.5	-47.0	-79.6	-175.9	-319.4
407	272	203	165	141	122	0	-4.1	-14.4	-31.8	-57.3	-92.0	0	-8.2	-23.5	-47.0	-79.6	-175.9	-319.4
1292	904	620	427	313	252	0.6	0	-3.1	-9.2	-19.0	-33.1	2.1	0	-5.1	-13.8	-27.0	-70.1	-142.0
1773	1380	1059	801	595	437	0.5	0.9	0	-2.3	-6.1	-11.8	2.0	1.7	0	-3.3	-8.4	-25.2	-53.4
1765	1351	1017	751	547	398	0.2	0	-1.6	-4.9	-10.0	-17.4	2.4	2.0	0	-3.9	-10.1	-30.5	-65.2
1015	586	317	176	122	95	0.3	0	-2.3	-7.3	-15.9	-29.6	1.5	0	-4.2	-12.1	-25.0	-72.1	-157.2
1941	1516	1171	890	666	491	0.4	0.8	0	-2.0	-5.5	-10.6	1.8	1.5	0	-3.0	-7.5	-22.7	-48.0
1867	1433	1084	805	588	427	0.6	1.0	0	-2.5	-6.9	-13.2	2.3	1.9	0	-3.7	-9.4	-28.6	-60.9
1824	1363	999	718	512	373	0.3	0	-1.9	-5.8	-11.9	-20.7	2.9	2.4	0	-4.7	-12.0	-36.7	-79.2
2447	1901	1461	1105	821	600	0.3	0.7	0	-1.8	-5.0	-9.7	2.7	3.0	2.2	0	-3.7	-16.6	-38.9
2854	2406	2018	1682	1389	1139	0.5	0.8	0	-2.0	-5.4	-10.2	1.8	1.5	0	-2.9	-7.2	-20.8	-42.2
2689	2088	1606	1219	909	664	0.3	0.6	0	-1.6	-4.5	-8.7	2.4	2.7	1.9	0	-3.3	-15.0	-35.2
2791	2343	1957	1622	1334	1087	0.4	0.7	0	-1.9	-5.1	-9.7	1.7	1.4	0	-2.7	-6.8	-19.9	-40.5
2791	2300	1883	1527	1226	974	0.4	0.8	0	-2.0	-5.3	-10.0	1.7	1.5	0	-2.8	-7.1	-20.8	-42.7
2801	2307	1886	1528	1225	973	0.6	0.9	0	-2.3	-6.1	-11.7	2.1	1.7	0	-3.3	-8.2	-24.1	-49.4
2736	2221	1788	1424	1121	871	0.4	0.8	0	-2.0	-5.3	-10.1	1.7	1.5	0	-2.8	-7.2	-21.1	-43.7
2724	2243	1830	1480	1185	940	0.6	1.0	0	-2.4	-6.3	-12.1	1.7	1.8	0	-3.4	-8.5	-24.8	-51.0
2313	1774	1340	998	742	563	0.4	0	-2.3	-6.8	-13.8	-23.7	1.5	0	-3.7	-10.0	-19.1	-48.1	-95.4
3040	2458	1972	1567	1230	952	0.3	0.6	0	-1.7	-4.7	-9.1	2.5	2.8	2.0	0	-3.4	-15.0	-34.5
3221	2667	2196	1792	1448	1160	0.4	0.8	0	-1.9	-5.2	-9.9	1.7	1.5	0	-2.8	-7.0	-20.5	-42.1
3178	2718	2313	1956	1644	1372	0.6	0.9	0	-2.3	-6.0	-11.3	2.0	1.7	0	-3.2	-7.9	-22.7	-45.8
967	600	373	262	208	173	0.9	0	-4.5	-13.5	-28.3	-49.9	0	-4.5	-13.5	-28.3	-49.9	-118.6	-228.2
967	622	399	280	221	185	0.9	0	-4.3	-13.0	-26.9	-47.4	2.9	0	-7.2	-19.7	-38.7	-100.4	-200.5
1902	1356	944	651	461	357	0.5	0	-2.6	-7.7	-16.0	-27.9	1.7	0	-4.3	-11.6	-22.7	-59.1	-120.5
1902	1356	944	651	461	357	0.5	0	-2.6	-7.7	-16.0	-27.9	1.7	0	-4.3	-11.6	-22.7	-59.1	-120.5
1902	1356	944	651	461	357	0.5	0	-2.6	-7.7	-16.0	-27.9	1.7	0	-4.3	-11.6	-22.7	-59.1	-120.5
1827	1355	989	720	535	425	0.6	0	-3.0	-8.9	-18.0	-31.1	2.0	0	-4.8	-13.0	-25.1	-63.6	-126.7
1827	1355	989	720	535	425	0.6	0	-3.0	-8.9	-18.0	-31.1	2.0	0	-4.8	-13.0	-25.1	-63.6	-126.7
1696	1253	913	666	502	405	0.7	0	-3.3	-9.7	-19.6	-33.8	2.2	0	-5.3	-14.1	-27.2	-69.0	-136.9
2790	1974	1366	915	595	388	0.4	0.7	0	-2.0	-5.6	-11.1	1.7	1.5	0	-3.1	-8.0	-25.5	-57.4
2736	2145	1662	1269	953	706	0.4	0.8	0	-2.1	-5.6	-10.7	1.8	1.5	0	-3.0	-7.7	-23.0	-48.5
2839	2217	1708	1295	967	716	0.6	1.0	0	-2.4	-6.6	-12.7	2.2	1.8	0	-3.5	-9.0	-27.0	-57.1
2820	2281	1827	1445	1131	876	0.6	0.9	0	-2.3	-6.3	-12.0	2.1	1.8	0	-3.3	-8.5	-25.0	-51.8
2913	2203	1635	1192	859	603	0.2	0	-1.8	-5.5	-11.2	-19.5	2.7	2.3	0	-4.4	-11.3	-34.4	-73.7
2913	2436	2023	1666	1362	1105	0.2	0	-1.6	-4.8	-9.7	-16.5	2.4	2.0	0	-3.7	-9.3	-27.0	-54.9
2837	2216	1708	1301	988	758	0.4	0	-2.3	-6.8	-13.8	-23.6	1.5	0	-3.7	-9.9	-19.0	-47.4	-93.1
2837	2347	1924	1567	1268	1024	0.4	0	-2.2	-6.4	-12.7	-21.6	1.5	0	-3.5	-9.1	-17.2	-41.8	-79.9

HSP-Hollow Soft Point PEP-Positive Expanding Point PSP-Pointed Soft Point PP(SP)-Power-Point Soft Point
FMC-Full Metal Case SP-Soft Point HP-Hollow Point OPE-Open Point Expanding ST-Silvertip
Specifications are nominal. Test barrels are used to determine ballistics figures. Individual firearms may differ from these test barrel statistics.

WINCHESTER-WESTERN CENTERFIRE RIFLE BALLISTICS

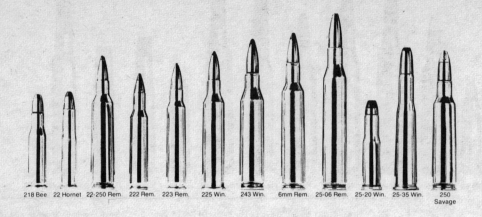

218 Bee | 22 Hornet | 22-250 Rem. | 222 Rem. | 223 Rem. | 225 Win. | 243 Win. | 6mm Rem. | 25-06 Rem. | 25-20 Win. | 25-35 Win. | 250 Savage

WINCHESTER FIREARM SELECTOR	CARTRIDGE	GAME SELECTOR GUIDE	BULLET WT. GRS.	BULLET TYPE	SYMBOL	PRIMER	BARREL LENGTH INCHES	MUZZLE	100	200	300 YARDS	400	500
	30-40 Krag Super-X	D	180	PP(SP)	X30401	8½-120	24	2430	2099	1795	1525	1298	1128
	30-40 Krag Super-X	D	180	ST	X30403	8½-120	24	2430	2213	2007	1813	1632	1468
	30-40 Krag Super-X	L	220	ST	X30404	8½-120	24	2160	1956	1765	1587	1427	1287
• 0	300 Winchester Mag. Super-X	D,0/P	150	PP(SP)	X30WM1	8½-120	24	3290	2951	2636	2342	2068	1813
• 0	300 Winchester Mag. Super-X	0/P,L	180	PP(SP)	X30WM2	8½-120	24	2960	2745	2540	2344	2157	1979
• 0	300 Winchester Mag. Super-X	L,XL	220	ST	X30WM3	8½-120	24	2680	2448	2228	2020	1823	1640
	300 H.&H. Magnum Super-X	0/P	150	ST	X300H1	8½-120	24	3130	2822	2534	2264	2011	1776
	300 H.&H. Magnum Super-X	0/P,L	180	ST	X300H2	8½-120	24	2880	2640	2412	2196	1991	1798
	300 H.&H. Magnum Super-X	L,XL	220	ST	X300H3	8½-120	24	2580	2341	2114	1901	1702	1520
	300 Savage Super-X	D,0/P	150	PP(SP)	X3001	8½-120	24	2630	2311	2015	1743	1500	1295
	300 Savage Super-X	D,0/P	150	ST	X3003	8½-120	24	2630	2354	2095	1853	1631	1434
	300 Savage Super-X	D	180	PP(SP)	X3004	8½-120	24	2350	2025	1728	1467	1252	1098
	300 Savage Super-X	D	180	ST	X3005	8½-120	24	2350	2137	1935	1745	1570	1413
	303 Savage Super-X	D	190	ST	X3032	8½-120	24	1940	1657	1410	1211	1073	982
	303 British Super-X	D	180	PP(SP)	X303B1	8½-120	24	2460	2233	2018	1816	1629	1459
■	308 Winchester Super-X	S	110	PSP	X3081	8½-120	24	3180	2666	2206	1795	1444	1178
■	308 Winchester Super-X	S	125	PSP	X3087	8½-120	24	3050	2697	2370	2067	1788	1537
■	308 Winchester Super-X	D,0/P	150	PP(SP)	X3085	8½-120	24	2820	2488	2179	1893	1633	1405
■	308 Winchester Super-X	D,0/P	150	ST	X3082	8½-120	24	2820	2533	2263	2009	1774	1560
■	308 Winchester Super-X	D,0/P,L	180	PP(SP)	X3086	8½-120	24	2620	2274	1955	1666	1414	1212
■	308 Winchester Super-X	D,0/P,L	180	ST	X3083	8½-120	24	2620	2393	2178	1974	1782	1604
■	308 Winchester Super-X	L	200	ST	X3084	8½-120	24	2450	2208	1980	1767	1572	1397
	32 Win. Special Super-X	D	170	PP(SP)	X32WS2	8½-120	24	2250	1870	1537	1267	1082	971
	32 Win. Special Super-X	D	170	ST	X32WS3	8½-120	24	2250	1870	1537	1267	1082	971
	32 Remington Super-X	D	170	ST	X32R2	8½-120	24	2140	1785	1475	1228	1064	963
	32-20 Winchester	S	100	SP	X32202	6½-116	24	1210	1021	913	834	769	712
	32-20 Winchester	S	100	Lead	X32201	6½-116	24	1210	1021	913	834	769	712
	8mm Mauser (8x57) Super-X	D	170	PP(SP)	X8MM	8½-120	24	2360	1969	1622	1333	1123	997
•	338 Winchester Mag. Super-X	D,0/P	200	PP(SP)	X3381	8½-120	24	2960	2658	2375	2110	1862	1635
•	338 Winchester Mag. Super-X	L,XL	225	SP	X3383	8½-120	24	2180	2572	2374	2184	2003	1832
•	338 Winchester Mag. Super-X	L,XL	250	ST	X3382	8½-120	24	2660	2395	2145	1910	1693	1497
	348 Winchester Super-X	D,L	200	ST	X3482	8½-120	24	2520	2215	1931	1672	1443	1253
	35 Remington Super-X	D	200	PP(SP)	X35R1	8½-120	24	2020	1646	1335	1114	985	901
	35 Remington Super-X	D	200	ST	X35R3	8½-120	24	2020	1646	1335	1114	985	901
	351 Winchester S.L.	D	180	SP	X351SL2	6½-116	20	1850	1556	1310	1128	1012	933
	358 Winchester Super-X	D,L	200	ST	X3581	8½-120	24	2490	2171	1876	1610	1379	1194
	358 Winchester Super-X	L	250	ST	X3582	8½-120	24	2230	1988	1762	1557	1375	1224
★	375 Winchester	D,L	200	PP(SP)	X375W	8½-120	24	2200	1841	1526	1268	1089	980
★	375 Winchester	D,L	250	PP(SP)	X375W1	8½-120	24	1900	1647	1424	1239	1103	1011
•	375 H.&H. Magnum Super-X	L,XL	270	PP(SP)	X375H1	8½-120	24	2690	2420	2166	1928	1707	1507
•	375 H.&H. Magnum Super-X	L,XL	300	ST	X375H2	8½-120	24	2530	2268	2022	1793	1583	1397
•	375 H.&H. Magnum Super-X	L,XL	300	FMC	X375H3	8½-120	24	2530	2171	1843	1551	1307	1126
	38-40 Winchester	D	180	SP	X3840	7-111	24	1160	999	901	827	764	710
★	38-55 Winchester	D	255	SP	X3855	8½-120	24	1320	1190	1091	1018	963	917
	44 Remington Magnum Super-X	D	240	HSP	X44MHSP	7M-111F	20	1760	1362	1094	953	861	789
	44-40 Winchester	D	200	SP	X4440	7-111	24	1190	1006	900	822	756	699
	45-70 Government	D,L	405	SP	X4570	8½-120	24	1330	1168	1055	977	918	869
•	458 Winchester Mag. Super-X	XL	500	FMC	X4580	8½-120	24	2040	1823	1623	1442	1287	1161
•	458 Winchester Mag. Super-X	L,XL	510	SP	X4581	8½-120	24	2040	1770	1527	1319	1157	1046

WINCHESTER FIREARMS SELECTOR CODE

■ = Models 70 XTR   • = Models 70 XTR Magnum   ★ = Model 94

□ = Model 70 XTR Varmint

WINCHESTER-WESTERN CENTERFIRE RIFLE BALLISTICS

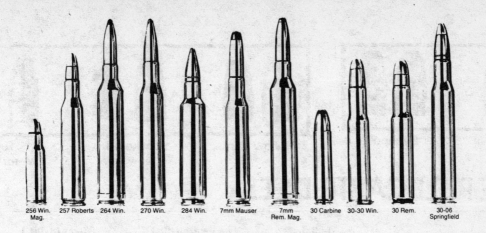

256 Win. Mag.   257 Roberts   264 Win.   270 Win.   284 Win.   7mm Mauser   7mm Rem. Mag.   30 Carbine   30-30 Win.   30 Rem.   30-06 Springfield

TRAJECTORY Inches above (+) or below (-) line of sight 0 = Indicates yardage at which rifle is sighted in.

| ENERGY IN FOOT POUNDS | | | | | | SHORT RANGE | | | | | | LONG RANGE | | | | | | |
MUZZLE	100	200	300 YARDS	400	500	50	100	150	200 YARDS	250	300	100	150	200 250 YARDS	300	400	500	
2360	1761	1288	929	673	508	0.4	0	-2.4	-7.1	-14.5	-25.0	1.6	0	-3.9	-10.5	-20.3	-51.7	-103.9
2360	1957	1610	1314	1064	861	0.4	0	-2.1	-6.2	-12.5	-21.1	1.4	0	-3.4	-8.9	-16.8	-40.9	-78.1
2279	1869	1522	1230	995	809	0.6	0	-2.9	-8.2	-16.4	-27.6	1.9	0	-4.4	-11.6	-21.9	-53.3	-101.8
3605	2900	2314	1827	1424	1095	0.3	0.7	0	-1.8	-4.8	-9.3	2.6	2.9	2.1	0	-3.5	-15.4	-35.5
3501	3011	2578	2196	1859	1565	0.5	0.8	0	-2.2	-5.5	-10.4	1.9	1.6	0	-2.9	-7.3	-20.9	-41.9
3508	2927	2424	1993	1623	1314	0.2	0	-1.7	-4.9	-9.9	-16.9	2.5	2.0	0	-3.8	-9.5	-27.5	-56.1
3262	2652	2138	1707	1347	1050	0.4	0.8	0	-2.0	-5.3	-10.1	1.7	1.5	0	-2.8	-7.2	-21.2	-43.8
3315	2785	2325	1927	1584	1292	0.6	0.9	0	-2.3	-6.0	-11.5	2.1	1.7	0	-3.2	-8.0	-23.3	-47.4
3251	2677	2183	1765	1415	1128	0.3	0	-1.9	-5.5	-11.0	-18.7	2.7	2.2	0	-4.2	-10.5	-30.7	-63.0
2303	1779	1352	1012	749	558	0.3	0	-1.9	-5.7	-11.6	-19.9	2.8	2.3	0	-4.5	-11.5	-34.4	-73.0
2303	1845	1462	1143	886	685	0.3	0	-1.8	-5.4	-11.0	-18.8	2.7	2.2	0	-4.2	-10.7	-31.5	-65.5
2207	1639	1193	860	626	482	0.5	0	-2.6	-7.7	-15.6	-27.1	1.7	0	-4.2	-11.3	-21.9	-55.8	-112.0
2207	1825	1496	1217	985	798	0.4	0	-2.3	-6.7	-13.5	-22.8	1.5	0	-3.6	-9.6	-18.2	-44.1	-84.2
1588	1158	839	619	486	407	0.9	0	-4.1	-11.9	-24.1	-41.4	2.7	0	-6.4	-17.3	-33.2	-83.7	-164.4
2418	1993	1627	1318	1060	851	0.3	0	-2.1	-6.1	-12.2	-20.8	1.4	0	-3.3	-8.8	-16.6	-40.4	-77.4
2470	1736	1188	787	509	339	0.5	0.9	0	-2.3	-6.5	-12.8	2.0	1.8	0	-3.5	-9.3	-29.5	-66.7
2582	2019	1559	1186	887	656	0.5	0.8	0	-2.2	-6.0	-11.5	2.0	1.7	0	-3.2	-8.2	-24.6	-51.9
2648	2061	1581	1193	888	657	0.2	0	-1.6	-4.8	-9.8	-16.9	2.4	2.0	0	-3.8	-9.8	-29.3	-62.0
2648	2137	1705	1344	1048	810	0.2	0	-1.5	-4.5	-9.3	-15.9	2.3	1.9	0	-3.6	-9.1	-26.9	-55.7
2743	2066	1527	1109	799	587	0.3	0	-2.0	-5.9	-12.1	-20.9	2.9	2.4	0	-4.7	-12.1	-36.9	-79.1
2743	2288	1896	1557	1269	1028	0.2	0	-1.8	-5.2	-10.4	-17.7	2.6	2.1	0	-4.0	-9.9	-28.9	-58.8
2665	2165	1741	1386	1097	867	0.4	0	-2.1	-6.3	-12.6	-21.4	1.4	0	-3.4	-9.0	-17.2	-42.1	-81.1
1911	1320	892	606	442	356	0.6	0	-3.1	-9.2	-19.0	-33.2	2.0	0	-5.1	-13.8	-27.1	-70.9	-144.3
1911	1320	892	606	442	356	0.6	0	-3.1	-9.2	-19.0	-33.2	2.0	0	-5.1	-13.8	-27.1	-70.9	-144.3
1728	1203	821	569	427	350	0.7	0	-3.4	-10.2	-20.9	-36.5	2.3	0	-5.6	-15.2	-29.6	-76.7	-154.5
325	231	185	154	131	113	0	-6.3	-20.9	-44.9	-79.3	-125.1	0	-11.5	-32.3	-63.6	-106.3	-230.3	-413.3
325	231	185	154	131	113	0	-6.3	-20.9	-44.9	-79.3	-125.1	0	-11.5	-32.3	-63.6	-106.3	-230.3	-413.3
2102	1463	993	671	476	375	0.5	0	-2.7	-8.2	-17.1	-29.8	1.8	0	-4.5	-12.4	-24.3	-63.8	-130.7
3890	3137	2505	1977	1539	1187	0.5	0.9	0	-2.3	-6.1	-11.6	2.0	1.7	0	-3.2	-8.2	-24.3	-50.4
3862	3306	2816	2384	2005	1677	1.2	1.3	0	-2.7	-7.1	-12.9	2.7	2.1	0	-3.6	-9.4	-25.0	-49.9
3927	3184	2554	2025	1591	1244	0.2	0	-1.7	-5.2	-10.5	-18.0	2.6	2.1	0	-4.0	-10.2	-30.0	-61.9
2820	2178	1656	1241	925	697	0.3	0	-2.1	-6.2	-12.7	-21.9	1.4	0	-3.4	-9.2	-17.7	-44.4	-87.9
1812	1203	791	551	431	360	0.9	0	-4.1	-12.1	-25.1	-43.9	2.7	0	-6.7	-18.3	-35.8	-92.8	-185.5
1812	1203	791	551	431	360	0.9	0	-4.1	-12.1	-25.1	-43.9	2.7	0	-6.7	-18.3	-35.8	-92.8	-185.5
1368	968	686	508	409	348	0	-2.1	-7.8	-17.8	-32.9	-53.9	0	-4.7	-13.6	-27.6	-47.5	-108.8	-203.9
2753	2093	1563	1151	844	633	0.4	0	-2.2	-6.5	-13.3	-23.0	1.5	0	-3.6	-9.7	-18.6	-47.2	-94.1
2760	2194	1723	1346	1049	832	0.5	0	-2.7	-7.9	-16.0	-27.1	1.8	0	-4.3	-11.4	-21.7	-53.5	-103.7
2150	1506	1034	714	527	427	0.6	0	-3.2	-9.5	-19.5	-33.8	2.1	0	-5.2	-14.1	-27.4	-70.1	-138.1
2005	1506	1126	852	676	568	0.9	0	-4.1	-12.0	-24.2	-40.9	2.7	0	-6.5	-17.2	-32.7	-80.6	-154.1
4337	3510	2812	2228	1747	1361	0.2	0	-1.7	-5.1	-10.3	-17.6	2.5	2.1	0	-3.9	-10.0	-29.4	-60.7
4263	3426	2723	2141	1669	1300	0.3	0	-2.0	-5.9	-11.9	-20.3	2.9	2.4	0	-4.5	-11.5	-33.8	-70.1
4263	3139	2262	1602	1138	844	0.3	0	-2.2	-6.5	-13.5	-23.4	1.5	0	-3.6	-9.8	-19.1	-49.1	-99.5
538	399	324	273	233	201	0	-6.7	-22.2	-47.3	-83.2	-130.8	0	-12.1	-33.9	-66.4	-110.6	-238.3	-425.6
987	802	674	587	525	476	0	-4.7	-15.4	-32.7	-57.2	-89.3	0	-8.4	-23.4	-45.6	-75.2	-158.8	-277.4
1650	988	638	484	395	232	0	-2.7	-10.2	-23.6	-44.2	-73.3	0	-6.1	-18.1	-37.4	-65.1	-150.3	-282.5
629	449	360	300	254	217	0	-6.5	-21.6	-46.3	-81.8	-129.1	0	-11.8	-33.3	-65.5	-109.5	-237.4	-426.2
1590	1227	1001	858	758	679	0	-4.7	-15.8	-34.0	-60.0	-94.5	0	-8.7	-24.6	-48.2	-80.3	-172.4	-305.9
4620	3689	2924	2308	1839	1496	0.7	0	-3.3	-9.6	-19.2	-32.5	2.2	0	-5.2	-13.6	-25.8	-63.2	-121.7
4712	3547	2640	1970	1516	1239	0.8	0	-3.5	-10.3	-20.8	-35.6	2.4	0	-5.6	-14.9	-28.5	-71.5	-140.4

GAME SELECTOR CODE

S = Small game
D = Deer

O/P = Open or Plains shooting
(i.e. Antelope, Deer)
L = Large game (i.e. Moose, Elk)

XL = Extra Large game
(i.e. Kodiak bear)

WINCHESTER-WESTERN RIMFIRE CARTRIDGE BALLISTICS

Lead   Dynapoint

Hollow Point   Jacketed Hollow Point   Full Metal Case

RIMFIRE RIFLE CARTRIDGES

Cartridge	Bullet		Velocity (ft/s)		Energy (ft. lbs.)		Nominal Mid-Range Traj. (In.)
	Wt. Grs.	Type	Muzzle	100 yds.	Muzzle	100 yds.	100 yds.
22 Short Super-X	29	L*	1095	902	77	52	4.5
22 Short H.P. Super-X	27	L*	1120	904	75	49	4.4
22 Long Super-X	29	L*	1240	961	99	59	3.9
22 Long Rifle Super-X	40	L*	1255	1016	140	92	3.6
22 Long Rifle DYNAPOINT Super-X	40	L*	1255	1016	140	92	3.6
22 Long Rifle H.P. Super-X	37	L*	1280	1013	135	84	3.5
22 Long Rifle Shot Super-X (#12 Shot)	—	—	—	—	—	—	—
22 Long Rifle Xpediter H.P.	29	L*	1680	1079	182	75	2.5
22 Winchester MAGNUM R.F. Super-X	40	JHP	1910	1326	324	156	1.7
22 Winchester MAGNUM R.F. Super-X	40	FMC	1910	1326	324	156	1.7
22 Short T22	29	Lead*	1045	872	70	49	4.8
22 Long Rifle T22	40	Lead*	1150	975	117	84	4.0
22 Short Blank	—	—	—	—	—	—	—
22 Short C.B.	29	Lead*	715	—	33	—	—

RIMFIRE PISTOL AND REVOLVER CARTRIDGES

Cartridge	Bullet		Barrel Length	Muzzle Velocity (ft/s)	Muzzle Energy (ft. lbs.)
	Wt. Grs.	Type			
22 Short Blank	—	—	—	—	—
22 Short Super-X	29	L*	6"	1010	66
22 Short T22	29	Lead*	6"	865	48
22 Long Super-X	29	L*	6"	1095	77
22 Long Rifle Super-X	40	L*	6"	1060	100
22 Long Rifle T22	40	Lead*	6"	950	80
22 Long Rifle Super-Match Mark IV	40	Lead*	6¾"	1060	100
22 Winchester MAGNUM Rimfire Super-X	40	JHP	6½"	1480	195
22 Winchester MAGNUM Rimfire Super-X	40	FMC	6½"	1480	195

FMC—Full Metal Case   *—Wax Coated   L—Lubaloy   JHP—Jacketed Hollow Point

Specifications are nominal. Test barrels are used to determine ballistics figures. Individual firearms may differ from these test barrel statistics.

Reloading

HORNADY RIFLE BULLETS

RIFLE BULLETS
"I" denotes interlock bullets.

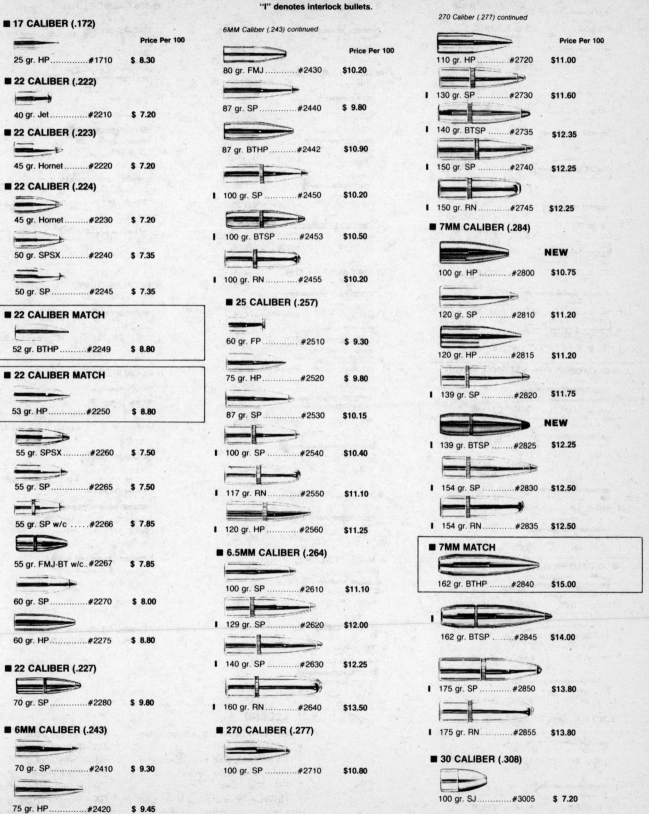

■ 17 CALIBER (.172)

Price Per 100

25 gr. HP.............#1710 $ 8.30

■ 22 CALIBER (.222)

40 gr. Jet.............#2210 $ 7.20

■ 22 CALIBER (.223)

45 gr. Hornet........#2220 $ 7.20

■ 22 CALIBER (.224)

45 gr. Hornet........#2230 $ 7.20

50 gr. SPSX.........#2240 $ 7.35

50 gr. SP.............#2245 $ 7.35

■ 22 CALIBER MATCH

52 gr. BTHP.........#2249 $ 8.80

■ 22 CALIBER MATCH

53 gr. HP.............#2250 $ 8.80

55 gr. SPSX.........#2260 $ 7.50

55 gr. SP.............#2265 $ 7.50

55 gr. SP w/c .....#2266 $ 7.85

55 gr. FMJ-BT w/c..#2267 $ 7.85

60 gr. SP.............#2270 $ 8.00

60 gr. HP.............#2275 $ 8.80

■ 22 CALIBER (.227)

70 gr. SP.............#2280 $ 9.80

■ 6MM CALIBER (.243)

70 gr. SP.............#2410 $ 9.30

75 gr. HP.............#2420 $ 9.45

6MM Caliber (.243) continued

Price Per 100

80 gr. FMJ...........#2430 $10.20

87 gr. SP.............#2440 $ 9.80

87 gr. BTHP.........#2442 $10.90

I   100 gr. SP ....#2450 $10.20

I   100 gr. BTSP ....#2453 $10.50

I   100 gr. RN ....#2455 $10.20

■ 25 CALIBER (.257)

60 gr. FP .... #2510 $ 9.30

75 gr. HP.............#2520 $ 9.80

87 gr. SP.............#2530 $10.15

I   100 gr. SP ....#2540 $10.40

I   117 gr. RN ....#2550 $11.10

I   120 gr. HP ....#2560 $11.25

■ 6.5MM CALIBER (.264)

100 gr. SP ....#2610 $11.10

I   129 gr. SP ....#2620 $12.00

I   140 gr. SP ....#2630 $12.25

I   160 gr. RN ....#2640 $13.50

■ 270 CALIBER (.277)

100 gr. SP ....#2710 $10.80

---

270 Caliber (.277) continued

Price Per 100

110 gr. HP ....#2720 $11.00

I   130 gr. SP ....#2730 $11.60

I   140 gr. BTSP ....#2735 $12.35

I   150 gr. SP ....#2740 $12.25

I   150 gr. RN ....#2745 $12.25

■ 7MM CALIBER (.284)

NEW

100 gr. HP ....#2800 $10.75

120 gr. SP ....#2810 $11.20

120 gr. HP ....#2815 $11.20

I   139 gr. SP ....#2820 $11.75

NEW

I   139 gr. BTSP ....#2825 $12.25

I   154 gr. SP ....#2830 $12.50

I   154 gr. RN ....#2835 $12.50

■ 7MM MATCH

162 gr. BTHP ....#2840 $15.00

I   162 gr. BTSP ....#2845 $14.00

I   175 gr. SP ....#2850 $13.80

I   175 gr. RN ....#2855 $13.80

■ 30 CALIBER (.308)

100 gr. SJ.............#3005 $ 7.20

HORNADY RIFLE BULLETS

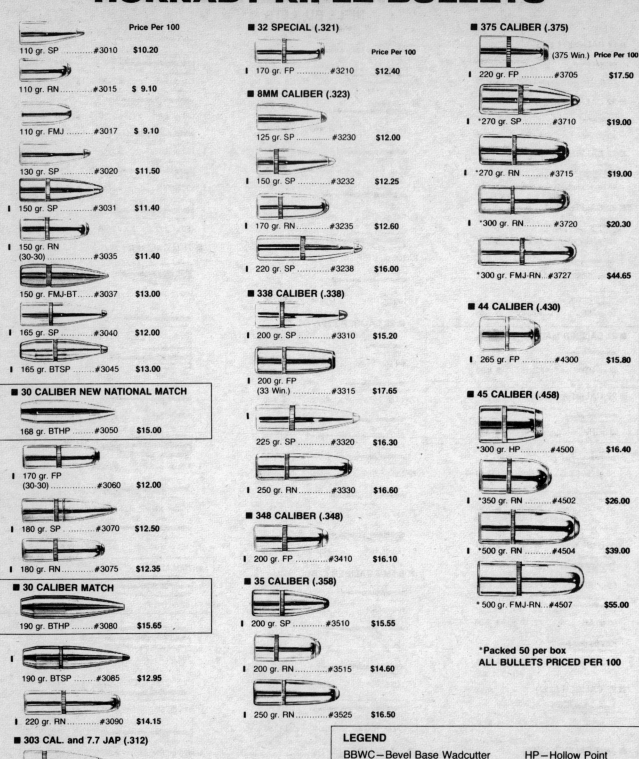

Price Per 100

110 gr. SP	#3010	$10.20
110 gr. RN	#3015	$ 9.10
110 gr. FMJ	#3017	$ 9.10
130 gr. SP	#3020	$11.50
150 gr. SP	#3031	$11.40
150 gr. RN (30-30)	#3035	$11.40
150 gr. FMJ-BT	#3037	$13.00
165 gr. SP	#3040	$12.00
165 gr. BTSP	#3045	$13.00

■ 30 CALIBER NEW NATIONAL MATCH

168 gr. BTHP	#3050	$15.00

170 gr. FP (30-30)	#3060	$12.00
180 gr. SP	#3070	$12.50
180 gr. RN	#3075	$12.35

■ 30 CALIBER MATCH

190 gr. BTHP	#3080	$15.65

190 gr. BTSP	#3085	$12.95
220 gr. RN	#3090	$14.15

■ 303 CAL. and 7.7 JAP (.312)

150 gr. SP	#3120	$12.50
174 gr. RN	#3130	$13.00

■ 32 SPECIAL (.321)

Price Per 100

170 gr. FP	#3210	$12.40

■ 8MM CALIBER (.323)

125 gr. SP	#3230	$12.00
150 gr. SP	#3232	$12.25
170 gr. RN	#3235	$12.60
220 gr. SP	#3238	$16.00

■ 338 CALIBER (.338)

200 gr. SP	#3310	$15.20
200 gr. FP (33 Win.)	#3315	$17.65
225 gr. SP	#3320	$16.30
250 gr. RN	#3330	$16.60

■ 348 CALIBER (.348)

200 gr. FP	#3410	$16.10

■ 35 CALIBER (.358)

200 gr. SP	#3510	$15.55
200 gr. RN	#3515	$14.60
250 gr. RN	#3525	$16.50

■ 375 CALIBER (.375)

(375 Win.) Price Per 100

220 gr. FP	#3705	$17.50
*270 gr. SP	#3710	$19.00
*270 gr. RN	#3715	$19.00
*300 gr. RN	#3720	$20.30
*300 gr. FMJ-RN	#3727	$44.65

■ 44 CALIBER (.430)

265 gr. FP	#4300	$15.80

■ 45 CALIBER (.458)

*300 gr. HP	#4500	$16.40
*350 gr. RN	#4502	$26.00
*500 gr. RN	#4504	$39.00
* 500 gr. FMJ-RN	#4507	$55.00

*Packed 50 per box
ALL BULLETS PRICED PER 100

LEGEND

BBWC—Bevel Base Wadcutter	HP—Hollow Point
BT—Boat Tail	RN—Round Nose
DEWC—Double End Wadcutter	SJ—Short Jacket
FMJ—Full Metal Jacket	SP—Spire Point
FP—Flat Point	SWC—Semi-Wadcutter
HBWC—Hollow Base Wadcutter	SX—Super Explosive

HORNADY BULLETS

JACKETED PISTOL BULLETS

■ 25 CALIBER (.251)

Price Per 100

50 gr. FMJ-RN.......#3545 $ 7.75

■ 9MM CALIBER (.355)

90 gr. HP.............#3550 $ 8.05

100 gr. FMJ ....#3552 $ 8.25

115 gr. HP ....#3554 $ 8.35

124 gr. FMJ-FP....#3556 $ 8.85

■ 38 CALIBER (.357)

110 gr. HP ....#3570 $ 8.35

125 gr. HP ....#3571 $ 8.55

125 gr. FP ....#3573 $ 8.55

140 gr. JHP..........#3574 $ 8.85

Price Per 100

158 gr. HP...........#3575 $ 8.90

158 gr. FP ....#3578 $ 8.90

160 gr. FMJ ....#3579 $10.30

180 gr. FMJ-FP......#3576 $10.95

■ 41 CALIBER (.410)

210 gr. HP ....#4100 $10.80

210 gr. FMJ/FP .....#4103 $11.65

■ 44 CALIBER (.430)

200 gr. HP ....#4410 $10.80

240 gr. HP ....#4420 $11.75

240 gr. FMJ-FP....#4427 $12.60

■ 45 CALIBER (.451)

Price Per 100

185 gr. HP, ACP ...#4510 $11.20

185 gr. Target
SWC, ACP...........#4513 $11.50

200 gr.
FMJ-C/T (Match) ..# 4515 $11.75

230 gr. FMJ-RN .....#4517 $11.75

230 gr. FMJ-FP......#4518 $11.75

■ 45 CALIBER (.452)

250 gr. Long
Colt HP ....#4520 $12.00

LEAD PISTOL BULLETS

Bulk lead bullets must be ordered in increments of carton quantities per bullet, 5000 bullets per carton except 44 caliber is 4000 per carton.

32 cal. (.314)

90 gr.   #3250 $ 5.00
SWC............ • #1000 $40.00

38 cal. (.358)

148 gr.   #3580 $ 5.75
BBWC...... • #1010 $45.35

38 cal. (.358)

148 gr.   #3582 $ 5.75
HBWC...... • #1020 $45.35

38 cal. (.358)

148 gr.   (Bulk only)
DEWC............ • #1030 $45.35

38 cal. (.358)

158 gr. RN .... #3586 $ 6.00
            • #1050 $48.60

38 cal. (.358)

158 gr. SWC .... #3588 $ 6.00
            • #1040 $48.60

44 cal. (.430)

240 gr. SWC .... #4430 $ 8.65
            • #1110 $71.30

45 cal. (.452)

200 gr. SWC .... #4526 $ 7.55
            • #1210 $65.40

500 Per Box except 44 cal. (400 Per Box)
• **Bulk Price Per 1000**

ROUND LEAD BALLS

Here is an item for Black Powder shooters. Round Lead Balls in 12 sizes, from .350 through .570.

Price Per 100

.310..............#6000 $ 4.20
.350 ....#6010   4.45
.375 ....#6020   4.70
.433 ....#6030   5.40
.440 ....#6040   5.50
.445 ....#6050   5.60
.451 ....#6060   5.80
.454 ....#6070   5.90
.457 ....#6080   6.00
.490 ....#6090   6.60
.530 ....#6100   7.45
.535 ....#6110   7.70
*.570 ....#6120   8.55

*Packed 50 per box—all others packed 100 per box

NOSLER BULLETS

NEW—Solid Base 6mm, 75 Gr: Spitzer; 7mm, 162 Gr. Spitzer

Nosler Trophy Grade Bullets

Whether your trophy is a bull elk of Boone and Crockett proportions or an engraved cup awarded in competitive shooting, the performance of every bullet you shoot has to measure up to the job at hand. Nosler designs and manufactures every bullet it makes, both Partition and Solid Base, to perform every time as if your target were a trophy. Because Nosler believes *every* shot you take is important, *every* Nosler bullet has trophy performance built in...in accuracy, in flight characteristics, in striking power. That is why Nosler bullets can truly be called "Trophy Grade" bullets.

Caliber	Diameter	Partition	Bullet Weight and Style	50 PER BOX
6mm	.243"		95 Gr. Spitzer	$ 13.90
	.243"		100 Gr. Semi Spitzer	14.10
.25	.257"		100 Gr. Spitzer	14.10
	.257"		115 Gr. Spitzer	N/A
	.257"		117 Gr. Semi Spitzer	14.90
6.5mm	.264"		125 Gr. Spitzer	15.10
	.264"		140 Gr. Spitzer	15.70
.270	.277"		130 Gr. Spitzer	15.25
	.277"		150 Gr. Spitzer	16.00
	.277"		160 Gr. Semi Spitzer	16.20
7mm	.284"		140 Gr. Spitzer	15.70
	.284"		150 Gr. Spitzer	16.00
	.284"		160 Gr. Spitzer	16.40
	.284"		175 Gr. Semi Spitzer	16.80
.30	.308"		150 Gr. Spitzer	15.90
	.308"		165 Gr. Spitzer	16.40
	.308"		180 Gr. Spitzer	17.10
	.308"		180 Gr. Protected Point	17.10
	.308"		200 Gr. Round Nose	17.40
.338	.338"		210 Gr. Spitzer	21.85
	.338"		250 Gr. Round Nose	23.40

Caliber	Diameter	Solid Base	Bullet Weight and Style	100 PER BOX
.22	.224"		50 Gr. Spitzer	$ 7.45
	.224"		50 Gr. Hollow Point	7.90
	.224"		50 Gr. Hollow Pt. Match	9.30
	.224"		52 Gr. Hollow Point	9.20
	.224"		52 Gr. Hollow Pt. Match	9.85
	.224"		55 Gr. Spitzer	7.60
	.224"		60 Gr. Spitzer	8.80
6mm	.243"		70 Gr. Hollow Point	9.50
	.243"		70 Gr. Hollow Pt. Match	11.45
	.243"		85 Gr. Spitzer	10.75
	.243"		100 Gr. Spitzer	11.00
.25	.257"		100 Gr. Spitzer	10.55
	.257"		120 Gr. Spitzer	12.45
6.5mm	.264"		120 Gr. Spitzer	11.90
.270	.277"		100 Gr. Spitzer	11.00
	.277"		130 Gr. Spitzer	12.45
	.277"		150 Gr. Spitzer	13.50
7mm	.284"		120 Gr. Spitzer	11.30
	.284"		140 Gr. Spitzer	11.90
	.284"		150 Gr. Spitzer	13.20
.30	.308"		150 Gr. Flat Point	11.60
	.308"		150 Gr. Spitzer	12.60
	.308"		150 Gr. Hollow Point	13.00
	.308"		150 Gr. Hollow Pt. Match	15.70
	.308"		165 Gr. Spitzer	13.20
	.308"		168 Gr. Hollow Point	14.30
	.308"		168 Gr. Hollow Pt. Match	16.20
	.308"		170 Gr. Flat Point	11.80
	.308"		180 Gr. Spitzer	14.10

REMINGTON BULLETS

"Core-Lokt® Bullets

The "Number One Mushroom"—a name given by hunters everywhere to the Remington center fire cartridges with "Core-Lokt" bullets.

Superior mushrooming and one-shot stopping power are the results of the advanced design of "Core-Lokt" bullets: metal jacket and lead core are locked together by the jacket's heavy mid-section. "Core-Lokt" bullets are available in a wide variety of types and weights.

Bronze Point Expanding Bullet

A top performing all-around bullet of a unique design for extra long range accuracy and controlled expansion. Travels in a flat trajectory and has great wind bucking qualities.

"Power-Lokt"® Bullets

Remington "Power-Lokt" bullets are uniquely designed with the core and jacket electrolytically bonded into a one-piece unit. This exclusive process produces a better balance and more concentric bullet of uniformly high performance, rapid expansion and amazing accuracy.

ABBREVIATIONS

BrPt—Bronze Point	PL—Power-Lokt
CL—Core-Lokt	PSP—Pointed Soft Point
GC—Gas Check	SJ—Semi-Jacketed
HP—Hollow Point	SP—Soft Point
J—Jacketed	WC—Wadcutter
LD—Lead	SWC—Semi-Wadcutter
MC—Metal Case	

NEW ORDER NO.	OLD ORDER NO.		DESCRIPTION	WT. (LBS.) PER 100
17 cal. (.172)				
B1705	B22936		25 gr. PLHP	0.3
22 cal. (.224)				
B2210	B22704		45 gr. SP	0.7
B2220	B27710		50 gr. PSP	0.7
B2230	B22708		50 gr. MC	0.7
B2240	B22950		50 gr. PLHP	0.7
B2250	B22956		50 gr. PL Match	0.7
B2260	B22948		52 gr. HPBR	0.8
B2270	B22924		55 gr. PSP	0.8
B2280	B22952		55 gr. PLHP	0.8
B2290	B22958		55 gr. PL Match	0.8
B2265	B23558		55 gr. MC WO/C	0.8
6mm (.243)				
B2420	B22966		80 gr. PSP	1.2
B2430	B22954		80 gr. PLHP	1.2
B2440	B22960		80 gr. PL Match	1.2
B2460	B22920		100 gr. PSPCL	1.5
25 cal. (.257)				
B2510	B22752		87 gr. PLHP	1.4
B2520	B22730		100 gr. PSPCL (25-06)	1.5
B2540	B22736		120 gr. PSPCL (25-06)	1.8
6.5mm (.264)				
B2610	B22926		120 gr. PSPCL	1.8
270 cal. (.277)				
B2710	B23744		100 gr. PSP	1.5
B2720	B22746		130 gr. PSPCL	1.9
B2730	B22748		130 gr. BrPt	1.9
B2740	B22750		150 gr. SPCL	2.2
7mm (.284)				
B2830	B22756		150 gr. PSPCL	2.2
B2850	B22918		175 gr. PSPCL 7mm Rem.	2.6
30 cal. (.308)				
B3010	B22796		110 gr. SP Carbine	1.6
B3020	B22770		150 gr. BrPt (30-06)	2.2
B3025	B22774		150 gr. SPCL (30-30)	2.2
B3030	B22776		150 gr. PSPCL	2.2
B3040	B23594		165 gr. PSPCL	2.4
B3050	B22782		170 gr. SPCL	2.5
B3060	B22784		180 gr. BrPt	2.6
B3070	B22786		180 gr. SPCL	2.6

NEW ORDER NO.	OLD ORDER NO.		DESCRIPTION	WT. (LBS.) PER 100
30 Cal. (.308) Cont'd				
B3080	B22788		180 gr. PSPCL	2.6
B3090	B22792		220 gr. SPCL	3.2
32 cal. (.320)				
B3250	B22828		170 gr. SPCL	2.5
8mm (.323)				
B3270	B22984		185 gr. PSPCL	2.8
B3280	B22986		220 gr. PSPCL	3.3
35 cal. (.358)				
B3510	B22868		200 gr. SPCL	2.9
9mm (.354)				
B3550	B22942		115 gr. JHP	1.8
B3552	B22842		124 gr. MC	1.9
38 cal.				
B3810	B22944		95 gr. SJHP	1.4
357/38 cal. (.357)				
B3570	B23586		110 gr. SJHP	1.6
B3572	B22866		125 gr. SJHP	1.9
B3574	B22846		158 gr. SP	2.3
B3576	B22938		158 gr. SJHP	2.3
357 cal. (.358)				
B3578	B22856		158 gr. LEAD SWC†	2.3
38 cal. (.360)*				
B3830	B22850		148 gr. LD WC†	2.2
38 cal. (.358)				
B3840	B22854		158 gr. LEAD†	2.3
B3850	B23568		158 gr. LEAD HP	2.3
41 mag. (.310)				
B4110	B22888		210 gr. SP	3.1
41 mag. (.411)				
B4120	B22922		210 gr. LEAD	3.1
44 cal. (.430)				
B4405	B23588		180 gr. SJHP	2.8
B4410	B22906		240 gr. SP	3.5
B4420	B22940		240 gr. SJHP	3.5
44 cal. (.432)				
B4430	B22884		240 gr. LEAD GC	3.5
B4440	B22768		240 gr. LEAD	3.5
45 cal. (.451)				
B4530	B22892		230 gr. MC†	3.4
B4510	B22890		185 gr. MCWC†	2.7
B4520	B22586		185 gr. JHP	2.7

* .360 dia. for best accuracy.   † Also available in bulk pack.

PRICES NOT AVAILABLE

SIERRA BULLETS

Stock No.	Description	Price
.22 Caliber (.224 Diameter)		
1100	40 gr. Hornet (.223 Dia.)	**$7.82**
1110	45 gr. Hornet (.223 Dia.)	7.82
1200	40 gr. Hornet	7.82
1210	45 gr. Hornet	7.82
1300	45 gr. SMP	7.82
1310	45 gr. SPT	7.82
1320	50 gr. SMP	7.91
1330	50 gr. SPT	7.91
1340	50 gr. Blitz	7.91
1410	52 gr. HPBT	10.64
1400	53 gr. HP	10.55
1345	55 gr. Blitz	8.00
1350	55 gr. SMP	8.00
1355	55 gr. FMJBT	7.91
1360	55 gr. SPT	8.00
1365	55 gr. SBT	9.09
1370	63 gr. SMP	8.36
6MM .243 Caliber (.243 Diameter)		
1500	60 gr. HP	$ 9.82
1505	70 gr. HPBT	12.27
1510	75 gr. HP	10.45
1520	85 gr. SPT	10.73
1530	85 gr. HPBT	11.73
1535	90 gr. FMJBT NEW	10.46
1540	100 gr. SPT	11.00
1550	100 gr. SMP	11.09
1560	100 gr. SBT	12.55
.25 Caliber 6.3MM (.257 Diameter)		
1600	75 gr. HP	$10.91
1610	87 gr. SPT	11.09
1615	90 gr. HPBT	12.09
1620	100 gr. SPT	11.36

Stock No.	Description	Price
1630	117 gr. SBT	**$13.45**
1640	117 gr. SPT	12.00
1650	120 gr. HPBT	13.55
6.5MM .264 Caliber (.264 Diameter)		
1700	85 gr. HP	**$11.64**
1710	100 gr. HP	12.18
1720	120 gr. SPT	12.45
1730	140 gr. SBT	14.82
1740	140 gr. HPBT	16.18
.270 Caliber 6.8MM (.277 Diameter)		
1800	90 gr. HP	**$11.82**
1810	110 gr. SPT	12.00
1820	130 gr. SBT	14.09
1830	130 gr. SPT	12.27
1835	140 gr. HPBT NEW	13.19
1840	150 gr. SBT	15.27
1850	150 gr. RN	13.00
7MM .284 Caliber (.284 Diameter)		
1900	120 gr. SPT	**$12.00**
1905	140 gr. SBT	14.36
1910	140 gr. SPT	12.73
1915	150 gr. HPBT	16.64
1920	160 gr. SBT	15.27
1930	168 gr. HPBT	17.18
1950	170 gr. RN	14.27
1940	175 gr. SBT	16.45
.30 Caliber (.308 Diameter)		
2020	125 gr. HP (30-30)	**$12.09**
2000	150 gr. FN (30-30)	12.36
2010	170 gr. FN (30-30)	12.91
2100	110 gr. RN	9.55
2105	110 gr. FMJ	9.55
2110	110 gr. HP	11.45

SIERRA BULLETS

Stock No.	Description		Price
2120	125 gr. SPT		$ 11.82
2130	150 gr. SPT		12.18
2125	150 gr. SBT		13.91
2190	150 gr. HPBT		16.55
2135	150 gr. RN		12.45
2145	165 gr. SBT		14.91
2140	165 gr. HPBT		14.91
2200	168 gr. HPBT		17.18
2150	180 gr. SPT		13.00
2160	180 gr. SBT		15.45
2220	180 gr. HPBT		18.27
2170	180 gr. RN		13.18
2210	190 gr. HPBT		18.64
2165	200 gr. SBT		17.55
2230	200 gr. HPBT		19.09
2240	220 gr. HPBT		21.55
2180	220 gr. RN		14.91

.303 Caliber 7.7MM (.311 Diameter)

Stock No.	Description		Price
2320	125 gr. FMJ	NEW	13.65
2300	150 gr. SPT		13.82
2310	180 gr. SPT		14.55

8MM .323 Caliber (.323 Diameter)

Stock No.	Description		Price
2400	150 gr. SPT		13.82
2410	175 gr. SPT		14.55
2420	220 gr. SBT		10.82

.338 Caliber 8.38MM (.338 Diameter)

Stock No.	Description		Price
2600	250 gr. SBT		11.36

.35 Caliber 8.9MM (.358 Diameter)

Stock No.	Description		Price
2800	200 gr. RN		7.73

.375 Caliber 9.3MM (.375 Diameter)

Stock No.	Description		Price
3000	300 gr. SBT		16.36

.45 Caliber (45-70) 11.4MM (.458 Diameter)

Stock No.	Description		Price
8900	300 gr. HP		11.82

.25 Caliber 6.35MM (.251 Diameter)

Stock No.	Description		Price
8000	50 gr. FMJ	NEW	7.91

.30 Caliber 7.65MM (.308 Diameter)

Stock No.	Description		Price
8020	93 gr. FMJ	NEW	14.56

.32 Caliber 7.65MM (.308 Diameter)

Stock No.	Description		Price
8010	71 gr. FMJ	NEW	8.46

9MM .355 Caliber (.355 Diameter)

Stock No.	Description		Price
8100	90 gr. JHP	NEW	8.46
8105	95 gr. FMJ	NEW	8.46
8110	115 gr. JHP	NEW	8.73

*50 bullets per box

Stock No.	Description		Price
8120	125 gr. FMJ		8.91
8345	130 gr. FMJ	NEW	10.95

.38 Caliber (.357 Diameter)

Stock No.	Description		Price
8300	110 gr. JHC Blitz	NEW	8.55
8310	125 gr. JSP		8.64
8320	125 gr. JHC		8.73
8325	140 gr. JHC		8.91
8360	158 gr. JHC	NEW	9.10
8340	158 gr. JSP		8.91
8365	170 gr. JHC	NEW	9.46
8350	170 gr. FMJ Match		11.91

.41 Caliber 10.2MM (.410 Diameter)

Stock No.	Description		Price
8500	170 gr. JHC		12.09
8520	210 gr. JHC		12.36
8530	220 gr. FPJ Match		13.09

.44 Magnum 10.7MM (.4295 Diameter)

Stock No.	Description		Price
8600	180 gr. JHC		12.36
8620	210 gr. JHC		12.55
8605	220 gr. FPJ Match		13.09
8610	240 gr. JHC		12.73

.45 Caliber 11.4MM (.4515 Diameter)

Stock No.	Description		Price
8800	185 gr. JHP	NEW	12.46
8810	185 gr. FPJ Match		12.91
8815	230 gr. FMJ Match		13.18
8820	240 gr. JHP		12.73

Accessories

Description	Price
Sierra Bullet Board with Real Redwood Frame	$75.00
Sierra Reloading Manual (700 pgs.)	13.95
Sierra Bullet Patch	1.50
Sierra Bullet Patch, Pin and Decal Set	4.50
Sierra Marksman Cap	8.00
Sierra Bullet Keychain	1.50
Sierra Solid Brass Belt Buckle	11.00
Sierra Bullet Paperweight	14.00
Sierra T-shirts	8.00
Sierra Counter Mats	
Distributor Price Lists	
Sierra Catalog	

SPEER BULLETS

22 CALIBER (.223)

1005 40 Gr. Spire Point

1011 45 Gr. Spitzer

22 CALIBER (.224)

1017 40 Gr. Spire

1023 45 Gr. Spitzer

1029 50 Gr. Spitzer

1035 52 Gr. Hollow Point

1045 55 Gr. FMJ

1047 55 Gr. Spitzer

1049 55 Gr. Spitzer

1053 70 Gr. Semi-Spitzer

6mm CALIBER (.243)

1205 75 Gr. Hollow Point

1211 80 Gr. Spitzer

1213 85 Gr. Boat Tail

1215 90 Gr. FMJ

1217 90 Gr. Spitzer

1223 105 Gr. Round Nose

1229 105 Gr. Spitzer

25 CALIBER (.257)

1241 87 Gr. Spitzer

1405 100 Gr. spitzer

1407 100 Gr. Hollow Point

1410 120 Gr. Boat Tail

1411 120 Gr. Spitzer

6.5mm CALIBER (.263)

1435 120 Gr. Spitzer

1441 140 Gr. Spitzer

270 CALIBER (.277)

1447 100 Gr. Hollow Point

1453 100 Gr. Spitzer

1458 130 Gr. Boat Tail

1459 130 Gr. Spitzer

1465 130 Gr. Grand Slam

1604 150 Gr. Boat Tail

1605 150 Gr. Spitzer

1608 150 Gr. Grand Slam

7mm CALIBER (.284)

1617 115 Gr. Hollow Point

1623 130 Gr. Spitzer

1628 145 Gr. Boat Tail

1629 145 Gr. Spitzer

1631 145 Gr. Match Boat Tail

1634 160 Gr. Boat Tail

1635 160 Gr. Spitzer

1637 160 Gr. Mag-Tip

1638 160 Gr. Grand Slam

1641 175 Gr. Mag-Tip

1643 175 Gr. Grand Slam

30 CALIBER (.308)

1805 100 Gr. Plinker ®

1835 110 Gr. Hollow Point

1845 110 Gr. Round Nose

1855 110 Gr. Spire Point

2005 130 Gr. Hollow Point

2007 130 Gr. Flat Point

2011 150 Gr. Flat Point

2017 150 Gr. Round Nose

2022 150 Gr. Boat Tail

2023 150 Gr. Spitzer

2025 150 Gr. Mag-Tip

2029 165 Gr. Round Nose

2034 165 Gr. Boat Tail

2035 165 Gr. Spitzer

2038 165 Gr. Grand Slam

2040 168 Gr. Match Boat Tail

2041 170 Gr. Flat Point

2047 180 Gr. Round Nose

2052 180 Gr. Boat Tail

2053 180 Gr. Spitzer

2059 180 Gr. Mag-Tip

2063 180 Gr. Grand Slam

2080 190 Gr. Match Boat Tail

2211 200 Gr. Spitzer

Prices not available

SPEER BULLETS

303 CALIBER (.311)

#2217
150 Grain
Spitzer

#2223
180 Grain
Round Nose

32 CALIBER (.321)

#2259
170 Grain
Flat Nose

8mm CALIBER (.323)

#2277
150 Grain
Spitzer

#2283
170
Semi-Spitzer

#2285
200 Grain
Spitzer

338 CALIBER (.338)

#2405
200 Grain
Spitzer

#2408
250 Grain
Grand Slam

#2411
275 Grain
Semi-Spitzer

35 CALIBER (.358)

#2435
180 Grain
Flat Nose

#2453
250 Grain
Spitzer

375 CALIBER (.375)

#2471
235 Grain
Semi-Spitzer

#2473
285 Grain
Grand Slam

45 CALIBER (.458)

#2479
400 Grain
Flat Nose

9mm CALIBER (.355)

#4000
88 Grain
Hollow Point

#3983
100 Grain
Hollow Point

#4005
125 Grain
Soft Point

38 CALIBER (.357)

#4007
110 Grain
Hollow Point

#4011
125 Grain
Soft Point

#4013
125 Grain
Hollow Point

#4203
140 Grain
Hollow Point

#4205
146 Grain
Hollow Point

#4211
158 Grain
J H P

#4217
158 Grain
Soft Point

#4223
160 Grain
Soft Point

41 CALIBER (.410)

#4405
200 Grain
Soft Point

#4417
220 Grain
Soft Point

44 CALIBER (.429)

#4425
200 Grain
Mag Hollow Point

#4435
225 Grain
Hollow Point

#4447
240 Grain
Soft Point

#4453
240 Grain
Mag
Hollow Point

#4457
240 Grain
Mag Soft Point

45 CALIBER (.451)

#4477
200 Grain
Hollow Point

#4479
225 Grain
Mag Hollow Point

#4481
260 Gr.
Hollow Point

(Lead)

9mm CALIBER (.356)

#4601
125 Grain
Round Nose

38 CALIBER (.358)

#4605
148 Grain
BBWC

#4617
148 Grain
HBWC

#4623
158 Grain
SWC

#4647
158 Grain
Round Nose

44 CALIBER (.430)

#4660
240 Grain
SWC

45 CALIBER (.452)

#4677
200 Grain
SWC

#4690
230 Grain
Round Nose

#4683
250 Grain
SWC

ROUND BALL

#5113 .375	#5135 .454"
#5127 .433"	#5137 .457"
#5129 .440"	#5139 .490"
#5131 .445"	#5142 .530"
#5133 .451"	#5180 .570"

FEDERAL PRIMERS

PRIMERS Non-Corrosive/Non-Mercuric

ITEM NUMBER	DESCRIPTION	NOMINAL DIAMETER IN INCHES	COLOR CODING	PACKAGED	WEIGHT PER CASE	PRICE Per 1000
100	Small Pistol	.175	Green		4.8 lbs.	$14.00
150	Large Pistol	.210	Green		6.1	14.00
155	Large Magnum Pistol	.210	Blue		6.7	16.00
200	Small Rifle & Mag. Pistol	.175	Red		4.9	14.00
205	Small Rifle	.175	Purple	100 per Box	4.9	14.00
210	Large Rifle	.210	Red	10 Boxes per ctn.,	6.5	14.00
215	Large Magnum Rifle	.210	Purple	5 ctn. per Case,	6.5	16.00
205M	Small Rifle Match	.175	Purple	of 5000	4.9	20.75
210M	Large Rifle Match	.210	Red		6.5	20.75
209	Shotshell	.243	—		16.7	25.00
410	Shotshell	.243	—		16.7	25.00

FEDERAL UNPRIMED CASES

UNPRIMED BRASS PISTOL CASES

ITEM NUMBER	DESCRIPTION	RECOMMENDED FEDERAL PRIMER NUMBER FOR HAND LOADS	PACKAGED	APPR. WEIGHT PER CASE	PRICE PER BOX
380UP	380 Auto	100		8.4 lbs.	$6.45
9UP	9mm Luger Auto	200	50 per Box,	10.0	9.60
38UP	38 Special	100	20 Boxes	10.6	6.75
357UP	357 Magnum	200	per Case of	12.4	7.45
44UP	44 Rem. Magnum	150 or 155	1000 Rounds	18.6	10.10
45UP	45 Auto	150		14.1	9.60
45LCAUP	45 Colt	150		19.6	10.10

UNPRIMED BRASS RIFLE CASES

ITEM NUMBER	DESCRIPTION	RECOMMENDED FEDERAL PRIMER NUMBER FOR HAND LOADS	PACKAGED	APPR. WEIGHT PER CASE	PRICE PER BOX
222UP	222 Remington	200 or 205		18.2 lbs.	$4.60
22250UP	22-250 Remington	210		29.4	6.55
223UP	223 Remington	200 or 205		18.3	5.65
243UP	243 Winchester	210		30.4	6.55
2506UP	25-06 Remington	210		34.0	6.90
270UP	270 Winchester	210	20 per Box,	34.2	6.90
7RUP	7mm Rem. Magnum	215	50 Boxes	40.5	8.60
30CUP	30 Carbine	200	per Case of	13.1	4.00
3030UP	30-30 Winchester	210	1000 Rounds	26.0	5.90
3006UP	30-06 Springfield	210		34.4	6.90
300WUP	300 Win. Magnum	215		42.0	8.60
308UP	308 Winchester	210		31.0	6.55
4570UP	4570 Government	210		16.1	6.35

UNPRIMED NICKEL PLATED MATCH RIFLE CASES

ITEM NUMBER	DESCRIPTION	RECOMMENDED FEDERAL PRIMER NUMBER FOR HAND LOADS	PACKAGED	APPR. WEIGHT PER CASE	PRICE PER BOX
222MUP	222 Remington Match	205M	20 per Box, 50 Boxes	18.5 lbs.	$5.60
308MUP	308 Winchester Match	210M	per Case of 1000 Rounds	30.6	7.60

REMINGTON CASES & PRIMERS

Remington brass cases with 5% more brass for extra strength in head section—annealed neck section for longer reloading life—primer pocket dimension controlled to .0005 inch to assure precise primer fit—heavier bridge and sidewalls—formed and machined to exacting tolerances for consistent powder capacity—choice of seventy-one center fire rifle, pistol and revolver cases—

Rifle Cases (Unprimed)

Case	QTY. PER BOX	"KLEANBORE" PRIMER NO.
17 REMINGTON • U17REM ★	20	7½
22 HORNET • U22HRN	50	6½
222 REMINGTON • U222R	20	7½
222 REMINGTON MAGNUM • U222MG	20	7½
22-250 REMINGTON • U22250	20	9½
223 REMINGTON • U223	20	7½
6mm REMINGTON • U6MM	20	9½
243 WINCHESTER • U243	20	9½
25-06 REMINGTON • U2506	20	9½
270 WINCHESTER • U270	20	9½
7mm-08 REMINGTON • U7MM08	20	9½
7mm EXPRESS REMINGTON • U7MM06 ‡	20	9½
7mm REMINGTON MAGNUM • U7MMMAG	20	9½M
30 CARBINE • U30CAR	50	6½
30-06 SPRINGFIELD • U3006	20	9½
30-30 WINCHESTER • U3030	20	9½
300 WINCHESTER MAGNUM • U300W	20	9½M
8mm REMINGTON MAGNUM • U8MMMAG	20	9½M
308 WINCHESTER • U308	20	9½
45-70 GOVERNMENT • U4570	20	9½

Pistol and Revolver Cases

Case	QTY. PER BOX	"KLEANBORE" PRIMER NO.
357 MAGNUM (BRASS) • U357B	50	5½
9mm LUGER AUTO PISTOL • U9MLUG	50	1½
38 SPECIAL (BRASS) • U38SPB	50	1½
41 REMINGTON MAGNUM • U41MAG	50	2½
44 REMINGTON MAGNUM • U44MAG	50	2½
45 COLT • U45CLT	50	2½
45 AUTO • U45AP	50	2½

* Designed for Remington No. 7½ primer only. Substitutions not recommended. U number is unprimed.

‡ Interchangeable with 280 Rem.

Bench Rest Cases

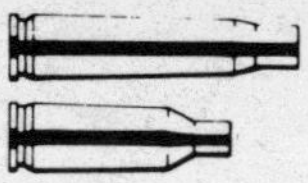

Case	QTY. PER BOX	"KLEANBORE" PRIMER NO.
	20	7½

Order No. URBR Remington .308 BR case ready for sizing, shortened and necked down to .224, 6mm, or 7mm.

Remington "Kleanbore" CENTER FIRE PRIMERS

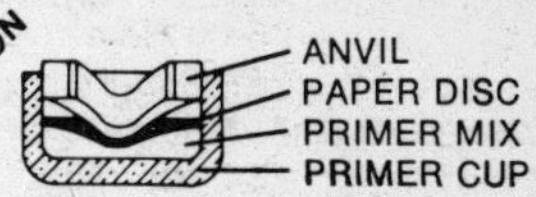

ANVIL
PAPER DISC
PRIMER MIX
PRIMER CUP

PRIMER NO.	ORDER NO.	DESCRIPTION
Small Pistol 1½	X 22600	Brass. Nickel-plated. For small revolver and pistol cartridges.
Large Pistol 2½	X 22604	Brass. Nickel-plated. For large revolver and pistol cartridges.
Small Pistol 5½	X 22626	Brass. Nickel-plated. Specially designed for 32 S & W and 357 Magnum cartridges.
Small Rifle 6½	X 22606	Brass. Nickel-plated. For small rifle cartridges other than those noted under Primer No. 7½.
Small Rifle Bench Rest 7½	X 22628	Brass. Copper-plated. Specially designed for 17 Rem., 221 Rem., "Fire Ball," 222 Rem., 222 Rem. Mag., 22 Rem. BR and 223 Rem. cartridges.
Large Rifle 9½	X 22608	Brass. For large rifle cartridges.
Magnum Rifle 9½M	X 22622	Brass. For use in belted magnum cartridges, 264 Win., 6.5mm Rem. Magnum., 7mm Rem. Magnum, 300 Win. Magnum, 300 H&H Magnum, 8mm Rem. Magnum, 350 Rem. Magnum, 375 H&H Magnum, 458 Win. Magnum cartridges.

PERCUSSION CAPS

SIZE	INSIDE DIA.	ORDER NO.	DESCRIPTION
10	.162"	X 22616	A hotter primer mix to assure more reliable ignition of both black powder and substitutes. Uniform, dependable performance. F.C. trimmed edge, foil-lined, center fire. Identical in length, priming mixture, weight of charge.
11	.167"	X 22618	

All Remington Center Fire Primers and Percussion Caps packed 100 per box (PC caps—tin), 1,000 per carton, 5,000 per case.

Prices not available

UNPRIMED CASES

SYMBOL	CALIBER	PER 100	SYMBOL	CALIBER	PER 100
U218	218 Bee	$20.00	U8mm	8mm Mauser	$39.25
U22H	22 Hornet	20.20	U338	338 Win Mag	45.55
U2250	22-250 Rem	34.65	U348	348 Win	48.20
U220S	220 Swift	34.65	U35R	35 Rem	37.30
U222R	222 Rem	24.25	U356	356 Win	40.10
U223R	223 Rem	29.95	U358	358 Win	39.25
U225	225 Win	29.95	U375H	375 H & H Mag	53.45
U243	243 Win	34.65	U375W	375 Win	45.45
U6mmR	6mmR	34.65	U3840	38-40 Win	23.20
U2520	25/20 Win	23.20	U3855	38-55 Win	44.45
U256	256 Win Mag	23.20	U440	44-40 Win	23.20
U250	250 Savage	37.30	U44M	44 Rem Mag	21.35
U2506	25-06 Rem	36.45	U4570	45-70 Govt	33.75
U257	257 Roberts	37.30	U458	458 Win Mag	53.45
U257F	257 Roberts +P	38.30	U25A	25 Auto	14.10
U264	204 Win Mag	45.45	U256	256 Win Mag	23.20
U270	270 Win	36.45	U32A	32 Auto	13.70
U284	284 Win	39.25	U32SW	32 S & W	12.20
U7mm	7mm Mauser	39.25	U32SWL	32 S & W Long	12.20
U7 Mag	7mm Rem Mag	45.55	U357	357 Mag (Nickel)	15.85
U30C	30 Carbine	21.05	U9mm	9mm Luger	20.30
U3030	30-30 Win	31.35	U38SW	38 S & W	13.70
U3006	30-06 Springfield	36.45	U38SP	38 Special	14.25
U3040	30-40 Krag	39.25	U38A	38 Auto	16.65
U300WM	300 Win Mag	45.45	U380A	380 Auto	13.70
U300H	300 H & H Mag	50.00	U41	41 Rem Mag	21.20
U300	300 Savage	37.30	U44S	44 S & W Special	17.90
U307	307 Win	35.45	U44M	44 Rem Mag	21.35
U308	308 Win	34.65	U45C	45 Colt	21.35
U303	303 British	39.25	U45A	45 Auto	20.30
U32W	32 Win Special	33.75			
U3220	32-20 Win	23.20			

PRIMERS

Symbol			Per 1000
W209	#W209	Shot Shell	$26.75
WLR	#8½-120	Large Rifle	14.20
WSR	#6½-116	Small Rifle	14.20
WSP	#1½-108	Small (Regular) Pistol	14.20
WLP	#7-111	Large (Regular) Pistol	14.20
WSPM	#1½M-108	Small (Mag) Pistol	16.15

PLASTIC WADS

	Per 1000
WAA 12	$26.40
WAA 12R	26.40
WAA 12F 114	26.40
WAA 12F 1	26.40
WAA 20	26.40
WAA 20F 1	26.40
WAA 28	26.40
WAA 41	26.40

NORMA EMPTY UNPRIMED RIFLE CASES

Caliber	Box 20	Caliber	Box 20	Caliber	Box 20
220 Swift	$9.35	30 U.S. Carbine	$6.47	358 Norma Belted Magnum	NA
222 Remington	7.75	7.62 Russian	11.00	9.3x57 Dual Core	NA
22 SAV High Power	NA	30-06 Springfield	7.65	9.3x62 Dual Core	NA
243 Winchester	7.60	22-250 Rem.	7.85		
6.5 Jap	9.75	30-30 WIN	9.35		
6.5 Norma (6.5x55)	9.75	308 Winchester	7.60		
6.5 Carcano	9.75	308 Norma Magnum	13.00		
270 Winchester	7.70	7.65 Argentine Mauser	10.00		
7mm Mauser	NA	303 British	9.45		
7x57 R (Rimmed)	NA	7.7mm Jap	10.50		
7mm Rem. Mag.	10.45	8x57J (.318 dia.)	NA		
7x64	NA	8mm Mauser (.323 dia.)	NA		
7.5x55 (7.5 Swiss)	9.75				

NORMA EMPTY UNPRIMED PISTOL CASES

Caliber	Box 50
32 S & W Long	$11.78
9mm Luger	11.78
38 Special	11.55
357 Magnum	13.05
44 Magnum	15.30
44 Auto Mag	NA

DU PONT SMOKELESS POWDERS

SHOTSHELL POWDER

Hi-Skor 700-X Double-Base Shotshell Powder. Specifically designed for today's 12-gauge components. Developed to give optimum ballistics at minimum charge weight (means more reloads per pound of powder). 700-X is dense, easy to load, clean to handle and loads uniformly.

PB Shotshell Powder. Produces exceptional 20- and 28-gauge skeet reloads; preferred by many in 12-gauge target loads,

it gives 3-dram equivalent velocity at relatively low chamber pressures.

SR-4756 Powder. Great all-around powder for target and field loads.

SR-7625 Powder. A fast growing "favorite" for reloading target as well as light and heavy field loads in 4 gauges. Excellent velocity-chamber pressure.

IMR-4227 Powder. Can be used effectively for reloading .410-gauge shotshell ammunition.

RIFLE POWDER

IMR-3031 Rifle Powder. Specifically recommended for medium-capacity cartridges.

IMR-4064 Rifle Powder. Has exceptionally uniform burning qualities when used in medium- and large-capacity cartridges.

IMR-4198. Made the Remington 222 cartridge famous. Developed for small- and medium-capacity cartridges.

IMR-4227 Rifle Powder. Fastest burning of the IMR Series. Specifically designed for the 22 Hornet class of cartridges.

SR-4759. Brought back by shooter demand. Available for Cast bullet loads.

IMR-4320. Recommended for high-velocity cartridges.

IMR-4350 Rifle Powder. Gives unusually uniform results when loaded in magnum cartridges. Slowest burning powder of the IMR series.

IMR-4831. Produced as a canister-grade handloading powder. Packaged in 1 lb. canister, 8 lb. caddy and 20 lb. kegs.

IMR-4895 Rifle Powder. The time-tested standard for caliber 30 military ammunition is now being manufactured again. Slightly faster than IMR-4320. Loads uniformly in all powder measures. One of the country's favorite powders.

PISTOL POWDER

PB Powder. Another powder for reloading a wide variety of center-fire handgun ammunition.

IMR-4227 Powder. Can be used effectively for reloading "magnum" handgun ammunition.

"Hi-Skor" 700-X Powder. The same qualities that make it a superior shotshell powder contribute to its excellent

performance in all the popular handguns.

SR-7625 Powder. For reloading a wide variety of center-fire handgun ammunition.

SR-4756, IMR-3031 and IMR-4198. Three more powders in a good selection—all clean burning and with uniform performance.

HERCULES SMOKELESS POWDERS

Eight types of Hercules smokeless sporting powders are available to the handloader. These have been selected from the wide range of powders produced for factory loading to provide at least one type that can be used efficiently and economically for each type of ammunition. These include:

Powder	Packaging				
	1-lb Canisters	4-lb Canisters	5-lb Canisters	8-lb Keg	15-lb Keg
Bullseye	X	X		X	X
Red Dot	X	X		X	X
Green Dot	X	X		X	X
Unique	X	X		X	X
Herco	X	X		X	X
Blue Dot	X		X		
Hercules 2400	X	X		X	X
Reloder 7	X				

BULLSEYE®

A high-energy, quick-burning powder especially designed for pistol and revolver. The most popular powder for .38 special target loads. Can also be used for 12 gauge-1 oz. shotshell target loads.

RED DOT®

The preferred powder for light-to-medium shotshells; specifically designed for 12-gauge target loads. Can also be used for handgun loads.

GREEN DOT®

Designed for 12-gauge medium shotshell loads. Outstanding in 20-gauge skeet loads.

UNIQUE®

Has an unusually broad application from light to heavy shotshell loads. As a handgun powder, it is our most versatile, giving excellent performance in many light to medium-heavy loads.

HERCO®

A long-established powder for high velocity shotshell loads. Designed for heavy and magnum 10-, 12-, 16-, and 20-gauge loads. Can also be used in high-performance handgun loads.

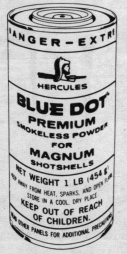

BLUE DOT®

Designed for use in magnum shotshell loads, 10-, 12-, 16-, 20- and 28-gauge. Also provides top performance with clean burning in many magnum handgun loads.

HERCULES 2400®

For use in small-capacity rifle cartridges and .410-Bore shotshell loads. Can also be used for large-caliber magnum handgun cartridges.

RELODER® 7

Designed for use in center-fire rifle cartridges. Has outstanding accuracy in small-capacity rifle cartridges used in bench rest shooting.

HODGDON SMOKELESS POWDER

RIFLE POWDER

H4227 and H4198

H4227 is the fastest burning of the IMR series. Well adapted to Hornet, light bullets in 222 and all bullets in 357 and 44 magnum pistols. Cuts leading with lead bullets. H4198 was developed especially for small and medium capacity cartridges.

1 lb. can $11.75; 8 lb. keg $88.50

H322

A new extruded bench-rest powder which has proved to be capable of producing fine accuracy in the .22 and .308 Bench-rest guns. This powder fills the gap between H4198 and BL-C(2). Performs best in small to medium capacity cases.

1 lb. can $11.75; 8 lb. keg $88.50

SPHERICAL BL-C®, Lot No. 2

A highly popular favorite of the Bench-rest shooters. Best performance is in the 222, and in other cases smaller than 30/06.

1 lb. can $10.95; 8 lb. keg $82.35

SPHERICAL H335®

Similar to BL-C(2), H335 is popular for its performance in medium capacity cases, especially in 222 and 308 Winchester.

1 lb. can $10.95; 8 lb. keg $82.35

4895®

4895 may well be considered the most versatile of all propellants. It gives desirable performance in almost all cases from 222 Rem. to 458 Win. Reduced loads, to as low as 3/5 of maximum, still give target accuracy.

1 lb. can $11.75; 8 lb. keg $88.50

SPHERICAL H380®

This number fills a gap between 4320 and 4350. It is excellent in 22/250, 220 Swift, the 6mm's, 257 and 30/06.

1 lb. can $10.95; 8 lb. keg $82.35

SPHERICAL H414®

A new development in spherical powder. In many popular medium to medium-large calibers, pressure velocity relationship is better.

1 lb. can $10.25; 8 lb. keg $75.00

SPHERICAL H870®

Very slow burning rate adaptable to overbore capacity magnum cases such as 257, 264, 270 and 300 mags with heavy bullets.

1 lb. can $5.95; 8 lb. keg $38.00

SPHERICAL H450®

A powder well adapted to maximum loads in most cartridges. Gives excellent performance in 30/06.

1 lb. can $10.25; 8 lb. keg $75.00

H4831®

Here is a new batch of the original 4831. The most popular of all powders. Use same loading data as our original surplus powder. Outstanding performance with medium and heavy bullets in the 6mm's, 25/06, 270 and magnum calibers.

1 lb. can $11.75; 8 lb. keg $88.50

SHOTGUN AND PISTOL POWDER

HP38

A fast pistol powder for most pistol loading. Especially recommended for mid-range 38 special.

12 oz. can $7.50; 8 lb. keg $67.50

TRAP 100

Trap 100 is a spherical trap and light field load powder, also excellent for target loads in centerfire pistol. Mild recoil.

8 oz. can $4.75; 8 lb. keg $64.75

HS-6 and HS-7

HS-6 and HS-7 for magnum field loads are unsurpassed since they do not pack in the measure. They deliver uniform charges and are dense so allow sufficient wad column for best patterns.

HS-6 and HS-7 1 lb. can $8.95; 8 lb. keg $64.75

H110

A spherical powder made especially for the 30 M1 carbine. H110 also does very well in 357, 44 Spec., 44 Mag. or 410 ga. Shotshell. Magnum primers are recommended for consistent ignition.

1 lb. can $8.95; 8 lb. keg $64.75

NORMA SMOKELESS POWDER
RIFLE POWDERS

NORMA 200

A fast-burning powder, for small capacity cartridge cases as the 222, but also for use with light bullets and/or light loads in larger calibers. **400 g. canister $24.95**

NORMA 204

A slow-burning powder, adapted for cartridges with a large case capacity and/or using heavy bullets in relation to the caliber.
500 g. canister

NORMA 201

Slower than the 200, used with lighter bullets in medium-size cases, or with big-caliber cartridges where a large bore volume is to be filled up quickly by expanding gases.
case capacity. **500 g. canister $24.95**

NORMA 202

A rifle powder of medium-burning rate that makes it the right choice for cartridges in the 6.5mm-7mm—30-06 caliber range of regular **500 g. canister $24.95**

NORMA MAGNUM RIFLE POWDER

Exceptionally slow-burning, high-energy powder for highest velocity with large capacity cases. A must for Magnums. **400 g. canister**

HANDGUN POWDERS

NORMA POWDER R-1

Is a fast-burning, easily ignited powder especially adapted for revolver cartridges with lead bullets, such as 38 Special target loads. It is clean burning, and the granules are of such size and shape that they flow easily in the powder measure and without binding the cylinder. It also handles very easily in the spoon or powder trickler for shooters who prefer weighing their loads. **200 g. canister $23.75**

NORMA POWDER R-123

Is a slow-burning handgun powder for heavier loads in cartridges such as 357 and 44 Magnum, especially when using jacketed bullets. This powder gives a lower breech pressure and the charge weight can therefore be increased for higher bullet velocities.
200 g. canister $23.75

NORMA RELOADING POWDERS

Rifle Powders/Pulver für Büchsenpatronen

Caliber	Bullet index no	Bullet weight (grains)	Max Cartridge length (inch)	(mm)	Norma primer	Norma powder	Load (grains)	(grams)	Muzzle vel Feet per sec	Meter per sec	Pressure psi	bar
220 Swift	65701	50	2.62	66.5	LR	202	39.3	2.55	3980	1213	53700	3700
222 Rem	65701 + 65702	50	2.11	53.5	SR	200	21.0	1.36	3200	975	46400	3200
						200	20.2	1.31	3000	914	46400	3200
						200	17.7	1.15	2790	850	46400	3200
	65704	53	2.16	55.0	SR	200	20.8	1.35	3115	950	46400	3200
22-250	65704	53	2.38	60.5	LR	202	36.6	2.37	3710	1130	53700	3700
5.6x52 R	65604	71	2.50	63.5	LR	202	27.0	1.75	2835	864	42100	2900
	65605	71	2.50	63.5	LR	202	27.0	1.75	2835	864	42100	2900
243 Win	66002 + 66003	100	2.62	66.5	LR	204	45.1	2.92	3070	936	52200	3600
						204	43.8	2.84	2870	875	52200	3600
						204	42.0	2.72	2670	814	52200	3600
6.5 Jap	66531	139	2.82	71.5	LR	202	30.9	2.00	2270	692	32200	2220
						201	28.2	1.83	2230	680	32200	2220
						200	24.0	1.55	2030	618	32200	2220
	66532	156	2.89	73.5	LR	202	28.2	1.83	2035	620	32200	2220
						201	24.7	1.60	1865	568	32200	2220
						200	20.5	1.33	1665	508	32200	2220
6.5x55	66551	77	2.62	66.5	LR	200	33.2	2.15	2725	830	45000	3100
						200	37.8	2.45	3115	950	45000	3100
						200	34.1	2.21	2915	889	45000	3100
	66512	139	2.99	76.0	LR	204	46.6	3.02	2790	850	45000	3100
						MRP	49.4	3.20	2815	858	45000	3100
						MRP	47.8	3.10	2740	835	45000	3100
	66532	156	3.07	78.0	LR	204	44.2	2.86	2495	760	45000	3100
						204	42.5	2.75	2295	700	45000	3100
						204	39.8	2.58	2095	639	45000	3100
6.5 Carc.	66532	156	2.97	75.5	LR	202	35.5	2.30	2340	713	37700	2600
						200	25.2	1.63	1800	549	37700	2600
270 Win	66902	130	3.15	80.0	LR	204	57.0	3.69	3140	957	52200	3600
						204	55.0	3.56	2940	896	52200	3600
						204	52.0	3.37	2740	835	52200	3600
	66903	150	3.23	82.0	LR	204	52.4	3.39	2800	853	52200	3600
						204	50.5	3.27	2600	792	52200	3600
						204	46.7	3.02	2400	731	52200	3600
7x57	67002	150	3.05	77.5	LR	202	44.0	2.85	2690	820	49300	3400
						201	40.0	2.59	2555	779	49300	3400
						201	36.5	2.36	2355	718	49300	3400
7x57 R	67002 + 67003	150	3.02	76.7	LR	202	42.9	2.78	2620	799	43500	3000
						201	36.3	2.35	2290	698	43500	3000
Super 7x61	67002	150	3.19	81.0	LR	MRP	67.4	4.37	3165	965	55100	3800
						204	58.5	3.79	2950	899	55100	3800
						204	55.3	3.58	2750	838	55100	3800
7 mm Rem. M	67002	150	3.25	82.5	LR	MRP	71.4	4.63	3250	990	55100	3800
						204	66.6	4.31	3060	933	55100	3800
						204	62.4	4.04	2860	872	55100	3800
7x64	67002	150	2.13	84.0	LR	204	57.1	3.70	2890	880	52200	3600
						204	52.9	3.43	2690	819	52200	3600
						204	49.5	3.21	2490	758	52200	3600
	67036	175	2.13	84.0	LR	MRP	56.6	3.67	2725	830	52200	3600
						MRP	51.7	3.35	2475	754	52200	3600
						MRP	48.3	3.13	2275	693	52200	3600
280 Rem	67002	150	3.29	83.5	LR	MRP	59.4	3.85	2980	910	50800	3500
7.5x55 Swiss	67625	180	2.91	74.0	LR	204	52.2	3.38	2650	808	45000	3100
						204	54.0	3.50	2690	820	45000	3100
7.62 Russ	67623	130	2.66	67.5	LR	201	51.4	3.33	3100	945	47900	3300
	67624	150	2.75	70.0	LR	201	47.8	3.10	2800	853	47900	3300
	67625	180	2.82	71.5	LR	202	47.1	3.05	2595	791	47900	3300
						201	37.2	2.41	2225	678	47900	3300
30 US Carb	67621	110	1.67	42.5	SR	–	–	–	1970	600	46400	3200
30-06	67621	110	2.87	73.0	LR	201	54.5	3.53	3280	1000	50800	3500
	67623	130	3.11	79.0	LR	202	56.3	3.65	3205	977	50800	3500
	67624	150	3.13	79.5	LR	202	52.5	3.40	2955	901	50800	3500
						MRP	62.4	4.04	2820	860	50800	3500
	67628	180	3.17	80.5	LR	204	56.3	3.65	2700	823	50800	3500
						202	48.5	3.14	2645	806	50800	3500
						201	41.6	2.69	2300	701	50800	3500
	67648	180	3.15	80.0	LR	204	56.3	3.65	2700	823	50800	3500
						202	48.5	3.14	2645	806	50800	3500
						201	41.6	2.69	2300	701	50800	3500
30-30 Win	67630	150	2.50	63.5	LR	201	35.5	2.30	2410	735	43500	3000
						201	32.5	2.10	2210	674	43500	3000
						200	26.1	1.69	2010	613	43500	3000
	67631	170	2.50	63.5	LR	201	32.4	2.10	2220	677	43500	3000
						200	26.3	1.70	2020	616	43500	3000
						200	23.3	1.51	1820	555	43500	3000
308 Win	67621	110	2.38	60.5	LR	200	40.1	2.60	2740	835	52200	3600
	67623	130	2.62	66.5	LR	200	40.6	2.63	2900	884	52200	3600
						200	38.2	2.47	2700	823	52200	3600
						200	35.1	2.27	2500	762	52200	3600
	67624	150	2.65	67.5	LR	201	45.5	2.95	2860	872	52200	3600
						201	43.3	2.80	2660	811	52200	3600
						201	40.6	2.63	2460	750	52200	3600
	67628	180	2.70	68.5	LR	202	42.1	2.73	2525	770	52208	3600
308 Norma M	67623	130	3.17	80.5	LR	204	78.4	5.08	3545	1080	55100	3800
	67624	150	3.21	81.5	LR	204	76.7	4.97	3330	1015	55100	3800
	67628	180	3.25	82.5	LR	MRP	74.3	4.81	3020	920	55100	3800
						204	71.8	4.65	2900	884	55100	3800
						204	70.0	4.53	2700	823	55100	3800
7.65 Arg	67701	150	2.85	72.5	LR	201	47.8	3.10	2920	890	49300	3400
						201	44.0	2.85	2720	829	49300	3400
						201	42.5	2.75	2520	768	49300	3400
303 British	67701	150	2.95	75.0	LR	201	44.6	2.89	2720	829	46400	3200
						201	41.4	2.68	2520	768	46400	3200
						200	33.9	2.19	2320	707	46400	3200
	67713	180	2.97	75.5	LR	202	43.0	2.79	2540	774	46400	3200
						202	43.5	2.82	2600	792	46400	3200
						201	36.2	2.34	2140	652	46400	3200
7.7 Jap.	67711	130	2.84	72.0	LR	202	51.7	3.35	3005	916	39200	2700
	67713	180	3.03	77.0	LR	202	46.0	2.98	2515	767	39200	2700
8x57 J	67901	196	2.97	75.5	LR	202	48.0	3.11	2485	757	48500	3300
						201	39.8	2.58	2125	648	48500	3300
8x57 JS	68003	196	2.95	75.0	LR	202	48.3	3.13	2485	757	49300	3400
						200	36.4	2.36	2125	648	49300	3400
	68007	196	2.97	75.5	LR	202	48.3	3.13	2485	757	49300	3400
						200	36.4	2.36	2125	648	49300	3400
358 Norma M	69001	250	3.23	82.0	LR	202	66.3	4.30	2710	826	53400	3700
						201	57.0	3.69	2400	731	53400	3700
9.3x57	69303	286	3.01	76.5	LR	201	44.6	2.89	2065	630	36300	2500
						201	40.6	2.63	1865	569	36300	2500
						200	34.2	2.22	1665	508	36300	2500
9.3x62	69303	286	3.23	82.0	LR	201	54.7	3.54	2360	720	49300	3400
						201	51.2	3.32	2160	659	49300	3400
						200	44.0	2.85	1960	598	49300	3400

MRP/Magnum Rifle Powder

An exceptionally slow burning, high-energy powder for highest velocity with large capacity cases. Replaces the famous Norma 205 powder. A must for magnums.

Caliber	Bullet index no.	Bullet weight grains	Max Cartridge length inch.	mm	Norma primer	Norma powder	Load grains	grams	Muzzle vel. Feet per sec.	Meter per sec.	Pressure[1] psi	bar
243 Win.	–	80	2.54	64.5	LR	MRP	50.6	3.28	3347	1020	52200	3600
243 Win.	66003	100	2.62	66.5	LR	MRP	49.2	3.19	3199	975	52200	3600
6 mm Rem.	66003	100	2.82	71.6	LR	MRP	46.4	3.01	3117	950	54400	3750
6 mm Rem.	66003	100	2.82	71.6	LR	MRP	48.2	3.12	3248	990	54400	3750
6.5 Carc.	66551	77	2.52	64.0	LR	MRP	46.5	3.01	2965	904	37700	2600
6.5 Carc.	66522	80	2.50	63.5	LR	MRP	46.6	3.02	2950	899	37700	2600
6.5 Carc.	66512	139	2.85	72.5	LR	MRP	43.2	2.80	2570	783	37700	2600
6.5 Carc.	66510	144	2.95	75.0	LR	MRP	43.2	280	2550	777	37700	2600
6.5 Carc.	66532	156	2.95	75.0	LR	MRP	42.4	2.75	2435	744	37700	2600
6.5 Jap.	66512	139	2.81	71.5	LR	MRP	37.7	2.44	2335	712	37700	2600
6.5 Jap.	66532	156	2.89	73.3	LR	MRP	38.1	2.47	2310	704	37700	2600
6.5x55	66531	139	2.99	76.0	LR	MRP	47.8	3.10	2740	835	45000	3100
6.5x55	66512	139	2.99	76.0	LR	MRP	49.4	3.20	2815	858	49300	3400[2]
6.5x55	66510	144	3.05	77.5	LR	MRP	48.6	3.15	2780	847	49300	3400[2]
6.5x55	66532	156	3.07	78.0	LR	MRP	48.0	3.11	2645	806	49300	3400[2]
270 Win.	–	110	3.15	80.0	LR	MRP	61.5	3.98	3166	965	52200	3600
270 Win.	66902	130	3.15	80.0	LR	MRP	60.9	3.95	3133	955	52200	3600
270 Win.	66903	150	3.23	82.0	LR	MRP	58.4	3.78	2969	905	52200	3600
7x57	67002	150	3.03	77.0	LR	MRP	50.9	3.30	2615	797	49300	3400
7x57 R	67002	150	3.02	76.7	LR	MRP	51.3	3.32	2690	820	43500	3000
7x57 R	–	160	3.06	77.7	LR	MRP	50.4	3.27	2608	795	43500	3000
7x61 Super	–	160	3.19	81.0	LR	MRP	66.5	4.31	3100	945	55100	3800
7x61 Super	–	175	3.19	81.0	LR	MRP	64.8	4.20	2904	885	55100	3800
7x64	67002	150	3.27	83.0	LR	MRP	59.6	3.86	2960	902	52200	3600
7 mm Rem.	–	160	3.19	81.0	LR	MRP	70.2	4.55	3166	965	55100	3800
7 mm Rem.	–	175	3.21	81.5	LR	MRP	68.0	4.41	2986	910	55100	3800
7.5x55	67621	110	2.56	65.0	LR	MRP	60.9	3.95	3085	940	45000	3100
7.5x55	67623	130	2.80	71.0	LR	MRP	60.2	3.90	3060	933	45000	3100
7.5x55	67602	146	2.81	71.5	LR	MRP	57.1	3.70	2920	890	45000	3100
7.5x55	67624	150	2.80	71.0	LR	MRP	57.1	3.70	2890	881	45000	3100
7.5x55	67625	180	2.80	71.0	LR	MRP	55.6	3.60	2730	832	45000	3100
30–06	67624	150	3.13	79.5	LR	MRP	62.4	4.04	2822	860	50800	3500
30–06	67628	180	3.17	80.5	LR	MRP	60.1	3.89	2658	810	50800	3500
30–06	–	200	3.23	82.0	LR	MRP	59.4	3.85	2608	795	50800	3500
30–06	67628	180	3.17	80.5	–	MRP	61.7	4.00	2790	850	50800	3500

Loading data for Weatherby Magnums/Ladedata für Weatherby Magnum Patronen

Caliber	Bullet index no.	Bullet weight grains	Max Cartridge length inch.	mm	Norma primer	Norma powder	Load grains	grams	Muzzle vel. Feet per sec.	Meter per sec.	Pressure[1] psi	bar
240 WM	–	70	3.15	80.0	–	MRP	59.4	3.85	3838	1170	55100	3800
240 WM	–	85	3.15	80.0	–	MRP	54.9	3.56	3497	1066	55100	3800
240 WM	–	87	3.15	80.0	–	MRP	54.5	3.53	3497	1066	55100	3800
240 WM	–	100	3.15	80.0	–	MRP	54.0	3.50	3395	1035	55100	3800
257 WM	–	87	3.42	87.0	–	MRP	74.1	4.80	3757	1145	55100	3800
257 WM	–	100	3.42	87.0	–	MRP	71.3	4.62	3555	1084	55100	3800
257 WM	–	117	3.42	87.0	–	MRP	67.1	4.35	3300	1006	55100	3800
270 WM	–	100	3.42	87.0	–	MRP	77.2	5.00	3760	1146	55100	3800
270 WM	–	130	3.42	87.0	–	MRP	73.3	4.75	3375	1029	55100	3800
270 WM	–	150	3.42	87.0	–	MRP	71.7	4.65	3245	990	55100	3800
7 mm WM	–	139	3.42	87.0	–	MRP	74.1	4.80	3300	1006	55100	3800
7 mm WM	–	154	3.42	87.0	–	MRP	72.8	4.72	3160	963	55100	3800
7 mm WM	–	160	3.42	87.0	–	MRP	72.5	4.70	3150	960	55100	3800
7 mm WM	–	175	3.42	87.0	–	MRP	71.0	4.60	3070	935	55100	3800
300 WM	–	110	3.58	91.0	–	MRP	81.0	5.25	3900	1189	55100	3800
300 WM	–	150	3.58	91.0	–	MRP	88.0	5.70	3545	1081	55100	3800
300 WM	–	180	3.58	91.0	–	MRP	83.3	5.40	3245	990	55100	3800
300 WM	–	200	3.58	91.0	–	MRP	78.7	5.10	3000	914	55100	3800
300 WM	–	220	3.58	91.0	–	MRP	79.2	5.13	2905	885	55100	3800
340 WM	–	200	3.70	94.0	–	MRP	91.0	5.90	3210	978	55100	3800
340 WM	–	210	3.70	94.0	–	MRP	91.0	5.90	3180	969	55100	3800
340 WM	–	250	3.70	94.0	–	MRP	85.2	5.52	2850	869	55100	3800
378 WM	–	270	3.70	94.0	–	MRP	115.5	7.48	3180	969	58785	4055
378 WM	–	300	3.70	94.0	–	MRP	111.8	7.20	2925	892	58785	4055

Handgun Powders

Caliber	Bullet index no.	Bullet weight grains	Max Cartridge length inch.	mm	Norma primer	Norma powder	Load grains	grams	Muzzle velocity Feet per sec.	Meter per sec.	Pressure[1] psi	bar
9 mm Luger	69010	116	1.16	29.5	SP	R-1	3.8	0.246	1115	340	36300	2500
38 Special	69110	148	1.16	29.5	SP	R-1	2.5	0.162	800	244	17000	1170
	69112	158	1.50	38.0	SP	R-1	3.5	0.227	870	265	20000	1380
	69107	158	1.48	37.5	SP	R-1	4.2	0.272	900	274	20000	1380
	69101	158	1.46	37.0	SP	R-1	4.2	0.272	900	274	20000	1380
357 Mag.	69101	158	1.59	40.5	SP	R-123	13.9	0.900	1450	442	40600	2800
	69107	158	1.59	40.5	SP	R-123	13.9	0.900	1450	442	40600	2800
38 S & W	–	146	1.16	29.5	SP	R-1	2.0	0.130	730	222	13800	950
44 Mag.	61103	240	1.61	41.0	LP	R-123	19.1	1.240	1675	511	40600	2800

BONANZA RELOADING TOOLS

CO-AX® PRESS

Snap-in and snap-out die change, positive spent primer catcher, automatic self-acting shell holder, floating guide rods, perfect alignment of die and case is assured, good for right- or left-handed operators, uses standard ⅞ x 14 dies.

MODEL 68 PRESS

No obstructions to visibility of operator, open working space, upright mounting, equal thrust distribution, simple in construction, heavy duty, constructed of automotive-type casting, ram is machined and fitted.

BONANZA MODEL 68 PRESS .... $ 70.00
BONANZA CO-AX PRESS (B-1) less dies 156.00
EXTRA SET JAWS for Co-Ax .... set 15.40

BONANZA B-Z PRESS (with new E-Z Just Shell Holder) $170.00
BONANZA "BLUE RIBBON" PRIMING CONVERSION UNIT FOR B-1 PRESS 28.00

PISTOL DIES

BONANZA PISTOL DIES are three-die sets. The 38 Spl. & 357 Mag., and the 44 Spl. & 44 Mag. are so designed that each set may be used to load the two calibers. You need not buy extra dies to load the magnums. The Bonanza Cross Bolt Lock Ring is standard on all Bonanza dies. A special taper crimp die is available for 45 ACP and 38-357 and 9mm Luger.

Bonanza Three-Die Pistol Set $32.00
Bonanza Taper Crimp Die 14.00
Bonanza Two-Die Pistol Set 27.00

CO-AX RIFLE DIES

All Bonanza Dies are made with ⅞ x 14 threads and can be used on various other makes of presses. The CO-AX SEATER can be adjusted to crimp or not to crimp. All calibers crimp. The Sizer, with elevated expander button, is the same as is supplied with the Bench Rest Dies. This "E-Z" OUT expander button is drawn through the case neck while the operator uses the full mechanical advantage of the press.

Bonanza CO-AX Die Set $27.00
Bonanza CO-AX Seating Dies only 14.00
Bonanza CO-AX Sizing Die only 18.00
Bonanza Three-Die Rifle Set 32.00

BONANZA RELOADING TOOLS

CO-AX®INDICATOR

Gives a reading of how closely the axis of the bullet corresponds with the axis of the cartridge case. Spring-loaded plunger holds against cartridges **a recessed, adjustable rod** supported in a "V" block.

BONANZA CO-AX INDICATOR, less Indicator Dial $37.00

Indicator Dial only 38.90

CASE TRIMMER MODEL "66"

Neck case pilot eliminates the need for a collet and shell holder. Reversible mandrell and four-blade case-mouth trimmer. Dull cutter is exchanged for a sharpened cutter.

BONANZA CASE TRIMMER, complete with Pilot (state caliber) $25.00
extra Pilots (state caliber) 1.60
extra Cutter 12.00
Cutter Sharpening "Exchange" 6.00

BONANZA BULLS-EYE PISTOL POWDER MEASURE

Measure has fixed-charge rotor. Supplied with a quick detachable bracket for use on a bench, or it can be held by hand.
Bonanza Pistol Powder Measure and One Rotor . . **$28.50**
Extra Rotor or Blank Rotor **5.00**

BONANZA BENCH REST®POWDER MEASURE

Powder is metered from the charge arm.
Measure will throw uniform charges from 2½-grains bulls-eye to 95-grains 4320.
Measure empties by removing charge bar from charge arm, letting contents flow through charge arm into powder container.
BBRPM Bonanza Bench Rest®Powder Measure **$51.50**
Stand (extra) fits either Pistol or Bench Rest Measure **14.50**

BONANZA RELOADING TOOLS

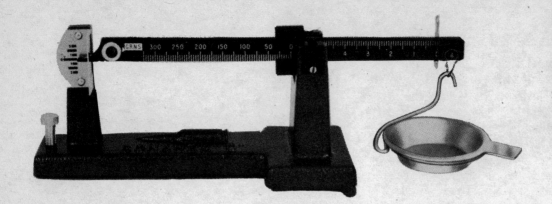

**BONANZA
POWDER
AND
BULLET
SCALE**

MODEL "D"™

Bonanza Powder and Bullet Scale Model "D"™ **$34.95**

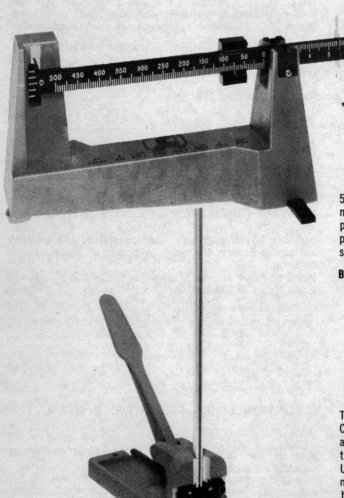

**BONANZA
"M" MAGNETIC
DAMPENED
SCALE**

505 grain capacity, tempered stainless steel right hand poise, diamond polished agate "V" bearings, non-glare white markings, three point suspension base, strengthened beam at pivot points, powder pan for right or left pouring, guaranteed accurate to 1/10 grain, sensitivity guaranteed to 1/20 grain.

Bonanza "M" Magnetic Dampened Scale **$55.00**

BONANZA BLUE RIBBON CO-AX® PRIMER SEATER

The Bonanza Primer Seater is designed so that primers are seated Co-Axially (primer in line with primer pocket). Mechanical leverage allows primers to be seated fully without crushing. With the addition of one extra set of Disc Shell Holders and one extra Primer Unit, all modern cases, rim or rimless, from .222 up to .458 Magnum can be primed. Shell Holders are easily adjusted to any case by rotating to contact rim or cannelure of the case.

Bonanza Primer Seater **$43.50**
Primer Tube **2.90**

BONANZA RELOADING TOOLS

CO-AX® CASE TRIMMER
Model 80000

The cutter shaft rides within a honed bearing for turning of the crank handle when trimming. Hardened and ground cutter teeth remove excess brass. Case to be trimmed is locked in a collet case holder, case is seated against the collet then locked, cases are trimmed to the same length regardless of rim thickness or head diameter. For accuracy of setting to proper trim length a collar stop is provided on the shaft. Cases may be trimmed to a tolerance of .001" or less.

Case Trimmer with one collet and one pilot	**$35.65**
Case Trimmer less collet and pilot	**29.00**
Case Trimmer Pilot 8009 (give caliber)	**1.40**
Case Trimmer Collet 0102-(No. 1, 2, or 3)	**4.35**
Case Trimmer Cutter Shaft 0107 (Standard)	**8.65**
Case Trimmer Cutter Shaft 0107 — .17 caliber	**8.65**
Case Trimmer Pilot for .17 caliber	**1.40**
(Above two items are accessories and not offered with a trimmer. Not interchangeable with standard shaft.)	
Short Base 0104-S	**6.10**
Long Base 0104-L	**6.10**

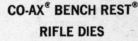

CO-AX® BENCH REST®
RIFLE DIES

BONANZA BENCH REST DIES are glass hard for long wear and minimum friction. Interiors are polished mirror smooth. Special attention is given to headspace, tapers and diameters so that brass will not be overworked when resized. Our sizing die has an elevated expander button which is drawn through the neck of the case at the moment of the greatest mechanical advantage of the press. Since most of the case neck is still in the die when expanding begins, better alignment of case and neck is obtained. **Our Bench Rest® Seating Die** is of the chamber type. The bullet is held in alignment in a close fitting channel. The case is held in a tight fitting chamber. Both bullet and case are held in alignment all the while the bullet is being seated. These dies represent the first improvement in design since 1924. The set costs less than some are charging for a straight line seater alone. As a bonus you get our cross bolt lock ring.

Bench Rest® Die Set	**$33.00**
Full Length Sizer	**18.00**
Bench Seating Die	**18.00**

C-H RELOADING TOOLS

C-H RELOADING DIES

C-H reloading dies are available in all popular calibers. The outside has a non-glare satin finish. The outside threads are ⅞ x 14 and will fit all standard presses. C-H die lock rings feature a nylon ball lock inside the set screw to prevent damage to the threads and facilitate readjustment.

C-H TRIM DIES

By using these C-H Trim Dies you can shorten the neck of your cases with a file or a fine-tooth hacksaw. Dies are hardened and will not be effected by the filing. Available in the following calibers: 222 Rem., 22-250, 225 Win., 243 Win., 6mm R, 257 Robts., 25-06, 257 Wea., 6.5x55, 270 Win., 7x57 Mauser, 7mm Rem. Mag., 7mm Wea., 308 Win., 30-06, 300 Win. Mag., 300 Wea., 8x57.
File Trim Die **$11.50**

AUTO CHAMPION MARK V- A

Available for 38 Special/357; 45 ACP; 44 Mag. and 9 mm Luger. Features: Reloading capability of 500 rounds per hour. Fully progressive loading. Powder measure cam allows you to "jog" the machine without dispensing powder. Simple powder measure emptying device included with each unit. Tungsten-carbide sizing die at no extra cost. Unit comes with your choice of powder bushing and seating stem (round nose, wadcutter or semi-wadcutter). Seating die cavity-tapered for automatic alignment of the bullet. One 100-capacity primer tube, two 15-capacity case tubes and tube coupling also included at no extra cost **$699.00**

STANDARD CALIBER DIE SETS

Series 'A' Full Length Sizer and Seater Die . **$23.65**
Series 'B' Sizer, Expander-Decapper and
    Seater Die 23.65
Series 'C' Sizer-Decapper, Expander and
    Seater Die 23.65
Series 'D' Neck Sizer and Seater Die 23.65
Series 'E' Full Length Sizer, Neck Sizer and
    Seater Die 29.70
Series 'F' Sizer, Expander-Decapper and
    Speed Seater Die 25.30
Series 'G' Carbide Sizer, Expander-Decapper and Seater Die 41.80
Series 'H' Carbide Sizer, Expander-Decapper and Speed Seater Die 42.00
Decapping Pin, Specify caliber (standard
    or heavy duty) 1.00
    pkg. of 5

C-H CHAMPION PRESS

Compound leverage press for all phases of re-loading. Heavyweight (26#) C-Hampion comes complete with primer arm, ⅞ x 14 bushing for use with all reloading dies. Spent primers fall through back of press into waste basket. 'O' frame design will not spring under any conditions. Ideal press for swaging bullets. Top of frame bored 1¼ x 18 for use with special dies and shot-shell dies.

                         $199.50

C-H TUNGSTEN CARBIDE EXPANDER BALLS

Now available as an accessory, the C-H Tungsten Carbide Expander Ball eliminates the need for lubricating the inside of the case neck.
Available in the following calibers: 22, 243, 25, 270, 7mm, 30, 320, 322. Calibers 7mm and larger have 10-32 inside threads, 243 to 270 have 8-32 inside threads and 22 has 6-32 inside threads. (270 will not fit RCBS)
C-H Carbide Expander Ball .. **$5.50**
For the RCBS 22 expander unit we can provide a complete rod with carbide expander that will fit their die body.
C-H Carbide Expander Ball to fit....
    22 cal. RCBS die **$6.50**

C-H RELOADING TOOLS

CHAMPION jr. RELOADING PRESS

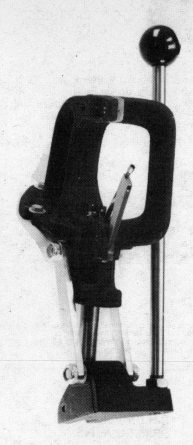

CHAMPION Jr. Heavy Duty Reloading Press— semi steel (cast iron) "O" press offset so the opening is 210 degrees for better access. Solid steel handle is offset to match opening.

Positioning of toggle pin provides maximum leverage—so powerful that a 30/06 case can be forced into a 250 full length resizing die. In addition to usual 2 bolt fastening we put a 3rd bolt so the "big" jobs using maximum power won't break off your bench.

Weight 13½ lbs.

Uses standard detachable shell holders.

Price complete w/primer arm and 1 shell holder $114.95

Price complete with 1 die set 133.60

C-H DIE BOX

Protect your dies from dust and damage with a C-H 3-compartment plastic Die Box. High-impact plastic—will not break. Easy to label and stack.
No. 700 C-H Die Box $1.50

FROM C-H 3/4 JACKETED PISTOL BULLET

SWAGING DIES

- Any bullet weight from 110 gr. to 250 gr. with same set of dies
- Can be used in any good ⅞ x 14 loading tool
- Absolutely no leading
- Complete — no extras to buy
- Increased velocity
- Solid Nose or hollow point (hollow point $2.50 extra)
- Available in 38/357, 41 S & W 44 Mag. and 45 colt calibers

PRICE
$38.45

BULLET SWAGING DIE EJECTOR

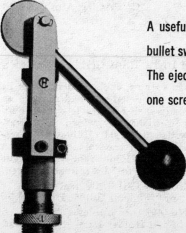

A useful accessory for use with the new C-H jacketed bullet swaging dies.

The ejector attaches easily to the swaging die body with one screw. Can be used with either the core seating die or the swage die. Ejects the seated core or finished bullet with ease. No more tapping the top of the die.

Price $24.65

FROM C-H NEW SOLID STEEL

CANNELURE TOOL

PRICE
$29.95

- Will work on all sizes of bullets, from 17 to 45
- Completely adjustable for depth and height
- One set will process thousands of bullets
- Necessary for rolling in grooves on bullets prior to crimping
- Hardened cutting wheel, precision machined throughout

C-H RELOADING ACCESSORIES

NO. 725 POWDER and BULLET SCALE

Chrome plated, brass beam. Graduated in 10 gr., 1 gr. and 1/10th gr. increments. Convenient pouring spout on pan. Leveling screw on base. All metal construction. 360 gr. capacity. **Price** **$33.95**

C-H POWDER MEASURE

The new steel drum is designed so the handle can be placed on either the right or left side, and the charge can be dropped on either the up or down stroke. Or reverse for use with micrometer either front or back. Base threads are ⅞ x 14. The rifle micrometer adjusts precisely and permits up to 100 grains of 4831. The Pistol micrometer permits up to 12 grains of Bullseye.

A baffle plate is supplied with the optional 10" production hopper.

No. 502 Powder Measure *Specify Rifle or Pistol* **$34.95**

No. 502-1 Stand ⅞" thread **6.95**

No. 502-2 Micrometer *Specify Rifle or Pistol* **9.75**

No. 592-3 10" Production Hopper (*with baffle*) **5.50**

C-H CARTRIDGE RACK TRAY

Holds 60 cartridges. Comes in black, white or red. It is handy for the reloader who works up cases for different loads, etc. Holes are 15/16" deep which is too deep for 38 Spl. Holes are not large enough for 45/70 or 348 but hold all sizes up to 375 H&H.

No. 403 Cartridge Rack Tray **$1.65**

C-H CASE TRIMMER No. 301

This design features a unique clamp to lock case holder in position. Ensures perfect uniformity from 22 cal. thru 45 cal. whether rifle or pistol cases. Complete including hardened case holder . . . **$21.95**
Extra case holders (hardened & hand-lapped) . . . **$3.50**

C-H UNIVERSAL PRIMING ARMS

Accommodates all standard rifle and pistol primers. Made of fine metal—not a stamping, for extra strength and dimensional stability. Packaged in clear acetate tube.

No. 414 C-H Universal "C" Priming Arm . . **$6.95**

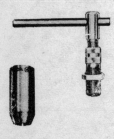

C-H BULLET PULLER

C-H Bullet Puller features positive die-locking action, removes the bullet easily without any damage to housing or bullet. The detachable handle is constructed of ⅜" stock and adjusts to any position. The hex nut for crescent wrench adjustment locks the die into firm position. Extra long internal thread for extra locking leeway.

No. 402 with Collet . **$10.50**
No. 402-1 Extra Collet **3.25**

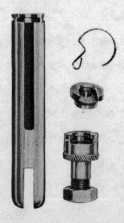

C-H UNIVERSAL SHELL HOLDERS

Up to now, shell holders came in one piece and you had to have as many shell holders as the calibers you wished to reload. However, with the C-H Universal Shell Holder all the reloader needs is the Shell Holder ram and then get the heads for the calibers desired.

No. 408 C-H Universal "C" or "H" Shell Holder Head **$4.00**

No. 407 C-H Universal "H" Shell Holder Ram **5.25**

No. 412 C-H Universal "C" Shell Holder Ram **5.50**

LYMAN RELOADING TOOLS

FOR RIFLE OR PISTOL CARTRIDGES

LYMAN 310 TOOL

The 310 Tool is a compact, portable reloading kit that can be used anywhere—home, hunting camp, in the field, on the range. Using the 310 Tool, the novice can start reloading with a small investment. The 310 Tool performs all the operations required for reloading metallic cartridges for handguns and rifles. It removes the old primer, resizes the cartridge neck, it inserts a new primer, and seats the new bullet. A practiced reloader can load, fire, adjust and reload his charge right on the range, test firing until he determines his best load.

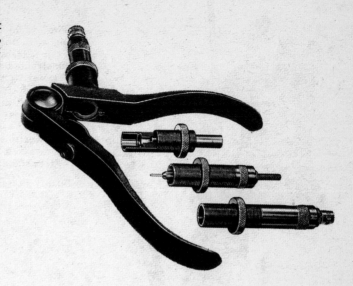

310 Tool Handles Only (large or small) **$24.95**

310 Dies (rifle or handgun)—Set consists of five pieces: Neck Resizing and Decapping Die, Priming Chamber, Neck Expanding Chamber, Bullet Seating Chamber and an Adapter Die **$29.95**

GROUP V AA BENCH REST 2-DIE SETS

Bench Rest Set includes a micrometer seating die for ultra-precise seating depth control and bullet to case alignment; a neck sizing die designed to consistently retain the cartridge's precise fire-formed dimensions and a true micrometer head. Micrometer head may be repositioned within the die body—no special shell holders are ever needed, no matter how short your cartridge. Because there's no port, the full contact alignment sleeve is precisely centered throughout the entire bullet seating operation. It cannot lose concentric alignment right at the point when alignment is critical. Sizing die only sizes the neck of the case so cartridges retain the exact fire-formed shape of the gun chamber. The die is machined to hold maximum concentricity between the neck of the shell and the body of the die.

Die Set	**$54.50**
Micrometer Seating Die	39.95
Neck Sizing Die	18.95

LYMAN SHOTSHELL HANDBOOK

The second edition of the Lyman Shotshell Handbook features an authoritative study devoted exclusively to shotshell reloading—a reloading handbook which covers every aspect of modern shotshell reloading. Dealing with the latest components it is an indispensable reference book which belongs on every reloading bench. Complete "How To Reload" section on choosing a load, factory velocities, assembling shotshells, etc. Reference section covers up-to-date pressure information, four color case identification chapter, plus chapters on wads, patterns, powder and primers. Over 1000 tested loads covering all gauges 10, 12, 16, 20, 28 and 410. Contains suggested reloads using modern components from all of the major manufacturers **$11.95**

LYMAN RELOADING TOOLS

FOR RIFLE OR PISTOL CARTRIDGES

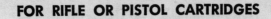

LYMAN SPAR-T TURRET PRESS

The Lyman Spar-T Press combines the maximum speed of turret loading with the operating ease, and strength of the ever popular C Frame Press. It's massive frame, and 6 station Turret, are ruggedly constructed of high-silicone, iron-steel castings (not aluminum alloy). It's Verti-Lock Turret is firmly secured to the frame by a heavy duty ¾" steel stud. Positive stop, audible click action insures foolproof cartridge to die alignment and rapid operation. Uses standard ⅞ x 14 dies.

Features: • Lock nut rigidly locks turret in one position for swaging. • Powerful toggle-link leverage (25 to 1) • UP or DOWN STROKE operation. • Alignment ramp positions Shell Holder at top of stroke. • Uses standard Spartan accessories.

Spar-T Press with ram and primer arm **$109.95**

SPAR-T SET: Consists of Spar-T Press, Spar-T Auto-Primer Feed, Spartan Primer Arm, Spartan Ram, Spartan Shell Holder Head, Complete set of All-American Dies. **$134.95**

SPAR-T ACCESSORIES

PRIMER CATCHER: Made of heavy-duty plastic, this unit may be used on either the Spartan or Spar-T Press. Locks securely to press, yet allows for easy removal when emptying primers. **$3.95**

DETACHABLE SHELL HOLDER: Precision cut and hardened to ensure perfect case fit. Used with the Spartan Ram on the Spartan Press and on many other presses. **$4.95**

UNIVERSAL PRIMING ARM: Seats all sizes and types of primers. Supplied with two priming sleeves (large and small), two flat priming punches (large and small), and two round priming punches (large and small). **$6.95**

TOP PUNCH AND SIZING DIES FOR LYMAN 450 SIZER/LUBRICATOR

Lyman sizing dies and top punches are made to exacting standards for accurate sizing and lubricating of lead alloy bullets in Lyman's 450 Sizer/Lubricator. The inside contour of each top punch is precisely machined to fit bullet nose shape exactly. This eliminates nose deformation when the top punch forces a bullet down into the sizing die. Refer to Lyman's bullet mould listing for suggested top punch number.

The sizing die's tapered mouth and hardened interior forms bullets to a perfect cylindrical shape and also holds them in place for Lyman lubricant. Interior dimensions of Lyman sizing dies correspond to the suggested diameters for all popular rifle and pistol calibers. Refer to the sizing die diameter chart on this page for the complete list of available dies.

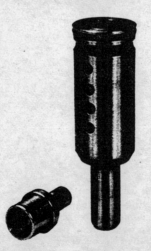

Price:
Top Punch (G) — specify number -see page 20 & 21 (½ oz.) **$4.50**
Sizing Die Assembly (H & I) - specify diameter - (2 oz.) **$11.95**

AUTO-PRIMER FEED: Eliminates handling of primer with oily fingers, speeds loading. Supplied with two tubes (large and small) Spartan and O-Mag. Spar-T **$13.95**

LYMAN RELOADING TOOLS
FOR RIFLE OR PISTOL CARTRIDGES

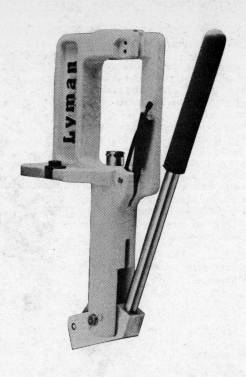

LYMAN O-MAG

Lyman has fitted its O-Mag with some unexpected extras that truly make it the magnum press for every serious reloader. These extras include a 4½-inch opening that easily accommodates even the largest cartridge, a longer, slip-free grip and a hole behind the mounting (in addition to the two conventional side holes) for an extra measure of stability and leverage. The Lyman O-Mag is also the first magnum press to introduce a flat work surface above and behind the die station for mounting racks and accessories. Set includes the O-Mag press and primer catcher, universal primer arm, ram, detachable shell holder and a complete set of standard AA dies (state caliber).

Also available as a companion to the Lyman O-Mag is the Powder Measure Stand, which features the standard ⅞″ x 14″ thread and raises any measure high enough to position cases beneath the powder drop tube.

O-Mag Set (18 lbs.)	**$109.95**
O-Mag Press only w/ram and universal primer arm .	89.95
Powder Measure Stand	14.95

T-MAG SET (shown)

Our T-Mag Set includes the T-Mag Press, plus the tools you need to turn out top-quality reloads for your rifle or handgun:

- T-Mag Press
- O-Mag Primer Catcher
- Universal Primer Arm
- Ram
- Detachable Shell Holder
- Complete Set of standard AA Dies (state caliber)

T-Mag Set (18 lbs.) **$164.95**

T-MAG TURRET RELOADING PRESS

With the T-Mag you can mount up to six different reloading dies on our turret. This means you can have all your dies set up, precisely mounted, locked in and ready to reload at all times. The T-Mag works with all ⅞ x 14 dies. It's built with O-Mag strength and uses standard O-Mag primer feed and O-Mag primer catcher. The T-Mag turret is held in rock-solid alignment by a ¾-inch steel stud.

T-Mag Press only with Ram and Universal Priming Arm (17 lbs.) **$139.95**

LYMAN RELOADING ACCESSORIES

PRIMER POCKET REAMER

Cleans and removes rough metal edges from a primer pocket. This tool is a must for military type primers. Available in large or small—see priming punch size in cartridge table.

Price $7.95

POWDER FUNNEL

This plastic powder funnel is designed to fill cases from 22 Hornet through 45-70 without inserts or adjustments.

Price: $2.50

Powder Dribbler $7.95

THE NO. 55 POWDER MEASURE

This Powder Measure and dispensing device charges any number of cases with black, or smokeless, powder loads that are consistent within a fraction of a grain. Its three-slide micrometer adjustable cavity adjusts the load accurately, and locks in place to provide accurate charging. The 2400 grain capacity plastic reservoir gives a clear view of the powder level. The reservoir is fabricated from blue-tinted polyvinyl-chloride plastic that resists chemical action of double base powders, and filters out light rays that would damage powders. An optional 7000 grain reservoir is available. The measure clamps securely to the loading bench, or mounts directly to any turret press by means of threaded drop tubes (supplied with measure). A knocker mounted on the side of the measure insures complete discharge of powder directly into the cartridge case. No funnel is required.

No. 55 POWDER MEASURE **$55.95**
Optional 7000 grain capacity reservoir . **9.95**
7/8" x 14 Adapter for Turret Mounting ... **2.00**

The unique three-slide micrometer adjustable cavity is the key to the unfailing accuracy of the 55 Powder Measure. Micrometer adjustments for both width and depth provide a dependable, consistent measure that minimizes cutting of coarse powder.

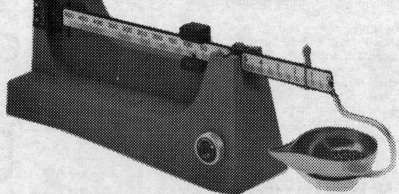

LYMAN M-500 SCALE

Dial markings are white on jet black for easy reading. The pointer, and dial, are placed on the same plane to eliminate parallax error. Its high capacity of up to 505 grains, permits the heaviest charges and even bullets to be weighed. Features magnetic damping. Genuine agate bearings guarantee one tenth of a grain of sensitivity.

Lyman M-500 Scale $44.95

LYMAN RELOADING DIES

The All-American Dies shown on this page are designed for use with the Lyman Spartan, Spar-T, AA Turret, and all other reloading presses having 7/8" x 14" thread die stations. AA die sets are offered in either 2 or 3 die combinations, depending on shape of cartridge case, and type of bullet to be loaded.

Outer surfaces of all dies are chrome-plated. All bullet seating dies are adjustable to crimp or not crimp the bullet. Sizing dies for bottleneck cartridges are vented to prevent air traps.

TWO-DIE RIFLE SET

These sets consist of two dies. The first die full-length resizes, decaps, and expands, while the second die seats the bullet and crimps when desired. Two die sets are specifically designed for loading bottleneck shape cartridge cases using jacketed bullets. These sets are not offered for straight-taper shape cases. They should not be used with cast bullets unless in conjunction with an "M" die (see below). Two-die rifle set **$27.50**

T-C* PISTOL DIE

*Tungsten Carbide Resizing & Decapping Die for handgun cartridges.

A lifetime of reloads, some 200,000 rounds can be pushed through this Full-Length Sizing and Decapping Die without a sign of wear. Its diamond-like sizing surface of polished tungsten carbide creates far less friction (75% less) than steel dies. With the Lyman T-C Die, cases need not be lubricated and even dirty cases come out of the die with a polished burnished appearance. T-C Dies are available for the following pistol cartridges.

38 S & W (also fits 38 ACP & 38 Super)	44 Special (also fits 44 Magnum)
38 Special (also fits 357 Magnum)	45 ACP
41 Magnum	45 Colt

T-C Pistol Die **$34.95**

THREE-DIE RIFLE SET

Required to load straight-taper cartridge cases, and all other cartridges when using cast bullets.

This set consists of: full-length resizing and decapping die, a 2-step neck expanding die, and a bullet seating and crimping die. The added advantage of the three-die set is in the use of the 2-step neck expanding die which allows the bullet to enter the case freely, without cutting or marring lead. This method of neck-expanding insures precise case neck tension on seated bullet.

Standard Three-die rifle set **$35.00**

THREE-DIE PISTOL SETS

Available for all pistol calibers this set can be used with either cast of jacketed bullets.

Set consists of: full-length resizing and decapping die, a 2-step neck expanding die, and a bullet seating and crimping die. Available for various bullet styles.

Standard Three-die pistol set **$29.50**

TWO-STEP "M" NECK-EXPANDING DIE FOR CAST RIFLE BULLETS

Available for all rifle cases this die is required when loading cast bullets, and will also improve the accuracy of jacketed bullet reloads. The first step expands the neck of the cartridge to slightly under bullet diameter. The second step expands the first 1/16" of the neck to slightly over bullet diameter, allowing the bullet to enter the case freely, without cutting lead. This die insures precise case neck tension on seated bullet. **$10.95**

LYMAN RELOADING

AA Bench Rest 2-Die Sets
(for jacketed bullets)

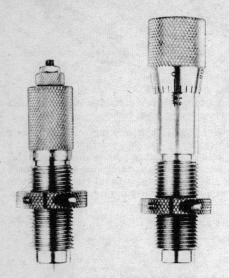

Cartridge	Die Set Number	Micrometer Seating Die	Neck Sizing Die
22-250 (22 Varminter)	7690012	7161012	7135012
220 Swift	7690013	7161013	7135013
222 Remington	7690005	7161005	7135005
223 Remington (5.56mm)	7690006	7161006	7135006
243 Winchester	7690015	7161015	7135015
6mm Remington (244 Rem.)	7690016	7161016	7135016
25-06	7690024	7161024	7135024
270 Winchester	7690033	7161033	7135033
7mm Remington Magnum	7690039	7161039	7135039
7mm Mauser (7 x 57mm)	7690035	7161035	7135035
30-06 (7.62 x 63mm)	7690049	7161049	7135049
300 Winchester Magnum	7690051	7161051	7135051
308 Winchester (7.62 x 51mm Nato)	7690047	7161047	7135047
Price:	$54.50	$39.95	$18.95

Match grade performance through the use of proven bench rest techniques. The set consists of a neck sizing die and our AA Micro-Seat Die. This combination enables you to get neck sizing and truly precise bullet seating from a traditional reloading press.

AA Multi-Deluxe Pistol Die Sets
Here's one innovative die set that does the reloading work of two, four or even six premium die sets. Bullet styles are changed quickly and easily because each set includes two or three seating screws that screw out of the top of the die. Multi-Deluxe Pistol Dies feature Tungsten-Carbide rings for friction-free sizing without the mess of lubrication, a two-step neck expanding die, which loads lead alloy bullets without lead shaving and distortion. A Special-Magnum advantage permits loading of the 38-Special and 357 Magnum with the same die set. Multi-Deluxe Pistol Die Set (1 lb. 10 oz.) **$52.50**

LYMAN RELOADING
DIE REFERENCE CHART

This handy chart can direct you to the correct die sets and accessories needed for reloading any of the cartridges listed.
Die Group column gives you the die set or sets that may be used for the cartridge.

Shell Holder column gives you correct number for appropriate caliber.
Primer column lets you know large or small size for choosing Primer Punches, pocket reamers and cleaners.

Trimmer Pilot column lists appropriate trimmer pilot. Lyman's Universal Trimmer requires no other collets — just the inexpensive pilot.

PISTOL CARTRIDGE	Die Group	Shell Holder Number	Primer Punch & Sleeve	Case Trimmer Pilot Number
25 ACP	NA	NA	small	25A
7mm TCU	V, VIII	26	small	28
30 Mauser	VIII	12	small	30
30 Herrett	VII	6	large	30
32 ACP	VIII	23	small	30
32 Smith & Wesson	VIII	9	small	31
38 Super Auto	VIII	12	small	9mm
38 Smith & Wesson	VIII	21	small	35
380 Auto	VIII	26	small	9mm
9mm Luger	VIII	12	small	9mm

PISTOL CARTRIDGE	Die Group	Shell Holder Number	Primer Punch & Sleeve	Case Trimmer Pilot Number
38 Special/357 Magnum	VII, IX	1	small	35
41 Magnum	VII, IX	30	small	41
44 Magnum/44 Special	VII, IX	7	large	44
44-40 Winchester	VII	14B	large	44A
45 ACP	VII, IX	2	large	45A
45 Colt	VII, IX	11	large	45A

RIFLE CARTRIDGE	Die Group	Shell Holder Number	Primer Punch & Sleeve	Case Trimmer Pilot Number
22 Hornet	II	4	small	22
22-250	I, V	2	large	22
220 Swift	II, V	5	large	22
221 Fireball	II	26	small	22
222 Remington	I, V	26	small	22
222 Remington Magnum	II	26	small	22
223 Remington (5.56mm)	I, V	26	small	22
243 Winchester	I, V	2	large	24
6mm Remington (244 Rem.)	II, V	2	large	24
25-06	I, V	2	large	25
250 Savage (250-3000 Sav.)	II	2	large	25
264 Winchester Magnum	II	13	large	26
6.5 x 55mm Swedish Mauser	II	27	large	26
270 Winchester	I, V	2	large	27
7mm Remington Magnum	I, V	13	large	28
7mm x 57 Mauser (7mm Mauser)	II, V	2	large	28
7mm Mauser (also loads 7 x 57R)	II, V	13	large	28
280 Remington (7mm Exp. Rem.)	II	2	large	28
30 M1 Carbine	III	19	small	30
30-30 Winchester (30 WCF)	I	6	large	30

RIFLE CARTRIDGE	Die Group	Shell Holder Number	Primer Punch & Sleeve	Case Trimmer Pilot Number
30-06 (7.62 x 63mm)	I, V	2	large	30
7.65 Argentine Mauser	II	2	large	31
30-40 Krag	II	7	large	30
300 H&H Magnum	II	13	large	30
300 Savage	II	2	large	30
300 Weatherby Magnum	II	13	large	30
300 Winchester Magnum	II, V	13	large	30
308 Winchester	I, V	2	large	30
303 British	II	7	large	31
32 Winchester Special	II	6	large	32
32-20 Winchester	III	10	small	32
32-40 Winchester	IV	6	large	32
8mm Mauser (8 x 57mm. 8 x 57JSmm. 7.9 x 57mm)	II	2	large	8mm
8mm Mauser (also loads 8 x 57JRSmm)	II	14B	large	8mm
8mm Remington Magnum	II	13	large	8mm
338 Winchester Magnum	II	13	large	33
35 Remington	II	8 or 2	large	35
375 Winchester	IV	6	large	37
375 H&H Magnum	II	13	large	37
444 Marlin	IV	14B	large	44
45-70 Government	IV	17	large	45
50-70 Government	IV	22	large	NA

LYMAN BULLET SIZING EQUIPMENT

**450
BULLET SIZER**

450 BULLET SIZER:

The 450 Bullet Sizer and Lubricator sizes the bullet to the correct diameter, forces lubricant under pressure into the bullet grooves, and will seat gas checks, if required—all in one rapid, accurate operation. Adaptable to all bullets by changing "G" and bullet sizing assembly "H & I". Use with Ideal Bullet Lubricant **$85.95**

G, H & I DIES "WITH SWAGING ACTION":

Cast bullets as much as ten thousandths oversize can be easily formed to size by the use of these dies. Lyman bullet sizing dies have been newly designed to supply a swaging rather than shearing action in reducing bullet diameters. The mouth of the "H" die contains a gentle taper which allows the gas check and bullet to start into the die easily. This tapering of the mouth combined with the exact tolerance and ultra-smoothness of the hardened inner chamber, completely eliminates shearing of lead and produces a perfectly cylindrical bullet. As this swaging action compresses and work hardens the alloy, a tougher, smoother, and more accurate bullet results.

"G"

"H"

"I"

IDEAL BULLET LUBRICANT . . . Special grease developed especially for use as a cast bullet lubricant. One stick lubricates 2500 small of 500 large bullets.
Ideal Bullet
    Lubricant **$2.50**
ALOX Bullet
    Lubricant 2.50

BASIC GROOVE DIAMETER FOR RIFLES

Caliber	Groove Dia.	Caliber	Groove Dia.
All 22 cal. (except 22 Hi-power)	.224	338 Win. & 33 Win.	.338
.22 Hi-Power	.226	348 Win.	.348
.243, .244, 6 M/M	.243	35 Win. S. L. & 351 S. L.	.352
.256 Win. & All 25 cals.	.257	9 x 56 M/M & 9 x 57 M/M	.354
.264 Win., 6.5 M/M	.264	35 cal.	.358
.270 Win.	.277	375 H & H Mag.	.375
7 M/M, .280- Rem., .284 Win.	.284	38/55	.379
7.35 Carcano	.299	38/40	.400
30 cals.	.308	401 S.L.	.406
7.62 Russian	.310	405 Win.	.412
32/20 Win.	.311	44/40 Win. Rifles	.428
7.65 Mauser	.311	44/40 Rem. Rifles	.425
.303 British, 7.7 M/M Jap.	.313	444 Marlin	.430
8 M/M Mauser (J.Bore)	.318	11 Mauser	.439
8 M/M Mauser (S Bore)	.323	45/70 & 458 Win.	.457
32 Win. Spec. 32 S.L. & 32 Rem.	.321		

BASIC GROOVE DIAMETER FOR PISTOLS

Caliber	Groove Dia.	Caliber	Groove Dia.
22 Jet	.222	38/40	.400
30 Mauser	.309	41 Colt	.406
30 Luger	.310	41 S.& W. Mag.	.410
32 Auto	.311	44/40 (revolver)	.425
32/20	.312	44 S & W Spec. & 44 Russian	.429
32 S & W & 32 Colt N.P.	.314	44 Mag. (S & W & Ruger)	.430
9 M/M Luger	.354	45 A.C.P.	.450
38 Special & 357 Mag. (Colt), 38 A.C.P. & 380 Auto	.355	45 Auto Rim	.451
38 Special & 357 Mag. (S & W)	.357	45 Colt (post-war)	.451
38 S & W	.360	45 Colt (pre-war)	.454
		.455 Webley	.457

SIZING DIE DIAMETERS

.224	.225	.243	.244	.251	.257	.258
.264	.277	.278	.280	.284	.285	.301
.308	.309	.310	.311	.312	.313	.314
.321	.322	.323	.325	.338	.350	.352
.354	.355	.356	.357	.358	.359	.360
.375	.377	.378	.379	.400	.401	.410
.427	.428	.429	.430	.431	.450	.451
.452	.454	.457	.458	.459	.509	.512

LYMAN BULLET SIZING EQUIPMENT

MOULD MASTER XX

Lyman's Mould Master XX electric casting furnace features greatly increased capacity with lighter overall weight. It operates on household current. The thermostat housing has been relocated to one side allowing the caster a better view of the bottom-pour spout. Furthermore, access to the pot for ladle casting has been improved by replacing the over-arm stop with a metering thumbscrew in the lever hinge. Other features include:
- 20 lb. pot capacity.
- Calibrated thermostat permits controlled heat throughout the casting spectrum.
- Available in 115V A.C.

Furnace w/mould guide **$179.95**

MOULD MASTER BULLET CASTING FURNACE—

Heavy-duty, 11 lb. capacity furnace. Operates on standard household power—115 volts, A.C. or D.C., 1000 Watts. Calibrated dial control heats from 450° to 850° F. within 20°. Discharge spout is controlled by a lever operated valve.

Mould Master Furnace complete with Ingot Mould and Mould Guide	**$139.95**
Extra Ingot Mould	**7.25**
Mould Guide	**15.95**

DEBURRING TOOL—

Lyman's deburring tool can be used for chamfering or deburring of cases up to 45 caliber. For precise bullet seating, use the pointed end of the tool to bevel the inside of new or trimmed cases. To remove burrs left by trimming, place the other end of the deburring tool over the mouth of the case and twist. The tool's centering pin will keep the case aligned **$9.50**

MOULD HANDLES—

These large hardwood handles are available in three sizes—single, double and four-cavity.

Single-cavity handles (for small block, black powder and specialty moulds) (9 oz.)	**$13.95**
Double-cavity handles (for two-cavity and large-block single-cavity moulds) (9 oz.)	**13.95**
Four-cavity handles (1 lb.)	**16.95**

RIFLE MOULDS—

All Lyman rifle moulds are available in double cavity only, except those moulds where the size of the bullet necessitates a single cavity (12 oz.) **$34.95**

HOLLOW-POINT BULLETS—

Hollow-point moulds are cut in single-cavity blocks only and require single-cavity handles (9 oz.) **$35.95**

COMPOSITE CAST PISTOL BULLETS—

Kit includes single-cavity moulds for the nose/core and jacket, a special nose punch designed to fit the jacket's cavity during resizing, basic casting instructions and special information on preparing these new two-piece bullets. Requires single-cavity handles (1 lb. 2 oz.) **$69.50**

SHOTGUN SLUG MOULDS—

Available in 12 or 20 gauge and do not require rifling. Moulds are single cavity only cut on the larger double-cavity block and require double-cavity handles (14 oz.) **$35.95**

LEAD DIPPER—

Dipper with cast iron head. Spout is shaped for easy, accurate pouring that prevents air pockets in the finished bullet. **$7.50**

INERTIA BULLET PULLER—

Quickly and easily removes bullets from cartridges **$19.95**

UNIVERSAL TRIMMER MULTI PILOT PAK

This trimmer with patented chuck head accepts all metallic rifle or pistol cases, regardless of rim thickness. To change calibers, simply change the case head pilot. Other features include coarse and fine cutter adjustments, an oil-impregnated bronze bearing, and a rugged cast base assures precision alignment and years of service.

Trimmer less pilot	**$47.95**
Extra pilot (state caliber)	**1.95**
Replacement cutter head	**3.95**

PILOTS AVAILABLE IN THE FOLLOWING SIZES $1.95

17	All 17 caliber rifle cases
22	All 22 caliber rifle cases
24	All 6 M M rifle cases
25A	25 ACP pistol cases
25	All 25 caliber rifle cases
26	All 6.5 M M and 264 caliber rifle cases
27	All 270 caliber rifle cases
28	All 7 M M and 284 caliber rifle cases
29	7.35 M M Italian rifle cases
30	All 30 caliber rifle plus 30 Mauser, 30 Luger and 32 Auto pistol cases
31	303 British, 7.65 M M Argentine, 7.7 M M Japanese, 32 20 rifle, plus 32 Colt and 32 S & W pistol cases
32	All 32 caliber rifle cases
8MM	8M M rifle (.323" dia.) cases
33	All 33 caliber rifle cases
9MM	9M M Luger, 38 ACP, 38 Super, 380 Auto pistol cases
34	348 Winchester rifle cases
35A	351 Winchester rifle cases
35	All 35 caliber rifle cases plus 38 Special 357, Magnum, 38 Colt and 38 S & W pistol cases
37	375 H & H, 378 Weatherby Mag., 38 55 rifle plus 41 Long Colt pistol cases
39	38 40, 301 Winchester rifle cases
41	41 S & W Magnum pistol plus 405 Winchester rifle cases
44A	44 40 rifle and pistol cases
44	44 Special, 44 Magnum pistol plus 444 Marlin and 43 Spanish rifle cases
45A	45 ACP, 45 A.R., 45 Colt, 455 Webley pistol, plus 11 M M Mauser rifle cases
45	45 70, 458 Winchester Mag., 460 Weatherby Mag. rifle cases

GAS CHECKS—

Gas checks are gilding metal caps which fit to the base of cast bullets. These caps protect the bullet base from the burning effect of hot powder gases and permit higher velocities. Easily seated during the bullet sizing operation, only Lyman gas checks should be used with Lyman cast bullets.
Note: .38 Special same as 35 caliber.

22 through 45 caliber (per 1000)......................	**$14.50**
Also available in 45 caliber	**11.50**

LEAD POT

Cast iron pot and holder for melting lead alloy using any source of heat. Pot capacity is 10 pounds of alloy. Holder keeps pot secure and level, prevents lead from splashing on stove or burner **$7.50**

MEC RELOADING

GRABBER 76

The Grabber grabs and squeezes the shell to dimensions well within commercial tolerances for new shells. Grabber resizing completely reforms the metal portion of the fired shotgun shell to factory standards in **all** respects. (Low brass 2¾" shells.) Resizing is done as an integral part of the reloading sequence and without undue agitation that might affect the uniformity of the charges. The measure assembly has been designed for strength and safety. Large capacity shot container holds 17+ pounds.

- AUTOMATIC PRIMER FEED
- GRABBER RESIZING
- EXCLUSIVE CHARGE BAR WINDOW
- FLIP TYPE MEASURE
- EXCLUSIVE PRIMER SEATING
- LARGE CAPACITY SHOT CONTAINER

12, 16, 20, 28 or 410 gauges fitted in durable chrome

price complete

$334.45

HUSTLER 76

The Grabber with its revolutionary resize chamber, combined with the MEC hydraulic system, becomes the Hustler. It gives you your own miniature reloading factory, but one that resizes to under industry standards for minimum chamber. The motor operates on regular 110 volt household current and the pump supplies instant, constant pressure. The entire downstroke and upstroke functions are utilized and synchronized to allow continuous action. Every stroke of the cylinder piston is positive and performs all operations at six reloading stations. Every downstroke of the reloader produces one finished shell.

Reloader less pump and hose **$369.63**

- ALL THE FINE FEATURES OF THE GRABBER PLUS HYDRAULIC POWER

12, 16, 20, 28 or 410 gauges fitted in durable chrome

price complete

$898.62

600 JR.
THE PLASTIC MASTER

Any MEC reloader can be used for reloading plastic shells, but the "600 jr." positively masters the process. The PLASTIC MASTER is a single stage tool, but is designed to permit rapid, progressive operation. Every step from fired shell to the fresh-crimped product is performed with a minimum of motion. An exclusive shell holder positions and holds the shell at each station. No transfer die is required . . . resizing dies at reconditioning and crimping stations give your shell its proper form.

- CAM-ACTUATED RECONDITIONING STATION
- SPINDEX STAR CRIMP HEAD
- ADJUSTA-GUIDE WAD FEED
- CAM-LOCK CRIMP
- HARDENED CHARGING BAR
- TOGGLE LINKAGE
- FLIP-TYPE MEASURE
- ALL STEEL CONSTRUCTION
- PRIMER CATCHER

Choice of 10, 12, 16, 20, 28 or 410 gauges— fitted in beautiful lifetime chrome

price complete

$120.40

700
VERSAMEC
THE SINGLE STAGE ULTIMATE

The exclusive Platform Cam which provides the longer ejection stroke necessary to eject existing field shells at the resize station. No adjustments or part changes are required, regardless of brass length. The Pro-Check, which programs the charge bar and wad guide. This ingenious device programs the measure assembly to position the charge bar in the correct sequence. Even the hunter who reloads once or twice a year cannot err . . . the Pro-Check eliminates mistakes . . . automatically. The paper crimp starter which assembles into the Spindex Crimper. Only seconds are required to change from the 6 or 8 point plastic crimp spinner to the smooth cone for fired paper shells.

- CAM-ACTUATED RECONDITIONING STATION
- PRO-CHECK
- SPINDEX STAR CRIMP HEAD
- ADJUSTA-GUIDE WAD FEED
- CAM LOCK CRIMP
- HARDENED CHARGING BAR
- TOGGLE LINKAGE
- FLIP TYPE MEASURE
- PRIMER CATCHER
- ALL STEEL CONSTRUCTION

Choice of 12, 16, 20, 28 or 410 gauges— fitted in beautiful lifetime chrome.

price complete

$139.07

MEC RELOADING

650 THE RELOADER WITH A MEMORY

Up to 12 operations on 6 individual shells are performed simultaneously with one stroke of the press handle. Outstanding features of each 650 include a revolutionary Star Crimp Head, Automatic Primer feeding, exclusive Resize-Deprime apparatus, Toggle linkage, cam operated crimping die and Auto-Cycle charging sequence. The Auto-Cycle charging sequence automatically maintains the correct operating sequence of the charge bar. The charge bar can be actuated only when a shell is properly located to receive the powder. The MEC 650 can even handle the 3 inch shells . . . high-base, low base and light or heavy plastics. It's all steel with an extra heavy base-column. Tool comes completely assembled, tested and ready to use . . . without adjustment.

- AUTOMATIC PRIMER FEED.
- AUTOMATIC POWDER AND SHOT CHARGING
- FLIP-TYPE MEASURE
- HARDENED CHARGING BAR
- OPEN BASE
- PRIMER CATCHER
- EXCLUSIVE CAM-OPERATED CRIMP
- EXCLUSIVE RESIZE-DEPRIME APPARATUS
- 12 OPERATIONS WITH 1 STROKE
- SPINDEX STAR CRIMP HEAD
- AUTO-CYCLE

Choice of 12, 16, 20, 28 or 410 gauges — fitted in beautiful lifetime chrome

price complete

$244.07

THE MINIATURE RELOADING FACTORY

Take the 650 or the Super 600 reloader and marry it to a hydraulic system . . . the result is the hydraMEC, today's most advanced concept in high-volume reloaders. The hydraulic system is compact, lightweight and designed for long, trouble-free service. The motor operates on regular 110 volt household current and the pump supplies instant, constant pressure . . . no slowdown, no misses. The entire downstroke and upstroke functions are utilized and synchronized to allow continuous action. Every stroke of the cylinder piston is positive and performs up to 12 operations on six reloading stations. Every downstroke of the reloader produces one finished shell. The operator inserts empty shells and wads . . . the hydraMEC does the rest . . . automatically.

Tool linked for hydraulic operation to include base and cylinder.
hydraMEC 650 .... **$349.48**

HYDRAULIC UNIT ONLY—Hydraulic unit to include pump, motor, cylinder, controls, base, links and bolts required to attach to reloader with instructions. **$613.63**

650 HYDRAMEC

- AUTOMATIC PRIMER FEED
- AUTOMATIC POWDER & SHOT CHARGING
- FLIP-TYPE MEASURE
- HARDENED CHARGING BAR
- PRIMER CATCHER
- EXCLUSIVE CAM-OPERATED CRIMP
- EXCLUSIVE RESIZE-DEPRIME APPARATUS
- TOGGLE LINKAGE
- FOOL PROOF HYDRAULIC SYSTEM
- 12 OPERATIONS WITH 1 STROKE

$808.70

Choice of 12, 16, 20, 28 or 410 gauges — fitted in beautiful lifetime chrome

---

ACCESSORY EQUIPMENT

SPINDEX STAR CRIMP HEAD

The SPINDEX STAR CRIMP HEAD is a revolutionary crimp starter that prepares plastic shells for a perfect crimp . . . everytime. The SPINDEX automatically engages the original folds of each shell. No prior indexing of the shell is required . . . even on some of the earlier, unskived plastics that show no impressions of the original crimp folds. Because it employs a pressed metal part that spins into alignment with the original folds, the SPINDEX starts every crimp perfectly. And even better . . . you have a choice of an 8-segment, 6-segment, or smooth crimp starter, depending on the shells you are reloading.

SPINDEX STAR CRIMP HEAD

Dual Purpose 6 & 8 Fold (specify gauge and model of press)
434 for Model 400	$7.55
534 for all Models 600 Jr., and 700	7.55
600 Super and 650	7.55

ACCESSORIES
301L13X BH & Cap Accy.	$1.51
453P Wad Finger Ptlc.	1.01
634P Crimp St. Paper	1.16
8042 Magnum Container	4.41
15CA Ez Pak Accy.	5.20

FOR THE MEC 600 JR.
741P Die Set (12, 16, 20, 28, 410) specify gauge	$41.91
741D-10 Die Set (Not Pie Set)	16.91
73 Kit VersaMEC 700 Modification	12.14
ProCheck	3.69
63 Kit for 3" shells (12 and 20 gauge)	4.53

FOR THE VERSAMEC 700
741V Die Set (10, 12, 16, 28, 410) specify gauge	$46.91

COMPLETELY AUTOMATIC PRIMER FEED

FROM CARTON TO SHELL WITH SECURITY, IT PROVIDES SAFE, CONVENIENT PRIMER POSITIONING AND INCREASES RATE OF PRODUCTION. REDUCES BENCH CLUTTER, ALLOWING MORE FREE AREA FOR WADS AND SHELLS.

- PRIMERS TRANSFER DIRECTLY FROM CARTON TO RELOADER — ELIMINATING TUBES AND TUBE FILLERS.
- POSITIVE MECHANICAL FEED (NOT DEPENDENT UPON AGITATION OF PRESS)
- VISIBLE SUPPLY
- AUTOMATIC — ELIMINATES HAND MOTION
- LESS SUSCEPTIBLE TO DAMAGE
- ADAPTS TO ALL DOMESTIC AND MOST FOREIGN PRIMERS WITH ADJUSTMENT OF THE COVER
- MAY BE PURCHASED SEPARATELY TO REPLACE TUBE TYPE PRIMER FEED OR TO UPDATE YOUR PRESENT RELOADER.

E-Z PRIME "V"

For 600 Jr. 700 Versamec

Sizemaster 77

$30.47

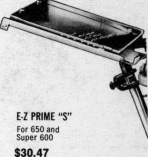

E-Z PRIME "S"

For 650 and Super 600

$30.47

MEC E-Z PAK

Here's how to pack shot shell reloads the easy way. As each shell is reloaded, they're placed in E-Z PAK, exactly as if they were being placed in the box. After each 25 shells, original box is slipped over E-Z PAK, which is then inverted, and removed. Nothing easier — nothing neater. Available in all gauges.

$5.20

MEC SIZEMASTER 77
- SINGLE-STAGE
- PRECISION SHELL HOLDER
- EXCLUSIVE RESIZING CHAMBER
- AUTOMATIC PRIMER FEED
- POSITIVE REPRIMING
- CHARGE BAR WINDOW
- PRO-CHECK
- ADJUSTA-GUIDE WAD FEED
- WAD PRESSURE GAUGE
- WAD HEIGHT GAUGE
- EXTRA CAPACITY SHOT CONTAINER
- SPINDEX CRIMP STARTER
- CAM-ACTUATED CRIMPING STATION

Size Master 77 (includes Primer Feed)	$186.13
77 Die Set 12, 16, 20, 28 and 410	70.08
77 10-gauge Die Set	82.26

MTM

CASE-GARD 50 SERIES RIFLE AMMO CASES

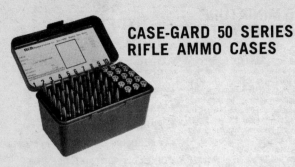

Features include
- versatility - cases for every caliber from 222 to 458 Win.
- durability - material doesn't warp, crack, chip, peel, expand, or contract.
- each case rests in its own individual compartment.
- unique hinge is designed to keep the cover in the open position when reloading.
- Snap-lok latch protects contents from inadvertent spilling.
- each CASE-GARD 50 ammo box is supplied with a form for recording load and sight data.

Available in MTM Green or Light Brown

RS-50 (Small Rifle)	.....222 to 222 Mag	$3.45
RM-50 (Medium Rifle)	.... 22-250 to 308 Win	3.45
RL-50 (Large Rifle)	....220 Swift to 458 Win	3.45
RS-S-50	22 & 6mm PPC's, 22 & 6mm Rem. BR's	3.45
22 Horn	......22 Hornet only	3.45

CASE-GARD H50 SERIES DELUXE AMMO CASE

Features include:
- handle for ease of carrying.
- scuff resistant, texturized finish.
- extra space between rounds to facilitate removal when wearing gloves.
- design that allows belted magnums to be carried rim up or down.

Available in MTM Green or Light Brown

H50-RS	...... 17 Rem. to 223 Rem.	$4.74
H50-RM	..... 22-250 to 308 Rem.	4.74
H50-RL	...... 6mm Rem. to 30-06	4.74
H50-R MAG	......264 Win. Mag to 470 KYNOCH	4.74

CASE-GARD 22 MATCH AMMO BOX

CASE-GARD® 22 Match Ammo Box— For the Small Bore Competitor. Precision molded body designed to hold 30 rounds - 3 strings - projectile-down for easy handling; plus box of ammo and loose rounds, if desired. Inside of lid equipped with supports for stop watch. The lid holds the watch at a 40° angle, for ease of reading by shooter. The Case-Gard 22 Match Ammo Box features Snap-lok latch, virtually indestructible integral hinge, and leather-like textured finish.

Available in MTM Green or Light Brown

SB-22	$5.51

CASE-GARD 9 AMMO WALLET

CASE-GARD 9 Ammo WalletT.M. ammunition carrier holds 9 rounds in pocket or saddlebag. Provides absolute protection for ammunition.
Available in Dark Brown

W-9 SM	......22-250 to 30-30	$3.35
W-9 LM	......22-250 to 375 Mag	3.35

CASE-GARD 50 SERIES HANDGUN AMMO CASES

Features include:
- versatility - cases for every caliber from 9mm to 44 Mag.
- durability - virtually indestructible material doesn't warp, crack, chip, peel, expand or contract.
- each round rests in its own individual compartment.
- unique hinge designed to keep the cover in the open position when reloading.
- Snap-lok latch protects contents from inadvertent spilling.

Available in MTM Green or Light Brown

50-9	...... 9mm	$1.61
PS-3	..... 38 to 357 Mag	1.61
PL-4	.....45, 41, and 44 Mag.	1.61

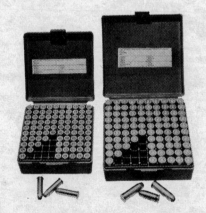

MAG 100 CASE-GARD AMMO BOXES

Features include:
- Snap-lok latch that protects loaded rounds from accidental spilling.
- integral hinge.
- molded of virtually indestructible high-impact polypropylene.
- pressure-sensitive label for reloading data included with each box.

Available in MTM Green or Light Brown

P-100-3	.... 38 Special and 357 Mag.	$3.19
P-100-4	.........45 Auto, 41 Mag. and 44 Mag.	3.19
P-100-9	.... 9mm Lugar	3.19

MTM

CASE-GARD AMMO WALLET
CASE-GARD 6, 12 AND 18

MTM offers 3 different models of varying capacity. All share common design features:
- textured finish looks like leather, and provides good gripping surface, even when wet.
- Snap-lok latch protects contents from damage, even if unit is dropped.
- integral hinge.
- contents are protected from dust and moisture.
- each round is carried securely in its own individual rattleproof recess.

Available in Dark Brown

CALIBER→ CAPACITY↓	380 Auto & 9mm	38 & 357 Mag	41 Mag	44 Mag	45 Auto
6 Round	W6-9 $2.69	W6-38 $2.69	W6-41 $2.69	W6-44 $2.69	W6-45 $2.69
12 Round	W12-9 $2.91	W12-38 $2.91	W12-41 $2.91	W12-44 $2.91	W12-45 $2.91
18 Round	18-9 $3.23	18-38 $3.23	18-41 $3.23	18-44 $3.23	18-45 $3.23

CASE-GARD AMMO WALLET
FOR 22's

Special **CASE-GARD Ammo Wallet** carrier holds 30 rounds, 22 Longs or 22 Mags . . . a convenient way to carry ammo to the range or field. Design features are:
- leather-like finish.
- Snap-lok latch protects case against inadvertent opening, even if dropped.
- each round is carried securely in its own recess.
- virtually indestructible hinge.

Available in Dark Brown
30-22M $3.35

MTM HANDLOADER'S LOG

MTM Handloader's Log. Space provided for 1,000 entries covering date, range, group size or score, components, and conditions. Book is heavy duty vinyl, reinforced 3-ring binder.

HL-74 .... $10.50
HL-50 extra pages 5.28

CASE-GARD 100 AMMO CARRIER
FOR SKEET AND TRAP

THE MTM^T.M. **CASE-GARD®** 100 Round Shotshell Case carries 100 rounds in 2 trays; or 50 rounds, plus 2 boxes of factory ammo; or 50 rounds plus sandwiches and insulated liquid container; or 50 rounds, with room left for fired hulls.
- stainless steel hinge pin
- center balanced handles facilitate carrying and can be padlocked for security
- high-impact material supports 300 pounds, and will not warp, split, expand or contract
- dustproof and rainproof

Each **CASE-GARD 100** Shotshell case is supplied with 2 50-round trays.

Available in Textured Black
S100-12   12 gauge $12.63
S100-16   16 gauge 12.63
S100-20   20 gauge 12.63

FUNNELS

MTM Benchrest Funnel Set designed specifically for the benchrest shooter. One fits 222 and 243 cases only; the other 7mm and 308 cases. Both can be used with pharmaceutical vials popular with benchrest competitors for storage of pre-weighed charges. Funnel design prevents their rolling off the bench.
BF-2 .... $2.58

MTM Universal Funnel fits all calibers from 222 to 45.
UF-1 .... $1.47

Patented MTM Adapt 5-in-1 Funnel Kit includes funnel, adapters for 17 Rem., 222 Rem. and 30 through 45. Long drop tube facilitates loading of maximum charges: 222 to 45.
AF-5 .... $3.19

PACIFIC

105 SHOTSHELL RELOADER

- All the features of expensive reloaders . . . without sacrificing quality.
- Crimps shells perfectly. Floating crimp starter automatically aligns with original crimp folds. Final crimp die is fully adjustable.
- Seats wads easily with built-in wad guide.
- Eliminates guesswork . . . all operations end on positive stop.

105 SHOTSHELL RELOADER	**$104.50**
Complete with charge bushings.	
105 DIE SET	32.50
For quick-change conversion to different gauge.	
105 MAGNUM CONVERSION SET	12.00
Converts 2¾" dies to load 3" shells of same gauge, or vice versa.	
105 CRIMP STARTER	2.75
(8-point crimp starter standard equipment with loader and with Die Sets).	
EXTRA CHARGE BUSHINGS	2.00

00-7 PRESS

- "Power-Pac" linkage multiplies lever-to-ram power.
- Frame of press angled 30° to one side, making the "0" area of press totally accessible.
- More mounting area for rock-solid attachment to bench.
- Special strontium-alloy frame provides greater stress, resistance—won't spring under high pressures needed for full-length resizing.

00-7 PRESS (does not include dies or shell holder) **$104.95**
00-7 AUTOMATIC PRIMER FEED (complete with large and small primer tubes) 12.50

0-7 PRESS

- Faster priming cycle. Prime during the normal stroke of the ram without hand operation of the primer arm.
- Auto primer feed permits fast and simple delivery of primers to the seating cup.
- Easier to use. The frame of the 0-7 Press is angled 30 degrees to one side to make the "0" area totally accessible.
- Delivers maximum energy with minimum effort during the critical final half-inch stroke.
- More mounting area for better attachment to bench.
- No springing or alignment problems.

0-7 PRESS (does not include dies or shellholder) **$82.50**
0-7 AUTOMATIC PRIMER FEED (complete with large and small primer tubes) 12.50

PACIFIC

155 SHOTSHELL RELOADER

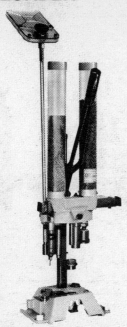

The 155 resizes entire length of the shell including head and rim. Spring-loaded finish die produces perfect tapered crimp. 113 interchangeable shot and powder bushings and handles both plastic and paper shells. Quick-change die sets let you load everything from 3-inch 12-gauge shells to 2½-inch .410 gauge shells. Dies are polished steel with deep blued finish. All operations end on a positive stop, including fully adjustable wad seating.

155 SHOTSHELL RELOADER 10 Ga. $176.00
155 SHOTSHELL RELOADER 12 & 20 Ga. $162.50
155 SHOTSHELL RELOADER 16, 28 & .410 Ga. $168.00
Complete with standard charge bushings. (Does not include automatic primer feed.)
155 APF SHOTSHELL RELOADER 12 & 20 Ga. $184.75
155 APF SHOTSHELL RELOADER 16, 28 & .410 Ga. $190.00
Complete with standard charge bushings.

155/155 APF DIE SET 12 & 20 Ga. $51.00
155 10 Ga. DIE SET (Special Order—Loader must be returned to factory.)
155/155 APF DIE SET 16, 28 & .410 Ga. $51.00
155/155 APF MAGNUM CONVERSION SET $22.50
Converts 2¾" dies to load 3" shells of same gauge, or vice versa.
AUTOMATIC PRIMER FEED CONVERSION UNIT $31.00
EXTRA CRIMP STARTERS 2.75
EXTRA CHARGE BUSHINGS 2.00

266 SHOTSHELL RELOADER

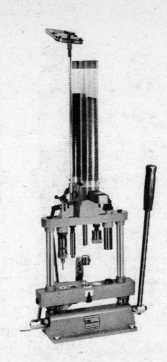

The most advanced loader in its price range. Right or left-hand operation to suit the operator. New wad guide with unbreakable spring fingers prevents wad tipping. Two-way adjustable crimper assures precise crimp depth and taper. Automatic primer feed automatically drops primer when preceding shell is powder charged.

SAFE AND CONVENIENT — Charging assembly constructed for no-spark safety. Shot and powder assembly removes completely for fast, easy load change.

266 SHOTSHELL RELOADER
Complete with charge bushings.
12 & 20 ga. $250.00; 16, 28 & .410 ga.* $263.50

266 DIE SET
For conversion to different gauge.
12, 16, 20 28 & .410 ga. $55.50

266 MAGNUM CONVERSION SET $22.50
Converts 2¾" dies to load 3" shells of same gauge, or vice versa.
EXTRA CRIMP STARTER $2.75
EXTRA CHARGE BUSHINGS 2.00
Automatic primer feed does not operate in .410.

366-AUTO SHOTSHELL RELOADER

The 366-Auto features full-length resizing with each stroke, automatic primer feed, swing-out wad guide, three stage crimping featuring Taper-Loc for factory tapered crimp, automatic advance to the next station and automatic ejection. The turntable holds 8 shells for 8 operations with each stroke. The primer tube filler is fast; automatic charge bar loads shot and powder; right or left hand operation; interchangeable charge bushings, die sets and magnum dies and crimp starters for 6 point, 8 point and paper crimps.

366-AUTO SHOTSHELL RELOADER 12, 16, 20 or 28 gauge $445.00
Complete with standard charge bushings.

366—AUTO ● ADVANCE
The Auto ● Advance automatically advances the shells to the next station. It is standard equipment on 366 loaders manufactured after November 1, 1975 and it can be added to any earlier models.
366—SHELL DROP
Makes it unnecessary to manually remove loaded shells from the shell plate. Standard on 366-Auto loaders manufactured after February 1, 1976. The shell drop can be installed on earlier models; please return your 366 to Pacific postpaid for factory installation (specify gauge).
366—SWING-OUT WAD GUIDE AND SHELL DROP COMBO
Return your 366 to Pacific postpaid (specify gauge).
366—SWING-OUT WAD GUIDE
Makes insertion of the wad easier. Return 366 to Pacific postpaid for installation.
366—SHOT/POWDER SHUTOFF $30.00
Now standard on Pacific's 366 loaders, the unit fits any 366 loader and can be purchased separately.

366-AUTO DIE SET 12, 20 or 28 $85.00
366-AUTO MAGNUM CONVERSION SET $25.00
Converts 2¾" dies to load 3" shells of same gauge, or vice versa.
EXTRA CRIMP STARTERS $2.75
EXTRA CHARGE BUSHINGS 2.00

PACIFIC

DURACHROME DIES
GUARANTEED FOR LIFE

For All Popular Rifle & Pistol Calibers

- **LIFETIME DURACHROME FINISH** — satin-hard chrome protection that keeps dies looking and working like new. Guaranteed never to chip, crack or peel.
- **HEXAGON SPINDLE HEADS** — for easy removal of stuck cases and more positive adjustment.
- **PRECISION-ROLLED** ⅞ x 14 threads held to perfect size and pitch. Fits most other tools because this pioneer Pacific development has been widely copied.
- **FAST CONVENIENT ADJUSTMENT** is made possible by Pacific's all-steel lock rings.
- **BUILT IN PROVISION FOR CRIMPING** provided on all bullet seating dies.
- **ALL STEEL CONSTRUCTION** — no inexpensive substitute metals.
- **PRECISE DIMENSIONS** — minimum tolerances maintained throughout. After chambering, dies are hardened for lifetime wear, then polished to insure perfect dimensions and smooth interior surfaces.
- **HEAVY DUTY STORAGE BOX,** sample of Pacific Die Lube and spare decap pin are included with each set.

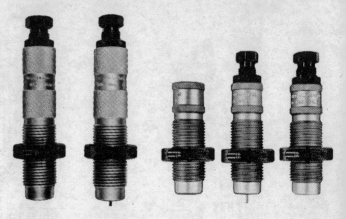

2 DIE SETS
(for bottleneck cases)

3 DIE SETS
(for straight sided cases)

Full-Length Sizing Sets
Series I **$27.50**
Series III **31.00**

Neck Sizing Set
Series I & III **$27.50**

For Series II Only
Standard	Carbide
$27.50	**$48.50**

#1 CARBIDE SIZE DIES
For 3 Die Sets
The ideal answer for large volume reloading. Diamond-hard finish won't scratch cases, no lubrication needed. Cases need not be cleaned.

METALLIC SILHOUETTE & BENCH REST DIE SETS
2 and 3 Die Sets **$31.00**

TAPER CRIMP DIE
The taper crimp die, used for applying proper crimp to auto-loading pistols, may be added to 3-die pistol sets, for improved feeding and functioning. **$12.00**

CUSTOM DIE SETS
Manufactured to order. See Die Reference Chart **$35.00**

FILE TYPE TRIM DIE
Uses a fine grade file to insure precision case length. The most inexpensive and practical way to trim and form rifle cases. Made of finest steel with lifetime Durachrome finish. Available in most rifle calibers. **$13.25**

REMOVABLE HEAD SHELL HOLDER
Precision machined from hardened steel then heat treated to prevent wear and give lifetime operation. Each Shell Holder is specifically designed for case to assure accurate alignment and eliminate tipping and side movement. Fits all tools using Pacific "C" design. **$5.00**

PACIFIC DIE REFERENCE CHART

2 DIE SETS (Rifle)

CARTRIDGE	Die Group	Primer Punch Size	Shell Holder	Trimmer Pilot	Bullet Puller Collet
17 Rem. [.172]	I*	Small	16	Order Pilot & Cutter as one unit for all 17 cal.	1
17/222 [.172]	Custom*	Small	16		1
17/223 [.172]	Custom*	Small	16		1
218 Bee [.224]	III	Small	7	1	2
219 Zipper [.224]	Custom	Large	2	1	2
221 Rem. [.224]	I	Small	16	1	2
222 Rem. [.224]	I*	Small	16	1	2
222 Rem. Mag. [.224]	I*	Small	16	1	2
22 Hornet [.224]	I	Small	3	1	2
22 K-Hornet [.224]	Custom	Small	3	1	2
22 RCFM-Jet [.224]	Custom	Small	6	1	2
22 PPC [.224]	Sil & BR Dies	Small	6	1	2
5.6 x 50 Mag. [.224]	Custom	Small	16	1	2
5.6 x 52R [.227]	Custom	Large	2	1	2
5.6 x 57 [.224]	Custom	Large	1	1	2
223 Rem. [.224]	I*	Small	16	1	2
22/250 [.224]	I*	Large	1	1	2
220 Swift [.224]	I*	Large	4	1	2
22 Sav. HP [.227]	Custom	Large	2	1	2
224 Wby. [.224]	Custom*	Large	17	1	2
225 Win. [.224]	III	Large	4	1	2
240 Wby. [.243]	III	Large	1	3	3
243 Win. [.243]	I*	Large	1	3	3
244/6MM [.243]	I	Large	1	3	3
6MM Int. [.243]	Sil & BR Dies*	Large	1	3	3
6MM/223 [.243]	Sil & BR Dies*	Small	16	3	3
6MM/PPC [.243]	Sil & BR Dies	Small	6	3	3
6MM/284 [.243]	Custom*	Large	1	3	3
6 x 47 Rem. [.243]	Sil & BR Dies*	Small	16	3	3
250 Sav. [.257]	III	Large	1	4	4
25/06 [.257]	I*	Large	1	4	4
257 Rbts. [.257]	III*	Large	1	4	4
25/20 Win. [.257]	Custom	Small	7	4	4
25/35 Win. [.257]	III	Large	2	4	4
256 Win. [.257]	Custom	Small	6	4	4
257 Wby. [.257]	III	Large	5	4	4
25 Rem. [.257]	Custom	Large	12	4	4
25/284 [.257]	Custom*	Large	1	4	4
6.5 x 55 [.264]	I*	Large	19	5	4
6.5/06 [.264]	Custom*	Large	1	5	4
6.5 Rem. Mag. [.264]	Custom*	Large	5	5	4
6.5 Mann. [.264]	Custom	Large	20	5	4
6.5 Carc. [.264]	Custom	Large	21	5	4
6.5 Jap. [.264]	Custom	Large	34	5	4
6.5 x 57 [.264]	III	Large	1	5	4
6.5 x 68 [.264]	III	Large	30	5	4
264 Win. Mag. [.264]	I	Large	5	5	4
270 Win. [.270]	I*	Large	1	6	5
270 Wby. [.270]	Custom	Large	5	6	5
7MM Mau. (7x57) [.284]	I	Large	1	7	6
7MM/08 [.284]	Sil & BR Dies	Large	1	7	6
7MM Rem. Mag. [.284]	I*	Large	5	7	6
7MM Rem. BR [.284]	Sil & BR Dies	Large	1	7	6
7MM TCU [.284]	Sil & BR Dies*	Large	16	16	9
7MM Merrill [.284]	Sil & BR Dies	Large	4	N/A	N/A
7 x 65R [.284]	Custom	Large	13	7	6
7MM Wby. [.284]	III*	Large	5	7	6
7 x 64 [.284]	Custom	Large	1	7	6
7MM/223 Ingram [.284]	Sil & BR Dies*	Small	16	7	6
7 x 47 Helm [.284]	Sil & BR Dies	Small	16	7	6
7 x 61 S & H [.284]	Custom*	Large	35	7	6
280 Rem. (7MM Rem. Exp.) [.284]	III*	Large	1	7	6
284 Win. [.284]	III*	Large	1	7	6
7.35 Carc. [.300]	Custom	Large	21	8	7
30/30 Win. [.308]	I*	Large	2	8	7
300 Sav. [.308]	I	Large	1	8	7
30 Luger [.308]	III	Large	8	8	7
30 Merrill [.308]	Sil & BR Dies	Large	4	N/A	N/A

*Neck size die available.

[Bullet Diameter]

2 DIE SETS (Rifle)

CARTRIDGE	Die Group	Primer Punch Size	Shell Holder	Trimmer Pilot	Bullet Puller Collet
30 Herrett [.308]	Sil & BR Dies*	Large	2	8	7
303 Sav. [.308]	Custom	Large	33	9	7
308 Win. [.308]	I*	Large	1	9	7
30/40 Krag [.308]	III	Large	11	9	7
30/06 [.308]	I*	Large	1	9	7
300 H & H [.308]	Custom	Large	5	9	7
300 Win. Mag. [.308]	I	Large	5	9	7
300 Wby. [.308]	III*	Large	5	9	7
308 Norma Mag. [.308]	Custom*	Large	5	9	7
7.62 Russ. [.308]	I	Large	23	9	7
7.5 Swiss [.308]	III	Large	30	9	7
7.7 Jap. [.312]	III	Large	1	10	7
303 Brit. [.312]	I*	Large	11	10	7
7.65 Belg. [.312]	III	Large	24	10	7
32 Win. Spl. [.321]	III	Large	2	11	8
32/20 Win. [.310]	Custom	Small	7	10	7
8MM Mau. [.323]	I*	Large	1	10	8
8MM/06 [.323]	Custom*	Large	1	10	8
8MM Rem. Mag. [.323]	III	Large	5	10	8
8 x 60S [.323]	Custom	Large	1	10	8
8 x 68S [.323]	Custom	Large	30	10	8
8.15 x 46R [.337]	Custom	Large	2	11	8
338 Win. Mag. [.338]	I	Large	5	13	8
33 Win. [.338]	I	Large	14	3	8
340 Wby. [.338]	III	Large	5	13	8
348 Win. [.348]	Custom	Large	25	14	9
35 Rem. [.358]	I*	Large	26	15	9
35 Whelen [.358]	Custom	Large	1	15	9
357 B & D [.358]	Sil & BR Dies	Large	30	15	9
350 Rem. Mag. [.358]	Custom*	Large	5	15	9
357 Herrett [.357]	Sil & BR Dies*	Large	2	15	9
358 Win. [.358]	III	Large	1	15	9
375 H & H [.375]	III*	Large	5	16	9
378 Wby. [.375]	Custom	Large	14	16	9
9.3 x 74R [.366]	Custom	Large	13	15	9
9.3 x 57 [.366]	Custom	Large	1	15	9
9.3 x 62 [.366]	Custom	Large	1	15	9
10.3 x 60 [.415]	Custom	Small	25	N/A	N/A
460 Wby. [.458]	Custom	Large	14	19	14

3 DIE SETS

CARTRIDGE	Die Group	Primer Punch Size	Shell Holder	Trimmer Pilot	Bullet Puller Collet
25 ACP [.251]	II	Small	37	4	4
30 M1 Carb. [.308]	II	Small	22	9	7
32 ACP [.312]	Custom	Small	22	10	7
32 S&W Long [.312]	II	Small	36	10	7
32 S&W Short [.312]	Custom	Small	36	10	7
9MM Luger [.355]	II	Small	8	15	9
380 Auto [.355]	II	Small	16	15	9
38 Super Auto [.357]	Custom	Small	8	15	9
38 S&W [.357]	Custom	Small	28	15	9
38 Spl. [.357]	II	Small	6	15	9
357 Mag. [.357]	II	Small	6	15	9
375 Win. [.375]	II	Large	2	16	9
38/40 Win. [.400]	Custom	Large	9	16	11
41 Mag. [.410]	II	Small	29	17	12
44 Spl. [.430]	II	Large	30	18	12
44 Mag. [.430]	II	Large	30	18	12
44 Auto Mag. [.430]	Custom	Large	1	18	12
44/40 Win. [.429]	Custom	Large	9	18	12
45 Auto Rim [.451]	Custom	Large	31	19	13
45 ACP [.451]	II	Large	1	19	13
45 Colt [.451]	II	Large	32	19	13
444 Marlin [.430]	II	Large	27	18	12
45/70 Govt. [.458]	II	Large	14	19	13
459 Win. [.458]	II	Large	5	19	13
45 Win. Mag. [.451]	Sil & BR Dies	Large	1	19	13

PACIFIC

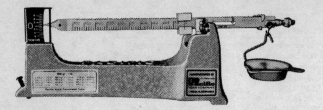

MAGNETIC PACIFIC DELUXE SCALE

Single balance beam teams with three counterpoises to give you added speed and accuracy. Graduated over/under scale lets you check powder charge or bullet weight variation without adjustments. Accepts weights up to 500 grains. Your choice of grain or gram measurements **$46.95**

MESUR-KIT™

An accurate, inexpensive portable measure at home, in the field or on the bench. Simple to use. Precise graduations make adjustable tube easy to set. Shearing action of Mesur-Kit arm gives precise charge leveling. Complete with chart for more than 1,000 load settings. Includes universal powder can. **$14.50**
Extra adjustable measure tube **12.00**

ALUMINUM POWDER FUNNEL

All-aluminum construction of Pacific's powder funnel eliminates the static electricity and powder clinging that occurs with plastic funnels. Available in 17, 22/270 and 28/45 calibers. **$2.75**

CASE CARE KIT

An invaluable aid in preparing deprimed cases for priming and loading. The kit contains a case lube pad with a reloading block in the lid, plus an assortment of popular case items including: accessory handle, three case neck brushes, large and small primer pocket cleaners, chamfering and deburring tool and bottle of case lube. **$23.75**

MULTI-DELUXE POWDER MEASURE

Fast, accurate measurement of all powder types. Standard 7/8-14 threads for mounting on reloading press or its bench stand. Includes both rifle and pistol metering assemblies, two powder-drop tubes (22-30 caliber and 30-45 caliber); large capacity hopper; blued-steel bench stand; Sure-Loc lock ring. Converts easily for left-hand operation.
Multi-Deluxe Powder Measure **$59.50**
Extra Rifle Metering Assembly **12.00**
Extra Pistol Metering Assembly **12.00**

PISTOL POWDER MEASURE

Sliding charge bar with interchangeable bushings gives a wide selection of loads. Standard 7/8 –14 threads for mounting on reloading press, bench or stand. Can be also hand held above loading block.
Pistol Powder Measure complete with stand and Sure-Loc lock ring. Does not include bushing **$27.00**
Bushings **2.00**

PISTOL POWDER MEASURE BUSHING CHART

Stock No.	Bushing Size No.	Dupont 700X	Dupont 4227	Dupont SR7625	Dupont SR4756	Dupont PB	Hercules Bullseye	Hercules 2400	Hercules Red Dot	Hercules Unique	Hercules Herco	Hercules Blue Dot	Hodgdon HP38	Hodgdon Trap 100	Hodgdon HS-5	Hodgdon HS-6	Hodgdon HS-7	Hodgdon H-110	Hodgdon H-4227	Norma R1	Norma R123	Winchester 231	Winchester 296	Winchester 630	Winchester 680
290006	1	2.0	NR	NR	NR	NR	2.6	NR	NR	NR	NR	NR	3.0	2.3	4.1	3.9	4.0	4.2	3.6	1.9	NR	3.0	NR	4.0	NR
290007	2	2.1	NR	NR	NR	NR	2.8	NR	NR	NR	NR	NR	3.2	2.5	4.5	4.2	4.4	4.5	3.9	2.0	NR	3.3	NR	4.2	NR
290008	3	2.3	NR	NR	NR	NR	3.0	NR	NR	NR	NR	NR	3.6	2.8	5.0	4.6	4.8	5.0	4.3	2.3	NR	3.6	NR	4.9	NR
290009	4	2.7	NR	NR	NR	NR	3.4	NR	NR	3.4	NR	NR	4.0	3.1	5.6	5.2	5.5	5.6	4.9	2.6	NR	4.1	NR	5.6	NR
290010	5	2.9	NR	3.1	NR	2.9	3.7	NR	NR	3.6	NR	NR	4.3	3.4	6.1	5.8	6.0	6.1	5.3	2.9	NR	4.5	NR	6.1	NR
290011	6	3.0	NR	3.5	NR	3.1	3.9	NR	NR	3.9	NR	NR	4.5	3.6	6.6	6.0	6.2	6.4	5.5	3.1	NR	4.6	NR	6.3	NR
290012	7	3.2	NR	3.6	NR	3.2	4.1	NR	NR	4.3	3.6	NR	4.8	3.9	6.9	6.3	6.7	6.9	6.0	3.2	NR	4.8	NR	6.5	NR
290013	8	3.5	NR	4.1	NR	3.3	4.4	NR	NR	4.5	3.8	NR	5.0	4.0	7.4	7.0	7.3	7.4	6.5	3.7	NR	5.3	NR	7.2	NR
290014	9	3.7	NR	4.2	3.7	3.4	4.5	NR	NR	4.6	3.9	NR	5.2	4.2	7.7	7.4	7.6	7.7	6.7	3.8	NR	5.5	NR	7.5	NR
290015	10	4.0	7.3	5.0	4.5	4.0	5.1	NR	NR	5.3	4.3	NR	6.1	4.9	8.5	7.9	8.4	8.6	7.5	4.3	NR	6.3	NR	8.4	NR
290016	11	4.3	7.5	5.1	4.6	4.6	5.2	7.3	NR	5.4	4.5	NR	6.4	5.1	8.9	8.2	8.8	9.0	7.7	4.5	NR	6.4	NR	8.7	8.8
290017	12	4.6	8.0	5.5	4.8	4.8	NR	7.9	2.2	5.8	4.8	NR	6.8	5.3	9.4	8.7	9.3	9.5	8.2	4.8	NR	6.9	NR	9.2	9.5
290018	13	5.0	8.8	6.0	5.6	5.3	NR	8.7	3.3	6.5	5.3	NR	7.6	5.8	10.3	9.7	10.1	10.4	9.0	5.3	NR	7.6	10.3	10.2	10.5
290019	14	5.5	9.4	6.4	6.0	5.8	NR	9.3	3.5	6.8	5.7	NR	8.1	6.4	11.1	10.5	11.0	11.1	9.6	5.7	NR	8.1	11.0	10.8	11.2
290020	15	5.8	9.9	6.8	6.4	6.0	NR	9.8	3.7	7.2	5.9	NR	8.5	6.7	11.8	11.1	11.6	11.8	10.2	6.0	NR	8.5	11.6	11.5	11.9
290021	16	6.1	10.3	7.1	6.7	6.4	NR	10.3	4.2	7.5	6.2	8.9	8.9	7.0	12.4	11.5	12.3	12.4	10.7	NR	NR	8.9	12.2	12.2	12.6
290022	17	6.5	11.5	7.9	7.6	7.0	NR	11.4	4.8	8.4	6.8	9.7	9.8	7.7	13.7	12.8	13.5	13.7	11.8	NR	NR	9.9	13.6	13.4	13.8
290023	18	NR	12.1	8.1	7.8	7.3	NR	12.0	5.3	8.7	7.3	10.1	10.2	8.4	15.0	13.9	14.0	14.0	12.2	NR	10.1	NR	13.8	14.2	14.3
290024	19	NR	12.3	8.6	8.3	7.6	NR	12.7	6.0	9.2	7.7	10.8	10.6	8.4	15.0	13.9	14.6	14.9	12.9	NR	10.8	NR	14.7	14.6	15.1
290025	20	NR	13.4	9.1	8.8	8.0	NR	13.4	6.4	9.7	8.1	11.4	11.4	8.8	15.7	14.9	15.6	15.6	13.6	NR	11.5	NR	15.6	15.5	16.0
290026	21	NR	14.7	9.9	9.7	8.9	NR	14.7	7.2	10.6	8.7	12.5	12.6	9.7	17.6	16.2	17.1	17.5	15.1	NR	12.5	NR	17.1	16.8	17.5
290027	22	NR	15.7	10.4	10.2	9.4	NR	15.5	7.5	11.4	9.5	13.2	13.2	10.4	18.3	17.0	17.7	17.9	15.9	NR	13.2	NR	17.9	18.0	18.3

NOTE: All Powder Designated in Grains.   NR = Not Recommended.

PONSNESS-WARREN

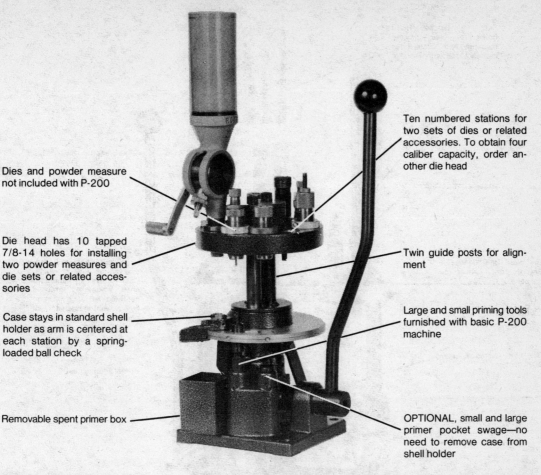

Dies and powder measure not included with P-200

Ten numbered stations for two sets of dies or related accessories. To obtain four caliber capacity, order another die head

Die head has 10 tapped 7/8-14 holes for installing two powder measures and die sets or related accessories

Twin guide posts for alignment

Case stays in standard shell holder as arm is centered at each station by a spring-loaded ball check

Large and small priming tools furnished with basic P-200 machine

Removable spent primer box

OPTIONAL, small and large primer pocket swage—no need to remove case from shell holder

METAL-MATIC P-200

Straight-wall case loader

The Metal-Matic P-200 has been designed to hold two calibers at one time. Conversion from one caliber to another is accomplished in less than five minutes. The P-200 uses standard 7/8-14 die sets and powder measure. Castings are heavy die cast aluminum coated with a silver vein black plastic applied with electrostatics and baked on for durability. Under normal conditions a person can load 200 rounds per hour, with some exceeding this average. The P-200 is designed for straight-wall cartridges.

Metal-Matic P-200 Complete (with small and large primer seating tools, less dies and powder measure)............ **$275.00**

Accessories:

Extra die head.................	**$12.50**
Large primer pocket swaging tool....	21.00
Small primer pocket swaging tool....	21.00
Case height stop assembly.........	20.00
Powder measure extension	19.00

METAL-MATIC P-200 PRIMER FEED

Primer feed fits standard 7/8-14 threads of the P-200 die head. Handles both large and small primers and has a shielded primer tube protector **$41.00**

PONSNESS-WARREN

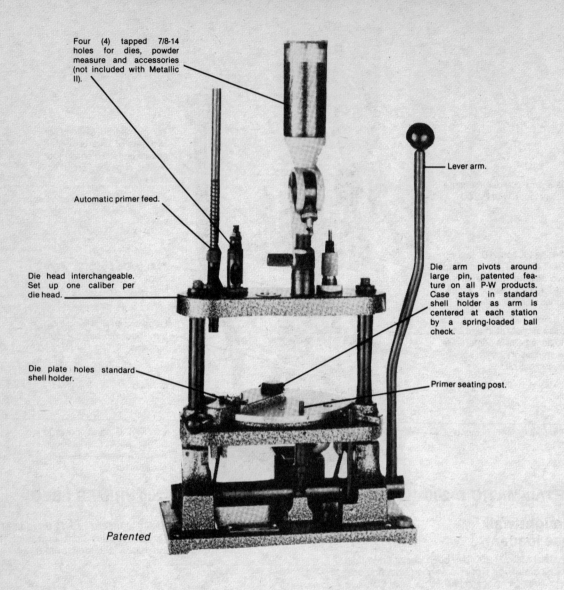

Four (4) tapped 7/8-14 holes for dies, powder measure and accessories (not included with Metallic II).

Automatic primer feed.

Die head interchangeable. Set up one caliber per die head.

Die plate holes standard shell holder.

Lever arm.

Die arm pivots around large pin, patented feature on all P-W products. Case stays in standard shell holder as arm is centered at each station by a spring-loaded ball check.

Primer seating post.

Patented

Metallic M-II   Rifle / pistol loader

The Metallic M-II is a totally unique and innovative loader capable of loading 150 rounds or more an hour with utmost precision. The Metallic M-II has power to spare for reforming brass, resizing cases, or loading tough calibers. The M-II uses standard dies, powder measure and shell holder. The die head has four tapped 7/8-14 holes to accept standard dies, powder measure and other accessories. Castings are heavy die case aluminum coated with a silver vein black plastic and baked on for durability.

Once the case is inserted into the shell holder, it is not removed until the case has been resized, new primer seated, powder dropped, and bullet seated and crimped. A depriming tube removes spent primer and residue, keeping the priming area clean. The Metallic M-II has an automatic primer feed. Optional features which can be purchased include additional die heads (for additional caliber capacity), and a powder measure extension to accommodate any standard powder measure.

Metallic M-II Complete (with small and large primer seating tools, automatic primer feed, large and small primer tubes, less dies, powder measure and shell holder) .. **$440.00**

Accessories:

Extra die head	$36.00
Powder measure extension ..	19.00
CAL-die, bullet seating die .	35.00
CAL-die, additional bullet retaining sleeves	7.00

PONSNESS-WARREN

Large shot and powder reservoirs.

Shot and powder baffles assure consistently precise loads.

Bushing access plug allows instant inspection or changing of bushings and also provides a direct shot drop for loading buck shot or granulated plastic.

Charging ring has positive lock to prevent accidental flow of powder.

Tool head can hold two gauges simultaneously.

Six and eight point crimp starters are ball bearing lined to give perfect crimp alignment every time.

Shot and powder may be drained out completely through shot and powder drop tube.

Double post construction for greater leverage and wear.

Absolute resizing, shell stays in full length sizing die through entire operation.

Trouble-free tip-out wad guide.

Sizing die is centered at each station by spring-loaded ball check.

Handy, removable spent-primer box.

Patented

DU-O-MATIC 375C

Precise reloading for field, trap or skeet

The Du-O-Matic 375C is the most versatile reloader made. It can hold tooling for one or two gauges simultaneously. With two gauges attached, it can be converted from one to the other in less than five minutes. Conversion kits for 3" can be installed in even less time. Factory-perfect reloads are made consistently by moving a shell encased in a full-length sizing die around the five station loading plate. The full-length sizing dies and tooling are precision ground, then polished or richly blued. All castings are of the finest grade aluminum, precision machined and handsomely finished. Under normal conditions, a person can load between 6 to 8 boxes of shells in an hour's time. The Du-O-Matic will handle all types of shells — paper or plastic, high or low base. Remember, all shells loaded on Ponsness-Warren tools are guaranteed to feed and chamber into any firearm.

Du-O-Matic 375C, one gauge complete; 12, 16, 20, 28 or .410 gauge (with 6 or 8 point crimp starter) **$299.99**

NOTE: 10 gauge available as accessory tooling set only.

Accessories Available:

375 Additional Tooling Set; 12, 16, 20, 28 or .410 gauge (Crimp starter included) **$349.99**

375 Special 10 gauge (3½") magnum additional tooling set (includes tool head, tooling and 6 point crimp starter) **$120.00**

375 3" Conversion Kit (12, 20 or .410 gauge) (For 20 gauge, brand of ammunition to be loaded should be specified) **$ 17.00**

375 2½", 12 gauge conversion kit (for international 65/67.5 mm 12 gauge shells only) **$ 33.00**

375 Tool Head (no tooling included) **$ 36.00**

Shot and Powder bushings

Our bushings are manufactured with extreme care to assure absolute accuracy and consistent performance. Shot and powder bushings are of different diameters to eliminate any possibility of their being reversed. Aluminum powder bushings absolutely eliminate sparking. All bushings are clearly and permanently marked.

Shot or Powder Bushing . . . . **$ 3.50**

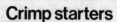

Crimp starters

Our six and eight point crimp starters are ball bearing lined and have sensitive automatic pick-up fingers to assure perfect crimp alignment every time. The crimp heads are interchangeable, so to broaden the loading capabilities of the tools, additional crimp heads can be attached to the original crimp starter housing.

Crimp Starter Complete (6 or 8 Point) . . . . **$ 20.00**
   (Specify model)
Crimp Starter Head Only (6 or 8 Point) . . . . **$ 11.00**

Special paper crimp assembly

This paper crimp conversion kit is intended for shooters who reload paper shells predominately. The crimp assembly which is standard on all Ponsness-Warren tools is designed primarily for plastic shells, and while paper shells can be loaded adequately, this special paper crimp assembly provides optimum appearance for paper shells. Installation can be accomplished easily in just a few minutes.

Special Paper Crimp Assembly **$17.00**
   (Specify gauge)

Wad guide fingers

Our engineers, taking advantage of recent developments in the plastics industry, have developed a wad guide finger with longer life and greater spring action than any available before. Our wad guide fingers handle all types of wad and are adaptable to most shotshell reloading tools. They are available in 10, 12, 16, 20, 28 and 410 gauge.

Wad Guide Fingers . . **$ 2.00**

PONSNESS-WARREN
SHOTSHELL RELOADING TOOLS

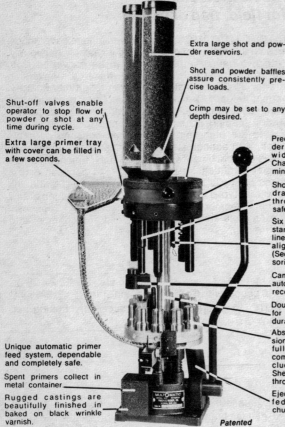

Extra large shot and powder reservoirs.

Shot and powder baffles assure consistently precise loads.

Crimp may be set to any depth desired.

Shut-off valves enable operator to stop flow of powder or shot at any time during cycle.

Extra large primer tray with cover can be filled in a few seconds.

Precision shot and powder bushings provide a wide range of loads. Changing takes but a few minutes.

Shot and powder may be drained out completely through drop tube for safety and convenience.

Six and eight point crimp starters are ball bearing lined to give perfect crimp alignment every time. (See illustration in Accessories section.)

Cam-operated wad carrier automatically tips out to receive all types of wads.

Double post construction for greater leverage and durability.

Absolute resizing — precision ground and polished full-length sizing dies completely resize case including brass and rim. Shell remains in sizing die through entire operation.

Ejected shells are gravity fed down handy shell chute.

Unique automatic primer feed system, dependable and completely safe.

Spent primers collect in metal container.

Rugged castings are beautifully finished in baked on black wrinkle varnish.

Patented

Large shot and powder reservoirs.

Shot and powder baffles assure consistently precise loads.

Bushing access plug allows instant inspection or changing of bushings and also provides a direct shot drop for loading buck shot or granulated plastic.

Charging ring has positive lock to prevent accidental flow of powder.

Tool head can hold two gauges simultaneously.

Six and eight point crimp starters are ball bearing lined to give perfect crimp alignment every time.

Shot and powder may be drained out completely through shot and powder drop tube.

Trouble-free tip-out wad guide.

Double post construction for greater leverage and wear.

Absolute resizing, shell stays in full length sizing die through entire operation.

Sizing die is centered at each station by spring-loaded ball check.

Handy, removable spent-primer box.

Photo shows Du-O-Matic with 12 and 20 gauge tooling attached.

Patented

Mult-O-Matic*
Model 600C

Mult-O-Matic 600B Complete (with 6 or 8 point crimp starter) 12, 16, 20, 28 or 410 gauge	**$579.00**

The 28 and 410 gauge 600's are designed primarily to load plastic casings using one piece plastic wads.

Accessories:

600B Additional Tooling Set Complete (with 6 or 8 point crimp starter) 12, 16, 20, 28 or 410 gauge	**$215.00**
600B 3″ Conversion Kit (12 and 20 gauge only)	195.00
(For 20 gauge, brand of ammunition to be loaded should be specified)	
Crimp Starter Head Only (6 or 8 point)	11.00
Special Paper Crimp Assembly (12 or 20 gauge only) ..	17.00
600B Crimp Starter Complete (6 or 8 point)	20.00

Du-O-Matic*
Model 375C

Du-O-Matic 375, One gauge complete; 12, 16, 20, 28 or 410 gauge, (with 6 or 8 point crimp starter)	**$299.00**
NOTE: 10 gauge available as accessory tooling set only.	
Du-O-Matic 375, 10 gauge complete with 6-point crimp starter	**$349.00**

Accessories:

375 Additional Tooling Set 12, 16, 20, 28 or 410 gauge ..	**$120.00**
(Crimp starter or head extra)	
375 Special 10 gauge (3½″) magnum additional tooling set	162.00
(Includes tool head, tooling and 6 point crimp starter)	
375 Crimp Starter Complete (6 or 8 point)	20.00
Crimp Starter Head Only (6 or 8 point)	11.00
375 3″ Conversion Kit (12, 20 or 410 gauge)	17.00
(For 20 gauge, brand of ammunition to be loaded should be specified)	
375 2½″, 12 gauge conversion kit	33.00
(for international 65/67.5mm 12 gauge shells only)	
375 Tool head (No tooling included)	36.00
Special Paper Crimp Assembly	17.00

PONSNESS-WARREN SHOTSHELL RELOADING TOOLS

Extra large shot & powder reservoirs.

Shot and powder baffles assure consistently precise loads.

Extra large primer tray with cover can be filled in a few seconds.

Precision bushings can be easily changed to vary shot and powder loads.

Shut off switches enable operator to stop flow of powder or shot at any time during the cycle. Switches include a drain feature which permits complete draining of reservoirs.

Cam operated wad carrier swings out to receive all types of wads.

Spent primers collect in convenient container.

Shot and powder are charged automatically and accurately.

Crimp may be set to any desired depth with handy adjustment screw.

Six and eight point crimp starters are ball bearing lined to assure perfect crimp alignment automatically.

Automatic taper crimp. Shell remains in precision die throughout the entire operation, eliminating feeding and chambering problems.

Cylinder indexes automatically. A factory perfect shell is produced with every pull of the handle.

Automatic primer feed.

Finished shell is automatically ejected down convenient shell chute at rear.

Rugged aluminum castings are finished in a handsome electro statically applied, baked on silver vein black plastic.

Patented

SILVER ST-800C

The ultimate shotshell reloader

This is the new Silver ST 800C shotshell reloader, the tool that automatically tapers the crimp while the shell remains in the precision die thoughout all operations. The same design perfection used in the Size-O-Matic 800B for over 17 years is now engineered for all cases — skived, straight wall, and paper. Available in all gauges. With the same high production as the 800B, the new ST 800C is engineered for outstanding ease of operation and is guaranteed to feed and chamber in any shotgun. The 800C has an automatic primer feed system with no tubes to fill and primers always in full view of the operator. A full box of 100 primers loads in just seconds. The 800C loads all plastic and paper shells, giving a beautiful tapered crimp automatically. The 800C is a quality product you would be proud to

Not convertible to other gauges.

No separate case resizer or conditioner needed

Size-O-Matic 800C Complete (with 6 or 8 point crimp starter) 12, 20, 28 or 410 gauge **$899.00**

The 28 and 410 gauge 800C's are designed primarily to load plastic casings using one piece plastic wads.

Accessories:

800C Crimp Starter Complete (6 or 8 point)	**$20.00**
Crimp Starter Head only (6 or 8 point)	11.00
Special Paper Crimp Assembly (12 or 20 gauge only)	17.00
Additional Shot or Powder Bushings	3.50
Additional Wad Guide Fingers	2.00
Wood grip shovel handle	27.00

PONSNESS-WARREN

Powder Measure Extension

CAL-die

The Ponsness/Warren Powder Measure Extension is designed for both the Metal-Matic P-200 and the Metallic M-II loaders.

This extension lifts the powder measure above the dies, thus enabling the loader to change or replace dies or powder measure without having to remove adjacent tooling.

The extension consists of three main parts: a spring (B-36-2) and a powder drop insert (PW-1-2 for large size, PW-1-3 for small size) which fit into the knurled housing (PW-1-1). Both large and small powder drop inserts are supplied with the extension.

Powder Measure Extension **$19.00**

Bullet Retaining Sleeve Diameter	Calibers*
.224	22
.243	243, 244, 6mm
.257	all 25
.264	6.5mm
.270	270
.284	280, 284, 7mm
.308	All 30, 30-06, 30-30
.32	32 Special, 8mm
.338	338
.358	All 35

*The list shows only the most generally used calibers and does not reflect the complete coverage of the sleeves shown.

The Ponsness-Warren CAL-die bullet seating dies for rifle cases is for use on P/W's new Metallic M-II rifle/pistol loader. The CAL-die has several unique features. Only one housing or die body is required for all diameters between .224 and .358 caliber. To change calibers, only the purchase of an inexpensive bullet retaining sleeve or collet is required (see chart) and is easily slipped into the housing. Another unusual feature of the CAL-die is that the bullet retaining sleeve holds the bullet until the case is pushed into the housing and the bullet is completely seated. Instead of having to hold the bullet during the seating operation, you merely drop the bullet through a port in the side of the housing where it is held in proper alignment until the bullet is seated.

Standard packaging of the CAL-die consists of the housing, a large bullet seating pin for calibers .30 and larger (installed in the housing), a small bullet seating pin for calibers under .30, and a bullet retaining sleeve in .308 diameter. This one .308 diameter sleeve will load all .30 caliber bullets including those shown in the chart below.

The addition of the CAL-die to your Metallic M-II rifle press, or any press threaded 7/8-14, will approximately double the volume output as compared to loading with a conventional bullet seating die.

CAL-die (complete with the housing, two bullet seating pins, and the .308 diameter bullet sleeve) . . . **$35.00**
Each additional sleeve **7.00**

PONSNESS-WARREN
Shot and Powder
BUSHINGS

SHOT BUSHINGS

1 – 1/2 oz.	4 – 7/8 oz.
2 – 5/8 oz.	5 – 1 oz.
3 – 3/4 oz.	6 – 1-1/8 oz.

7 – 1-1/4 oz.	10 – 1-5/8 oz.
8 – 1-3/8 oz.	11 – 1-3/4 oz.
9 – 1-1/2 oz.	12 – 1-7/8 oz.

13 – 2 oz.	
14 – 2-1/4 oz.	

POWDER BUSHINGS
(UNITS SHOWN IN GRAINS)

THIS IS NOT A LOADING TABLE, BUT RATHER A CHART BASED ON RELATIVE HOLE SIZES, SHOWING THE APPROXIMATE NUMBER OF GRAINS DROPPED BY PONSNESS-WARREN POWDER BUSHINGS.
(All shot bushings meet N.S.S.A. and A.T.A. requirements)

	DU PONT						HERCULES							WINCHESTER					HODGDON			ALCAN		
	800-X	700-X	PB	SR 7625	SR 4756	IMR 4227	BULLSEYE	RED DOT	GREEN DOT	BLUE DOT	HERCO	UNIQUE	2400	296	452AA	473AA	540	571	HS-5	HS-6	H-110	AL-5	AL-7	AL-8
1A						12.1							12.1	13.7							13.7			
2A						12.6							12.6	14.8							14.8			
3A						14.0							13.9	15.6		15.3					15.6			
A		8.8	9.3	10.0	10.5	15.9		8.0	8.0		10.0	11.3	15.8	17.5			16.8	17.1	18.2	16.8	17.5	13.2	13.2	
B		9.5	9.7	11.0	11.0	16.8		8.5	8.5		10.6	12.1	16.7	18.8			17.6	18.2	19.5	17.7	18.8	14.1	14.1	
C		10.0	10.3	11.5	12.0	17.8		9.3	9.3		11.3	12.7	17.7	20.0			18.5	18.8	20.7	18.8	20.0	14.6	14.6	
C1		10.3	10.4	11.9	12.4	18.2		9.5	9.5		11.7	13.2	18.0				19.6	20.1	21.1	19.2	20.6	14.9	14.9	
D	12.7	10.8	11.1	12.5	13.0	19.1		9.8	9.8		12.1	13.8	19.2				20.4	21.0	22.3	20.5	21.5	16.0	16.0	
D1	13.0	11.4	12.3	13.6	13.7	19.9		10.7	10.7		13.2	14.5	20.0			15.5	21.3	22.4	23.4	21.9		16.8	16.8	
E	14.6	12.4	13.1	15.0	15.0	22.6	15.0	11.5	11.5		14.6	16.2	22.5			16.8	23.5	24.2	25.5	24.2		18.7	18.7	
E1	15.2	12.9	13.8	15.6	15.8	23.9	15.3	12.1	12.1	19.1	15.3	17.0	23.7			17.1	24.0	24.7	28.3	25.5		19.7	19.7	
E2	16.2	13.6	14.5	16.8	16.6	25.2	17.0	12.8	12.8	21.7	16.0	17.9	25.3		15.0	18.0	26.1	26.5	28.9	26.8		20.8	20.8	
F	16.9	14.5	15.3	18.0	17.5	26.5	17.5	13.5	13.5	22.0	16.7	18.8	26.3		15.6	19.6	27.5	28.5	30.4	28.0		21.9	21.9	17.8
F1	17.2	15.0	16.1	19.2	18.4	27.9	18.0	14.1	14.1	22.4	17.7	19.7	27.7		16.4	20.1	28.3	29.3	31.5	29.4		23.0	23.0	18.6
G	18.9	16.3	17.0	20.5	19.5	29.3	19.5	14.7	14.7	24.5	18.6	20.6	29.0		18.3	22.7	31.2	32.3	33.6	30.7		24.1	24.1	19.5
G1	19.1	17.0	18.4	21.7	21.1	31.5	20.2	15.9	15.9	26.2	19.9	22.6	31.4		19.0	23.0	32.7	33.4	36.4	33.1		26.1	26.1	21.4
H	20.7	17.9	18.8	22.0	21.5	32.1	21.4	16.5	16.5	27.0	20.2	23.1	32.1		19.9	24.1	34.0	34.8	37.0	33.6		26.7	26.7	21.9
I	21.1	18.5	19.2	22.5	22.0	33.0		17.0	17.0	27.8	20.7	23.5	33.0		20.3	24.7	34.4	36.5	38.3	35.0		27.3	27.3	22.4
J	22.4	19.0	19.7	23.0	22.5	34.0		17.2	17.2	28.2	21.5	24.4	34.0		21.5	25.4	35.5	37.1	39.5	36.2		28.2	28.2	23.2
J1	22.8	19.6	20.3	24.2	23.2	35.4		17.9	17.9	29.3	22.2	25.4	35.4		22.3	26.8	36.9	38.8	40.7	37.2		29.1	29.1	23.7
K	23.3	20.0	20.9	24.5	24.0	35.9		18.2	18.2	29.5	22.7	25.8	36.0		22.5	27.0	37.1	39.0	41.9	38.3		29.9	29.9	24.2
L	24.5	21.0	21.7	26.3	25.5	37.4		19.0	19.0	31.3	24.2	27.3	37.5		23.4		39.5	41.1	43.8	39.4		31.0	31.0	25.3
M	25.6	22.0	23.0	27.3	26.5	39.6		19.9	19.9	32.7	25.3	28.1	39.5		24.0		41.2	42.8	45.9	41.8		32.9	32.9	26.8
N	27.3	23.5	24.5	28.8	28.0	42.0		21.2	21.2	35.0	26.4	30.3	41.8		26.5		44.7	46.4	48.7	44.6		34.8	34.8	28.5
O	27.9	24.0	24.7	29.3	28.5	42.4		21.5	21.5	35.5	26.8	30.5	42.5				45.5	46.9	49.4	45.3		35.4	35.4	28.7
P	28.3	24.5	25.8	30.3	29.5	43.8		22.0	22.0	36.0	27.1	30.9	43.8				46.4	48.0	49.9	45.5		36.0	36.0	29.5
Q	28.8	25.0	26.2	30.8	30.0	44.8		22.8	22.8	37.5	28.1	32.2	45.0				47.7	49.3	52.4			37.4	37.4	30.3
R	29.8	25.5	26.6	31.3	3.05	45.4		23.3	23.3	38.5	29.3	32.8	45.5						53.0	49.5		38.3	38.3	31.0
S	30.4	26.5	27.7	32.8	32.0	47.2		23.8	23.8	39.2	29.9	33.8	47.2						54.7	49.9		38.9	38.9	32.2
T	32.7	28.0	29.2	33.8	33.5	49.9		25.2	25.2	42.0	31.6	36.1	49.9						57.8	52.6		41.7	41.7	33.8
U	34.5	29.5	30.9	36.3	35.5	52.8		26.7	26.7	45.1	32.7	38.1	52.8						61.4	56.9		43.8	43.8	35.8
V	35.2	30.5	31.9	36.8	36.5	54.5		27.5	27.5	46.3	33.7	38.9	54.5						63.0	57.4		45.0	45.0	37.1
W	36.0	32.5	33.7	39.3	39.0	57.5		28.9	28.9	48.1	35.9	41.8	57.5						66.8	61.2		47.8	47.8	39.3
X	38.2	33.0	34.1	39.8	39.5	58.1		29.4	29.4	48.7	36.4	42.1	58.1									48.5	48.5	39.6
Y		34.0	35.7	41.3	41.0	60.6		30.8	30.8	50.3	37.9	43.7	60.6									50.5	50.5	41.3
Z		38.0	39.3	45.8	45.5	67.2		33.9	33.9	56.3	46.0	48.2	67.2									55.5	55.5	46.1
AA		41.0	42.2	49.3	49.0	72.4		37.1	37.1	60.6	46.0	52.2	72.4									60.4	60.4	49.6

All Ponsness-Warren reloaders and additional tooling sets come with one shot bushing and one powder bushing included. If you have need to vary your loads, additional bushings are available.

The above data has been obtained by methods and from sources that are normally reliable. Since Ponsness-Warren has no control over the actual loading, choice or condition of firearms and components, no responsibility for any use of this data is assumed or implied.

Drops from powder bushings will vary slightly depending on the model of tool, the stability of the loading bench and the individual operator as well as for the reasons stated below. *We recommend that you weigh a powder charge prior to each reloading session so that you can be assured of the exact powder drop you are getting.*

RCBS RELOADING TOOLS

RCBS AUTOMATIC PRIMING TOOL

Precision-engineered to provide fast, accurate and uniform seating of primers in one simple step. Single-stage leverage system is so sensitive it enables you to actually "feel" the primer being seated to the bottom of the primer pocket. This priming tool permits you to visually check each primer pocket before seating the primer; thus eliminating wasted motion or slowing down the reloading process.

Primers are released one at a time through the RCBS automatic primer feed, eliminating contamination caused by handling primers with oily fingers.

Both primer rod assemblies furnished with this tool will handle all large and small American-made Boxer-type rifle and pistol primers.

ECONOMY FEATURES: If you already have RCBS automatic primer feed tubes, and RCBS shell holders, they will fit this RCBS Priming Tool—thus eliminating the need to buy extras.

BERDAN PRIMER ROD ASSEMBLIES

Optional Berdan Primer Rod Assemblies are available in the three sizes shown below, and are interchangeable with the American Boxer-type Primer Rod Assemblies, furnished with the Priming Tool.

PART NO.	DESCRIPTION	PRICE
09460	Priming Tool (less Shell Holder)	$46.50

RCBS AUTOMATIC PRIMER FEED

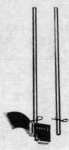

Stop misfires — greasy hands never need to touch primers. Automatically drops primers one at a time into the Primer Plug and Sleeve of the Primer Arm. Adjustable Primer Stop Pin eliminates jamming found in other Automatic Primer Feeds. Easily mounted on RCBS and most "C" type Presses. The Primer Tubes for large and small primers are completely interchangeable with the Body.

PART NO.	AUTO. PRIMER FEED	PRICE
09589	Combo for large and small primers	$14.50

RCBS PRIMER POCKET SWAGER

For fast, precision removal of primer pocket crimp from military cases. Leaves primer pocket perfectly rounded and with correct dimensions for seating of American Boxer-type primers. Will not leave oval-shaped primer pocket that reaming produces. Swager Head Assemblies furnished for large and small primer pockets — no need to buy a complete unit for each primer size. For use with all presses with standard ⅞"-14 top thread, except RCBS "A-3" Press. The RCBS "A-2" Press requires the optional Case Stripper Washer.

PART NO.	POCKET SWAGER	PRICE
09495	Combo for large and small primers	$16.00

RCBS UNIVERSAL PRIMER ARM

ONE PRIMER ARM HANDLES ALL PRIMERS

RCBS Primer Arms are designed for fast, accurate seating of primers. Interchangeable Primer Plugs and Sleeves eliminate necessity of having to buy a complete new Primer Arm for each primer size. Primer Plugs and Sleeves furnished for large and small primers. Body cast of rust-resistant zinc alloy. The Universal Primer Arm is designed for use with RCBS Rock Chucker and J.R. as well as most "C" type Presses.

PART NO.	UNIVERSAL PRIMER ARM	PRICE
9550	For large and small primers	$7.00
9552	Plug and Sleeve for large primers	2.20
9553	Plug and Sleeve for small primers	2.20

RCBS PRIMER TRAY

For fast, easy handling of primers and loading Automatic Primer Feed Tubes, place primers in this tray, shake tray horizontally, and primers will automatically position themselves anvil side up. Sturdy plastic case.

PART NO.	PRIMER TRAY	PRICE
09477	Single Tray	$2.00

RCBS PRIMER POCKET BRUSH

A slight twist of this tool thoroughly cleans residue out of primer pockets. Interchangeable stainless steel brushes, for large and small primer pockets, attaches easily to Accessory Handle.

PART NO.	PRIMER POCKET BRUSH	PRICE
09574	Complete, Combo	$9.00

RCBS RELOADING TOOLS

RCBS CASE LUBE KIT

Everything you need for proper case lubrication! Kit contains RCBS Case Lube Pad, 2 ounce tube RCBS Resizing Lubricant and RCBS Accessory Handle with .22 and .30 caliber Case Neck Brushes. See descriptions of items below.

PART NO.	DESCRIPTION	PRICE
09335	Case Lube Kit	$11.00

RCBS RESIZING LUBRICANT

A must for proper lubrication of cases before sizing or forming. Easily applied to cases with an RCBS Case Lube Pad. Packaged in convenient 2 ounce tube.

PART NO.	RESIZING LUBRICANT	PRICE
09300	Single Tube	$1.60

RCBS CASE NECK BRUSH

A handy tool for removing dirt and powder residue, and for lightly lubricating the insides of case necks to ease neck expanding operation. Accessory Handle accepts interchangeable nylon bristle Case Neck Brushes in the calibers shown below. Order Accessory Handle, and Brush in caliber of your choice.

SMALL	22- 25 caliber	$1.50
MEDIUM	270- 30 caliber	1.50
LARGE	35- 45 caliber	1.50

RCBS CASE LUBE PAD

This companion to RCBS Resizing Lubricant is ideal for lubricating cases before sizing or forming. Cases rolled lightly across Pad pick up just the right amount of lubricant. Plastic cover to protect pad.

PART NO	CASE LUBE PAD	PRICE
09307	1 Pad	$5.30

RCBS MODEL 5-10 SCALE

A major improvement in reloading scales. Gives fast, accurate weighings of powder charges and cartridge components, from 1/10th to 510 grains. **NEW Micrometer Poise** permits fast precision adjustments from 1/10th to 10 grains by merely rotating micrometer-type cylinder. **NEW Approach-to-Weight** Feature visually tells reloader when he is approaching the pre-set weight. **Easy-to-read scale beam** is graduated in 1/10th grain increments; has conventional large poise and extra-deep notches. **Magnetic Damper** eliminates beam oscillation. All-metal base and extra-large leveling foot reduce tipping. Weighted, anti-tip pan hanger, and pan platform accommodate long cartridges and components.

PART NO.	DESCRIPTION	PRICE
09070	Reloading Scale	$67.00
09072	Metric	77.00

RCBS POWDER TRICKLER

For fast, easy balancing of scales with precision powder charges. Merely twist knob and powder trickles into the scale pan a kernel at a time. Has large capacity powder reservoir. Extra large base minimizes tipping.

PART NO.	DESCRIPTION	PRICE
09094	Powder Trickler	$8.00

RCBS POWDER MEASURE STAND

Now more height — a full seven inches from the reloading bench to the bottom of the threads! The ideal accessory for raising Powder Measure to proper working height. Permits placing of Reloading Scale or cases in loading block under Powder Measure Drop Tube. Easily bolts to loading bench. For all Powder Measures with standard ⅞" - 14 thread.

PART NO.	DESCRIPTION	PRICE
09030	Powder Measure Stand	$14.50

RCBS UNIFLOW POWDER MEASURE

This tool saves the time of having to weigh every powder charge when reloading a quantity of cases. With it you will be able to throw consistently accurate and uniform powder charges directly into cases. RCBS Precisioneered Measuring Cylinder pours powder into case to eliminate clogging that occurs in powder measures that "dump" charges. Adjusts quickly and easily from one charge to another without emptying powder hopper. Powder level visible at all times. Includes stand plate for mounting on press or bench, and two drop tubes to fit from .22 to .45 caliber cases. Optional .17 caliber drop tube also available. Choice of large measuring cylinder for rifle cases, or small measuring cylinder for bench rest or pistol cases.

PART NO.	POWDER MEASURE	PRICE
09001	With Large Measuring Cylinder	$46.00
09002	With Small Measuring Cylinder	46.00
09000	Combo with Large & Small Measuring Cylinders	56.00
09003	Large Measuring Cylinder Assembly*	14.50
09004	Small Measuring Cylinder Assembly*	14.50
09028	Drop Tube .17 caliber	4.60

*Consists of Measuring Cylinder and Measuring Screw.

RCBS POWDER FUNNEL

For powder charging just a few cases at a time. Large, easy-to-use, plastic Powder Funnel in two sizes: .22 to .45 calibers, and .17 caliber. Specially designed drop tube prevents powder spills around case mouths. Antistatic treatment prevents powder from sticking. Square lip stops Funnel from rolling.

PART NO.	POWDER FUNNEL	PRICE
09087	22-45 calibers	$2.40
09086	17 caliber	2.40

RCBS RELOADING TOOLS

RELOADER SPECIAL
RCBS R.S. PRESS COMBINATION OFFER

Costs less than
9 boxes of
.30-06 cartridges

This RCBS J.R. Press is the ideal setup to get started reloading your own rifle and pistol ammo — from the largest Magnums down to .22 Hornets. This Press develops ample leverage and pressure to perform all reloading tasks including (1) resizing cases their full length, (2) forming cases from one caliber into another, (3) making bullets. Rugged Block "O" Frame, designed by RCBS, prevents Press from springing out of alignment — even under tons of pressure. Extra-long ram-bearing surface minimizes wobble and side play. Comfort grip handle. Converts to up or down stroke in minutes. Standard ⅞"-14 thread accepts all popular dies and reloading accessories. Price includes: PRIMER CATCHER, to collect ejected primers; RCBS UNIVERSAL PRIMER ARM with large and small primer plugs and sleeves; RCBS SHELL HOLDER; one set of RCBS DIES in choice of calibers shown below.

PART NO.	R.S. PRESS, LESS DIES	PRICE
09356	Less Shell Holder	$71.50

Combo $100.00

ROCK CHUCKER "COMBO"
RCBS R.C. PRESS COMBINATION OFFER

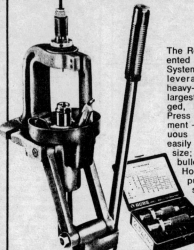

U.S. Pat. No. 2,847,895

The Rock Chucker Press, with Patented RCBS Compound Leverage System, delivers up to 200% more leverage than most presses for heavy-duty reloading of even the largest rifle and pistol cases. Rugged, Block "O" Frame prevents Press from springing out of alignment — even under the most strenuous operations. It case-forms as easily as most presses full-length size; it full-length sizes and makes bullets with equal ease. Shell Holders snap into sturdy, all-purpose shell holder ram. Non-slip handle with convenient grip. Operates on down-stroke for increased leverage. Standard ⅞"-14 thread. Price includes: PRIMER CATCHER to collect spent primers; RCBS UNIVERSAL PRIMER ARM with large and small primer plugs and sleeves; one RCBS SHELL HOLDER; one set of RCBS DIES in choice of calibers shown below.

PART NO.	ROCK CHUCKER PRESS, LESS DIES	PRICE
09366	Less Shell Holder	$110.00

Combo $137.50

PART NUMBERS FOR RELOADER SPECIAL COMBO & ROCK CHUCKER COMBO.

Reloader Special Combo	Rock Chucker Combo	Caliber	Reloader Special Combo	Rock Chucker Combo	Caliber
RIFLE CALIBERS			15371	15381	300 Winchester Magnum
10671	10681	22-250	15571	15581	308 Winchester
10971	10981	222 Reminaton			
11171	11181	223 Rem (5.6mm Rem.)	18278	18288	357 Magnum/38 Special (RN) (SWC) (WC)
11471	11481	243 Winchester			
13571	13581	270 Winchester			
13671	13681	7mm Rem. Magnum	18678	18688	44 Magnum/44 Special (RN) (SWC)
14671	14681	30-30 Winchester			
14871	14881	30-06 Springfield			
			18978	18988	45 Auto (45 ACP) (RN) (SWC)

NOTE: The following abbreviations are used to indicate bullet seater plug types: (RN) Roundnose, (SWC) Semi-Wadcutter, (WC) Wadcutter.

RCBS RELOADING TOOLS

IMPORTANT
Before checking these tables for the Die Set you require, refer to Die Reference Table. When you find the caliber you want, note the letter in Die Group column. This letter tells you which Group your caliber will be listed under in this section (Group A, B, C, etc.).

Each of these Full Length Die Sets includes a Full Length Sizer Die with Expander-Decapping Assembly and a Seater Die with built-in crimper.

GROUP A — $29.00 — Full Length Die Set 1½ lbs.

.17 Remington	17201
.218 Bee	10001
.22 Hornet	10201
.22 Remington Jet	10401
.22-250 (.22 Varminter)	10601
.220 Swift	10701
.221 Remington Fire Ball	10801
.222 Remington	10901
.222 Remington Magnum	11001
.223 Remington (5.56mm)	11101
.243 Winchester	11401
6mm Remington (.244 Remington)	11501
.25-06	12001
.25-20 Winchester	11801
.25-35 Winchester	12101
.250 Savage (.250-3000 Savage)	12201
.257 Roberts	12501
.257 Weatherby Magnum	12601
.264 Winchester Magnum	12701
6.5mmx55 Swedish Mauser	13201
.270 Weatherby Magnum	13401
.270 Winchester	13501
7mm Remington Magnum	13601
7mm Weatherby Magnum	13701
7mmx57 Mauser (7mm Mauser)	13801
.280 Remington	14001
.284 Winchester	14101
7.65mmx53 Mauser (Belgian)	14301
7.7mmx58 Japanese Arisaka	14401
.30-30 Winchester	14601
.30-40 Krag	14701
.30-06 Springfield	14801
.300 Holland & Holland Magnum	15001
.300 Savage	15101
.300 Weatherby Magnum	15201
.300 Winchester Magnum	15301
.303 British	15401
.308 Winchester	15501
.308 Norma Magnum	15601
.32 Winchester Special	15701
8mmx57 Mauser (8mm Mauser)	15901
8mm Remington Magnum	16001
.338 Winchester Magnum	16301
.35 Remington	16501
.375 Holland & Holland Magnum	16901
.30 Herrett	**17401**

GROUP B — $31.00 — 3-Die Set 1½ lbs.

.30 M1 Carbine (RN)	18005
.32-20 Winchester (RN)	18105
.357 Magnum (RN)	18205
.357 Magnum (SWC)	18206
.357 Magnum (WC)	18207
.38 Special (RN)	18305
.38 Special (SWC)	18306
.38 Special (WC)	18307
.41 Magnum (RN)	18505
.41 Magnum (SWC)	18506
.41 Magnum (WC)	18507
.44 Magnum (RN)	18605
.44 Magnum (SWC)	18606
.44 Magnum (WC)	18607
.44 Special (SWC)	18706
.44-40 Winchester (.44 Win.) (RN)	18805
.45 Automatic (.45 ACP) (RN)	18905
.45 Automatic (.45 ACP) (SWC)	18906
.45 Automatic (.45 ACP) (WC)	18907
.45 Colt (RN)	19105
.45 Colt (SWC)	19106

(RN) — Roundnose, (SWC) — Semi-Wadcutter, (WC) — Wadcutter.

GROUP D — $38.00 — Full Length Die Set 1½ lbs.

.219 Zipper	26001
.22 K-Hornet	26201
.224 Weatherby Magnum	32301
.240 Weatherby Magnum	33201
.256 Winchester Magnum	33301
.257 Improved (40°)	32201
6.5mm Remington Magnum	33401
6.5mm-06	27801
6.5mmx50 Japanese Arisaka	32401
6.5mmx52 Carcano	27601
6.5mmx54 Mannlicher-Schoenauer	27701
6.5mmx57	32801
7mmx64 Brenneke	34001
7.5mm Schmidt-Rubin	33501
7.62mm Russian	29001
7.62mmx39	32901
.30 Remington	29201
.30-338 Winchester Magnum	29401
.303 Savage	29601
.32-40 Winchester	32501
8mm-06	32601
.33 Winchester	30501
.340 Weatherby Magnum	30601
.348 Winchester	33601
.22 Savage High Power	**33801**
.225 Winchester	**33901**
.35 Whelen	30701
.350 Remington Magnum	33701
.358 Norma Magnum	31001
.358 Winchester	32701
.30 Luger (7.65mm Luger)	25001
.30 Mauser (7.63mm Mauser)	25101

These 3-Die Sets include a Sizer Die with Decapping Unit, Expander Die with Expander and Seater Die with built-in Crimper.

GROUP C — $35.00 — 3-Die Set 1½ lbs.

.444 Marlin	20704
.458 Winchester Magnum	20804
.45-70 U.S. Government	20904
.25ACP (.25 Automatic)	21004
.32 ACP (7.65mm Automatic)	20004
.32 Smith & Wesson, Long (RN)	20104
.32 Smith & Wesson, Long (WC)	20107
.38 Colt Super Automatic	20204
.38 Smith & Wesson	20304
.380 Auto Pistol	20404
9mm Luger	20504

GROUP F — $44.00 — 3-Die Set 1½ lbs.

.38-55 Winchester & Ballard	36504
.50-70 U.S. Government	38704
8mm Nambu	36404

RCBS originated 3-Die (and 4-Die) sets for straight wall rifle and pistol cases to avoid "overworking" of the brass case. Sizing is done in one Die, expanding in another, and seating in the final die.

The 3-Die Sets include a Sizer Die, Expander Die with Expander-Decapping Assembly and Seater Die with built-in crimper.

GROUP E — $38.00 — 3-Die Set 1½ lbs.

.357 Auto Magnum	35505
.38-40 Winchester (RN)*	35605
.45 Auto Rim (RN)	35705

*Jacketed bullets only — others on Special Order at extra cost.

RCBS RELOADING TOOLS

SMALL BASE DIES
GROUP A

A must for sizing small base cases to minimum dimensions, thereby ensuring smooth functioning in the actions of automatic, pump, slide and some lever action rifles. Each Small Base Die Set includes a Small Base Sizer Die with Expander-Decapping Assembly and a Seater Die with built-in crimper.

GROUP A Caliber	Small Base Die Set 1 ½ lbs. $29.00	Small Base Sizer Die ¾ lb. $19.00
.223 Remington (5.6mm) (SB)	11103	11131
.243 Winchester (SB)	11403	11431
6mm Remington (.244 Remington) (SB)	11503	11531
.270 Winchester (SB)	13503	13531
.280 Remington (SB)	14003	14031
.284 Winchester (SB)	14103	14131
.30-06 Springfield (SB)	14803	14831
.300 Savage (SB)	15103	15131
.308 Winchester (SB)	15503	15531
7mm Remington Magnum (SB)	13603	13631
300 Winchester Magnum (SB)	15303	15331

NECK DIES
GROUP A

These Dies size only the neck of the case, not the shoulder or body, just enough to grip the bullet. Each Neck Die Set includes a Neck Sizer Die with Expander-Decapping Assembly and a Seater Die with built-in crimper.

GROUP A Caliber	Neck Die Set 1 ½ lbs. $29.00	Neck Sizer Die ¾ lb. $19.00
.22-250 (.22 Varminter)	10602	10630
.222 Remington	10902	10930
.223 Remington (5.56mm)	11102	11130
.243 Winchester	11402	11430
6mm Remington (.244 Remington)	11502	11530
.25-06	12002	12030
.270 Winchester	13502	13530
7mm Remington Magnum	13602	13630
7mmx57 Mauser (7mm Mauser)	13802	13830
.30-06 Springfield	14802	14830
.300 Winchester Magnum	15302	15330
.308 Winchester	15502	15530
17 Remington	17202	17230
220 Swift	10702	10730

RCBS TRIM DIE
TO CUT CASES DOWN TO SIZE.

A sure way of checking and adjusting case lengths. Insert a case into this Trim Die and if it sticks out above the top it's too long. So simply file case down until it is flush with Die top. Don't worry about ruining Die with file – it's been specially heat treated to withstand a file bearing against the top.

After filing, just remove the burrs from outside of case and bevel the inside with an RCBS Burring Tool.

These Dies have precision-machined Sizer Die Chambers, but with slightly larger necks, to guarantee accuracy in gauging case lengths. Headspace is kept to minimum tolerances to avoid accidentally changing the case length when it's run into the Trim Die.

Caliber	Trim Die 1/2 lb. $16.00 Part No.
GROUP A	
.22-250 (.22 Varminter)	10665
.220 Swift	10765
.222 Remington	10965
.223 Remington (5.56mm)	11165
.243 Winchester	11465
6mm Remington (.244 Remington)	11565
.25-06	12065
.270 Winchester	13565
7mm Remington Magnum	13665
7mmx57 Mauser (7mm Mauser)	13865
.30 Herrett	17465
.30-30 Winchester	14665
.30-06 Springfield	14865
.300 Winchester Magnum	15365
.308 Winchester	15565
8mmx57 Mauser (8mm Mauser)	15965
GROUP B	
.357 Magnum (RN, SWC, WC)†	18265
.38 Special (RN, SWC, WC)†	18365
.44 Magnum (RN, SWC, WC)†	18665
.45 Automatic (45 ACP) (RN, SWC, WC)†	18965

†Extended shell holder required for trimming or forming.

NOTE: Trim dies other than those listed are available in any caliber on special order.

RCBS RELOADING TOOLS

TUNGSTEN CARBIDE DIES
GROUP B

The most extravagant Dies made, these are for the perfectionist who loads large quantities on a regular basis and wants to eliminate the need for lubing cases. Each 3-Die Carbide Set, 4-Die Carbide Set and 4-Die Carbide Set with Tamper Crimp includes a Carbide Sizer Die, Expander Die with Expander-Decapping Assembly. The 3-Die Carbide Set has Seater Die with built-in crimper, while the 4-Die Carbide Sets have a Seater Die without crimper and therefore a separate roll Crimper Die. Either roll or taper. The 4-Die Carbide Sets with Taper Crimp have a Seater Die without crimper and a Taper Crimp Die.

GROUP B Caliber	Carbide Sizer Die ½ lb.	4-Die Carbide Set 1½ lbs.	4-Die Carbide Set With Taper Crimp 1½ lbs.	Taper Crimp Die ½ lb.
30 M-1 Carbine (RN)	18037	—		—
357 Magnum (RN)	18237	18217		18264
357 Magnum (SWC)	18237	18218		18264
357 Magnum (WC)	18237	18219		18264
38 Special (RN)	18237	18317		18264
38 Special (SWC)	18237	18318		18264
38 Special (WC)	18237	18319		18264
41 Magnum (RN)	18537	18517		—
41 Magnum (SWC)	18537	18518		—
41 Magnum (WC)	18537	18519		—
44 Auto Magnum (SWC)	—	—		19264
44 Auto Magnum (WC)	—	—		19264
44 Magnum (RN)	18637	18617		—
44 Magnum (SWC)	18637	18618		—
44 Magnum (WC)	18637	18619		—
44 Special (SWC)	18637	18718		—
45 Automatic (RN)	18937	18917		18964
45 Automatic (SWC)	18937	18918		18964
45 Automatic (WC)	18937	18919		18964
45 Colt (RN)	19137	19117		—
45 Colt (SWC)	19137	19118		—
44 Auto Magnum (SWC)			*19226	
44 Auto Magnum (WC)			*19227	

*4-Die set includes regular sizer die. Tungsten Carbide sizer die not available in this caliber.

TUNGSTEN CARBIDE DIES
GROUP C

Identical to above Carbide Dies but for Group C calibers. Each 3-Die Carbide Set includes a Carbide Sizer Die with Decapping Assembly, Expander Die with Expander, and Seater Die with built-in crimper. The 3-Die Set is easily converted to a 4-Die Set by purchasing the optional Taper Crimp Die.

GROUP C Caliber	Carbide Sizer Die ½ lb.	3-Die Carbide Set 1½ lbs.	Taper Crimp Die ½ lb.
32 ACP (7.65mm Automatic)	20037	20009	—
32 Smith & Wesson Long (RN)	20137	20109	20164
32 Smith & Wesson Long (WC)	20137	20111	20164
38 Colt Super Automatic	20237	20209	—
380 Auto Pistol	20437	20409	20464
9mm Luger	20537	20509	20564

Note: Browning Automatic Rifles in .243 Winchester, .270 Winchester, .30-06 and .308 Winchester calibers require *Small Base Dies* shown above. The .338 caliber rifle requires *Standard Dies.*

(RN) = Roundnose, (SWC) = Semi-Wadcutter, (WC) = Wadcutter.

RCBS RELOADING TOOLS

MODEL 5-10

The model number has changed but this is the same scale that reloaders have been using for years. Weighs powder, bullets or complete cartridges up to 510 grains instantly and accurately thanks to a micrometer poise, an approach-to-weight indicator system, large easy-to-read graduations, magnetic dampening, agate bearings and an anti-tip pan. Guaranteed to 0.1 grain sensitivity. Also available in metric readings.

Model 5-10 Scale	09070	2 lbs.
Model 5-10 Metric Scale	09072	2 lbs.

A smart investment to protect the model 5-0-5 or 5-10 scale when not in use. Soft, vinyl dust cover folds easily to stow away, or has loop for hanging up.

Scale Cover	09075	1/8 lb.

Model 5-0-5	$49.00
Model 5-10	67.00
Model 5-10 Metric	77.00
Model 10-10	78.00

Du-O-Measure, 5-0-5 and 10-10 are Registered Trademarks of Ohaus Scale Corporation.

MODEL 5-0-5

This 511 grain capacity scale has a three poise system with widely spaced, deep beam notches to keep them in place. Two smaller poises on right side adjust from 0.1 to 10 grains, larger one on left side adjusts in full 10 grain steps. The first scale to use magnetic dampening to eliminate beam oscillation, the 5-0-5 also has a sturdy die cast base with large leveling legs for stability. Self-aligning agate bearings support the hardened steel beam pivots for a guaranteed sensitivity to 0.1 grains.

Model 5-0-5 Scale	09071	1½ lbs.

MODEL 10-10

UP TO 1010 GRAIN CAPACITY.

Normal capacity is 510 grains, which can be increased, without loss in sensitivity, by attaching the included extra weight.

Features include micrometer poise for quick, precise weighing, special approach-to-weight indicator, easy-to-read graduations, magnetic dampener, agate bearings anti-tip pan. and dustproof lid snaps on to cover scale for storage. Sensitivity is guaranteed to 0.1 grains.

Model 10-10 Scale	09073	3 lbs.

RCBS ROTARY CASE TRIMMER
PRECISIONEERED®
09369 CASE TRIMMER WITHOUT COLLET OR PILOT $33.00

CASE TRIMMER PILOT
$2.20

PART NO.	PILOT CAL.	PART NO.	PILOT CAL.
09377	.17	09387	.33
09378	.22	09388	.34
09379	.24	09390	.36
09380	.25	09391	.37
09381	.26	09392	.40
09382	.27	09393	.41
09383	.28	09394	.44
09384	.30	09395	.45
09385	.31	09396	.45-R
09386	.32		

This tool is used to (1) trim to standard length those cases which have stretched after repeated firings; (2) to trim a quantity of cases to the same length for uniform bullet seating; (3) to correct uneven case mouths.

The RCBS Rotary Case Trimmer works just like a lathe. To trim a brass case to the desired length — quickly, easily, and accurately — you lock the case into the trimmer collet. Then adjust the cutting blade to the length you wish case trimmed . . . turn the handle a few times . . . and your case is trimmed. Neatly and accurately. Bevel and deburr the trimmed case mouth with an RCBS Burring Tool and you're ready to reload it!

Interchangeable quick-release collets, available for all popular calibers (.17 to .45), lock cases securely into place for trimming. Trimmer Pilots are Precisioneered to the exact dimension of the case mouth, and lock into the cutter with a setscrew. This eliminates wobbling and ensures perfect vertical and horizontal alignment of case. Pilots are inter-

CASE TRIMMER COLLET
$5.50

PART NO.	COLLET NO.	PART NO.	COLLET NO.
09371	1	09373	3
09372	2	09374	4

changeable and available in twenty sizes to fit from .17 to .45 caliber cases.

Double lock rings on the cutting assembly permit any quantity of cases to be trimmed to the same length with a single adjustment. Cutter blades are made of hardened mill-type steel for extended service life, and removable for sharpening.

The RCBS Case Trimmer is 100 percent metal — no wood or plastic. Has slots for holding extra collets and pilots. Base can be secured to bench with screws.

RCBS RELOADING TOOLS

MODEL 304 SCALE

PART NO.	DESCRIPTION	SHPG. WT.	PRICE
09074	Model 304 Scale	4¾ lbs.	$195.00

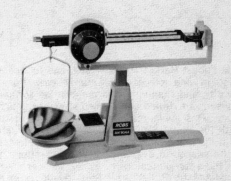

The 304 is a laboratory-quality scale offering an easy-to-set **direct reading** dial in values from 0.1 to 10 grains. Instead of the usual single beam, it has **two** tiered beams (10 to 100 grains and 100 to 1000 grains). Both beams have center-reading poises. The magnetic damper, plus agate bearings provide both speed of operation and accuracy. Guaranteed sensitivity 0.1 grain. Includes platform for holding powder trickler.

RCBS STUCK CASE REMOVER

Removes stuck cases from Sizer Dies quickly and efficiently. To use, back Die Expander-Decapping unit away from case head, drill case head and tap. Then place RCBS Stuck Case Remover on top of case head and turn hexhead screw until stuck case pulls free!

PART NO.	DESCRIPTION	PRICE
09340	STUCK CASE REMOVER	$9.50

RCBS BULLET PULLER

A valuable tool for pulling bullets from cases that have wrong powder charges, or for salvaging bullets from old ammo. Pulls bullets of any length or shape without damaging or marking them. Soft lead bullets may distort. Interchangeable Bullet Puller Collets work like a draw collet on a lathe, securely holding the bullet as the case is pulled away. Each Collet is precision-machined internally to the exact bullet diameter. Fits all reloading presses with standard ⅞"-14 thread. Order Bullet Puller plus one Collet in caliber of your choice from chart below.

RCBS BURRING TOOL

For beveling and removing burrs from case mouths of new factory cases, newly formed and trimmed cases. To bevel, insert pointed end of tool into case mouth and twist slightly. To remove burrs, place other end of tool over case mouth and twist. Centering pin keeps case aligned during deburring. Precision-machined and hardened for years of usage. Knurled for use by hand or in lathe. For .17 to .45 calibers.

PART NO.	DESCRIPTION	PRICE
09349	Burring Tool	$9.50

RCBS SETSCREW WRENCH

Here's a handy item for every reloading bench. The convenient hexagonal plastic handle will not roll off bench. Size is stamped in large easy-to-read numbers for quick identification. Available in two sizes to fit all popular RCBS products as shown below:

3/32″ Dies/Trim Dies/Case Forming Dies/Automatic Primer Feed attaching screws, bullet molds.

5/64″ Universal Primer Arm (new)•Case Trimmer

PART NO.	SETSCREW WRENCH	PRICE
09646	Combo	$5.00

PART NO.	DESCRIPTION		PRICE
09440	BULLET PULLER (less Collet)		$10.00
	BULLET PULLER COLLETS		$6.00

PART NO.	CALIBER	PART NO.	CALIBER
09419	.17	09428	32/8mm
09420	.22	09429	348
09421	6mm	09430	35/ 38 Spec.
09422	.25	09431	375
09423	6.5mm	09432	40
09424	.270	09433	41
09425	7mm	09435	44/11mm
09426	.30/7.35 Carc	09436	45
09427	.338		

RCBS RELOADING TOOLS

LUBE-A-MATIC Lubricator

The Lube-A-Matic frame, housing, and lubricant reservoir are cast in one piece—from sturdy cast iron—for strength, rigidity, and simplicity. The ram-bearing surface, and the Die housing, are drilled and reamed straight through, in one operation. This guarantees perfect alignment of the Top Punch with the Bullet Sizer Die below. The construction, combined with the link-leverage system, permits the largest cast bullets to be swaged in one short, continuous stroke, without strain on the sizer-lubricator.

Lube-A-Matic Bullet Sizer Dies—available in many different bullet diameters—lock firmly into the Die housing with a hexagonal Locking Cap.

Intercangeable Top Punches are available to fit the nose of any bullet design, and lock rigidly into the steel ram with an Allen set-screw.

The Lube-A-Matic Bullet Sizer-Lubricator is available completely equipped as shown. Lube-A-Matic Bullet Sizer Dies and Top Punches available separately—are listed below.

PART NO.	DESCRIPTION	SHPG. WT.	PRICE
80060	Lube-A-Matic—less Sizer Die and Top Punch	8 lbs.	$86.00

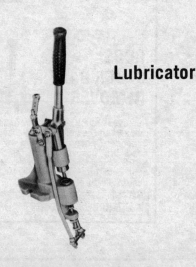

Lubricator

LUBE-A-MATIC BULLET SIZER DIES

Lube-A-Matic Sizer Dies are designed to swage bullets—with or without gas checks—to their correct diameters without shaving lead. This swaging action work-hardens the alloy through compression and produces a perfectly cylindrical bullet of increased strength, smoothness and accuracy.

BULLET SIZER DIE
SHPG. WT. ¼ lb. **$12.00**

Part No.	Sizer Die	Part No.	Sizer Die
82200	.224″	82222	.357″
82236	.228″	82223	.358″
82201	.243″	82224	.375″
82203	.257″	82225	.400″
82204	.264″	82238	.406″
82205	.277″	82226	.410″
82208	.284″	82227	.427″
82211	.308″	82228	.429″
82212	.309″	82230	.439″
82213	.310″	82239	.446″
82217	.321″	82231	.450″
82237	.323″	82232	.451″
82218	.338″	82233	.452″
82219	.354″	82234	.454″
82220	.355″	82235	.457″
82221	.356″	82240	.512″

LUBE-A-MATIC TOP PUNCHES

These Top Punches are designed for use in the RCBS Lube-A-Matic Bullet Sizer-Lubricator or with most other popular sizer-lubricators. Each Top Punch is precision machined for a perfect fit to the contour of the bullet nose. Locks into Bullet Sizer-Lubricator ram with Allen setscrew.

LUBE-A-MATIC TOP PUNCH
SHPG. WT. ⅛ lb. **$4.50**

Part No.	Top Punch	Part No.	Top Punch	Part No.	Top Punch	Part No.	Top Punch
82504	#115	82534	#460	85535	#535	85585	#585
82506	#190	82536	#465	85540	#540	85590	#590
82513	#311	82541	#495	85546	#546	85595	#595
82515	#344	85500	#500	85550	#550	85600	#600
82519	#374	85505	#505	85555	#555	85605	#605
82522	#402	85510	#510	85560	#560	82544	#610
82527	#421	85516	#516	85565	#565	85615	#615
82528	#424	85520	#520	85570	#570	85620	#620
82529	#429	85525	#525	85575	#575	82545	#680
82543	#445	85530	#530	85580	#580		

REDDING RELOADING TOOLS

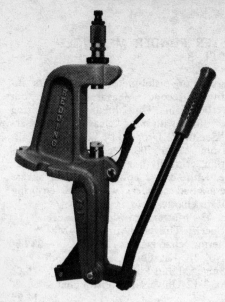

IMPROVED "C" PRESS
MODEL No. 7

New improvements include: Stronger frame (ASTM 30 alloy) for the heaviest reloading task; extremely shallow throat eliminates deflection; stronger (alloy steel) lower linkage; added rear mounting lug—prevents springing and "bench splitting;" snap-in shell holder may be rotated to any position; accepts all standard ⅞-14 threaded dies and all universal shell holders. Press includes primer arm for seating both large and small primers.

No. 7 "C" Press, complete	$ 75.95
No. 7K Kit includes press, shell holder, and one set of dies	103.95
No. 19 Automatic Primer Feeder	12.95
No. 20 Primer Catcher	6.00
No. 11 Shellholders (Universal Snap-in)	5.75

ULTRAMAG
MODEL NO. 700

A totally new concept in reloading presses.

Unlike other reloading presses which connect the linkage to the lower half of the press, the ULTRAMAG'S compound leverage system is connected at the top of the press frame. This allows the reloader to develop tons of pressure without the usual concern about press frame deflection. The strongest, most powerful press we've ever built. Huge frame opening will handle 50 x 3¼-inch Sharps with ease.

No. 700 Press complete	$171.95
No. 700K Kit, includes shellholder and one set of dies	199.95

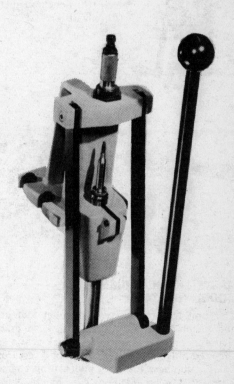

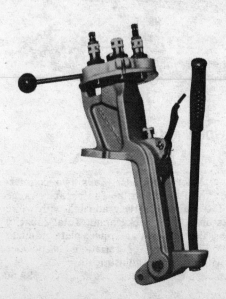

TURRET RELOADING PRESS
MODEL 25

Extremely rugged, ideal for production reloading. Choice of four or six Station Turrets. No need to move shell, just rotate turret head to positive alignment. Ram accepts any standard snap-in shell holder. Includes primer arm for seating both small and large primers.

No. 25 Press, complete	$198.50
No. 25K Kit, includes press, shell holder, and one set of dies	225.95
No. 25T Extra Turret (6 Station)	45.00
No. 19T Automatic Primer Feeder	14.95

REDDING RELOADING TOOLS

BENCHREST POWDER MEASURE
MODEL NO. 3BR

Designed for the most demanding reloaders — Benchrest, Silhouette and Varmint Shooters. The Model No. 3BR is unmatched for its precision and repeatability. Its special features include a powder baffle and zero backlash micrometer.

No. 3BR with Universal or Pistol
Metering Chamber **$75.00**
No. 3BRK includes both metering
chambers 92.50
No. 3-30 Benchrest metering chambers
(fit only 3BR) 19.95

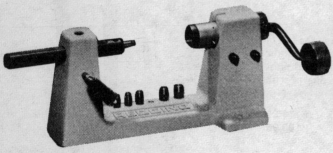

MASTER CASE TRIMMER
MODEL No. 1400

This unit features a universal collet that accepts all rifle and pistol cases. This trimmer is also unique in that it chamfers and deburrs the case neck at the same time it is trimmed to length. The frame is solid cast iron with storage holes in the base for extra pilots. Both coarse and fine adjustments are provided for case length.

The case-neck cleaning brush and primer pocket cleaners attached to the frame of this tool make it a very handy addition to the reloading bench.

Trimmer comes complete with the following:
* New speed cutter shaft
* Two pilots (.22 cal. and .30 cal.)
* Universal collet
* Two neck cleaning brushes (.22 thru .30 cal.)
* Two primer pocket cleaners (Large and Small)

No. 1400 Master Case Trimmer complete **$49.95**
No. 1500 Pilots 2.00

MASTER POWDER MEASURE
MODEL 3

Universal- or pistol-metering chambers interchange in seconds. Measures charges from ½ to 100 grains. Unit fitted with lock ring for fast dump with large "clear" plastic reservoir. "See-thru" Drop Tube accepts all calibers from .22 to .600. Precision-fitted rotating drum, critically honed to prevent powder escape. Knife-edged powder chamber shears coarse-grained powders with ease, ensuring accurate charges.

No. 3 Master Powder Measure,
(Specify Universal- or Pistol-Metering chamber) **$62.50**
No. 3K Kit Form, includes both
Universal and Pistol chambers. .. 75.00
No. 3-12 Universal or Pistol chamber. 14.95

POWDER TRICKLER
MODEL No. 5

Brings underweight charges up to accurate reading, adding powder to scale pan a granule or two at a time by rotating knob. Speeds weighing of each charge. Solid steel, low center of gravity. "Companion" height to all reloading scales; weighs a full pound

No. 5 Powder Trickler. **$12.95**

STANDARD POWDER AND BULLET SCALE
MODEL No. RS-1

For the beginner or veteran reloader. Only two counterpoises need to be moved to obtain the full capacity range of 1/10 grain to 380 grains. Clearly graduated with white numerals and lines on a black background. Total capacity of this scale is 380 grains. An over and under plate graduate in 10th grains allows checking of variations in powder charges or bullets without further adjustments.

Model No. RS-1 .... **$39.50**

REDDING RELOADING TOOLS

Guaranteed accurate to less than 1/10 grain. Master model has magnetic dampening for fast readings. 1/10 grain graduated over/under plate permits checking powder charge variations without moving counterpoises. Features also include: 505-grain capacity; high-visibility graduated beam; pour-spout pan; stable cast base; large convenient leveling screw; hardened and honed, self-aligning beam bearings for lifetime accuracy.

No. 2 Scale $49.50

RELOADING DIES
MODEL No. 10

Redding dies are made from alloy steels heat treated and hand polished. All Redding dies are lifetime guaranteed and use no aluminum parts or plating. Standard ⅞-14 thread to fit most presses. Available in 2 Or 3 die rifle sets, 3 die pistol sets and 4 die pistol sets with taper crimp.

Series A	**$29.00**
Series B	34.95
Series C	41.00
Series D	46.50

All Redding dies are packaged in the combination plastic storage box/loading block.

Neck sizing dies are available in most bottleneck calibers for those who wish to resize only the necks for longer case life and better accuracy.

Custom made dies are available on special order.

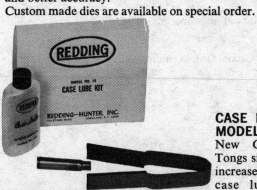

CASE LUBE KIT
MODEL No. 12

New Case Lube Tongs simplify and increase speed of case lubrication. Conforms to all cartridge cases, especially useful to ensure proper case neck lubrication. Eliminates stuck cases and pulled rims. Prolongs life of dies and simplifies case reforming. Includes 2 oz. plastic bottle of Redding case lube.

No. 12 Case Lube Kit $8.95
No. 21 Case Lube only, 2 oz. Bottle 2.50

"SUPERCHARGER"
POWDER MEASURE KITS
MODEL No. 101 AND 102

Supercharger Kit No. 101
Contains: Model No. RS-1 Standard Powder and Bullet Scale, Model No. 3 Master Powder Measure, Model No. 5 Powder Trickler and Model No. RS-6 Bench Stand.

No. 101 . . . . **$119.00**

Supercharger Kit No. 102
Contains: Model No. 2 Master Powder and Bullet Scale, Model No. 3 Powder Measure, Model No. 5 Powder Trickler and Model No. RS-6 Bench Stand.

No. 102 . . . . **$128.00**

TITANIUM CARBIDE PISTOL Dies

Model No. 10-TIC

Titanium carbide has the highest hardness of any readily available carbide yet is not as brittle. Its smooth, rounded micrograins present a slippery, nongalling surface, unattainable with other carbides. Lubrication is a thing of the past and the inserts are tapered, to prevent belts or shoulders on your cases.

No. 10-TIC Pistol Die Sets **$72.50**
No. 10-TIC Sizing Die Complete 56.00
No. 1021 R Decapping Rod Assembly 7.00

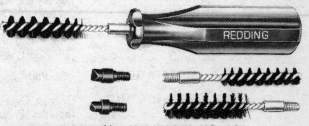

BENCH STAND
MODEL RS-6

Convenient bench stand for Redding Master Powder Measure. Stand is not threaded. Powder measure is secured with a lock ring permitting quick dump of reservoir. Fits all powder measures with ⅞-14 thread mounting.
$15.95

CASE PREPARATION KIT MODEL NO. 18

All the tools you need in one package for removing dirt and powder residue from the inside of case necks and primer pockets. Kit comes complete with accessory handle, large and small primer pocket cleaners and three case neck brushes to handle all cartridges from 22 thru 45 caliber.
$10.95

TEXAN RELOADING TOOLS

MODEL RT 6-STATION

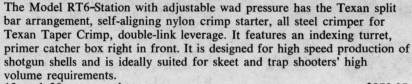

The Model RT6-Station with adjustable wad pressure has the Texan split bar arrangement, self-aligning nylon crimp starter, all steel crimper for Texan Taper Crimp, double-link leverage. It features an indexing turret, primer catcher box right in front. It is designed for high speed production of shotgun shells and is ideally suited for skeet and trap shooters' high volume requirements.

12 and 20 gauge only **$259.95**
Crimp Starter (specify gauge and number of points) may be used on
FW, GT, AP and DP Models **6.75**

MODEL M-IV

The MIV has a smooth self-indexing action which moves cases through all stations to produce a completed shell for each pull of the handle. The automatic priming system functions only if there is a case in position to be reprimed. It features a wad guide, which prevents deformed cases, easy to adjust and read wad pressure system, shell retention system, self-aligning crimp starter. It includes 6- and 8-point* crimp starters, shell ejector, cam, shell catcher, primer catcher, automatic primer feed and shot and powder bushings for both target and field loads.

RT-6

MIV

MV	New Loader with Brass Resizing station plus all features of MIV Complete with primer feed, shell ejector and catcher and automatic index. 12, 16, 20, 28 410 gauges **$599.00**
MIV	Loader 12, 16, 20, 28, 410 gauges with primer feed, shell ejector, and catcher **499.00**
MIV	Loader - "Basic" without primer feed, ejector or shell catcher 12, 16, 20, 28, 410 ga. **365.00**
MIV-CS	Crimp Starter. (Specify gauge and number of points) **6.75**

MODIFICATIONS
Modernize the Texan systems of the MV. The following systems may be installed without drilling, reaming or otherwise modifying the basic tool:

MIV-APF*	Complete Priming System .... **125.90** *Red Model M requires additional deprime punch for Primer Feed conversion **4.00**
MIV-WG	Complete Self Lowering Wad Guide System, including Nylon Wad Guide Finger .... **19.95** (Specify Gauge)
MIV-WP	Complete Wad Pressure System .... **25.00** (Specify Gauge)
MIV-STAGE	with Plate, Springs and Ejection Cam **75.00**
MII, MIIA/MIV	Change Over Package (Specify Gauge) Complete— Includes Priming, Wad Guide, Wad Pressure, and Stage **200.00**
MV, MIV	New Sizer Package to fit Models MIIA and MII (Press Head, Measure Cam holder, and All sizer parts) **200.00**

Factory overhaul of any Model M, MII, MIIA or MIV for parts and transportation, $25.00 flat rate labor.

TEXAN RELOADING TOOLS

MODEL 101-T-11

The 101T11 is a seven-station turret-type press that provides space for three two-die rifle sets or two three-die pistol sets plus one station for powder measure or other accessory. All stations threaded ⅞-14 to accept all popular rifle and pistol die sets. Interchangeable universal shell holder heads allow fast easy caliber changes. Rugged cast iron base and powerful leverage plus rigid two-post construction to insure ease of operation. Optional primer feed eliminates handling of primers and speeds up reloading operation.

101-T-II Press with primer feed $235.00
101-T-II Press without primer feed 210.00
191-PF Primer feed complete 34.95
101-T Primer post, large or small 6.00
191-T Primer feed post, large or small 6.00

101-T-11

301-H3

MODEL 301-H3

Uses 3-die pistol or 2-die rifle sets in one press without changing dies during the reloading operation. Stations are threaded ⅞-14 to accept all standard rifle and pistol dies. Uses H-type Universal rams and Universal shellholder heads. Three-column design maintains positive alignment for exacting reloading and smooth operation. Includes both large and small primer seating posts and three Universal H-type rams. Heavy-duty cast metal brass drilled for bench mounting.

Press with handle, 3 Universal H-type Shellholder
  Rams, large and small primer seating posts $134.95
H-3 Primer Post, large or small 6.00

MODEL 256 DOUBLE C PRESS

The Model 256 double C press is a heavy duty press with a rugged malleable cast frame. Precise alignment of the die and ram is insured by precision broaching. Threaded ⅞-14 to accept all popular dies. Universal primer arm includes cups and punches to seat both large and small primers. Equipped with universal shell holder ram and primer arm.

Model 256 C Press $62.95
  (with primer arm and ram)

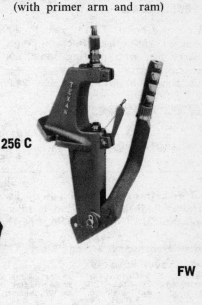

256 C

FW

MODEL FW

The FW features rugged aluminum castings and two column design plus double, toggle-action linkage. Cam action ejects high or low brass cases from resize die without adjustment. Repriming is positive with full base wad support to eliminate concaving case head. Shell mouth spreader opens shell mouth to aid in effortless seating of all types of wads through the self-lowering wad guide. Wad pressure is completely adjustable for all type wads. Self-aligning crimp starter seeks out original folds and final crimp die produces "Taper Crimp." Swivel top allows easy draining of powder or shot and convenient changing of powder or shot bushings. Unique base design allows operation without being bolted to bench or table. Conversion to other gauges is simple. All parts, including shot and powder bushings, are included in kit.

FW Loader, 12, 16, 20, 28, 410 gauge $129.95
FW Loader, 12, 20, or 410 gauge 3″ 135.95
FW-CK 2¾″ Conversion Kit,
    12, 16, 20, 28, 410 gauge 44.95
FW-SPL-CK Conversion Kit, 2¾″ to 3″,
    12, 16, 20, 28, 410 gauge 50.95
FW-CK 3″ Conversion Kit,
    12, 20 or 410 ga. 3″ regular 24.95

TEXAN RELOADING TOOLS

MODEL R-1 SHOTSHELL RECONDITIONER

Recommended for use in conjunction with the Texan models M-IV and other automatic reloaders. Reconditions both plastic and paper cases to fit all makes of shotguns. One pull of the handle resizes, deprimes, flattens bulged or concaved case head and reseats base wad. Makes possible reloads that look and perform like new.

Model R1 12, 16, 20, 28 or 410 guage $49.95
Model R1-CK Conversion Kit 12, 16, 20, 28 or
   410 gauge 13.25

POWDER SCALE

With magnetic or oil damped beam. Tenth grain to 500 grain graduation. Hardened knife-edged fulcrum points, three counterpoises, large pan with pouring spout and leveling screw. Rugged cast base.

No. 304 with magnetic damped beam 34.95

RELOADING ACCESSORIES

DEBURRING TOOL. Chamfers or deburrs mouth of cartridge cases to clean, smooth edge.

No. 259 .... 9.75

TEXAN DIE LUBE. Specially formulated lubricant. Exacting companion to Texan Micro-Bore dies.

2 oz. $2.00

BULLET PULLER. Will not mar or scratch bullet. Standard ⅞-14 thread.

No. 302 Bullet Puller without collet 13.95
No. 302 Collet of Special Caliber (specify) 6.00

CASE LUBE PAD. The fast, easy way to lubricate. Eliminates dents caused by excess lube.

Use with Texan die lube 6.95

"C" TYPE PRIMER ARM. For No. 256 "C" press. Fits most standard "C" presses or other makes.

No. 255 .... 4.95

ACCESSORIES INCLUDED WITH "C" TYPE PRIMER ARM. Large primer pin, concave; large primer pin, flat; small primer pin, concave; small primer pin, large sleeve and small sleeve 2.95

SHELLHOLDER

Texan Shellholder heads and rams are made of high quality steel. The No. 214 Universal Shellholder Head is interchangeable between both No. 214 C-type and No. 214 H-type Shellholder Rams.

The No. 214 C-type fits Texan Model "C" and other "C" presses. No. 214 H-type fits Texan Model 101-T-II, 301-H3 and other make H-type presses. When ordering rams, specify No. 214-C or No. 214-H type.

No. 214   Universal Head (specify number) $5.00
No. 214-H   Universal Ram, H-Type 9.00
No. 214-C   Universal Ram, C-Type 9.00

NO. 214 SHELLHOLDER HEAD GROUP NUMBERS

GROUP NO. 1		GROUP NO. 2	
225 Win.	7mm - 270	219 Zipper	30 Remington
22/250 (22 Var.)	280 Remington	219 Donaldson	32 Remington
243 Winchester	7.7 Jap	22 Sav. Hi-Power	351 Winchester
243 Rockchucker	30 - 06	25-35	
244 Remington	300 Savage	30-30	GROUP NO. 6
6mm Remington	308 Winchester	32 Special	257 Wea. Mag.
228 Ack. Mag.	7.9 Mauser	32 - 40	264 Winchester
257 Roberts	284 Winchester	38 - 55	264 - 270
250/3000 (250 Sav.)	8mm Mauser		270 Wea. Mag.
250 Donaldson	8 x 51	GROUP NO. 3	275 H & H Mag.
25/06	8 x 60	218 Bee	276 Dubiel
6.5 x 57	8mm - 06	25 - 20 Repeater	7 x 61 Sharpe & Hart
6.5 x 06	333 OKH	32 - 20	7mm Wea. Mag.
6mm - 06	35 Whelen		7 mm Rem. Mag.
256 Newton	358 Winchester	GROUP NO. 4	300 Wea. Mag.
270 WCF	9mm Mauser	220 Swift	300 H & H Mag.
7mm Mauser	9mm Mann. Sch.	220 Rocket	300 Winchester
7 x 57	9.3 x 72	240 Cobra	300 Norma Mag.
7 x 64	45 ACP	GROUP NO. 5	30 - 338
		25 Remington	30 Newton

8mm - 338	30 - 40 Krag	38 Super Auto	GROUP NO. 15
338 Winchester	303 British	GROUP NO. 12	221
35 Newton	35 WCF	22 Super Jet	222 Rem.
358 Norma Mag.	44 Special	22 Rem. Jet	222 Rem. Mag.
375 Wea. Mag.	44 Magnum	256 Win. Mag.	223 Rem.
375 H & H Mag.	44 Russian	357 Magnum	380 Auto
11mm Mauser	.444 Marlin	38 Special	9 MM Short
458 Winchester	ALL Ack. Sh. Mag.	GROUP NO. 9	GROUP NO. 16
6.5 Rem. Mag.	38 - 40	38 Long Colt	9 MM Luger
350 Rem. Mag.	44 - 40	GROUP NO. 13	GROUP NO. 17
GROUP NO. 7	GROUP NO. 10	6.5 x 55	41 Mag.
32 Long Colt	7.65 Belgian	GROUP NO. 18	
8 x 57 Rimmed	32 S & W	Mauser	45 Auto Rim.
GROUP NO. 8	GROUP NO. 11	GROUP NO. 14	SPECIALS
25 - 303	30 Luger	.35 Rem.	45 Long Colt
	30 Mauser	6.5 Carcano	30 M1 or 32 ACP
		7.35 Italian	

All other shellholder heads must be ordered by caliber as they are not interchangeable with this group of calibers.

MICRO-BORE PISTOL AND RIFLE DIES

Texan two-die sets, for bottle neck cases, and three-die sets for straight wall cases are constructed from special alloy steel, micro-bored and polished to rigid specifications. Each die body is treated inside and out, for protection against wear, rust or corrosion. Precision dies that feature the hex body design and double hex lock rings for secure, mar-free wrench adjustment. Every set packaged in attractive plastic display and storage box.

2 Die Rifle Set $28.95
3 Die Pistol Set 28.95
Plastic Die Storage Box Only 2.00

Caliber Available	No. Dies in Set	Shell Holder	Caliber Available	No. Dies in Set	Shell Holder	Caliber Available	No. Dies in Set	Shell Holder
222 Rem.	2	15	280 Rem.	2	1	350 Rem. Mag.	2	6
222 Rem. Mag.	2	15	284 Win.	2	1	38 S&W	3	SPL
223 Rem. (AR)	2	15	7MM Rem. Mag.	2	6	38 Super Auto.	3	11
22-250 Rem.	2	1	30 MI. Car.	3	SPL 30 MI	380 Auto.	3	15
243 Win.	2	1	30-30	2	2	9MM Luger	3	16
244 Rem.	2	1	300 Savage	2	1	38 Special	3	12
6MM Rem.	2	1	308 Win.	2	1	357 Mag.	3	12
257 Roberts	2	1	30-06	2	1	41 Mag.	3	17
25-06 Rem.	2	1	300 Win. Mag.	2	6	44 Special	3	8
264 Win.	2	6	303 British	2	8	44 Mag.	3	8
6.5 Rem. Mag.	2	6	8MM Mauser (8 x 57)	2	1	45 Auto. Rim.	3	18
270 Win.	2	1	338 Win. Mag.	2	1	45 A.C.P.	3	1
7MM Mauser (7 x 57)	2	1	35 Rem.	2	14	45 Long Colt	3	SPL 45 LC

Directory of Manufacturers and Suppliers

Abilene *(handguns)*
(available through Mossberg)

Action Arms. Ltd. (UZI)
P.O. Box 9573
Philadelphia, Pennsylvania 19124
(215) 744-0100

Anschutz
(rifles available through Talo Distributors;
air guns available through Talo Distributors
and Beeman's)

Armsport, Inc. *(rifles, shotguns)*
3590 NW 49th Street
Miami, Florida 33142
(305) 635-7850

Astra
(handguns available through Interarms; shotguns
available through L. Joseph Rahn, Inc.)

Auto-Ordnance Corporation *(rifles)*
Box 588
West Hurley, New York 12491

BSA *(air guns)*
(available through Precision Sports)

Baikal International Trading Corp.
(shotguns)
12 Farview Terrace
Paramus, New Jersey 07652
(201) 845-8710

Bauer Firearms Corporation *(handguns, rifles)*
34750 Klein Avenue
Fraser, Michigan 48026
(313) 294-9130

Beeman's Precision Air Guns, Inc. *(also*
Anschutz, Feinwerkbau, Webley, Weihrauch,
Wischo air guns)
47 Paul Drive
San Rafael, California 94903
(415) 472-7121

Benjamin Air Rifle Company
3205 Sheridan Road
Racine, Wisconsin 53403
(414) 633-5424

Beretta U.S.A. Corp. *(handguns,*
shotguns)
17601 Indianhead Highway
Acco Keck, Maryland 20607
(301) 283-2191

Bernardelli *(handguns)*
(available through Interarms)

Bersa *(handguns)*
(available through Interarms)

Bonanza Sports Manufacturing Co.
(reloading tools)
412 Western Avenue
Faribault, Minnesota 55021
(507) 332-8676

Browning *(handguns, rifles, shotguns*
black powder guns)
Route 1
Morgan, Utah 84050
(801) 876-2711

Maynard P. Buehler, Inc. *(mounts, screws)*
17 Orinda Highway
Orinda, California 94563
(415) 254-3201

Burris Company, Inc. *(scopes, mounts)*
331 East Eighth Street
Greeley, Colorado 80632
(303) 356-1670

Bushnell Optical Company *(scopes)*
(Div. of Bausch & Lomb)
2828 East Foothill Boulevard
Pasadena, California 91107
(213) 577-1500

CCI *(ammunition, primers)*
(see Omark Industries, Inc.)

CVA *(black powder guns)*
Connecticut Valley Arms, Inc.
Saybrook Road
Haddam, Connecticut 06438
(203) 345-8511

C-H Tool & Die Corporation
(reloading)
P.O. Box L
Owen, Wisconsin 54460
(715) 229-2146

Charter Arms Corporation *(handguns,*
rifles)
430 Sniffens Lane
Stratford, Connecticut 06497
(203) 377-8080

Colt Industries, Firearms Division
(handguns, rifles, black powder guns)
150 Huyshope Avenue
Hartford, Connecticut 06102
(203) 236-6311

Crosman Air Guns
980 Turk Hill Road
Fairport, New York 14450
(716) 223-6000

Daisy *(air guns; also Power Line)*
P.O. Box 220
Rogers, Arkansas 72756
(501) 636-1200

Dakota *(handguns)*
(see E.M.F. Company, Inc.)

Detonics Manufacturing Corporation *(handguns)*
2500 Seattle Tower
Seattle, Washington 98101
(206) 747-2100

Dixie Gun Works, Inc. *(black powder guns)*
Gunpowder Lane
Union City, Tennessee 38261
(901) 885-0561

E.I. Du Pont de Nemours & Co., Inc.
(gunpowder)
Explosives Department
1007 Market Street
Wilmington, Delaware 19898
(302) 774-1000

Dynamit Nobel of America, Inc. *(Rottweil*
shotguns)
105 Stonehurst Court
Northvale, New Jersey 07647
(201) 767-1660

E.M.F. Company, Inc. *(Dakota handguns)*
1900 East Warner Avenue, One D
Santa Ana, California 92705
(714) 966-0202

Euroarms of America *(black powder guns)*
1501 Lenoir Drive
Winchester, Virginia 22601
(703) 662-1863

Fabrique Nationale Sports *(rifles)*
(available through Steyr Daimler Puch)

Federal Cartridge Corporation
(ammunition, primers, cases)
2700 Foshay Tower
Minneapolis, Minnesota 55402
(612) 333-8255

Feinwerkbau *(air guns)*
(available through Beeman's)

FIAS *(shotguns)*
(available through Kassnar Imports)

FIE *(shotguns, black powder guns)*
P.O. Box 4866 Hialeah Lakes
Hialeah, Florida 33014
(305) 685-5966

Fox *(rifles, shotguns)*
(see Savage Arms)

Franchi *(shotguns)*
(available through International
Distributors)

Freedom Arms *(handguns)*
One Freedom Lane
Freedom, Wyoming 83120
(307) 883-2468

J.L. Galef & Son, Inc. *(shotguns)*
85 Chamers Street
New York, New York 10007
(212) 267-6727

Renato Gamba *(rifles, shotguns)*
(available through Steyr Daimler Puch)

Gamo *(air guns)*
(available through Stoeger Industries)

Garbi *(shotguns)*
(available through L.Joseph Rahn, Inc.)

Griffin & Howe, Inc. *(sights, mounts)*
589 Broadway
New York, New York 10012
(212) 966-5323

Harrington & Richardson, Inc.
(handguns, rifles, shotguns)
Industrial Rowe
Gardner, Massachusetts 01440
(617) 632-9600

Heckler & Koch *(handguns, rifles*
shotguns)
933 North Kenmore Street, Suite 218
Arlington, Virginia 22201
(703) 243-3700

Hercules, Inc. *(gunpowder)*
910 Market Street
Wilmington, Delaware 19899
(302) 575-5000

High Standard, Inc. *(handguns)*
31 Prestige Park Circle
East Hartford, Connecticut 06108
(203) 289-9531

Hodgdon Powder Co., Inc.
7710 West 63rd Street
Shawnee Mission, Kansas 66202
(913) 362-5410

Hopkins & Allen Arms *(black powder guns)*
3 Ethel Avenue
Hawthorne, New Jersey 07507
(201) 427-1165

Hornady Manufacturing Company *(reloading, ammunition)*
P.O. Box 1848
Grand Island, Nebraska 68801
(308) 382-1390

IGA *(available through Stoeger Industries)*

Interarms *(handguns, also Astra handguns, Bernardelli, Bersa, Star, Walther)*
10 Prince Street
Alexandria, Virginia 22313
(703) 548-1400

International Distributors, Inc.
(Taurus handguns)
7290 S.W. 42nd Street
Miami, Florida 33155
(305) 264-9321

Ithaca Gun Company, Inc. *(shotguns)*
123 Lake Street
Ithaca, New York 14850
(607) 273-0200

Paul Jaeger, Inc. *(mounts)*
211 Leedom Street
Jenkintown, Pennsylvania 19046
(215) 884-6920

Iver Johnson's Arms, Inc. *(handguns, rifles)*
Wilton Avenue off South Avenue
Middlesex, New Jersey 08846
(201) 752-4994

Kahles of America *(scopes)*
Main Street
Margaretsville, New York 12455
(914) 586-4103

Kassnar Imports *(rifles, black powder guns; Kassnar/Zabala, FIAS shotguns, Parker-Hale rifles)*
P.O. Box 6097
Harrisburg, Pennsylvania 17112
(717) 652-6101

Kimber *(rifles)*
9039 S.E. Jannsen Road
Clackamas, Oregon 97015
(503) 656-1704

Kleinguenther's Inc. *(rifles)*
P.O. Box 1261
Seguin, Texas 78155
(512) 379-8141

Krieghoff Gun Company *(shotguns)*
P.O. Box 52-3367
Miami, Florida 33152
(305) 871-6550
(Other Krieghoff shotguns available through
Shotguns of Ulm)

Leupold & Stevens, Inc. *(scopes, mounts; Nosler bullets)*
P.O. Box 688
Beaverton, Oregon 97075
(503) 646-9171

Llama *(handguns)*
(available through Stoeger Industries)

London Guns *(sights, mounts)*
1528 20th Street
Santa Monica, California 90404
(213) 828-8486

Luger *(handguns)*
(see Stoeger Industries)

Lyman Products Corporation *(black powder guns, sights, scopes, reloading tools)*
Route 147
Middlefield, Connecticut 06455
(203) 349-3421

MEC, Inc. *(reloading tools)*
Mayville Engineering Company, Inc.
P.O. Box 267
Mayville, Wisconsin 53050
(414) 387-4500

MTM Molded Products Company
(reloading tools)
5680 Webster Street
Dayton, Ohio 45414
(513) 890-7461

Mandall Shooting Supplies, Inc.
(Sig-Hammerli air guns)
7150 East Fourth Street
Scottsdale, Arizona 85252
(602) 945-2553

Mannlicher *(rifles)*
(see Steyr Daimler Puch)

Marksman Products, Inc. *(air guns)*
2133 Dominguez Street
Torrance, California 90509
(213) 775-8847

Marlin Firearms Company *(rifles, shotguns)*
100 Kenna Drive
North Haven, Connecticut 06473
(203) 239-5621

Merit Gunsight Company *(optical aids)*
318 Sunnyside North
Sequim, Washington 98382
(206) 683-6127

The Merrill Company *(handguns)*
704 East Commonwealth
Fullerton, California 92631
(714) 870-8530

Micro Sight Company *(sights)*
242 Harbor Boulevard
Belmont, California 94002
(415) 591-0760

O.F. Mossberg & Sons, Inc.
(rifles, shotguns)
7 Grasso Avenue
North Haven, Connecticut 06473
(203) 288-6491

Navy Arms Company *(handguns, black powder guns, replicas; Parker-Hale black powder guns)*
689 Bergen Boulevard
Ridgefield, New Jersey 07657
(201) 945-2500

Norma Precision *(ammunition, gunpowder, reloading cases)*
(see Outdoor Sports Headquarters, Inc.)

Nosler Bullets, Inc.
(available through Leupold & Stevens, Inc.)

ODI *(see Omega Defensive Industries*

Olin Industries, Inc.
(ammunition, primers, cases, imported shotguns)
East Alton, Illinois 62024
(618) 258-2000

Omark Industries, Inc. *(CCI, RCBS, Speer)*
Box 856
Lewiston, Idaho 83501
(208) 746-2351

Omega Defensive Industries *(handguns)*
124A Greenwood Avenue
Midland Park, NJ 07432

Outdoor Sports Headquarters, Inc.
(Norma)
P.O. Box 1327
Dayton, Ohio 45401
(513) 294-2811

Pachmayr Gun Works, Inc. *(scope mounts)*
1220 South Grand Avenue
Los Angeles, California 90015
(213) 748-7271

Pacific Tool Company *(reloading tools)*
(Div. of Hornady Manufacturing Company)

Parker-Hale
(black powder guns available through Navy Arms;
rifles available through Kassnar Imports)

Ponsness-Warren, Inc. *(reloading tools)*
P.O. Box 8
Rathdrum, Idaho 83858
(208) 687-1331

Power Line *(air guns)*
(see Daisy)

Precise International *(air guns)*
3 Chestnut Street
Suffern, New York 10901
(914) 357—6200

Precision Sports *(BSA, Norma)*
(Div. of General Sporting Goods Corporation)
798 Cascadilla Street
Ithaca, New York 14850
(607) 273-2993

RCBS, Inc. *(reloading tools)*
(see Omark Industries, Inc.)

L. Joseph Rahn, Inc. *(Astra, Garbi, Secolo shotguns)*
201 South Main Street
First National Building, Room 502
Ann Arbor, Michigan 48104
(313) 994-5089

Redding-Hunter, Inc. *(reloading tools)*
114 Starr Road
Cortland, New York 13045
(607) 753-3331

Redfield *(sights, scopes)*
5800 East Jewell Avenue
Denver, Colorado 80224
(303) 757-6411

Remington Arms Company, Inc. *(rifles, shotguns, ammunition, primers)*
939 Barnum Avenue
Bridgeport, Connecticut 06602
(203) 333-1112

Rossi *(handguns, rifles, shotguns)*
(available through Interarms)

Rottweil *(shotguns)*
(available through Dynamit Nobel of America, Inc.)

Ruger *(handguns, rifles, shotguns, black powder guns)*
(see Sturm, Ruger & Company, Inc.)

Sako *(rifles, scope mounts)*
(available through Stoeger Industries)

Savage Arms *(shotguns, rifles; also Fox, Stevens)*
Springdale Road
Westfield, Massachusetts 01085
(413) 562-2361

Secolo *(shotguns)*
(available through L. Joseph Rahn, Inc.)

Sheridan Products, Inc. *(air guns)*
3205 Sheridan Road
Racine, Wisconsin 53403
(414) 633-5424

Shiloh Products Co., Inc. *(black powder guns)*
37 Potter Street
Farmingdale, New York 11735
(516) 249-2801

Shotguns of Ulm *(also Krieghoff)*
P.O. Box 253
Milltown, New Jersey 08850
(201) 297-0573

Sierra Bullets
10532 South Painter Avenue
Santa Fe Springs, California 90670
(213) 941-0251

Sig-Hammerli *(air guns)*
(available through Mandall Shooting Supplies, Inc.)

Smith & Wesson *(handguns, shotguns)*
2100 Roosevelt Avenue
Springfield, Massachusetts 01101
(413) 781-8300

Speer *(bullets)*
(see Omark Industries, Inc.)

Springfield Armory *(rifles)*
420 West Main Street
Geneseo, Illinois 61254
(309) 944-5138

Star *(handguns)*
(available through Interarms)

Sterling Arms Corporation *(handguns)*
211 Grand Street
Lockport, New York 14094
(716) 434-6631

Stevens *(rifles, shotguns)*
(see Savage Arms)

Steyr *(handguns)*
(See Steyr Daimler Puch)

Steyr Mannlicher *(rifles)*
(See Steyr Daimler Puch)

Steyr Daimler Puch of America Corporation *(AKM, Fabrique Nationale, Steyr, Steyr Mannlicher)*
Sporting Arms Division
85 Metro Way
Secaucus, New Jersey 07094
(201) 865-2284

Stoeger Industries *(Gamo, IGA, Llama, Luger, Sako)*
55 Ruta Court
South Hackensack, New Jersey 07606
(201) 440-2700

Sturm, Ruger & Company, Inc.
(Ruger firearms)
Lacey Place
Southport, Connecticut 06490
(203) 259-7843

Talo Distributors, Inc.
(Anschutz rifles and air rifles)
P.O. Box 177
Westfield, Massachusetts 01086
(413) 562-9921

Tasco *(scopes)*
7600 N.W. 26th Street
Miami, Florida 33122
(305) 591-3670

Taurus International, Inc. *(Taurus handguns)*
4563 Southwest 71st Avenue
Miami, Florida 33155
(305) 662-2529

Texan Reloaders, Inc. *(reloading tools)*
444 Cips Street
Watseka, Illinois 60970
(815) 432-5065

Thompson/Center Arms *(black powder guns, handguns)*
Farrington Road
Rochester, New Hampshire 03867
(603) 332-2333

Tikka *(see Armsport, Inc.)* *(rifles, shotguns)*
SF-41160
Tikkakoski, Finland

U.S. Repeating Arms Co. *(domestic rifles, shotguns)*
275 Winchester Avenue
New Haven, Connecticut 06504
(203) 789-5000

Valment, Inc. *(rifles, shotguns)*
7 Westchester Plaza
Elmsford, New York 10523
(914) 347-4440

Ventura Imports *(shotguns)*
P.O. Box 2782
Seal Beach, California 90740
(213) 596-5372

Walther *(air guns, handguns)*
(available through Interarms)

Weatherby, Inc. *(rifles, shotguns, scopes, ammunition)*
2781 Firestone Boulevard
South Gate, California 90280
(213) 569-7186

W.R. Weaver Company *(sights, scopes, mounts)*
P.O. Box 20010
El Paso, Texas 79998
(915) 778-5281

Webley *(air guns)*
(available through Beeman's)

Weihrauch *(air guns)*
(available through Beeman's)

Dan Wesson Arms, Inc. *(handguns)*
293 Main Street
Monson, Massachusetts 01057
(413) 267-4081

Williams Gun Sight Company *(sights, scopes, mounts)*
7389 Lapeer Road
Davison, Michigan 48423
(313) 653-2131

Winchester *(domestic rifles, shotguns)*
(see U.S. Repeating Arms Co.)

Winchester-Western *(rifles, imported shotguns, ammunition, primers, cases)*
(see Olin Industries)

Winslow Arms Company *(rifles)*
P.O. Box 783
Camden, South Carolina 29020
(803) 432-2938

Wischo *(air guns)*
(available through Beeman's)

SHOTGUNS

AUTOLOADING

Beretta
Model A302 ... 304, 305

Browning
Auto-5 Hunting Models ... 310
Auto-5 Skeet Models ... 310
B-80 Gas Automatic Hunting Models ... 310
B-80 Superlight Models ... 310

Franchi
Hunter Model ... 313
Magnum Automatic ... 313
Standard Automatic ... 313
Spas-12 ... 313

Heckler & Koch
Benelli Model SL 121V ... 318
Benelli Model 121V, Slug ... 318
Benelli Model SL 123V ... 318
Benelli Model SL 201 ... 318

Ithaca
Model 51 ... 320
Model 51 Deerslayer ... 320

Remington
Model 1100D ... 326
Model 1100F ... 326
Model 1100 Deer Gun ... 326
Model 1100 Field Gun ... 326
Model 1100 Left Hand ... 326
Model 1100 LT-20 ... 325
Model 1100 LT-20 Limited ... 325
Model 1100 Magnum ... 326
Model 1100 Magnum, The Mississippi ... 327
Model 1100SA Skeet Gun ... 325
Model 1100 SA Skeet LT-20 ... 325
Model 1100SA Skeet Small Gauge ... 325
Model 1100 Small Gauge ... 325
Model 110TA Trap ... 331
Model 1100TA Left-Hand Trap Gun ... 331
Model 1100 Tournament Skeet ... 331
Model 1100 Tournament Trap ... 331

Smith & Wesson
Model 1000 ... 338

Weatherby
Eighty-Two Automatic ... 341

Winchester
Model 1500 XTR Winchoke ... 342

BOLT ACTION

Marlin
Original Goose Gun ... 320
Supergoose 10 ... 320

Mossberg
Model 183K ... 322
Model 385K ... 322
Model 395K ... 322
Model 395SPL ... 322

OVER-UNDER

Armsport
Single Selective Trigger Models ... 302

Astra
Model 650 ... 303
Model 650E ... 303
Model 750 ... 303
Model 750E ... 303
Model 750 Skeet ... 303
Model 750 Trap ... 303

Beretta
Model 685 Field Grade ... 305
Model 686 Field Grade ... 306
Model 680 Combo ... 306
Model 680 Skeet ... 306
Model 680 Trap ... 306

Browning
Citori Combo Trap Set ... 311
Citori Hunting Models ... 311
Citori Skeet Models ... 311
Citori Trap Models ... 311
Limited Edition Waterfowl Superposed ... 308
Presentation Superposed Hunting Model
Lightning 12 and 20 ... 307, 308
Lightning 28 and .410 ... 307, 308
Super Light 12 and 20 ... 307, 308
Presentation Superposed Skeet Model
Lightning 12 and 20 ... 307, 308
Lightning 28 and .410 ... 307, 308
Presentation Superposed Trap Model
Broadway 12 ... 307, 308
Lightning 12 ... 307, 308

Franchi
Alcione SL ... 313
Falconet S ... 313
Diamond ... 313

IGA
Single Trigger Models ... 317
Double Trigger Models ... 316

Remington
3200 Competition Skeet ... 327
3200 Competition Trap ... 327
3200 Live Bird ... 327
3200 Skeet Set ... 327

Rottweil
American Skeet ... 332
American Trap Combo ... 333
Montreal Trap ... 333
Olympia '72 Skeet ... 333
Supreme Field O/U ... 332

Ruger
Over & Under Shotgun ... 334

Shotguns of Ulm
K-80 Over & Under Trap and Skeet ... 337
K-80 Special Hunting Model ... 337

Valmet
412K Series ... 339
412KE Series ... 339
412KE Target Series ... 339

Weatherby
Orion Over/Under ... 342
Athena Shotgun ... 341

SIDE-BY-SIDE DOUBLE BARREL

Armsport
1040 Series ... 303
Holland & Holland ... 302
Premier Slug ... 302
Western Double ... 303

Beretta
Model 424 ... 304
Model 426 ... 304

Browning
B-SS Side-by-Side ... 312

Garbi
Model 51 ... 314
Model 60-A ... 314
Model 60-B ... 314
Model 62-A ... 314
Model 62-B ... 314

IGA
Side by Side ... 316

Rossi
Overland Model 11 ... 332
Squire Model 14 ... 332

Savage
Fox Model B-SE ... 335
Stevens Model 311 ... 335

Ventura
Model 51 ... 340
Model 53 ... 340
Model 66 ... 340

SINGLE BARREL

Armsport
Deluxe Goose Gun ... 303
Deluxe Turkey Gun ... 303
Premier Skeet ... 302
Premier Trap ... 302

Browning
BT-99 Trap Special ... 312

IGA
Coach Gun ... 317

Harrington & Richardson
Model 088 and 088JR ... 314
Model 098 ... 315
Model 099 Deluxe ... 315
Model 162 ... 314
Model 176 ... 315
Model 490 ... 315

Savage
Stevens Model 94-C ... 334
Stevens Model 94-Y ... 334
Stevens Model 9478 ... 334
Stevens Model 9478 10 Gauge Waterfowl ... 334
Stevens Model 9478-Y Youth Model ... 334

SLIDE ACTION

Browning
BPS Pump Shotgun ... 309

Ithaca
Model 37 ... 318
Model 37 Deerslayer ... 320
Model 37 M & P ... 319
Model 37 Ultra Featherweight ... 318

Marlin
Glenfield 778 12 Gauge Pump ... 321
Model 120 Magnum Pump ... 321

Mossberg
Model 500 ... 323, 324

Remington
Model 870 Brushmaster ... 328
Model 870 Standard ... 328
Model 870 20 Gauge Lightweight ... 330
Model 870 20 Gauge Lightweight
Magnum ... 330
Model 870 28 and .410 Gauges ... 329
Model 870 Competition Trap ... 329
Model 870 Deer Gun ... 328
Model 870 Field Gun
Wingmaster, Left hand ... 330
Model 870 Magnum ... 328
Model 870D High Grade ... 329
Model 870F High Grade ... 329
Model 870TA Trap Gun ... 329

Smith & Wesson
Model 3000 ... 338

Weatherby
Ninety-Two ... 341

Winchester
Model 1200 ... 343
Model 1200 Defender ... 343
Model 1200 Police ... 343
Model 1200 Stainless ... 343
Model 1300 XTR Deer Gun ... 343
Model 1300 XTR Waterfowl ... 343
Model 1300 XTR Winchoke ... 343
Ranger ... 344

PARAMILITARY

Index